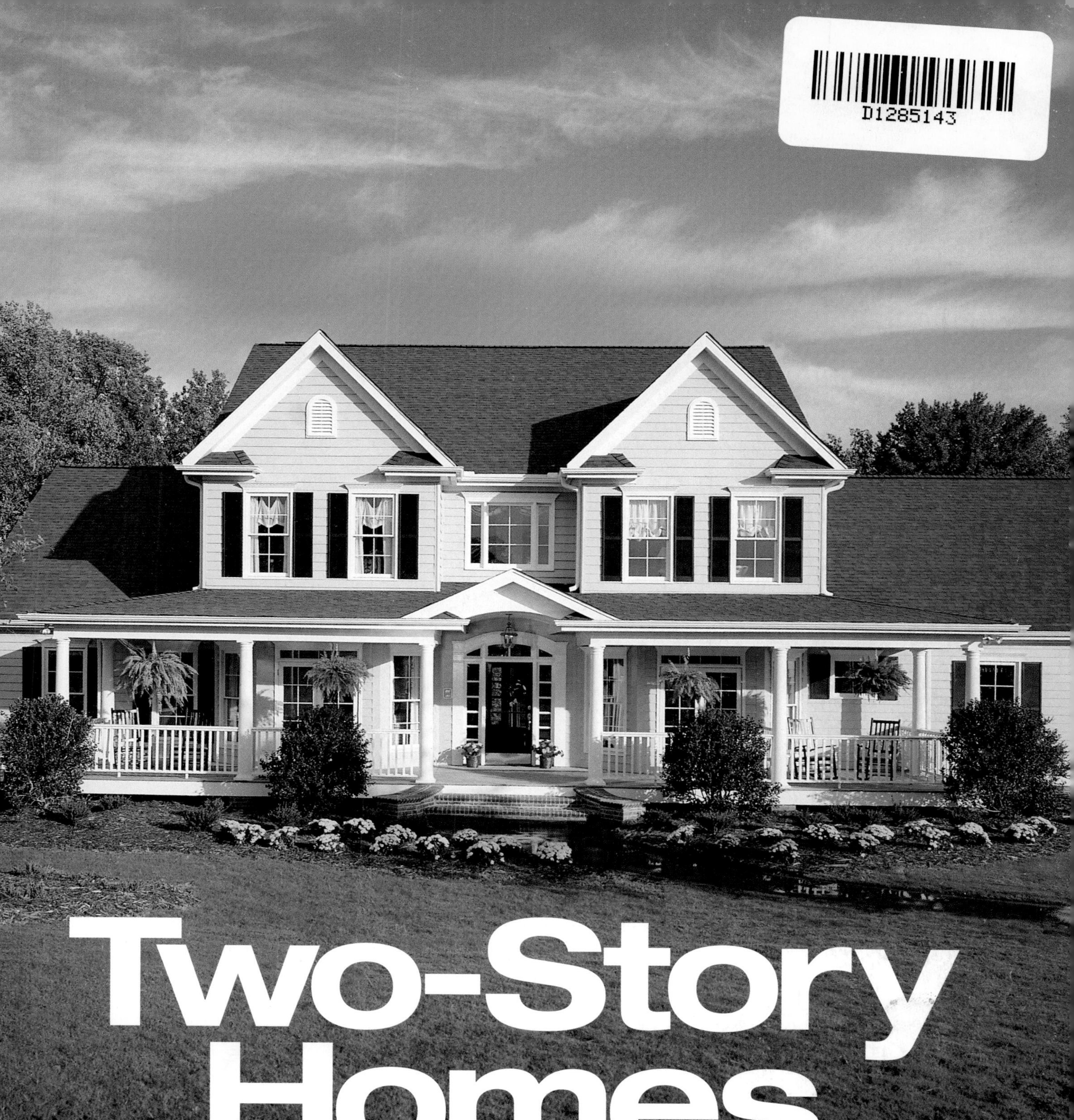

Two-Story Homes

DESIGN HPT930004, PAGE 8

450 Best-Selling Designs

HOME PLANNERS, LLC
Wholly owned by Hanley-Wood, LLC

TABLE OF CONTENTS

Design HPT930020, page 24

Two-Story Homes
450 Best-Selling Designs

Two-Story Homes
450 Best-Selling Designs

Published by Home Planners, LLC
Wholly owned by Hanley-Wood, LLC
3275 W. Ina Road, Suite 220
Tucson, Arizona 85741

Distribution Center
29333 Lorie Lane
Wixom, Michigan 48393

Photo Credits

Front Cover: Design HPT930354,
for details see page 358.
Photo courtesy of: Terrebonne Photography.

Back Cover: Design HPT930007,
for details see page 11.

10 9 8 7 6 5 4 3 2 1

Printed in the United States of America
Library of Congress Control Number: 2002115917
ISBN: 1-931131-15-5

Find Your Dream House

Two-Story Homes has the house for you – whether you are a retiree, just starting out, or somewhere in between! Choose among tried-and-true blueprints for every price range, style, and size home.

Have you dreamed of a balcony or loft overlooking a glorious great room? Or an elegant staircase that winds its way up through your foyer?

Take the first steps towards realizing those dreams through the plans in this book. Leaf through these pages and discover the efficiency, convenience, and timeless style of two-story homes. We've gathered a collection of 450 plans that is the definitive resource for someone looking to build a two-story home.

Two-story homes provide the maximum living space while minimizing the house's footprint - they're perfect if you have a small or narrow lot, or if you just want as large a yard as possible. Enjoy the privacy and security of an upstairs bedroom, or the convenience of a home office or recreation room near the master suite. Lots of other special features abound as well, including second-floor decks and balconies, beautiful lofts, and plenty of room to expand as your family grows.

Two-story homes also have a timeless quality, regardless of the architectural style. A wide variety of styles are represented in these pages, including:

■ **Farmhouses & Cottages:** Rural relaxation is the rule in this section of country designs.
■ **Retreats & Bungalows:** Get away from it all in these two-story versions of the popular bungalow style.
■ **Victorians & Tudors:** Discover English architectural influences like the towers and decorative facades that characterize Victorian- and Tudor-style homes.
■ **Cape Cods & Colonials:** Adapted from the first American homes, these styles possess a definite historic charm.
■ **French Country Chateaux:** Distinctive rooflines and open floor plans help define this popular style.
■ **Mediterranean Manors:** Find the high style of Europe in these luxurious homes.
■ **21st Century Styles:** These plans offer the latest in innovative design.

But first browse our Best-Selling section, where you'll discover the very best plans from the nation's top designers. These are time-tested homes that are offered in various sizes and styles.

Once you've found one you like, turn to the back of the book or visit eplans.com for ordering information. With complete construction blueprints are available for every home, you can be on the way to enjoying your dream home. ■

ALTERNATE EXTERIOR

SECOND FLOOR

FIRST FLOOR

plan# HPT930001

- Style: Traditional
- First Floor: 1,675 sq. ft.
- Second Floor: 448 sq. ft.
- Total: 2,123 sq. ft.
- Bonus Space: 345 sq. ft.
- Bedrooms: 4
- Bathrooms: 3
- Width: 53'-8"
- Depth: 69'-8"

SEARCH ONLINE @ EPLANS.COM

This attractive three-bedroom house offers a touch of country with its covered front porch. The foyer, flanked by the dining room and the bedroom/study, leads to the spacious great room. Here, a fireplace and window wall enhance any gathering. The U-shaped kitchen features a window over the sink and a serving counter to the breakfast room. The dining room and breakfast room have cathedral ceilings with arched windows that fill the house with natural light. The master bedroom boasts a cathedral ceiling and a bath with a whirlpool tub, shower and double-bowl vanity. Two family bedrooms reside upstairs.

THIS HOME, AS SHOWN IN THE PHOTOGRAPH, MAY DIFFER FROM THE ACTUAL BLUEPRINTS. FOR MORE DETAILED INFORMATION, PLEASE CHECK THE FLOOR PLANS CAREFULLY. DESIGN BASICS INC. PHOTO BY CARL SAPORITI

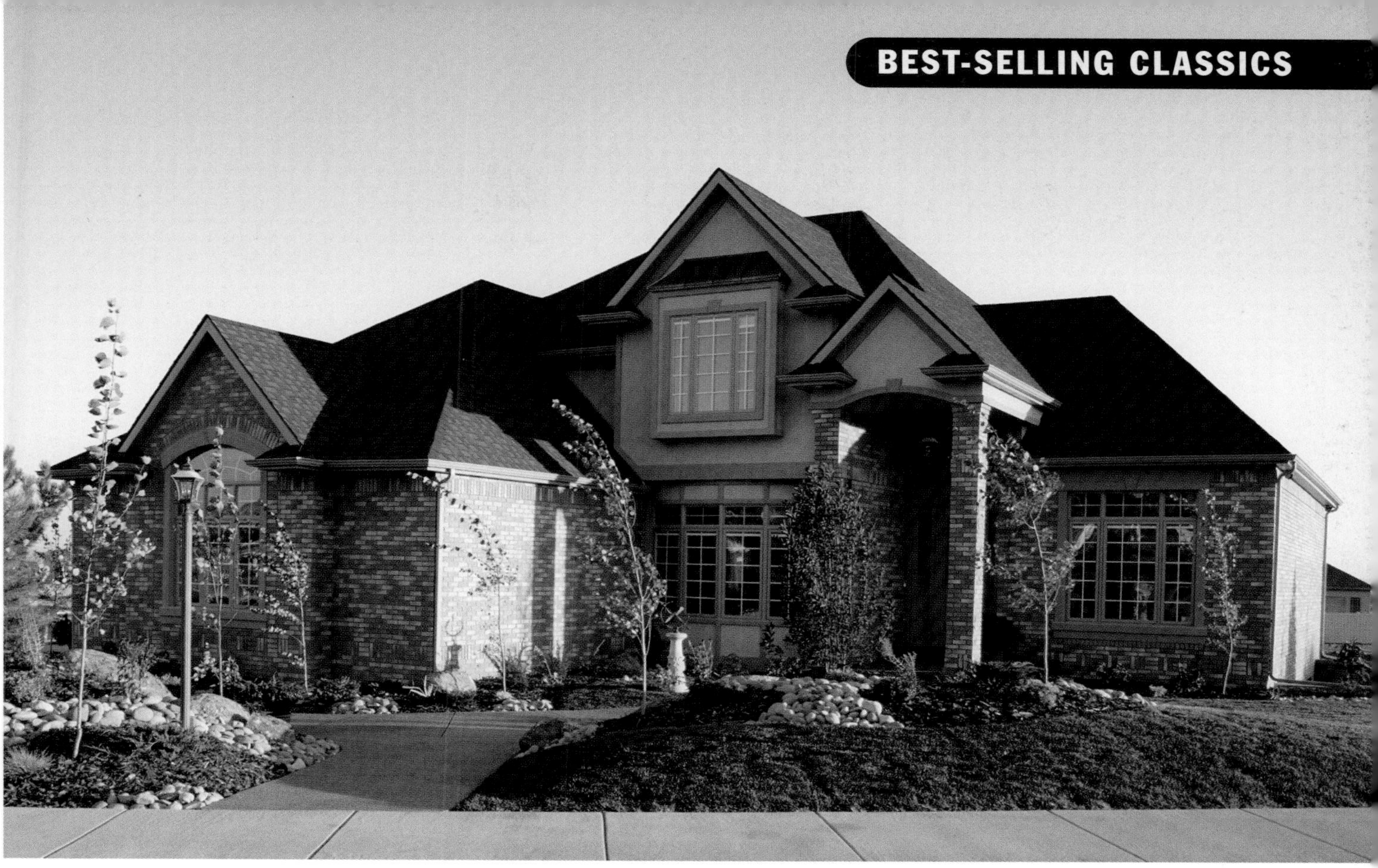

plan# HPT930429

- Style: Traditional
- First Floor: 1,860 sq. ft.
- Second Floor: 848 sq. ft.
- Total: 2,708 sq. ft.
- Bedrooms: 4
- Bathrooms: 3½
- Width: 56'-0"
- Depth: 59'-4"

SEARCH ONLINE @ EPLANS.COM

The gorgeous entry of this traditional home opens to a formal dining room, which offers hutch space, and a volume living room with a see-through fireplace to the spacious family room. Adjacent is the bayed breakfast area and the island kitchen with a wrap-around counter and a walk-in pantry. The master suite is highlighted with a formal ceiling in the bedroom and a bath with a two-person whirlpool tub, bayed windows and a double vanity. Upstairs, two bedrooms share private access to a compartmented bath; another bedroom has a private bath.

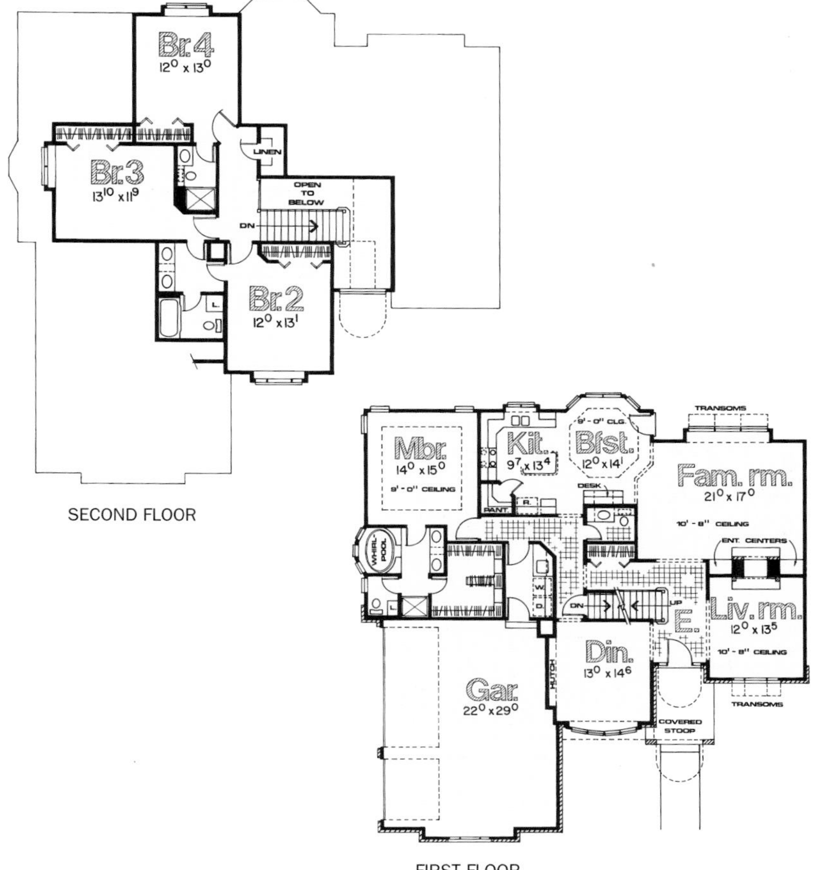

SECOND FLOOR

FIRST FLOOR

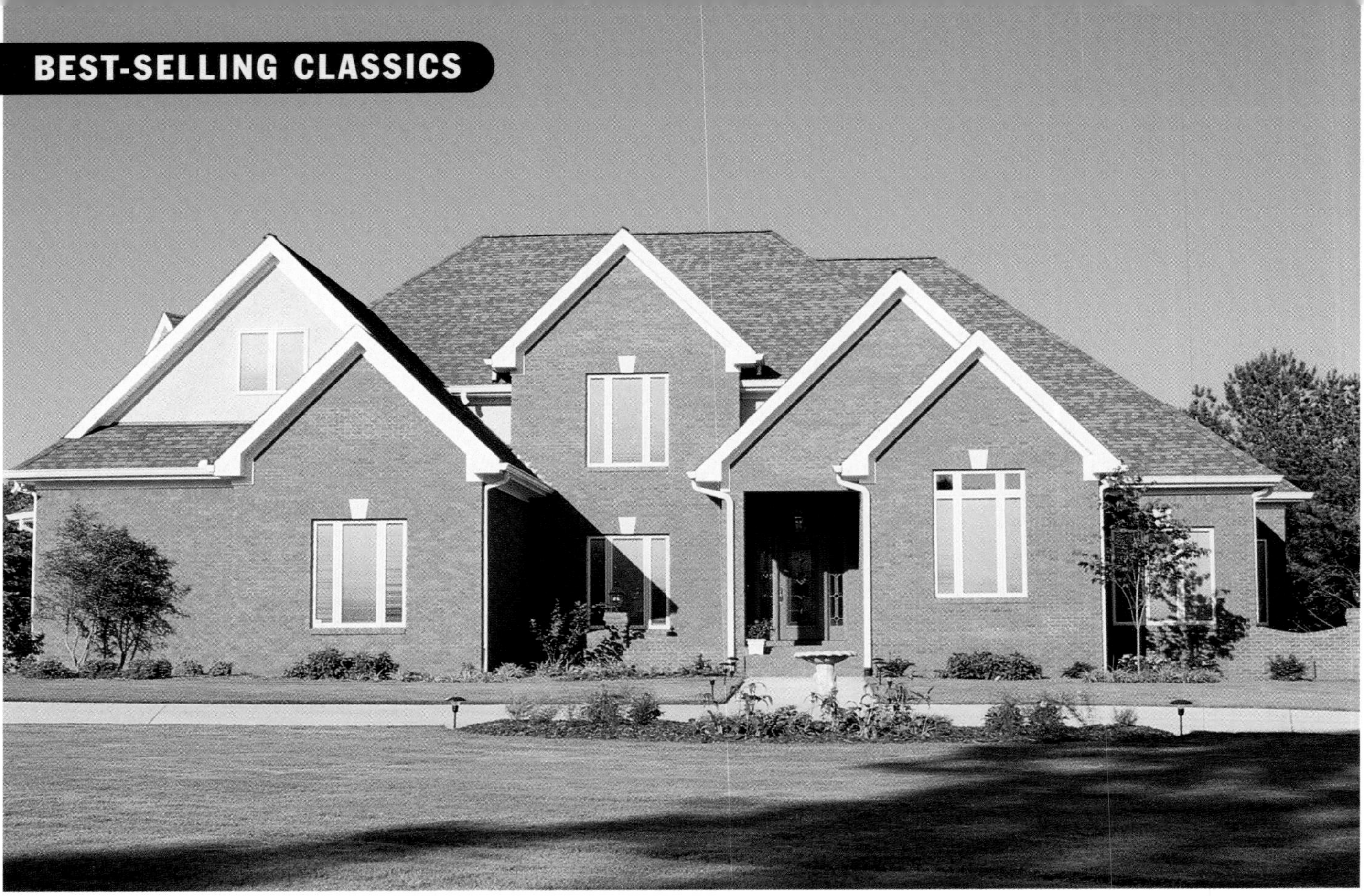

Keystone lintels and an arched transom over the entry spell classic design for this four-bedroom home. The tiled foyer offers entry to any room you choose, whether it be the secluded den with its built-in bookshelves, the formal dining room, the formal living room with its fireplace, or the spacious rear family room and kitchen area with a sunny breakfast nook. The first-floor master suite features a sitting room with bookshelves, two walk-in closets and a private bath with a corner whirlpool tub. Upstairs, two family bedrooms share a bath and enjoy separate vanities. A third family bedroom features its own full bath and a built-in window seat in a box-bay window.

plan# HPT930002

- Style: Traditional
- First Floor: 2,813 sq. ft.
- Second Floor: 1,091 sq. ft.
- Total: 3,904 sq. ft.
- Bedrooms: 4
- Bathrooms: 3½
- Width: 85'-5"
- Depth: 74'-8"

SEARCH ONLINE @ EPLANS.COM

FIRST FLOOR

SECOND FLOOR

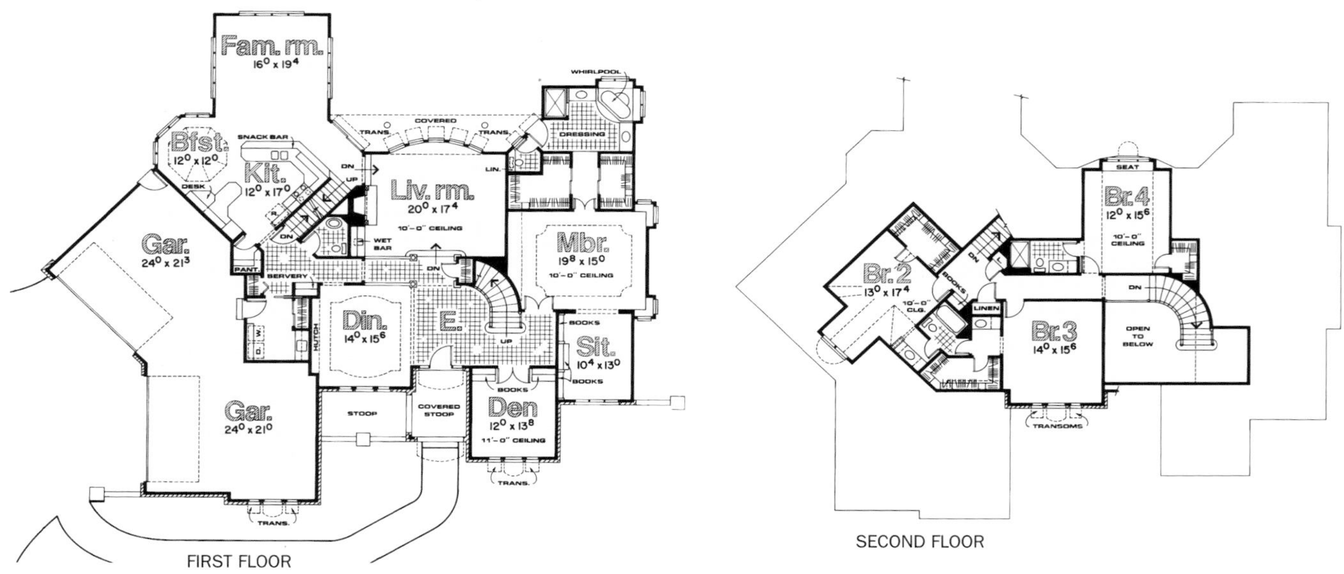

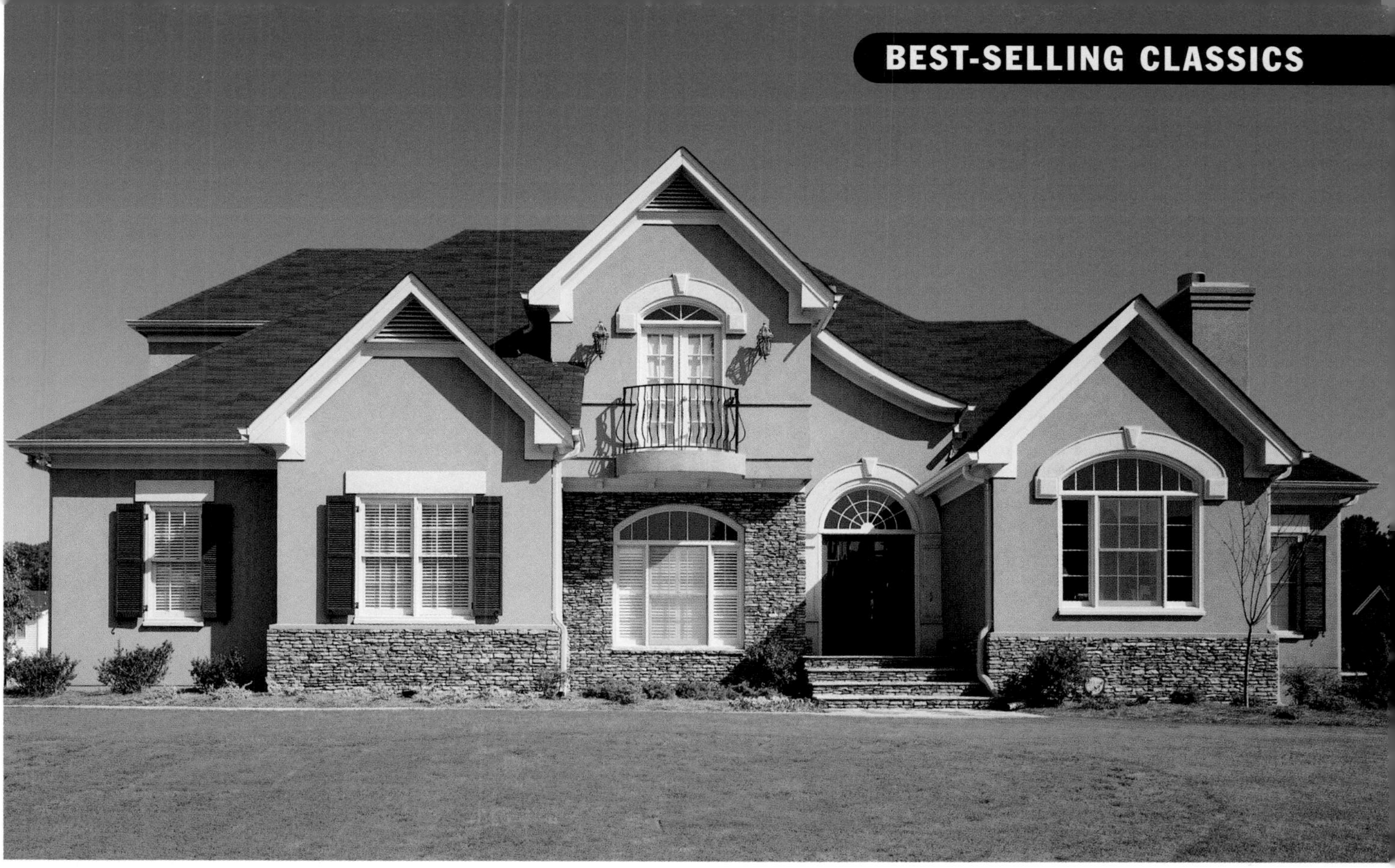

plan# HPT930003

- Style: French
- First Floor: 1,900 sq. ft.
- Second Floor: 800 sq. ft.
- Total: 2,700 sq. ft.
- Bedrooms: 4
- Bathrooms: 2½
- Width: 63'-0"
- Depth: 51'-0"
- Foundation: Walkout Basement

SEARCH ONLINE @ EPLANS.COM

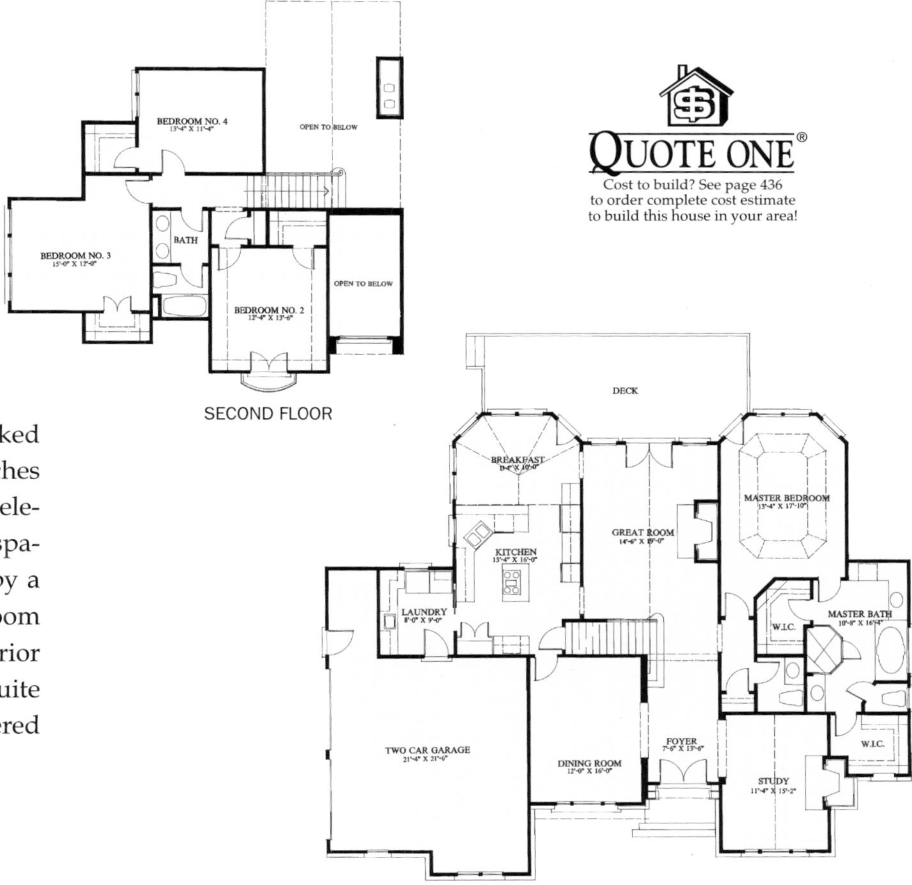

SECOND FLOOR

QUOTE ONE®
Cost to build? See page 436 to order complete cost estimate to build this house in your area!

A perfect blend of stucco and stacked stone sets off keystones, transoms and arches in this French country facade to inspire an elegant spirit. The foyer is flanked by the spacious dining room and study, accented by a vaulted ceiling and a fireplace. A great room with a full wall of glass connects the interior with the outdoors. A first-floor master suite offers both style and intimacy with a coffered ceiling and a secluded bath.

FIRST FLOOR

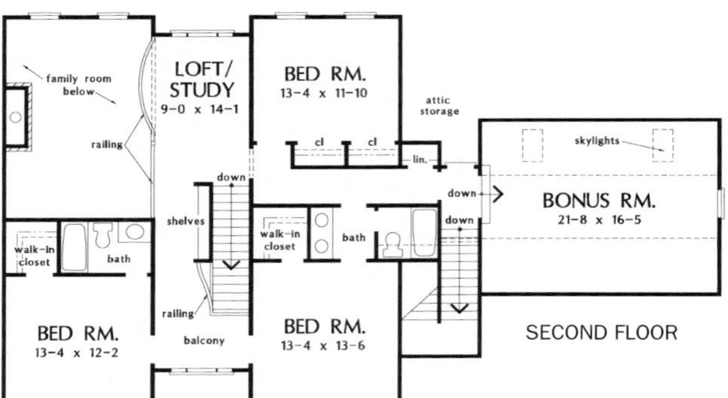

plan# HPT930004

- Style: Country Cottage
- First Floor: 2,086 sq. ft.
- Second Floor: 1,077 sq. ft.
- Total: 3,163 sq. ft.
- Bonus Space: 403 sq. ft.
- Bedrooms: 4
- Bathrooms: 3½
- Width: 81'-10"
- Depth: 51'-8"

SEARCH ONLINE @ EPLANS.COM

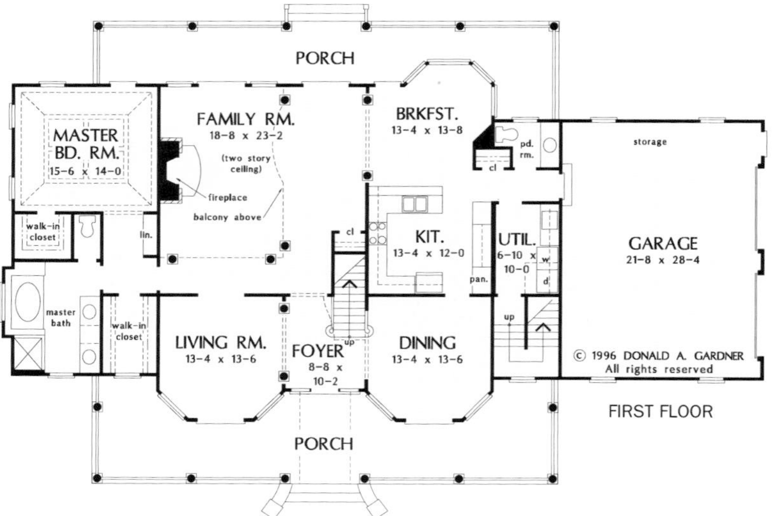

This beautiful farmhouse, with its prominent twin gables and bays, adds just the right amount of country style. The master suite is quietly tucked away downstairs with no rooms directly above. The family cook will love the spacious U-shaped kitchen and adjoining bayed breakfast nook. A bonus room is easily accessible from the back stairs or from the second floor, where three large bedrooms share two full baths. Storage space abounds with walk-ins, half-shelves and linen closets. A curved balcony borders a versatile loft/study, which overlooks the stunning two-story family room.

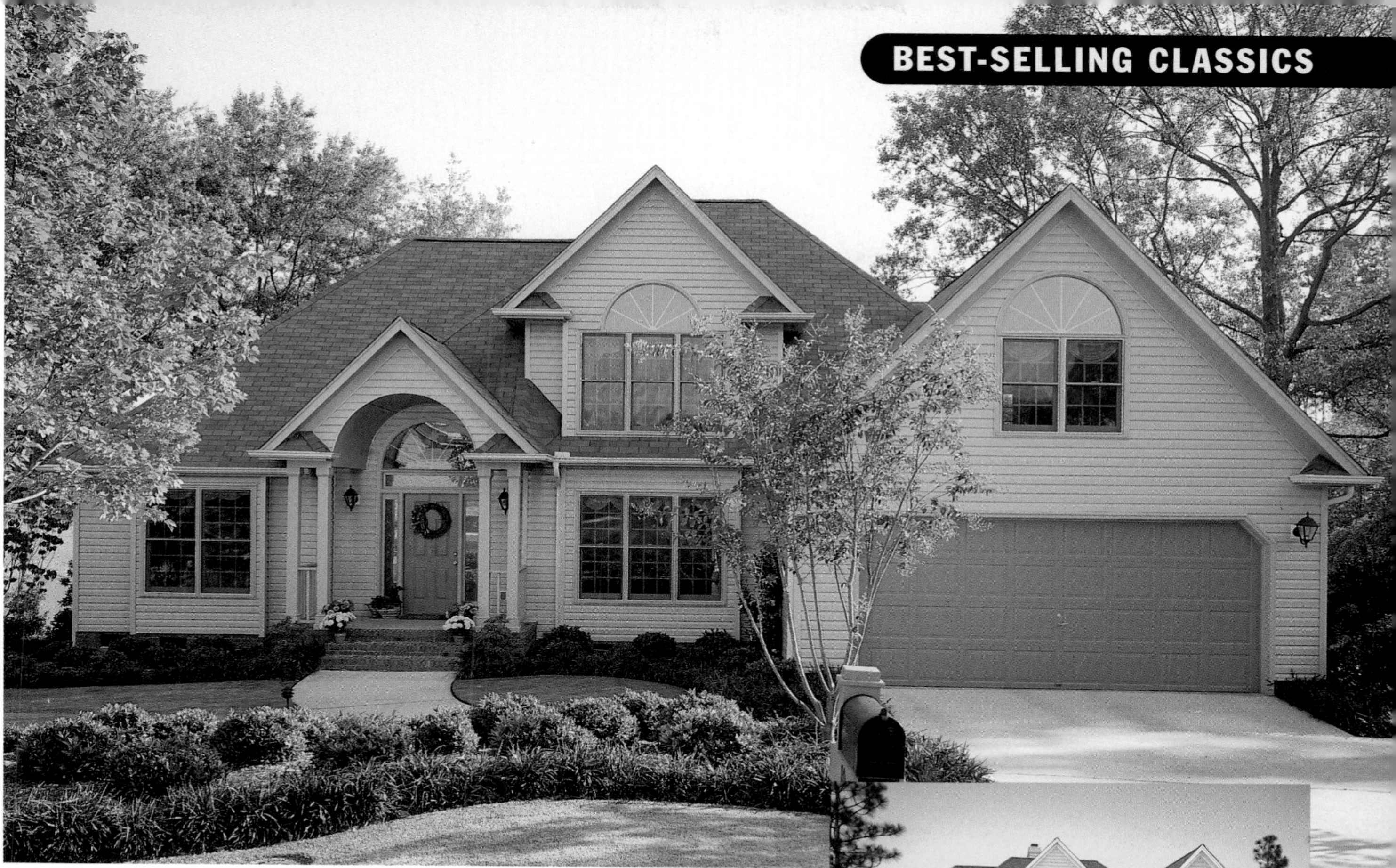

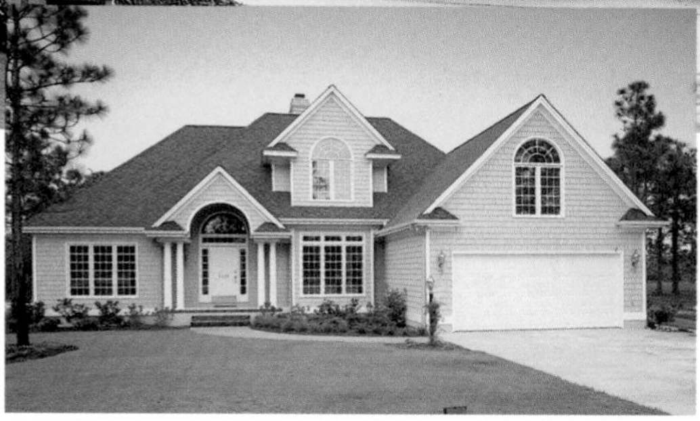

ALTERNATE EXTERIOR

plan# HPT930005

- Style: Bungalow
- First Floor: 1,416 sq. ft.
- Second Floor: 445 sq. ft.
- Total: 1,861 sq. ft.
- Bonus Space: 284 sq. ft.
- Bedrooms: 3
- Bathrooms: 2½
- Width: 58'-3"
- Depth: 68'-6"

SEARCH ONLINE @ EPLANS.COM

QUOTE ONE®
Cost to build? See page 436 to order complete cost estimate to build this house in your area!

Arched windows and triple gables provide a touch of elegance to this traditional home. A barrel-vaulted entrance supported by columns welcomes family and guests inside. On the main level, the dining room offers round columns at the entrance, while the great room boasts a cathedral ceiling, a fireplace, and an arched window over the doors to the deck. The kitchen features an island cooktop and an adjoining breakfast nook for informal dining. The master suite offers twin walk-in closets and a lavish bath that includes a whirlpool tub and a double-basin vanity.

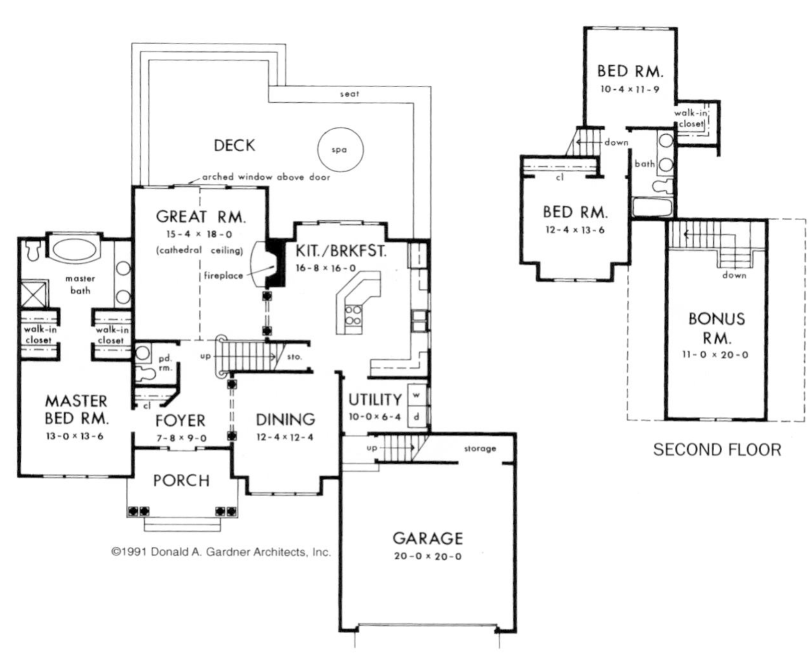

FIRST FLOOR

SECOND FLOOR

INTERIOR PHOTOGRAPHY COURTESY OF HICKORY CHAIR FURNITURE, EXTERIOR PHOTOGRAPHY BY JEFFERY S. OTTO
THIS HOME, AS SHOWN IN THE PHOTOGRAPH, MAY DIFFER FROM THE ACTUAL BLUEPRINTS.
FOR MORE DETAILED INFORMATION, PLEASE CHECK THE FLOOR PLANS CAREFULLY.

With Regency and Colonial Revival architectural characteristics, this home is elegant and comfortable. It combines the best of architecture and design. The master bedroom is complete with a master-suite library featuring one of the two fireplaces in this home. The other fireplace is conveniently located in the keeping room. Three sets of French doors open to the rear terrace. On the second floor, three bedrooms with individual bathrooms make every occupant feel like royalty.

plan# HPT930006

- Style: Georgian
- First Floor: 3,463 sq. ft.
- Second Floor: 1,924 sq. ft.
- Total: 5,387 sq. ft.
- Bedrooms: 4
- Bathrooms: 5½
- Width: 88'-6"
- Depth: 98'-0"
- Foundation: Basement

SEARCH ONLINE @ EPLANS.COM

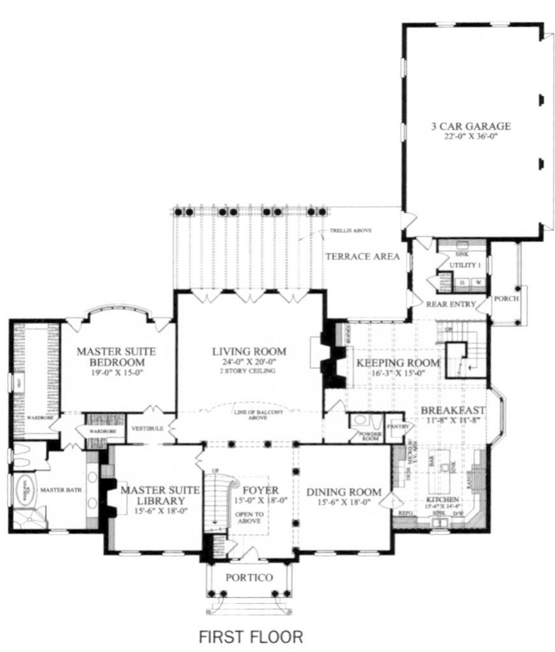

FIRST FLOOR

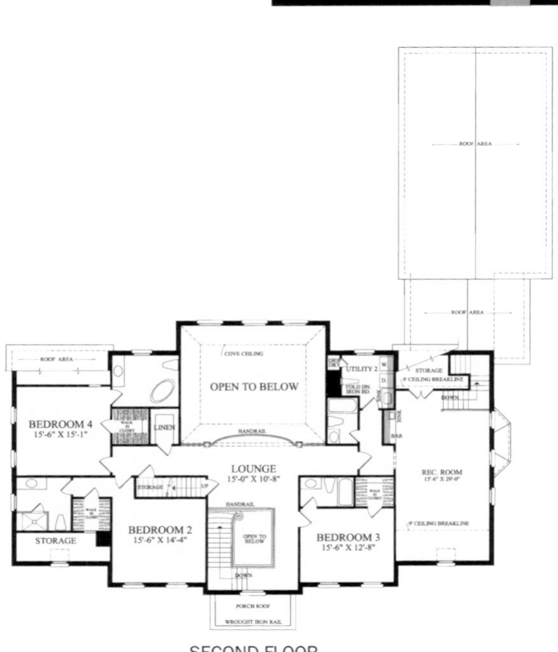

SECOND FLOOR

plan# HPT930007

- Style: Traditional
- First Floor: 2,270 sq. ft.
- Second Floor: 685 sq. ft.
- Total: 2,955 sq. ft.
- Bonus Space: 563 sq. ft.
- Bedrooms: 3
- Bathrooms: 2½
- Width: 75'-1"
- Depth: 53'-6"

SEARCH ONLINE @ EPLANS.COM

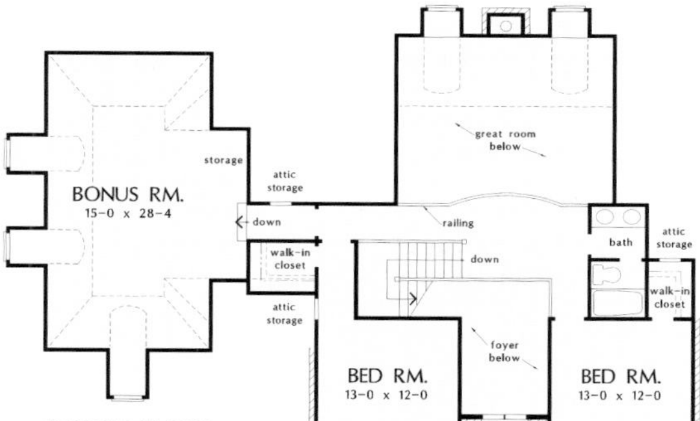

SECOND FLOOR

Hipped rooflines, sunburst windows and French-style shutters are the defining elements of this home's exterior. Inside, the foyer is flanked by the dining room and the study. Further on, the lavish great room can be entered through two stately columns, and is complete with a fireplace, built-in shelves, a vaulted ceiling and views to the rear patio. The island kitchen easily accesses a pantry and a desk and flows into the bayed breakfast area. The first-floor master bedroom enjoys a fireplace, two walk-in closets and an amenity-filled private bath. Two additional bedrooms reside upstairs, along with a sizable bonus room.

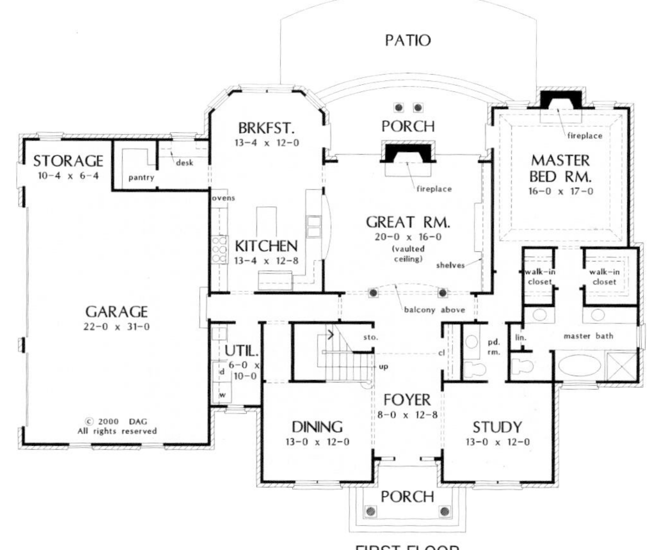

FIRST FLOOR

QUOTE ONE®

Cost to build? See page 436 to order complete cost estimate to build this house in your area!

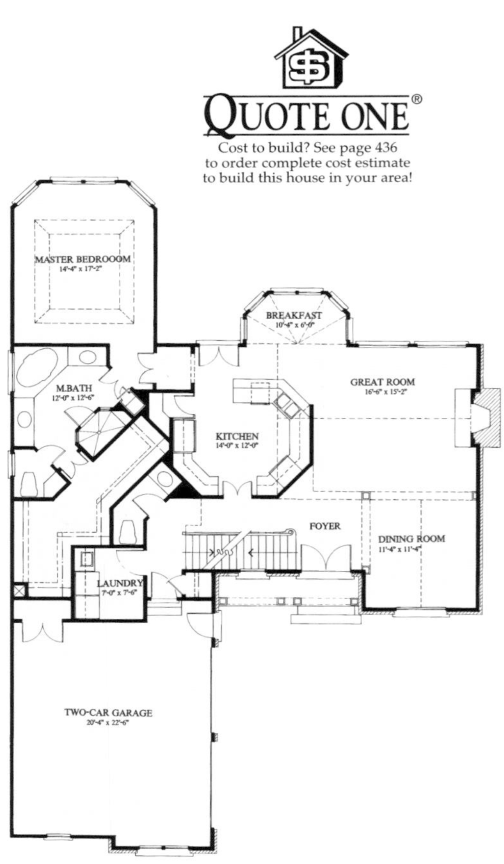

FIRST FLOOR

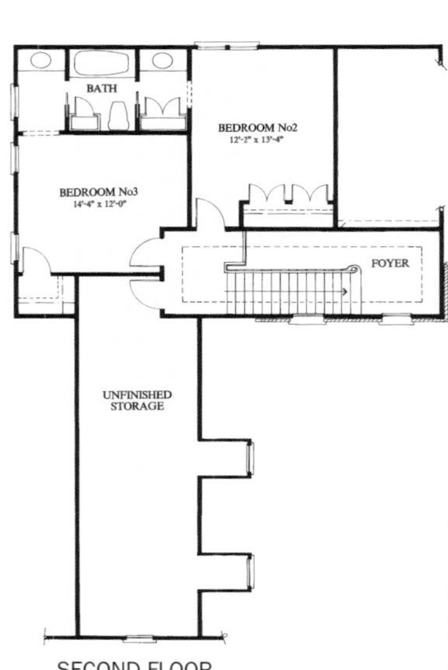

SECOND FLOOR

plan# HPT930008

- Style: Traditional
- First Floor: 1,580 sq. ft.
- Second Floor: 595 sq. ft.
- Total: 2,175 sq. ft.
- Bedrooms: 3
- Bathrooms: 2½
- Width: 50'-2"
- Depth: 70'-11"
- Foundation: Walkout Basement

SEARCH ONLINE  EPLANS.COM

This home is a true Southern original. Inside, the spacious foyer leads directly to a large vaulted great room with its handsome fireplace. The dining room, just off the foyer, features a dramatic vaulted ceiling. The spacious kitchen offers both storage and large work areas opening up to the breakfast room. At the rear of the home, you will find the master suite with its garden bath, His and Hers vanities and an oversized closet. The second floor provides two additional bedrooms with a shared bath and a balcony overlook to the foyer below.

THIS HOME, AS SHOWN IN THE PHOTOGRAPH, MAY DIFFER FROM THE ACTUAL BLUEPRINTS. FOR MORE DETAILED INFORMATION, PLEASE CHECK THE FLOOR PLANS CAREFULLY.

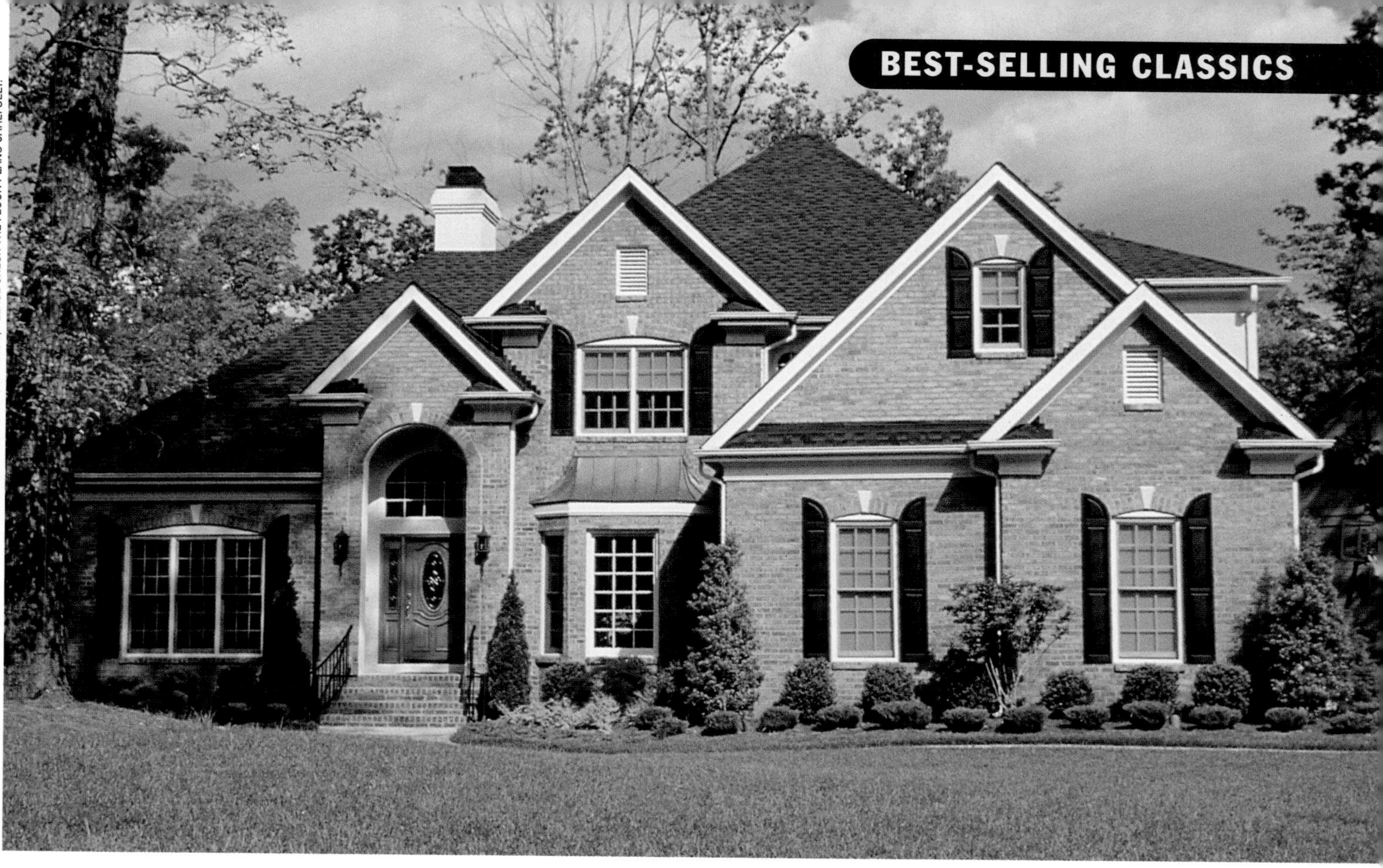

plan# HPT930009

- Style: Traditional
- First Floor: 1,878 sq. ft.
- Second Floor: 886 sq. ft.
- Total: 2,764 sq. ft.
- Bedrooms: 4
- Bathrooms: 3½
- Width: 67'-10"
- Depth: 56'-4"
- Foundation: Basement

SEARCH ONLINE @ EPLANS.COM

This distinguished brick home with traditional stucco accents includes a spectacular, two-story foyer and grand room featuring a dramatic Palladian window. The grand room also opens to the kitchen and morning room. The master suite and morning room create matching bay wings to form a beautiful rear facade. A deck/terrace is accessible from both wings. The master suite features a tray ceiling in the bedroom, a large walk-in closet and a bath with dual vanities and a garden tub. Upstairs, three additional suites share two baths. This design offers a basement plan that includes a guest suite and recreation area.

BASEMENT

SECOND FLOOR

FIRST FLOOR

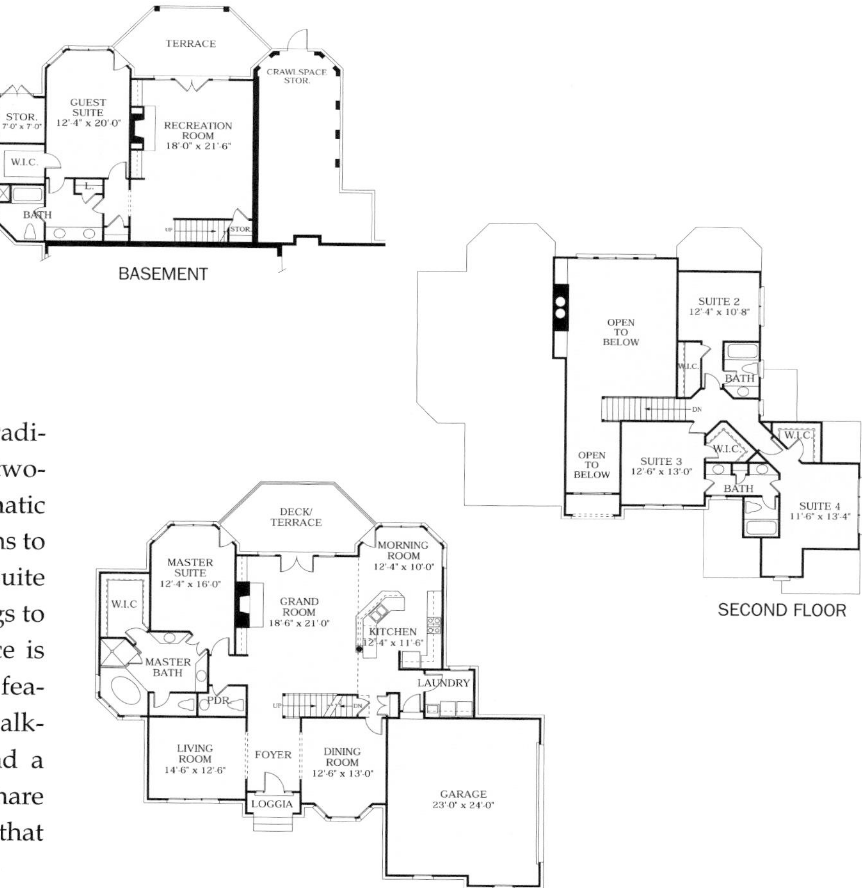

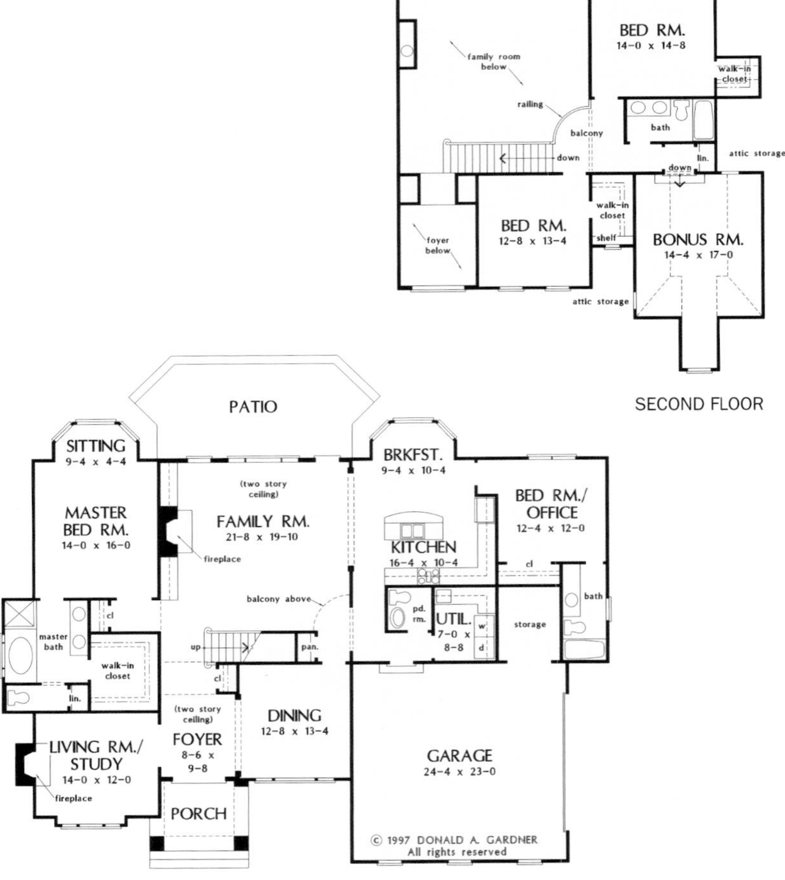

SECOND FLOOR

FIRST FLOOR

plan# HPT930010

- Style: Traditional
- First Floor: 2,249 sq. ft.
- Second Floor: 620 sq. ft.
- Total: 2,869 sq. ft.
- Bonus Space: 308 sq. ft.
- Bedrooms: 4
- Bathrooms: 3½
- Width: 69'-6"
- Depth: 52'-0"

SEARCH ONLINE @ EPLANS.COM

An impressive two-story entrance welcomes you to this stately home. Massive chimneys and pillars and varying rooflines add interest to the stucco exterior. The foyer, lighted by a clerestory window, opens to the formal living and dining rooms. The living room—which could also serve as a study—features a fireplace, as does the family room. Both rooms access the patio. The L-shaped island kitchen opens to a bay-windowed breakfast nook, which is echoed by the sitting area in the master suite. A room next to the kitchen could serve as a bedroom or a home office. The second floor contains two family bedrooms plus a bonus room for future expansion.

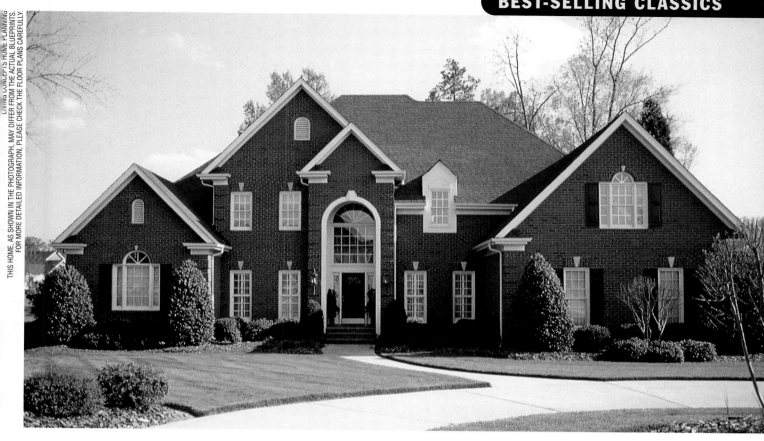

plan# HPT930011

- Style: Transitional
- First Floor: 2,198 sq. ft.
- Second Floor: 1,028 sq. ft.
- Total: 3,226 sq. ft.
- Bonus Space: 466 sq. ft.
- Bedrooms: 4
- Bathrooms: 3½
- Width: 72'-8"
- Depth: 56'-6"
- Foundation: Crawlspace

SEARCH ONLINE @ EPLANS.COM

Designed for active lifestyles, this home caters to homeowners who enjoy dinner guests, privacy, luxurious surroundings and open spaces. The foyer, parlor and dining hall are defined by sets of columns and share a gallery hall that runs through the center of the plan. The grand room opens to the deck/terrace, which is also accessed from the sitting area and morning room. The right wing of the plan contains the well-appointed kitchen. The left wing is dominated by the master suite with its sitting bay, fireplace, two walk-in closets and compartmented bath.

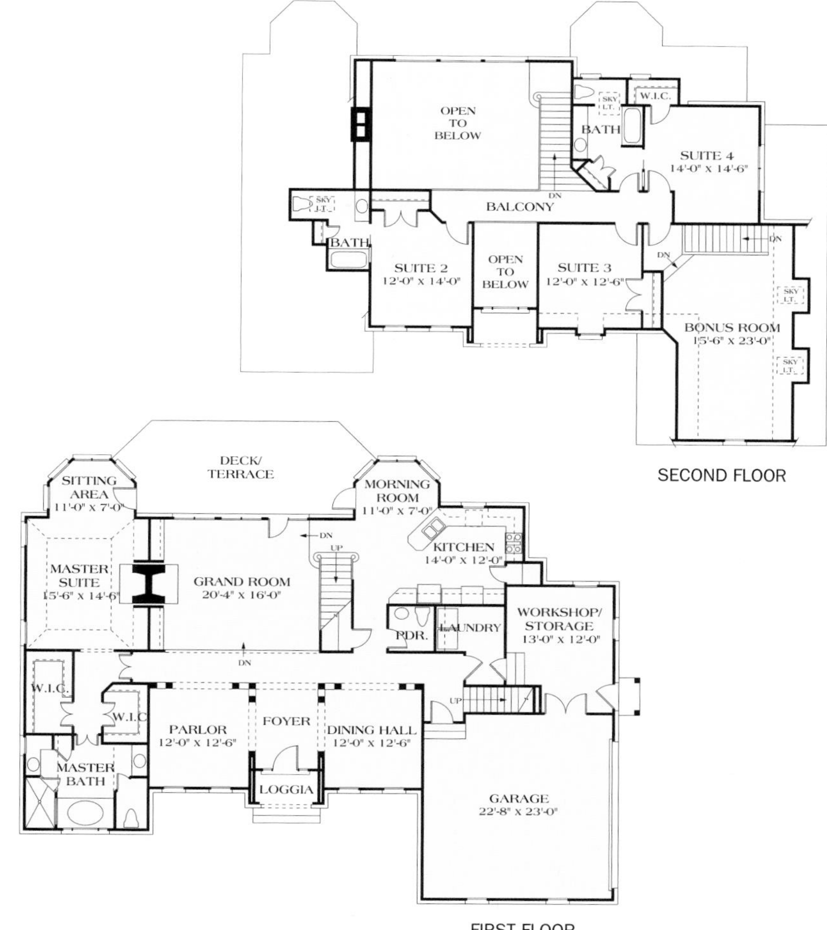

SECOND FLOOR

FIRST FLOOR

©LAURENCE TAYLOR PHOTOGRAPHY
THIS HOME, AS SHOWN IN THE PHOTOGRAPH, MAY DIFFER FROM THE ACTUAL BLUEPRINTS.
FOR MORE DETAILED INFORMATION, PLEASE CHECK THE FLOOR PLANS CAREFULLY.

QUOTE ONE®

Cost to build? See page 436 to order complete cost estimate to build this house in your area!

SECOND FLOOR

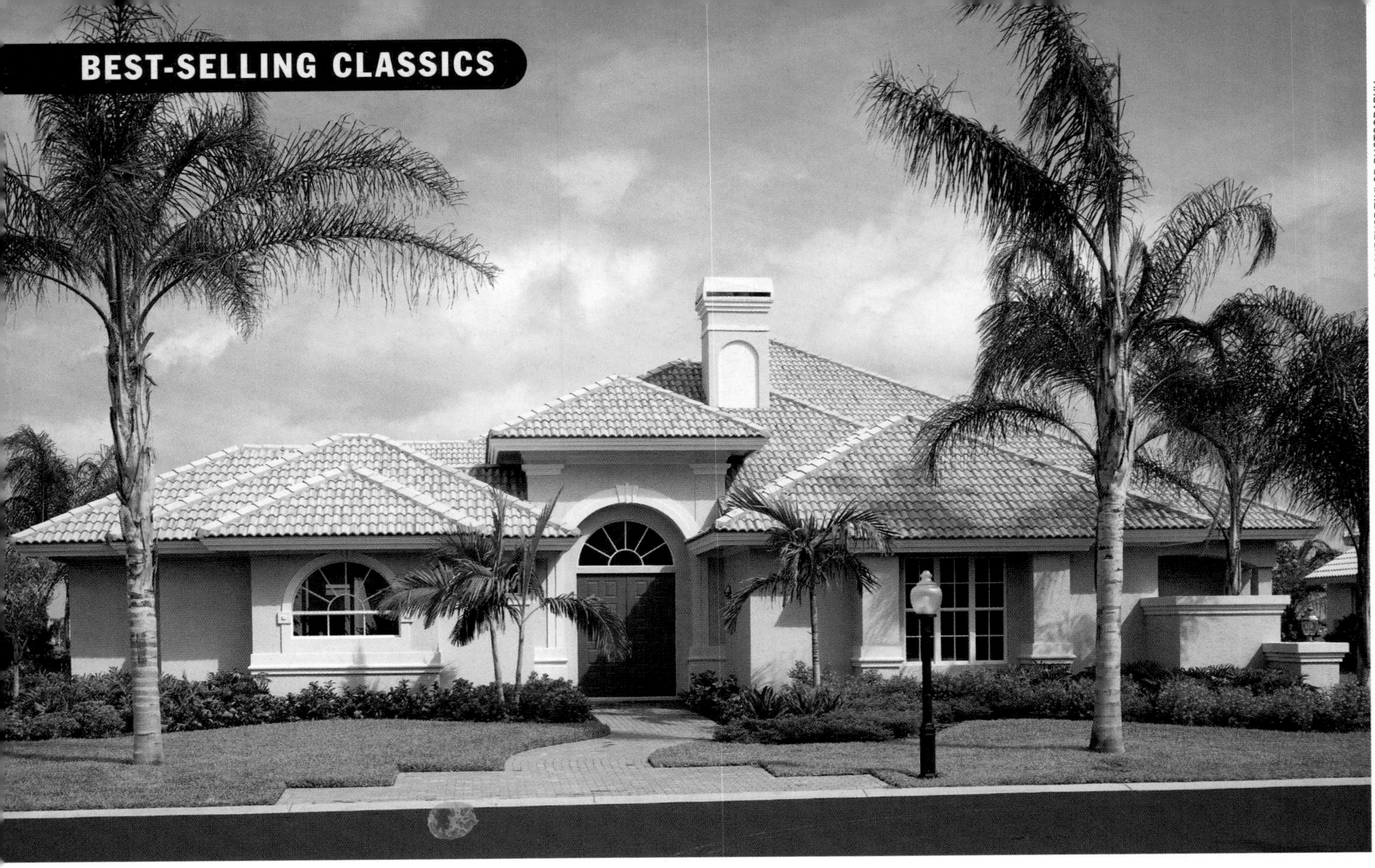

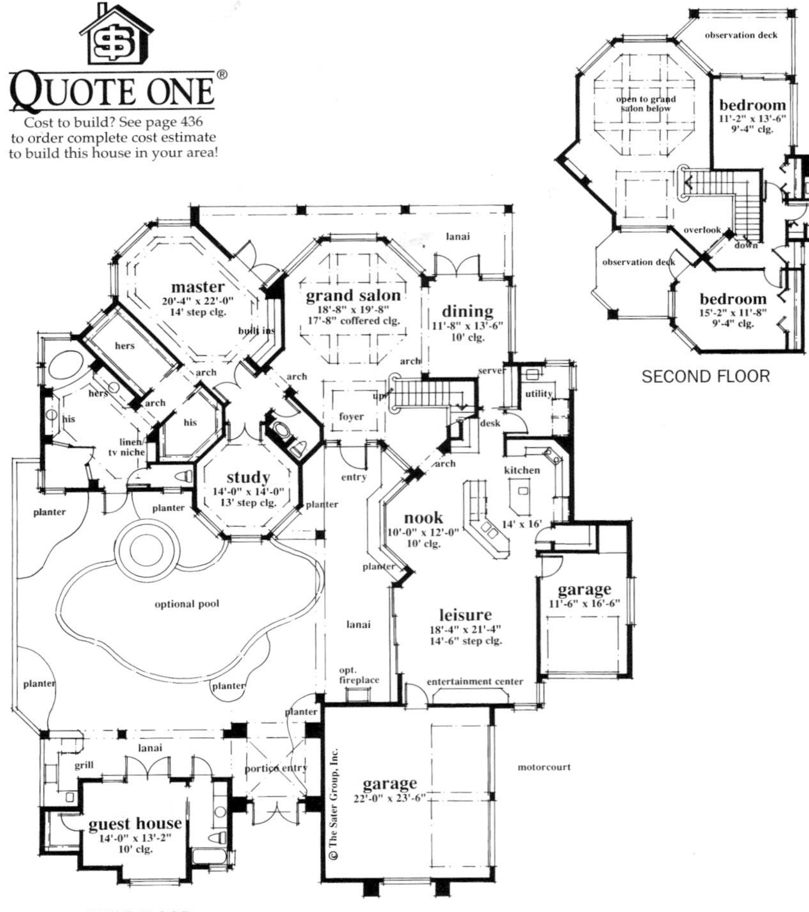

plan# HPT930012 L

- Style: Floridian
- First Floor: 2,853 sq. ft.
- Second Floor: 627 sq. ft.
- Total: 3,480 sq. ft.
- Bedrooms: 3
- Bathrooms: 3½
- Width: 80'-0"
- Depth: 96'-0"
- Foundation: Slab

SEARCH ONLINE @ EPLANS.COM

FIRST FLOOR

A unique courtyard provides a happy marriage of indoor/outdoor relationships for this design. Inside, the foyer opens to a grand salon with a wall of glass, providing unobstructed views of the backyard. Informal areas include a leisure room with an entertainment center and glass doors that open to a covered poolside lanai. An outdoor fireplace enhances casual gatherings. The master suite is filled with amenities that include a bayed sitting area, access to the rear lanai, His and Hers closets and a soaking tub. Upstairs, two family bedrooms—both with private decks—share a full bath. A detached guest house has a cabana bath and an outdoor grill area.

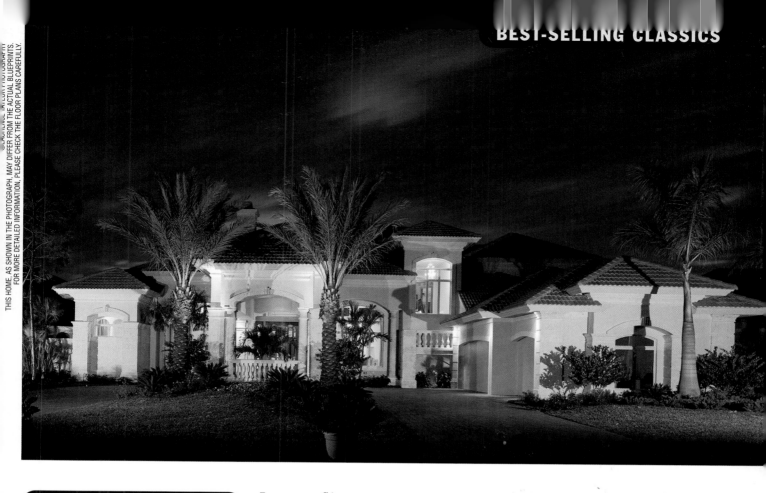

plan# HPT930013

- Style: Mediterranean
- First Floor: 3,852 sq. ft.
- Second Floor: 903 sq. ft.
- Total: 4,755 sq. ft.
- Bedrooms: 5
- Bathrooms: 6
- Width: 81'-10"
- Depth: 104'-0"
- Foundation: Slab

SEARCH ONLINE @ EPLANS.COM

Low rooflines and grand arches lend a Mediterranean flavor to this contemporary estate. Lovely glass-paneled doors lead to an open interior defined by decorative columns, stone arches and solid coffered ceilings. A formal living room boasts a fireplace and amazing views. Leisure space invites casual gatherings and allows the family to kick off their shoes and relax. A favorite feature, the outdoor kitchen encourages dining alfresco. A secluded master suite rambles across the right wing and includes a quiet study with a vintage high-beam ceiling, a sitting area, splendid bath and access to the veranda.

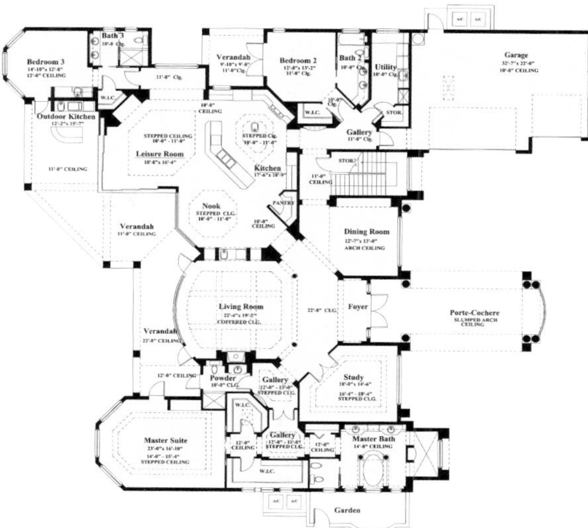

FIRST FLOOR

SECOND FLOOR

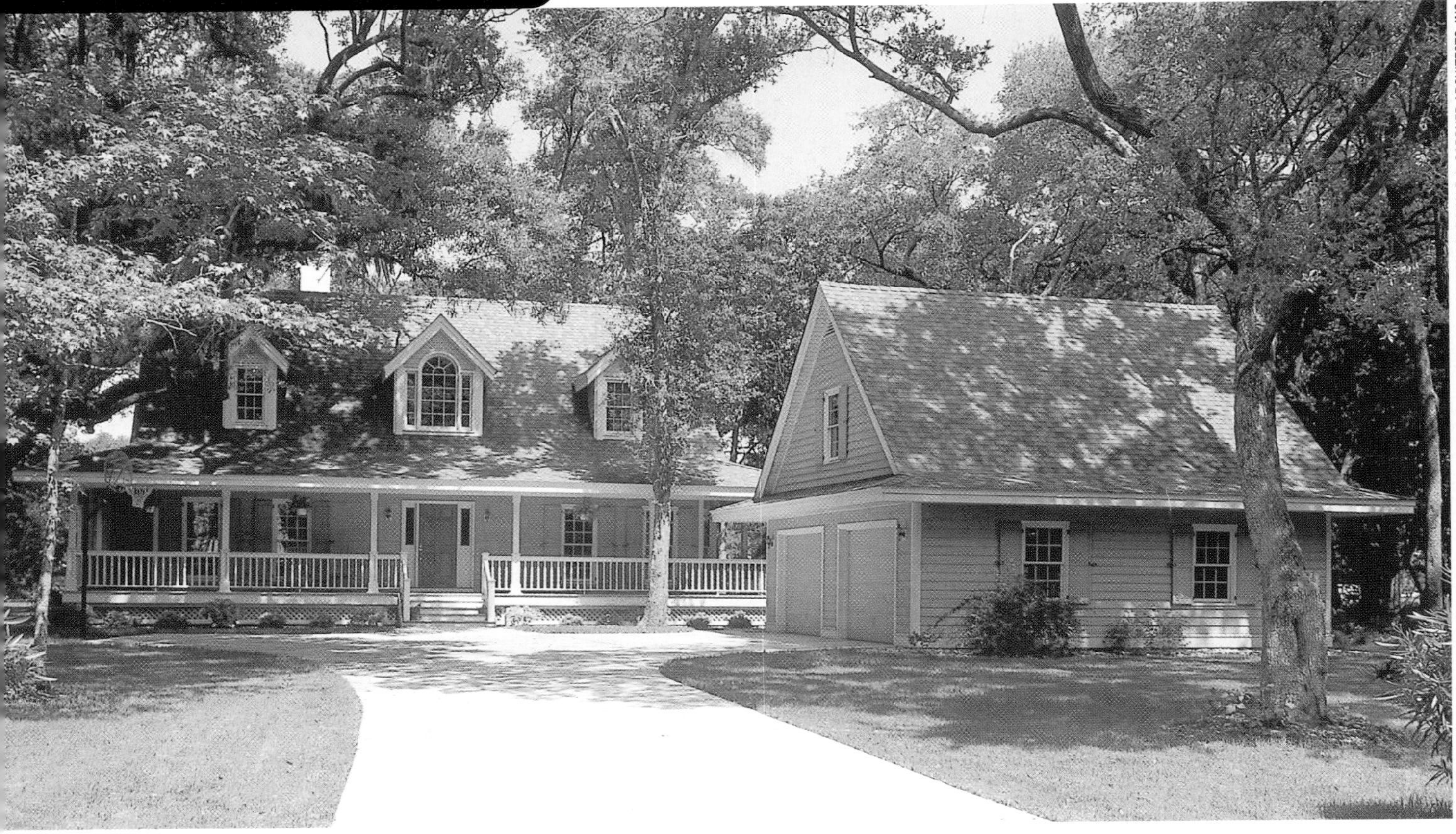

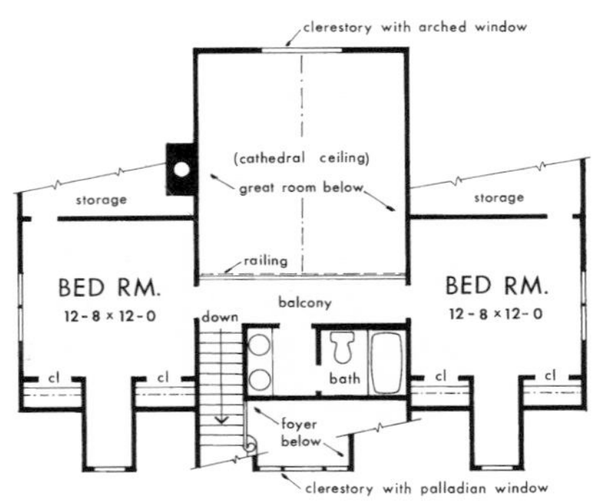

SECOND FLOOR

plan# HPT930014

- Style: Farmhouse
- First Floor: 1,651 sq. ft.
- Second Floor: 567 sq. ft.
- Total: 2,218 sq. ft.
- Bedrooms: 3
- Bathrooms: 2½
- Width: 55'-0"
- Depth: 53'-10"

SEARCH ONLINE @ EPLANS.COM

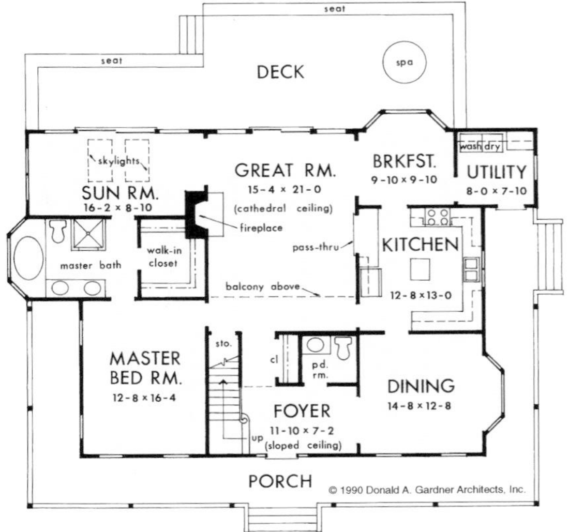

FIRST FLOOR

A wonderful wraparound covered porch at the front and sides of this house and the open deck with a spa at the back provide plenty of outside living area. Inside, the spacious great room is appointed with a fireplace, cathedral ceiling and clerestory with an arched window. The kitchen is centrally located for maximum flexibility in layout and features a food-preparation island for convenience. In addition to the master bedroom, with access to the sun room, there are two second-level bedrooms that share a full bath.

plan# HPT930015

- Style: Country
- First Floor: 1,293 sq. ft.
- Second Floor: 629 sq. ft.
- Total: 1,922 sq. ft.
- Bonus Space: 342 sq. ft.
- Bedrooms: 3
- Bathrooms: 2½
- Width: 58'-0"
- Depth: 55'-0"
- Foundation: Basement

SEARCH ONLINE @ EPLANS.COM

Country finesse and stylish charm present a lovely siding and stone exterior. The rear of the house encourages outdoor relaxation with abundant porches, an elegant bayed turret and a graceful curved stairway cascading from a second-floor porch to the rear patio. Inside, the family room is warmed by a large fireplace, while the dining room is illuminated by the spectacular turret bay. The first-floor master suite is enchanting with a walk-in closet and a private bath. Upstairs, three family bedrooms share a full hall bath and a study loft area.

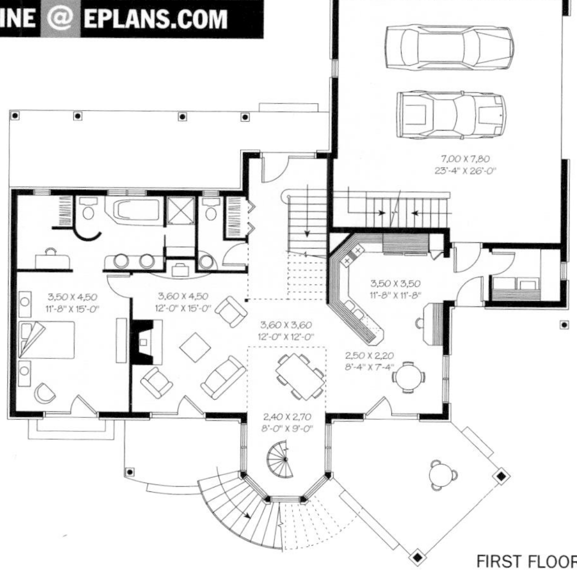

FIRST FLOOR

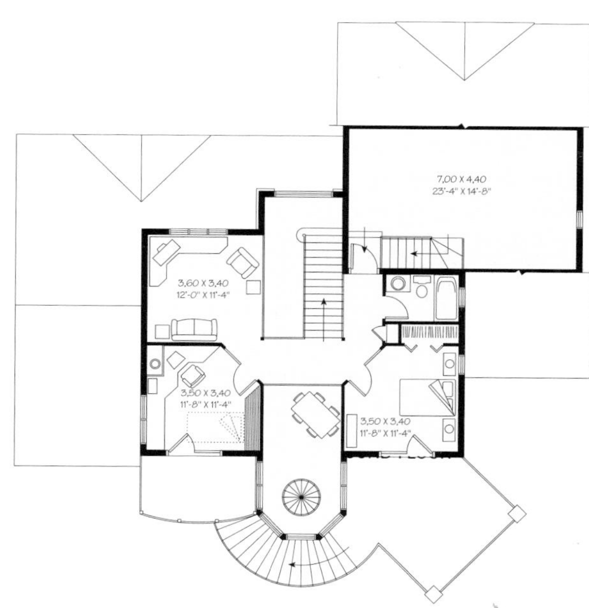

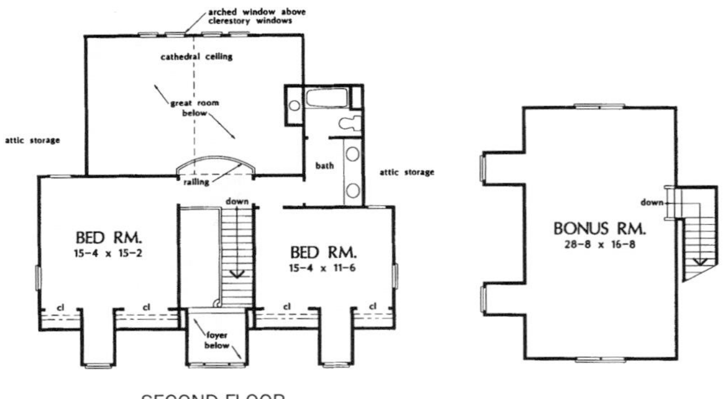

SECOND FLOOR

plan# HPT930016

- Style: Farmhouse
- First Floor: 2,316 sq. ft.
- Second Floor: 721 sq. ft.
- Total: 3,037 sq. ft.
- Bonus Space: 545 sq. ft.
- Bedrooms: 4
- Bathrooms: 3½
- Width: 95'-4"
- Depth: 54'-10"

SEARCH ONLINE @ EPLANS.COM

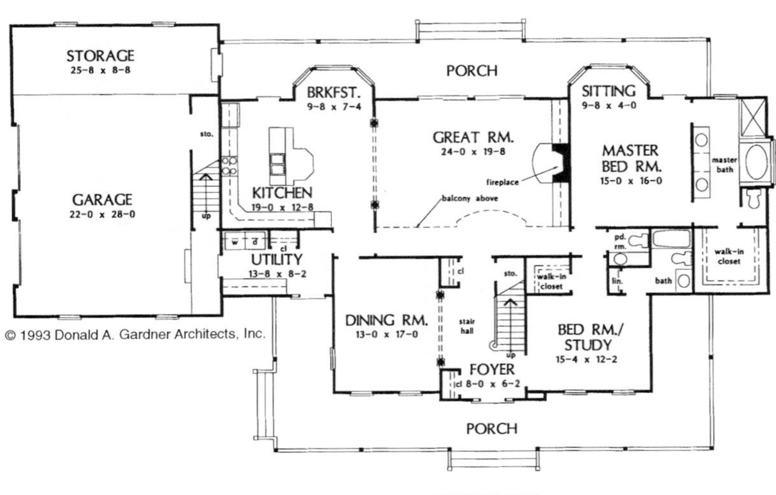

FIRST FLOOR

Three dormers top a very welcoming covered wraparound porch on this attractive country home. The entrance enjoys a Palladian clerestory window, lending an abundance of natural light to the foyer. The great room furthers this feeling of airiness with a balcony above and two sets of sliding glass doors leading to the back porch. For privacy, the master suite occupies the right side of the first floor. With a sitting bay and all the amenities of a modern master bath, this lavish retreat will be a welcome haven for the homeowner. Two family bedrooms reside upstairs, sharing a balcony over look into the great room.

THIS HOME, AS SHOWN IN THE PHOTOGRAPH, MAY DIFFER FROM THE ACTUAL BLUEPRINTS.
FOR MORE DETAILED INFORMATION, PLEASE CHECK THE FLOOR PLANS CAREFULLY.

ALTERNATE EXTERIOR

plan# HPT930017

- Style: Farmhouse
- First Floor: 1,356 sq. ft.
- Second Floor: 542 sq. ft.
- Total: 1,898 sq. ft.
- Bonus Space: 393 sq. ft.
- Bedrooms: 3
- Bathrooms: 2½
- Width: 59'-0"
- Depth: 64'-0"

SEARCH ONLINE @ EPLANS.COM

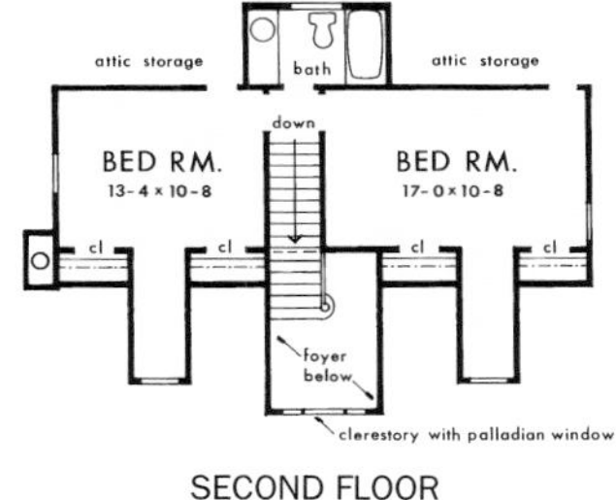

SECOND FLOOR

The welcoming charm of this country farmhouse is expressed by its many windows and its covered wraparound porch. A two-story entrance foyer is enhanced by a Palladian window in a clerestory dormer above to let in natural lighting. The first-floor master suite allows privacy and accessibility. The master bath includes a whirlpool tub, separate shower, double-bowl vanity and walk-in closet. The first floor features nine-foot ceilings throughout with the exception of the kitchen area, which sports an eight-foot ceiling. The second floor contains two additional bedrooms, a full bath and plenty of storage space. The bonus room provides room to grow.

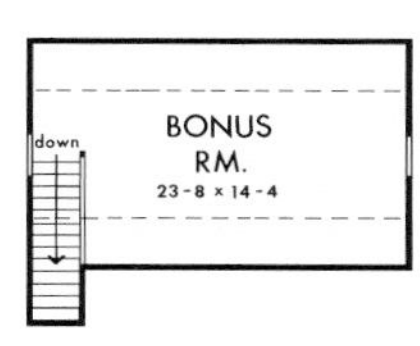

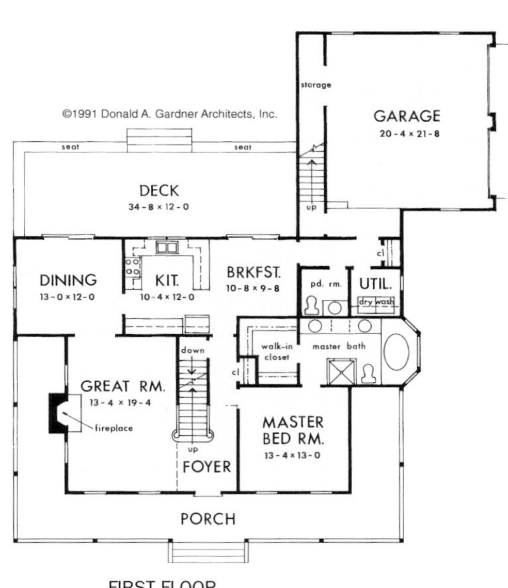

FIRST FLOOR

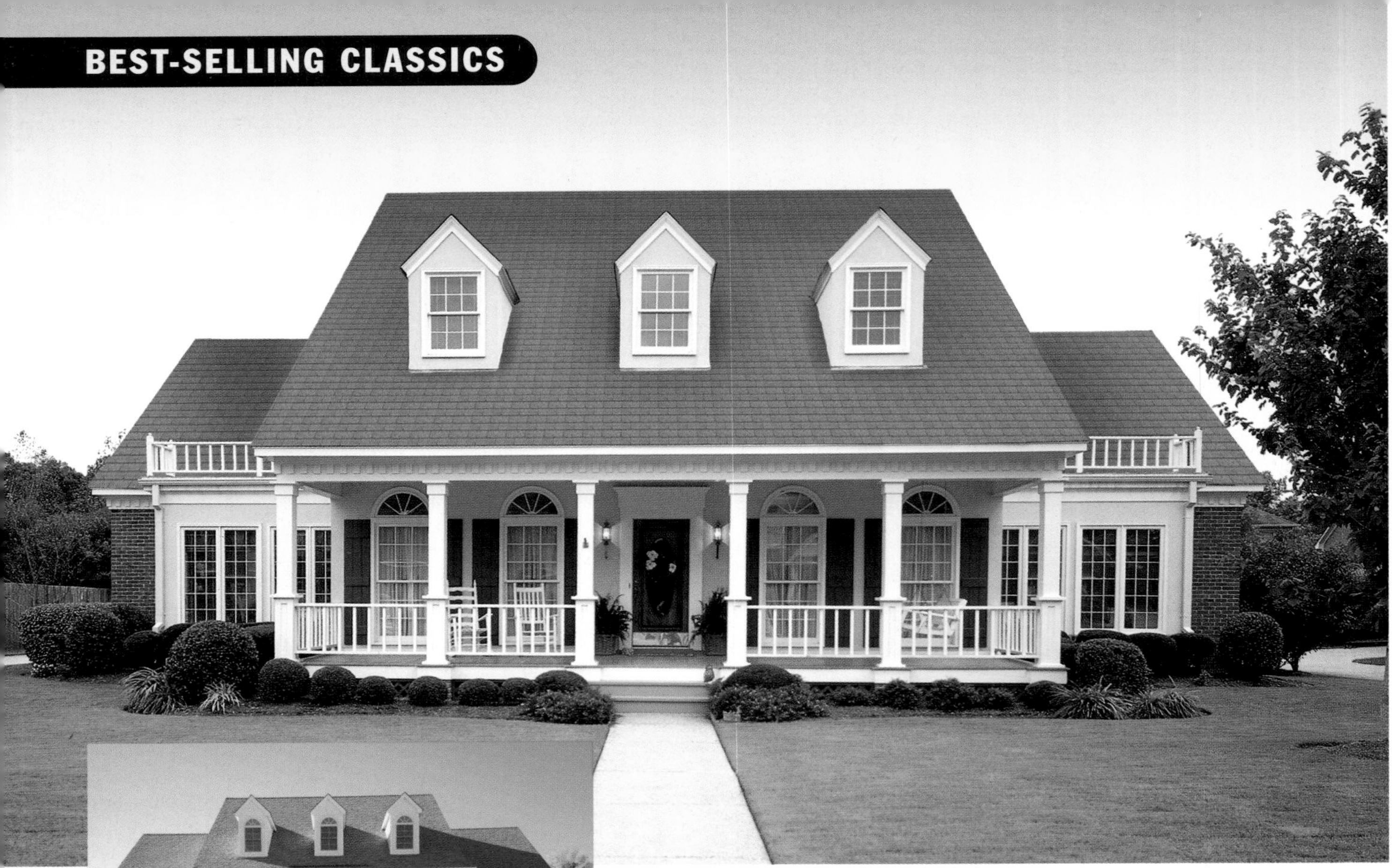

BRELAND & FARMER
THIS HOME, AS SHOWN IN THE PHOTOGRAPH, MAY DIFFER FROM THE ACTUAL BLUEPRINTS.
FOR MORE DETAILED INFORMATION, PLEASE CHECK THE FLOOR PLANS CAREFULLY.

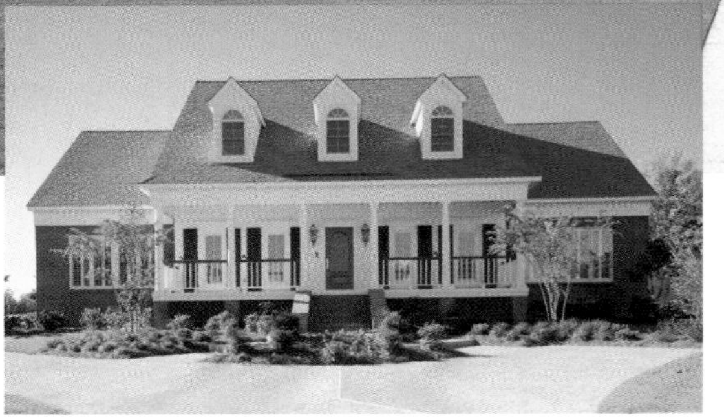

ALTERNATE EXTERIOR

plan# HPT930018

- Style: Plantation
- First Floor: 2,092 sq. ft.
- Second Floor: 1,027 sq. ft.
- Total: 3,119 sq. ft.
- Bedrooms: 4
- Bathrooms: 3½
- Width: 66'-0"
- Depth: 80'-0"
- Foundation: Crawlspace

SEARCH ONLINE @ EPLANS.COM

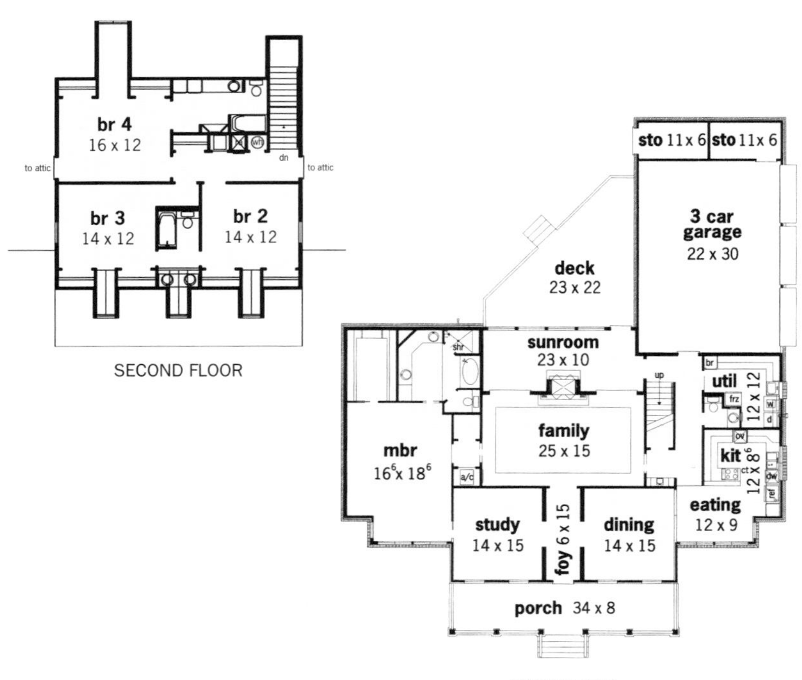

SECOND FLOOR

FIRST FLOOR

This Southern plantation home, featuring traditional accents such as front-facing dormers, a covered front porch and a stucco-and-brick facade, will be the delight of any fine neighborhood. Inside, a study and formal dining room flank the foyer. The family room shares a two-sided fireplace with the refreshing sun room, which overlooks the rear deck. The kitchen shares space with an eating area overlooking the front yard. The first-floor master suite features a large closet and a private bath. Three additional bedrooms and two baths are located upstairs.

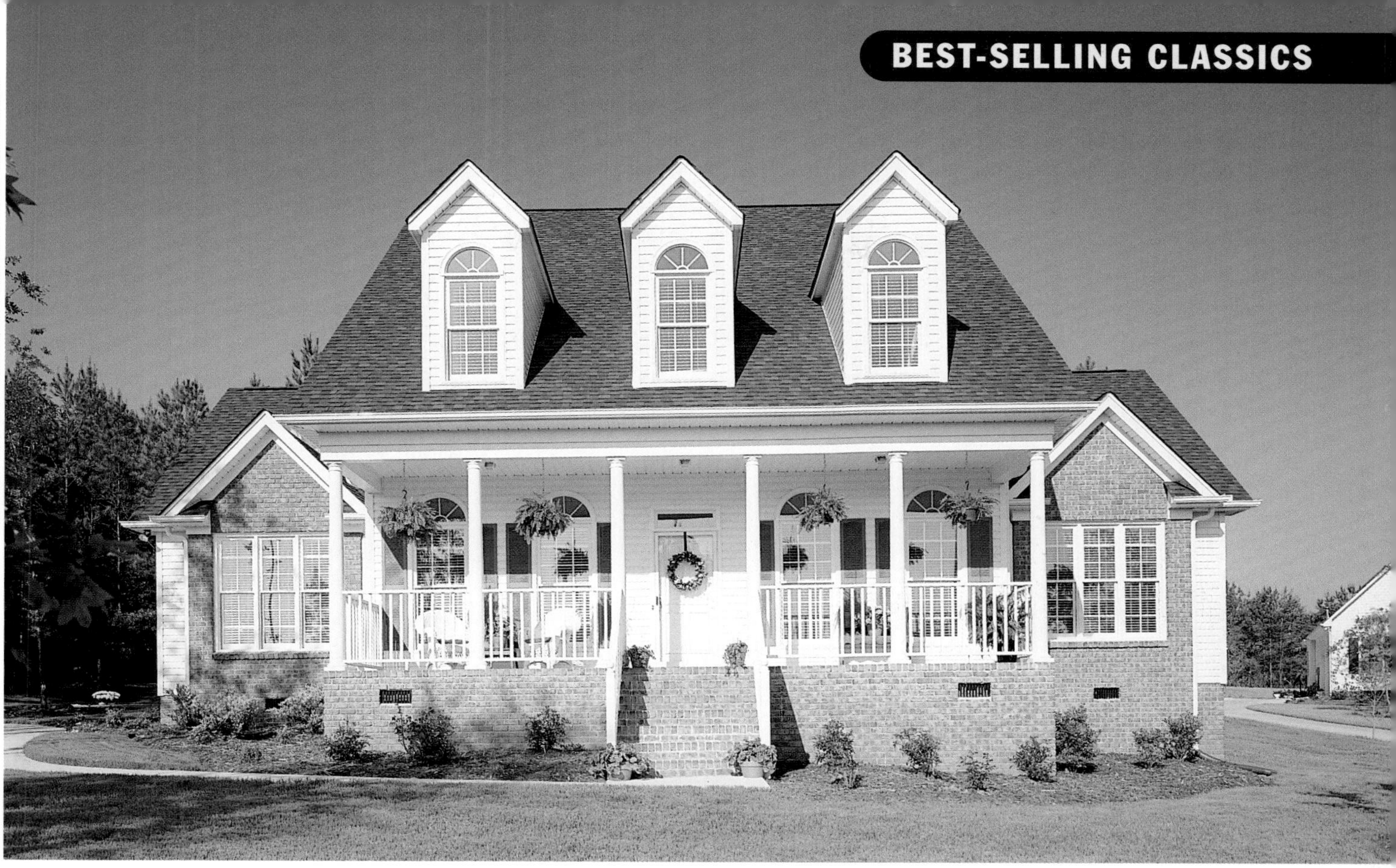

plan# HPT930019

- Style: Farmhouse
- First Floor: 1,783 sq. ft.
- Second Floor: 611 sq. ft.
- Total: 2,394 sq. ft.
- Bedrooms: 4
- Bathrooms: 3
- Width: 70'-0"
- Depth: 79'-2"

SEARCH ONLINE @ EPLANS.COM

Onlookers will delight in the symmetry of this facade's arched windows and dormers. The interior offers a great room with a cathedral ceiling. This open plan is also packed with the latest design features, including a kitchen with a large island, a wet bar in the great room, a bedroom/study combination on the first floor and a gorgeous master suite with a spa-style bath. Upstairs, two family bedrooms share a compartmented hall bath. An expansive rear deck and generous covered front porch offer maximum outdoor livability.

SECOND FLOOR

FIRST FLOOR

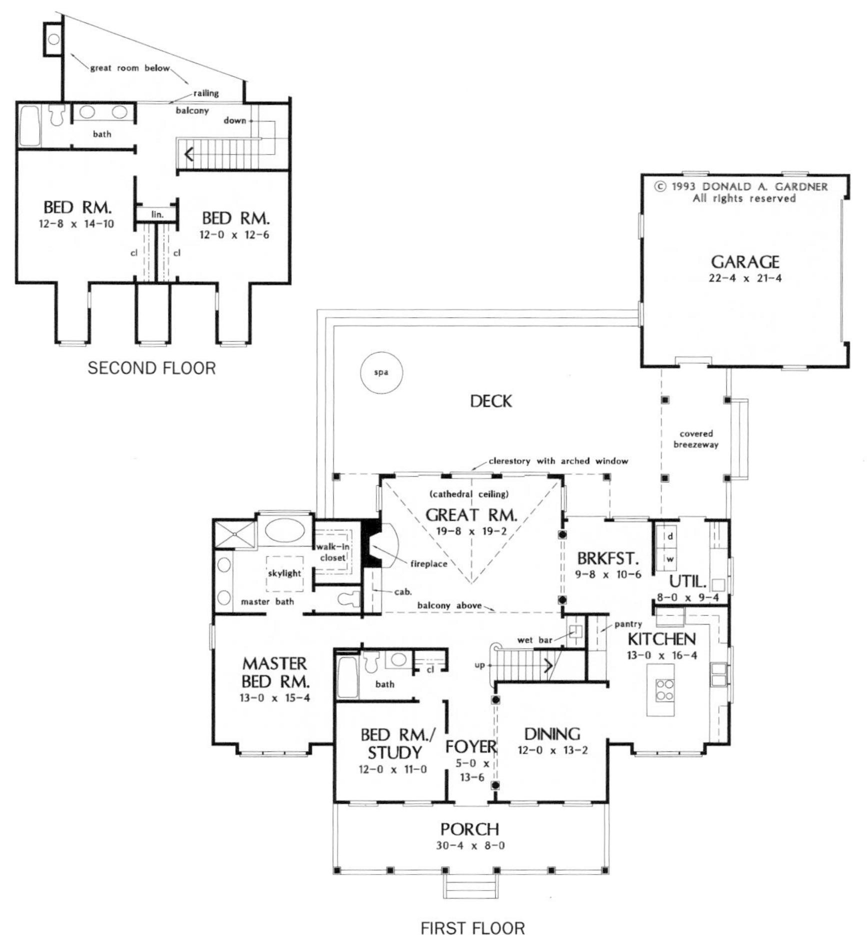

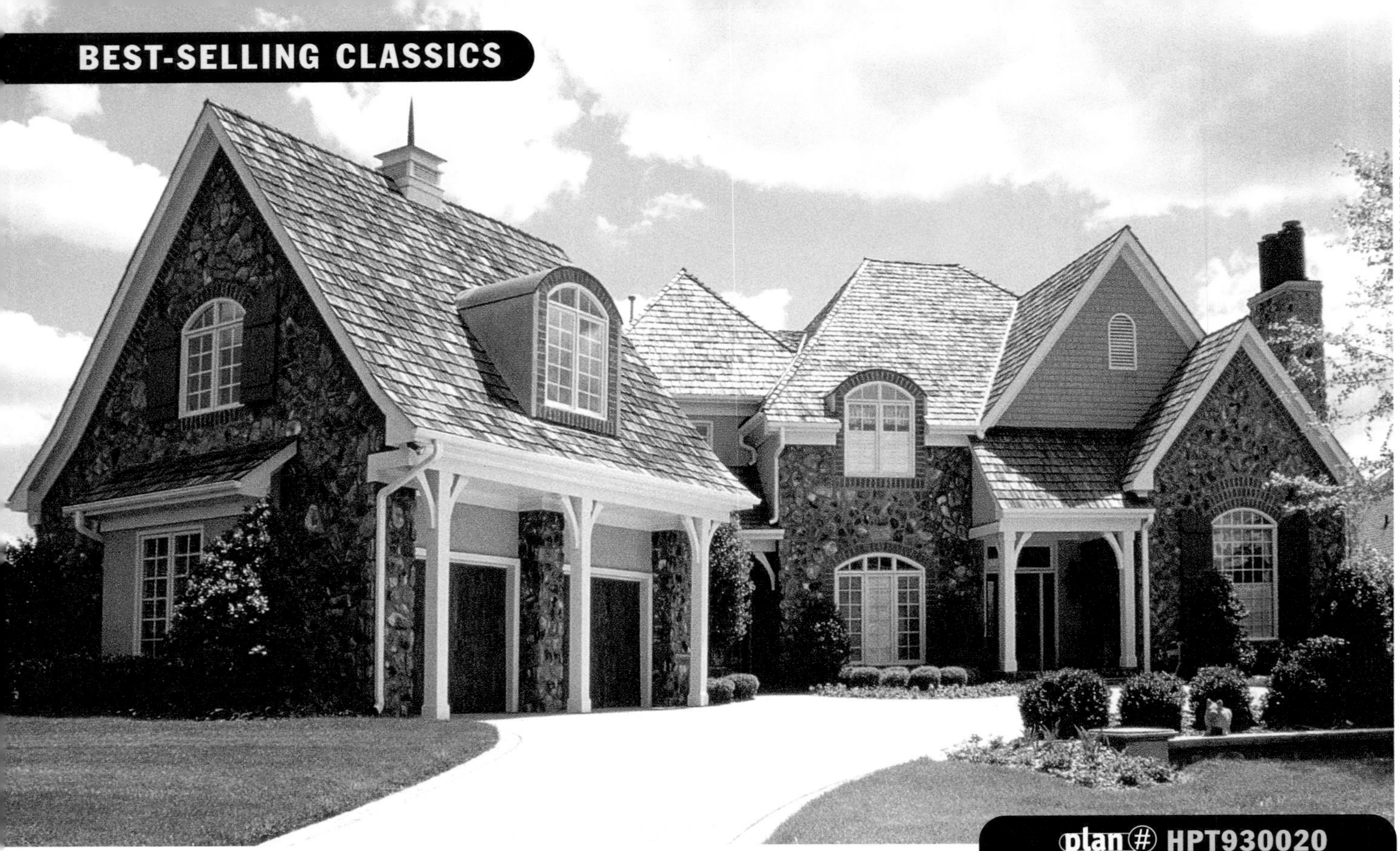

plan# HPT930020

- Style: French Country
- First Floor: 2,390 sq. ft.
- Second Floor: 765 sq. ft.
- Total: 3,155 sq. ft.
- Bonus Space: 433 sq. ft.
- Bedrooms: 3
- Bathrooms: 3½
- Width: 87'-11"
- Depth: 75'-2"
- Foundation: Crawlspace

SEARCH ONLINE @ EPLANS.COM

SECOND FLOOR

FIRST FLOOR

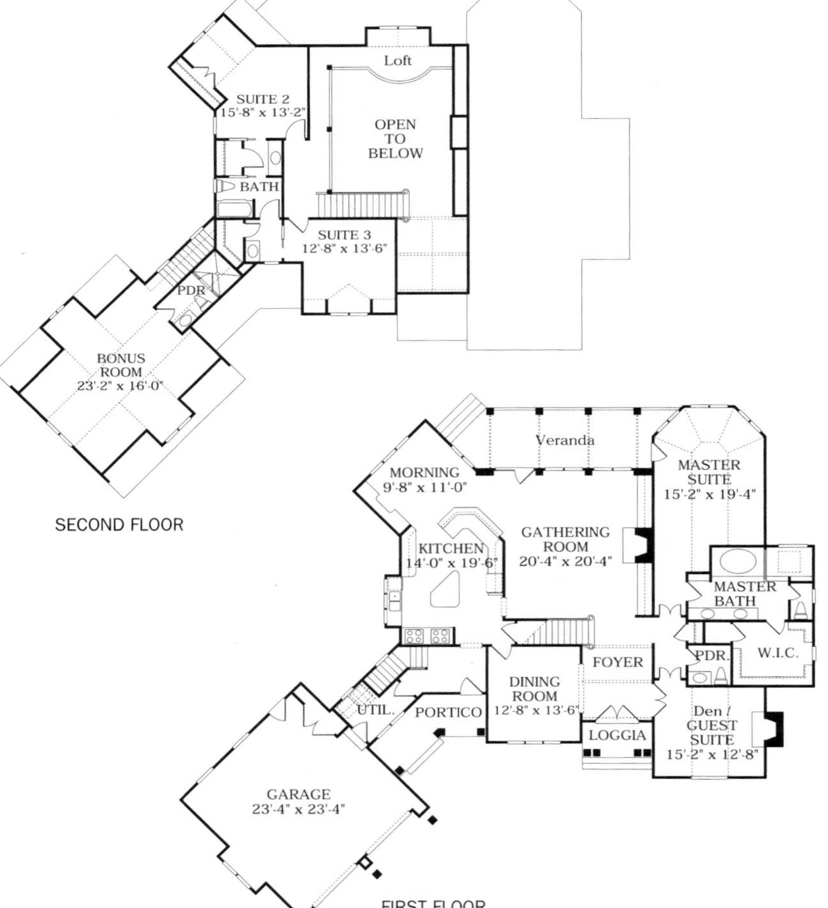

The grand exterior of this Normandy country design features a steeply pitched gable roofline. Arched dormers repeat the window accents. Inside, the promise of space is fulfilled with a large gathering room that fills the center of the house and opens to a long trellised veranda. The den or guest suite with a fireplace, the adjacent powder room and the master suite with a vaulted ceiling and access to the veranda reside in the right wing. Two additional bedrooms with two baths and a loft overlooking the gathering room are upstairs. A large bonus room is found over the garage and can be developed later as office or hobby space.

plan# HPT930021

- Style: Country Cottage
- First Floor: 1,874 sq. ft.
- Second Floor: 901 sq. ft.
- Total: 2,775 sq. ft.
- Bonus Space: 382 sq. ft.
- Bedrooms: 3
- Bathrooms: 3½
- Width: 90'-0"
- Depth: 58'-6"
- Foundation: Crawlspace

SEARCH ONLINE @ EPLANS.COM

From the wraparound porch to the gabled dormer windows, this sweet cottage is pure country. Inside, an open floor plan lends a spacious appeal. The formal dining room is defined by a pentagonal stepped ceiling. To the right, the study has unique angles and a sophisticated coffered ceiling. The two-story vaulted octagonal great room is brimming with architectural interest. Three sets of French doors extend to the rear porch; a lateral fireplace can be viewed from the gourmet kitchen with a cooktop island. An outdoor grill invites dining alfresco. The master suite is designed to pamper, with French doors and a plush bath. Two bedroom suites and bonus space reside on the second level and enjoy upper-deck access.

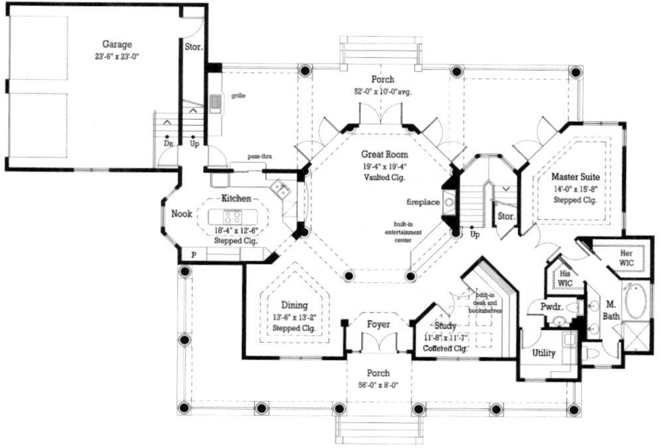

FIRST FLOOR

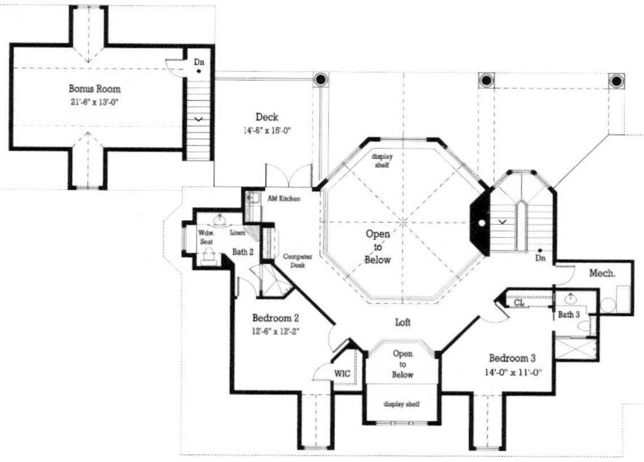

SECOND FLOOR

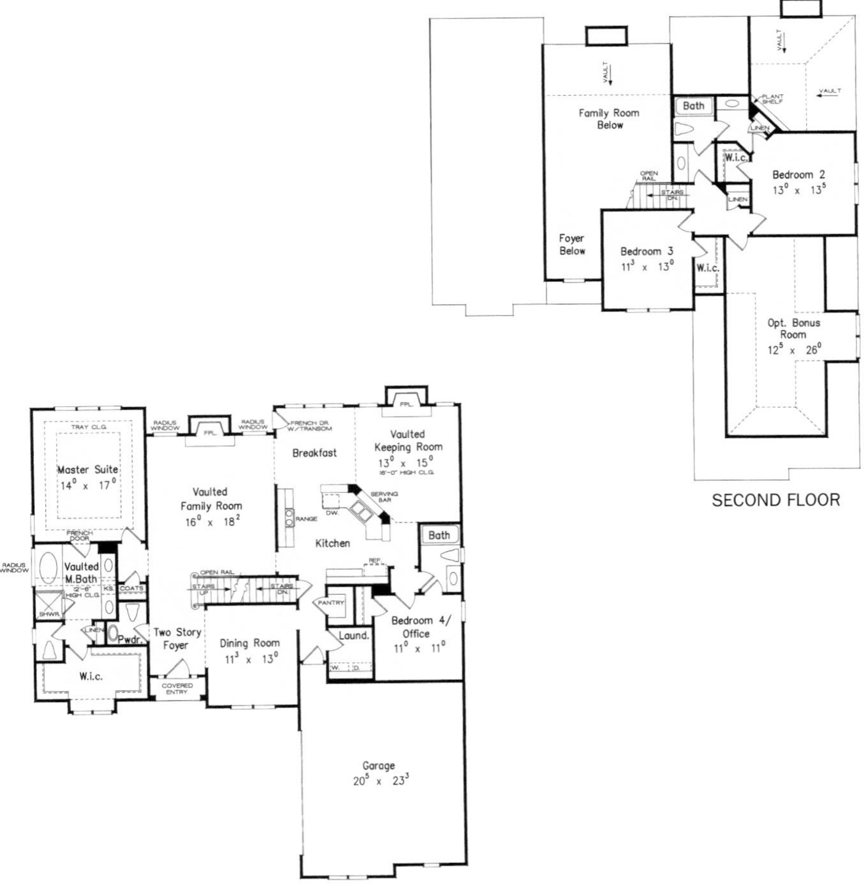

SECOND FLOOR

FIRST FLOOR

plan# HPT930022

- Style: French Country
- First Floor: 1,946 sq. ft.
- Second Floor: 562 sq. ft.
- Total: 2,508 sq. ft.
- Bonus Space: 366 sq. ft.
- Bedrooms: 4
- Bathrooms: 3½
- Width: 54'-0"
- Depth: 63'-4"
- Foundation: Crawlspace, Walkout Basement

SEARCH ONLINE @ EPLANS.COM

The hipped roof, gable accents and side-entry garage make this a striking home. The vaulted family room features a central fireplace for maximum comfort. The kitchen is open to the breakfast area and the vaulted keeping room. The master suite features a tray ceiling and a vaulted bath with an oval tub under a radius window. Two family bedrooms and an optional bonus room are located on the second level.

plan# HPT930023

- Style: Country Cottage
- First Floor: 2,495 sq. ft.
- Second Floor: 1,233 sq. ft.
- Total: 3,728 sq. ft.
- Bonus Space: 351 sq. ft.
- Bedrooms: 4
- Bathrooms: 3½
- Width: 66'-10"
- Depth: 57'-6"
- Foundation: Crawlspace, Walkout Basement

SEARCH ONLINE @ EPLANS.COM

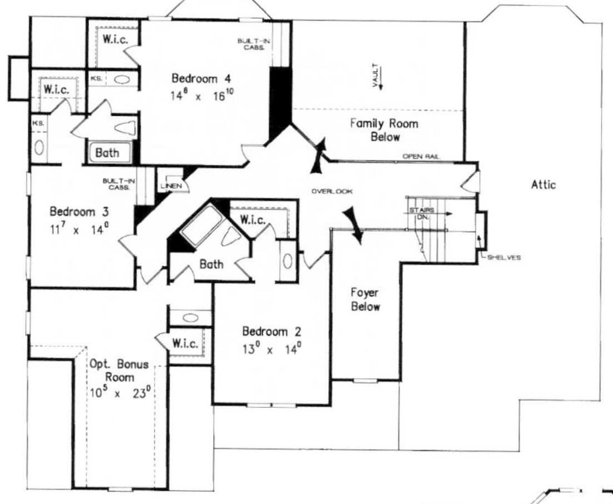

SECOND FLOOR

The brick-and-siding exterior and hipped roof lend a country aura to this home. Amenities abound inside, including a walk-in pantry in the island kitchen and fireplaces in the family and keeping rooms. Vaulted ceilings enhance the family and living rooms, and the keeping room features a lovely bay window. Note the elegant master suite on the first floor and three family bedrooms on the second. An optional bonus room offers plenty of space for future expansion.

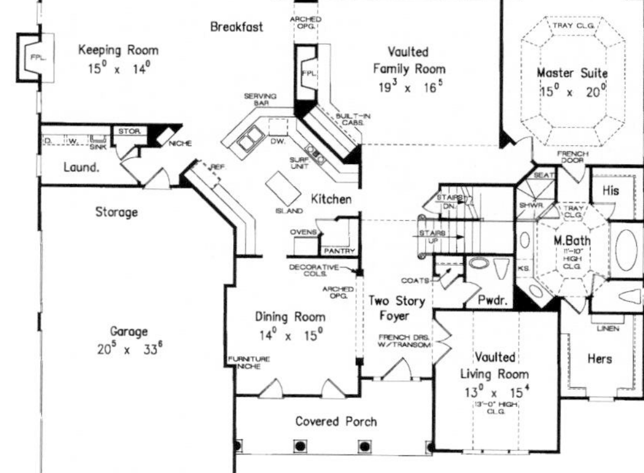

FIRST FLOOR

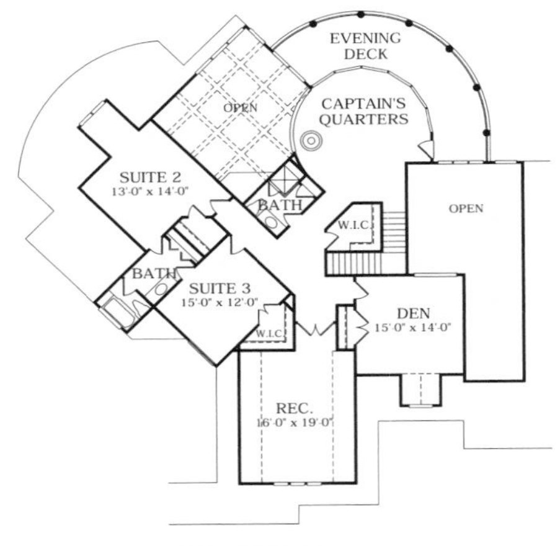

SECOND FLOOR

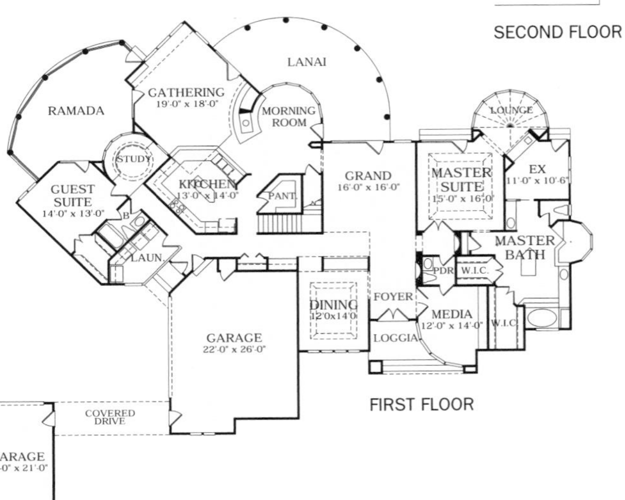

FIRST FLOOR

plan# HPT930024

- Style: Mediterranean
- First Floor: 3,329 sq. ft.
- Second Floor: 1,485 sq. ft.
- Total: 4,814 sq. ft.
- Bonus Space: 300 sq. ft.
- Bedrooms: 4
- Bathrooms: 4½
- Width: 106'-6"
- Depth: 89'-10"
- Foundation: Crawlspace

SEARCH ONLINE @ EPLANS.COM

A curved wall of windows leads to the entrance of this fine home. The lavish master suite features two walk-in closets, a deluxe bath with a separate tub and shower and two vanities, a separate lounge and an exercise room. On the other end of the home, find the highly efficient kitchen, a spacious gathering room, a round morning room and study and a quiet guest suite. The second level is equally deluxe with two suites, a recreation room, a quiet den and a large open area called the captain's quarters that opens to an evening deck.

plan# HPT930025

- Style: French
- First Floor: 2,608 sq. ft.
- Second Floor: 1,432 sq. ft.
- Total: 4,040 sq. ft.
- Bedrooms: 4
- Bathrooms: 3½
- Width: 89'-10"
- Depth: 63'-8"
- Foundation: Crawlspace, Slab

SEARCH ONLINE @ EPLANS.COM

A distinctively French flair is the hallmark of this European design. Inside, the two-story foyer provides views to the huge great room beyond. A well-placed study off the foyer provides space for a home office. The kitchen, breakfast room and sun room are adjacent to lend a spacious feel. The great room is visible from this area through decorative arches. The master suite includes a roomy sitting area and a lovely bath with a centerpiece whirlpool tub flanked by half-columns. Upstairs, Bedrooms 2 and 3 share a bath that includes separate dressing areas.

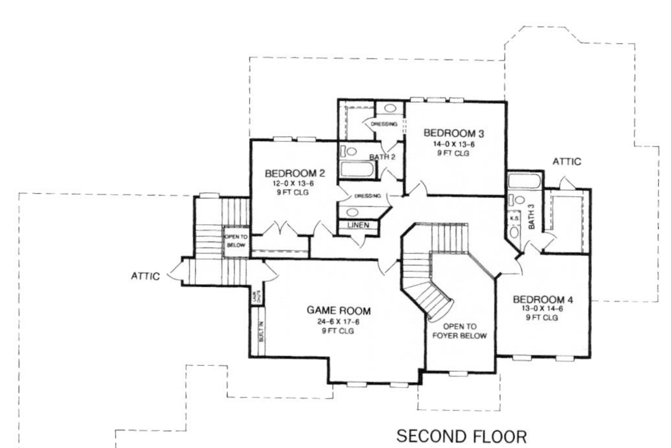

SECOND FLOOR

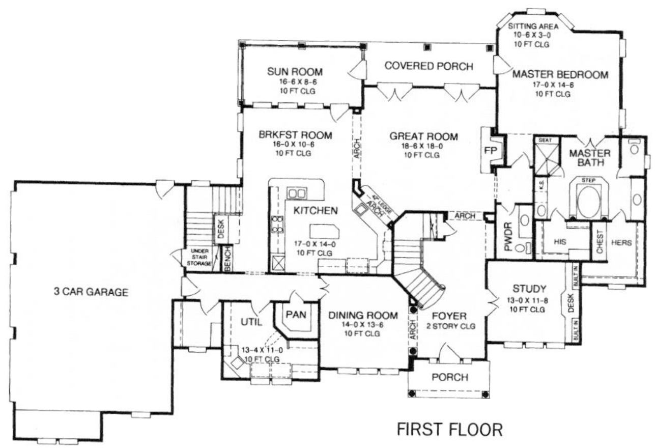

FIRST FLOOR

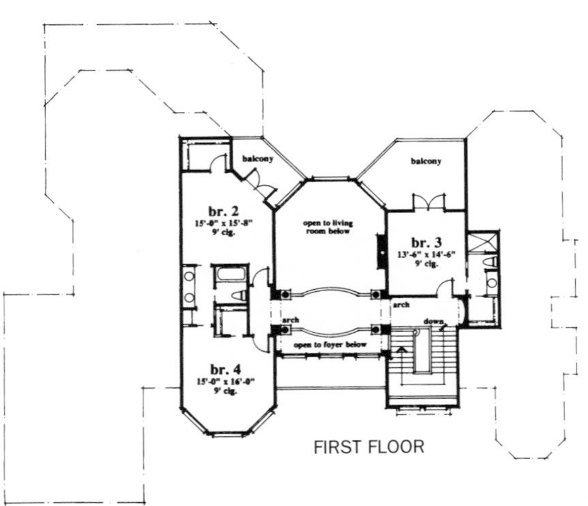

FIRST FLOOR

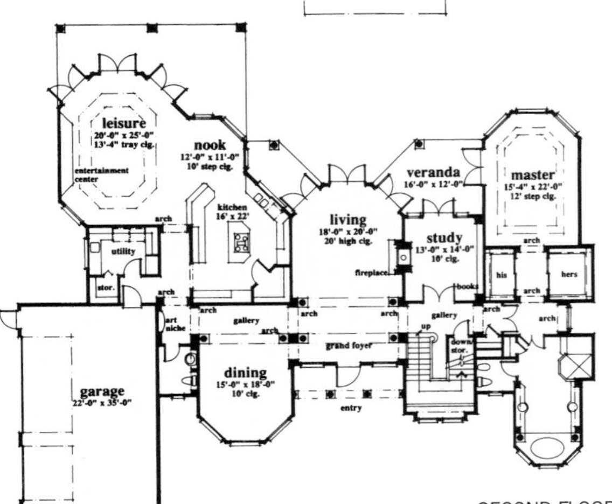

SECOND FLOOR

plan# HPT930026

- Style: Traditional
- First Floor: 3,546 sq. ft.
- Second Floor: 1,213 sq. ft.
- Total: 4,759 sq. ft.
- Bedrooms: 4
- Bathrooms: 3½
- Width: 96'-0"
- Depth: 83'-0"
- Foundation: Basement

SEARCH ONLINE @ EPLANS.COM

This grand traditional home offers an elegant, welcoming residence. Beyond the grand foyer, the spacious living room provides views of the rear grounds and opens to the veranda and rear yard through three pairs of French doors. An arched galley hall leads past the formal dining room to the family areas. Here, an ample gourmet kitchen easily serves the nook and the leisure room. The master wing includes a study or home office. Upstairs, each of three secondary bedrooms features a walk-in closet, and two bedrooms offer private balconies.

plan# HPT930027

- Style: French Country
- First Floor: 3,027 sq. ft.
- Second Floor: 1,079 sq. ft.
- Total: 4,106 sq. ft.
- Bedrooms: 4
- Bathrooms: 3½
- Width: 87'-4"
- Depth: 80'-4"
- Foundation: Basement

SEARCH ONLINE @ EPLANS.COM

The inside of this design is just as majestic as the outside. The grand foyer opens to a two-story living room with a fireplace and magnificent views. Dining in the bayed formal dining room will be a memorable experience. A well-designed kitchen is near a sunny nook and a leisure room with a fireplace and outdoor access. The master wing includes a separate study and an elegant private bath. The second level features a guest suite with its own bath and deck, two family bedrooms (Bedroom 3 also has its own deck) and a gallery loft with views to the living room below.

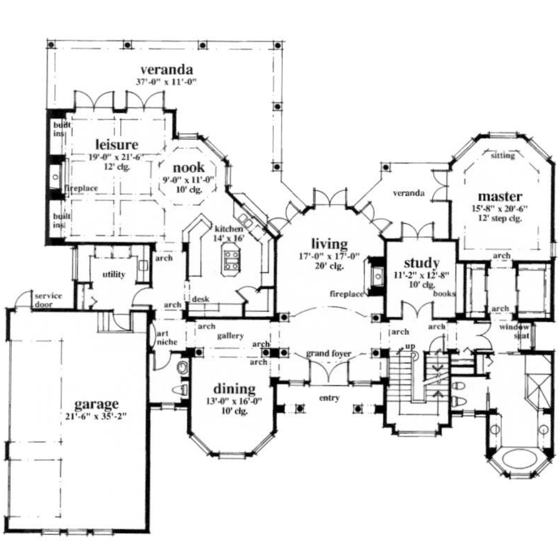

FIRST FLOOR

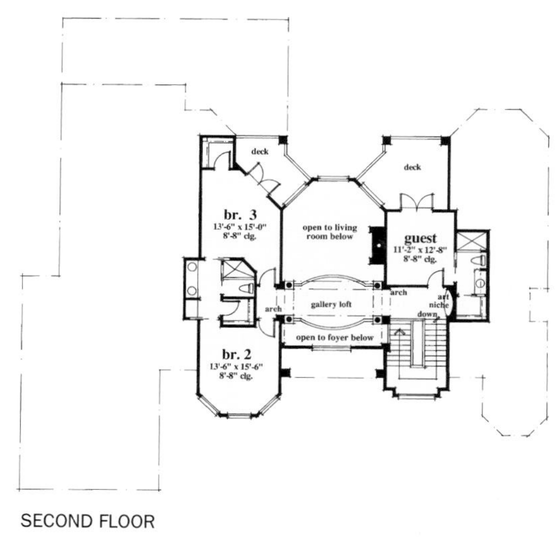

SECOND FLOOR

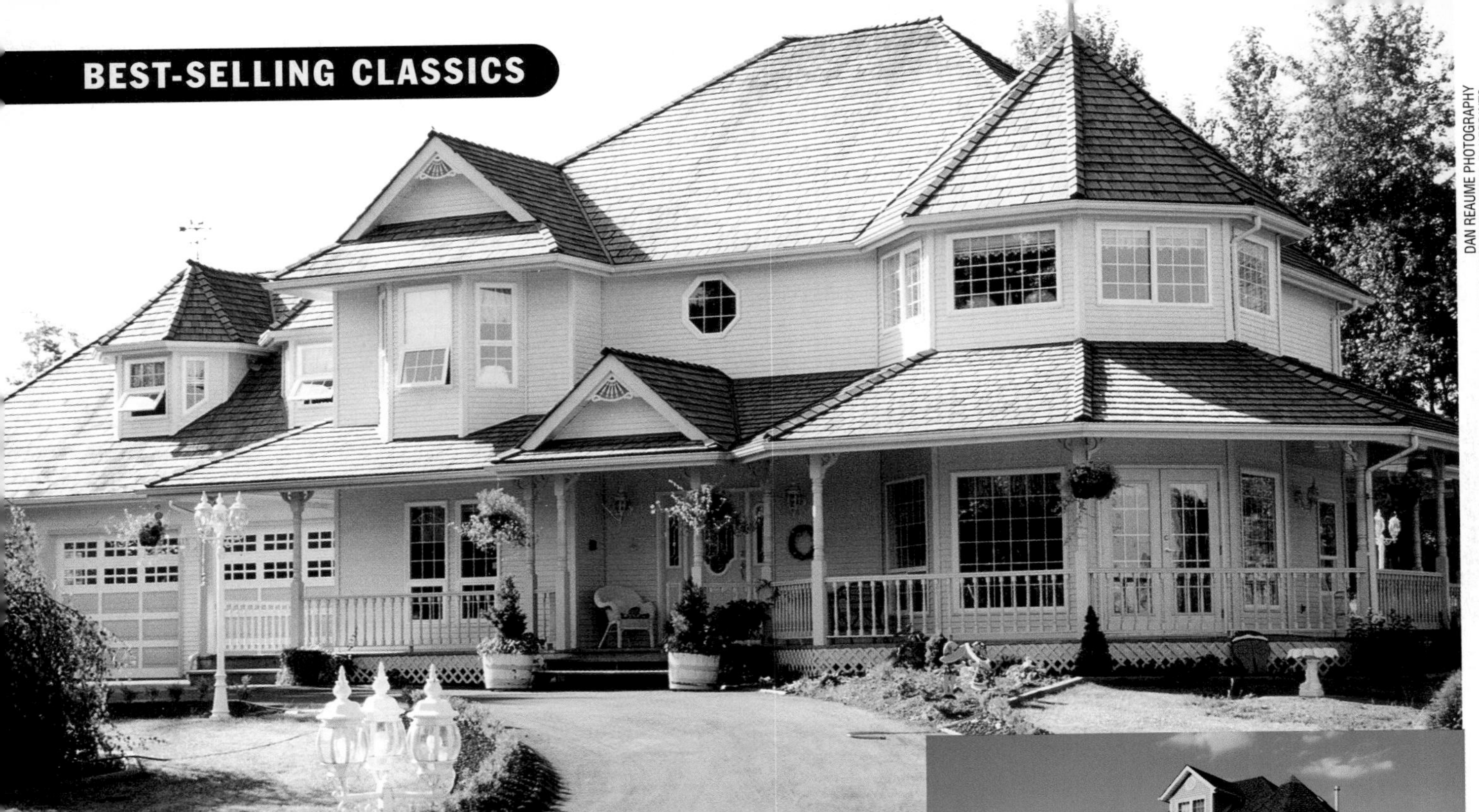

DAN REAUME PHOTOGRAPHY
THIS HOME, AS SHOWN IN THE PHOTOGRAPH, MAY DIFFER FROM THE ACTUAL BLUEPRINTS.

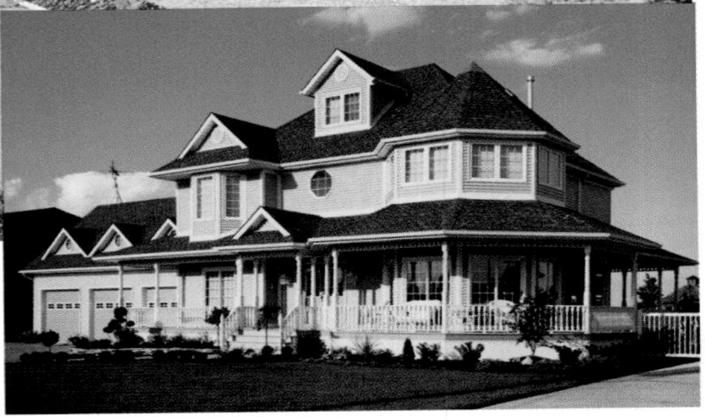

ALTERNATE EXTERIOR

plan# HPT930028

- Style: Country Cottage
- First Floor: 1,462 sq. ft.
- Second Floor: 1,288 sq. ft.
- Total: 2,750 sq. ft.
- Bedrooms: 4
- Bathrooms: 2½
- Width: 70'-8"
- Depth: 54'-0"
- Foundation: Basement, Crawlspace

SEARCH ONLINE @ EPLANS.COM

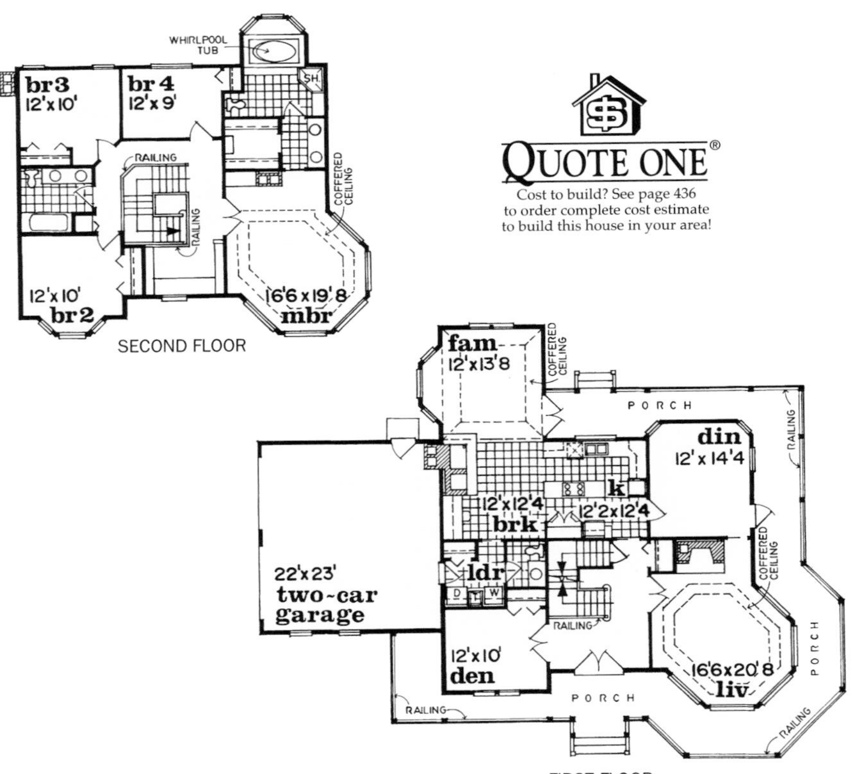

A touch of Victoriana enhances the facade of this home: a turret roof over a wraparound porch with turned wood spindles. Special attractions on the first floor include a tray ceiling in the octagonal living room, fireplaces in the country kitchen and the living room, a coffered ceiling in the family room, and double-door access to the cozy den. The master suite, set in the second-floor section of the turret, boasts a coffered ceiling, walk-in closet and whirlpool tub. Three family bedrooms and a full hall bath join the master suite on the second floor.

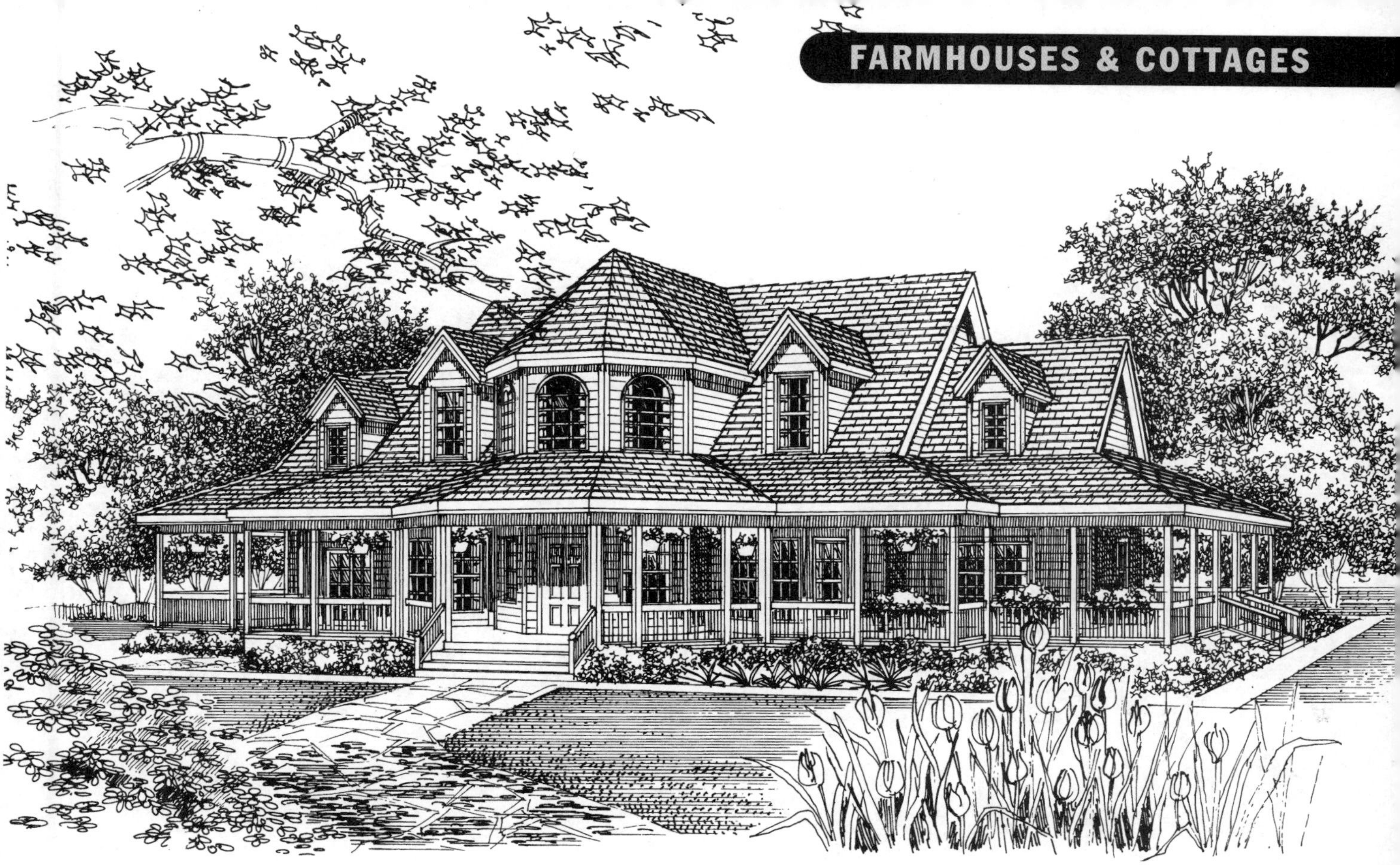

plan# HPT930029

- Style: Farmhouse
- First Floor: 1,752 sq. ft.
- Second Floor: 906 sq. ft.
- Total: 2,658 sq. ft.
- Bedrooms: 4
- Bathrooms: 3½
- Width: 74'-0"
- Depth: 51'-7"
- Foundation: Basement

L D

SEARCH ONLINE @ EPLANS.COM

Delightfully proportioned and superbly symmetrical, this Victorian farmhouse has lots of curb appeal. The wraparound porch offers rustic columns and railings, and broad steps present easy access to the front, rear and side yards. Archways, display niches and columns help define the great room, which offers a fireplace framed by views to the rear property. A formal parlor and a dining room flank the reception hall, and each offers a bay window. The master suite boasts two sets of French doors to the wraparound porch, and a private bath with a clawfoot tub, twin lavatories, a walk-in closet and a stall shower. Upstairs, a spacious office/den adjoins two family bedrooms, each with a private bath.

FIRST FLOOR

QUOTE ONE®

Cost to build? See page 436 to order complete cost estimate to build this house in your area!

SECOND FLOOR

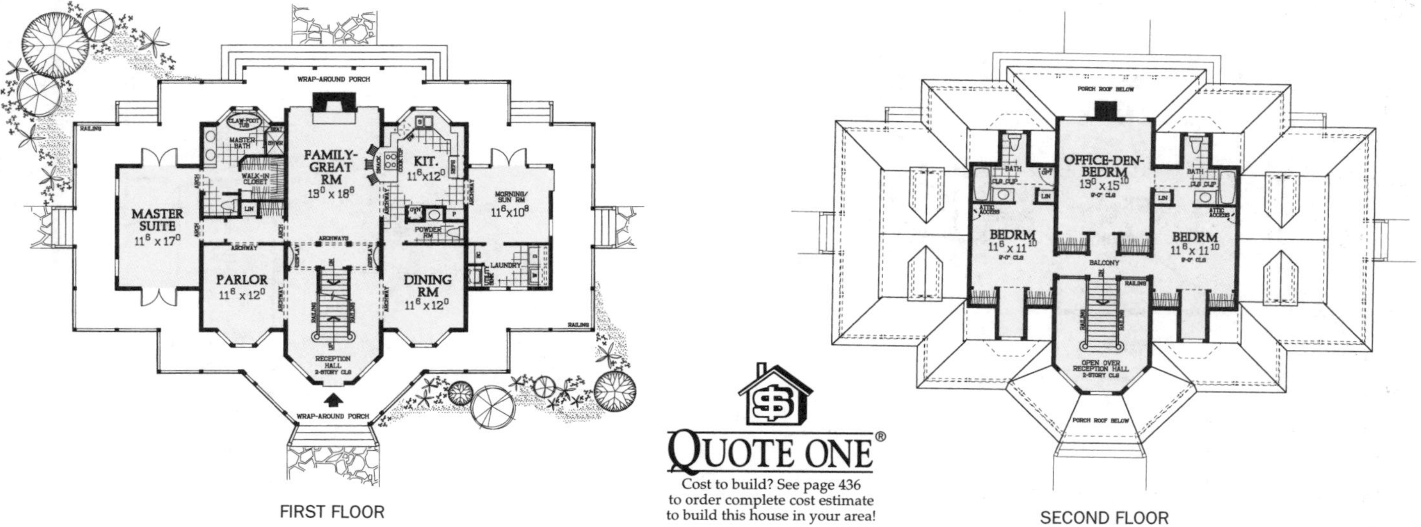

Balustrades and brackets, dual balconies and a wraparound porch create a country-style exterior reminiscent of soft summer evenings spent watching fireflies and sipping sun tea. The tiled foyer opens to the two-story great room filled with light from six windows and a fireplace. The sunny bayed nook shares its natural light with the snack counter and kitchen. A spacious master suite occupies a bay window and offers a sumptuous bath. Upstairs, two family bedrooms—each with a private balcony and a walk-in closet—share a full bath.

plan# HPT930030

L D

- Style: Farmhouse
- First Floor: 1,374 sq. ft.
- Second Floor: 600 sq. ft.
- Total: 1,974 sq. ft.
- Bedrooms: 3
- Bathrooms: 2½
- Width: 51'-8"
- Depth: 50'-8"
- Foundation: Basement

SEARCH ONLINE @ EPLANS.COM

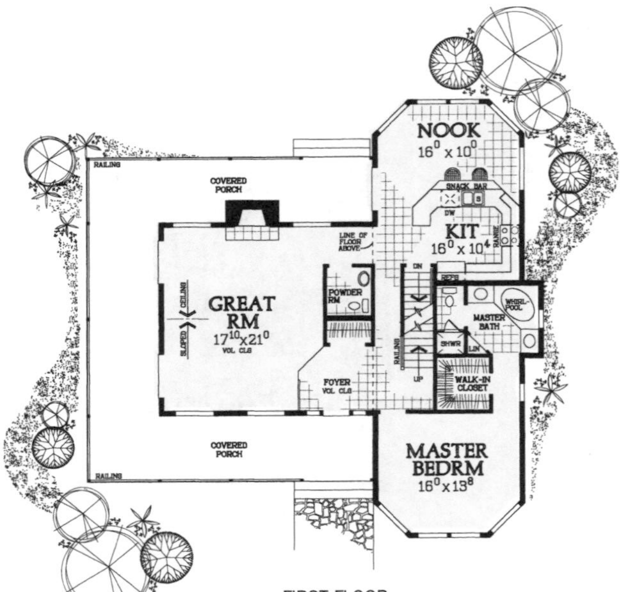

FIRST FLOOR

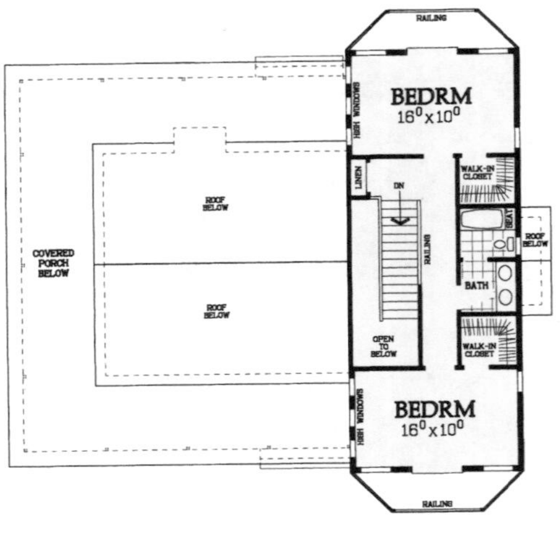

SECOND FLOOR

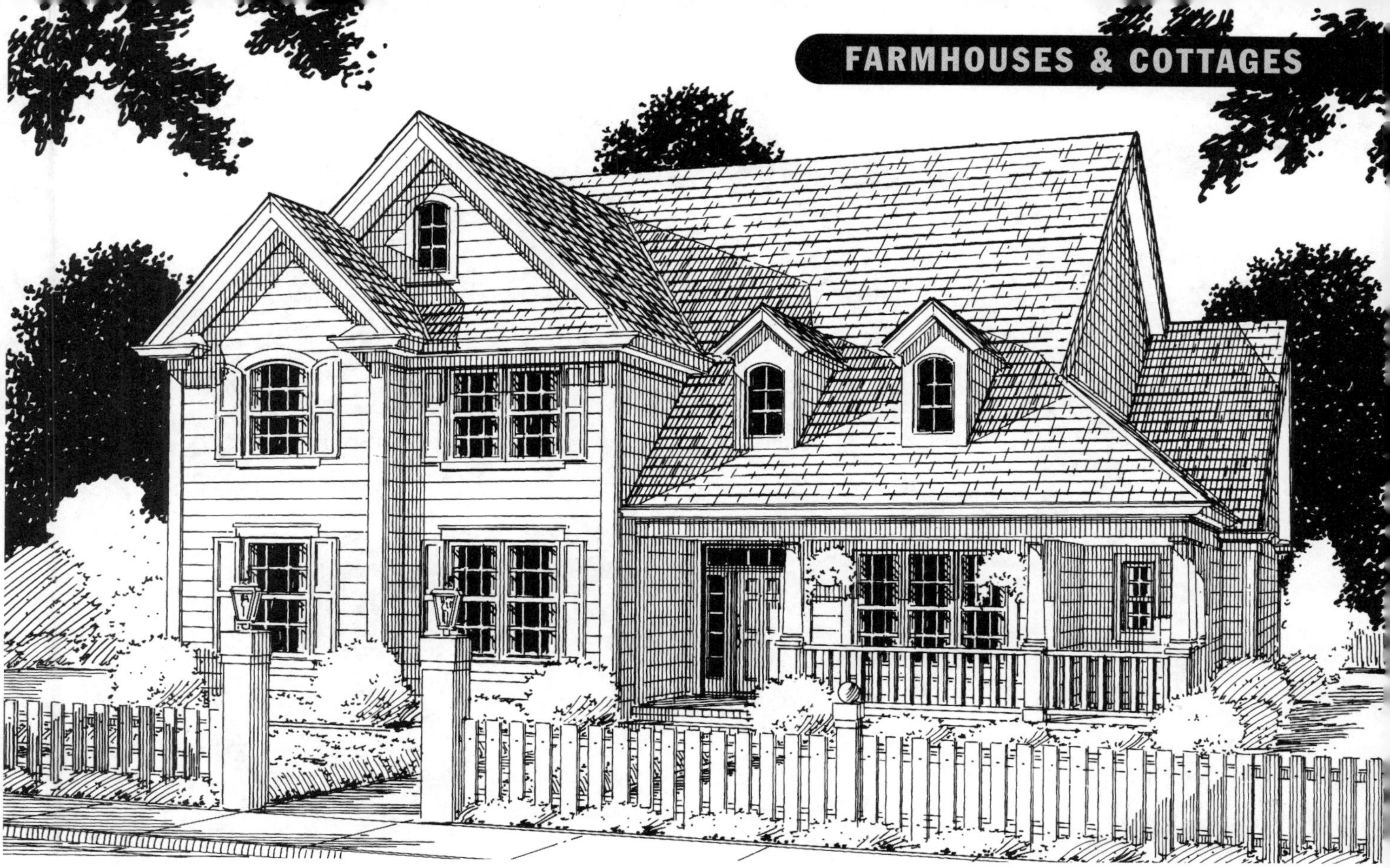

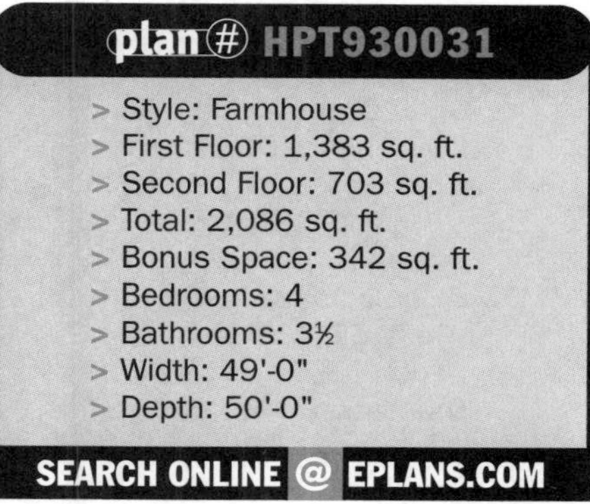

plan# HPT930031

- Style: Farmhouse
- First Floor: 1,383 sq. ft.
- Second Floor: 703 sq. ft.
- Total: 2,086 sq. ft.
- Bonus Space: 342 sq. ft.
- Bedrooms: 4
- Bathrooms: 3½
- Width: 49'-0"
- Depth: 50'-0"

SEARCH ONLINE @ EPLANS.COM

BEDROOM 2
11'6" X 12'8"
DESK
DN
OPTIONAL FUTURE SPACE
19' X 18'
AC
BEDROOM 4
10'8" X 11'6"
BEDROOM 3
10'4" X 11'6"

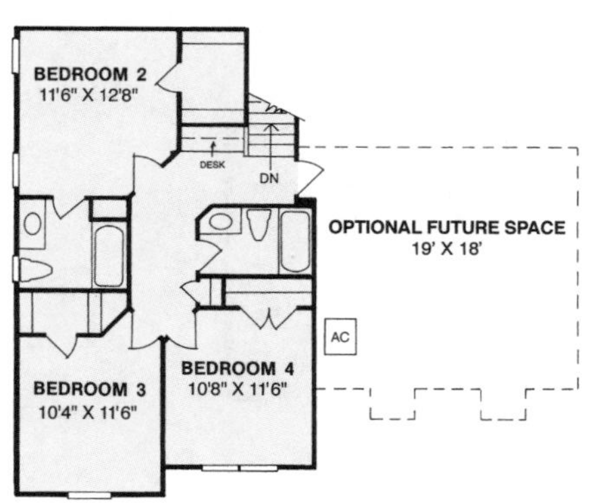

SECOND FLOOR

Gables, dormers and a corner porch define the facade of this traditional farmhouse design. The front entry opens on the right to the dining room and through a barrel arch to the living room straight ahead. This room features a fireplace, a built-in entertainment center and rear views through a wall of windows. The amenity-filled kitchen contains an eating bar, a pantry and a nearby breakfast nook. Sleeping quarters include a first-floor master suite and, upstairs, three family bedrooms sharing two full baths.

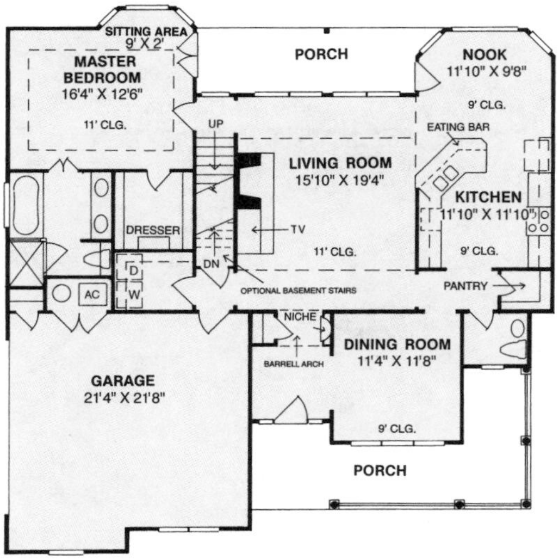

SITTING AREA
9' X 2'
MASTER
BEDROOM
16'4" X 12'6"
11' CLG.
PORCH
NOOK
11'10" X 9'8"
9' CLG.
EATING BAR
UP
LIVING ROOM
15'10" X 19'4"
KITCHEN
11'10" X 11'10"
DRESSER
TV
11' CLG.
9' CLG.
D
W
DN
AC
OPTIONAL BASEMENT STAIRS
PANTRY
NICHE
DINING ROOM
11'4" X 11'8"
BARRELL ARCH
GARAGE
21'4" X 21'8"
9' CLG.
PORCH

FIRST FLOOR

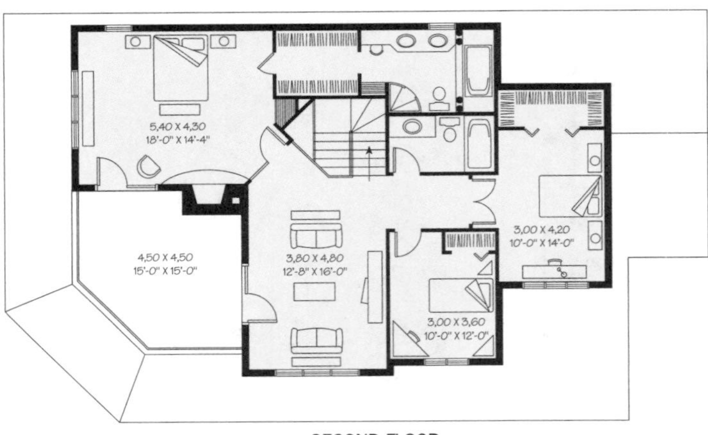

SECOND FLOOR

FIRST FLOOR

plan# HPT930032

- Style: Country
- First Floor: 1,067 sq. ft.
- Second Floor: 1,233 sq. ft.
- Total: 2,300 sq. ft.
- Bedrooms: 3
- Bathrooms: 2½
- Width: 58'-0"
- Depth: 33'-0"
- Foundation: Basement

SEARCH ONLINE @ EPLANS.COM

A wraparound porch and a second-floor deck add to the warmth and livability of this splendid two-story Victorian home. A large angled kitchen with an adjoining dining area are the hub around which all activity will revolve. A delightful fireplace adds warmth to the living room where French doors lead to the front porch. A utility room and half-bath are tucked away behind the staircase. The family room resides on the second-floor landing and shares the deck with the master suite. Two additional bedrooms and a full bath complete the second floor.

plan# HPT930033

- Style: Country Cottage
- First Floor: 1,050 sq. ft.
- Second Floor: 1,085 sq. ft.
- Total: 2,135 sq. ft.
- Bedrooms: 4
- Bathrooms: 2½
- Width: 50'-8"
- Depth: 39'-4"
- Foundation: Basement

SEARCH ONLINE @ EPLANS.COM

This lovely country design features a stunning wrapping porch and plenty of windows to provide the interior with natural light. The living room boasts a centered fireplace, which helps to define this spacious open area. A nine-foot ceiling on the first floor adds a sense of spaciousness and light. The casual living room leads outdoors to a rear porch. Upstairs, four bedrooms cluster around a central hall. The master suite sports a walk-in closet and a deluxe bath with an oval tub and a separate shower.

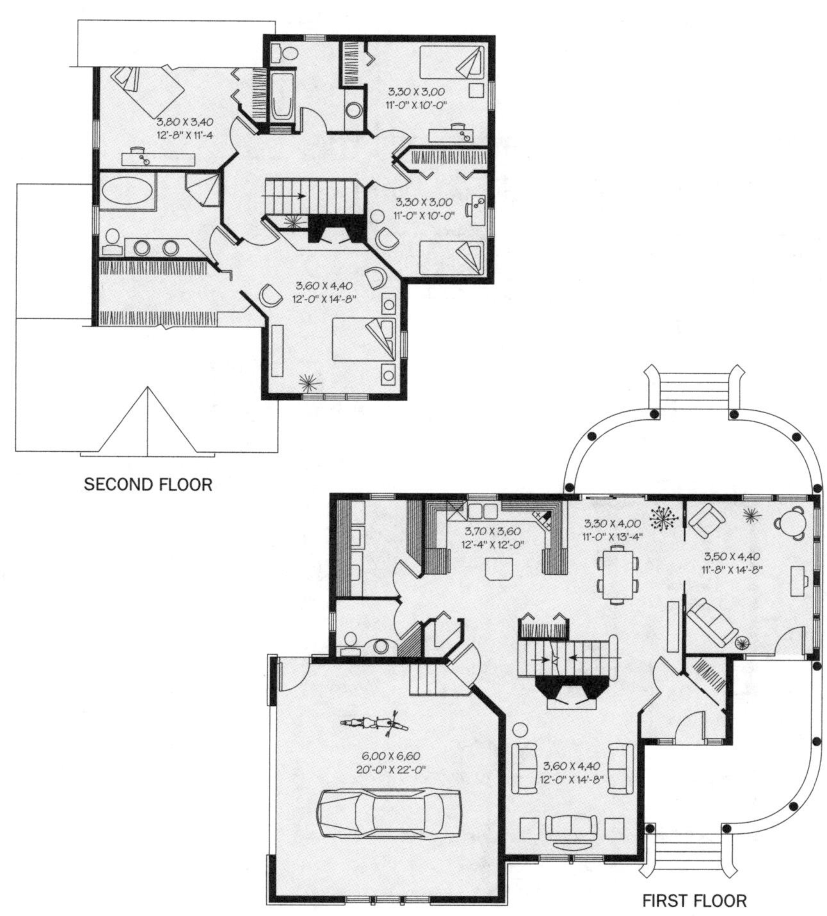

SECOND FLOOR

FIRST FLOOR

SECOND FLOOR

FIRST FLOOR

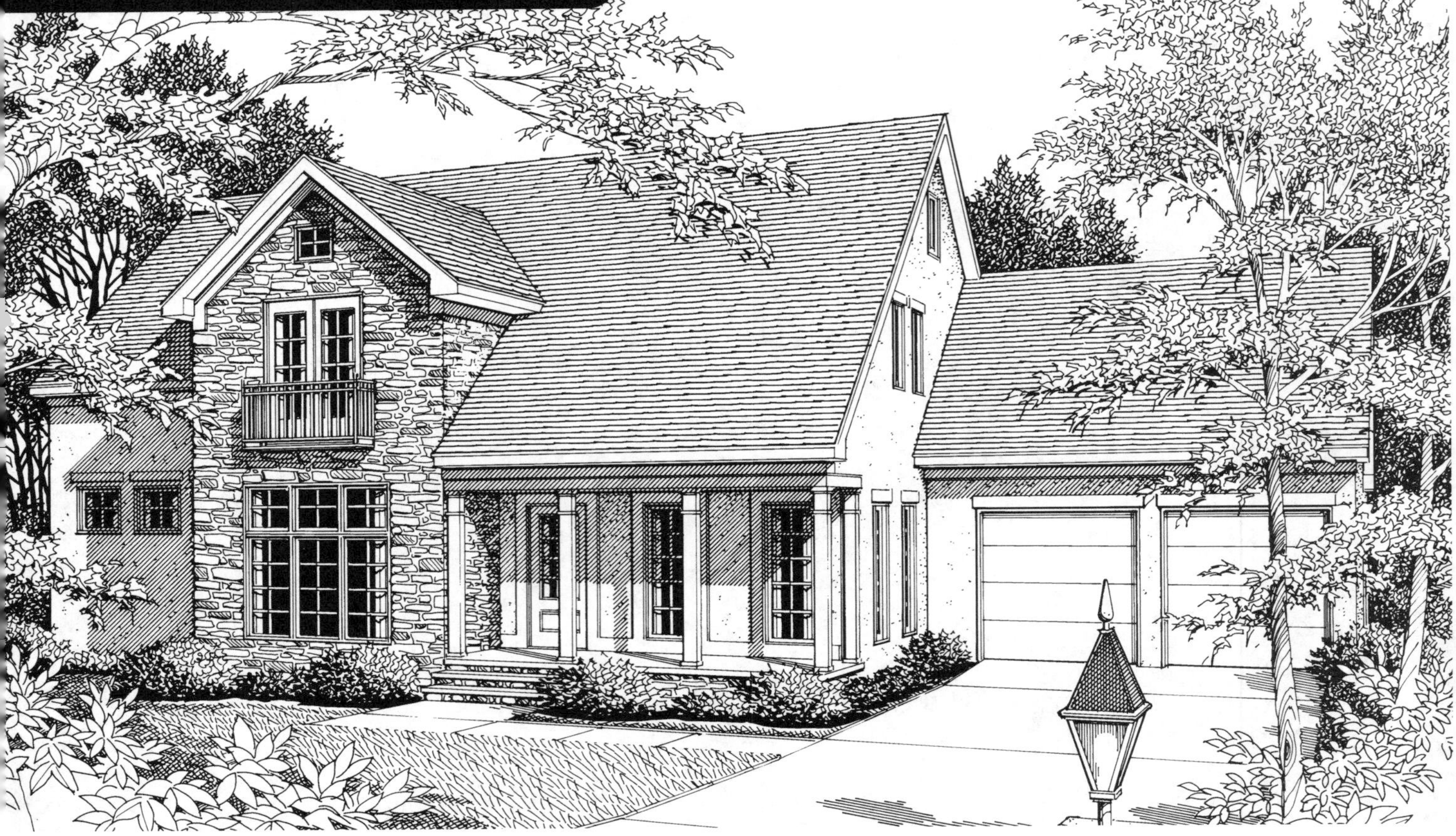

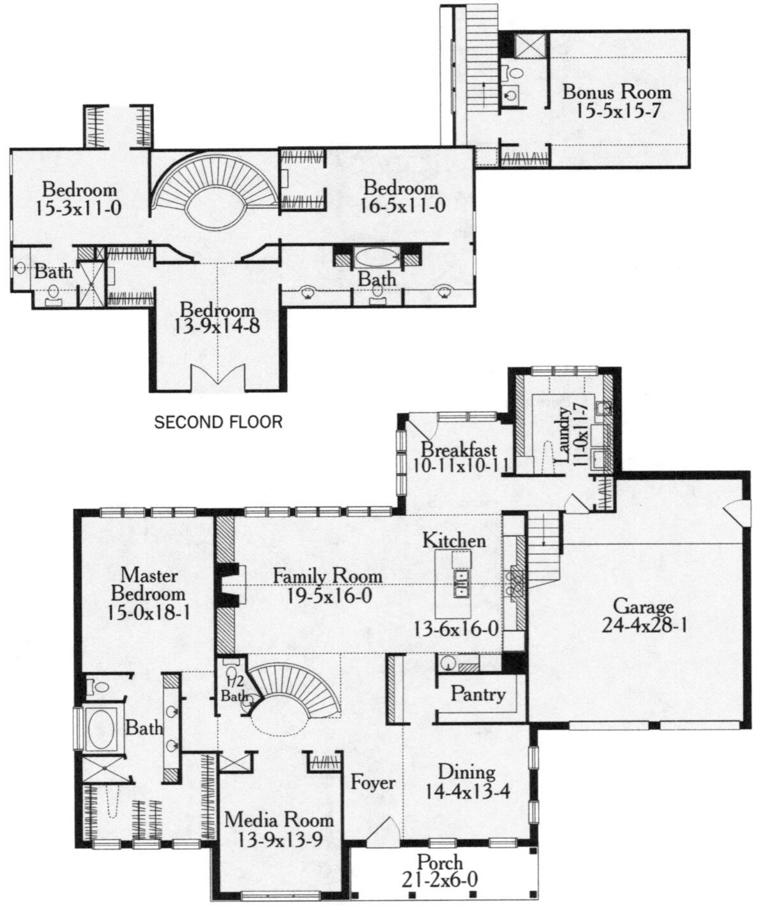

plan# HPT930034

- Style: Farmhouse
- First Floor: 2,458 sq. ft.
- Second Floor: 1,483 sq. ft.
- Total: 3,941 sq. ft.
- Bonus Space: 240 sq. ft.
- Bedrooms: 4
- Bathrooms: 4½
- Width: 76'-6"
- Depth: 61'-8"
- Foundation: Slab

SEARCH ONLINE @ EPLANS.COM

This stunning four-bedroom home offers an exciting facade that combines stone and stucco. The foyer opens to a grand and elegant circular staircase that rises to a circular overlook. Magnificent views to the rear are beheld from the family, breakfast and utility rooms in addition to the master suite. In the era of electronics, the library has become the media room where full-length windows adorn the front wall. The master suite is on the first floor with three additional bedrooms upstairs—note the Jack-and-Jill bath on the right. Additional space is found above the two-car garage for future development.

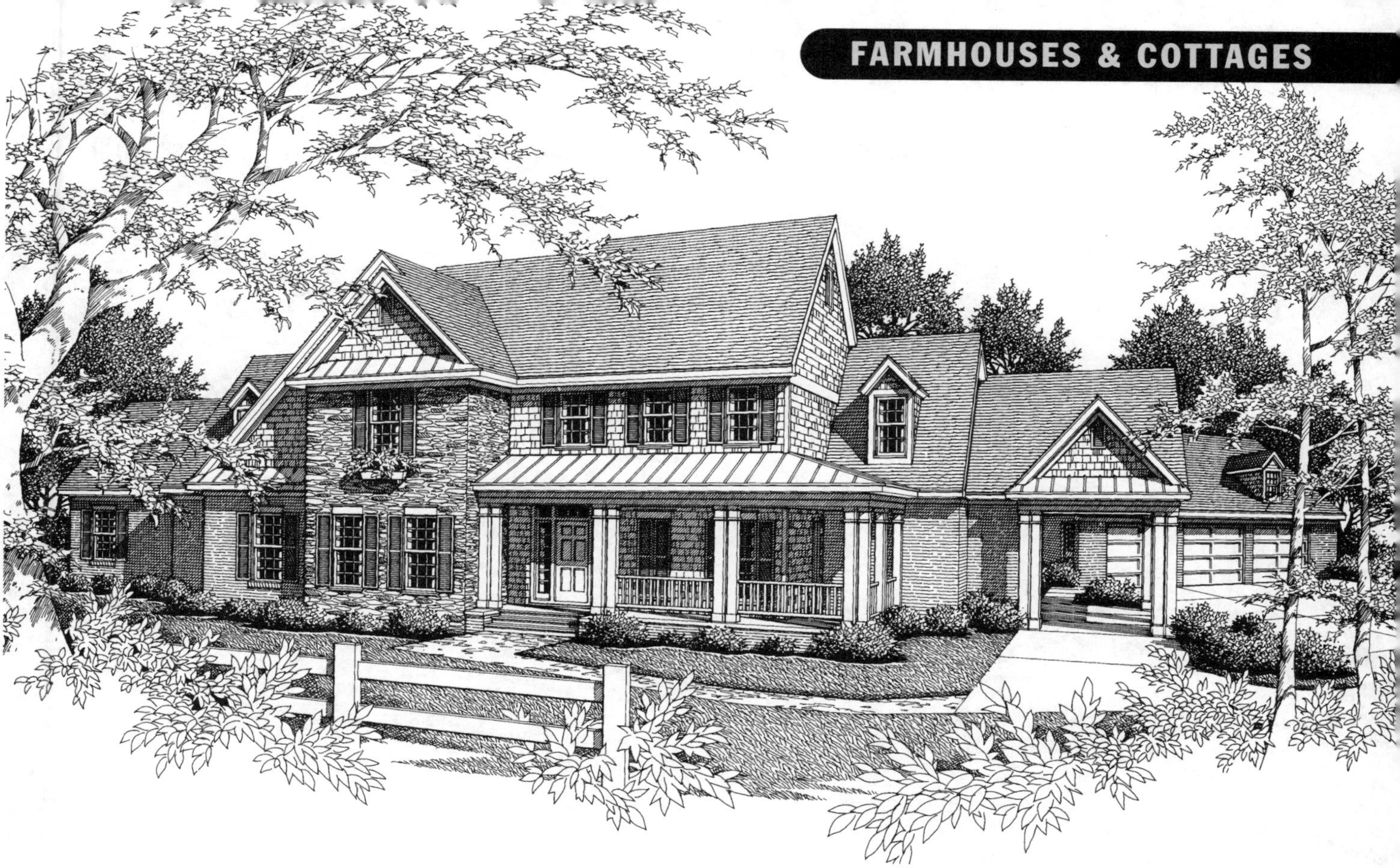

plan# HPT930035

- Style: Farmhouse
- First Floor: 3,120 sq. ft.
- Second Floor: 1,083 sq. ft.
- Total: 4,203 sq. ft.
- Bedrooms: 4
- Bathrooms: 5½
- Width: 118'-1"
- Depth: 52'-2"
- Foundation: Crawlspace, Slab

SEARCH ONLINE @ EPLANS.COM

SECOND FLOOR

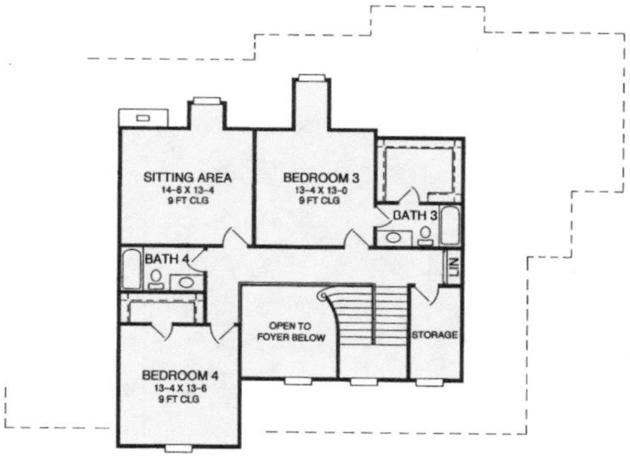

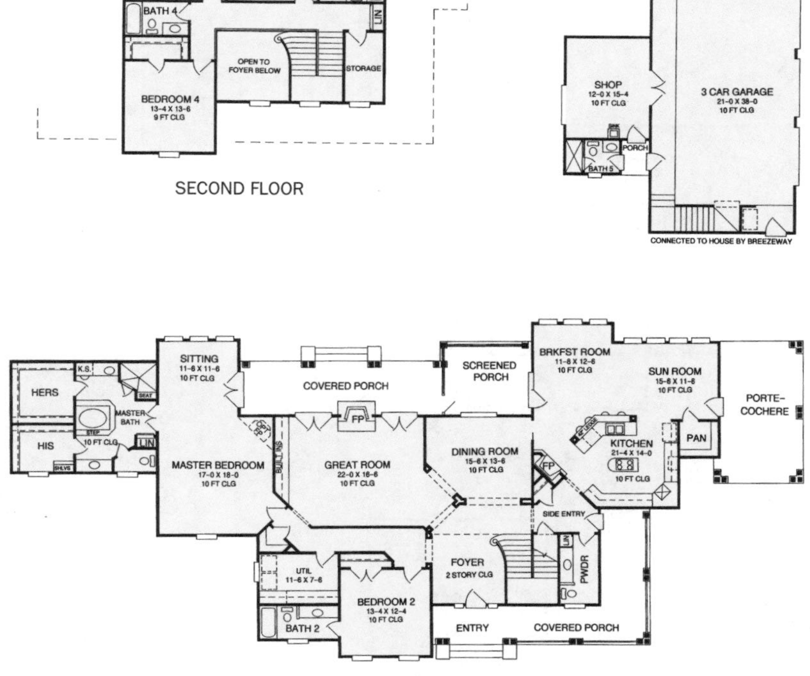

The blending of natural materials and a nostalgic farmhouse look give this home its unique character. Inside, a sophisticated floor plan includes all the amenities demanded by today's upscale family. Three large covered porches—one on the front and two on the rear—provide outdoor entertaining areas. The kitchen features a built-in stone fireplace visible from the breakfast and sun rooms. The master suite includes a large sitting area and a luxurious bath. Upstairs, two additional bedrooms and a large sitting room will please family and guests.

FIRST FLOOR

SECOND FLOOR

FIRST FLOOR

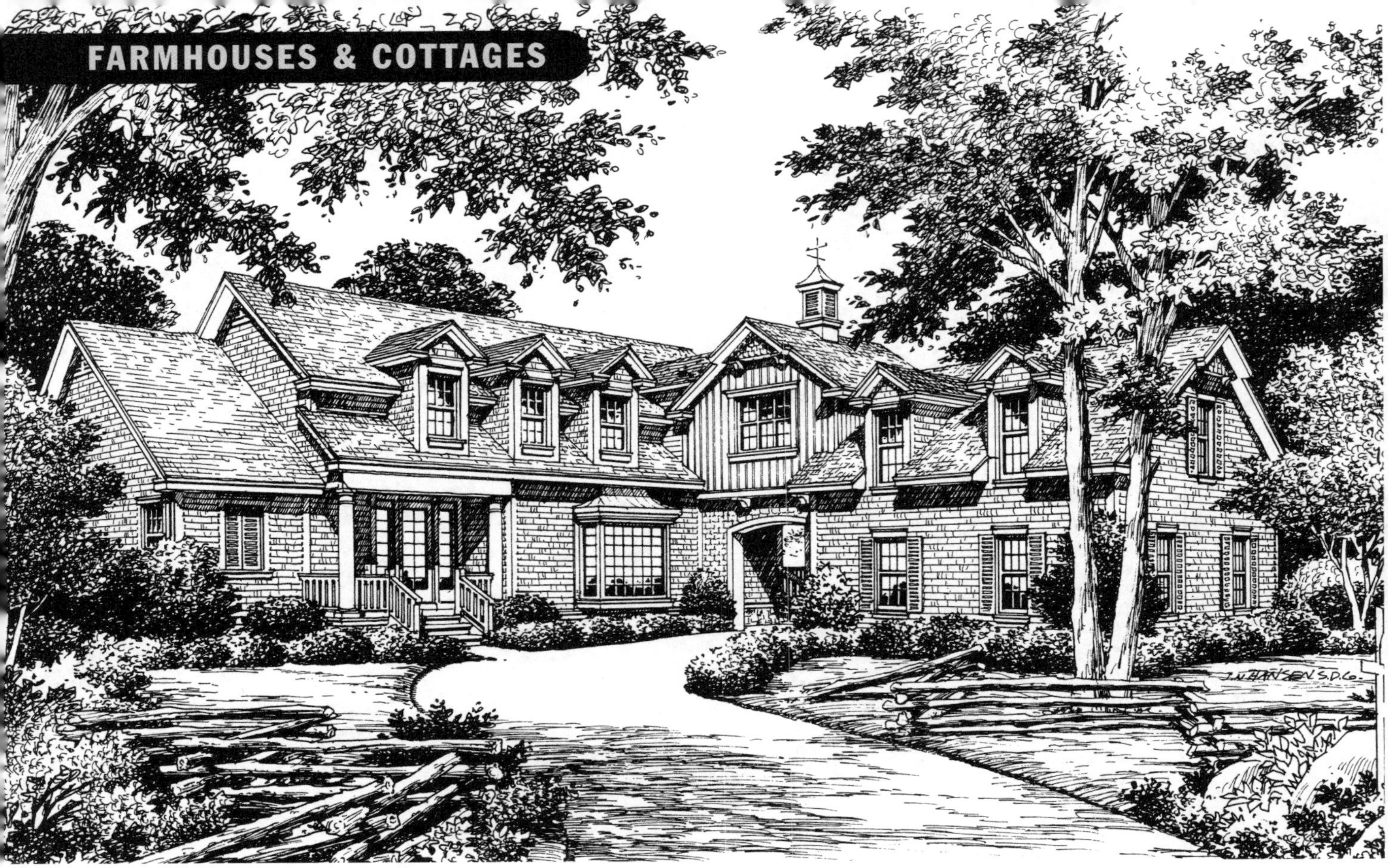

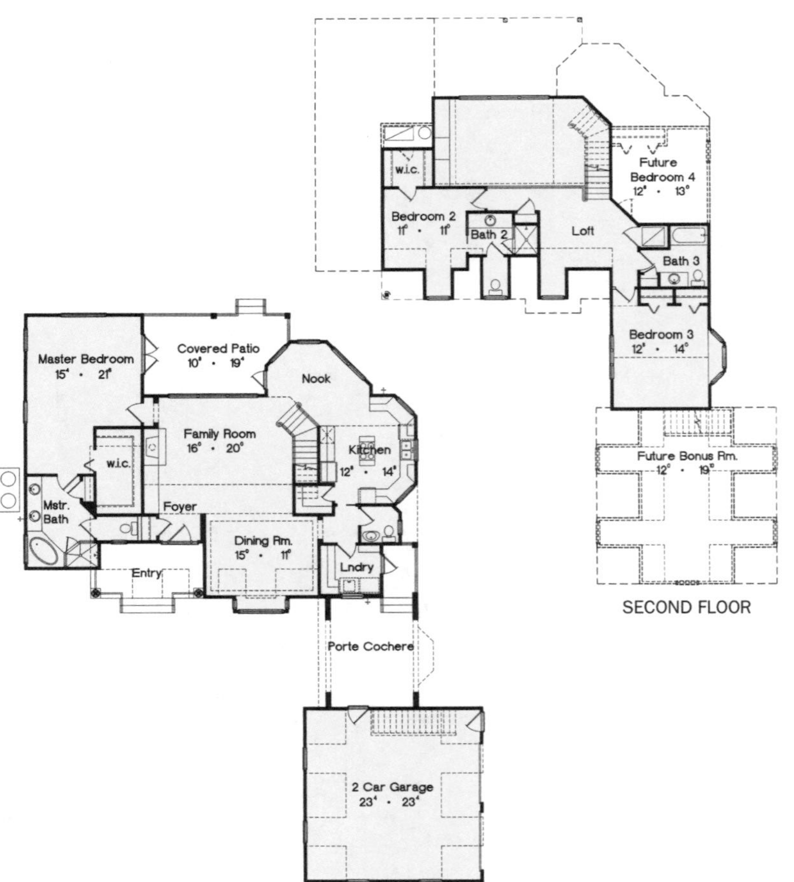

plan# HPT930036

- Style: Farmhouse
- First Floor: 1,530 sq. ft.
- Second Floor: 777 sq. ft.
- Total: 2,307 sq. ft.
- Bonus Space: 528 sq. ft.
- Bedrooms: 3
- Bathrooms: 3½
- Width: 61'-4"
- Depth: 78'-0"
- Foundation: Slab

SEARCH ONLINE @ EPLANS.COM

Five dormer windows adorn this L-shaped three-bedroom design. The dining room sits to the right of the foyer and showcases a beautiful box-bay window. Nearby, the family room features a warming fireplace. To the right of the family room, the master bedroom enjoys French-door access to the rear patio, an oval tub and a separate shower. Conveniently near the garage, the kitchen provides a walk-in pantry, cooktop island, bayed nook and powder room. The second floor includes two family bedrooms, two baths and the possibility for a future bonus room and future bedroom when space is needed.

plan# HPT930037

- Style: Farmhouse
- First Floor: 2,088 sq. ft.
- Second Floor: 1,074 sq. ft.
- Total: 3,162 sq. ft.
- Bedrooms: 4
- Bathrooms: 3½
- Width: 58'-0"
- Depth: 78'-0"
- Foundation: Basement, Crawlspace, Slab

SEARCH ONLINE @ EPLANS.COM

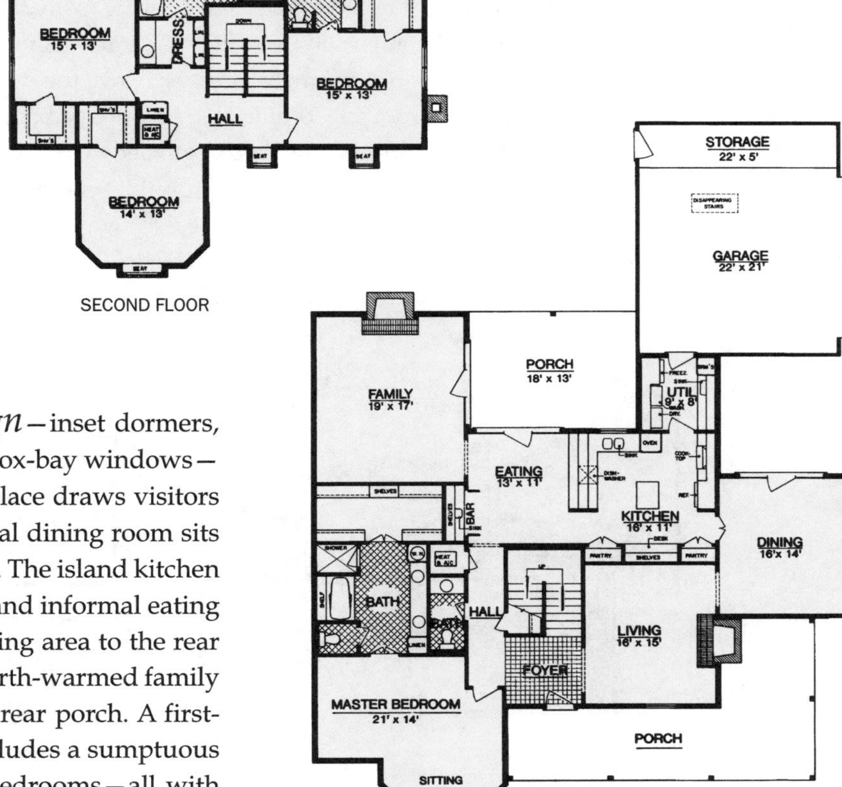

SECOND FLOOR

FIRST FLOOR

The hallmarks of fine country design—inset dormers, fish-scale shingles, a wraparound porch and box-bay windows—adorn this four-bedroom home. A warm fireplace draws visitors from the foyer into the living room. The formal dining room sits conveniently near the living room and kitchen. The island kitchen enjoys easy access to the utility room, garage and informal eating area. French doors lead from the informal eating area to the rear porch—a perfect place for a barbecue! The hearth-warmed family room also features French-door access to the rear porch. A first-floor master suite completes this level and includes a sumptuous bath, walk-in closet and sitting area. Three bedrooms—all with walk-in closets!—and two baths fill the second floor. Note the wonderful window seats, built within the inset dormers.

PHOTO BY: DESIGN BASICS, INC.
THIS HOME, AS SHOWN IN THE PHOTOGRAPH, MAY DIFFER FROM THE ACTUAL BLUEPRINTS.

Lap siding, special windows and a covered porch enhance the elevation of this popular-style home. The spacious two-story entry surveys the formal dining room, which includes hutch space. An entertainment center, a through-fireplace and bayed windows add appeal to the great room. Families will love the spacious kitchen with its breakfast and hearth rooms. Comfortable secondary bedrooms and a sumptuous master bedroom feature privacy by design. Bedroom 3 is highlighted by a half-round window, volume ceiling and double closets, while Bedroom 4 contains a built-in desk. The master suite possesses a vaulted ceiling, large walk-in closet, His and Hers vanities and an oval whirlpool tub.

plan# HPT930038

- Style: Farmhouse
- First Floor: 1,150 sq. ft.
- Second Floor: 1,120 sq. ft.
- Total: 2,270 sq. ft.
- Bedrooms: 4
- Bathrooms: 2½
- Width: 46'-0"
- Depth: 48'-0"

SEARCH ONLINE @ EPLANS.COM

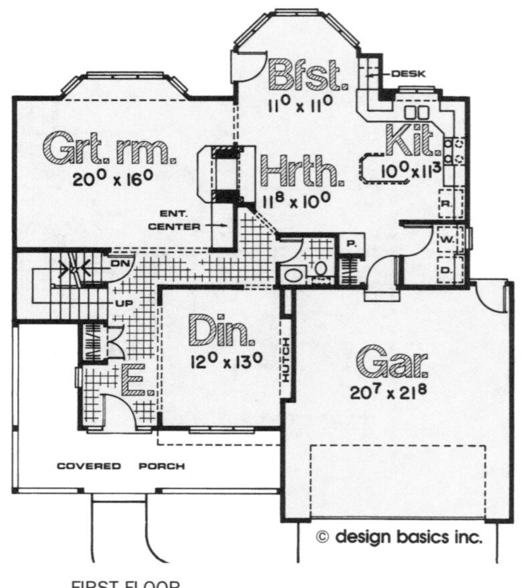

FIRST FLOOR

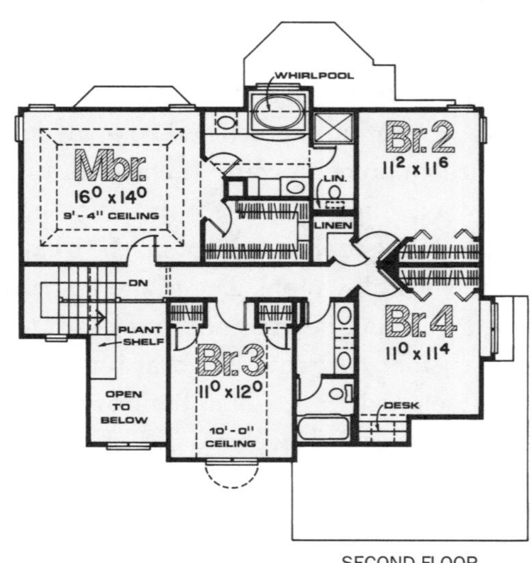

SECOND FLOOR

plan# HPT930039

- Style: Country
- First Floor: 1,278 sq. ft.
- Second Floor: 1,390 sq. ft.
- Total: 2,668 sq. ft.
- Bonus Space: 203 sq. ft.
- Bedrooms: 3
- Bathrooms: 2½
- Width: 60'-0"
- Depth: 44'-0"
- Foundation: Basement

SEARCH ONLINE @ EPLANS.COM

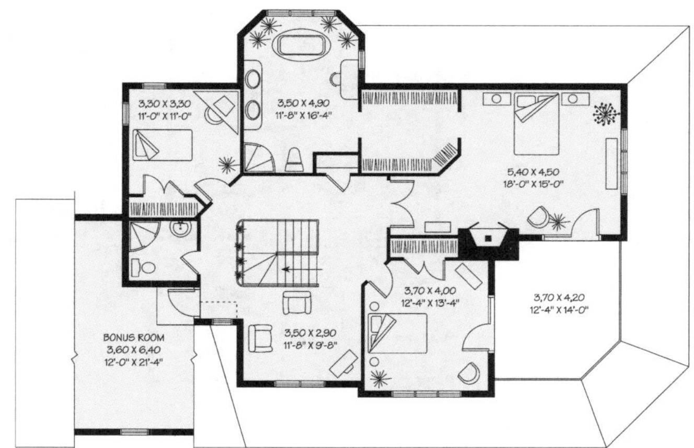

SECOND FLOOR

A truly lavish master suite resides on the second floor of this complex two-story farmhouse. The recessed entry opens to the dining room and kitchen with the family room on the right. The massive wraparound porch can be accessed from the family room, living room and the sunny breakfast bay. The island kitchen is conveniently placed between the dining room and the well-equipped utility room. On the second floor, the master suite enjoys a fireplace, a pampering bath and access to the second-floor deck.

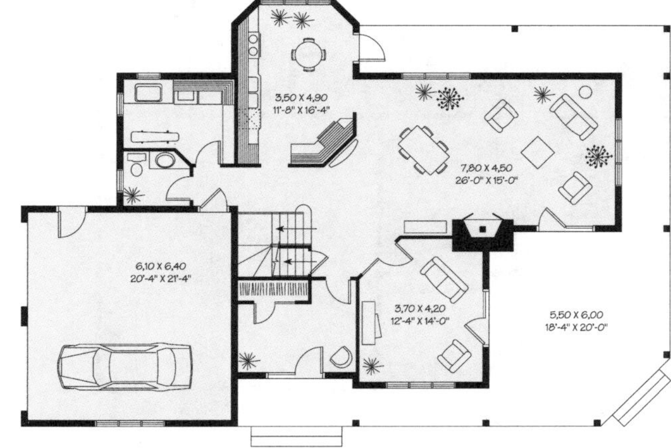

FIRST FLOOR

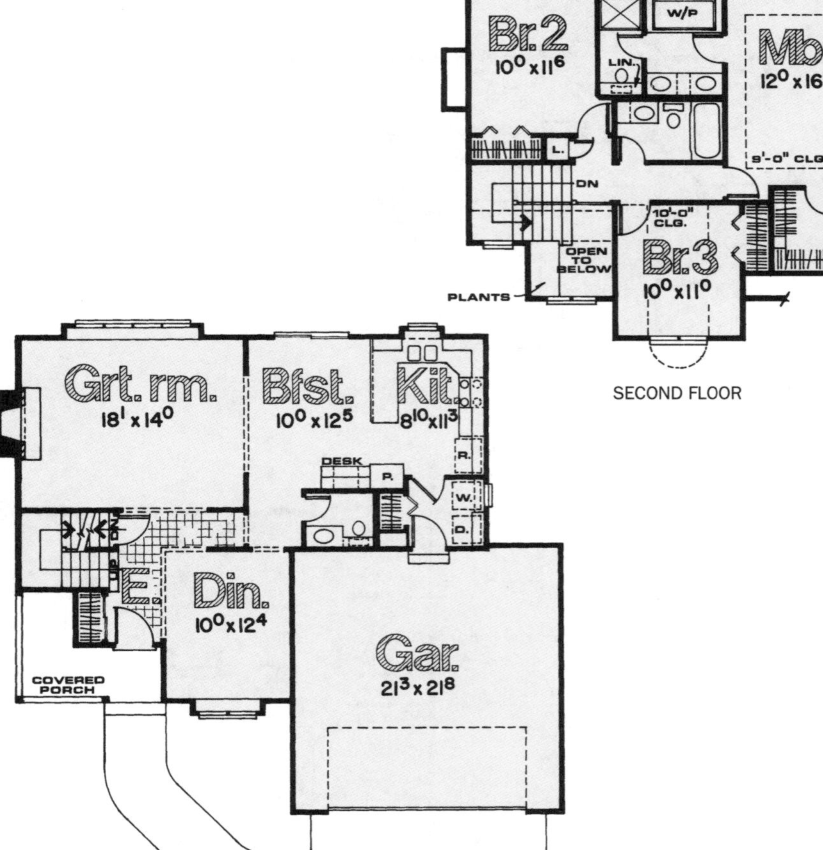

SECOND FLOOR

FIRST FLOOR

plan# HPT930040

- Style: Farmhouse
- First Floor: 891 sq. ft.
- Second Floor: 759 sq. ft.
- Total: 1,650 sq. ft.
- Bedrooms: 3
- Bathrooms: 2½
- Width: 44'-0"
- Depth: 40'-0"

SEARCH ONLINE @ EPLANS.COM

This modestly sized home provides a quaint covered front porch that opens to a two-story foyer. The formal dining room features a boxed window that can be seen from the entry. A fireplace in the great room adds warmth and coziness to the attached breakfast room and the well-planned kitchen. A powder room is provided nearby for guests. Three bedrooms occupy the second floor; one of these includes an arched window under a vaulted ceiling. The deluxe master suite provides a large walk-in closet and a dressing area with a double vanity and a whirlpool tub.

plan# HPT930041
L
> Style: Traditional
> First Floor: 1,930 sq. ft.
> Second Floor: 791 sq. ft.
> Total: 2,721 sq. ft.
> Bedrooms: 4
> Bathrooms: 3
> Width: 64'-4"
> Depth: 62'-0"
> Foundation: Basement, Crawlspace, Slab
SEARCH ONLINE @ EPLANS.COM

SECOND FLOOR

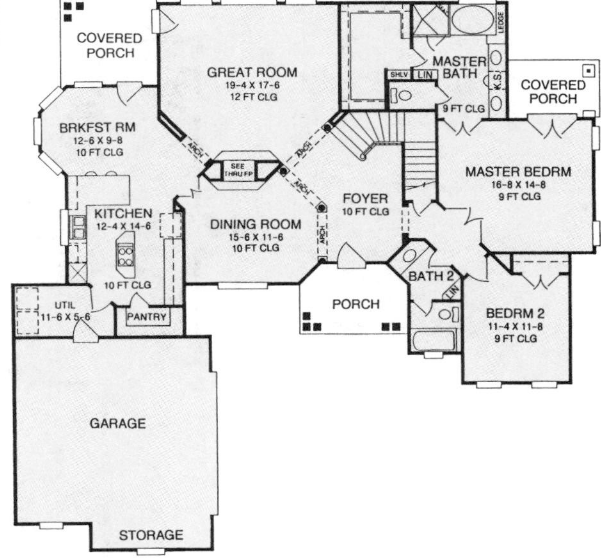

FIRST FLOOR

A delightful elevation with a swoop roof captures the eye and provides just the right touch for this inviting home. Inside, an angled foyer with a volume ceiling directs attention to the enormous great room. The detailed dining room includes massive round columns connected by arches and shares a through-fireplace with the great room. The master suite includes an upscale bath and access to a private covered porch. Nearby, Bedroom 2 is perfect for a nursery or home office/study. The kitchen features a large cooktop island and walk-in pantry. The second floor is dominated by an oversized game room. Two family bedrooms, a bath and a linen closet complete the upstairs.

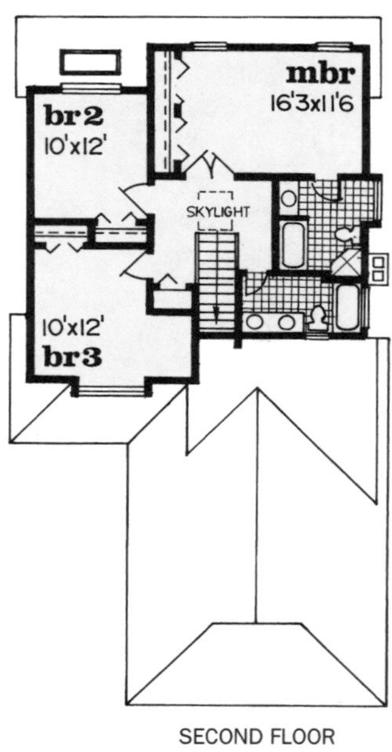

SECOND FLOOR

ALTERNATE EXTERIOR

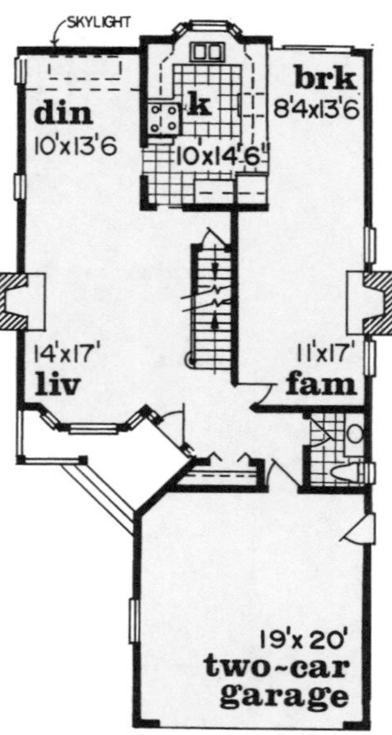

FIRST FLOOR

plan# HPT930042

- Style: Country Cottage
- First Floor: 1,084 sq. ft.
- Second Floor: 840 sq. ft.
- Total: 1,924 sq. ft.
- Bedrooms: 3
- Bathrooms: 2½
- Width: 30'-0"
- Depth: 60'-0"
- Foundation: Basement, Crawlspace

SEARCH ONLINE @ EPLANS.COM

With two exteriors to choose from—one a country cousin and one a Tudor version—this narrow lot home is designed for flexibility. Inside, the floor plan accommodates both formal and casual get-togethers. To the left, a bayed living room with a fireplace extends into a skylit dining room. Informal spaces are to the right: a cozy family room with fireplace flows into a breakfast room with sliding glass doors to the rear yard. The kitchen is conveniently central, and has a step-saving U-shaped work area. Three bedrooms are on the second floor: two family bedrooms share a full bath, and a master suite enjoys a private bath. The second-floor hall is brightened by a skylight.

plan# HPT930043

- Style: Cottage
- First Floor: 1,626 sq. ft.
- Second Floor: 1,789 sq. ft.
- Total: 3,415 sq. ft.
- Bedrooms: 4
- Bathrooms: 2½ + ½
- Width: 76'-8"
- Depth: 37'-8"
- Foundation: Basement, Crawlspace

SEARCH ONLINE @ EPLANS.COM

ALTERNATE ELEVATION

This cottage may be designed as a four- or a five-bedroom home. You'll also have the choice of a stucco or a brick exterior. The first floor holds living and dining space for both formal and informal occasions. A hearth warms the family room; you may also choose a hearth for the formal living room. The kitchen is large enough to suit the family and features an island work center. A large laundry/sewing room connects the first floor to the two-car garage. Bedrooms on the second floor include three family bedrooms and a master suite with an outside deck. The master bath is appointed with a corner whirlpool tub, double sinks and a separate shower. A den on the second floor can become a fifth bedroom.

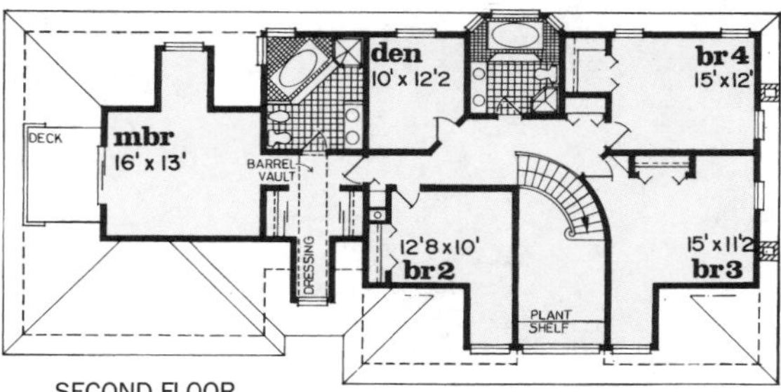

SECOND FLOOR

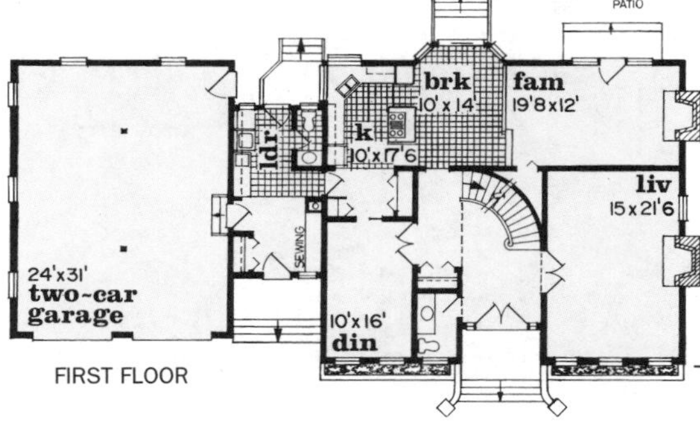

FIRST FLOOR

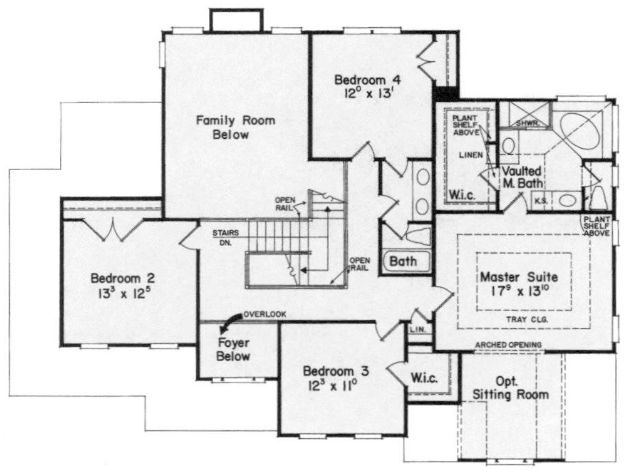

SECOND FLOOR

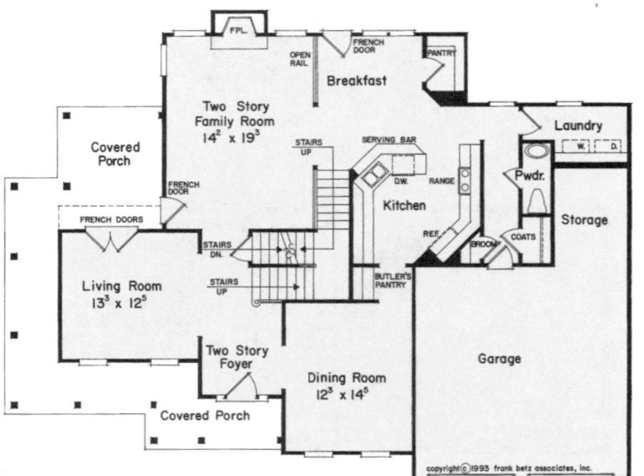

FIRST FLOOR

plan# HPT930044

- Style: Farmhouse
- First Floor: 1,351 sq. ft.
- Second Floor: 1,257 sq. ft.
- Total: 2,608 sq. ft.
- Bonus Space: 115 sq. ft.
- Bedrooms: 4
- Bathrooms: 2½
- Width: 60'-0"
- Depth: 46'-4"
- Foundation: Crawlspace, Walkout Basement

SEARCH ONLINE @ EPLANS.COM

Here's a new country home with a fresh face and a dash of Victoriana. Inside, the foyer leads to an elegant dining room and a spacious living room with French doors to the covered rear porch. The heart of the home is a two-story family room with a focal-point fireplace and its own French door to the rear property. A breakfast room offers a walk-in pantry and shares a snack bar with the kitchen, which in turn leads to the formal dining room through a butler's pantry. The second-floor master suite features an impressive private bath with a vaulted ceiling and an optional sitting room.

plan# HPT930045

- Style: Country Cottage
- First Floor: 1,475 sq. ft.
- Second Floor: 1,460 sq. ft.
- Total: 2,935 sq. ft.
- Bedrooms: 4
- Bathrooms: 3½
- Width: 57'-6"
- Depth: 46'-6"
- Foundation: Walkout Basement

SEARCH ONLINE @ EPLANS.COM

SECOND FLOOR

Cost to build? See page 436 to order complete cost estimate to build this house in your area!

Quaint keystones and shutters offer charming accents to the stucco-and-stone exterior of this stately English country home. The two-story foyer opens through decorative columns to the formal living room, which offers a wet bar. The nearby media room shares a through-fireplace with the two-story great room, which has double doors that lead to the rear deck. A bumped-out bay holds a breakfast area that shares its light with an expansive cooktop-island kitchen. This area opens to the formal dining room through a convenient butler's pantry. One wing of the second floor is dedicated to the rambling master suite, which boasts unusual amenities with angled walls, a tray ceiling and a bumped-out bay with a sitting area in the bedroom.

FIRST FLOOR

SECOND FLOOR

FIRST FLOOR

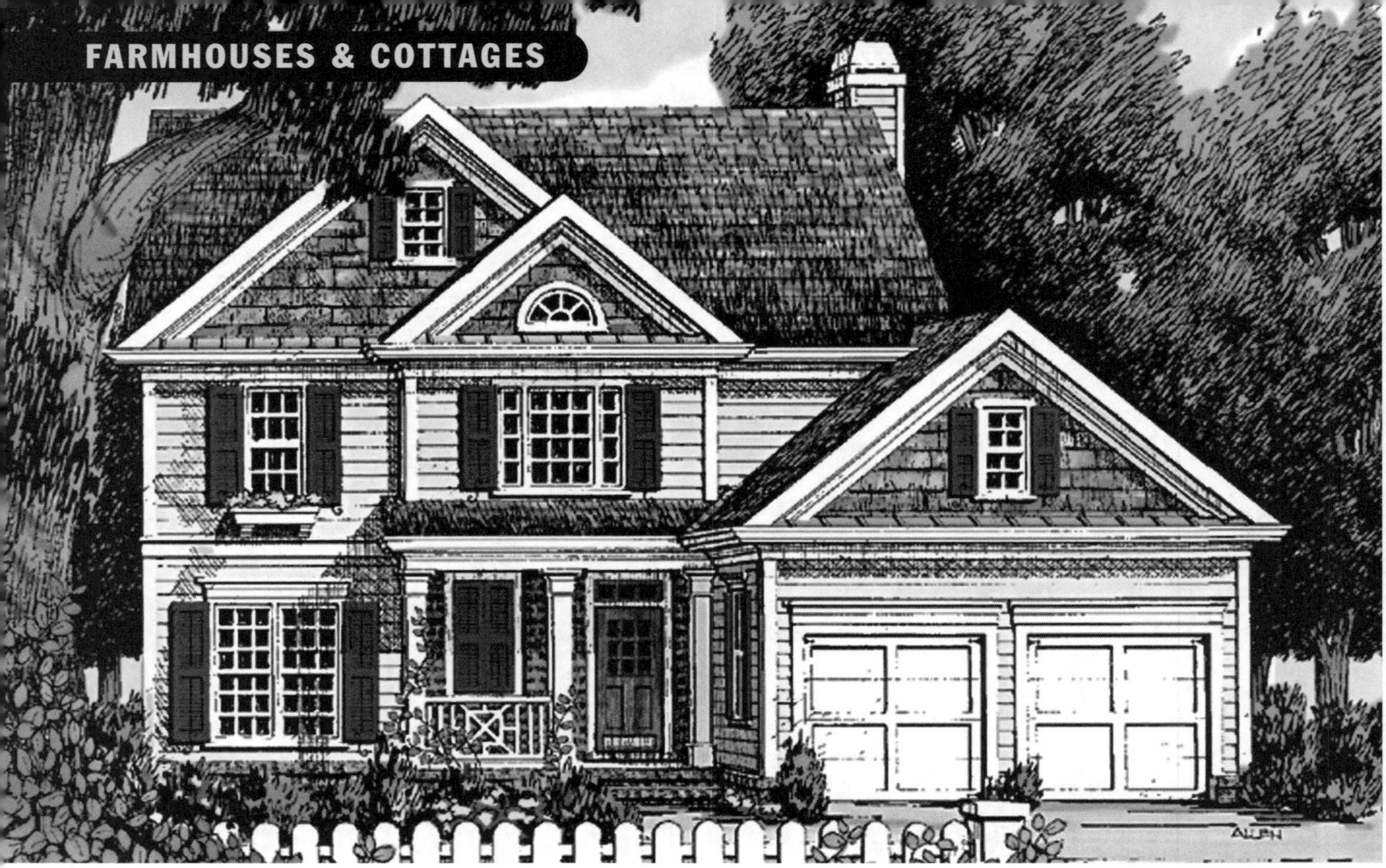

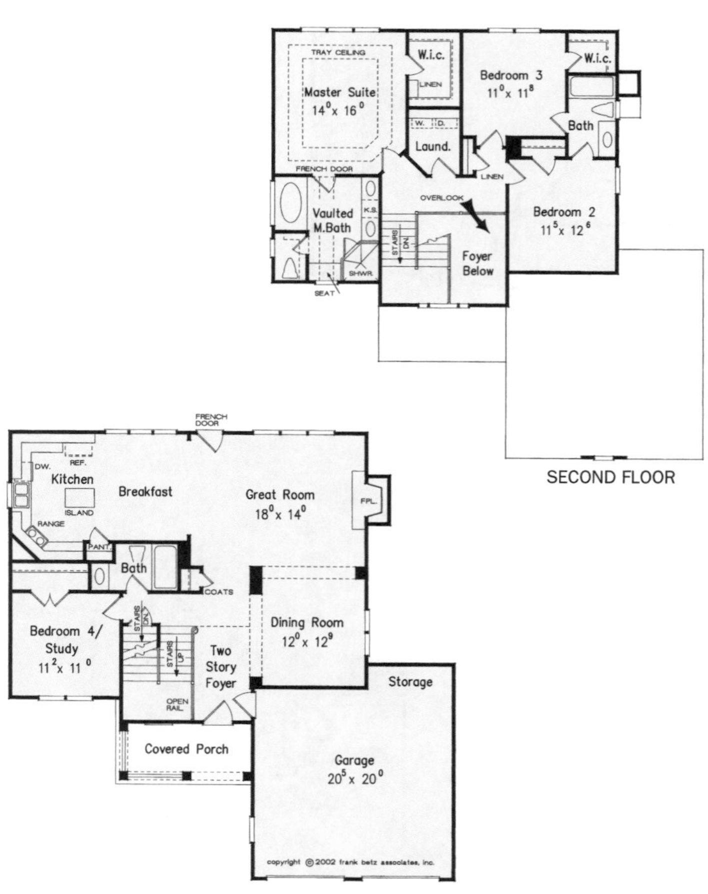

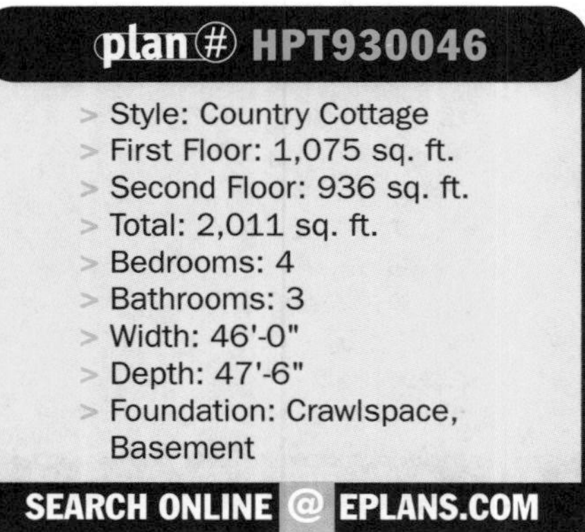

plan# HPT930046

- Style: Country Cottage
- First Floor: 1,075 sq. ft.
- Second Floor: 936 sq. ft.
- Total: 2,011 sq. ft.
- Bedrooms: 4
- Bathrooms: 3
- Width: 46'-0"
- Depth: 47'-6"
- Foundation: Crawlspace, Basement

SEARCH ONLINE @ EPLANS.COM

This country cottage is sure to warm the souls of all who enter. Pedimented arches and shuttered windows give this home a feeling of casual country. The covered porch opens to the two-story foyer where the formal dining area is surrounded by columns. The great room is open to the breakfast nook and kitchen area. An island in the kitchen makes this a great home to have either a formal or casual gathering. A master suite with a vaulted bath is located on the second floor. Two family bedrooms and a bath are also located on the second floor to complete the comfortable sleeping quarters.

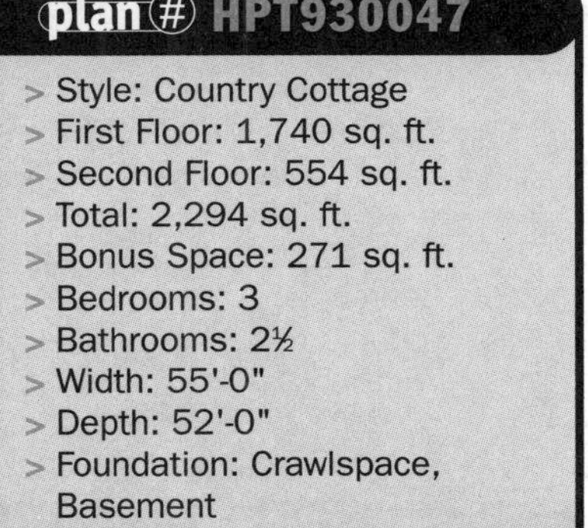

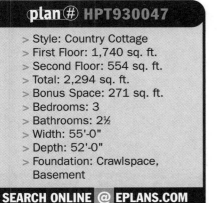

plan# HPT930047

- Style: Country Cottage
- First Floor: 1,740 sq. ft.
- Second Floor: 554 sq. ft.
- Total: 2,294 sq. ft.
- Bonus Space: 271 sq. ft.
- Bedrooms: 3
- Bathrooms: 2½
- Width: 55'-0"
- Depth: 52'-0"
- Foundation: Crawlspace, Basement

SEARCH ONLINE @ EPLANS.COM

The sharp pedimented arches and decorative covered porch make this home a country treat. Windows align the exterior of this home brightening the rooms at every angle. The two-story foyer opens to the vaulted living room. The breakfast nook and kitchen are well-lit with the surrounding windows. The master suite features a tray ceiling and a ribbon of windows. Two family bedrooms on the second floor overlook the family and dining rooms.

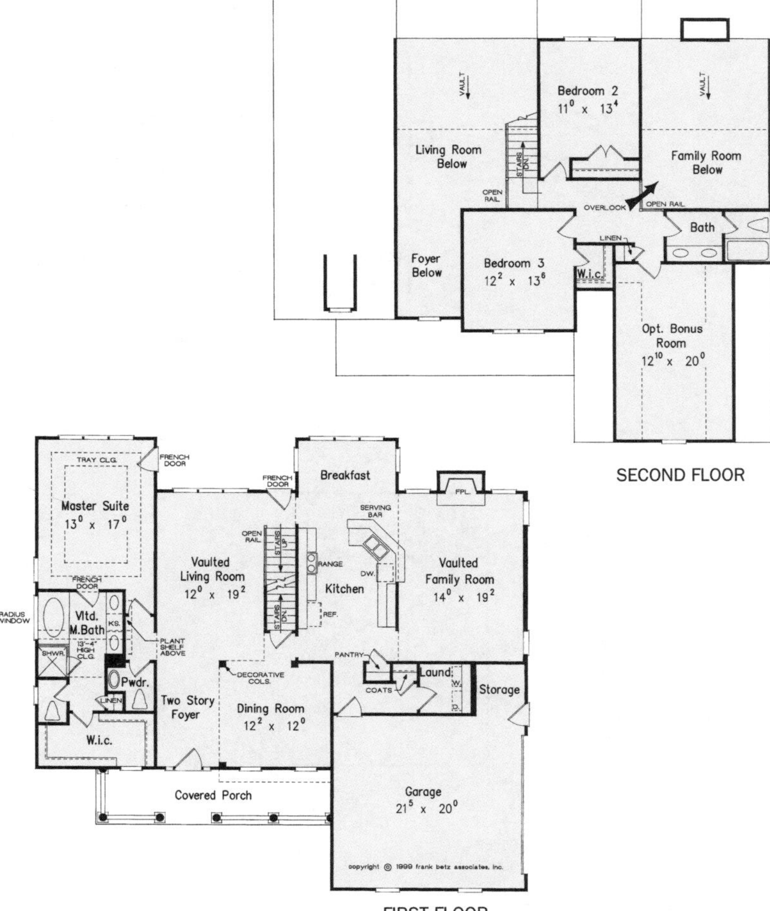

SECOND FLOOR

FIRST FLOOR

plan# HPT930048

- Style: Farmhouse
- First Floor: 1,169 sq. ft.
- Second Floor: 1,034 sq. ft.
- Total: 2,203 sq. ft.
- Bonus Space: 347 sq. ft.
- Bedrooms: 3
- Bathrooms: 2½
- Width: 55'-4"
- Depth: 52'-0"
- Foundation: Crawlspace

SEARCH ONLINE @ EPLANS.COM

This fashionable farmhouse shows off the height of style, but never at the expense of comfort. Clapboard siding sets off a lighthearted symmetry on this country elevation that braces an Early American flavor with new spirit. Inside, formal rooms flank the foyer and lead to casual living space. An expansive family room with a focal-point fireplace opens to a wide-open breakfast area and gourmet kitchen. The rear covered porch invites enjoyment of the outdoors and adjoins an entertainment porch. Upstairs, the lavish master suite offers twin vanities and a generous walk-in closet. Two additional bedrooms share a hall bath. A sizable bonus room includes a walk-in closet.

plan# HPT930049

- Style: Farmhouse
- First Floor: 959 sq. ft.
- Second Floor: 833 sq. ft.
- Total: 1,792 sq. ft.
- Bonus Space: 344 sq. ft.
- Bedrooms: 3
- Bathrooms: 2½
- Width: 52'-6"
- Depth: 42'-8"

SEARCH ONLINE @ EPLANS.COM

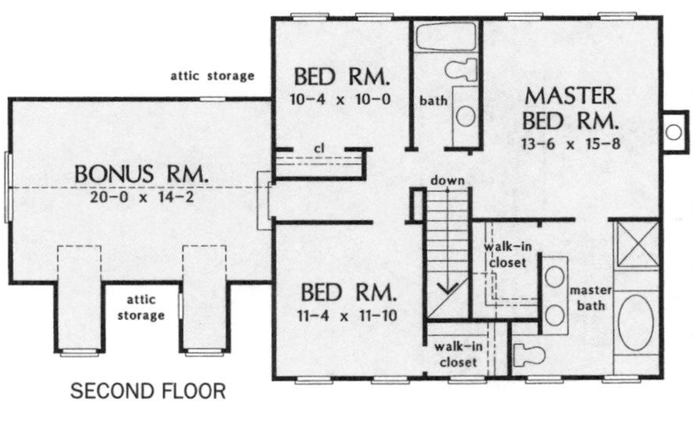

SECOND FLOOR

From its covered front porch to its covered rear porch, this farmhouse is a real charmer. The formal dining room is filled with light from a bay window. A matching bay is found in the cozy breakfast room. The large great room is graced with a warming fireplace and even more windows. The master suite offers a private bath with an array of luxuries. A bonus room extending over the garage can be developed into a game room, a fourth bedroom or a study at a later date.

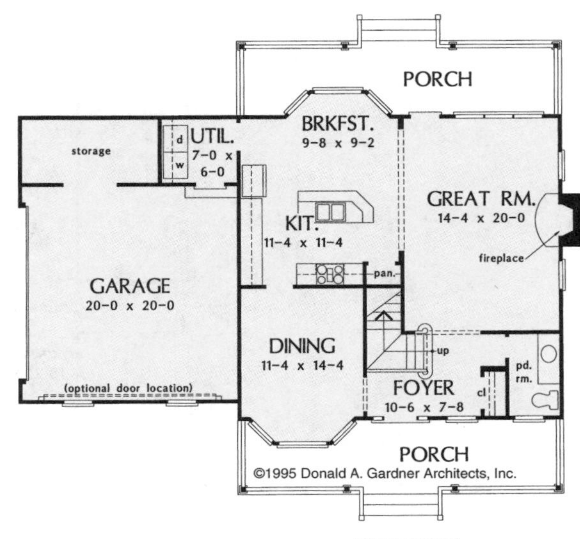

FIRST FLOOR

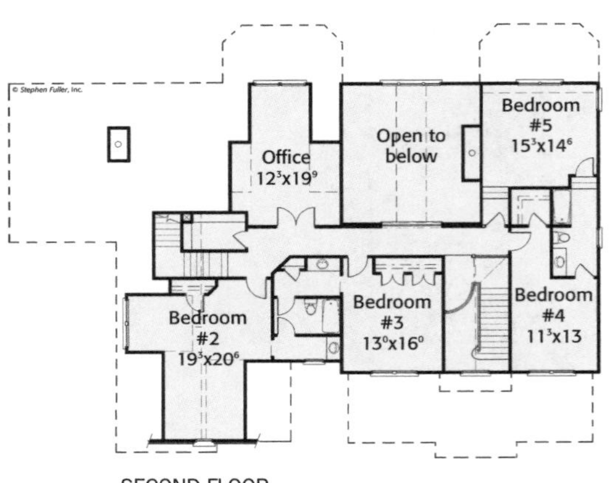

SECOND FLOOR

plan# HPT930050

- Style: Farmhouse
- First Floor: 2,628 sq. ft.
- Second Floor: 1,775 sq. ft.
- Total: 4,403 sq. ft.
- Bedrooms: 5
- Bathrooms: 3½
- Width: 79'-6"
- Depth: 65'-1"
- Foundation: Walkout Basement

SEARCH ONLINE @ EPLANS.COM

With five bedrooms and a wonderful stone-and-siding exterior, this country home will satisfy every need. Two sets of French doors provide access to the dining room and foyer. The great room enjoys a warming fireplace and deck access. The kitchen, breakfast bay and keeping room feature an open floor plan. A charming sitting area in a bay window sets off the master bedroom. The master bath features a large walk-in closet, two-sink vanity, separate tub and shower and compartmented toilet. Four bedrooms, an office and two full baths complete the upper level.

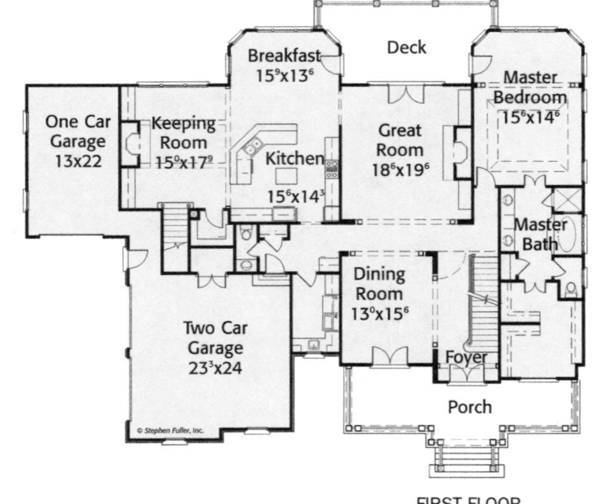

FIRST FLOOR

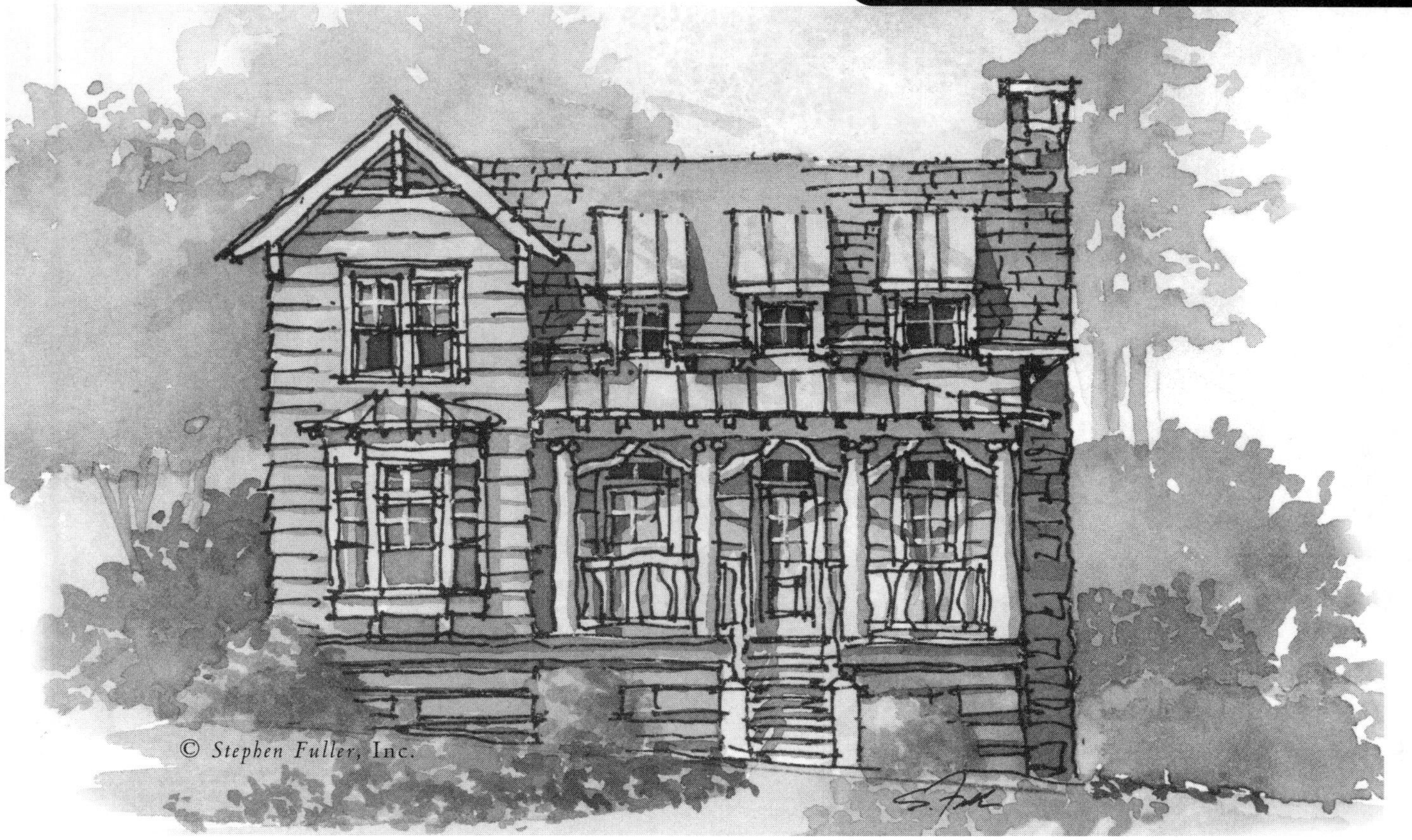

© Stephen Fuller, Inc.

plan# HPT930051

- Style: Farmhouse
- First Floor: 862 sq. ft.
- Second Floor: 654 sq. ft.
- Total: 1,516 sq. ft.
- Bedrooms: 3
- Bathrooms: 2
- Width: 34'-0"
- Depth: 39'-6"
- Foundation: Crawlspace

SEARCH ONLINE @ EPLANS.COM

The rustic simplicity of this country design is perfect for just about any setting. A covered front porch welcomes you inside to a spacious great room warmed by a fireplace. The kitchen is compact and features direct access to the rear covered porch. The first-floor bedroom is enhanced by a bayed window and is located next to a hall bath. Upstairs, two additional bedrooms share the second floor with a hall bath.

BEDROOM #3
20⁹ X 12⁹
BEDROOM #2
12⁶ X 11⁰
© Stephen Fuller, Inc.

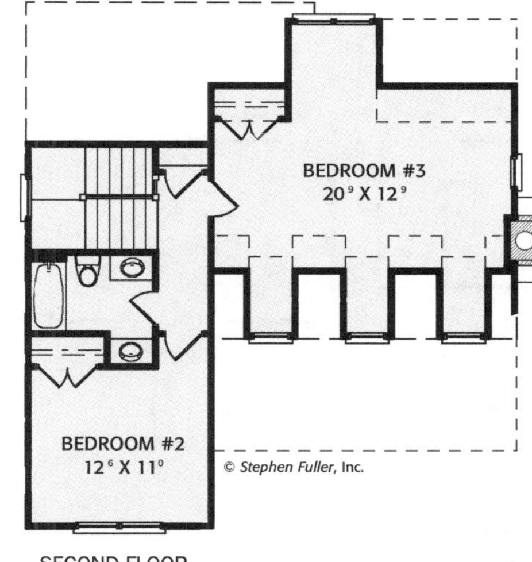

SECOND FLOOR

KITCHEN
15⁹ X 9⁹
COVERED PORCH
GREAT ROOM
20⁹ X 13⁶
COVERED PORCH
BEDROOM #1
12⁶ X 11⁶
© Stephen Fuller, Inc.

FIRST FLOOR

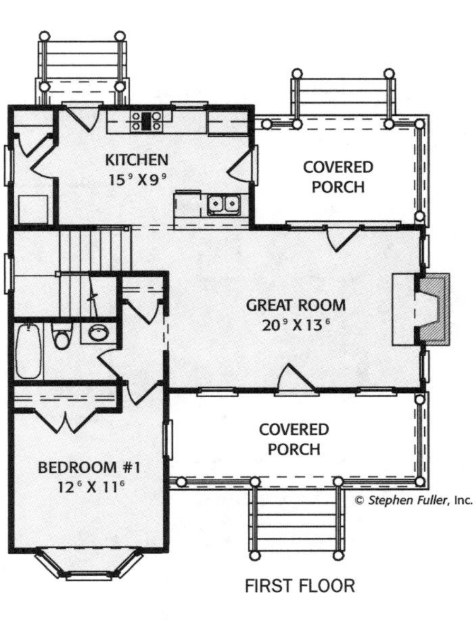

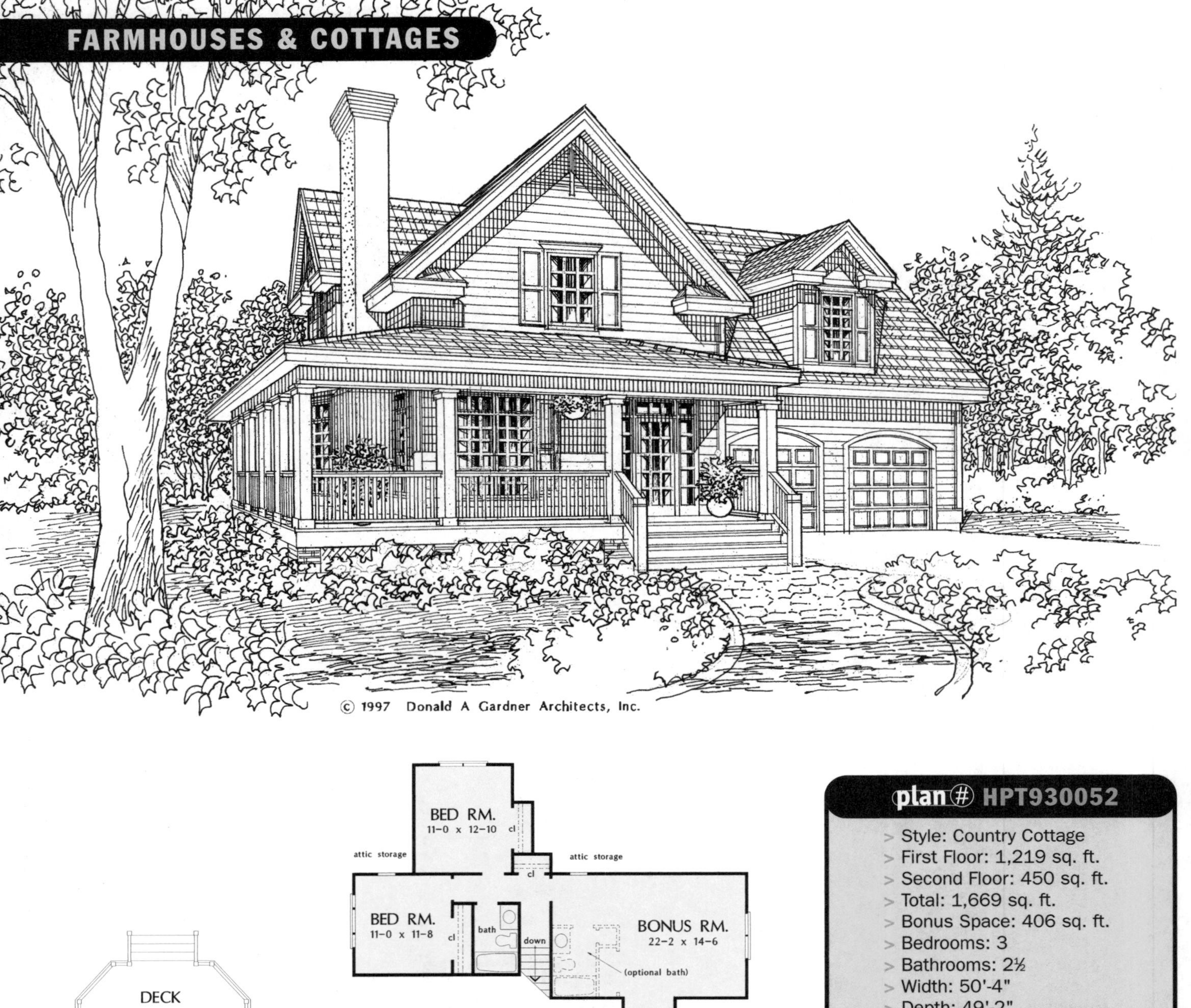

plan# HPT930052

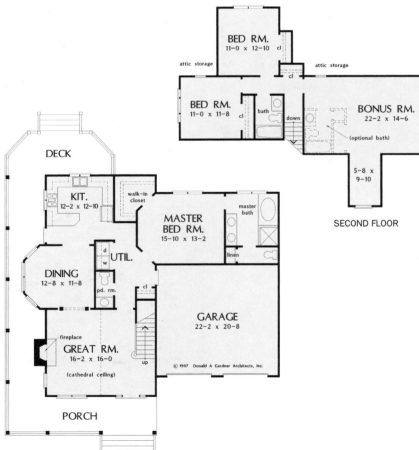

- Style: Country Cottage
- First Floor: 1,219 sq. ft.
- Second Floor: 450 sq. ft.
- Total: 1,669 sq. ft.
- Bonus Space: 406 sq. ft.
- Bedrooms: 3
- Bathrooms: 2½
- Width: 50'-4"
- Depth: 49'-2"

SEARCH ONLINE @ EPLANS.COM

This three-bedroom narrow-lot home offers some of the extras usually reserved for wider lots, such as a wraparound porch and a two-car garage. A vaulted ceiling adds volume to the great room, while columns and a bay window add distinction to the dining room. The kitchen is designed for efficiency and offers access to the side porch and rear deck for outdoor dining options. The master bedroom sits behind the two-car garage to shield it from noise while two family bedrooms, a full bath and the bonus room reside upstairs. The large bonus room can be adapted to serve additional family needs.

B. NATHAN

plan# HPT930053

- Style: Country
- First Floor: 1,293 sq. ft.
- Second Floor: 528 sq. ft.
- Total: 1,821 sq. ft.
- Bonus Space: 355 sq. ft.
- Bedrooms: 3
- Bathrooms: 2½
- Width: 48'-8"
- Depth: 50'-0"

SEARCH ONLINE @ EPLANS.COM

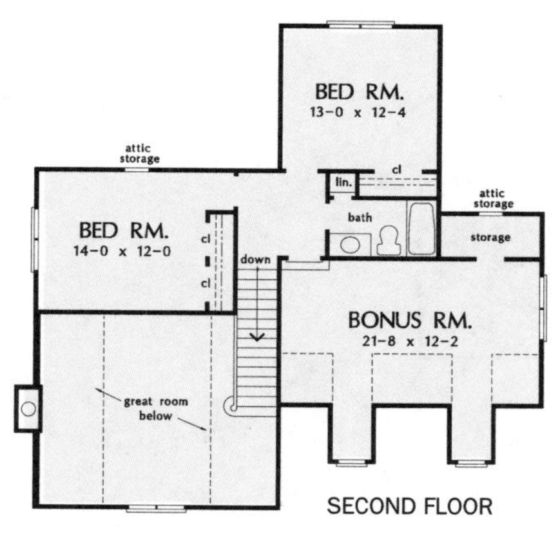

SECOND FLOOR

This nostalgic bungalow's facade is enhanced by a charming gable, twin dormers and a wrapping front porch. Bay windows enlarge both the dining room and the master bedroom, while the vaulted great room receives additional light from a front clerestory window. The kitchen features a practical design and includes a handy pantry and ample cabinets. A nearby utility room boasts a sink and additional cabinet and countertop space. Located on the first floor for convenience, the master suite enjoys a private bath and a walk-in closet. Upstairs, two more bedrooms and a generous bonus room share a full bath.

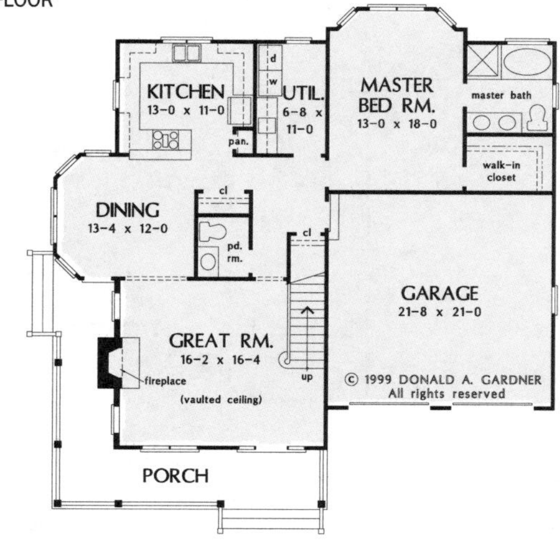

FIRST FLOOR

SECOND FLOOR

FIRST FLOOR

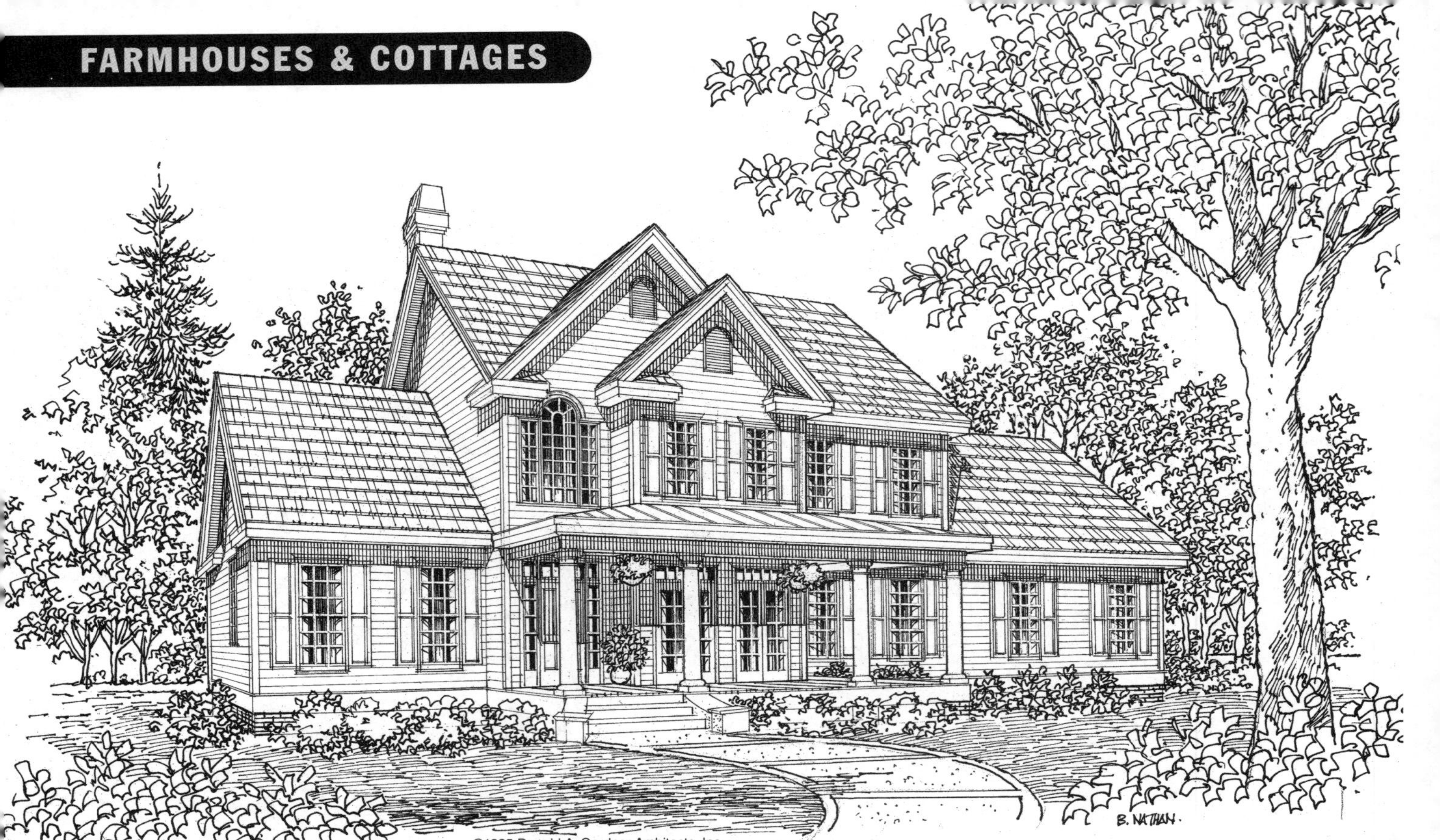

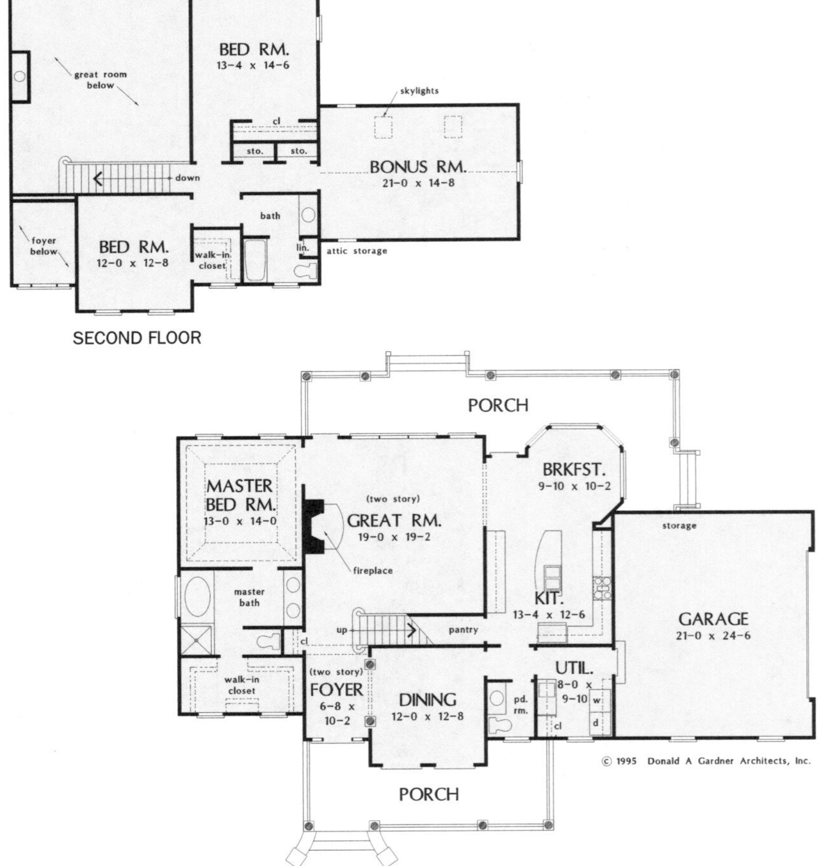

plan# HPT930054

- Style: Country Cottage
- First Floor: 1,561 sq. ft.
- Second Floor: 642 sq. ft.
- Total: 2,203 sq. ft.
- Bonus Space: 324 sq. ft.
- Bedrooms: 3
- Bathrooms: 2½
- Width: 68'-0"
- Depth: 50'-4"

SEARCH ONLINE @ EPLANS.COM

Traditional detailing, such as the covered porch with brick steps and a metal roof, gives this relaxed farmhouse extra finesse. A Palladian window, transoms over French doors, and large windows brighten the rooms, while nine-foot ceilings add volume and drama throughout the first floor. The master suite features a tray ceiling, and two second-floor bedrooms enjoy ample closet space and share a roomy bath.

plan# HPT930055

- Style: Country
- First Floor: 1,412 sq. ft.
- Second Floor: 506 sq. ft.
- Total: 1,918 sq. ft.
- Bonus Space: 320 sq. ft.
- Bedrooms: 3
- Bathrooms: 2½
- Width: 49'-8"
- Depth: 52'-0"

SEARCH ONLINE @ EPLANS.COM

Here's a country home with plenty of open interior space. Just off the foyer, a powder room and coat closet are thoughtfully placed to accommodate guests. A fireplace and built-ins highlight the great room. A formal dining room adjoins the kitchen and breakfast area, which features a triple window. Wrapping counter space in the kitchen provides enough food-preparation space for two cooks. The master suite includes a walk-in closet, well-appointed bath and additional linen storage. Upstairs, two family bedrooms share a hall bath and access to a spacious bonus room.

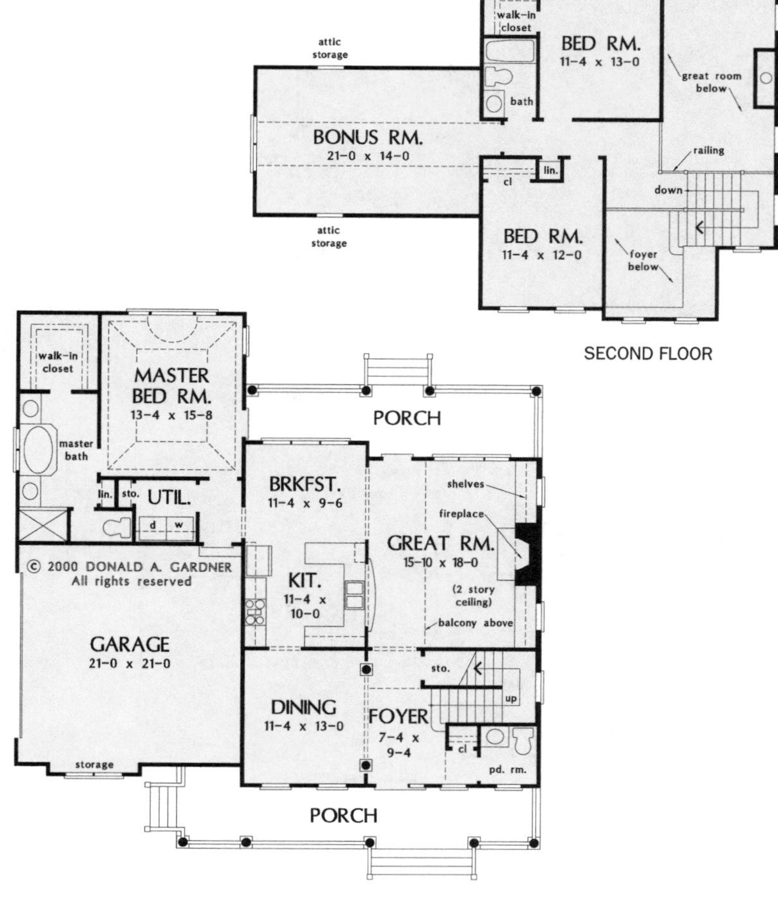

SECOND FLOOR

FIRST FLOOR

B. NATHAN

© 1997 Donald A. Gardner Architects, Inc.

SECOND FLOOR

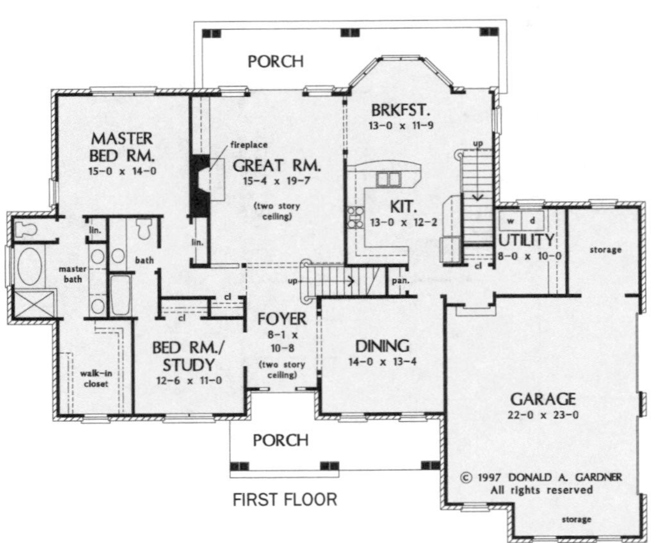

FIRST FLOOR

plan# HPT930056

- Style: Traditional
- First Floor: 2,067 sq. ft.
- Second Floor: 615 sq. ft.
- Total: 2,682 sq. ft.
- Bonus Space: 394 sq. ft.
- Bedrooms: 4
- Bathrooms: 3
- Width: 73'-0"
- Depth: 60'-6"

SEARCH ONLINE @ EPLANS.COM

Multiple gables, columns and a balustrade add stature to the facade of this four-bedroom traditional home. Both the foyer and great room have impressive two-story ceilings and clerestory windows. The great room is highlighted by built-in bookshelves and French doors that lead to the back porch. The breakfast bay features a rear staircase to the upstairs bedrooms and the bonus room. Downstairs, the master suite enjoys an indulgent bath with a large walk-in closet, and a nearby bedroom/study offers flexibility.

plan# HPT930057

- Style: Farmhouse
- First Floor: 1,483 sq. ft.
- Second Floor: 1,349 sq. ft.
- Total: 2,832 sq. ft.
- Bonus Space: 486 sq. ft.
- Bedrooms: 4
- Bathrooms: 2½
- Width: 66'-10"
- Depth: 47'-8"

SEARCH ONLINE @ EPLANS.COM

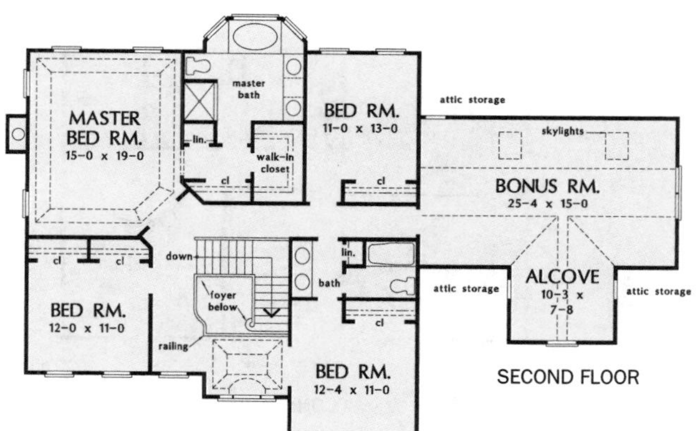

SECOND FLOOR

With two covered porches to encourage outdoor living, multi-pane windows and an open layout, this farmhouse has plenty to offer. Columns define the living room/study area. The family room is accented by a fireplace and accesses the rear porch. An adjacent sunny bayed breakfast room is convenient to the oversized island kitchen. Four bedrooms upstairs include a deluxe master suite with a lush bath and walk-in closet. Three family bedrooms have plenty of storage space and share a full hall bath.

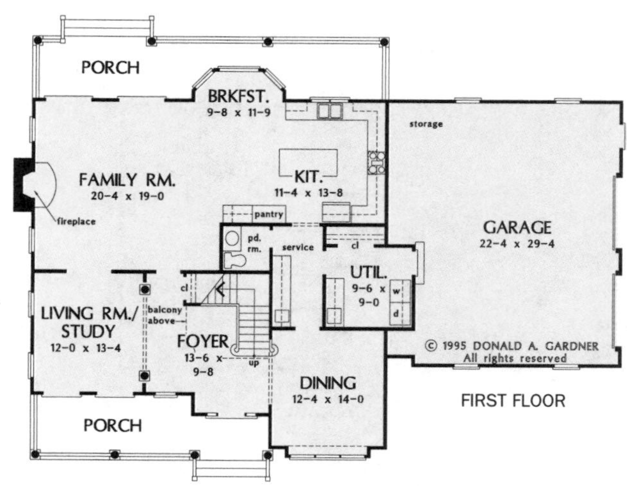

FIRST FLOOR

Basement Stair Location

SECOND FLOOR

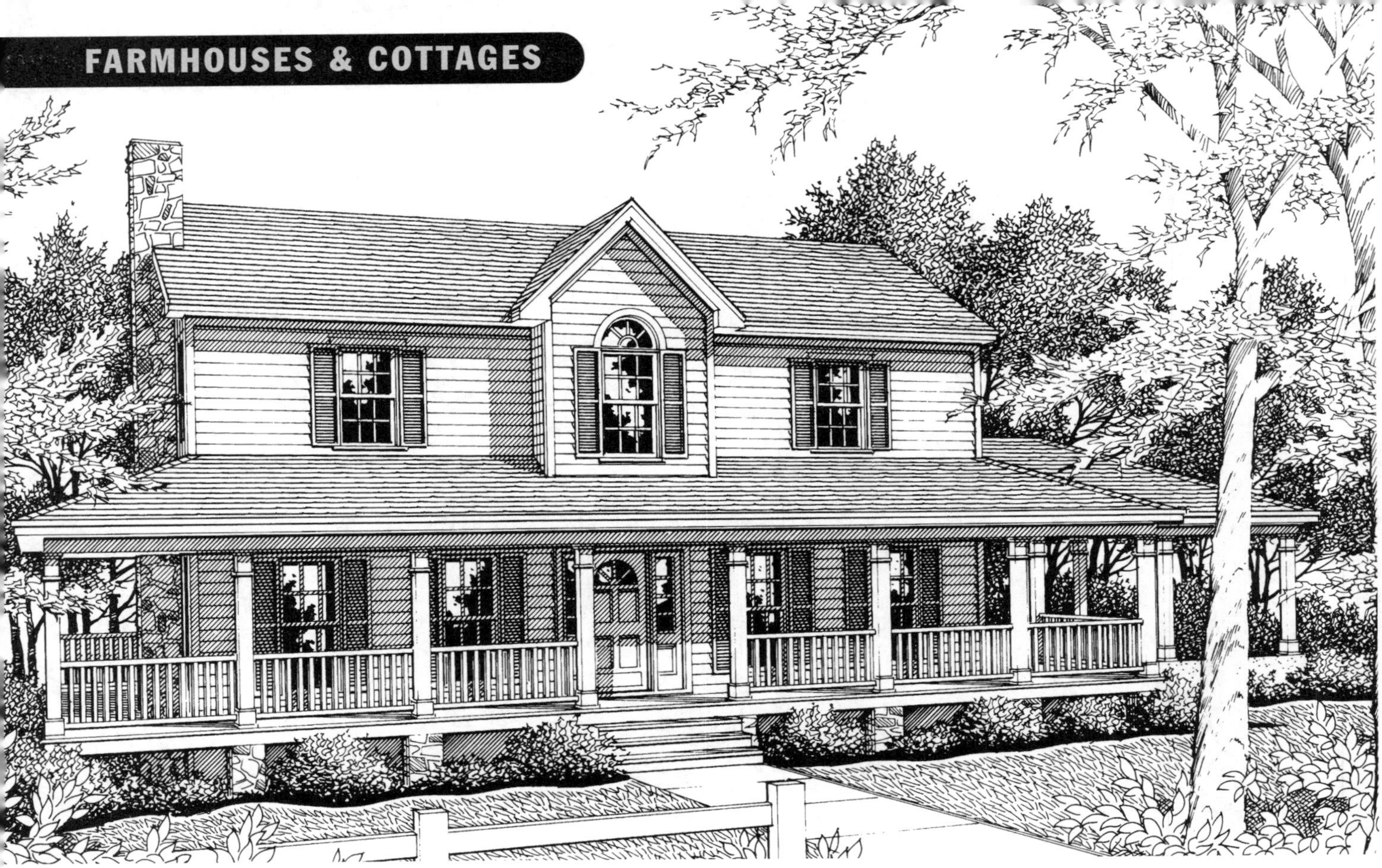

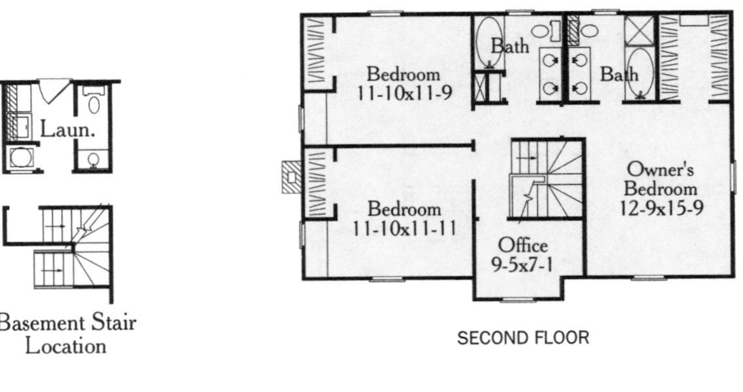

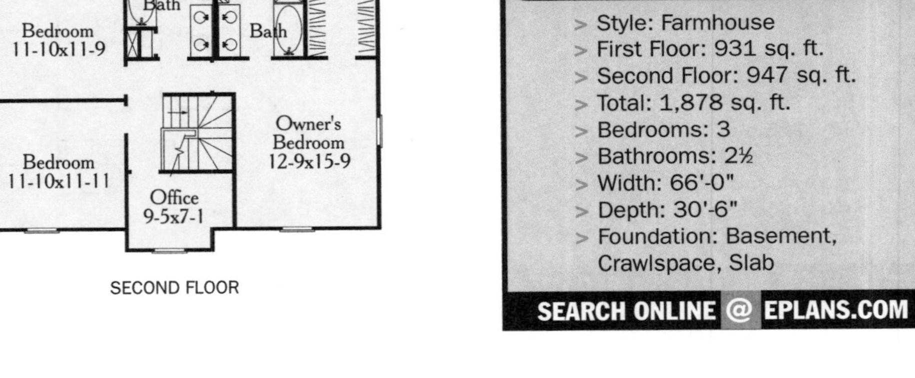

plan# HPT930058

- Style: Farmhouse
- First Floor: 931 sq. ft.
- Second Floor: 947 sq. ft.
- Total: 1,878 sq. ft.
- Bedrooms: 3
- Bathrooms: 2½
- Width: 66'-0"
- Depth: 30'-6"
- Foundation: Basement, Crawlspace, Slab

SEARCH ONLINE @ EPLANS.COM

FIRST FLOOR

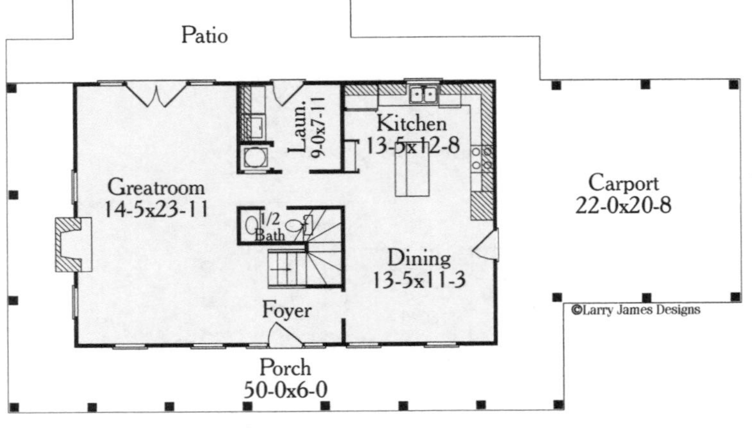

A full wraparound porch and an open layout make this farmhouse a delightful place to call home. Inside, the foyer opens on the left to a spacious great room, complete with a fireplace and outdoor access. The L-shaped kitchen offers a work island and easy access to the dining room. Upstairs, the master suite features a large walk-in closet and a private bath, while two family bedrooms share a hall bath and access to a small office.

B. NATHAN

A wraparound covered porch at the front and sides of this home and the open deck with a spa and seating provide plenty of outside living area. A central great room features a vaulted ceiling, fireplace and clerestory windows above. The loft/study on the second floor overlooks this gathering area. Besides a formal dining room, kitchen, breakfast room and sun room on the first floor, there is also a generous master suite with a garden tub. Three second-floor bedrooms complete the sleeping accommodations.

plan# HPT930059

- Style: Farmhouse
- First Floor: 1,734 sq. ft.
- Second Floor: 958 sq. ft.
- Total: 2,692 sq. ft.
- Bedrooms: 4
- Bathrooms: 3½
- Width: 55'-0"
- Depth: 59'-10"

SEARCH ONLINE 

seat
DECK
spa
SUN RM. 16-2 × 10-4
skylights
clerestory above
fireplace
pass-thru
BRKFST. 9-10 × 10-6
UTIL. 8-0 × 8-6
wash dry
sto.
GREAT RM. 15-4 × 23-2 (high ceiling)
loft above
KITCHEN 12-8 × 14-2
master bath
walk-in closet
MASTER BED RM. 12-8 × 16-4
sto.
cl
pd. rm.
FOYER 11-10 × 7-0
up
DINING 14-8 × 12-4
PORCH

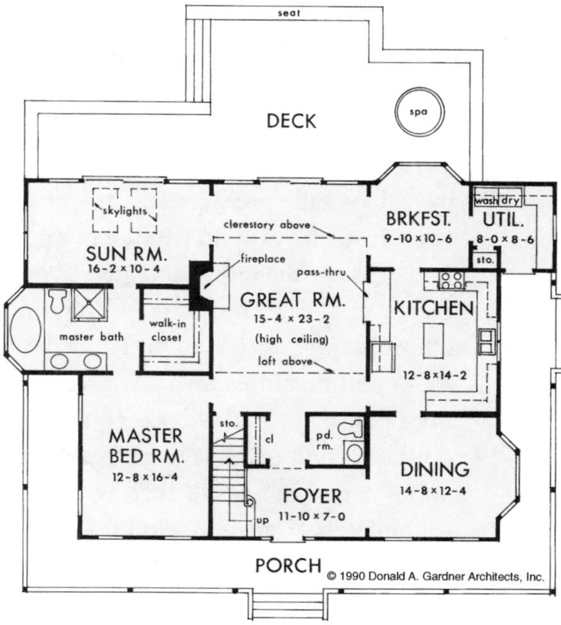

FIRST FLOOR

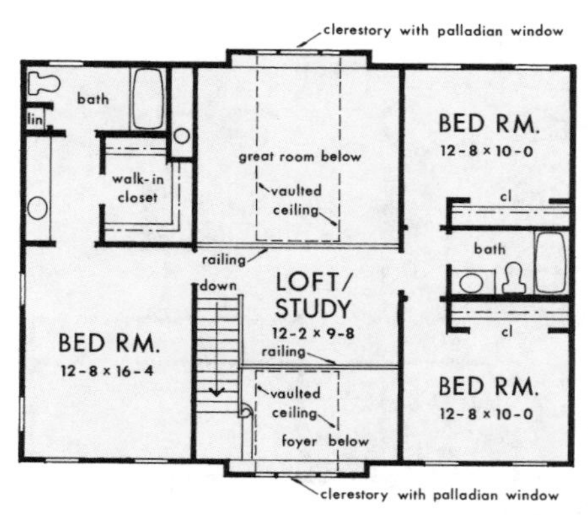

SECOND FLOOR

SECOND FLOOR

FIRST FLOOR

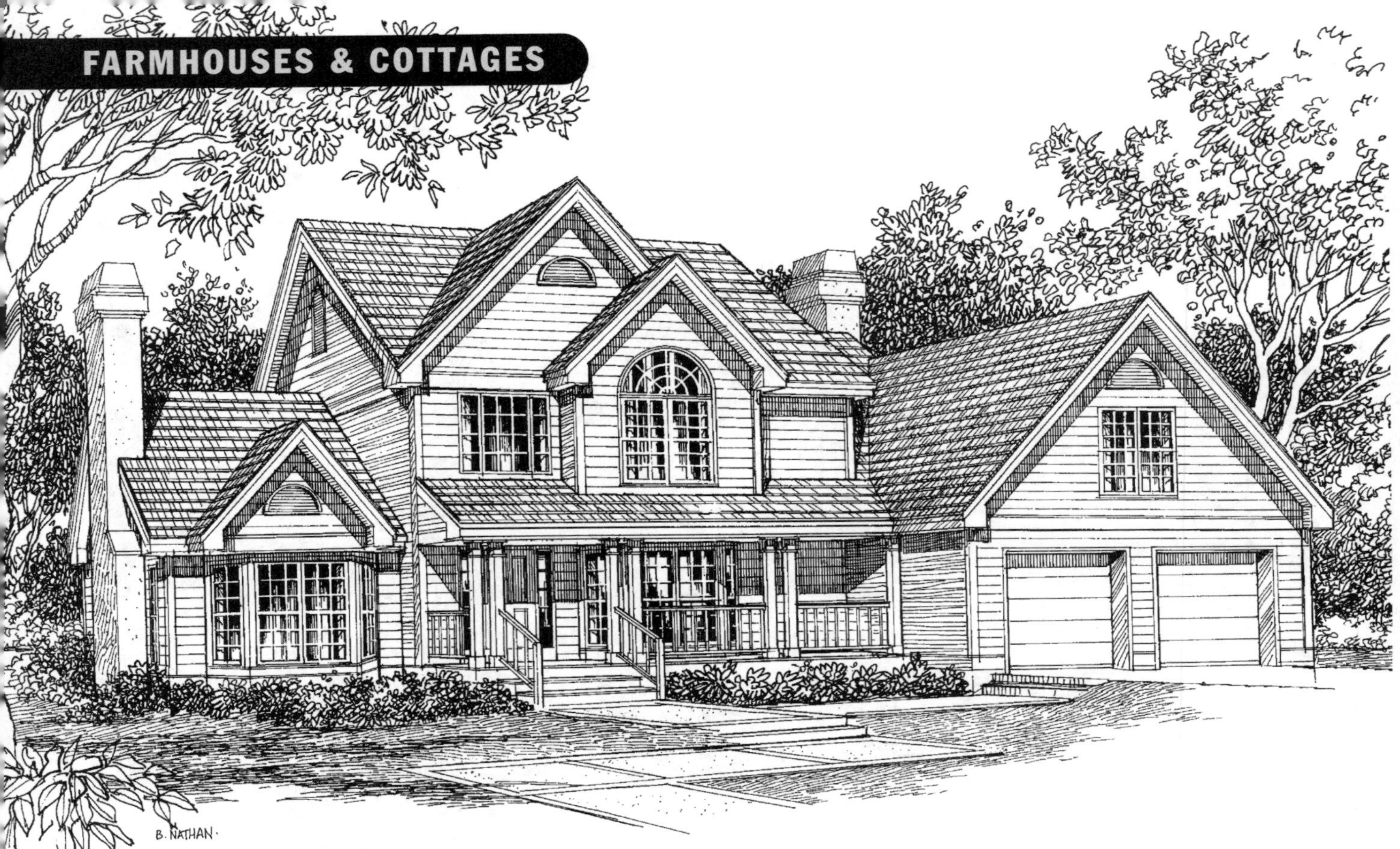

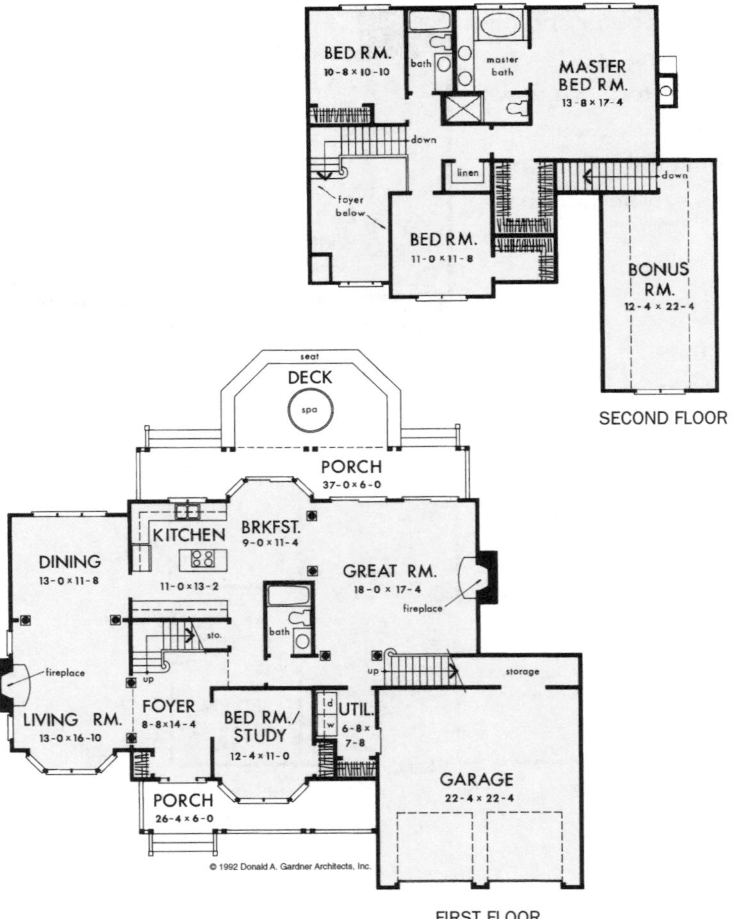

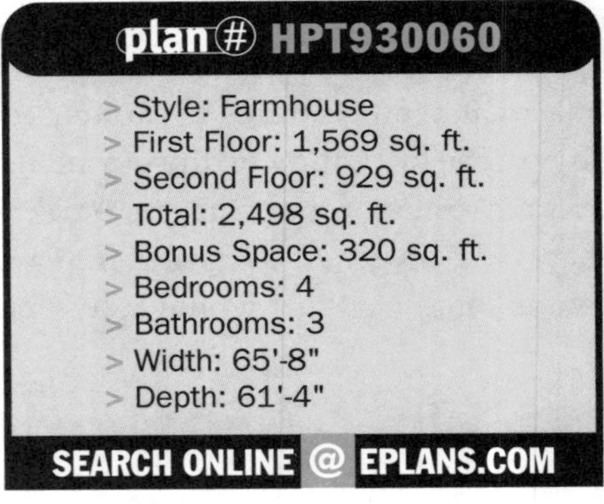

plan# HPT930060

- Style: Farmhouse
- First Floor: 1,569 sq. ft.
- Second Floor: 929 sq. ft.
- Total: 2,498 sq. ft.
- Bonus Space: 320 sq. ft.
- Bedrooms: 4
- Bathrooms: 3
- Width: 65'-8"
- Depth: 61'-4"

SEARCH ONLINE @ EPLANS.COM

This home's striking exterior is reinforced by its gables and arched-glass window. The central foyer leads to all spaces in the home's open layout. Both the living room and great room boast fireplaces and round columns. The efficient kitchen offers a cooking island to serve both the dining room and breakfast area. With four bedrooms, the floor plan calls for the master bedroom to be placed on the second level. It holds a large walk-in closet and a generous master bath with a whirlpool tub, separate shower and double-bowl vanity. Two additional bedrooms on this floor share a full bath. A bedroom on the first level can double as a study.

plan# HPT930061

- Style: Farmhouse
- First Floor: 1,439 sq. ft.
- Second Floor: 1,419 sq. ft.
- Total: 2,858 sq. ft.
- Bonus Space: 241 sq. ft.
- Bedrooms: 4
- Bathrooms: 2½
- Width: 63'-10"
- Depth: 40'-4"
- Foundation: Crawlspace

SEARCH ONLINE @ EPLANS.COM

Choose from one of two exteriors for this grand design—a lovely wood-sided farmhouse or a stately brick traditional. Plans include details for both facades. Special moldings and trim add interest to the nine-foot ceilings on the first floor. The dining room features a tray ceiling and is separated from the hearth-warmed living room by decorative columns. A study is secluded behind double doors just off the entry. The centrally located kitchen features a large cooking island, pantry, telephone desk and ample cupboard and counter space. The family room has a decorative beam ceiling and fireplace. The private master bedroom has a most exquisite bath with His and Hers walk-in closets, a soaking tub, separate shower and make-up vanity. An optional exercise/sitting room adds 241 square feet to the total. Family bedrooms share a full bath.

ALTERNATE EXTERIOR

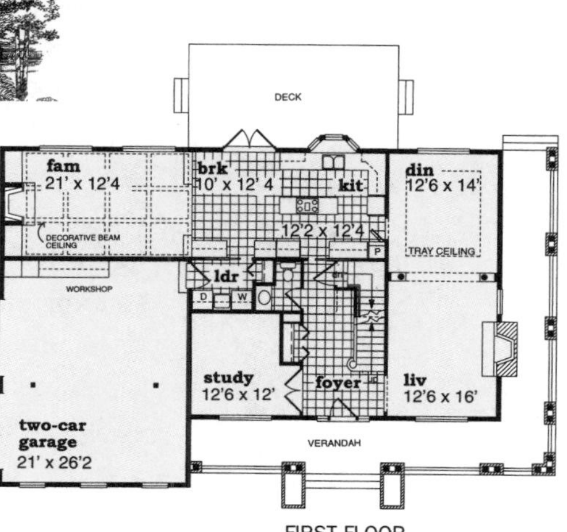

FIRST FLOOR

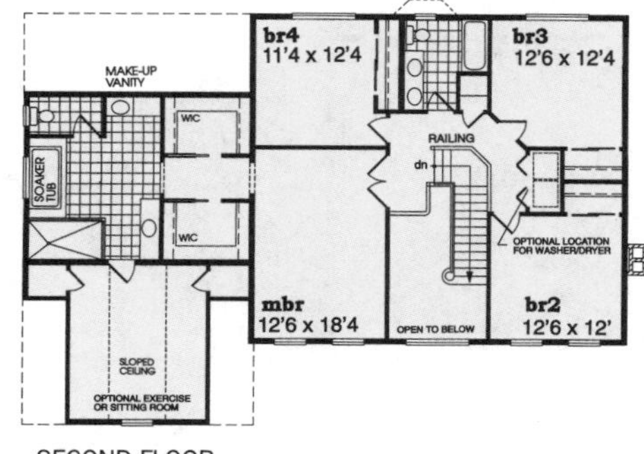

SECOND FLOOR

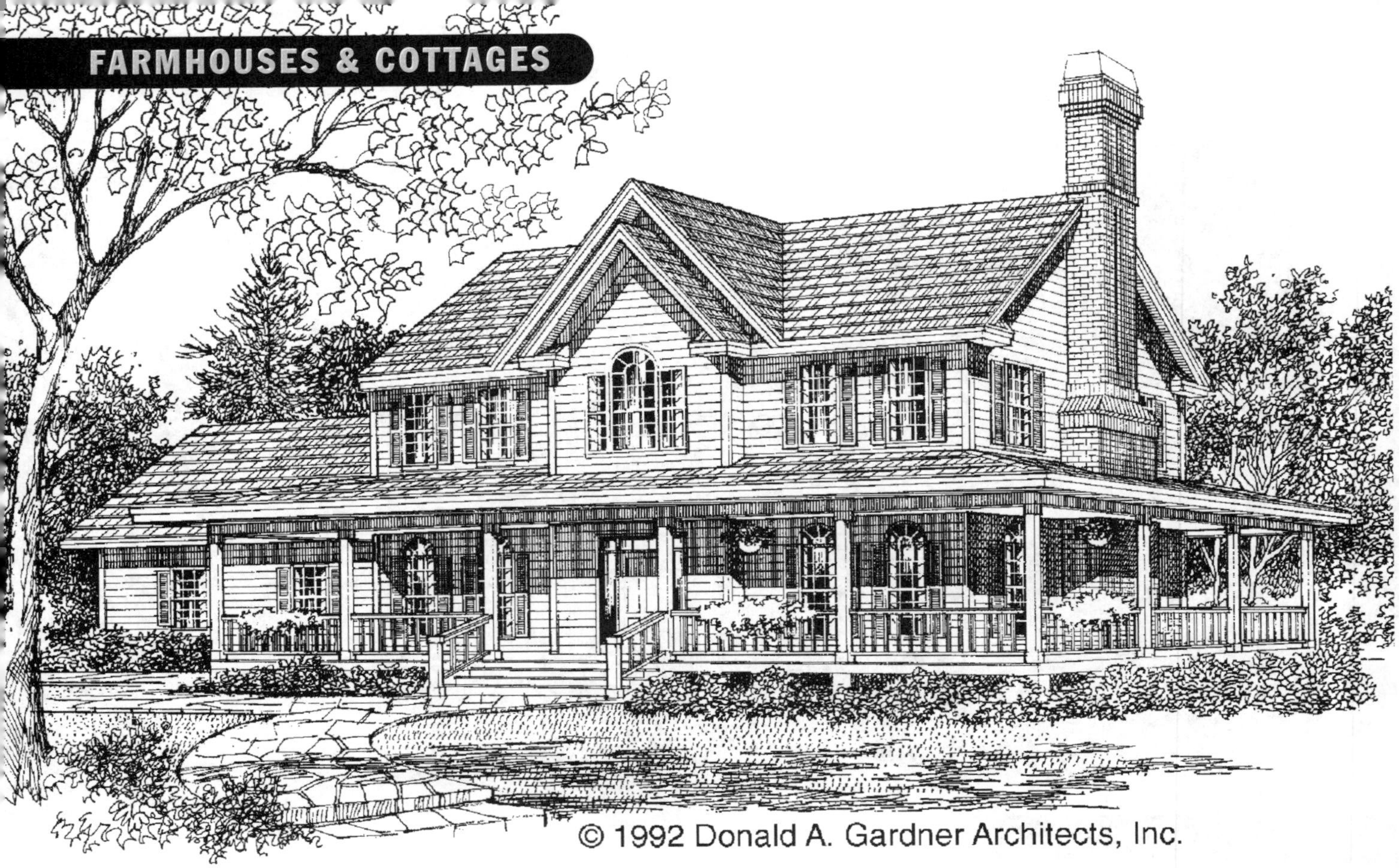

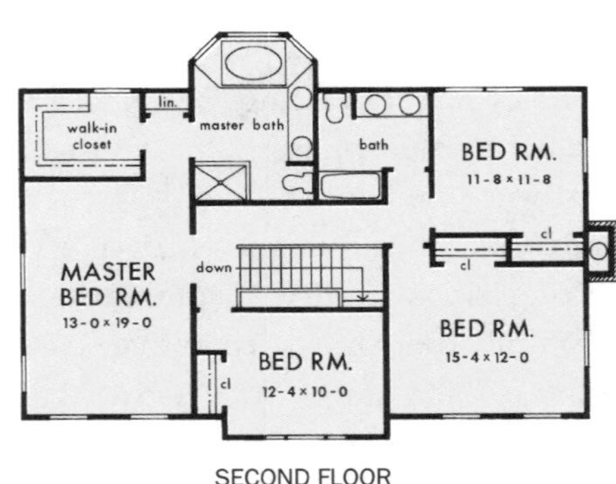

SECOND FLOOR

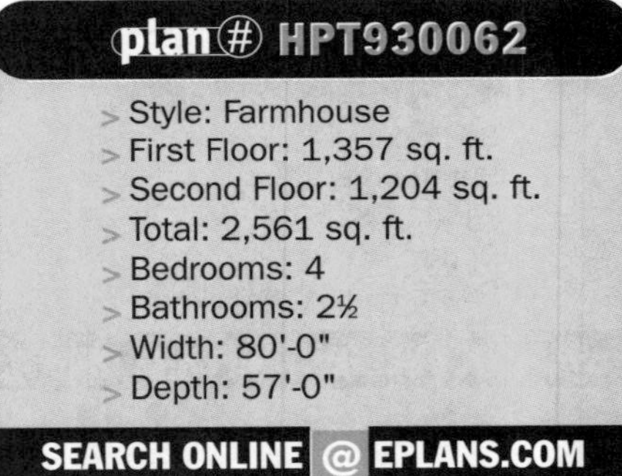

plan# HPT930062

- Style: Farmhouse
- First Floor: 1,357 sq. ft.
- Second Floor: 1,204 sq. ft.
- Total: 2,561 sq. ft.
- Bedrooms: 4
- Bathrooms: 2½
- Width: 80'-0"
- Depth: 57'-0"

SEARCH ONLINE @ EPLANS.COM

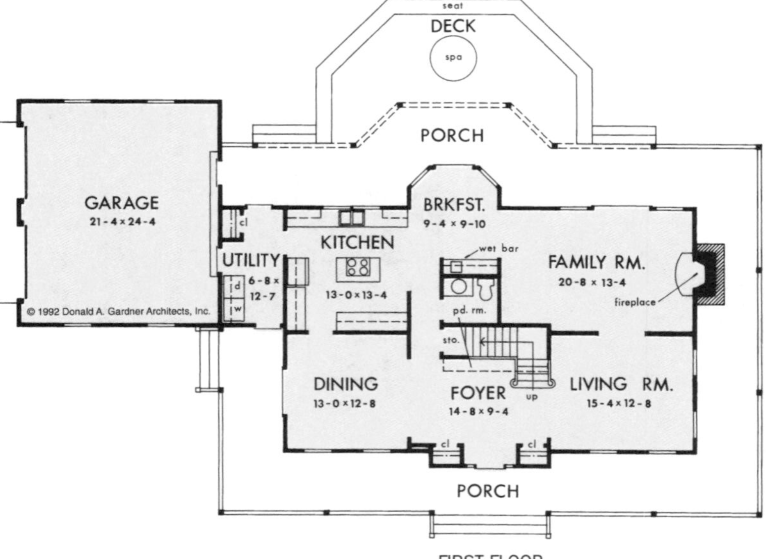

FIRST FLOOR

This grand farmhouse features a double-gabled roof, a Palladian window and an intricately detailed brick chimney. The foyer opens to the living room for formal entertaining, while the family room offers a fireplace, wet bar and direct access to the porch. The lavish kitchen boasts a cooking island and serves the dining room, breakfast nook and porch. The master suite on the second level has a large walk-in closet and a master bath with a whirlpool tub, separate shower and double-bowl vanity. Three additional bedrooms share a full bath.

plan# HPT930063

- Style: Farmhouse
- First Floor: 2,347 sq. ft.
- Second Floor: 1,087 sq. ft.
- Total: 3,434 sq. ft.
- Bedrooms: 4
- Bathrooms: 2½
- Width: 93'-6"
- Depth: 61'-0"
- Foundation: Basement

L

SEARCH ONLINE @ EPLANS.COM

Dutch-gable rooflines and a gabled wraparound porch provide an extra measure of farmhouse style. The foyer opens on the left to the study or guest bedroom that leads to the master suite. To the right is the formal dining room; the massive great room is in the center. The kitchen combines with the great room, the breakfast nook and the dining room for entertaining options. The master suite includes access to the covered patio, a spacious walk-in closet and a full bath with a whirlpool tub.

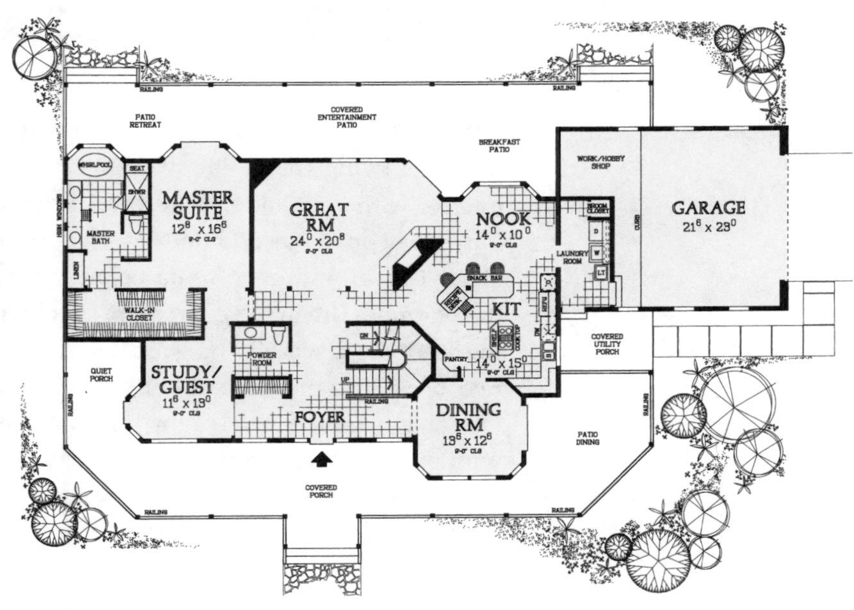

FIRST FLOOR

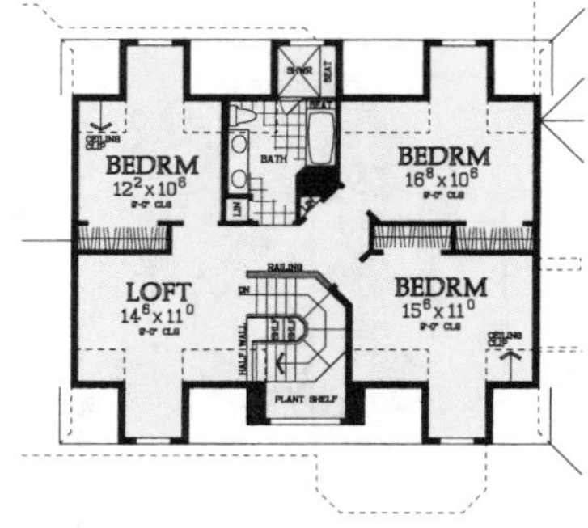

SECOND FLOOR

Cost to build? See page 436 to order complete cost estimate to build this house in your area!

© 1993 Donald A. Gardner Architects, Inc.

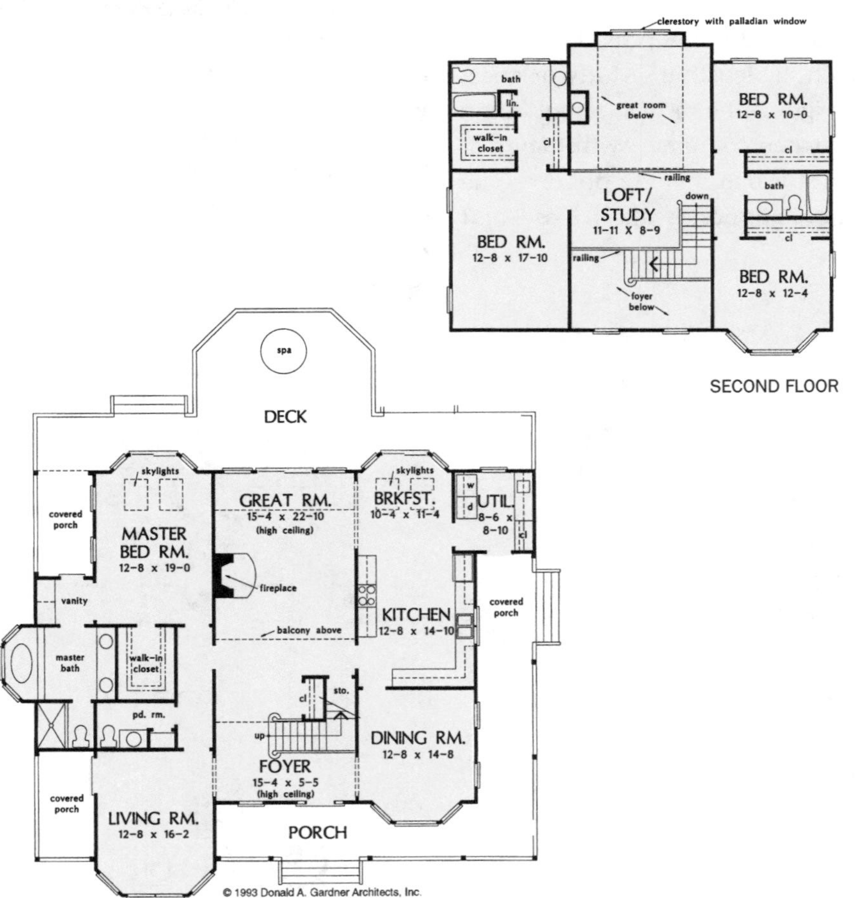

SECOND FLOOR

FIRST FLOOR

plan# HPT930064

- Style: Farmhouse
- First Floor: 1,976 sq. ft.
- Second Floor: 970 sq. ft.
- Total: 2,946 sq. ft.
- Bedrooms: 4
- Bathrooms: 3½
- Width: 58'-8"
- Depth: 66'-4"

SEARCH ONLINE @ EPLANS.COM

This stylish country farmhouse offers plenty of living space. Bay windows fill the interior with light and picturesque views. A loft/study on the second floor overlooks the elegant foyer and great room below. Sit by the warming fire in the great room or join in the outdoor fun via sliding glass doors to the rear deck. The master bedroom and breakfast area admit natural light through bay windows and skylights. Private covered porches are accessible from the master bedroom and the living room. Three bedrooms and two full baths occupy the second floor.

plan# HPT930065

- Style: Farmhouse
- First Floor: 1,346 sq. ft.
- Second Floor: 836 sq. ft.
- Total: 2,182 sq. ft.
- Bedrooms: 4
- Bathrooms: 3½
- Width: 49'-5"
- Depth: 45'-4"

SEARCH ONLINE @ EPLANS.COM

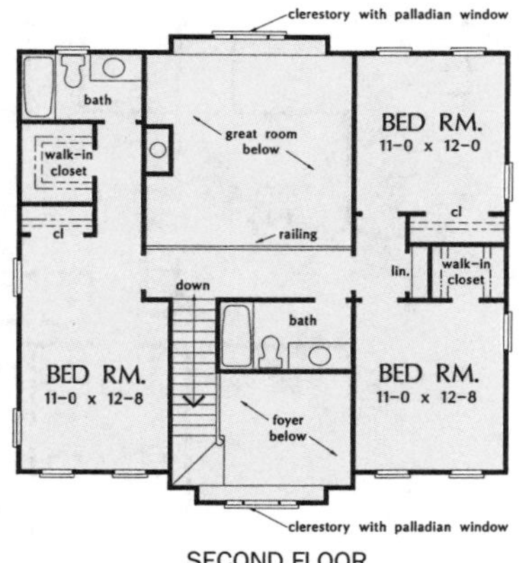

SECOND FLOOR

This classy, two-story home with a wraparound covered porch offers a dynamic open floor plan. The entrance foyer and the spacious great room both rise to two stories—a Palladian window at the second level floods these areas with natural light. The kitchen is centrally located for maximum flexibility in layout and, as an added feature, also has a breakfast bar. The large dining room delights with a bay window. The generous master suite has plenty of closet space as well as a bath with a whirlpool tub, a shower and a double-bowl vanity. On the second level, three bedrooms branch off the balcony that overlooks the great room. One large bedroom contains a private bath and a walk-in closet, while the other bedrooms share a full bath.

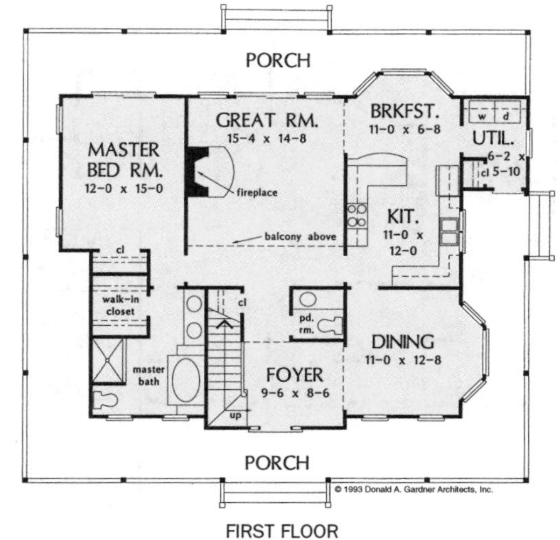

FIRST FLOOR

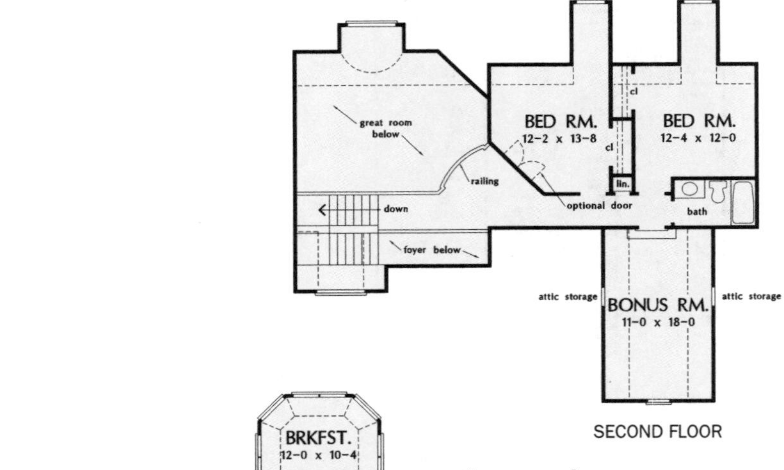

SECOND FLOOR

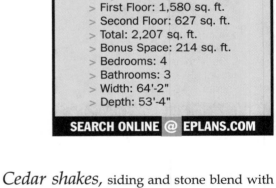

plan# HPT930066

- Style: Country
- First Floor: 1,580 sq. ft.
- Second Floor: 627 sq. ft.
- Total: 2,207 sq. ft.
- Bonus Space: 214 sq. ft.
- Bedrooms: 4
- Bathrooms: 3
- Width: 64'-2"
- Depth: 53'-4"

SEARCH ONLINE @ EPLANS.COM

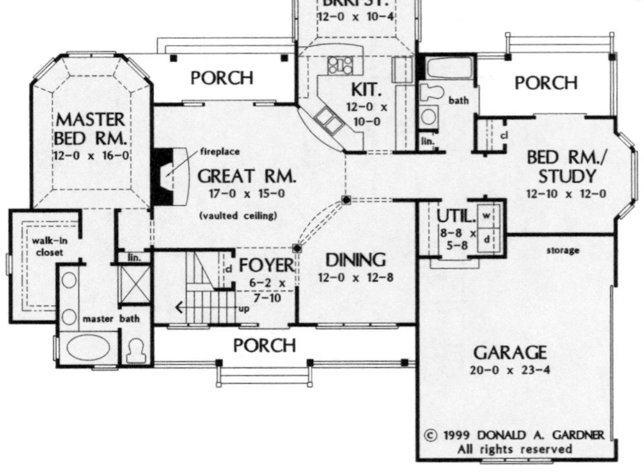

FIRST FLOOR

Cedar shakes, siding and stone blend with the Craftsman details of a custom design in this stunning home. The plan's open design and non-linear layout is refreshing and functional. The second-floor loft overlooks a centrally located and vaulted great room, and the breakfast area with a tray ceiling is virtually surrounded by windows to enhance the morningís light. The secluded first-floor master suite features a bay window, tray ceiling, walk-in closet and private bath. The second-floor family bedrooms are illuminated by rear dormers.

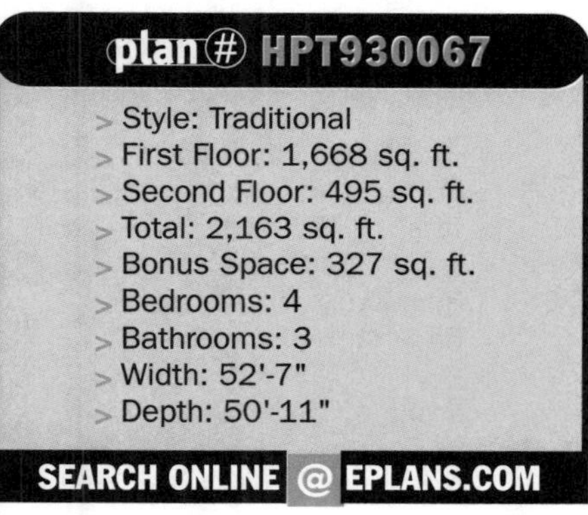

plan# HPT930067

- Style: Traditional
- First Floor: 1,668 sq. ft.
- Second Floor: 495 sq. ft.
- Total: 2,163 sq. ft.
- Bonus Space: 327 sq. ft.
- Bedrooms: 4
- Bathrooms: 3
- Width: 52'-7"
- Depth: 50'-11"

SEARCH ONLINE @ EPLANS.COM

Four gables, a Palladian window and an admirable transom with a sunburst are eye-catching additions to this plan's exterior. On the first floor, rounded columns present the dining room, which also sports a tray ceiling. The vaulted great room accesses the rear deck and features a warming fireplace. Set at an angle, the kitchen's serving bar allows the cook to keep up with activities in both the breakfast and great rooms. The master suite includes a walk-in closet, tray ceiling and sumptuous bath. Note the triangular shape of the tub and separate shower. Upstairs, two family bedrooms share a full bath.

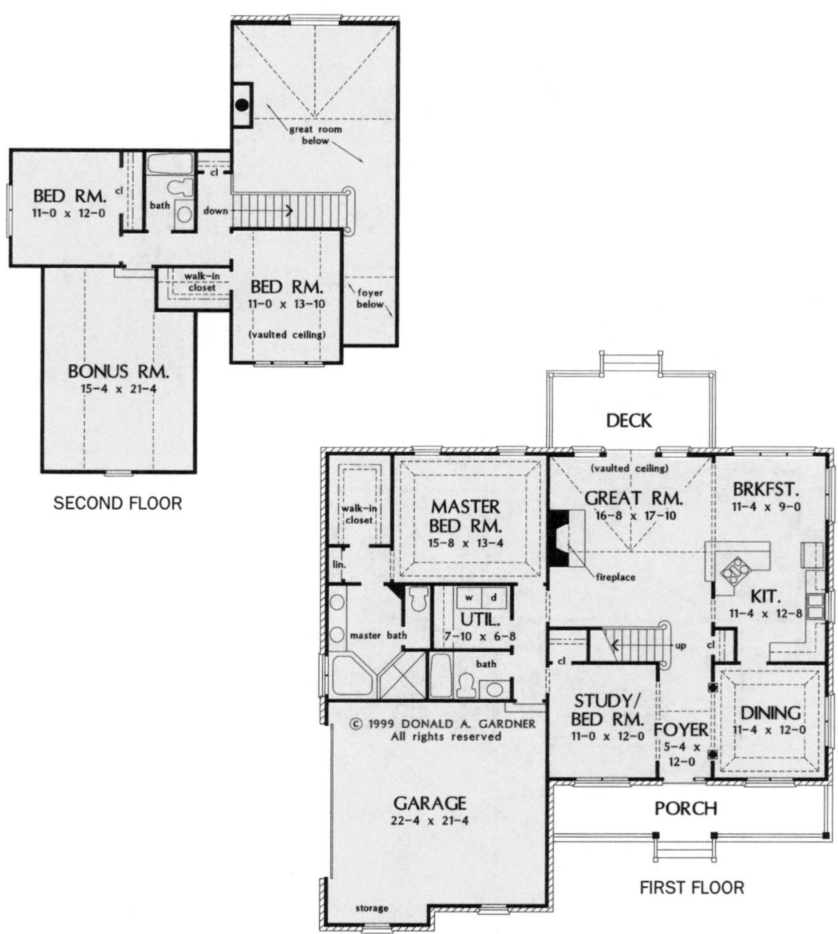

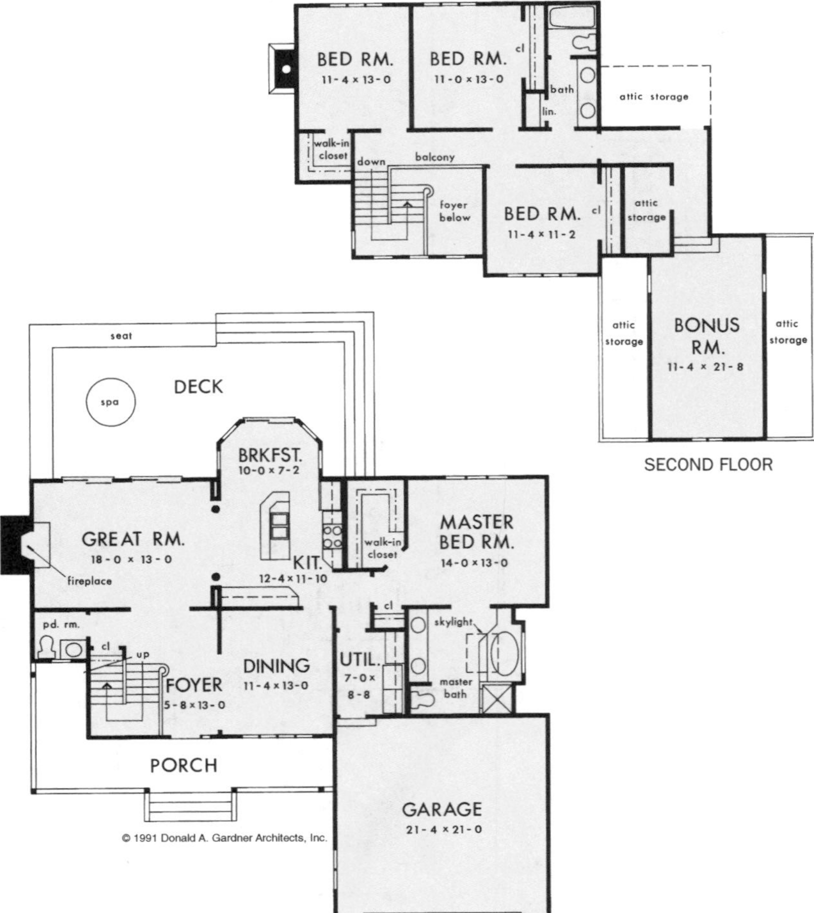

SECOND FLOOR

FIRST FLOOR

plan# HPT930068

- Style: Farmhouse
- First Floor: 1,377 sq. ft.
- Second Floor: 714 sq. ft.
- Total: 2,091 sq. ft.
- Bonus Space: 375 sq. ft.
- Bedrooms: 4
- Bathrooms: 2½
- Width: 55'-8"
- Depth: 62'-4"

SEARCH ONLINE @ EPLANS.COM

An inviting covered porch and a Palladian window offer an irresistible appeal to this four-bedroom plan. The great room with a fireplace and the breakfast bay both provide access to a rear deck. A work island with a sink adds plenty of work space to the kitchen. The master bedroom, located on the first level for privacy, has a walk-in closet and a bath consisting of a shower and a garden tub with a skylight overhead. The second level contains three bedrooms and a bath. There is room to grow with a bonus room upstairs.

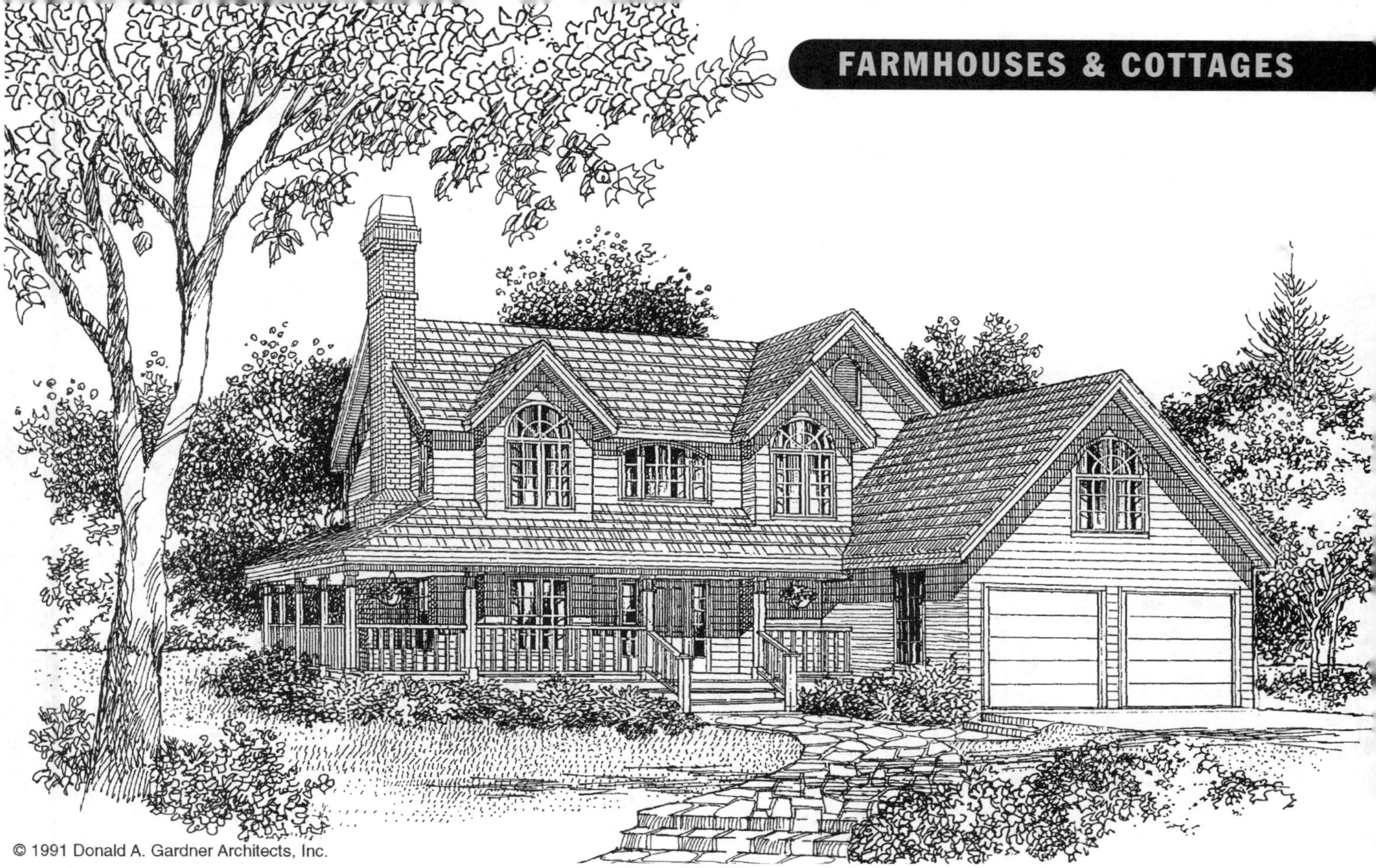

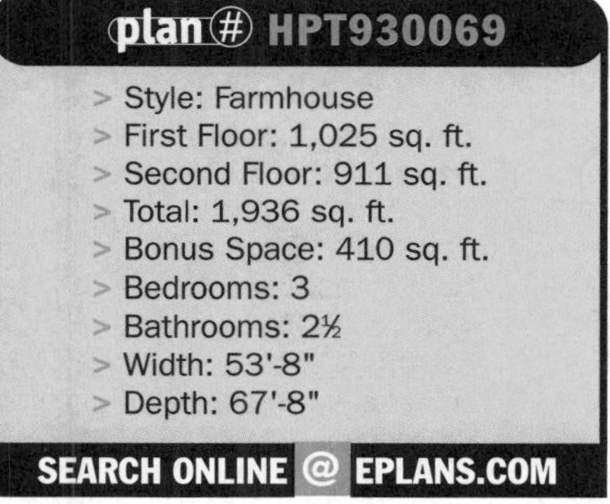

plan# HPT930069

- Style: Farmhouse
- First Floor: 1,025 sq. ft.
- Second Floor: 911 sq. ft.
- Total: 1,936 sq. ft.
- Bonus Space: 410 sq. ft.
- Bedrooms: 3
- Bathrooms: 2½
- Width: 53'-8"
- Depth: 67'-8"

SEARCH ONLINE @ EPLANS.COM

The exterior of this three-bedroom home is enhanced by its many gables, arched windows and the wraparound porch. The entry leads to the foyer, which extends to the left into the great room. The great room—with an impressive fireplace—leads to both the dining room and the screened porch, which accesses the deck. An open kitchen offers a country atmosphere. The second-floor master suite has two walk-in closets and a luxurious bath. Two family bedrooms share a full bath and plenty of storage. There is also bonus space over the garage.

SECOND FLOOR

FIRST FLOOR

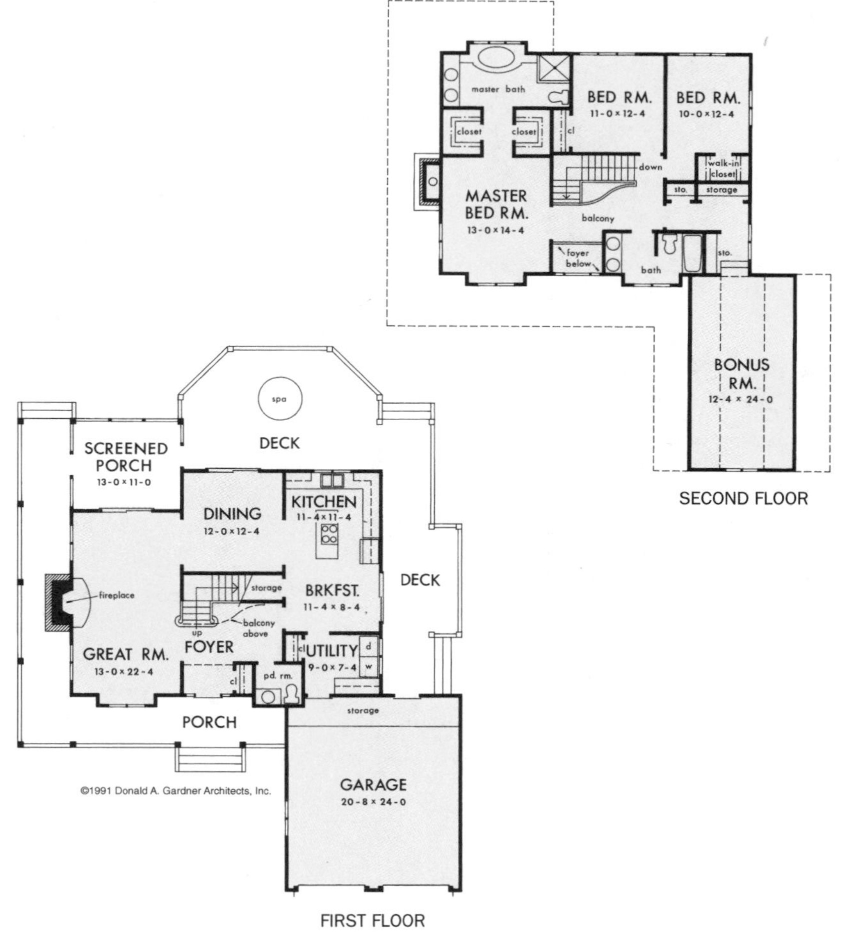

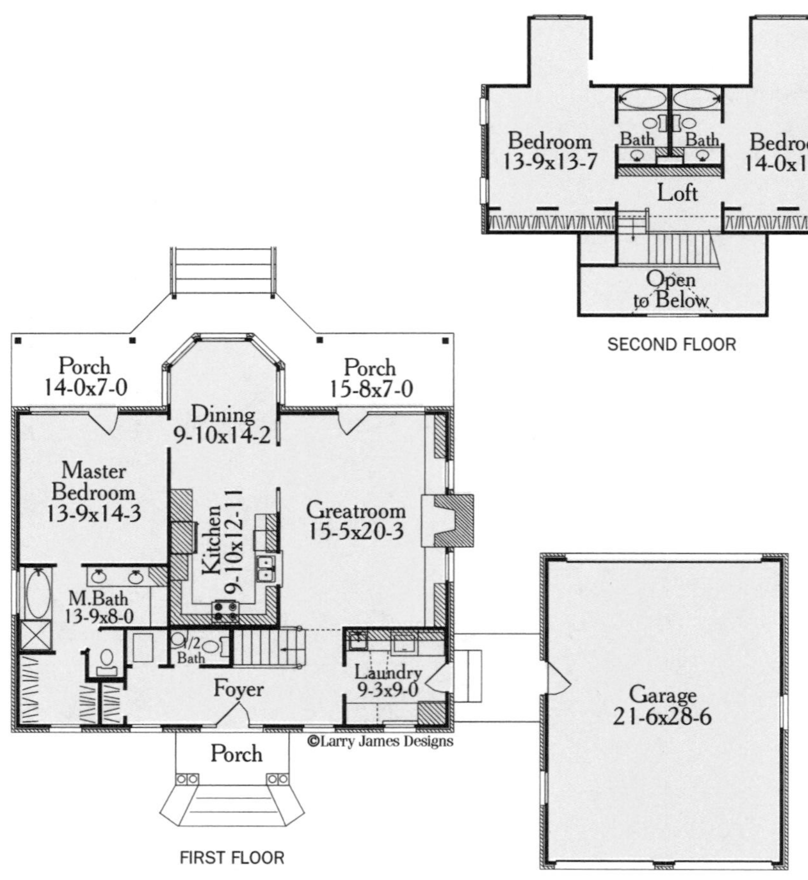

plan# HPT930070

- Style: Traditional
- First Floor: 1,351 sq. ft.
- Second Floor: 794 sq. ft.
- Total: 2,145 sq. ft.
- Bedrooms: 3
- Bathrooms: 3½
- Width: 72'-0"
- Depth: 51'-0"
- Foundation: Basement, Crawlspace, Slab

SEARCH ONLINE @ EPLANS.COM

With a seemingly traditional facade, one look inside will tell you that this floor plan is anything but cookie-cutter. A covered entry leads to an elongated two-story foyer with a coat closet and powder room. Past the laundry, the great room is cozy and warm with an extended-hearth fireplace and built-ins. Rear windows and porch access extend this room outdoors. A large bay, surrounded with windows, houses the dining area. The first-floor master suite has porch access and a lovely private bath. Upstairs, each bedroom enjoys a private bath and dormer windows.

plan# HPT930071

- Style: Country Cottage
- First Floor: 1,001 sq. ft.
- Second Floor: 466 sq. ft.
- Total: 1,467 sq. ft.
- Bonus Space: 292 sq. ft.
- Bedrooms: 3
- Bathrooms: 2½
- Width: 42'-0"
- Depth: 42'-0"
- Foundation: Crawlspace, Basement

SEARCH ONLINE @ EPLANS.COM

Arched transoms set off by keystones add the final details to the traditional exterior of this home. The foyer opens to a vaulted family room, which enjoys a warm fireplace and leads to a two-story dining area with built-in plant shelves and to a U-shaped kitchen with an angled countertop and spacious pantry. Down the hall, the abundant master suite boasts a tray ceiling and can be found in its own secluded area. Upstairs, two additional bedrooms are found sharing a full bath—note both bedrooms enjoy French doors. An optional bonus room with a walk-in closet is included in this plan.

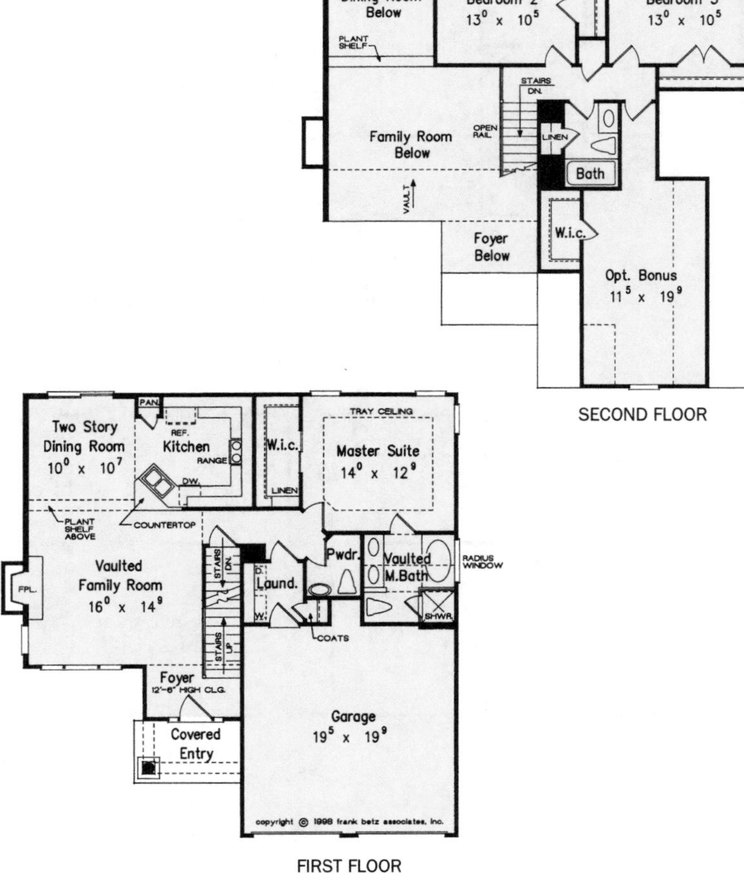

SECOND FLOOR

FIRST FLOOR

SECOND FLOOR

FIRST FLOOR

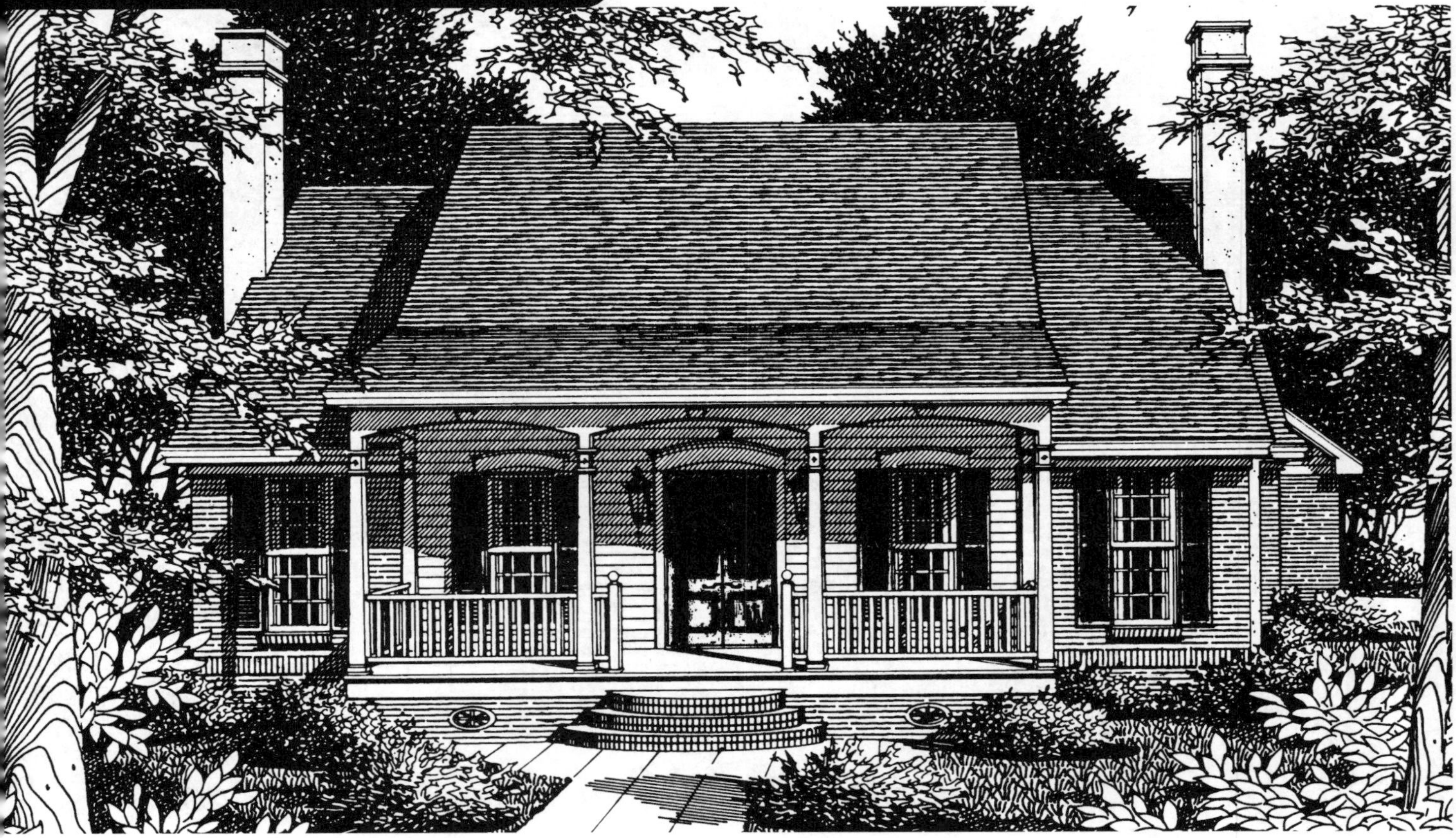

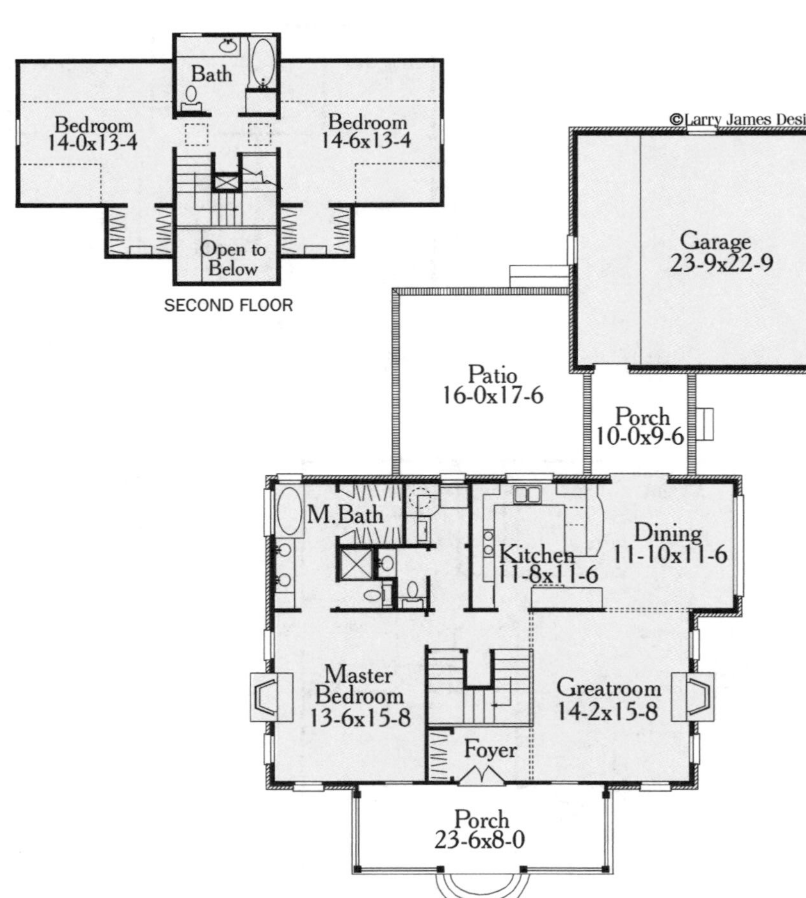

plan# HPT930072

- Style: Traditional
- First Floor: 1,173 sq. ft.
- Second Floor: 602 sq. ft.
- Total: 1,775 sq. ft.
- Bedrooms: 3
- Bathrooms: 2½
- Width: 51'-5"
- Depth: 69'-6"
- Foundation: Basement, Crawlspace, Slab

SEARCH ONLINE @ EPLANS.COM

Symmetry and rustic country charm provide a carefully designed floor plan that gets the most out of a modest square footage. The two-story foyer opens to the right to the great room with a cozy fireplace. A dining area with a serving bar from the kitchen is perfect for formal dinners or casual meals. Porch and patio access invite dining alfresco. The master bedroom is romantic with a fireplace and private bath with a spa tub. Two bedrooms upstairs share a full bath.

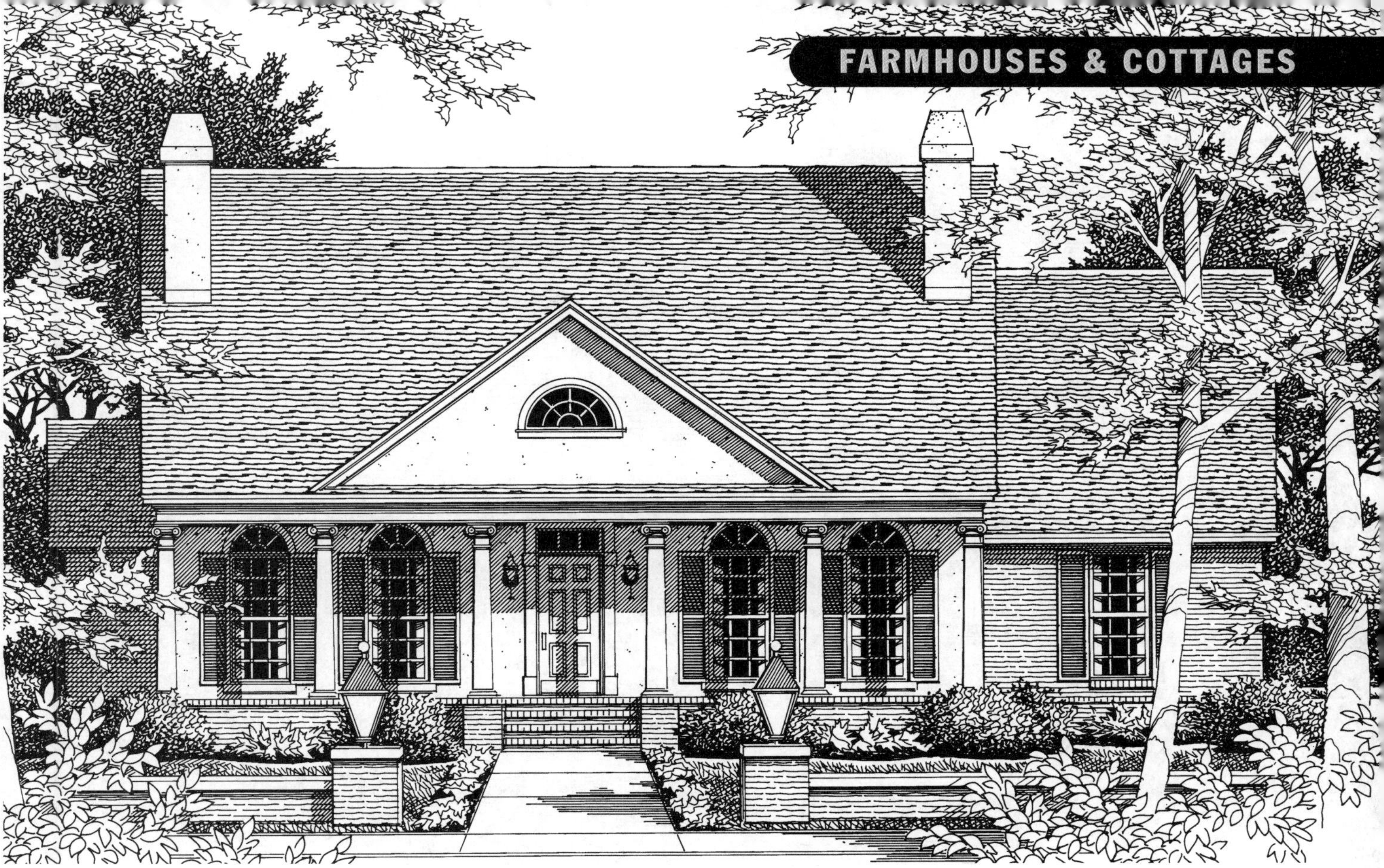

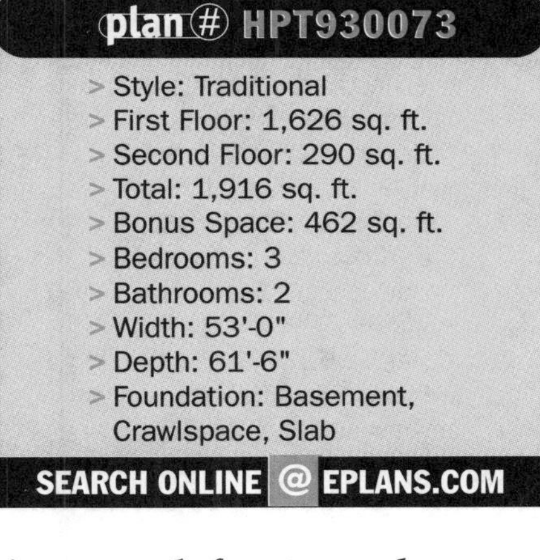

plan# HPT930073

- Style: Traditional
- First Floor: 1,626 sq. ft.
- Second Floor: 290 sq. ft.
- Total: 1,916 sq. ft.
- Bonus Space: 462 sq. ft.
- Bedrooms: 3
- Bathrooms: 2
- Width: 53'-0"
- Depth: 61'-6"
- Foundation: Basement, Crawlspace, Slab

SEARCH ONLINE @ EPLANS.COM

SECOND FLOOR

FIRST FLOOR

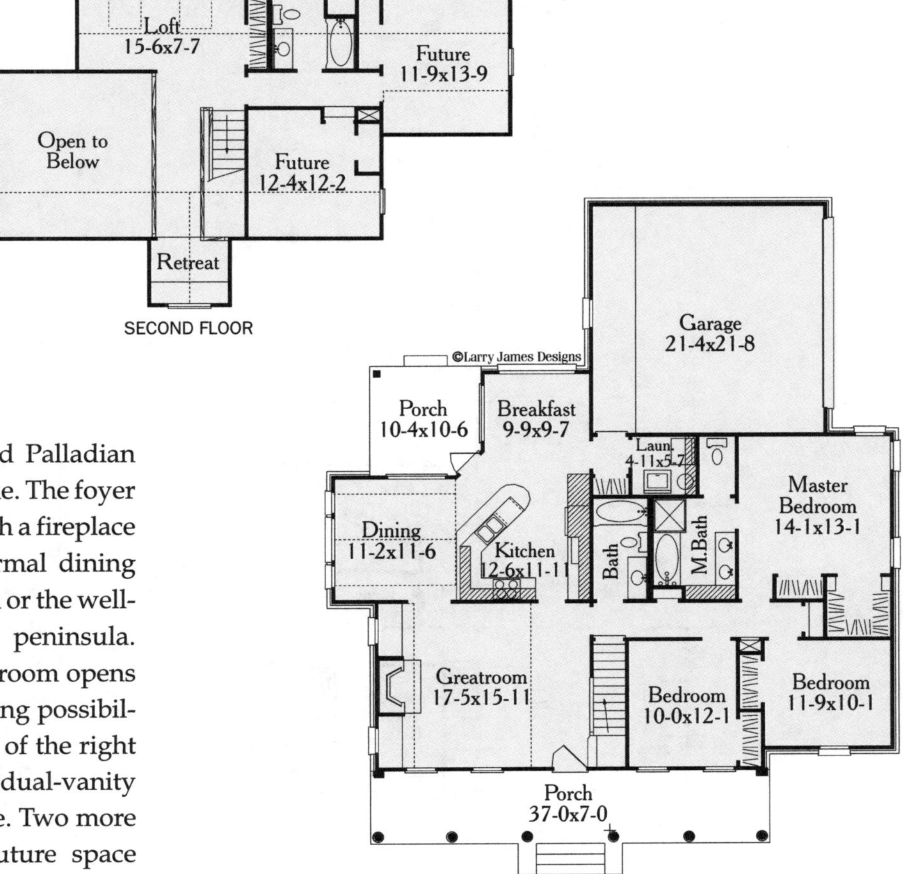

A covered front porch and shuttered Palladian windows grace this functional country home. The foyer opens to an ample great room, complete with a fireplace and lots of natural light. The vaulted formal dining room can be entered through the great room or the well-appointed kitchen with a serving-bar peninsula. Adjacent to the kitchen, a sunny breakfast room opens to the screened porch, extending entertaining possibilities. The master suite enjoys the seclusion of the right rear corner. With a pampering spa tub and dual-vanity counter, this room is certain to be a favorite. Two more bedrooms share a full bath. Upstairs, future space makes a great playroom, office, or home gym.

Garage
21-4x21-8
Porch
10-4x10-6
Breakfast
9-9x9-7
M.Bath
9-7x6-9
Master
Bedroom
14-1x13-1
Dining
11-2x11-6
Kitchen
12-6x11-11
Bath
Laun.
7-7x5-1
Greatroom
17-7x16-3
Bedroom
10-0x12-1
Bedroom
11-9x10-1
Porch
9-6x4-2
©Larry James Designs
FIRST FLOOR

plan# HPT930074

- Style: Traditional
- First Floor: 1,646 sq. ft.
- Second Floor: 247 sq. ft.
- Total: 1,893 sq. ft.
- Bonus Space: 365 sq. ft.
- Bedrooms: 3
- Bathrooms: 2
- Width: 53'-0"
- Depth: 62'-0"
- Foundation: Basement, Crawlspace, Slab

SEARCH ONLINE @ EPLANS.COM

A stately facade introduces a modern floor plan in this Southern plantation cottage. Enter to find a great room, with a balcony above and a sloped ceiling, that invites family and friends to gather around the fireplace. A unique angled kitchen allows effortless service to the sunny breakfast nook and cathedral dining room. Laundry facilities are central to the bedrooms for ultimate convenience. Two family bedrooms share a full bath; the master suite enjoys His and Hers closets and a private bath with a garden tub. A loft and future space upstairs are ready for expansion.

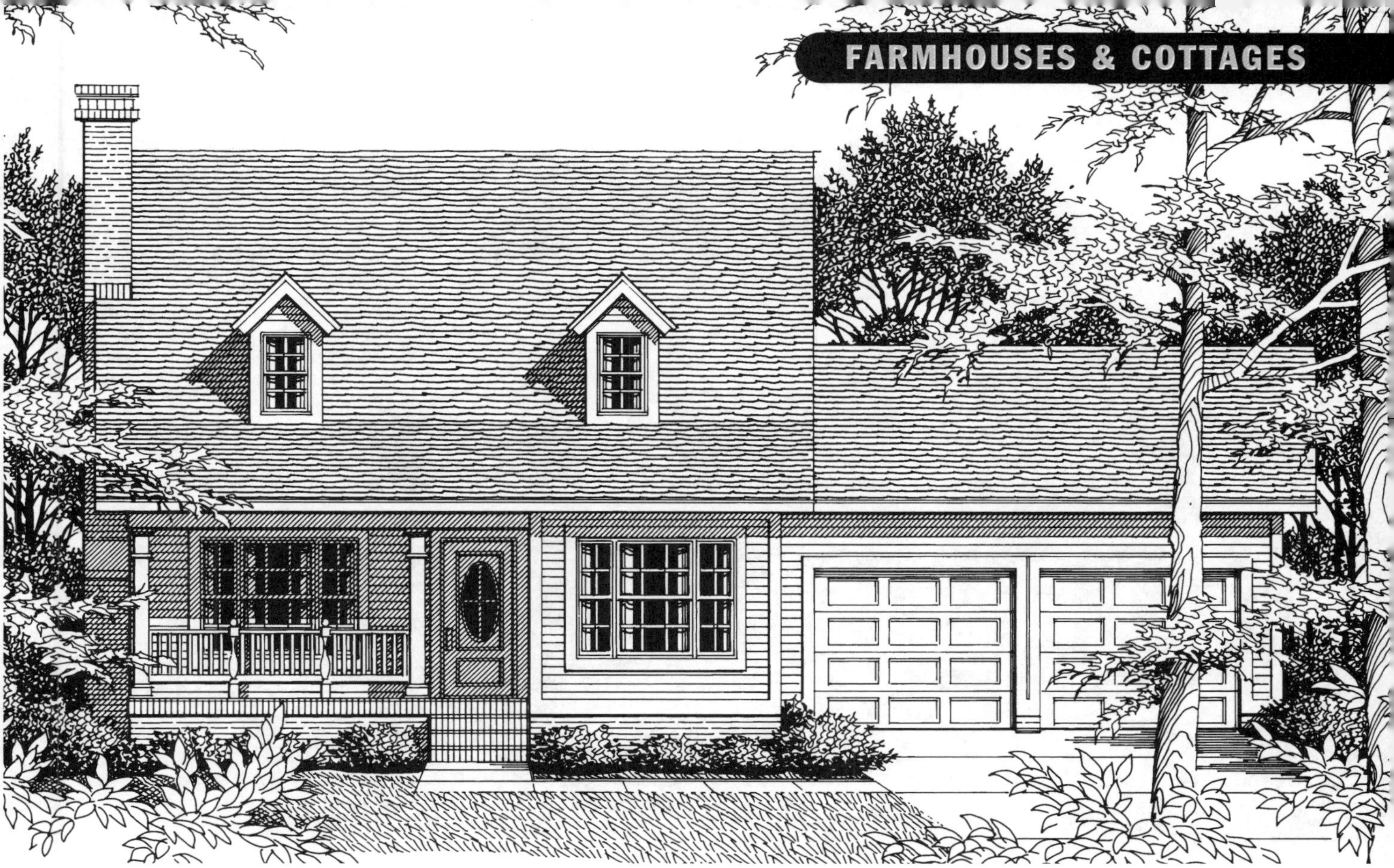

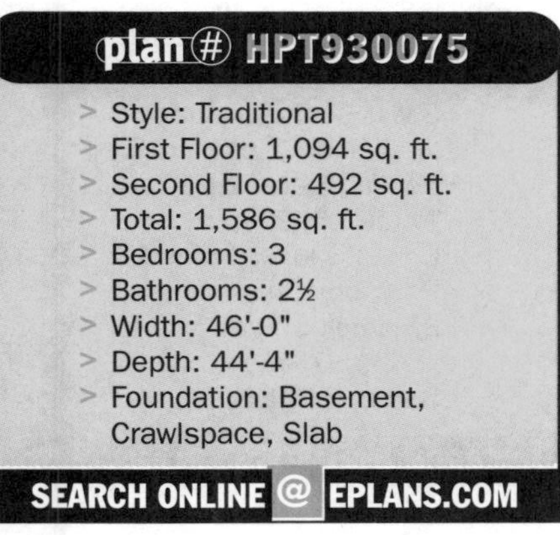

plan# HPT930075

- Style: Traditional
- First Floor: 1,094 sq. ft.
- Second Floor: 492 sq. ft.
- Total: 1,586 sq. ft.
- Bedrooms: 3
- Bathrooms: 2½
- Width: 46'-0"
- Depth: 44'-4"
- Foundation: Basement, Crawlspace, Slab

SEARCH ONLINE @ EPLANS.COM

Despite a modest square footage, this charming country home is adorned with all the features you expect from a quality family home. A covered front porch opens up to the great room, inviting with a cozy fireplace. A pass-through to the kitchen is great for entertaining. The dining area is flooded with natural light and flows effortlessly into the kitchen for easy serving. Tucked to the rear, the master suite includes a pampering bath with a spa tub, dual vanities and His and Hers walk-in closets. Twin bedrooms upstairs share a full bath.

SECOND FLOOR

FIRST FLOOR

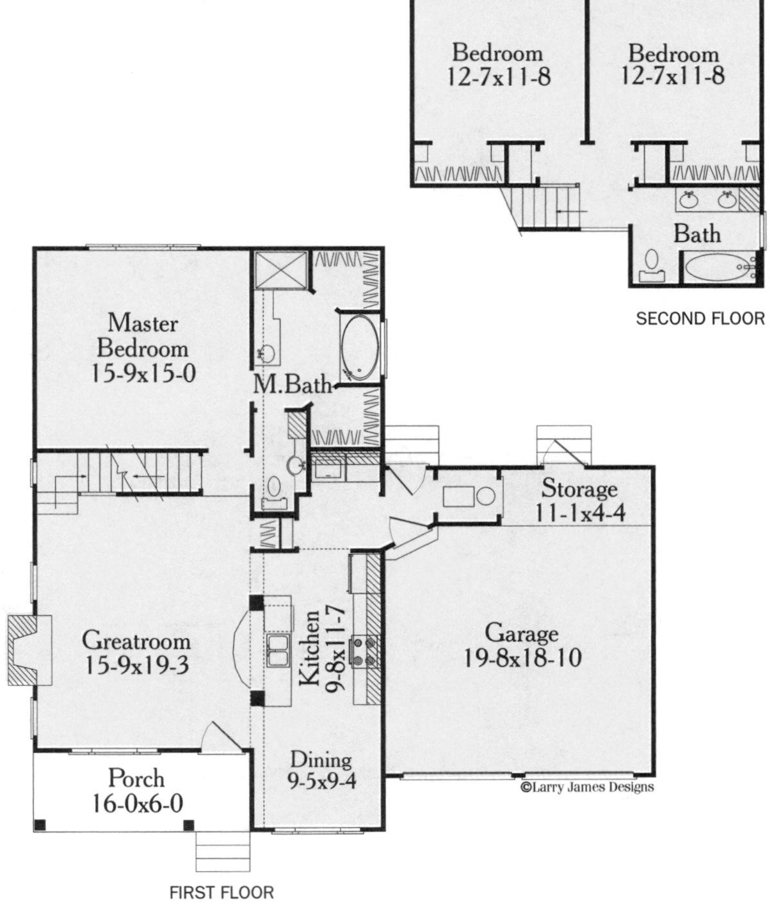

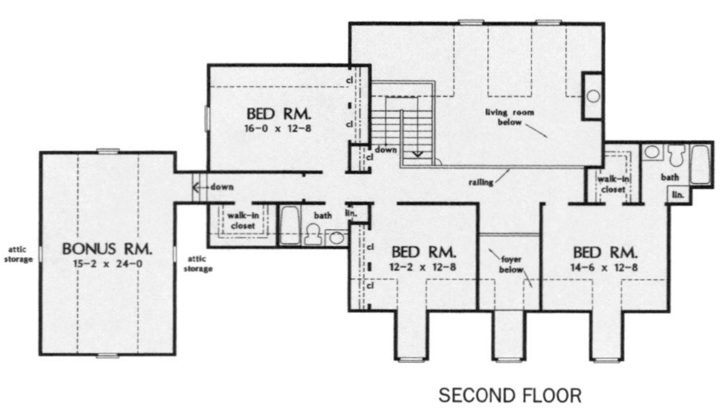

SECOND FLOOR

plan# HPT930076

- Style: Country Cottage
- First Floor: 2,676 sq. ft.
- Second Floor: 1,023 sq. ft.
- Total: 3,699 sq. ft.
- Bonus Space: 487 sq. ft.
- Bedrooms: 4
- Bathrooms: 3½
- Width: 87'-8"
- Depth: 63'-0"

SEARCH ONLINE @ EPLANS.COM

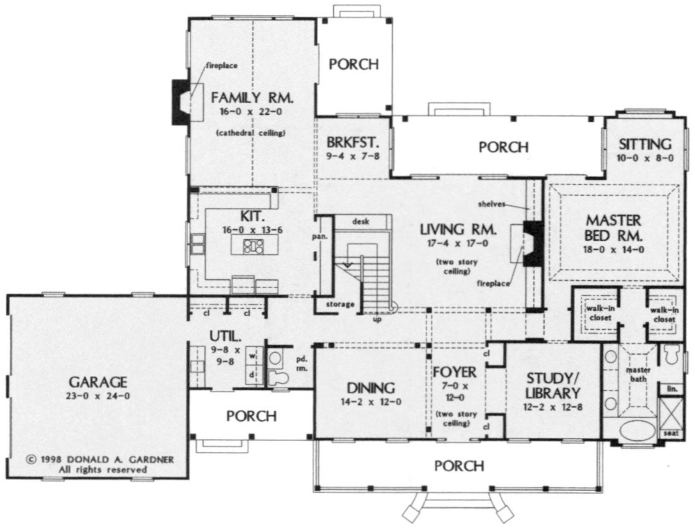

FIRST FLOOR

Brimming with luxury and style, this gracious country estate features spacious rooms, volume ceilings and four porches for extended outdoor living. Fireplaces in the living and family rooms grant warmth and character to these spacious gathering areas, while columns add definition to the open living and dining rooms. Built-in bookshelves in the living room are both attractive and functional, as is the built-in desk adjacent to the open U-shaped staircase. The master suite is a haven with a tray ceiling, a sitting alcove, dual walk-in closet and a luxurious bath. The upstairs balcony overlooks both the foyer and living room while serving as an open, central hallway for the home's three family bedrooms and bonus room.

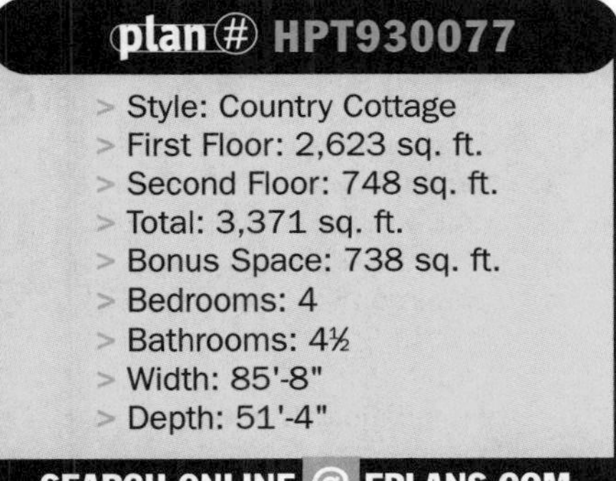

plan# HPT930077

- Style: Country Cottage
- First Floor: 2,623 sq. ft.
- Second Floor: 748 sq. ft.
- Total: 3,371 sq. ft.
- Bonus Space: 738 sq. ft.
- Bedrooms: 4
- Bathrooms: 4½
- Width: 85'-8"
- Depth: 51'-4"

SEARCH ONLINE @ EPLANS.COM

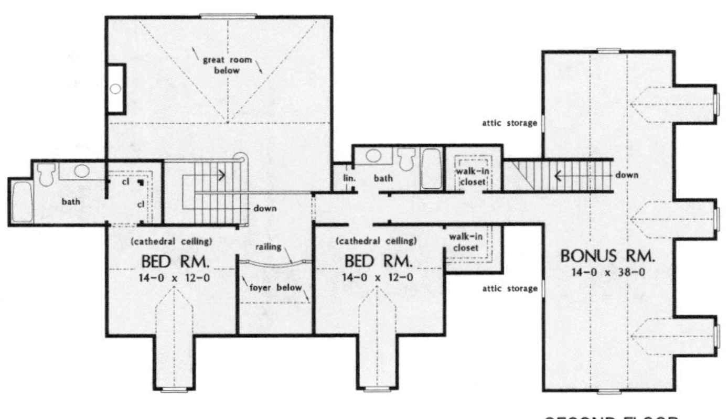

SECOND FLOOR

With a front porch that's perfect for sipping lemonade, this charming country estate is a welcome retreat with plenty of room for everyone. Marked by columns, the formal living and dining rooms are positioned up front, while the family gathering areas are open and casual at the back. The vaulted foyer and generous great room with its cathedral ceiling receive added drama from a second-floor balcony that overlooks both. The master suite features an elegant tray ceiling, and a bayed sitting area offers a private spot for relaxation. Upstairs, two family bedrooms feature cathedral ceilings. The bonus room provides future possibilities.

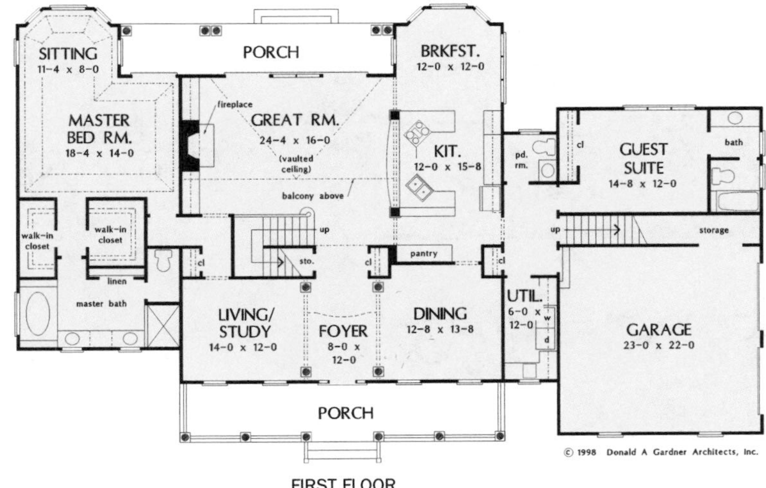

FIRST FLOOR

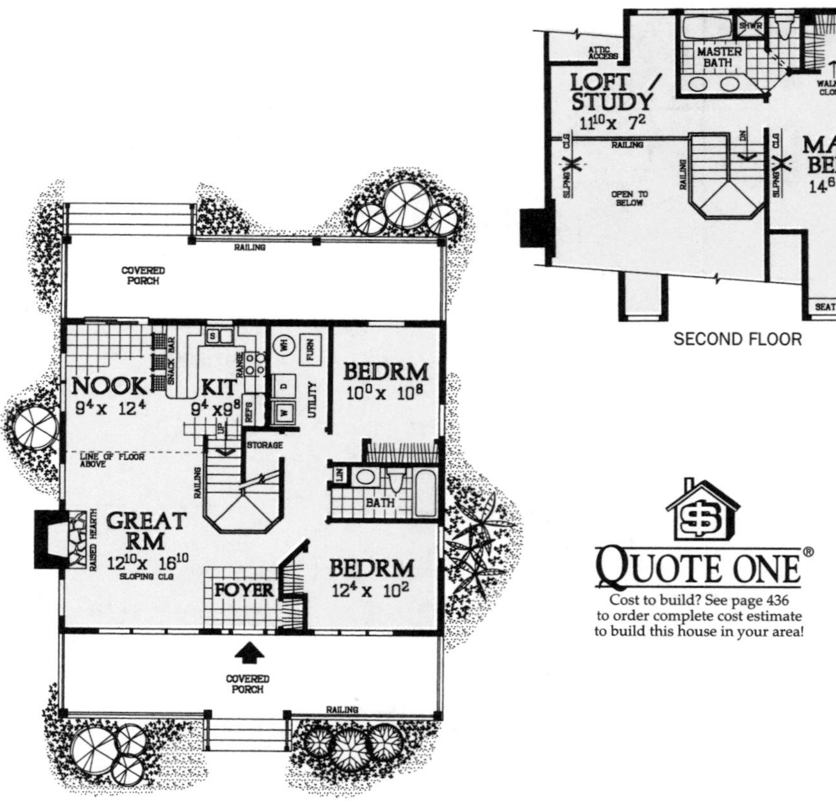

SECOND FLOOR

FIRST FLOOR

plan# HPT930078

- Style: Farmhouse
- First Floor: 1,093 sq. ft.
- Second Floor: 580 sq. ft.
- Total: 1,673 sq. ft.
- Bedrooms: 3
- Bathrooms: 2
- Width: 36'-0"
- Depth: 52'-0"
- Foundation: Crawlspace

L D

SEARCH ONLINE @ EPLANS.COM

QUOTE ONE®
Cost to build? See page 436 to order complete cost estimate to build this house in your area!

Brackets and balustrades on front and rear covered porches spell old-fashioned country charm on this rustic retreat. Warm evenings will invite family and guests outdoors for watching sunsets and stars. In cooler weather, the raised-hearth fireplace will make the great room a cozy place to gather. The nearby kitchen serves both a snack bar and a breakfast nook. Two family bedrooms and a full bath complete the main level. Upstairs, a master suite with a sloped ceiling offers a window seat and a complete bath. The adjacent loft/study overlooks the great room.

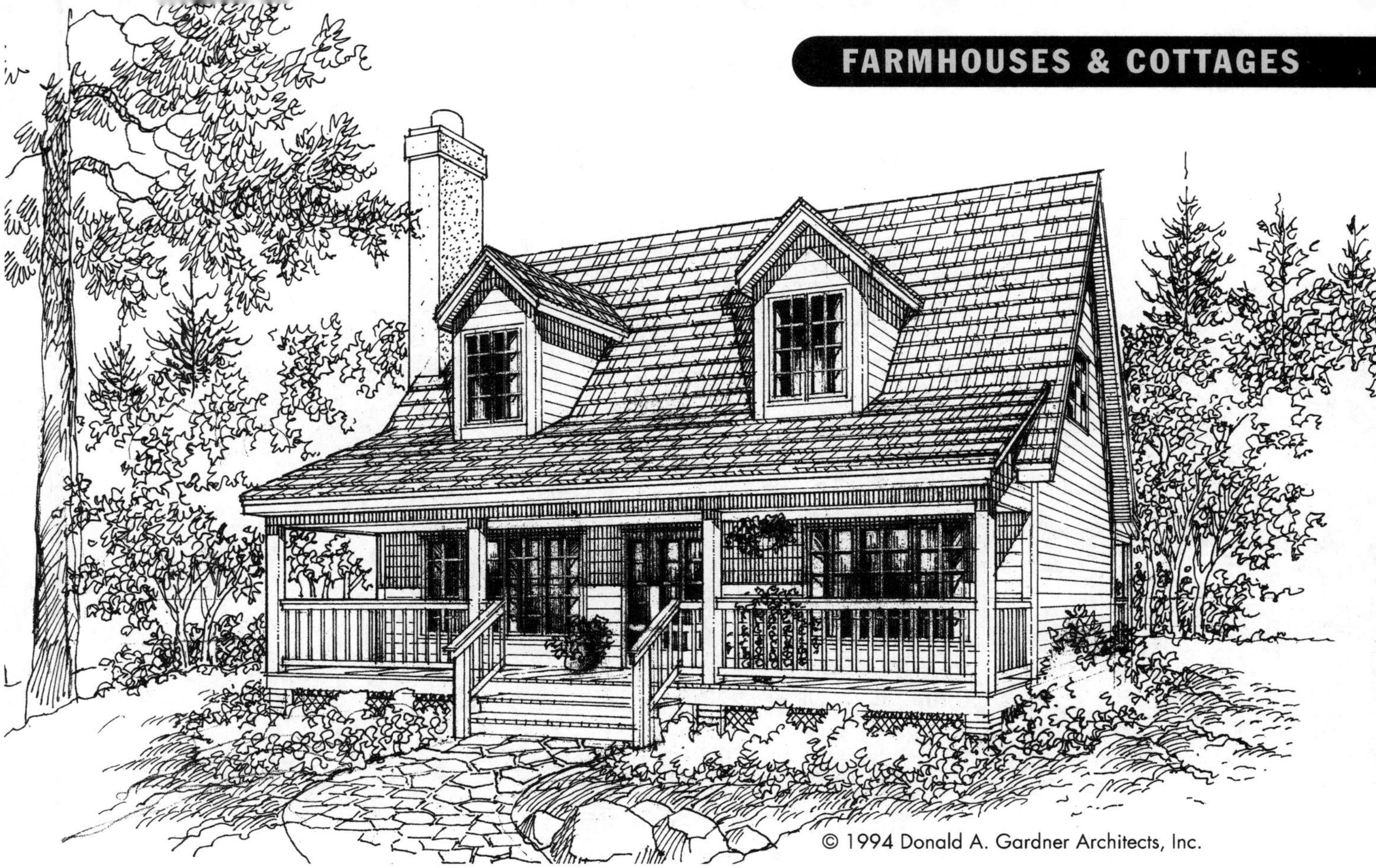

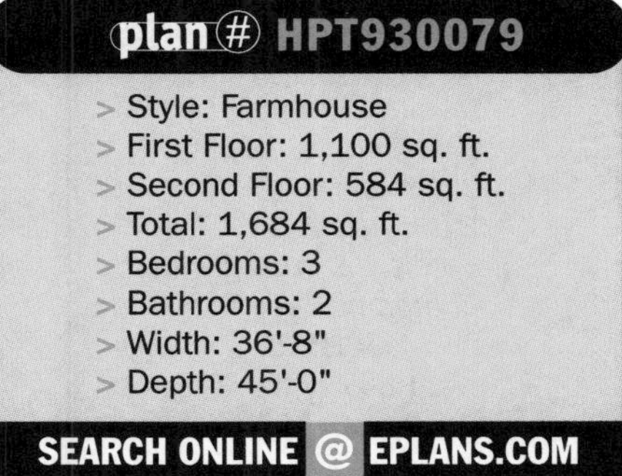

plan# HPT930079

- Style: Farmhouse
- First Floor: 1,100 sq. ft.
- Second Floor: 584 sq. ft.
- Total: 1,684 sq. ft.
- Bedrooms: 3
- Bathrooms: 2
- Width: 36'-8"
- Depth: 45'-0"

SEARCH ONLINE @ EPLANS.COM

SECOND FLOOR

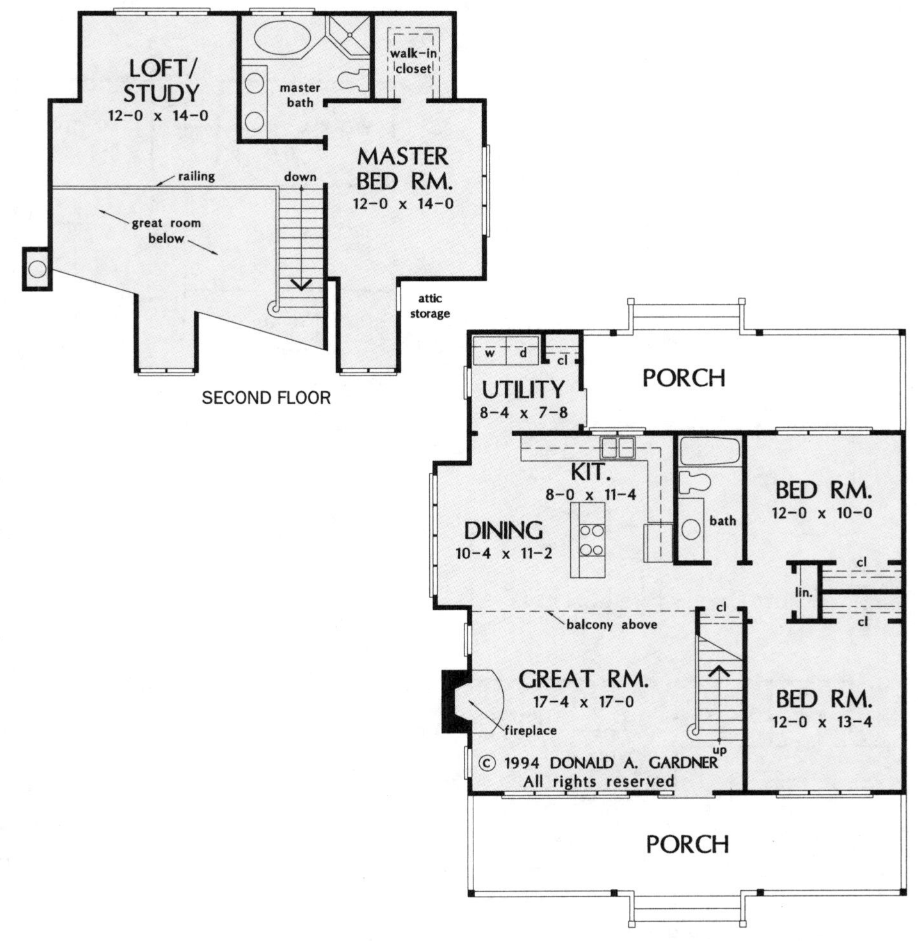

A relaxing country image projects from the front and rear covered porches of this rustic three-bedroom home. Open planning extends to the great room, the dining room, and the efficient kitchen. A shared cathedral ceiling creates an impressive space. Completing the first floor are two family bedrooms, a full bath, and a handy utility area. The second floor contains the master suite featuring a spacious walk-in closet and a master bath with a whirlpool tub and a separate corner shower. A generous loft/study overlooks the great room below.

FIRST FLOOR

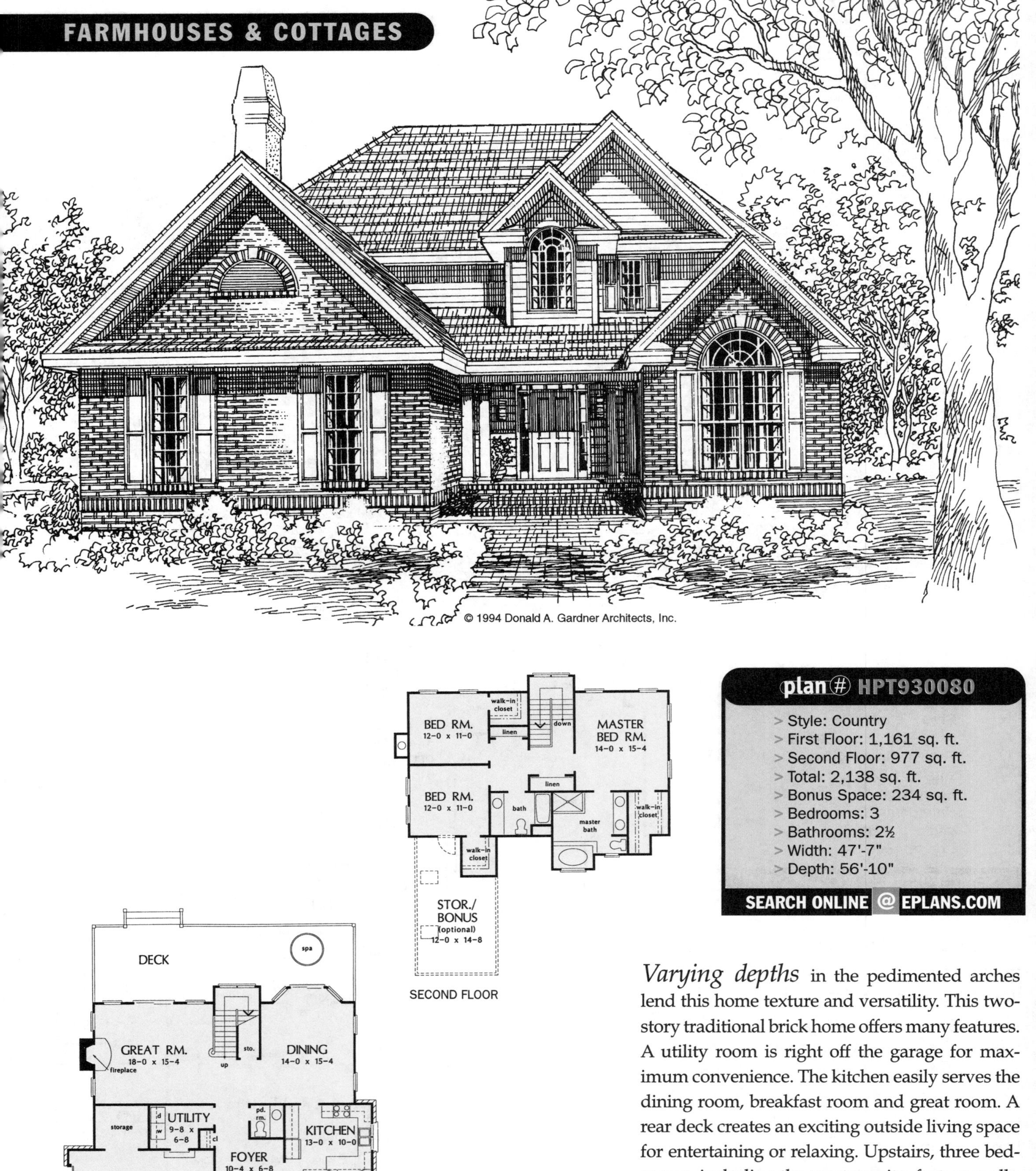

plan# HPT930080

- Style: Country
- First Floor: 1,161 sq. ft.
- Second Floor: 977 sq. ft.
- Total: 2,138 sq. ft.
- Bonus Space: 234 sq. ft.
- Bedrooms: 3
- Bathrooms: 2½
- Width: 47'-7"
- Depth: 56'-10"

SEARCH ONLINE @ EPLANS.COM

Varying depths in the pedimented arches lend this home texture and versatility. This two-story traditional brick home offers many features. A utility room is right off the garage for maximum convenience. The kitchen easily serves the dining room, breakfast room and great room. A rear deck creates an exciting outside living space for entertaining or relaxing. Upstairs, three bedrooms, including the master suite, feature walk-in closets. The master bedroom enjoys a luxurious bath with a whirlpool tub.

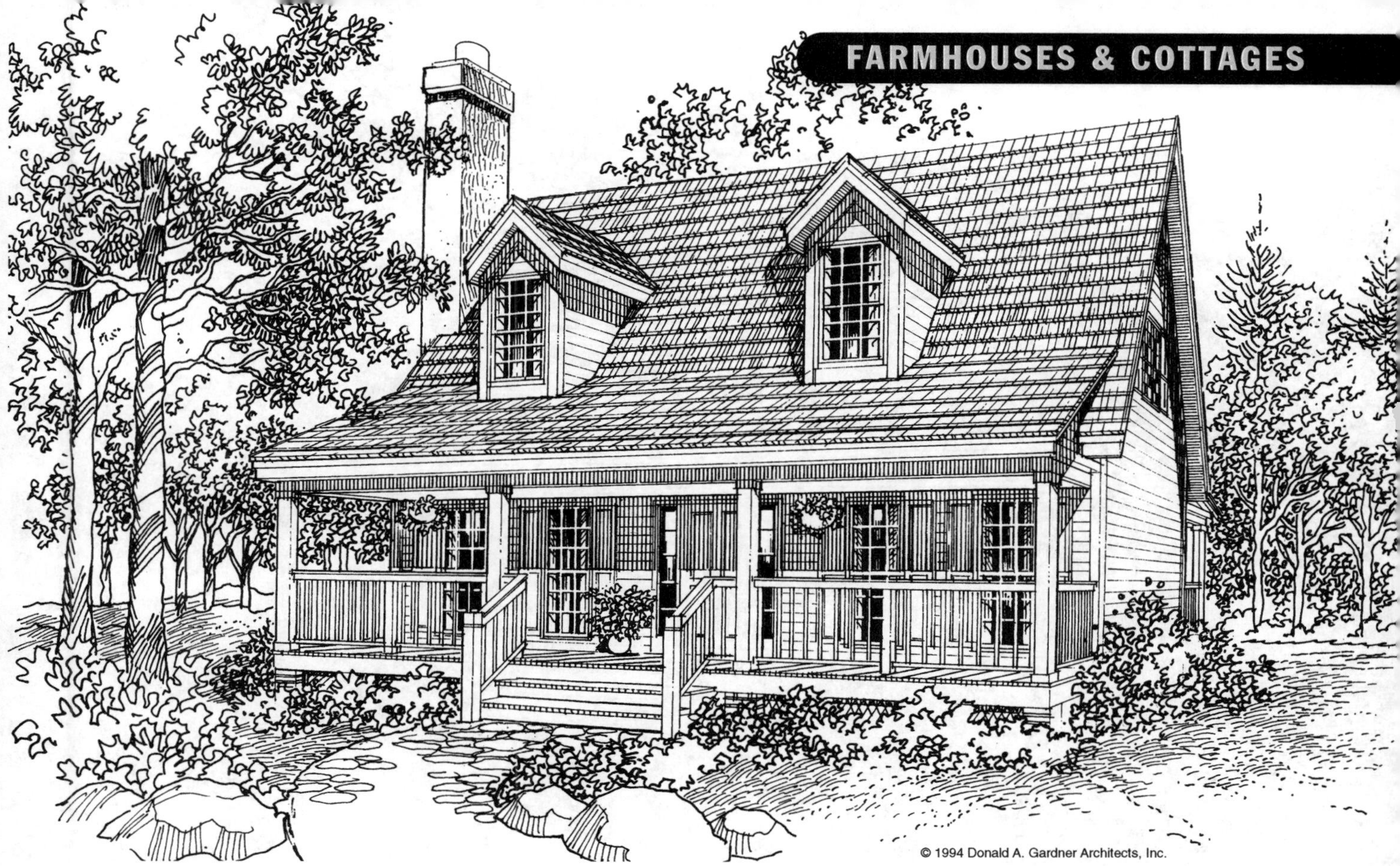

plan# HPT930081

- Style: Farmhouse
- First Floor: 966 sq. ft.
- Second Floor: 584 sq. ft.
- Total: 1,550 sq. ft.
- Bedrooms: 2
- Bathrooms: 2
- Width: 35'-9"
- Depth: 43'-0"

SEARCH ONLINE @ EPLANS.COM

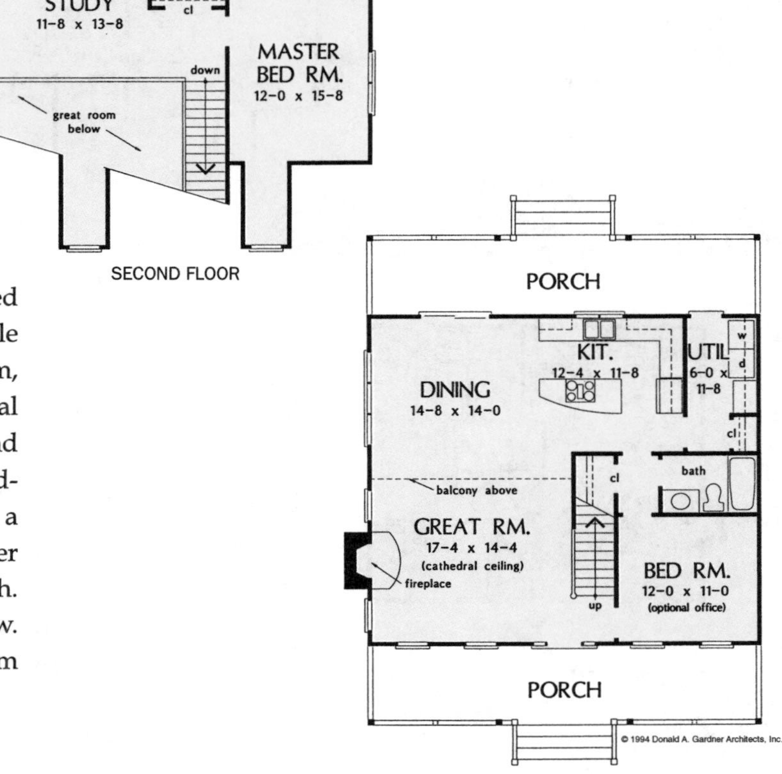

A country farmhouse exterior combined with an open floor plan creates a comfortable home or vacation getaway. The great room, warmed by a fireplace and opened by a cathedral ceiling, combines well with the dining room and the kitchen. Flexibility is offered in a front bedroom with a full bath that easily doubles as a home office. The second floor contains the master bedroom with a walk-in closet and a private bath. The loft/study overlooks the great room below. Front and rear porches provide plenty of room for outdoor enjoyment.

SECOND FLOOR

FIRST FLOOR

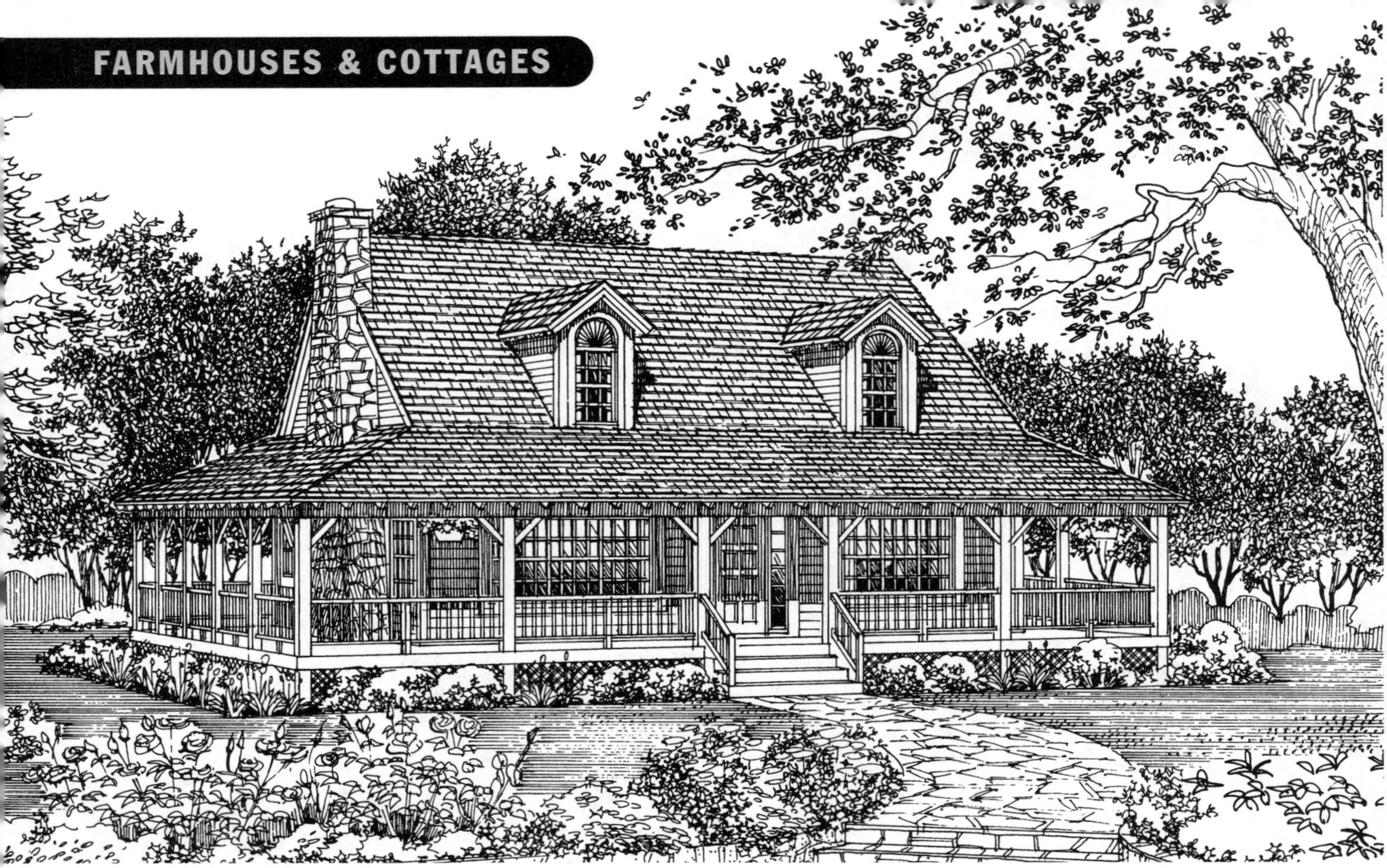

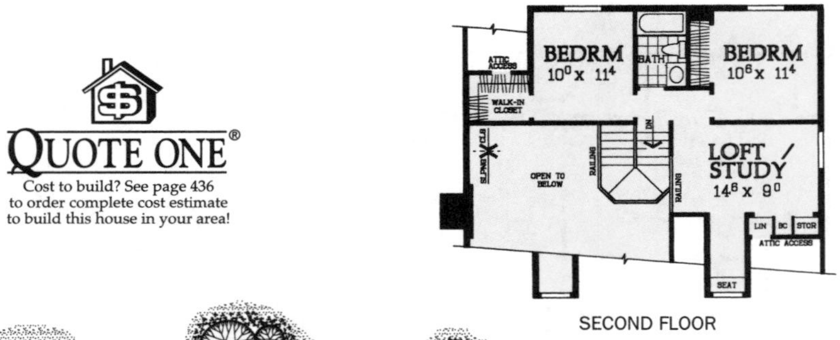

SECOND FLOOR

plan# HPT930082

- Style: Farmhouse
- First Floor: 1,093 sq. ft.
- Second Floor: 603 sq. ft.
- Total: 1,696 sq. ft.
- Bedrooms: 3
- Bathrooms: 2½
- Width: 46'-0"
- Depth: 52'-0"
- Foundation: Crawlspace

SEARCH ONLINE @ EPLANS.COM

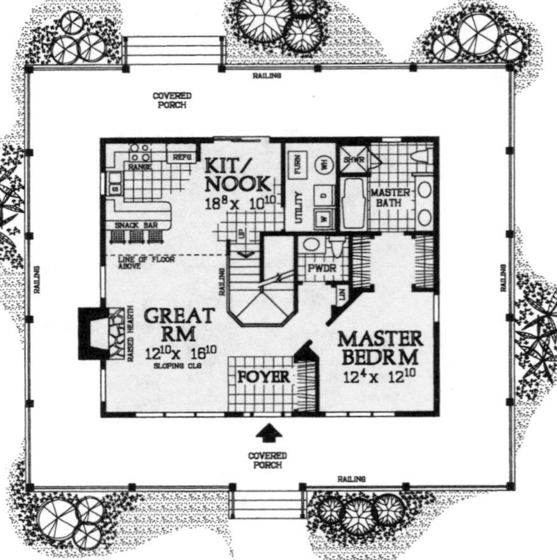

FIRST FLOOR

This two-story home's rustic design reflects thoughtful planning, including a porch that fully wraps the house in comfort and provides lots of room for rocking. A stone chimney and arched windows set in dormers further enhance this home's country appeal. Inside, the floor plan is designed for maximum efficiency. A great room with a sloped ceiling enjoys a raised-hearth fireplace whose warmth radiates into the kitchen/nook. The master suite is located on the first floor and includes plenty of closet space and a private bath filled with amenities. A utility room and a powder room complete this level. The second floor contains two secondary bedrooms, a full bath and a loft/study with a window seat.

- Style: Traditional
- First Floor: 1,093 sq. ft.
- Second Floor: 580 sq. ft.
- Total: 1,673 sq. ft.
- Bedrooms: 3
- Bathrooms: 2
- Width: 52'-0"
- Depth: 52'-0"
- Foundation: Crawlspace

L D

SEARCH ONLINE @ EPLANS.COM

QUOTE ONE®

Cost to build? See page 436 to order complete cost estimate to build this house in your area!

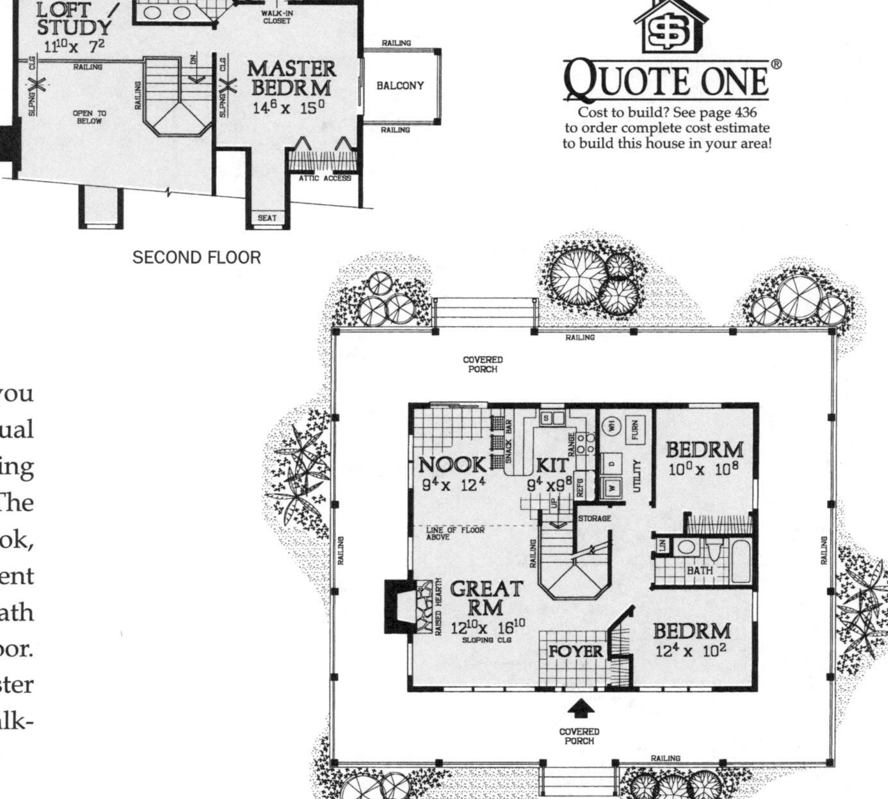

Comfortable covered porches lead you into a home that's tailor-made for casual living. The foyer offers access to a front-facing great room with a raised-hearth fireplace. The great room then flows into the breakfast nook, with outdoor access, and on to the efficient kitchen. Two family bedrooms, a shared bath and a utility room complete the first floor. Curved stairs lead you to the upstairs master bedroom with its private balcony, large walk-in closet and amenity-filled bath.

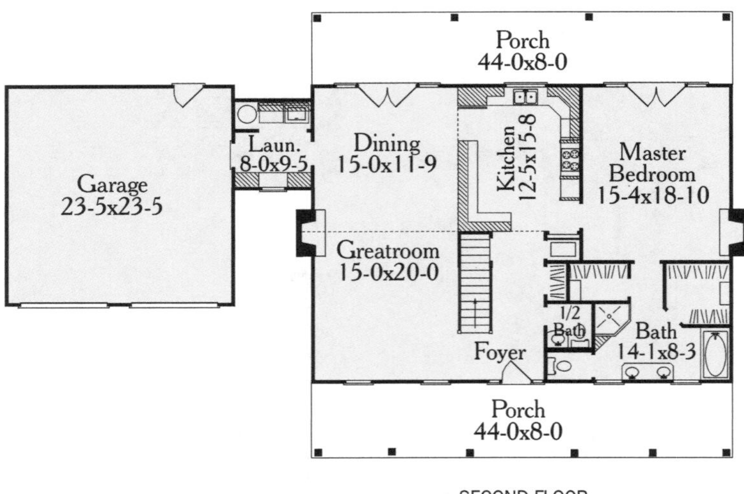

SECOND FLOOR

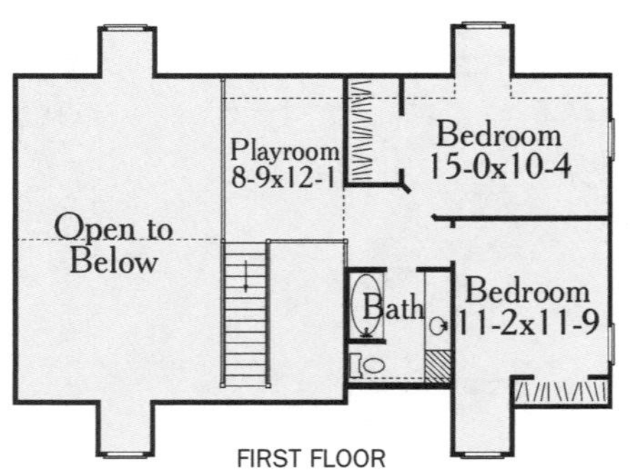

FIRST FLOOR

This home reveals its rustic charm with a metal roof, dormers and exposed-column rafters. The full-length porch is an invitation to comfortable living inside. The great room shares a fireplace with the spacious dining room that has rear-porch access. The kitchen is this home's focus, with plenty of counter and cabinet space, a window sink and an open layout. The first-floor master suite features two walk-in closets and a grand bath. Two family bedrooms and a playroom reside on the second floor.

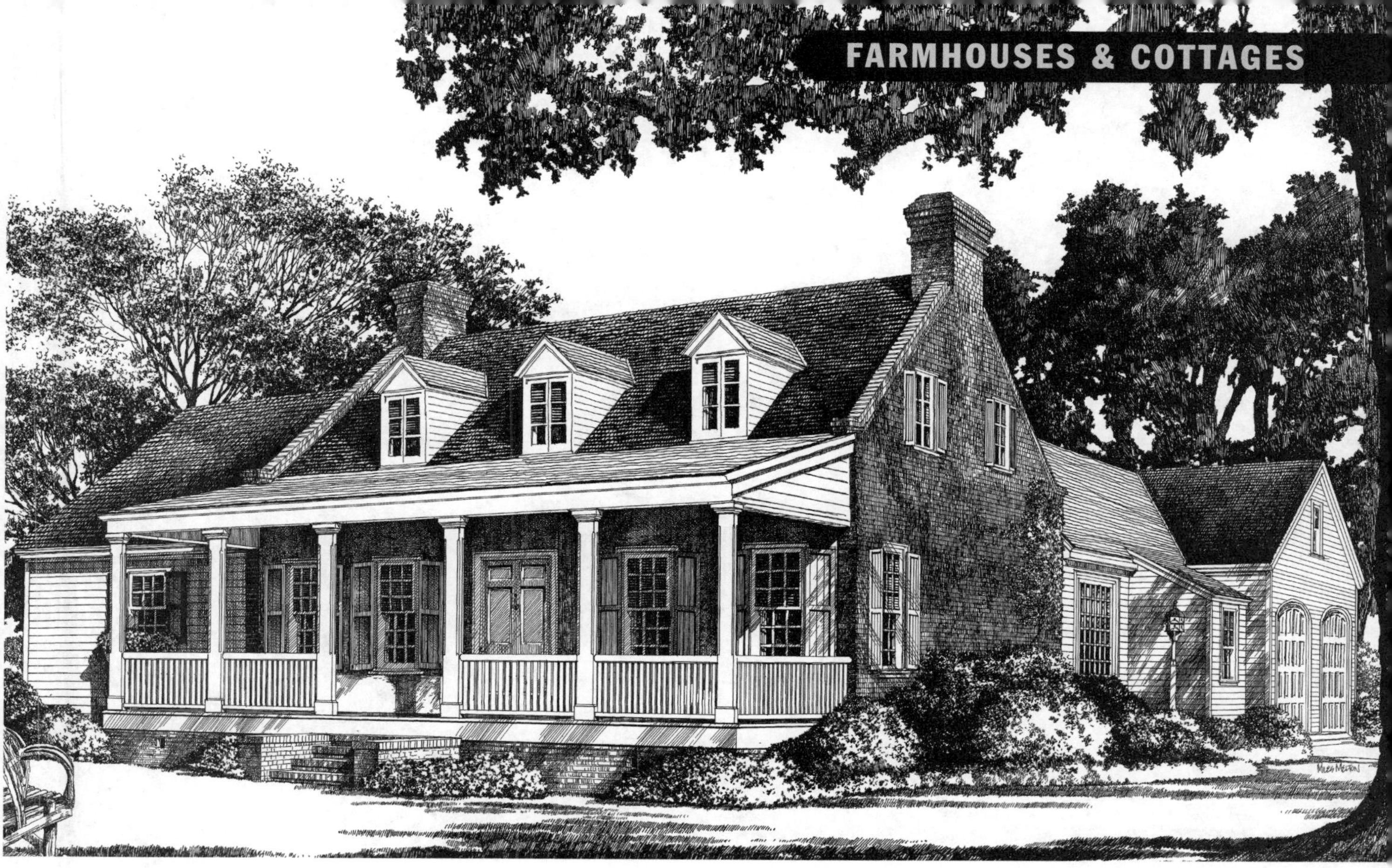

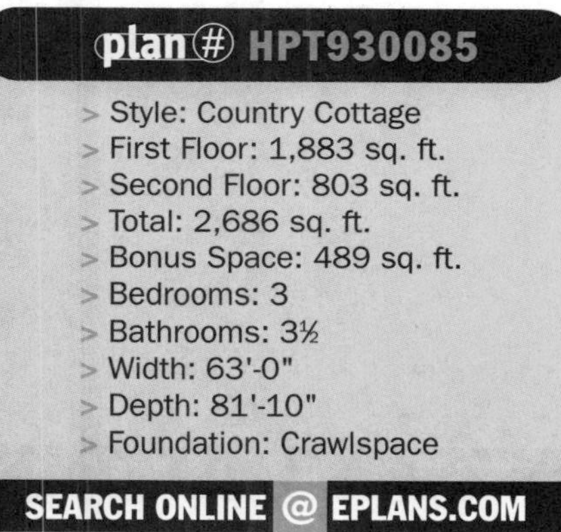

plan# HPT930085

- Style: Country Cottage
- First Floor: 1,883 sq. ft.
- Second Floor: 803 sq. ft.
- Total: 2,686 sq. ft.
- Bonus Space: 489 sq. ft.
- Bedrooms: 3
- Bathrooms: 3½
- Width: 63'-0"
- Depth: 81'-10"
- Foundation: Crawlspace

SEARCH ONLINE @ EPLANS.COM

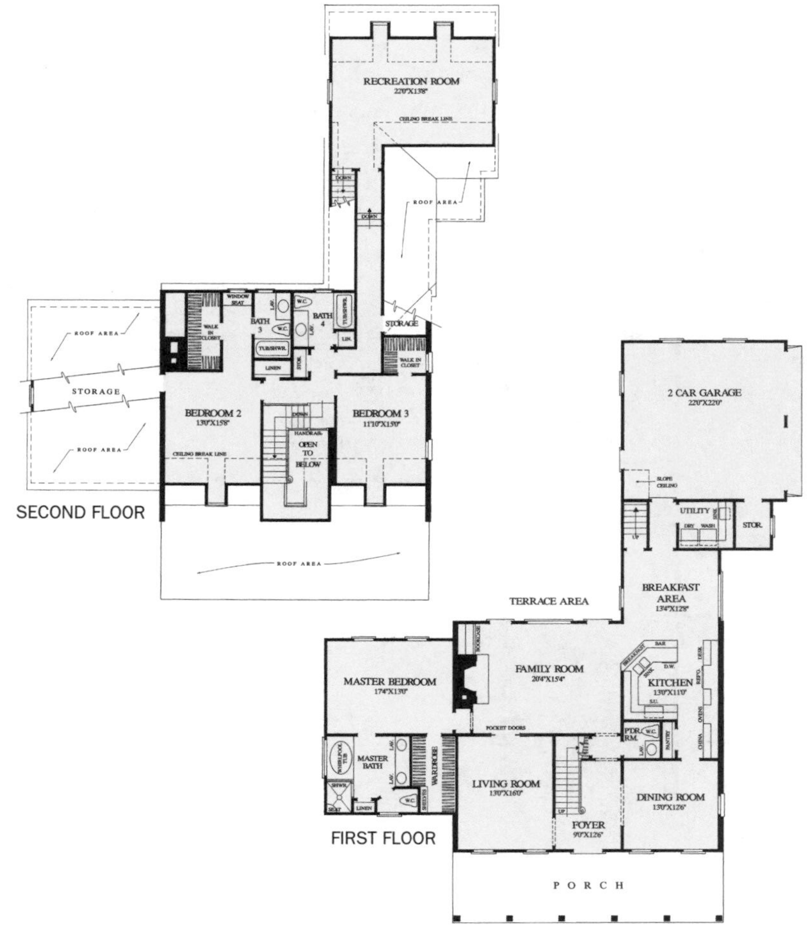

Where creeks converge and marsh grasses sway in gentle breezes, this is a classical low country home. Steep rooflines, high ceilings, front and back porches plus long and low windows are typical details of these charming planters' cottages. The foyer is flanked by the formal dining room and the living room, which opens to the family room. Here several windows look out to the terrace and a fireplace removes the chill on a winter's night. The sunny breakfast room, which adjoins the kitchen, offers a wonderful space for casual dining. Two bedrooms, the lavish master suite and the two-car garage complete the floor plan.

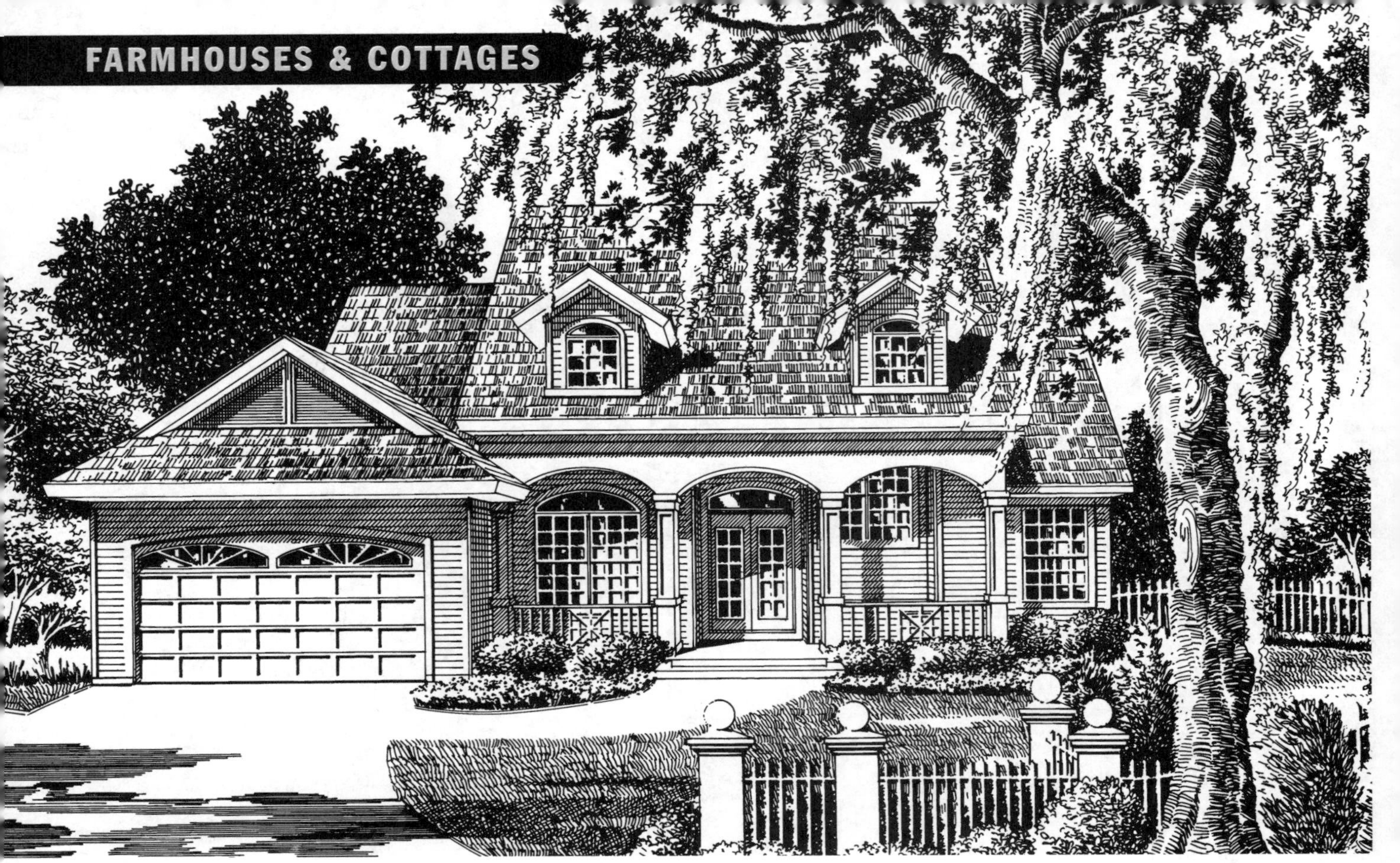

Muntin windows and gentle arches decorate the exterior of this traditional home. Living spaces consist of a formal dining room, a kitchen with an adjacent breakfast bay, and a great room with access to the rear veranda. A private study or guest suite in the rear left corner of the plan offers its own door to the veranda. The master suite enjoys a spacious bath with twin lavatories, a dressing area and two walk-in closets. A gallery hall on the second floor leads to a computer loft with built-ins for books and software.

plan# HPT930086

- Style: Farmhouse
- First Floor: 1,676 sq. ft.
- Second Floor: 851 sq. ft.
- Total: 2,527 sq. ft.
- Bedrooms: 4
- Bathrooms: 2½
- Width: 55'-0"
- Depth: 50'-0"
- Foundation: Slab

SEARCH ONLINE @ EPLANS.COM

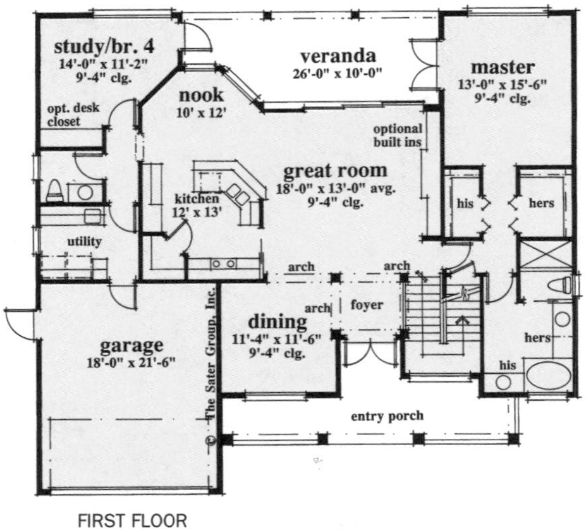

study/br. 4
14'-0" x 11'-2"
9'-4" clg.
veranda
26'-0" x 10'-0"
master
13'-0" x 15'-6"
9'-4" clg.
nook
10' x 12'
opt. desk
closet
optional
built ins
great room
18'-0" x 13'-0" avg.
9'-4" clg.
kitchen
12' x 13'
his
hers
utility
arch
arch
arch
foyer
dining
11'-4" x 11'-6"
9'-4" clg.
garage
18'-0" x 21'-6"
hers
his
entry porch
© The Sater Group, Inc.

FIRST FLOOR

balcony
br. 2
11'-10" x 11'-0"
8' clg.
br. 3
15'-0" x 10'-0"
8' clg
attic room
computer loft/
built ins
books
br. 1
11'-8" x 14'-4"
8' clg.
open to
foyer
below
wdw.
seat

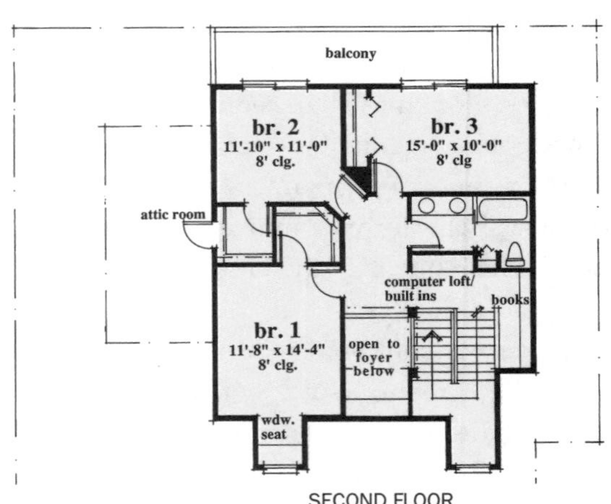

SECOND FLOOR

plan# HPT930087

- Style: Farmhouse
- First Floor: 1,335 sq. ft.
- Second Floor: 488 sq. ft.
- Total: 1,823 sq. ft.
- Bedrooms: 3
- Bathrooms: 2½
- Width: 61'-6"
- Depth: 54'-0"

SEARCH ONLINE @ EPLANS.COM

Elegant dormers and arch-topped windows offer a charming facade for this traditional design, with plenty of fabulous amenities to be found within. Lead guests leisurely through the foyer and central hall to a magnificent great room with vaulted ceiling and skylight, centered fireplace, decorative plant shelf and access to the rear deck. Attached to the nearby kitchen, a breakfast nook opens to a screened porch, perfect for informal alfresco dining. The well-appointed kitchen also serves the adjacent dining room for more formal occasions. A secluded main-floor master suite introduces high elegance with a cathedral ceiling and a Palladian-style window. A spacious walk-in closet, a whirlpool tub and a separate shower complete the comforts of this suite. Upstairs, a balcony hall connects two additional bedrooms that share a full bath.

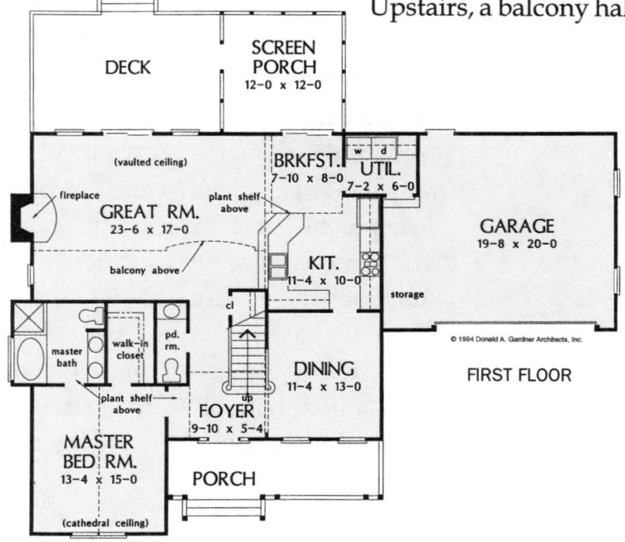

FIRST FLOOR

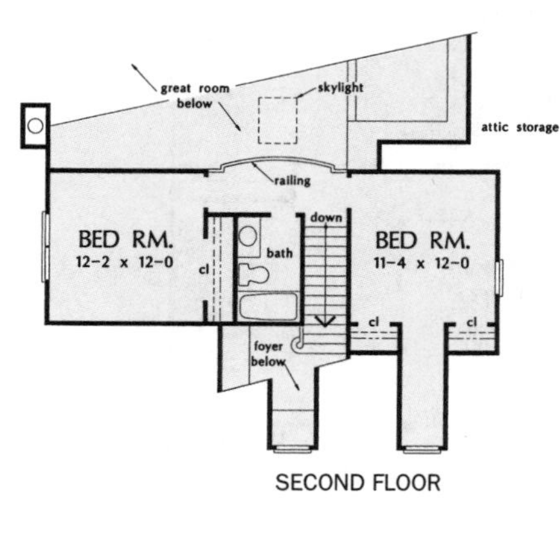

SECOND FLOOR

B.NATHAN

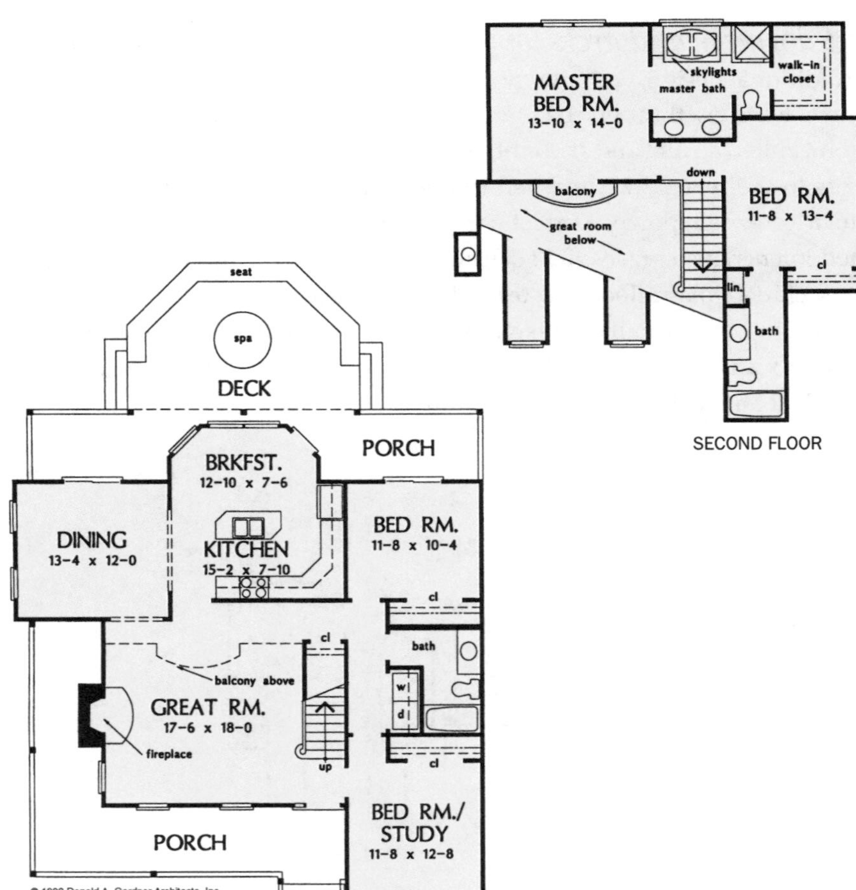

SECOND FLOOR

FIRST FLOOR

plan# HPT930088

- Style: Farmhouse
- First Floor: 1,271 sq. ft.
- Second Floor: 665 sq. ft.
- Total: 1,936 sq. ft.
- Bedrooms: 4
- Bathrooms: 3
- Width: 41'-6"
- Depth: 44'-8"

SEARCH ONLINE @ EPLANS.COM

This gabled and dormered country home with an L-shaped wrapping porch fits unexpected luxury into this compact plan. A balcony adds drama to the vaulted great room, and the large, center-island kitchen opens to rear porches and a deck with a spa area for great entertaining. Two bedrooms reside on the first floor and share a bath, while an additional bedroom has its own full bath on the second floor. The second-floor master bedroom features a bath with all of the extras including a walk-in closet, dual sinks, skylights and a separate tub and shower.

© 1998 Donald A Gardner, Inc.

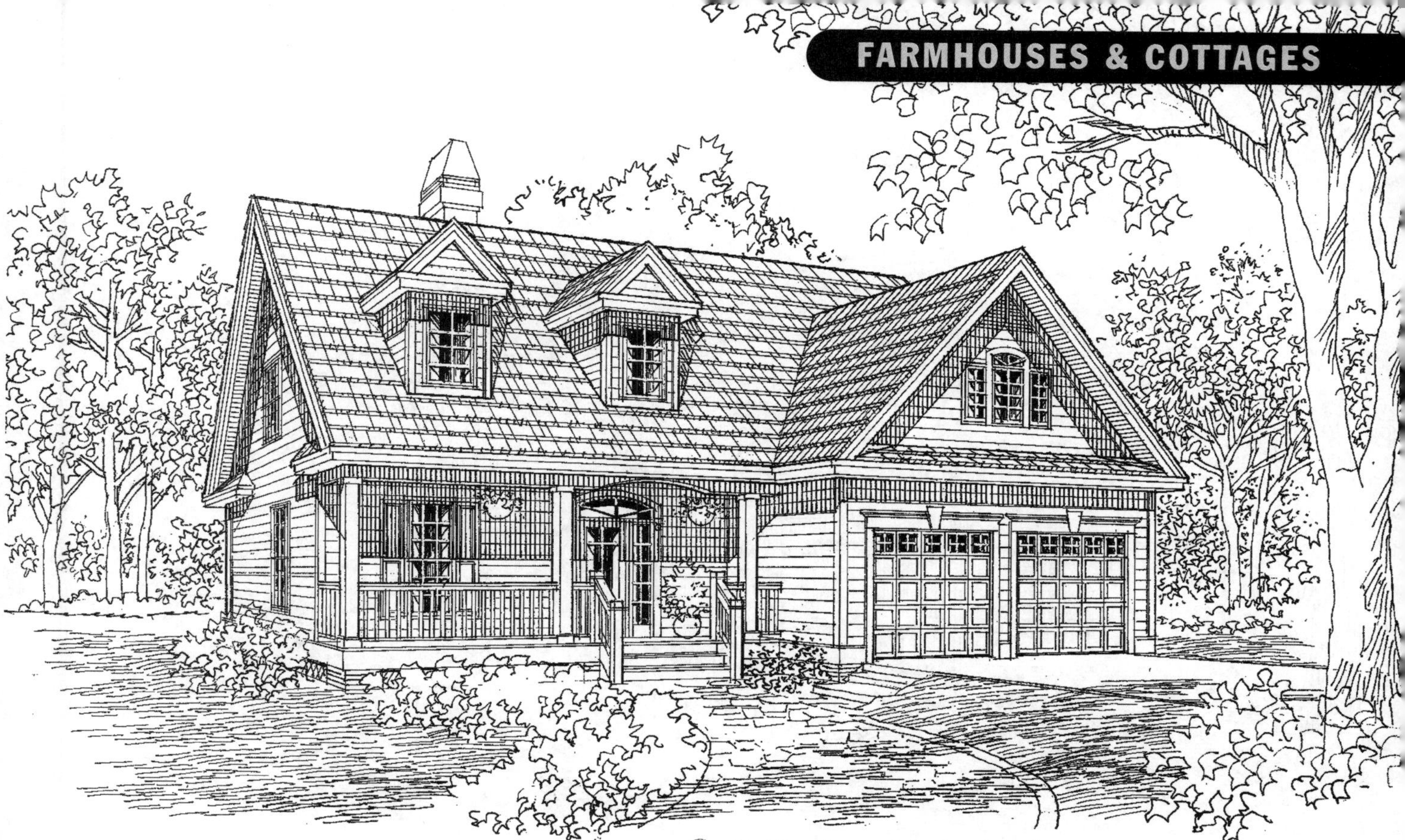

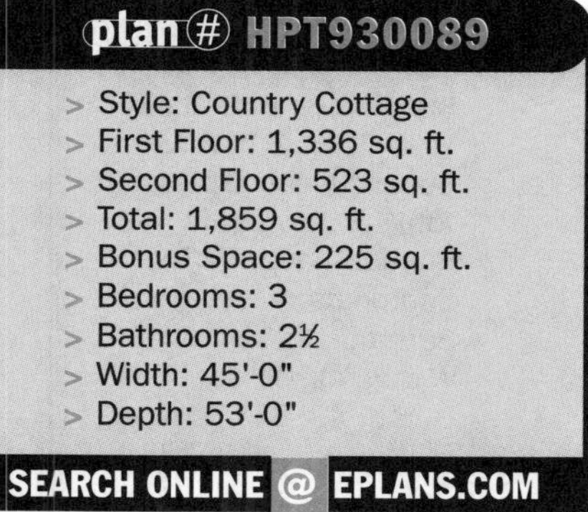

plan# HPT930089

- Style: Country Cottage
- First Floor: 1,336 sq. ft.
- Second Floor: 523 sq. ft.
- Total: 1,859 sq. ft.
- Bonus Space: 225 sq. ft.
- Bedrooms: 3
- Bathrooms: 2½
- Width: 45'-0"
- Depth: 53'-0"

SEARCH ONLINE @ EPLANS.COM

Gable treatments along with stone and horizontal siding give a definite country flavor to this two-story home. The formal dining room is accented with decorative columns that define its perimeter. The great room boasts a fireplace, built-ins and a magnificent view of the backyard beyond the rear porch. The master suite boasts two walk-in closets and a private bath. Two bedrooms share a full bath on the second floor.

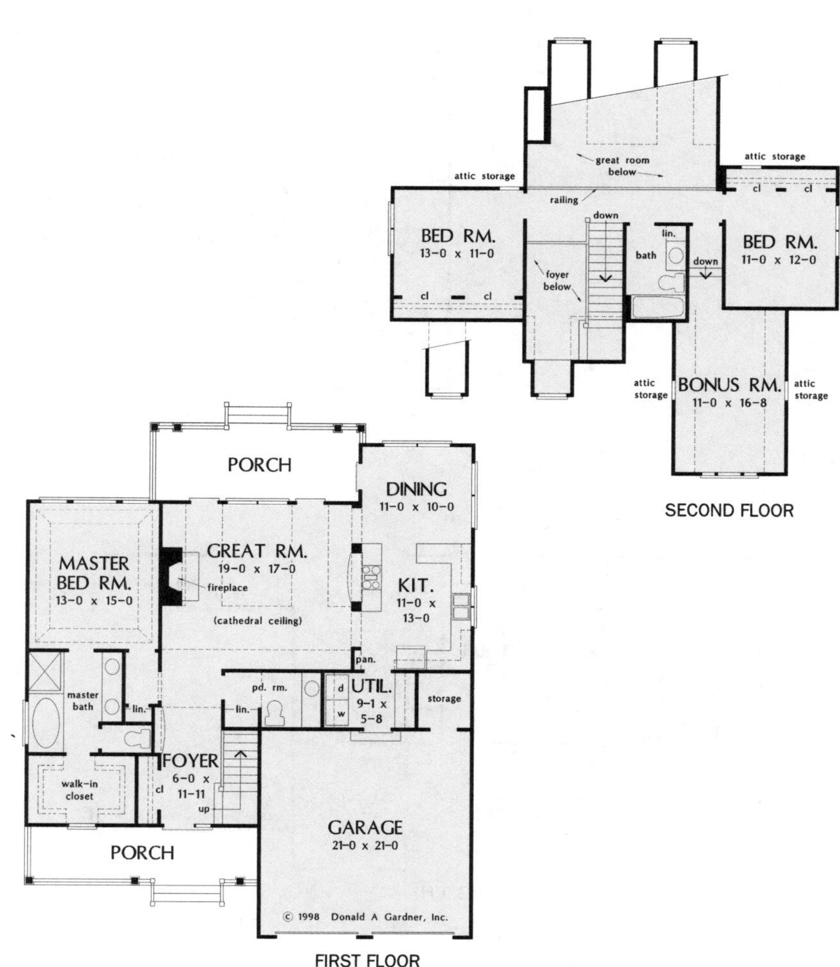

SECOND FLOOR

FIRST FLOOR

B. NATHAN

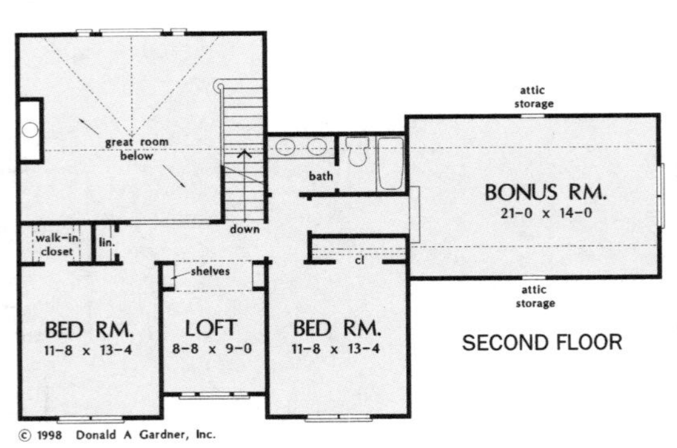

plan# HPT930090

- Style: Country Cottage
- First Floor: 1,718 sq. ft.
- Second Floor: 638 sq. ft.
- Total: 2,356 sq. ft.
- Bonus Space: 348 sq. ft.
- Bedrooms: 4
- Bathrooms: 3
- Width: 71'-0"
- Depth: 42'-8"

SEARCH ONLINE @ EPLANS.COM

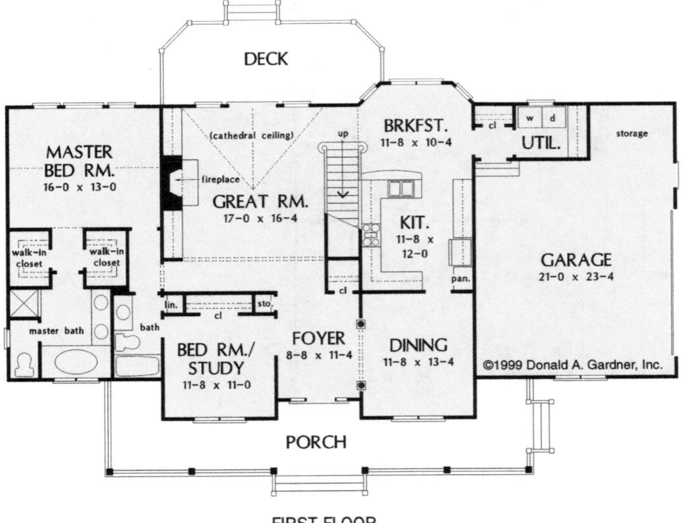

Twin gables and a generous front porch give this graceful farmhouse stature and appeal. A rear deck adds outdoor expansion to the great room, which features a fireplace, built-ins, a convenient rear staircase and an overlooking balcony. The first-floor master suite enjoys His and Hers walk-in closets and a private bath with a garden tub. A versatile bedroom/study and full bath are nearby. Located upstairs are two family bedrooms, a loft with built-in bookshelves, an ample second-floor bath and a bonus room.

B.NATHAN

plan# HPT930091

- Style: Country Cottage
- First Floor: 1,614 sq. ft.
- Second Floor: 892 sq. ft.
- Total: 2,506 sq. ft.
- Bonus Space: 341 sq. ft.
- Bedrooms: 4
- Bathrooms: 2½
- Width: 71'-10"
- Depth: 50'-0"

SEARCH ONLINE @ EPLANS.COM

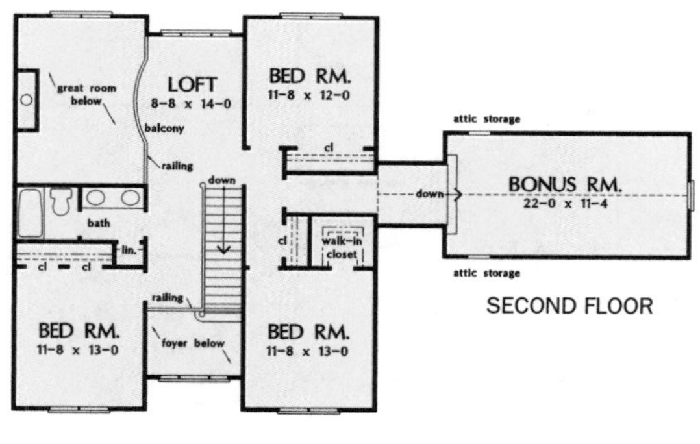

SECOND FLOOR

At the front of this farmhouse design, the master suite includes a sitting bay, two walk-in closets, a door to the front porch and a compartmented bath with a double-bowl vanity. The formal dining room in the second bay also features a door to the front porch. Access the rear porch from the great room, which is opens to the breakfast room under the balcony. On the second floor, three family bedrooms share a bath that has a double-bowl vanity. One of the family bedrooms offers a walk-in closet. A bonus room over the garage can be used as a study or game room.

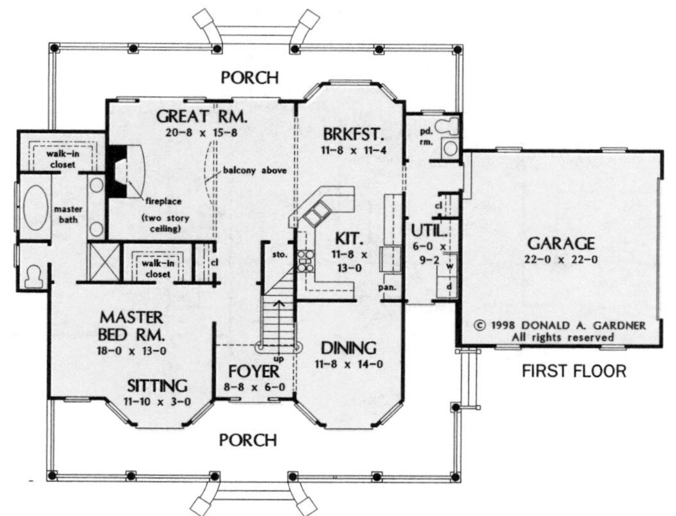

FIRST FLOOR

B. NATHAN

SECOND FLOOR

plan# HPT930092

- Style: Country Cottage
- First Floor: 1,914 sq. ft.
- Second Floor: 597 sq. ft.
- Total: 2,511 sq. ft.
- Bonus Space: 487 sq. ft.
- Bedrooms: 3
- Bathrooms: 2½
- Width: 79'-2"
- Depth: 51'-6"

SEARCH ONLINE @ EPLANS.COM

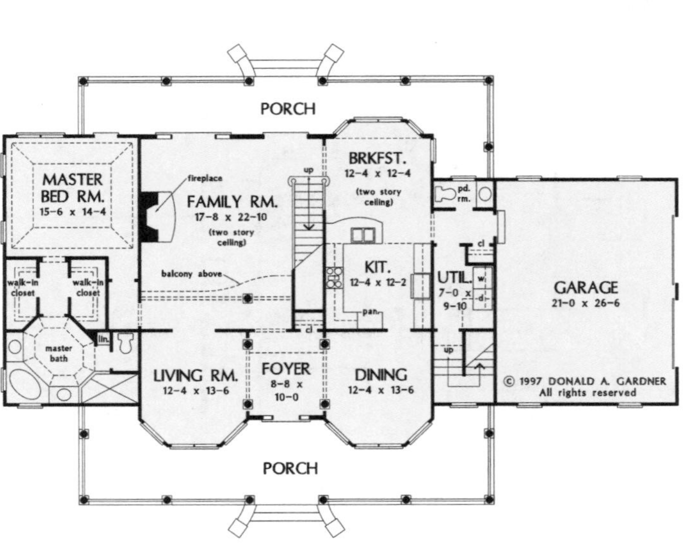

FIRST FLOOR

Filled with the charm of farmhouse details, such as twin dormers and bay windows, this design begins with a classic covered porch. The entry leads to a foyer flanked by columns that separate it from the formal dining and living rooms. The U-shaped kitchen separates the dining room from the bayed breakfast room. The first-floor master suite features a bedroom with a tray ceiling and a luxurious private bath.

plan# HPT930093

- Style: Country Cottage
- First Floor: 1,943 sq. ft.
- Second Floor: 1,000 sq. ft.
- Total: 2,943 sq. ft.
- Bonus Space: 403 sq. ft.
- Bedrooms: 4
- Bathrooms: 2½
- Width: 79'-10"
- Depth: 51'-8"

SEARCH ONLINE @ EPLANS.COM

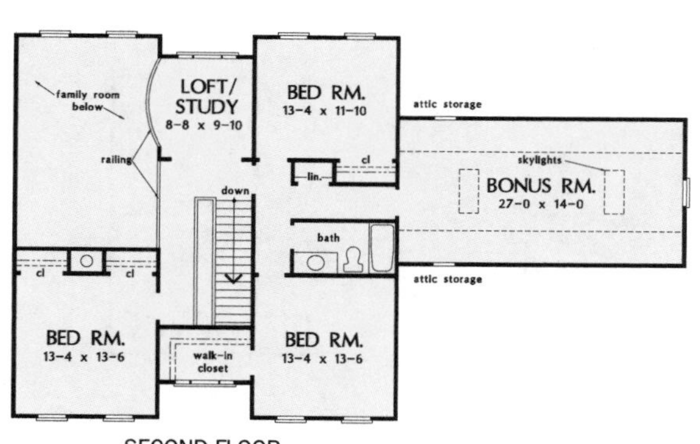

SECOND FLOOR

Two symmetrical bay windows accent the formal living room and dining room of this design. The foyer leads straight back to the family room and rear porch. A fireplace, built-ins and an overhead balcony grace the family room. Between the dining room and kitchen, there's a handy pantry area. The utility room and a powder room are to the right of the breakfast room. The master suite is off the family room and includes a walk-in closet and a bath with a double-bowl vanity. Upstairs, three bedrooms share a hall bath and a loft/study that overlooks the family room.

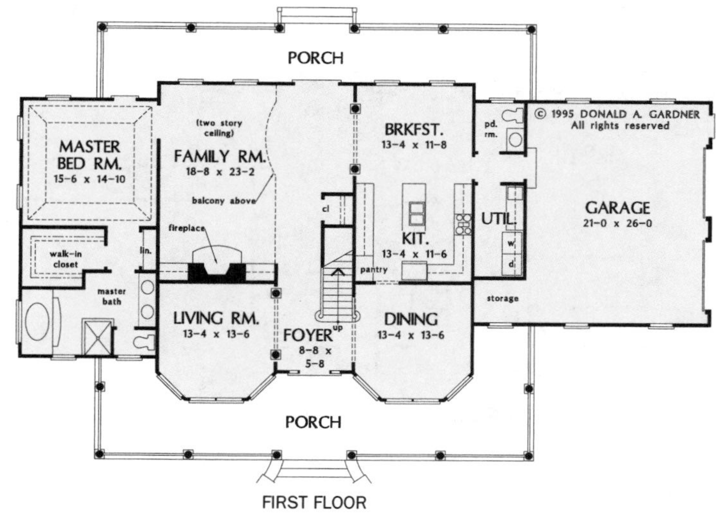

FIRST FLOOR

SECOND FLOOR

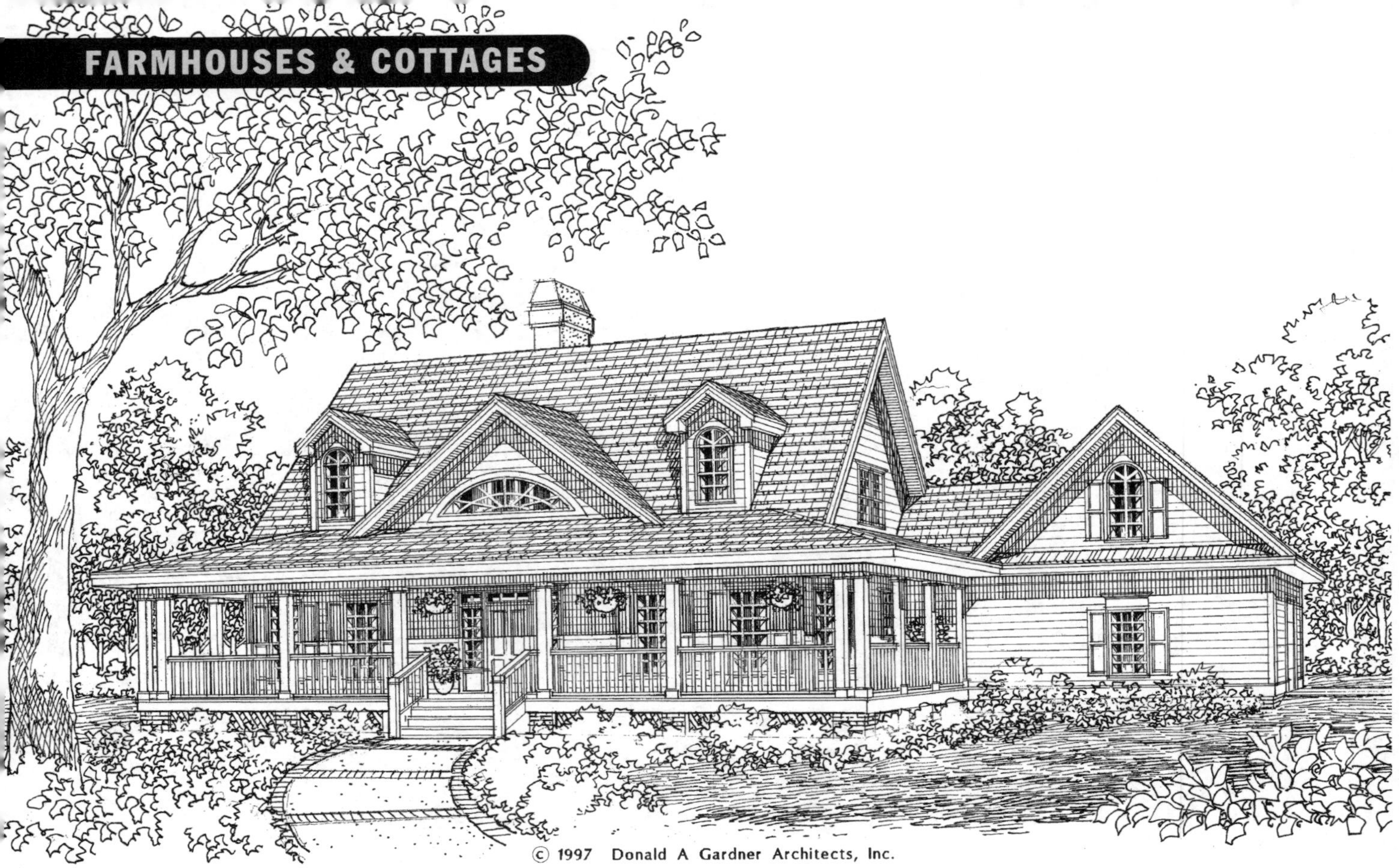

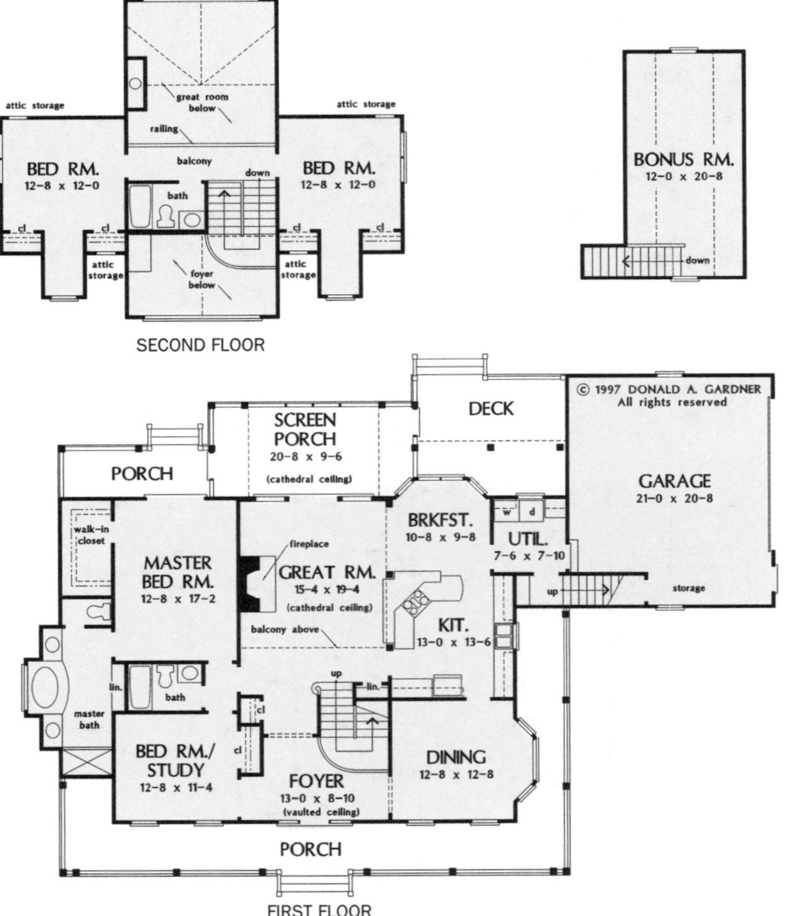

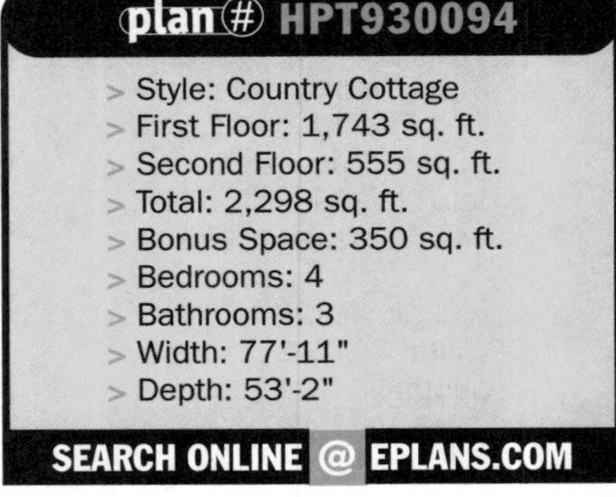

plan# HPT930094

- Style: Country Cottage
- First Floor: 1,743 sq. ft.
- Second Floor: 555 sq. ft.
- Total: 2,298 sq. ft.
- Bonus Space: 350 sq. ft.
- Bedrooms: 4
- Bathrooms: 3
- Width: 77'-11"
- Depth: 53'-2"

SEARCH ONLINE @ EPLANS.COM

FIRST FLOOR

A lovely arch-top window and a wraparound porch set off this country exterior. Inside, formal rooms open off the foyer, which leads to a spacious great room. This living area provides a fireplace and access to a screened porch with a cathedral ceiling. Bay windows allow natural light into the breakfast area and formal dining room. The master suite features a spacious bath and access to a private area of the rear porch. Two second-floor bedrooms share a bath and a balcony hall that offers an overlook to the great room.

B. NATHAN

plan# HPT930095

- Style: Farmhouse
- First Floor: 1,499 sq. ft.
- Second Floor: 665 sq. ft.
- Total: 2,164 sq. ft.
- Bonus Space: 380 sq. ft.
- Bedrooms: 4
- Bathrooms: 2½
- Width: 69'-8"
- Depth: 40'-6"

SEARCH ONLINE @ EPLANS.COM

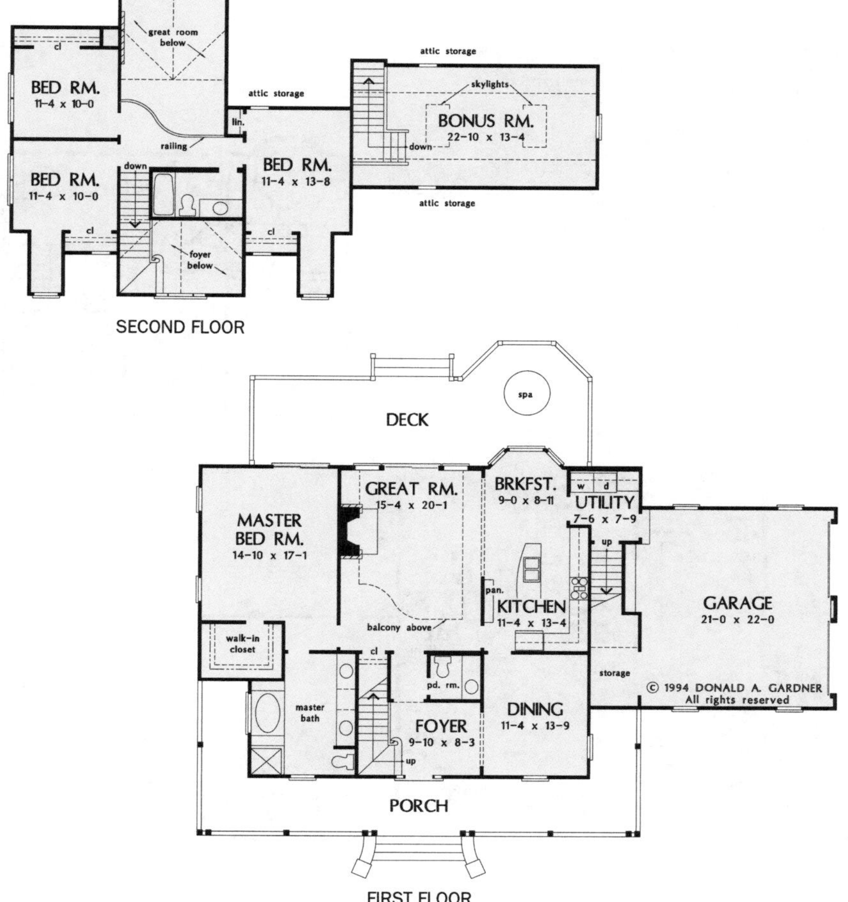

The warm down-home appeal of this country house is as apparent inside as it is out. Inside, a two-story foyer and a great room with a hearth give the home an open feel. The great room leads to the breakfast area and the efficient kitchen with an island work area and a large pantry. The master bedroom is situated on the left side of the house for privacy. It features deck access, a large walk-in closet and a bath that includes dual vanities, a whirlpool tub and a separate shower. Three additional bedrooms, a full bath and bonus space are located upstairs.

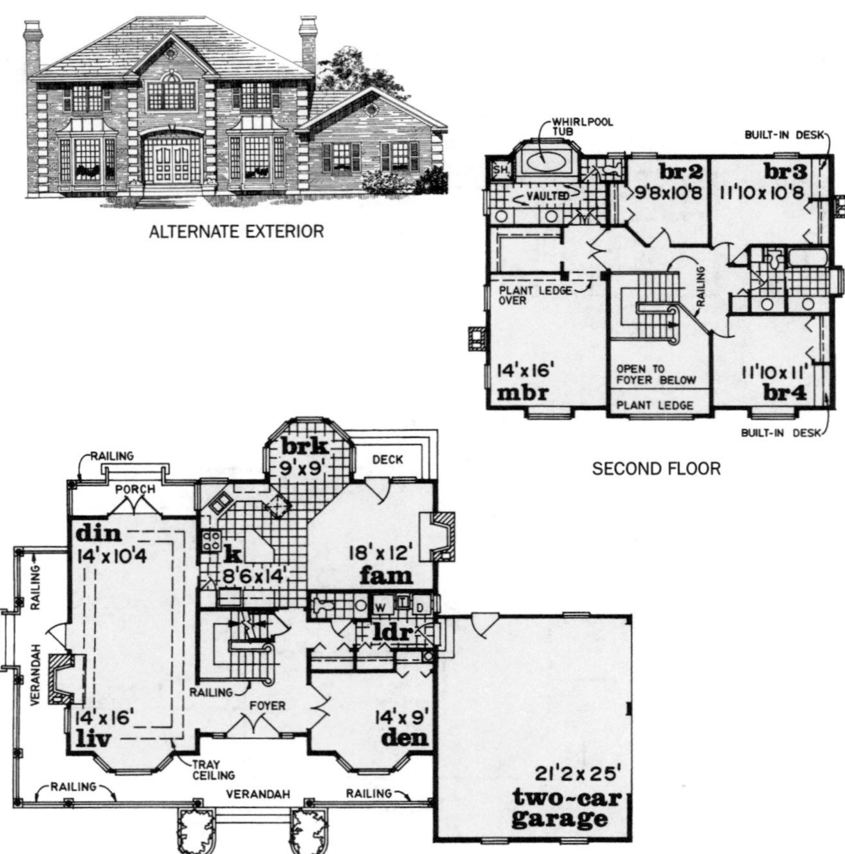

ALTERNATE EXTERIOR

SECOND FLOOR

FIRST FLOOR

plan# HPT930096

- Style: Country Cottage
- First Floor: 1,324 sq. ft.
- Second Floor: 1,206 sq. ft.
- Total: 2,530 sq. ft.
- Bedrooms: 4
- Bathrooms: 2½
- Width: 69'-6"
- Depth: 48'-4"
- Foundation: Basement, Crawlspace

SEARCH ONLINE @ EPLANS.COM

This design may be finished in brick or horizontal siding with a wrapping veranda. Details for both options are included in the plans. From the wide foyer, the plan stretches to a living/dining room combination with a tray ceiling, fireplace and French doors to the covered porch at the back. The family room has a fireplace and access to a private deck. The vaulted master suite enjoys a vaulted bath with a whirlpool tub and double sinks.

plan# HPT930097

- Style: Farmhouse
- First Floor: 1,109 sq. ft.
- Second Floor: 2,044 sq. ft.
- Total: 3,153 sq. ft.
- Bedrooms: 4
- Bathrooms: 3½
- Width: 66'-0"
- Depth: 74'-0"
- Foundation: Crawlspace, Slab, Basement

SEARCH ONLINE @ EPLANS.COM

Fish-scale shingles and horizontal siding team up with the detailed front porch to create the look of yesteryear. Brickwork enriches the sides and rear of the home. The main level features high ceilings throughout the central living space. The front-oriented formal areas merge with the family room via three sets of French doors. The island kitchen and skylit eating area have sloped ceilings. A breezeway off the deck connects the house to a roomy workshop. The main-floor master suite offers an opulent skylit bath with a garden vanity, a spa tub, a separate shower and a high sloped ceiling. The upper floor offers three more bedrooms, two full baths and a balcony that looks to the backyard.

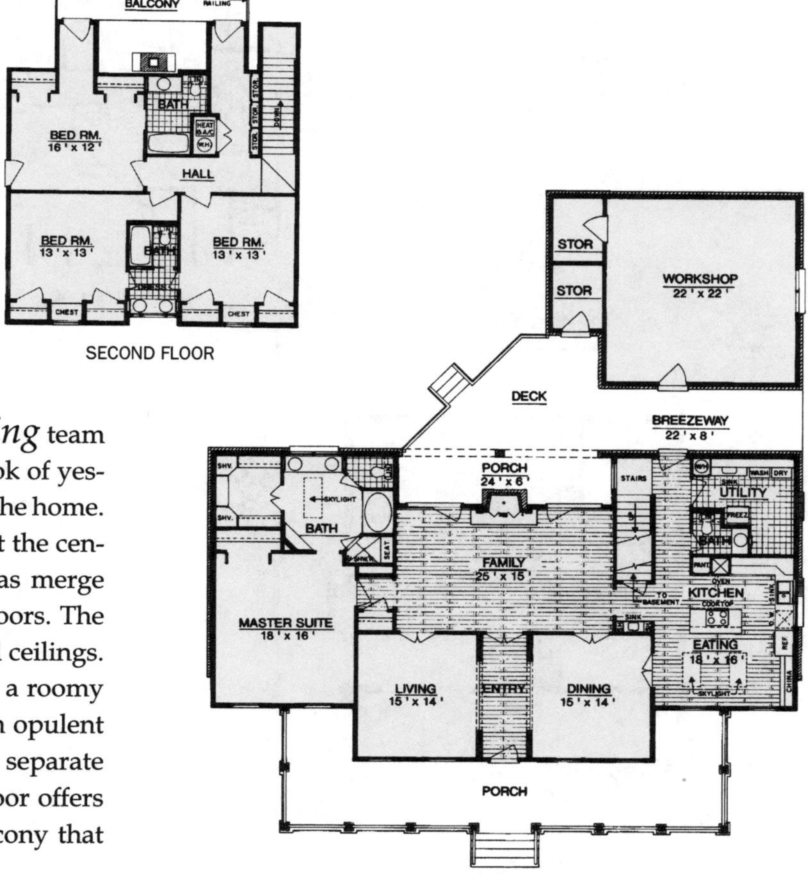

SECOND FLOOR

FIRST FLOOR

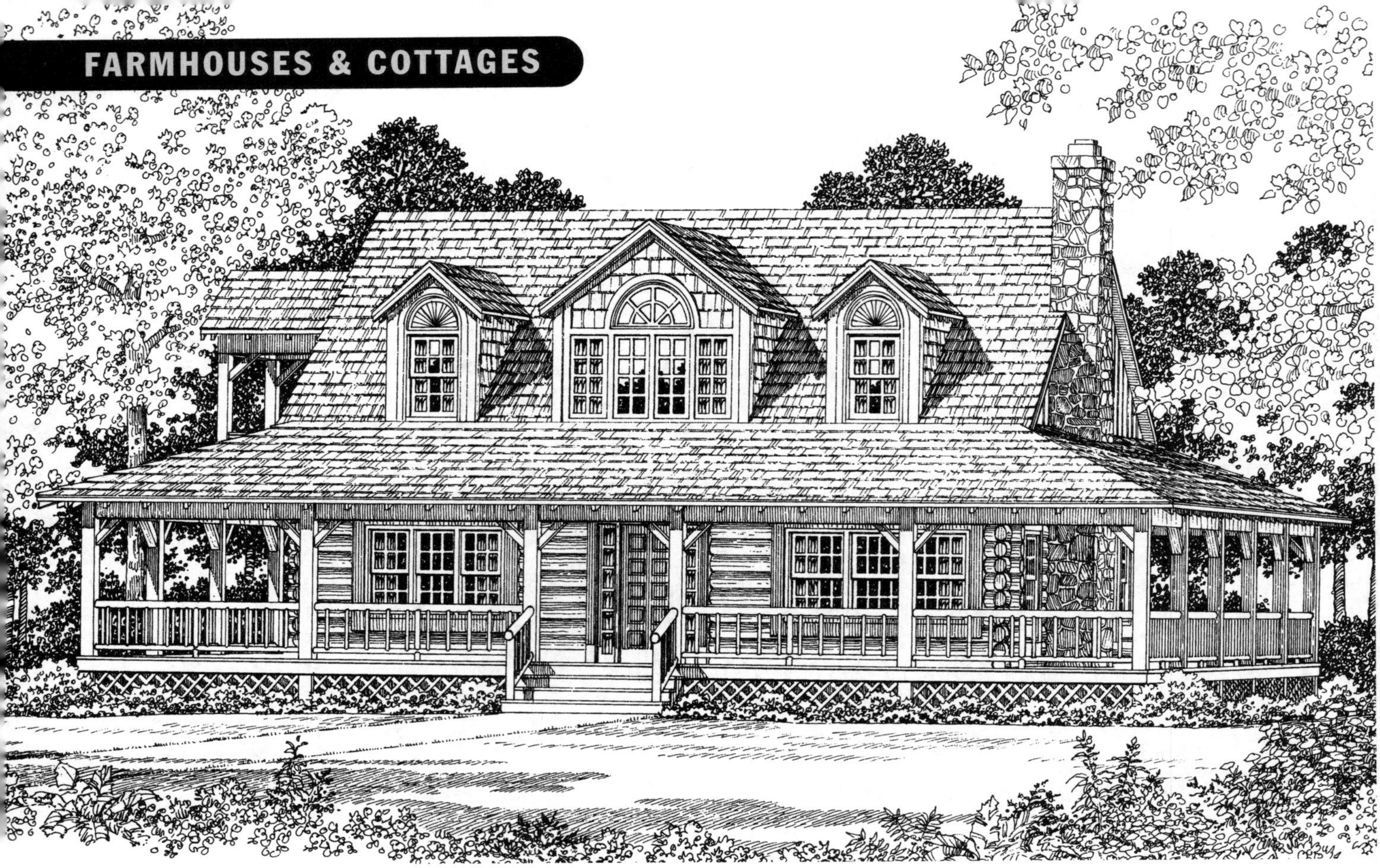

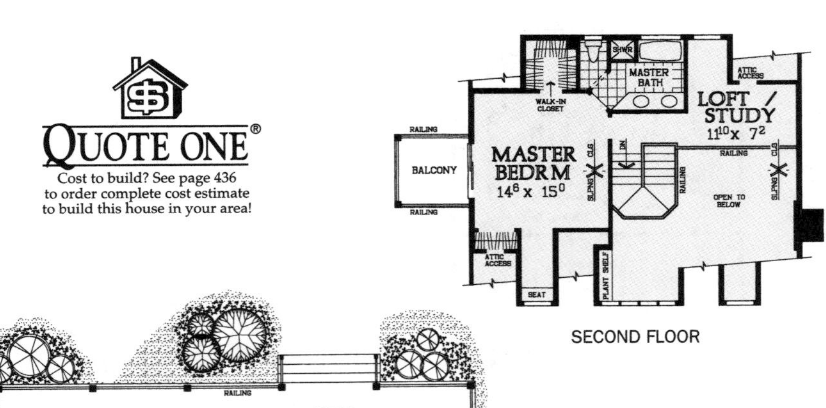

SECOND FLOOR

FIRST FLOOR

plan# HPT930098

- Style: Farmhouse
- First Floor: 1,139 sq. ft.
- Second Floor: 576 sq. ft.
- Total: 1,715 sq. ft.
- Bedrooms: 3
- Bathrooms: 2
- Width: 52'-0"
- Depth: 46'-0"
- Foundation: Crawlspace

SEARCH ONLINE @ EPLANS.COM

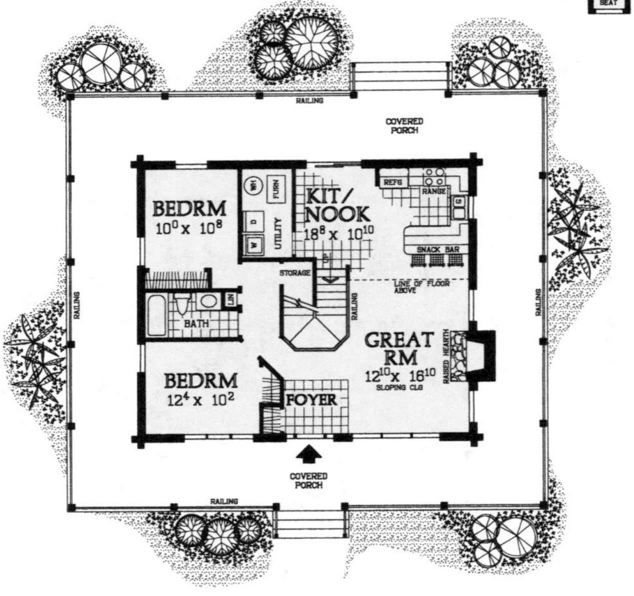

A grand wraparound porch invites outdoor enjoyment, even during a rainstorm! The entrance to this fine log home is highlighted by a Palladian window above. Inside, a two-story great room to the right offers a warming fireplace, setting a spirited country mood. Nearby, a snack bar joins the living area with the U-shaped kitchen and attached nook. Two family bedrooms, a full bath and a utility room complete the first floor. The second-floor master suite is filled with amenities. Curl up in the window seat with a good book or enjoy fresh air from your own private balcony. A walk-in closet, a master bath and a loft/study complete this special retreat.

plan# HPT930099

- Style: Farmhouse
- First Floor: 1,526 sq. ft.
- Second Floor: 635 sq. ft.
- Total: 2,161 sq. ft.
- Bonus Space: 355 sq. ft.
- Bedrooms: 3
- Bathrooms: 2½
- Width: 76'-4"
- Depth: 74'-2"

SEARCH ONLINE @ EPLANS.COM

QUOTE ONE®
Cost to build? See page 436 to order complete cost estimate to build this house in your area!

BED RM. 12-4 × 11-8
LOFT/ STUDY 9-0 × 10-8
BED RM. 12-4 × 10-4
BONUS RM. 27-0 × 12-0

SECOND FLOOR

GARAGE 23-4 × 21-4
DECK
SCREENED PORCH 16-0 × 10-6
GREAT RM. 16-0 × 19-2
BRKFST. 12-4 × 10-2
KITCHEN 12-4 × 11-0
MASTER BED RM. 12-4 × 16-0
FOYER 12-6 × 8-0
DINING 14-4 × 12-4
PORCH

FIRST FLOOR

This beautiful farmhouse boasts all the extras! Clerestory windows with arched tops enhance the exterior both front and back as well as allow natural light to penetrate into the foyer and the great room. A kitchen with an island counter and breakfast area accesses the spacious great room through a cased opening with a colonnade. The exquisite master suite boasts a generous bedroom, a large walk-in closet and a dramatically designed bath with emphasis on the whirlpool tub flanked by double columns. Access to the rear deck is possible from the screened porch, the master bath and the breakfast area. The second level includes two bedrooms sharing a full bath and a loft/study area overlooking the great room.

© 1998 Donald A Gardner, Inc.

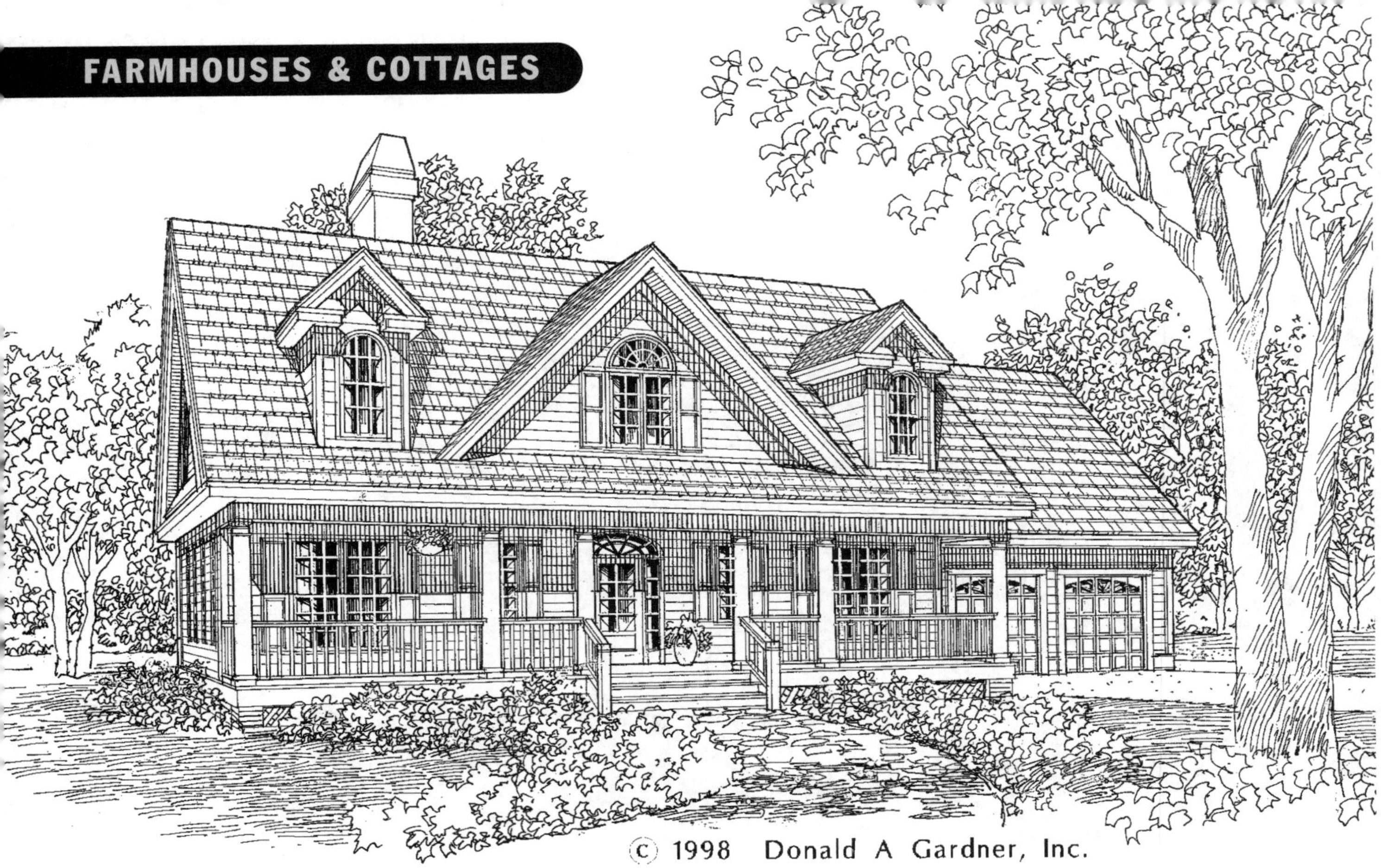

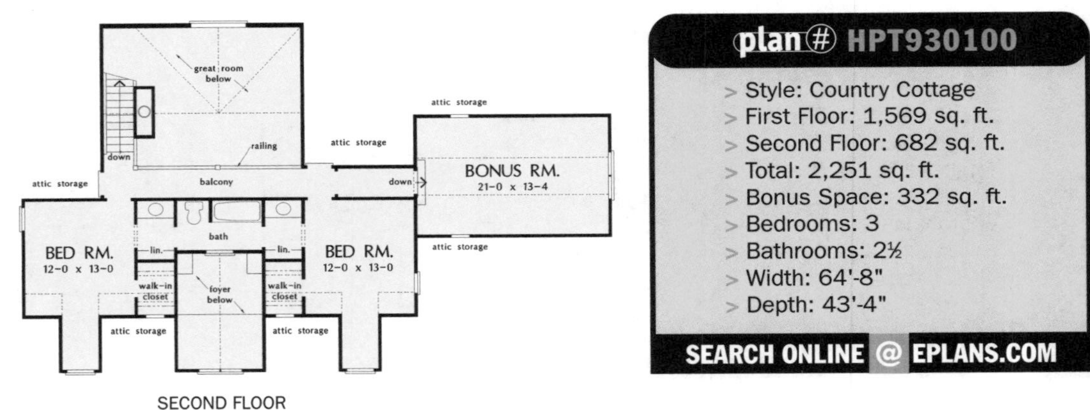

SECOND FLOOR

plan# HPT930100

- Style: Country Cottage
- First Floor: 1,569 sq. ft.
- Second Floor: 682 sq. ft.
- Total: 2,251 sq. ft.
- Bonus Space: 332 sq. ft.
- Bedrooms: 3
- Bathrooms: 2½
- Width: 64'-8"
- Depth: 43'-4"

SEARCH ONLINE @ EPLANS.COM

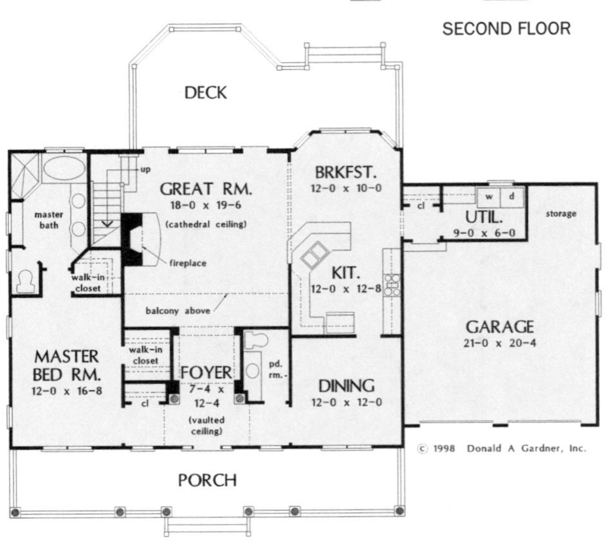

FIRST FLOOR

The wide porch across the front and the deck off the great room in back allow as much outdoor living as the weather permits. The foyer opens through columns off the front porch to the dining room, with a nearby powder room, and to the great room. The breakfast room is open to the great room and the adjacent kitchen. The utility room adjoins this area and accesses the garage. On the opposite side of the plan, the master suite offers a compartmented bath and two walk-in closets. A staircase leads upstairs to two family bedrooms—one at each end of a balcony that overlooks the great room. Each bedroom contains a walk-in closet, a dormer window and private access to the bath through a private vanity area.

©2000 Donald A. Gardner, Inc.

B. NATHAN

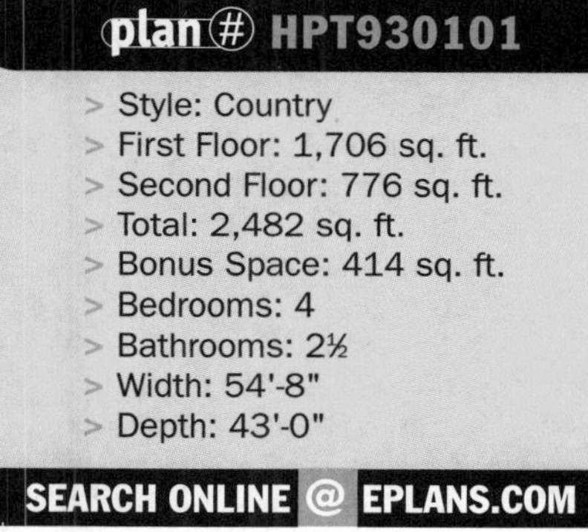

plan# HPT930101

- Style: Country
- First Floor: 1,706 sq. ft.
- Second Floor: 776 sq. ft.
- Total: 2,482 sq. ft.
- Bonus Space: 414 sq. ft.
- Bedrooms: 4
- Bathrooms: 2½
- Width: 54'-8"
- Depth: 43'-0"

SEARCH ONLINE @ EPLANS.COM

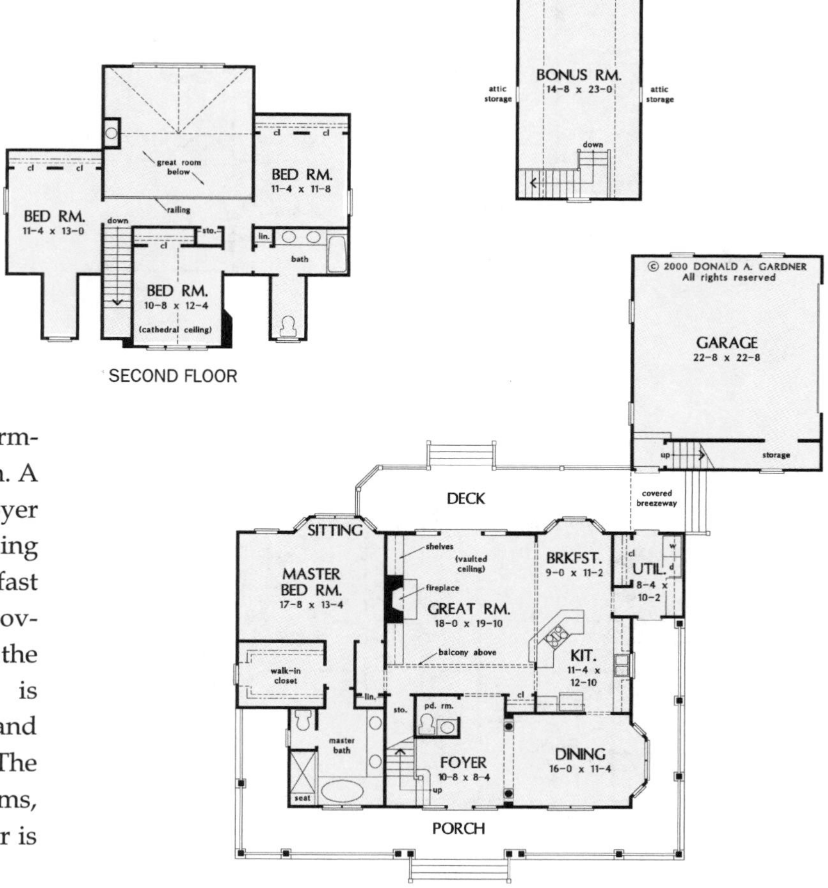

SECOND FLOOR

FIRST FLOOR

The small appearance of this country farmhouse belies the spaciousness that lies within. A large great room lies directly beyond the foyer and boasts a fireplace, shelves, a vaulted ceiling and a door to the rear deck. A bayed breakfast room, located just off the kitchen, looks to a covered breezeway that leads from the house to the garage. The first-floor master bedroom is enhanced with a sitting area, walk-in closet and full bath with a garden tub and dual sinks. The second floor includes three additional bedrooms, one with a cathedral ceiling. The second floor is also open to the great room below.

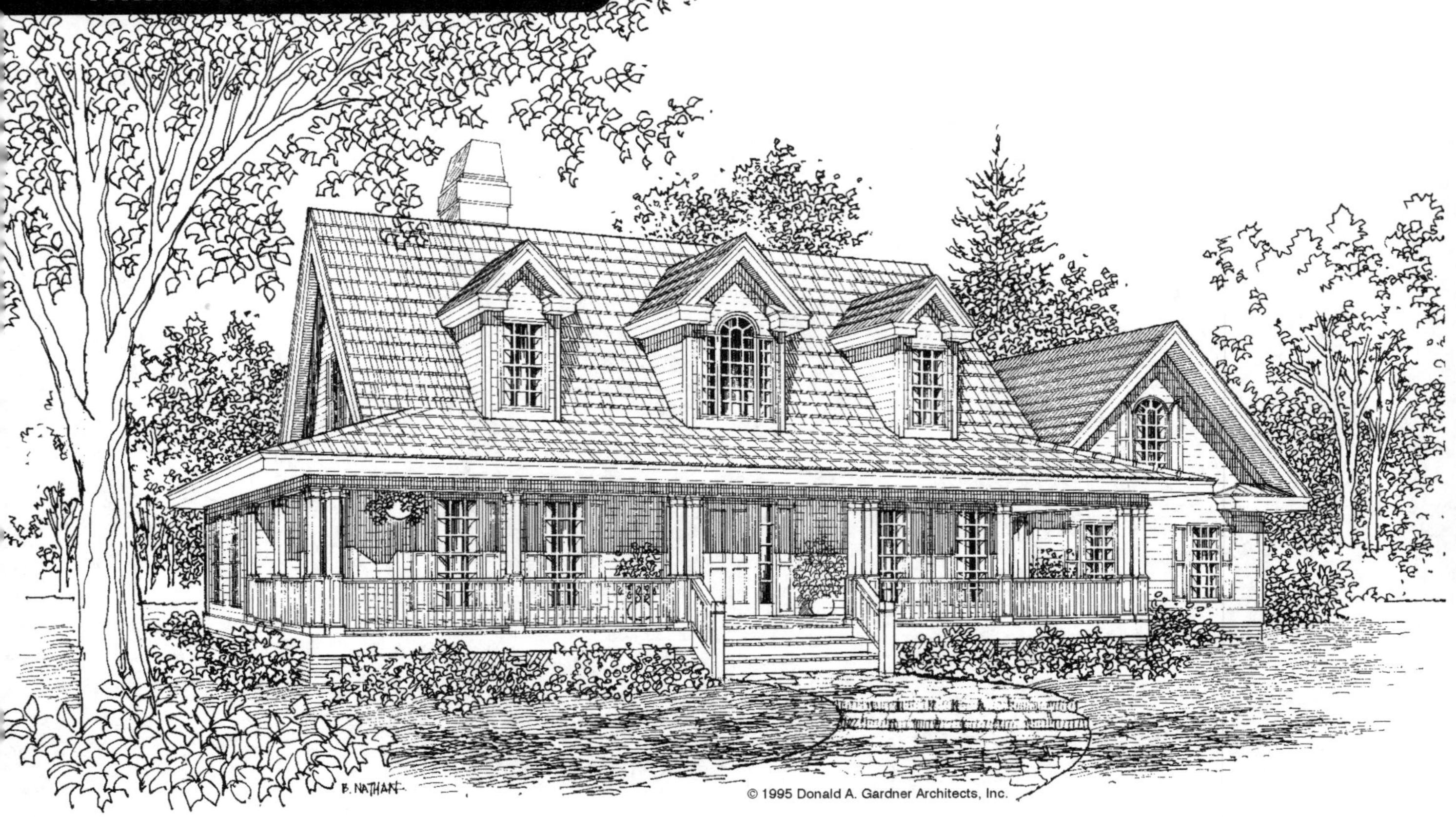

B. NATHAN

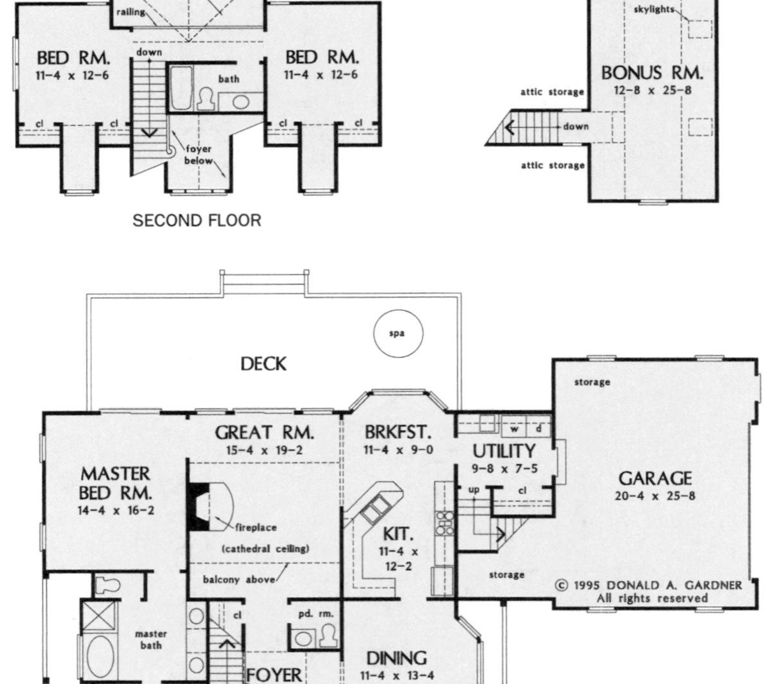

plan# HPT930102

- Style: Farmhouse
- First Floor: 1,480 sq. ft.
- Second Floor: 511 sq. ft.
- Total: 1,991 sq. ft.
- Bonus Space: 363 sq. ft.
- Bedrooms: 3
- Bathrooms: 2½
- Width: 73'-0"
- Depth: 51'-10"

SEARCH ONLINE @ EPLANS.COM

This farmhouse has plenty to offer, from its covered front porch to its rear deck with a spa. Inside, the amenities continue, including a bayed formal dining room, a great room—with both a fireplace and direct access to the rear deck—and a bayed breakfast nook. A nearby kitchen is spacious and shares a snack bar with the breakfast/great room area. A deluxe master bedroom pampers you with access to the rear deck and a luxurious bath. Upstairs, two family bedrooms share a full hall bath and a balcony overlooking the great room.

© 1993 Donald A. Gardner Architects, Inc.

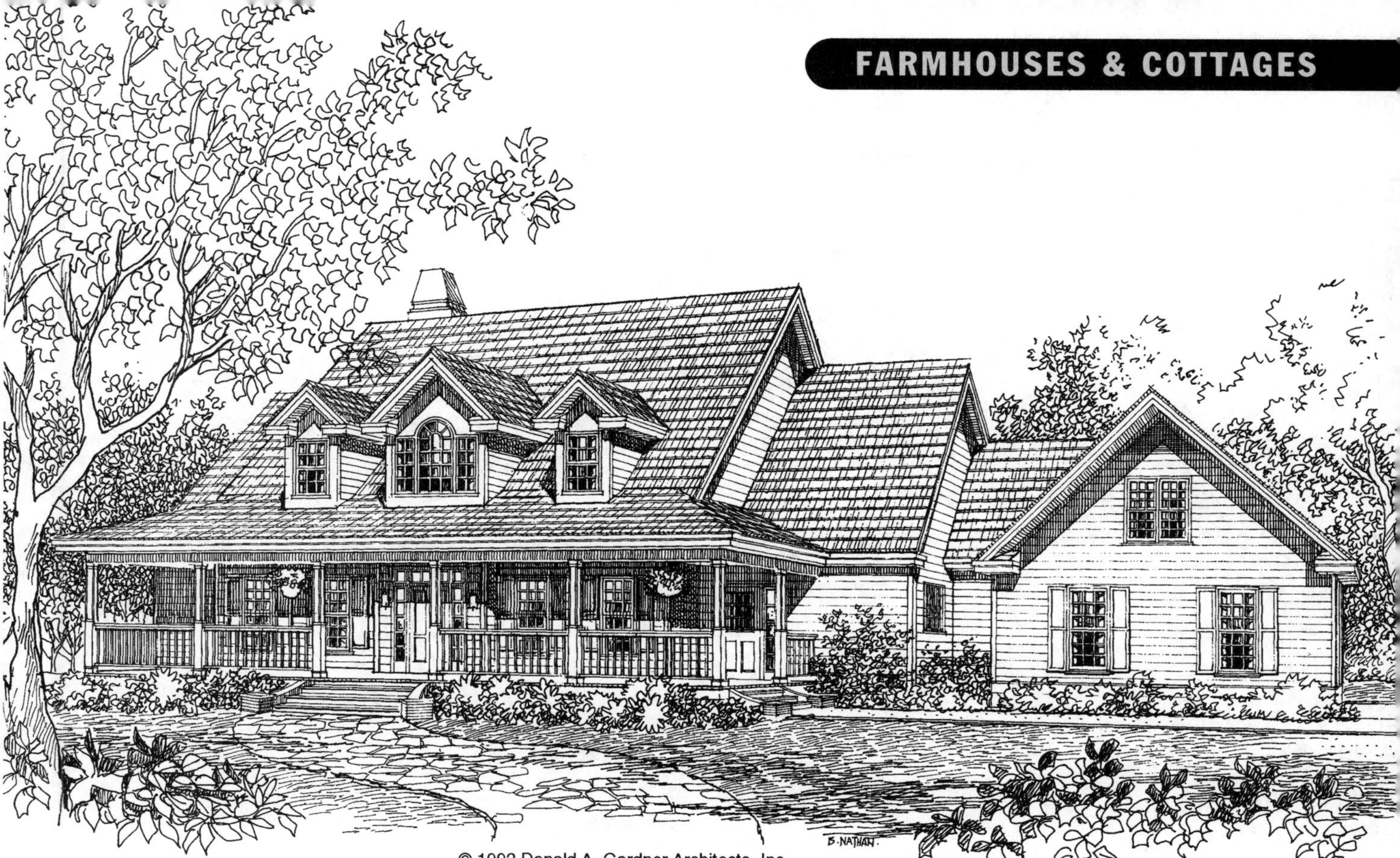

plan# HPT930103

- Style: Farmhouse
- First Floor: 2,064 sq. ft.
- Second Floor: 594 sq. ft.
- Total: 2,658 sq. ft.
- Bonus Space: 483 sq. ft.
- Bedrooms: 4
- Bathrooms: 3½
- Width: 92'-0"
- Depth: 57'-8"

SEARCH ONLINE @ EPLANS.COM

You'll find country living at its best when meandering through this four-bedroom farmhouse with its wraparound porch. A front Palladian dormer window and rear clerestory windows in the great room add exciting visual elements to the exterior while providing natural light to the interior. The large great room boasts a fireplace, bookshelves and a raised cathedral ceiling, allowing a curved balcony overlook above. The great room, master bedroom and breakfast room are accessible to the rear porch for greater circulation and flexibility. Special features such as the large cooktop island in the kitchen, the wet bar, the bedroom/study, the generous bonus room over the garage and ample storage space set this plan apart.

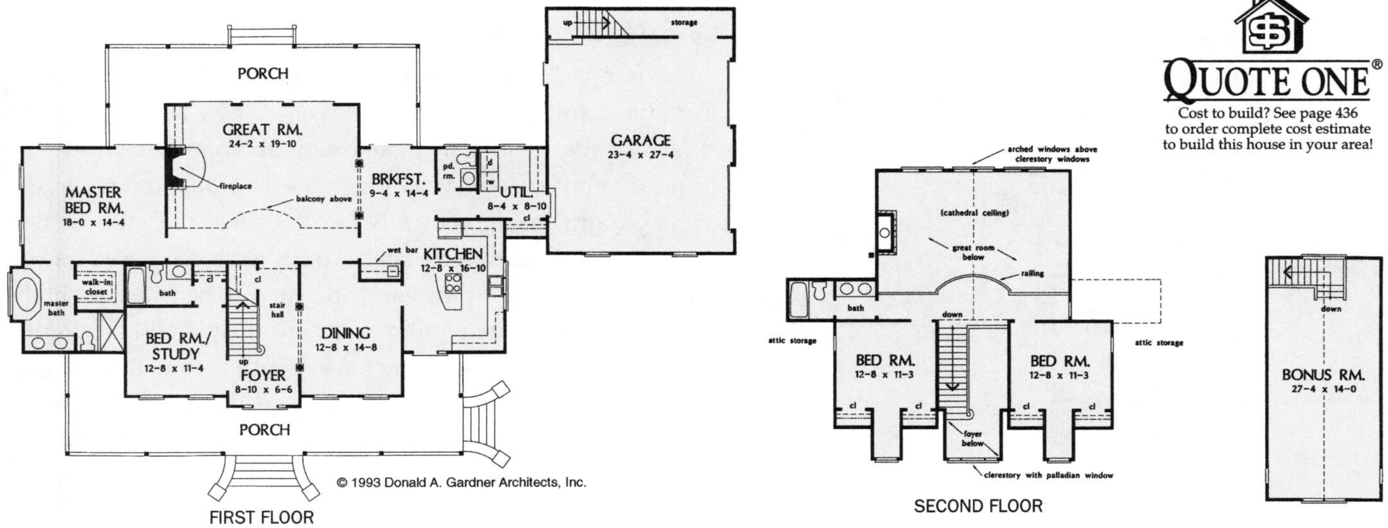

QUOTE ONE®

Cost to build? See page 436 to order complete cost estimate to build this house in your area!

© 1993 Donald A. Gardner Architects, Inc.

FIRST FLOOR

SECOND FLOOR

B NATHAN

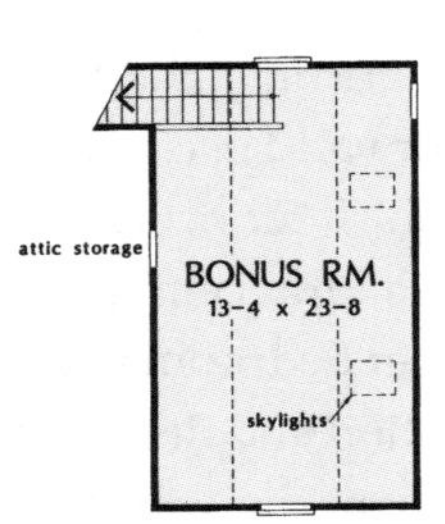

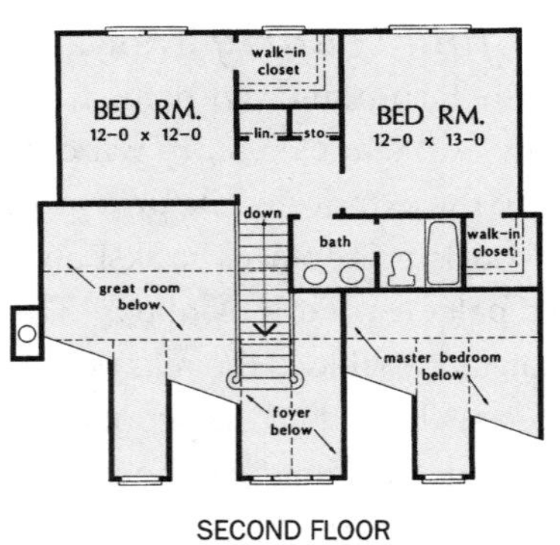

SECOND FLOOR

plan# HPT930104

- Style: Farmhouse
- First Floor: 1,313 sq. ft.
- Second Floor: 525 sq. ft.
- Total: 1,838 sq. ft.
- Bonus Space: 367 sq. ft.
- Bedrooms: 3
- Bathrooms: 2½
- Width: 66'-4"
- Depth: 41'-2"

SEARCH ONLINE @ EPLANS.COM

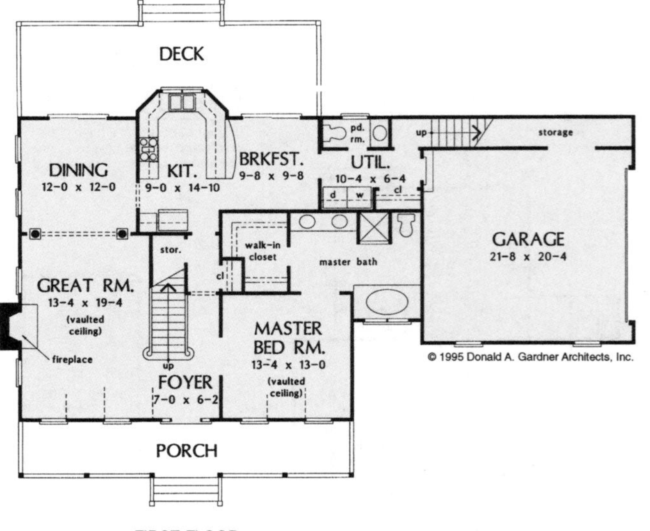

FIRST FLOOR

Vaulted ceilings and beautiful dormers will welcome your family home to open, contemporary living with comfortable country style. An airy foyer, emphasized by a grand staircase, flows into a great room differentiated from the dining room by accent columns. The breakfast room and the dining room are conveniently located adjacent to the kitchen and expand entertaining space to the deck. Split away from family bedrooms for privacy, the master bedroom is highlighted by a vaulted ceiling. A garden tub with a double window enhances a relaxing master bath that includes a spacious walk-in closet. Upstairs, two secondary bedrooms—both with walk-in closets—share a bath that includes a double-bowl vanity. A bonus room may be developed as additional space is needed.

plan# HPT930105

- Style: Country Cottage
- First Floor: 1,454 sq. ft.
- Second Floor: 1,258 sq. ft.
- Total: 2,712 sq. ft.
- Bonus Space: 401 sq. ft.
- Bedrooms: 4
- Bathrooms: 2½
- Width: 79'-6"
- Depth: 40'-0"

SEARCH ONLINE @ EPLANS.COM

SECOND FLOOR

Surrounded by a graceful wraparound porch, this home boasts formal rooms at the front and a wonderfully open casual area at the back for family gatherings. The foyer, living room and dining room welcome all into this gracious four-bedroom farmhouse. The generous island kitchen and breakfast area with a bay window open to the spacious family room with a fireplace and built-ins. Upstairs, the master suite features a tray ceiling, two walk-in closets and a marvelous bath. The family bedrooms utilize a segmented hall bath with dual sinks and a linen closet. The recreation room/bedroom offers an optional fourth wall or railing for added openness.

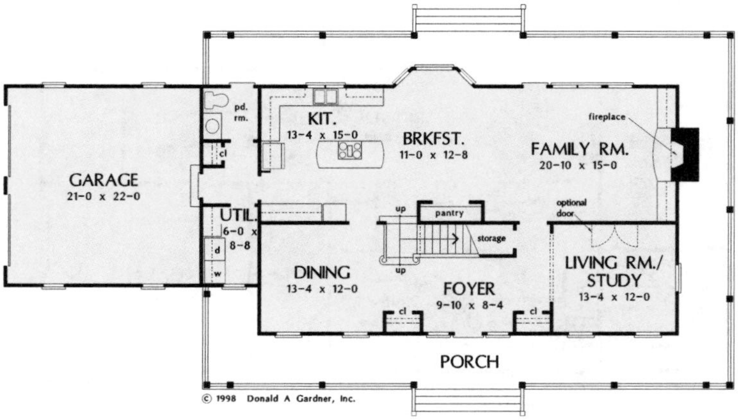

FIRST FLOOR

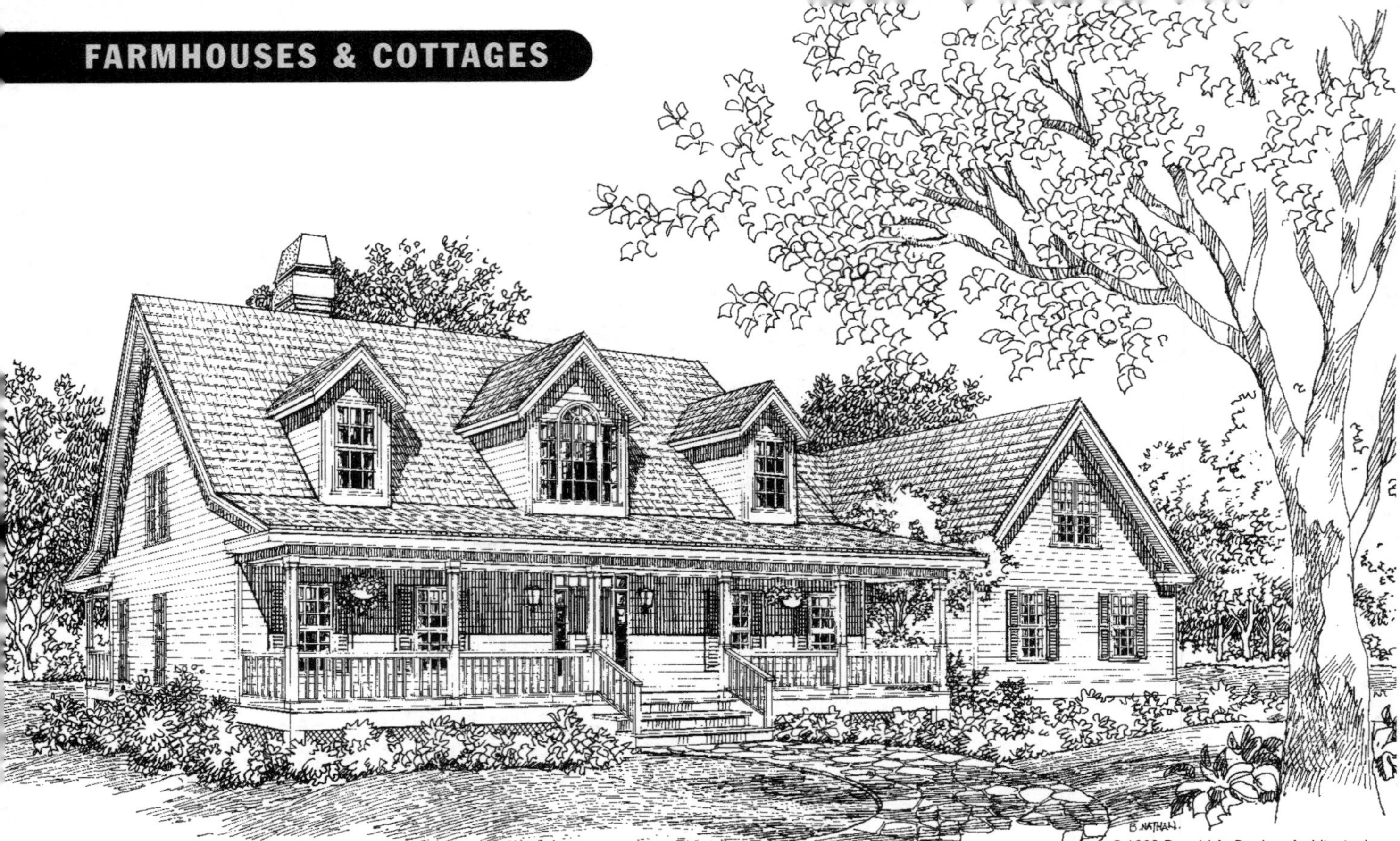

clerestory with arched window
great room below
railing
BED RM. 13-2 × 15-4
balcony
BED RM. 12-4 × 15-4
storage
down
bath
foyer below
clerestory with palladian window
BONUS RM. 13-0 × 33-2

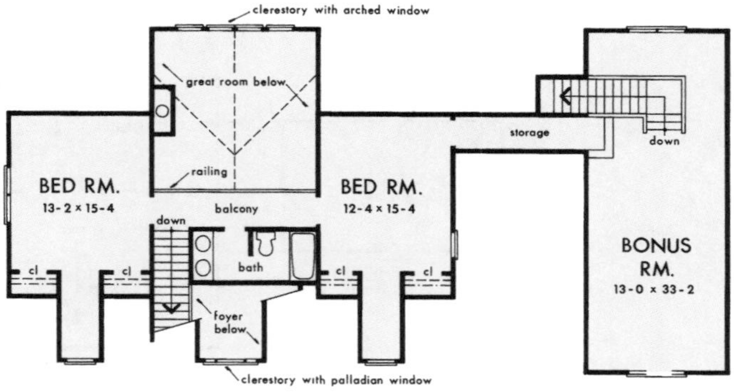

SECOND FLOOR

plan# HPT930106

- Style: Farmhouse
- First Floor: 1,632 sq. ft.
- Second Floor: 669 sq. ft.
- Total: 2,301 sq. ft.
- Bonus Space: 528 sq. ft.
- Bedrooms: 3
- Bathrooms: 2½
- Width: 72'-6"
- Depth: 46'-10"

SEARCH ONLINE @ EPLANS.COM

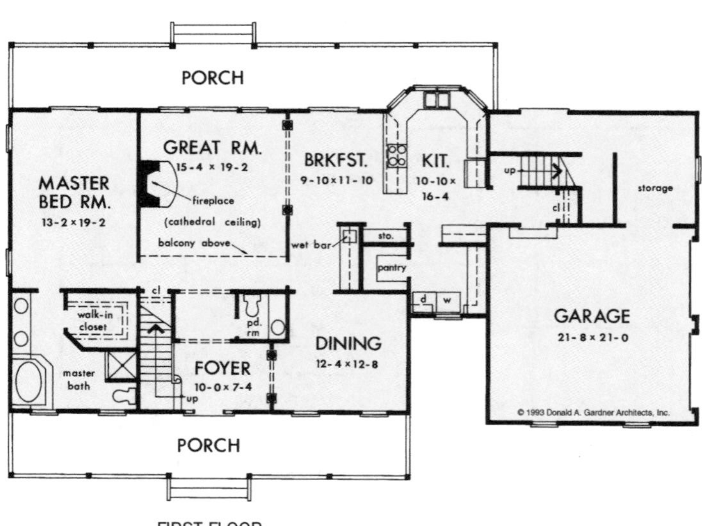

FIRST FLOOR

This open country plan boasts front and rear covered porches and a bonus room for future expansion. The foyer has a sloped ceiling and a Palladian window clerestory to let in natural light. The spacious great room presents a fireplace, cathedral ceiling and clerestory with arched windows. The second-floor balcony overlooks the great room. A U-shaped kitchen provides the ideal layout for food preparation. For flexibility, access is provided to the bonus room from both the first and second floors. The first-floor master bedroom features a bath with dual lavatories, a separate tub and shower and a walk-in closet. Two large bedrooms and a full bath are located on the second floor.

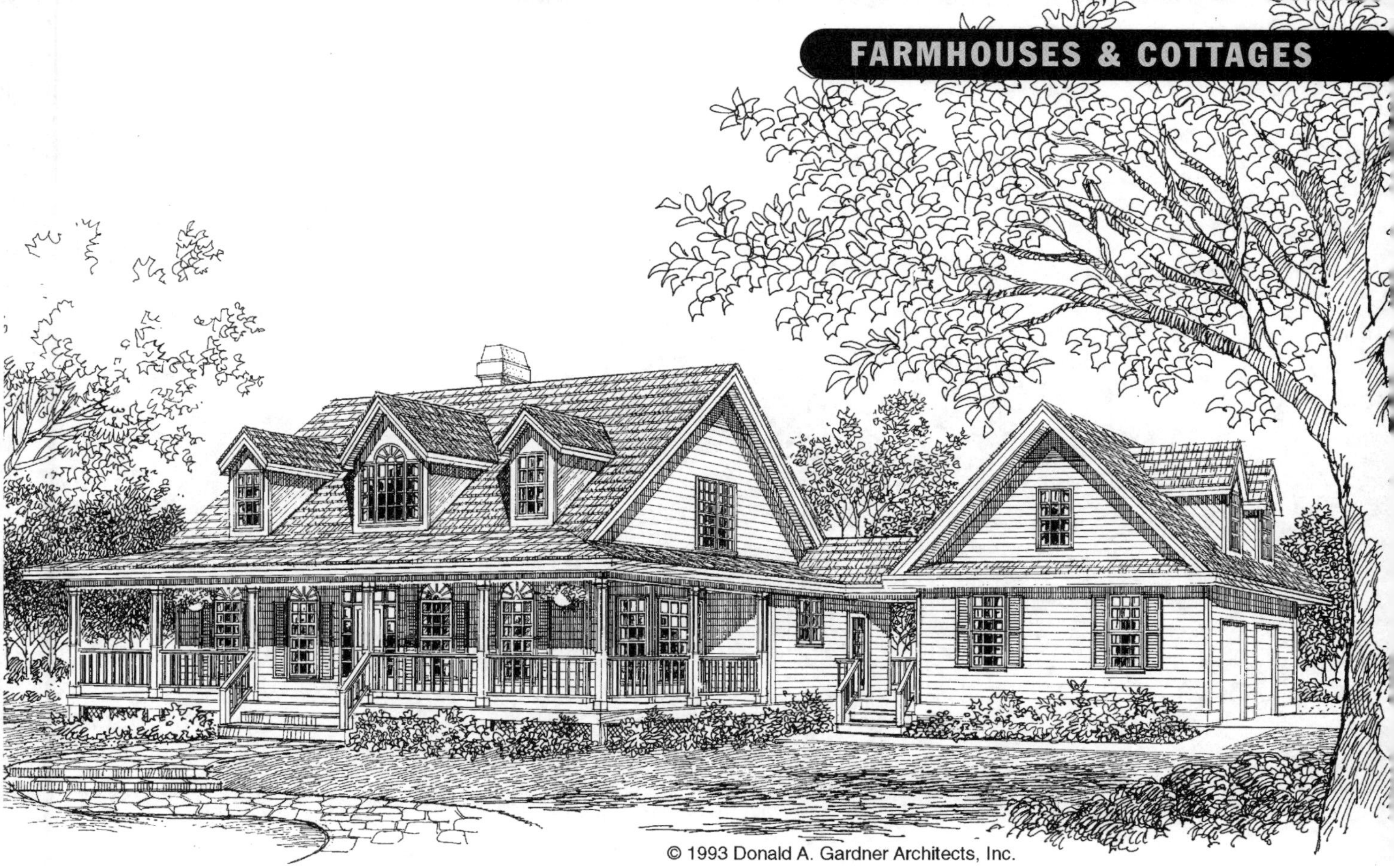

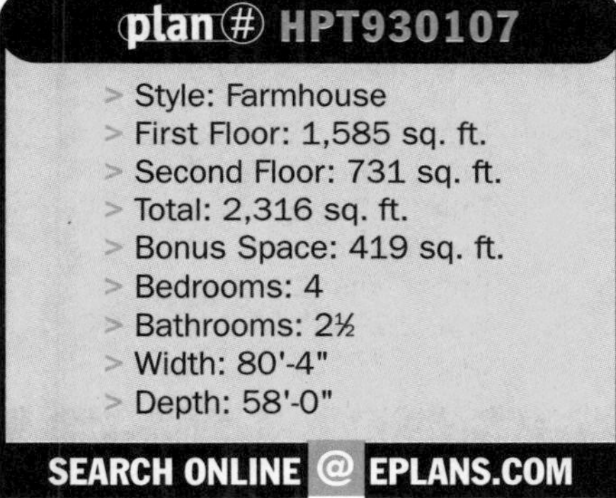

plan# HPT930107

- Style: Farmhouse
- First Floor: 1,585 sq. ft.
- Second Floor: 731 sq. ft.
- Total: 2,316 sq. ft.
- Bonus Space: 419 sq. ft.
- Bedrooms: 4
- Bathrooms: 2½
- Width: 80'-4"
- Depth: 58'-0"

SEARCH ONLINE @ EPLANS.COM

SECOND FLOOR

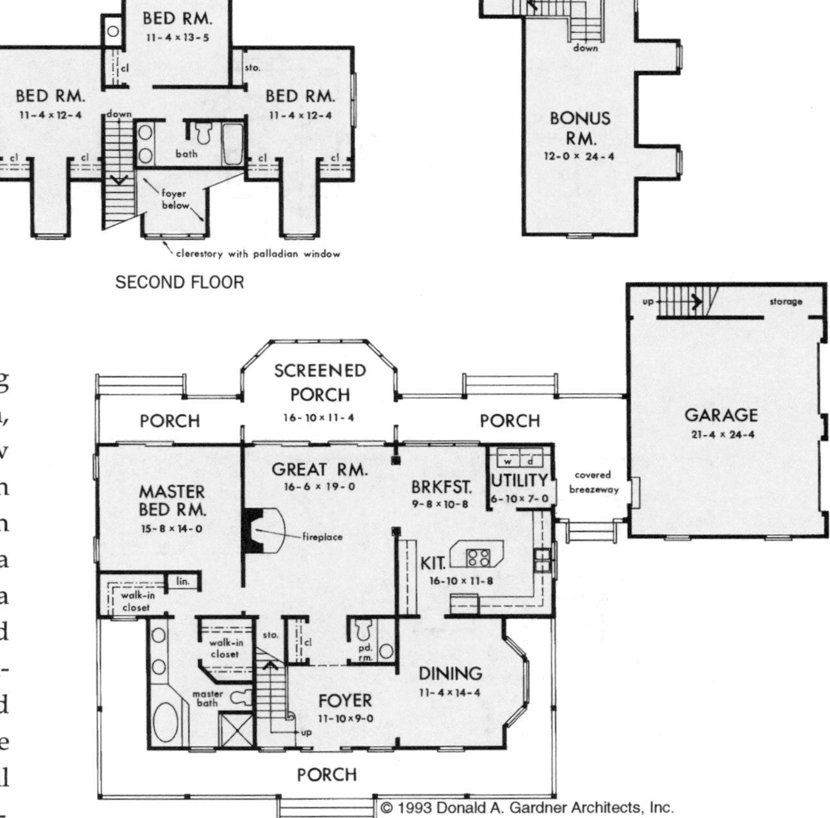

This complete farmhouse projects an exciting and comfortable feeling with its wraparound porch, arched windows and dormers. A Palladian window in the clerestory above the entrance foyer allows an abundance of natural light. The large kitchen with a cooking island easily services the breakfast area and dining room. The generous great room with a fireplace offers access to the spacious screened porch for carefree outdoor living. The master bedroom suite, located on the first level for privacy and convenience, has a luxurious master bath. The second level allows for three bedrooms and a full bath. Don't miss the garage with a bonus room—both meet the main house via a covered breezeway.

FIRST FLOOR

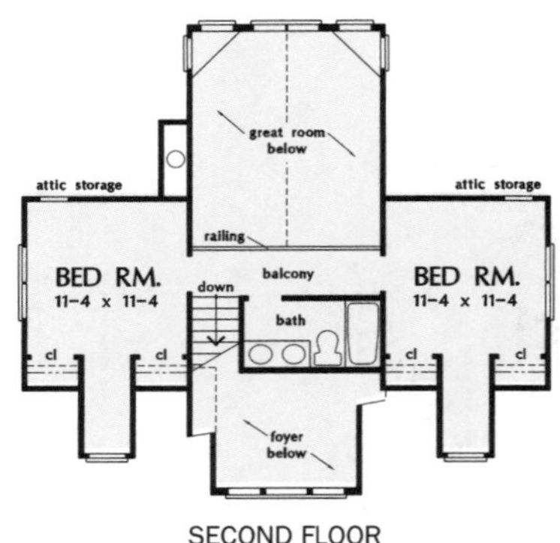

SECOND FLOOR

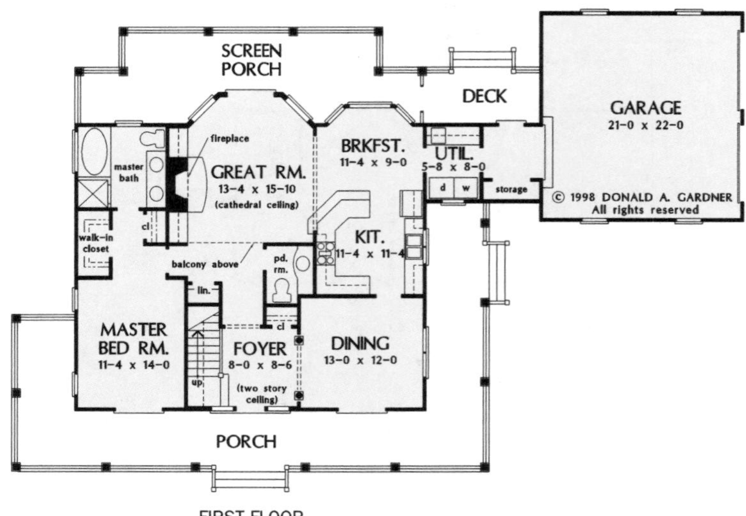

FIRST FLOOR

plan# HPT930108

- Style: Country Cottage
- First Floor: 1,271 sq. ft.
- Second Floor: 490 sq. ft.
- Total: 1,761 sq. ft.
- Bedrooms: 3
- Bathrooms: 2½
- Width: 77'-8"
- Depth: 50'-0"

SEARCH ONLINE @ EPLANS.COM

This farmhouse looks and lives larger than its square footage, courtesy of a wrapping front porch and generous screened back porch.The compact design possesses all the amenities available in larger homes. The large center dormer directs light through clerestory windows into the dramatic two-story foyer, where interior columns mark the entrance to the formal dining room. The heart of the home is the central great room, where a fireplace is the focal point. The master suite occupies one entire wing of the first floor, while two bedrooms share a full bath upstairs.

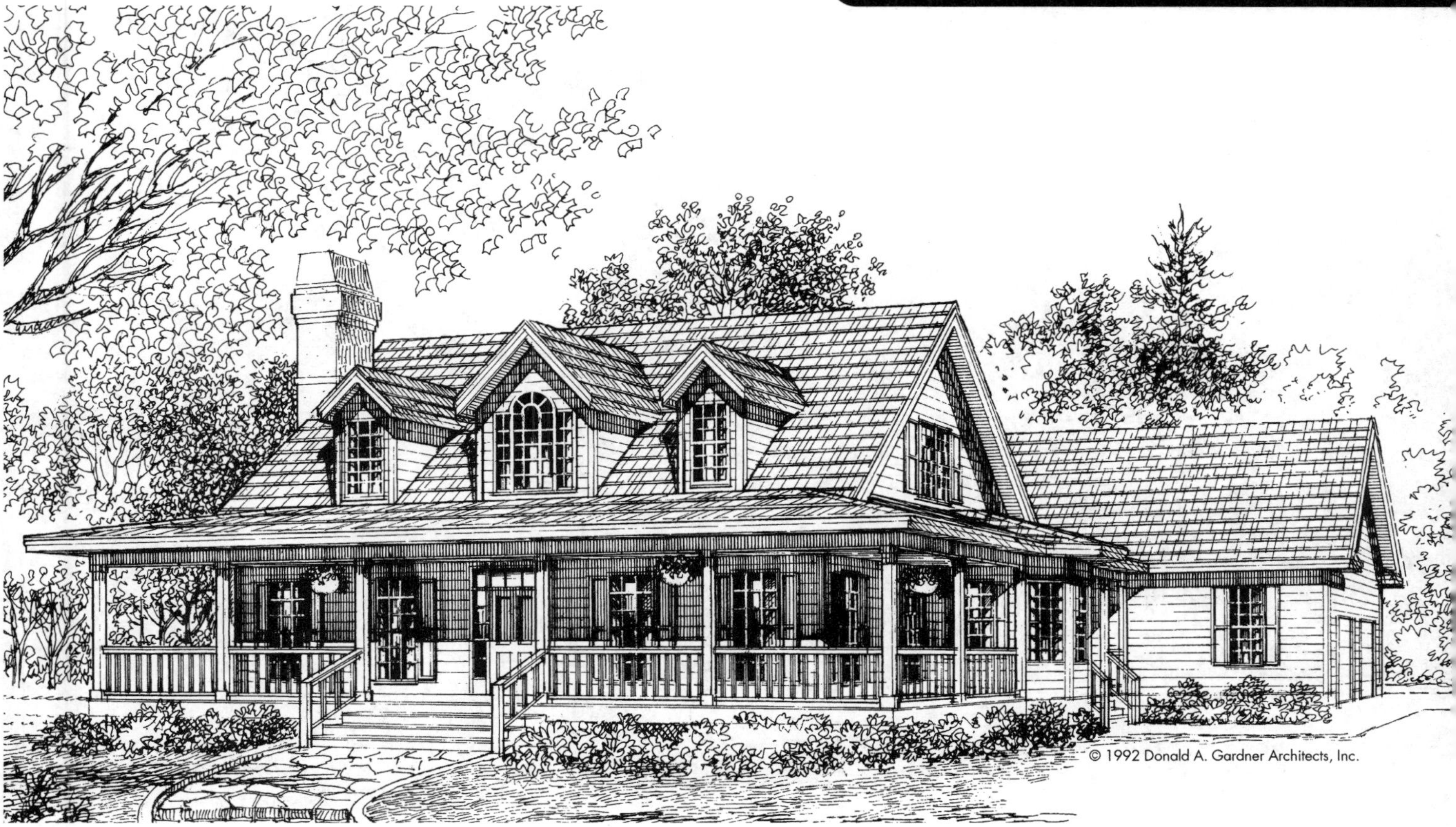

plan# HPT930109

- Style: Country
- First Floor: 1,537 sq. ft.
- Second Floor: 641 sq. ft.
- Total: 2,178 sq. ft.
- Bonus Space: 418 sq. ft.
- Bedrooms: 3
- Bathrooms: 2½
- Width: 65'-8"
- Depth: 70'-0"

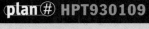

SEARCH ONLINE @ EPLANS.COM

The welcoming charm of this farmhouse is expressed by its many windows and its covered wraparound porch. The two-story entrance foyer offers a Palladian window in a clerestory dormer that casts warm natural light on a wood-trimmed interior. The first-floor master suite, thoughtfully positioned for privacy and accessibility, features a U-shaped walk-in closet and a private bath with a bumped-out tub and twin vanities. The second floor has two bedrooms, a full bath and plenty of storage.

SECOND FLOOR

FIRST FLOOR

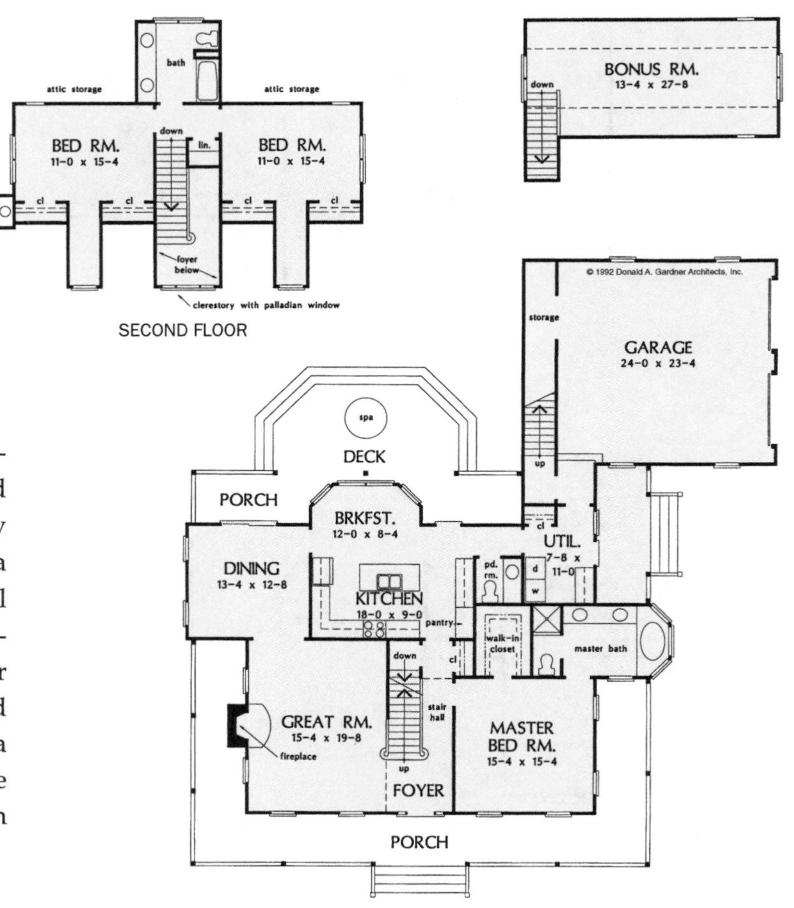

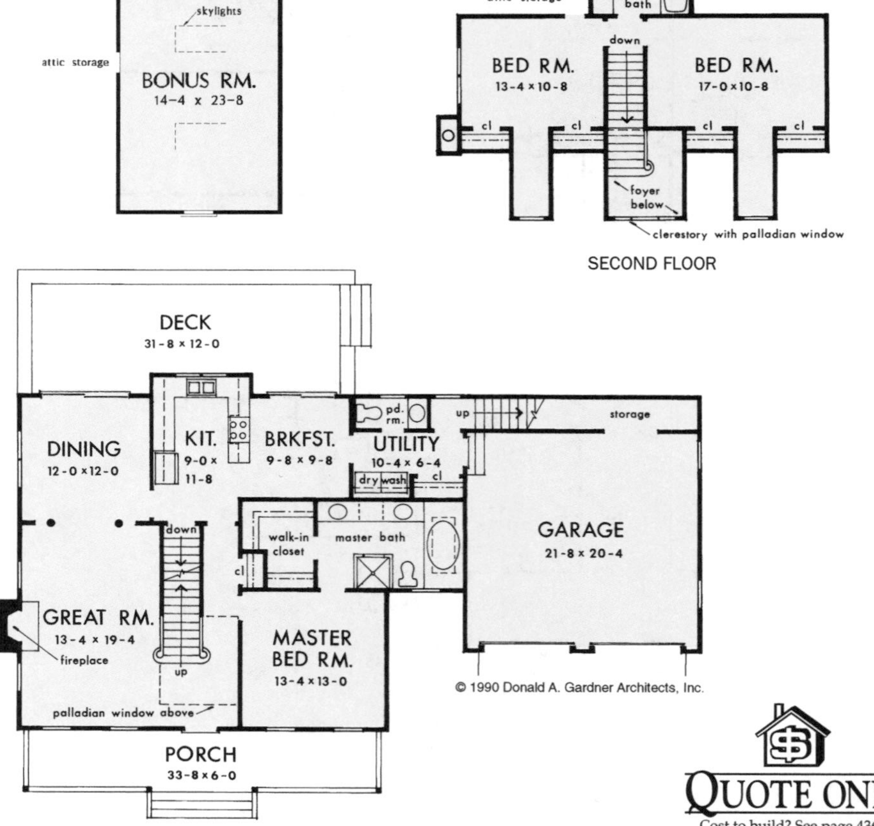

plan# HPT930110

- Style: Farmhouse
- First Floor: 1,289 sq. ft.
- Second Floor: 542 sq. ft.
- Total: 1,831 sq. ft.
- Bonus Space: 393 sq. ft.
- Bedrooms: 3
- Bathrooms: 2½
- Width: 66'-4"
- Depth: 40'-4"

SEARCH ONLINE @ EPLANS.COM

This cozy country cottage is perfect for the growing family. Enter through the two-story foyer with a Palladian window in a clerestory dormer above. The master suite is on the first floor for privacy and accessibility. Its accompanying bath boasts a whirlpool tub with a skylight above and a double-bowl vanity. The second floor contains two bedrooms, a full bath and plenty of storage.

QUOTE ONE®

Cost to build? See page 436 to order complete cost estimate to build this house in your area!

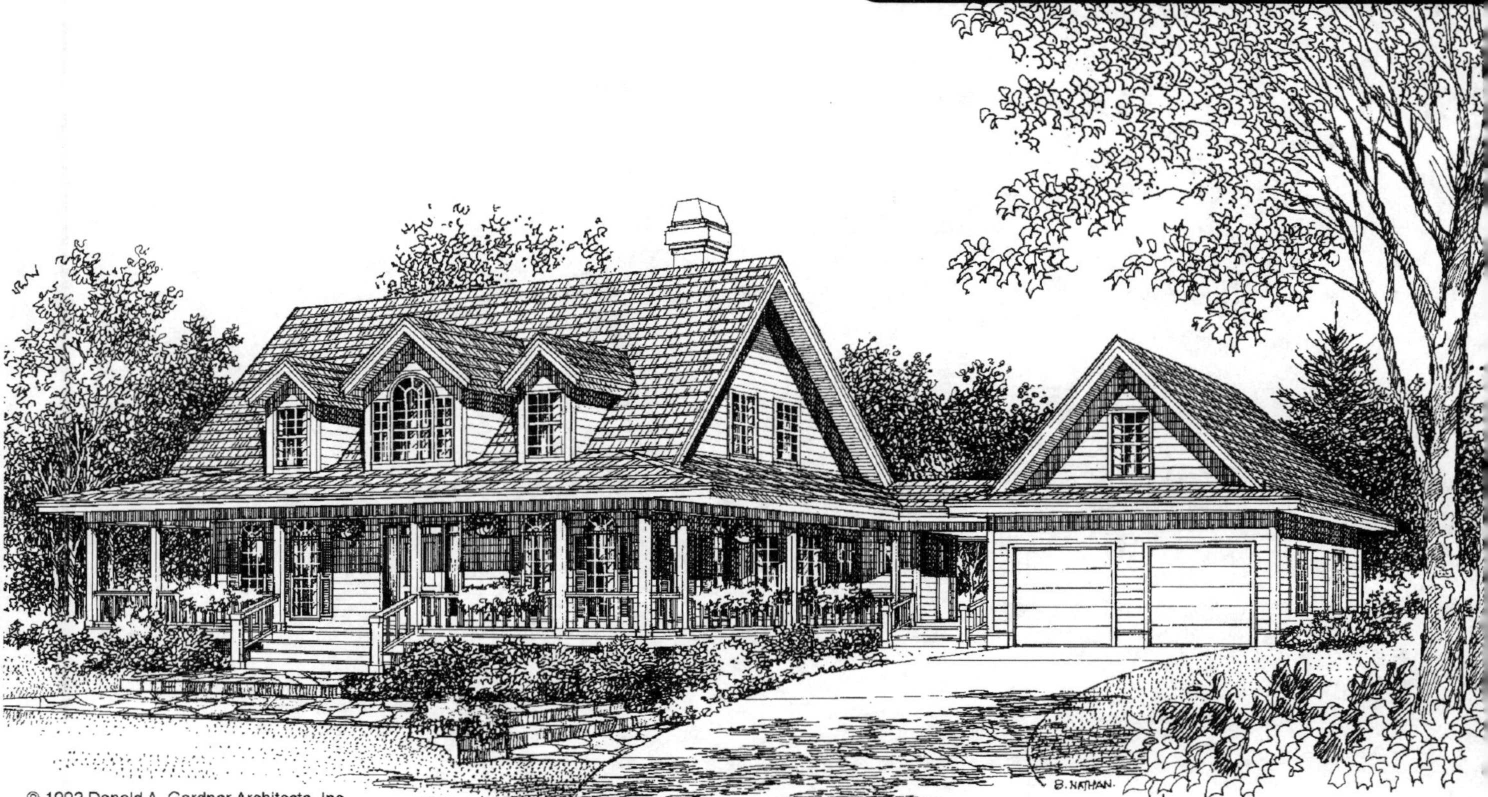

B. NATHAN

plan# HPT930111

- Style: Farmhouse
- First Floor: 1,759 sq. ft.
- Second Floor: 888 sq. ft.
- Total: 2,647 sq. ft.
- Bonus Space: 324 sq. ft.
- Bedrooms: 4
- Bathrooms: 3½
- Width: 85'-0"
- Depth: 67'-4"

SEARCH ONLINE @ EPLANS.COM

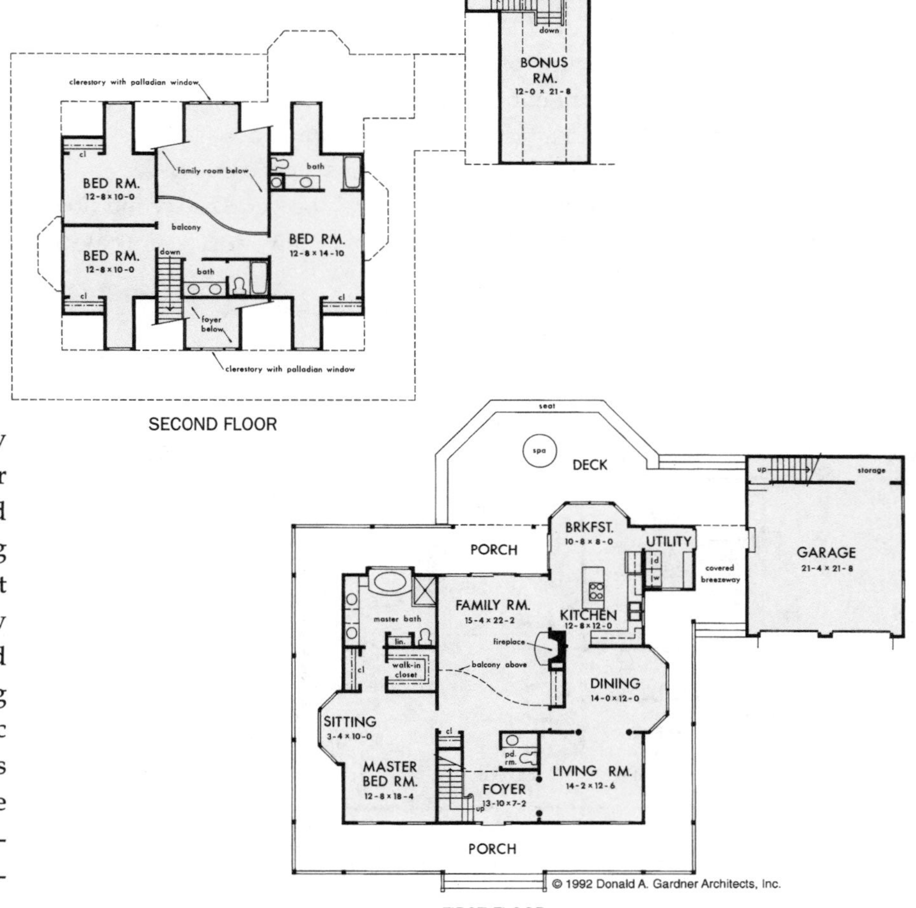

This complete four-bedroom country farmhouse ignites a passion for both indoor and outdoor living with the well-organized open layout and the continuous flowing porch and deck encircling the house. Front and rear Palladian window dormers allow natural light to penetrate the foyer and family room below as well as adding exciting visual elements to the exterior. The dramatic family room with sloped ceiling envelopes the curved balcony. The master suite includes a large walk-in closet, a special sitting area and a bath with whirlpool tub, separate shower and double-bowl vanity.

A wraparound covered porch at the front and sides of this house and an open deck at the back provide plenty of outside living area. The spacious great room features a fireplace, cathedral ceiling and clerestory with an arched window. The island kitchen offers an attached skylit breakfast room complete with a bay window. The first-floor master bedroom contains a generous closet and a master bath with a garden tub, double-bowl vanity and shower. The second floor sports two bedrooms and a full bath with a double-bowl vanity. An elegant balcony overlooks the great room.

plan# HPT930112

- Style: Farmhouse
- First Floor: 1,756 sq. ft.
- Second Floor: 565 sq. ft.
- Total: 2,321 sq. ft.
- Bedrooms: 4
- Bathrooms: 3
- Width: 56'-8"
- Depth: 54'-4"

SEARCH ONLINE @ EPLANS.COM

QUOTE ONE®
Cost to build? See page 436 to order complete cost estimate to build this house in your area!

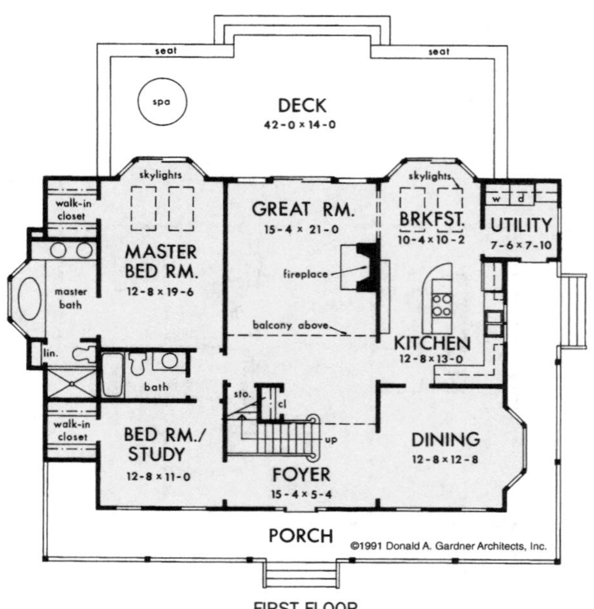

FIRST FLOOR

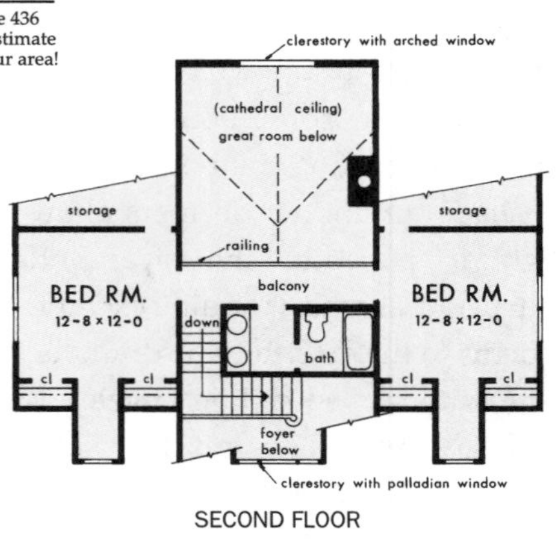

SECOND FLOOR

plan# HPT930113

- Style: Farmhouse
- First Floor: 1,325 sq. ft.
- Second Floor: 453 sq. ft.
- Total: 1,778 sq. ft.
- Bedrooms: 3
- Bathrooms: 2½
- Width: 48'-4"
- Depth: 51'-10"

SEARCH ONLINE  EPLANS.COM

Cost to build? See page 436 to order complete cost estimate to build this house in your area!

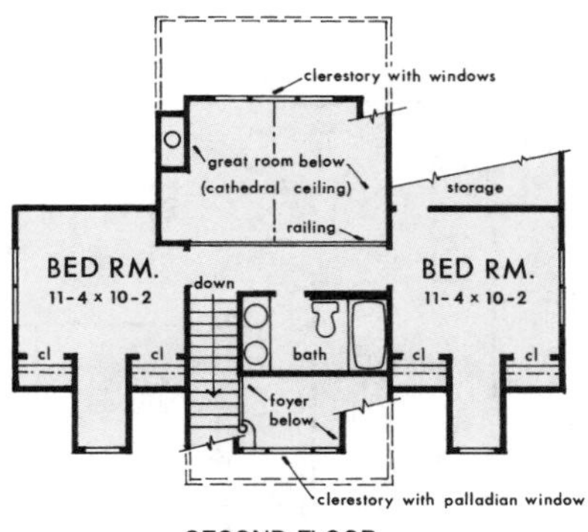

SECOND FLOOR

This compact design has all the amenities available in larger plans with little wasted space. In addition, a wraparound covered porch, a front Palladian window, dormers and rear arched windows provide exciting visual elements to the exterior. The spacious great room has a fireplace, a cathedral ceiling and clerestory windows. A second-level balcony overlooks this gathering area. The kitchen is centrally located for maximum flexibility in layout and features a pass-through to the great room. Besides the generous master suite with a pampering bath, two family bedrooms located on the second level share a full bath.

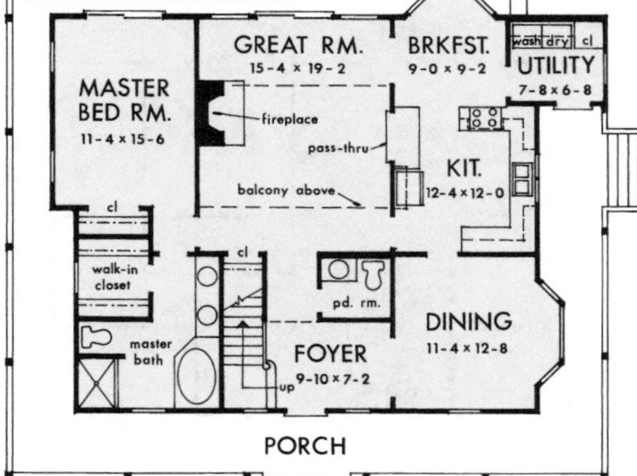

FIRST FLOOR

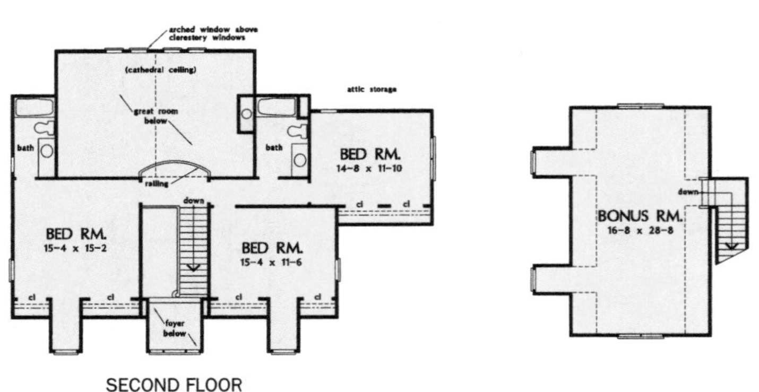

SECOND FLOOR

plan# HPT930114

- Style: Country Cottage
- First Floor: 2,357 sq. ft.
- Second Floor: 995 sq. ft.
- Total: 3,352 sq. ft.
- Bonus Space: 545 sq. ft.
- Bedrooms: 4
- Bathrooms: 3½
- Width: 95'-4"
- Depth: 54'-10"

SEARCH ONLINE @ EPLANS.COM

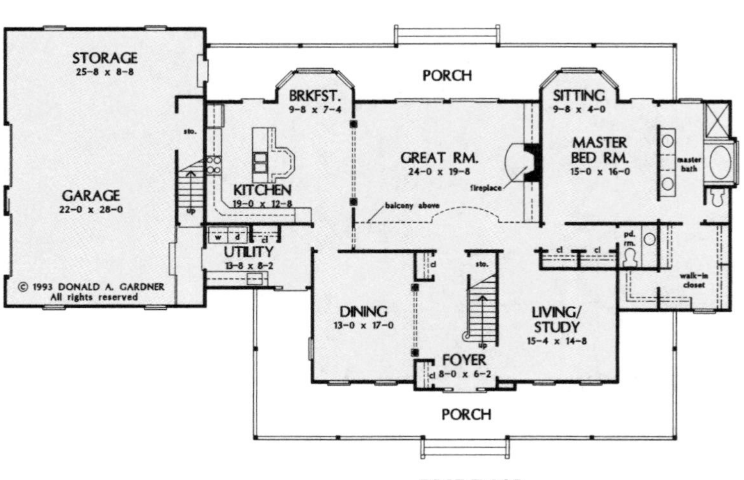

FIRST FLOOR

From the two-story foyer with a Palladian clerestory window and graceful stairway to the large great room with a cathedral ceiling and curved balcony, impressive spaces prevail in this open plan. A columned opening from the great room introduces the spacious family kitchen with a center island counter and breakfast bay. The master suite, privately located at the opposite end of the first floor, features a sitting bay, an extra-large walk-in closet and a bath with every possible luxury. Three bedrooms and two full baths make up the second floor, perfect for friends and family. A bonus room and attic storage offer expansion opportunities for the future.

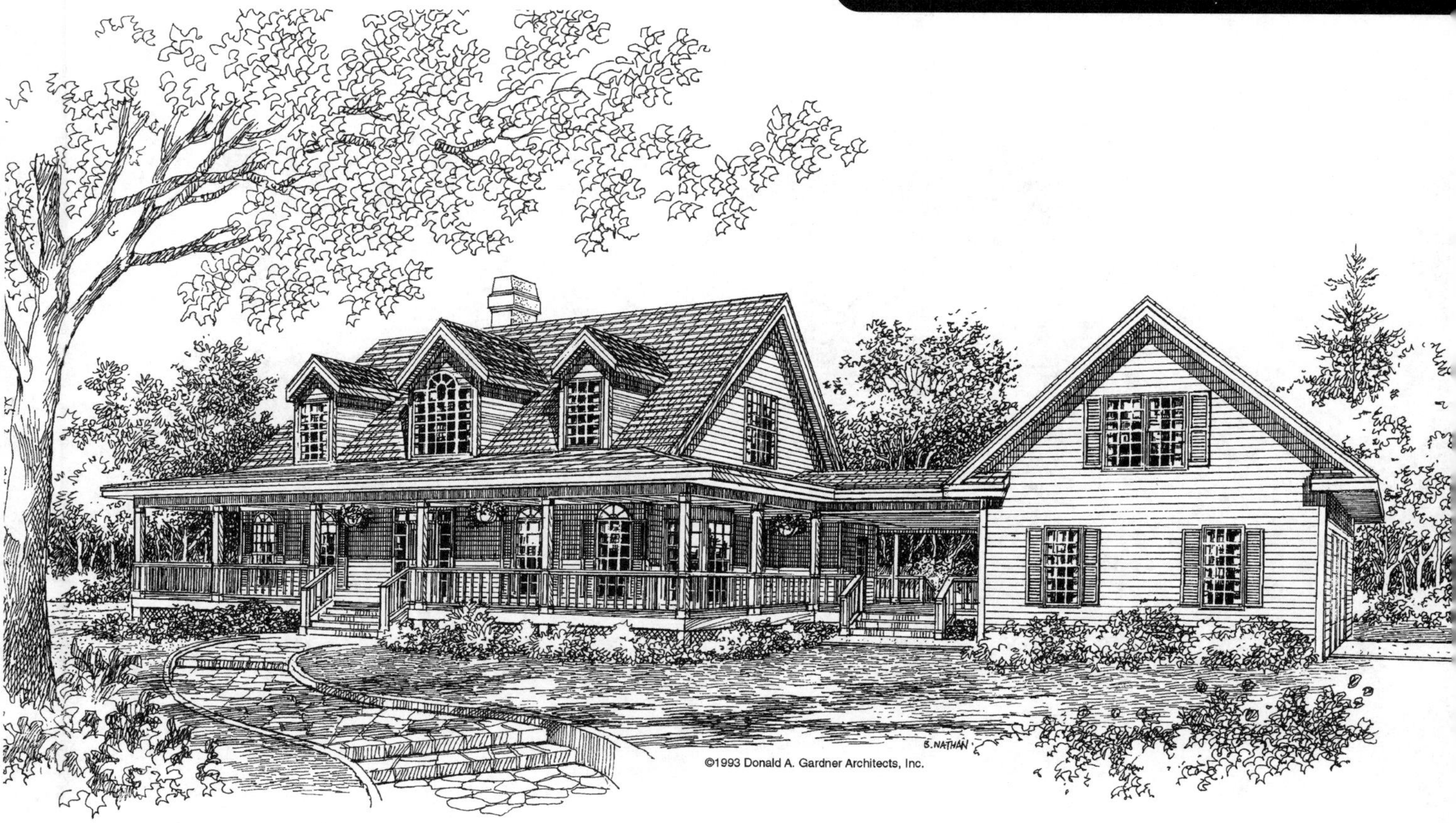

plan# HPT930115

- Style: Farmhouse
- First Floor: 1,618 sq. ft.
- Second Floor: 570 sq. ft.
- Total: 2,188 sq. ft.
- Bonus Space: 495 sq. ft.
- Bedrooms: 3
- Bathrooms: 2½
- Width: 87'-0"
- Depth: 57'-0"

SEARCH ONLINE @ EPLANS.COM

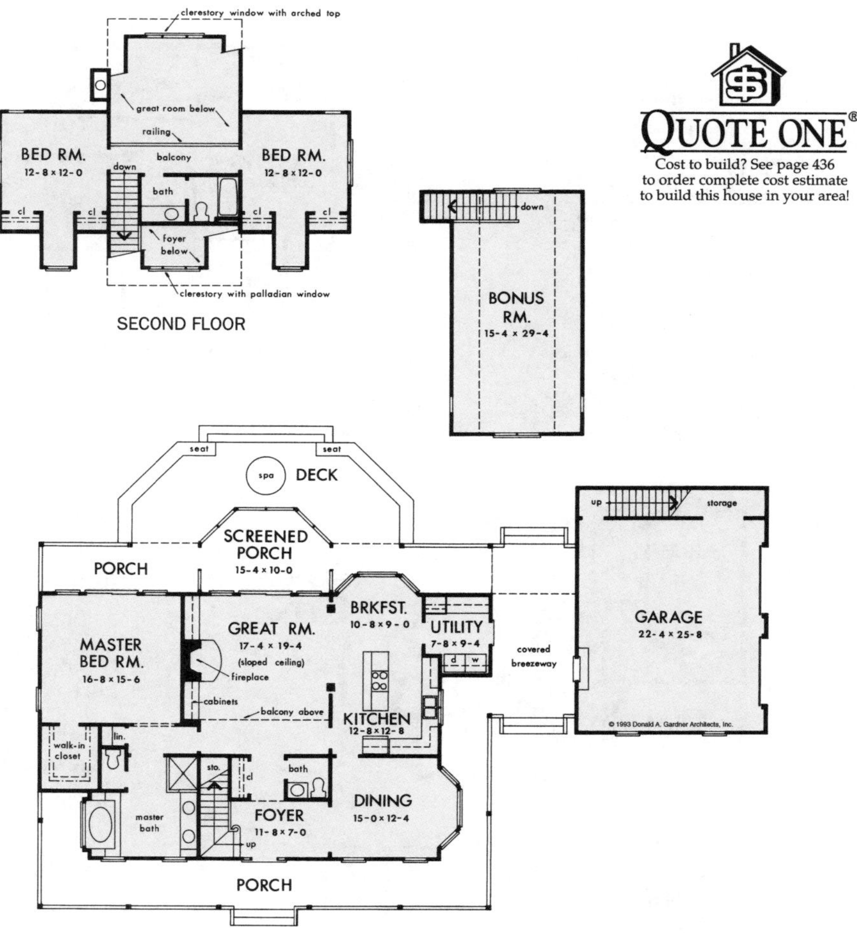

The entrance foyer and great room with sloped ceilings have Palladian window clerestories to allow natural light to enter. All other first-floor spaces have nine-foot ceilings. The spacious great room boasts a fireplace, cabinets and bookshelves. The second-floor balcony overlooks the great room. The kitchen with a cooking island is conveniently located between the dining room and the breakfast room with an open view of the great room. A generous master bedroom has plenty of closet space as well as an exceptional master bath. A bonus room over the garage allows for expansion.

QUOTE ONE®

Cost to build? See page 436 to order complete cost estimate to build this house in your area!

SECOND FLOOR

plan# HPT930116

- Style: Farmhouse
- First Floor: 1,093 sq. ft.
- Second Floor: 576 sq. ft.
- Total: 1,669 sq. ft.
- Bedrooms: 3
- Bathrooms: 2
- Width: 52'-0"
- Depth: 46'-0"
- Foundation: Crawlspace

SEARCH ONLINE @ EPLANS.COM

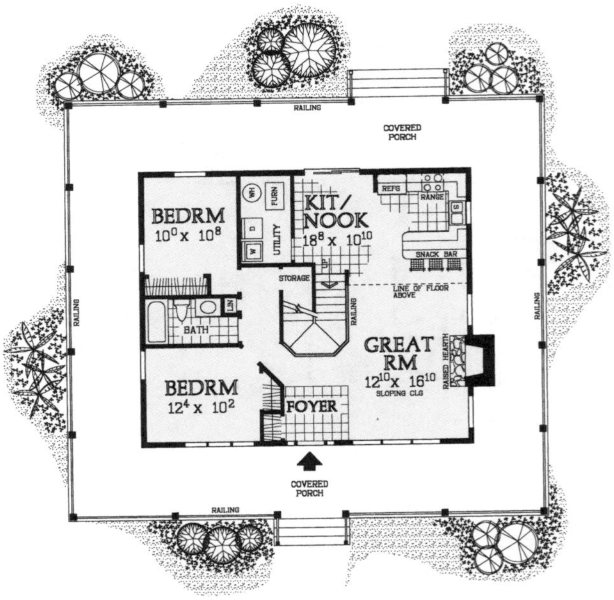

FIRST FLOOR

Here's a great country farmhouse with a lot of contemporary appeal. The generous use of windows—including two sets of triple muntin windows in the front—adds exciting visual elements to the exterior as well as plenty of natural light to the interior. An impressive tiled entry opens to a two-story great room with a raised hearth and views to the front and side grounds. The U-shaped kitchen conveniently combines with this area and offers a snack counter in addition to a casual dining nook with rear-porch access. The family bedrooms reside on the main level, while an expansive master suite with an adjacent study creates a resplendent retreat upstairs, complete with a private balcony, walk-in closet and bath.

© 1994 Donald A. Gardner Architects, Inc.

plan# HPT930117

- Style: Farmhouse
- First Floor: 1,841 sq. ft.
- Second Floor: 594 sq. ft.
- Total: 2,435 sq. ft.
- Bonus Space: 391 sq. ft.
- Bedrooms: 4
- Bathrooms: 3
- Width: 82'-2"
- Depth: 48'-10"

SEARCH ONLINE @ EPLANS.COM

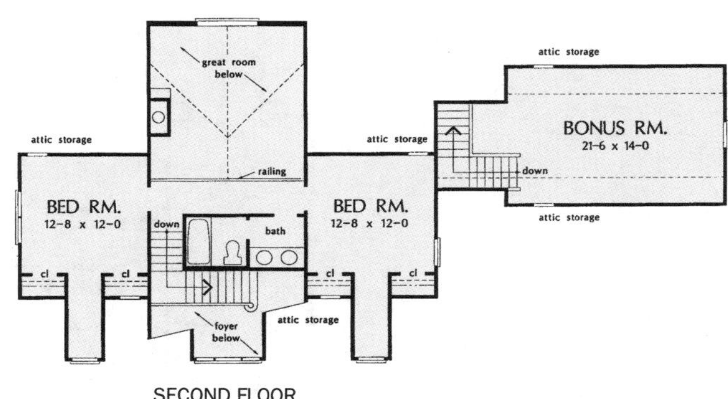

SECOND FLOOR

Spaciousness and lots of amenities earmark this design as a family favorite. The front wraparound porch leads to the foyer where a bedroom/study and dining room open. The central great room presents a warming fireplace, a two-story cathedral ceiling and access to the rear porch. The kitchen features an island food-prep counter and opens to a bayed breakfast area, which conveniently accesses the garage through a side utility room. In the master suite, a private bath with a bumped-out tub and a walk-in closet are extra enhancements. Upstairs, two bedrooms flank a full bath. A bonus room over the garage allows for future expansion.

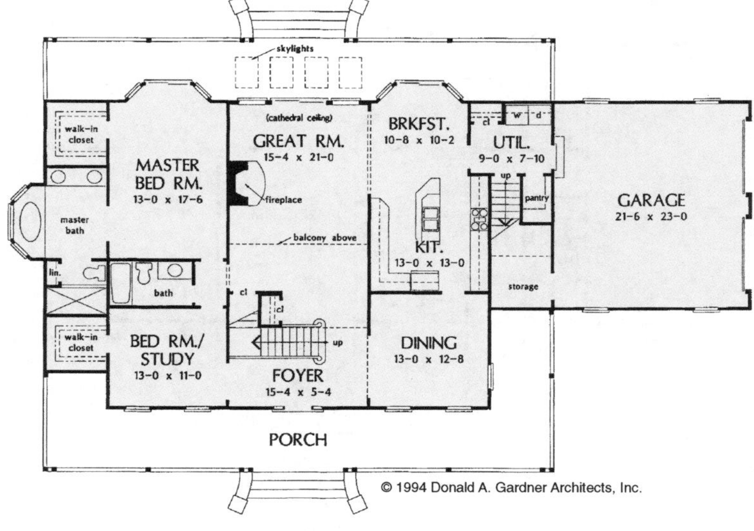

© 1994 Donald A. Gardner Architects, Inc.

FIRST FLOOR

B. NATHAN

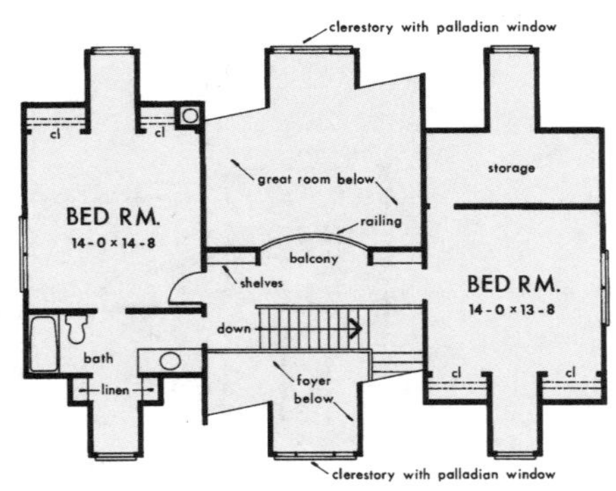

SECOND FLOOR

plan# HPT930118

- Style: Farmhouse
- First Floor: 2,238 sq. ft.
- Second Floor: 768 sq. ft.
- Total: 3,006 sq. ft.
- Bedrooms: 4
- Bathrooms: 3½
- Width: 94'-1"
- Depth: 59'-10"

SEARCH ONLINE @ EPLANS.COM

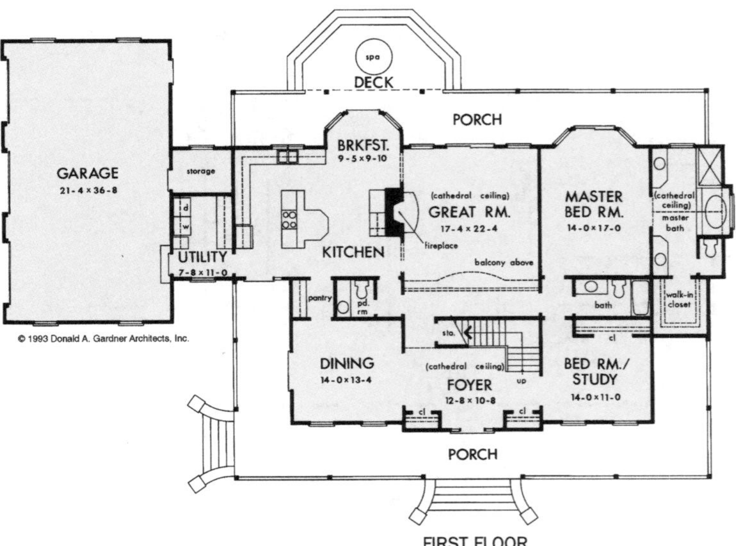

FIRST FLOOR

This grand country farmhouse with a wraparound porch offers comfortable living at its finest. The open floor plan is accented by the great room's cathedral ceiling and the entrance foyer with clerestory windows. The large kitchen has lots of counter space, a sunny breakfast nook and a cooktop island with a bumped-out snack bar. The master suite has beautiful bay windows, a well-designed private bath and a spacious walk-in closet. The second level has two large bedrooms, a full bath and plenty of attic storage.

plan# HPT930119

- Style: Country Cottage
- First Floor: 2,357 sq. ft.
- Second Floor: 995 sq. ft.
- Total: 3,352 sq. ft.
- Bonus Space: 545 sq. ft.
- Bedrooms: 5
- Bathrooms: 4½
- Width: 95'-4"
- Depth: 54'-10"

SEARCH ONLINE @ EPLANS.COM

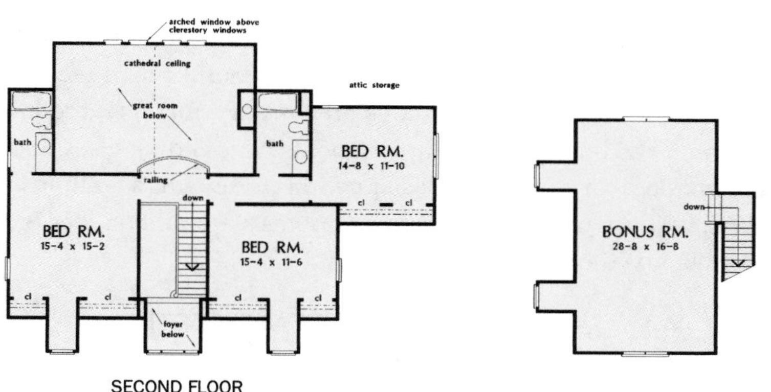

SECOND FLOOR

This five-bedroom, four-and-a-half bath home is the classic sprawling farmhouse, elegantly refined. The two-story foyer with a Palladian clerestory window and the large great room with cathedral ceiling and balcony make dramatic statements. A bedroom/study with a private full bath on the first floor offers a double master suite option. The master suite features a bayed sitting area, a walk-in closet and a lavish bath. The island kitchen has access to the rear covered porch as well as a sunny breakfast area. Upstairs, three bedrooms share two full baths. Note the extra storage above the garage.

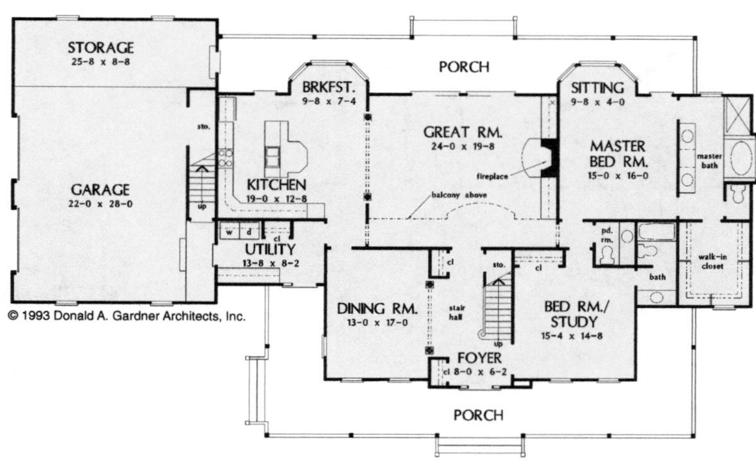

FIRST FLOOR

Look this plan over and you'll be amazed at how much livability can be found in less than 2,000 square feet. A wraparound porch welcomes visitors, who can step right into the enormous fireplace-warmed great room. To the rear of the home, the breakfast and dining rooms have sliding glass doors to a large deck with room for a spa. The master bedroom contains a walk-in closet and an airy bath with a whirlpool tub. Two bedrooms are found on the second floor, as well as a bonus room over the garage.

plan# HPT930120

- Style: Farmhouse
- First Floor: 1,145 sq. ft.
- Second Floor: 518 sq. ft.
- Total: 1,663 sq. ft.
- Bonus Space: 380 sq. ft.
- Bedrooms: 3
- Bathrooms: 2½
- Width: 59'-4"
- Depth: 56'-6"

SEARCH ONLINE @ EPLANS.COM

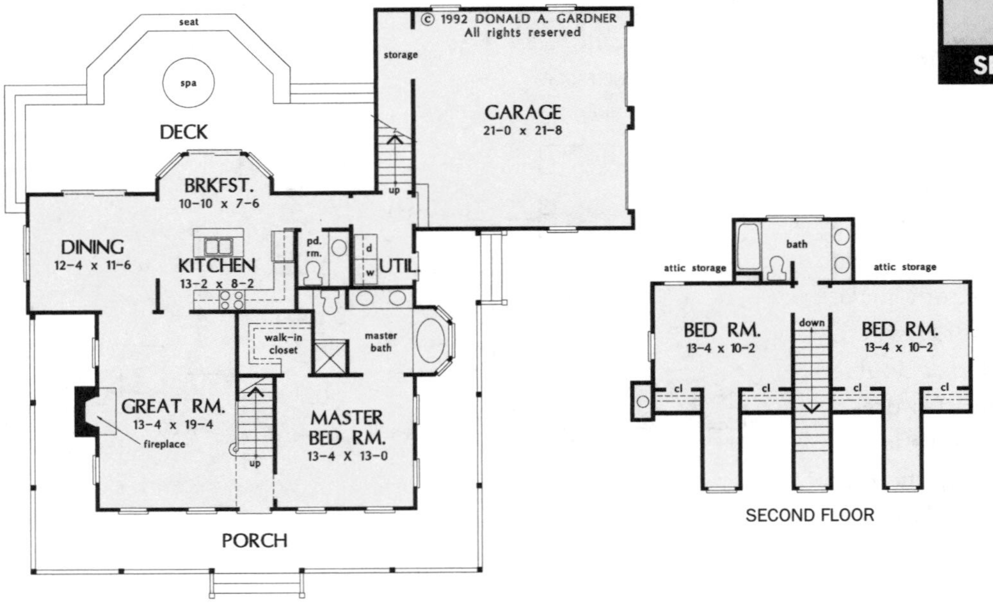

FIRST FLOOR

SECOND FLOOR

Cost to build? See page 436 to order complete cost estimate to build this house in your area!

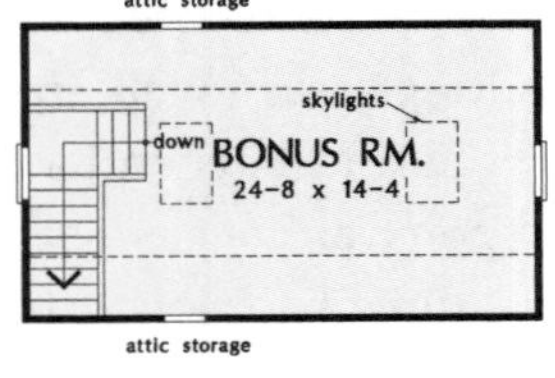

plan# HPT930121

- Style: Farmhouse
- First Floor: 1,766 sq. ft.
- Second Floor: 670 sq. ft.
- Total: 2,436 sq. ft.
- Bedrooms: 4
- Bathrooms: 3½
- Width: 59'-10"
- Depth: 53'-4"

SEARCH ONLINE @ EPLANS.COM

This farmhouse celebrates sunlight with a Palladian window dormer, a skylit screened porch and a rear arched window. The clerestory window in the foyer throws natural light across the loft to a great room with a fireplace and a cathedral ceiling. The central island kitchen and the breakfast area are open to the great room. The master suite is a calm retreat and opens to the screened porch through a bay area. Upstairs, a loft overlooking the great room connects two family bedrooms, each with a private bath.

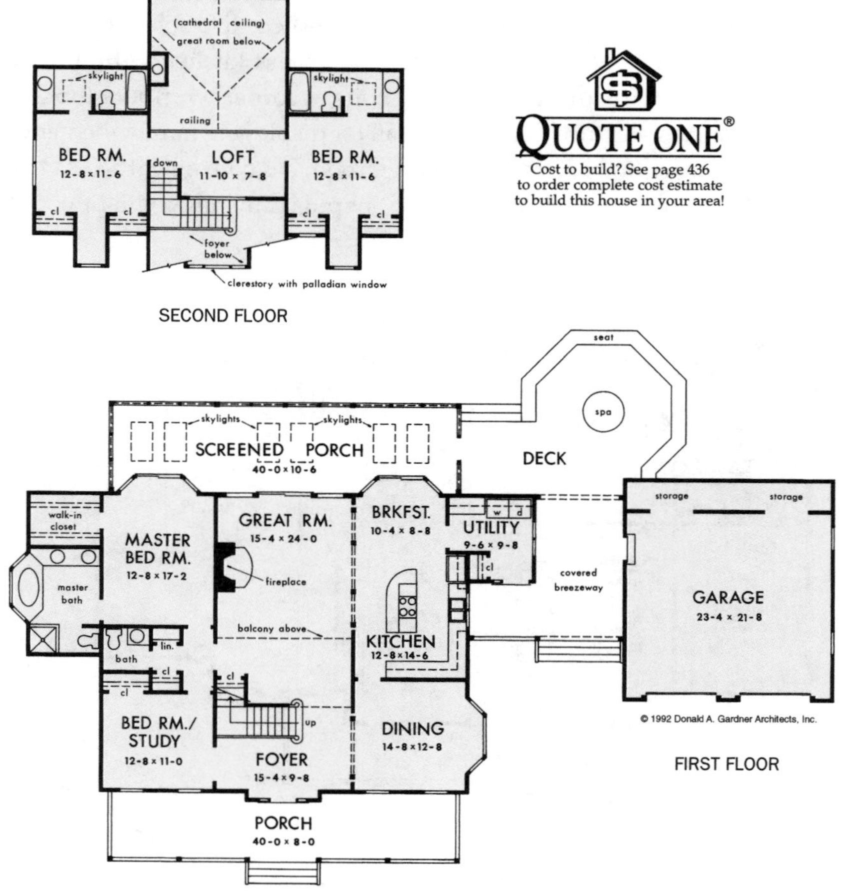

SECOND FLOOR

FIRST FLOOR

QUOTE ONE®
Cost to build? See page 436 to order complete cost estimate to build this house in your area!

Oval windows and an appealing covered porch lend character to this 11/2-story home. Three large windows and a raised-hearth fireplace flanked by bookcases highlight a volumed great room. An island kitchen with a huge pantry serves a gazebo dinette. In the master suite, a corner whirlpool tub and roomy dressing area are featured. A gallery wall for displaying family mementos graces the upstairs corridor. Each secondary bedroom has convenient access to the bathrooms. This home's charm and blend of popular amenities will fit your lifestyle.

plan# HPT930122

- Style: Farmhouse
- First Floor: 1,881 sq. ft.
- Second Floor: 814 sq. ft.
- Total: 2,695 sq. ft.
- Bedrooms: 4
- Bathrooms: 3½
- Width: 72'-0"
- Depth: 45'-4"

SEARCH ONLINE @ EPLANS.COM

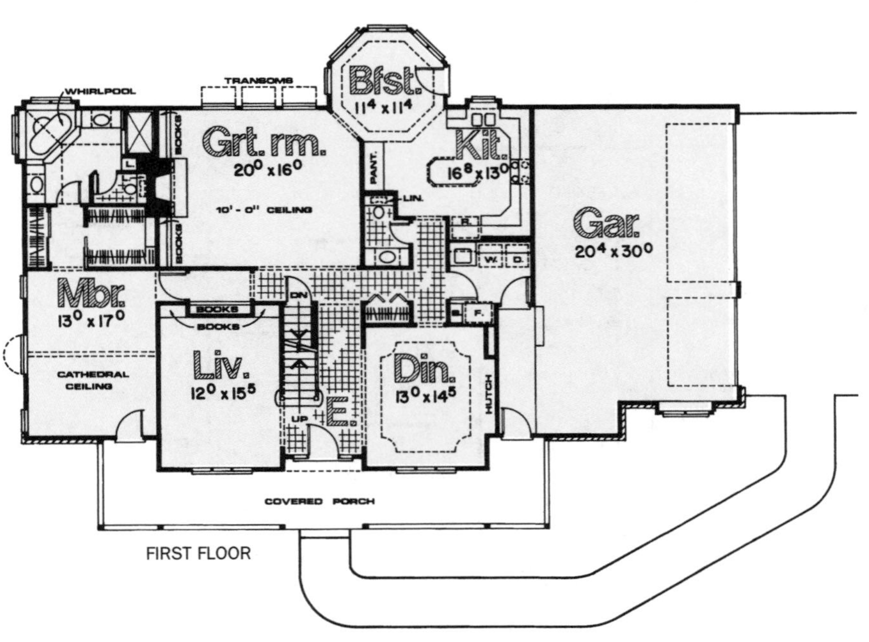

FIRST FLOOR

QUOTE ONE®

Cost to build? See page 436 to order complete cost estimate to build this house in your area!

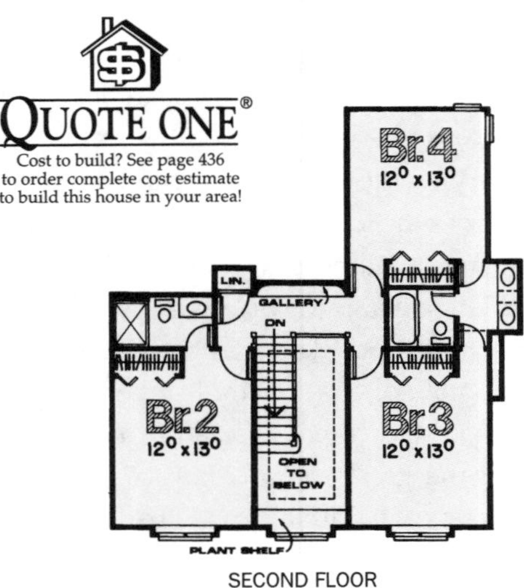

SECOND FLOOR

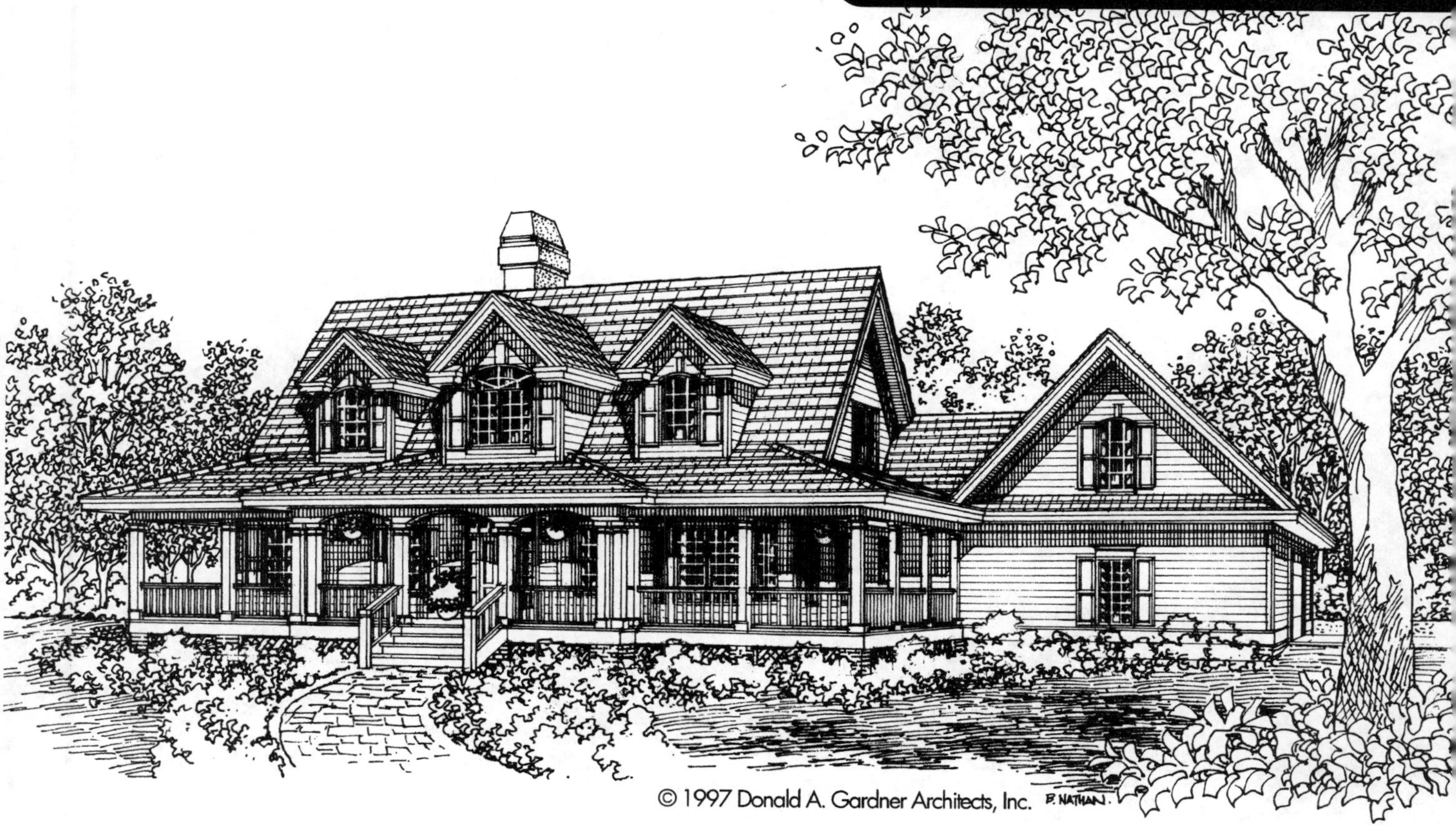

plan# HPT930123

- Style: Country Cottage
- First Floor: 1,471 sq. ft.
- Second Floor: 577 sq. ft.
- Total: 2,048 sq. ft.
- Bonus Space: 368 sq. ft.
- Bedrooms: 3
- Bathrooms: 2½
- Width: 75'-5"
- Depth: 52'-0"

SEARCH ONLINE @ EPLANS.COM

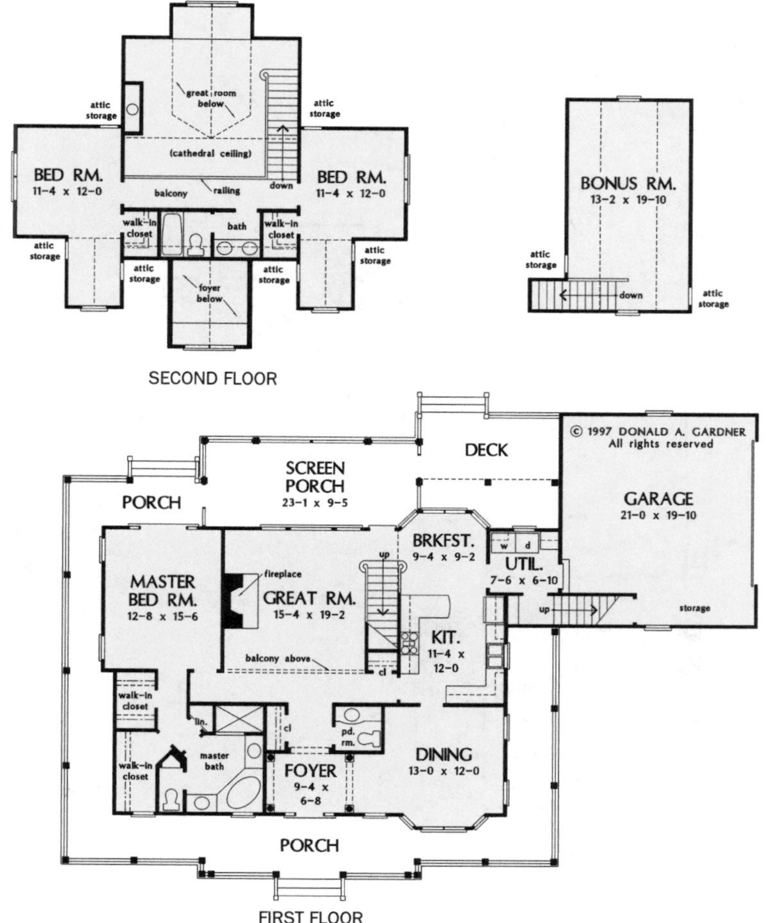

For the family that enjoys outdoor living, this wraparound porch that leads to a screened porch and then to a deck is the best of all worlds! At the front, the dining room features a bay window and mirrors the breakfast bay at the back, with the kitchen in between. On the opposite side of the plan, the master suite, with two walk-in closets and a deluxe bath, accesses the rear porch. Two family bedrooms share a full bath on the second floor.

SECOND FLOOR

FIRST FLOOR

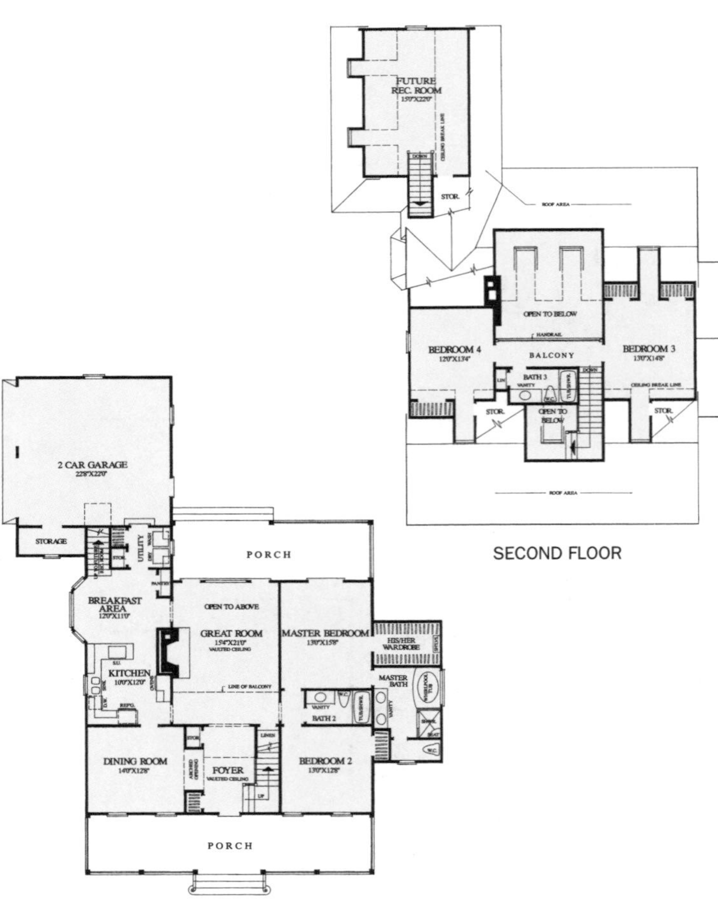

SECOND FLOOR

FIRST FLOOR

plan# HPT930124

- Style: Farmhouse
- First Floor: 1,776 sq. ft.
- Second Floor: 643 sq. ft.
- Total: 2,419 sq. ft.
- Bonus Space: 367 sq. ft.
- Bedrooms: 4
- Bathrooms: 3
- Width: 61'-8"
- Depth: 74'-4"
- Foundation: Basement, Crawlspace

SEARCH ONLINE @ EPLANS.COM

A covered porch that stretches the entire width of the house welcomes friends and family to this fine four-bedroom home. Inside, the foyer is flanked by the staircase to the right and an arched opening into the formal dining room to the left. Next, the great room, with a two-story ceiling, fireplace and wall of windows, has easy access to the bayed breakfast area and the efficient kitchen. Two bedrooms occupy this level—one a lavish master suite complete with a walk-in closet and pampering bath, and the other a family bedroom with easy access to a full bath. Upstairs, two more bedrooms share a hall bath and a balcony overlooking the great room.

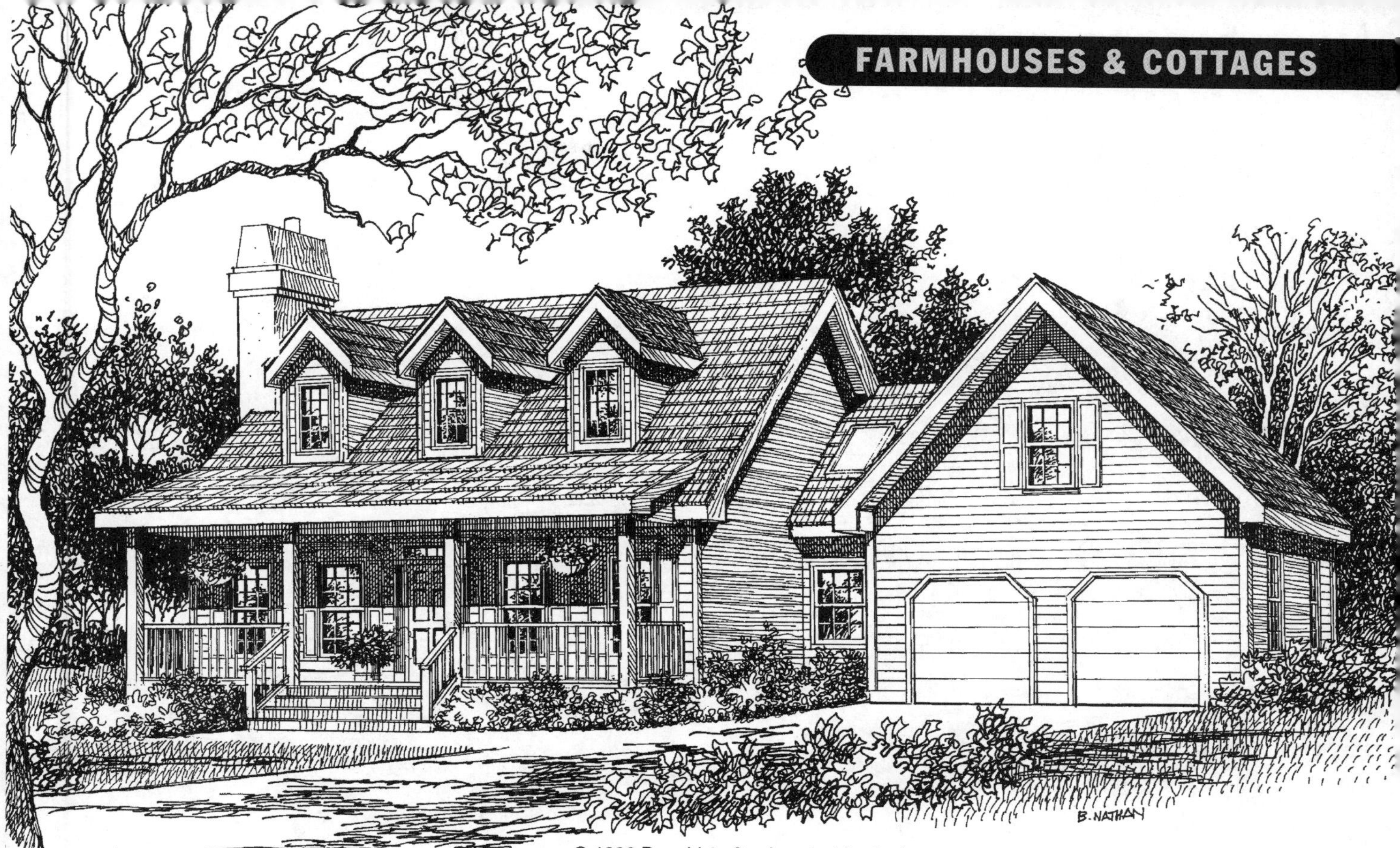

B. NATHAN

plan# HPT930125

- Style: Farmhouse
- First Floor: 1,057 sq. ft.
- Second Floor: 500 sq. ft.
- Total: 1,557 sq. ft.
- Bonus Space: 342 sq. ft.
- Bedrooms: 3
- Bathrooms: 2½
- Width: 59'-4"
- Depth: 50'-0"

SEARCH ONLINE @ EPLANS.COM

This cozy country cottage is perfect for the economically conscious family. Its entrance foyer is highlighted by a clerestory dormer for natural light. Entertaining will be a breeze and a delight. The great room has a grand fireplace and is separated from the formal dining room by a pair of decorative columns. The kitchen leads to a utility room and a half-bath. The master suite is conveniently located on the first level for privacy and accessibility. The master bath boasts a skylight and lush amenities. Second-level bedrooms share a full bath. The bonus room above the garage is available for future expansion.

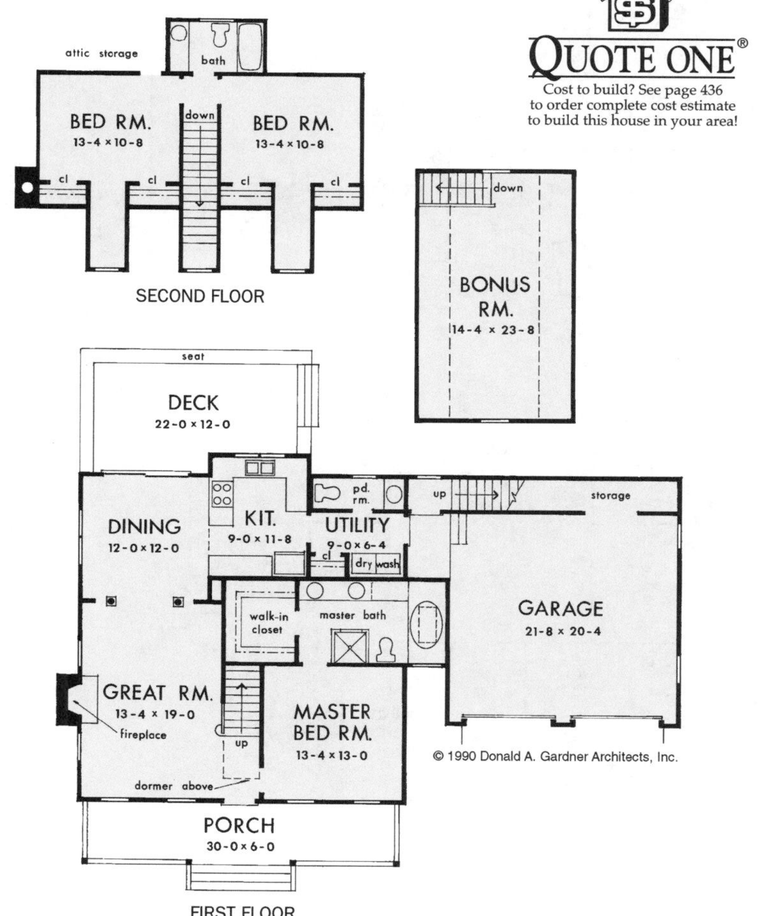

SECOND FLOOR

FIRST FLOOR

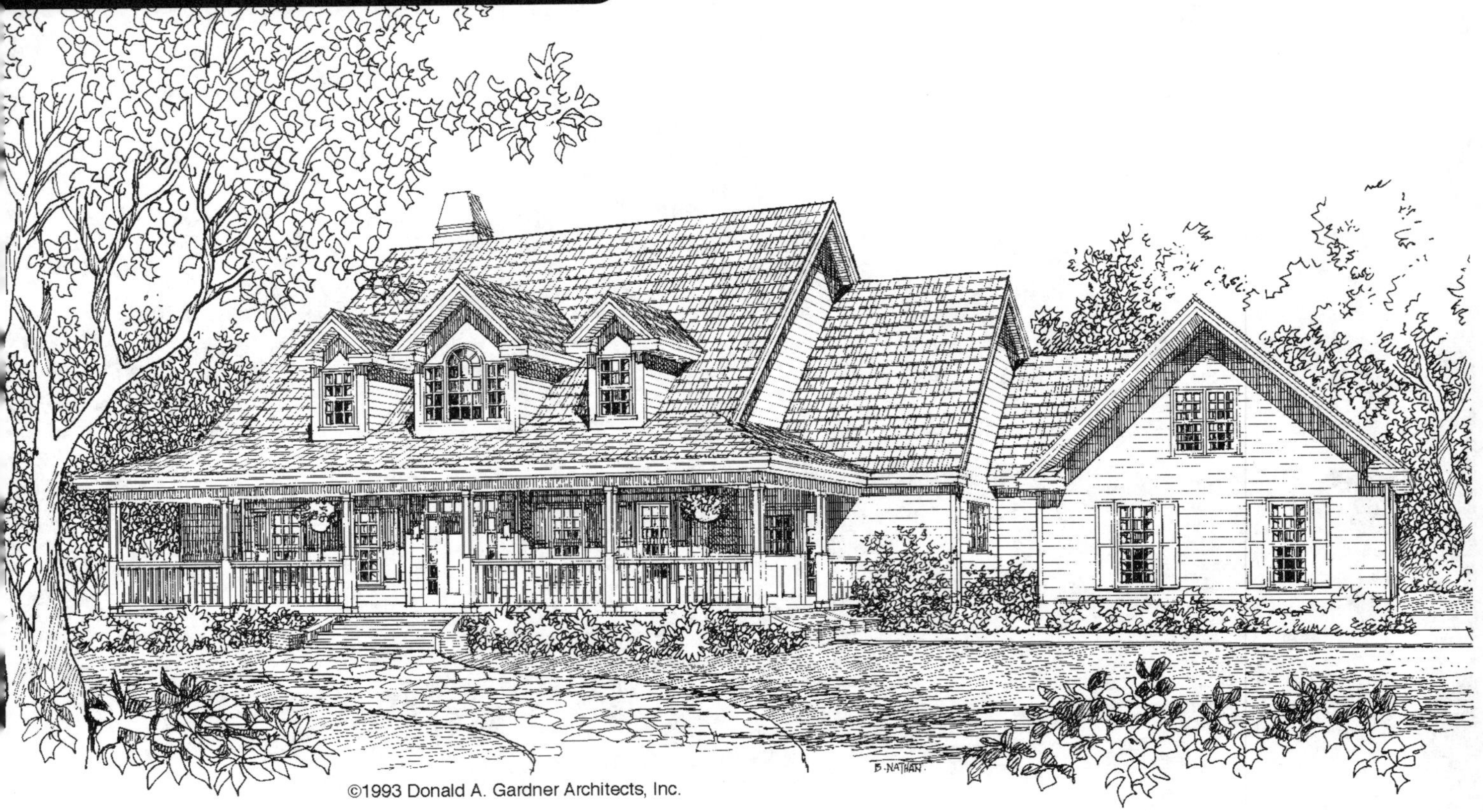

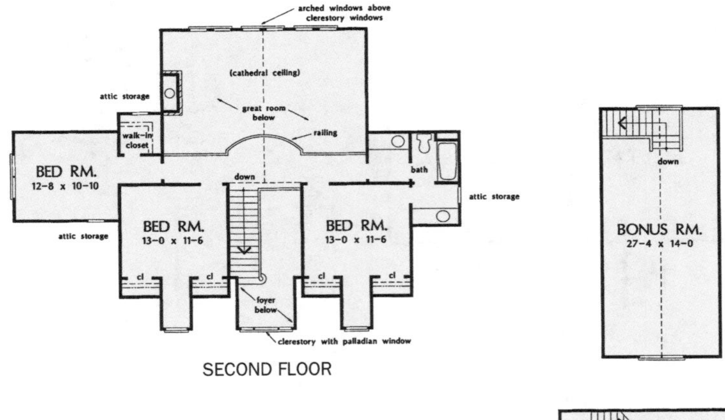

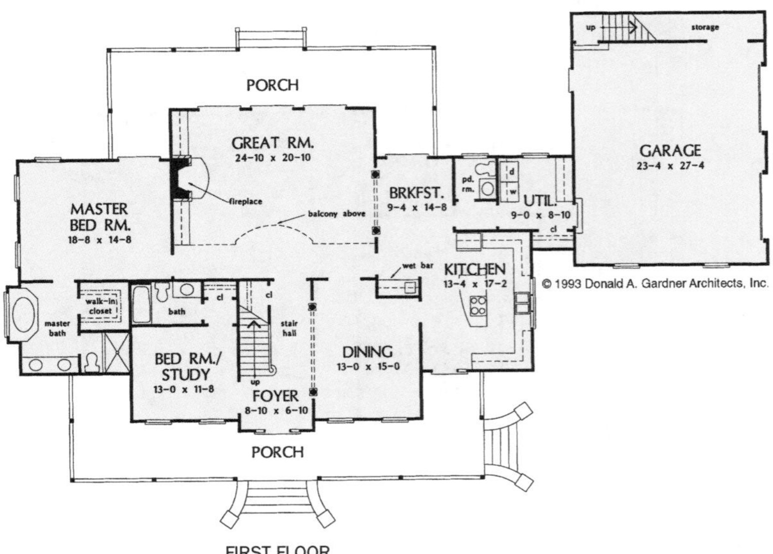

plan# HPT930126

- Style: Farmhouse
- First Floor: 2,176 sq. ft.
- Second Floor: 861 sq. ft.
- Total: 3,037 sq. ft.
- Bonus Space: 483 sq. ft.
- Bedrooms: 5
- Bathrooms: 3½
- Width: 94'-0"
- Depth: 58'-4"

SEARCH ONLINE @ EPLANS.COM

Country living is at its best in this spacious five-bedroom farmhouse with a wraparound porch. A front Palladian window dormer and rear clerestory windows add exciting visual elements to the exterior and provide natural light to the interior. The large great room boasts a fireplace, bookshelves and a raised cathedral ceiling, allowing the curved balcony to overlook from above. Special features such as a large cooktop island in the kitchen, a wet bar, a bedroom/study combination and a generous bonus room over the garage set this plan apart from the rest.

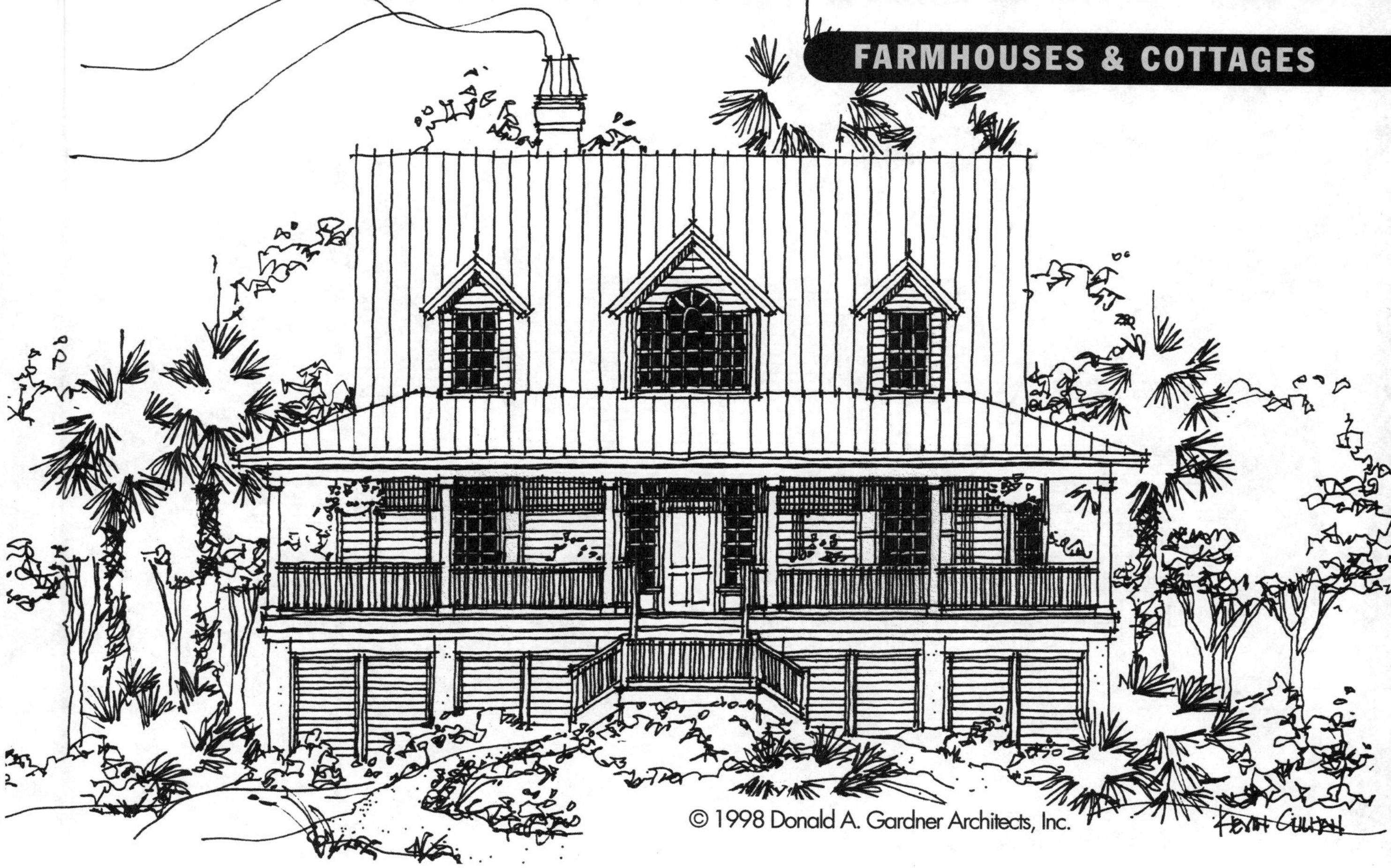

plan# HPT930127

- Style: Country Cottage
- First Floor: 1,362 sq. ft.
- Second Floor: 481 sq. ft.
- Total: 1,843 sq. ft.
- Bedrooms: 3
- Bathrooms: 2½
- Width: 49'-4"
- Depth: 44'-10"

SEARCH ONLINE @ EPLANS.COM

An enchanting wraparound porch, delightful dormers and bright bay windows create excitement inside and out for this coastal home. The large center dormer brightens the vaulted foyer, while the great room enjoys added light from a trio of rear clerestory windows. A balcony dividing the second-floor bedrooms overlooks the great room and visually connects the two floors. The master suite is located on the first floor and features back-porch access, a walk-in closet and a private bath with a garden tub and separate shower. The second-floor bedrooms, each with a dormer alcove, share a hall bath that includes a dual-sink vanity.

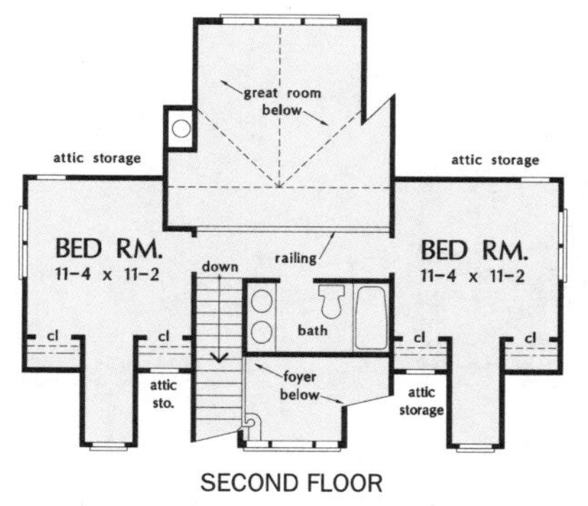

SECOND FLOOR

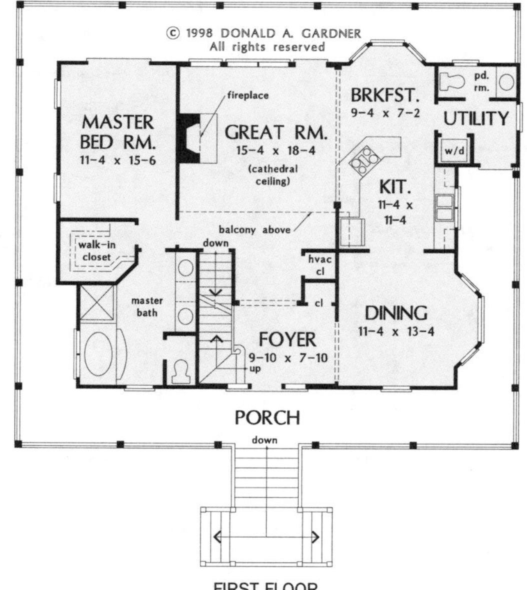

FIRST FLOOR

SECOND FLOOR

FIRST FLOOR

plan# HPT930128

- Style: Farmhouse
- First Floor: 2,008 sq. ft.
- Second Floor: 1,027 sq. ft.
- Total: 3,035 sq. ft.
- Bedrooms: 4
- Bathrooms: 3½
- Width: 66'-0"
- Depth: 74'-0"
- Foundation: Basement, Crawlspace, Slab

SEARCH ONLINE @ EPLANS.COM

A porch with wood railings borders the facade of this plan, lending a farmhouse or country feel. The family room includes a fireplace and French doors to the porch, which opens further to the deck area. The master bedroom is filled with luxuries, from the walk-in closet with shelves, and full bath with a skylight, sloped ceiling and vanity, to the shower with a convenient seat. Three additional bedrooms upstairs share two full baths between them. A breezeway, placed between the garage and the house, leads easily to the deck area. Extras include a large utility room, pantry, half-bath downstairs and two storage areas.

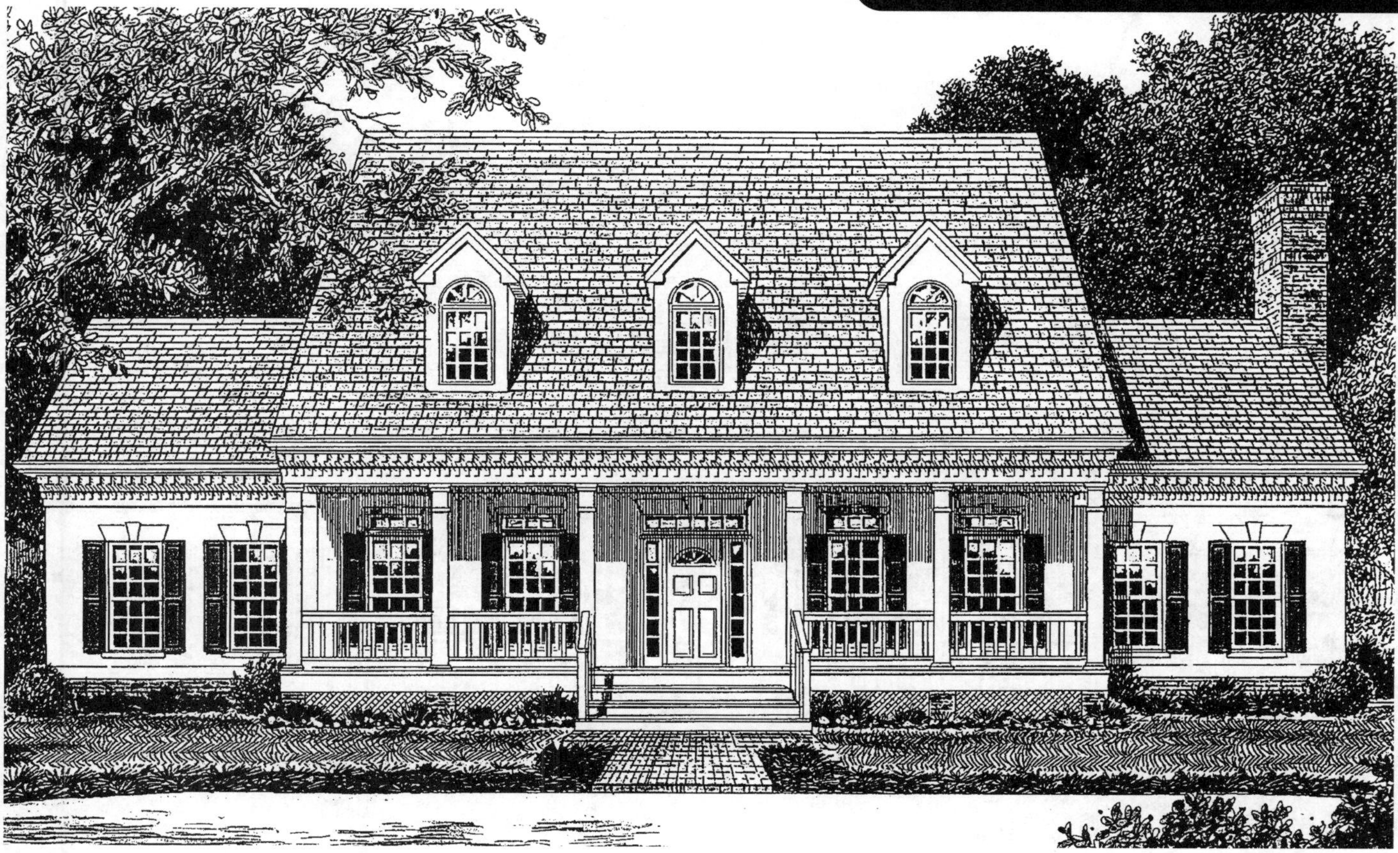

plan# HPT930129

- Style: Plantation
- First Floor: 2,159 sq. ft.
- Second Floor: 1,179 sq. ft.
- Total: 3,338 sq. ft.
- Bonus Space: 360 sq. ft.
- Bedrooms: 4
- Bathrooms: 3½
- Width: 68'-0"
- Depth: 69'-0"
- Foundation: Crawlspace

SEARCH ONLINE @ EPLANS.COM

This attractive Plantation-style home exhibits a floor plan that is completely up-to-date, beginning with the secluded master suite and its lavish bath. The foyer is flanked by the living room and the dining room and leads ahead to the morning room. The family chef will enjoy the open kitchen and its nearby pantry and wet bar. The family room features a fireplace and built-ins. The second floor contains three bedrooms, two baths, a bonus room and attic storage.

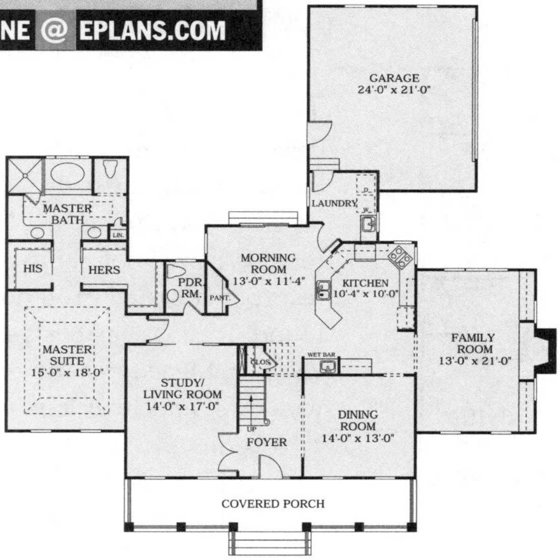

GARAGE 24'-0" x 21'-0"
LAUNDRY
MASTER BATH
LIN
HIS
HERS
PDR. RM.
PANT.
MORNING ROOM 13'-0" x 11'-4"
KITCHEN 10'-4" x 10'-0"
FAMILY ROOM 13'-0" x 21'-0"
MASTER SUITE 15'-0" x 18'-0"
CLOS.
WET BAR
STUDY/ LIVING ROOM 14'-0" x 17'-0"
UP
FOYER
DINING ROOM 14'-0" x 13'-0"
COVERED PORCH

FIRST FLOOR

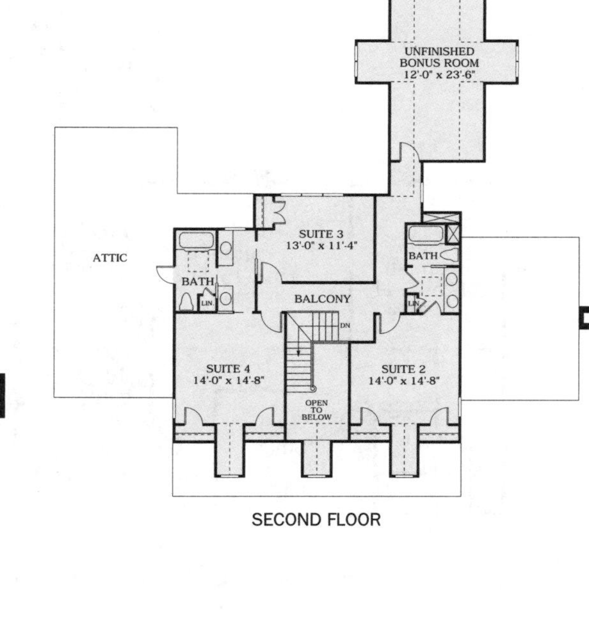

SECOND FLOOR

SECOND FLOOR

FIRST FLOOR

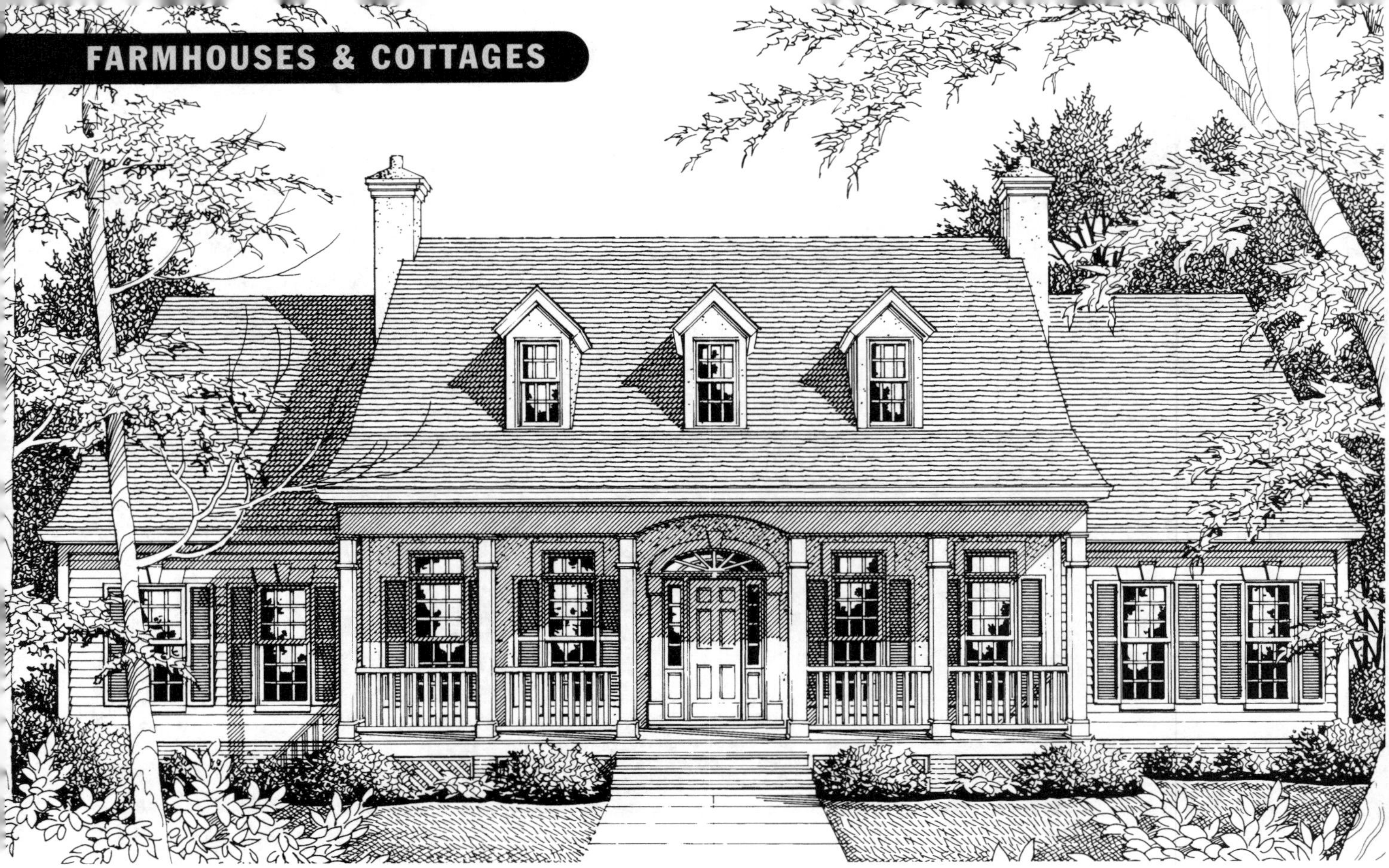

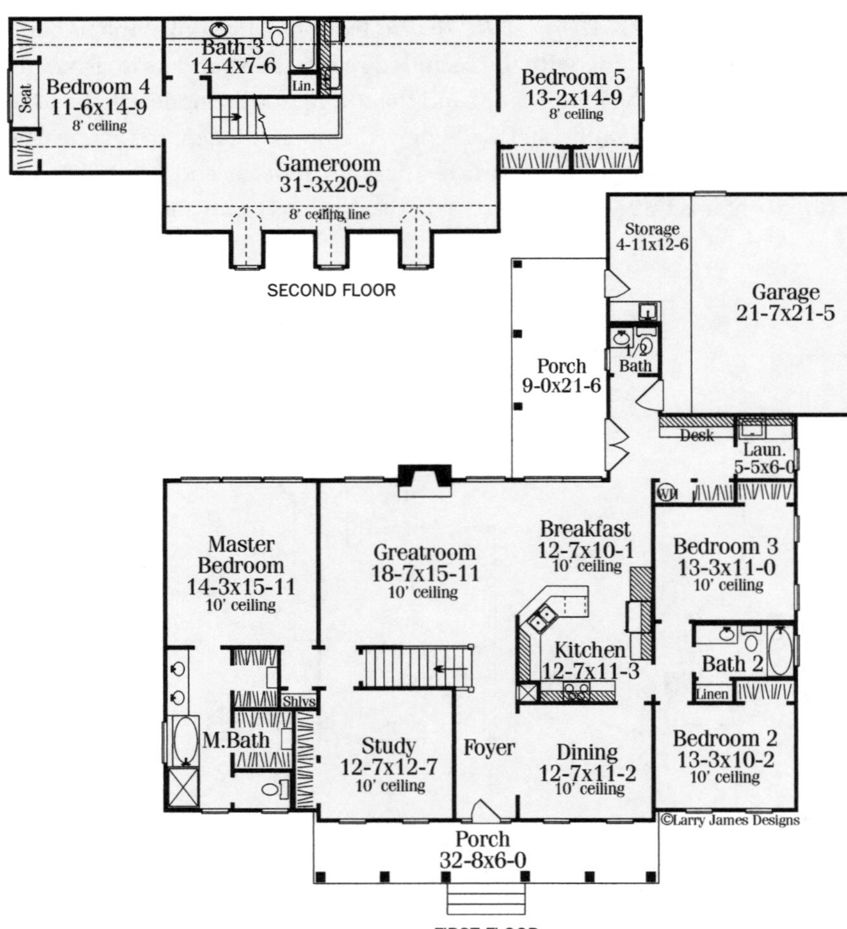

plan# HPT930130

- Style: Traditional
- First Floor: 2,127 sq. ft.
- Second Floor: 1,110 sq. ft.
- Total: 3,237 sq. ft.
- Bedrooms: 5
- Bathrooms: 3½
- Width: 69'-0"
- Depth: 67'-4"
- Foundation: Basement, Crawlspace, Slab

SEARCH ONLINE @ EPLANS.COM

This beautiful Bayou cottage was designed for family living! Ten-foot ceilings throughout the first floor are elegant and tasteful. A warming fireplace in the great room is perfect for chilly nights; front and rear porches invite outdoor living year-round. The master suite is separated for privacy, brightened by a triplet of double-hung windows, and luxurious with a spa bath. Two bedrooms share a bath on the main level. An upper-level game room separates two additional bedrooms, one of which has a window seat, and provides a full bath.

plan# HPT930131

- Style: Traditional
- First Floor: 2,082 sq. ft.
- Second Floor: 1,013 sq. ft.
- Total: 3,095 sq. ft.
- Bedrooms: 4
- Bathrooms: 3½
- Width: 70'-6"
- Depth: 57'-10"
- Foundation: Basement, Crawlspace, Slab

SEARCH ONLINE @ EPLANS.COM

Share the intriguing floorplan of this brick Bayou home with family and friends—there's room for everyone! The front porch is lovely with balcony-style apertures framing two sets of French doors, and a paneled front door framed by sidelights and a sunburst. Inside, the dining room is set off from the foyer by decorative columns. The great room enjoys a fireplace and a snack bar pass-through to the island kitchen. Two bedrooms, one with porch access, share a full bath. The master suite is tucked away with a spa bath and twin walk-in closets. Upstairs, a fourth bedroom, media room and game room share a full bath.

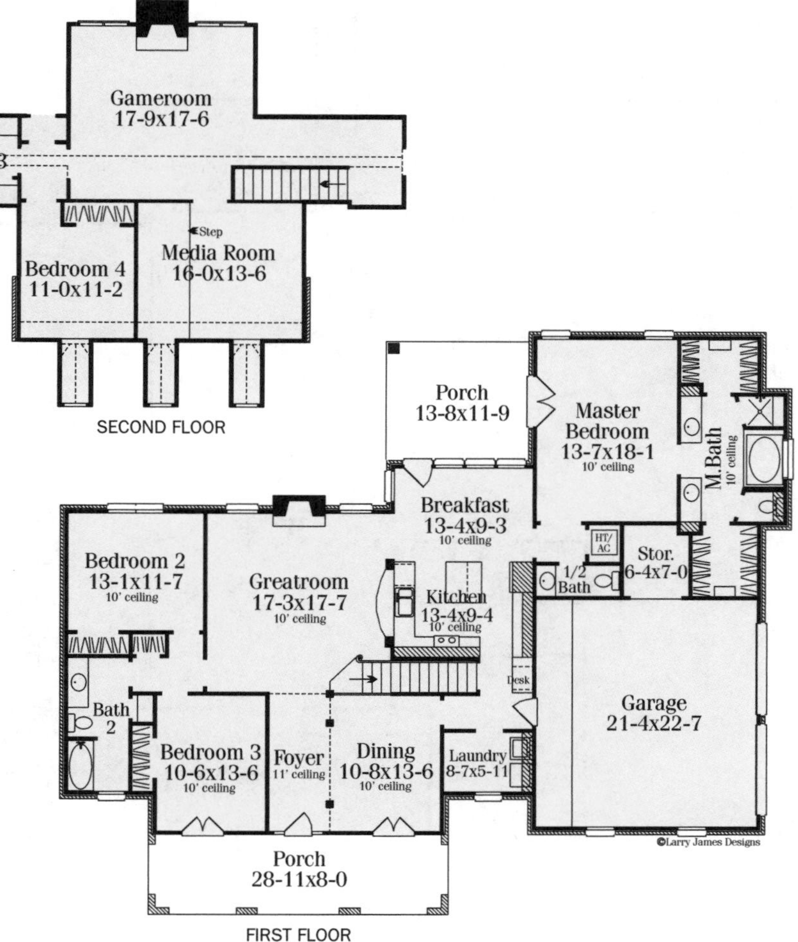

SECOND FLOOR

FIRST FLOOR

SECOND FLOOR

FIRST FLOOR

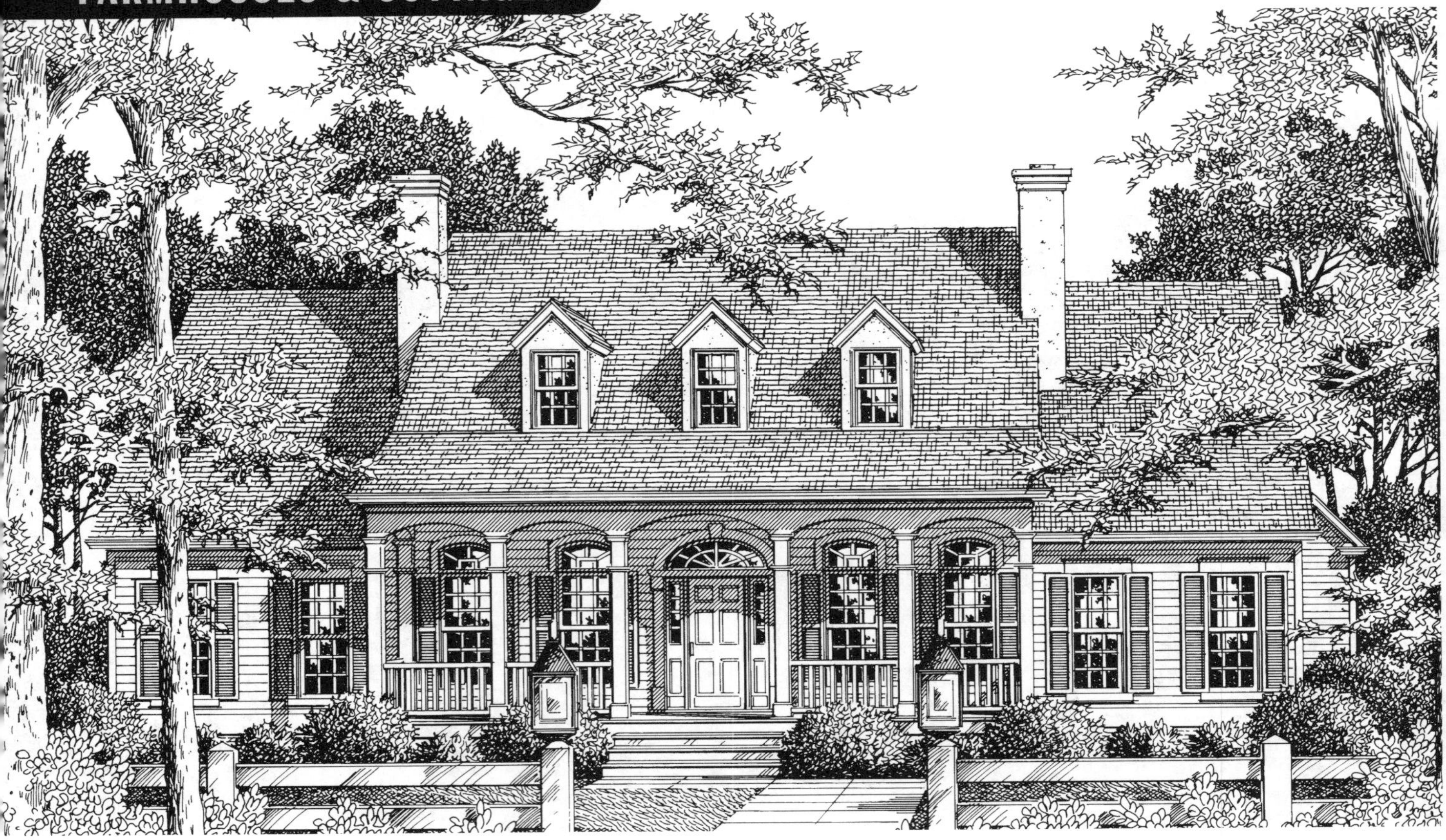

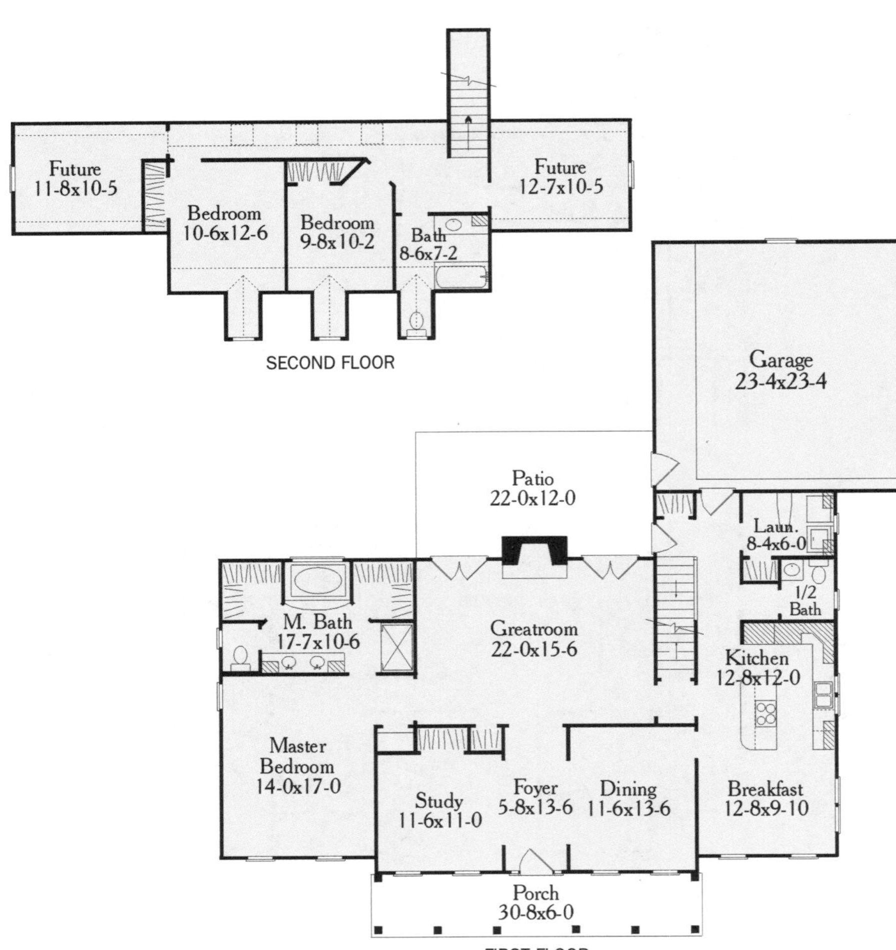

plan# HPT930132

- Style: Transitional
- First Floor: 1,791 sq. ft.
- Second Floor: 553 sq. ft.
- Total: 2,344 sq. ft.
- Bonus Space: 284 sq. ft.
- Bedrooms: 3
- Bathrooms: 2½
- Width: 64'-4"
- Depth: 66'-1"
- Foundation: Basement, Crawlspace, Slab

SEARCH ONLINE @ EPLANS.COM

Symmetry is the key to the classic appeal of this home, with a traditional elevation fronted by an expansive covered porch. A study and a formal dining room flank the entry leading into the great room with its centered fireplace and double sets of French doors. The opulent master suite is secluded for privacy on one side of the plan, while the kitchen and breakfast room bring balance on the other. The second floor includes two bedrooms, a full bath and two future rooms.

plan# HPT930133

- Style: Traditional
- First Floor: 1,768 sq. ft.
- Second Floor: 707 sq. ft.
- Total: 2,475 sq. ft.
- Bedrooms: 3
- Bathrooms: 2½
- Width: 66'-0"
- Depth: 52'-8"
- Foundation: Basement, Crawlspace, Slab

SEARCH ONLINE @ EPLANS.COM

Classic good looks and a fun country flair have made this charming home one of our favorites. Inside, the great room welcomes family and friends with a warming fireplace and an elegant columned archway leading to the dining room. Just off the gourmet island kitchen, a home office/bonus room is filled with natural light. In the master suite, a cathedral ceiling and French doors add grandeur and a private bath will soothe. Two bedrooms, one lit by triplet dormers, reside upstairs and share a playroom and a full bath.

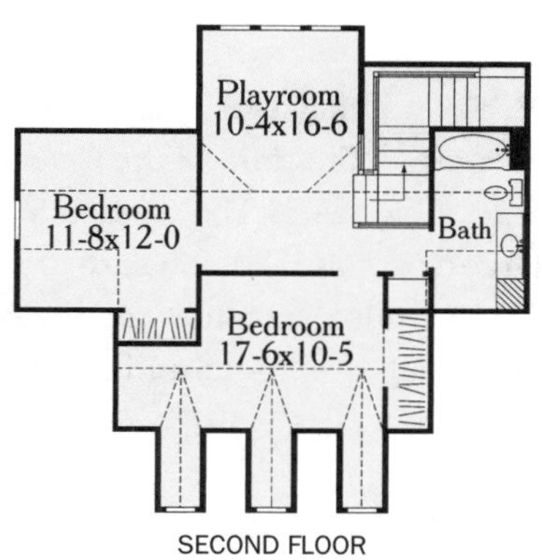

SECOND FLOOR

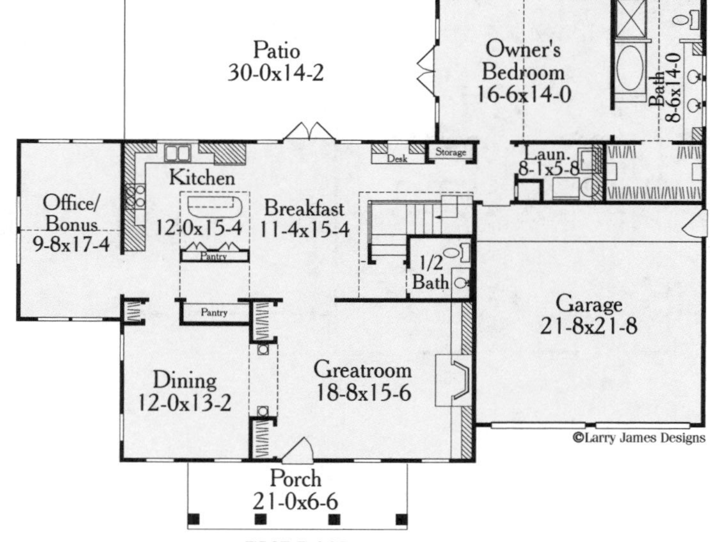

FIRST FLOOR

Dormers and transom windows lend charm to this Colonial design. Inside, columns define the formal dining room to the right of the foyer, while the study to the left of the foyer is accessed by double doors. The vaulted family room offers a corner fireplace. A bay window, large closet and spacious private bath highlight the first-floor master suite; a bay window also decorates the breakfast area. Upstairs are three family bedrooms, all with walk-in closets, and two full baths.

plan# HPT930134

- Style: Colonial
- First Floor: 1,907 sq. ft.
- Second Floor: 908 sq. ft.
- Total: 2,815 sq. ft.
- Bedrooms: 4
- Bathrooms: 3½
- Width: 64'-8"
- Depth: 51'-0"

SEARCH ONLINE @ EPLANS.COM

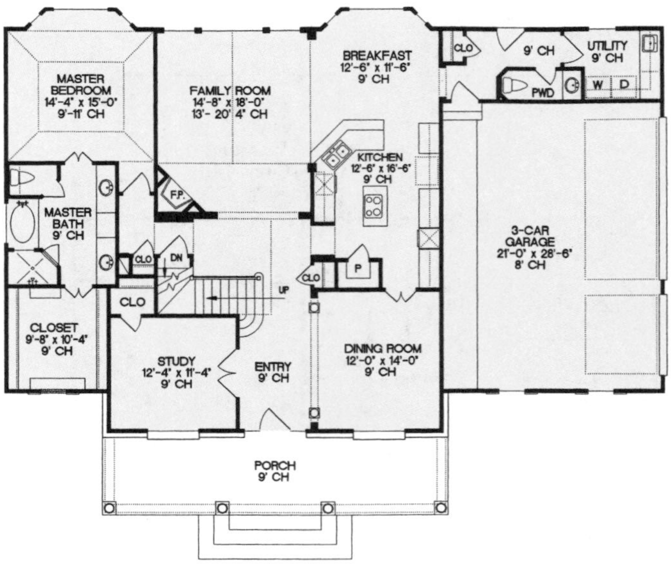

FIRST FLOOR

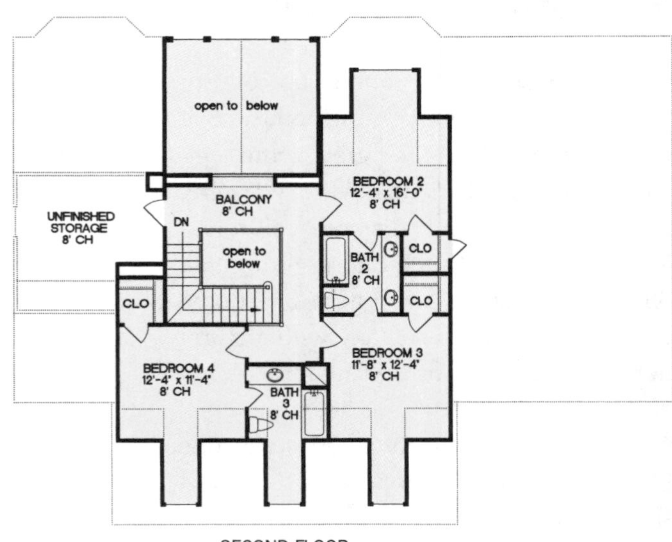

SECOND FLOOR

plan# HPT930135

- Style: Farmhouse
- First Floor: 1,765 sq. ft.
- Second Floor: 595 sq. ft.
- Total: 2,360 sq. ft.
- Bedrooms: 3
- Bathrooms: 2½
- Width: 68'-0"
- Depth: 74'-0"
- Foundation: Basement, Crawlspace, Slab

SEARCH ONLINE @ EPLANS.COM

Dormer windows and a covered front porch lend a Southern country flavor to the exterior of this fine home. The interior is well planned and spacious. The living areas are open to one another and are comprised of a formal dining room, a family room with a sloped ceiling and fireplace, and a kitchen with an eating area. A huge pantry offers convenience to the kitchen. The master suite features a sitting area and large garden bath. The second floor holds two family bedrooms and a full bath. The balcony overlooks the family room below.

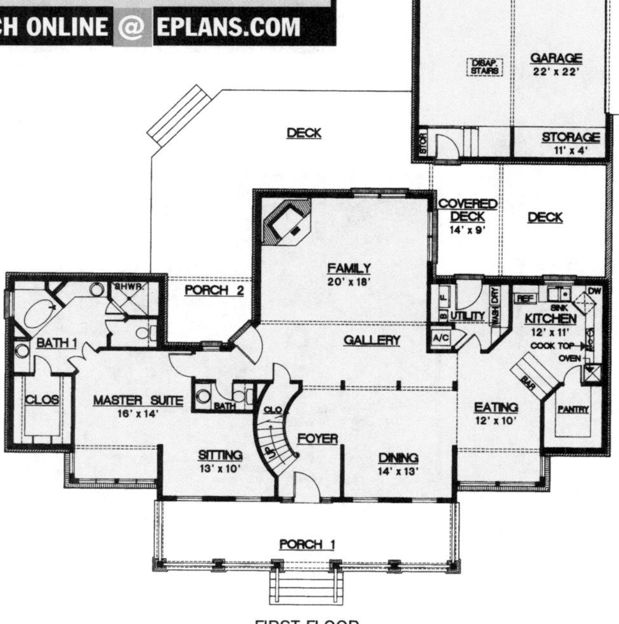

FIRST FLOOR

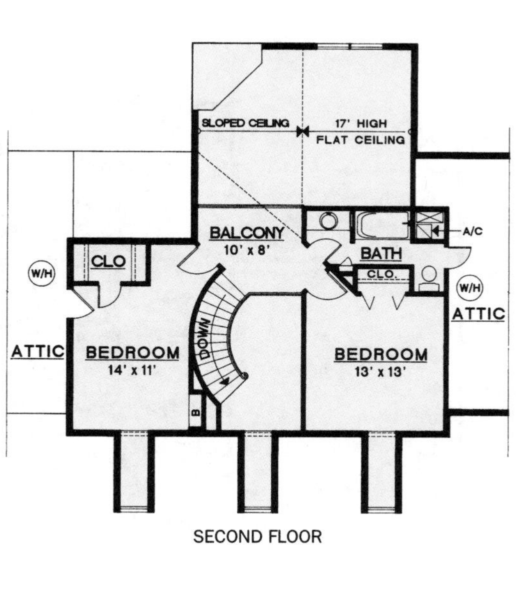

SECOND FLOOR

This home's distinctive design personality is complemented by a large covered porch with a wood railing. The living room is distinguished by the warmth of a bay window and French doors leading to the family room. Hutch space adds interest to the formal dining room. A large laundry room provides practical access to the garage, the outdoors and the kitchen. In the well-appointed kitchen, an island cooktop will save you steps. The master suite on the second floor delights with special ceiling treatment and a spacious bath.

plan# HPT930136

- Style: Farmhouse
- First Floor: 1,093 sq. ft.
- Second Floor: 905 sq. ft.
- Total: 1,998 sq. ft.
- Bedrooms: 3
- Bathrooms: 2½
- Width: 55'-4"
- Depth: 37'-8"

SEARCH ONLINE @ EPLANS.COM

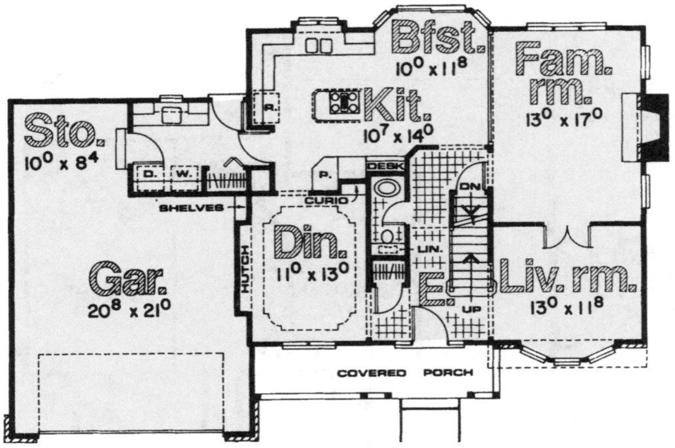

FIRST FLOOR

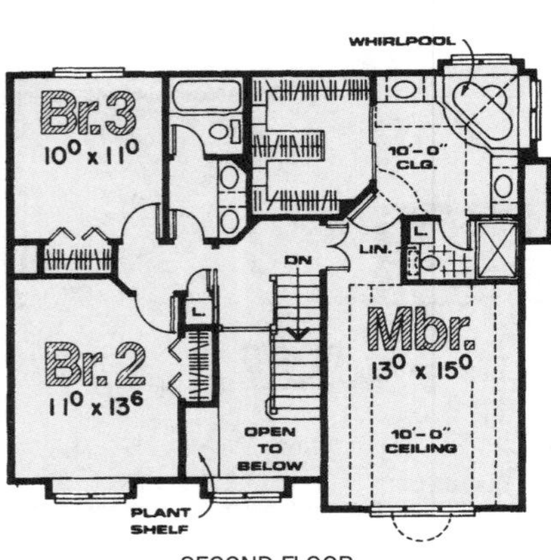

SECOND FLOOR

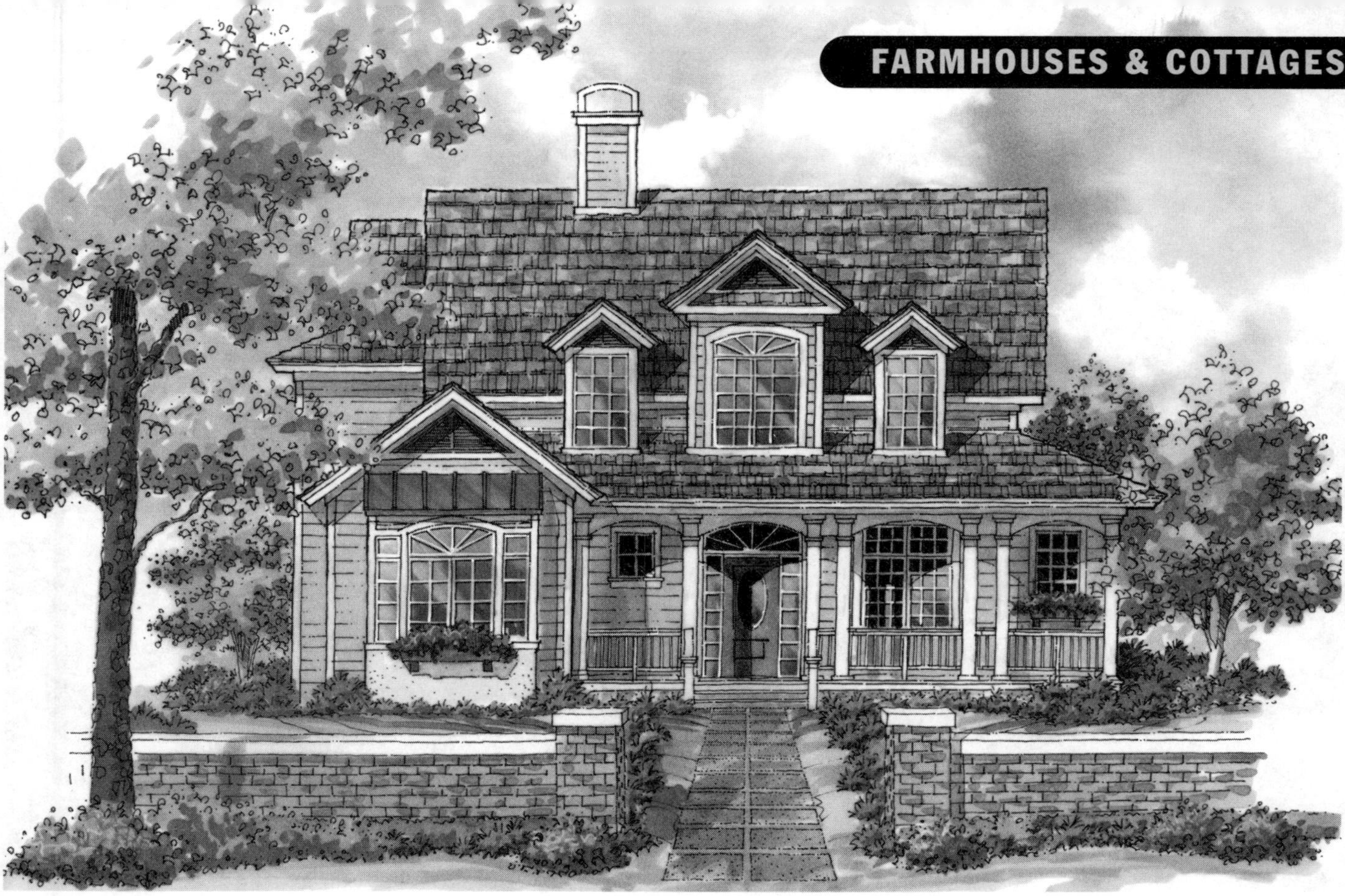

plan# HPT930137

- Style: Country Cottage
- First Floor: 1,716 sq. ft.
- Second Floor: 618 sq. ft.
- Total: 2,334 sq. ft.
- Bedrooms: 3
- Bathrooms: 3
- Width: 47'-0"
- Depth: 50'-0"
- Foundation: Crawlspace

SEARCH ONLINE @ EPLANS.COM

This country farmhouse enjoys special features such as gables, dormers, plenty of windows, and a covered front porch. Columns adorn the home throughout for an extra touch of elegance. The formal dining room enjoys a tray ceiling and is open to the kitchen, which enjoys access to either a utility room or to the breakfast nook with a bay window. The massive great room enjoys a vaulted ceiling, a cozy fireplace, and built-ins—French doors tie this room to a vaulted rear porch. On the left of this home is a study/office along with the sumptuous master suite. The second floor holds two family bedrooms—both with walk-in closets and built-in desks—sharing a full bath.

FIRST FLOOR

SECOND FLOOR

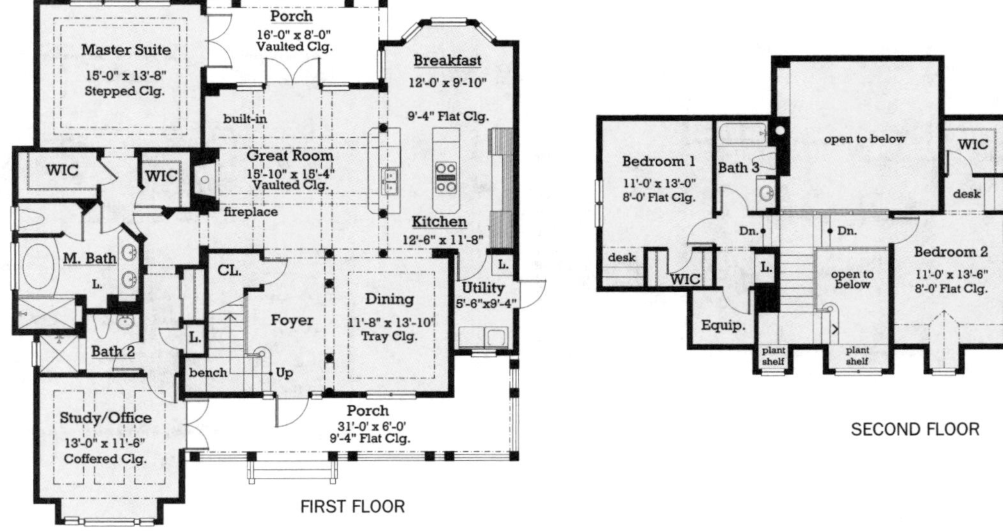

COURTESY OF DESIGN BASICS, INC.
THIS HOME, AS SHOWN IN THE PHOTOGRAPH, MAY DIFFER FROM THE ACTUAL BLUEPRINTS

Beginning with the interest of a wraparound porch, there's a feeling of country charm in this two-story plan. Formal dining and living rooms, visible from the entry, offer ample space for gracious entertaining. The large family room is truly a place of warmth and welcome with its gorgeous bay window, fireplace and French doors to the living room. The kitchen, with an island counter, pantry and desk, makes cooking a delight. Upstairs, the secondary bedrooms share an efficient compartmented bath. The expansive master bedroom has its own luxury bath with a double vanity, whirlpool tub, walk-in closet and dressing area.

plan# HPT930138

- Style: Farmhouse
- First Floor: 1,188 sq. ft.
- Second Floor: 1,172 sq. ft.
- Total: 2,360 sq. ft.
- Bedrooms: 4
- Bathrooms: 2½
- Width: 58'-0"
- Depth: 40'-0"

SEARCH ONLINE @ EPLANS.COM

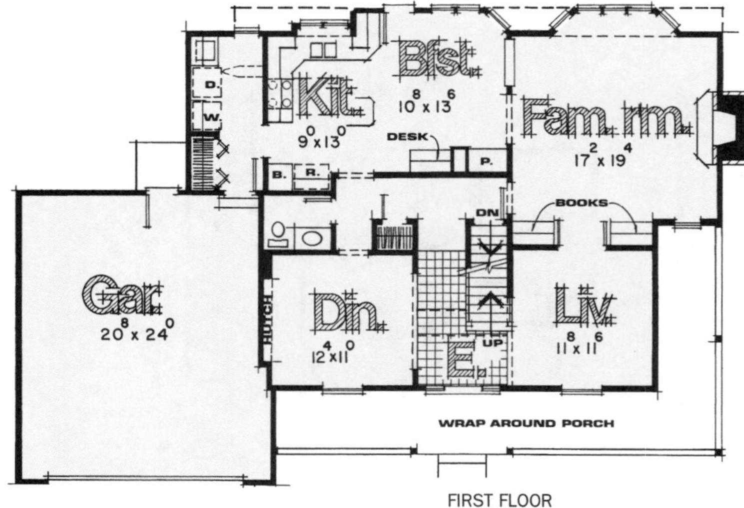

FIRST FLOOR

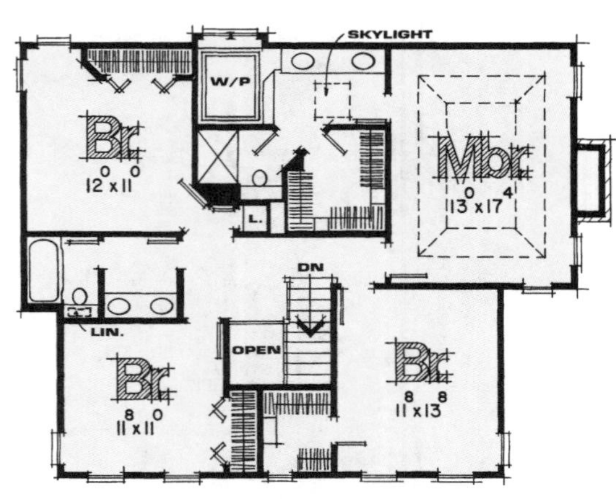

SECOND FLOOR

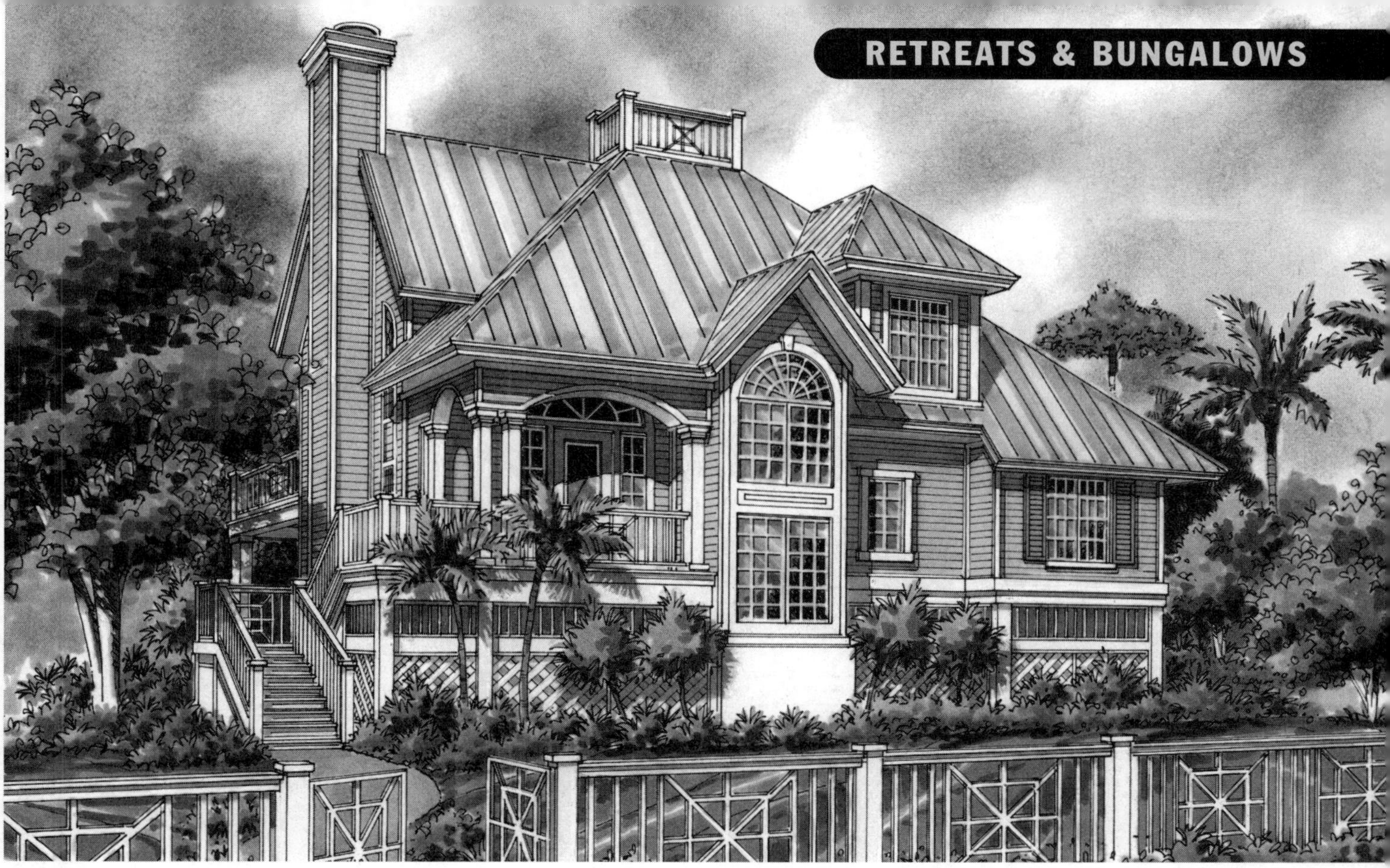

plan# HPT930139

- Style: Seaside
- First Floor: 1,342 sq. ft.
- Second Floor: 511 sq. ft.
- Total: 1,853 sq. ft.
- Bedrooms: 3
- Bathrooms: 2
- Width: 44'-0"
- Depth: 40'-0"
- Foundation: Island Basement

SEARCH ONLINE @ EPLANS.COM

Detailed fretwork complements a standing-seam roof on this tropical cottage. An arch-top transom provides an absolutely perfect highlight to the classic clapboard facade. An unrestrained floor plan offers cool digs for kicking back, and a sensational retreat for guests—whether the occasion is formal or casual. French doors open to a rear porch from the great room letting in fresh air and the sights and sounds of the great outdoors. Inside, the master bedroom leads to a dressing space with linen storage and a walk-in closet. The lavish bath includes a garden tub, oversized shower and a wraparound vanity with two lavatories. Two secondary bedrooms on the upper level share a spacious loft that overlooks the great room. One of the bedrooms opens to a private deck.

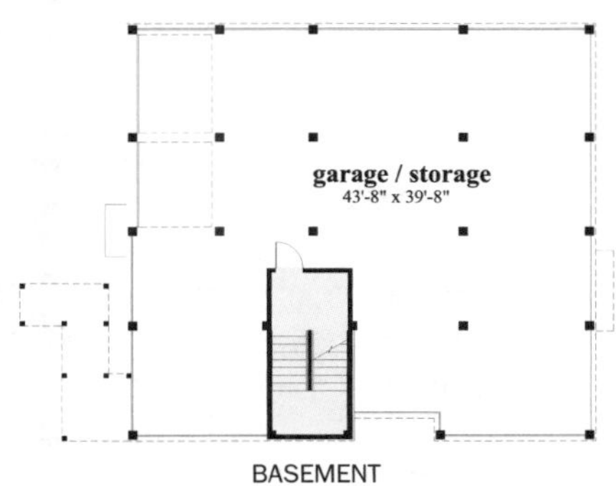

BASEMENT

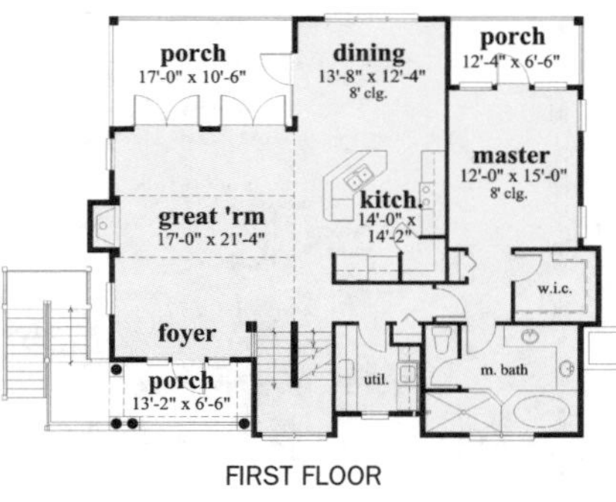

FIRST FLOOR

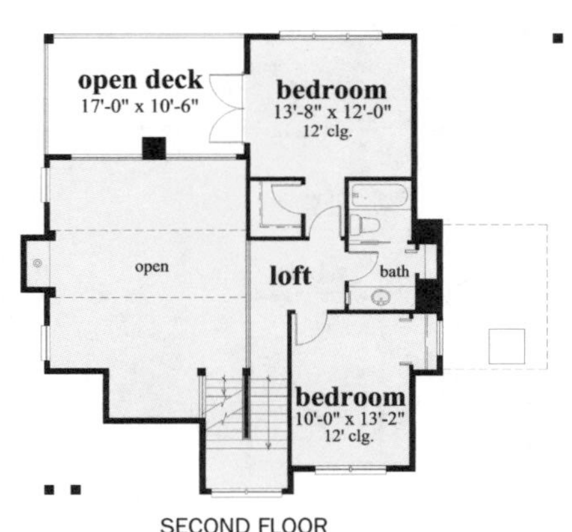

SECOND FLOOR

Variable rooflines, a tower and a covered front porch all combine to give this home a wonderful ambiance. Enter through the mid-level foyer and head either up to the main living level or down to the garage. On the main level, find a spacious light-filled great room sharing a fireplace with the dining room. A study offers access to the rear covered veranda. The efficient island kitchen is open to the dining room, offering ease in entertaining. A guest suite with a private full bath completes this level. Upstairs, a second guest suite with its own bath and a deluxe master suite with a covered balcony, sun deck, walk-in closet and lavish bath are sure to please.

plan# HPT930140

- Style: European Cottage
- First Floor: 1,637 sq. ft.
- Second Floor: 1,022 sq. ft.
- Total: 2,659 sq. ft.
- Bonus Space: 532 sq. ft.
- Bedrooms: 3
- Bathrooms: 3½
- Width: 50'-0"
- Depth: 53'-0"
- Foundation: Pier

SEARCH ONLINE @ EPLANS.COM

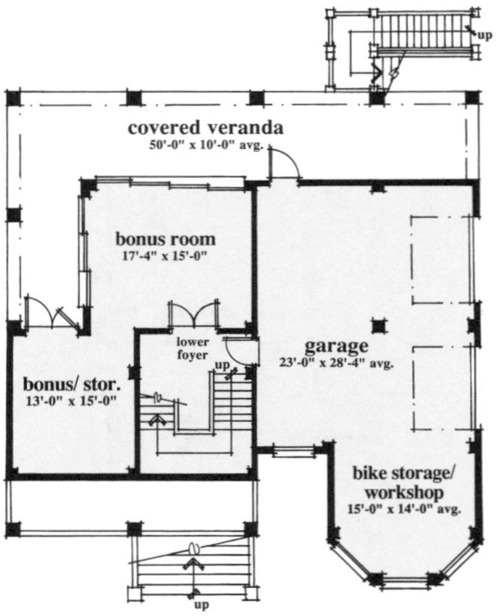

BASEMENT

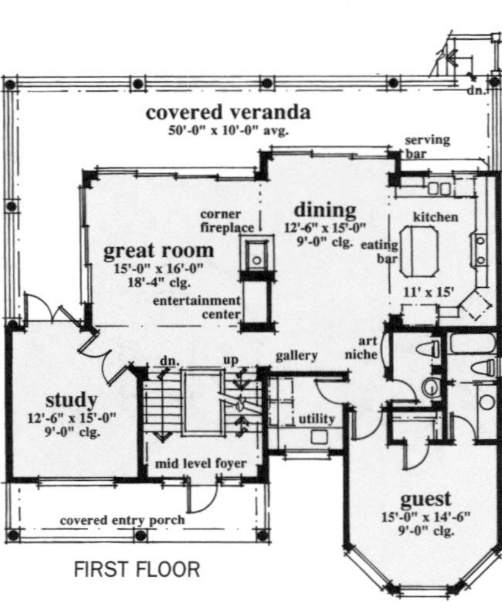

FIRST FLOOR

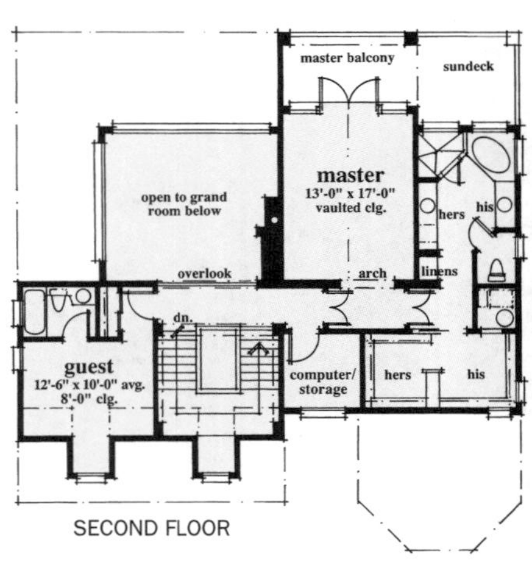

SECOND FLOOR

plan# HPT930141

- Style: Vacation
- First Floor: 1,586 sq. ft.
- Second Floor: 601 sq. ft.
- Total: 2,187 sq. ft.
- Bedrooms: 3
- Bathrooms: 2
- Width: 50'-0"
- Depth: 44'-0"
- Foundation: Pier

SEARCH ONLINE @ EPLANS.COM

Lattice walls, pickets and horizontal siding complement a relaxed Key West design that's perfect for waterfront properties. The grand room with a fireplace, the dining room and Bedroom 2 open through French doors to the veranda. The master suite occupies the entire second floor and features access to a private balcony through double doors. This pampering suite also includes a spacious walk-in closet and a full bath with a whirlpool tub. Enclosed storage/bonus space and a garage are available on the lower level.

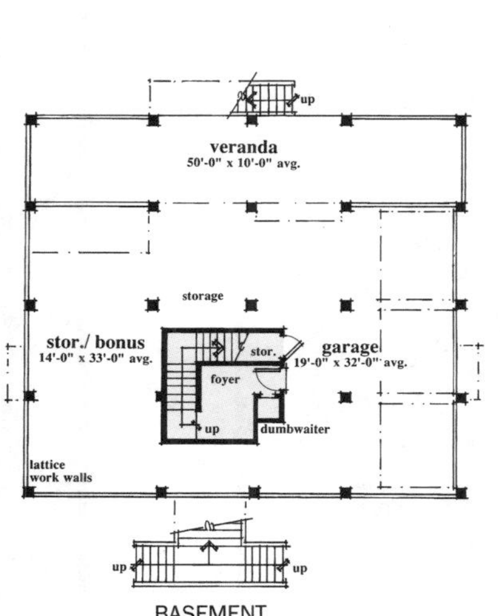

BASEMENT

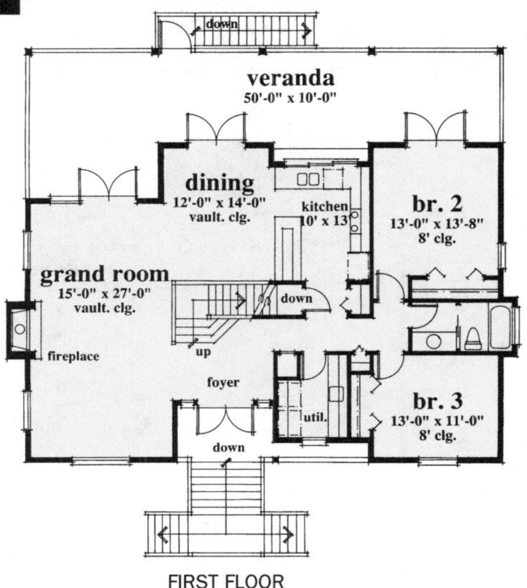

FIRST FLOOR

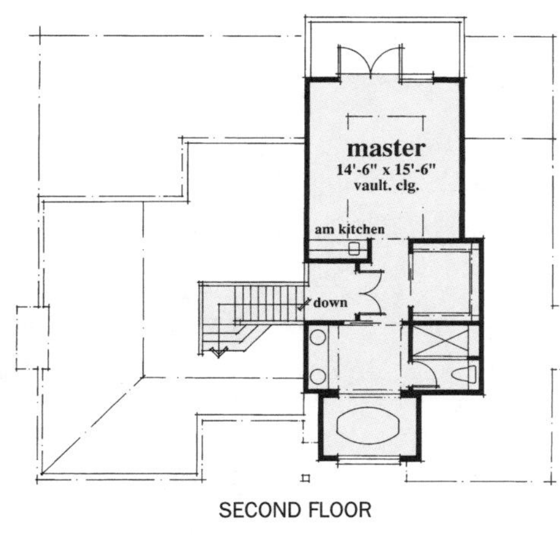

SECOND FLOOR

Amenities abound in this delightful two-story home. The foyer opens directly into the fantastic grand room, which offers a warming fireplace and two sets of double doors to the rear deck. The dining room also accesses this deck and a second deck shared with Bedroom 2. A convenient kitchen and another bedroom also reside on this level. Upstairs, the master bedroom reigns supreme. Entered through double doors, it pampers with a luxurious bath, walk-in closet, morning kitchen and private observation deck.

plan# HPT930142

- Style: Floridian
- First Floor: 1,342 sq. ft.
- Second Floor: 511 sq. ft.
- Total: 1,853 sq. ft.
- Bedrooms: 3
- Bathrooms: 2
- Width: 44'-0"
- Depth: 40'-0"
- Foundation: Pier

SEARCH ONLINE @ EPLANS.COM

SECOND FLOOR

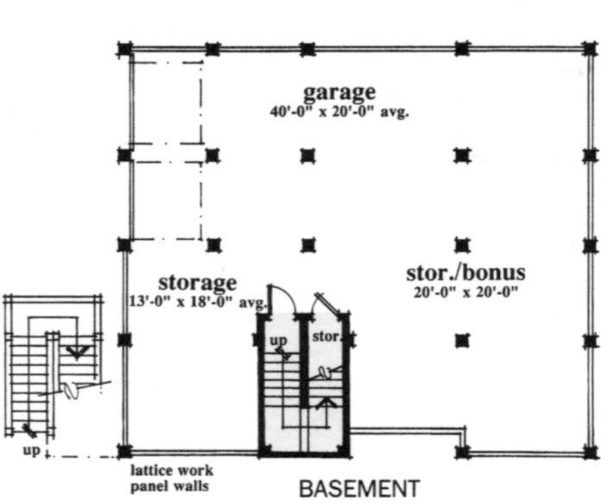

BASEMENT

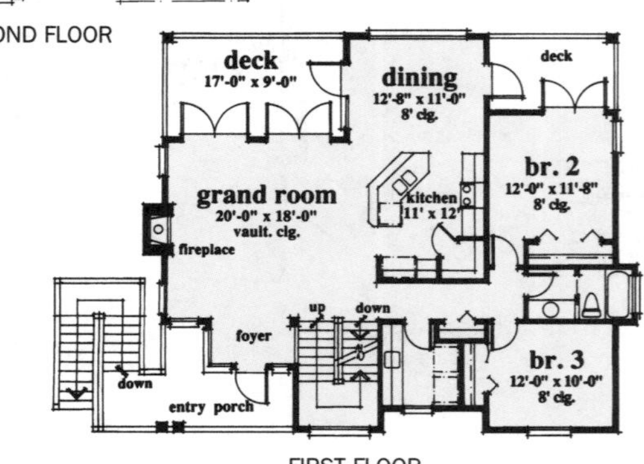

FIRST FLOOR

plan# HPT930143

- Style: Floridian
- First Floor: 2,725 sq. ft.
- Second Floor: 1,418 sq. ft.
- Total: 4,143 sq. ft.
- Bedrooms: 4
- Bathrooms: 5½
- Width: 61'-4"
- Depth: 62'-0"
- Foundation: Slab

L

SEARCH ONLINE @ EPLANS.COM

Florida living takes off in this grand design. A grand room gains attention as a superb entertaining area. A see-through fireplace here connects this room to the dining room. In the study, quiet time is assured—or slip out the doors and onto the veranda for a breather. A full bath connects the study and Bedroom 2. Bedroom 3 sits on the opposite side of the house and enjoys its own bath. The kitchen features a large work island and a connecting breakfast nook. Upstairs, the master bedroom suite contains His and Hers baths, a see-through fireplace and access to an upper deck. A guest bedroom suite is located on the other side of the upper floor.

Cost to build? See page 436 to order complete cost estimate to build this house in your area!

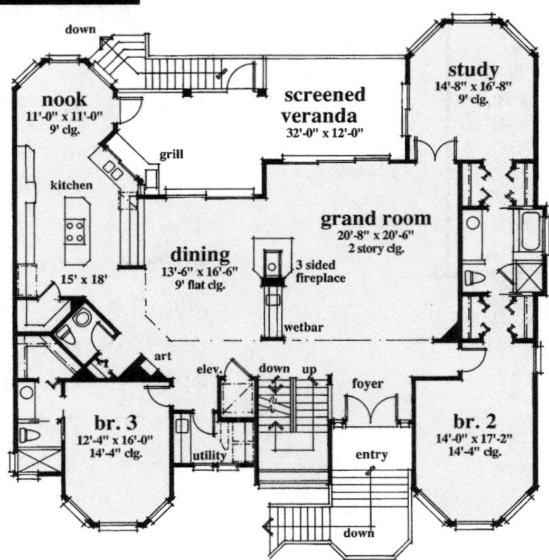

FIRST FLOOR

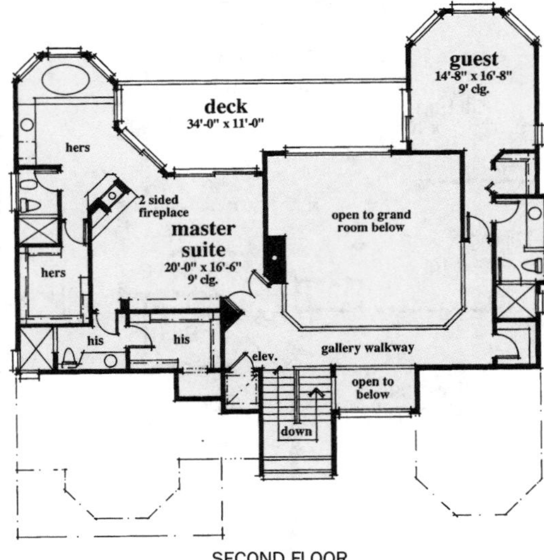

SECOND FLOOR

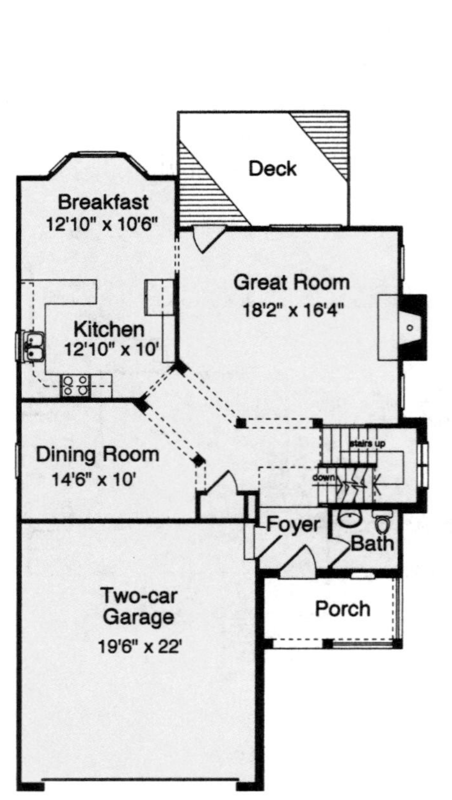

FIRST FLOOR

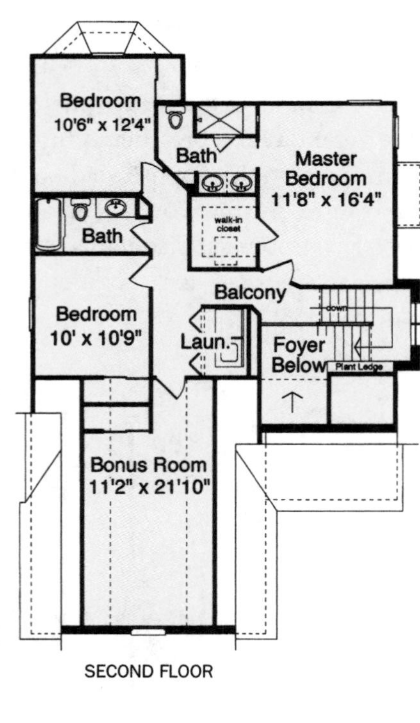

SECOND FLOOR

plan# HPT930144

- Style: Retreat
- First Floor: 939 sq. ft.
- Second Floor: 788 sq. ft.
- Total: 1,727 sq. ft.
- Bonus Space: 210 sq. ft.
- Bedrooms: 3
- Bathrooms: 2½
- Width: 34'-0"
- Depth: 52'-0"
- Foundation: Walkout Basement

SEARCH ONLINE @ EPLANS.COM

Designed for a narrow lot, this two-story home creates a package that offers maximum living space in a small footprint. The large great room features a fireplace and multiple windows. A delightful place to start the day, the bayed breakfast area enjoys plenty of sunshine. The formal dining room opens to the great room and is adorned with columns. On the second level, a master bedroom with a large walk-in closet and private bath is joined by two family bedrooms, a laundry and a hall bath. Note the bonus room available for future expansion.

plan# HPT930145

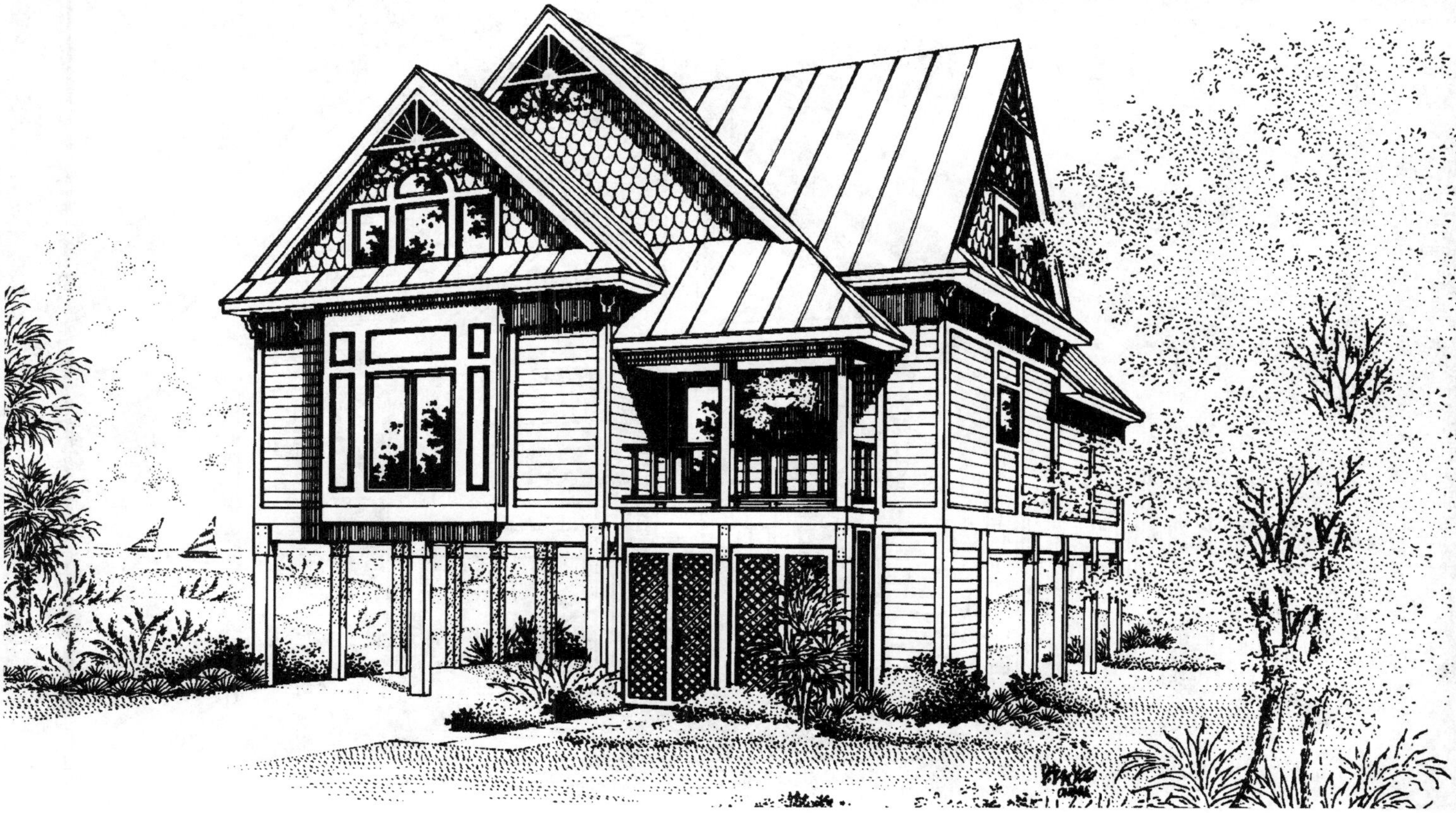

- > Style: Retreat
- > First Floor: 1,182 sq. ft.
- > Second Floor: 838 sq. ft.
- > Total: 2,020 sq. ft.
- > Bedrooms: 4
- > Bathrooms: 3
- > Width: 34'-0"
- > Depth: 52'-0"
- > Foundation: Pier

SEARCH ONLINE @ EPLANS.COM

This two-story coastal home finds its inspiration in a Craftsman style that's highlighted by ornamented gables. Open planning is the key with the living and dining areas sharing the front of the first floor with the U-shaped kitchen and stairway. Both the dining room and the living room access the second porch. The master suite boasts a walk-in closet, private vanity and angled tub. The utility room is efficiently placed between the kitchen and bath. Bedrooms 2 and 3 share a bath while Bedroom 4 enjoys a private bath.

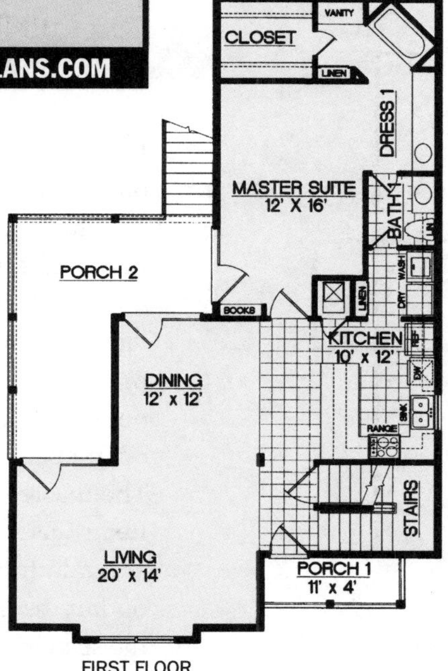

FIRST FLOOR

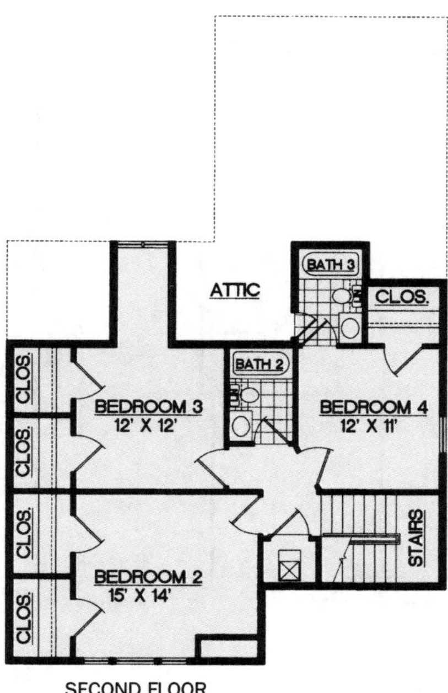

SECOND FLOOR

FIRST FLOOR

SECOND FLOOR

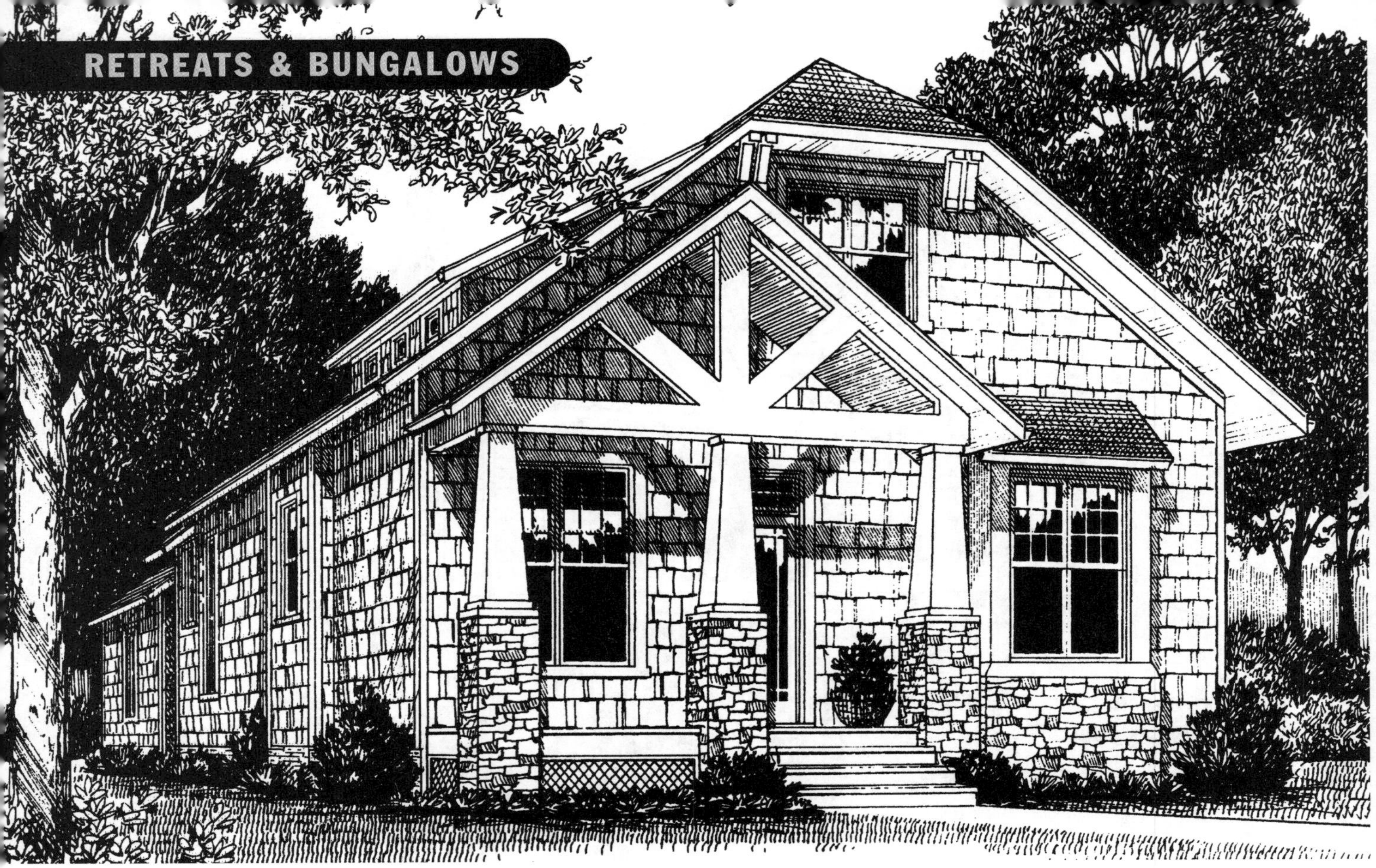

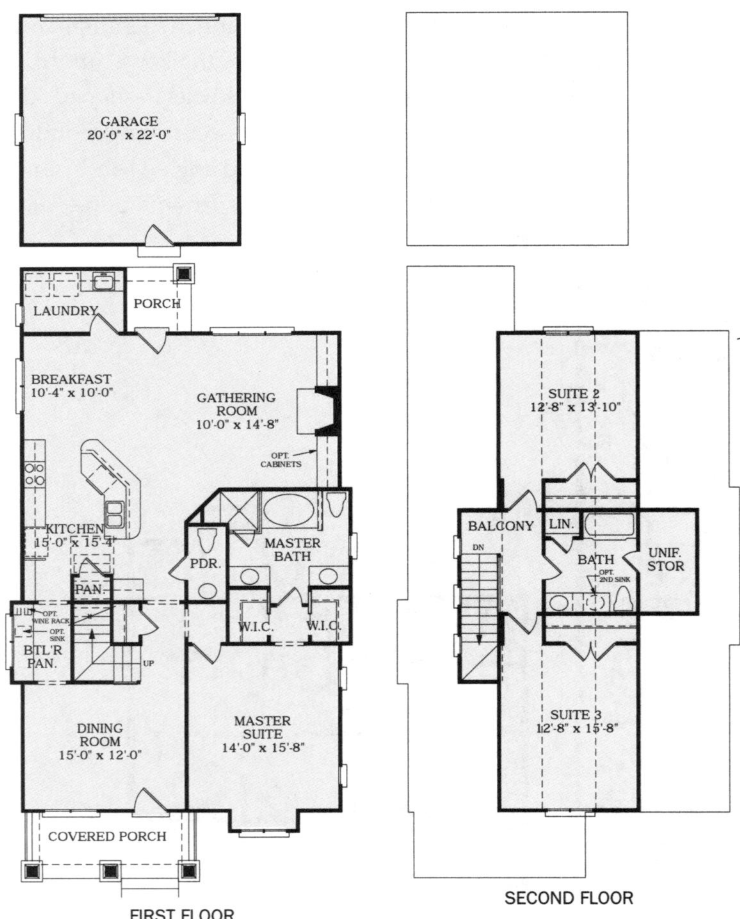

plan# HPT930146

- Style: Bungalow
- First Floor: 1,478 sq. ft.
- Second Floor: 629 sq. ft.
- Total: 2,107 sq. ft.
- Bedrooms: 3
- Bathrooms: 2½
- Width: 32'-0"
- Depth: 59'-0"
- Foundation: Crawlspace

SEARCH ONLINE @ EPLANS.COM

With its shingle siding and decorative front porch, this Craftsman delight willshine in any neighborhood. The spacious dining room is accessed by the well-equipped kitchen via the butler's pantry. In the rear, the more private and casual breakfast nook and gathering room create an open space for intimate entertaining. The master suite on the right offers a luxurious bath, twin walk-in closets and a bumped-out window. Two secondary bedrooms share a full bath on the second floor.

plan# HPT930147

- Style: European Cottage
- First Floor: 756 sq. ft.
- Second Floor: 580 sq. ft.
- Total: 1,336 sq. ft.
- Bedrooms: 2
- Bathrooms: 2½
- Width: 32'-0"
- Depth: 36'-9"
- Foundation: Crawlspace

SEARCH ONLINE @ EPLANS.COM

This sweet Tudor cottage offers a petite design with plenty of family appeal. Mixed materials enhance the exterior and a quaint covered porch welcomes you inside. The first floor offers a two-sided fireplace that warms the living and dining rooms. The main level is completed by a U-shaped kitchen, powder room, laundry and plenty of outdoor porch space. Upstairs, the master bedroom features a private bath and walk-in closet, while the guest bedroom also features a private bath and a bayed wall of windows.

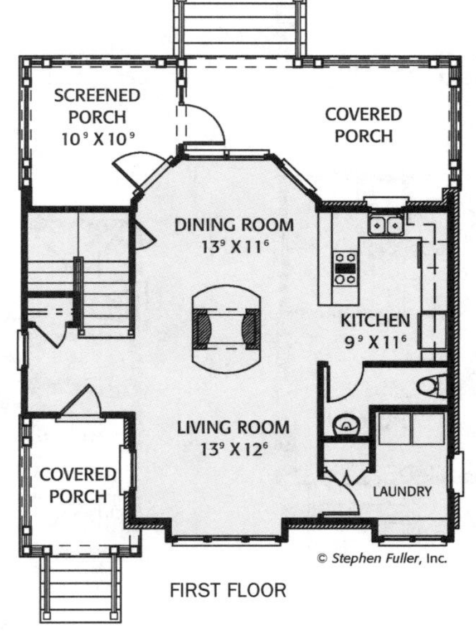

FIRST FLOOR

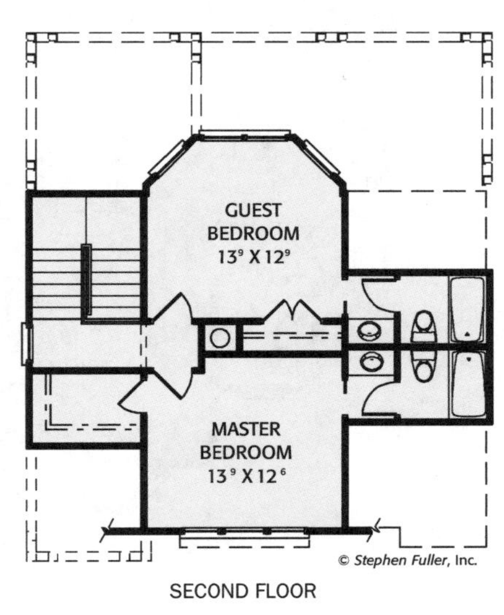

SECOND FLOOR

This charming cottage design is perfect for a vacation by the lake or in the country. European details and a bayed living-room window enhance the exterior. A petite covered front porch welcomes you inside where a two-sided fireplace warms the living and dining rooms. The kitchen is compact yet efficient and accesses a rear grilling porch. A powder bath is located nearby. Upstairs, two family bedrooms feature ample closet space—and each bedroom features its own private bath.

plan# HPT930148

- Style: European Cottage
- First Floor: 617 sq. ft.
- Second Floor: 474 sq. ft.
- Total: 1,091 sq. ft.
- Bedrooms: 2
- Bathrooms: 2½
- Width: 32'-0"
- Depth: 31'-0"
- Foundation: Crawlspace

SEARCH ONLINE @ EPLANS.COM

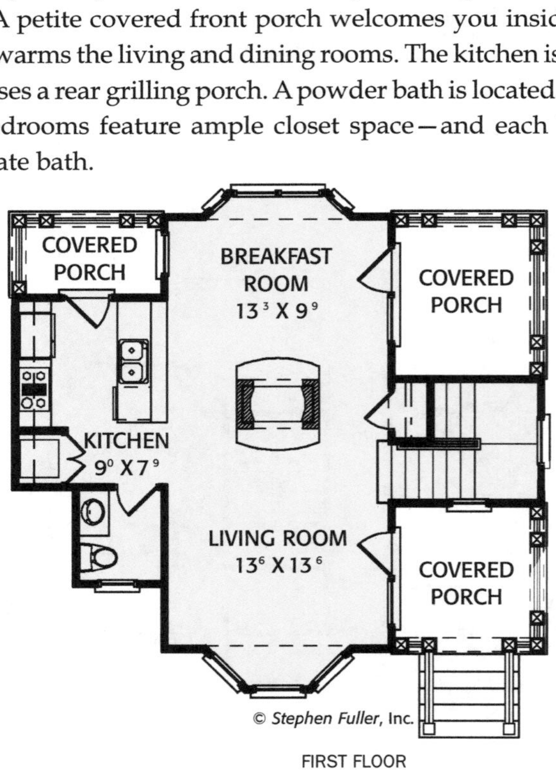

COVERED PORCH
BREAKFAST ROOM 13^{3} X 9^{9}
COVERED PORCH
KITCHEN 9^{0} X 7^{9}
LIVING ROOM 13^{6} X 13^{6}
COVERED PORCH

FIRST FLOOR

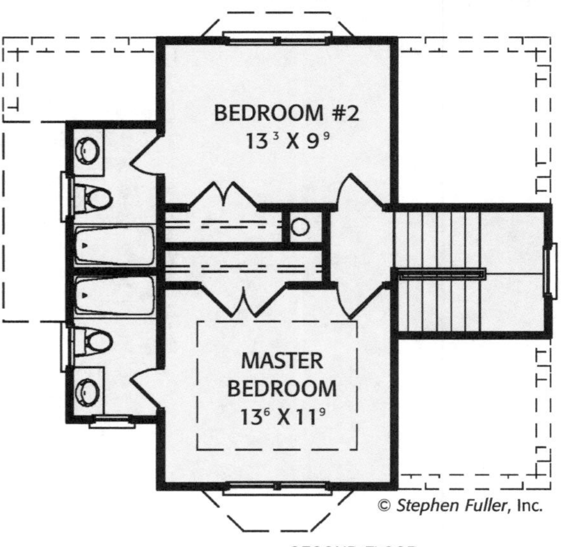

SECOND FLOOR

plan# HPT930149

- Style: European Cottage
- First Floor: 648 sq. ft.
- Second Floor: 683 sq. ft.
- Total: 1,331 sq. ft.
- Bedrooms: 2
- Bathrooms: 2½
- Width: 42'-0"
- Depth: 29'-6"
- Foundation: Crawlspace

SEARCH ONLINE @ EPLANS.COM

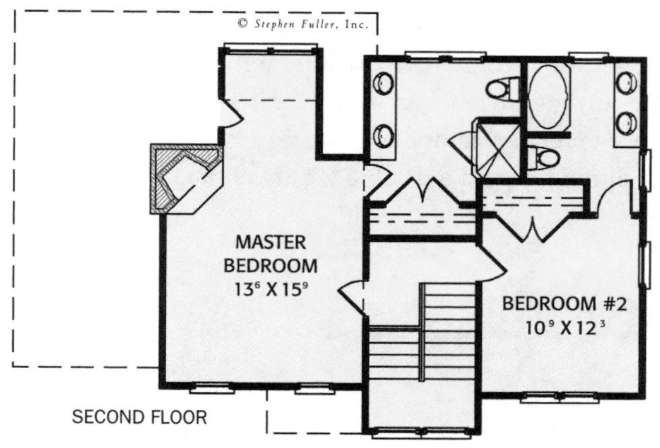

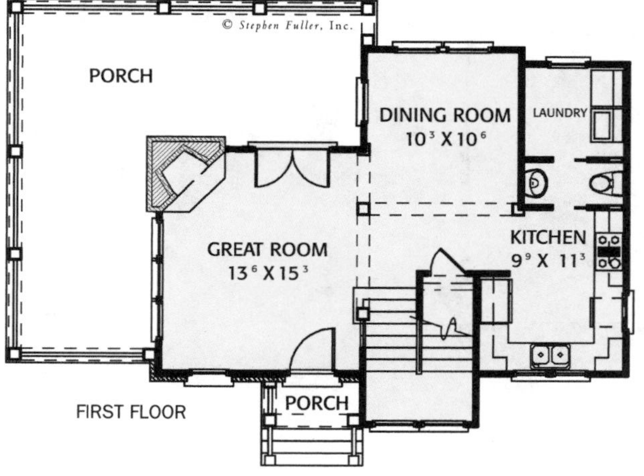

Half timbers and stucco in combination with the elaborate two-story facade create a fairytale-like attitude. The covered porch opens to the sunny great room with a corner fireplace situated between a window wall and French doors that lead out to the covered porch. Columns and archways keep the first floor open and airy. The dining room sits opposite the elegant staircase with the U-shaped kitchen residing on the right along with a half-bath and the utility room. Upstairs, the master bedroom boasts a corner fireplace hearth, a sitting area and an adjoining private bath. Bedroom 2, on the right, enjoys a private bath as well.

Arch-top windows offer charming accents to this distinctive contemporary exterior. The entry leads to the living room, which has a fireplace and a cathedral ceiling. A gourmet kitchen serves the dining room, which opens to the outdoors. The upper-level mezzanine offers a reading area plus space for lounging. An angled whirlpool tub and a double vanity enhance the master suite.

plan# HPT930150

- Style: Contemporary
- First Floor: 917 sq. ft.
- Second Floor: 742 sq. ft.
- Total: 1,659 sq. ft.
- Bedrooms: 3
- Bathrooms: 1½
- Width: 38'-0"
- Depth: 36'-0"
- Foundation: Basement

SEARCH ONLINE @ EPLANS.COM

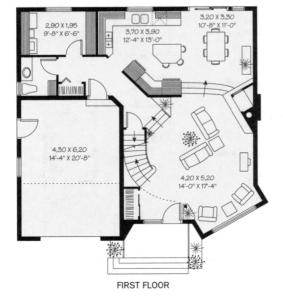

2,90 X 1,95
9'-8" X 6'-6"
3,70 X 3,90
12'-4" X 13'-0"
3,20 X 3,30
10'-8" X 11'-0"
4,30 X 6,20
14'-4" X 20'-8"
4,20 X 5,20
14'-0" X 17'-4"

FIRST FLOOR

3,10 X 2,90
10'-4" X 9'-8"
3,00 X 3,90
10'-0" X 13'-0"
4,40 X 3,60
14'-8" X 12'-0"

SECOND FLOOR

plan# HPT930151

- Style: Lakefront
- First Floor: 728 sq. ft.
- Second Floor: 442 sq. ft.
- Total: 1,170 sq. ft.
- Bedrooms: 2
- Bathrooms: 1½
- Width: 28'-0"
- Depth: 26'-0"
- Foundation: Basement

SEARCH ONLINE @ EPLANS.COM

This petite vacation design features contemporary accents and comfortable accommodations for any lakefront setting. A wall of windows and brilliant skylights fill the front of the home with sensational light. Double doors open inside to a combined living and dining room, overlooked by a second-floor sitting area. A compact U-shaped kitchen, a full bath and laundry facilities are located at the rear on the first level. Upstairs, the second floor hosts two bedrooms with ample closet space, a powder room and a sitting area.

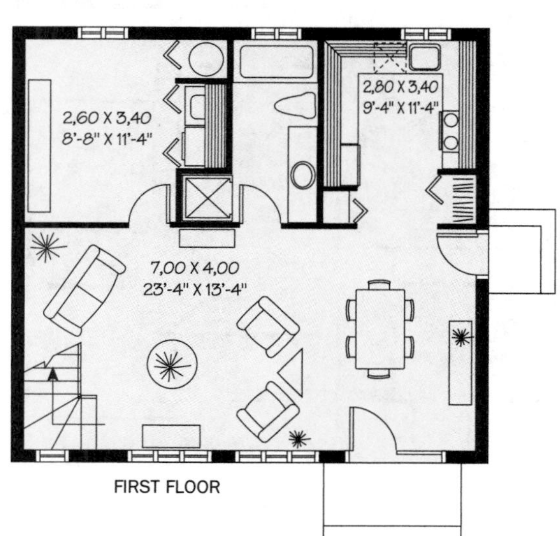

FIRST FLOOR

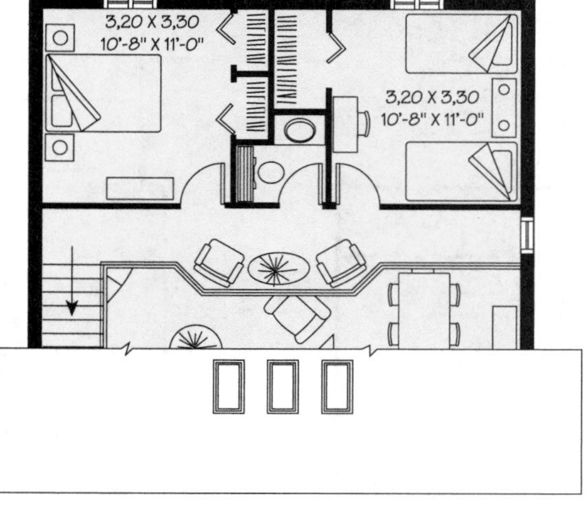

SECOND FLOOR

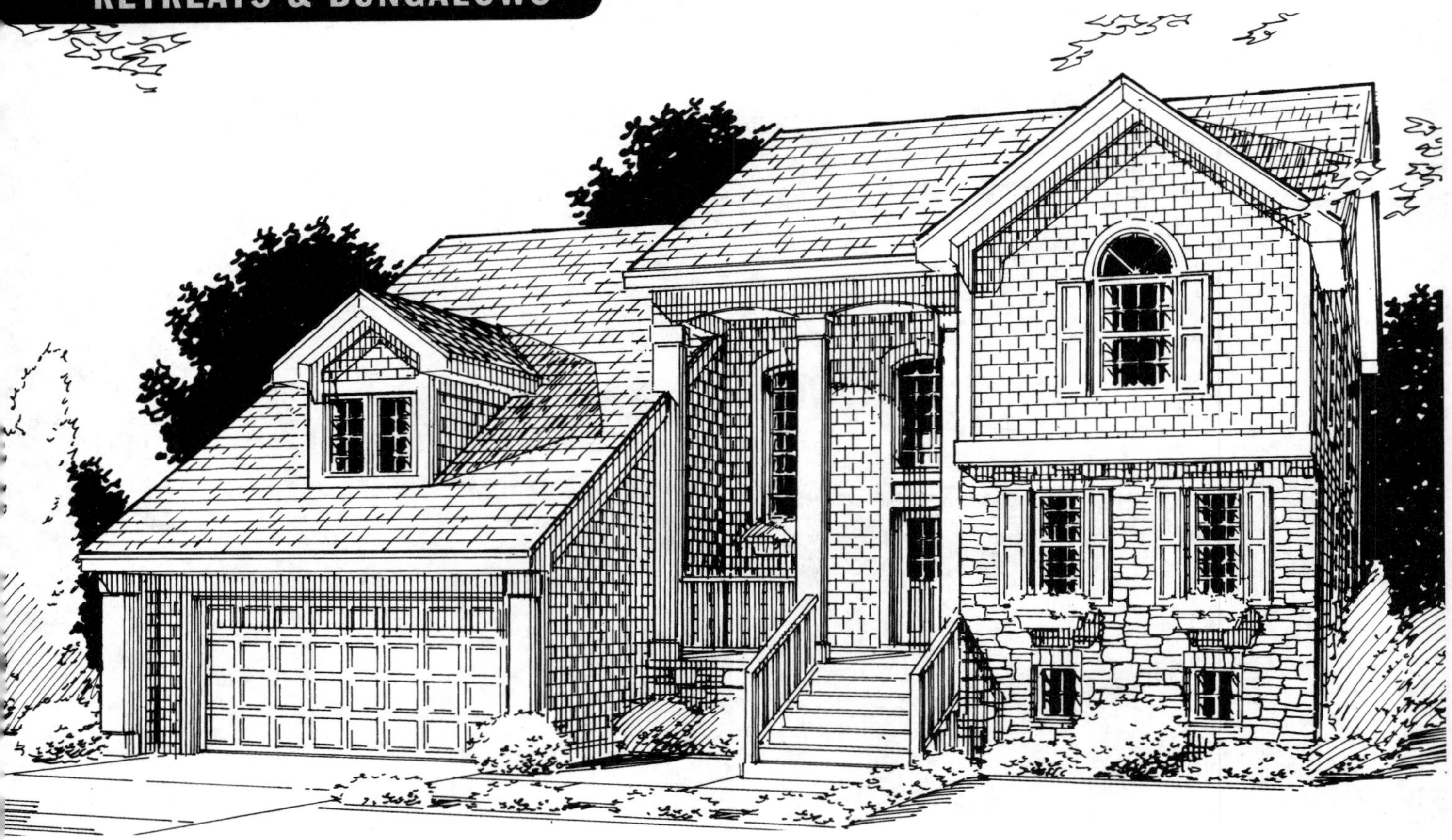

A rich, stately appearance is created by the raised elevation and the cedar shakes and stone facade of this unique multi-level home. At the foyer, you are presented with a view to the spectacular great room, with high windows, a warm fireplace and a raised ceiling. An island and sliding doors to the rear yard decorate the kitchen. The master bedroom suite is located on the main level. Two family bedrooms and an optional bonus space or guest room are located on the second floor.

plan# HPT930152

- Style: Bungalow
- First Floor: 1,333 sq. ft.
- Second Floor: 512 sq. ft.
- Total: 1,845 sq. ft.
- Bonus Space: 373 sq. ft.
- Bedrooms: 3
- Bathrooms: 2½
- Width: 50'-10"
- Depth: 51'-0"
- Foundation: Basement

SEARCH ONLINE @ EPLANS.COM

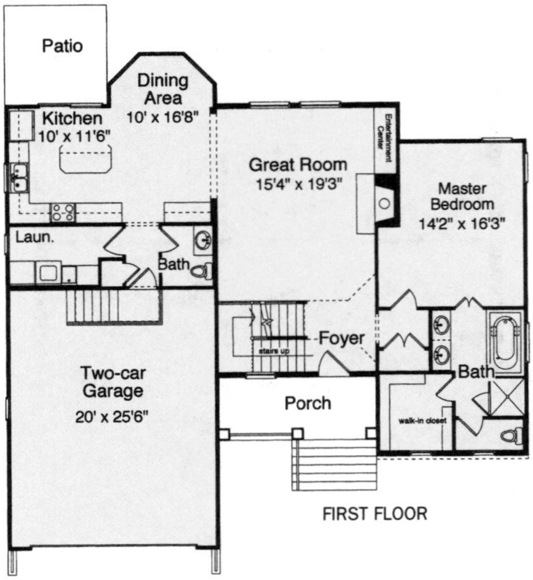

Patio
Dining Area 10' x 16'8"
Kitchen 10' x 11'6"
Entertainment Center
Great Room 15'4" x 19'3"
Master Bedroom 14'2" x 16'3"
Laun.
Bath
stairs up
Foyer
Bath
Two-car Garage 20' x 25'6"
Porch
walk-in closet

FIRST FLOOR

Great Room Below
Bedroom 11'10" x 12'8"
Bath
Balcony
Foyer Below
Bonus Room Guest Room 14'7" x 11'3"
Bath
Bedroom 13'10" x 12'8"

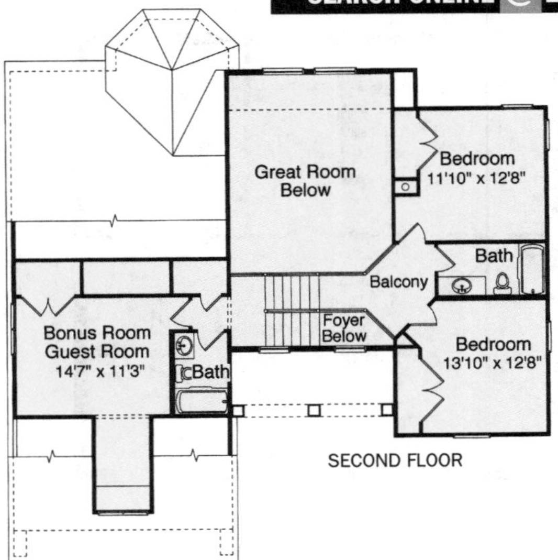

SECOND FLOOR

plan# HPT930153

- Style: Cape Cod
- First Floor: 2,015 sq. ft.
- Second Floor: 777 sq. ft.
- Total: 2,792 sq. ft.
- Bedrooms: 3
- Bathrooms: 2½
- Width: 58'-4"
- Depth: 59'-10"
- Foundation: Basement

SEARCH ONLINE @ EPLANS.COM

A covered porch, boxed window and dormer decorate the exterior of this delightfully designed home. At the foyer, an impressive view is offered to the formal dining room and through to the large great room. The great room lives up to its name with a high ceiling, fireplace and French doors that expand the living space to a covered porch. Angled walls wrap around the breakfast room and a counter with seating at the kitchen—adding a delightful transition between the great room and breakfast room. A cozy area adjoining the breakfast room could provide a flexible family center with a built-in desk. The master bedroom suite offers luxury to the homeowners and access to the laundry room from the closet. Rear stairs lead to a second-floor bedroom and loft, providing a dramatic view to the great room.

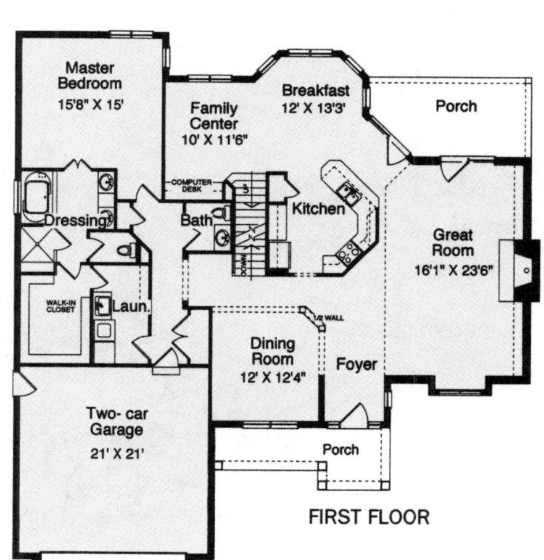

FIRST FLOOR

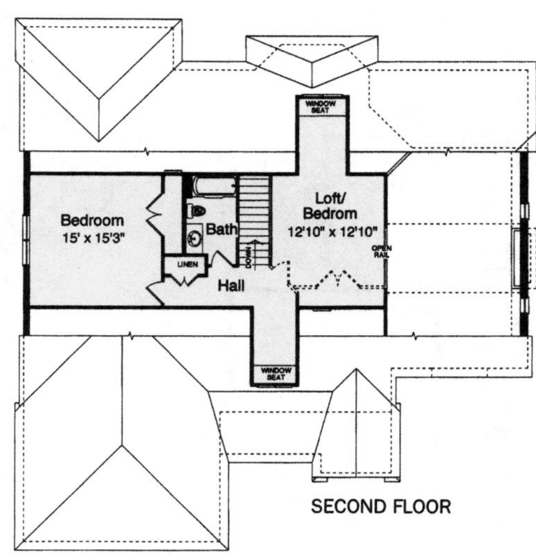

SECOND FLOOR

This design may be finished in either horizontal siding or stucco, with distinct window treatments. Inside, a fine floor plan reigns. A floor-to-ceiling window wall accentuates the vaulted ceiling in the living room and carries light into the open dining room nearby. The living room is further graced by a fireplace; the dining room has buffet space and a box-bay window. Second-floor bedrooms include a master suite with a large wall closet, window seats in the bedroom and bath, and a whirlpool tub. Blueprints include plans for both exteriors.

plan# HPT930154

- Style: Traditional
- First Floor: 1,019 sq. ft.
- Second Floor: 750 sq. ft.
- Total: 1,769 sq. ft.
- Bedrooms: 3
- Bathrooms: 2½
- Width: 47'-0"
- Depth: 41'-6"
- Foundation: Basement, Crawlspace

SEARCH ONLINE @ EPLANS.COM

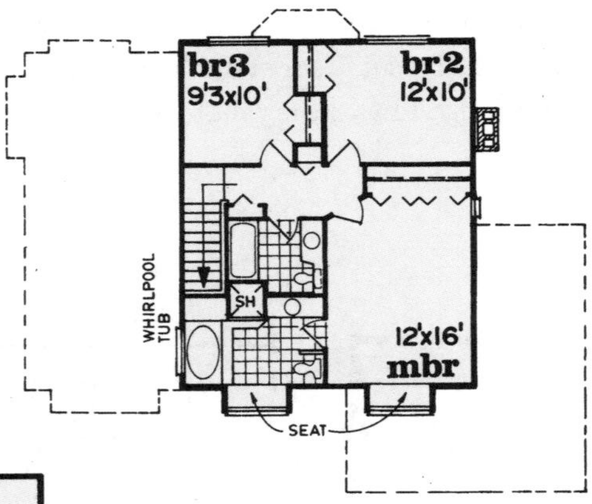

SECOND FLOOR

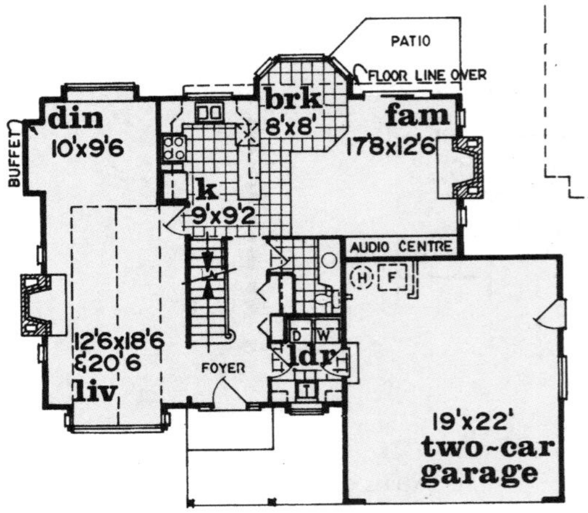

FIRST FLOOR

ALTERNATE EXTERIOR

plan# HPT930155

- Style: Traditional
- First Floor: 1,353 sq. ft.
- Second Floor: 899 sq. ft.
- Total: 2,252 sq. ft.
- Bonus Space: 183 sq. ft.
- Bedrooms: 3
- Bathrooms: 3
- Width: 38'-0"
- Depth: 59'-0"
- Foundation: Basement, Crawlspace

SEARCH ONLINE @ EPLANS.COM

This three-bedroom plan has bonus space and offers horizontal siding with brick, or if you'd like, a stucco version is also available. Note the fireplace and window seat in the living room. The nearby L-shaped kitchen, with a center cooking island, adjoins a sunny breakfast room and large family room. On the second floor are three bedrooms and bonus space to develop into a fourth bedroom if needed. The master suite has a coffered ceiling and a bath with a raised tub and separate shower.

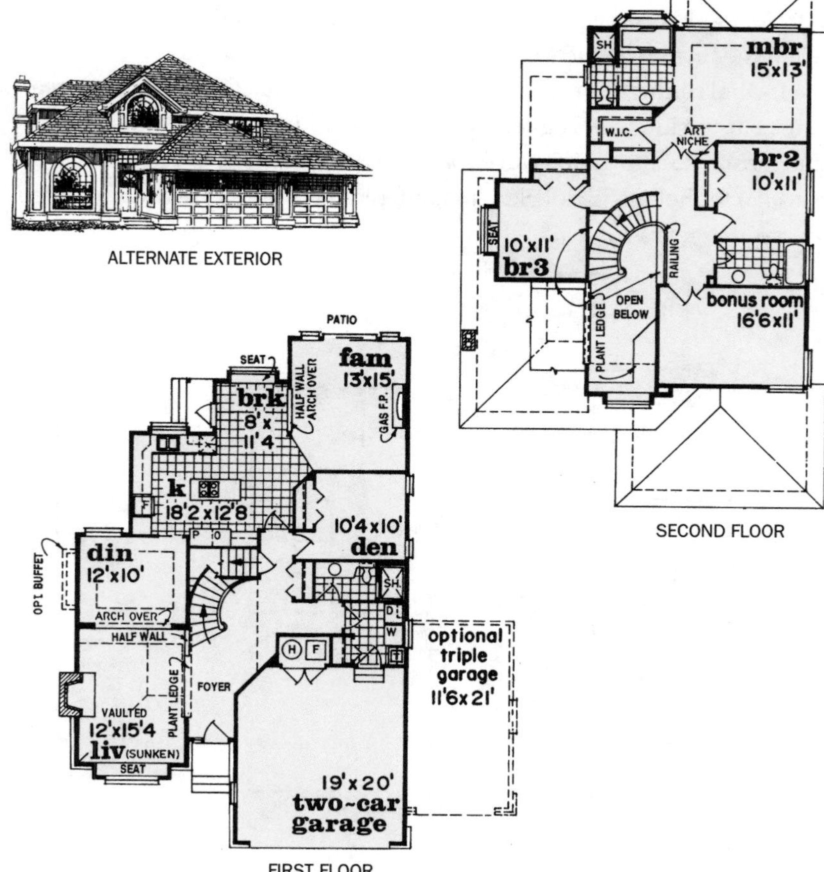

ALTERNATE EXTERIOR

SECOND FLOOR

FIRST FLOOR

The striking combination of wood framing, shingles and glass creates the exterior of this classic cottage. The foyer opens to the main-level layout. To the left of the foyer is a study with a warming hearth and vaulted ceiling; to the right is a formal dining room. A great room with an attached breakfast area sits to the rear near the kitchen. A guest room is nestled in the rear of the plan for privacy. The master suite provides an expansive tray ceiling, a glass sitting area and easy passage to the outside deck. Upstairs, two bedrooms are accompanied by a loft for a quiet getaway.

plan# HPT930156

- Style: Traditional
- First Floor: 2,070 sq. ft.
- Second Floor: 790 sq. ft.
- Total: 2,860 sq. ft.
- Bedrooms: 4
- Bathrooms: 3½
- Width: 58'-4"
- Depth: 54'-10"
- Foundation: Walkout Basement

SEARCH ONLINE @ EPLANS.COM

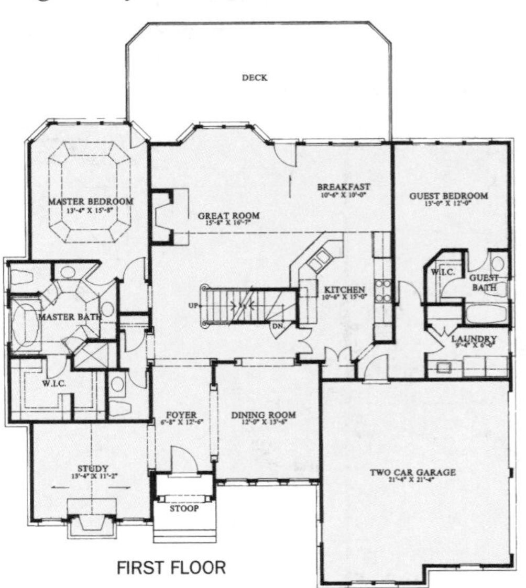

FIRST FLOOR

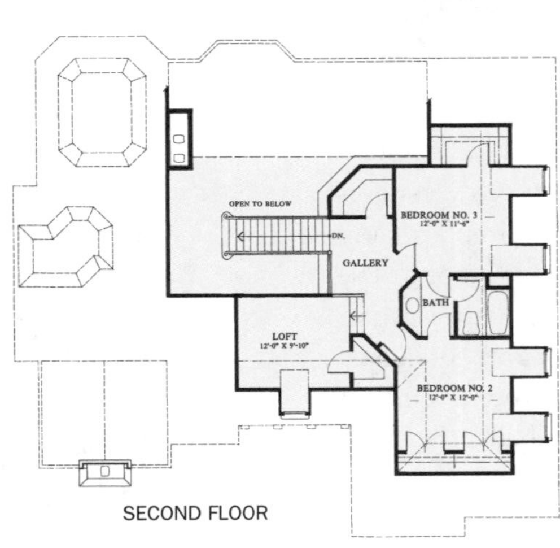

SECOND FLOOR

Cost to build? See page 436 to order complete cost estimate to build this house in your area!

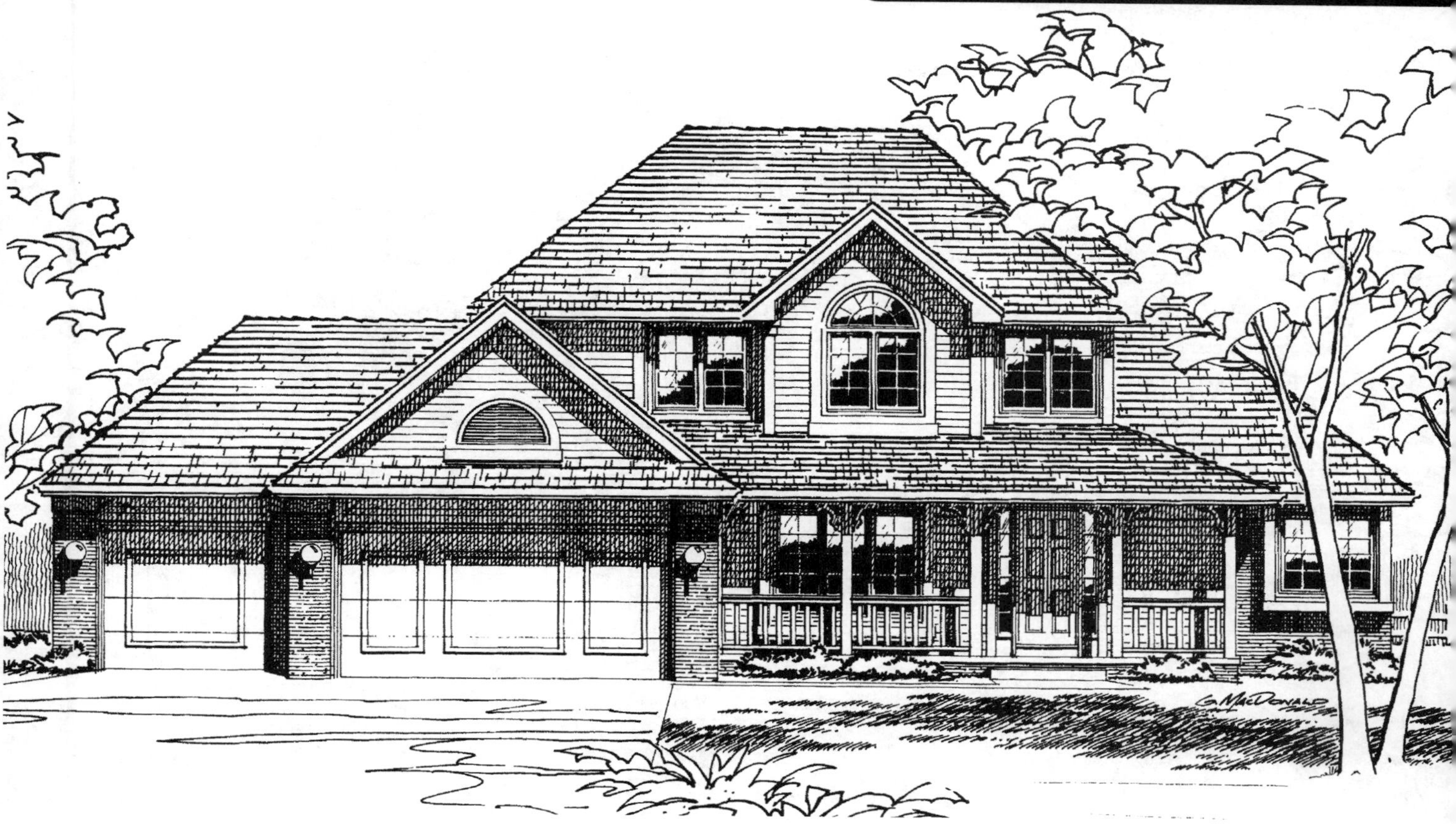

plan# HPT930157

- Style: Farmhouse
- First Floor: 1,505 sq. ft.
- Second Floor: 610 sq. ft.
- Total: 2,115 sq. ft.
- Bedrooms: 4
- Bathrooms: 2½
- Width: 64'-0"
- Depth: 52'-0"

SEARCH ONLINE @ EPLANS.COM

Farmhouse style is updated and improved on this home by a high roofline and a central arched window. The formal dining room with hutch space is conveniently located near the island kitchen. A main-floor laundry room with a sink is discreetly located next to the bright breakfast area with a desk and pantry. Highlighting the spacious great room are a raised-hearth fireplace, a cathedral ceiling and trapezoid windows. Special features in the master suite include a large dressing area with a double vanity, skylight, step-up corner whirlpool tub and generous walk-in closet. Upstairs, the three secondary bedrooms are separated from the master bedroom and share a hall bath.

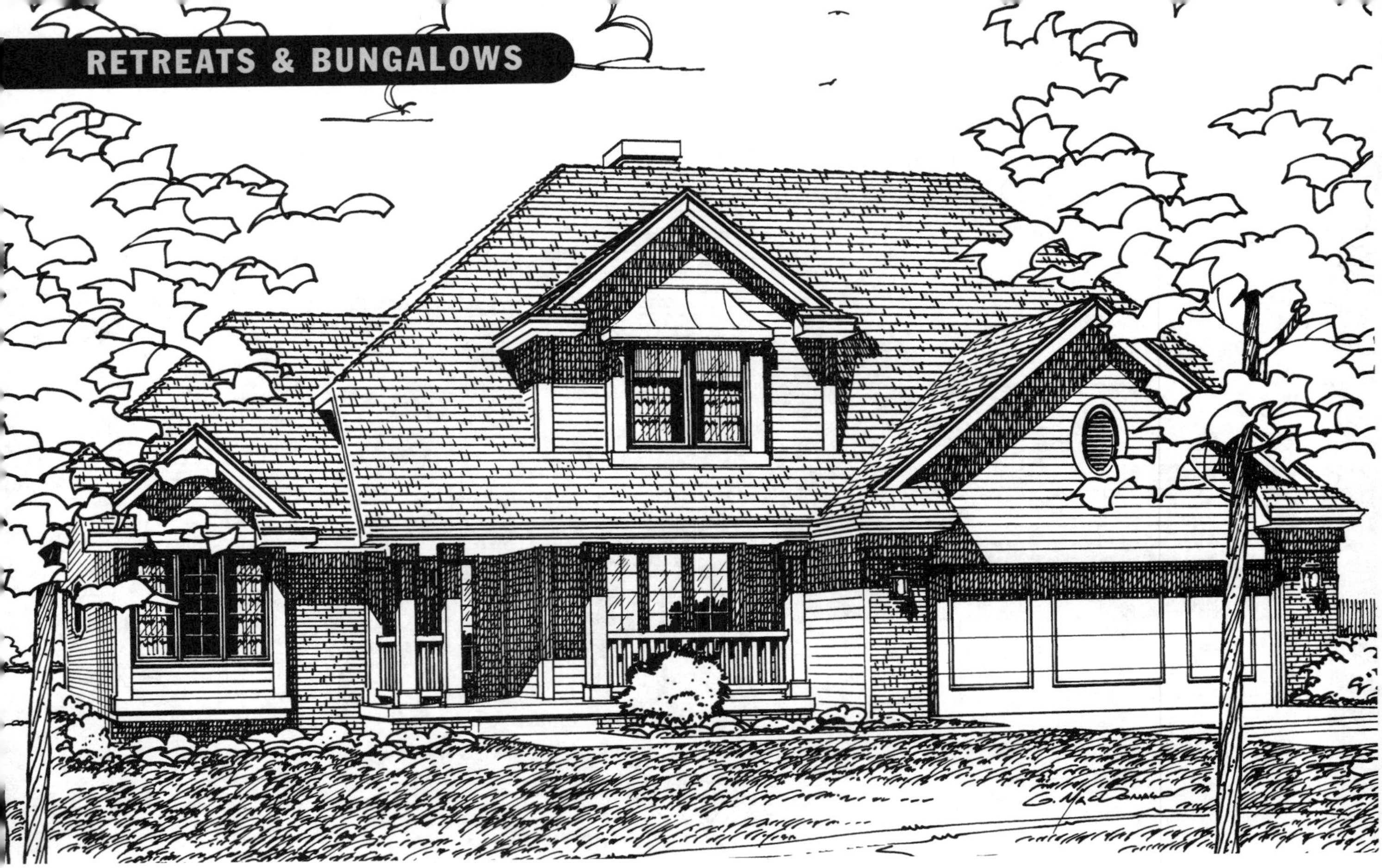

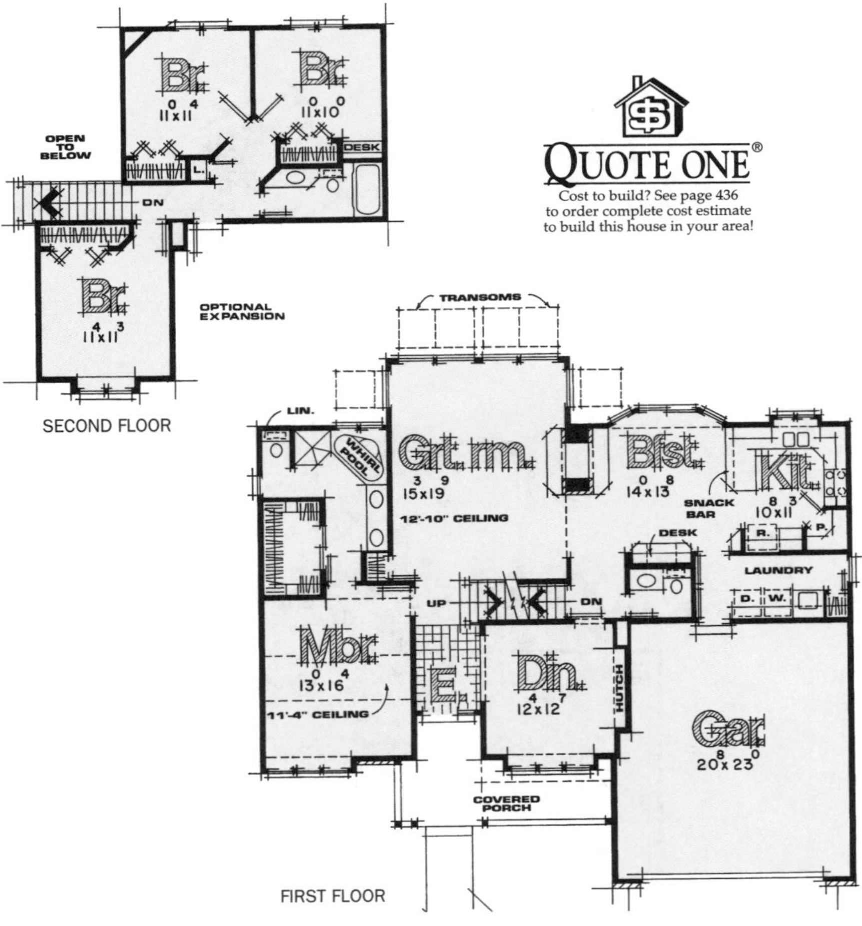

plan# HPT930158

- Style: Traditional
- First Floor: 1,421 sq. ft.
- Second Floor: 578 sq. ft.
- Total: 1,999 sq. ft.
- Bedrooms: 4
- Bathrooms: 2½
- Width: 52'-0"
- Depth: 47'-4"

SEARCH ONLINE @ EPLANS.COM

Growing families will love this unique plan. Start with the living areas—a spacious great room with high ceilings, windows overlooking the backyard, a see-through fireplace to the kitchen area and access to the rear deck. The dining room with hutch space accommodates formal occasions. The hearth kitchen features a well-planned work space and a bayed breakfast area. The master suite with a whirlpool tub and walk-in closet is found downstairs, while three family bedrooms are upstairs. A two-car garage and handy laundry room complete the plan.

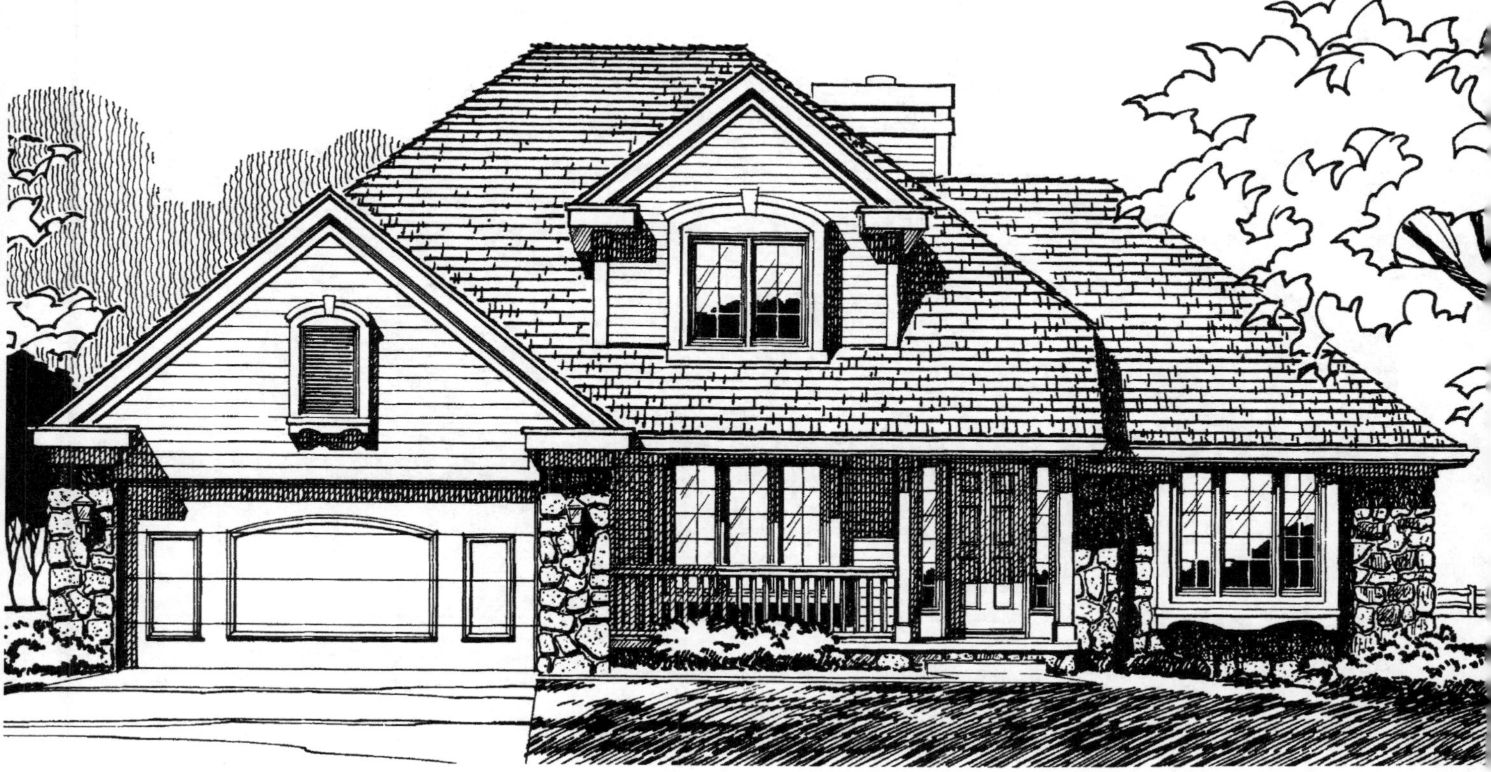

plan# HPT930159

- Style: Traditional
- First Floor: 1,297 sq. ft.
- Second Floor: 388 sq. ft.
- Total: 1,685 sq. ft.
- Bedrooms: 3
- Bathrooms: 2½
- Width: 52'-0"
- Depth: 45'-4"

SEARCH ONLINE @ EPLANS.COM

A lovely covered porch welcomes family and guests to this delightful 1 1/2-story home. The formal dining room with boxed windows and the great room with fireplace are visible from the entry. A powder room for guests is located just beyond the dining room. An open kitchen/dinette features a pantry, planning desk and a snack-bar counter. The elegant master suite is appointed with a formal ceiling and a window seat. A skylight above the whirlpool tub, a decorator plant shelf and double sinks dress up the master bath. Two family bedrooms on the second floor share a centrally located bath.

SECOND FLOOR

QUOTE ONE®

Cost to build? See page 436 to order complete cost estimate to build this house in your area!

FIRST FLOOR

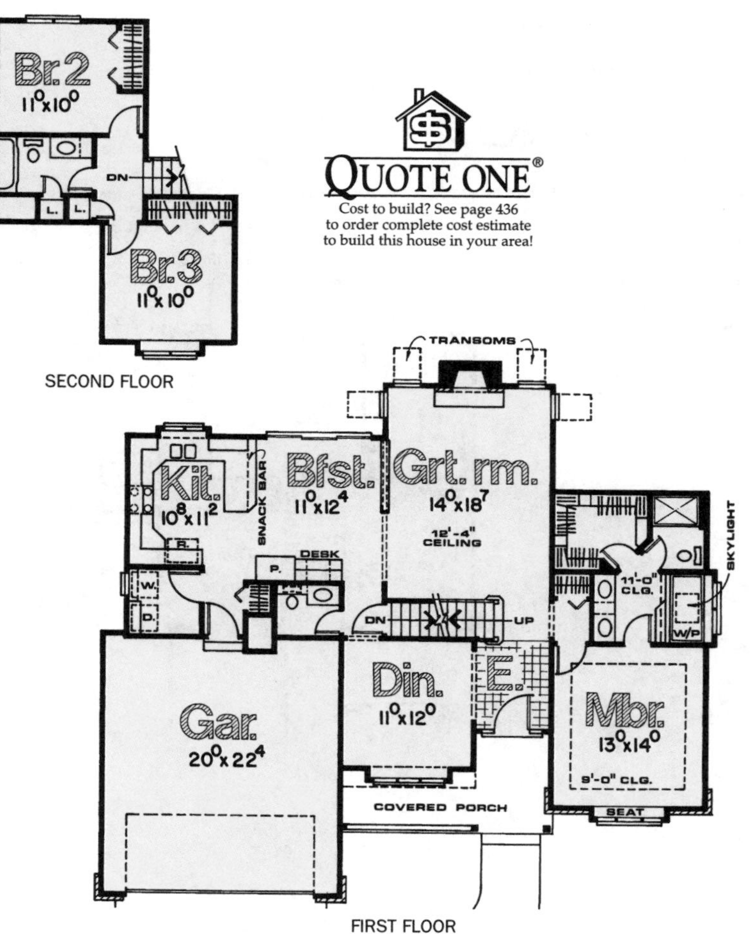

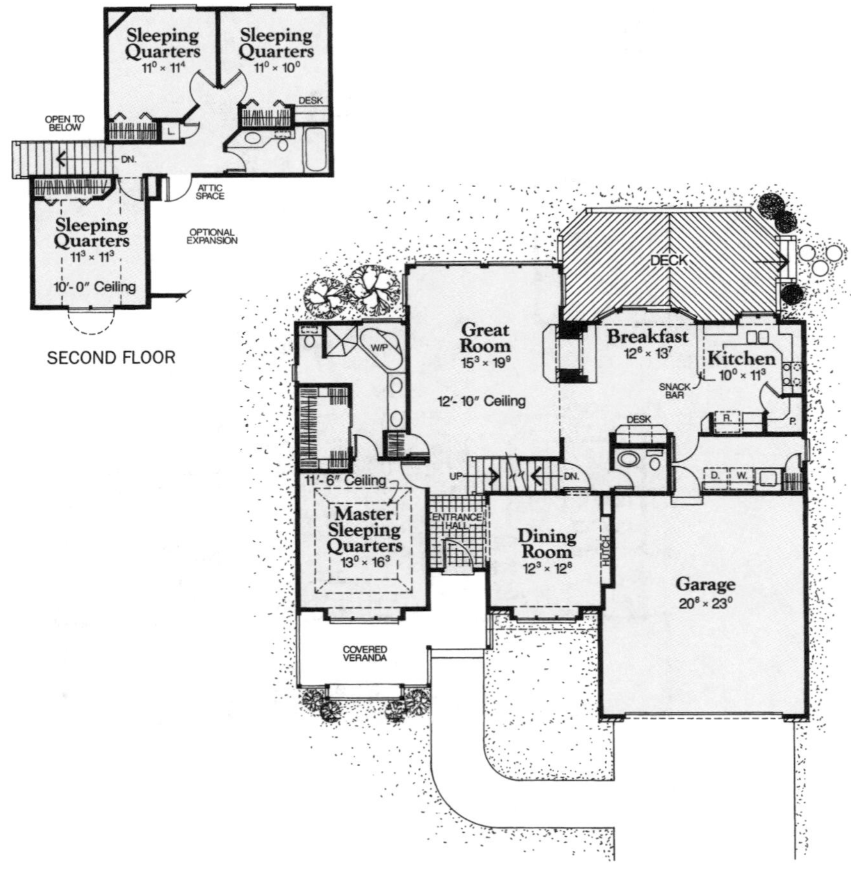

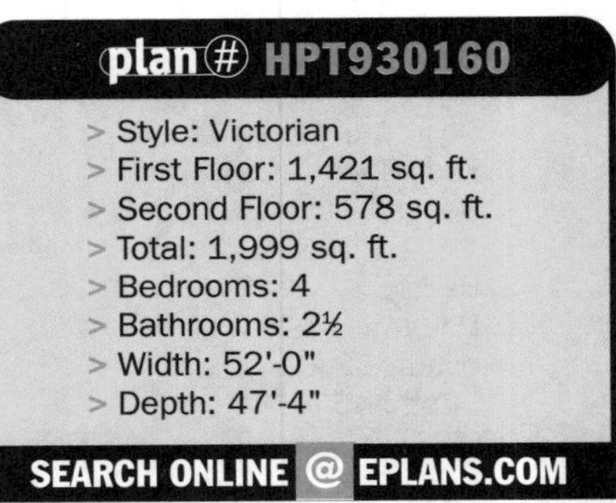
plan# HPT930160

- Style: Victorian
- First Floor: 1,421 sq. ft.
- Second Floor: 578 sq. ft.
- Total: 1,999 sq. ft.
- Bedrooms: 4
- Bathrooms: 2½
- Width: 52'-0"
- Depth: 47'-4"

SEARCH ONLINE @ EPLANS.COM

Victorian details and a covered veranda lend a peaceful flavor to the elevation of this popular home. A volume entry hall views the formal dining room and luxurious great room. Imagine the comfort of relaxing in the great room, which features a volume ceiling and abundant windows. The kitchen and breakfast area includes a through-fireplace, snack bar, walk-in pantry and wrapping counters. The secluded master suite features a vaulted ceiling, luxurious dressing/bath area and corner whirlpool tub. Upstairs, the family sleeping quarters contain special amenities unique to each.

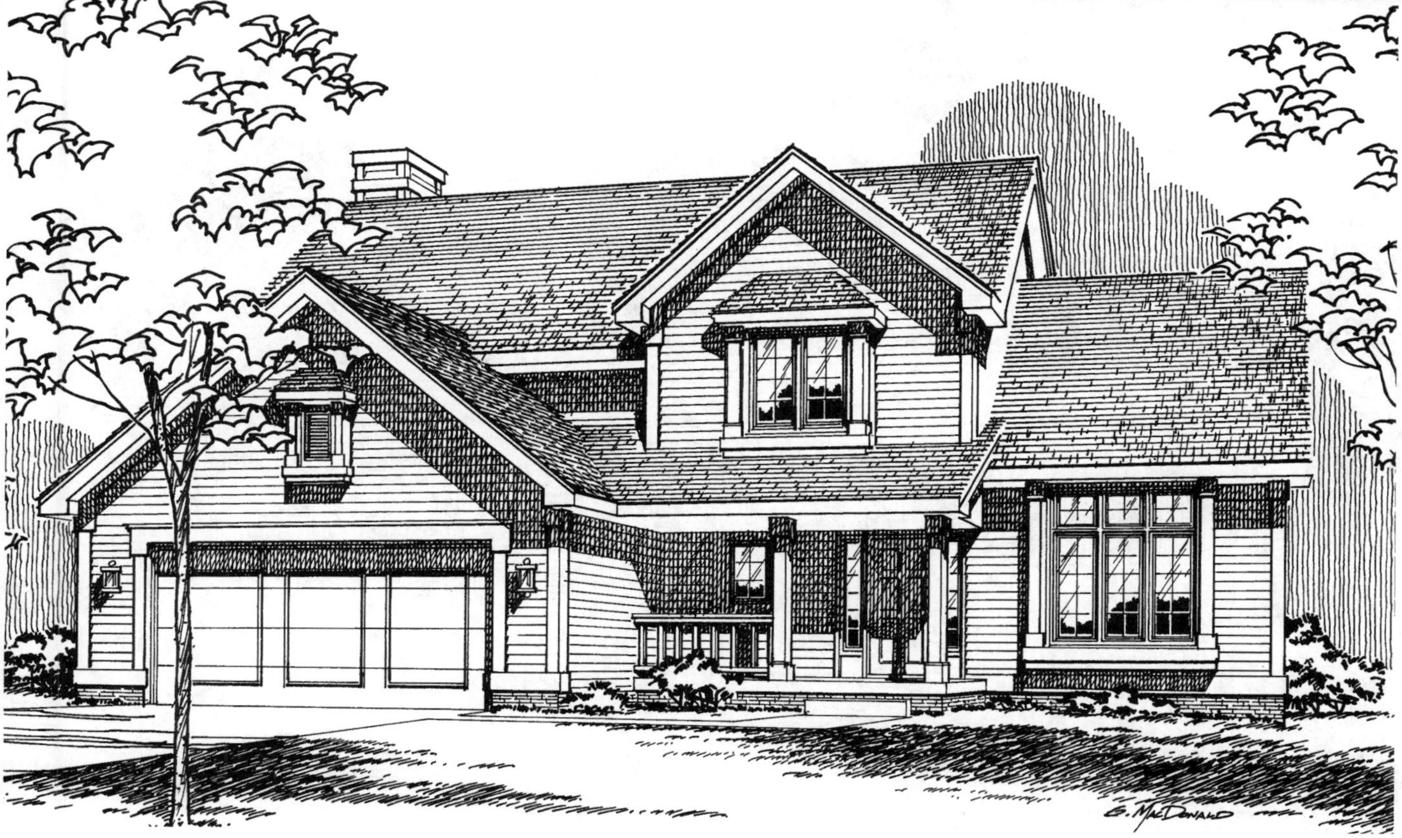

plan# HPT930161

- Style: Traditional
- First Floor: 1,042 sq. ft.
- Second Floor: 803 sq. ft.
- Total: 1,845 sq. ft.
- Bedrooms: 3
- Bathrooms: 2½
- Width: 48'-0"
- Depth: 40'-0"

SEARCH ONLINE @ EPLANS.COM

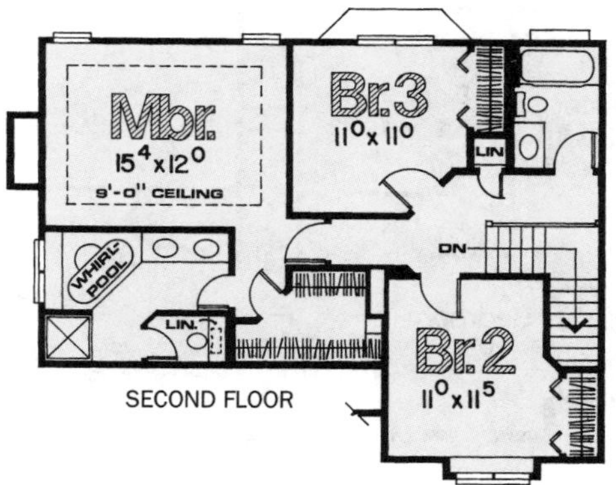

This classic two-story home is perfect for a variety of lifestyles. To the right of the entry is a formal living room with a ten-foot ceiling. Nearby, the formal dining room enjoys a bright window. Serving the dining room and bright bayed dinette, the kitchen features a pantry, Lazy Susan and window sink. Off the breakfast area, step down into the family room with a handsome fireplace and a wall of windows. Upstairs, two secondary bedrooms share a hall bath. The private master bedroom contains a boxed ceiling, walk-in closet and a pampering dressing area with a double vanity and whirlpool tub.

SECOND FLOOR

FIRST FLOOR

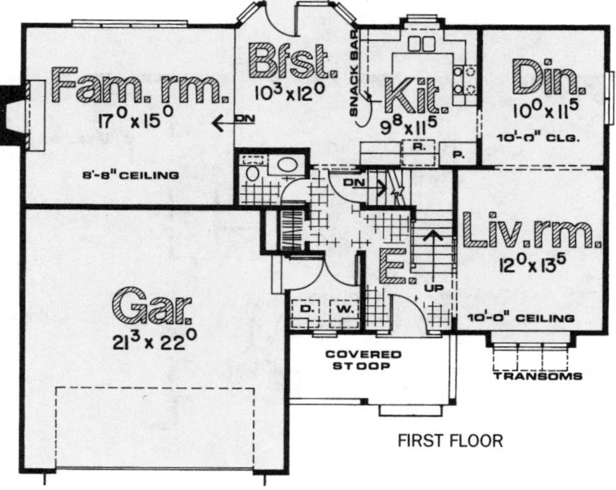

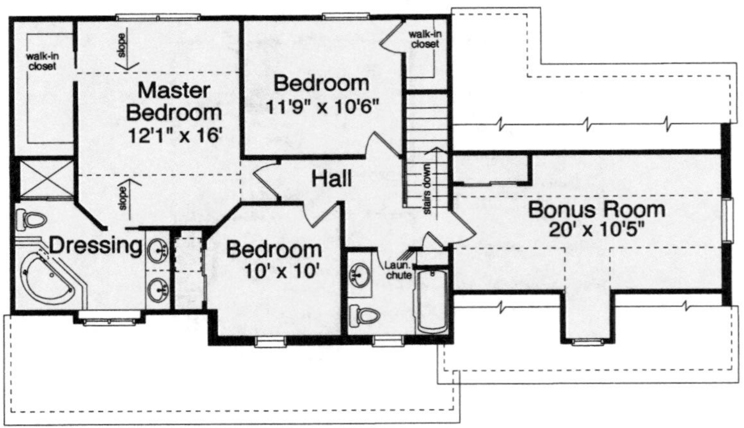

SECOND FLOOR

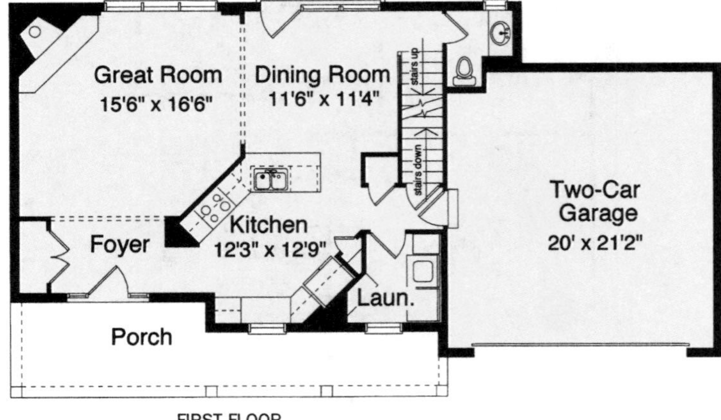

FIRST FLOOR

plan# HPT930162

- Style: Traditional
- First Floor: 798 sq. ft.
- Second Floor: 777 sq. ft.
- Total: 1,575 sq. ft.
- Bonus Space: 242 sq. ft.
- Bedrooms: 3
- Bathrooms: 2½
- Width: 53'-6"
- Depth: 27'-4"
- Foundation: Basement

SEARCH ONLINE @ EPLANS.COM

A covered front porch offers a warm and welcoming appearance to this charming two-story home. An open floor plan offers step-saving convenience, while a corner fireplace, angles and a high percentage of windows across the rear wall create a stylish setting for a relaxing lifestyle. The kitchen serves the dining room with ease. The second-floor master bedroom offers the luxury of a whirlpool tub, separate shower, double-bowl vanity and large walk-in closet. A bonus room above the garage makes this home expandable to four bedrooms or a game room or study.

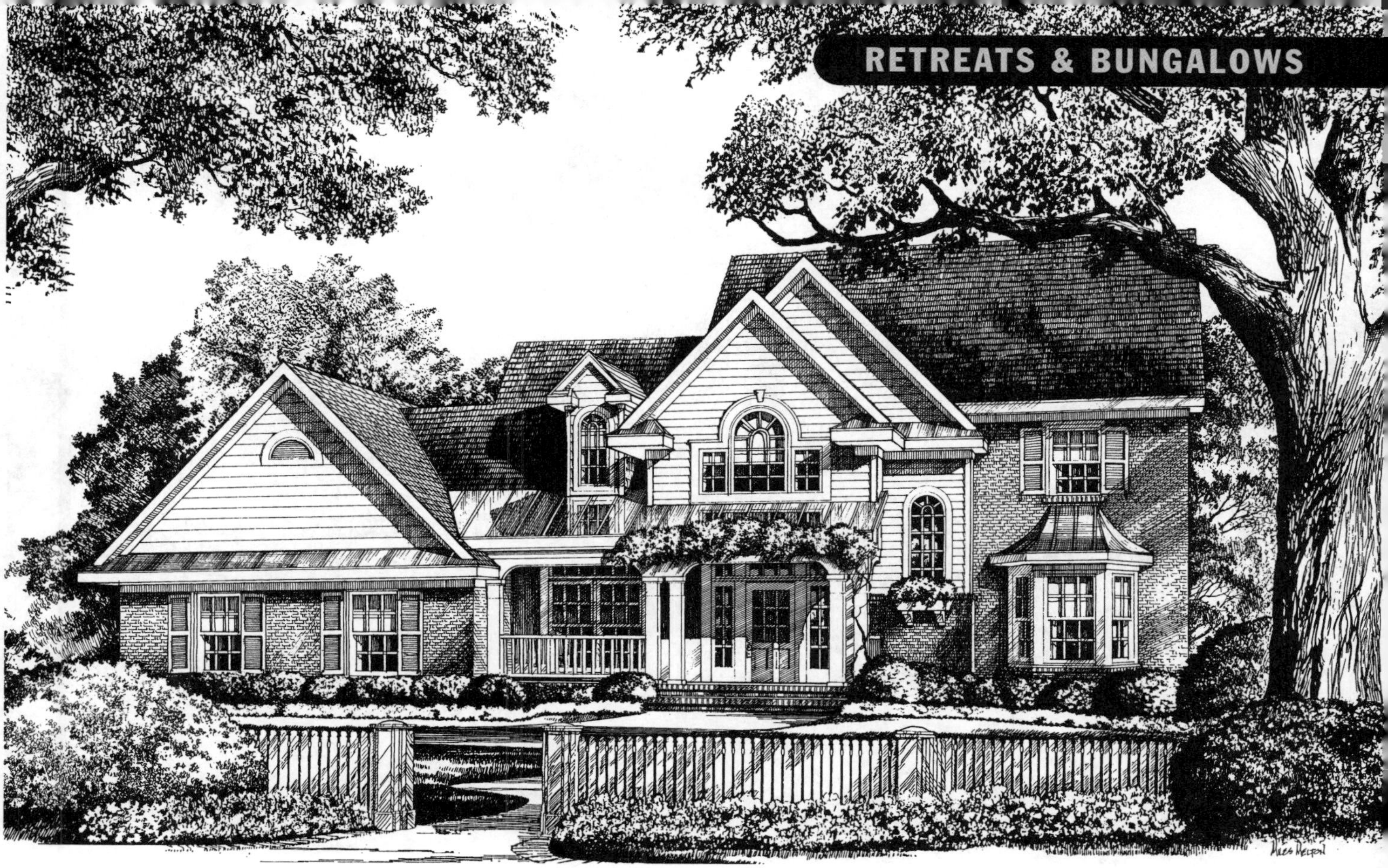

plan# HPT930163

- Style: Traditional
- First Floor: 2,028 sq. ft.
- Second Floor: 558 sq. ft.
- Total: 2,586 sq. ft.
- Bonus Space: 272 sq. ft.
- Bedrooms: 4
- Bathrooms: 3
- Width: 64'-10"
- Depth: 61'-0"
- Foundation: Basement

SEARCH ONLINE @ EPLANS.COM

Double columns and an arch-top clerestory window create an inviting entry to this fresh interpretation of traditional style. Decorative columns and arches open to the formal dining room and to the octagonal great room, which has a ten-foot tray ceiling. The U-shaped kitchen looks over an angled counter to a breakfast bay that brings in the outdoors and shares a through-fireplace with the great room. A sitting area and a lavish bath set off the secluded master suite. A nearby secondary bedroom with its own bath could be used as a guest suite, while upstairs two family bedrooms share a full bath and a hall that leads to an expandable area.

SECOND FLOOR

FIRST FLOOR

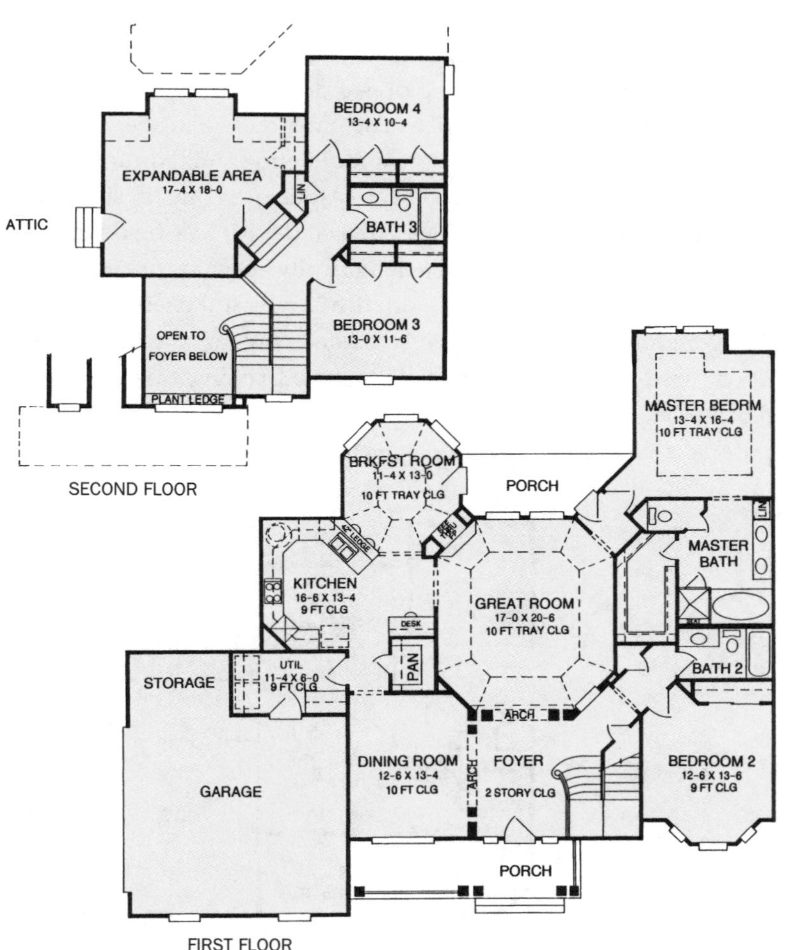

A covered front porch, angled walls, dormers and a brick facade create a rich, solid look to this exciting one-and-a-half-story home. Angles continue to be a delightful design element as you enter the foyer. Separated by columns and varied ceiling treatments, the great room and formal dining room create a functional gathering area that serves the casual everyday lifestyle equally as well as your special-occasion festivities. An island with seating defines the food preparation area of the kitchen and a delightfully spacious breakfast area with sloped ceiling and multiple windows offers a bright and cheery place to start the day. A covered rear porch offers a relaxed getaway for enjoying the outdoors. A first floor master bedroom suite with a raised ceiling treatment and deluxe bath dazzle the homeowner. Two additional bedrooms on the second floor, a computer alcove and rich wooden stair rails complete this exciting home.

plan# HPT930164

- Style: Retreat
- First Floor: 1,925 sq. ft.
- Second Floor: 524 sq. ft.
- Total: 2,449 sq. ft.
- Bedrooms: 3
- Bathrooms: 2½
- Width: 56'-4"
- Depth: 53'-4"
- Foundation: Basement

SEARCH ONLINE @ EPLANS.COM

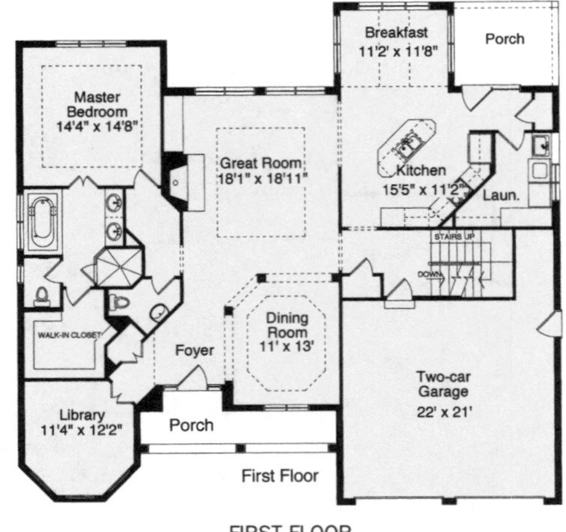

FIRST FLOOR

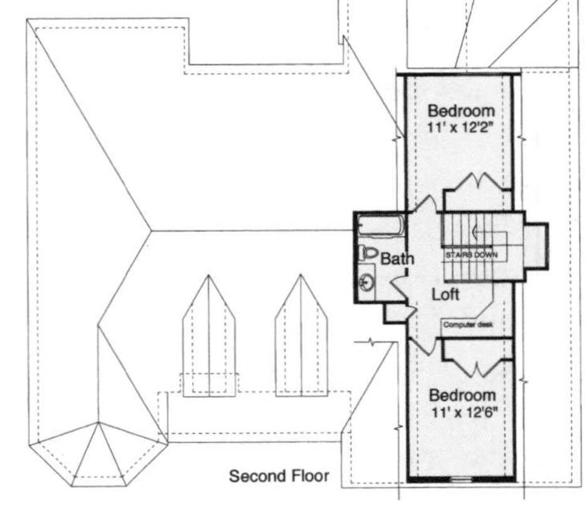

SECOND FLOOR

plan# HPT930165

- Style: Retreat
- First Floor: 1,432 sq. ft.
- Second Floor: 464 sq. ft.
- Total: 1,896 sq. ft.
- Bonus Space: 153 sq. ft.
- Bedrooms: 3
- Bathrooms: 2½
- Width: 49'-6"
- Depth: 53'-6"
- Foundation: Basement

SEARCH ONLINE @ EPLANS.COM

A combination of exterior materials is artistically showcased on this exciting home, offering impressive curb appeal. Amenities such as a covered porch, sloped ceilings, angles, skylights, a snack bar in the spacious kitchen, and a deluxe bath in the master suite offer stylish luxury to this moderate-sized home. The bonus room above the garage offers the option of creating a second-story game room, home office or fourth bedroom.

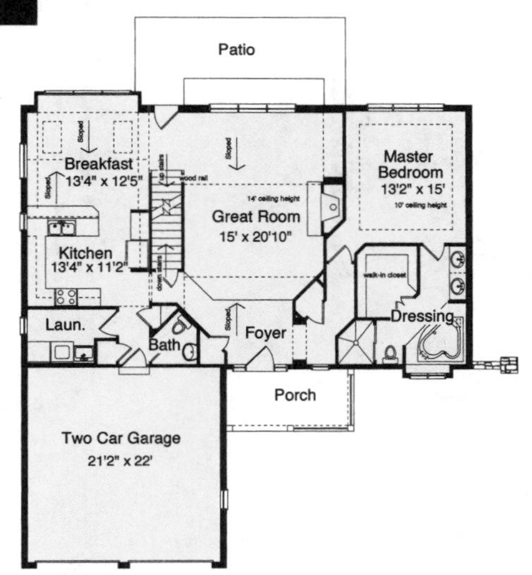

FIRST FLOOR

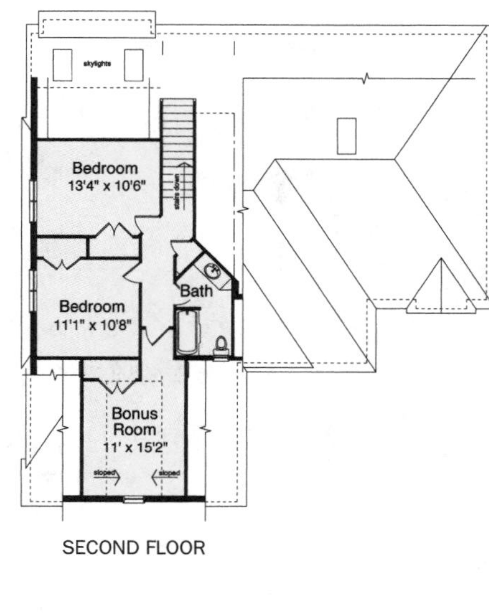

SECOND FLOOR

This fine cottage design offers two levels of livability. The front porch invites you inside to a foyer introducing a graceful staircase to the second floor. The island kitchen easily serves the breakfast and dining rooms. The two-story great room is warmed by a fireplace. The master bedroom offers a whirlpool bath with a walk-in closet. A laundry room and two-car garage complete the plan. Upstairs, two additional family bedrooms share a loft and hall bath with the bonus room—great for attic space, a home office or another bedroom.

plan# HPT930166

- Style: Retreat
- First Floor: 1,633 sq. ft.
- Second Floor: 705 sq. ft.
- Total: 2,338 sq. ft.
- Bonus Space: 203 sq. ft.
- Bedrooms: 3
- Bathrooms: 2½
- Width: 58'-6"
- Depth: 49'-0"
- Foundation: Basement

SEARCH ONLINE @ EPLANS.COM

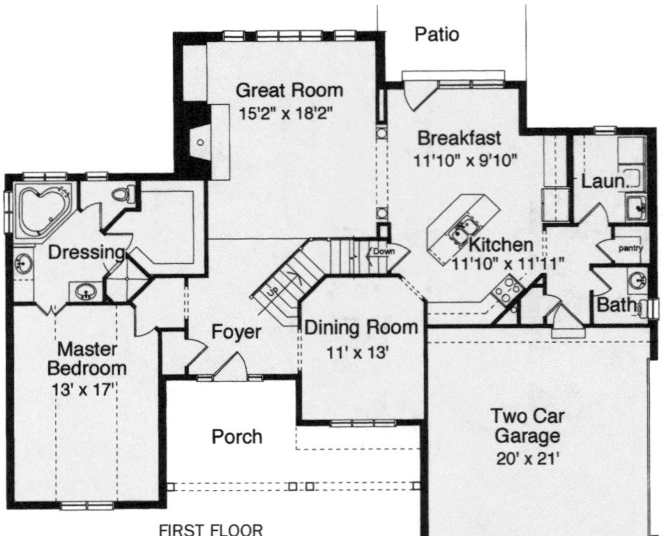

Patio
Great Room 15'2" x 18'2"
Breakfast 11'10" x 9'10"
Laun.
Dressing
Kitchen 11'10" x 11'11"
Down
pantry
Up
Bath
Master Bedroom 13' x 17'
Foyer
Dining Room 11' x 13'
Two Car Garage 20' x 21'
Porch

FIRST FLOOR

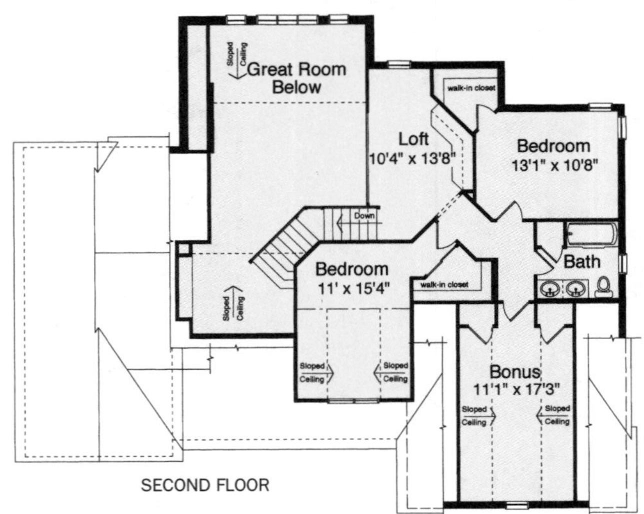

SECOND FLOOR

plan# HPT930167

- Style: Retreat
- First Floor: 1,263 sq. ft.
- Second Floor: 434 sq. ft.
- Total: 1,697 sq. ft.
- Bedrooms: 3
- Bathrooms: 2½
- Width: 55'-2"
- Depth: 57'-3"
- Foundation: Basement

SEARCH ONLINE @ 

A covered porch and siding facade add color and dimension to this delightful one-and-a-half-story home. A convenient floor plan offers a favorable first impression. Turned stairs with rich wood finishes, a grand opening to the great room, fireplace wall as a focal point and the introduction of natural light with the multiple windows combine to add spectacular design elements. A secondary hall offers convenient access to the kitchen and master suite. The large breakfast area and open kitchen, with island, create a lively family work and gathering area. A first floor master bedroom with raised ceiling, super bath and walk-in closet create a luxurious retreat. The second floor balcony offers a breathtaking view to the open foyer and leads to two additional bedrooms, bath and storage space.

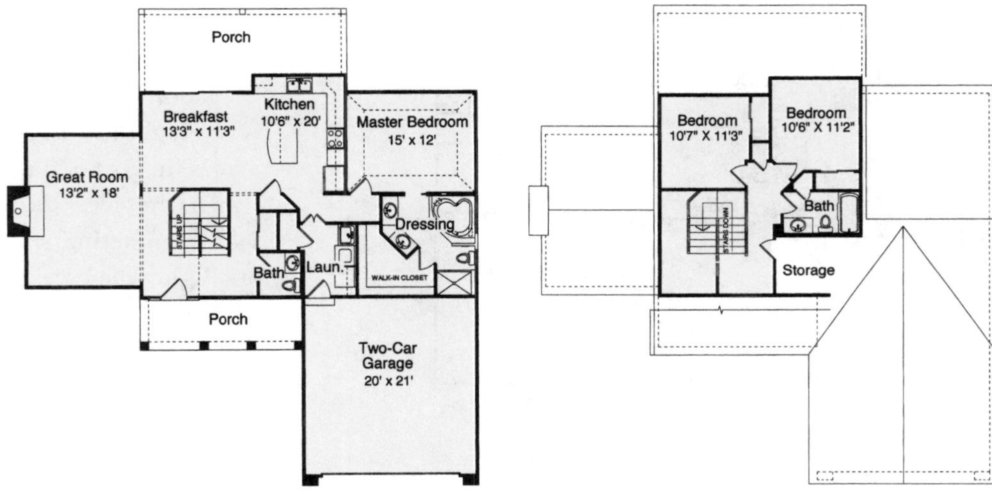

plan# HPT930168

- Style: Retreat
- First Floor: 2,141 sq. ft.
- Second Floor: 923 sq. ft.
- Total: 3,064 sq. ft.
- Bedrooms: 4
- Bathrooms: 2½
- Width: 65'-0"
- Depth: 56'-6"
- Foundation: Basement

SEARCH ONLINE @ EPLANS.COM

A stone-and-siding exterior, arched windows and multiple gables create an exquisite appearance for this transitional home. Dual French doors with high arched-topped windows across the rear of the great room and a warm fireplace decorate this captivating gathering space with warmth and light. The breakfast room delivers a panoramic view in three directions and creates a sun-room effect for the family eating area.

plan# HPT930169

- Style: Traditional
- First Floor: 1,112 sq. ft.
- Second Floor: 882 sq. ft.
- Total: 1,994 sq. ft.
- Bedrooms: 3
- Bathrooms: 2½
- Width: 40'-0"
- Depth: 43'-0"
- Foundation: Crawlspace

SEARCH ONLINE @ EPLANS.COM

In just under 2,000 square feet, this traditional family home shines with Palladian windows and a brilliant floor plan. The entry leads to a vaulted living room, bathed in light, or ahead, to the family room, warmed by a corner fireplace. The kitchen features an island cooktop with a serving bar and easy access to the bayed breakfast nook and the formal dining room. A private den makes a great home office or gym. Located on the upper level, two secondary bedrooms (one vaulted) share a full bath. The master suite revels in a vaulted bedroom, private spa bath and large walk-in closet.

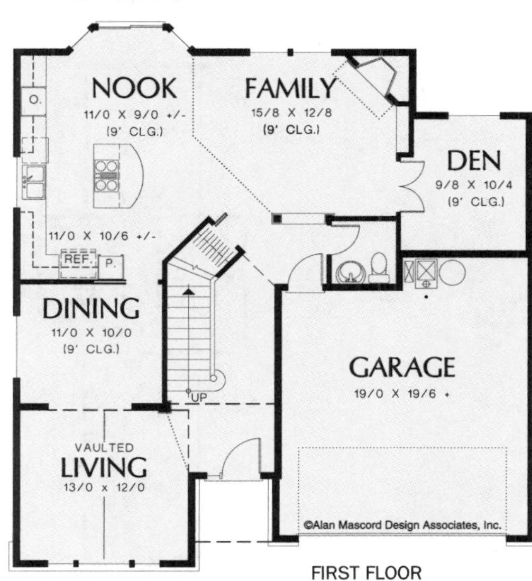

FIRST FLOOR

SECOND FLOOR

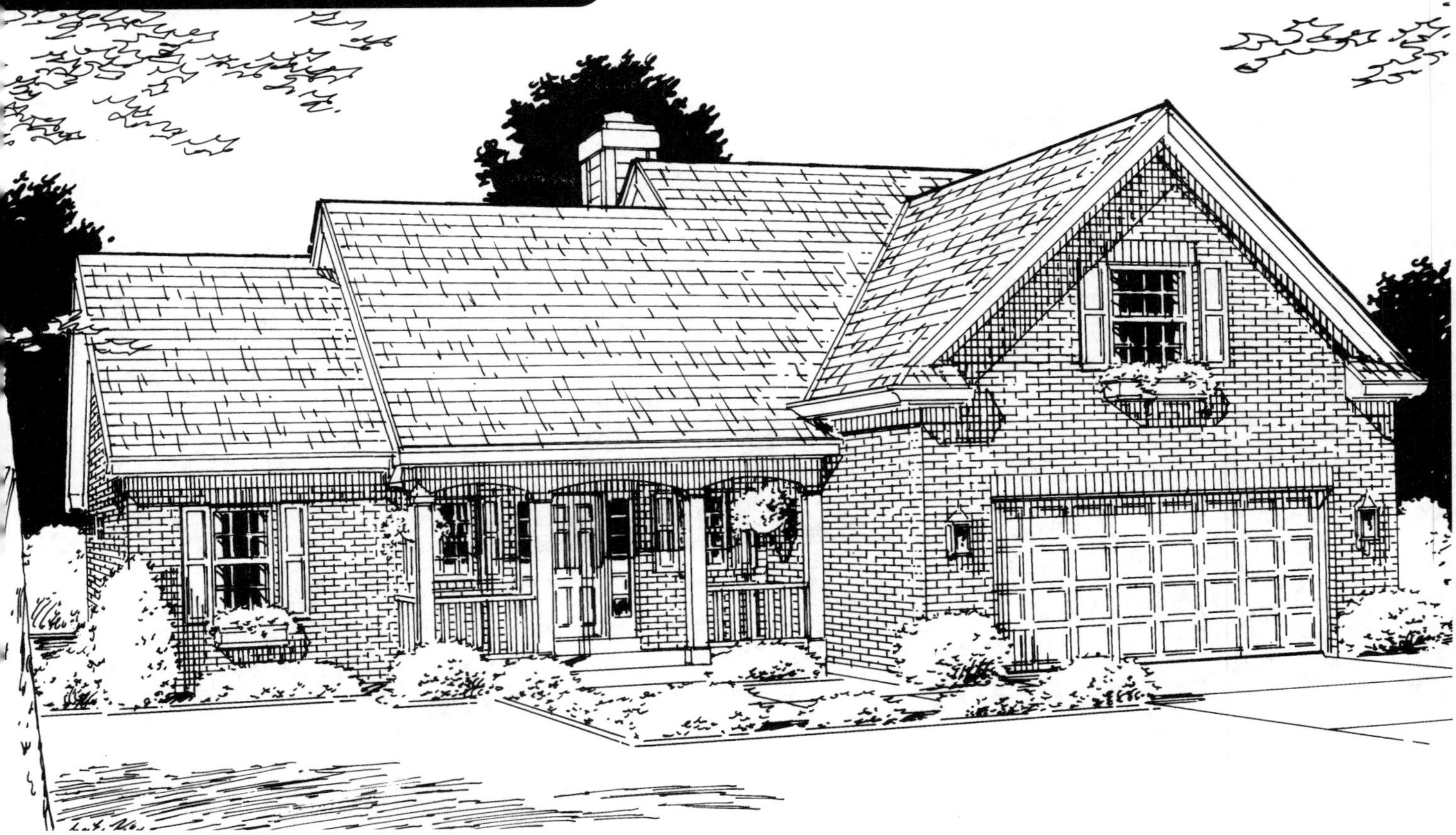

An open and casual floor plan combined with a first-floor master bedroom offers a relaxed lifestyle and stylish amenities for this exciting home. A sloped ceiling that expands through the great room and dining area adds volume. The warmth of the fireplace radiates throughout the living space, and a view from the kitchen allows this room to share in the cozy atmosphere. A first-floor master suite, secluded for privacy, is complemented by a whirlpool tub, double-bowl vanity, linen closet, compartmented shower and commode, and large walk-in closet. Split stairs lead to a second floor, which offers additional bedrooms and a computer loft.

plan# HPT930170

- Style: Cape Cod
- First Floor: 1,399 sq. ft.
- Second Floor: 671 sq. ft.
- Total: 2,070 sq. ft.
- Bedrooms: 3
- Bathrooms: 2½
- Width: 49'-8"
- Depth: 52'-0"
- Foundation: Walkout Basement

SEARCH ONLINE @ EPLANS.COM

FIRST FLOOR

SECOND FLOOR

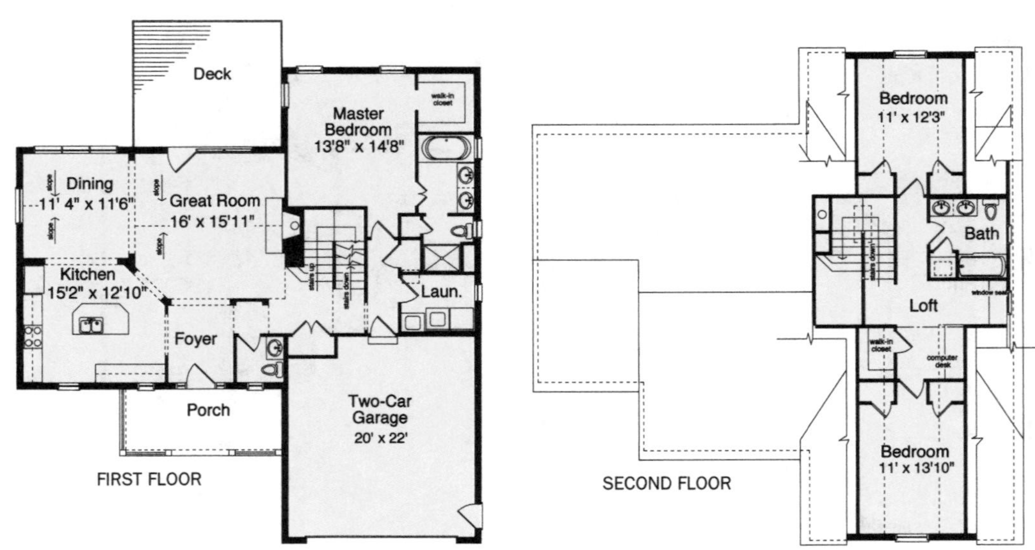

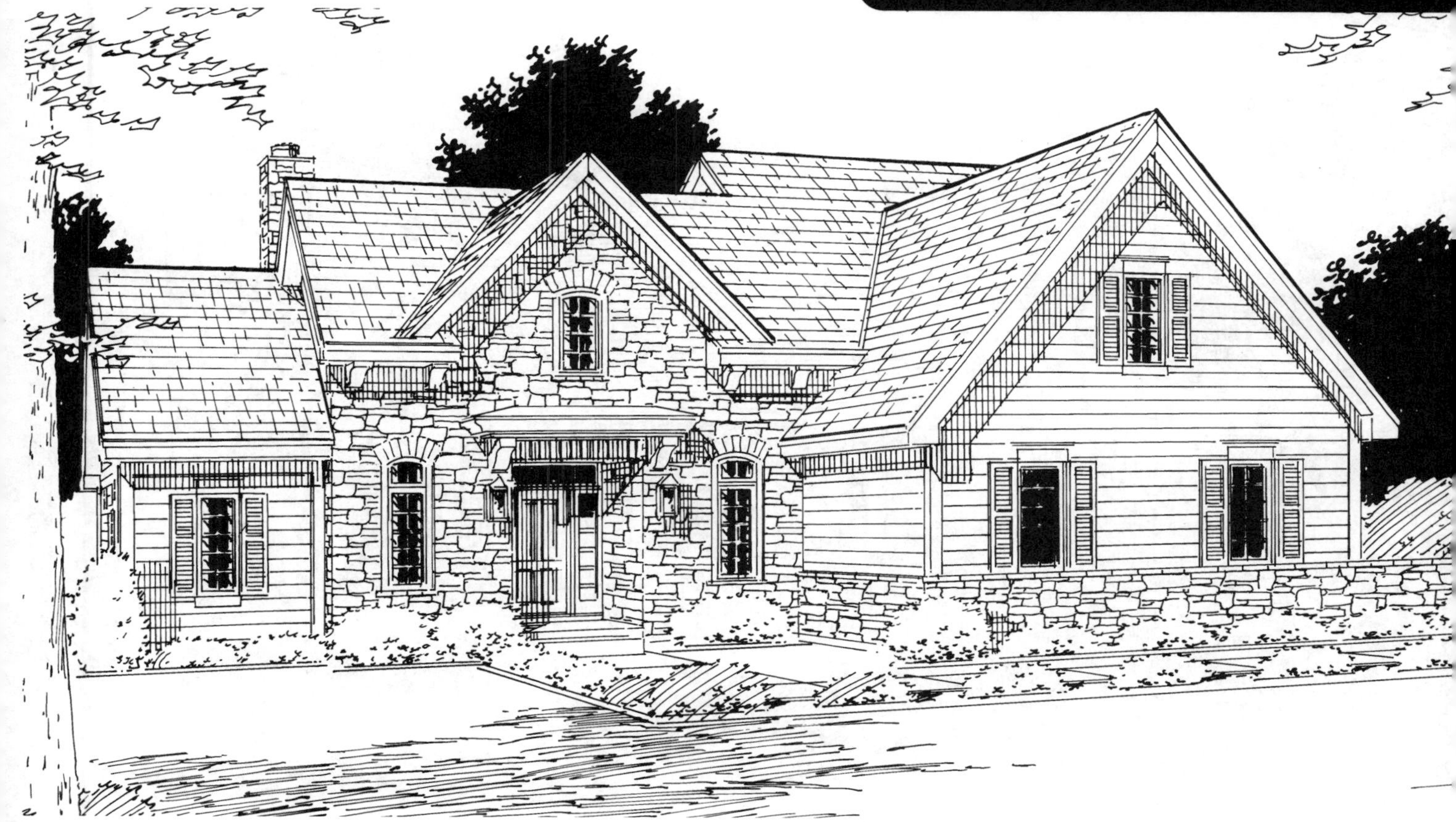

plan# HPT930171

- Style: Retreat
- First Floor: 1,250 sq. ft.
- Second Floor: 411 sq. ft.
- Total: 1,661 sq. ft.
- Bonus Space: 207 sq. ft.
- Bedrooms: 3
- Bathrooms: 2½
- Width: 60'-0"
- Depth: 41'-6"
- Foundation: Basement

SEARCH ONLINE @ EPLANS.COM

This is a transitional vacation home—perfect for a lakefront. A stone and siding exterior provides texture and color to this exciting two-story home. Decorating the great room is a sloped ceiling, boxed window, fireplace and alcove that accommodates an entertainment center. The adjacent dining area visually expands the great room and creates a stylish transition to a delightful covered rear porch. Positioned to offer order in the home, the kitchen features a corner sink and an open abundance of counter space and cabinets. Offering luxury and convenience to the homeowner, the master bedroom suite provides a sloped ceiling, whirlpool tub, dual vanities and a decorative plant shelf. An open rail frames the stairs leading to two additional bedrooms and an added bonus room.

FIRST FLOOR

SECOND FLOOR

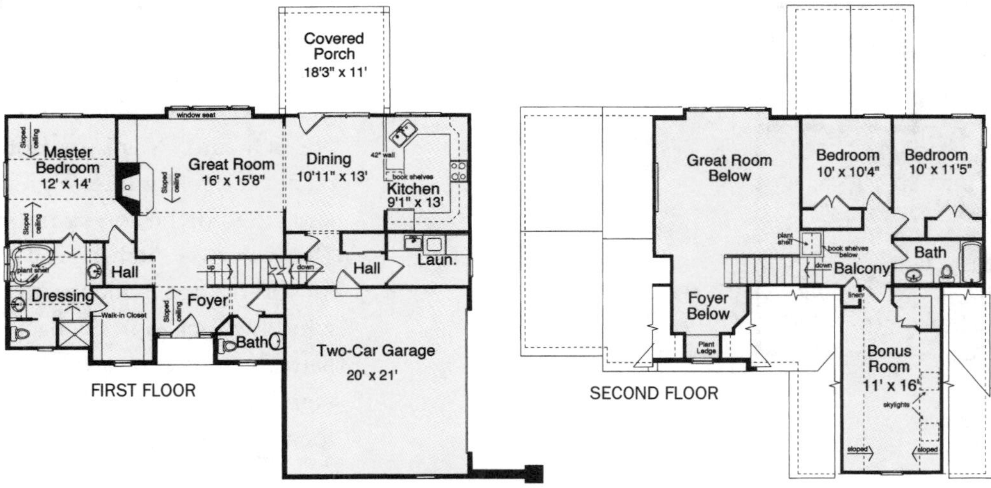

plan# HPT930172

- Style: Traditional
- First Floor: 707 sq. ft.
- Second Floor: 148 sq. ft.
- Total: 855 sq. ft.
- Bedrooms: 1
- Bathrooms: 1
- Width: 26'-0"
- Depth: 50'-2"
- Foundation: Basement, Crawlspace, Slab

SEARCH ONLINE @ EPLANS.COM

In the wilderness of everyday life, wouldn't it be nice to come home to this cabin retreat? Perfect for retirees or as a mountain getaway, this one-bedroom, one-bath home is one of a kind. Nestle in- front of the stone fireplace on a cold winter night, or enjoy the front and side porches on starry summer evenings. The L-shaped kitchen—with island—opens to the dining area, which is framed by a Palladian window. Tucked in the back, the bedroom and bath are quite comfortable. On the second level you will find a loft with overlooks to the great room and dining room below.

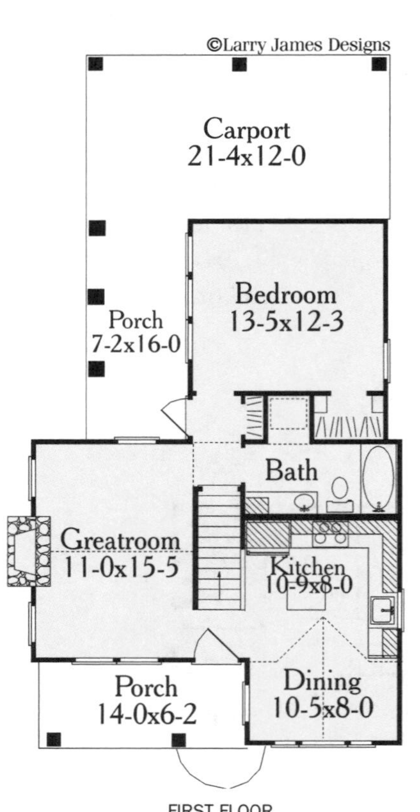

FIRST FLOOR

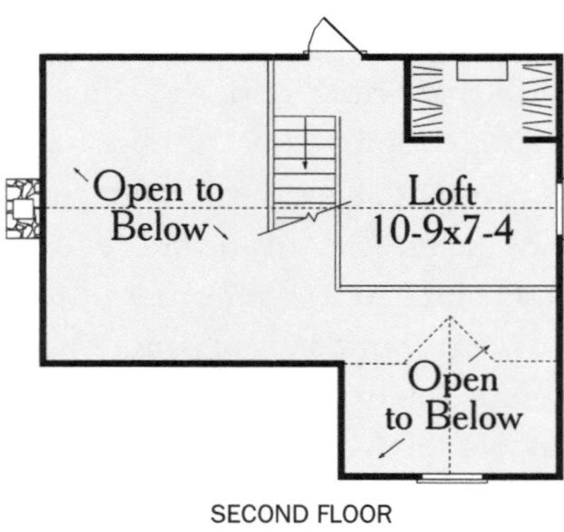

SECOND FLOOR

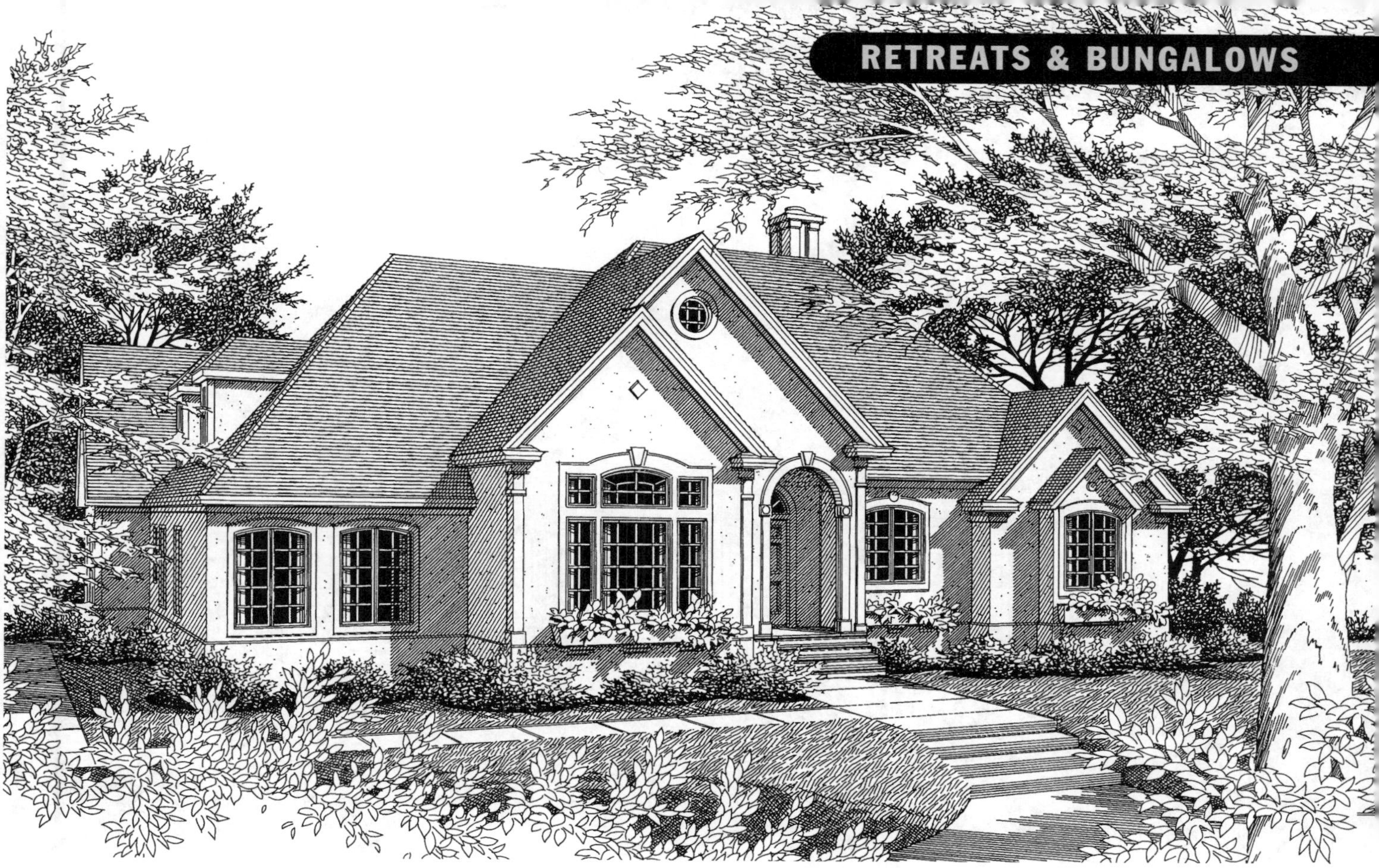

plan# HPT930173

- Style: European Cottage
- First Floor: 2,094 sq. ft.
- Second Floor: 264 sq. ft.
- Total: 2,358 sq. ft.
- Bonus Space: 498 sq. ft.
- Bedrooms: 3
- Bathrooms: 2½
- Width: 65'-6"
- Depth: 62'-7"
- Foundation: Basement, Crawlspace, Slab

SEARCH ONLINE @ EPLANS.COM

This stucco home with careful details and all the most-wanted amenities will delight at every turn. Open planning defines the dining room with a cathedral ceiling and a single column. The two-story great room has a cathedral ceiling and a brick extended-hearth fireplace. From here, expansive rear views continue to the sunny breakfast nook. An angled galley kitchen is made for gourmet meals. Two left-wing bedrooms share a full bath. In the right wing, the master suite revels in a cathedral bath and a bumped-out Roman tub. His and Hers closets are a wonderful convenience.

SECOND FLOOR

FIRST FLOOR

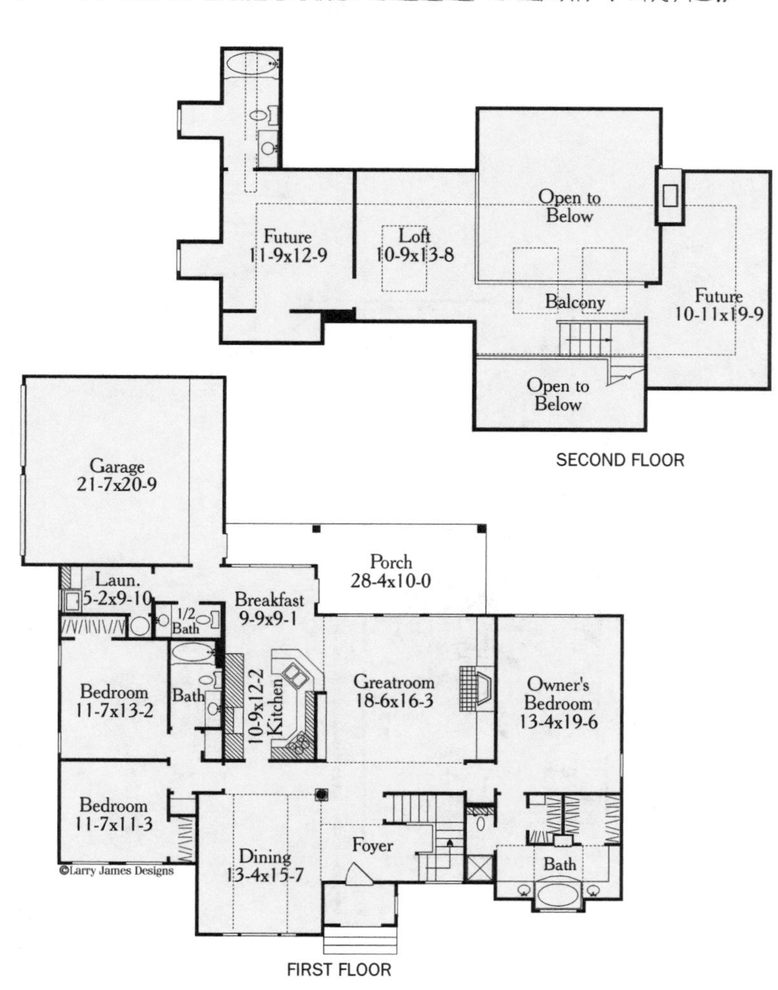

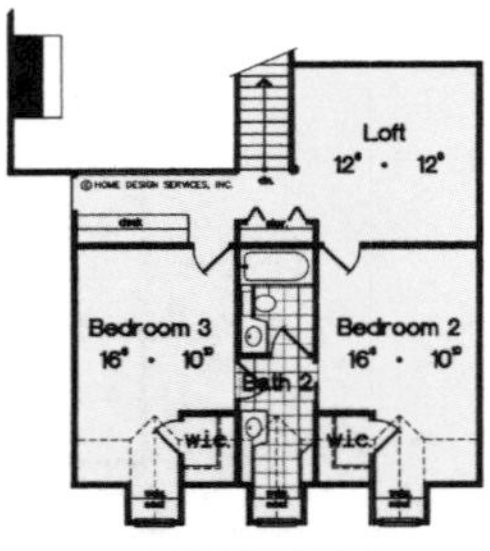

Loft
12' · 12'
Bedroom 3
16' · 10'
Bedroom 2
16' · 10'
Bath 2
w.i.c.
w.i.c.

SECOND FLOOR

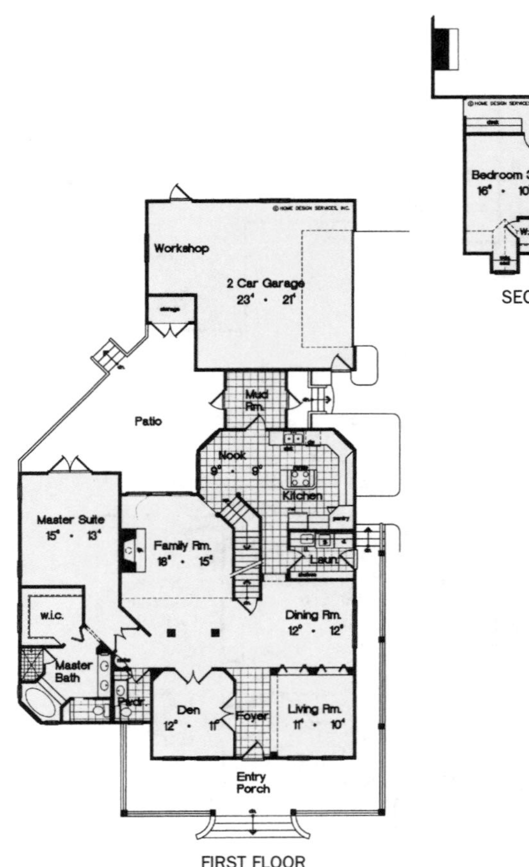

FIRST FLOOR

plan# HPT930174

- Style: Retreat
- First Floor: 1,907 sq. ft.
- Second Floor: 758 sq. ft.
- Total: 2,665 sq. ft.
- Bedrooms: 3
- Bathrooms: 2½
- Width: 50'-0"
- Depth: 86'-0"
- Foundation: Slab

SEARCH ONLINE @ EPLANS.COM

An inviting entry porch on this fine home impresses with a warm welcome. Upon entering the foyer, notice the formal living room to the right and a casual den area to the left. The open family room boasts a fireplace and overlooks the rear patio. An island cooktop kitchen is conveniently located between the dining room and the breakfast nook. A laundry room is available on the first floor, and a workshop area sits inside the two-car garage. Secluded on the first floor for privacy, the master suite provides a luxurious private bath, a spacious walk-in closet and private access to the rear patio. On the second floor, two additional family bedrooms, each with walk-in closets, share access to a bathroom. A spacious loft area completes the upper floor.

plan# HPT930175

- Style: European Cottage
- First Floor: 1,998 sq. ft.
- Second Floor: 1,898 sq. ft.
- Total: 3,896 sq. ft.
- Bedrooms: 4
- Bathrooms: 2½
- Width: 60'-0"
- Depth: 56'-4"
- Foundation: Crawlspace

SEARCH ONLINE @ EPLANS.COM

Elegant details on this four-bedroom home include a trio of dormers, an attractive bay window and graceful rooflines. Inside, the two-story foyer presents the formal living room, complete with a warming fireplace, a bay window and a vaulted ceiling. The formal dining room opens directly off this room, and offers easy access to the spacious island kitchen via a butler's pantry. The family room features a built-in media center and shares a fireplace with the cozy den. A wet bar is conveniently located between the family room, kitchen and dining room. Up the curved staircase, three family bedrooms share a hall bath with twin vanities. A large game room provides built-in storage and privacy for the children. The master suite is full of amenities, including a huge walk-in closet, separate tub and shower, twin vanities and a vaulted ceiling.

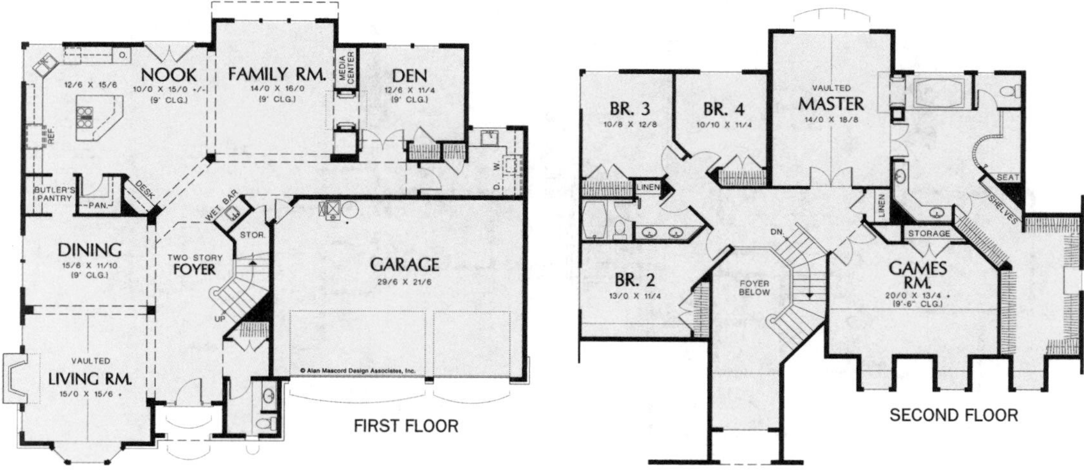

Horizontal siding, plentiful windows and a wraparound porch grace this comfortable home. The great room is aptly named, with a fireplace, built-in seating and access to the rear deck. Meal preparation is a breeze with a galley kitchen designed for efficiency. A screened porch is available for sipping lemonade on warm summer afternoons. The first floor contains two bedrooms and a unique bath to serve family and guests. The second floor offers a private getaway with a master suite that supplies panoramic views from its adjoining sitting area. A master bath with His and Hers walk-in closets and a private deck completes the second floor.

plan# HPT930176

- Style: Vacation
- First Floor: 1,341 sq. ft.
- Second Floor: 598 sq. ft.
- Total: 1,939 sq. ft.
- Bedrooms: 3
- Bathrooms: 2
- Width: 50'-3"
- Depth: 46'-3"
- Foundation: Crawlspace

SEARCH ONLINE @ EPLANS.COM

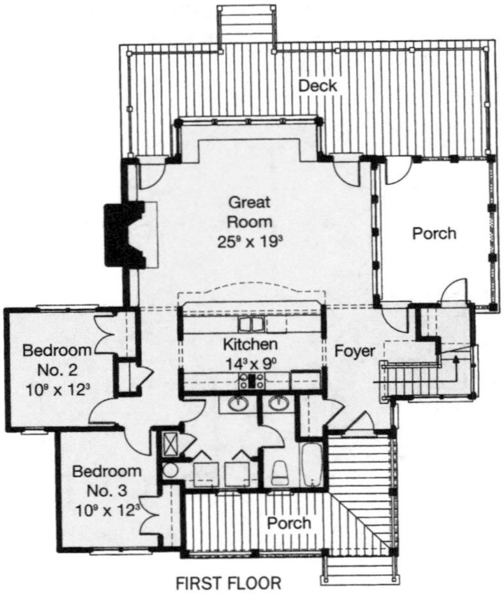

FIRST FLOOR

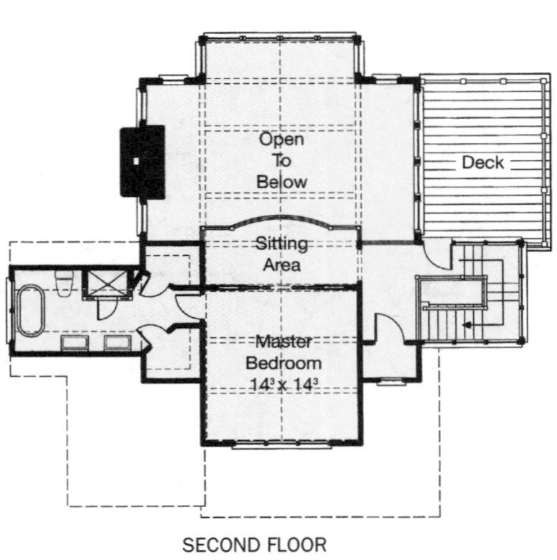

SECOND FLOOR

plan# HPT930177

- Style: Victorian
- First Floor: 2,041 sq. ft.
- Second Floor: 1,098 sq. ft.
- Total: 3,139 sq. ft.
- Bonus Space: 385 sq. ft.
- Bedrooms: 4
- Bathrooms: 3½
- Width: 76'-6"
- Depth: 62'-2"
- Foundation: Slab

SEARCH ONLINE @ EPLANS.COM

The turret and the circular covered porch of this Victorian home make a great impression. The foyer carries you past a library and dining room to the hearth-warmed family room. A spacious kitchen with an island acts as a passageway to the nook and dining area. The master bedroom is located on the first floor and offers its own French doors to the rear covered porch. The master bath is designed to cater to both His and Her needs with two walk-in closets, separate vanities, a garden tub and separate shower. On the second floor, an enormous loft gives each bedroom its own private space.

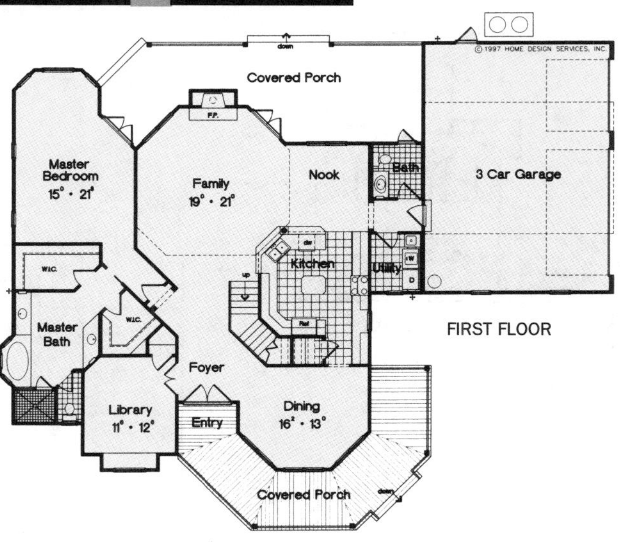

FIRST FLOOR

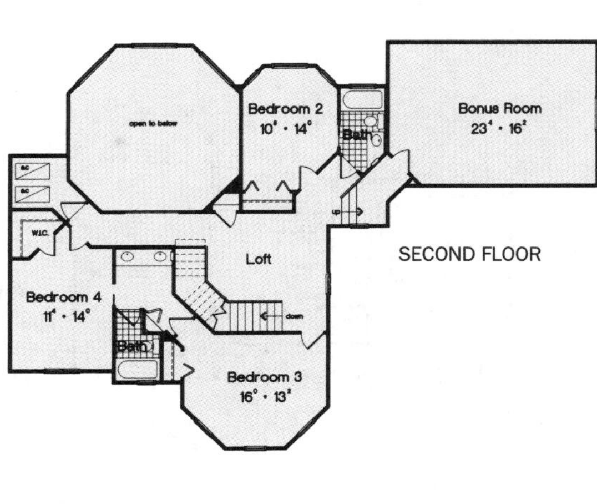

SECOND FLOOR

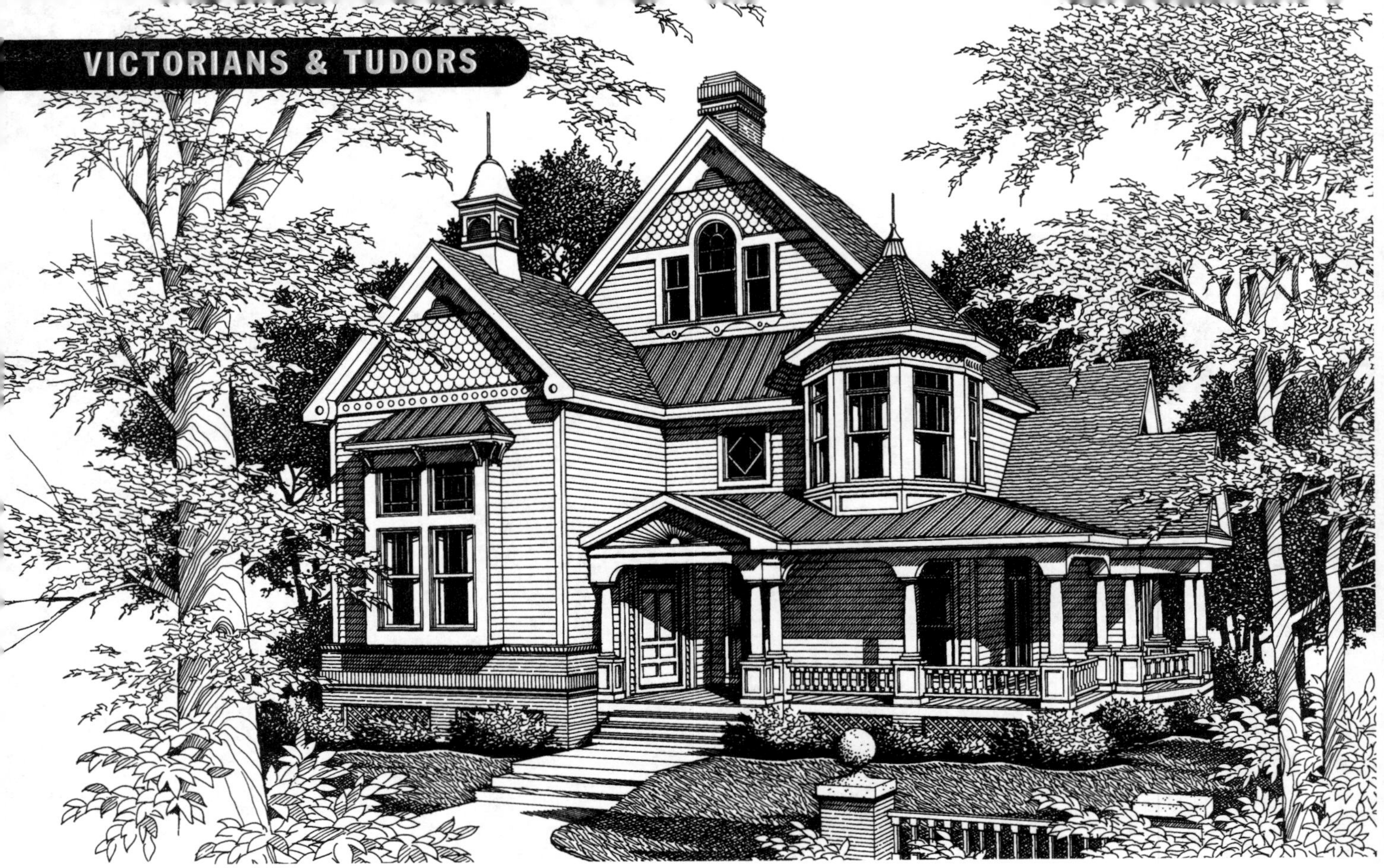

With equally appealing front and side entrances, a charming Victorian facade invites entry to this stunning home. The foyer showcases the characteristic winding staircase and opens to the large great room with masonry fireplace. An enormous kitchen features a cooktop island and a breakfast bar large enough to seat four. A lovely bay window distinguishes the nearby dining room. The master suite with masonry fireplace is located on the first floor. The amenity-filled master bath features double vanities, a whirlpool tub, a separate shower and a gigantic walk-in closet with an additional cedar closet. The second floor contains two bedrooms—one with access to the outdoor balcony on the side of the home. The third floor is completely expandable.

plan# HPT930178 L

- Style: Victorian
- First Floor: 2,194 sq. ft.
- Second Floor: 870 sq. ft.
- Total: 3,064 sq. ft.
- Bonus Space: 251 sq. ft.
- Bedrooms: 3
- Bathrooms: 2½
- Width: 50'-11"
- Depth: 91'-2"
- Foundation: Crawlspace, Slab

SEARCH ONLINE @ EPLANS.COM

FIRST FLOOR

SECOND FLOOR

OPTIONAL LAYOUT

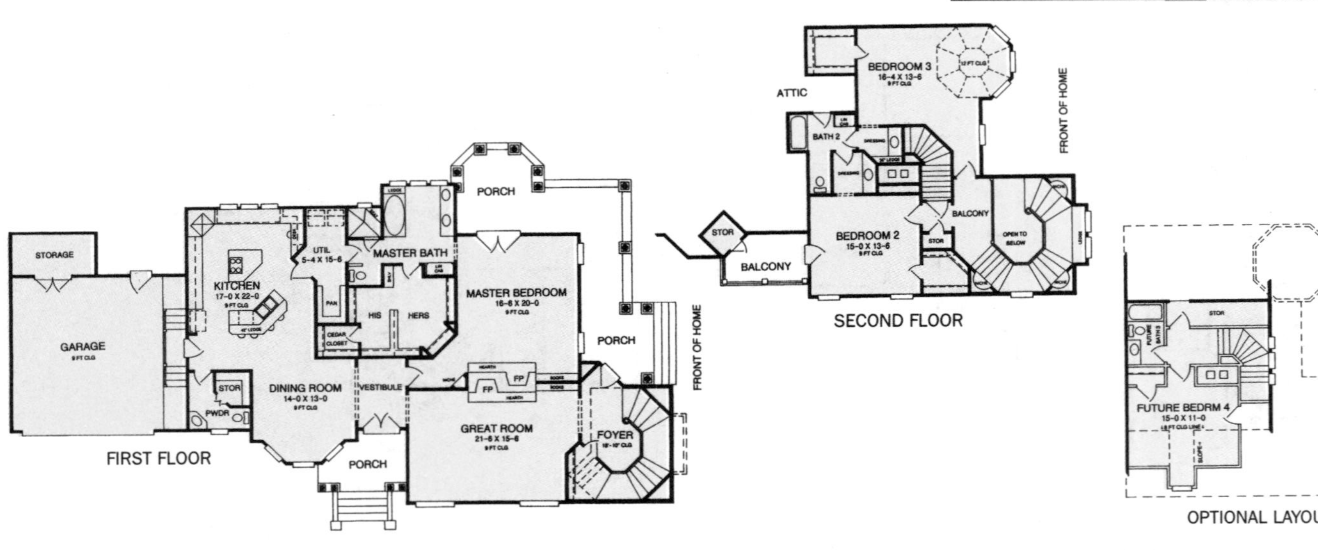

plan# HPT930179

- Style: Victorian
- First Floor: 1,329 sq. ft.
- Second Floor: 1,917 sq. ft.
- Total: 3,246 sq. ft.
- Loft: 189 sq. ft.
- Bedrooms: 3
- Bathrooms: 2½
- Width: 40'-4"
- Depth: 62'-0"
- Foundation: Crawlspace

SEARCH ONLINE @ EPLANS.COM

While speaking clearly of the past, the inside of this Victorian home coincides with the open, flowing interiors of today. Dine in the elegant dining room with its tray ceiling, or move through the double French doors between the formal living room and informal family room to sense the livability of this charming home. The kitchen boasts a large pantry and a corner sink with a window. The lovely master suite resides upstairs. The raised sitting area off the master bedroom provides the owner with a mini-retreat for reading and relaxing. The second floor also includes two large bedrooms and a library/music room.

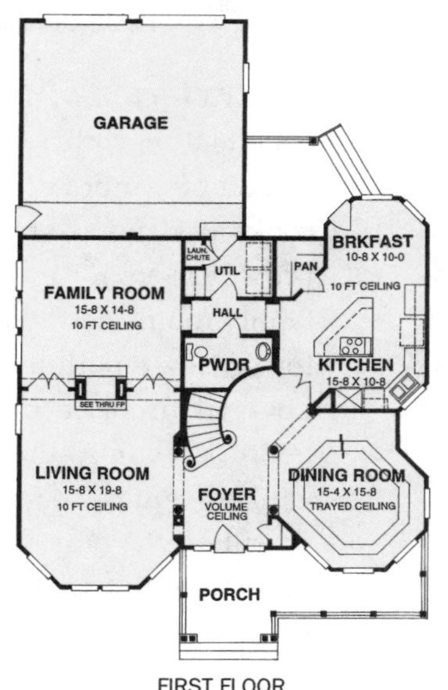

FIRST FLOOR

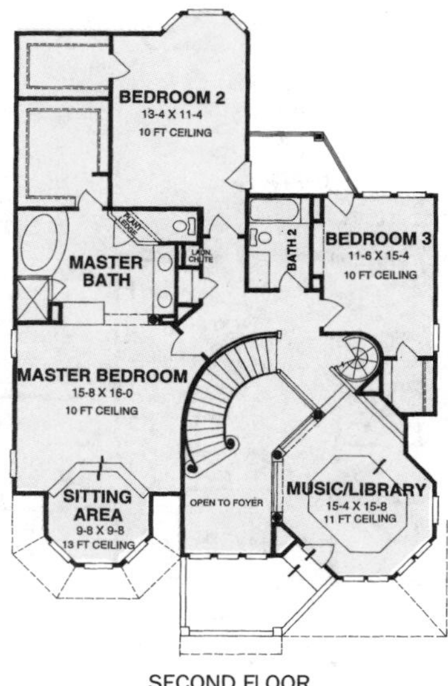

SECOND FLOOR

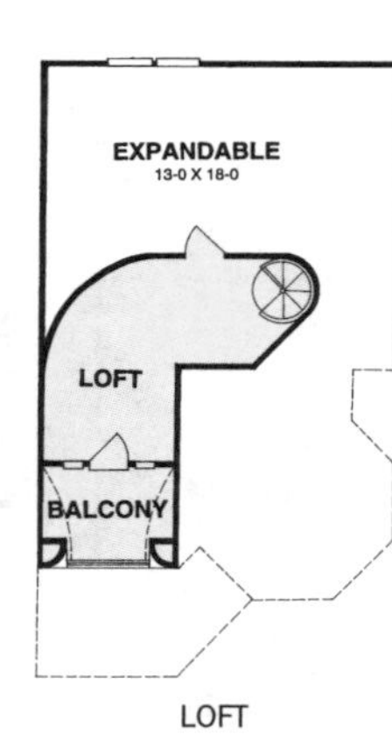

LOFT

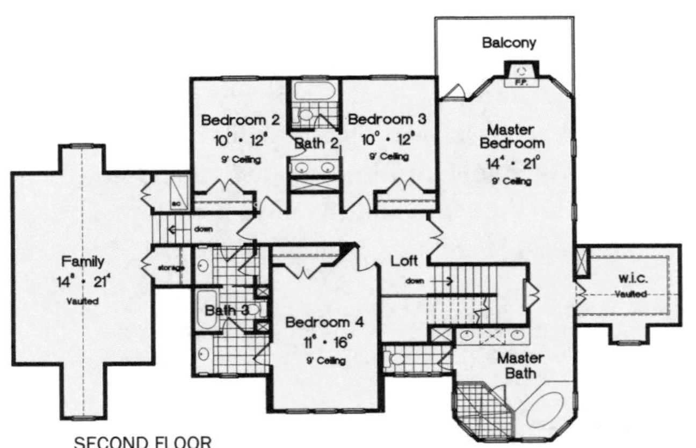

SECOND FLOOR

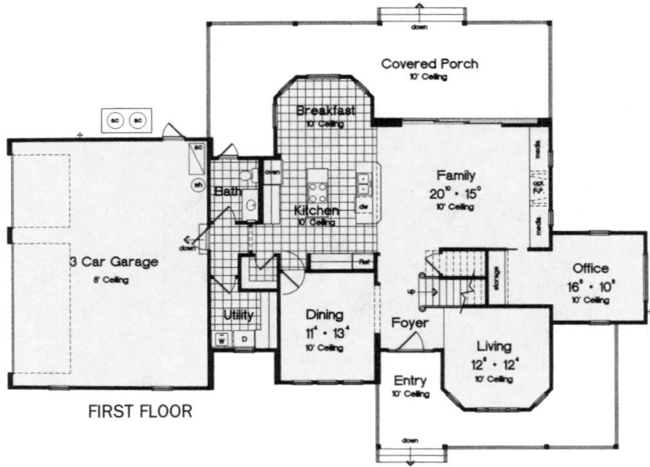

FIRST FLOOR

plan# HPT930180

- Style: Victorian
- First Floor: 1,474 sq. ft.
- Second Floor: 1,554 sq. ft.
- Total: 3,028 sq. ft.
- Bonus Space: 436 sq. ft.
- Bedrooms: 4
- Bathrooms: 3½
- Width: 76'-8"
- Depth: 52'-8"
- Foundation: Slab

SEARCH ONLINE @ EPLANS.COM

The exterior of this home is sure to get attention with a Victorian turret and its ribbon of windows. Inside the kitchen, a cooktop island and plenty of counter space provide room for meal preparation. In the family room—located near the entrance to the office—a built-in media center and an optional fireplace provide a focal point. Four bedrooms, three full baths and a vaulted family room occupy the second floor. French doors open to the master bedroom where a fireplace and private balcony satisfy a high standard of living.

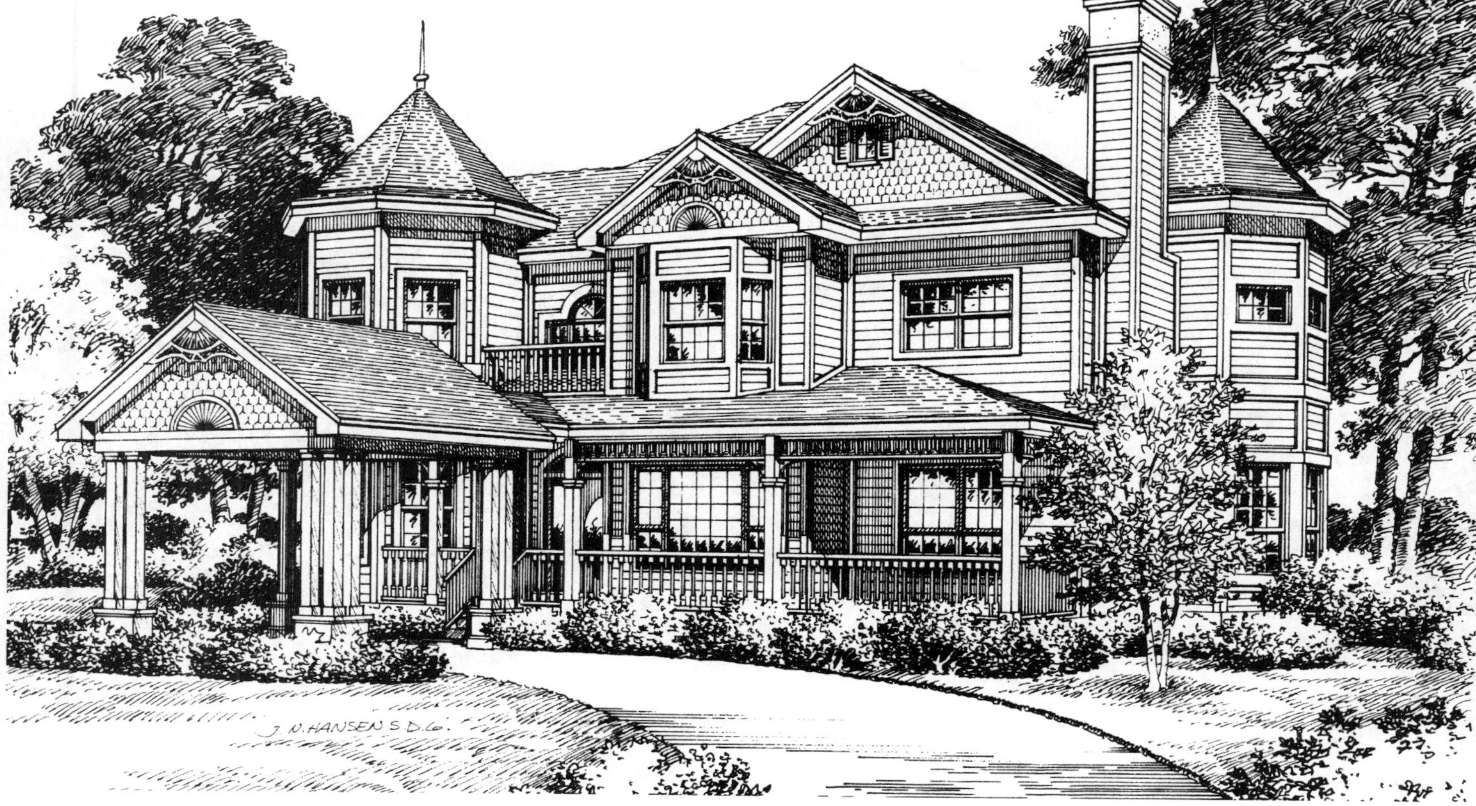

plan# HPT930181

- Style: Victorian
- First Floor: 1,379 sq. ft.
- Second Floor: 1,304 sq. ft.
- Total: 2,683 sq. ft.
- Bedrooms: 4
- Bathrooms: 2½
- Width: 54'-8"
- Depth: 61'-4"
- Foundation: Slab

SEARCH ONLINE @ EPLANS.COM

SECOND FLOOR

FIRST FLOOR

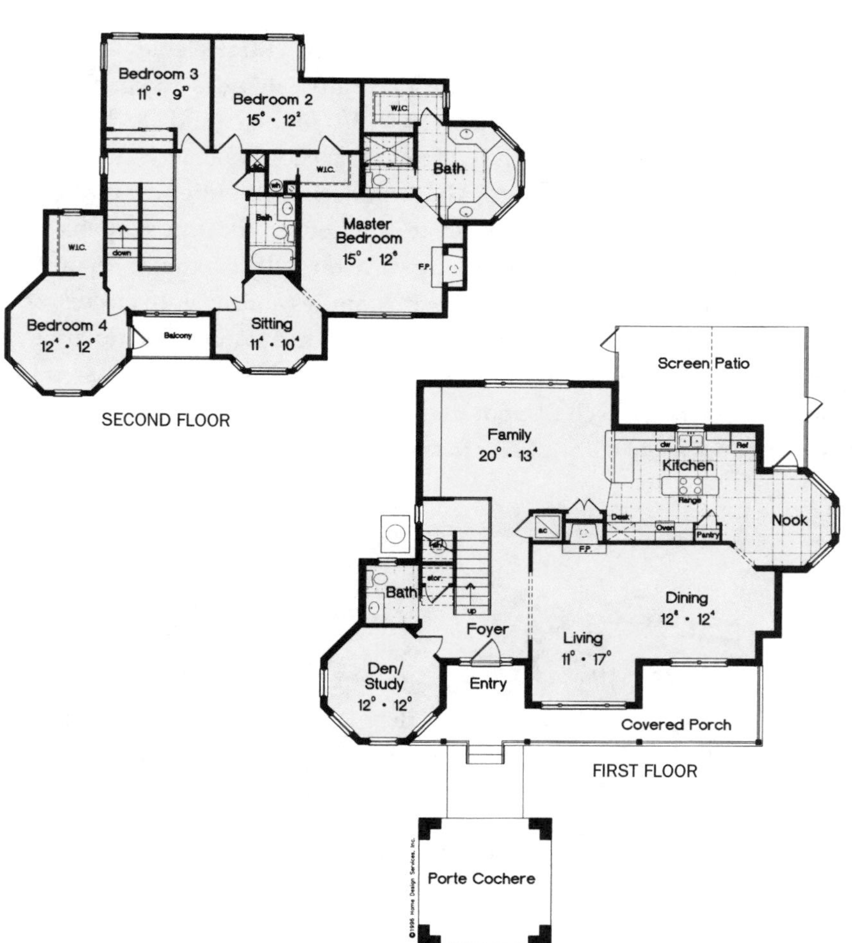

Two turrets, scalloped shingles and gingerbread trim enhance this majestic Queen Anne design. A welcoming covered porch gives way to the foyer, which is flanked by an expansive living/dining area and a den that doubles as a study. The galley-style kitchen offers an island work counter and adjoins a breakfast bay that opens to a screened patio. Sleeping quarters are thoughtfully placed upstairs, away from the main living area. An indulgent master suite features a sitting area, a fireplace and a full bath encircled by a turret. Three additional bedrooms, two with walk-in closets, share a second full bath.

This enchanting manor displays architectural elements typical of the Victorian style: asymmetrical facade, decorative shingles and gables, and a covered porch. The two-story living room with a fireplace and wet bar opens to the glass-enclosed rear porch with skylights. A spacious kitchen is filled with amenities including an island cooktop, built-in desk, and butler's pantry connecting to the dining room. The master suite, adjacent to the study, opens to the rear deck; a cozy fireplace keeps the room warm on chilly evenings. Separate His and Hers dressing rooms are outfitted with vanities and walk-in closets, and a luxurious whirlpool tub connects the baths. The second floor opens to a large lounge with built-in cabinets and bookshelves. Three bedrooms and two full baths complete the second-floor living arrangements. The three-car garage contains disappearing stairs to an attic storage area.

plan# HPT930182

L

- Style: Victorian
- First Floor: 3,079 sq. ft.
- Second Floor: 1,461 sq. ft.
- Total: 4,540 sq. ft.
- Bedrooms: 4
- Bathrooms: 4½ + ½
- Width: 118'-4"
- Depth: 54'-6"
- Foundation: Basement

SEARCH ONLINE @ EPLANS.COM

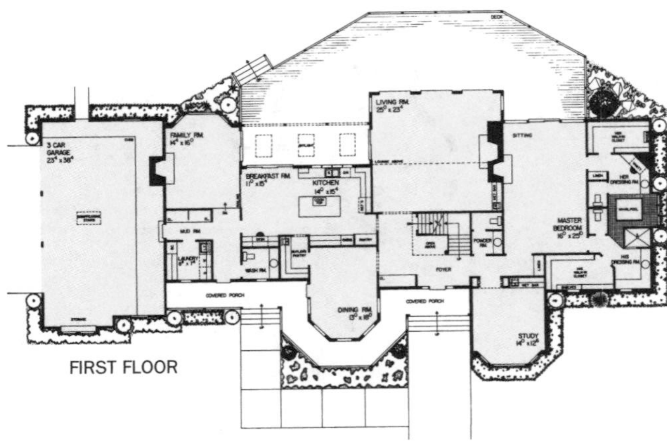

FIRST FLOOR

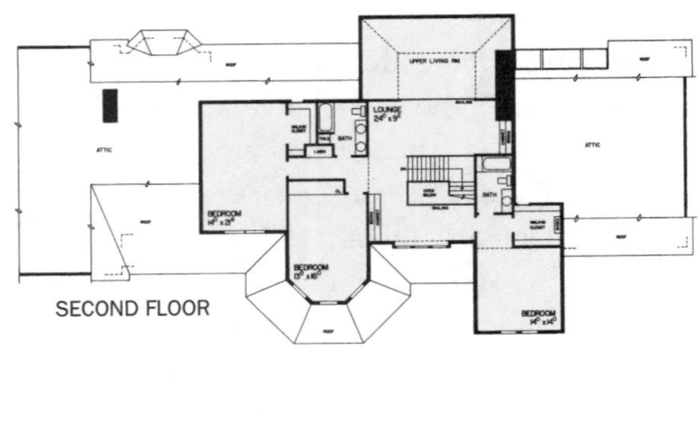

SECOND FLOOR

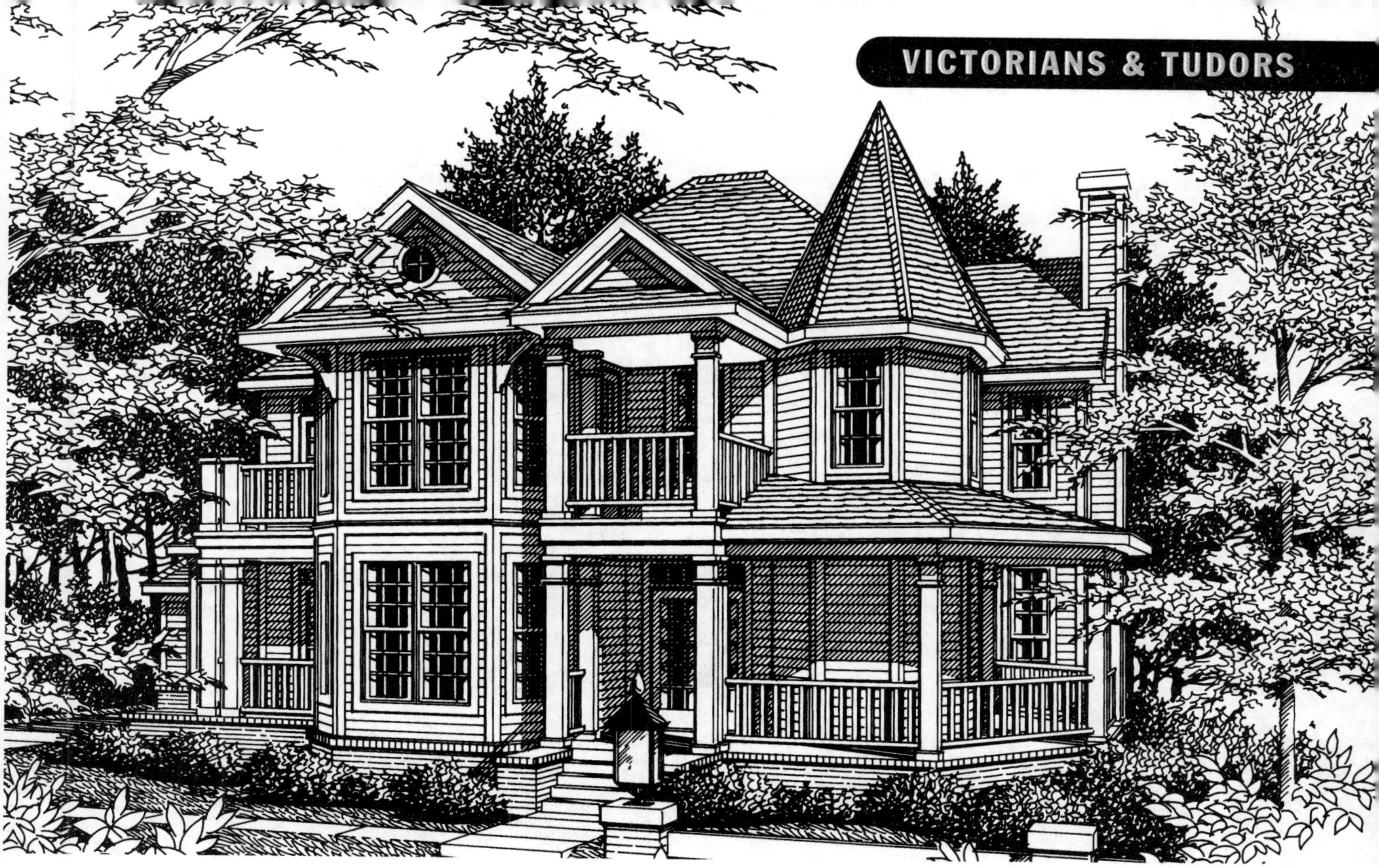

plan# HPT930183

- Style: Victorian
- First Floor: 1,718 sq. ft.
- Second Floor: 1,089 sq. ft.
- Total: 2,807 sq. ft.
- Bedrooms: 3
- Bathrooms: 2
- Width: 63'-10"
- Depth: 62'-6"
- Foundation: Crawlspace, Slab

SEARCH ONLINE @ EPLANS.COM

The impressive entrance of this Victorian home welcomes guests to the formal areas—the dining room to the left and the living room straight ahead. The covered porch opening off the living room provides a pleasant sitting space in warm weather, while a fireplace is appreciated on cool evenings. A side-porch entry opens to the breakfast room. On this level, the master suite offers a sitting bay, two walk-in closets, a bath with separate vanities and a private entrance from the rear porch. Two bedrooms upstairs share a bath and a game room. Each bedroom includes a private balcony and a walk-in closet.

SECOND FLOOR

FIRST FLOOR

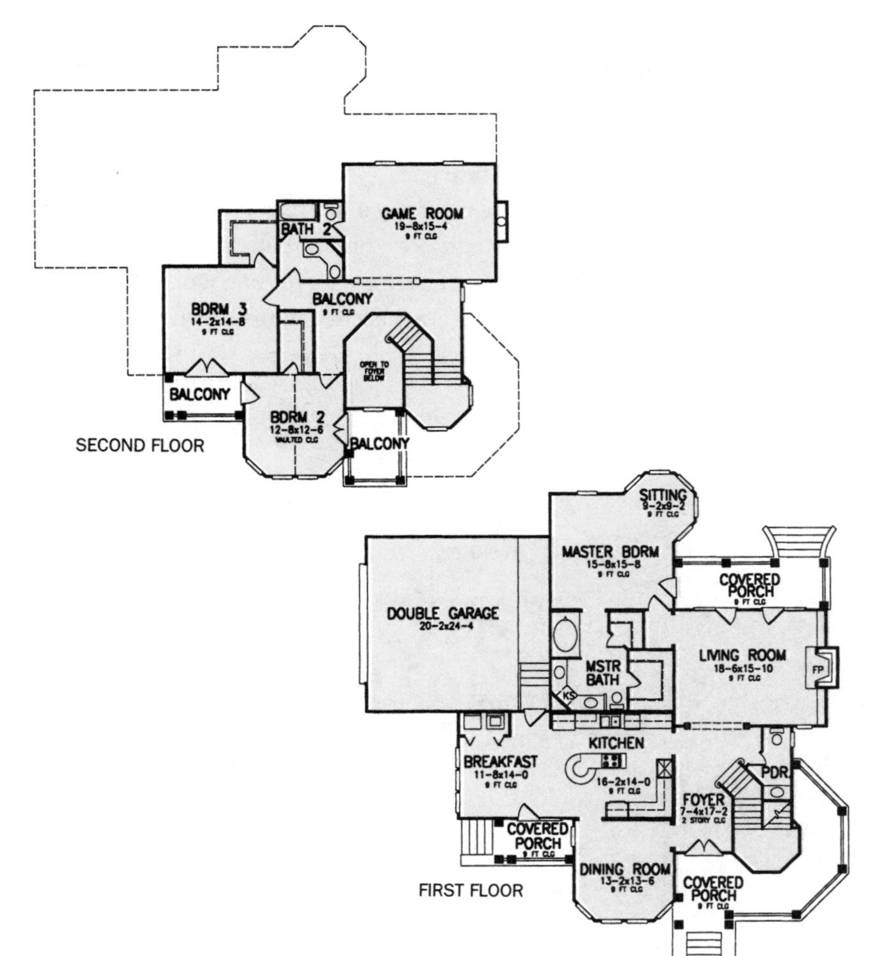

This two-story beauty is rich in luxurious style. A dramatic entrance welcomes you to the foyer, where a stunning curved staircase greets you. A turret-style dining room is flooded with light from the bayed windows. Across the gallery, the living room features a through-fireplace to the family room. The island kitchen is open to the breakfast room, which accesses the rear porch and the family room, which features built-ins. The first-floor master bedroom offers a bath with a whirlpool tub, two walk-in closets and a dressing room. Two additional bedrooms, a study and a game room with sun-deck access all reside on the second floor.

plan# HPT930184

- Style: Victorian
- First Floor: 2,144 sq. ft.
- Second Floor: 1,253 sq. ft.
- Total: 3,397 sq. ft.
- Bedrooms: 3
- Bathrooms: 3½
- Width: 64'-11"
- Depth: 76'-7"
- Foundation: Slab

SEARCH ONLINE @ EPLANS.COM

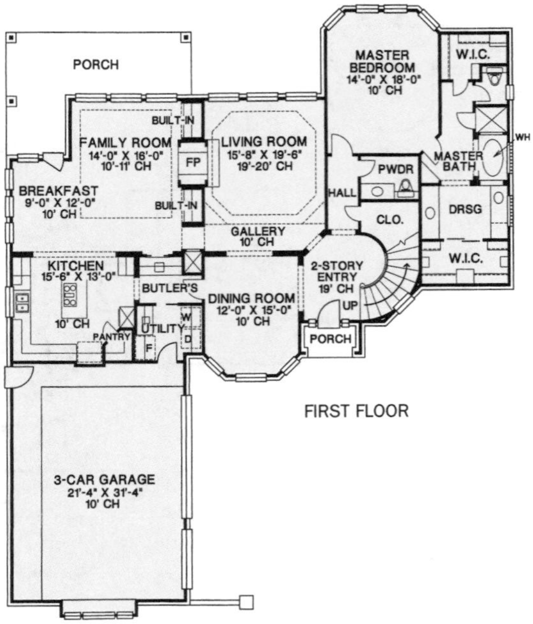

FIRST FLOOR

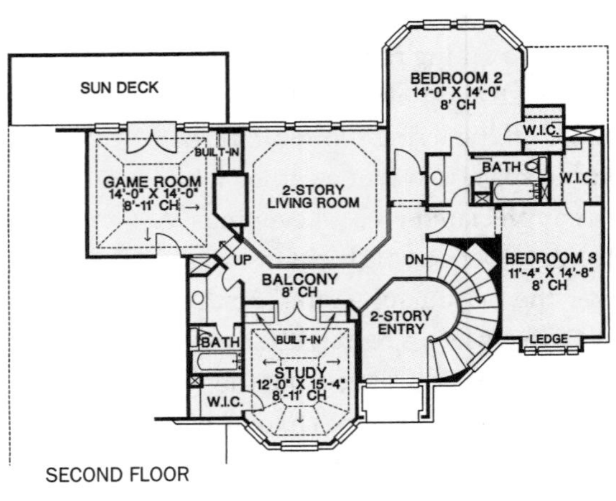

SECOND FLOOR

FOR MORE DETAILED INFORMATION, PLEASE CHECK THE FLOOR PLANS CAREFULLY.

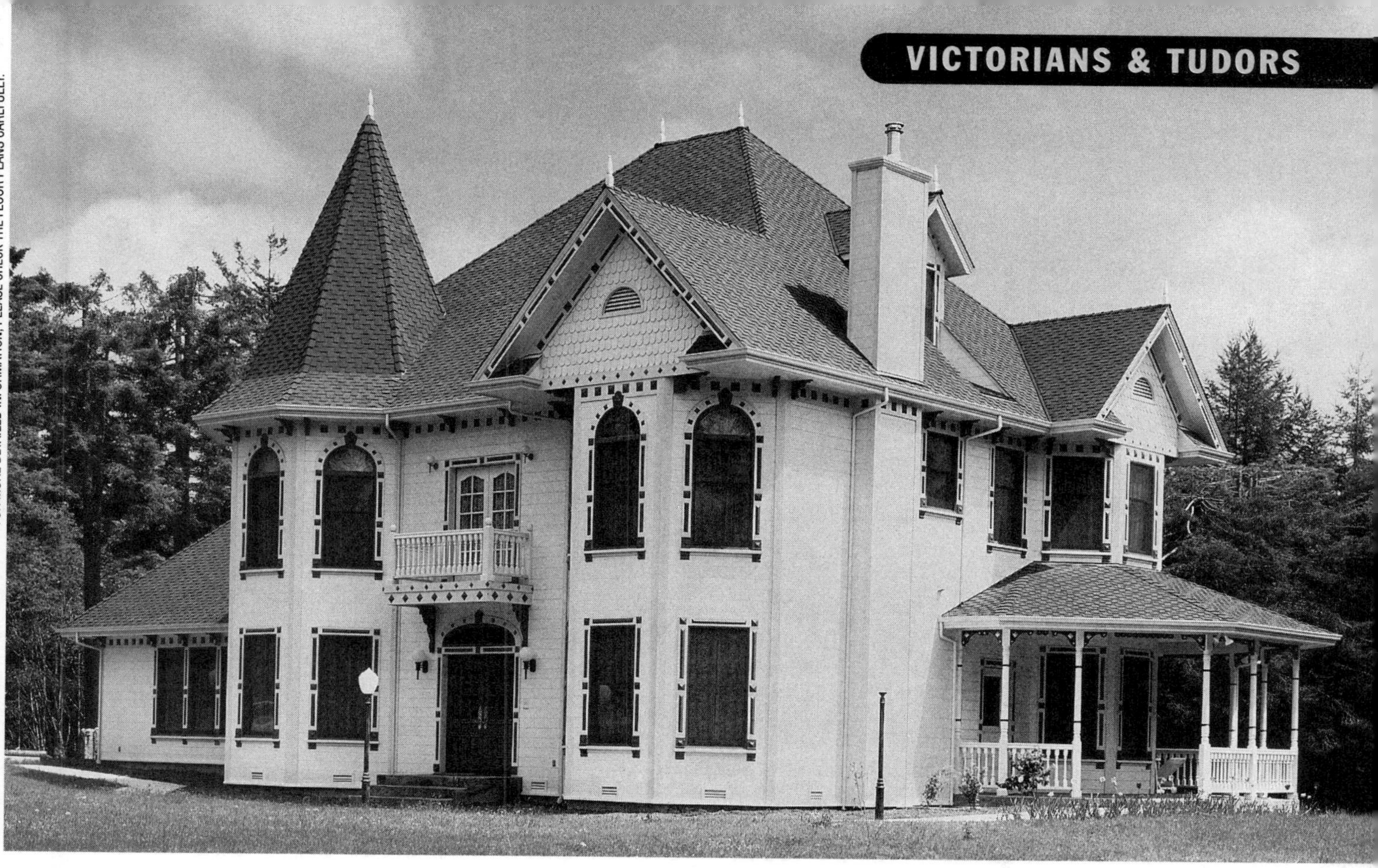

plan# HPT930185

- Style: Victorian
- First Floor: 1,766 sq. ft.
- Second Floor: 1,519 sq. ft.
- Total: 3,285 sq. ft.
- Bedrooms: 4
- Bathrooms: 2½
- Width: 77'-7"
- Depth: 44'-2"
- Foundation: Basement

SEARCH ONLINE @ EPLANS.COM

SECOND FLOOR

QUOTE ONE®

Cost to build? See page 436 to order complete cost estimate to build this house in your area!

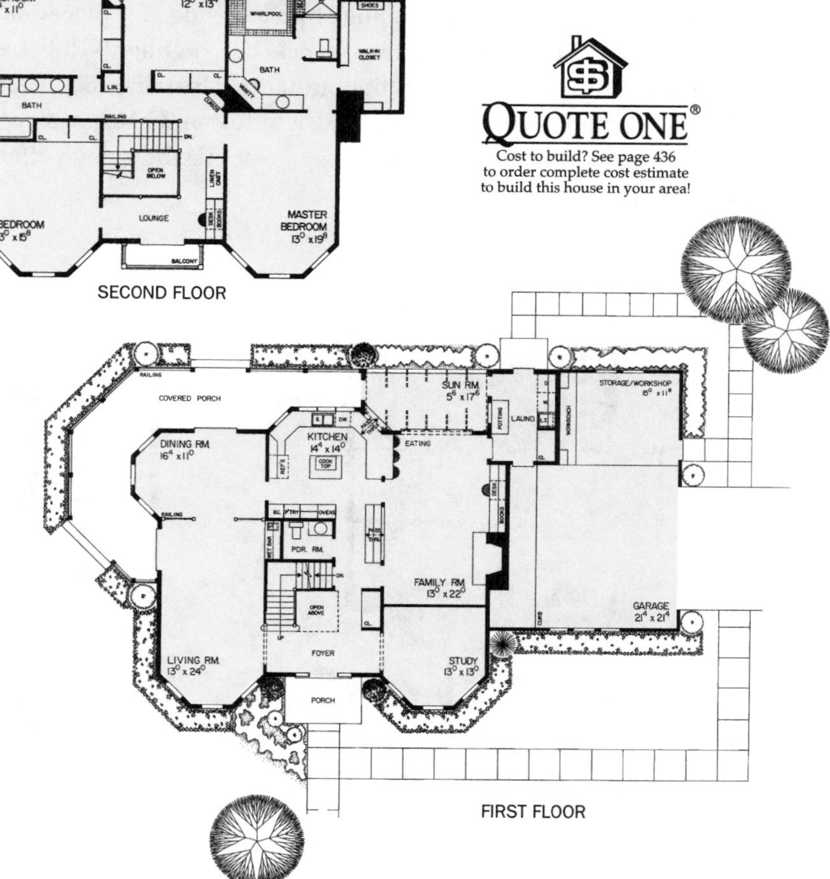

The stately proportions and exquisite Victorian detailing of this home are exciting indeed. Like so many Victorian houses, interesting rooflines set the character of this design. Observe the delightful mixture of gabled roof, hipped roof and dramatic turret. The kitchen features a center island cooktop and shares a wide counter for casual dining with the adjoining family room. A bayed dining room with access to the rear porch is available for more formal occasions. Upstairs, each of the four bedrooms offers a bay area and plenty of closet space. Don't miss the spacious master bath.

FIRST FLOOR

This country Victorian design comes loaded with charm and amenities. The entry leads to open living space, defined by a two-sided fireplace and a large bay window. An island counter with a snack bar highlights the L-shaped kitchen. A quiet sitting area opens to the outdoors. Upstairs, the master suite allows plenty of sunlight from the turret's bay window and boasts a step-up tub, dual vanities and a separate shower. Bonus space above the garage offers room for future expansion.

plan# HPT930186

- Style: Victorian
- First Floor: 880 sq. ft.
- Second Floor: 880 sq. ft.
- Total: 1,760 sq. ft.
- Bonus Space: 256 sq. ft.
- Bedrooms: 3
- Bathrooms: 2½
- Width: 42'-0"
- Depth: 40'-0"
- Foundation: Basement

SEARCH ONLINE @ EPLANS.COM

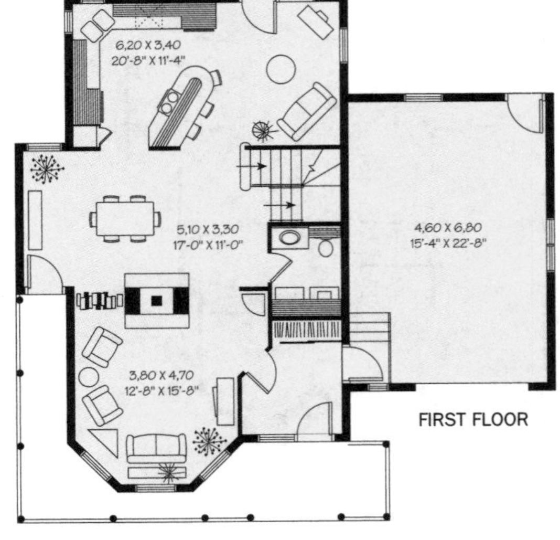

FIRST FLOOR

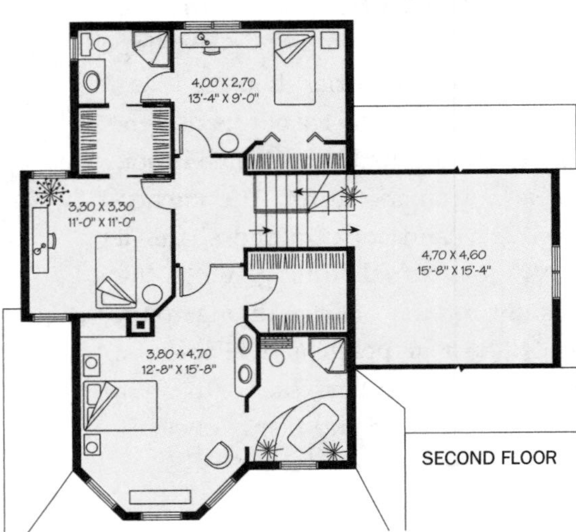

SECOND FLOOR

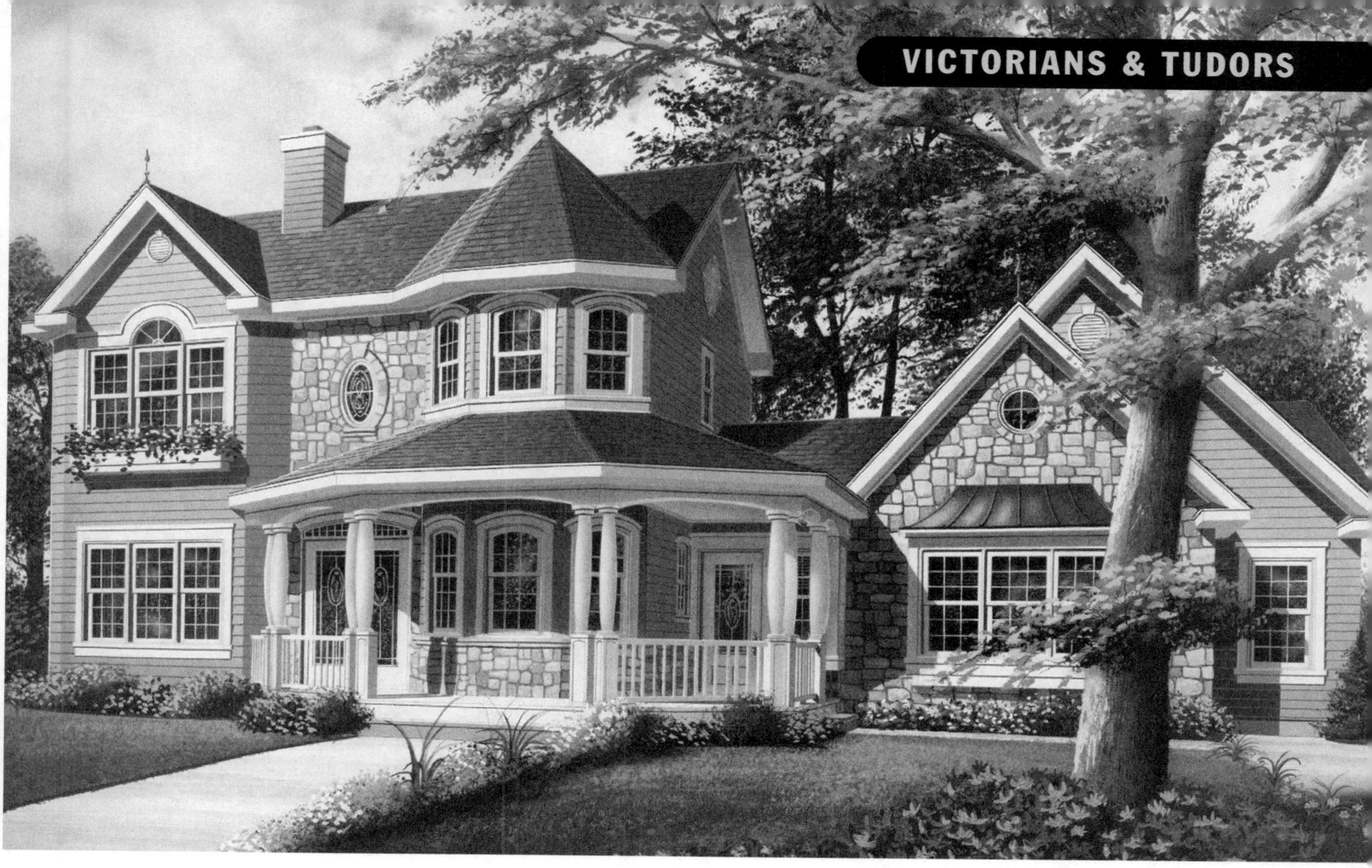

plan# HPT930187

- Style: Victorian
- First Floor: 1,358 sq. ft.
- Second Floor: 894 sq. ft.
- Total: 2,252 sq. ft.
- Bonus Space: 300 sq. ft.
- Bedrooms: 4
- Bathrooms: 3½
- Width: 58'-0"
- Depth: 58'-4"
- Foundation: Basement

SEARCH ONLINE @ EPLANS.COM

From the wraparound covered porch, enter this attractive home to find the roomy master suite on the left and the formal dining room on the right. Leading through double doors from the dining area is a sunlit U-shaped kitchen with a breakfast island. This room then flows into a comfortable family room featuring a fireplace. Separate access to the garage and upstairs completes the first floor. The second floor is reserved for three family bedrooms that share a full bath.

FIRST FLOOR

SECOND FLOOR

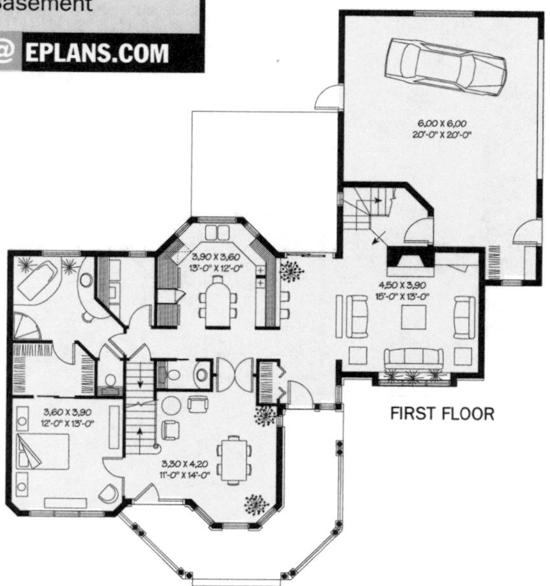

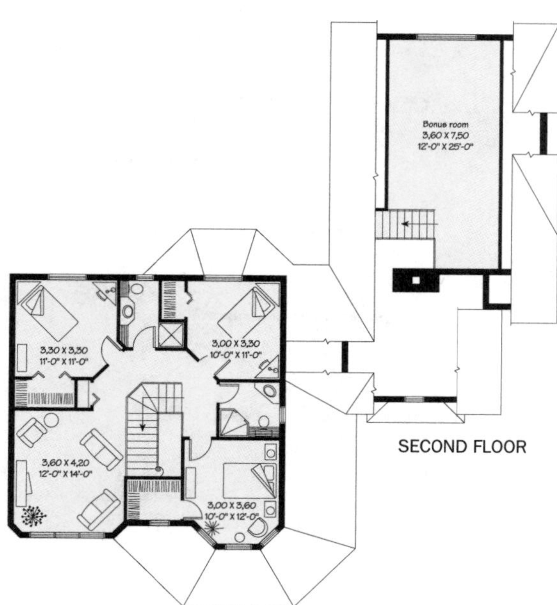

Special attention to exterior details and interior nuances gives this relaxed farmhouse fine distinction on any street. From the large covered porch, enter to find a spacious, thoughtful plan. A striking central staircase separates the first-floor living area, which boasts a home office and a cathedral ceiling in the living room. The second floor includes a master suite, two secondary bedrooms that share a full bath, and a flexible upstairs sitting area. The master suite contains a bath with double-bowl vanities and a walk-in closet.

plan# HPT930188

- Style: Victorian
- First Floor: 1,274 sq. ft.
- Second Floor: 983 sq. ft.
- Total: 2,257 sq. ft.
- Bedrooms: 3
- Bathrooms: 2½
- Width: 50'-0"
- Depth: 46'-0"
- Foundation: Walkout Basement

SEARCH ONLINE @ EPLANS.COM

FIRST FLOOR

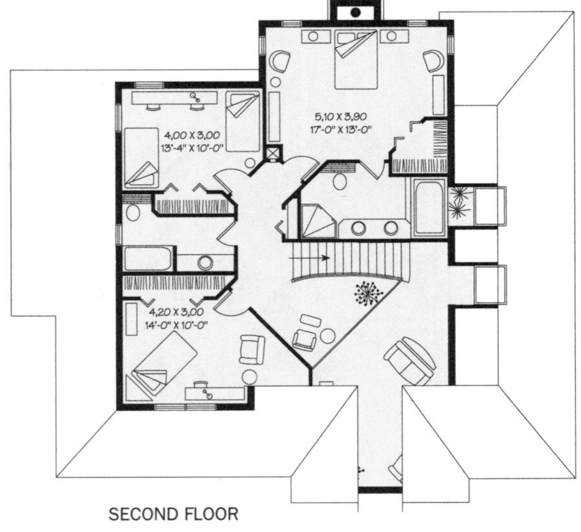

SECOND FLOOR

plan# HPT930189

- Style: Victorian
- First Floor: 1,146 sq. ft.
- Second Floor: 943 sq. ft.
- Total: 2,089 sq. ft.
- Bonus Space: 324 sq. ft.
- Bedrooms: 3
- Bathrooms: 2½
- Width: 56'-0"
- Depth: 38'-0"
- Foundation: Basement

SEARCH ONLINE @ EPLANS.COM

This beautiful three-bedroom home boasts many attractive features. Two covered porches will entice you outside, while inside, a special sun room on the first floor brings the outdoors in. The foyer opens on the right to a comfortable family room that may be used as a home office. On the left, the living area is warmed by the sun room and a cozy corner fireplace. A formal dining area lies adjacent to an efficient kitchen with a central island and breakfast nook overlooking the back porch. The second level offers two family bedrooms served by a full bath. A spacious master suite with a walk-in closet and luxurious bath completes the second floor.

FIRST FLOOR

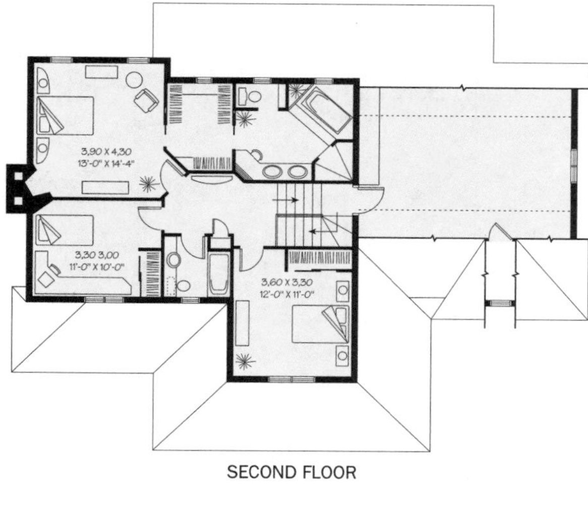

SECOND FLOOR

Graceful details combine with a covered entryway to welcome friends and family to come on in. The canted bay sitting area in the master suite provides sunny respite and quiet solitude. To be the center of attention, invite everyone to party in the vaulted great room, which spills over into the big airy kitchen. Guests can make use of the optional study/bedroom. Upstairs, secondary bedrooms share a full bath and a balcony overlook. A spacious central hall leads to a bonus room that provides wardrobe space.

plan# HPT930190

- Style: Victorian
- First Floor: 1,688 sq. ft.
- Second Floor: 558 sq. ft.
- Total: 2,246 sq. ft.
- Bonus Space: 269 sq. ft.
- Bedrooms: 4
- Bathrooms: 3
- Width: 54'-0"
- Depth: 48'-0"
- Foundation: Crawlspace, Slab, Basement

SEARCH ONLINE @ EPLANS.COM

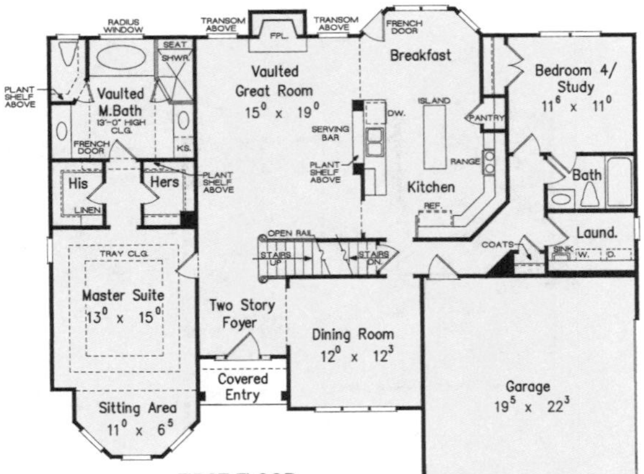

FIRST FLOOR

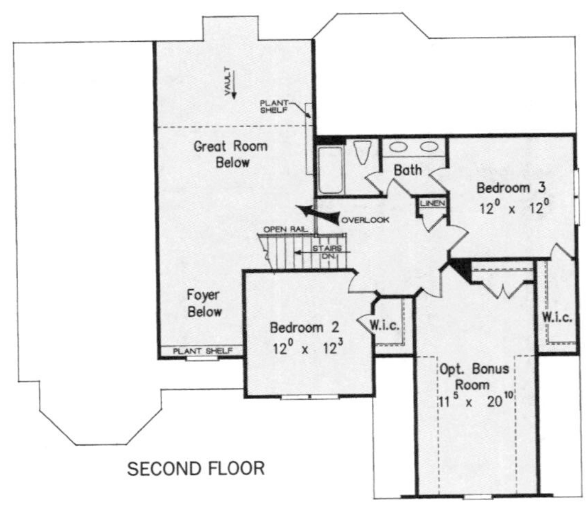

SECOND FLOOR

plan# HPT930191

- Style: Victorian
- First Floor: 2,294 sq. ft.
- Second Floor: 869 sq. ft.
- Total: 3,163 sq. ft.
- Bonus Space: 309 sq. ft.
- Bedrooms: 4
- Bathrooms: 3½
- Width: 63'-6"
- Depth: 63'-0"
- Foundation: Crawlspace, Basement

SEARCH ONLINE @ EPLANS.COM

A turreted living room adds a special touch to this four-bedroom home. From the pleasing covered porch, the two-story foyer leads through an arched opening to the formal dining room and also to the charming bayed living room. The master suite is tucked away on the first floor, with its own vaulted sitting room, walk-in closet and spacious bath. The two-story family room with a fireplace and rear views rounds out the main level. Three more bedrooms and two baths, plus an optional bonus room, complete the upper level.

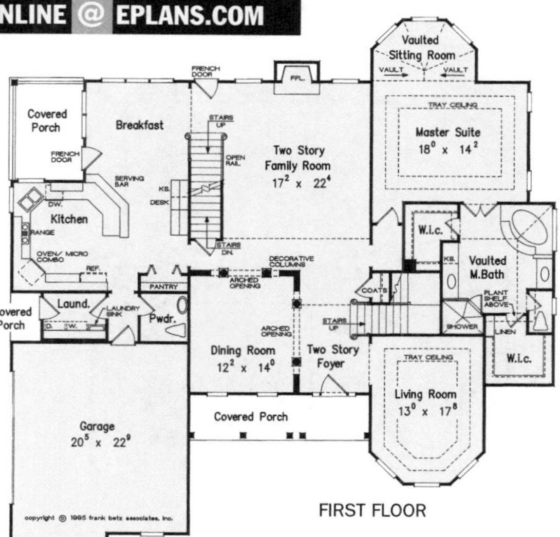

FIRST FLOOR

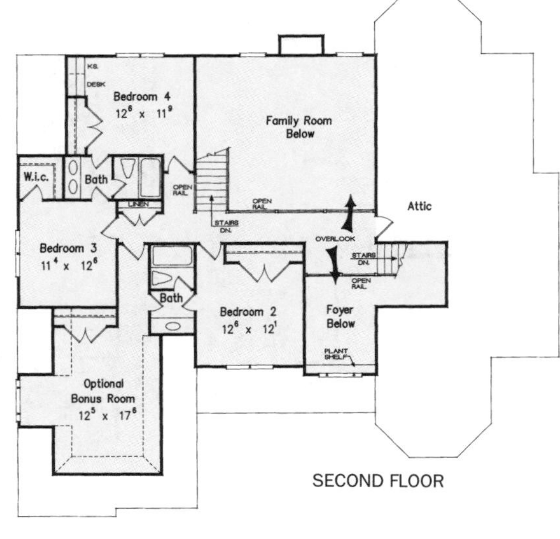

SECOND FLOOR

A gracious front porch off the formal dining room and a two-story entry set the tone for this elegant home. The living room is set to the front of the plan, thoughtfully separated from casual family areas that radiate from the kitchen. The two-story family room is framed by a balcony hall and accented with a fireplace and serving bar. The first-floor master suite features a sitting area, lush bath and walk-in closet. Upstairs, two family bedrooms share a full bath while a third enjoys a private bath.

plan# HPT930192

- Style: French Country
- First Floor: 2,044 sq. ft.
- Second Floor: 896 sq. ft.
- Total: 4,984 sq. ft.
- Bonus Space: 197 sq. ft.
- Bedrooms: 4
- Bathrooms: 3½
- Width: 63'-0"
- Depth: 54'-0"
- Foundation: Crawlspace, Slab, Basement

SEARCH ONLINE @ EPLANS.COM

FIRST FLOOR

SECOND FLOOR

plan# HPT930193

- Style: Victorian
- First Floor: 1,398 sq. ft.
- Second Floor: 515 sq. ft.
- Total: 1,913 sq. ft.
- Bonus Space: 282 sq. ft.
- Bedrooms: 3
- Bathrooms: 2½
- Width: 48'-0"
- Depth: 50'-10"
- Foundation: Crawlspace, Slab, Basement

SEARCH ONLINE @ EPLANS.COM

Varied rooflines, keystones and arches set off a stucco exterior that's highlighted by a stone turret and a bay window. Inside, the formal dining room leads to a private covered porch for after-dinner conversation on pleasant evenings. The central kitchen boasts a built-in planning desk, an ample pantry and an angled counter that overlooks the breakfast room. Sleeping quarters include a first-floor master suite with a vaulted bath and a plant shelf, and two second-floor family bedrooms that share a balcony overlook and a full bath.

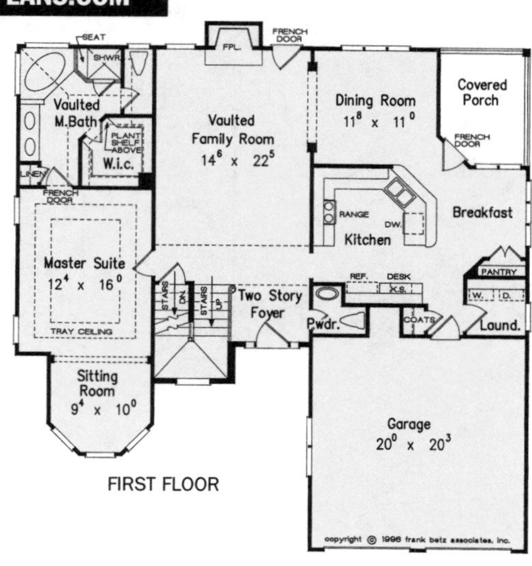

FIRST FLOOR

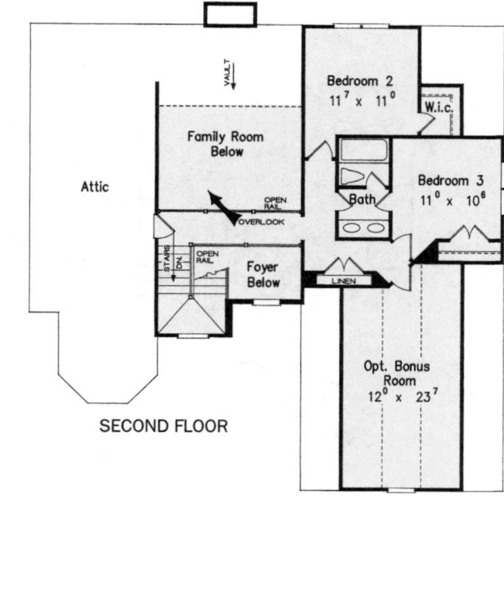

SECOND FLOOR

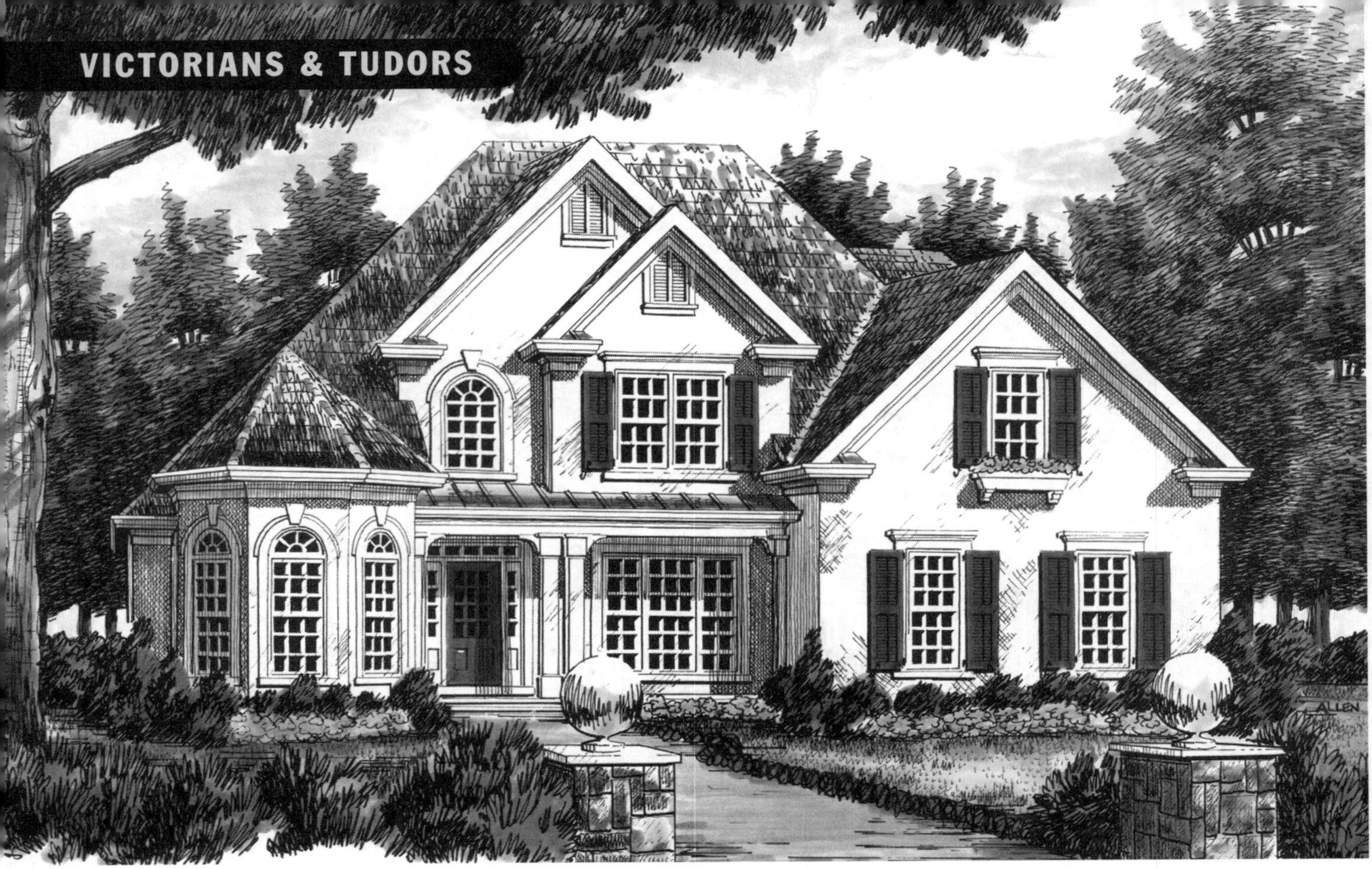

This beautiful one-story turret accompanied by arched windows and a stucco facade. A terrific casual combination of kitchen, breakfast area and a vaulted keeping room provide a space for family gatherings. Both the keeping room and great room sport cheery fireplaces. The master suite is secluded on the first floor. This relaxing retreat offers a sitting room, His and Hers walk-in closets, dual vanities and compartmented toilet. Two family bedrooms share a full bath on the second floor. An optional bonus room can be used as a game room or home office.

plan# HPT930194

- Style: Victorian
- First Floor: 1,972 sq. ft.
- Second Floor: 579 sq. ft.
- Total: 2,551 sq. ft.
- Bonus Space: 256 sq. ft.
- Bedrooms: 3
- Bathrooms: 2½
- Width: 57'-4"
- Depth: 51'-2"
- Foundation: Crawlspace, Slab, Basement

SEARCH ONLINE @ EPLANS.COM

FIRST FLOOR

SECOND FLOOR

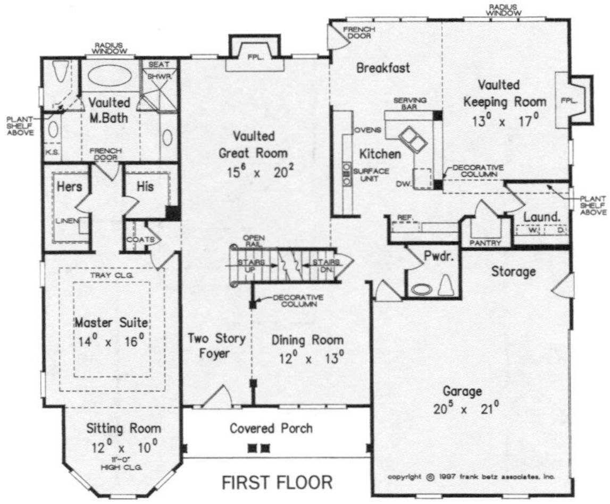

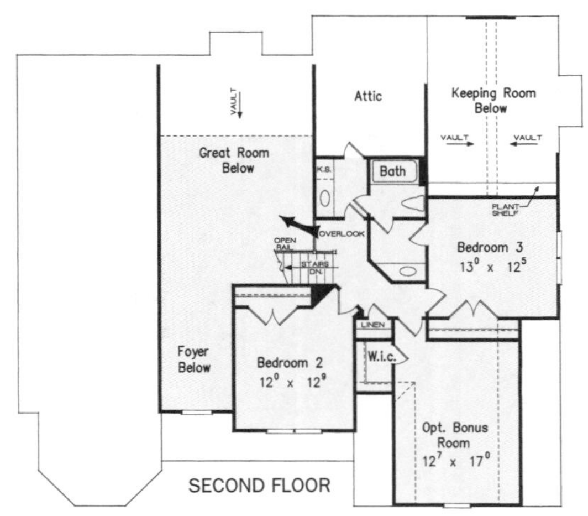

plan# HPT930195

- Style: Victorian
- First Floor: 2,302 sq. ft.
- Second Floor: 845 sq. ft.
- Total: 3,147 sq. ft.
- Bonus Space: 247 sq. ft.
- Bedrooms: 4
- Bathrooms: 3½
- Width: 64'-0"
- Depth: 59'-4"
- Foundation: Crawlspace, Basement

SEARCH ONLINE @ EPLANS.COM

The arched front doorway bids a warm welcome to this spacious home. The formal dining room, outlined by decorative columns, opens to the right. Both the family and keeping rooms feature a fireplace and vaulted ceiling, while the large kitchen offers a work island and a serving bar to make mealtimes in the breakfast nook a cinch. On the left side of the plan are a gazebo-shaped formal living room and the elegant master suite with a bayed sitting area. Two staircases lead to three family bedrooms and the optional bonus room.

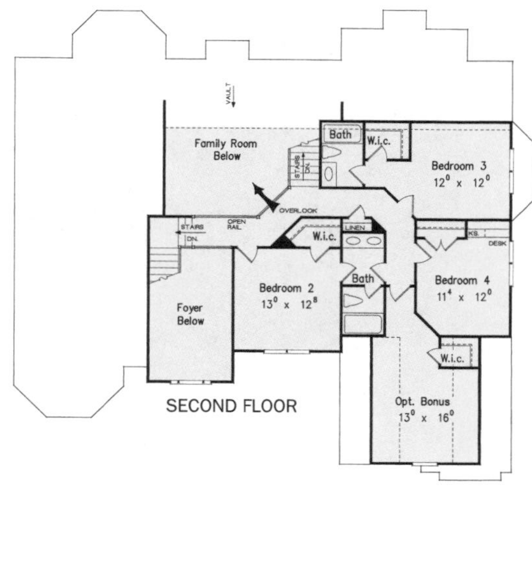

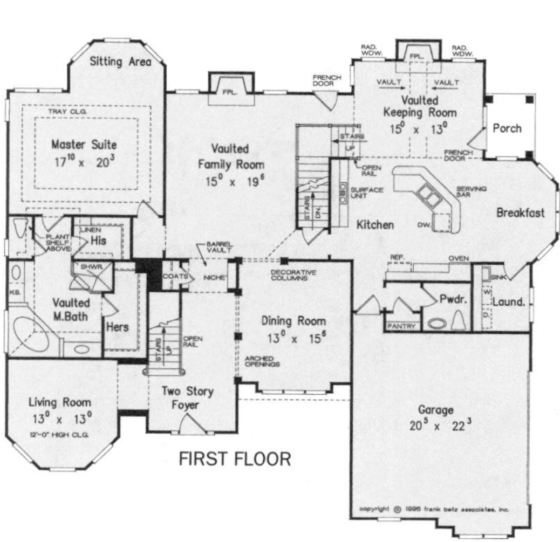

Keystones that cap each window, a terrace that dresses up the entrance, and a bay-windowed turret add up to a totally refined exterior of this home. Inside, open planning employs columns to define the foyer, dining room and two-story family room. The first-floor master suite is designed with every amenity to answer your needs. Rounding out the first floor are the kitchen, breakfast nook and keeping room. The second floor contains two bedrooms, each with a private bath and walk-in closet, and an optional bonus room.

plan# HPT930196

- Style: Victorian
- First Floor: 2,429 sq. ft.
- Second Floor: 654 sq. ft.
- Total: 3,083 sq. ft.
- Bonus Space: 420 sq. ft.
- Bedrooms: 3
- Bathrooms: 3½
- Width: 63'-6"
- Depth: 71'-4"
- Foundation: Crawlspace, Slab, Basement

SEARCH ONLINE @ EPLANS.COM

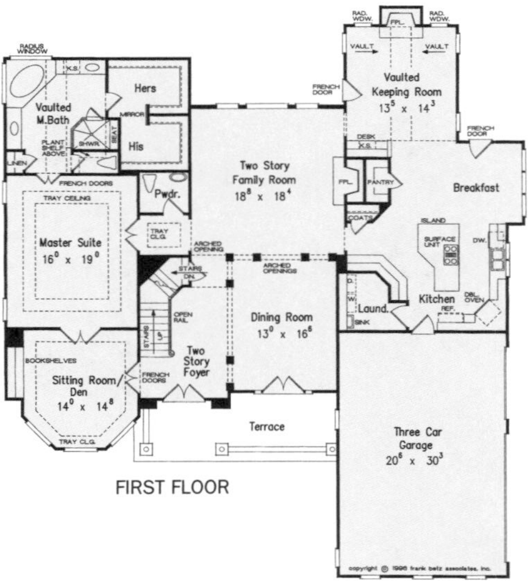

FIRST FLOOR

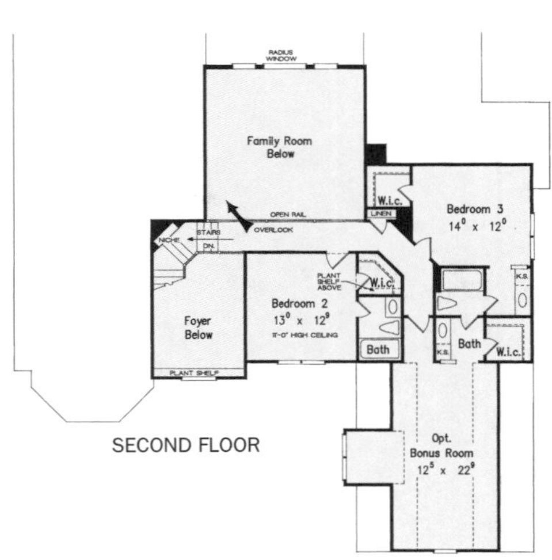

SECOND FLOOR

plan# HPT930197

- Style: Traditional
- First Floor: 1,551 sq. ft.
- Second Floor: 725 sq. ft.
- Total: 2,276 sq. ft.
- Bedrooms: 4
- Bathrooms: 2½
- Width: 54'-0"
- Depth: 50'-0"

SEARCH ONLINE @ EPLANS.COM

This narrow-lot plan features a wraparound porch at the two-story entry, which opens to the formal dining room with beautiful bay windows. The great room features a handsome fireplace and a ten-and-a-half foot ceiling. A well-equipped island kitchen with a pantry and built-in desk is designed for the serious cook. The large master bedroom enjoys a vaulted ceiling and a luxurious master bath. Upstairs, three secondary bedrooms with ample closet space share a compartmented bath.

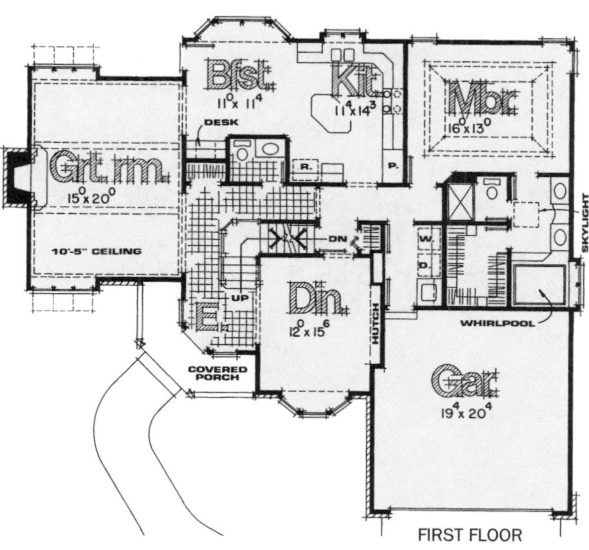

FIRST FLOOR

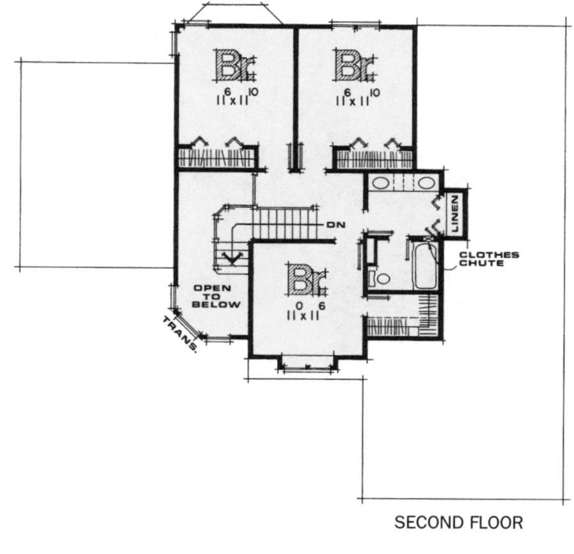

SECOND FLOOR

SECOND FLOOR

FIRST FLOOR

plan# HPT930198

- Style: Traditional
- First Floor: 2,084 sq. ft.
- Second Floor: 848 sq. ft.
- Total: 2,932 sq. ft.
- Bedrooms: 4
- Bathrooms: 3½
- Width: 68'-8"
- Depth: 60'-0"

SEARCH ONLINE @ EPLANS.COM

The combination of brick, stucco and elegant detail provides this home with instant curb appeal. The entry is flanked by the formal dining room and the den, with a fireplace and an intriguing ceiling pattern. The great room offers a through-fireplace to the hearth room and French doors to a covered veranda. A sunny breakfast room and kitchen feature an island with a snack bar, wrapping counters and a pantry. The first-floor master suite affords luxury accommodations with two closets, a whirlpool tub, His and Hers vanities and access to the covered veranda. Three secondary bedrooms on the second floor offer walk-in closets and easy bathroom access.

plan# HPT930199

- Style: Victorian
- First Floor: 946 sq. ft.
- Second Floor: 923 sq. ft.
- Total: 1,869 sq. ft.
- Bedrooms: 3
- Bathrooms: 2½
- Width: 42'-0"
- Depth: 51'-0"
- Foundation: Crawlspace, Basement

SEARCH ONLINE @ EPLANS.COM

Choose one of two exteriors for this lovely plan—both are included in the plans package. The floor plan is the same—open and accommodating. The large living room may be built with or without a bay window and is warmed by a fireplace. The dining room is connected and has buffet space. On the opposite side of the plan is the more casual family room, also with a fireplace, which leads to the rear yard through sliding glass doors. The kitchen and bayed breakfast nook sit between the two living areas. An open-railed gallery on the second floor connects the two family bedrooms and the master suite. The master bedroom has a walk in closet and private bath. Family bedrooms share a full bath with linen closet.

ALTERNATE EXTERIOR

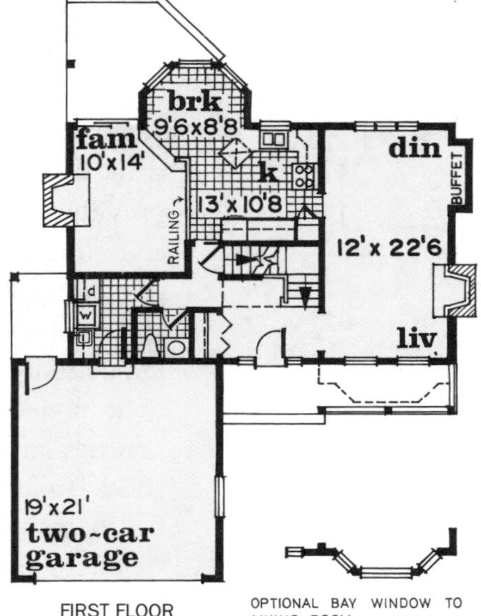

FIRST FLOOR

OPTIONAL BAY WINDOW TO LIVING ROOM

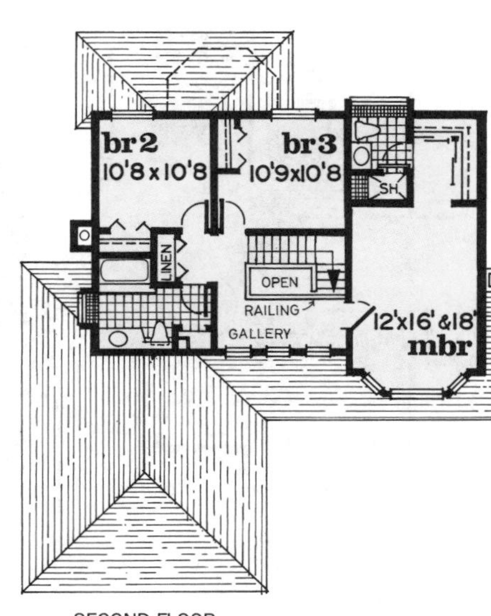

SECOND FLOOR

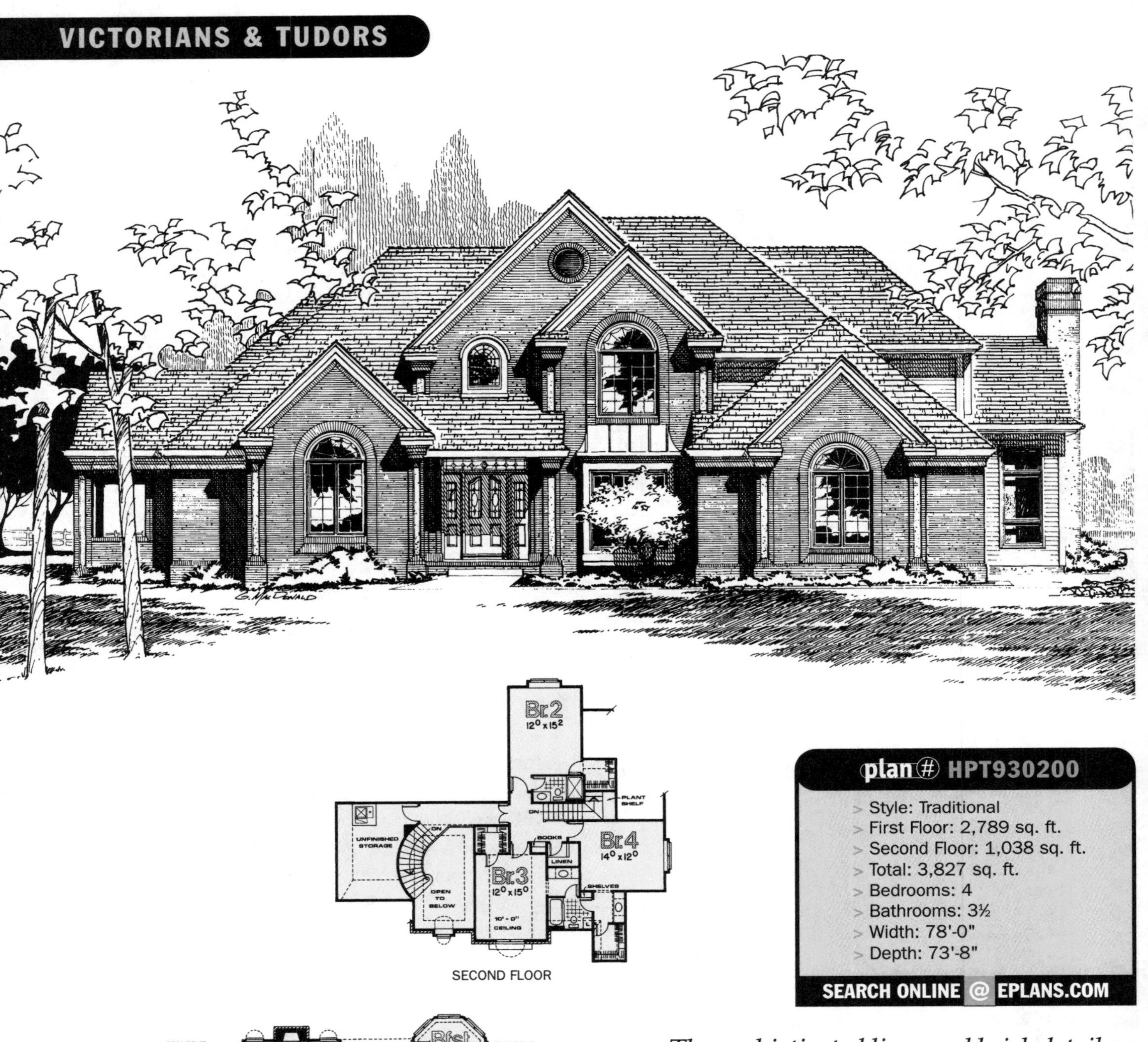

plan# HPT930200

- Style: Traditional
- First Floor: 2,789 sq. ft.
- Second Floor: 1,038 sq. ft.
- Total: 3,827 sq. ft.
- Bedrooms: 4
- Bathrooms: 3½
- Width: 78'-0"
- Depth: 73'-8"

SEARCH ONLINE @ EPLANS.COM

The sophisticated lines and brick details of this house are stunning enhancements. The entry surveys a dramatic curved staircase. French doors open to the den, where a tiered ceiling and a bookcase wall provide a lofty ambiance. Large gatherings are easily accommodated in the dining room. The living room enjoys an eleven-foot ceiling and a fireplace flanked by transom windows. For more casual living, the family room includes a raised-hearth fireplace and a built-in desk. The gourmet kitchen provides two pantries, an island cooktop, a wrapping counter, a snack bar and private stairs to the second level. Four bedrooms include a pampering master suite on the first floor and three family bedrooms upstairs.

plan# HPT930201

- Style: Traditional
- First Floor: 1,829 sq. ft.
- Second Floor: 657 sq. ft.
- Total: 2,486 sq. ft.
- Bedrooms: 4
- Bathrooms: 2½
- Width: 68'-8"
- Depth: 47'-8"

SEARCH ONLINE @ EPLANS.COM

Elegant windows and trim details highlight the exterior of this traditional home. In the living room, transom windows let in plenty of light. The formal dining room features hutch space. Casual living is the focus in the heartwarming kitchen and gathering room. Wrapping counters, a cooktop island with snack bar and an angular breakfast nook nicely balance the large gathering room that's accented with a fireplace. The secluded master suite includes a nine-foot ceiling, pocket door to the den, corner whirlpool tub and huge walk-in closet. Three family bedrooms are on the second floor.

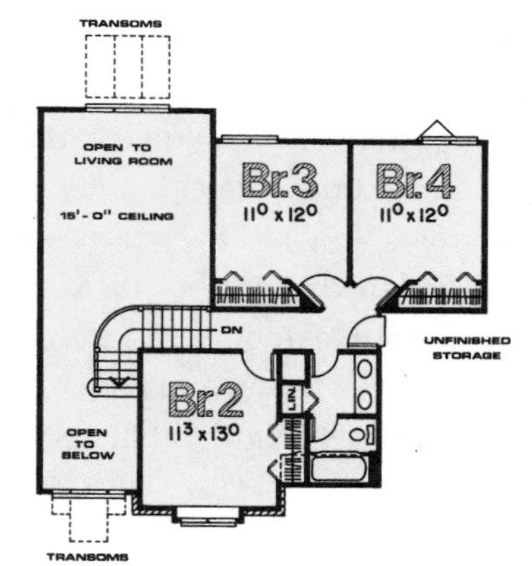

SECOND FLOOR

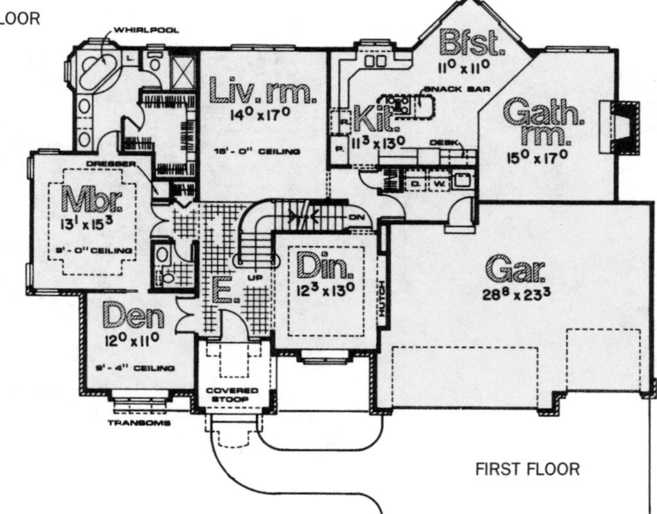

FIRST FLOOR

A dramatic elevation with bright windows hints at the luxurious floor plan of this four-bedroom, two-story home. Upon entry, a beautiful staircase and formal living spaces are in sight. To the right, transom windows and a volume ceiling grace the living room. The dining room accommodates a hutch. The large family room includes elegant bowed windows and a showy three-sided fireplace. A bright dinette and snack bar are served by the open island kitchen. Step up a half-flight of stairs to a private den with double doors and a special ceiling treatment. All secondary bedrooms access either a Hollywood bath or a private bath. A tiered ceiling, sumptuous bath and two closets highlight the master suite.

plan# HPT930202

- Style: Traditional
- First Floor: 1,583 sq. ft.
- Second Floor: 1,331 sq. ft.
- Total: 2,914 sq. ft.
- Bedrooms: 4
- Bathrooms: 3½
- Width: 58'-0"
- Depth: 59'-4"

SEARCH ONLINE @ EPLANS.COM

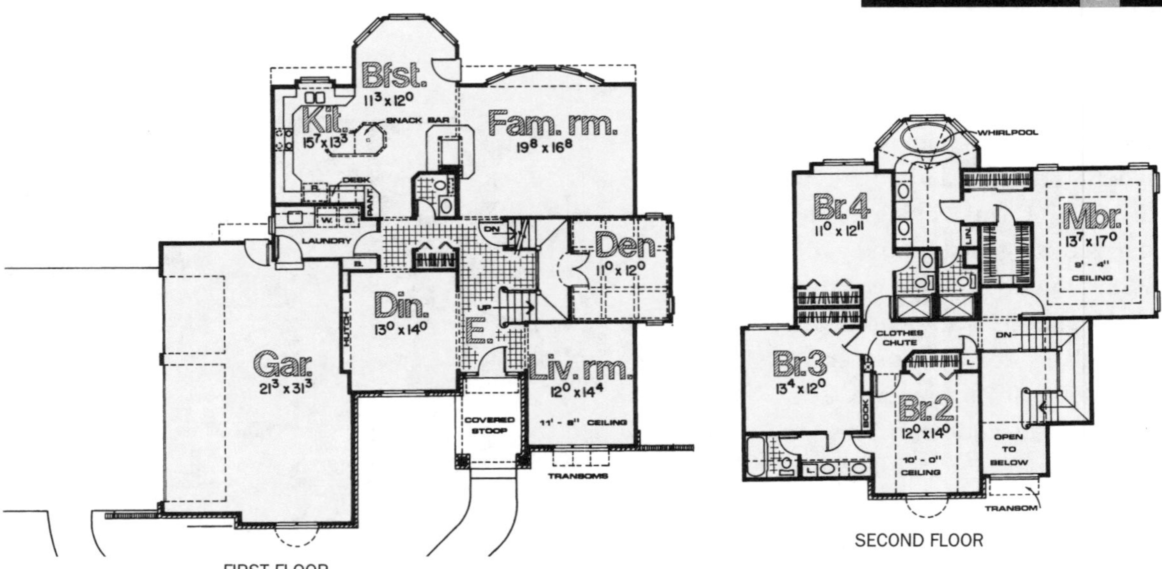

FIRST FLOOR

SECOND FLOOR

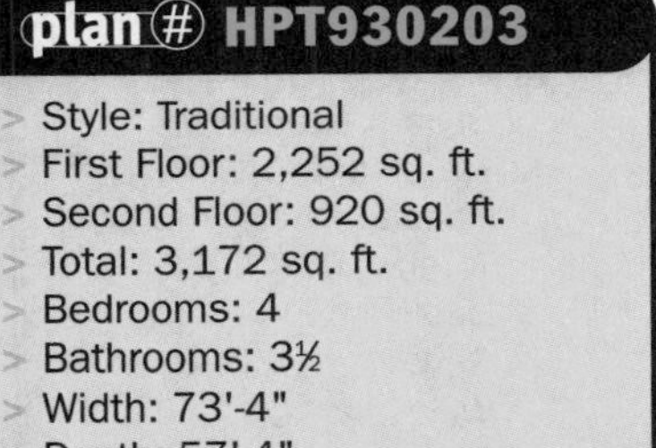
plan# HPT930203

- Style: Traditional
- First Floor: 2,252 sq. ft.
- Second Floor: 920 sq. ft.
- Total: 3,172 sq. ft.
- Bedrooms: 4
- Bathrooms: 3½
- Width: 73'-4"
- Depth: 57'-4"

SEARCH ONLINE @ EPLANS.COM

A curving staircase graces the entry to this beautiful home. Besides an oversized great room with a fireplace and arched windows, there's a cozy hearth room with its own fireplace. The gourmet kitchen has a work island and breakfast area. A secluded den contains bookcases and an arched transom above double doors. The master suite is on the first floor, thoughtfully separated from three family bedrooms upstairs. Bedrooms 2 and 4 share a full bath, while Bedroom 3 has its own private bath. Note the informal second stair to the second floor originating in the hearth room.

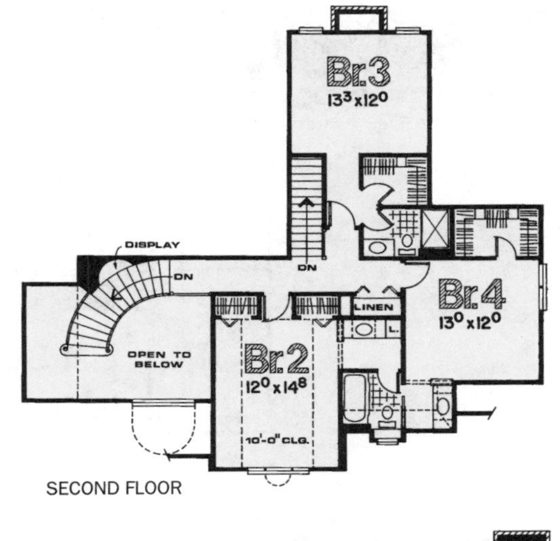

SECOND FLOOR

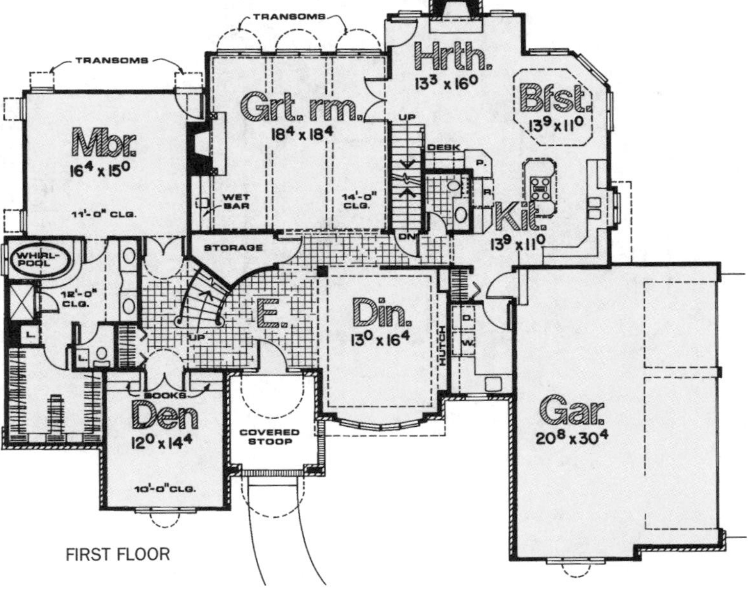

FIRST FLOOR

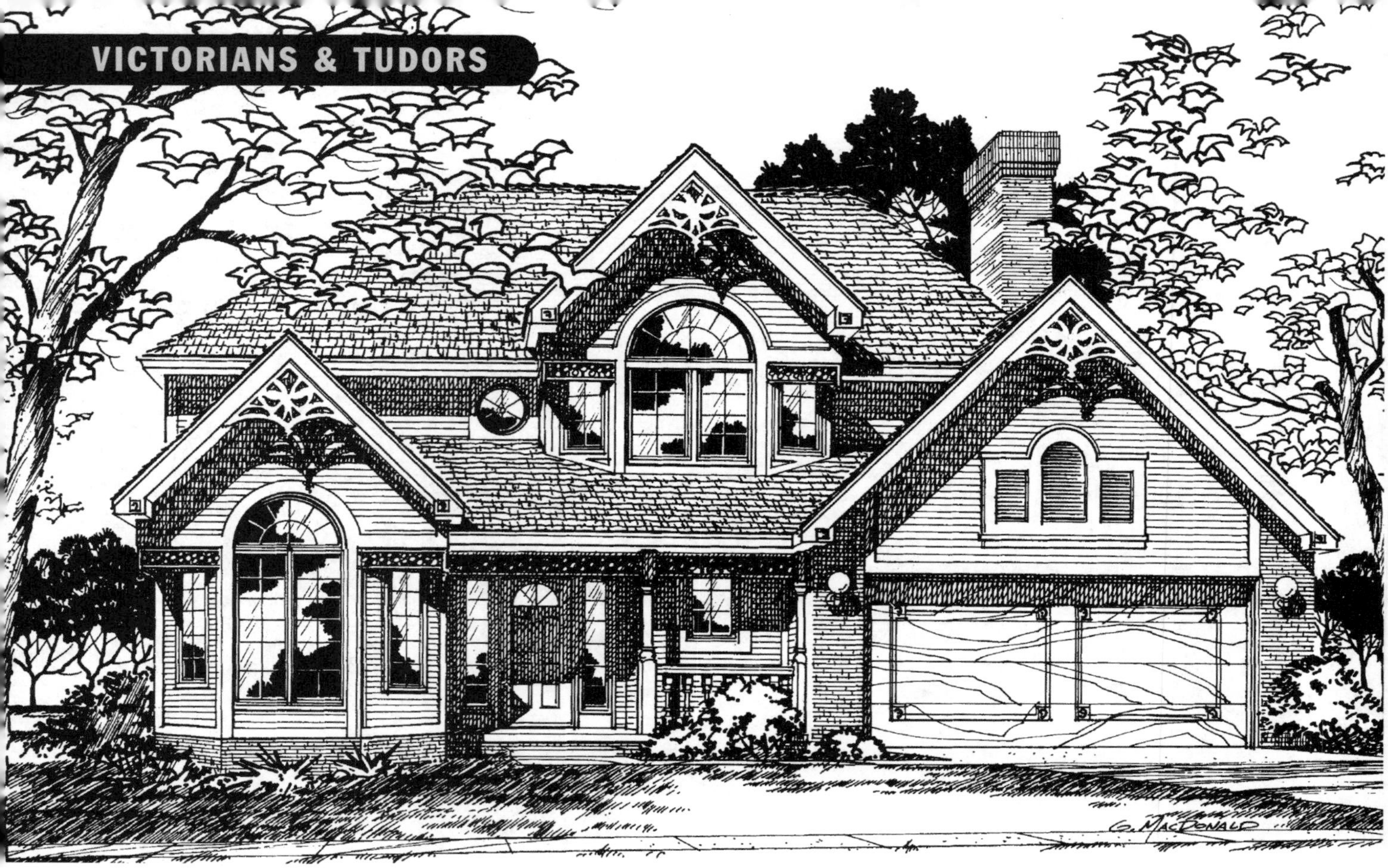

plan# HPT930204

- Style: Victorian
- First Floor: 1,113 sq. ft.
- Second Floor: 965 sq. ft.
- Total: 2,078 sq. ft.
- Bedrooms: 4
- Bathrooms: 2½
- Width: 46'-0"
- Depth: 41'-5"

SEARCH ONLINE @ EPLANS.COM

Yesterday's simpler lifestyle is reflected throughout this plan. From the large bayed parlor with sloped ceiling to the sunken gathering room with fireplace, there's plenty to appreciate about the floor plan. The formal dining room opens to the parlor for convenient entertaining. An L-shaped kitchen with attached breakfast room is nearby. Upstairs quarters include a master suite with private dressing area and whirlpool bath, and three family bedrooms.

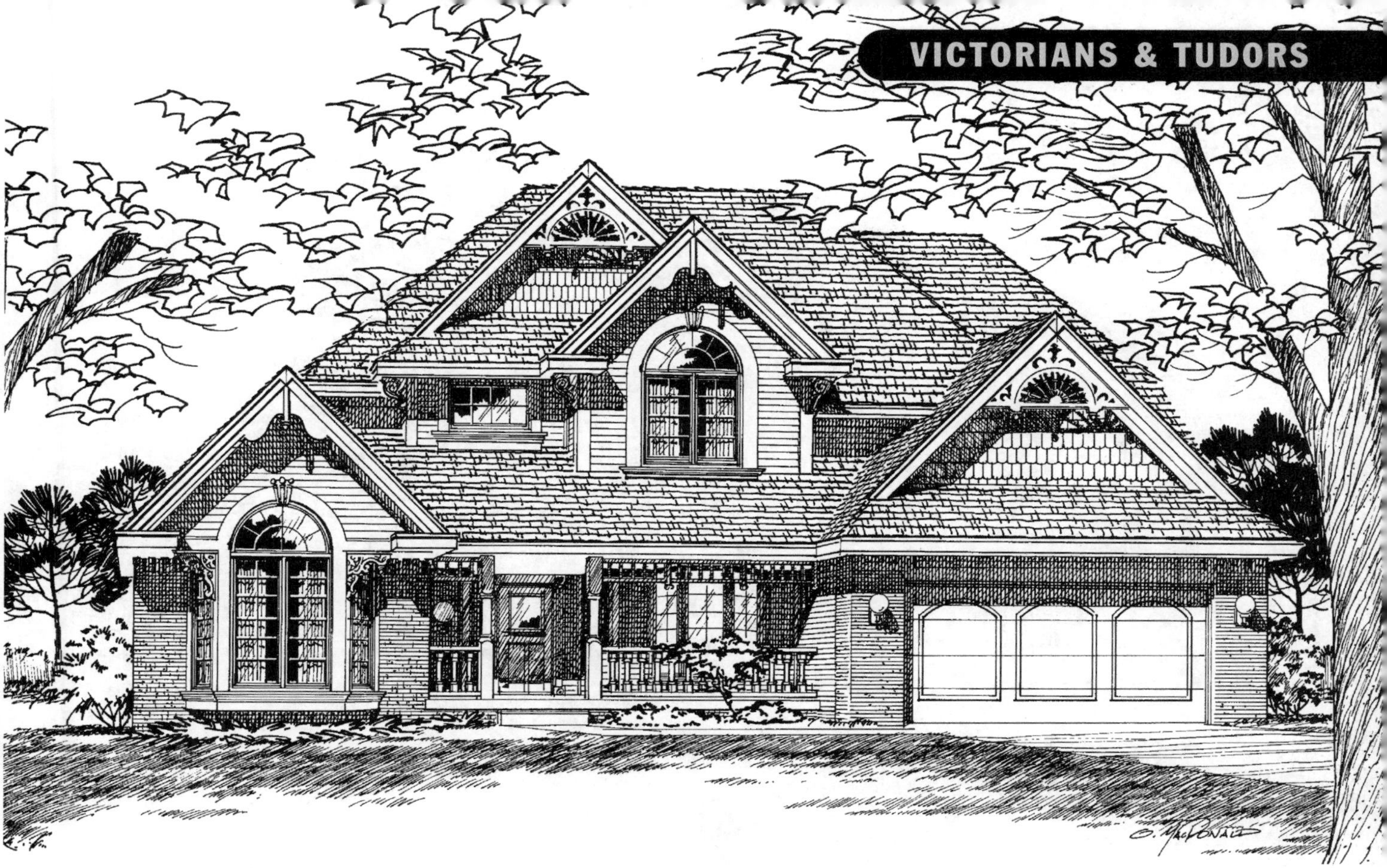

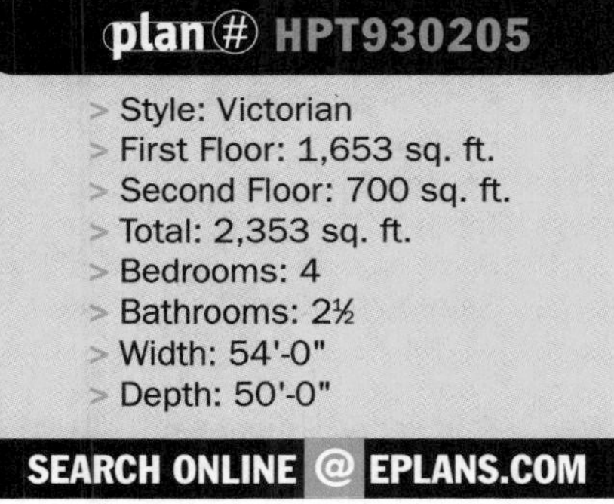

plan# HPT930205

- Style: Victorian
- First Floor: 1,653 sq. ft.
- Second Floor: 700 sq. ft.
- Total: 2,353 sq. ft.
- Bedrooms: 4
- Bathrooms: 2½
- Width: 54'-0"
- Depth: 50'-0"

SEARCH ONLINE @ EPLANS.COM

SECOND FLOOR

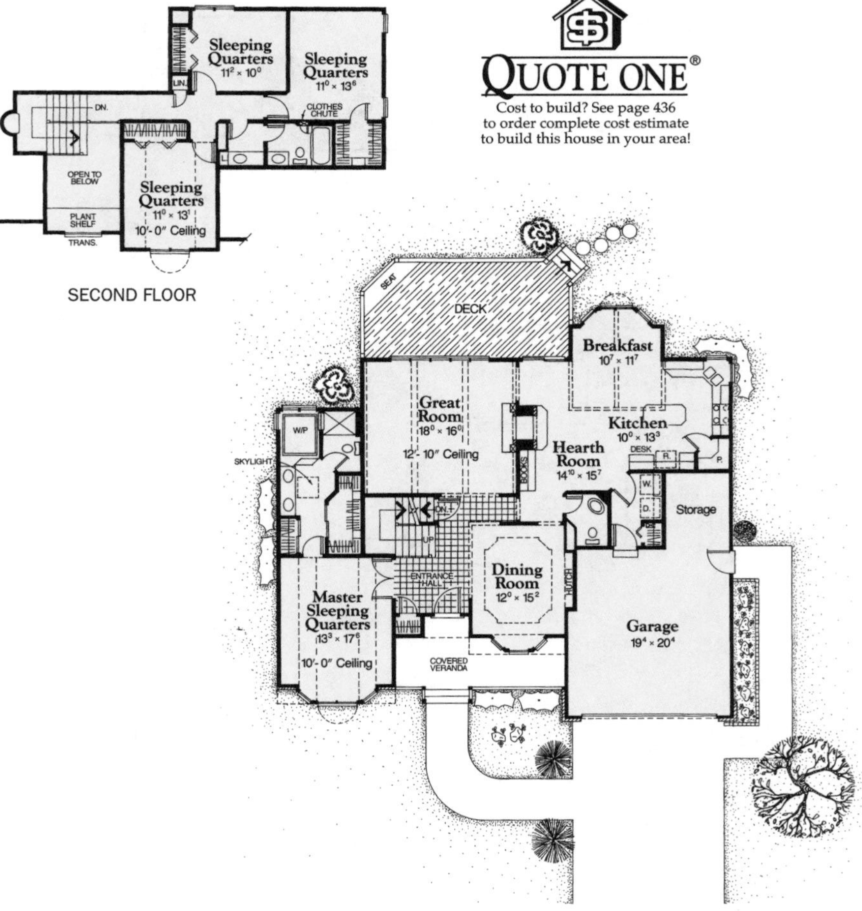

QUOTE ONE®

Cost to build? See page 436 to order complete cost estimate to build this house in your area!

Beautiful arches and elaborate detail give the elevation of this four-bedroom home an unmistakable elegance. Inside, the floor plan is equally appealing. Note the formal dining room with a bay window, visible from the entrance hall. The large great room has a fireplace and a wall of windows with views of the rear property. A hearth room with a built-in bookcase adjoins the kitchen, which boasts a corner walk-in pantry and a spacious breakfast nook with a bay window. The first-floor master suite features His and Hers wardrobes and a large whirlpool tub.

FIRST FLOOR

SECOND FLOOR

FIRST FLOOR

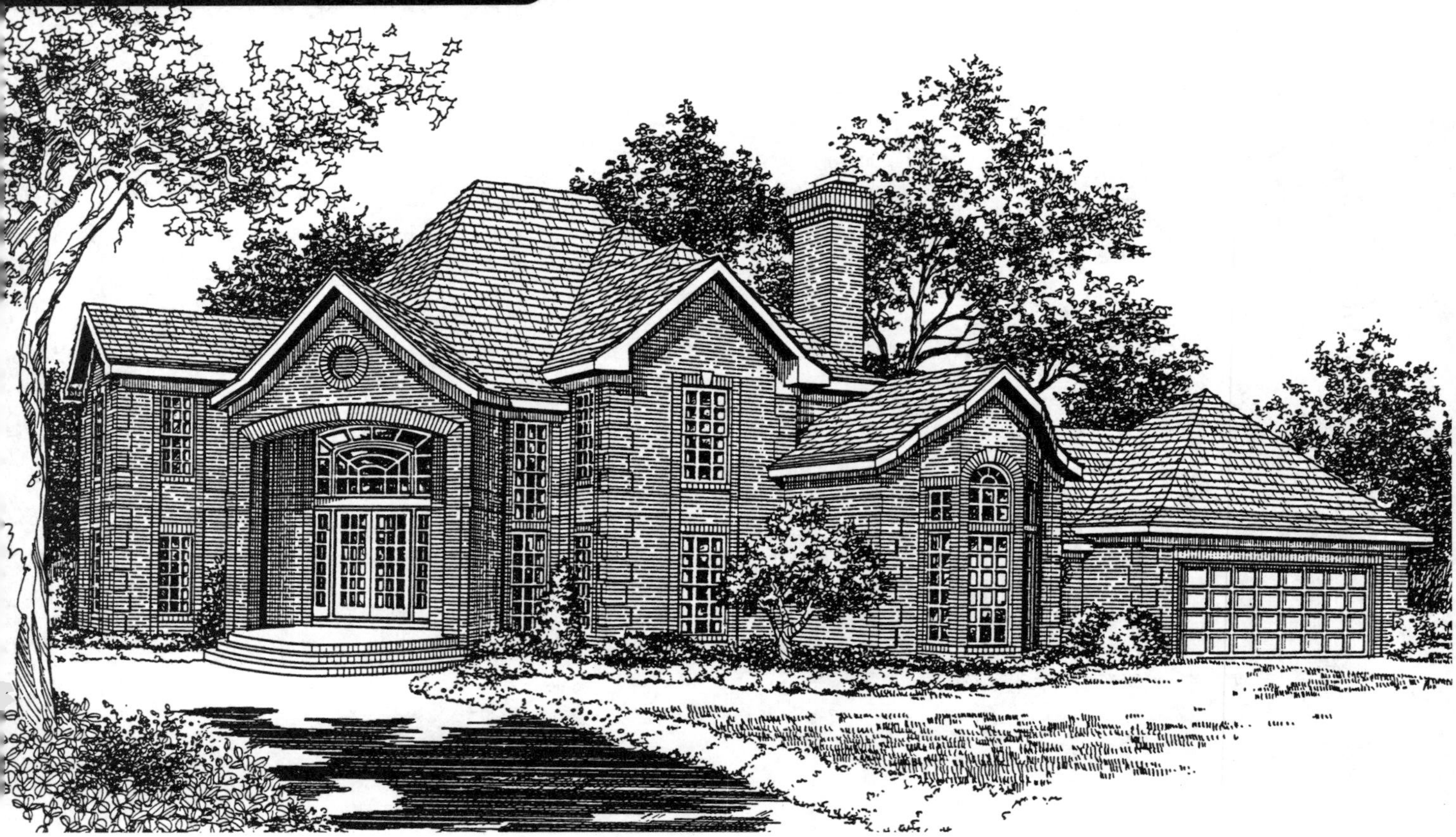

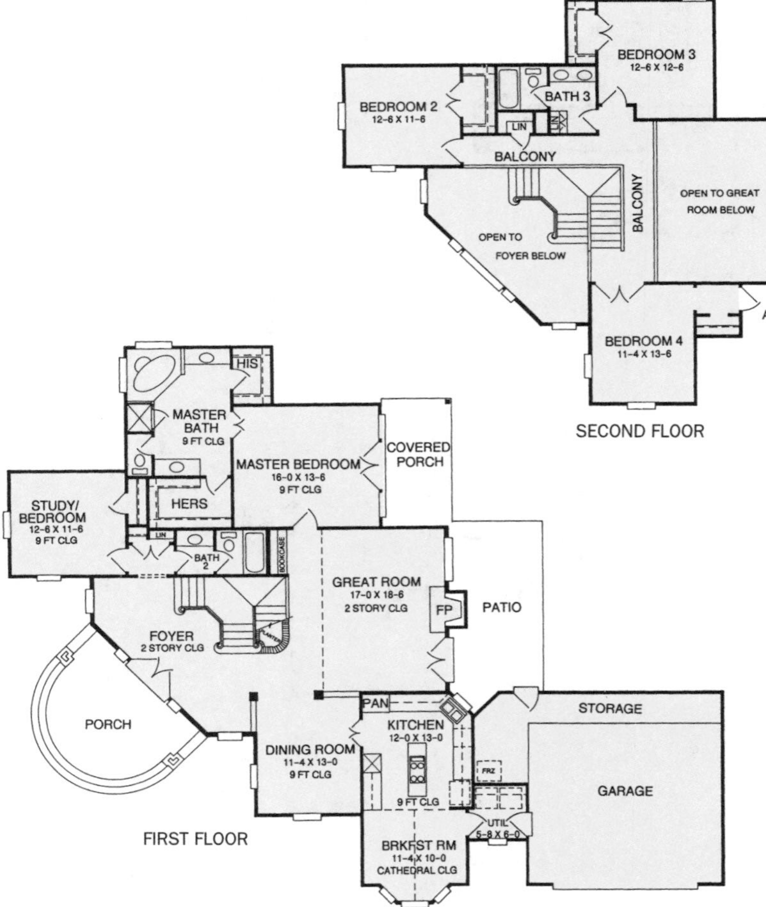

plan# HPT930206

- Style: Traditional
- First Floor: 1,966 sq. ft.
- Second Floor: 872 sq. ft.
- Total: 2,838 sq. ft.
- Bedrooms: 4
- Bathrooms: 3
- Width: 63'-10"
- Depth: 79'-10"
- Foundation: Basement, Crawlspace, Slab

SEARCH ONLINE @ EPLANS.COM

This elegant brick two-story home, with its corner quoins, varied rooflines and multi-pane windows, has so many amenities to offer! Enter into the two-story foyer graced by an elegant, curved staircase. The formal dining room, defined by columns, is nearby and has double-door access to the efficient island kitchen. The large great room is enhanced by a warming fireplace and direct access to the rear patio. The first-floor master bedroom suite is nicely secluded for privacy and pampers with its own covered porch, His and Hers walk-in closets and a lavish bath. Upstairs, all three family bedrooms have walk-in closets and share a full hall bath.

plan# HPT930207

- Style: Traditional
- First Floor: 1,709 sq. ft.
- Second Floor: 1,597 sq. ft.
- Total: 3,306 sq. ft.
- Bedrooms: 4
- Bathrooms: 3½
- Width: 62'-0"
- Depth: 55'-4"

SEARCH ONLINE @ EPLANS.COM

An attractive facade and amenity-filled interior make this home a showplace both outside and in. Immediately off the two-story foyer is the living room and formal dining room, both with interesting ceiling details, and the quiet library with built-in bookcases. The enormous gourmet kitchen features a large island work counter/snack bar, pantry, desk and gazebo breakfast room. Just steps away is the spacious family room with a grand fireplace and windows overlooking the backyard. Upstairs are three family bedrooms served by two baths and a luxurious master suite with a bay-windowed sitting room, detailed ceiling and skylit bath with a whirlpool tub.

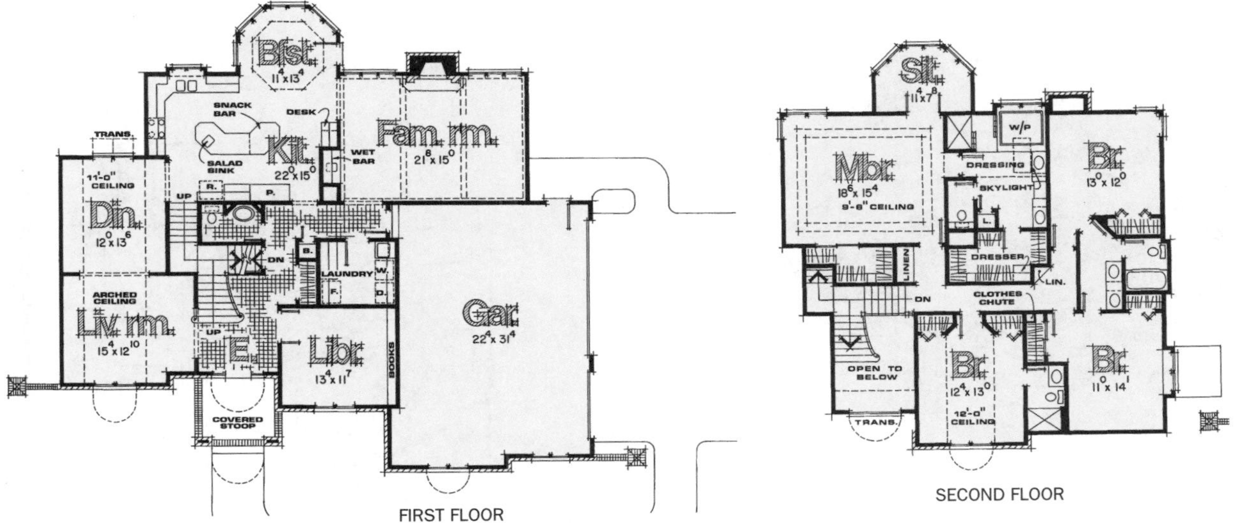

FIRST FLOOR

SECOND FLOOR

A richly detailed entrance sets the elegant tone of this luxurious design. Rising gracefully from the two-story foyer, the staircase is a fine prelude to the great room beyond, where a fantastic span of windows on the back wall overlooks the rear grounds. The dining room is located off the entry and has a lovely coffered ceiling. The kitchen, breakfast room and sun room are conveniently grouped for casual entertaining. The elaborate master suite enjoys a coffered ceiling, private sitting room and spa-style bath. The second level consists of four bedrooms with private baths and a large game room featuring a rear stair.

plan# HPT930208 L

- Style: Traditional
- First Floor: 3,722 sq. ft.
- Second Floor: 1,859 sq. ft.
- Total: 5,581 sq. ft.
- Bedrooms: 5
- Bathrooms: 4½
- Width: 127'-10"
- Depth: 83'-9"
- Foundation: Slab

SEARCH ONLINE @ EPLANS.COM

FIRST FLOOR

SECOND FLOOR

plan# HPT930209

- Style: Victorian
- First Floor: 1,741 sq. ft.
- Second Floor: 1,884 sq. ft.
- Total: 3,625 sq. ft.
- Bedrooms: 5
- Bathrooms: 4
- Width: 61'-9"
- Depth: 48'-10"
- Foundation: Crawlspace

SEARCH ONLINE @ EPLANS.COM

Corner quoins, gabled rooflines and attractive shutters give this four-bedroom home plenty of curb appeal. Inside, the floor plan is designed for entertaining. For formal occasions, there is the living/dining room combination, separated by graceful columns. Casual gatherings will be welcomed in the spacious family room, which features a fireplace, built-ins and direct access to the rear deck. A sunny breakfast room is easily served by the efficient kitchen. A guest room/study with a walk-in closet and a full bath complete this level. Upstairs, three bedrooms share two baths and access to a large playroom/loft. The master bedroom suite is sure to please with a tray ceiling, two walk-in closets and a luxurious bath.

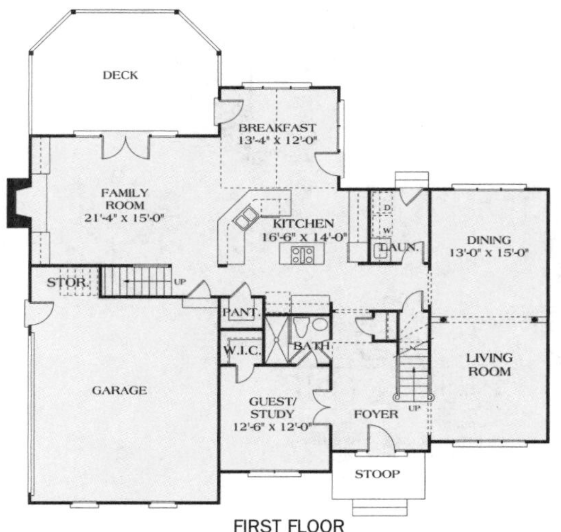

FIRST FLOOR

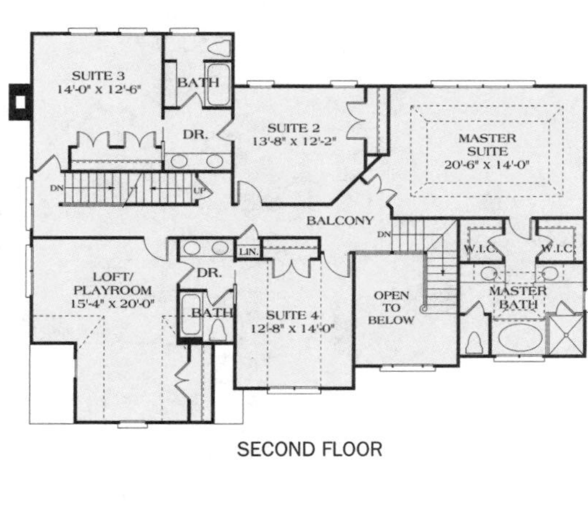

SECOND FLOOR

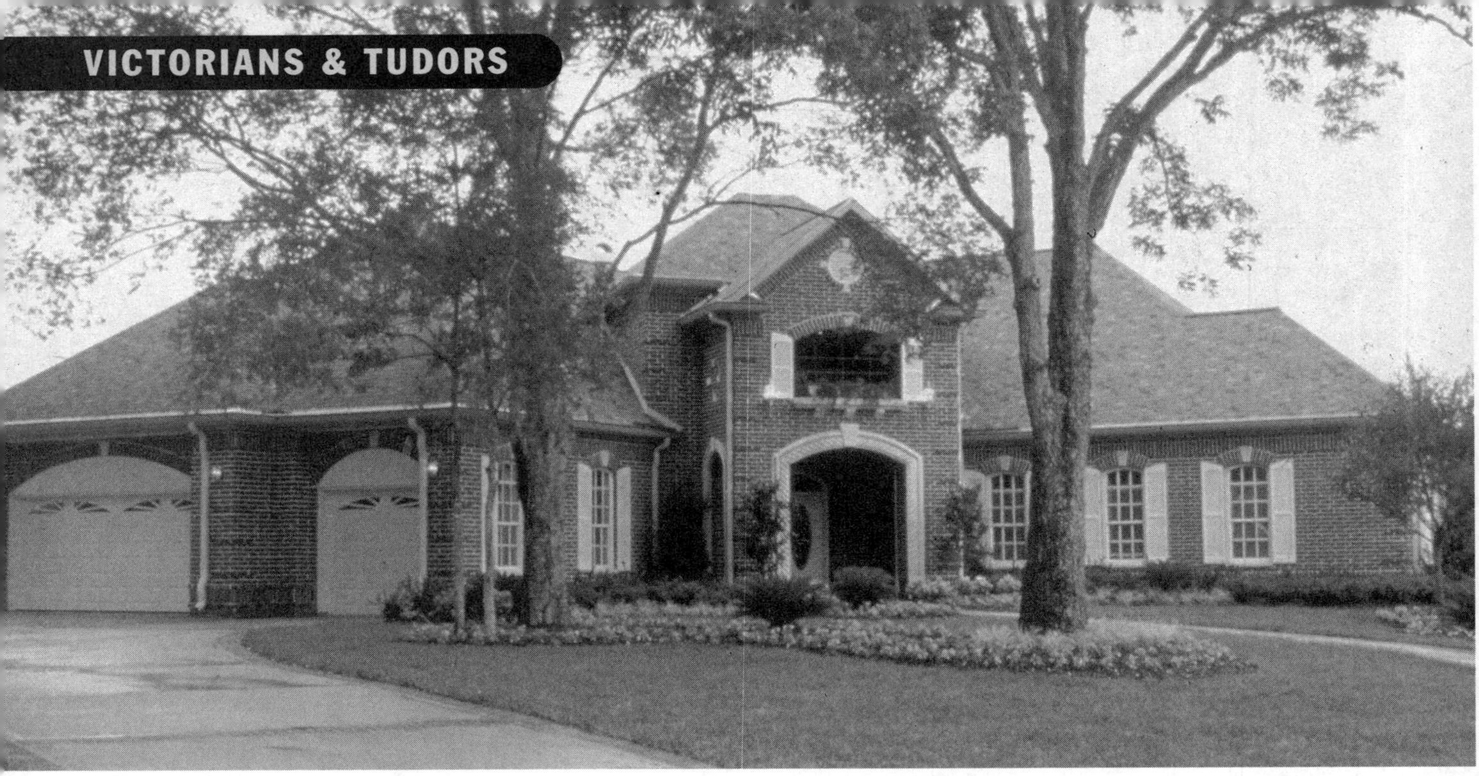

This elegant home combines a traditional exterior with a contemporary interior and provides a delightful setting for both entertaining and individual solitude. A living room and bay-windowed dining room provide an open area for formal entertaining, which can spill outside to the entertainment terrace or to the nearby gathering room with its dramatic fireplace. On the opposite side of the house, French doors make it possible for the study/guest room to be closed off from the rest of the first floor. The master suite is also a private retreat, offering a fireplace as well as an abundance of natural light, and a bath designed to pamper. The entire family will enjoy the second-floor media loft from which a balcony overlooks the two-story gathering room below.

plan# HPT930210

- Style: Traditional
- First Floor: 3,297 sq. ft.
- Second Floor: 1,453 sq. ft.
- Total: 4,750 sq. ft.
- Bedrooms: 5
- Bathrooms: 4½
- Width: 80'-10"
- Depth: 85'-6"
- Foundation: Slab

SEARCH ONLINE @ EPLANS.COM

FIRST FLOOR

QUOTE ONE®
Cost to build? See page 436 to order complete cost estimate to build this house in your area!

SECOND FLOOR

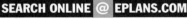

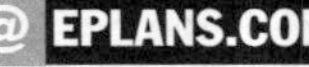

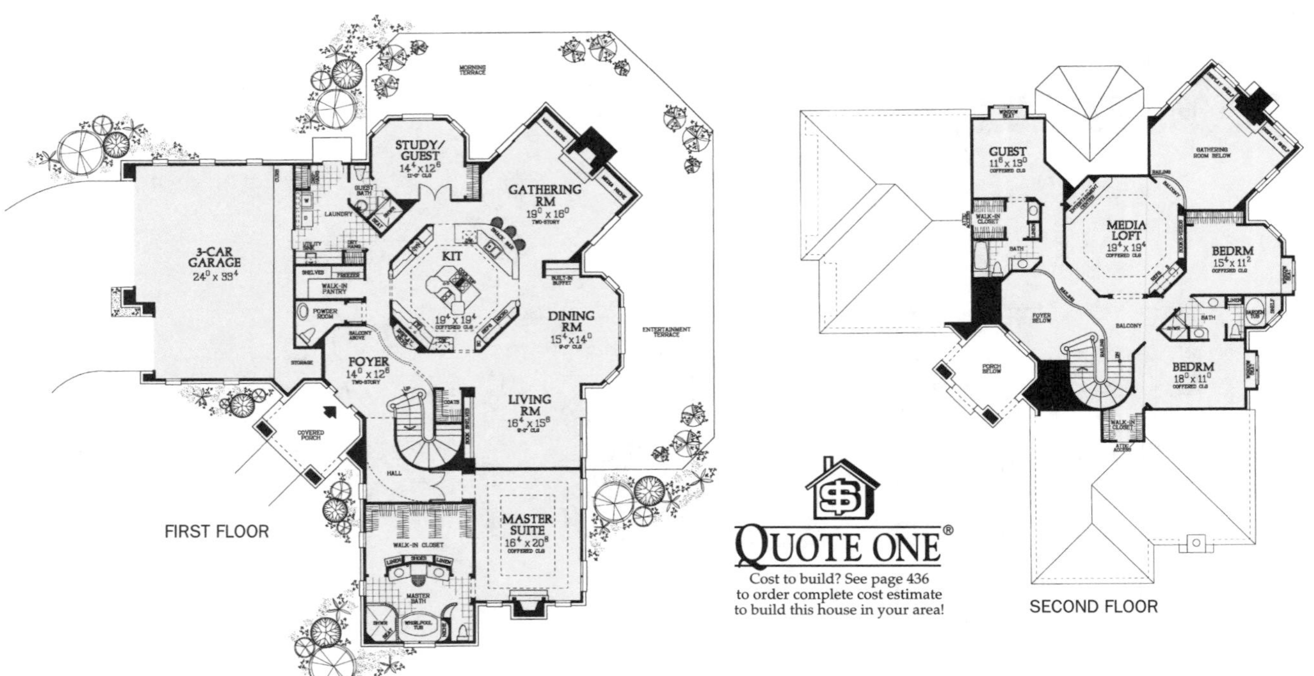

plan# HPT930211

- Style: European Cottage
- First Floor: 2,356 sq. ft.
- Second Floor: 1,450 sq. ft.
- Total: 3,806 sq. ft.
- Bonus Space: 261 sq. ft.
- Bedrooms: 5
- Bathrooms: 4
- Width: 67'-0"
- Depth: 82'-0"
- Foundation: Crawlspace

SEARCH ONLINE @ EPLANS.COM

With sturdy brick detailing, sweeping rooflines and a turret that settles seamlessly into the facade, this fine five-bedroom home will be a winner in any neighborhood. Inside, the two-story foyer leads directly to the spacious great room. A study hides to the right of the foyer, offering privacy. The formal dining room is graced with a ten-foot ceiling, a pass-through to the kitchen and direct access to the backyard. The C-shaped kitchen features a six-burner stove, work island, large walk-in pantry and a nearby octagonal nook. An option for two lavish master suites is available, one on the first floor and one replacing Bedrooms 4 and 5 on the second floor. Each suite includes a decadent bath; the second-floor master bedroom has a romantic fireplace.

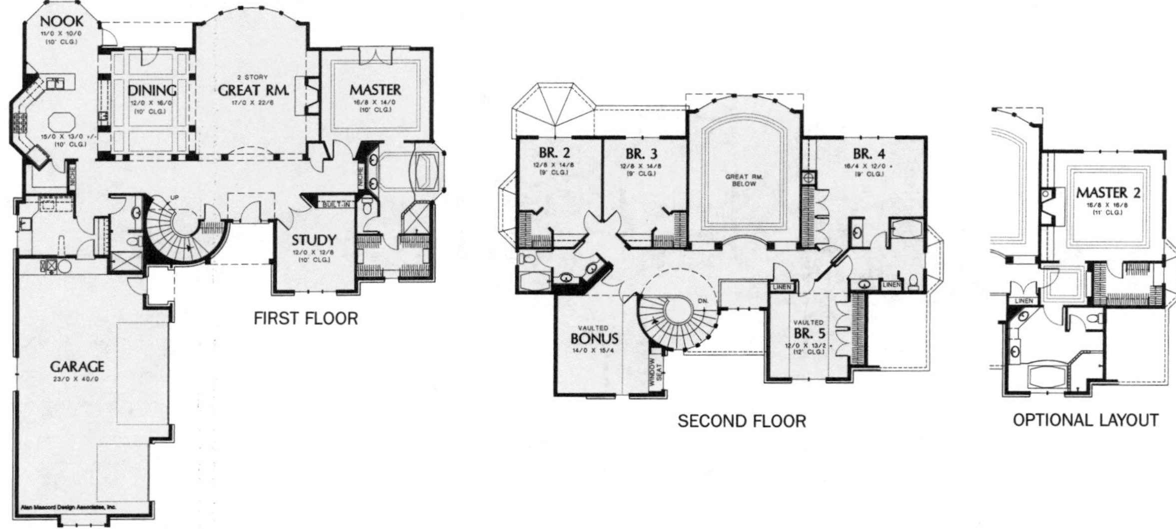

FIRST FLOOR

SECOND FLOOR

OPTIONAL LAYOUT

Suited for a narrow lot, this design may also be finished with brick if you prefer. It features a flawless floor plan with space for both formal and informal occasions. The living/dining room area is warmed by a fireplace and has large window areas overlooking the front yard. The smaller, cozier den can be reached from either the family room or the foyer. Look for another fireplace in the family room, as well as sliding glass doors to the rear yard. The kitchen and breakfast area separate the formal from the informal living areas. The second floor holds two family bedrooms and a master suite with private bath. There is also a gallery with corner windows and a storage closet, plus a bonus room, which can become a fourth bedroom

plan# HPT930212

- Style: Tudor
- First Floor: 1,100 sq. ft.
- Second Floor: 1,157 sq. ft.
- Total: 2,257 sq. ft.
- Bonus Space: 204 sq. ft.
- Bedrooms: 3
- Bathrooms: 2½
- Width: 30'-0"
- Depth: 60'-0"
- Foundation: Basement

SEARCH ONLINE @ EPLANS.COM

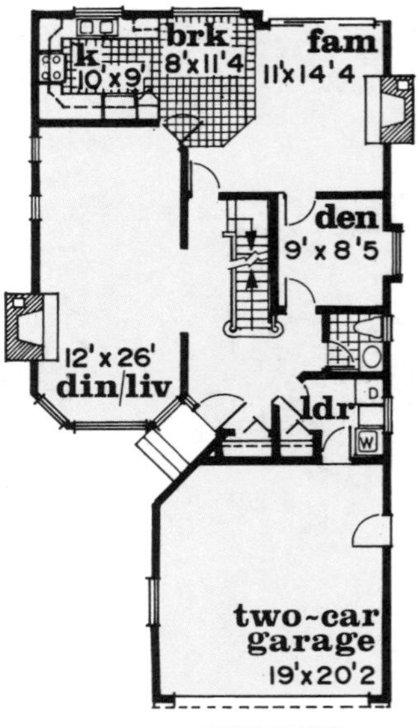

k 10'x9'
brk 8'x11'4
fam 11'x14'4
den 9'x8'5
12'x26' din/liv
ldr
two-car garage 19'x20'2

FIRST FLOOR

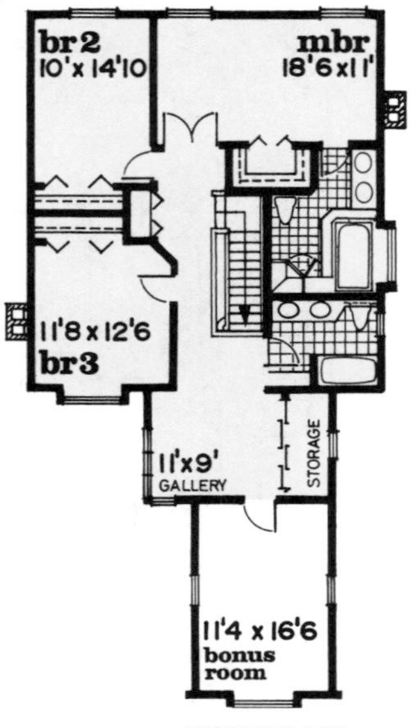

br2 10'x14'10
mbr 18'6x11'
11'8x12'6 br3
11'x9' GALLERY
STORAGE
11'4 x 16'6 bonus room

SECOND FLOOR

ALTERNATE EXTERIOR

plan# HPT930213

- Style: Farmhouse
- First Floor: 1,182 sq. ft.
- Second Floor: 838 sq. ft.
- Total: 2,020 sq. ft.
- Bedrooms: 4
- Bathrooms: 3
- Width: 62'-0"
- Depth: 52'-0"
- Foundation: Basement, Crawlspace, Slab

SEARCH ONLINE @ EPLANS.COM

Behind this intriguing exterior sits a brilliant plan with open living areas and a secluded master suite on the first floor. The entry introduces the combined living and dining rooms, both featuring French-door access to the back porch—the perfect recipe for entertaining large and small groups. The master suite also enjoys a private entrance to the porch. The second floor holds three bedrooms that feature lots of closet space. Bedroom 4 contains its own private bath and is accessible to the attic. An efficient kitchen, powder room and laundry area complete the plan.

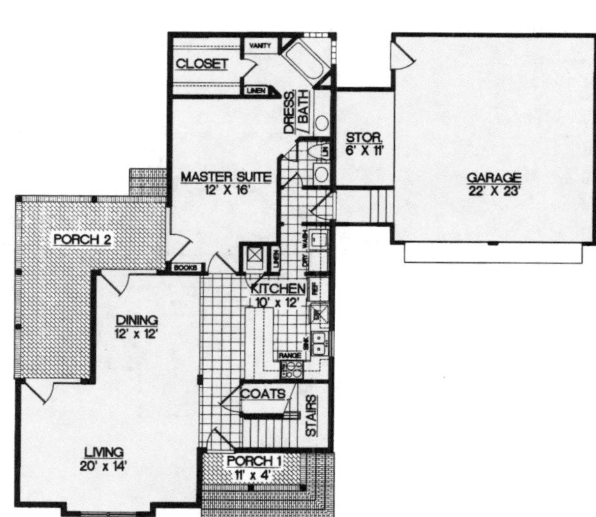

FIRST FLOOR

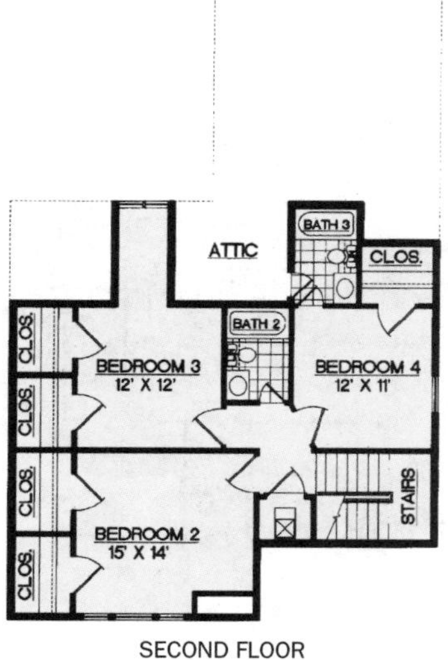

SECOND FLOOR

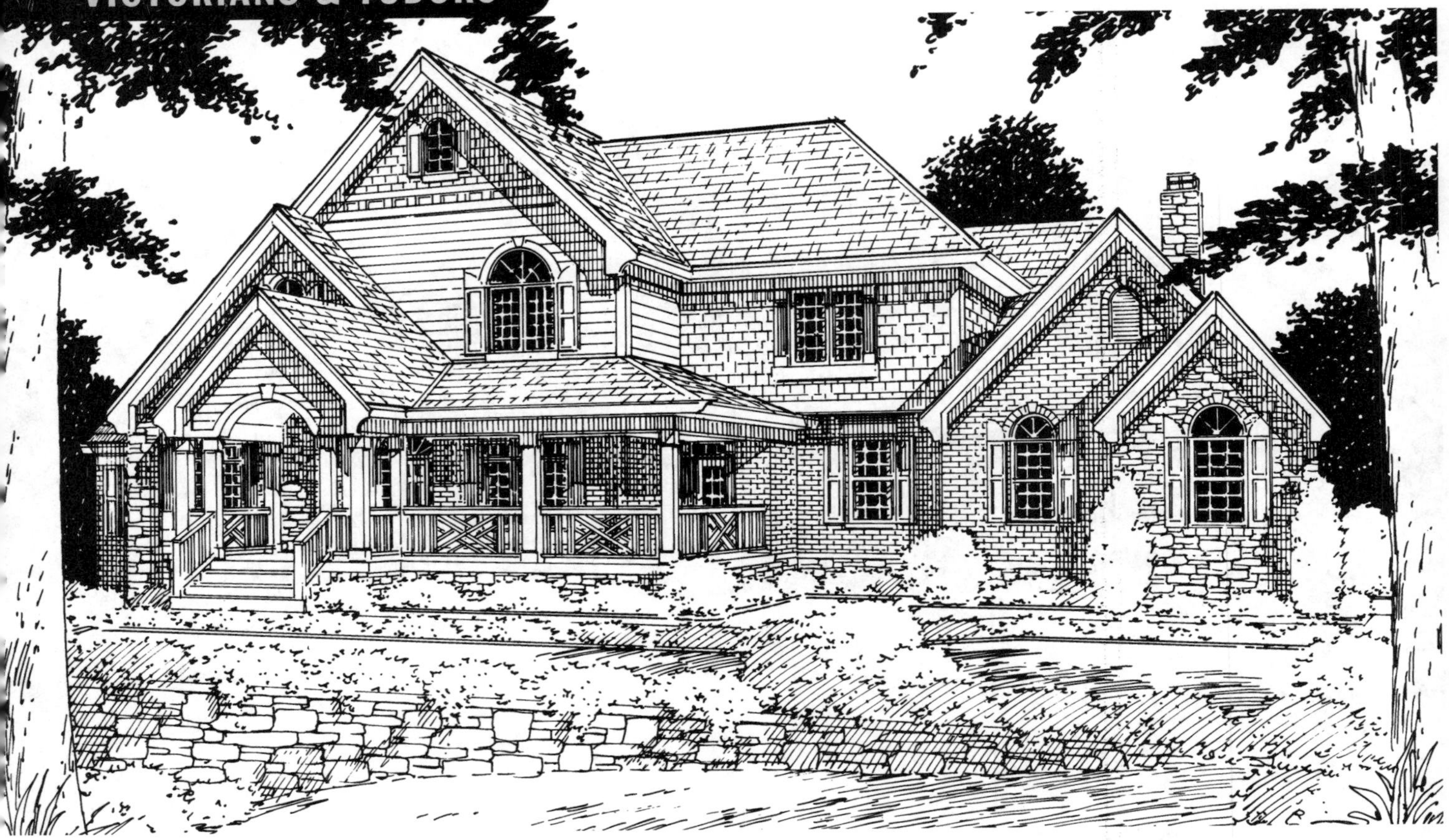

This lovely plan steps into the future with an exterior mix of brick, stone and cedar siding. With a large front porch, the home appears as if it should be located in a quaint oceanfront community. Comfortable elegance coupled with modern-day amenities and nostalgic materials makes this home a great choice. The large great room and hearth room/breakfast area offer grand views to the rear yard, where a large deck complements outdoor activities.

plan# HPT930214

- Style: Tudor
- First Floor: 2,665 sq. ft.
- Second Floor: 1,081 sq. ft.
- Total: 3,746 sq. ft.
- Bedrooms: 4
- Bathrooms: 3½
- Width: 88'-0"
- Depth: 52'-6"
- Foundation: Walkout Basement

SEARCH ONLINE @ EPLANS.COM

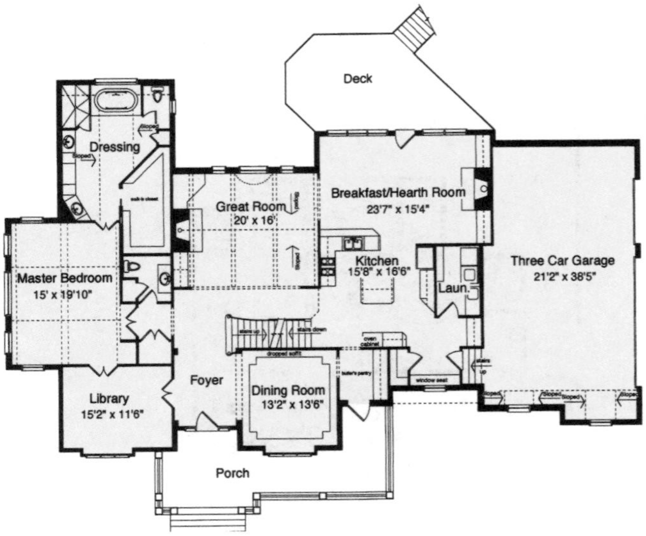

Deck
Dressing
Great Room
20' x 16'
Breakfast/Hearth Room
23'7" x 15'4"
Kitchen
15'8" x 16'6"
Laun.
Three Car Garage
21'2" x 38'5"
Master Bedroom
15' x 19'10"
Library
15'2" x 11'6"
Foyer
Dining Room
13'2" x 13'6"
Porch

FIRST FLOOR

Great Room
Below
Computer
Loft
Bedroom
13'6" x 16'2"
Bath
Bedroom
13'6" x 14'5"
Foyer
Below
Bedroom
13'6" x 13'10"
Bath

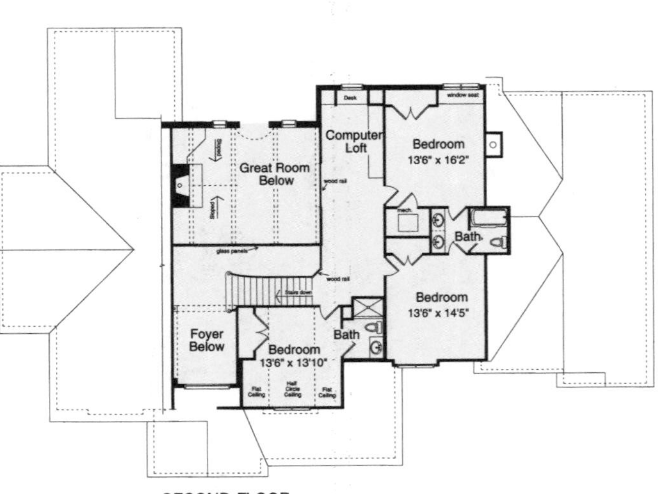

SECOND FLOOR

plan# HPT930215

- Style: Southern Colonial
- First Floor: 1,305 sq. ft.
- Second Floor: 1,052 sq. ft.
- Total: 2,357 sq. ft.
- Bonus Space: 430 sq. ft.
- Bedrooms: 3
- Bathrooms: 2½
- Width: 69'-4"
- Depth: 35'-10"
- Foundation: Crawlspace, Basement

SEARCH ONLINE @ EPLANS.COM

With a hipped roofline, whitewashed brick and attractive shutters, this fine Colonial will dress up any neighborhood. Inside, the foyer introduces the formal living room to the right, which is separated from the formal dining room by graceful columns—a perfect layout for dinner parties. The spacious family room offers a warming fireplace, built-ins and backyard access. Designed with an efficient island, the kitchen easily serves the formal dining room as well as the sunny breakfast area. Upstairs, two family bedrooms share a hall bath, and the master suite provides privacy with a lavish bath and His and Hers walk-in closets.

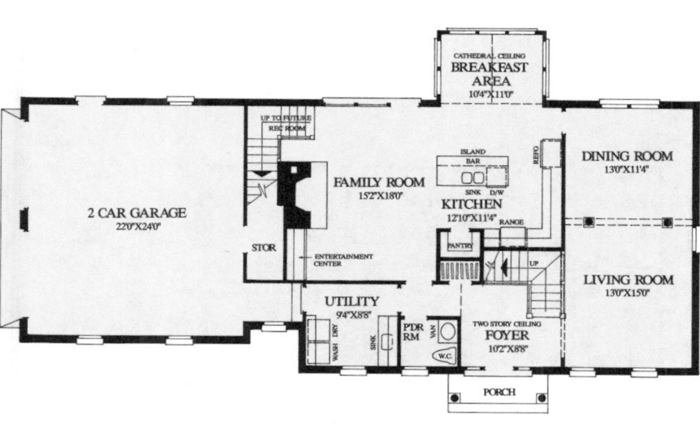

FIRST FLOOR

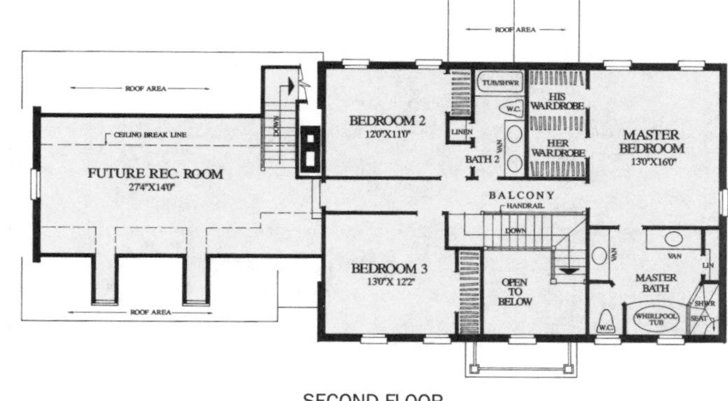

SECOND FLOOR

The grandeur of this Southern estate belies the practical floor plan within. An elegant foyer joins the dining room and oversized living room—both with fireplaces—to welcome guests. The left wing comprises a gourmet kitchen with a walk-in pantry, two powder rooms and a utility area featuring a mud-room and a separate entrance. The two-story family room, with porch access and a fireplace, is central, while the right wing is devoted to a luxurious master suite and a private study, each with a fireplace. An expansive upper level includes three family suites, a balcony overlook and future space for a fifth bedroom and bath, as well as a game room.

plan# HPT930216

- Style: Plantation
- First Floor: 3,635 sq. ft.
- Second Floor: 1,400 sq. ft.
- Total: 5,035 sq. ft.
- Bonus Space: 789 sq. ft.
- Bedrooms: 4
- Bathrooms: 4½ + ½
- Width: 121'-6"
- Depth: 59'-5"
- Foundation: Basement, Crawlspace

SEARCH ONLINE @ EPLANS.COM

FIRST FLOOR

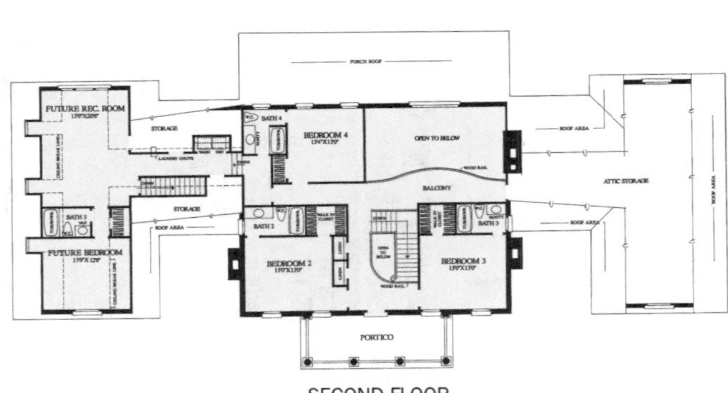

SECOND FLOOR

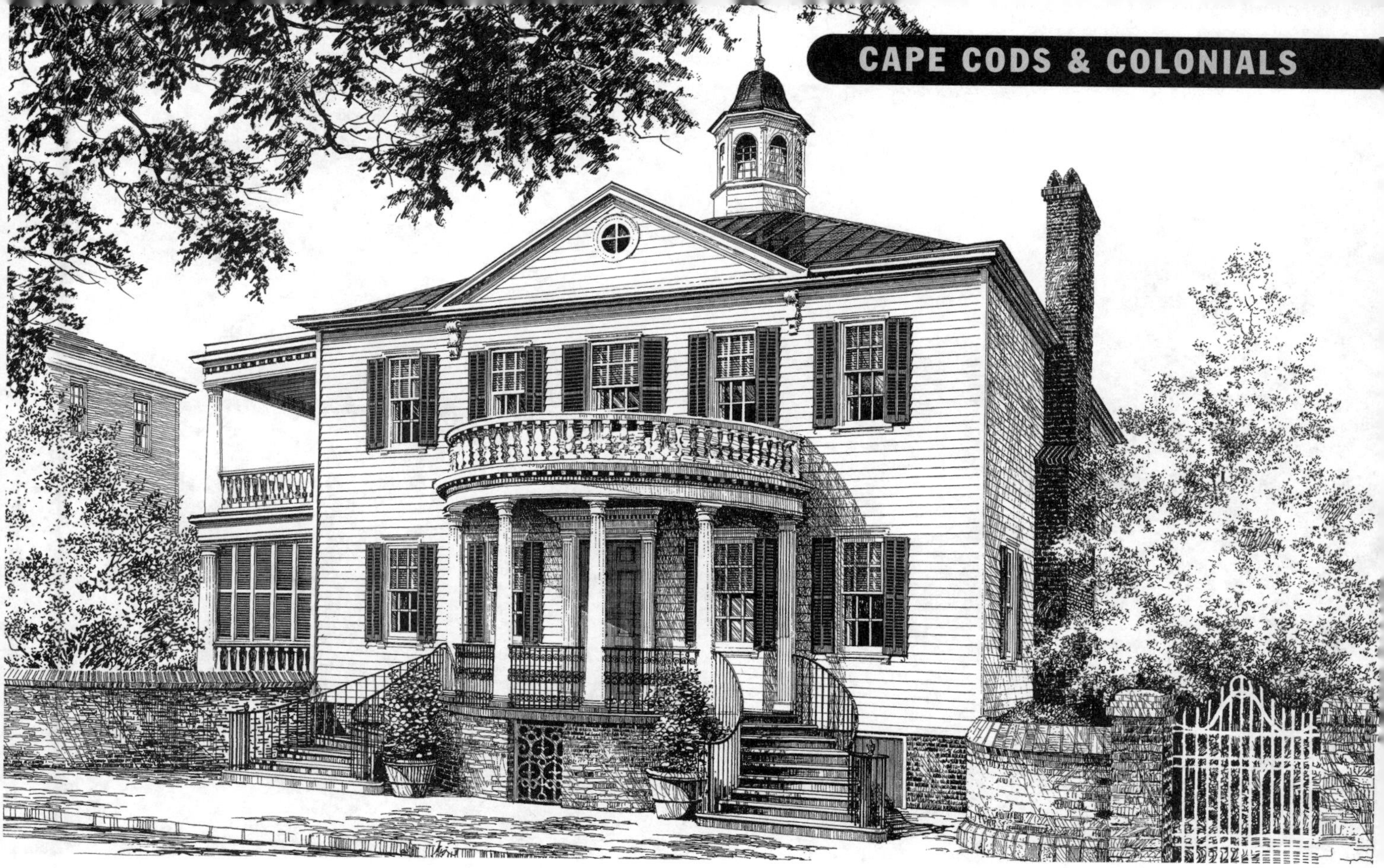

plan# HPT930217

- Style: Georgian
- First Floor: 2,064 sq. ft.
- Second Floor: 1,521 sq. ft.
- Total: 3,585 sq. ft.
- Bonus Space: 427 sq. ft.
- Bedrooms: 4
- Bathrooms: 3
- Width: 84'-8"
- Depth: 65'-0"
- Foundation: Crawlspace

SEARCH ONLINE @ EPLANS.COM

This home has a very stately, southern appeal. The two-story portico adds great depth and appeal to this home's feel. Windows align the first and second floor of this beautiful home. The expansive interior offers the homeowner many options in a way of decorating and designing. The room just left of the two-story foyer can either be a fourth bedroom or a library. Fireplaces warm both the family room and living room. A sunroom is just off the kitchen to make cooking in any season a bright occasion. The master bedroom and two family bedrooms are located on the second floor.

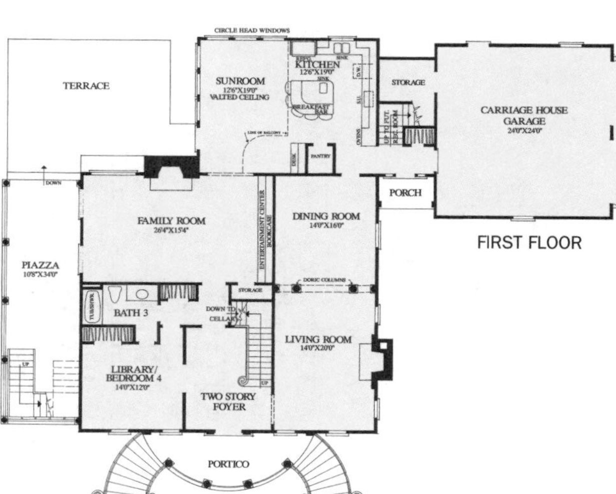

FIRST FLOOR

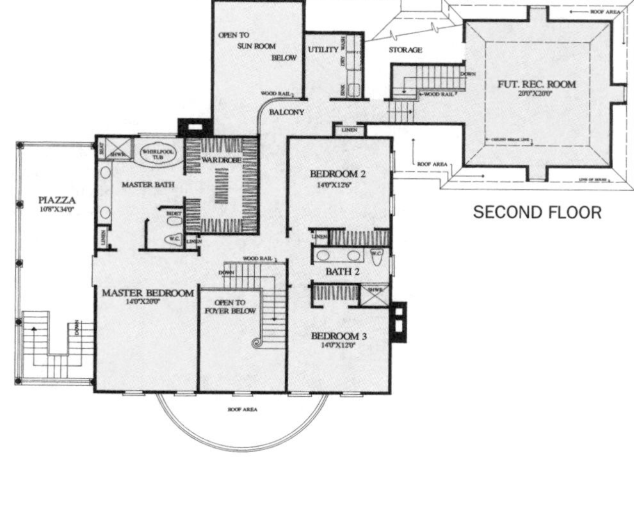

SECOND FLOOR

This magnificent estate is detailed with exterior charm: a porte cochere connecting the detached garage to the house, a covered terrace and oval windows. The first floor consists of a lavish master suite, a cozy library with a fireplace, a grand room/solarium combination and an elegant formal dining room with another fireplace. Three bedrooms dominate the second floor—each features a walk-in closet. For the kids, there is a playroom and, up another flight of stairs, is a room for future expansion into a deluxe studio with a fireplace. Over the three-car garage, there is a room for a future mother-in-law or maid's suite.

plan# HPT930218

- Style: Colonial
- First Floor: 3,703 sq. ft.
- Second Floor: 1,427 sq. ft.
- Total: 5,130 sq. ft.
- Bonus Space: 1,399 sq. ft.
- Bedrooms: 4
- Bathrooms: 4½ + ½
- Width: 125'-2"
- Depth: 58'-10"
- Foundation: Walkout Basement

SEARCH ONLINE @ EPLANS.COM

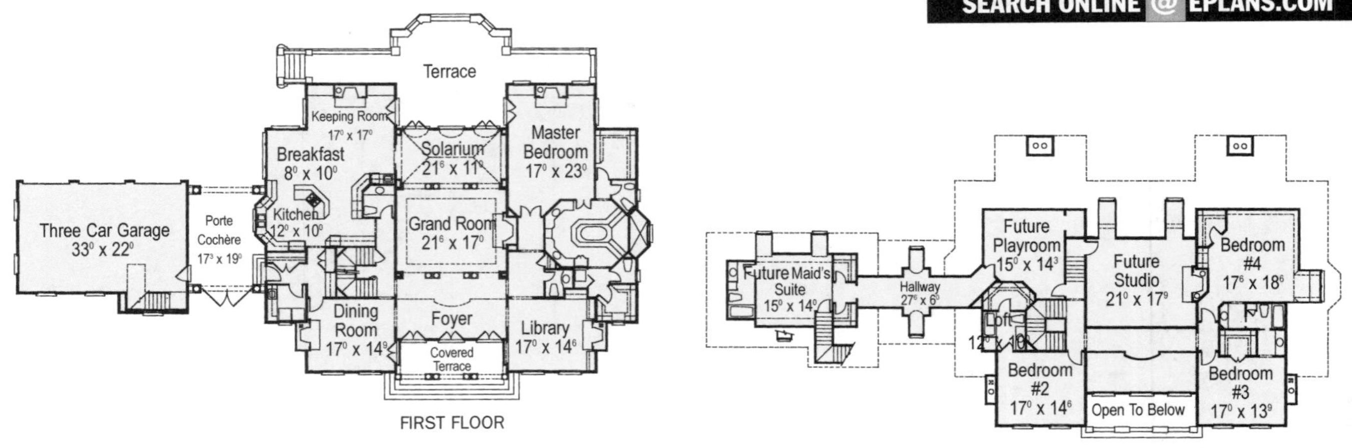

FIRST FLOOR

SECOND FLOOR

plan# HPT930219

- Style: Federal
- First Floor: 3,294 sq. ft.
- Second Floor: 1,300 sq. ft.
- Total: 4,594 sq. ft.
- Bedrooms: 5
- Bathrooms: 3½
- Width: 106'-10"
- Depth: 52'-10"
- Foundation: Basement

SEARCH ONLINE @ EPLANS.COM

The charm of the Old South is designed into this stately Federal manor. A round entry portico leads to the two-story foyer with a circular staircase. The formal living room, dining room and family room each feature a distinctive fireplace; the latter is also highlighted by a built-in entertainment center, walk-in wet bar, beamed cathedral ceiling and access to a rear covered patio. Impressive ten-foot ceilings grace the entire first floor. The secluded master bedroom has a vaulted ceiling, three walk-in closets and porch access. Four additional bedrooms on the second floor share adjoining baths.

FIRST FLOOR

SECOND FLOOR

The dazzling exterior of this Southern estate is true to form with six magnificent columns creating an awe-inspiring facade. The foyer leads to the living room with its fifteen-foot ceiling and paired window walls. Access to both the rear covered porch and the side courtyard is gained from the living room. The angled kitchen is flanked by the sunny eating bay and the convenient utility room. The side-loading, two-car garage at the rear contains an expansive storage area. The second floor holds the game room, an ancillary kitchen and three bedrooms while the master suite finds seclusion on the first floor. Bedroom 4 includes a dressing area, a private bath and access to the balcony.

plan# HPT930220

- Style: Greek Revival
- First Floor: 1,944 sq. ft.
- Second Floor: 1,427 sq. ft.
- Total: 3,371 sq. ft.
- Bedrooms: 4
- Bathrooms: 3½
- Width: 52'-0"
- Depth: 84'-0"
- Foundation: Basement, Crawlspace, Slab

SEARCH ONLINE @ EPLANS.COM

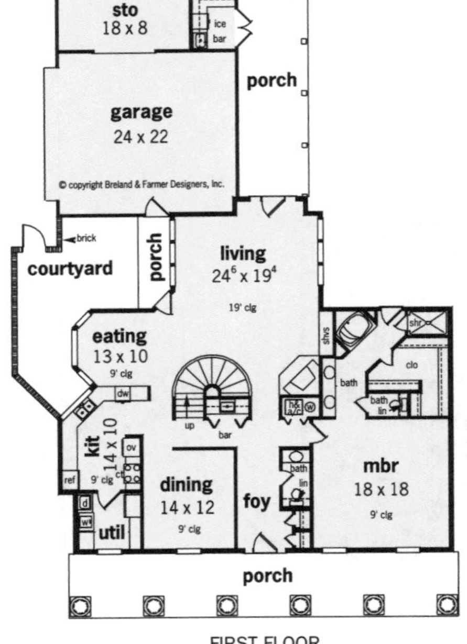

FIRST FLOOR

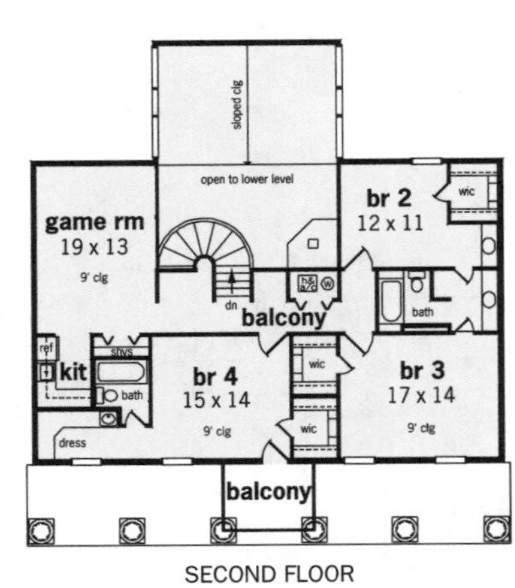

SECOND FLOOR

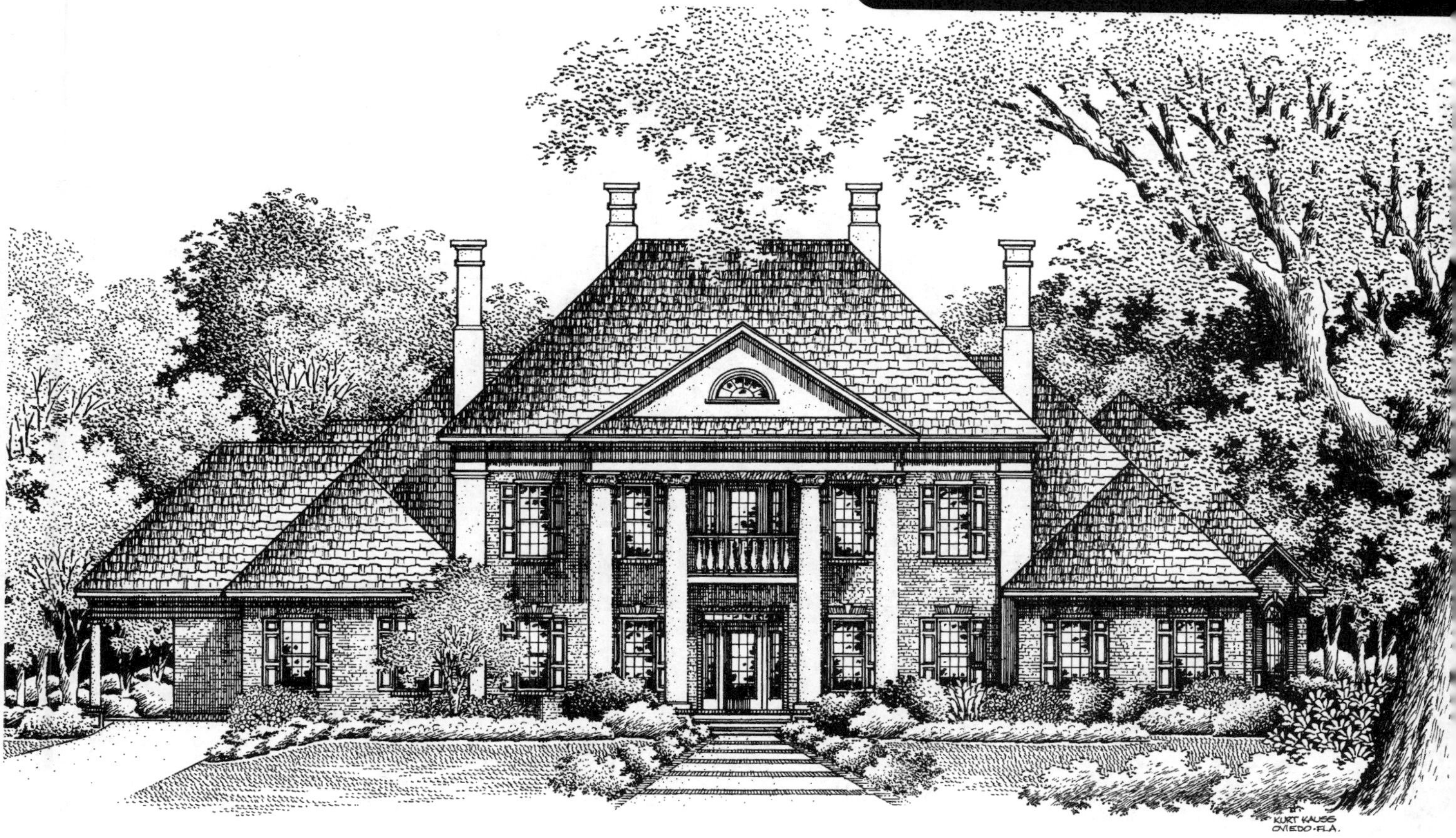

plan# HPT930221

- Style: Southern Colonial
- First Floor: 3,439 sq. ft.
- Second Floor: 803 sq. ft.
- Total: 4,242 sq. ft.
- Bedrooms: 4
- Bathrooms: 4½ + ½ + ½
- Width: 95'-0"
- Depth: 90'-0"
- Foundation: Slab

SEARCH ONLINE @ EPLANS.COM

Although the exterior of this classic estate is pure Colonial, the floor plan is anything but old fashioned. The grand foyer opens up to the sunken two-story living room, detailed with columns, a fireplace and access to the rear property. To the left, a sunny bayed eating area joins a unique kitchen (with a butler's pantry) and the formal dining room for casual or formal meals. The veranda includes an outdoor grill and bar, perfect for dining alfresco. The right wing is devoted to sumptuous living: enter the master bedroom through a private sitting room with a two-sided fireplace. The sunken sleeping area flows into a pampering bath. Upstairs, dual central staircases present two generous bedrooms, each with a private bath and study area, and a balcony designed to accommodate a library.

FIRST FLOOR

SECOND FLOOR

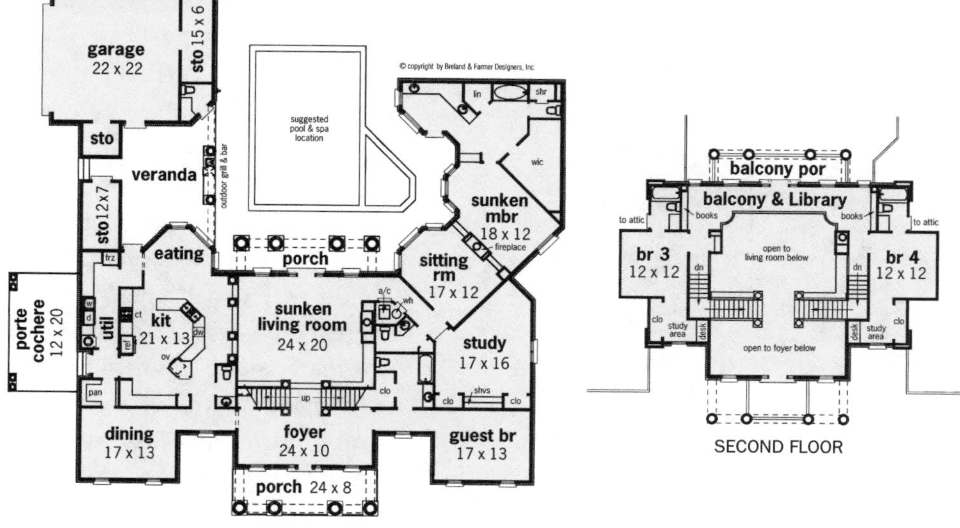

FIRST FLOOR

SECOND FLOOR

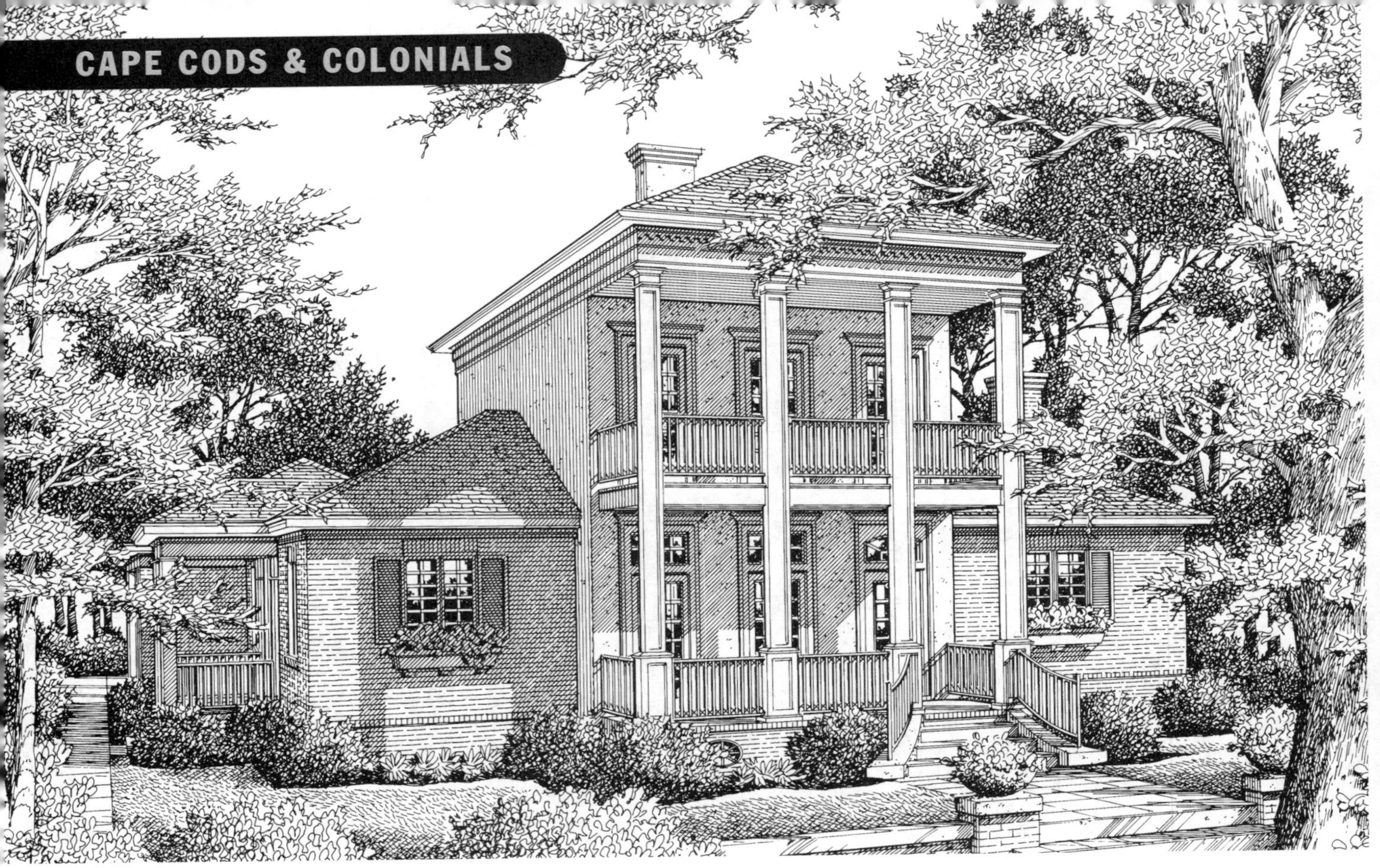

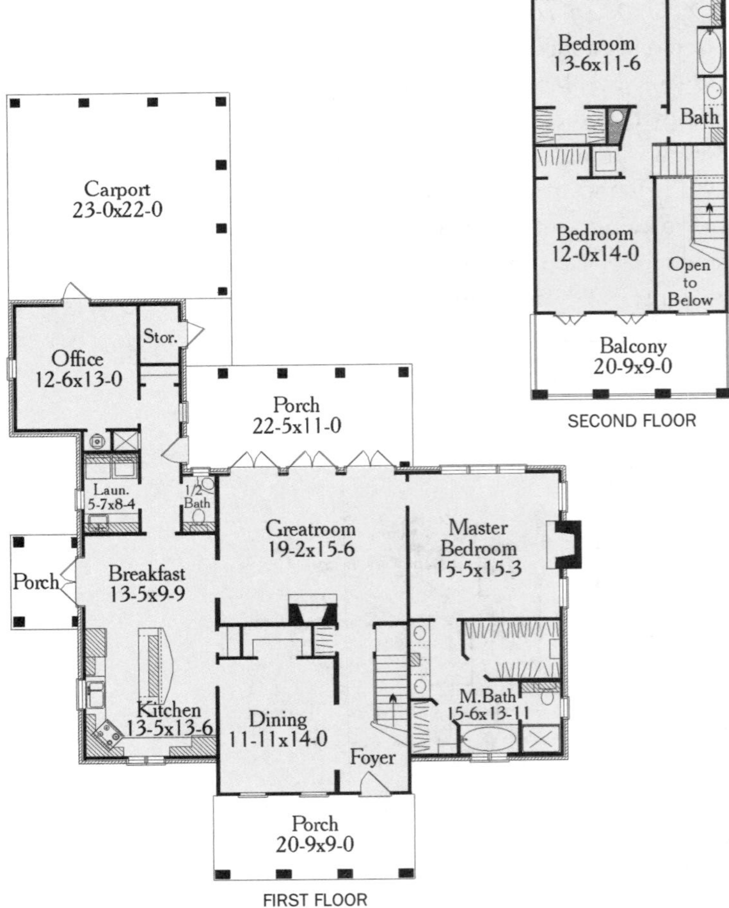

plan# HPT930222

- Style: Southern Colonial
- First Floor: 1,907 sq. ft.
- Second Floor: 551 sq. ft.
- Total: 2,458 sq. ft.
- Bedrooms: 3
- Bathrooms: 2½
- Width: 58'-10"
- Depth: 83'-7"
- Foundation: Crawlspace, Slab

SEARCH ONLINE @ EPLANS.COM

Straight from the South, this home sets a country tone. This Southern Colonial design boasts decorative two-story columns and large windows that enhance the front porch and balcony. Enter through the foyer—notice that the formal dining room on the left connects to the island kitchen. The kitchen opens to a breakfast room, which accesses a side porch that's perfect for outdoor grilling. The great room features a warming fireplace and accesses a rear porch. The master bedroom also includes a fireplace, as well as a private bath with a whirlpool tub and a walk-in closet. A home office, laundry room and carport complete the first floor. Upstairs, two additional bedrooms share a full hall bath.

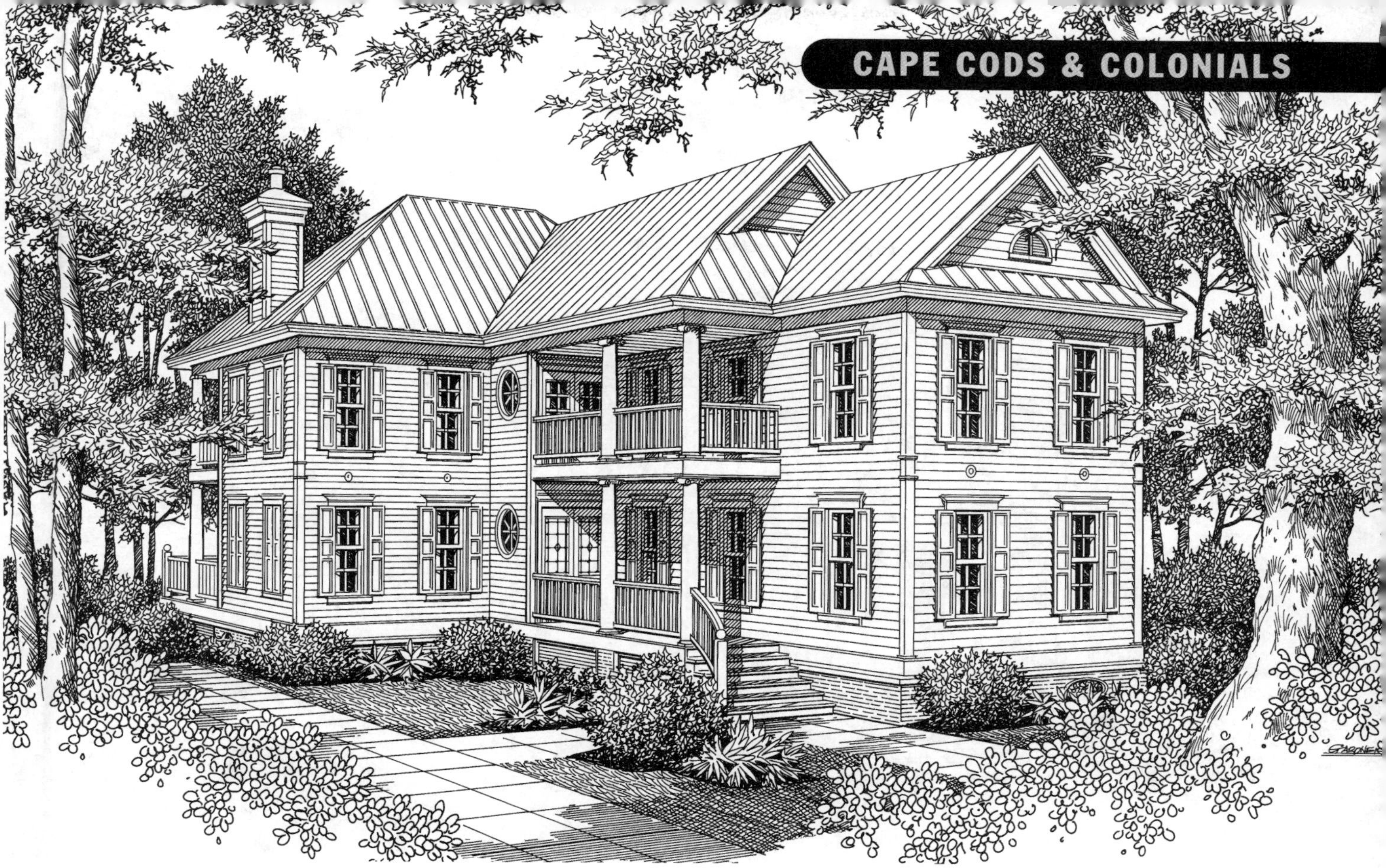

plan# HPT930223

- Style: Southern Colonial
- First Floor: 1,742 sq. ft.
- Second Floor: 1,624 sq. ft.
- Total: 3,366 sq. ft.
- Bedrooms: 4
- Bathrooms: 3
- Width: 42'-10"
- Depth: 77'-0"
- Foundation: Pier

SEARCH ONLINE @ EPLANS.COM

Elegant Southern living is the theme of this seaside townhouse. The narrow-lot design allows for comfortable urban living. Inside, the living room is warmed by a fireplace, while the island kitchen serves the breakfast room and casual den. A first-floor guest bedroom is located at the front of the design. The dining room is reserved for more formal occasions. Upstairs, the gracious master suite features a private second-floor porch, two walk-in closets and a private bath. Two additional bedrooms share a hall bath on this floor.

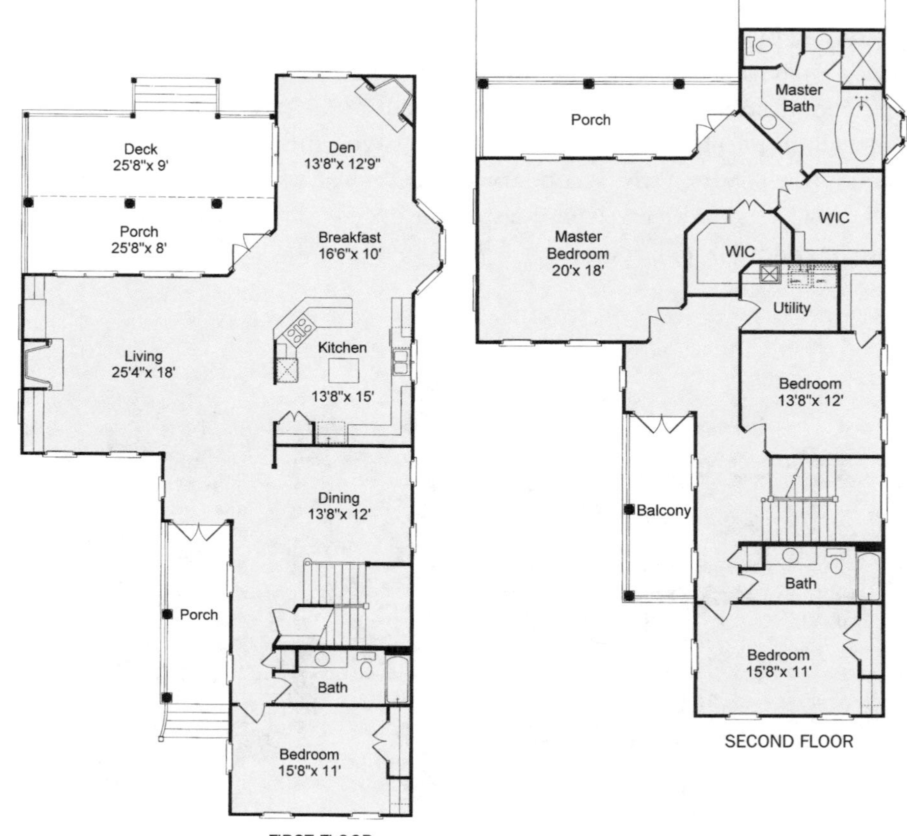

A grand facade detailed with brick corner quoins, stucco flourishes, arched windows and an elegant entrance presents this home. A spacious foyer is accented by curving stairs and flanked by a formal living room and a formal dining room. For cozy times, a through-fireplace is located between a large family room and a quiet study. The master bedroom is designed to pamper, with two walk-in closets, a two-sided fireplace, a bayed sitting area and a lavish private bath. Upstairs, three secondary bedrooms each have a private bath and walk-in closet. Also on this level is a spacious recreation room, perfect for a game room or children's playroom.

plan# HPT930224

- Style: Georgian
- First Floor: 3,599 sq. ft.
- Second Floor: 1,621 sq. ft.
- Total: 5,220 sq. ft.
- Bonus Space: 356 sq. ft.
- Bedrooms: 4
- Bathrooms: 5½
- Width: 108'-10"
- Depth: 53'-10"
- Foundation: Basement, Slab

SEARCH ONLINE @ EPLANS.COM

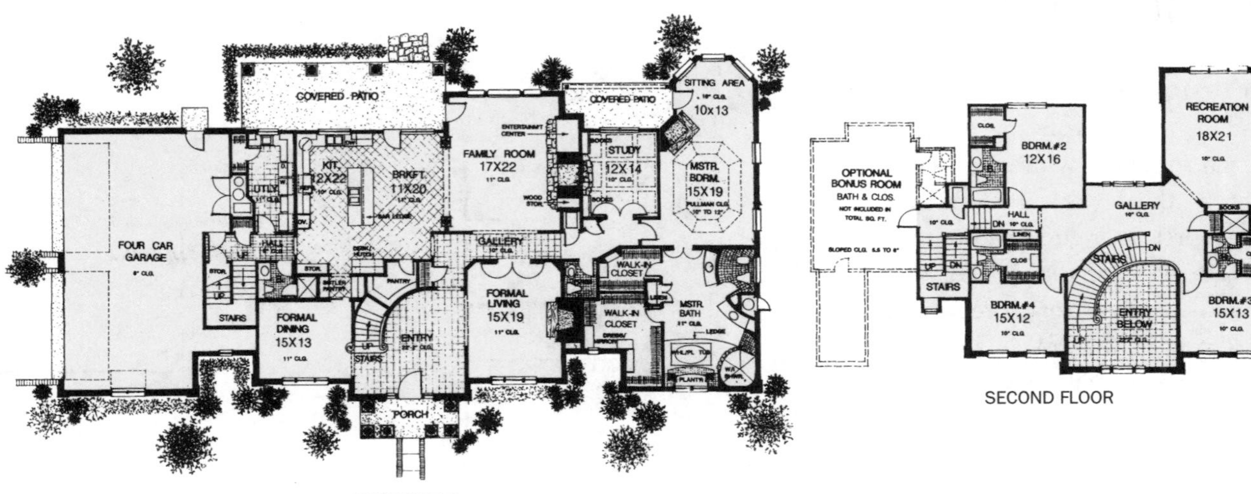

SECOND FLOOR

FIRST FLOOR

plan# HPT930225

- Style: Traditional
- First Floor: 2,814 sq. ft.
- Second Floor: 979 sq. ft.
- Total: 3,793 sq. ft.
- Bedrooms: 4
- Bathrooms: 3½
- Width: 98'-0"
- Depth: 45'-10"
- Foundation: Basement, Slab

SEARCH ONLINE @ EPLANS.COM

A covered, columned porch and symmetrically placed windows welcome you to this elegant brick home. The formal living room offers built-in bookshelves and one of two fireplaces, the other being found in the spacious family room. A gallery running between these rooms leads to the sumptuous master suite, which includes a sitting area, a private covered patio, and a bath with two walk-in closets, dual vanities, a large shower and a garden tub. The step-saving kitchen features a work island and a snack bar. The breakfast and family rooms offer doors to the large covered veranda. Upstairs you'll find three bedrooms and attic storage space. The three-car garage even has room for a golf cart.

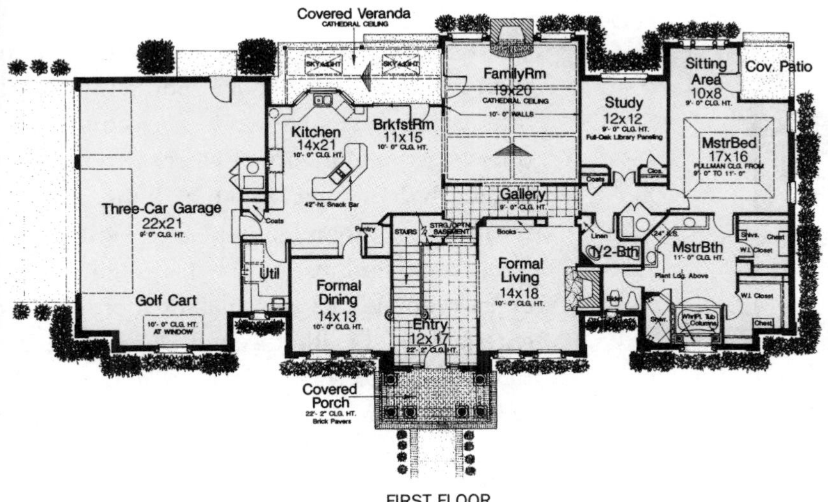

FIRST FLOOR

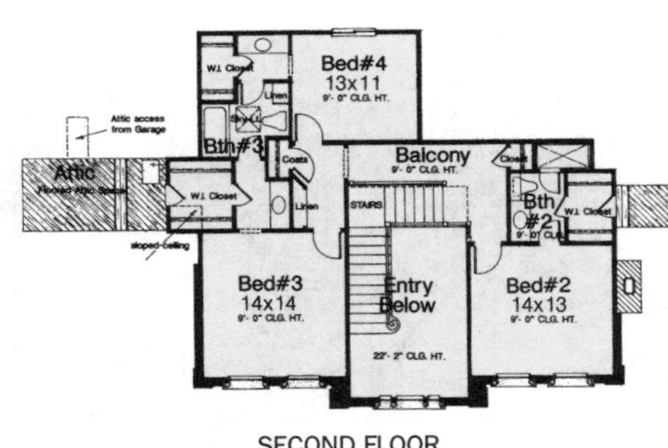

SECOND FLOOR

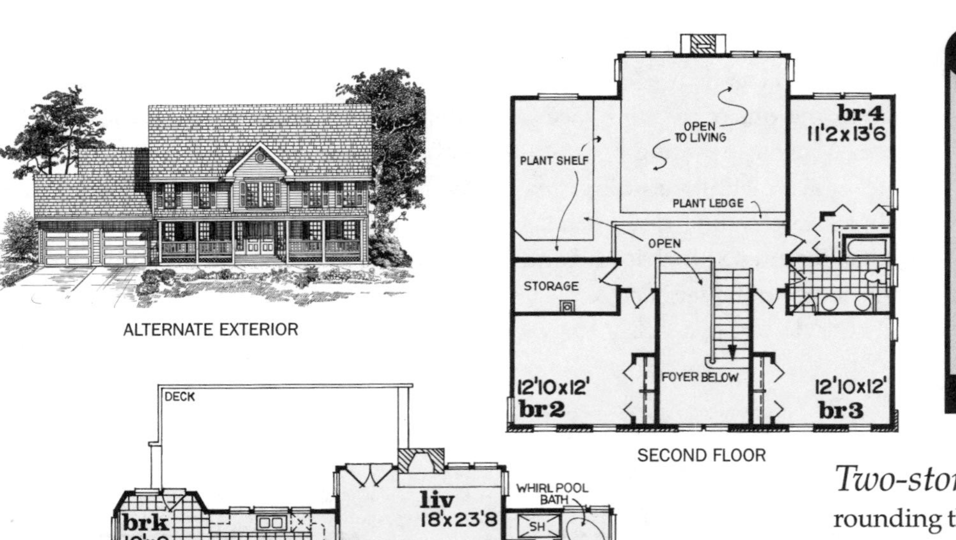

ALTERNATE EXTERIOR

SECOND FLOOR

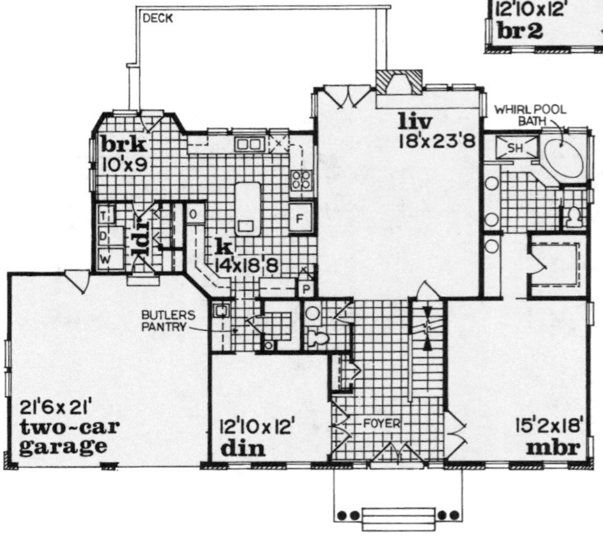

FIRST FLOOR

plan# HPT930226

- Style: Colonial
- First Floor: 1,929 sq. ft.
- Second Floor: 975 sq. ft.
- Total: 2,904 sq. ft.
- Bedrooms: 4
- Bathrooms: 2½
- Width: 64'-8"
- Depth: 49'-6"
- Foundation: Basement, Crawlspace

SEARCH ONLINE @ EPLANS.COM

Two-story pillars create a majestic aura surrounding this Colonial home. Shutters adorn the facade to give it that down-home feeling. French doors open into the foyer where two more sets of French doors open into the dining room and the master bedroom. A fireplace is located in the living room for those cozy winter nights. A deck opens onto the backyard making more space for entertaining. On the second floor three bedrooms overlook the family room and foyer. The floor plans offer an alternate elevation that is the essence of country. Both elevations are included with the floor plans for convenience.

plan# HPT930227

- Style: Georgian
- First Floor: 1,452 sq. ft.
- Second Floor: 1,100 sq. ft.
- Total: 2,552 sq. ft.
- Bonus Space: 687 sq. ft.
- Bedrooms: 4
- Bathrooms: 2½
- Width: 62'-0"
- Depth: 48'-0"
- Foundation: Crawlspace

SEARCH ONLINE @ EPLANS.COM

Choose between a country feel, with the wraparound porch, and a stately feel, with the brick exterior, when constructing this home. An alternate elevation is included in the floor plans.Enter the foyer and you'll be greeted by double doors opening to a den on the left and a spacious living room with a fireplace on the right. The dining room is separated from the living room by a plant bridge and pair of columns. The full-sized family room features a three-sided fireplace and a corner media center, plus access to the rear yard. A staircase from the family room leads to bonus space over the garage. Four bedrooms on the second floor cluster around a center hall. The master suite and one family bedroom have walk-in closets.

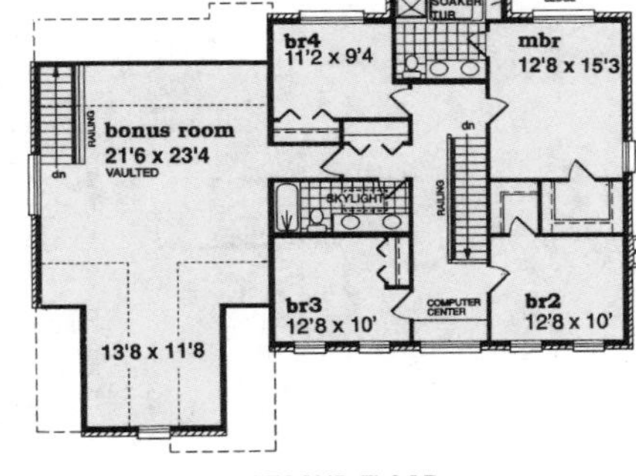

SECOND FLOOR

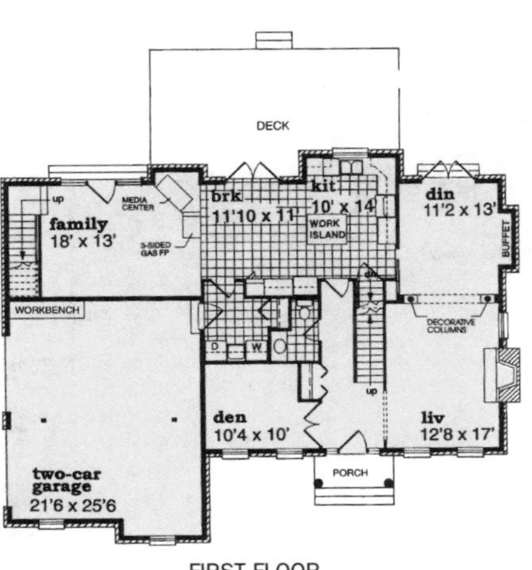

FIRST FLOOR

ALTERNATE EXTERIOR

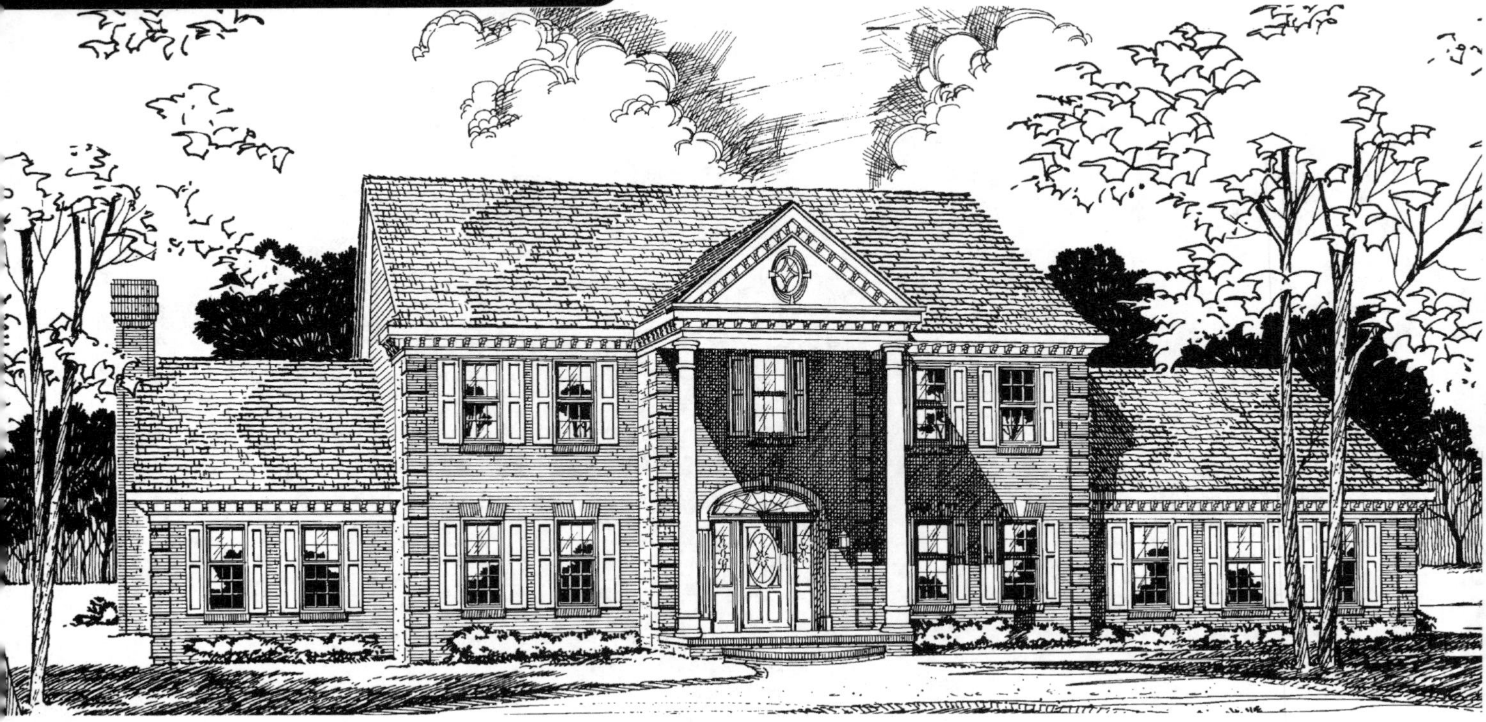

Stately columns highlight the facade of this beautiful Southern Colonial home. The open entry allows for views into formal areas and up the tapering staircase. The dining room joins the kitchen through double doors. The living room can be divided from the sunken family room by pocket doors. Step down into the huge family room to find large windows, a fireplace, a built-in entertainment center and bookcases. The kitchen features a gazebo breakfast area, serving bar and cooktop island. Upstairs, three family bedrooms share two full baths. The private master suite features a tiered ceiling, two walk-in closets and a roomy bayed sitting area.

plan# HPT930228

- Style: Colonial
- First Floor: 1,717 sq. ft.
- Second Floor: 1,518 sq. ft.
- Total: 3,235 sq. ft.
- Bedrooms: 4
- Bathrooms: 3½
- Width: 78'-0"
- Depth: 42'-0"

SEARCH ONLINE @ EPLANS.COM

FIRST FLOOR

QUOTE ONE®
Cost to build? See page 436 to order complete cost estimate to build this house in your area!

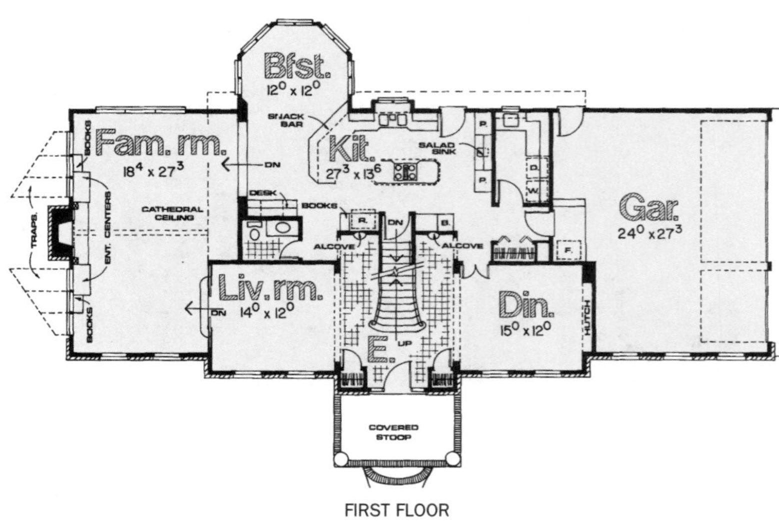

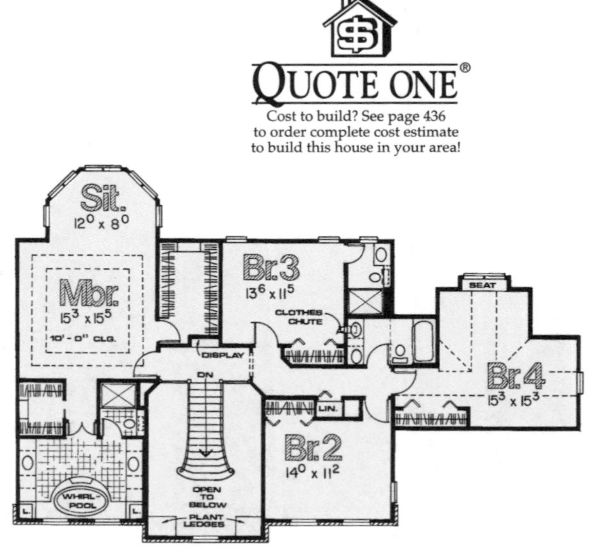

SECOND FLOOR

 HPT930229

- Style: Colonial
- First Floor: 1,675 sq. ft.
- Second Floor: 1,605 sq. ft.
- Total: 3,280 sq. ft.
- Bedrooms: 4
- Bathrooms: 3½
- Width: 65'-0"
- Depth: 46'-0"

SEARCH ONLINE @ EPLANS.COM

A grand and glorious split staircase makes a lasting first impression in this stately two-story home. The impressive family room is lit by a beveled wall of windows, a wet bar, built-in bookcases and entertainment center provide the finishing touches. The spacious kitchen is sure to please, featuring an island cooktop/snack bar, a planning desk and a sunny bayed breakfast area. Upstairs, each secondary bedroom enjoys a walk-in closet; two bedrooms share a Hollywood bath while a third includes a private bath. The master suite offers uncommon elegance with French doors opening to the master bedroom with tray ceiling, gazebo sitting area and a separate off-season closet. Enter the master bath through French doors and enjoy its relaxing whirlpool tub, open shower and built-in dressers in the large walk-in closet.

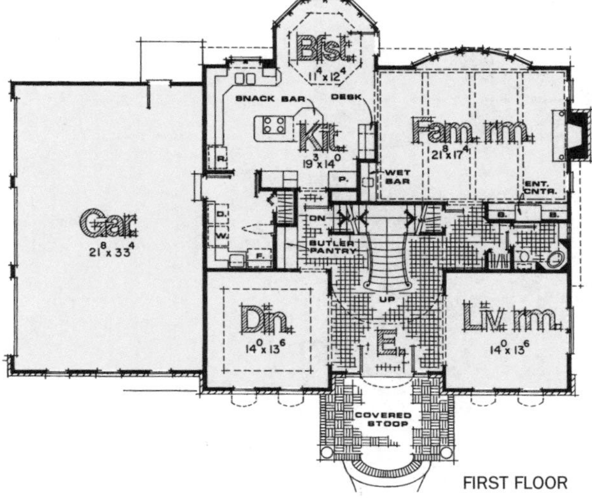

FIRST FLOOR

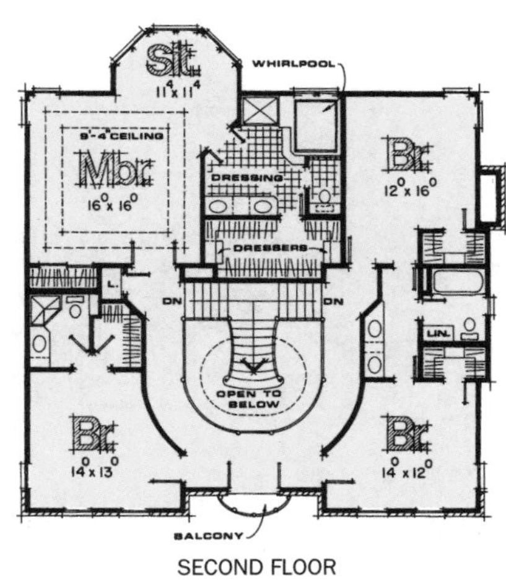

SECOND FLOOR

Two upper-level floor plan options are included with this delightful design. Both options include space for two family bedrooms, a full bath and a master suite with a tray ceiling and a lavish private bath. The second option adds an upper-level laundry room and a bonus room with a walk-in closet. Downstairs, the large family room, bayed breakfast room and efficient kitchen cater to comfort.

plan# HPT930230

- Style: Traditional
- First Floor: 1,068 sq. ft.
- Second Floor: 977 sq. ft.
- Total: 2,045 sq. ft.
- Bonus Space: 412 sq. ft.
- Bedrooms: 3
- Bathrooms: 2½
- Width: 56'-4"
- Depth: 43'-0"
- Foundation: Crawlspace, Basement

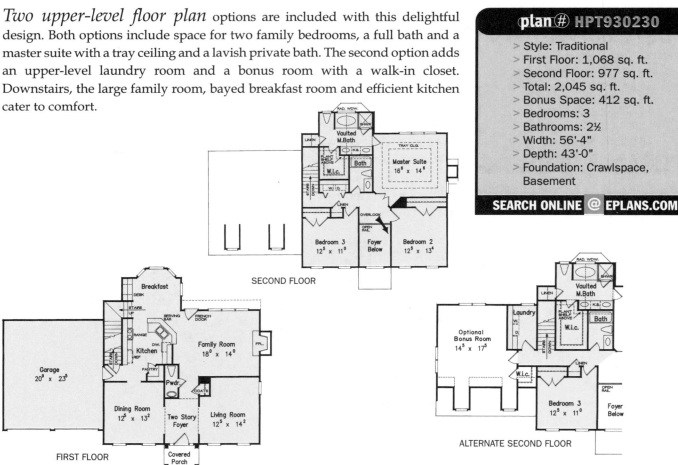

SEARCH ONLINE @ EPLANS.COM

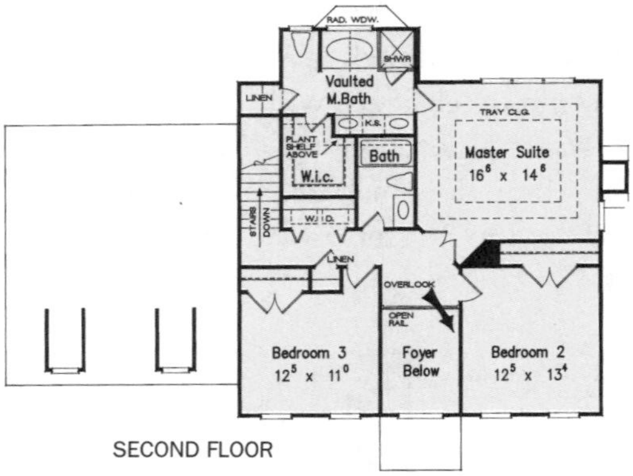

SECOND FLOOR

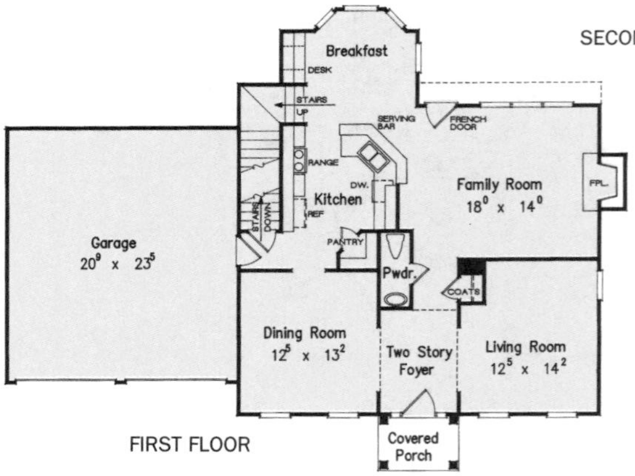

FIRST FLOOR

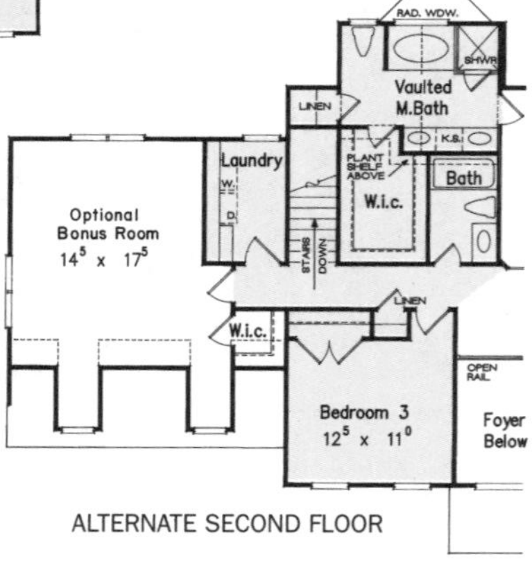

ALTERNATE SECOND FLOOR

plan# HPT930231

- Style: Georgian
- First Floor: 1,848 sq. ft.
- Second Floor: 1,111 sq. ft.
- Total: 2,959 sq. ft.
- Bedrooms: 4
- Bathrooms: 3½
- Width: 73'-4"
- Depth: 44'-1"
- Foundation: Basement, Crawlspace, Slab

SEARCH ONLINE @ EPLANS.COM

Every homeowner's wish is granted with a floor plan designed to enchant family members and guests. Relish the master bedroom privileged with patio access and a divine master bath. The great room, with a hearth, is fit for casual gatherings, while the formal living and dining rooms are savored for special occasions. Outdoor relaxing and entertaining are effortless with an extended patio and a covered area. Three bedrooms, two full baths and a loft occupy the second floor. The three-car garage enters through the utility room and leads to the island kitchen.

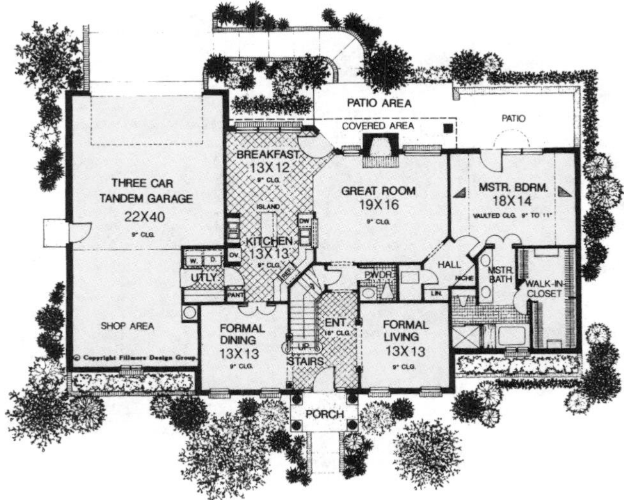

FIRST FLOOR

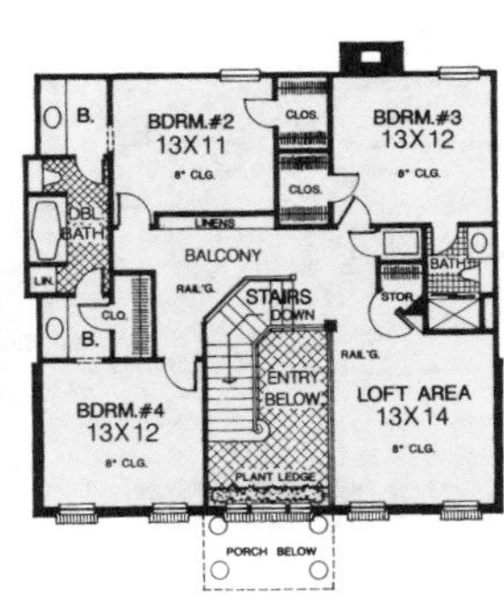

SECOND FLOOR

With a gazebo-style covered porch and careful exterior details, you can't help but imagine tea parties, porch swings and lazy summer evenings. Inside, a living room/library will comfort with its fireplace and built-ins. The family room is graced with a fireplace and a curved, two-story ceiling with an overlook above. The master bedroom is a private retreat with a lovely bath, twin walk-in closets and rear-porch access. Upstairs, three bedrooms with sizable closets—one bedroom would make an excellent guest suite or alternate master suite—share access to expandable space.

plan# HPT930232

- Style: Farmhouse
- First Floor: 2,442 sq. ft.
- Second Floor: 1,286 sq. ft.
- Total: 3,728 sq. ft.
- Bonus Space: 681 sq. ft.
- Bedrooms: 4
- Bathrooms: 3½ + ½
- Width: 89'-4"
- Depth: 60'-0"
- Foundation: Crawlspace

SEARCH ONLINE @ EPLANS.COM

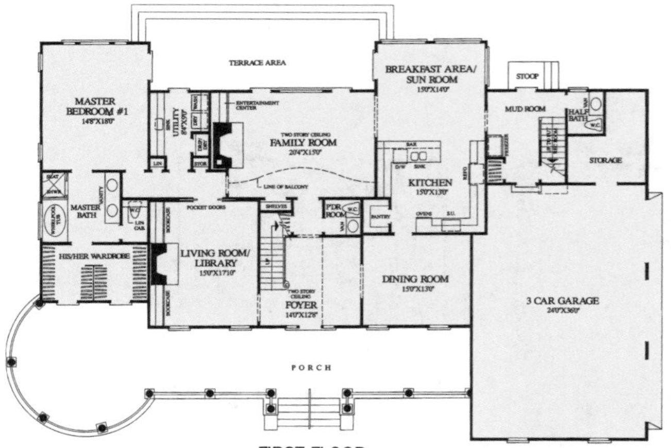

FIRST FLOOR

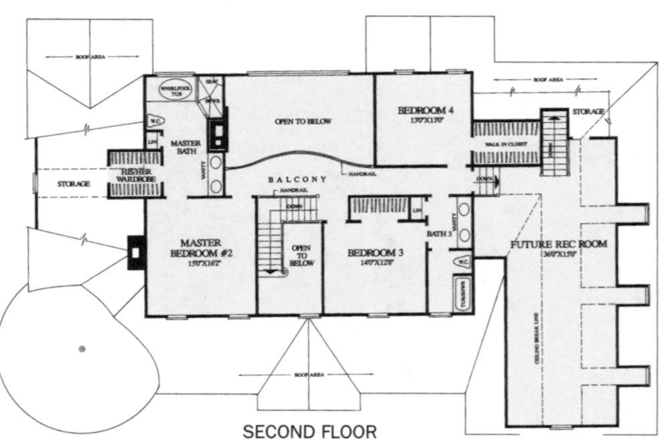

SECOND FLOOR

plan# HPT930233

- Style: Georgian
- First Floor: 2,081 sq. ft.
- Second Floor: 940 sq. ft.
- Total: 3,021 sq. ft.
- Bedrooms: 4
- Bathrooms: 3½
- Width: 69'-9"
- Depth: 65'-0"
- Foundation: Walkout Basement

SEARCH ONLINE @ EPLANS.COM

This Georgian country-style home displays an impressive appearance. The front porch and columns frame the elegant elliptical entrance. Georgian symmetry balances the living room and dining room off the foyer. The first floor continues into the two-story great room, which offers built-in cabinetry, a fireplace and a large bay window that overlooks the rear deck. A dramatic tray ceiling, a wall of glass and access to the rear deck complete the master bedroom. To the left of the great room, a large kitchen opens to a breakfast area with walls of windows. Upstairs, each of three family bedrooms features ample closet space as well as direct access to a bathroom.

QUOTE ONE®

Cost to build? See page 436 to order complete cost estimate to build this house in your area!

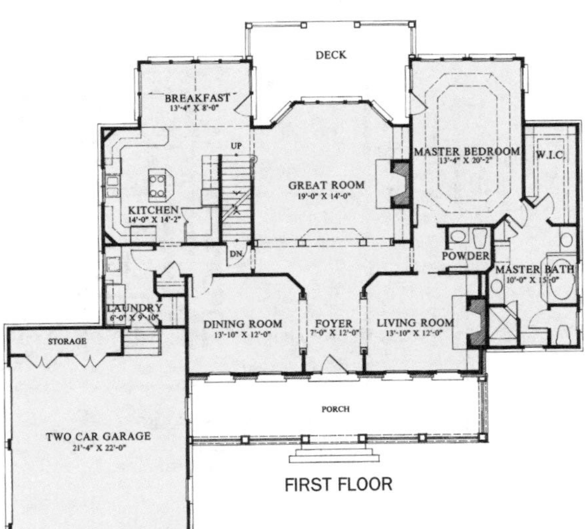

FIRST FLOOR

SECOND FLOOR

At less than 2,000 square feet, this plan captures the heritage and romance of an authentic Colonial home with many modern amenities. A central hall leads to the formal rooms at the front where the homeowner can display showpiece furnishings. For daily living, the informal rooms can't be beat. The master suite shows further evidence of tasteful design. A volume ceiling, large walk-in closet and whirlpool tub await the fortunate homeowner. Each secondary bedroom includes bright windows to add natural lighting and comfort.

plan# HPT930234

- Style: Colonial
- First Floor: 1,000 sq. ft.
- Second Floor: 993 sq. ft.
- Total: 1,993 sq. ft.
- Bedrooms: 4
- Bathrooms: 2½
- Width: 56'-0"
- Depth: 30'-0"

SEARCH ONLINE @ EPLANS.COM

FIRST FLOOR

QUOTE ONE®

Cost to build? See page 436 to order complete cost estimate to build this house in your area!

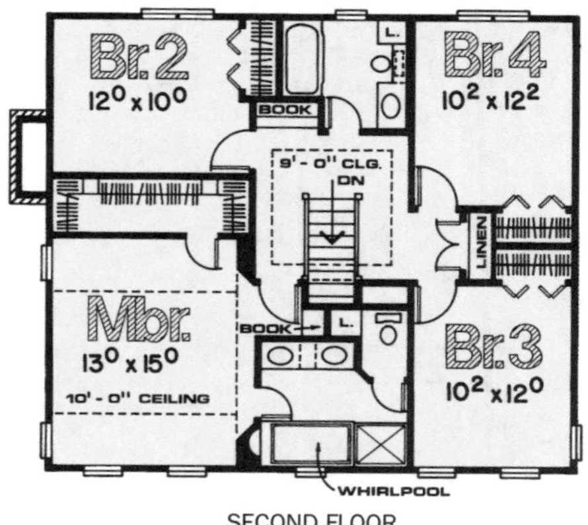

SECOND FLOOR

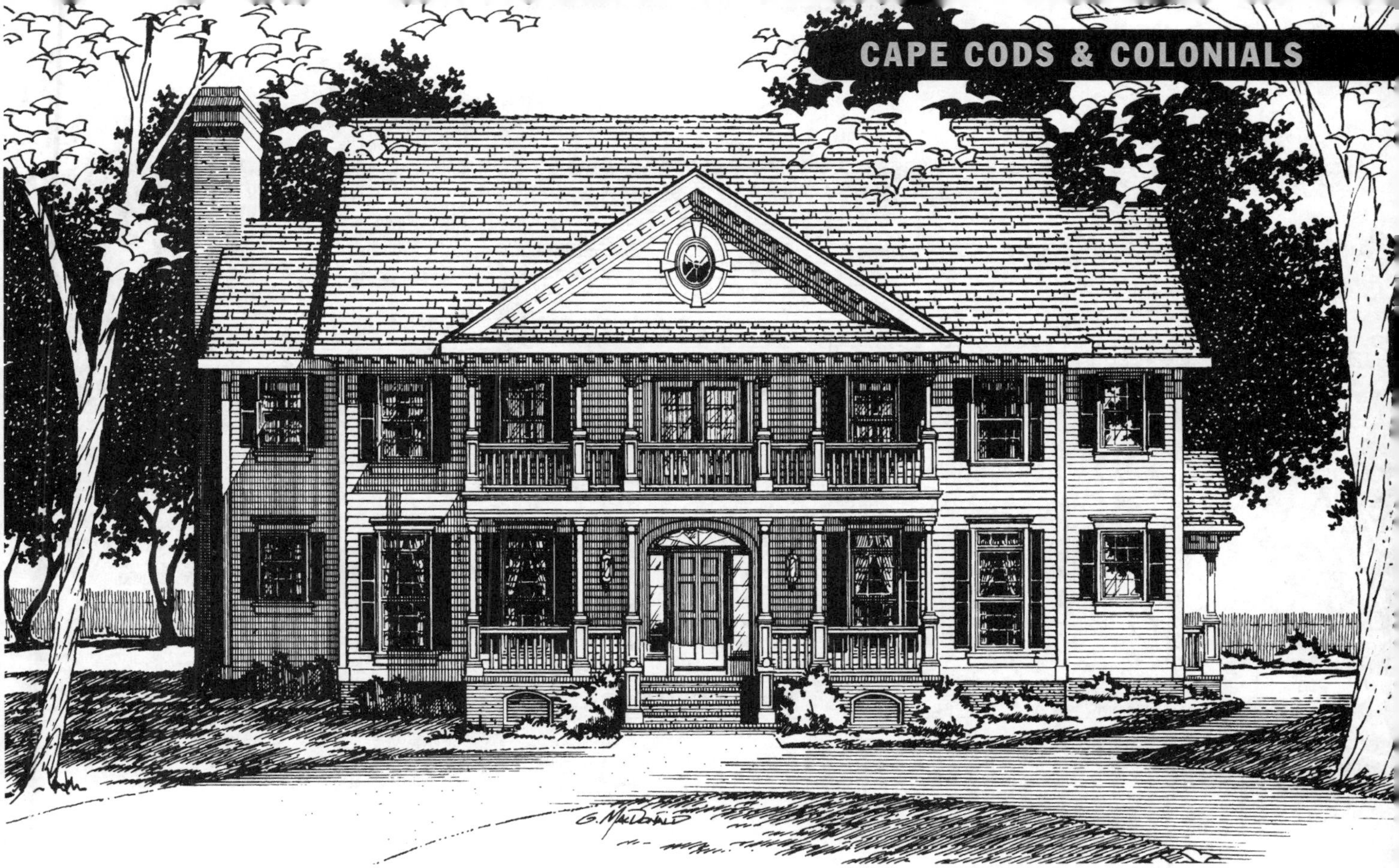

plan# HPT930235

- Style: Colonial
- First Floor: 1,598 sq. ft.
- Second Floor: 1,675 sq. ft.
- Total: 3,273 sq. ft.
- Bonus Space: 534 sq. ft.
- Bedrooms: 4
- Bathrooms: 3½
- Width: 54'-8"
- Depth: 68'-0"

SEARCH ONLINE @ EPLANS.COM

First- and second-level covered porches, accompanied by intricate detailing, and many multi-pane windows create a splendid Southern mansion. The prominent entry opens to formal dining and living rooms. The grand family room is warmed by a fireplace and views a screened porch with a cozy window seat. The roomy breakfast area provides access to the porch and the three-car garage. French doors open to the second-floor master suite, which features decorative ceiling details, His and Hers walk-in closets, a large dressing area, dual vanities, a whirlpool bath and a separate shower area.

FIRST FLOOR

SECOND FLOOR

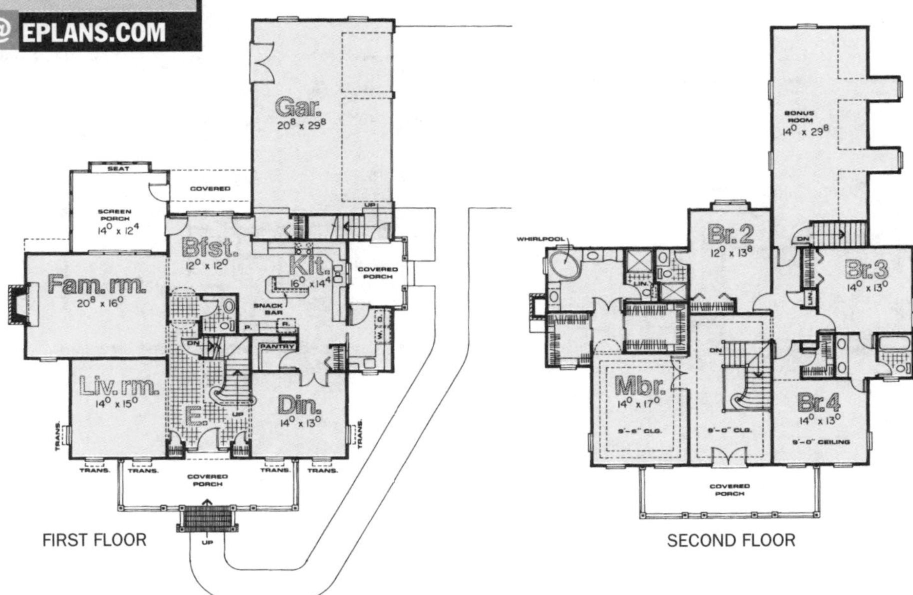

An arched entry, shutters and a brick facade highlight the exterior of this two-story modern Colonial home. Living and dining rooms at the front of the plan accommodate formal occasions. The rear of the plan is designed for informal gatherings, such as the generous family room, which includes a warming fireplace and bayed conversation area. The bright breakfast area is open to an efficient U-shaped kitchen with a snack bar. Bright windows and French doors add appeal to the living room. Upstairs, a U-shaped balcony hall overlooks the entry below and connects four bedrooms, including a master suite. This retreat features a private sitting room, two walk-in closets, a compartmented bath, separate vanities and a window-brightened whirlpool tub.

plan# HPT930236

- Style: Colonial
- First Floor: 1,000 sq. ft.
- Second Floor: 1,345 sq. ft.
- Total: 2,345 sq. ft.
- Bedrooms: 4
- Bathrooms: 3½
- Width: 57'-4"
- Depth: 30'-0"

SEARCH ONLINE @ EPLANS.COM

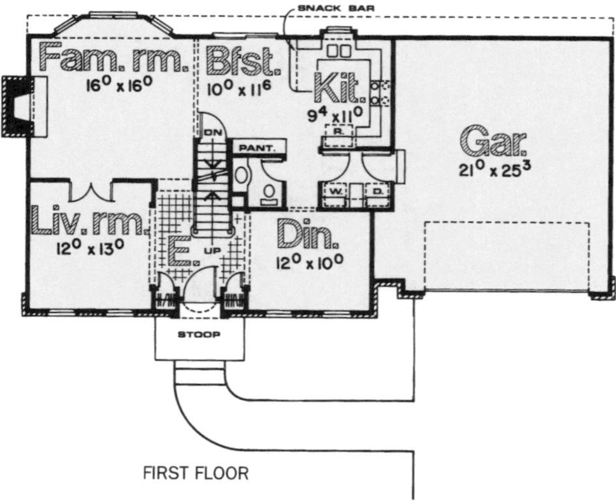

FIRST FLOOR

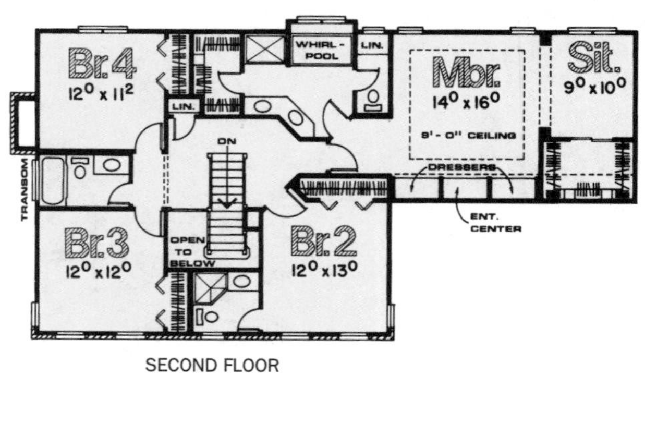

SECOND FLOOR

plan# HPT930237

- Style: Colonial
- First Floor: 2,063 sq. ft.
- Second Floor: 894 sq. ft.
- Total: 2,957 sq. ft.
- Bedrooms: 4
- Bathrooms: 4½
- Width: 72'-8"
- Depth: 51'-4"

SEARCH ONLINE @ EPLANS.COM

An elegant brick elevation and rows of shuttered windows lend timeless beauty to this two-story Colonial design. The volume entry opens to the formal dining and living rooms and the magnificent great room. Sparkling floor-to-ceiling windows flank the fireplace in the great room, which offers a cathedral ceiling. French doors, bay windows, a wet bar and a decorative ceiling highlight the private den. Special lifestyle amenities in the kitchen and bayed breakfast area include a built-in desk, wrapping counters and an island. In the master bath/dressing area, note the large walk-in closet, built-in dresser, His and Hers vanities, oval whirlpool tub and plant shelves. Upstairs, each secondary bedroom contains a roomy closet and private bath.

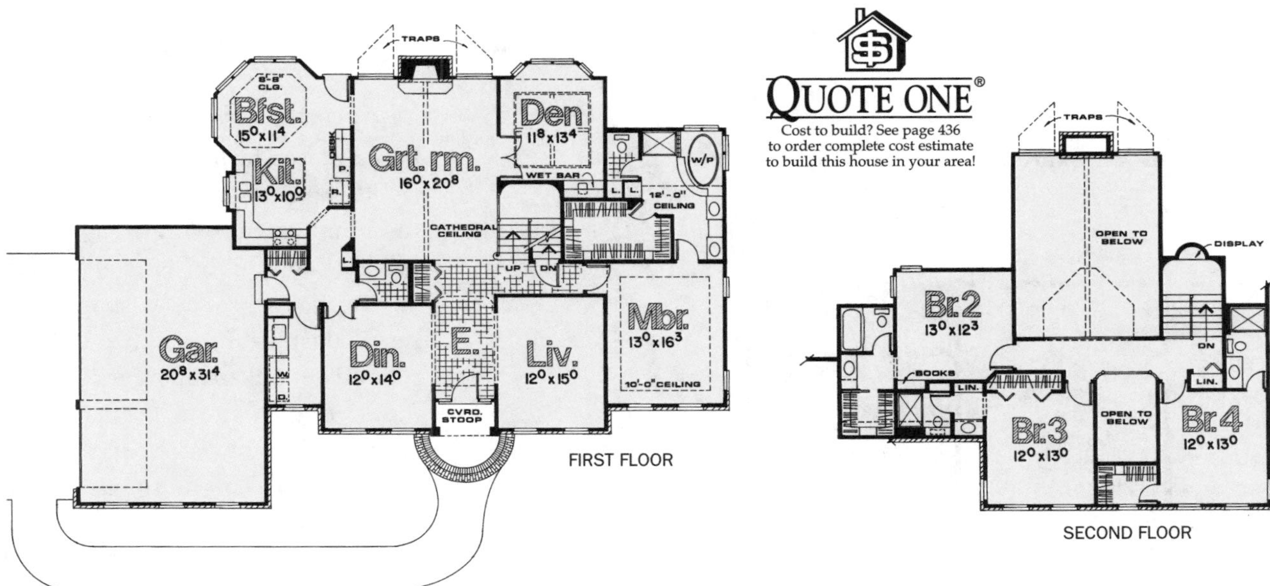

FIRST FLOOR

SECOND FLOOR

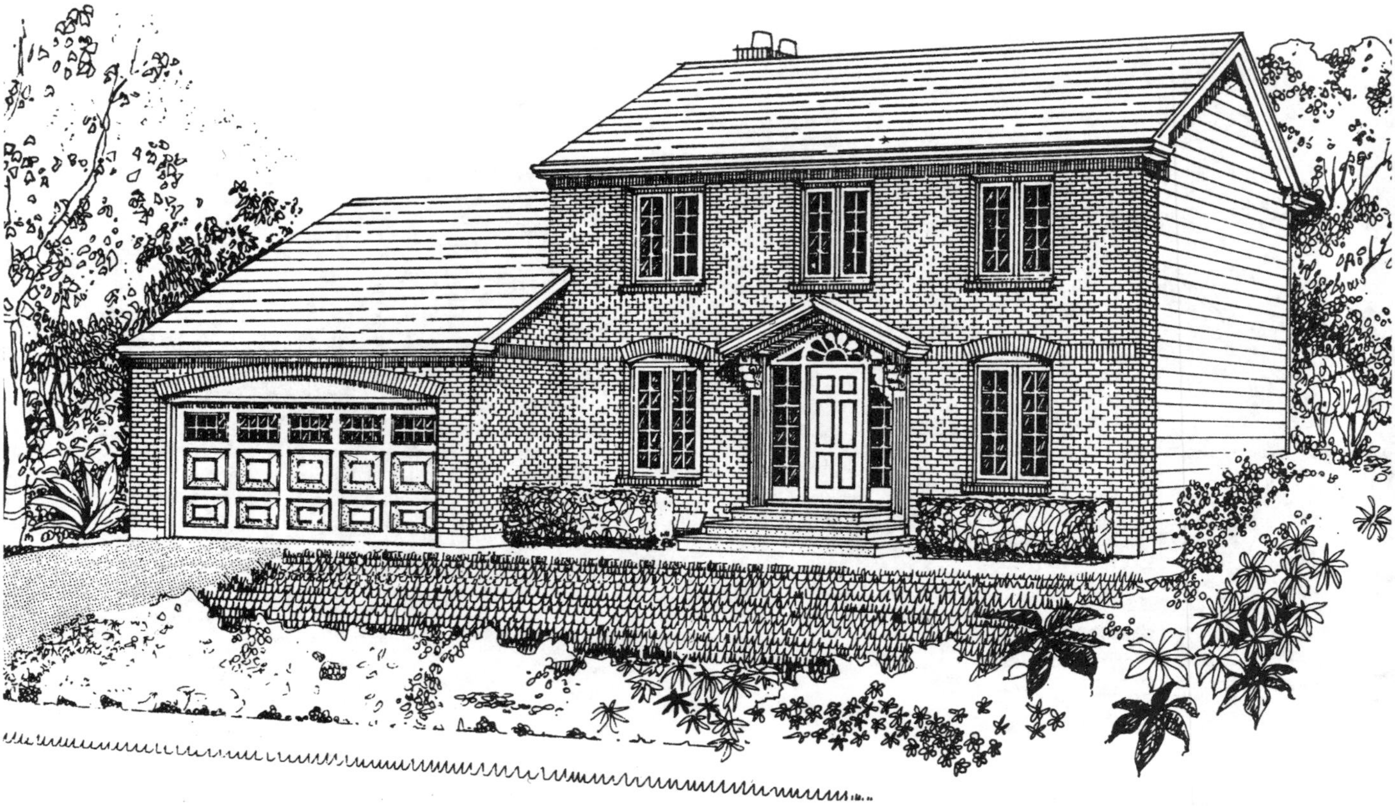

ALTERNATE EXTERIOR

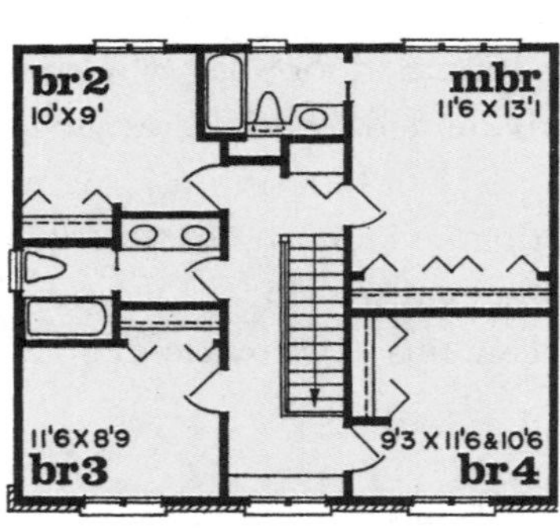

SECOND FLOOR

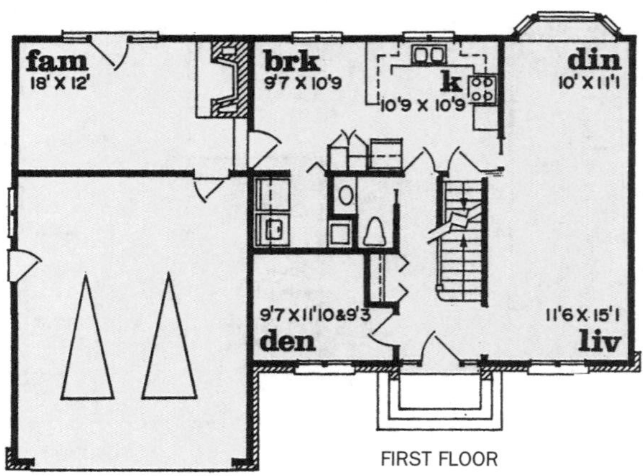

FIRST FLOOR

The commodious floor plan of this home places formal living areas on the right. The living room flows directly into the dining room with a bay window.A private den is to the left, near a half-bath off the hallway. The U-shaped kitchen serves the breakfast room and the dining room. The sunken family room features a fireplace and a door to the rear yard. Four corner bedrooms are located on the second floor. The master suite offers a large wall closet and a private bath. Three family bedrooms share a full bath.

plan# HPT930239

- Style: Colonial
- First Floor: 1,437 sq. ft.
- Second Floor: 1,138 sq. ft.
- Total: 2,575 sq. ft.
- Bedrooms: 3
- Bathrooms: 2½ + ½
- Width: 56'-0"
- Depth: 44'-10"
- Foundation: Basement, Crawlspace

SEARCH ONLINE  **EPLANS.COM**

This Colonial-style home offers three bedrooms on the second floor. The crowning glory is the bayed whirlpool spa in the master bath, with decorative columns adding a romantic accent. The master suite also includes a sitting area and a walk-in closet with a dressing area and vanity counter. On the first floor, the family room features a fireplace and a coffered ceiling. The kitchen is a gourmet cook's delight: it offers a center cooktop island, a breakfast bar, a walk-in pantry, a built-in desk and a breakfast bay. The powder room has dual access, from the entry hall and from the laundry room. The den opens through French doors from the entry hall and offers a built-in bookshelf.

ALTERNATE EXTERIOR

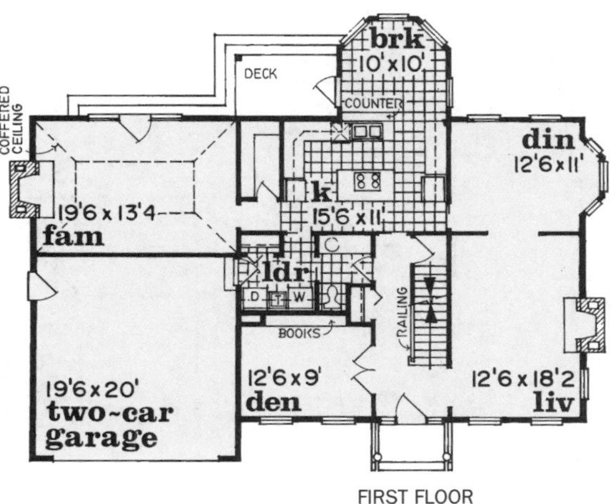

FIRST FLOOR

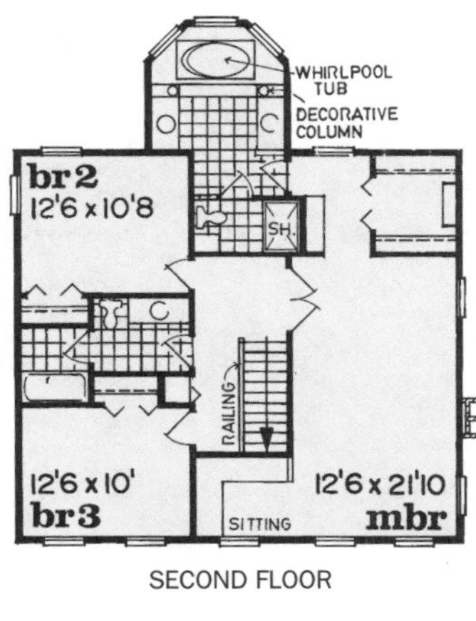

SECOND FLOOR

The exterior of this expansive home is both elegant and simple, much like the spacious interior. Two bayed windows, one in the dining room and the other in the living room, accent the front of the home. The two-story foyer opens up to the two-story family room, where a fireplace awaits guests and family members alike. The breakfast nook opens to a rear porch. There are three bedrooms and a master suite with a vaulted master bath and sitting room on the second floor.

plan# HPT930240

- Style: Colonial
- First Floor: 2,002 sq. ft.
- Second Floor: 1,947 sq. ft.
- Total: 3,949 sq. ft.
- Bedrooms: 5
- Bathrooms: 4½
- Width: 60'-4"
- Depth: 63'-6"
- Foundation: Crawlspace, Basement

SEARCH ONLINE @ EPLANS.COM

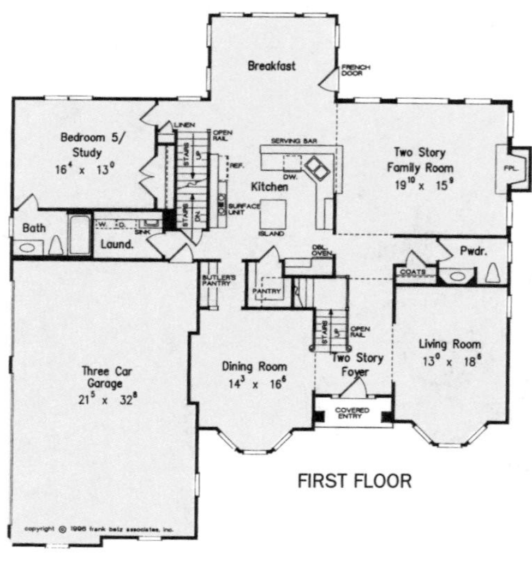

FIRST FLOOR

SECOND FLOOR

plan# HPT930241

- Style: Colonial
- First Floor: 1,135 sq. ft.
- Second Floor: 917 sq. ft.
- Total: 2,052 sq. ft.
- Bonus Space: 216 sq. ft.
- Bedrooms: 4
- Bathrooms: 3
- Width: 52'-4"
- Depth: 37'-6"
- Foundation: Basement, Crawlspace, Slab

SEARCH ONLINE @ EPLANS.COM

This grand two-story home proves that tried-and-true traditional style is still the best! Thoughtful planning brings formal living areas to the forefront and places open, casual living areas to the rear of the plan. Bedroom 4 serves as a multi-purpose room, providing the flexibility desired by today's homeowner. The second floor is devoted to the relaxing master suite, two secondary bedrooms, a full hall bath and a balcony overlook.

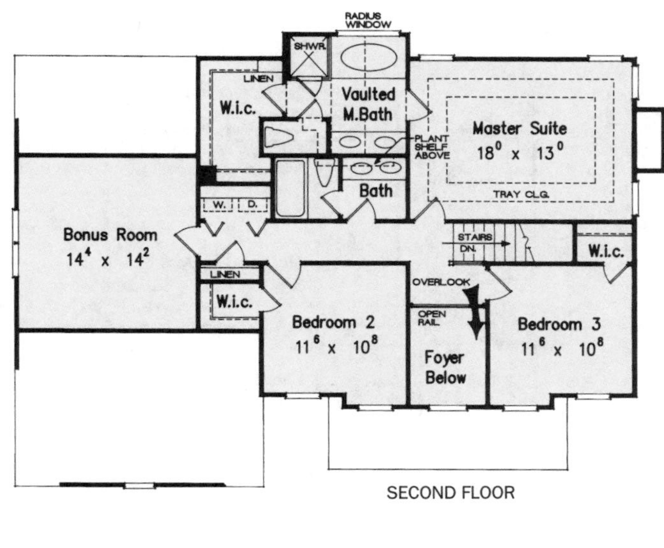

SECOND FLOOR

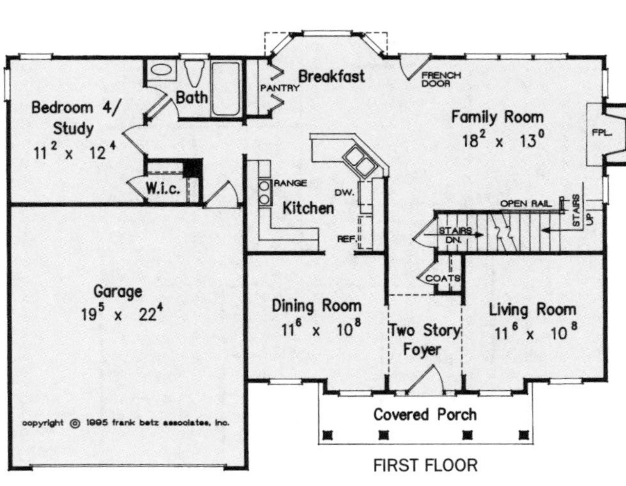

FIRST FLOOR

A dash of Victorian elegance brings new light to a traditional country home. Inside, decorative columns help define an elegant dining room, but the heart of the home is the vaulted family room with a radius window and a French door to the rear property. The first-floor master suite features a private bath with a vaulted ceiling and a whirlpool tub set off with a radius window. The second floor boasts two bedrooms—each with walk-in closets—a shared bath and an open hallway that overlooks that family room and foyer below.

plan# HPT930242

- Style: Colonial
- First Floor: 1,583 sq. ft.
- Second Floor: 543 sq. ft.
- Total: 3,709 sq. ft.
- Bonus Space: 251 sq. ft.
- Bedrooms: 4
- Bathrooms: 3
- Width: 53'-0"
- Depth: 47'-0"
- Foundation: Basement, Crawlspace, Slab

SEARCH ONLINE @ EPLANS.COM

copyright © 1996 frank betz associates, inc.

FIRST FLOOR

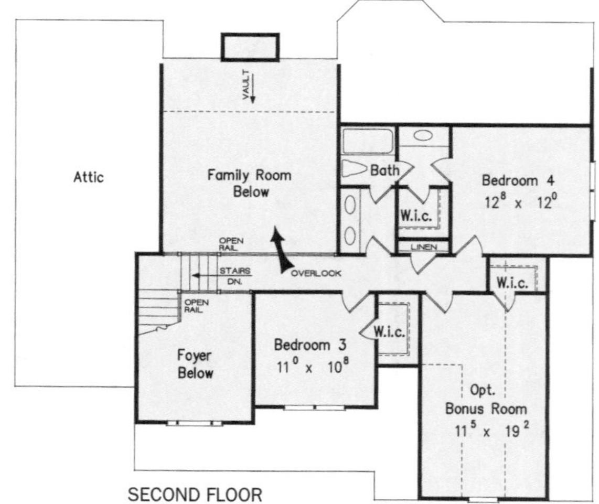

SECOND FLOOR

plan# HPT930243

- Style: Colonial
- First Floor: 1,415 sq. ft.
- Second Floor: 1,015 sq. ft.
- Total: 2,430 sq. ft.
- Bonus Space: 169 sq. ft.
- Bedrooms: 4
- Bathrooms: 3½
- Width: 54'-0"
- Depth: 43'-4"
- Foundation: Crawlspace, Basement

SEARCH ONLINE @ EPLANS.COM

This striking design is reminiscent of the grand homes of the past century. Its wood siding and covered porch are complemented by shuttered windows and a glass-paneled entry. Historic design is updated in the floor plan to include a vaulted living room, a two-story family room and a den that doubles as a guest suite on the first floor. Second-floor bedrooms feature a master suite with tray ceiling and vaulted bath. An optional loft on the second floor may be finished as a study area.

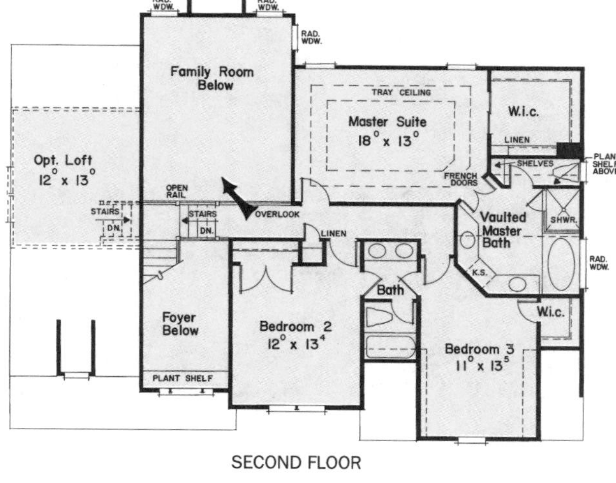

SECOND FLOOR

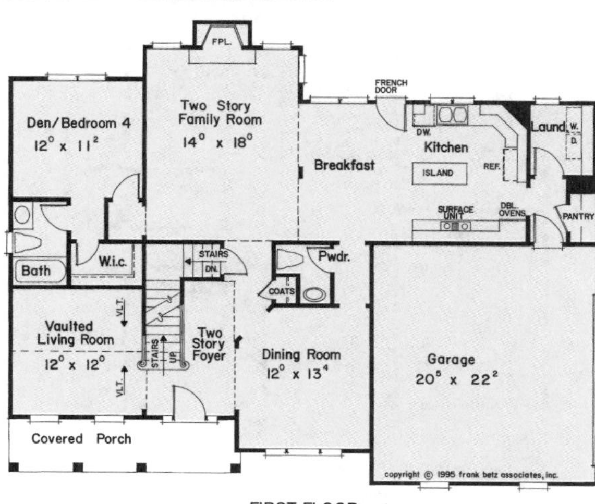

FIRST FLOOR

This home's facade is well defined with sharp arches, symmetrical windows and steep rooflines. The columned porch complements its definition with sophistication. A two-story foyer is flanked by a living room and a dining room. The family room has a cozy hearth and an open view of the kitchen area and breakfast nook. All the bedrooms are located on the second floor, as well as a bonus space. A master bath and shared bath, both with dual vanities, complete the sleeping quarters.

plan# HPT930244

- Style: Cape Cod
- First Floor: 1,319 sq. ft.
- Second Floor: 1,181 sq. ft.
- Total: 2,500 sq. ft.
- Bonus Space: 371 sq. ft.
- Bedrooms: 4
- Bathrooms: 2½
- Width: 60'-0"
- Depth: 42'-0"
- Foundation: Crawlspace

SEARCH ONLINE @ EPLANS.COM

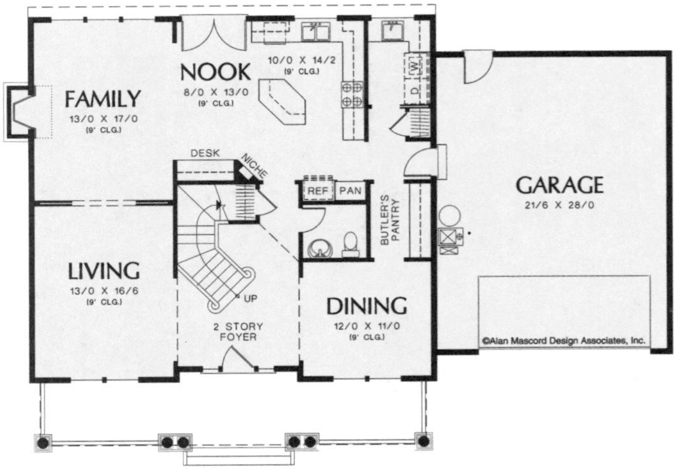

FIRST FLOOR

SECOND FLOOR

plan# HPT930245

- Style: Southern Colonial
- First Floor: 2,113 sq. ft.
- Second Floor: 2,098 sq. ft.
- Total: 4,211 sq. ft.
- Bedrooms: 5
- Bathrooms: 4½
- Width: 68'-6"
- Depth: 53'-0"
- Foundation: Crawlspace, Slab, Basement

SEARCH ONLINE @ EPLANS.COM

This two-story Colonial has much to offer, with the most exciting feature being the opulent master suite, which takes up almost the entire width of the upper level. French doors access the large master bedroom with its coffered ceiling. Steps lead to a separate sitting room with a fireplace and sun-filled bay window. His and Hers walk-in closets lead the way to a vaulted private bath with separate vanities and a lavish whirlpool tub. On the first floor, an island kitchen and a bayed breakfast room flow into a two-story family room with a raised-hearth fireplace, built-in shelves and French-door access to the rear yard.

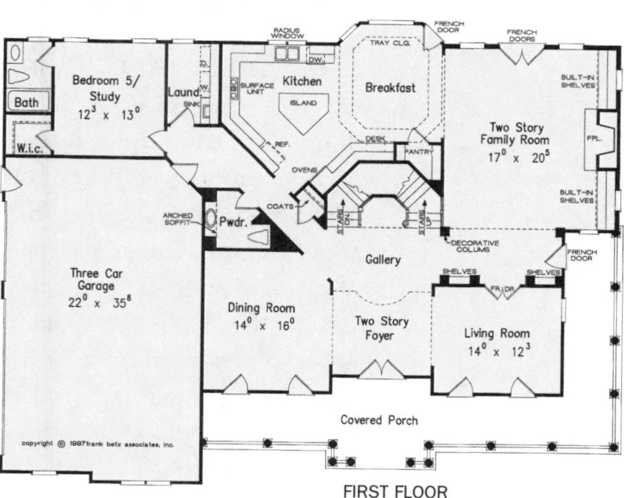

FIRST FLOOR

SECOND FLOOR

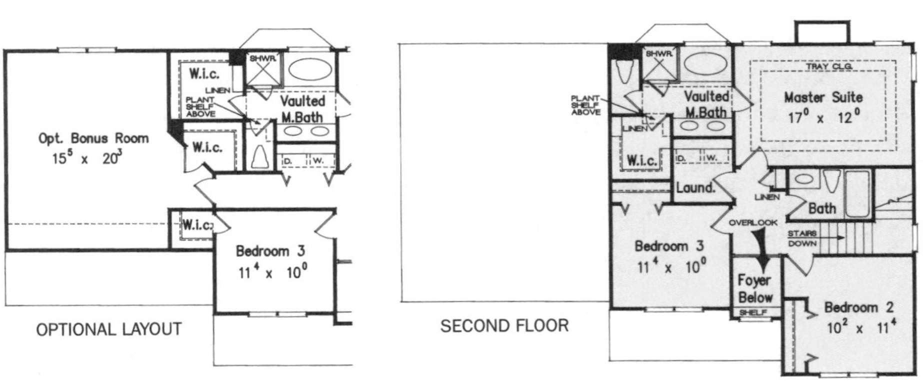

OPTIONAL LAYOUT

SECOND FLOOR

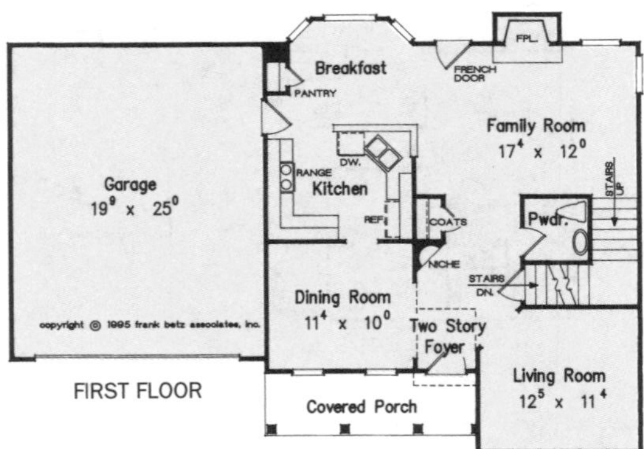

FIRST FLOOR

plan# HPT930246

- Style: Southern Colonial
- First Floor: 882 sq. ft.
- Second Floor: 793 sq. ft.
- Total: 1,675 sq. ft.
- Bonus Space: 416 sq. ft.
- Bedrooms: 3
- Bathrooms: 2½
- Width: 49'-6"
- Depth: 35'-4"
- Foundation: Basement, Crawlspace, Slab

SEARCH ONLINE @ EPLANS.COM

A cozy and inviting facade promises a great place to live. This fetching country home features a second-floor room-to-grow option that is both savvy and stylish. The first floor places formal living spaces to the front of the design and casual living spaces to the rear of the plan. The bayed breakfast nook will be a great place to relax in the sun. Upstairs, the master suite is enhanced with a bath that contains a walk-in closet.

plan# HPT930247

- Style: Southern Colonial
- First Floor: 1,142 sq. ft.
- Second Floor: 1,004 sq. ft.
- Total: 2,146 sq. ft.
- Bonus Space: 156 sq. ft.
- Bedrooms: 4
- Bathrooms: 3
- Width: 52'-4"
- Depth: 38'-6"
- Foundation: Crawlspace, Slab, Basement

SEARCH ONLINE @ EPLANS.COM

This traditional home enjoys shingles, gables and muntin windows. Some amenities include the two-story family room and a kitchen with an island counter. The master suite enjoys a tray ceiling with a French door leading to a vaulted bath. The master bath features a radius window by the soaking tub, a separate shower, compartmented toilet, two-sink vanity and plant shelf. Note the convenient second-floor laundry between Bedrooms 2 and 3.

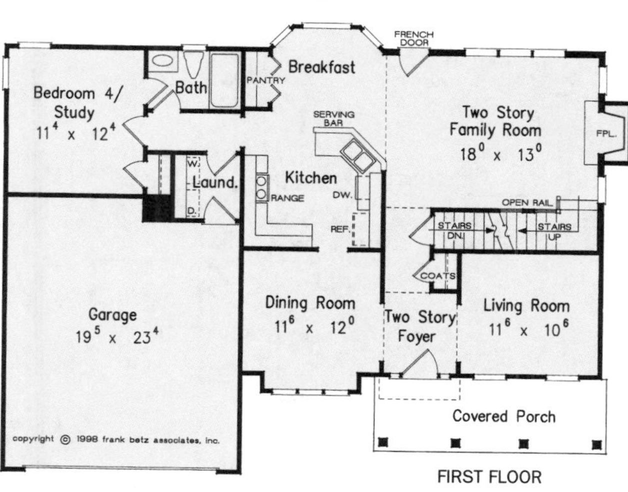

FIRST FLOOR

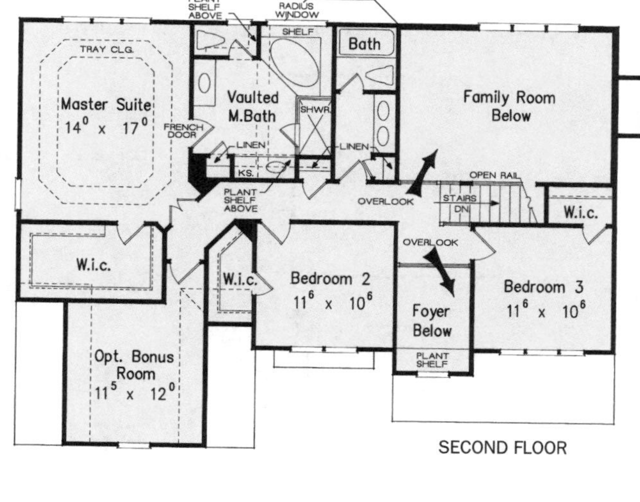

SECOND FLOOR

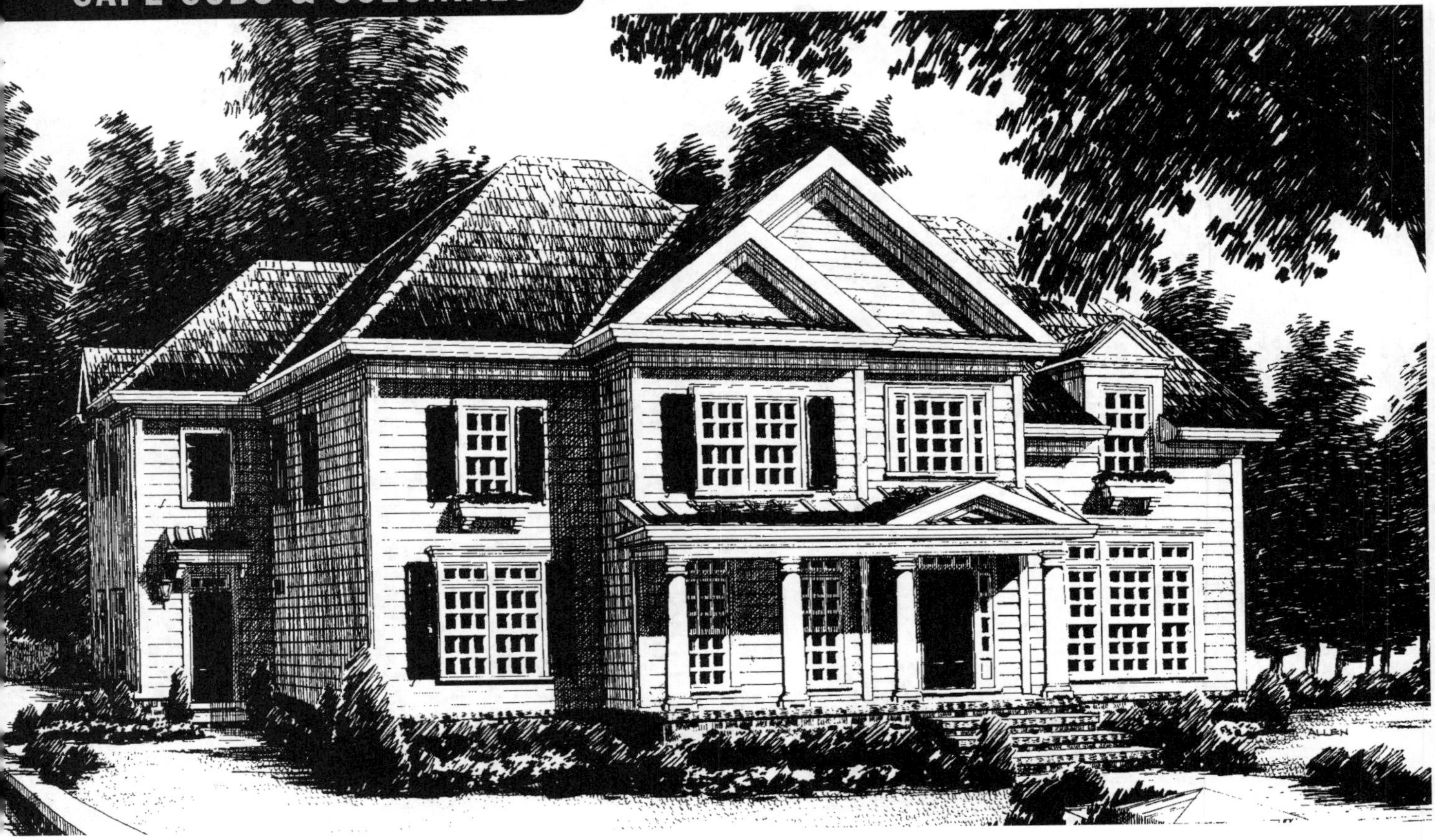

Two gables set in the multi-level hipped roof create appeal for the exterior of this modified Colonial home. The two-story foyer introduces a V-shaped stairway leading up to a bridge overlook, four bedrooms and a laundry room. Bedroom 2 enjoys a private bath and walk-in closet. The master suite, adorned with a tray ceiling, features a plush vaulted bath. An open floor plan expands the first floor. A study and dining room face one another across the foyer. A butler's pantry connects the dining room to the kitchen. Note the wonderful series of windows facing the backyard from the breakfast nook and family room. Bedroom 5 includes access to a full bath—a wonderful location for a guest suite.

plan# HPT930248

- Style: Cape Cod
- First Floor: 1,560 sq. ft.
- Second Floor: 1,522 sq. ft.
- Total: 3,082 sq. ft.
- Bedrooms: 5
- Bathrooms: 4
- Width: 56'-4"
- Depth: 52'-0"
- Foundation: Crawlspace, Basement

SEARCH ONLINE @ EPLANS.COM

FIRST FLOOR

SECOND FLOOR

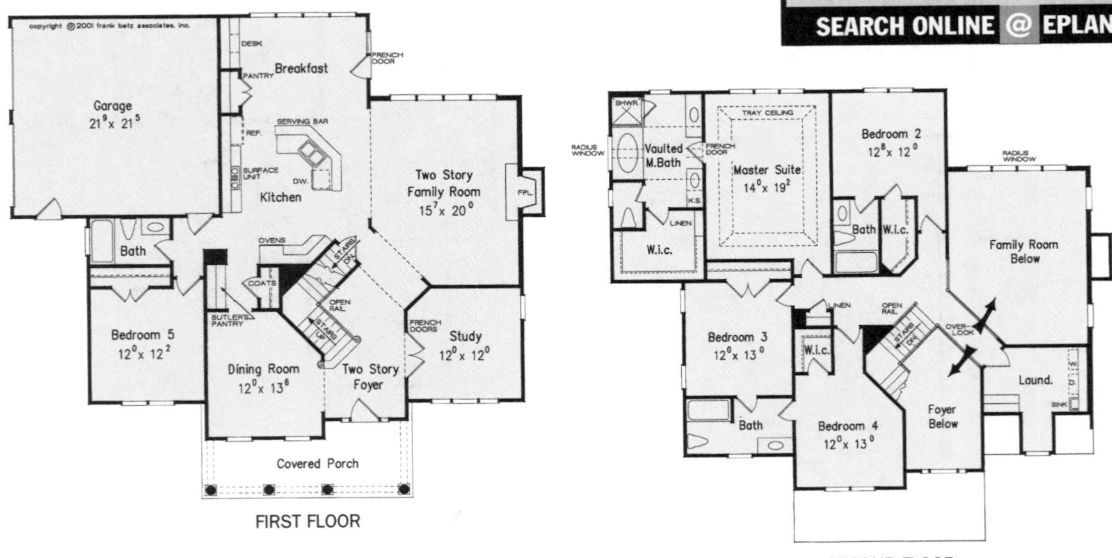

plan# HPT930249

- Style: Southern Colonial
- First Floor: 1,306 sq. ft.
- Second Floor: 1,276 sq. ft.
- Total: 2,582 sq. ft.
- Bedrooms: 5
- Bathrooms: 3
- Width: 50'-0"
- Depth: 45'-4"
- Foundation: Basement, Crawlspace, Slab

SEARCH ONLINE @ EPLANS.COM

Siding and shutters add a charming country style to this traditional home. The family room is flanked by the kitchen/breakfast area and a bedroom that doubles as a den. Upstairs, four bedrooms overlook the family room and foyer. Bedroom 3 features a window seat. Adorned with a tray ceiling and a ribbon of windows, the master suite enjoys many amenities including a plant shelf, vaulted bath, garden tub set in a box-bay window, separate shower and walk-in closet. A second-floor laundry ensures that wash day will be a breeze.

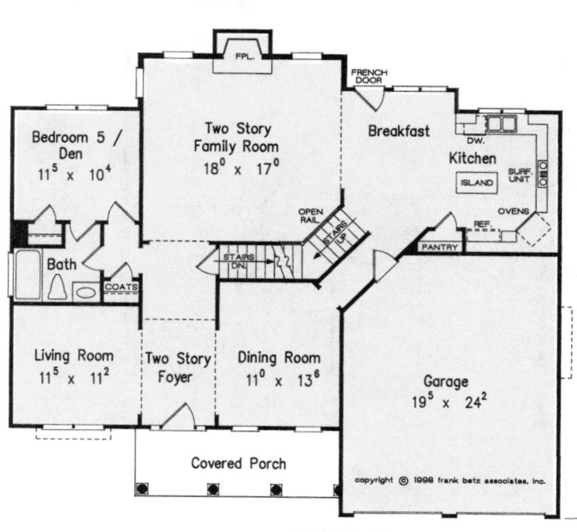

FIRST FLOOR

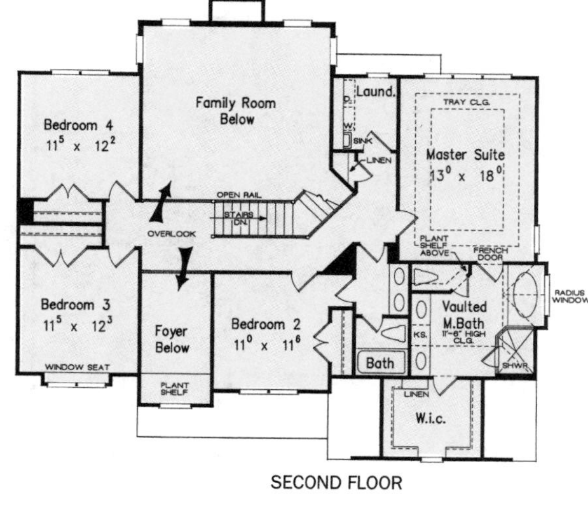

SECOND FLOOR

An array of multiple rooflines and double gables set a gratifying tone to this stone and siding exterior. Under the covered porch and through the foyer is the dining room and stairs to the second floor. The two-story family room, with a hearth, is open to the breakfast area and island kitchen. French doors open the master suite that includes a vaulted bath, sitting area and tray ceiling. Two famliy bedrooms are located in the second floor and reside on the first floor near the full hall bath.

plan# HPT930250

- Style: Colonial
- First Floor: 1,277 sq. ft.
- Second Floor: 1,173 sq. ft.
- Total: 2,450 sq. ft.
- Bedrooms: 4
- Bathrooms: 3
- Width: 42'-0"
- Depth: 52'-10"
- Foundation: Crawlspace, Basement

SEARCH ONLINE @ EPLANS.COM

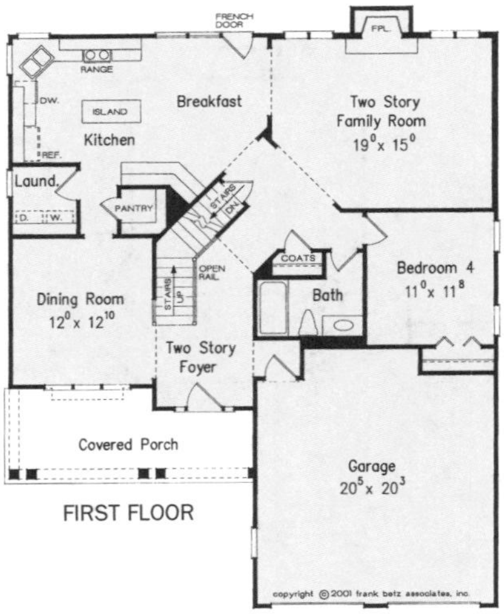

FIRST FLOOR

SECOND FLOOR

plan# HPT930251

- Style: Southern Colonial
- First Floor: 1,103 sq. ft.
- Second Floor: 759 sq. ft.
- Total: 1,862 sq. ft.
- Bonus Space: 342 sq. ft.
- Bedrooms: 4
- Bathrooms: 3
- Width: 50'-4"
- Depth: 35'-0"
- Foundation: Basement, Crawlspace, Slab

SEARCH ONLINE @ EPLANS.COM

This charming country home speaks well of an American vernacular, with classic clapboard siding, shutters and sash windows—all dressed up for 21st-Century living. A flex room on the first floor can be a study, playroom or fourth bedroom. The casual living space enjoys a fireplace, wide views of the rear property, and a French door to the outside. Upstairs, the master suite features a vaulted bath with separate shower, dual vanity and walk-in closet with linen storage.

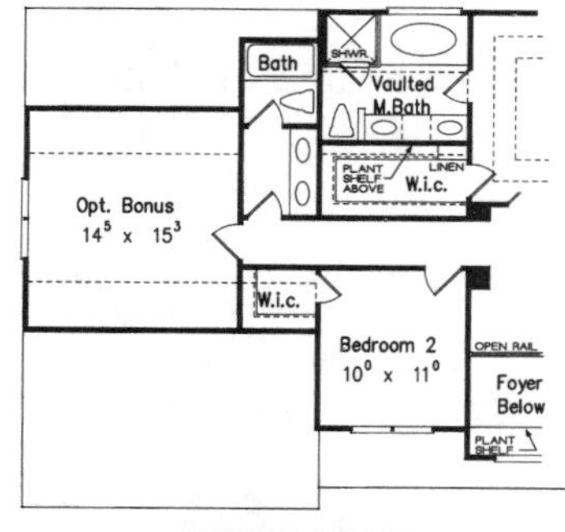

OPTIONAL LAYOUT

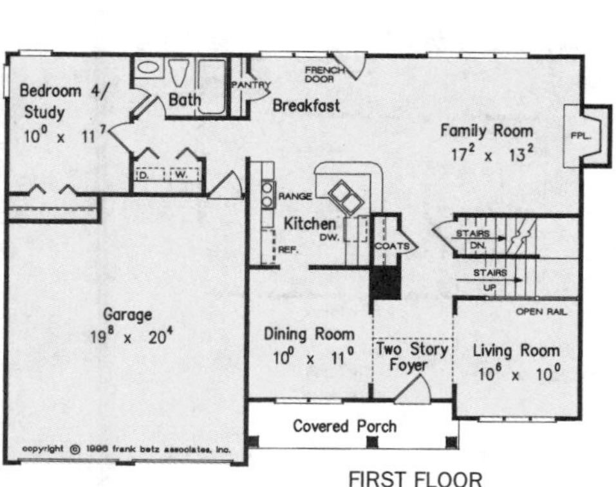

FIRST FLOOR

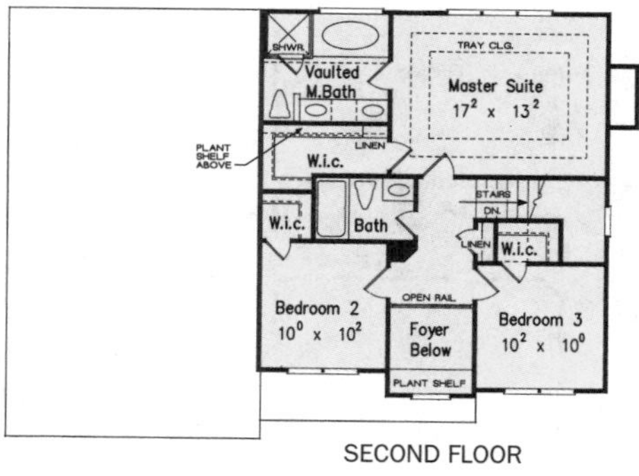

SECOND FLOOR

Classic capstones and arched windows complement rectangular shutters and pillars on this traditional facade. The family room offsets a formal dining room and shares a see-through fireplace with the keeping room. The gourmet kitchen boasts a food-preparation island with a serving bar, a generous pantry and French-door access to the rear property. Upstairs, a sensational master suite—with a tray ceiling and a vaulted bath with a plant shelf, whirlpool spa and walk-in closet—opens from a gallery hall with a balcony overlook. Bonus space offers the possibility of an adjoining sitting room. Three additional bedrooms share a full bath.

plan# HPT930252

- Style: Colonial
- First Floor: 1,223 sq. ft.
- Second Floor: 1,163 sq. ft.
- Total: 3,609 sq. ft.
- Bonus Space: 204 sq. ft.
- Bedrooms: 4
- Bathrooms: 2½
- Width: 50'-0"
- Depth: 48'-0"
- Foundation: Crawlspace, Basement

SEARCH ONLINE @ EPLANS.COM

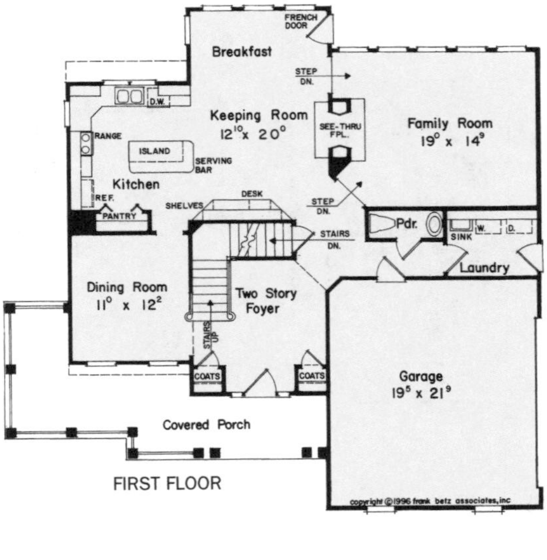

FIRST FLOOR

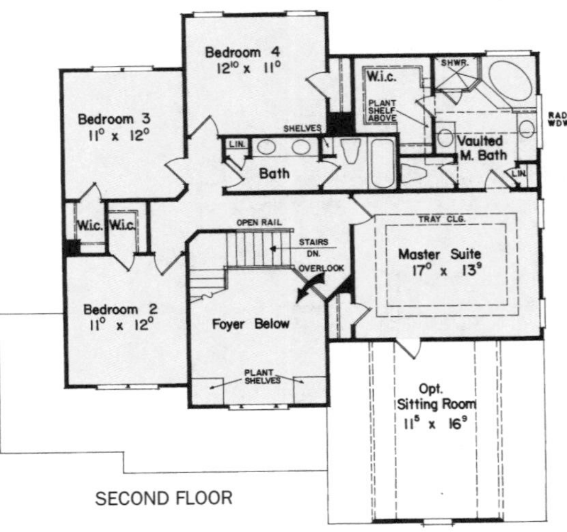

SECOND FLOOR

plan# HPT930253

- Style: Colonial
- First Floor: 1,679 sq. ft.
- Second Floor: 1,605 sq. ft.
- Total: 3,284 sq. ft.
- Bedrooms: 5
- Bathrooms: 4
- Width: 57'-0"
- Depth: 45'-4"
- Foundation: Crawlspace, Basement

SEARCH ONLINE @ EPLANS.COM

A columned porch highlights the Colonial beauty of this home. Windows decorate the facade and flood the interior with natural light. An elegant two-story foyer is flanked by the study and the dining room. Bayed windows off the breakfast nook and two-story family room decorate the rear of this home. Three bedrooms and a master suite occupy the second floor. Another bayed window is found in the sitting area of the master suite.

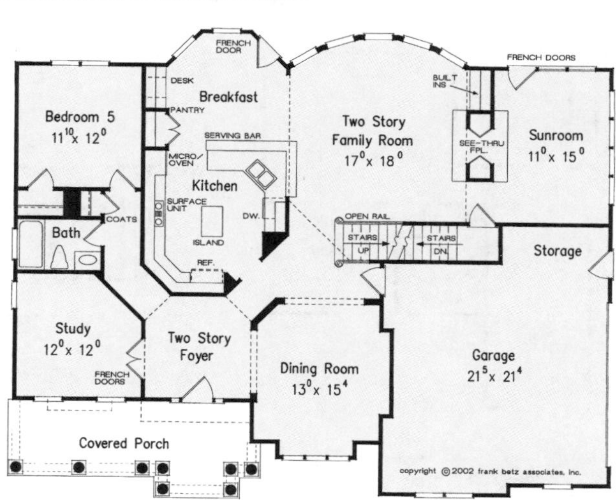

FIRST FLOOR

SECOND FLOOR

A brick garage with a flower box window lends this two-story home a cottage feel. Inside, efficient use of space and flexibility add to the appeal. A formal dining room opens from the two-story foyer, and leads to a cleverly designed kitchen. A serving bar connects the kitchen and breakfast nook. The hearth-warmed family room is just steps away. Four bedrooms—three family bedrooms and a master suite—fill the second level. Note the option of turning Bedroom 4 into a sitting area for the master suite.

plan# HPT930254

- Style: Colonial
- First Floor: 947 sq. ft.
- Second Floor: 981 sq. ft.
- Total: 1,928 sq. ft.
- Bedrooms: 4
- Bathrooms: 2½
- Width: 41'-0"
- Depth: 39'-4"
- Foundation: Crawlspace, Basement

SEARCH ONLINE @ EPLANS.COM

FRENCH DOORS
FPL.
SERVING BAR
RANGE DW.
Kitchen
Breakfast
Family Room $19^0 \times 13^5$
REF.
PANT.
LIN.
DECORATIVE COLUMN OVER KNEEWALL
Pwdr.
Laund.
COATS
D. W.
STAIRS DN.
Dining Room $11^7 \times 12^0$
STAIRS UP
Two Story Foyer
Garage $19^5 \times 22^9$
Covered Porch

FIRST FLOOR

Bedroom 3 $11^0 \times 11^6$
Bedroom 4 $10^0 \times 10^0$
TRAY CEILING
Master Suite $16^7 \times 13^5$
Bath
OPEN RAIL
LINEN
STAIRS DN.
SHWR.
W.i.c.
Vaulted M.Bath
RADIUS WINDOW
LINEN
K.S.
Bedroom 2 $11^7 \times 11^0$
Foyer Below
PLANT SHELF

SECOND FLOOR

Sitting Area $10^0 \times 10^0$
Master Suite $16^7 \times 13^5$

OPTIONAL LAYOUT

plan# HPT930255

- Style: Southern Colonial
- First Floor: 1,488 sq. ft.
- Second Floor: 1,551 sq. ft.
- Total: 3,039 sq. ft.
- Bedrooms: 5
- Bathrooms: 4
- Width: 55'-0"
- Depth: 57'-4"
- Foundation: Crawlspace, Slab, Basement

SEARCH ONLINE @ EPLANS.COM

Traditional lines accentuate the powerful brick facade of this home. Flanked by the formal dining and living rooms, the two-story foyer features a handsome staircase. To the rear of the plan, windows frame the fireplace in the family room, while both the dining room and living room feature tall windows. A guest room is near the full bath on the right of the plan. A roomy island kitchen handles casual to formal meals with ease. On the second floor, the master suite includes a vaulted bath with a radius window over the tub. Three family bedrooms—one with a private bath—complete the living quarters.

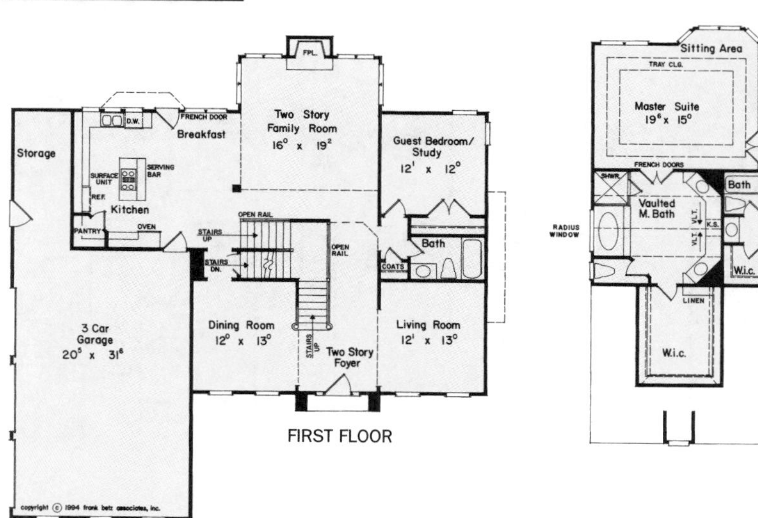

FIRST FLOOR

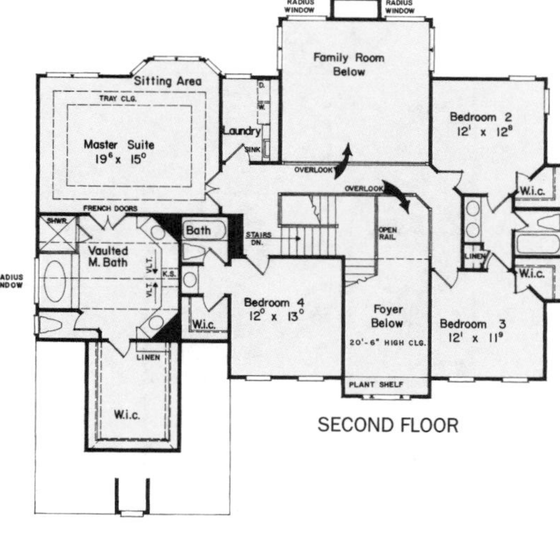

SECOND FLOOR

The nearly octagonal shape of the kitchen, with its long work island, will please the family's gourmet cook. The breakfast room, which opens to the back through a French door, flows into the two-story family room. To the right, leads a butler's pantry to the dining room. The formal living room is on the other side of the two-story foyer. A bedroom with a private bath and walk-in closet could be an in-law suite, study or home office. The other four bedrooms are upstairs off a balcony overlooking the family room. The laundry room is also on this floor. The master suite includes a sitting room, a walk-in closet and a luxurious bath.

plan# HPT930256

- Style: Southern Colonial
- First Floor: 1,463 sq. ft.
- Second Floor: 1,490 sq. ft.
- Total: 2,953 sq. ft.
- Bedrooms: 5
- Bathrooms: 4½
- Width: 54'-0"
- Depth: 51'-6"
- Foundation: Crawlspace, Slab, Basement

SEARCH ONLINE @ EPLANS.COM

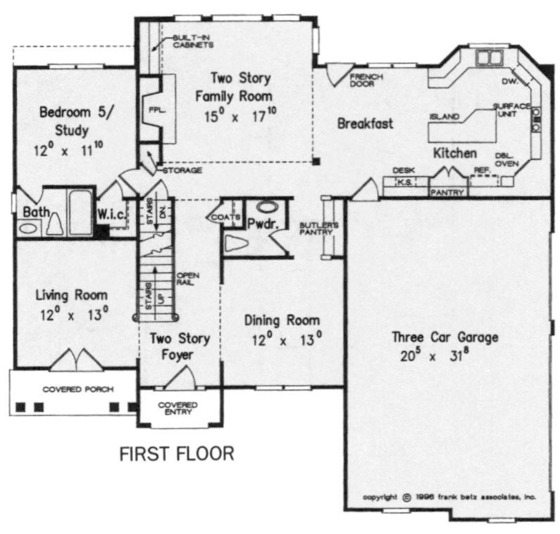

FIRST FLOOR

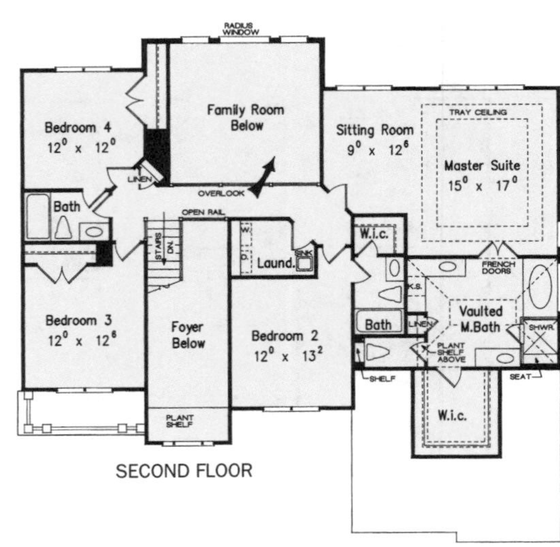

SECOND FLOOR

plan# HPT930257

- Style: Southern Colonial
- First Floor: 1,665 sq. ft.
- Second Floor: 1,554 sq. ft.
- Total: 3,219 sq. ft.
- Bedrooms: 5
- Bathrooms: 4
- Width: 58'-6"
- Depth: 44'-10"
- Foundation: Crawlspace, Basement

SEARCH ONLINE @ EPLANS.COM

This stately transitional home focuses on family living. The formal living areas are traditionally placed flanking the two-story foyer. The two-story family room has a lovely fireplace and windows to the rear yard. The remarkable kitchen features wraparound counters, a breakfast nook and a cooktop island/serving bar. A bedroom and full bath would make a comfortable guest suite or a quiet den. A balcony hall leads to two bedrooms that share a bath; a third bedroom has its own bath and walk-in closet. The master suite is designed with a tray ceiling and a sitting room with a through-fireplace to the vaulted bath.

FIRST FLOOR

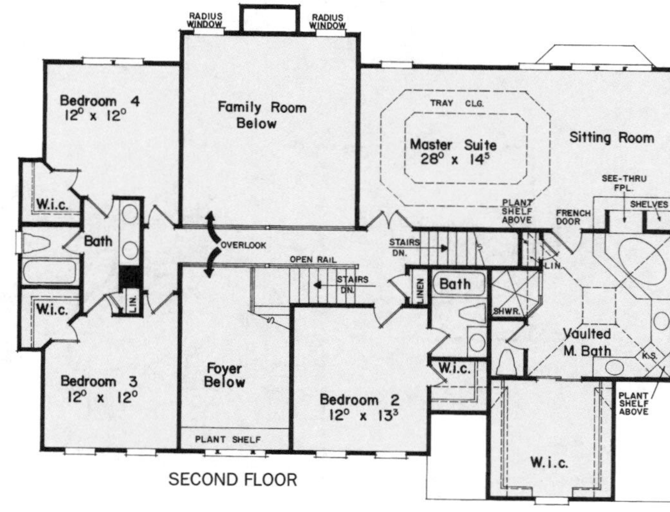

SECOND FLOOR

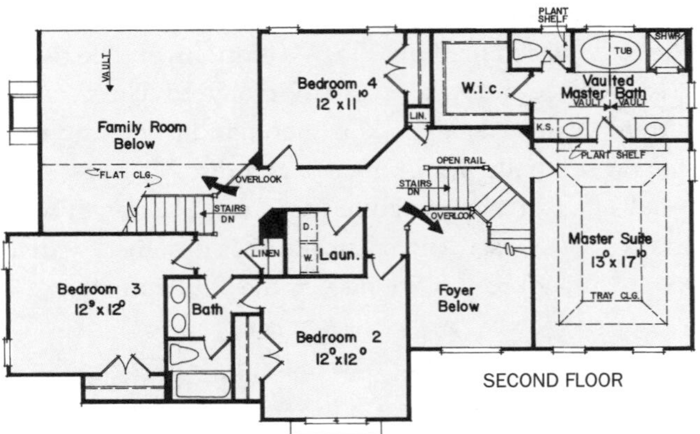

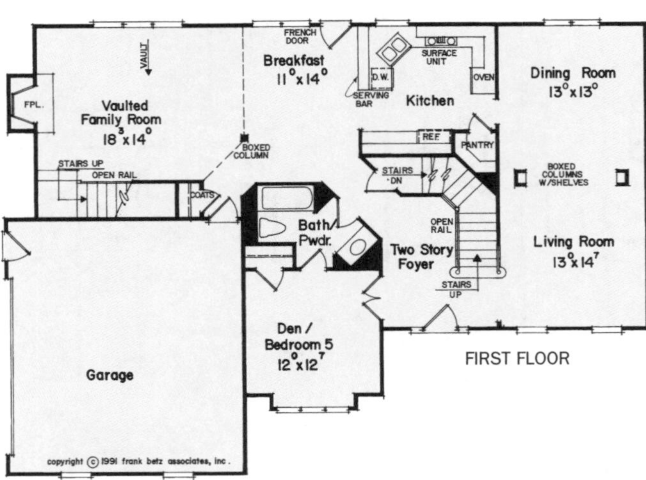

plan# HPT930258

- Style: Colonial
- First Floor: 1,424 sq. ft.
- Second Floor: 1,256 sq. ft.
- Total: 2,680 sq. ft.
- Bedrooms: 4
- Bathrooms: 3
- Width: 57'-0"
- Depth: 41'-0"
- Foundation: Basement, Crawlspace, Slab

SEARCH ONLINE @ EPLANS.COM

A grand two-story foyer takes its charm from a bright clerestory window. Just off the foyer lies the formal living area, where the living room joins the dining room with twin boxed columns that are personalized with shelves. The kitchen is placed to easily serve the dining room while remaining open to the breakfast area and vaulted family room. Upstairs, the master suite and bath are nicely balanced with three family bedrooms, a full hall bath and a convenient laundry room.

plan# HPT930259

- Style: Southern Colonial
- First Floor: 1,294 sq. ft.
- Second Floor: 1,058 sq. ft.
- Total: 2,352 sq. ft.
- Bonus Space: 168 sq. ft.
- Bedrooms: 4
- Bathrooms: 3
- Width: 54'-4"
- Depth: 37'-6"
- Foundation: Crawlspace, Basement

SEARCH ONLINE @ EPLANS.COM

Traditional stylings—pilaster and sidelight accents at the front entry and keystone jack-arched windows with shutters—present a home with class and appeal. The two-story foyer is flanked by the formal dining room and the living room. Beyond the enclosed staircase, the family room, warmed with a fireplace, offers a cozy environment for intimate gatherings. The angled kitchen enjoys a serving bar, and is situated between the dining room and breakfast area for convenience. Note the home office/bedroom, tucked away on the left, with its private entrance to the full bath. The lavish master suite resides on the second floor along with two additional bedrooms, a full bath, laundry and a bonus room.

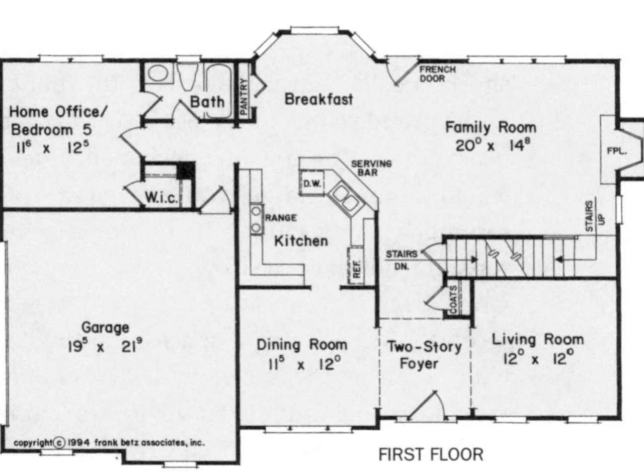

FIRST FLOOR

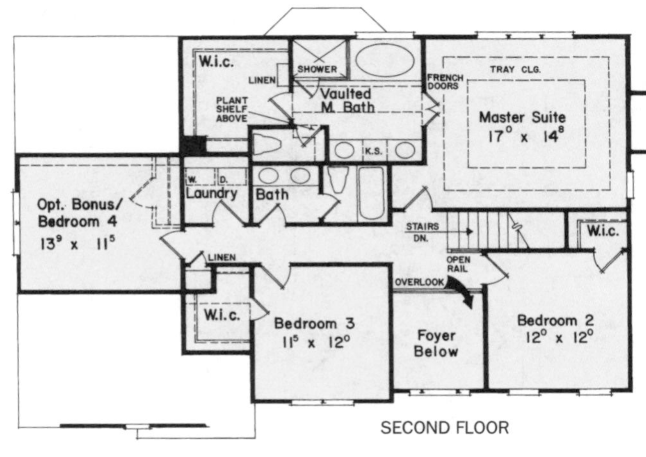

SECOND FLOOR

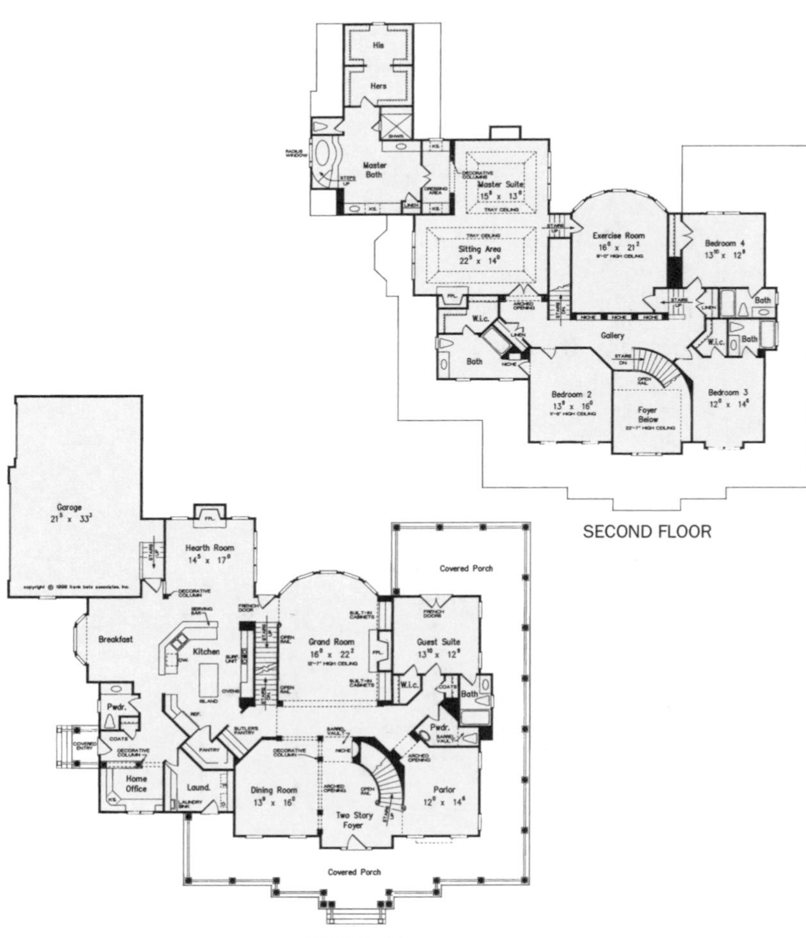

SECOND FLOOR

FIRST FLOOR

plan# HPT930260

- Style: Plantation
- First Floor: 2,732 sq. ft.
- Second Floor: 2,734 sq. ft.
- Total: 5,466 sq. ft.
- Bedrooms: 5
- Bathrooms: 5½ + ½
- Width: 85'-0"
- Depth: 85'-6"
- Foundation: Crawlspace, Slab, Basement

SEARCH ONLINE  EPLANS.COM

A wraparound covered porch adds plenty of outdoor space to this already impressive home. Built-in cabinets flank the fireplace in the grand room; a fireplace also warms the hearth room. The gourmet kitchen includes an island counter, large walk-in pantry and serving bar. A secluded home office, with a separate entrance nearby, provides a quiet work place. The master suite dominates the second floor, offering a spacious sitting area with an elegant tray ceiling, a dressing area and a luxurious bath with two walk-in closets, double vanities and a raised garden tub.

plan# HPT930261

- Style: Colonial
- First Floor: 2,024 sq. ft.
- Second Floor: 958 sq. ft.
- Total: 2,982 sq. ft.
- Bedrooms: 4
- Bathrooms: 3½
- Width: 62'-0"
- Depth: 50'-4"
- Foundation: Crawlspace, Basement

SEARCH ONLINE @ EPLANS.COM

Windows illuminate this home's exterior as well as its interior, and shutters add a dimension of coziness. The covered porch opens to the foyer where the dining room resides on the left and the study is placed on the right. Straight back is the vaulted family room with a magnificent hearth. The master suite is just to the right of the family room complete with its bayed window and vaulted bath. A vaulted keeping room has its own fireplace. On the second floor are two bedrooms and two baths, perfect for a family.

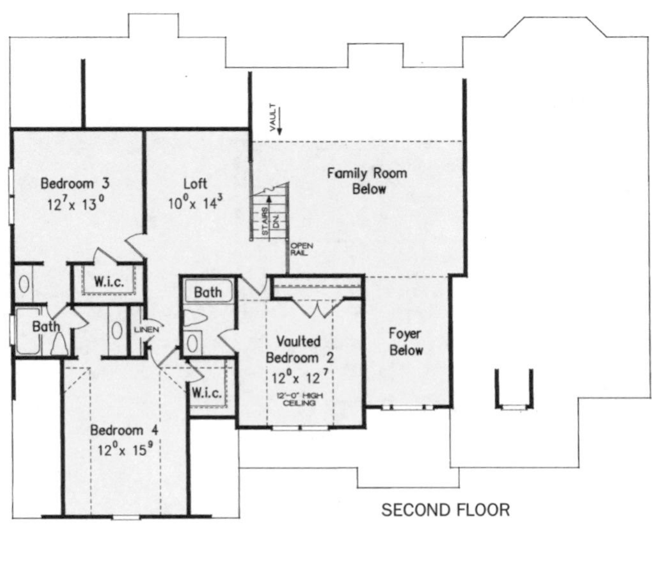

SECOND FLOOR

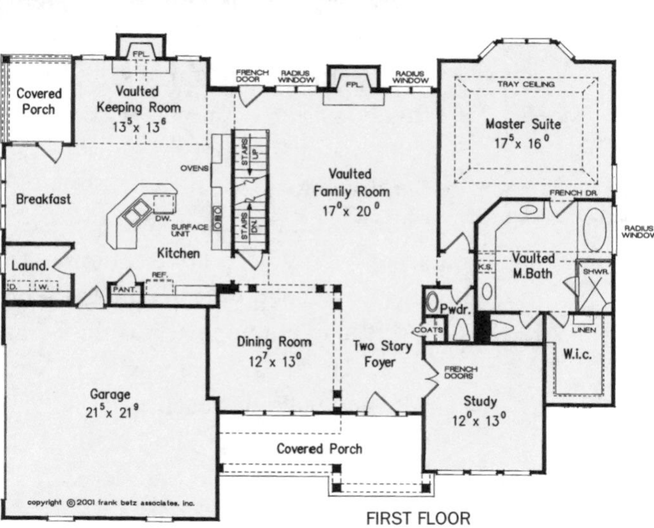

FIRST FLOOR

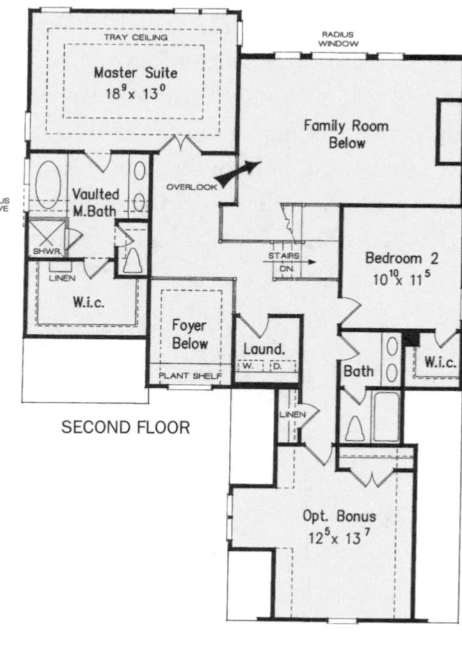

SECOND FLOOR

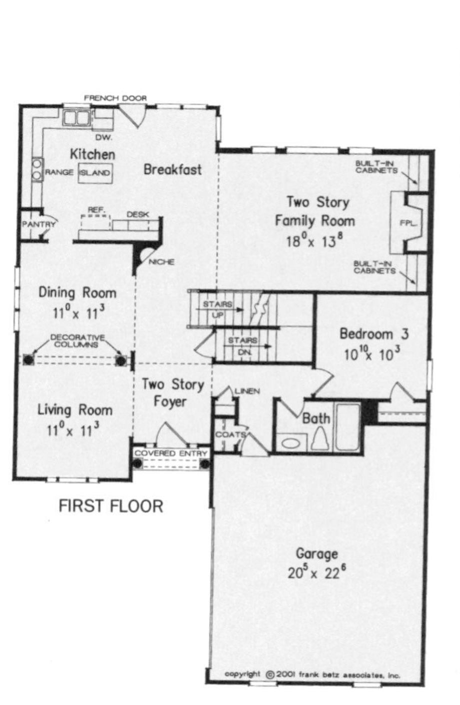

FIRST FLOOR

plan# HPT930262

- Style: Colonial
- First Floor: 1,293 sq. ft.
- Second Floor: 922 sq. ft.
- Total: 2,215 sq. ft.
- Bonus Space: 235 sq. ft.
- Bedrooms: 3
- Bathrooms: 3
- Width: 40'-0"
- Depth: 57'-0"
- Foundation: Crawlspace, Basement

SEARCH ONLINE @ EPLANS.COM

The shingle and rock exterior of this home offer a timeless and sophisticated look. The covered entry leads into the two-story foyer where the living room and dining room are accessed and separated by decorative columns. The L-shaped kitchen offers extra space on the island and convenience to the breakfast nook. The master suite with its vaulted bath and walk-in closet, along with a separate bedroom, bath and walk-in closet, are located on the second floor.

plan# HPT930263

- Style: Colonial
- First Floor: 1,969 sq. ft.
- Second Floor: 894 sq. ft.
- Total: 2,863 sq. ft.
- Bonus Space: 213 sq. ft.
- Bedrooms: 4
- Bathrooms: 2½
- Width: 55'-0"
- Depth: 54'-0"
- Foundation: Crawlspace, Basement

SEARCH ONLINE @ EPLANS.COM

The low rooflines and high arches create a dramatic contrast on this home. The covered porch is a great place to relax on sunny afternoons. With decorative columns throughout this home any get-together is sure to be one of simple elegance. The grand master bedroom is complete with tray ceilings and a bayed sitting area. The breakfast nook also has a bayed window and plenty of sunlight. Three bedrooms and plenty of storage space are available on the second floor.

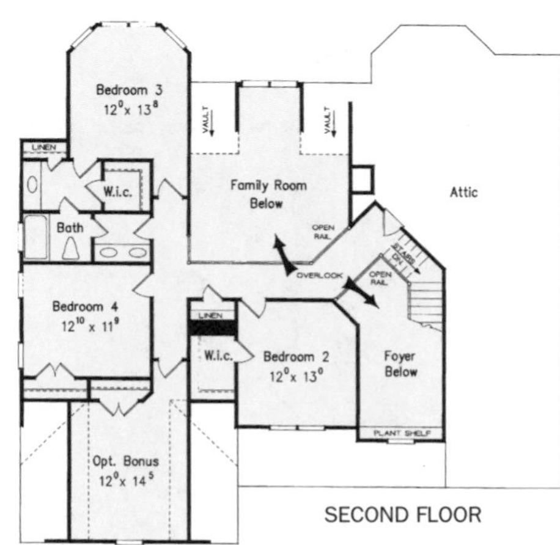

SECOND FLOOR

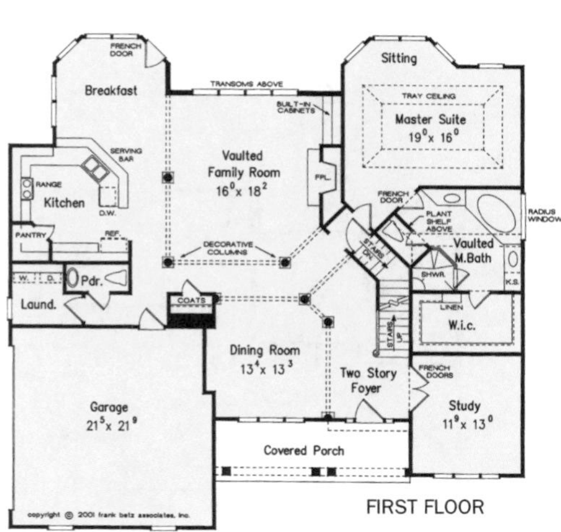

FIRST FLOOR

Colonial details and a covered porch combine to give this home plenty of curb appeal. Inside, a formal dining room presides at the front of the plan, while more casual rooms wait in the back. Here, a family room with a fireplace works well with the C-shaped kitchen and adjacent breakfast area. The first-floor master suite ensures privacy and offers two walk-in closets and a lavish bath, as well a private access to the rear porch. Upstairs, three spacious bedrooms provide plenty of storage—Bedrooms 2 and 4 share a large bath, while Bedroom 3 is all about privacy. The two-car garage is wonderfully convenient to the kitchen, making unloading groceries a breeze.

plan# HPT930264

- Style: NE Colonial
- First Floor: 1,832 sq. ft.
- Second Floor: 973 sq. ft.
- Total: 2,805 sq. ft.
- Bedrooms: 4
- Bathrooms: 3½
- Width: 49'-0"
- Depth: 66'-0"
- Foundation: Walkout Basement

SEARCH ONLINE @ EPLANS.COM

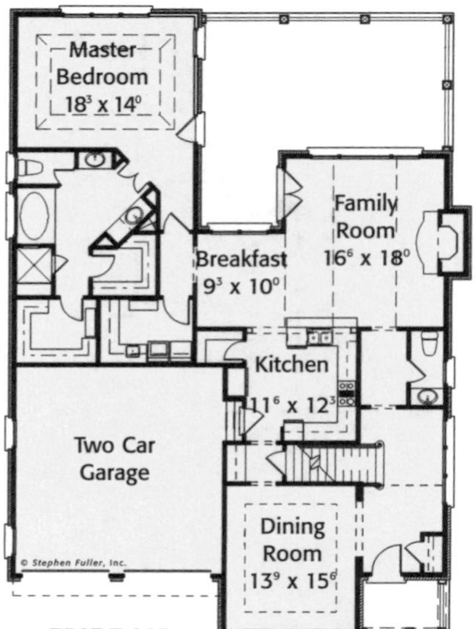

Master Bedroom 18^{3} x 14^{0}
Family Room 16^{6} x 18^{0}
Breakfast 9^{3} x 10^{0}
Kitchen 11^{6} x 12^{3}
Two Car Garage
Dining Room 13^{9} x 15^{6}
© Stephen Fuller, Inc.
FIRST FLOOR

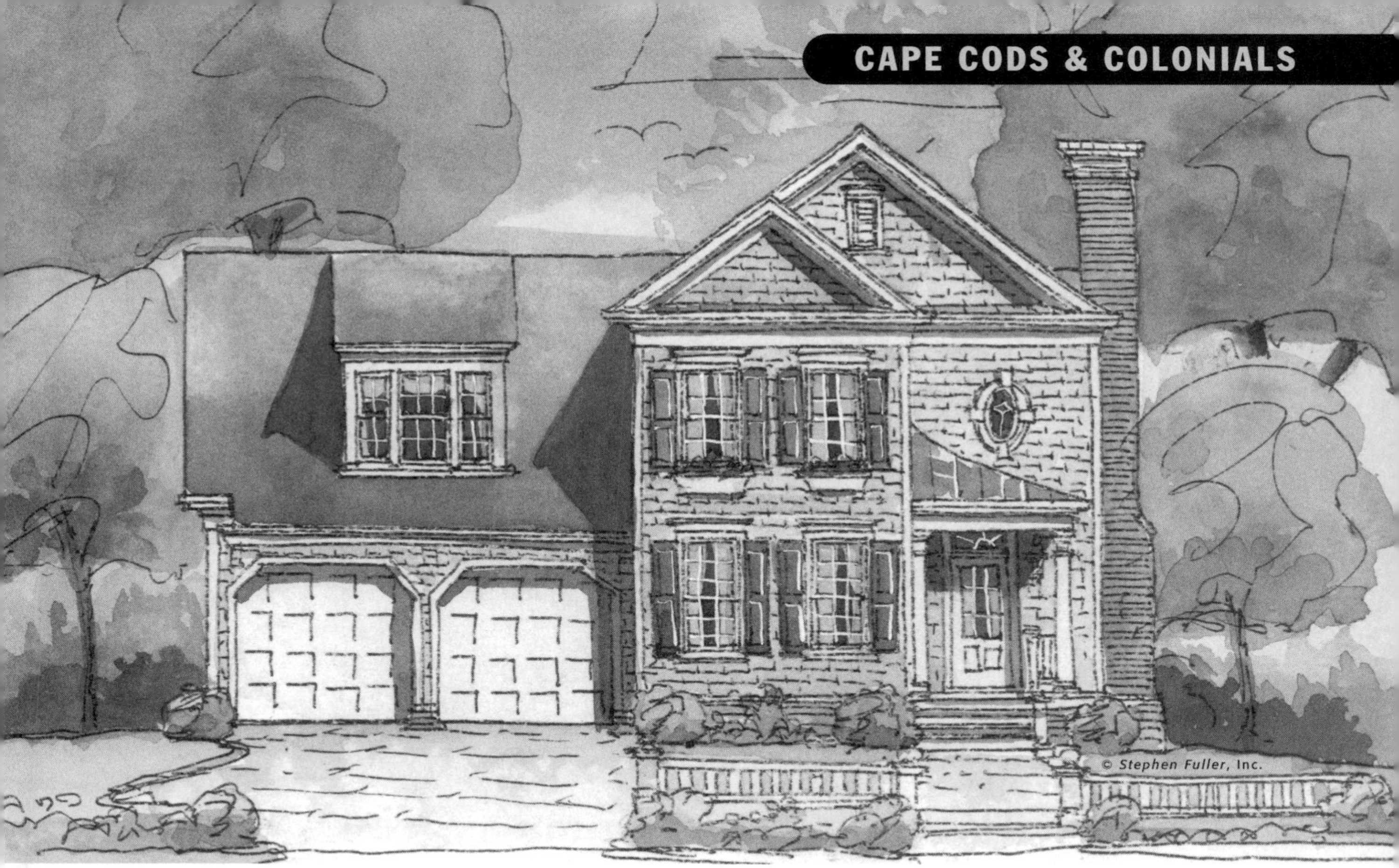

plan# HPT930265

- Style: Cape Cod
- First Floor: 1,872 sq. ft.
- Second Floor: 643 sq. ft.
- Total: 2,515 sq. ft.
- Bonus Space: 328 sq. ft.
- Bedrooms: 3
- Bathrooms: 3½
- Width: 46'-0"
- Depth: 66'-0"
- Foundation: Basement

SEARCH ONLINE @ EPLANS.COM

This enchanting design offers a touch of Arts and Crafts with porch details and an accent window. Inside, the formal dining room includes a tray ceiling. The spacious family room is warmed by a massive hearth and accesses the rear porch. The island kitchen is set between the dining room and breakfast room. The master bedroom, secluded on the first floor, features a tray ceiling, private access to the rear porch, a whirlpool tub and His and Hers walk-in closets. Two additional family bedrooms reside upstairs, along with a bonus room that easily converts to a fourth bedroom, home office or playroom.

FIRST FLOOR

SECOND FLOOR

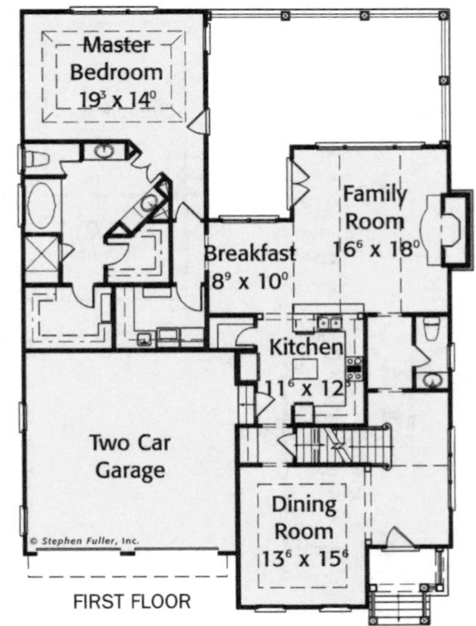

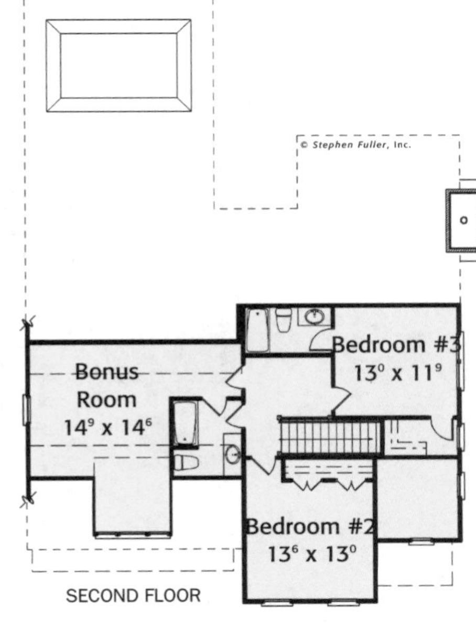

© Stephen Fuller, Inc.

A beautiful brick Georgian from one of our top designers, this three-bedroom plan is a pleasure to call home. The two-story foyer and family room have balcony overlooks from above, adding architectural interest. To the left of the foyer, the study opens with French doors; to the right, the dining room features butler's pantry access to the country kitchen, complete with a cooktop island. The breakfast nook opens to a vaulted sun room. The master suite enjoys peace and quiet, along with an enormous walk-in closet and sumptuous bath with a corner tub. Two upstairs bedrooms, each with private baths and walk-in closets, share a bonus room.

plan# HPT930266

- Style: Georgian
- First Floor: 2,719 sq. ft.
- Second Floor: 929 sq. ft.
- Total: 3,648 sq. ft.
- Bonus Space: 530 sq. ft.
- Bedrooms: 3
- Bathrooms: 4
- Width: 62'-8"
- Depth: 83'-0"
- Foundation: Walkout Basement

SEARCH ONLINE @ EPLANS.COM

FIRST FLOOR

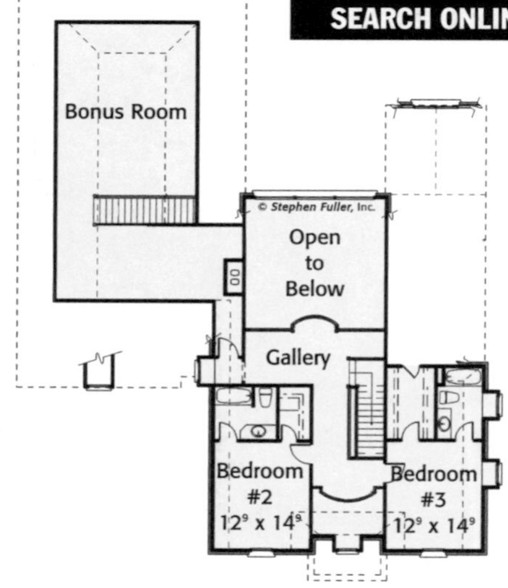

SECOND FLOOR

plan# HPT930267

- Style: Georgian
- First Floor: 1,981 sq. ft.
- Second Floor: 1,935 sq. ft.
- Total: 3,916 sq. ft.
- Bedrooms: 5
- Bathrooms: 4
- Width: 65'-0"
- Depth: 64'-10"
- Foundation: Walkout Basement

SEARCH ONLINE @ EPLANS.COM

Take one look at this Early American Colonial home and you'll fall in love with it's beauty, functionality and luxuries. From the covered front porch, continue to the great room, where a fireplace and a bay window with wonderful rear-property views await. The kitchen will delight, with a wraparound counter that provides plenty of workspace for easy meal preparation. Up the grand staircase, the master suite revels in a private deck and pampering spa bath. Three additional bedrooms complete this level. Don't miss the first-floor guest room with an adjacent full bath.

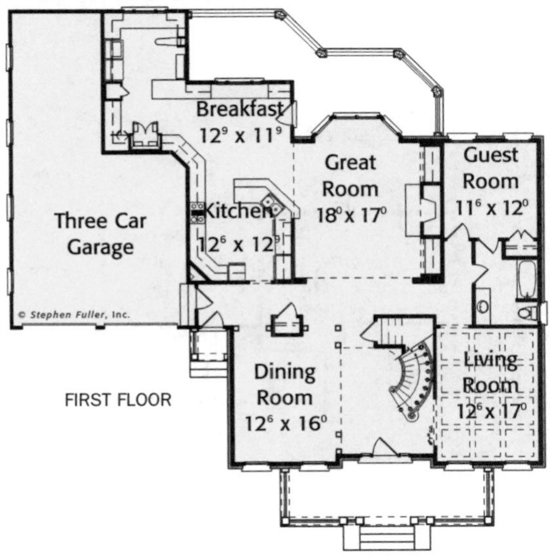

FIRST FLOOR

SECOND FLOOR

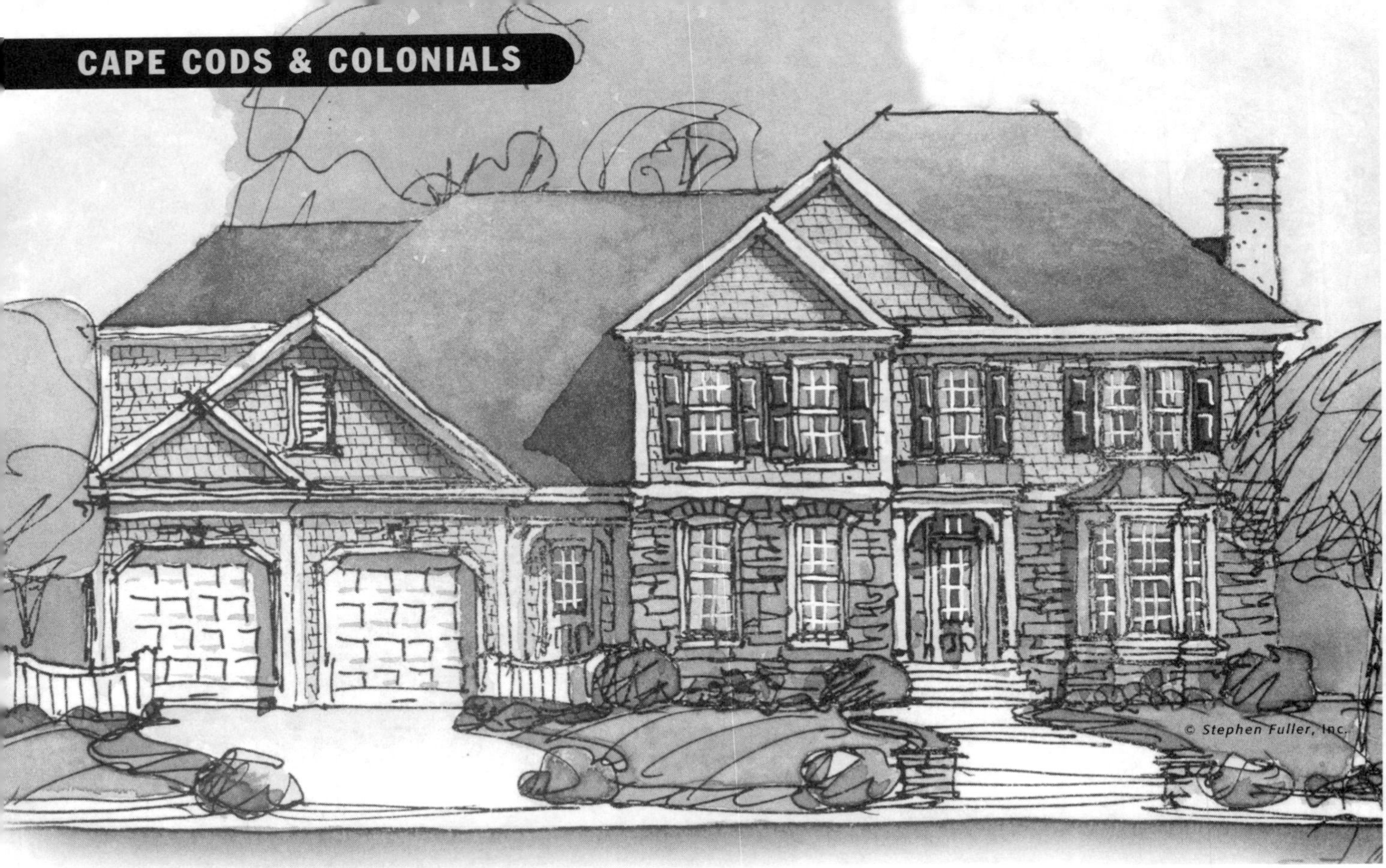

This classic North Eastern Colonial home is a dream to own, with shingle and stone outside, and a comfortable family plan inside. In the two-story great room, a fireplace warms, while French doors invite outdoor living. To the left of the island kitchen, the office accesses a private porch. The aptly named sun room is accessed from the breakfast nook, or through French doors from the guest room, complete with a private bath. Upstairs, the deluxe master suite includes a sitting area, vaulted bath and Z-shaped walk-in closet. Two additional bedrooms share a full bath.

plan# HPT930268

- Style: Cape Cod
- First Floor: 2,194 sq. ft.
- Second Floor: 1,695 sq. ft.
- Total: 3,889 sq. ft.
- Bedrooms: 4
- Bathrooms: 3½
- Width: 64'-4"
- Depth: 63'-0"
- Foundation: Walkout Basement

SEARCH ONLINE @ EPLANS.COM

FIRST FLOOR

SECOND FLOOR

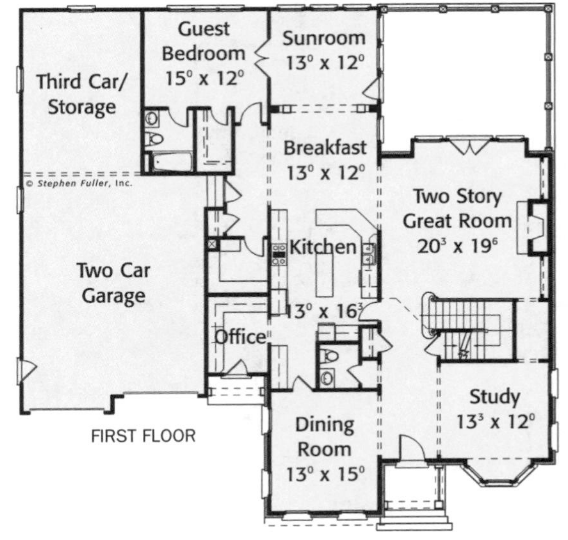

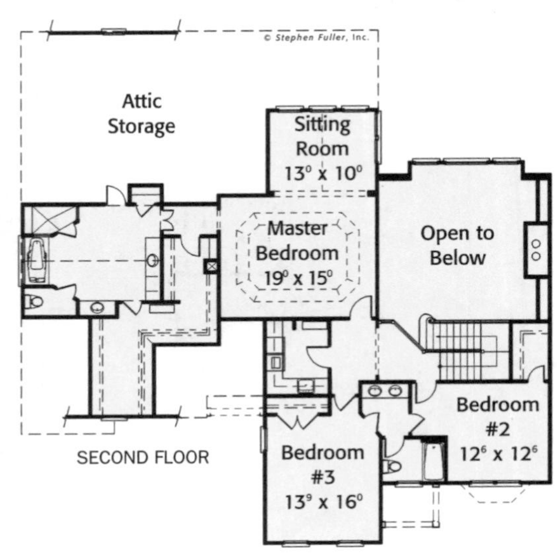

plan# HPT930269

- Style: Southern Colonial
- First Floor: 2,175 sq. ft.
- Second Floor: 1,647 sq. ft.
- Total: 3,822 sq. ft.
- Bedrooms: 4
- Bathrooms: 3½
- Width: 64'-4"
- Depth: 63'-0"
- Foundation: Walkout Basement

SEARCH ONLINE @ EPLANS.COM

Step into comfort in this beautiful brick Southern Colonial. Enter to find a plan designed with you in mind. The dining room and study allow plenty of natural light at the front of the home. Continue to the great room, offering an extended-hearth fireplace and French doors to the rear patio. The guest suite is tucked away with a private bath and French-door access to the sun room. Upstairs, the master bedroom will surround you in luxury, with a sitting room bathed in light, a vaulted bath with a spa tub, and a Z-shaped walk-in closet. Two additional bedrooms share a full bath.

FIRST FLOOR

SECOND FLOOR

A brick facade with the charm of a Cape Cod cottage, this home is designed for flexibility and family living. The formal living and dining rooms flank the entry, which leads to the vaulted great room. A lateral fireplace is surrounded by built-in shelving; access to the sun room assures year-round enjoyment. The gourmet island kitchen serves a sunny breakfast nook and accesses the dining room through a butler's pantry. The master suite is tucked to the rear of the plan, with a bay window, and a fabulous bath with a spa tub. Unfinished areas upstairs allow room to grow. Don't miss the optional office/third-car garage addition.

plan# HPT930270

- Style: Cape Cod
- First Floor: 3,081 sq. ft.
- Second Floor: 622 sq. ft.
- Total: 3,703 sq. ft.
- Bonus Space: 1,437 sq. ft.
- Bedrooms: 3
- Bathrooms: 2½
- Width: 65'-0"
- Depth: 78'-6"
- Foundation: Walkout Basement

SEARCH ONLINE @ EPLANS.COM

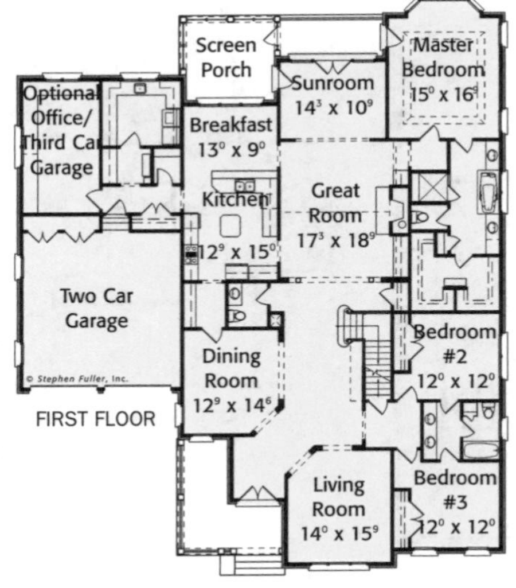

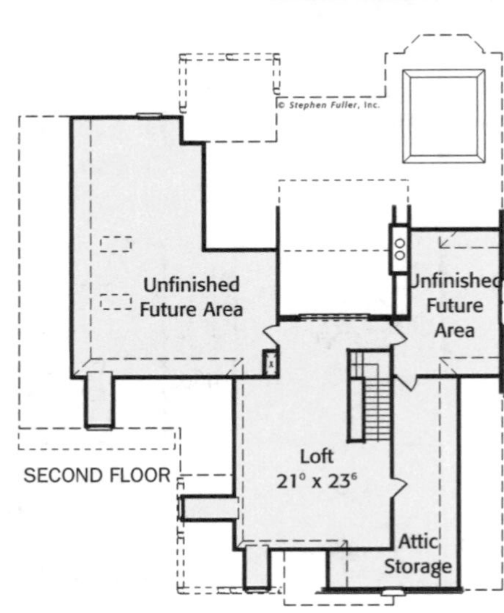

© Stephen Fuller, Inc.

plan# HPT930271

- Style: Cape Cod
- First Floor: 3,108 sq. ft.
- Second Floor: 512 sq. ft.
- Total: 3,620 sq. ft.
- Bonus Space: 605 sq. ft.
- Bedrooms: 3
- Bathrooms: 2½
- Width: 65'-0"
- Depth: 81'-0"
- Foundation: Walkout Basement

SEARCH ONLINE @ EPLANS.COM

A sweet, traditional neighborhood home with eclectic touches, this spacious plan is sure to please. The formal spaces, including the bayed living room, are located near the entry, defined by arches. The gourmet kitchen serves the dining room through a butler's pantry, and opens to a bright breakfast nook. The vaulted great room features a fireplace for those chilly nights, and a sun room for warm, lazy days. Twin bedrooms toward the front of the plan share a full bath; the master suite is tucked to the rear with a tray ceiling and a sumptuous bath. Bonus space is limited only by your imagination.

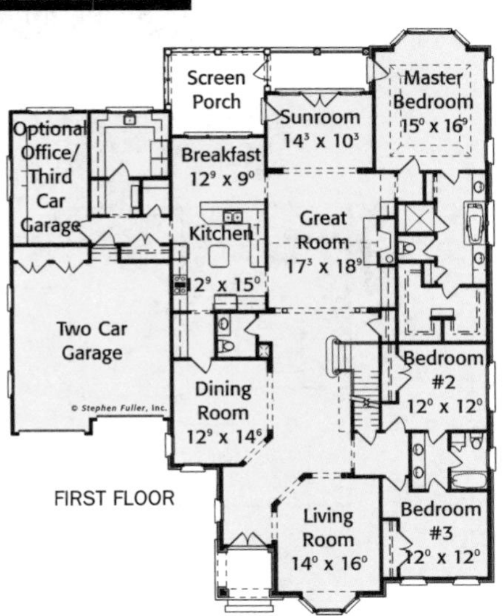

FIRST FLOOR

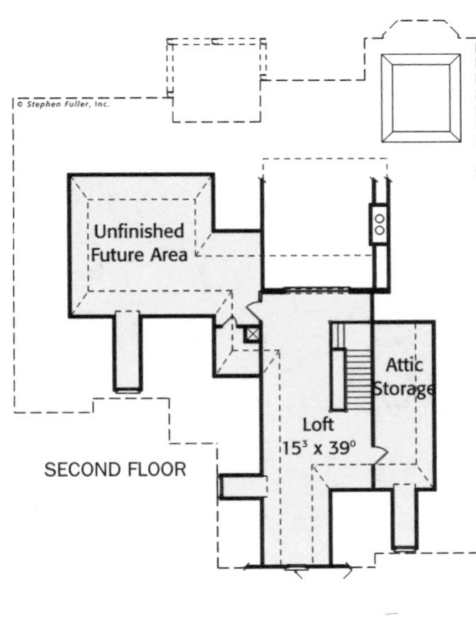

SECOND FLOOR

This enchanting farmhouse brings the past to life with plenty of modern amenities. An open-flow kitchen/breakfast area and family room combination is the heart of the home, opening up to the screened porch and enjoying the warmth of a fireplace. For more formal occasions, the foyer is flanked by a living room on the left and a dining room on the right. An elegant master bedroom, complete with a super-size walk-in closet, is tucked away quietly behind the garage. Three more bedrooms reside upstairs, along with two full baths and a future recreation room.

plan# HPT930272

- Style: Colonial
- First Floor: 1,913 sq. ft.
- Second Floor: 997 sq. ft.
- Total: 2,910 sq. ft.
- Bonus Space: 377 sq. ft.
- Bedrooms: 4
- Bathrooms: 3½
- Width: 63'-0"
- Depth: 59'-4"
- Foundation: Basement, Crawlspace

SEARCH ONLINE @ EPLANS.COM

FIRST FLOOR

SECOND FLOOR

plan# HPT930273

- Style: Colonial
- First Floor: 1,804 sq. ft.
- Second Floor: 1,041 sq. ft.
- Total: 2,845 sq. ft.
- Bedrooms: 4
- Bathrooms: 3½
- Width: 57'-3"
- Depth: 71'-0"
- Foundation: Walkout Basement

SEARCH ONLINE @ EPLANS.COM

There's a feeling of old Charleston in this stately home—particularly on the quiet side porch that wraps around the kitchen and breakfast room. The interior of this home revolves around a spacious great room with a welcoming fireplace. The left wing is dedicated to the master suite, which boasts wide views of the rear property. A corner kitchen easily serves planned events in the formal dining room, as well as family meals in the breakfast area. Three family bedrooms, one with a private bath and the others sharing a bath, are tucked upstairs.

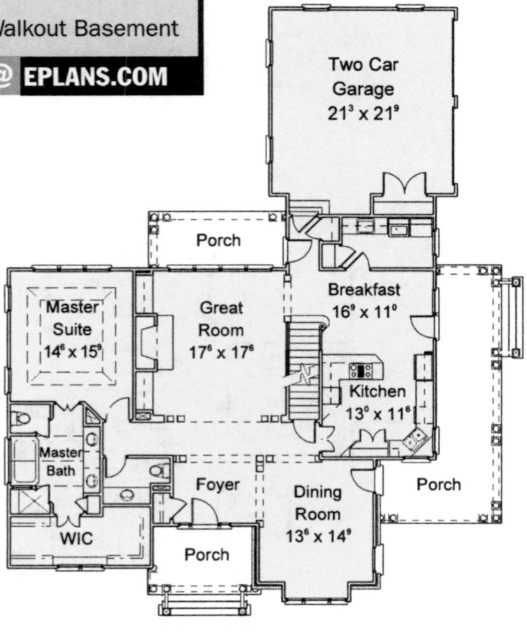

FIRST FLOOR

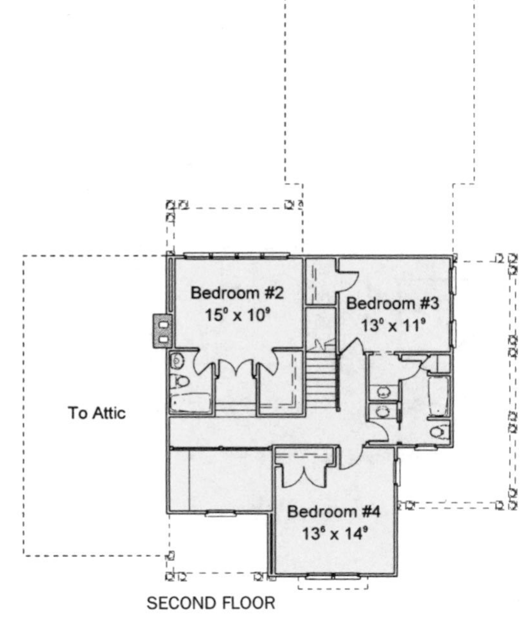

SECOND FLOOR

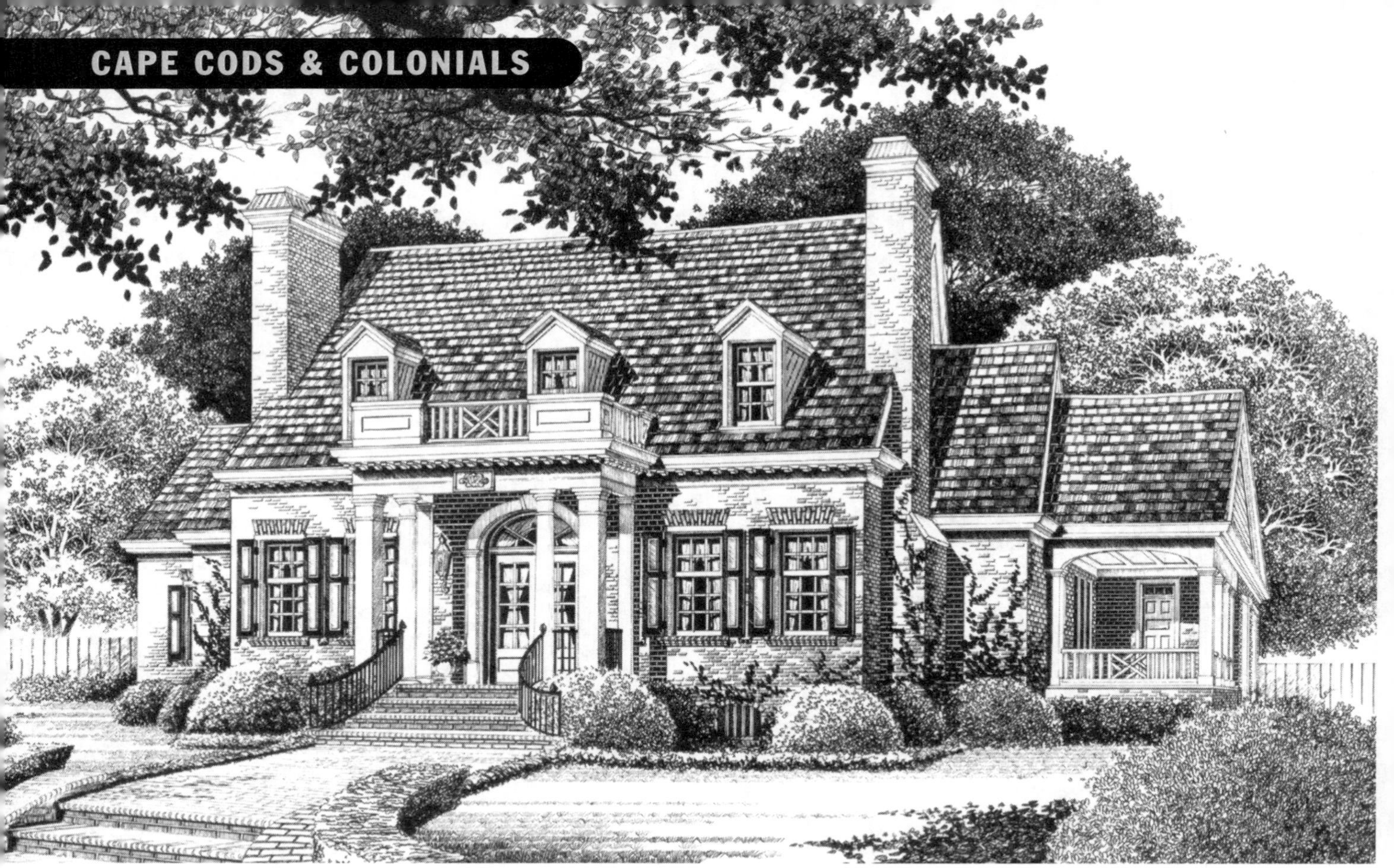

Finely crafted porches—front, side and rear—make this home a classic in traditional Southern living. Past the large French doors, the impressive foyer is flanked by the formal living and dining rooms. Beyond the stair is a vaulted great room with an expanse of windows, a fireplace and built-in bookcases. From here, the breakfast room and kitchen are easily accessible and open to a private side porch. The master suite provides a large bath, two spacious closets and a fireplace. The second floor contains three bedrooms with private bath access and a playroom.

plan# HPT930274

- Style: Plantation
- First Floor: 2,380 sq. ft.
- Second Floor: 1,295 sq. ft.
- Total: 3,675 sq. ft.
- Bedrooms: 4
- Bathrooms: 3½
- Width: 77'-4"
- Depth: 58'-4"
- Foundation: Walkout Basement

SEARCH ONLINE @ EPLANS.COM

FIRST FLOOR

QUOTE ONE®
Cost to build? See page 436 to order complete cost estimate to build this house in your area!

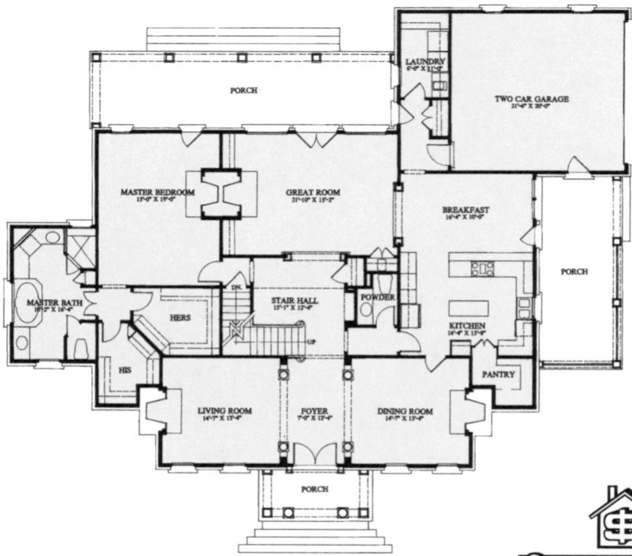

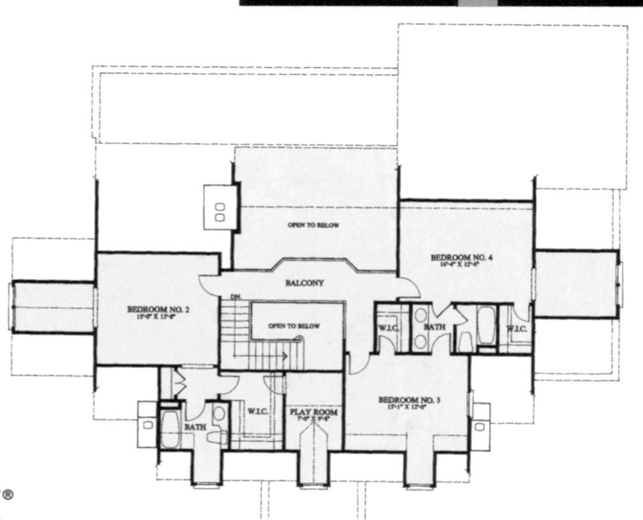

SECOND FLOOR

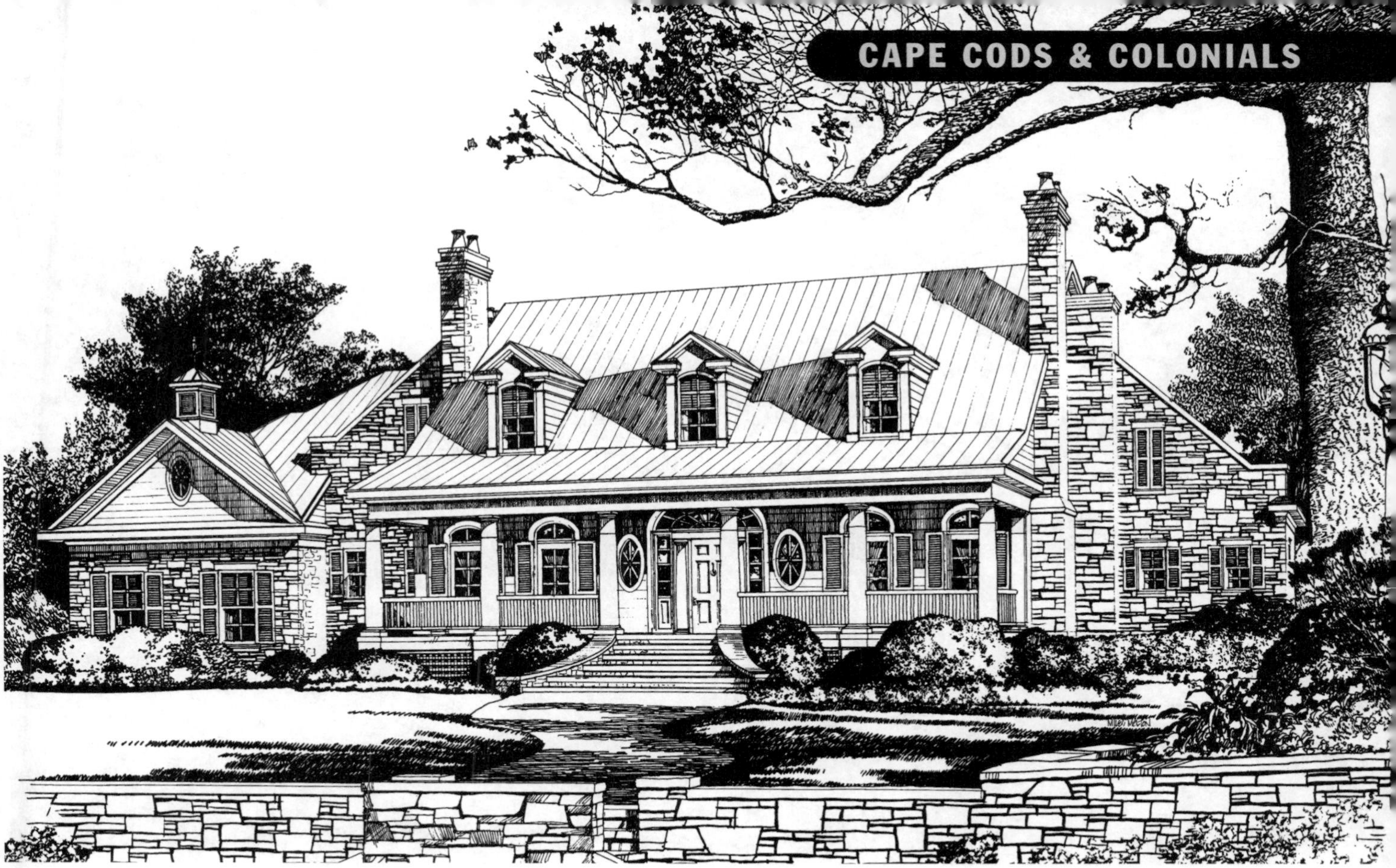

plan# HPT930275

- Style: Southern Colonial
- First Floor: 3,170 sq. ft.
- Second Floor: 1,914 sq. ft.
- Total: 5,084 sq. ft.
- Bonus Space: 445 sq. ft.
- Bedrooms: 4
- Bathrooms: 3½
- Width: 100'-10"
- Depth: 65'-5"
- Foundation: Crawlspace

SEARCH ONLINE @ EPLANS.COM

SECOND FLOOR

This elegantly appointed home is a beauty inside and out. A centerpiece stair rises gracefully from the two-story grand foyer. The kitchen, breakfast room and family room provide open space for the gathering of family and friends. The beam-ceilinged study and the dining room flank the grand foyer and each includes a fireplace. The master bedroom features a cozy sitting area and a luxury master bath with His and Hers vanities and walk-in closets. Three large bedrooms and a game room complete the second floor. A large expandable area is available at the top of the rear stair.

FIRST FLOOR

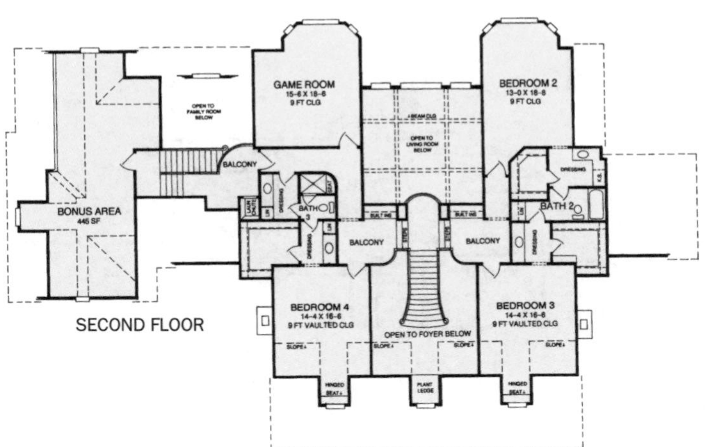

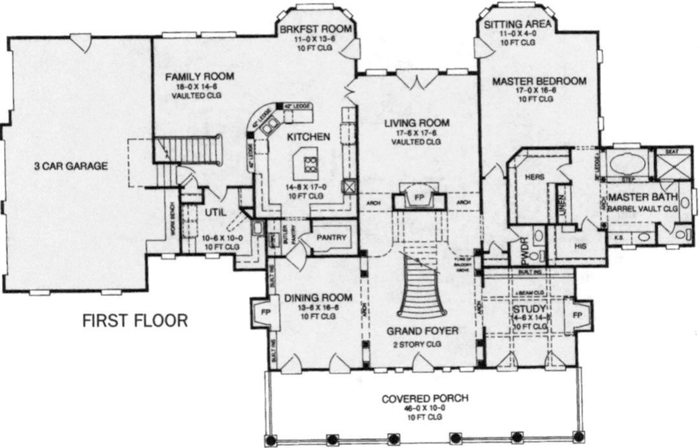

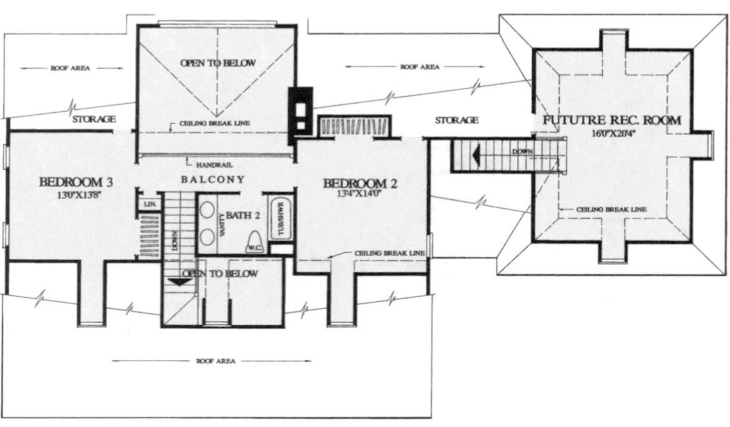

SECOND FLOOR

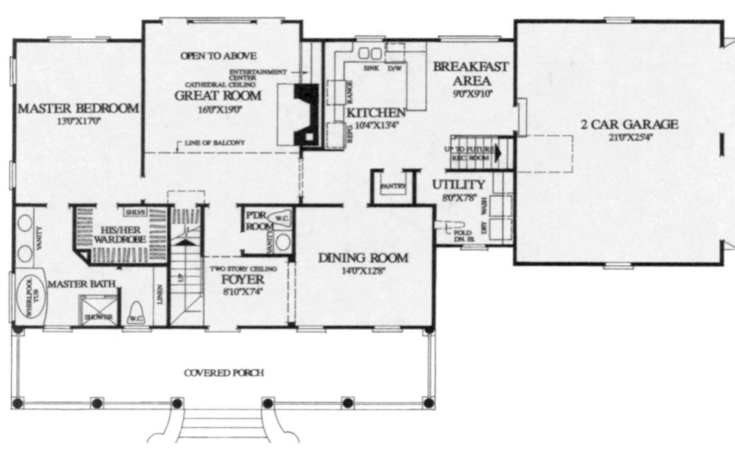

FIRST FLOOR

plan# HPT930276

- Style: Colonial
- First Floor: 1,556 sq. ft.
- Second Floor: 623 sq. ft.
- Total: 2,179 sq. ft.
- Bonus Space: 368 sq. ft.
- Bedrooms: 3
- Bathrooms: 2½
- Width: 73'-4"
- Depth: 41'-4"
- Foundation: Basement, Crawlspace

SEARCH ONLINE @ EPLANS.COM

This charming farmhouse starts out with a welcoming front porch, lined with columns. Inside, the foyer opens to the right to the formal dining room. At the rear of the home, a two-story great room provides a fireplace, built-ins and direct access to the backyard. The nearby kitchen is complete with a walk-in pantry and an adjacent breakfast area. The first-floor master suite offers a large walk-in closet and a pampering bath. Upstairs, two family bedrooms share a hall bath.

plan# HPT930277

- Style: Colonial
- First Floor: 2,191 sq. ft.
- Second Floor: 1,220 sq. ft.
- Total: 5,602 sq. ft.
- Bonus Space: 280 sq. ft.
- Bedrooms: 4
- Bathrooms: 3½
- Width: 75'-8"
- Depth: 54'-4"
- Foundation: Basement, Crawlspace

SEARCH ONLINE @ EPLANS.COM

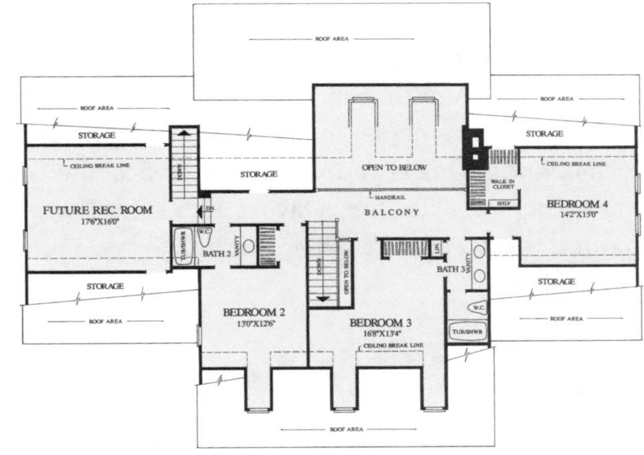

SECOND FLOOR

The shingled exterior of this home adds comfort along with elegance to this spacious home. Triple dormers and a columned front porch create a very country, yet Colonial feel. Walk into the home through the foyer and find the living room and the dining room on either side. A well-lit breakfast nook is right next to the back porch which is nothing short of comfortable outdoor living. Three bedrooms and lots of extra storage space is located on the second floor with room for growth.

FIRST FLOOR

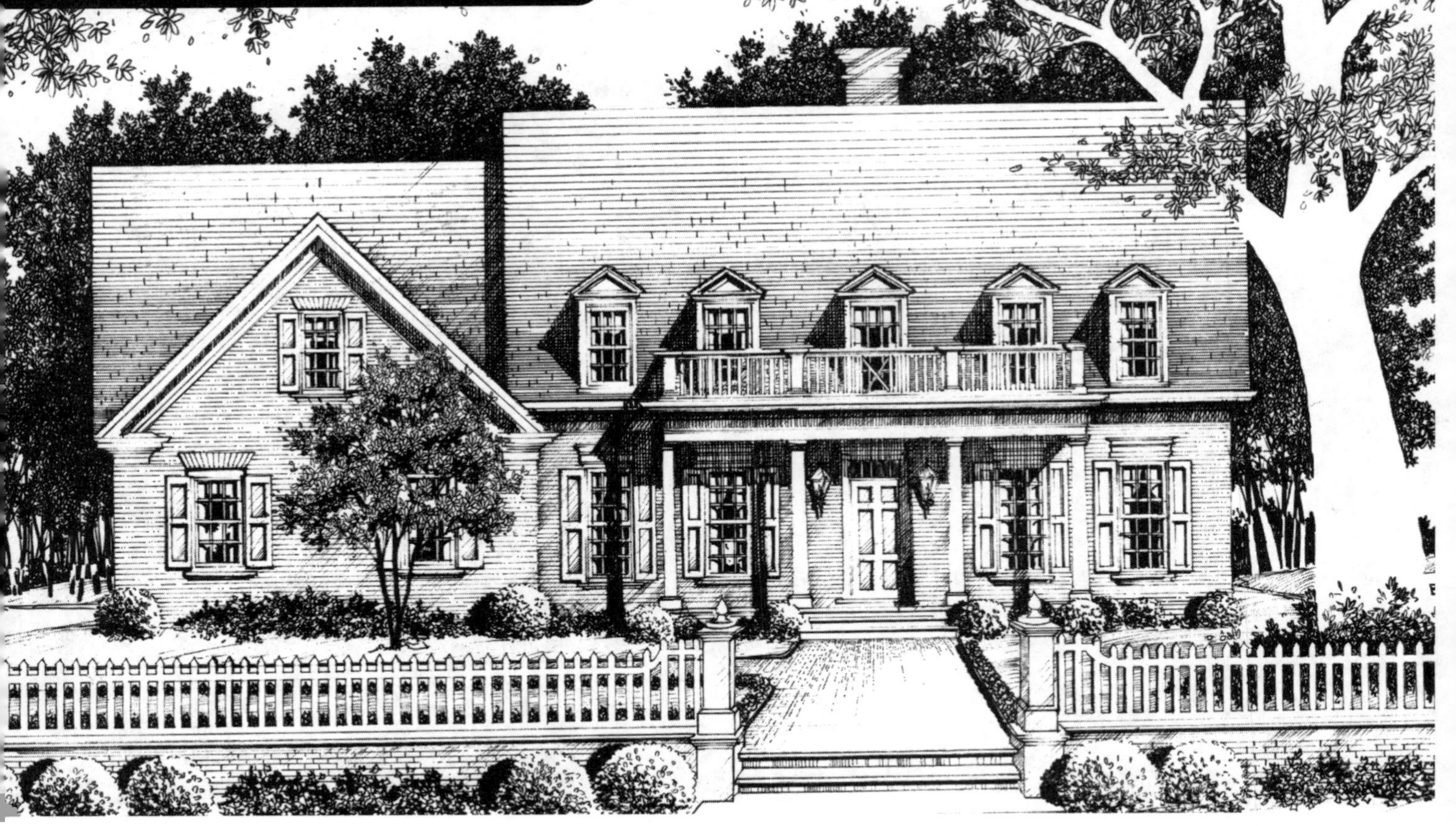

The covered front porch of this home warmly welcomes family and visitors. To the right of the foyer is a versatile option room. On the other side is the formal dining room. A comfortable great room boasts French doors to a rear deck and easy access to a large breakfast area and sun room. The adjacent kitchen includes a cooking island/breakfast bar. Secluded on the main level for privacy, the master suite features a lavish bath loaded with amenities. Just off the bedroom is a private deck. Three additional bedrooms and two baths occupy the second level.

plan# HPT930278

- Style: Southern Colonial
- First Floor: 2,199 sq. ft.
- Second Floor: 1,235 sq. ft.
- Total: 3,434 sq. ft.
- Bedrooms: 4
- Bathrooms: 4
- Width: 62'-6"
- Depth: 54'-3"
- Foundation: Walkout Basement

SEARCH ONLINE @ EPLANS.COM

QUOTE ONE®
Cost to build? See page 436 to order complete cost estimate to build this house in your area!

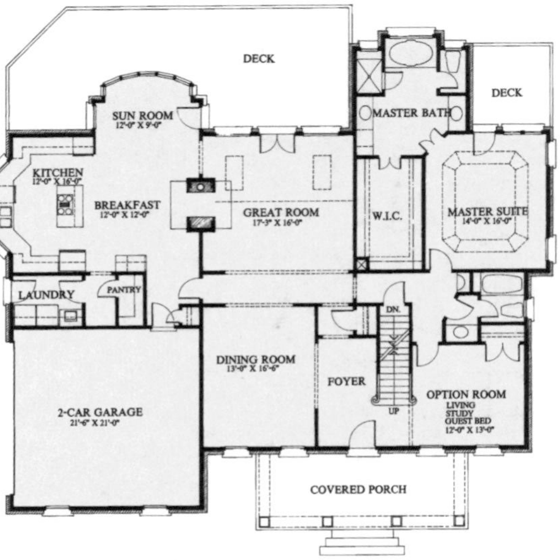

DECK
SUN ROOM 12'-0" X 9'-0"
MASTER BATH
DECK
KITCHEN 12'-0" X 16'-0"
BREAKFAST 12'-0" X 12'-0"
GREAT ROOM 17'-3" X 16'-0"
W.I.C.
MASTER SUITE 14'-0" X 16'-0"
LAUNDRY
PANTRY
DN.
DINING ROOM 13'-0" X 16'-6"
FOYER
UP
OPTION ROOM
LIVING STUDY GUEST BED 12'-0" X 13'-0"
2-CAR GARAGE 21'-6" X 21'-0"
COVERED PORCH

FIRST FLOOR

1/2 VAULT OPEN TO BELOW
W.I.C.
BATH
W.I.C.
BEDROOM NO. 4 14'-0" X 13'-0"
W.I.C.
BEDROOM NO. 3 13'-0" X 13'-0"
DN
OPEN TO BELOW
BEDROOM NO. 2 13'-0" X 16'-9"
W.I.C.
BATH
UNFINISHED STORAGE

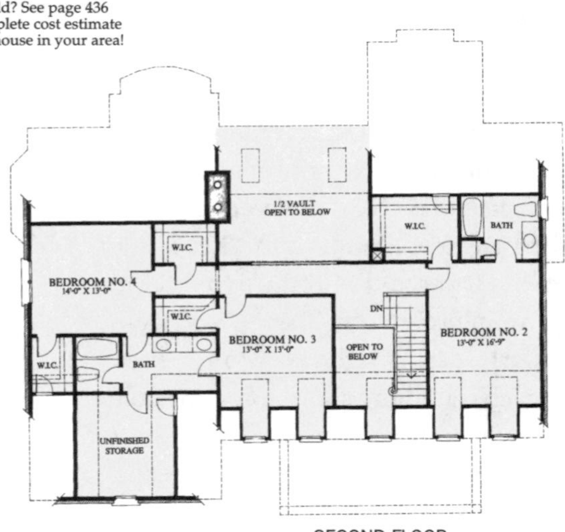

SECOND FLOOR

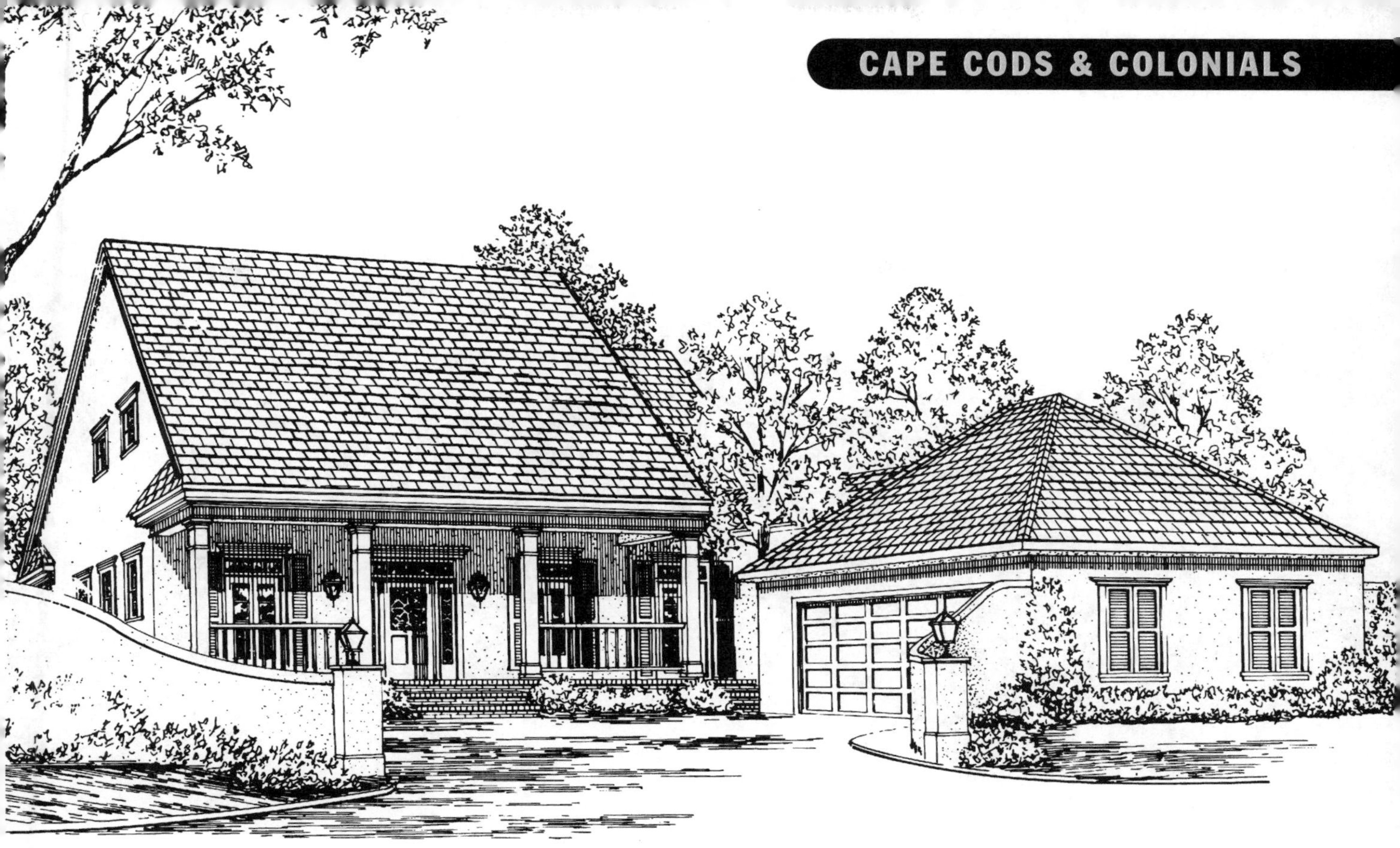

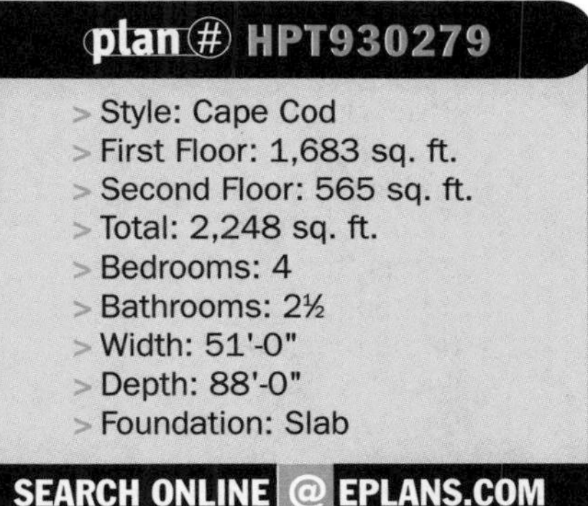

plan# HPT930279

- Style: Cape Cod
- First Floor: 1,683 sq. ft.
- Second Floor: 565 sq. ft.
- Total: 2,248 sq. ft.
- Bedrooms: 4
- Bathrooms: 2½
- Width: 51'-0"
- Depth: 88'-0"
- Foundation: Slab

SEARCH ONLINE @ EPLANS.COM

Defined in cool stucco, this petite two-story plan features a separate two-car garage reached via a walkway from the main house. The interior includes a formal dining room just to the right of the entry. A family room with a corner fireplace has sliding glass doors leading out to a covered porch. A bayed breakfast nook adjoins the kitchen. The master bedroom and private bath and one additional bedroom line the left side of the first floor. Upstairs are two additional bedrooms and a full bath.

FIRST FLOOR

SECOND FLOOR

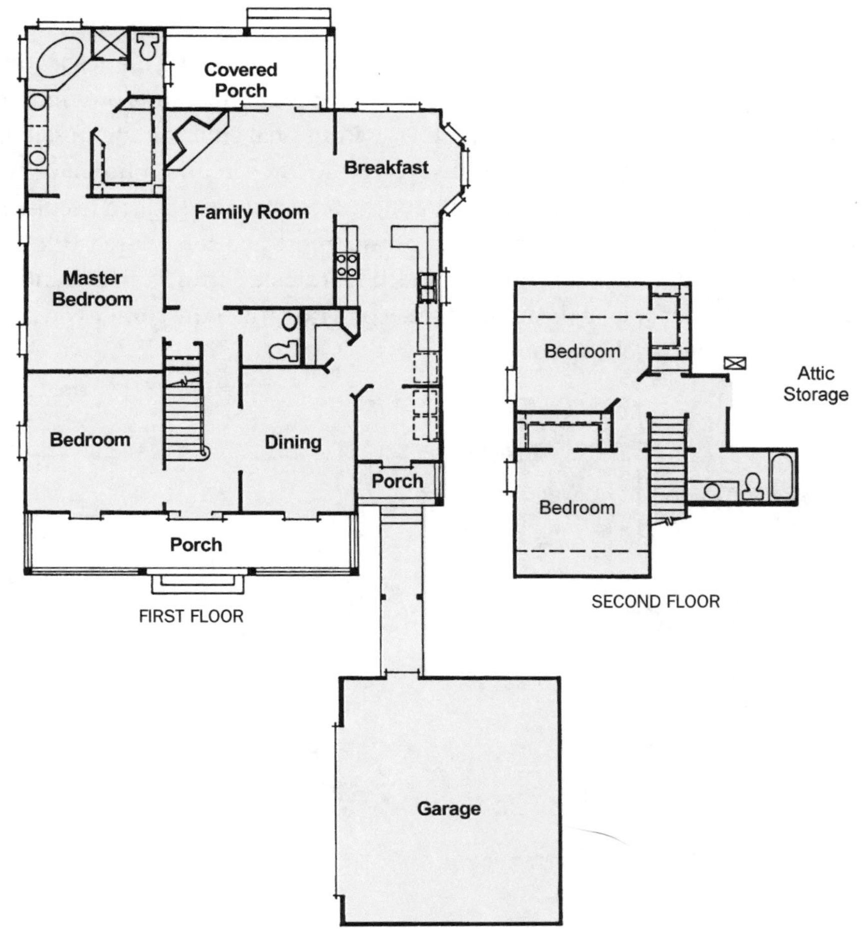

The origin of this house dates back to 1787 and George Washington's stately Mount Vernon. The unusual design features curved galleries leading to matching wings. In the main house, the living and dining rooms provide a large open area, with access to the rear porch for additional entertaining possibilities. A keeping room features a pass-through to the kitchen and a fireplace with a built-in wood box. Four bedrooms, including a master suite with a fireplace, are found upstairs. One wing contains separate guest quarters with a full bath, a lounge area and an upstairs studio, which features a spiral staircase and a loft area. On the other side of the house, the second floor over the garage can be used for storage or as a hobby room.

plan# HPT930280

- Style: Georgian
- First Floor: 1,992 sq. ft.
- Second Floor: 1,458 sq. ft.
- Total: 3,450 sq. ft.
- Bonus Space: 380 sq. ft.
- Bedrooms: 5
- Bathrooms: 3½
- Width: 108'-0"
- Depth: 64'-0"
- Foundation: Basement

SEARCH ONLINE @ EPLANS.COM

OPTIONAL LAYOUT

FIRST FLOOR

SECOND FLOOR

QUOTE ONE®

Cost to build? See page 436 to order complete cost estimate to build this house in your area!

plan# HPT930281

- Style: Plantation **L D**
- First Floor: 1,969 sq. ft.
- Second Floor: 660 sq. ft.
- Total: 2,629 sq. ft.
- Bonus Space: 360 sq. ft.
- Bedrooms: 3
- Bathrooms: 3
- Width: 90'-8"
- Depth: 80'-4"
- Foundation: Basement

SEARCH ONLINE @ EPLANS.COM

Varying roof planes, gables and dormers help create the unique character of this house. Inside, the family/great room gains attention with its high ceiling, fireplace/media-center wall, view of the upstairs balcony and French doors to the sun room. In the U-shaped kitchen, an island work surface, a planning desk and pantry are added conveniences. The spacious master suite can function with the home office, library or private sitting room. Its direct access to the huge raised veranda provides an ideal private outdoor haven for relaxation. The second floor contains two bedrooms and a bath. The garage features a workshop area and stairway to a second-floor storage or multi-purpose room.

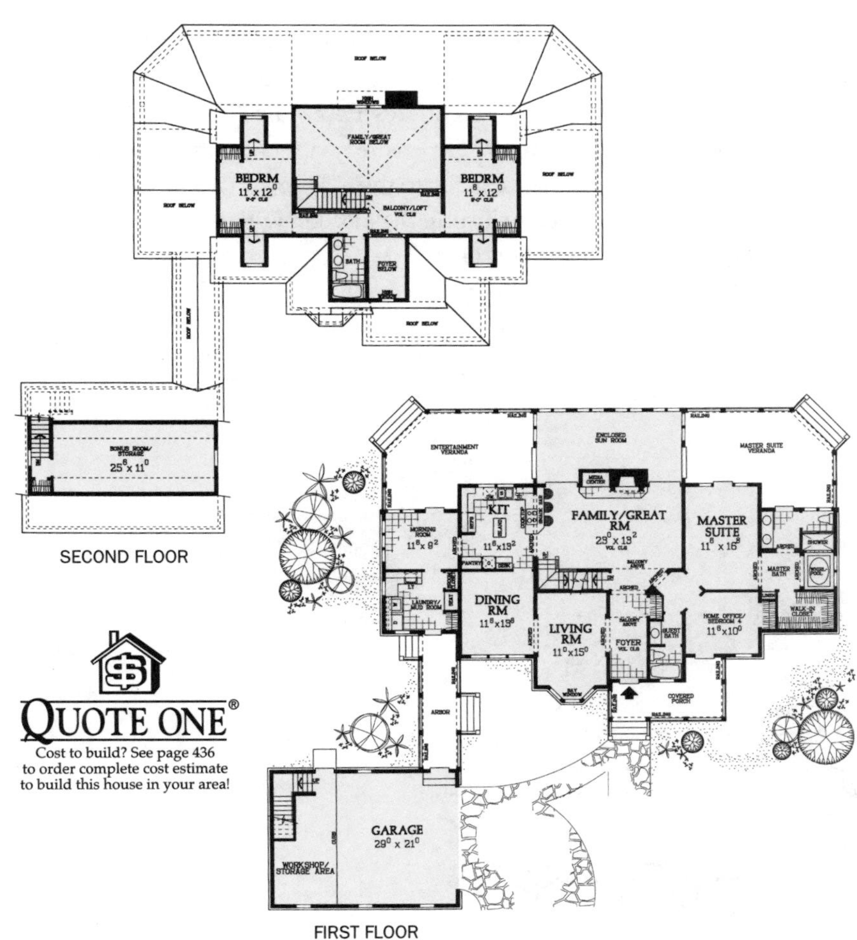

SECOND FLOOR

FIRST FLOOR

QUOTE ONE®
Cost to build? See page 436 to order complete cost estimate to build this house in your area!

From its dramatic front entry to its rear twin-bay turret, this design is as traditional as it is historic. A two-story foyer opens through a gallery to an expansive gathering room, which shares its natural light with a bumped-out morning nook. A formal living room or study offers a coffered ceiling and a private door to the gallery hall that leads to the master suite. The dining room opens to more casual living space, including the kitchen with its angled island counter. Bonus space may be developed later.

plan# HPT930282

- Style: Traditional
- First Floor: 2,293 sq. ft.
- Second Floor: 901 sq. ft.
- Total: 3,194 sq. ft.
- Bonus Space: 265 sq. ft.
- Bedrooms: 3
- Bathrooms: 3½
- Width: 82'-6"
- Depth: 67'-2"
- Foundation: Walkout Basement

SEARCH ONLINE @ EPLANS.COM

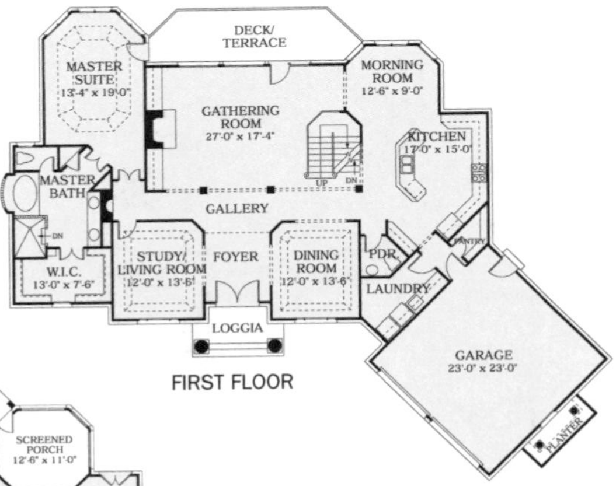

FIRST FLOOR

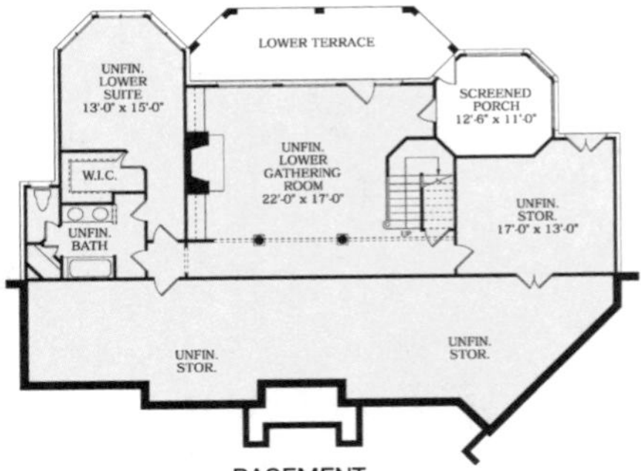

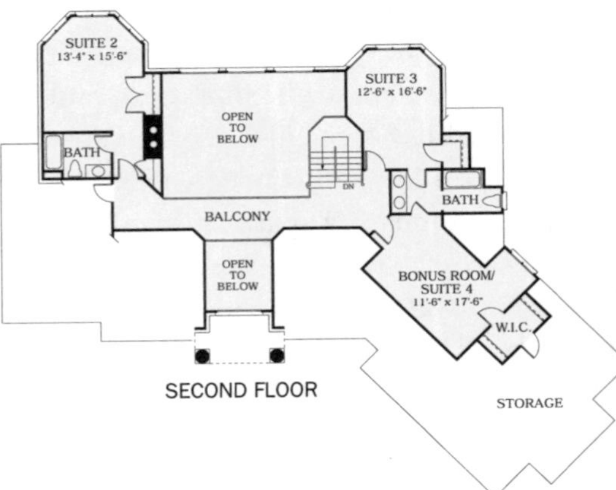

SECOND FLOOR

BASEMENT

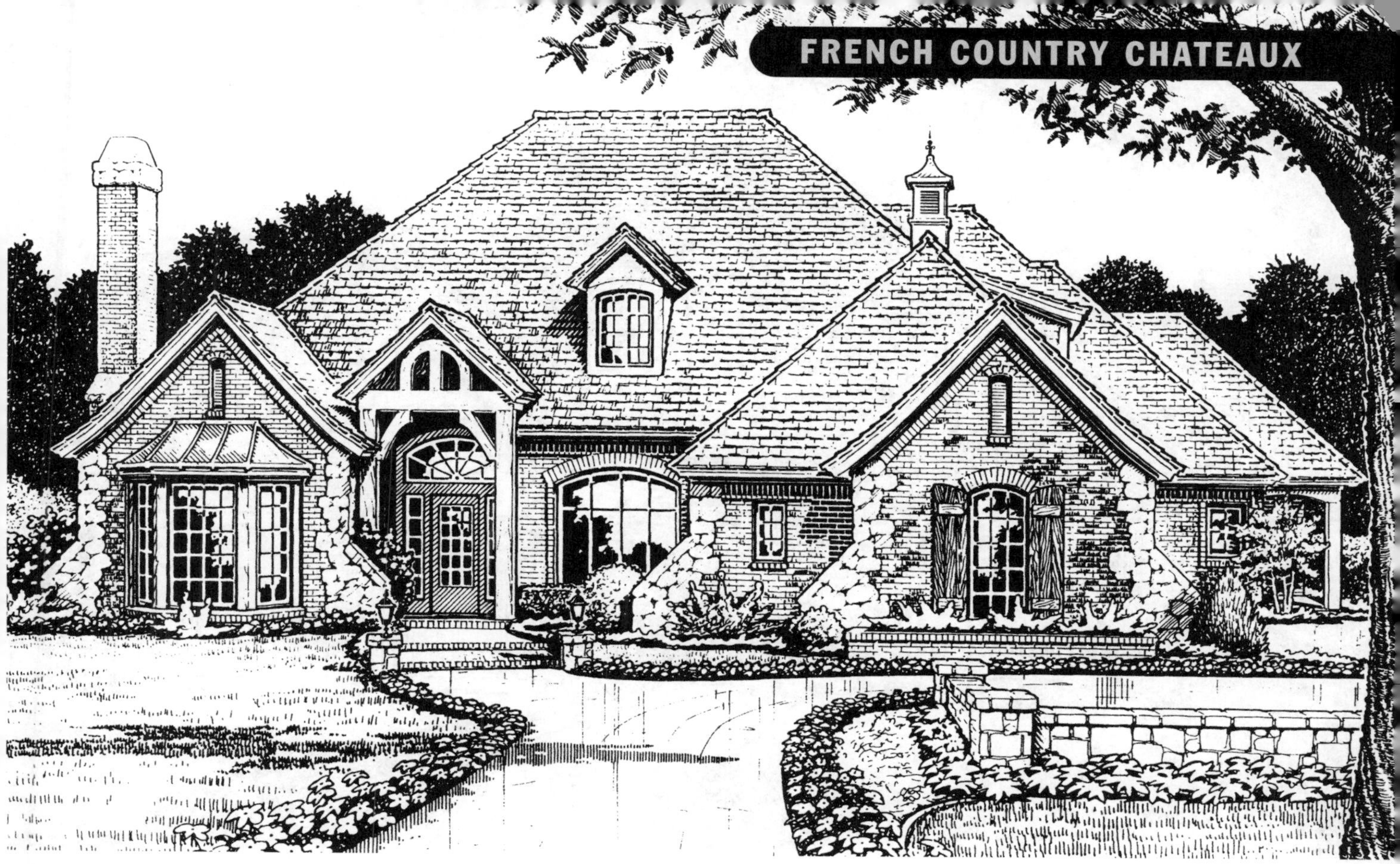

plan# HPT930283

- Style: French
- First Floor: 2,438 sq. ft.
- Second Floor: 882 sq. ft.
- Total: 3,320 sq. ft.
- Bonus Space: 230 sq. ft.
- Bedrooms: 4
- Bathrooms: 4½
- Width: 70'-0"
- Depth: 63'-2"
- Foundation: Basement, Slab

SEARCH ONLINE @ EPLANS.COM

Wonderful rooflines top a brick exterior with cedar and stone accents and lots of English country charm. The two-story entry reveals a graceful curving staircase and opens to the formal living and dining rooms. Fireplaces are found in the living room as well as the great room, which also boasts built-in bookcases and access to the rear patio. The kitchen and breakfast room add to the informal area and include a snack bar. A private patio is part of the master suite, which also offers a lavish bath, a large walk-in closet and a nearby study. Three family bedrooms and a bonus room complete the second floor.

SECOND FLOOR

FIRST FLOOR

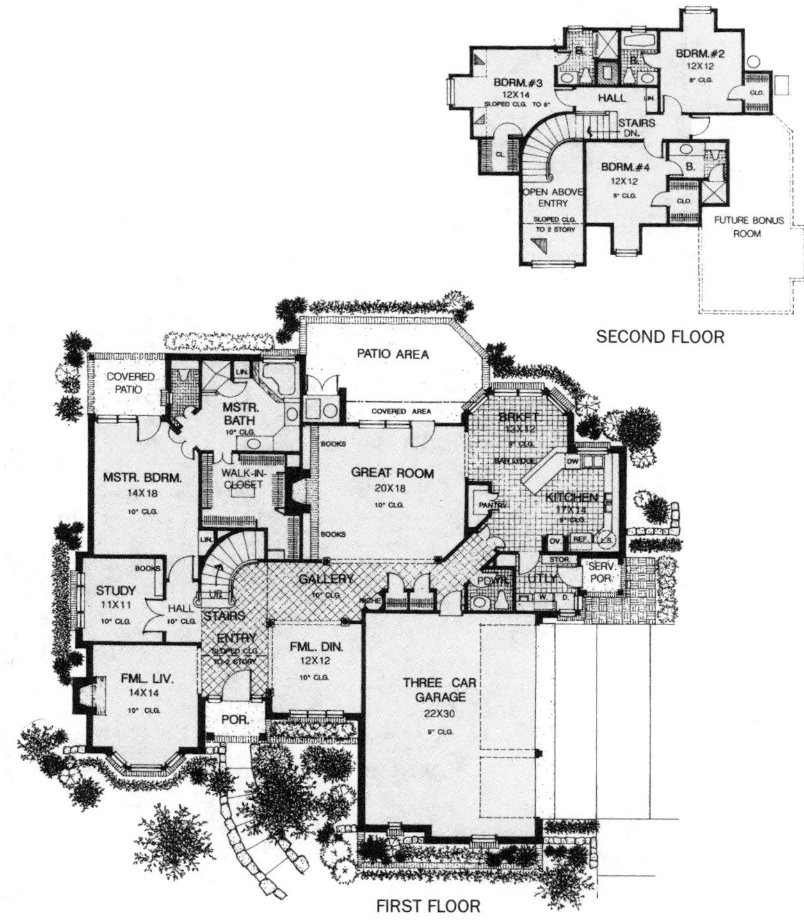

SECOND FLOOR

FIRST FLOOR

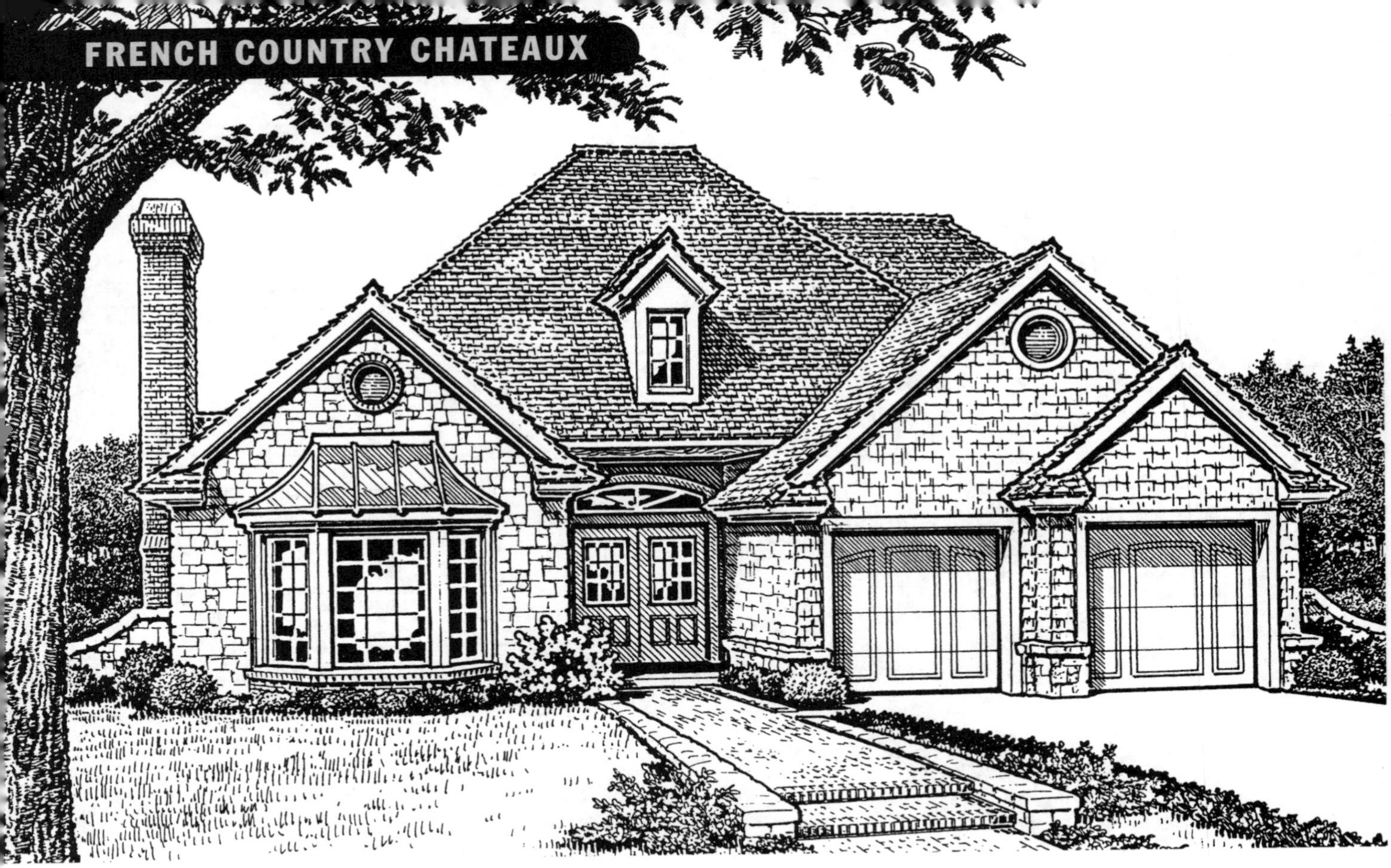

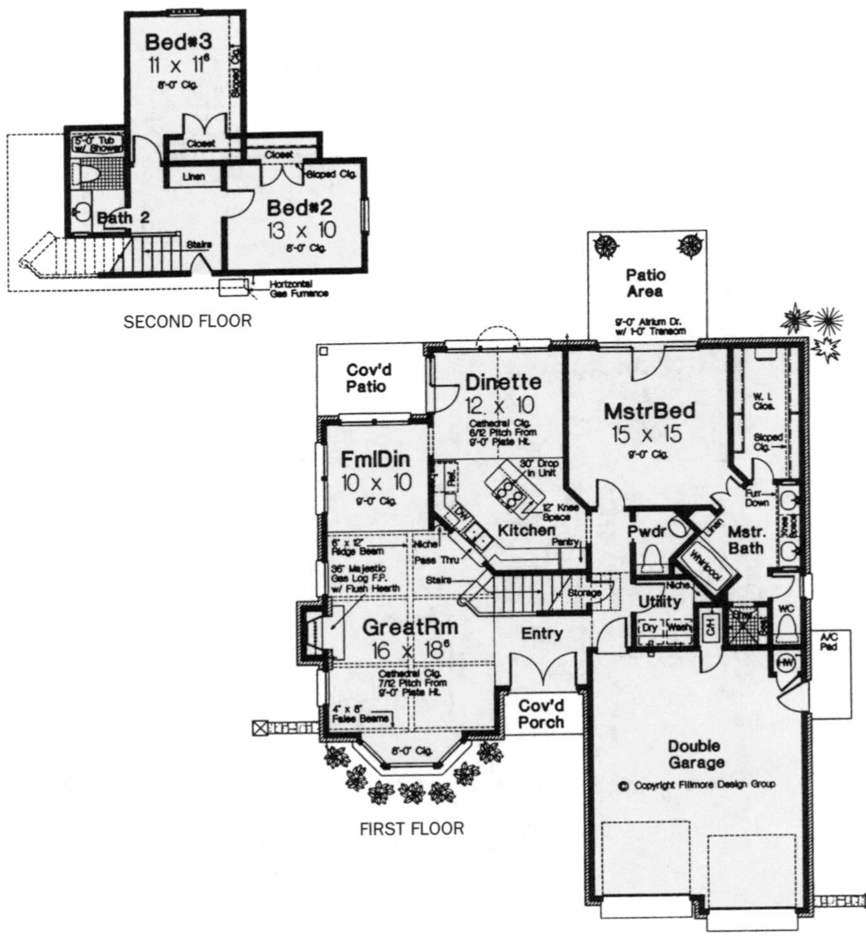

plan# HPT930284

- Style: Country Cottage
- First Floor: 1,375 sq. ft.
- Second Floor: 446 sq. ft.
- Total: 1,821 sq. ft.
- Bedrooms: 3
- Bathrooms: 2½
- Width: 44'-10"
- Depth: 52'-11"
- Foundation: Slab

SEARCH ONLINE @ EPLANS.COM

A bay window with copper flashing above brings French country charm to this stone and shingle home. The entry leads to the great room, breathtaking with an exposed-beam cathedral ceiling, gas log fireplace and a bay that would make a perfect window seat. In the kitchen, a cooktop island makes preparation a breeze, with easy service to the sunburst-lit dinette and dining room. The master suite features a resplendent bath and access to a private patio. Upstairs, two bedrooms share a full bath.

plan# HPT930285

- Style: European Cottage
- First Floor: 2,039 sq. ft.
- Second Floor: 772 sq. ft.
- Total: 2,811 sq. ft.
- Bonus Space: 480 sq. ft.
- Bedrooms: 4
- Bathrooms: 3½
- Width: 56'-0"
- Depth: 63'-6"
- Foundation: Crawlspace, Slab

SEARCH ONLINE @ EPLANS.COM

Enjoy the quiet elegance of stone and brick in this French country home. Beautiful flooring makes a lovely entrance; a formal living room with a fireplace and bay window, and a dining room defined by columns welcome guests. The family room inspires gatherings around the extended brick fireplace, while outdoor spaces invite summer fun. The vaulted master suite has a spa bath with French doors and a whirlpool tub. Upstairs, three bedrooms, all with sloped ceilings and dormer windows, share a bonus room.

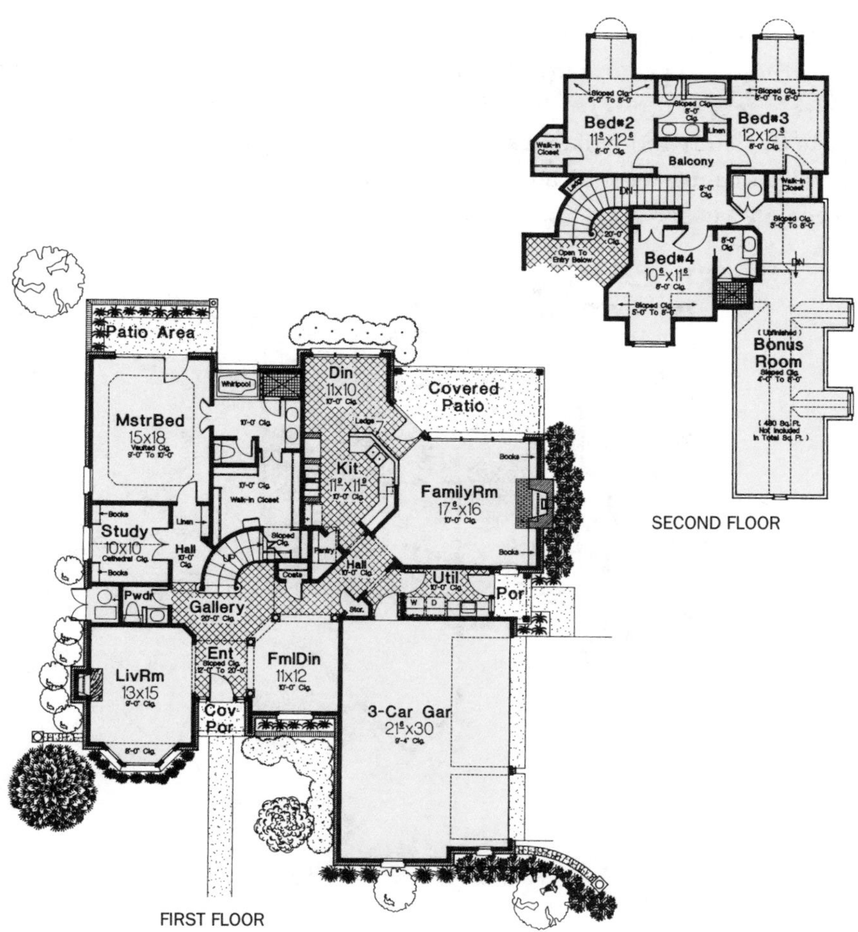

SECOND FLOOR

FIRST FLOOR

This magnificent French Country Chateaux has amazing details throughout. The courtyard off the covered porch really makes entering this home a treat in itself. The bayed window, French doors, and cathedral ceiling make the study more than just a place to work; it's a place to enjoy. Two bedrooms and a master suite are located on the first floor. A studio apartment and a separate kitchen are a fine use of space on the second floor.

plan# HPT930286

- Style: French Country
- First Floor: 2,387 sq. ft.
- Second Floor: 509 sq. ft.
- Total: 2,896 sq. ft.
- Bedrooms: 3
- Bathrooms: 2½
- Width: 82'-3"
- Depth: 86'-6"
- Foundation: Slab

SEARCH ONLINE @ EPLANS.COM

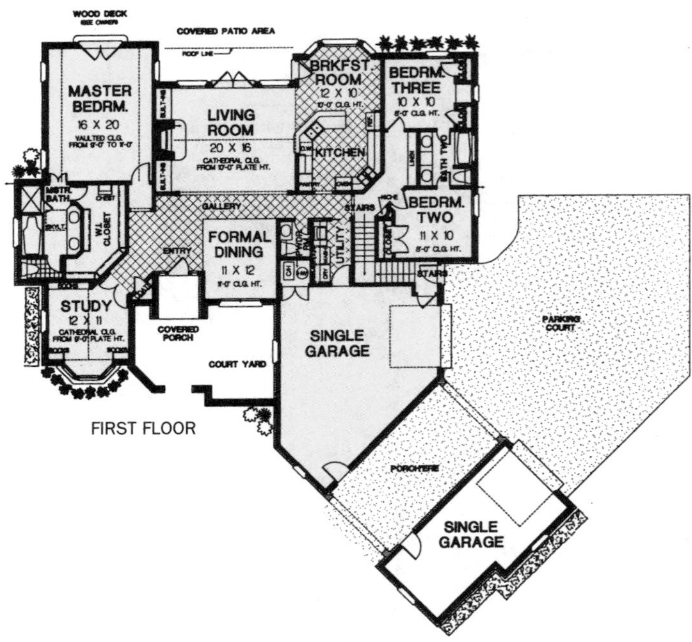

FIRST FLOOR

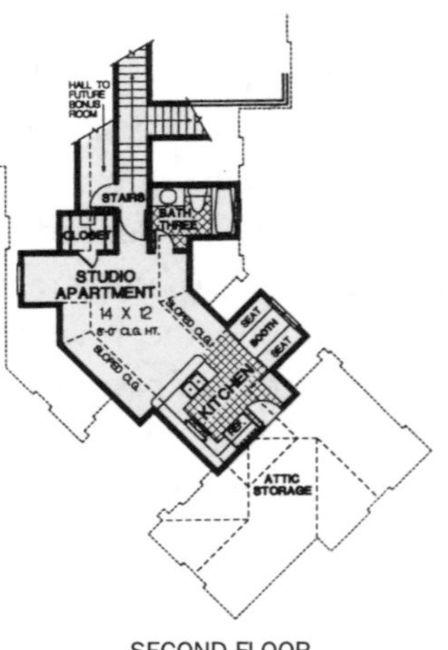

SECOND FLOOR

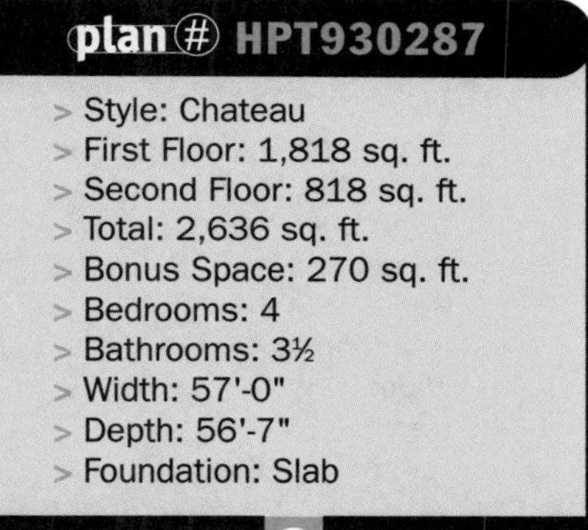

plan# HPT930287

- Style: Chateau
- First Floor: 1,818 sq. ft.
- Second Floor: 818 sq. ft.
- Total: 2,636 sq. ft.
- Bonus Space: 270 sq. ft.
- Bedrooms: 4
- Bathrooms: 3½
- Width: 57'-0"
- Depth: 56'-7"
- Foundation: Slab

SEARCH ONLINE @ EPLANS.COM

An alluring chateau with all the modern comforts you've come to expect from our top designers, this beautiful home will be a joy for years to come. Brick and stonework usher you into the entry, bordered by a study and bayed dining room. A stylish gallery presents the great room, with a distinctive brick fireplace and built-in entertainment center. In the refined master suite, an indulgent bath will soothe and pamper. Upstairs, three bedrooms—one with a private bath and dormer window—share a playroom and study area.

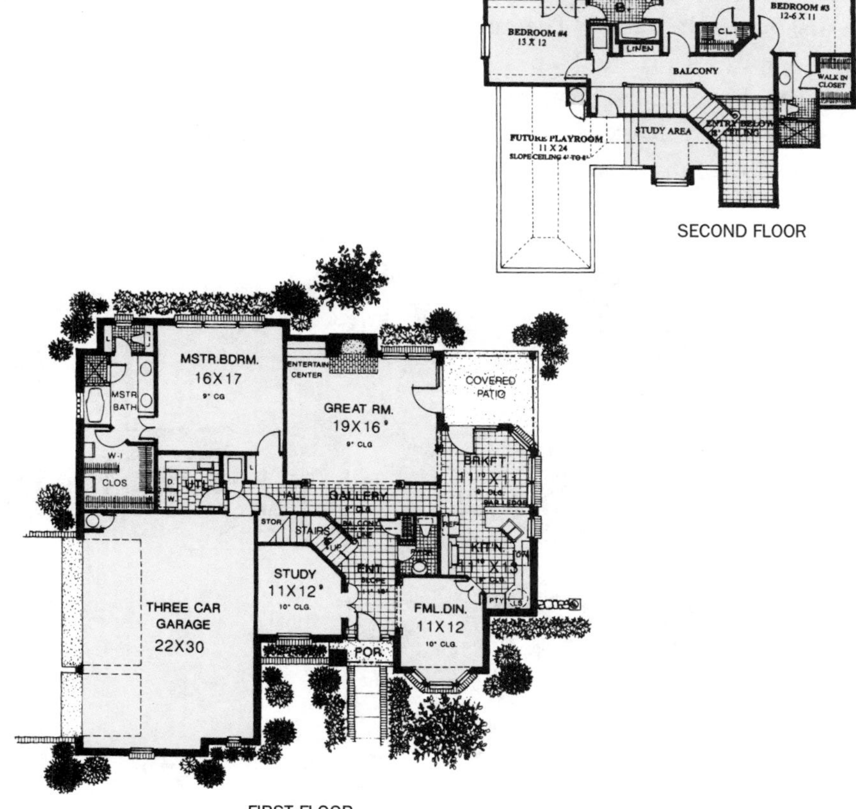

SECOND FLOOR

FIRST FLOOR

This dazzling and majestic European design features a stucco and stone facade, French shutters and castle-like rooflines. The entry is flanked by a study with a fireplace and a formal dining room. A formal living room with a fireplace is just across the gallery. The master wing is brightened by a bayed sitting area and features a private bath that extends impressive closet space. The island kitchen overlooks the breakfast and great rooms. A guest suite is located on the first floor for privacy, while two additional family bedrooms reside upstairs, along with a future playroom.

plan# HPT930288

- Style: Chateau
- First Floor: 3,030 sq. ft.
- Second Floor: 848 sq. ft.
- Total: 3,878 sq. ft.
- Bonus Space: 320 sq. ft.
- Bedrooms: 4
- Bathrooms: 4½
- Width: 88'-0"
- Depth: 72'-1"
- Foundation: Slab

SEARCH ONLINE @ EPLANS.COM

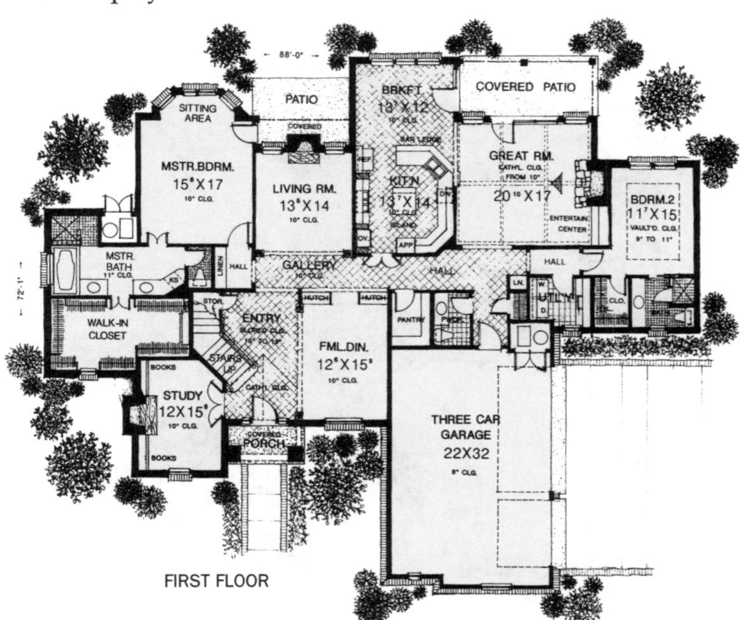

FIRST FLOOR

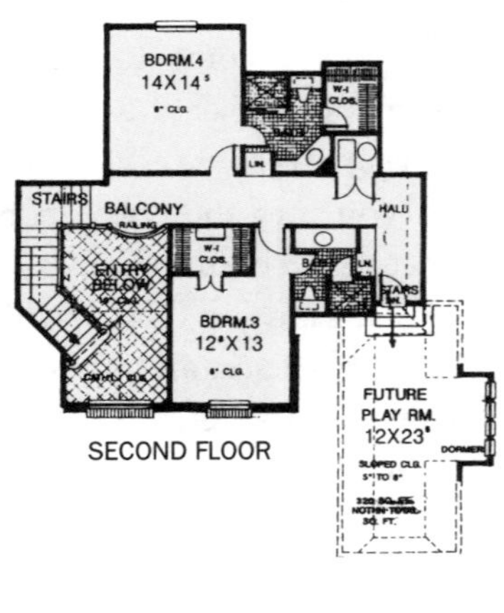

SECOND FLOOR

plan# HPT930289

- Style: Chateau
- First Floor: 2,237 sq. ft.
- Second Floor: 931 sq. ft.
- Total: 3,168 sq. ft.
- Bonus Space: 304 sq. ft.
- Bedrooms: 4
- Bathrooms: 3½
- Width: 68'-0"
- Depth: 55'-6"
- Foundation: Slab

SEARCH ONLINE @ EPLANS.COM

This majestic estate has palatial inspiration, with a plan any modern family will love. A hardwood entry leads to brick flooring in the kitchen and breakfast nook, for vintage appeal. The family room and vaulted living room warm heart and soul with extended-hearth fireplaces. For a quiet retreat, the study opens with French doors from the hall, and leads out to the walled lanai courtyard through another set of French doors. The vaulted master suite is impressive, with a bay window, a sumptuous bath and His and Hers walk-in closets. Upstairs, three ample bedrooms will access the future playroom.

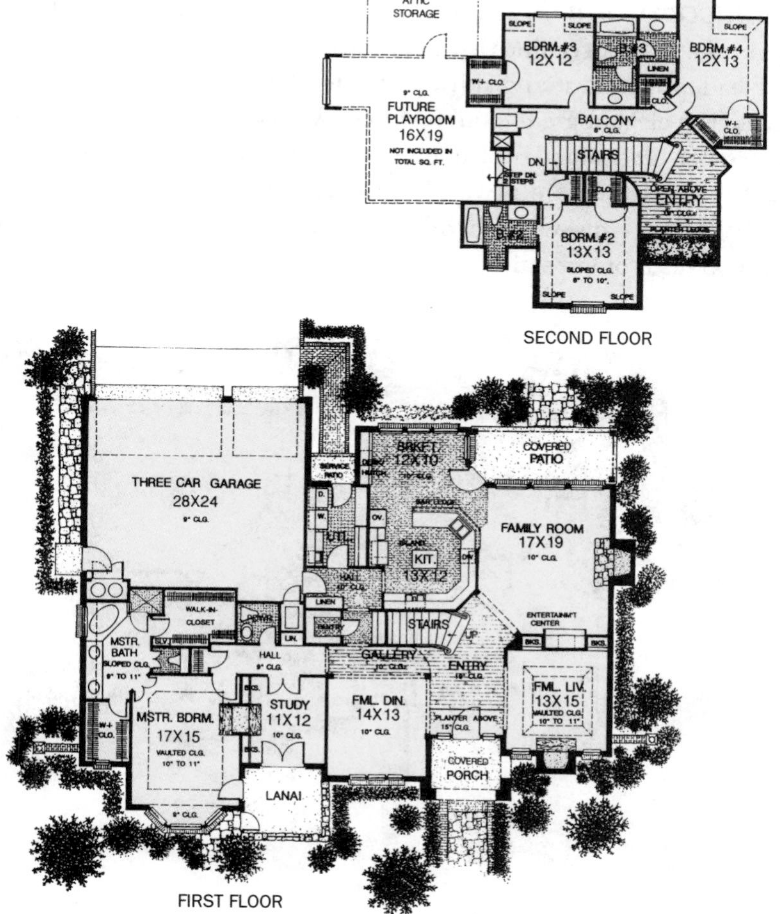

SECOND FLOOR

FIRST FLOOR

Reminiscent of a French country manor, this exquisite home will inspire you. Ten-foot ceilings heighten the first floor. From the tiled entry, French doors lead to a grand study with an extended-hearth fireplace and built-in bookshelves. The elegant great room features a wall of windows, built-in entertainment center, and stone-hearth fireplace. The master suite is romantic and splendid, with a fireplace, private lanai access and a sumptuous bath. Three generous bedrooms—one with a barrel-vault ceiling and two with sloped ceilings—share a bonus room upstairs.

plan# HPT930290

- Style: Chateau
- First Floor: 2,246 sq. ft.
- Second Floor: 966 sq. ft.
- Total: 3,212 sq. ft.
- Bonus Space: 250 sq. ft.
- Bedrooms: 4
- Bathrooms: 3½
- Width: 68'-10"
- Depth: 60'-1"
- Foundation: Basement, Slab

SEARCH ONLINE @ EPLANS.COM

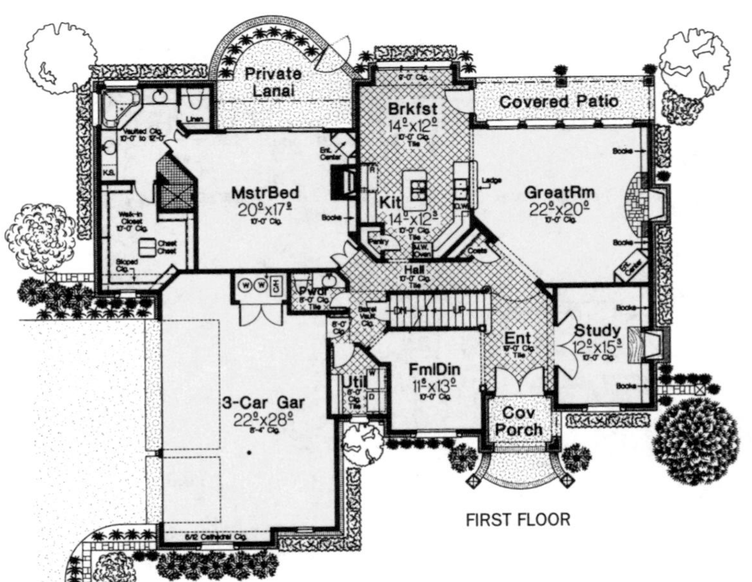

FIRST FLOOR

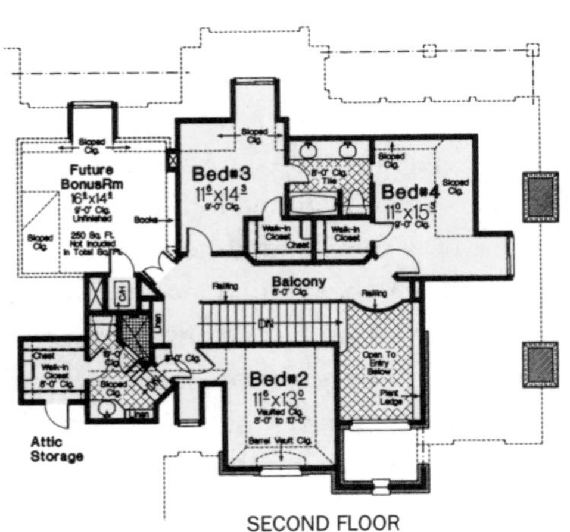

SECOND FLOOR

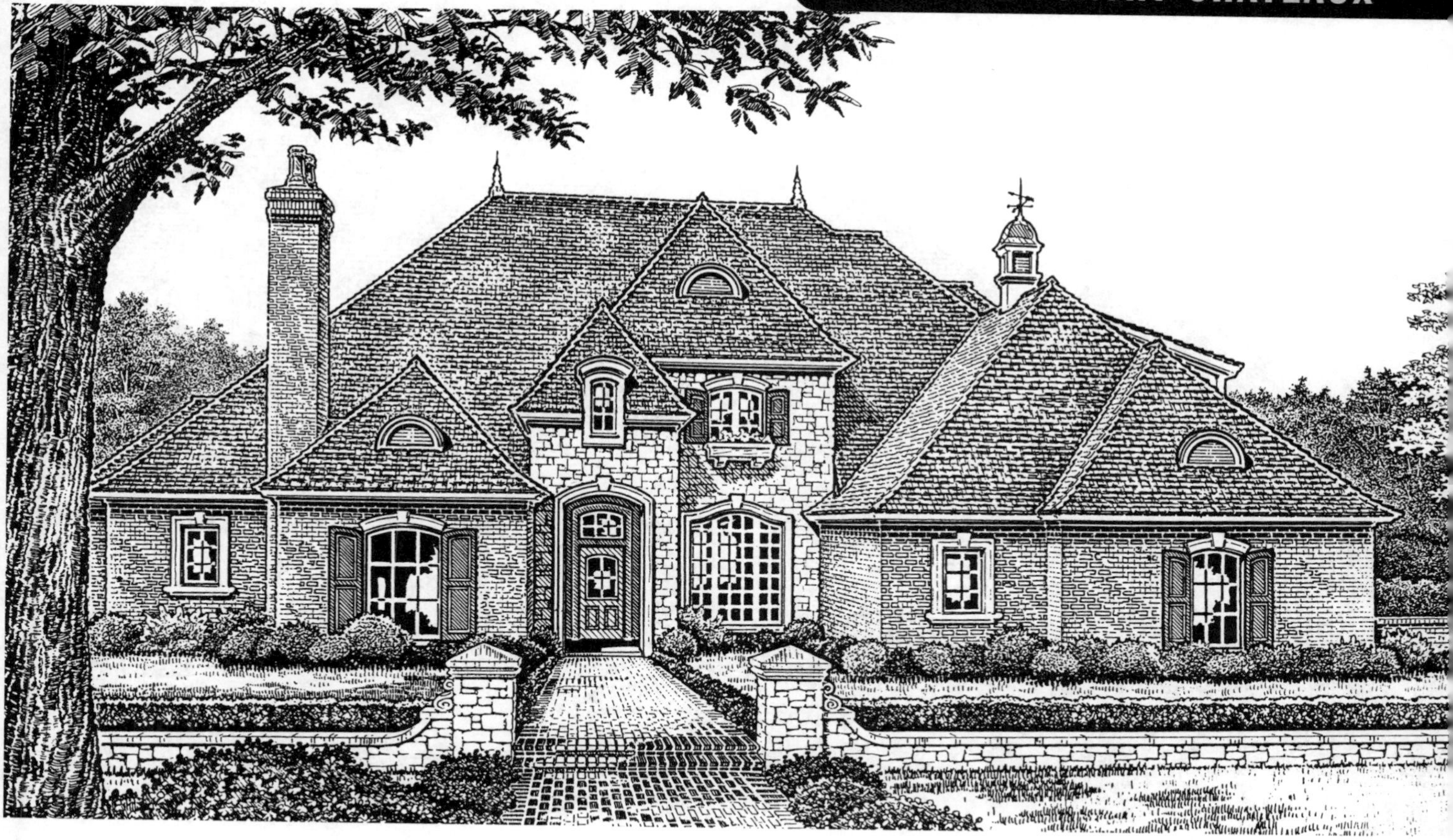

plan# HPT930291

- Style: Chateau
- First Floor: 2,907 sq. ft.
- Second Floor: 1,148 sq. ft.
- Total: 4,055 sq. ft.
- Bonus Space: 543 sq. ft.
- Bedrooms: 4
- Bathrooms: 4½
- Width: 79'-11"
- Depth: 79'-1"
- Foundation: Slab

SEARCH ONLINE @ EPLANS.COM

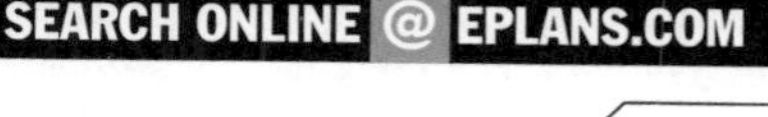

This chateau estate will be the envy of neighbors, friends and passers-by. Inside, stylish tile flooring runs throughout the home, from the entry to the kitchen and bayed breakfast nook. The living room entertains with a fireplace and natural light; the family room is a showpiece, with an exposed beam cathedral ceiling, access to the rear patio and an extended-hearth fireplace. The master suite revels in a tiled bath with a whirlpool tub and an enormous walk-in closet. Three upstairs bedrooms all have private baths and share a sitting area and future space.

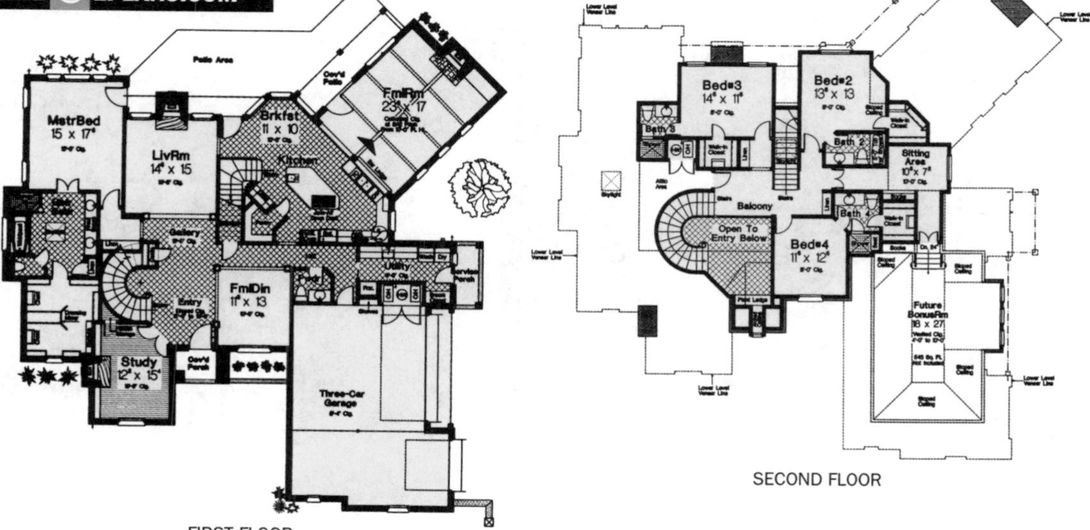

FIRST FLOOR

SECOND FLOOR

With the perfect balance of grandeur and functionality, this stunning English manor inspires luxury at every turn, and is built with the needs of an active family in mind. A tiled entry opens to the formal dining room and quiet study. Just ahead, the great room hosts a warming fireplace and great views. The gourmet kitchen effortlessly serves a sunny breakfast nook. The vast master suite includes a turret-style sitting area, lavish bath and private lanai. Overlooking the great room, three upstairs bedrooms are situated for privacy and share a playroom and computer room.

plan# HPT930292

- Style: European Cottage
- First Floor: 2,509 sq. ft.
- Second Floor: 1,629 sq. ft.
- Total: 4,138 sq. ft.
- Bedrooms: 4
- Bathrooms: 3½
- Width: 83'-0"
- Depth: 56'-5"
- Foundation: Slab

SEARCH ONLINE @ EPLANS.COM

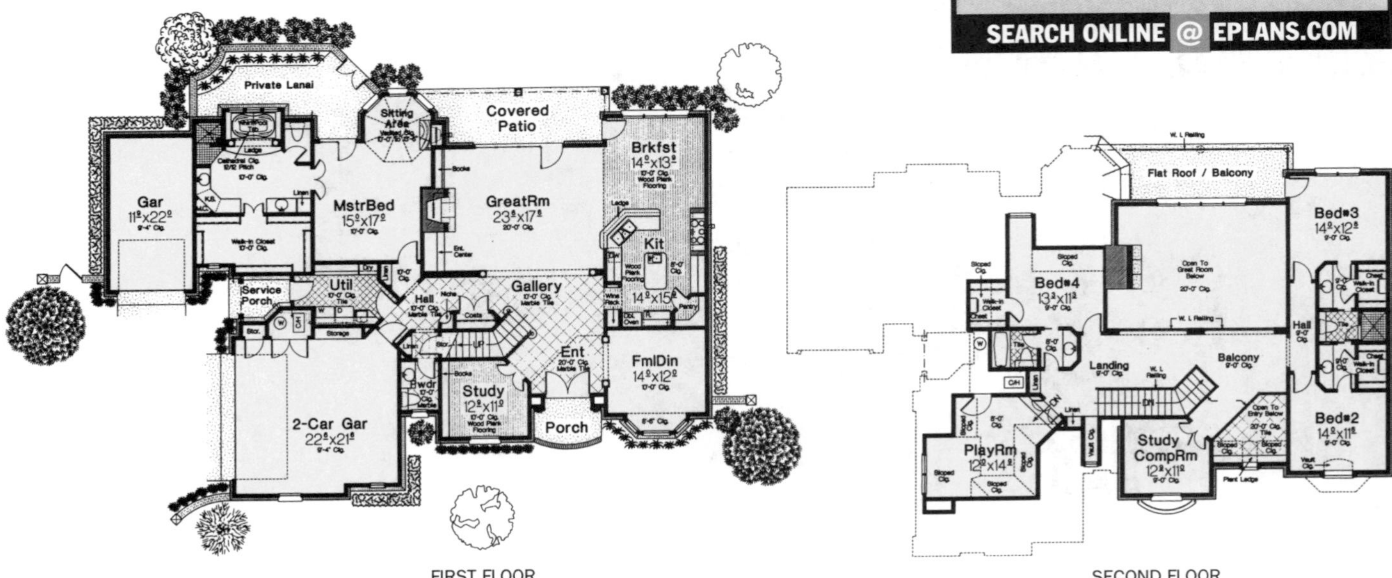

FIRST FLOOR

SECOND FLOOR

plan# HPT930293

- Style: French Country
- First Floor: 2,672 sq. ft.
- Second Floor: 1,586 sq. ft.
- Total: 4,258 sq. ft.
- Bonus Space: 650 sq. ft.
- Bedrooms: 5
- Bathrooms: 4½ + ½ + ½
- Width: 89'-6"
- Depth: 63'-0"
- Foundation: Basement, Crawlspace

SEARCH ONLINE @ EPLANS.COM

Windows, stone, and flower boxes create many dimensions for this French country chateau. Windows spread across this home's facade to shed light inside. The kitchen and breakfast nook invite visitors and homeowners alike. A rear terrace area is a great place for outdoor entertaining. The family room offers warmth through the great hearth. A master suite with His and Hers walk-in closet is found on the first floor. On the second floor four more family bedrooms are found.

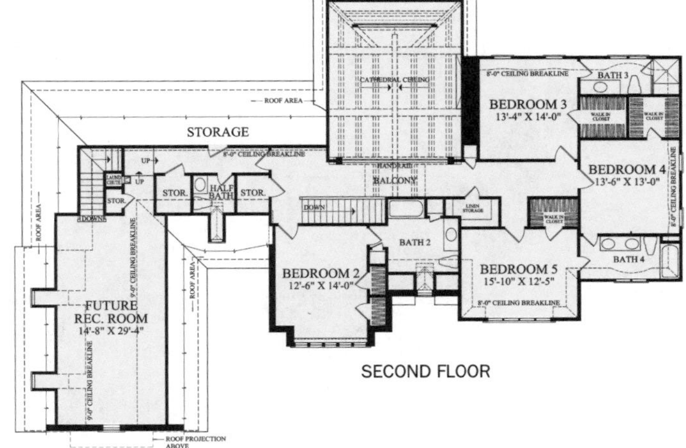

SECOND FLOOR

FIRST FLOOR

This sprawling chateau estate encompasses over 5,000 square feet, yet the delicate touches and handsome details lend a lived-in, personal quality. Stretching throughout the entry, gallery, island kitchen, bayed breakfast nook and utility areas, tile flooring is both elegant and easy to maintain. The formal dining room and the living room, with its extended stone fireplace, are graced with hardwood floors. From the living room, the trellis patio transforms to wrap around the entire right side of the home. The left wing is devoted to the master suite, grand with a Pullman ceiling, entertainment center, dual walk-in closets, fabulous bath and private exercise room. Upstairs, three large bedrooms, a recreation room and a future bonus room allow plenty of room for family and friends.

plan# HPT930294

- Style: Chateau
- First Floor: 3,617 sq. ft.
- Second Floor: 1,542 sq. ft.
- Total: 5,159 sq. ft.
- Bonus Space: 450 sq. ft.
- Bedrooms: 4
- Bathrooms: 3½ + ½
- Width: 108'-11"
- Depth: 88'-7"
- Foundation: Slab

SEARCH ONLINE @ EPLANS.COM

plan# HPT930295

- Style: French
- First Floor: 5,152 sq. ft.
- Second Floor: 726 sq. ft.
- Total: 5,878 sq. ft.
- Bedrooms: 4
- Bathrooms: 5½
- Width: 146'-7"
- Depth: 106'-7"
- Foundation: Slab

SEARCH ONLINE @ EPLANS.COM

Luxury abounds in this graceful manor. The formal living and dining rooms bid greeting as you enter, and the impressive great room awaits more casual times with its cathedral ceiling and raised-hearth fireplace. A gallery hall leads to the kitchen and the family sleeping wing on the right and to the study, guest suite and master suite on the left. The large island kitchen offers a sunny breakfast nook. The master suite includes a bayed sitting area, a dual fireplace shared with the study, and a luxurious bath. Each additional bedroom features its own bath and sitting area. Upstairs is a massive recreation room with a sunlit studio area and a bridge leading to an attic over the garage.

SECOND FLOOR

FIRST FLOOR

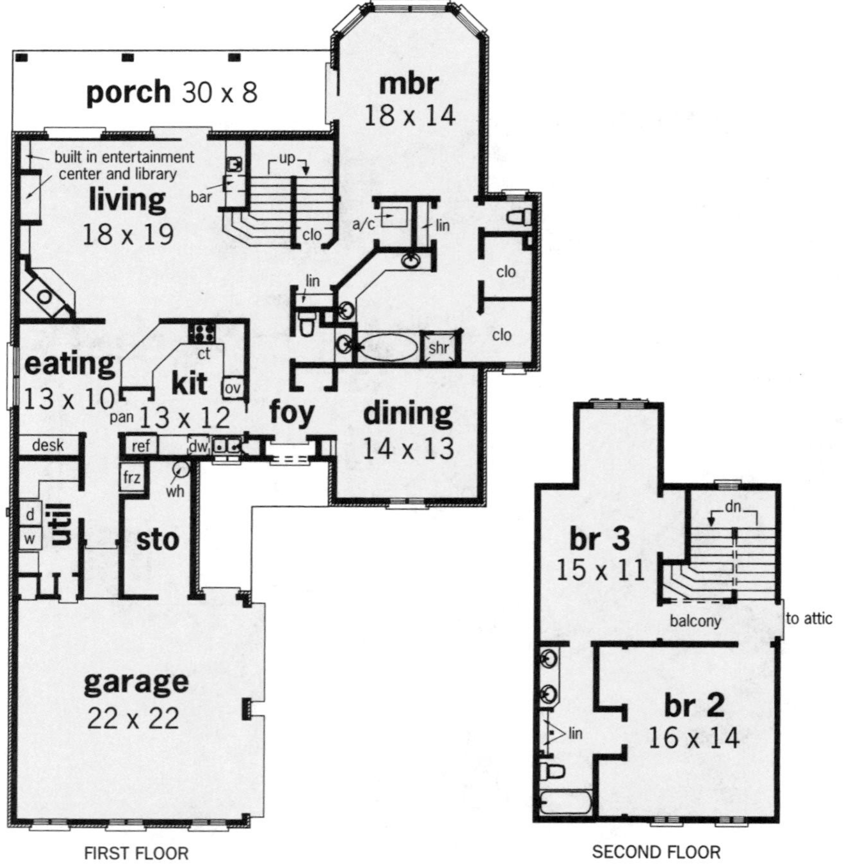

FIRST FLOOR

SECOND FLOOR

plan# HPT930296

- Style: European Cottage
- First Floor: 1,802 sq. ft.
- Second Floor: 670 sq. ft.
- Total: 2,472 sq. ft.
- Bedrooms: 3
- Bathrooms: 2½
- Width: 49'-0"
- Depth: 79'-0"
- Foundation: Crawlspace

SEARCH ONLINE @ EPLANS.COM

With all the charm and romance of the French countryside, this European design features great amenities for today's modern family. French shutters and a stucco facade dazzle the exterior. Inside, the foyer is flanked by the efficient kitchen and formal dining room. The kitchen serves the petite eating nook with ease. The living room is enhanced by a corner fireplace, wet bar and a built-in entertainment center complete with library shelves. The first-floor master suite features a bay-windowed wall, a private bath and two walk-in closets. Two additional bedrooms are located upstairs, sharing a bath.

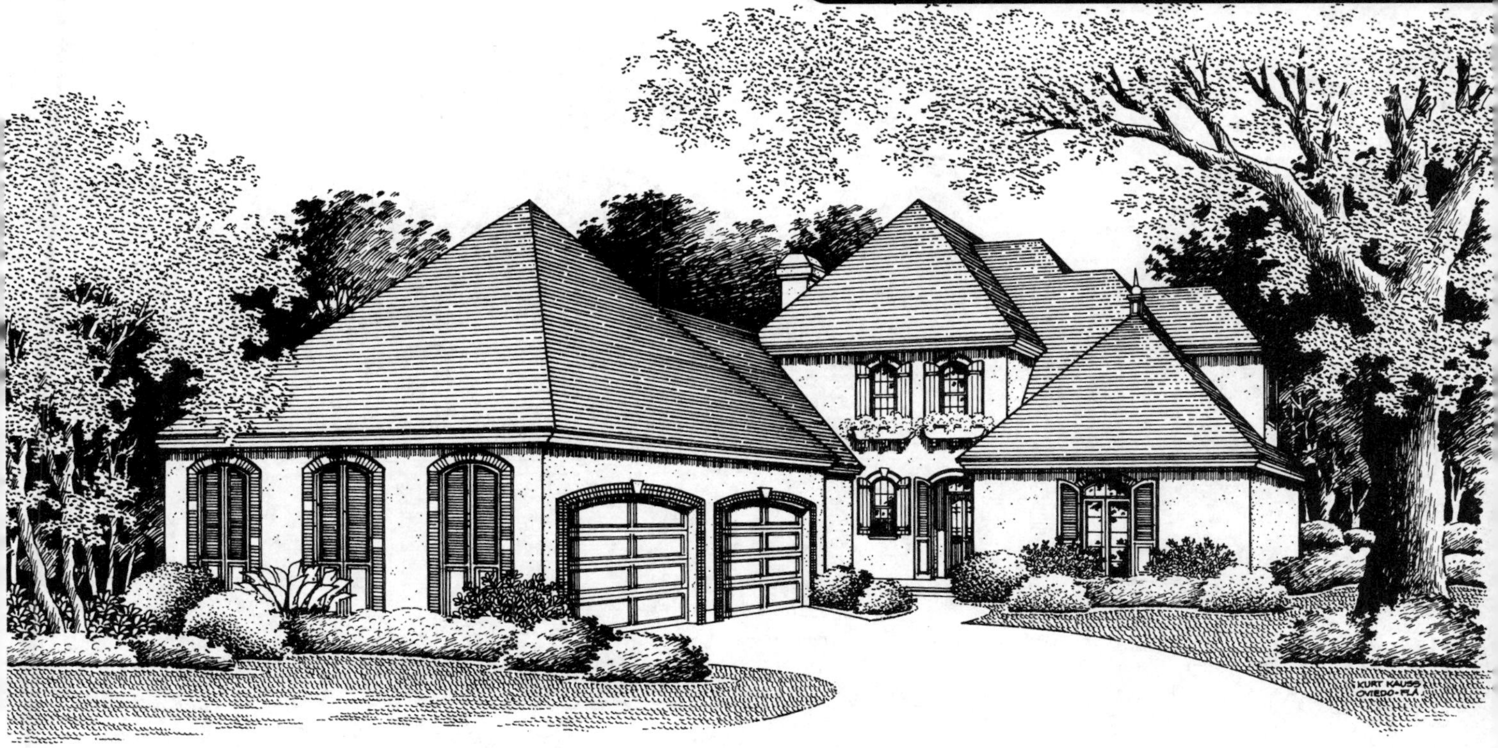

plan # HPT930297

- Style: European Cottage
- First Floor: 1,884 sq. ft.
- Second Floor: 1,034 sq. ft.
- Total: 2,918 sq. ft.
- Bedrooms: 4
- Bathrooms: 3½
- Width: 49'-0"
- Depth: 79'-0"
- Foundation: Slab

SEARCH ONLINE @ EPLANS.COM

FIRST FLOOR

SECOND FLOOR

This lovely home features capped, hipped rooflines that capture a French fairy-tale appeal. Inside, the formal dining room is separated from the hardworking kitchen by the foyer. An eating nook is a perfect spot for casual meals. The living room boasts a built-in entertainment center, bookshelves, a wet bar and a warm, cozy fireplace. The master bedroom is secluded to the rear right. Two walk-in closets, dual vanities, a separate tub and shower and a compartmented toilet pamper homeowners. Three spacious family bedrooms—one with its own bath—encompass the second floor.

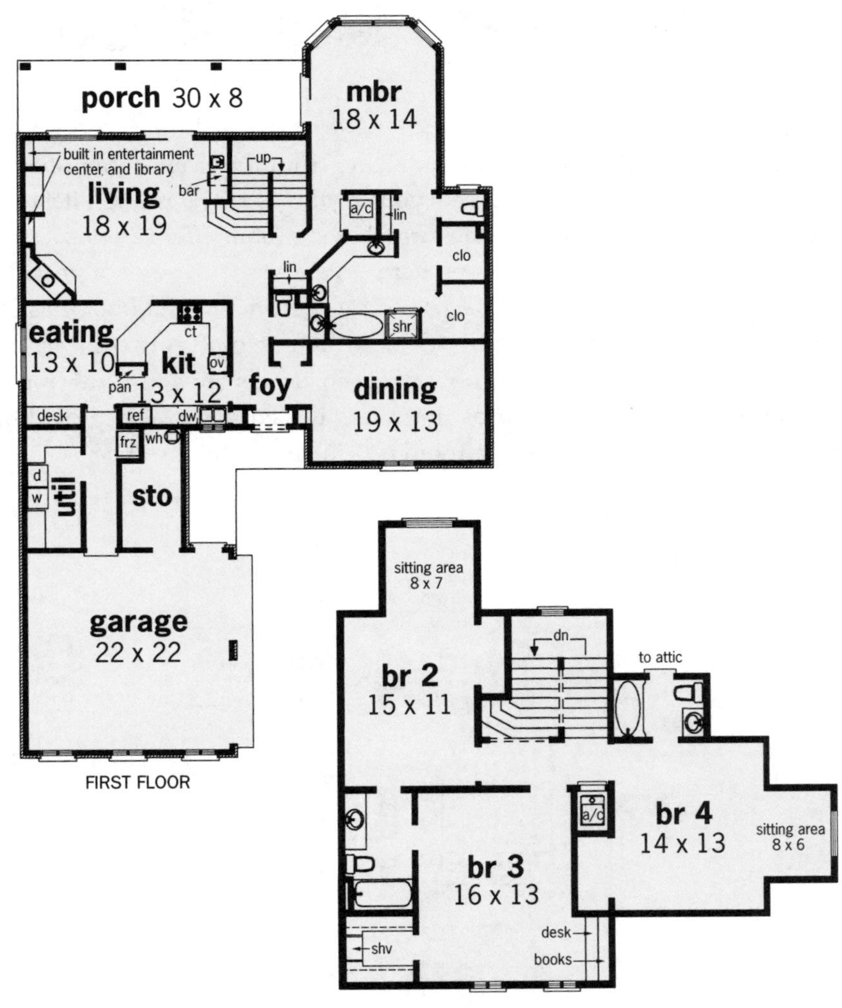

This contemporary, European-style cottage offers a fresh look for new neighborhoods. Elegant double doors from the front porch open inside, where a formal dining room greets you to your left. The island kitchen serves the breakfast room with ease. The formal living room offers an impressive fireplace with flanking built-ins. From here, access to the rear porch provides outdoor entertainment. The porch is also accessed from the first-floor master suite, which enjoys a private bath and double walk-in closet. A two-car garage and utility room complete the first floor. Walk-in closets are abundant in the three second-floor bedrooms—two of these family bedrooms also provide sitting areas for study space. The game room is flexible as a home office.

plan# HPT930298

- Style: French Country
- First Floor: 2,170 sq. ft.
- Second Floor: 1,098 sq. ft.
- Total: 3,268 sq. ft.
- Bedrooms: 4
- Bathrooms: 3½
- Width: 53'-10"
- Depth: 71'-10"
- Foundation: Slab

SEARCH ONLINE @ EPLANS.COM

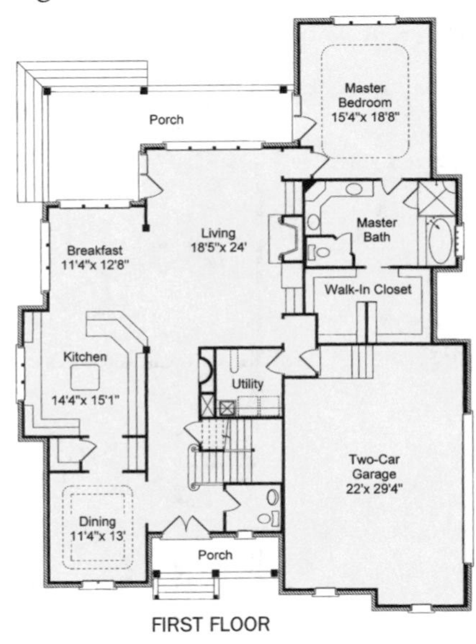

FIRST FLOOR

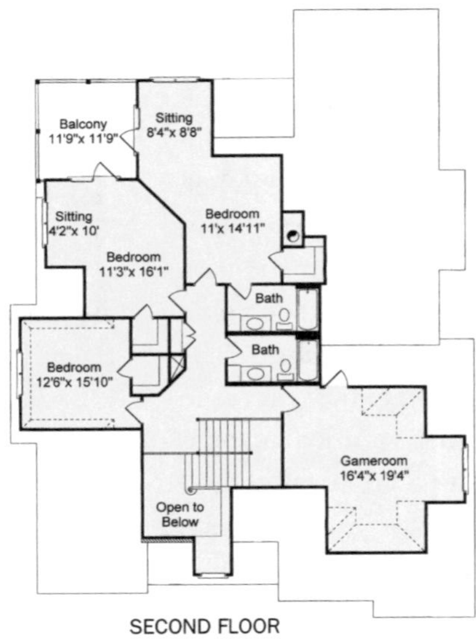

SECOND FLOOR

plan# HPT930299

- Style: French Country
- First Floor: 2,000 sq. ft.
- Second Floor: 934 sq. ft.
- Total: 2,934 sq. ft.
- Bonus Space: 363 sq. ft.
- Bedrooms: 3
- Bathrooms: 2½
- Width: 42'-0"
- Depth: 94'-8"
- Foundation: Crawlspace

SEARCH ONLINE @ EPLANS.COM

This enchanting stone cottage is a beautiful example of French country living. Inside, a dining room and study/guest suite flank the foyer. A hall niche is ready to display your treasures. Past the powder room, the gathering room is comfortable and inviting with a fireplace and French door access to the terrace. An angled kitchen has an island cooktop for the ultimate in convenience. Separated for privacy, the master suite pampers with a soothing spa bath. Upstairs, two bedroom suites have private toilets and vanities and a shared shower/tub. A studio suite can be added as your family grows.

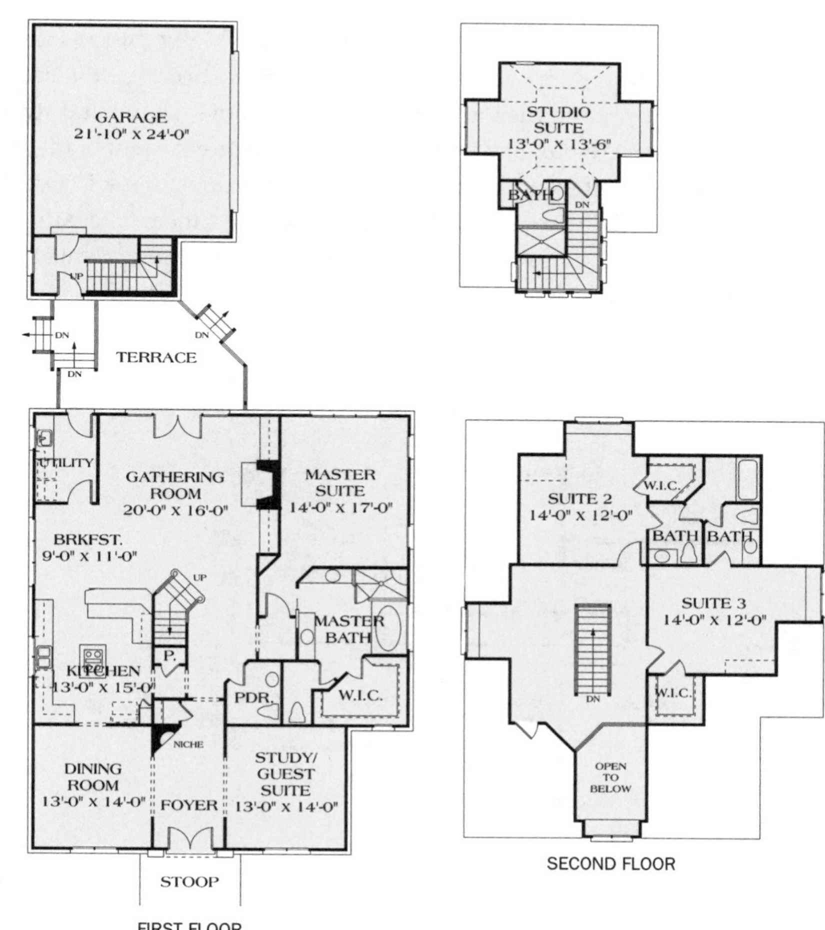

FIRST FLOOR

SECOND FLOOR

Stone accents and a second-floor turret highlight the facade of this four-bedroom home. The split-descending staircase accesses the second floor from both the foyer and the kitchen. The library enjoys a bay window while the dining room boasts a box-bay window. The sunken great room holds an impressive fireplace and offers access to the deck. The breakfast nook is awash in sunlight with views of the backyard. On the second floor, the master suite pampers with a bay window, massive walk-in closet and a luxurious private bath. Three additional bedrooms reside here along with two full baths.

plan# HPT930300

- Style: Tudor; Traditional
- First Floor: 1,678 sq. ft.
- Second Floor: 1,766 sq. ft.
- Total: 3,444 sq. ft.
- Bedrooms: 4
- Bathrooms: 3½
- Width: 72'-6"
- Depth: 55'-8"
- Foundation: Basement

SEARCH ONLINE @ EPLANS.COM

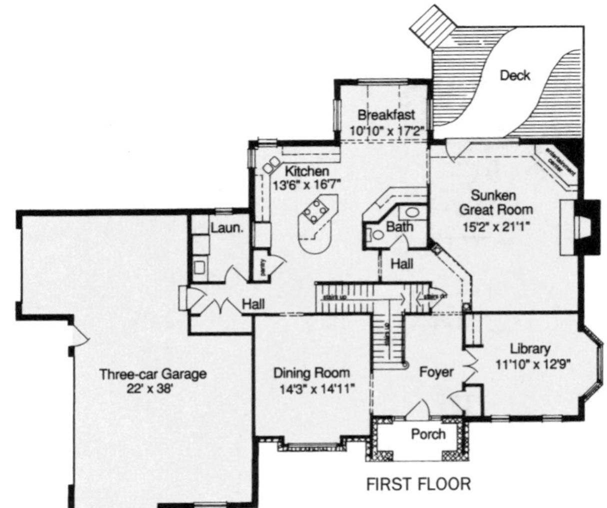

Deck
Breakfast 10'10" x 17'2"
Kitchen 13'6" x 16'7"
Sunken Great Room 15'2" x 21'1"
Laun.
Bath
Hall
Hall
Three-car Garage 22' x 38'
Dining Room 14'3" x 14'11"
Foyer
Library 11'10" x 12'9"
Porch

FIRST FLOOR

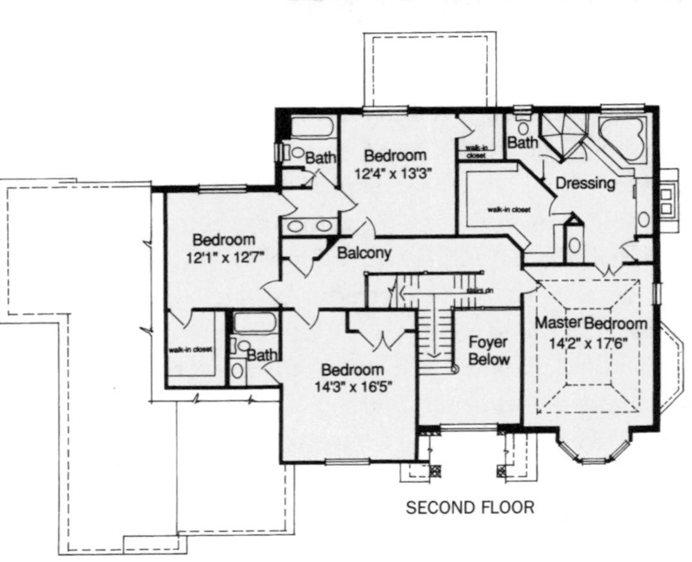

SECOND FLOOR

plan# HPT930301

- Style: European Cottage
- First Floor: 1,836 sq. ft.
- Second Floor: 775 sq. ft.
- Total: 2,611 sq. ft.
- Bedrooms: 3
- Bathrooms: 2½
- Width: 54'-10"
- Depth: 56'-7"
- Foundation: Crawlspace

SEARCH ONLINE @ EPLANS.COM

Exterior details are only the beginning. This breathtaking European cottage packs abundant living space in less than 2,000 square feet. Enter through the covered front porch; the formal dining room and study are on either side of the foyer. Continue to the family room, featuring an extended-hearth fireplace and built-ins, and out to the patio—perfect for summer barbecues. The master suite includes a separate tub and shower and dual vanities. Two upstairs bedrooms are lit by flower-box windows and share a full bath.

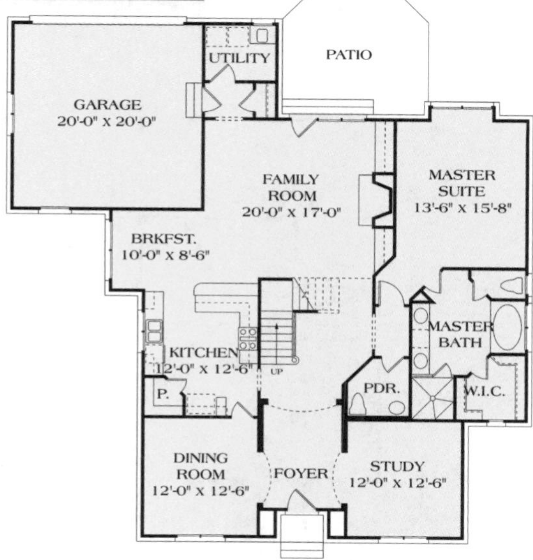

FIRST FLOOR

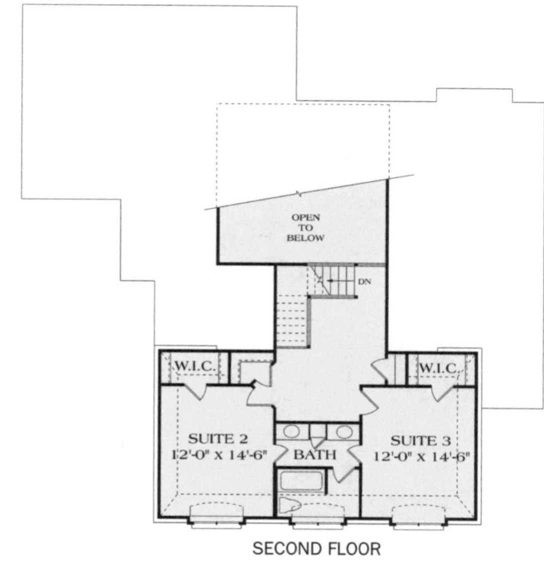

SECOND FLOOR

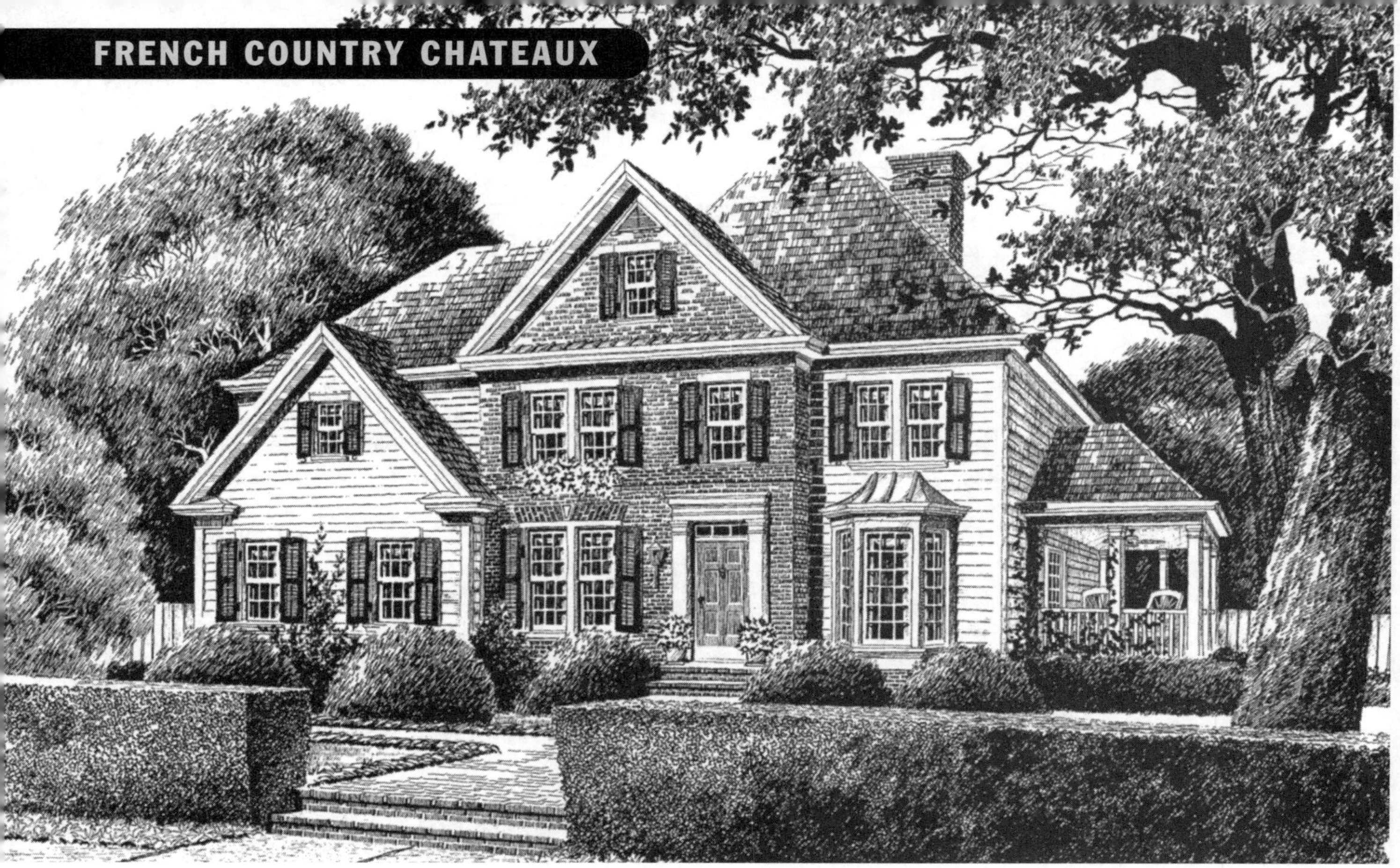

This charming exterior conceals a perfect family plan. The formal dining and living rooms reside on either side of the foyer. At the rear of the home is a family room with a fireplace and access to a deck and veranda. The modern kitchen features a sunlit breakfast area. The second floor provides four bedrooms, one of which may be finished at a later date and used as a guest suite. Note the extra storage space in the two-car garage.

plan# HPT930302

- Style: French Country
- First Floor: 1,205 sq. ft.
- Second Floor: 1,160 sq. ft.
- Total: 2,365 sq. ft.
- Bonus Space: 350 sq. ft.
- Bedrooms: 3
- Bathrooms: 3½
- Width: 52'-6"
- Depth: 43'-6"
- Foundation: Walkout Basement

SEARCH ONLINE @ EPLANS.COM

QUOTE ONE®

Cost to build? See page 436 to order complete cost estimate to build this house in your area!

FIRST FLOOR

SECOND FLOOR

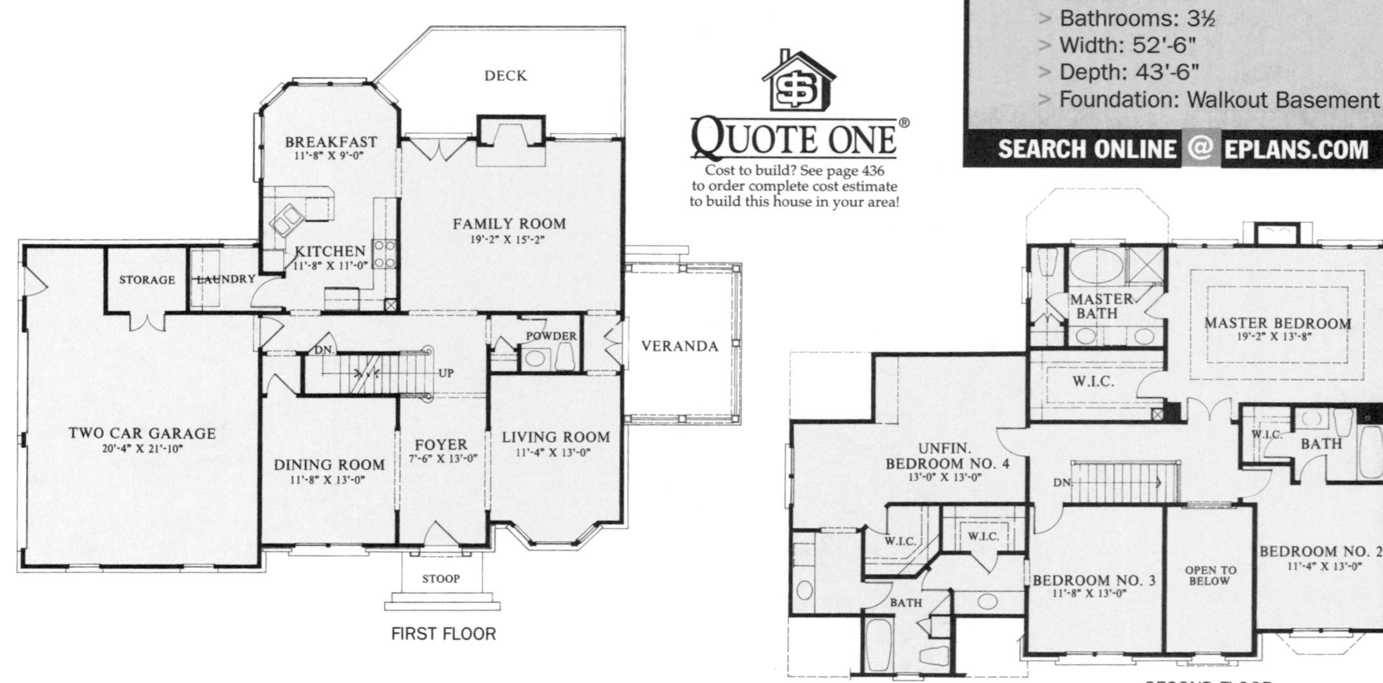

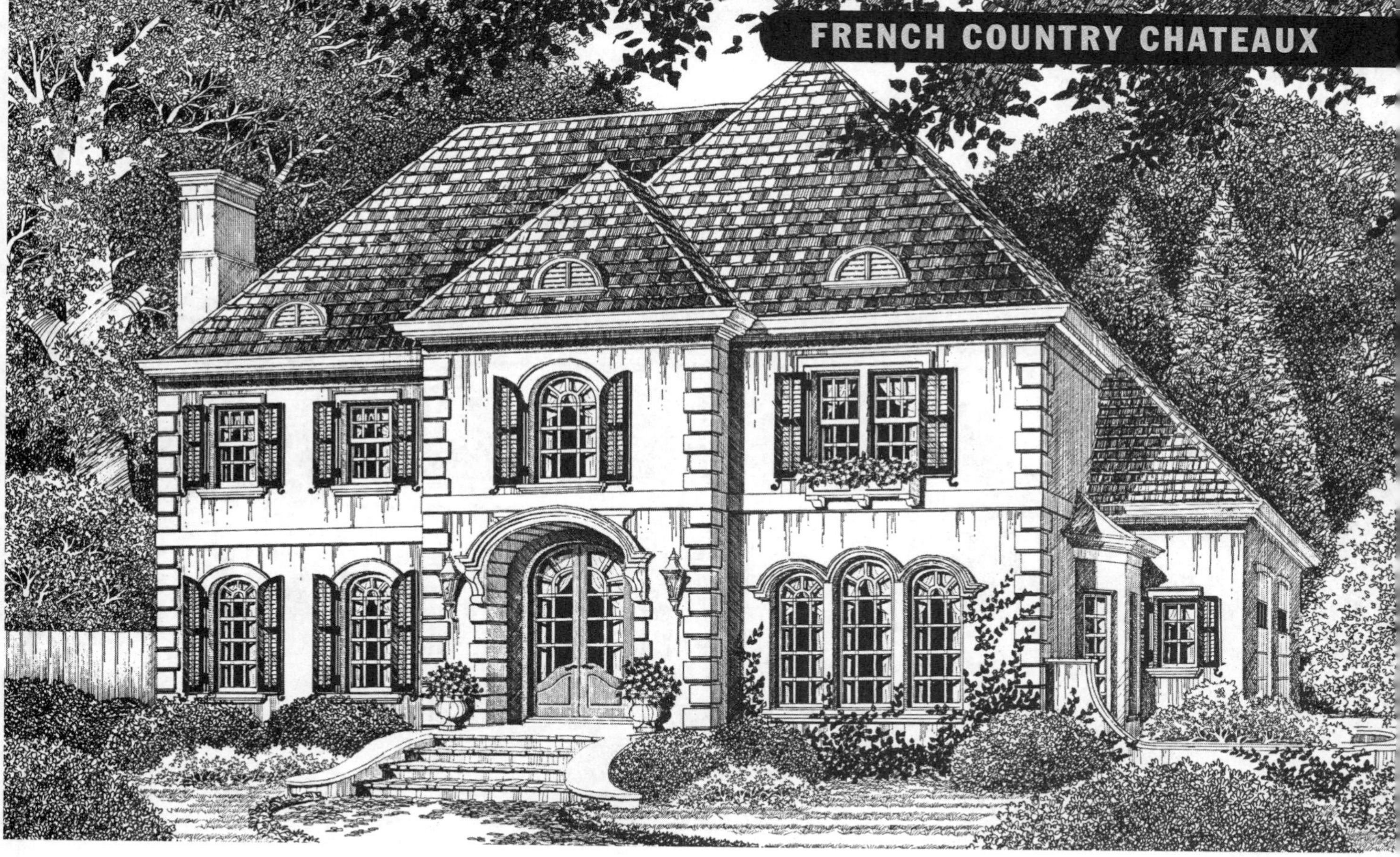

plan# HPT930303

- Style: Norman
- First Floor: 1,360 sq. ft.
- Second Floor: 1,400 sq. ft.
- Total: 2,760 sq. ft.
- Bedrooms: 4
- Bathrooms: 3½
- Width: 52'-0"
- Depth: 49'-0"
- Foundation: Walkout Basement

SEARCH ONLINE @ EPLANS.COM

The appeal of this home is definitely European, with an interior that is open and inviting. Decorative columns separate the formal living room and dining room. To the left of the foyer, the comfortable family room boasts a large fireplace and open-rail detailing and allows access to the breakfast room and kitchen. An open staircase to the gallery above leads to a grand master suite with a tray ceiling and a luxurious private bath with a whirlpool tub, His and Hers vanities and a walk-in closet. Two bedrooms with a connecting bath and a third bedroom with a private bath complete the room arrangements.

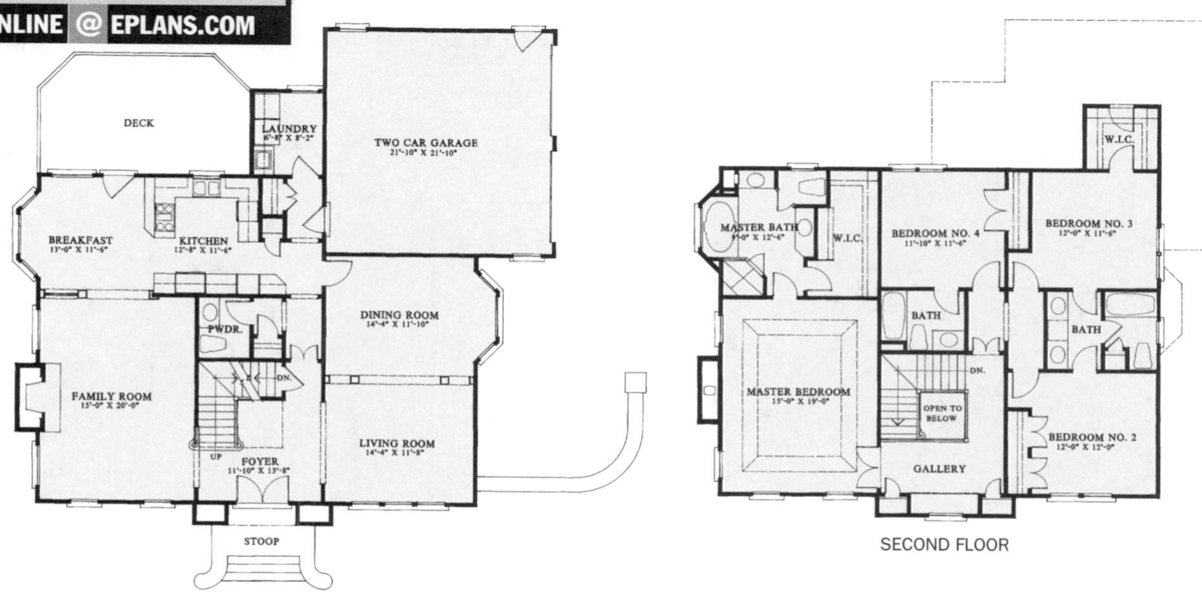

FIRST FLOOR

SECOND FLOOR

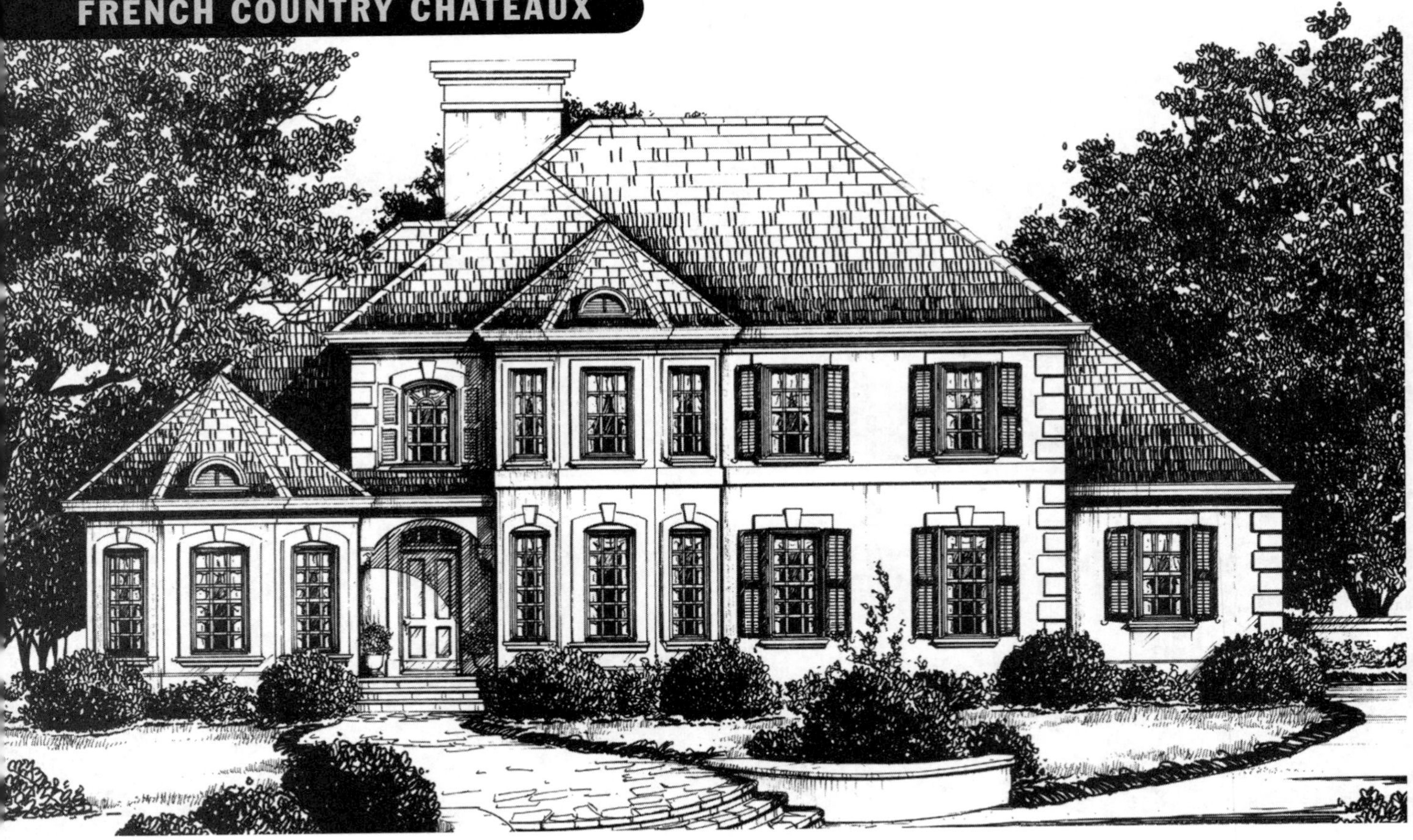

This European design is filled with space for formal and informal occasions. Informal areas include an open kitchen, breakfast room and family room with a fireplace. Formal rooms surround the foyer, with the living room on the left and dining room on the right. The master suite is conveniently placed on the first floor, with a gorgeous private bath and a walk-in closet. Each of the family bedrooms upstairs features a sizable walk-in closet and access to a full bath. Additional storage space is found in the hallway. A fourth bedroom, not included in the square footage, is optional.

plan# HPT930304

- Style: French
- First Floor: 1,660 sq. ft.
- Second Floor: 665 sq. ft.
- Total: 2,325 sq. ft.
- Bonus Space: 240 sq. ft.
- Bedrooms: 4
- Bathrooms: 3½
- Width: 64'-0"
- Depth: 48'-6"
- Foundation: Walkout Basement

SEARCH ONLINE @ EPLANS.COM

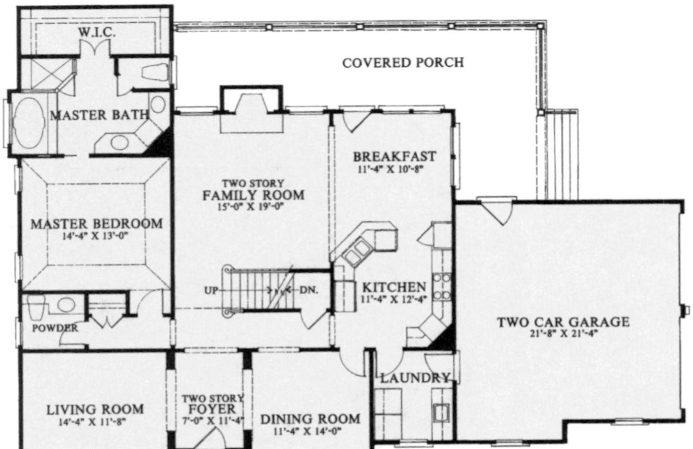

W.I.C.
COVERED PORCH
MASTER BATH
BREAKFAST 11'-4" X 10'-8"
TWO STORY FAMILY ROOM 15'-0" X 19'-0"
MASTER BEDROOM 14'-4" X 13'-0"
UP
DN.
KITCHEN 11'-4" X 12'-4"
TWO CAR GARAGE 21'-8" X 21'-4"
POWDER
LAUNDRY
LIVING ROOM 14'-4" X 11'-8"
TWO STORY FOYER 7'-0" X 11'-4"
DINING ROOM 11'-4" X 14'-0"

FIRST FLOOR

OPEN TO BELOW
BEDROOM NO. 3 11'-4" X 14'-0"
BATH
FUTURE BEDROOM NO. 4 10'-6" X 14'-0"
W.I.C.
DN.
W.I.C.
FUTURE W.I.C.
OPEN TO BELOW
BEDROOM NO. 2 11'-4" X 15'-0"
BATH

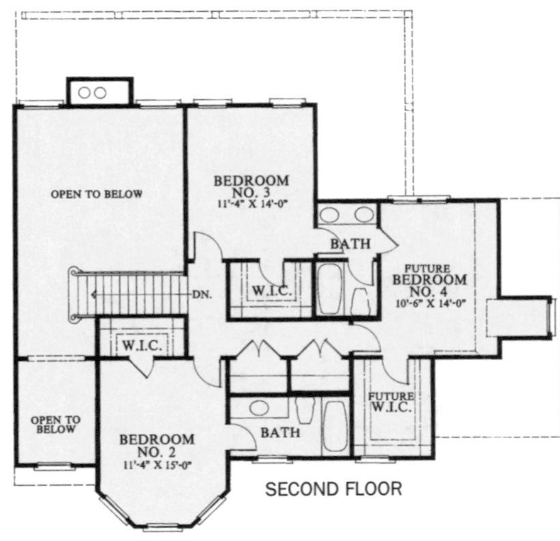

SECOND FLOOR

© Stephen Fuller, Inc.

plan# HPT930305

- Style: Norman
- First Floor: 1,660 sq. ft.
- Second Floor: 665 sq. ft.
- Total: 2,325 sq. ft.
- Bonus Space: 240 sq. ft.
- Bedrooms: 3
- Bathrooms: 3½
- Width: 64'-0"
- Depth: 48'-6"
- Foundation: Walkout Basement

SEARCH ONLINE @ EPLANS.COM

Stately brick and jack-arch detailing create an exterior with an established look, yet the floor plan offers 21st-Century livability. A dramatic two-story entry is framed by formal living and dining areas. The cheery breakfast nook allows rear covered porch access and opens to a kitchen loaded with modern amenities. A coffered ceiling, His and Hers vanities and a walk-in closet highlight the master suite.

QUOTE ONE®
Cost to build? See page 436 to order complete cost estimate to build this house in your area!

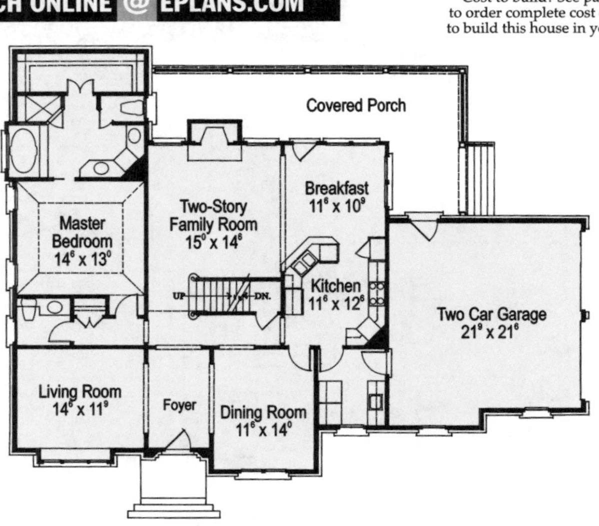

FIRST FLOOR

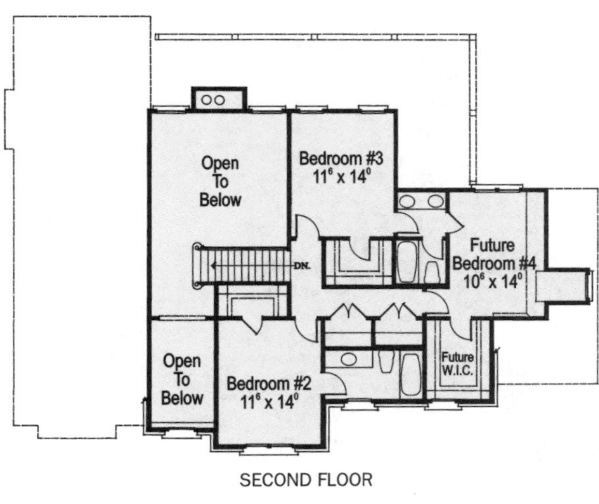

SECOND FLOOR

This astonishing traditional home looks great with its gables, muntin windows, keystone lintels and turret-style bay. Inside, the heart of the home is the vaulted family room with a fireplace. The kitchen conveniently connects to the dining room, breakfast room and garage. The master bath leads into a walk-in closet. The home office or nursery near the hall bath is illuminated by a bayed wall of windows and could become an additional family bedroom. Family bedrooms upstairs share a loft that overlooks the family room.

plan# HPT930306

- Style: French Country
- First Floor: 2,247 sq. ft.
- Second Floor: 637 sq. ft.
- Total: 2,884 sq. ft.
- Bonus Space: 235 sq. ft.
- Bedrooms: 4
- Bathrooms: 4
- Width: 64'-0"
- Depth: 55'-2"
- Foundation: Crawlspace, Basement

SEARCH ONLINE @ EPLANS.COM

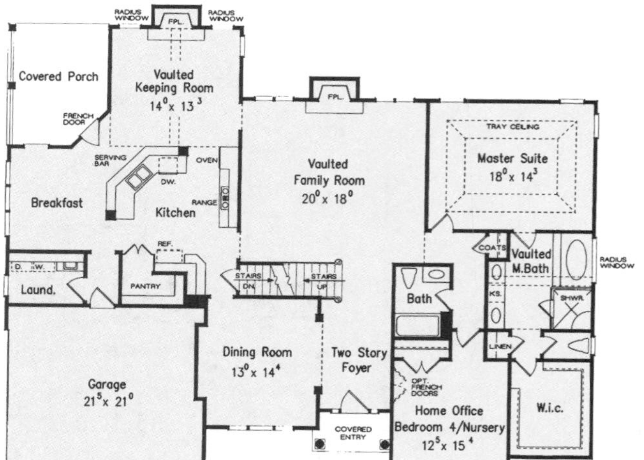

Covered Porch
Vaulted Keeping Room 14⁰ x 13³
Vaulted Family Room 20⁰ x 18⁰
Master Suite 18⁰ x 14³
Breakfast
Kitchen
Laund.
Bath
Vaulted M.Bath
Garage 21⁵ x 21⁰
Dining Room 13⁰ x 14⁴
Two Story Foyer
Home Office Bedroom 4/Nursery 12⁵ x 15⁴
W.i.c.

FIRST FLOOR

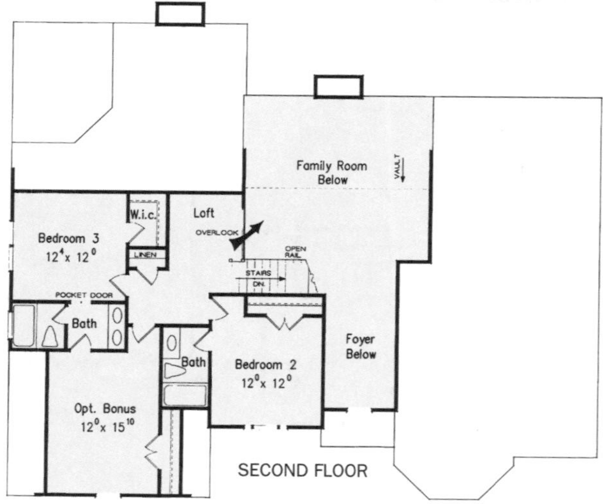

SECOND FLOOR

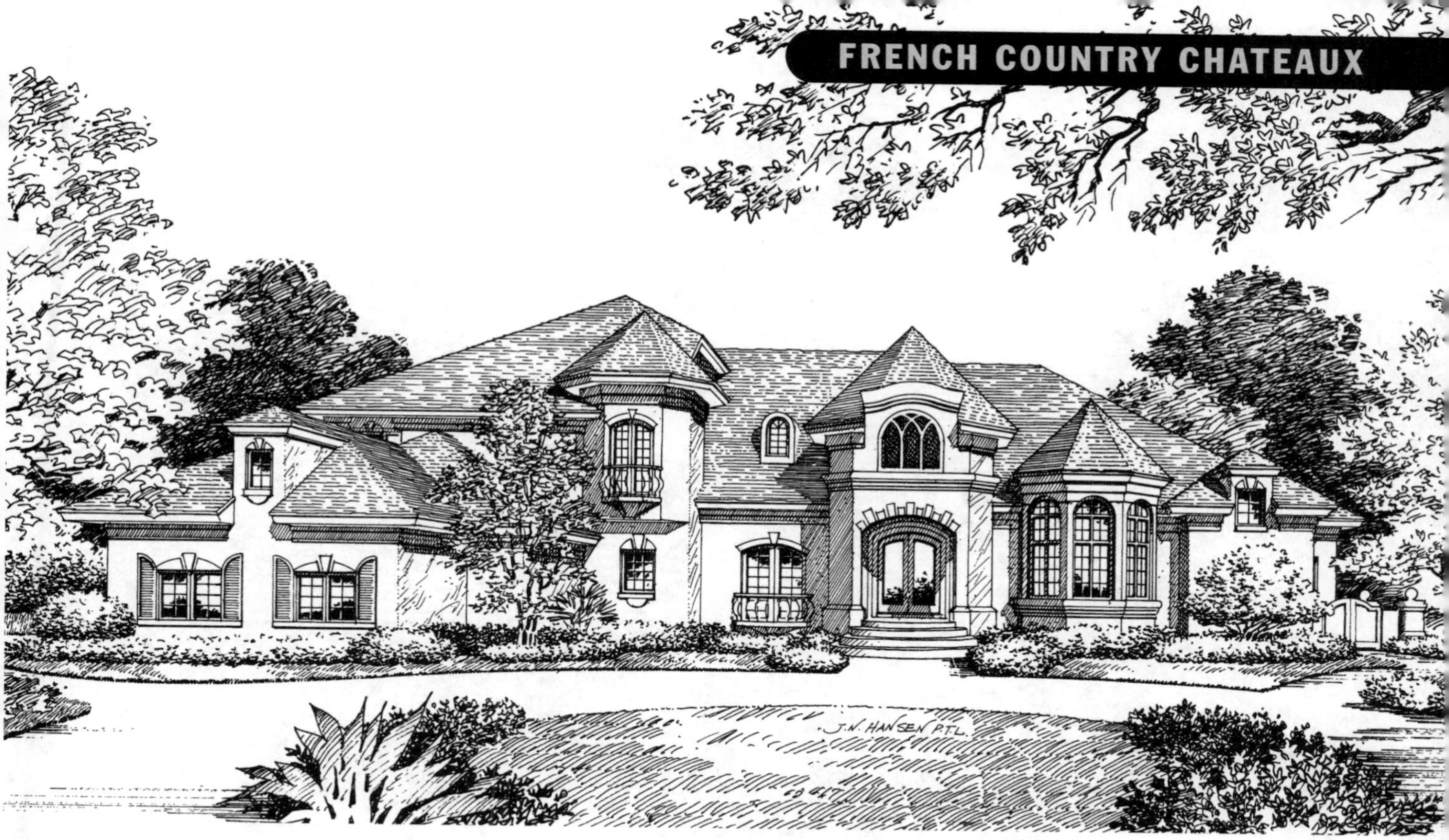

plan# HPT930307

- Style: French
- First Floor: 3,739 sq. ft.
- Second Floor: 778 sq. ft.
- Total: 4,517 sq. ft.
- Bedrooms: 4
- Bathrooms: 5½ + ½
- Width: 105'-0"
- Depth: 84'-0"
- Foundation: Slab

SEARCH ONLINE @ EPLANS.COM

This estate embraces the style of an elegant region—Southern France. Double doors open to a formal columned foyer and give views of the octagonal living room beyond. To the left is the formal dining room that connects to the kitchen via a butler's pantry. To the right is an unusual den with octagonal reading space. The master wing is immense. It features a wet bar, private garden and exercise area. Two secondary bedrooms have private baths; Bedroom 2 has a private terrace. An additional bedroom with a private bath resides on the second floor, making it a perfect student's retreat. Also on the second floor is a game loft and storage area.

FIRST FLOOR

SECOND FLOOR

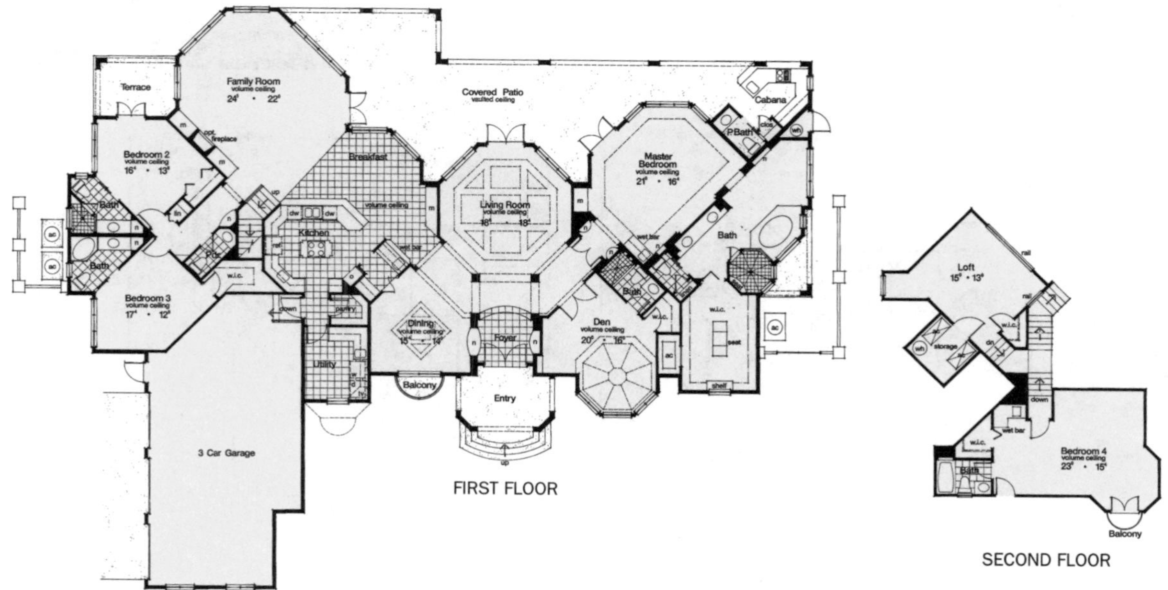

The French country facade of this lovely design hints at the enchanting amenities found within. A two-story foyer welcomes you inside. To the right, a bayed living room is separated from the formal dining room by graceful columns. A butler's pantry leads to the gourmet island kitchen. The breakfast room accesses a rear covered porch and shares a casual area with the two-story family room. Here, a fireplace flanked by built-ins adds to the relaxing atmosphere. Bedroom 5 with a private bath converts to an optional study. Upstairs, the master suite offers palatial elegance. Here, the sitting room is warmed by a fireplace flanked by built-ins, and the suite accesses a private second-floor porch. A dressing room leads to the vaulted master bath and enormous His and Hers walk-in closets. Three additional bedrooms are available on the second floor.

plan# HPT930308

- Style: French Country
- First Floor: 2,095 sq. ft.
- Second Floor: 1,954 sq. ft.
- Total: 4,049 sq. ft.
- Bedrooms: 5
- Bathrooms: 4½
- Width: 56'-0"
- Depth: 63'-0"
- Foundation: Crawlspace, Basement

SEARCH ONLINE @ EPLANS.COM

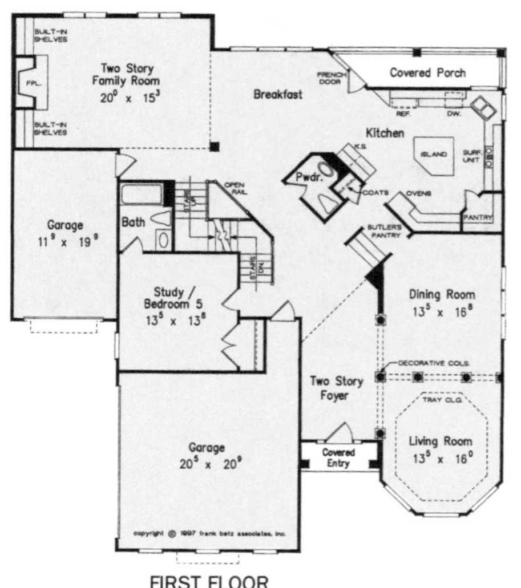

FIRST FLOOR

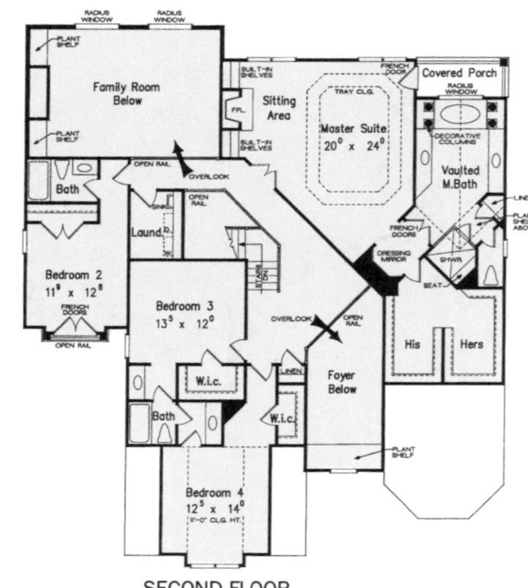

SECOND FLOOR

plan# HPT930309

- Style: French Country
- First Floor: 2,384 sq. ft.
- Second Floor: 1,234 sq. ft.
- Total: 3,618 sq. ft.
- Bonus Space: 314 sq. ft.
- Bedrooms: 5
- Bathrooms: 4½
- Width: 64'-6"
- Depth: 57'-10"
- Foundation: Crawlspace, Slab, Basement

SEARCH ONLINE @ EPLANS.COM

Stucco and stone, French shutters, a turret-style bay and lovely arches create a magical timeless style. A formal arch romanticizes the front entry, which opens to a two-story foyer. A bayed living room resides to the right, while a formal dining room is set to the left. Straight ahead, the vaulted two-story family room is warmed by an enchanting fireplace. The island kitchen is set between the breakfast and dining rooms. The master suite is enhanced by a tray ceiling and offers a lavish master bath with a whirlpool tub. Upstairs, Bedroom 2 offers another private bath and a walk-in closet. Bedrooms 3 and 4 each provide their own walk-in closets and share a full bath between them. The bonus room is perfect for a future home office or playroom.

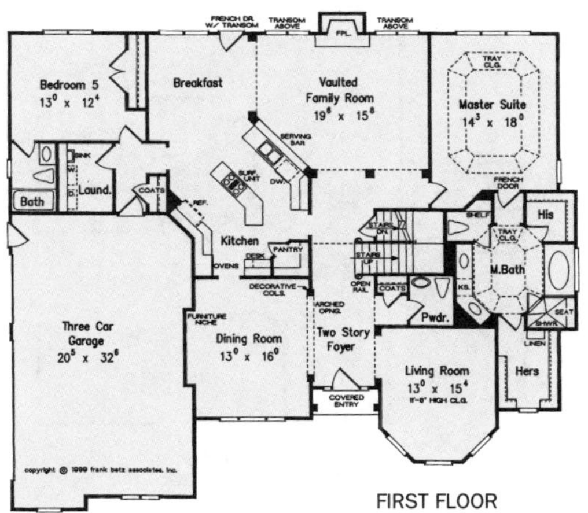

FIRST FLOOR

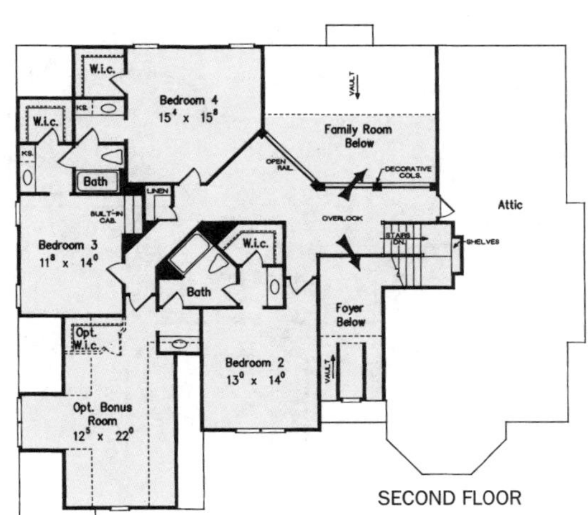

SECOND FLOOR

COPYRIGHT LARRY E. BELK

This majestic storybook cottage, from the magical setting of rural Europe, provides the perfect home for any large family with a wealth of modern comforts within. A graceful staircase cascades from the two-story foyer. To the left, a sophisticated study offers a wall of built-ins. To the right, a formal dining room is easily served from the island kitchen. The breakfast room accesses the rear screened porch. Fireplaces warm the great room and keeping room. Two sets of double doors open from the great room to the rear covered porch. The master bedroom features private porch access, a sitting area, lavish bath and two walk-in closets. Upstairs, three additional family bedrooms offer walk-in closet space galore! The game room is great entertainment for both family and friends. A three-car garage with golf-cart storage completes the plan.

plan# HPT930310

- Style: European Cottage
- First Floor: 3,033 sq. ft.
- Second Floor: 1,545 sq. ft.
- Total: 4,578 sq. ft.
- Bedrooms: 4
- Bathrooms: 3½ + ½
- Width: 91'-6"
- Depth: 63'-8"
- Foundation: Basement, Crawlspace, Slab

SEARCH ONLINE  **EPLANS.COM**

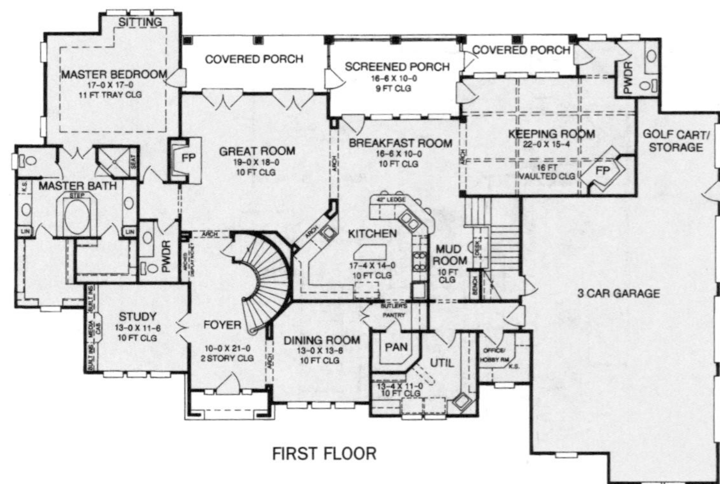

FIRST FLOOR

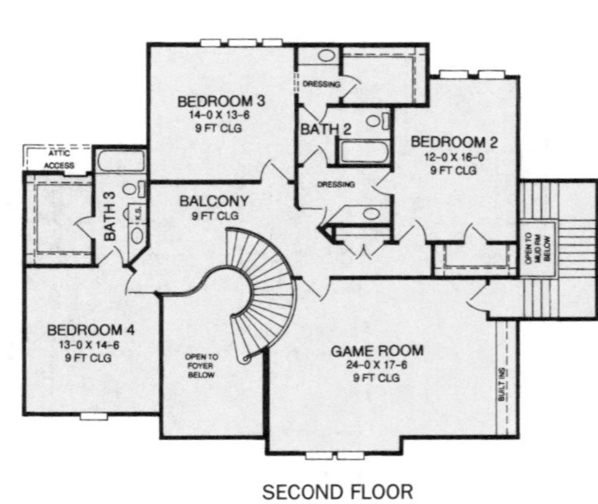

SECOND FLOOR

plan# HPT930311

- Style: Chateau
- First Floor: 3,058 sq. ft.
- Second Floor: 2,076 sq. ft.
- Total: 5,134 sq. ft.
- Bedrooms: 4
- Bathrooms: 4½
- Width: 79'-6"
- Depth: 73'-10"
- Foundation: Basement, Crawlspace, Slab

SEARCH ONLINE @ EPLANS.COM

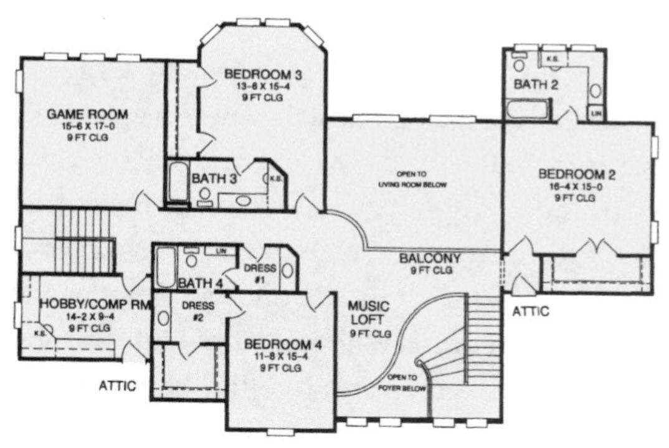

SECOND FLOOR

This sweeping European facade, featuring a majestic turret-style bay, will be a stand-out in the neighborhood and a family favorite. The foyer opens to a spacious formal receiving area. Double doors from the living room open to the rear porch for outdoor activities. The master wing features a sitting area, a luxurious master bath and two walk-in closets. The spacious island kitchen works with the bayed breakfast room for more intimate meals. The family room offers a warm and relaxing fireplace. A private, raised study, three-car garage and utility room complete the first floor. Upstairs, three additional family bedrooms share the second floor with a music loft, hobby room and game room.

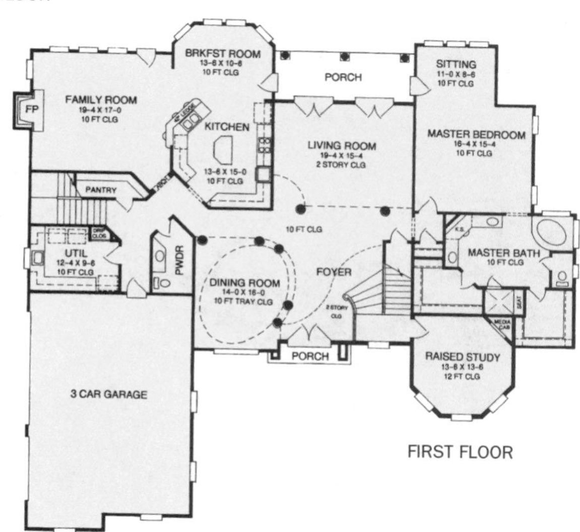

FIRST FLOOR

Be the owner of your own country estate—this two-story home gives the look and feel of grand-style living without the expense of large square footage. The entry leads to a massive foyer and great hall. There's space enough here for living and dining areas.Two window seats in the great hall overlook the rear veranda. One fireplace warms the living area, while another looks through the dining room to the kitchen and breakfast nook. A screened porch offers casual dining space for warm weather. The master suite has another fireplace and a window seat and adjoins a luxurious master bath with a separate tub and shower. The second floor contains three family bedrooms and two full baths. A separate apartment over the garage includes its own living room, kitchen and bedroom.

plan# HPT930312

L

- Style: French
- First Floor: 1,566 sq. ft.
- Second Floor: 837 sq. ft.
- Total: 2,403 sq. ft.
- Apartment: 506 sq. ft.
- Bedrooms: 4
- Bathrooms: 3½
- Width: 116'-3"
- Depth: 55'-1"
- Foundation: Basement

SEARCH ONLINE @ EPLANS.COM

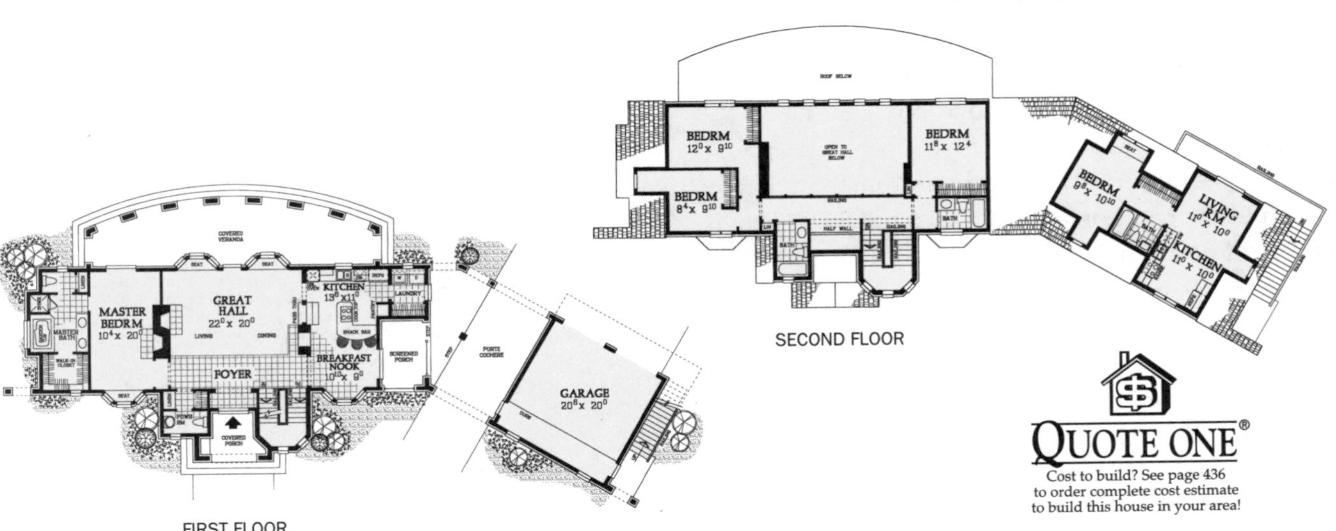

QUOTE ONE®

Cost to build? See page 436 to order complete cost estimate to build this house in your area!

plan# HPT930313

- Style: French Country
- First Floor: 4,565 sq. ft.
- Second Floor: 4,008 sq. ft.
- Total: 8,573 sq. ft.
- Bedrooms: 6
- Bathrooms: 6½ + ½
- Width: 128'-4"
- Depth: 71'-2"
- Foundation: Crawlspace

SEARCH ONLINE @ EPLANS.COM

This luxurious French country estate is a palace full of comforts and amenities. A portico welcomes you into an elegant foyer flanked by a dining room and a study with a fireplace and built-ins. A graceful curving staircase is introduced in the gallery. The living room is warmed by an enormous hearth. The kitchen is open to a breakfast room accessing a rear patio, and the family room warmed by a fireplace. The master wing is an impressive retreat filled with a wealth of amenities. The suite accesses the rear lanai, while a hearth-warmed sitting room leads through a trellis into the private gardens. The suite also features His and Hers baths with walk-in closets and an exercise room with a sauna. Upstairs, three additional suites share the second level with a guest room, recreation room, theater and a nanny's suite that includes a kitchenette and living room.

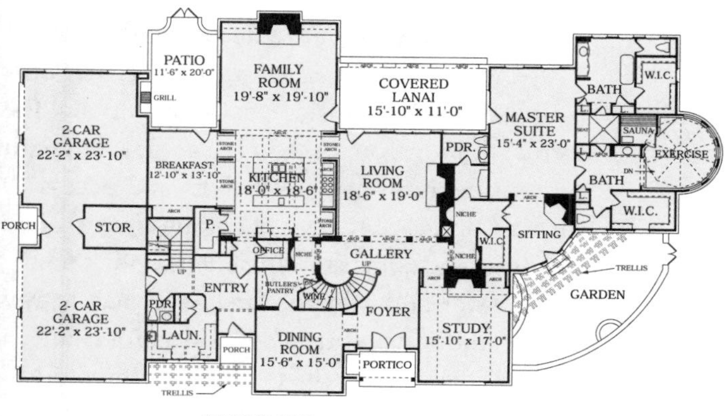

FIRST FLOOR

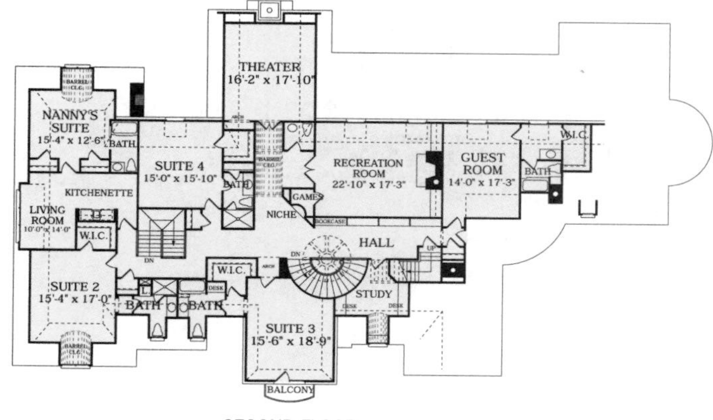

SECOND FLOOR

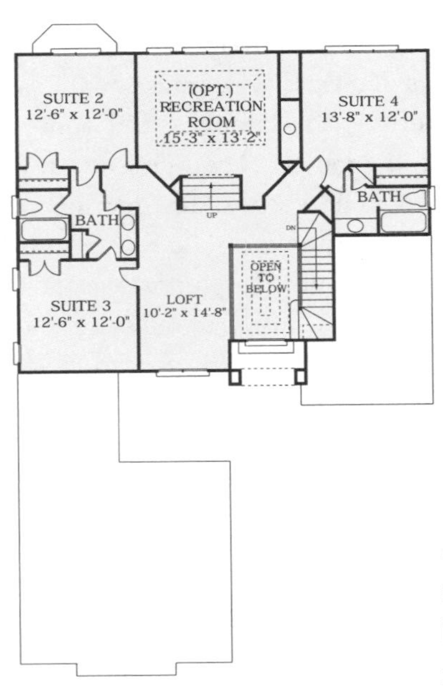

SECOND FLOOR

plan# HPT930314

- Style: Transitional
- First Floor: 1,751 sq. ft.
- Second Floor: 1,043 sq. ft.
- Total: 2,794 sq. ft.
- Bonus Space: 200 sq. ft.
- Bedrooms: 4
- Bathrooms: 3½
- Width: 45'-0"
- Depth: 69'-6"
- Foundation: Crawlspace

SEARCH ONLINE @ EPLANS.COM

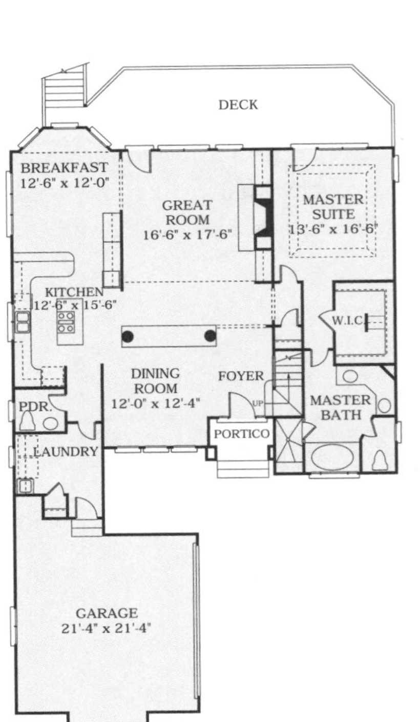

FIRST FLOOR

Stately pilasters and a decorative balcony at a second-level window adorn this ornate four-bedroom design. Inside, columns define the formal dining room. Ahead is a great room with a fireplace, built-in bookshelves and access to the rear deck. A breakfast nook nestles in a bay window and joins an efficient island kitchen. The master suite on the first level has a tray ceiling and a walk-in closet and garden tub in the bath. Upstairs, a versatile loft, three additional bedrooms and two baths are connected by a hallway open to the great room below.

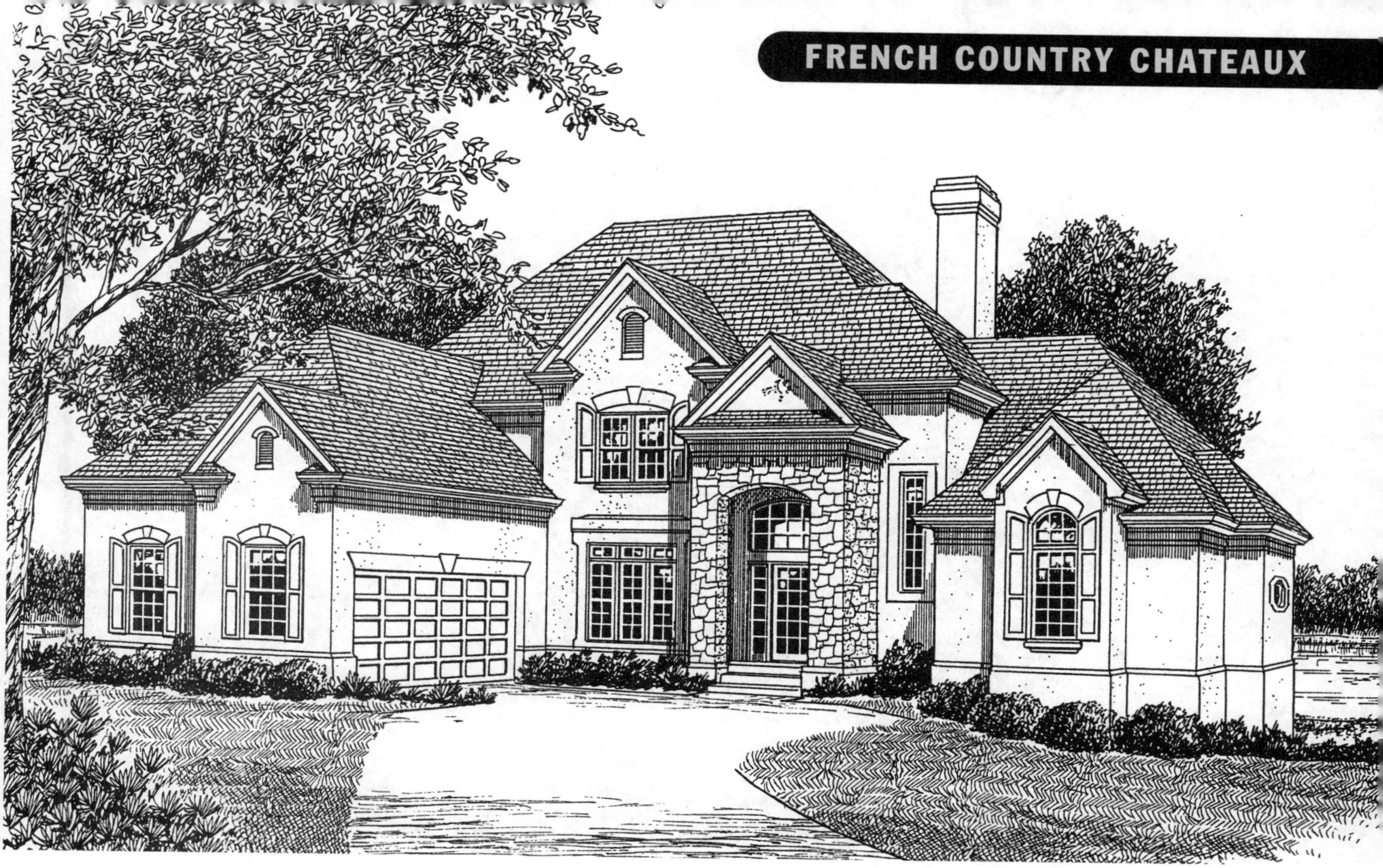

plan# HPT930315

- Style: French
- First Floor: 2,075 sq. ft.
- Second Floor: 859 sq. ft.
- Total: 2,934 sq. ft.
- Bonus Space: 262 sq. ft.
- Bedrooms: 3
- Bathrooms: 3½
- Width: 70'-4"
- Depth: 67'-4"
- Foundation: Basement, Crawlspace

SEARCH ONLINE @ EPLANS.COM

This open, airy design is one that seems much larger than it actually is. A large, two-story great room, which can be viewed from the balcony above, opens into the dining room. Master suite boasts a terrific walk-in closet and bath with dual lavatories. A breakfast area that opens onto a deck, and corner windows at the kitchen sink help bring the outdoors in. There's plenty of storage, including an ample pantry, a two-car garage and bonus room that can double as a fourth suite. Special features include a plant ledge over the great room and an arched, copper dormer.

SECOND FLOOR

FIRST FLOOR

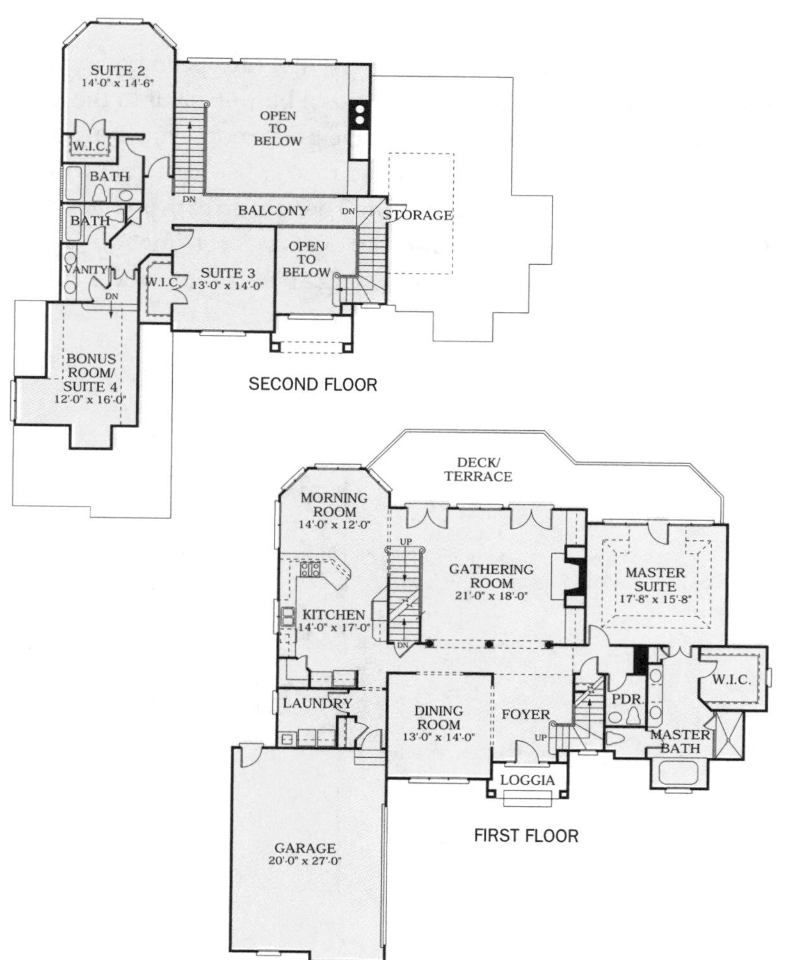

The brick accents of this home give it a European flavor.The vaulted foyer introduces the formal dining room plus a built-in shelf to the right and the den and Bedroom 4 to the left. The massive great room enjoys a vaulted ceiling and includes a cozy fireplace. The vaulted master bedroom features a walk-in closet and private access to the utility room. The private bath is entered through French doors and boasts dual vanities and an oversized soaking tub. Upstairs, two additional bedrooms share a hall with a large bonus room and a full bath with dual vanities—Bedroom 2 features a walk-in closet.

plan# HPT930316

- Style: French
- First Floor: 1,658 sq. ft.
- Second Floor: 538 sq. ft.
- Total: 2,196 sq. ft.
- Bonus Space: 496 sq. ft.
- Bedrooms: 4
- Bathrooms: 2½
- Width: 50'-0"
- Depth: 56'-0"
- Foundation: Crawlspace

SEARCH ONLINE @ EPLANS.COM

FIRST FLOOR

SECOND FLOOR

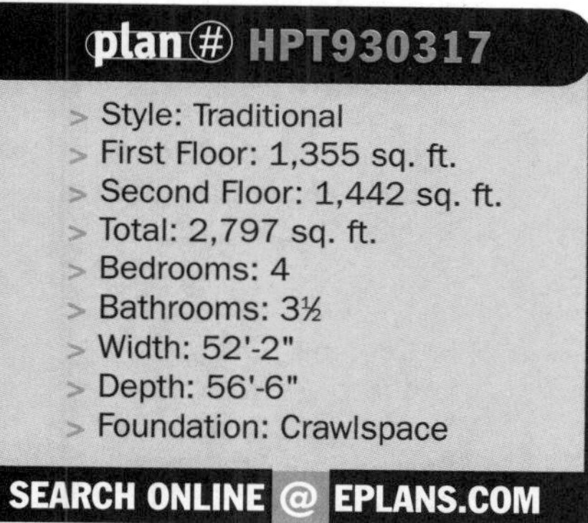

plan# HPT930317

- Style: Traditional
- First Floor: 1,355 sq. ft.
- Second Floor: 1,442 sq. ft.
- Total: 2,797 sq. ft.
- Bedrooms: 4
- Bathrooms: 3½
- Width: 52'-2"
- Depth: 56'-6"
- Foundation: Crawlspace

SEARCH ONLINE @ EPLANS.COM

This Southern design begins with a spacious gathering room, complete with an extended-hearth fireplace and lovely French doors. The gathering room opensto a sunny breakfast area, with its own French door to the back terrace and deck. Upstairs, the master suite features a coffered ceiling, two walk-in closets and a lavish bath with separate vanities. Three family bedrooms, one with a private bath, share a hall that opens to a generous sitting area with space for books and computers.

SECOND FLOOR

FIRST FLOOR

The handsome facade of this outstanding two-story traditional home is equaled by its efficient interior design. A library with multi-pane windows sits to the right of the entryway. The living room on the left adjoins a formal dining room with an octagonal tray ceiling. The island kitchen fills a bay window that looks out to the rear deck. A large breakfast room is adjacent to the family room with a fireplace and hearth. The master suite, with a cove ceiling, private bath and walk-in closet, resides on the second floor. Three family bedrooms and a bonus room complete this floor.

plan# HPT930318

- Style: Traditional
- First Floor: 1,426 sq. ft.
- Second Floor: 1,315 sq. ft.
- Total: 2,741 sq. ft.
- Bonus Space: 200 sq. ft.
- Bedrooms: 4
- Bathrooms: 2½
- Width: 57'-7"
- Depth: 44'-10"
- Foundation: Crawlspace

SEARCH ONLINE @ EPLANS.COM

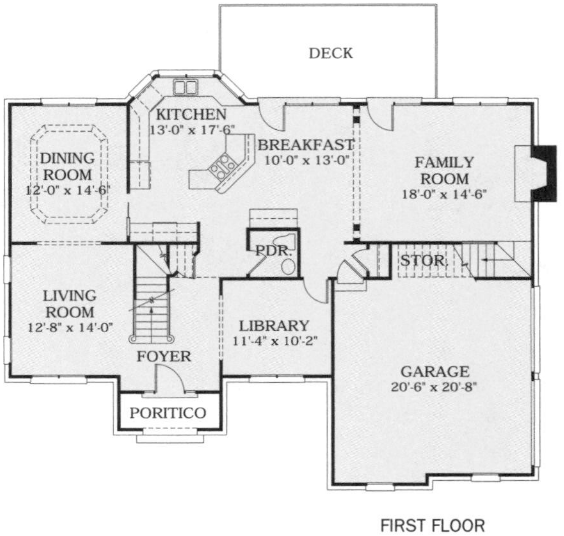

FIRST FLOOR

SECOND FLOOR

plan# HPT930319

- Style: French
- First Floor: 1,706 sq. ft.
- Second Floor: 791 sq. ft.
- Total: 2,497 sq. ft.
- Bonus Space: 644 sq. ft.
- Bedrooms: 3
- Bathrooms: 2½
- Width: 53'-4"
- Depth: 63'-4"
- Foundation: Crawlspace, Basement

SEARCH ONLINE @ EPLANS.COM

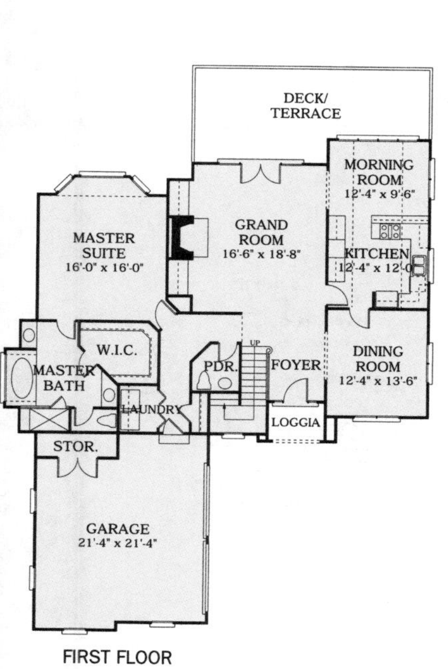

FIRST FLOOR

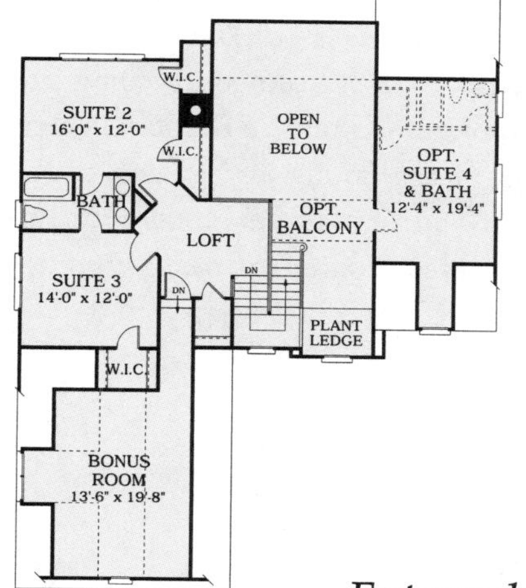

SECOND FLOOR

Extremely cost effective to build, this house makes great use of interior space. The foyer opens to a two-story grand room, which features a fireplace and an elegant Palladian window. A full kitchen connects the dining room and brightly lit morning room. The master suite overlooks the backyard through a bay window. An expansive walk-in closet and garden tub grace the master bath. A U-shaped staircase leads up to a loft and two additional suites that share a bath. The bonus room provides space for a home office or playroom.

This beautiful European estate, with corner quoins, high arched windows and a grand brick facade, will be the envy of any neighborhood. The entry is bordered by the bayed dining room and the living room, with a cathedral ceiling and a warming fireplace. The family room is ideal for entertaining; a fireplace, entertainment center and covered-patio access will please family and guests. In the island kitchen, space enough for two exuberant chefs makes meal preparation fun and easy. Past the study, French doors lead to the master suite, luxurious with private patio access and a spa bath. Upstairs, three generous bedrooms and a playroom will delight.

plan# HPT930320

- Style: French
- First Floor: 2,223 sq. ft.
- Second Floor: 1,163 sq. ft.
- Total: 3,386 sq. ft.
- Bedrooms: 4
- Bathrooms: 3½
- Width: 68'-10"
- Depth: 58'-1"
- Foundation: Crawlspace, Slab

SEARCH ONLINE @ EPLANS.COM

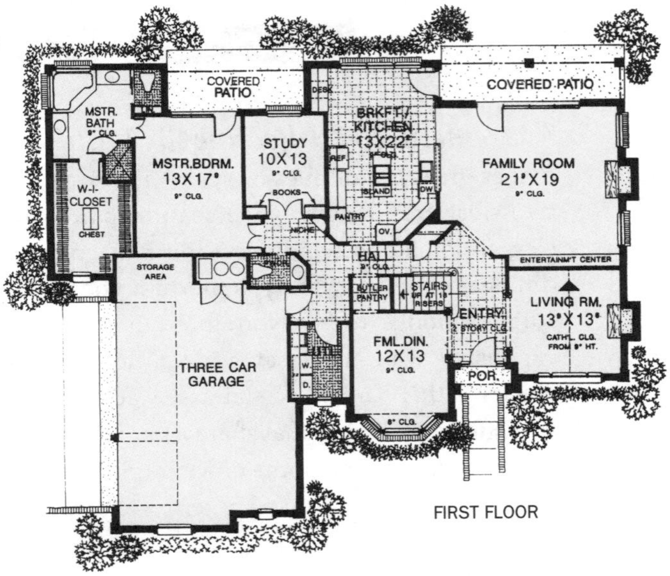

FIRST FLOOR

SECOND FLOOR

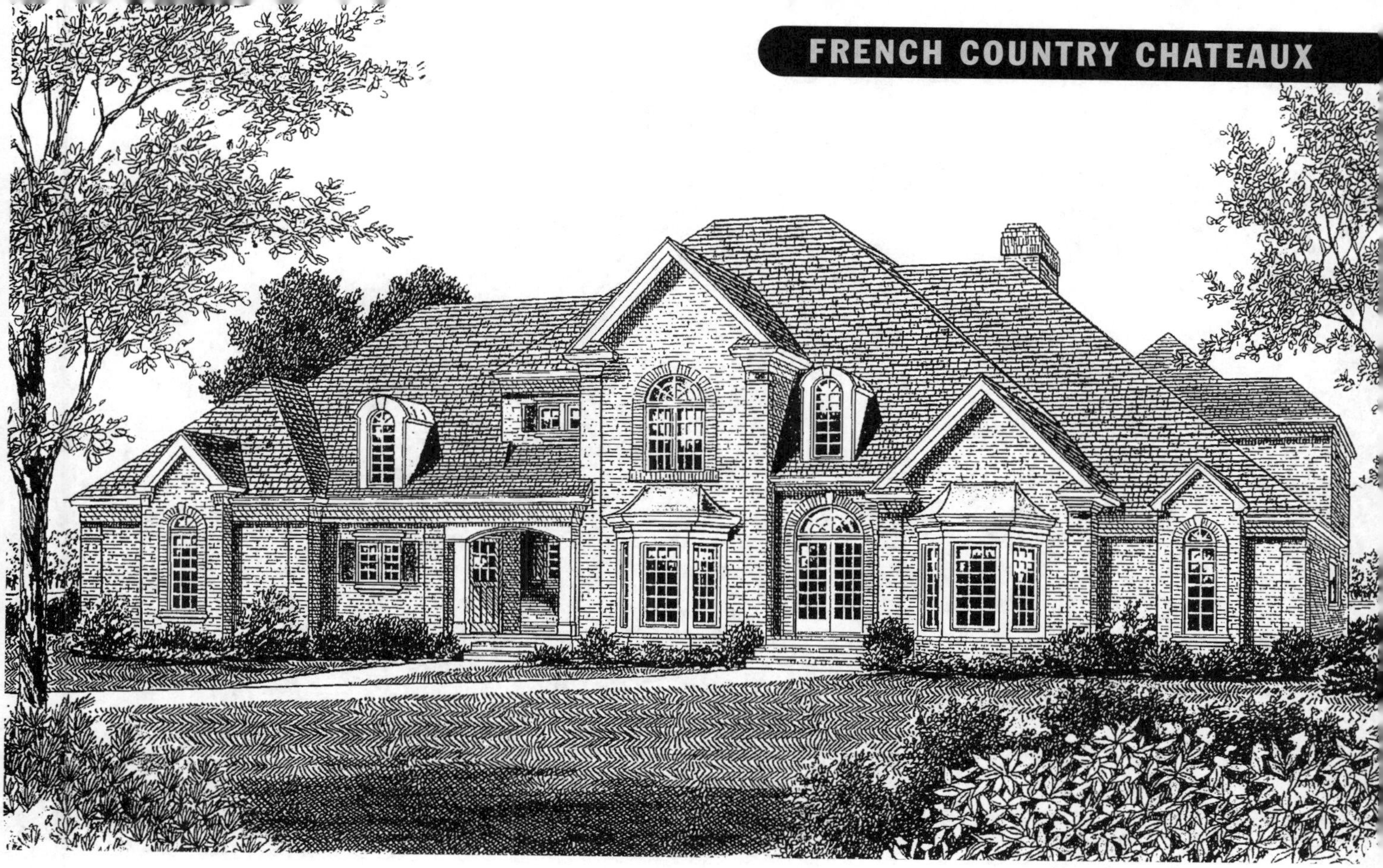

plan# HPT930321

- Style: Transitional
- First Floor: 2,588 sq. ft.
- Second Floor: 1,375 sq. ft.
- Total: 3,963 sq. ft.
- Bonus Space: 460 sq. ft.
- Bedrooms: 4
- Bathrooms: 3½
- Width: 91'-4"
- Depth: 51'-10"
- Foundation: Crawlspace

SEARCH ONLINE @ EPLANS.COM

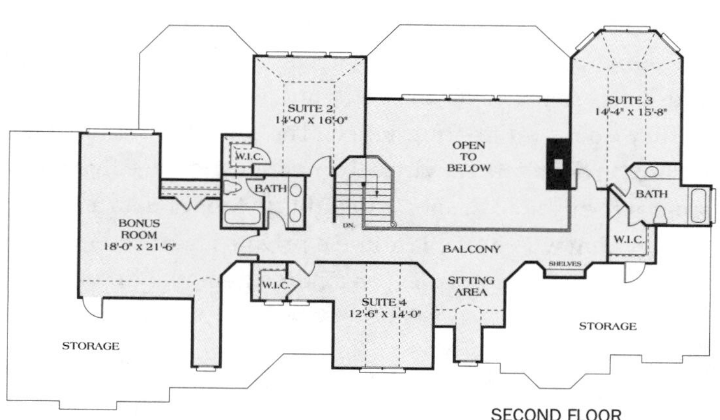

SECOND FLOOR

Though there are two entrances to this fine home, the one on the right is where friends and family should enter to truly absorb the grandeur of this design. The foyer is flanked by a bayed formal dining room and a bayed formal living room. Directly ahead is the lake gathering room, a spacious room with a welcoming fireplace and access to the rear veranda. Located on the first floor for privacy, the master suite is complete with a huge dressing closet, access to the veranda, and a lavish bath.

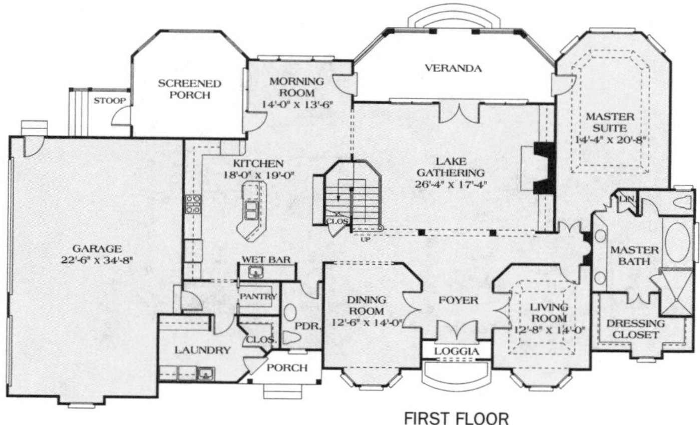

FIRST FLOOR

Storybook style lends irresistible charm to this captivating estate. Inside, vintage detailing blends artistically with modern amenities for a perfect balance. Hard-wood floors cover the entry and living areas; in the great room, a warming fireplace is an inviting touch. The kitchen and breakfast nook are accented with brick pavers for virtually maintenance-free flooring. A secluded master suite at the front of the home delights in tons of natural light, a splendid bath, a sitting room with a fireplace and a private lanai. Three upper-level bedrooms share a bonus room, perfect as a home gym, playroom or studio.

plan# HPT930322

- Style: Chateau
- First Floor: 2,431 sq. ft.
- Second Floor: 952 sq. ft.
- Total: 3,383 sq. ft.
- Bedrooms: 4
- Bathrooms: 3½
- Width: 70'-0"
- Depth: 64'-3"
- Foundation: Slab

SEARCH ONLINE @ EPLANS.COM

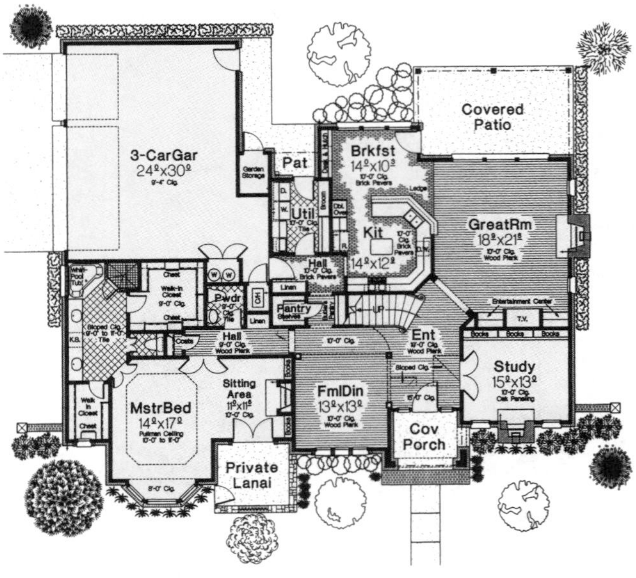

FIRST FLOOR

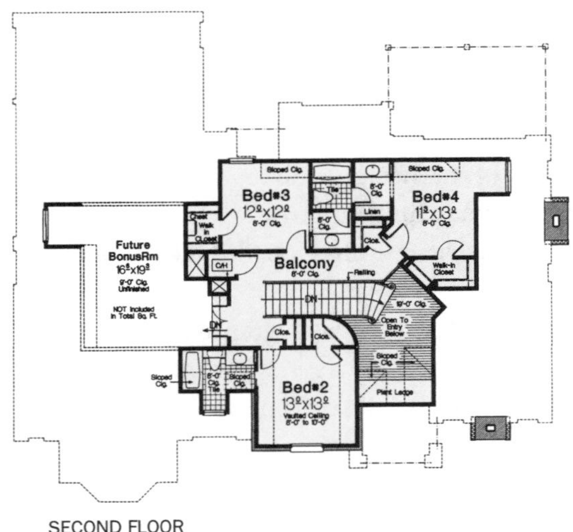

SECOND FLOOR

plan# HPT930323

- Style: European Cottage
- First Floor: 2,317 sq. ft.
- Second Floor: 1,302 sq. ft.
- Total: 3,619 sq. ft.
- Bedrooms: 4
- Bathrooms: 3½
- Width: 74'-0"
- Depth: 56'-4"
- Foundation: Slab

SEARCH ONLINE @ EPLANS.COM

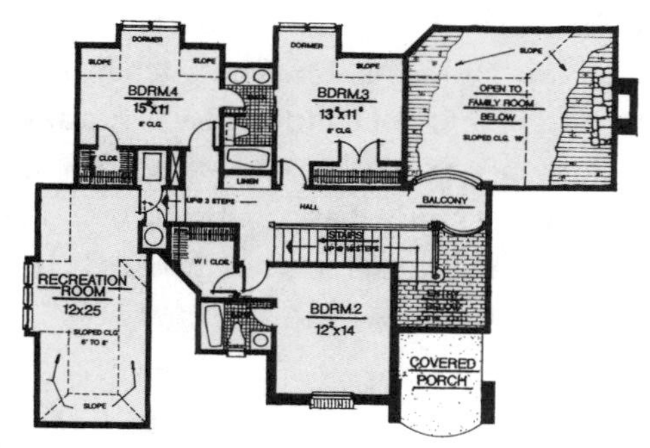

SECOND FLOOR

Stone and brick combine with gables and arches on the facade of this fine English manor. A grand arched doorway welcomes friends and family alike to this delightful design. Inside, the two-story foyer is flanked by the formal dining room to the left and a cozy study with a fireplace and built-in bookcases to the right. Directly ahead, the great room features a sloped ceiling and a stone hearth. The spacious kitchen offers a worktop island, a walk-in pantry and a serving counter to the sunny breakfast room. Separated for privacy, the first-floor master suite is complete with two walk-in closets, a lavish bath and a private patio area. Upstairs, Bedrooms 3 and 4 share a bath, while Bedroom 2 insists on privacy. The large recreation room is perfect for kids. A three-car garage will easily handle the family fleet.

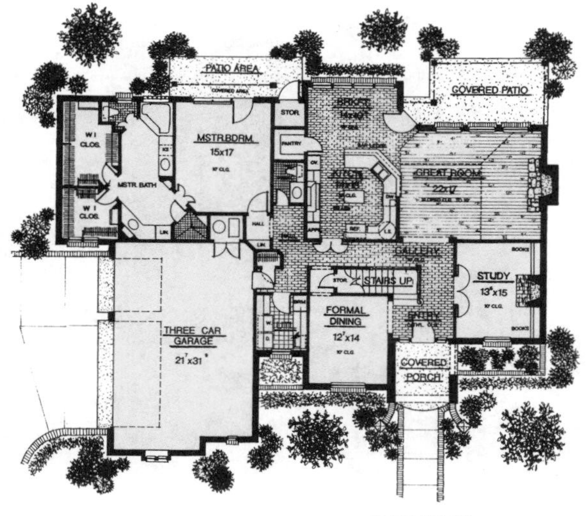

FIRST FLOOR

Multiple rooflines, a stone, brick and siding facade and an absolutely grand entrance combine to give this home the look of luxury. A striking family room showcases a beautiful fireplace framed with built-ins. The nearby breakfast room streams with light and accesses the rear patio. The kitchen features an island workstation, walk-in pantry and plenty of counter space. A guest suite is available on the first floor, perfect for when family members visit. The first-floor master suite enjoys easy access to a large study, bayed sitting room and luxurious bath. Private baths are also included for each of the upstairs bedrooms.

plan# HPT930324

- Style: French
- First Floor: 3,248 sq. ft.
- Second Floor: 1,426 sq. ft.
- Total: 4,674 sq. ft.
- Bedrooms: 5
- Bathrooms: 5½ + ½
- Width: 99'-10"
- Depth: 74'-10"
- Foundation: Basement

SEARCH ONLINE @ EPLANS.COM

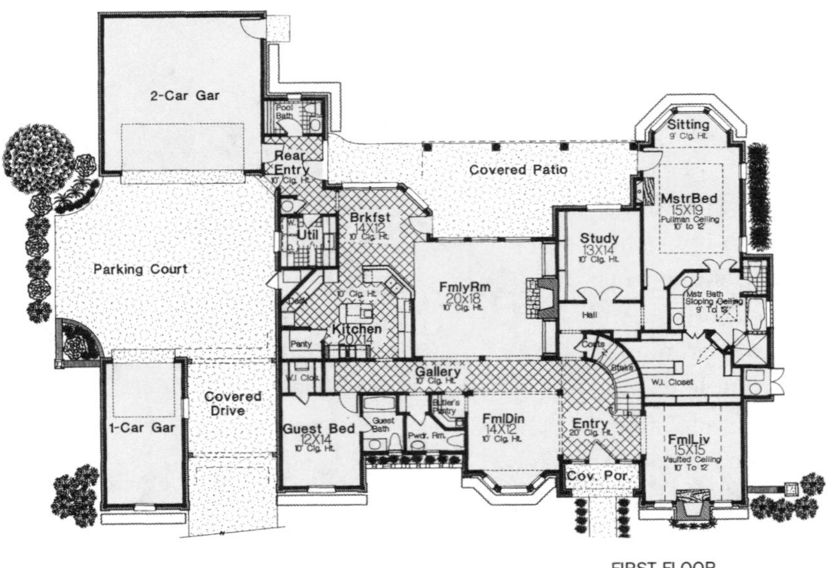

FIRST FLOOR

SECOND FLOOR

plan# HPT930325

- Style: French Country
- First Floor: 3,261sq. ft.
- Second Floor: 1,920 sq. ft.
- Total: 5,181 sq. ft.
- Bedrooms: 4
- Bathrooms: 3½
- Width: 86'-2"
- Depth: 66'-10"
- Foundation: Basement, Crawlspace

SEARCH ONLINE @ EPLANS.COM

This home is elegantly styled in the French country tradition. A large dining room and a study open off the two-story grand foyer. The large formal living room accesses the covered patio. A more informal family room is conveniently located off the kitchen and breakfast room. The master suite includes a sitting area, a luxurious private bath and its own entrance to the study. The second floor can be reached from the formal front stair or a well-placed rear staircase. Three large bedrooms and a game room are located on this floor.

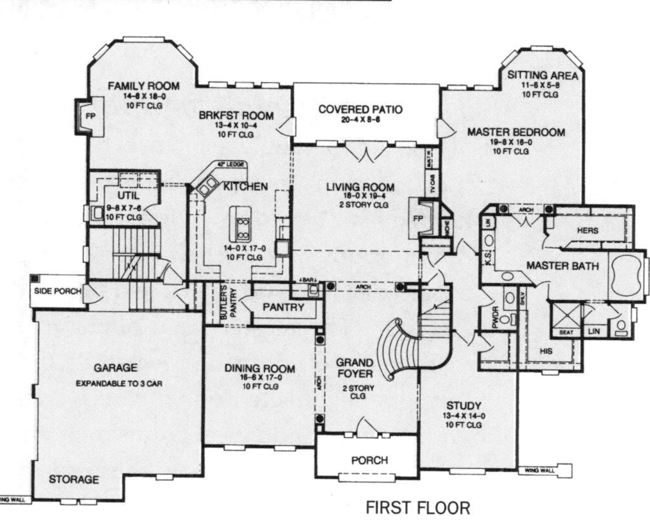

FIRST FLOOR

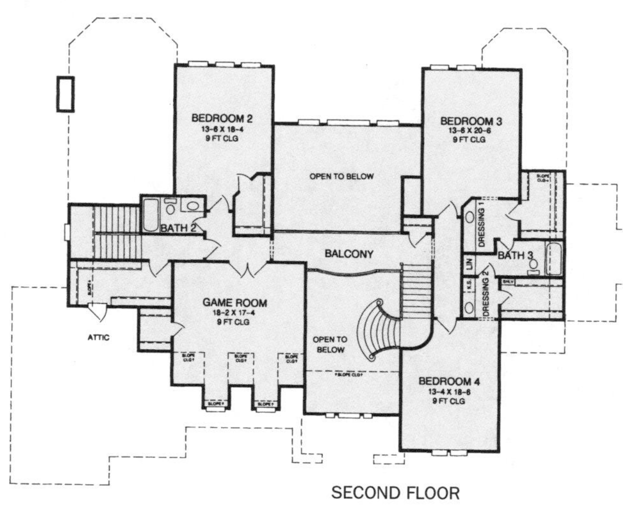

SECOND FLOOR

SECOND FLOOR

FIRST FLOOR

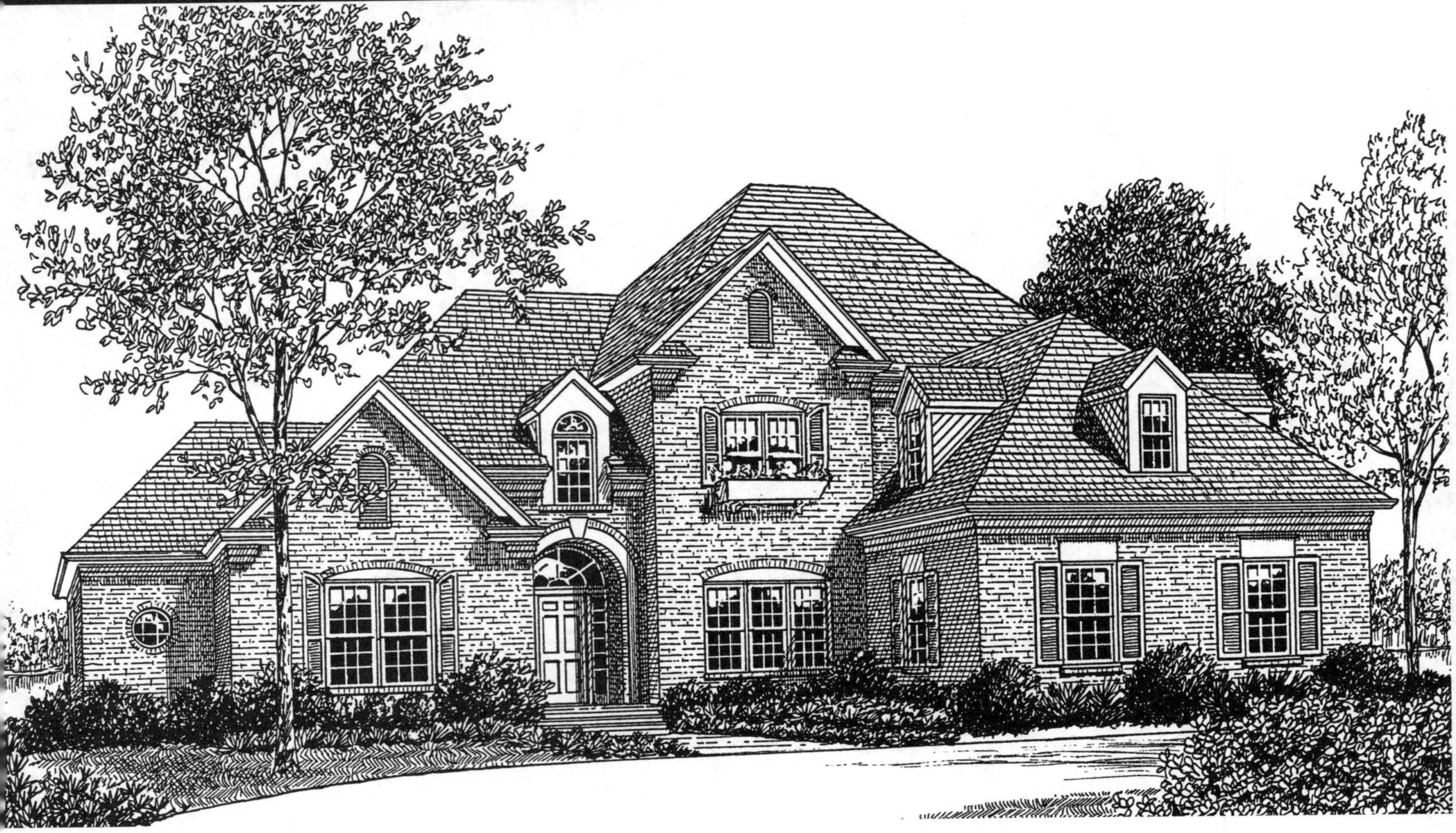

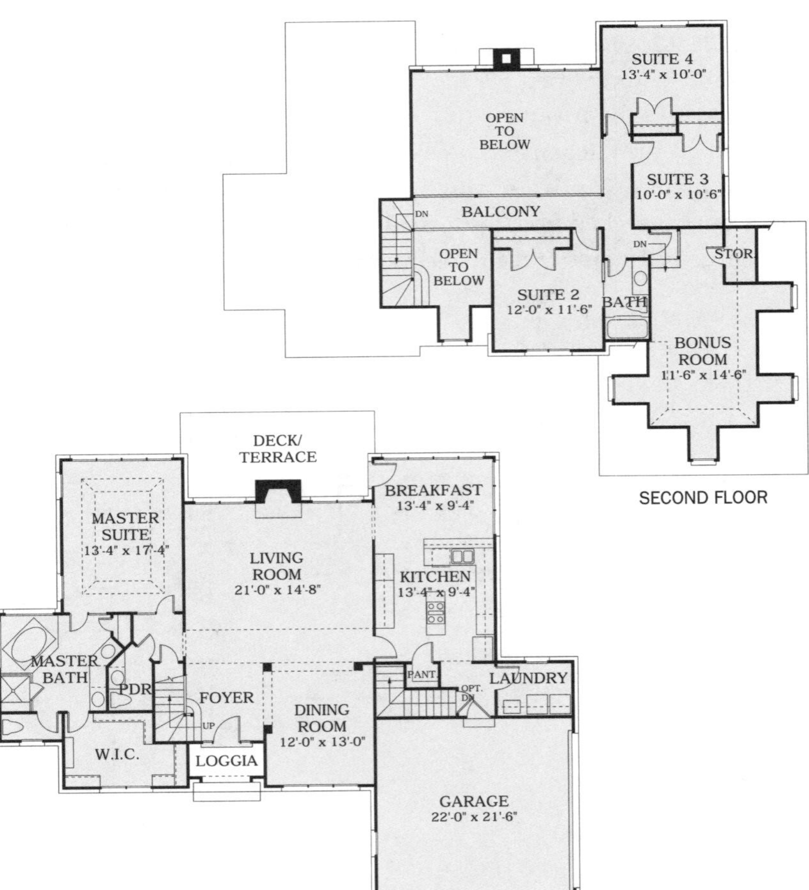

plan# HPT930326

- Style: Transitional
- First Floor: 1,737 sq. ft.
- Second Floor: 727 sq. ft.
- Total: 2,464 sq. ft.
- Bonus Space: 376 sq. ft.
- Bedrooms: 4
- Bathrooms: 2½
- Width: 65'-6"
- Depth: 53'-0"
- Foundation: Basement, Crawlspace

SEARCH ONLINE @ EPLANS.COM

The beauty and warmth of a brick facade adds stately elegance to this traditional design. Its open floor plan is highlighted by a two-story living room and open dining room. The kitchen includes a central cooking island, and opens to a bright breakfast area. The master suite offers an ample walk-in closet/dressing area and a bath featuring an exquisite double vanity and a tub with corner windows. A bonus room over the two-car garage offers room for expansion.

plan# HPT930327

- Style: French
- First Floor: 2,302 sq. ft.
- Second Floor: 1,177 sq. ft.
- Total: 3,479 sq. ft.
- Bedrooms: 4
- Bathrooms: 3½
- Width: 66'-3"
- Depth: 57'-9"
- Foundation: Walkout Basement

SEARCH ONLINE @ EPLANS.COM

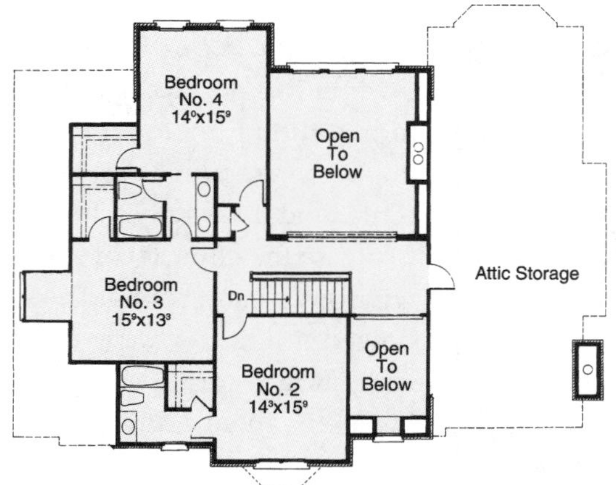

SECOND FLOOR

Gently arched cornices and keystones call up a sense of history with this traditional home. Formal rooms flank the two-story foyer, which leads to comfortably elegant living space with an extended-hearth fireplace. A sizable kitchen serves the formal dining room through a butler's pantry and overlooks the breakfast room. A secluded home office is a quiet place for business conversations. The master suite nestles to the rear of the plan and offers luxurious amenities. Upstairs, Bedrooms 3 and 4 share a full bath that includes two lavatories, while Bedroom 2 enjoys a private bath.

FIRST FLOOR

plan# HPT930328

- Style: French Country
- First Floor: 2,181 sq. ft.
- Second Floor: 710 sq. ft.
- Total: 2,891 sq. ft.
- Bonus Space: 240 sq. ft.
- Bedrooms: 3
- Bathrooms: 3
- Width: 66'-4"
- Depth: 79'-0"
- Foundation: Basement, Slab

SEARCH ONLINE @ EPLANS.COM

An arched, covered porch presents fine double doors leading to a spacious foyer in this decidedly European home. A two-story tower contains an elegant formal dining room on the first floor and a spacious bedroom on the second floor. The grand room is aptly named with a fireplace, a built-in entertainment center and three sets of doors opening onto the veranda. A large kitchen is ready to please the gourmet of the family with a big walk-in pantry and a sunny, bay-windowed eating nook. The secluded master suite is luxury in itself. A bay-windowed sitting area, access to the rear veranda, His and Hers walk-in closets and a lavish bath are all set to pamper you. Upstairs, two bedrooms, both with walk-in closets, share a full hall bath that includes twin vanities.

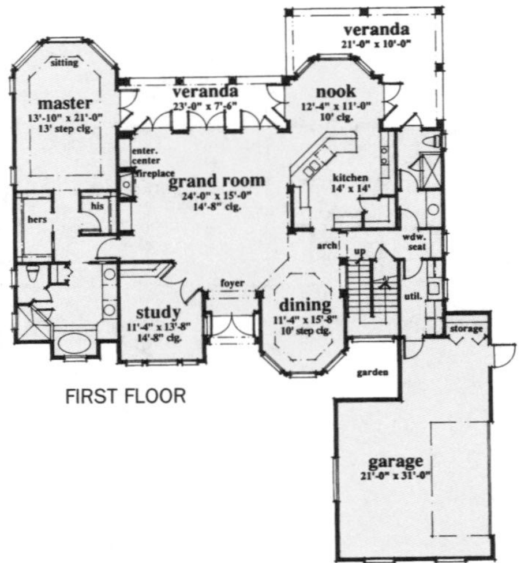

FIRST FLOOR

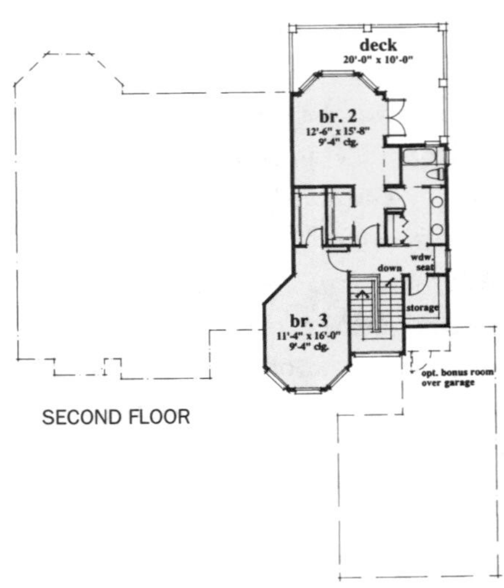

SECOND FLOOR

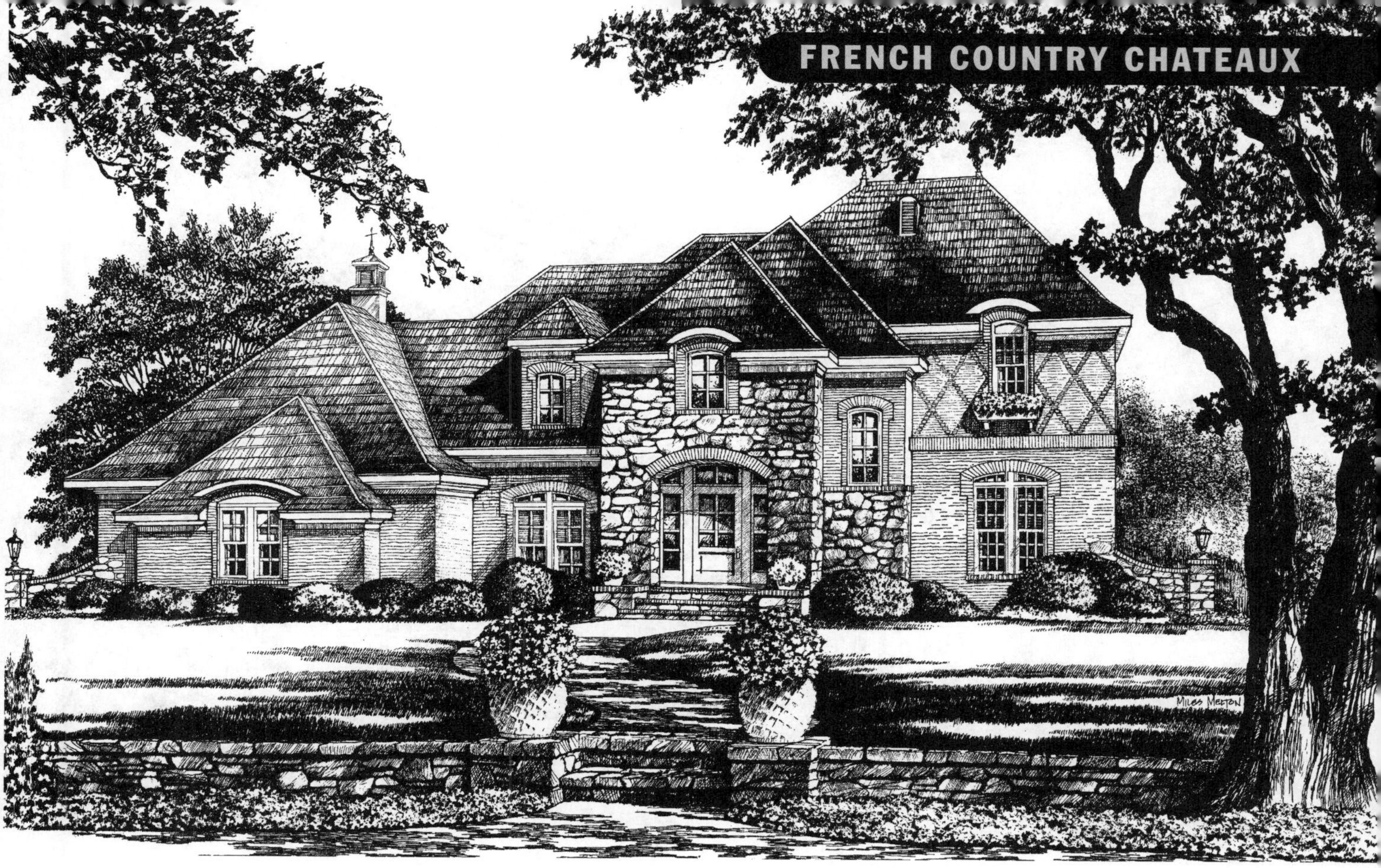

plan# HPT930329

- Style: European Cottage
- First Floor: 2,050 sq. ft.
- Second Floor: 561 sq. ft.
- Total: 2,611 sq. ft.
- Bonus Space: 272 sq. ft.
- Bedrooms: 4
- Bathrooms: 3
- Width: 64'-10"
- Depth: 64'-0"
- Foundation: Basement, Crawlspace, Slab

SEARCH ONLINE @ EPLANS.COM

Old World ambiance characterizes this European-style home. The elegant stone entrance opens to the two-story foyer. A well-proportioned dining room is viewed through an arch flanked by columns. The oversized great room features a coffered ceiling and a see-through fireplace that can be seen from the kitchen, breakfast room and great room. The master suite includes a luxury bath and a cozy sitting area off the bedroom. A second bedroom on this floor acts as a nursery, guest room or study. Upstairs, two roomy bedrooms share a bath, and an expandable area is available for future use.

SECOND FLOOR

FIRST FLOOR

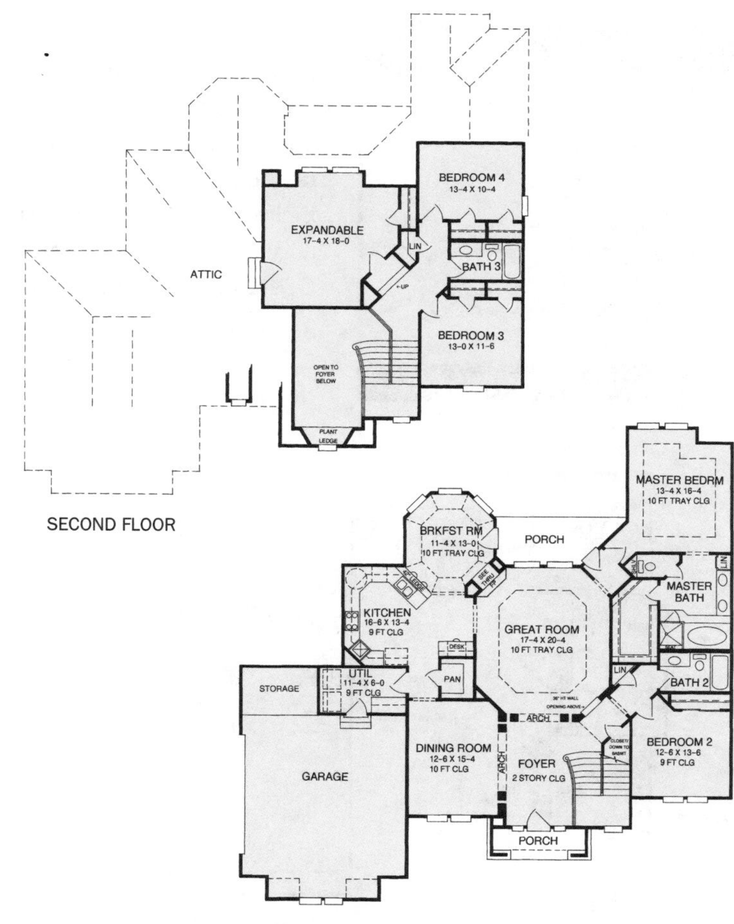

plan# HPT930330

- Style: French Country
- First Floor: 2,182 sq. ft.
- Second Floor: 856 sq. ft.
- Total: 3,038 sq. ft.
- Bedrooms: 4
- Bathrooms: 3½
- Width: 62'-0"
- Depth: 54'-0"
- Foundation: Crawlspace, Basement

SEARCH ONLINE @ EPLANS.COM

Arched windows, shutters and lintels add a touch of European flavor to this two-story, four-bedroom home. To the right of the two-story foyer is a living room, and to the left a spacious dining area. The vaulted great room is immense, and includes a see-through fireplace to the cooktop-island kitchen and the keeping room. A bayed breakfast area—accessible to a covered porch—is also included in this area of the home. The master bedroom features a tray ceiling and French doors opening to a luxurious private bath and a vast walk-in closet. Upstairs, each family bedroom is complete with an individual walk-in closet—one bedroom also contains a private full bath.

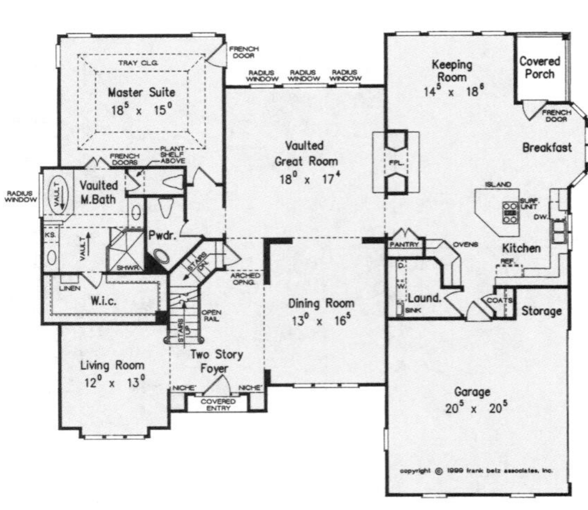

FIRST FLOOR

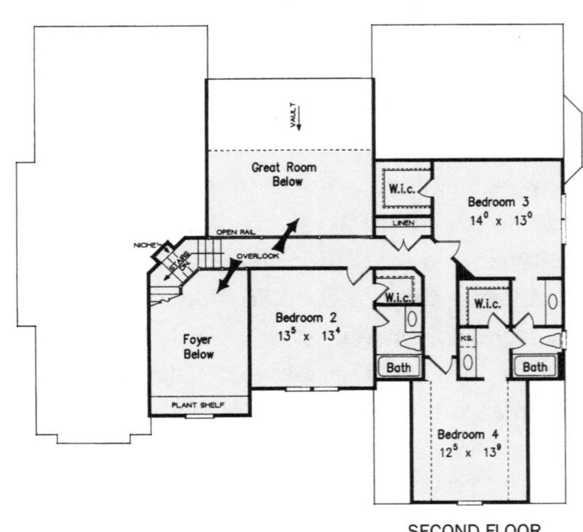

SECOND FLOOR

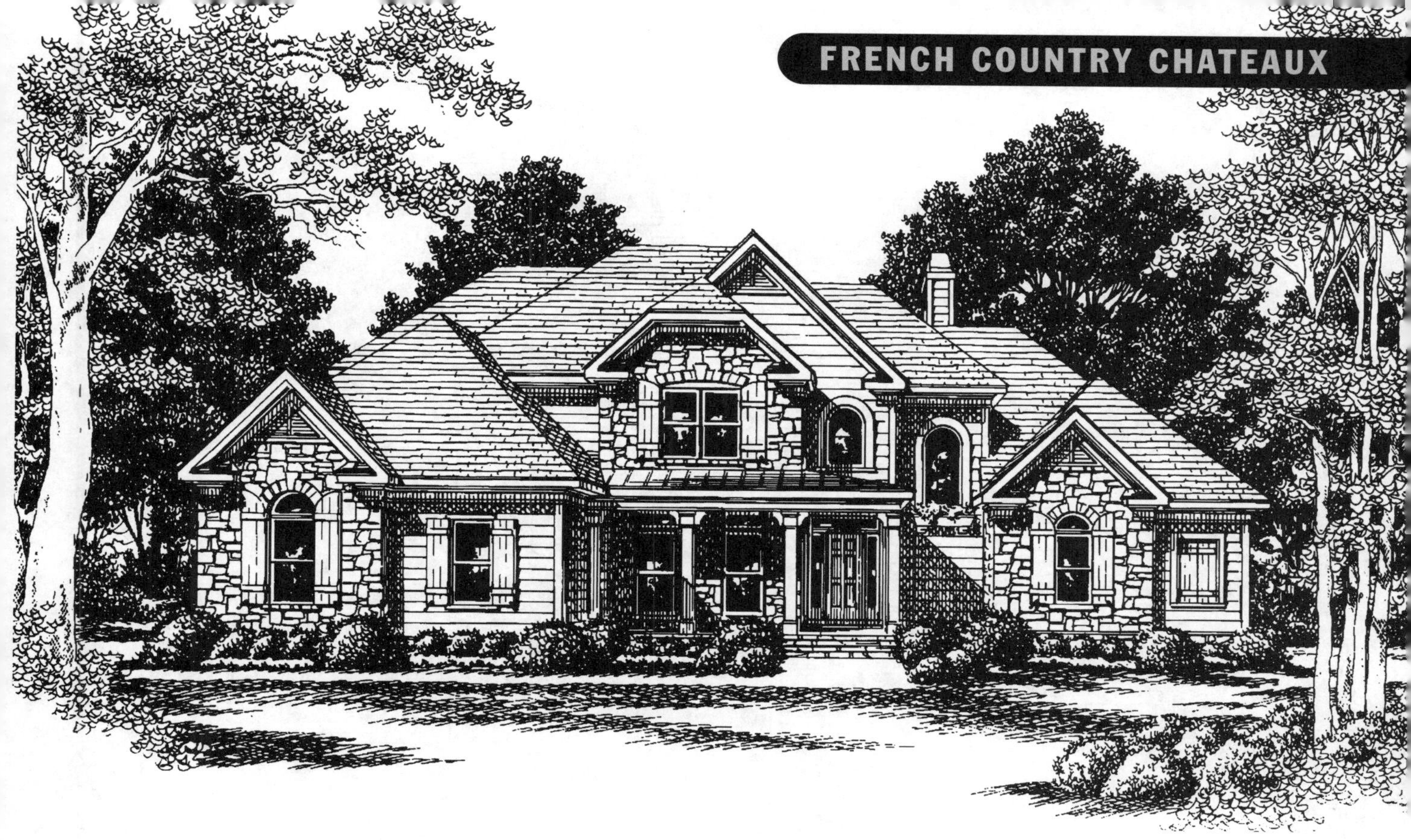

plan# HPT930331

- Style: French Country
- First Floor: 2,293 sq. ft.
- Second Floor: 992 sq. ft.
- Total: 3,285 sq. ft.
- Bonus Space: 131 sq. ft.
- Bedrooms: 4
- Bathrooms: 3½
- Width: 71'-0"
- Depth: 62'-0"
- Foundation: Crawlspace, Basement

SEARCH ONLINE @ EPLANS.COM

SECOND FLOOR

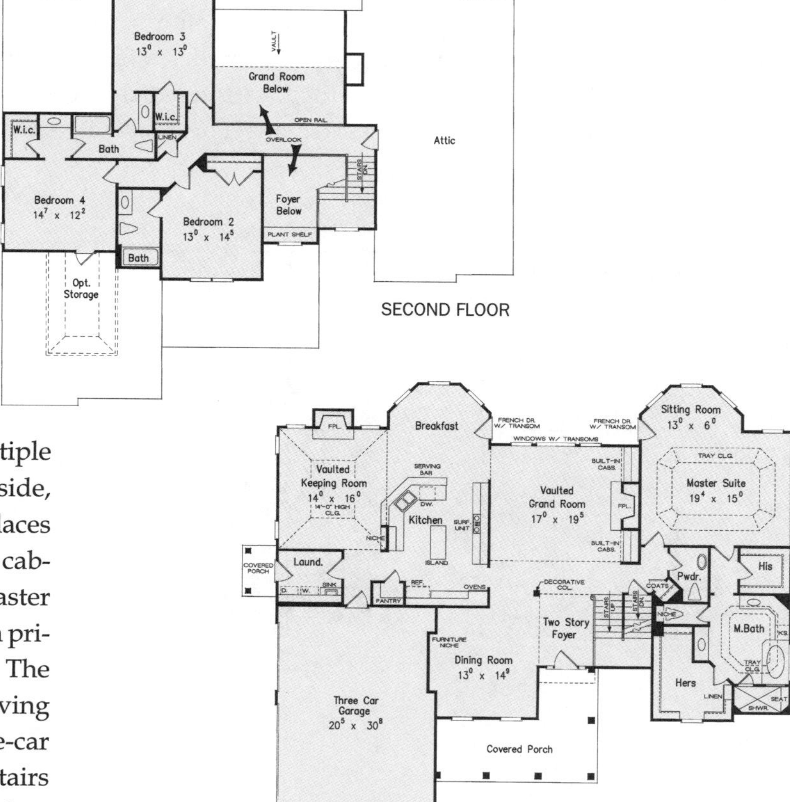

A combination of stone, siding and multiple rooflines creates a cottage feel to this large home. Inside, the grand room and keeping room both feature fireplaces and vaulted ceilings—the grand room adds built-in cabinets and windows with transoms. A sumptuous master suite enjoys a sitting room, a tray ceiling, and a lavish private bath featuring a shower with a built-in seat. The gourmet kitchen enjoys an island countertop, a serving bar, and a walk-in pantry which accesses the three-car garage. Three additional bedrooms are found upstairs with two full baths—Bedrooms 3 and 4 each include a large walk-in closet.

FIRST FLOOR

This stately home provides the owners with the winning combination of efficiency and extravagance. The interior features columns that add sophistication and comfort. The vaulted family room provides a fireplace and built-in shelves. Highly efficient and spacious, the U-shaped kitchen easily serves the bayed breakfast nook. The relaxing master suite offers a vaulted sitting room.

plan# HPT930332

- Style: French Country
- First Floor: 1,626 sq. ft.
- Second Floor: 541 sq. ft.
- Total: 2,167 sq. ft.
- Bonus Space: 256 sq. ft.
- Bedrooms: 3
- Bathrooms: 2½
- Width: 53'-0"
- Depth: 43'-4"
- Foundation: Crawlspace, Slab, Basement

SEARCH ONLINE @ EPLANS.COM

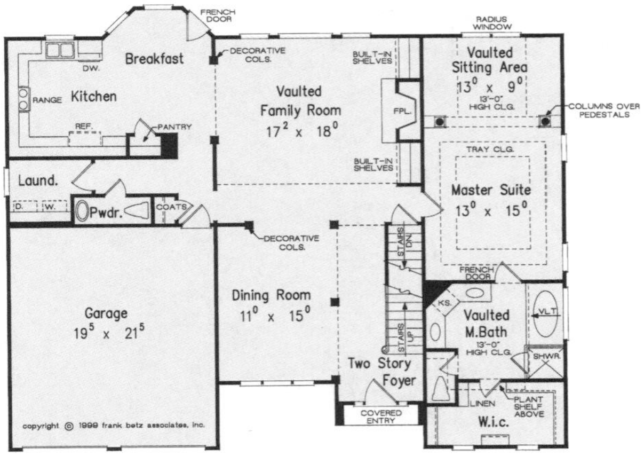

FIRST FLOOR

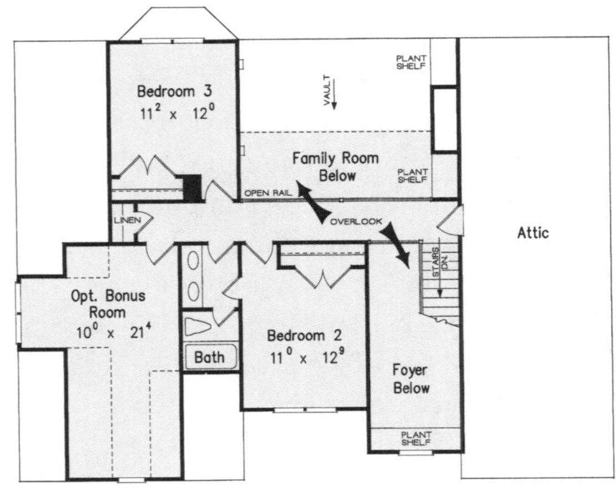

SECOND FLOOR

plan# HPT930333

- Style: French Country
- First Floor: 1,628 sq. ft.
- Second Floor: 527 sq. ft.
- Total: 2,155 sq. ft.
- Bonus Space: 207 sq. ft.
- Bedrooms: 3
- Bathrooms: 2½
- Width: 54'-0"
- Depth: 46'-10"
- Foundation: Crawlspace, Slab, Basement

SEARCH ONLINE @ EPLANS.COM

Multiple rooflines, charming stonework and a covered entryway all combine to give this home plenty of curb appeal. Inside, the two-story foyer leads to either the formal dining room on the right or the spacious vaulted great room at the back. Here, a fireplace waits to warm cool evenings and a French door gives access to the rear yard. The large efficient kitchen offers plenty of counter and cabinet space and works well with the vaulted breakfast room and nearby vaulted keeping room. Sleeping quarters are split for privacy, with the deluxe master suite located on the first floor and two secondary bedrooms sharing a full bath on the second floor.

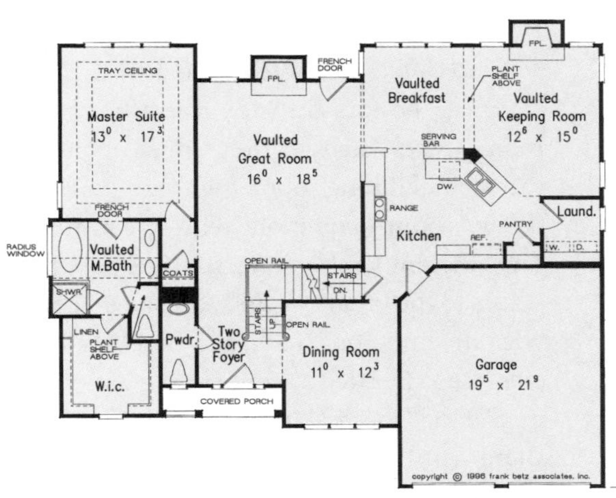

FIRST FLOOR

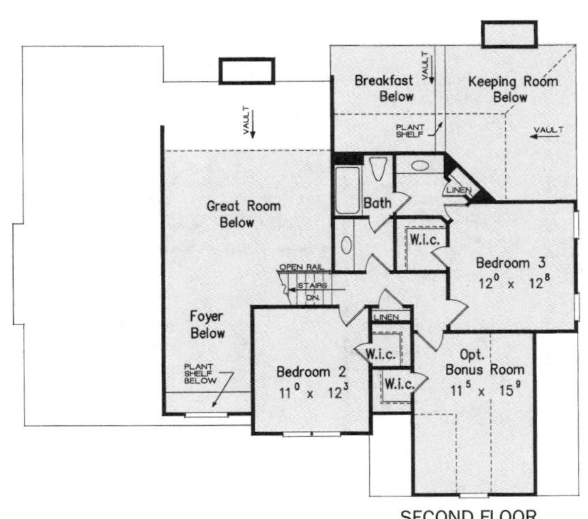

SECOND FLOOR

plan# HPT930334

- Style: French Country
- First Floor: 1,382 sq. ft.
- Second Floor: 436 sq. ft.
- Total: 3,200 sq. ft.
- Bonus Space: 298 sq. ft.
- Bedrooms: 3
- Bathrooms: 2½
- Width: 52'-4"
- Depth: 45'-10"
- Foundation: Crawlspace, Slab, Basement

SEARCH ONLINE @ EPLANS.COM

Variety in the facade is just a prelude to the charm to be found inside this attractive three-bedroom home. The two-story foyer opens on the right to a formal dining room, then leads back to a vaulted family room—complete with a warming fireplace. The efficient kitchen offers a breakfast bar and easy access to the breakfast area. The master suite is lavish with its amenities. Included here is a huge walk-in closet, a separate tub and shower, and a tray ceiling in the bedroom. Upstairs, two family bedrooms share a full hall bath. An optional bonus room is available for future development.

plan# HPT930335

- Style: French Country
- First Floor: 1,418 sq. ft.
- Second Floor: 1,844 sq. ft.
- Total: 3,262 sq. ft.
- Bedrooms: 4
- Bathrooms: 3½
- Width: 63'-0"
- Depth: 41'-0"
- Foundation: Crawlspace, Slab, Basement

SEARCH ONLINE @ EPLANS.COM

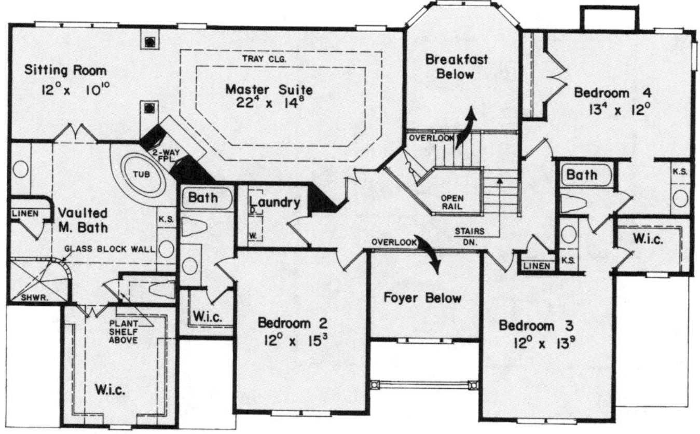

SECOND FLOOR

Hipped rooflines, lintels and French-style shutters give this home a taste of Europe. The two-story foyer is flanked by the formal living and dining rooms, and the living room opens through French doors to a private covered porch. A spacious, sunken family room features a warming fireplace framed by windows. The second floor has an overlook to the breakfast area and foyer. The lavish master bedroom provides a tray ceiling, a sitting room, a through-fireplace and a sumptuous bath. Three family bedrooms and two full baths complete this level.

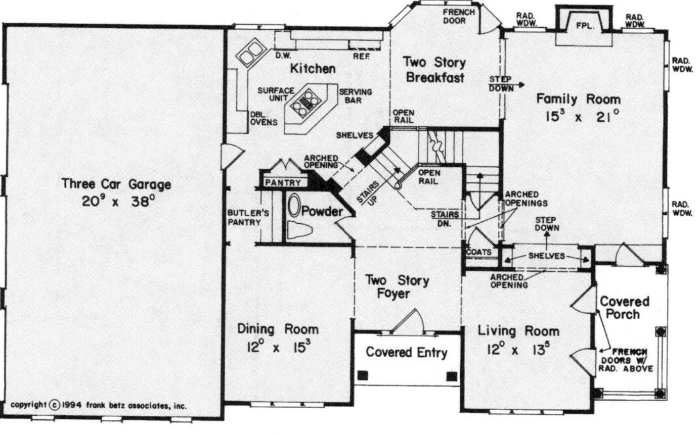

FIRST FLOOR

SECOND FLOOR

FIRST FLOOR

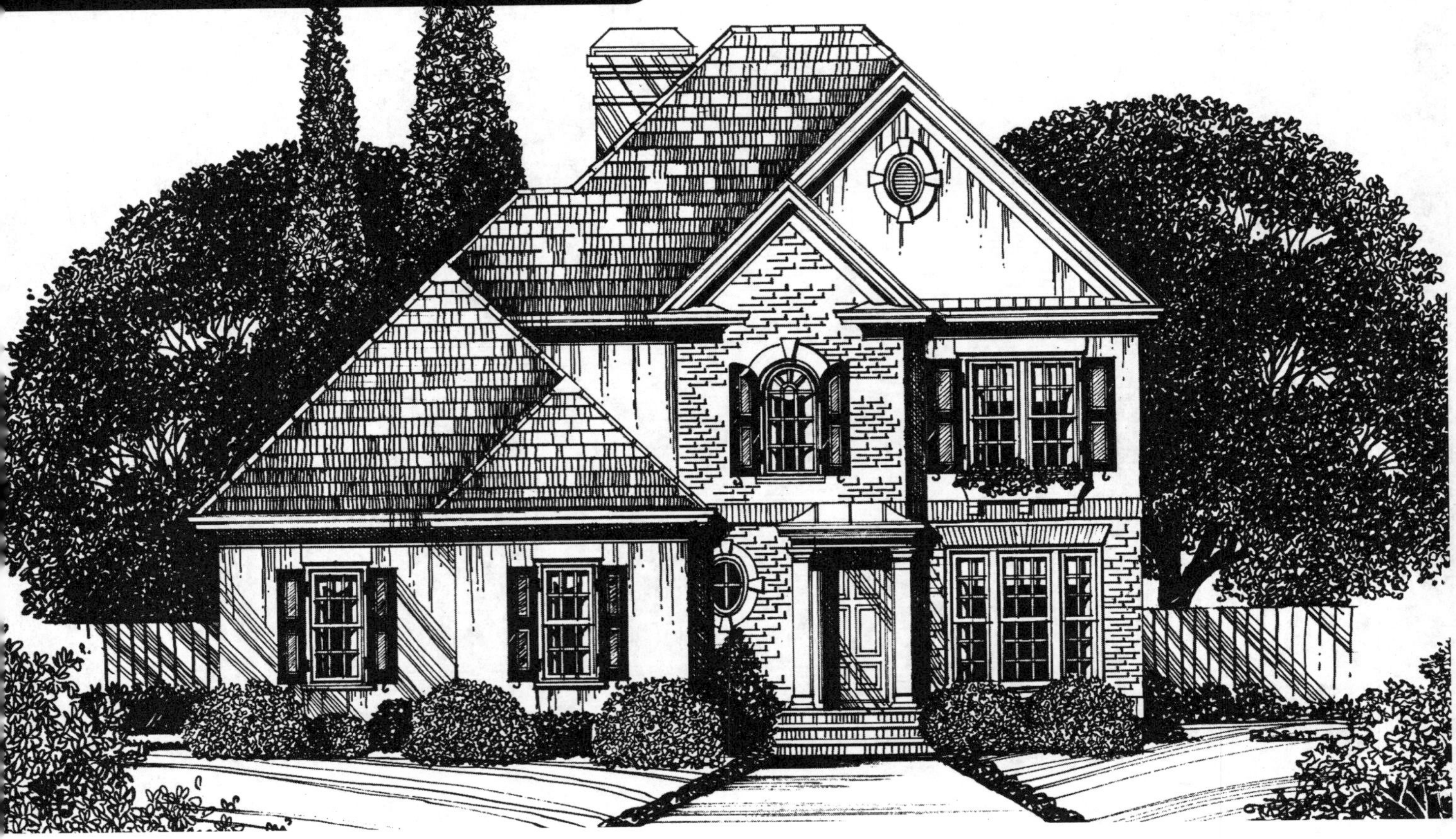

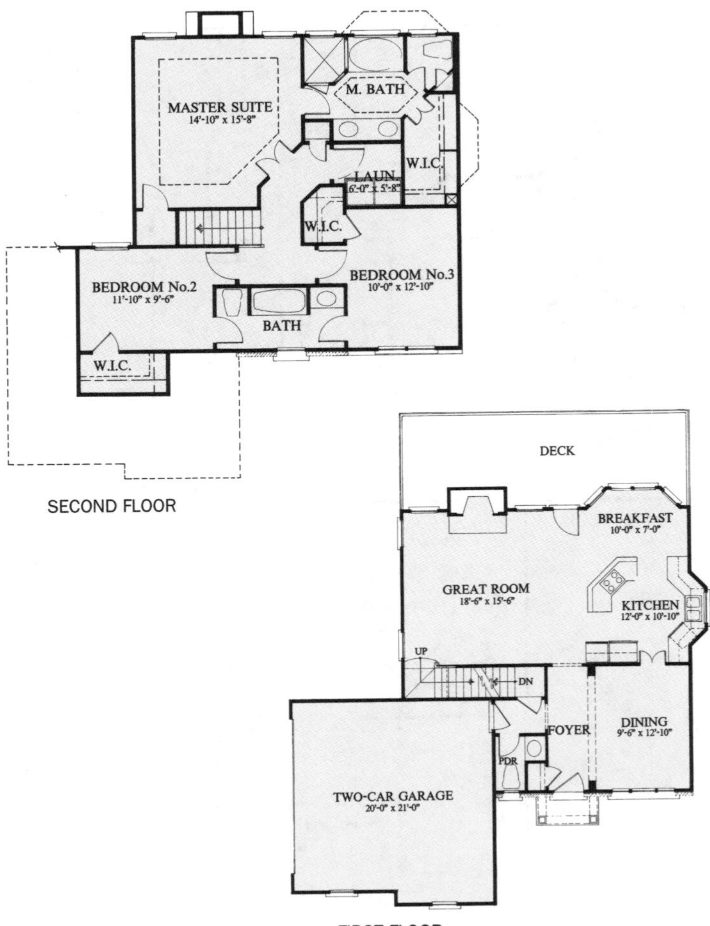

plan# HPT930336

- Style: French Country
- First Floor: 780 sq. ft.
- Second Floor: 915 sq. ft.
- Total: 1,695 sq. ft.
- Bedrooms: 3
- Bathrooms: 2½
- Width: 41'-0"
- Depth: 41'-0"
- Foundation: Walkout Basement

SEARCH ONLINE @ EPLANS.COM

Columns, brickwork and uniquely shaped windows and shutters remind us of the best homes of turn-of-the-century America. Inside, contemporary priorities reign. To the right of the foyer is a formal dining room with a passage to the kitchen, which is open to the breakfast area and great room. This area is particularly well-suited to entertaining both formally and informally, with an open, airy design. The large fireplace, framed by windows, creates a lovely focal point in the great room. Upstairs, double doors lead to the lavish master suite, which features a tray ceiling. The adjoining bath and walk-in closet complement this area. Bedrooms 2 and 3 complete this floor, with a shared bath featuring private entrances.

SECOND FLOOR

FIRST FLOOR

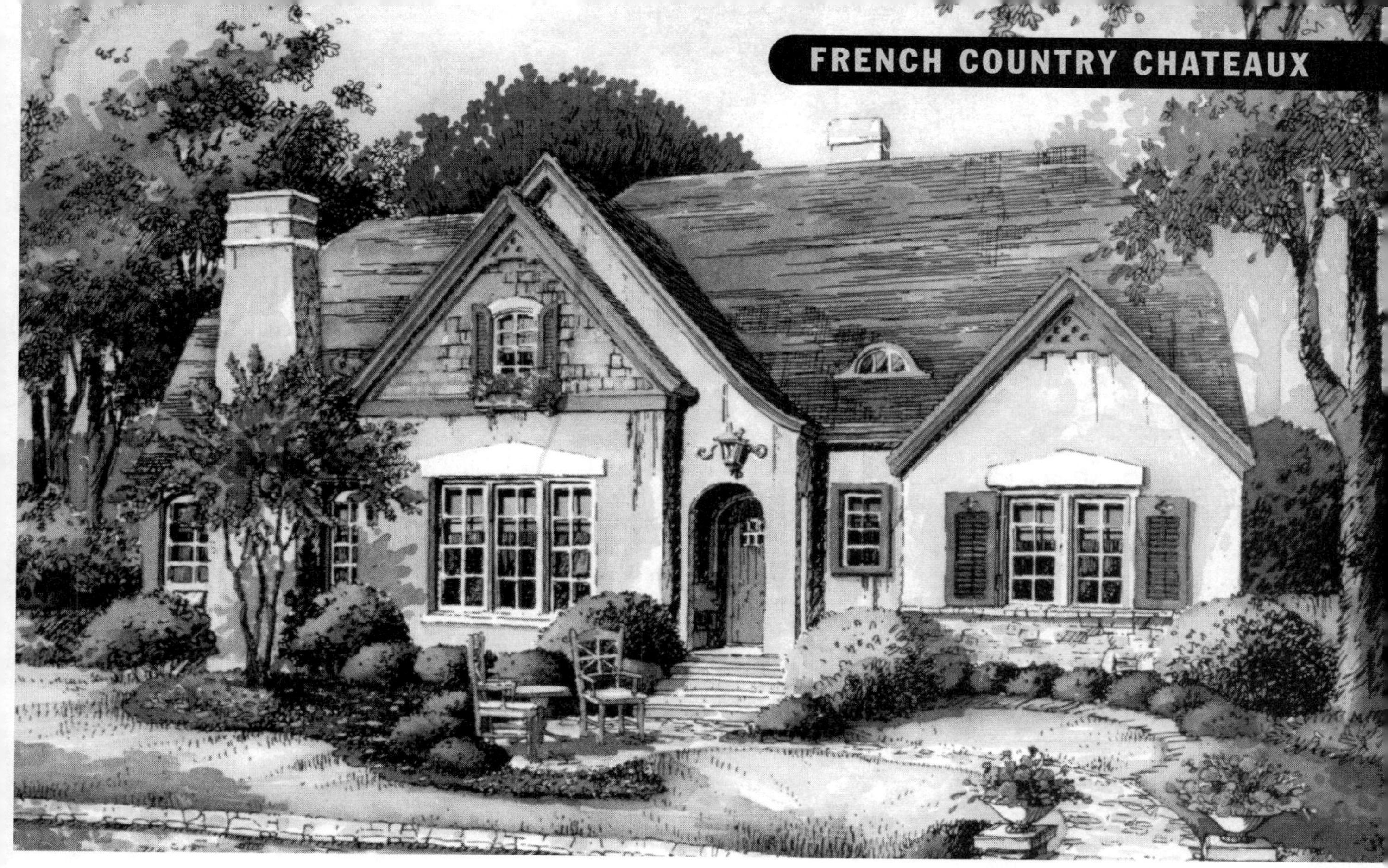

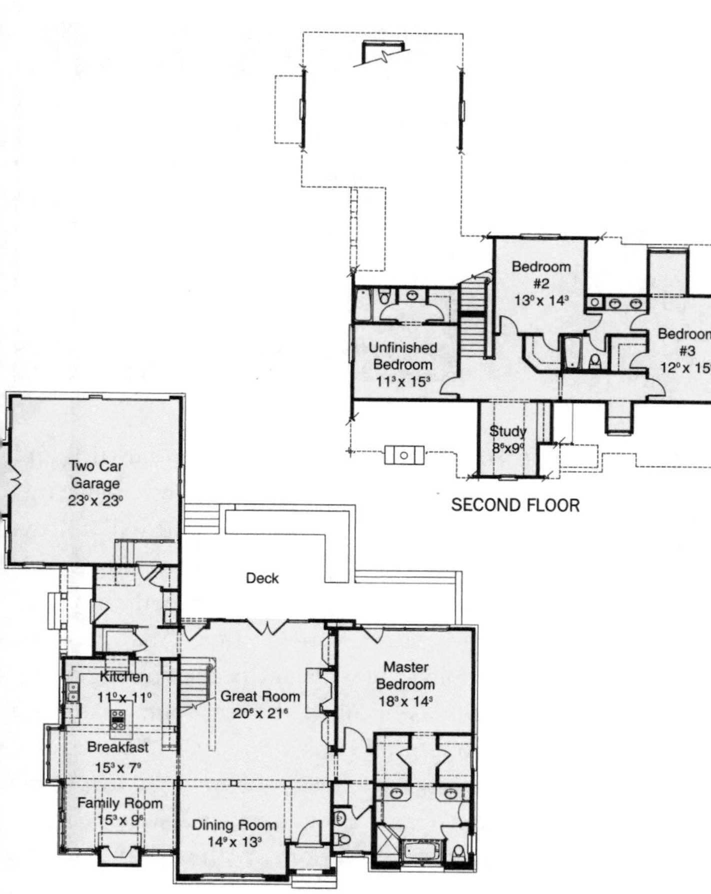

plan# HPT930337

- Style: European Cottage
- First Floor: 1,840 sq. ft.
- Second Floor: 840 sq. ft.
- Total: 2,680 sq. ft.
- Bonus Space: 295 sq. ft.
- Bedrooms: 3
- Bathrooms: 2½
- Width: 66'-0"
- Depth: 65'-10"
- Foundation: Crawlspace

SEARCH ONLINE @ EPLANS.COM

Multi-pane windows, shutters and shingle accents adorn the stucco facade of this wonderful French country home. Inside, the foyer introduces the hearth-warmed great room that features French-door access to the rear deck. The dining room, defined from the foyer and great room by columns, enjoys front-yard views. The master bedroom includes two walk-in closets, rear-deck access and a dual vanity bath. The informal living areas have an open plan. The box-bayed breakfast nook joins the cooktop-island kitchen and hearth-warmed family room. The second floor holds two bedrooms with walk-in closets, a study and an unfinished bedroom for future expansion.

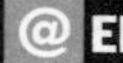

SECOND FLOOR

FIRST FLOOR

plan# HPT930338

- Style: French
- First Floor: 1,724 sq. ft.
- Second Floor: 700 sq. ft.
- Total: 2,424 sq. ft.
- Bedrooms: 3
- Bathrooms: 2½
- Width: 47'-10"
- Depth: 63'-8"
- Foundation: Walkout Basement

SEARCH ONLINE @ EPLANS.COM

All the charm of gables, stonework and multi-level rooflines combine to create this home. To the left of the foyer, you will see the dining room highlighted by a tray ceiling. This room and the living room flow together to form one large entertainment area. The gourmet kitchen holds a work island and adjoining octagonal breakfast room. The great room features a pass-through wet bar, a fireplace and bookcases. The master suite enjoys privacy at the rear of the home. An open-rail loft above the foyer leads to two additional bedrooms with walk-in closets, private vanities and a shared bath.

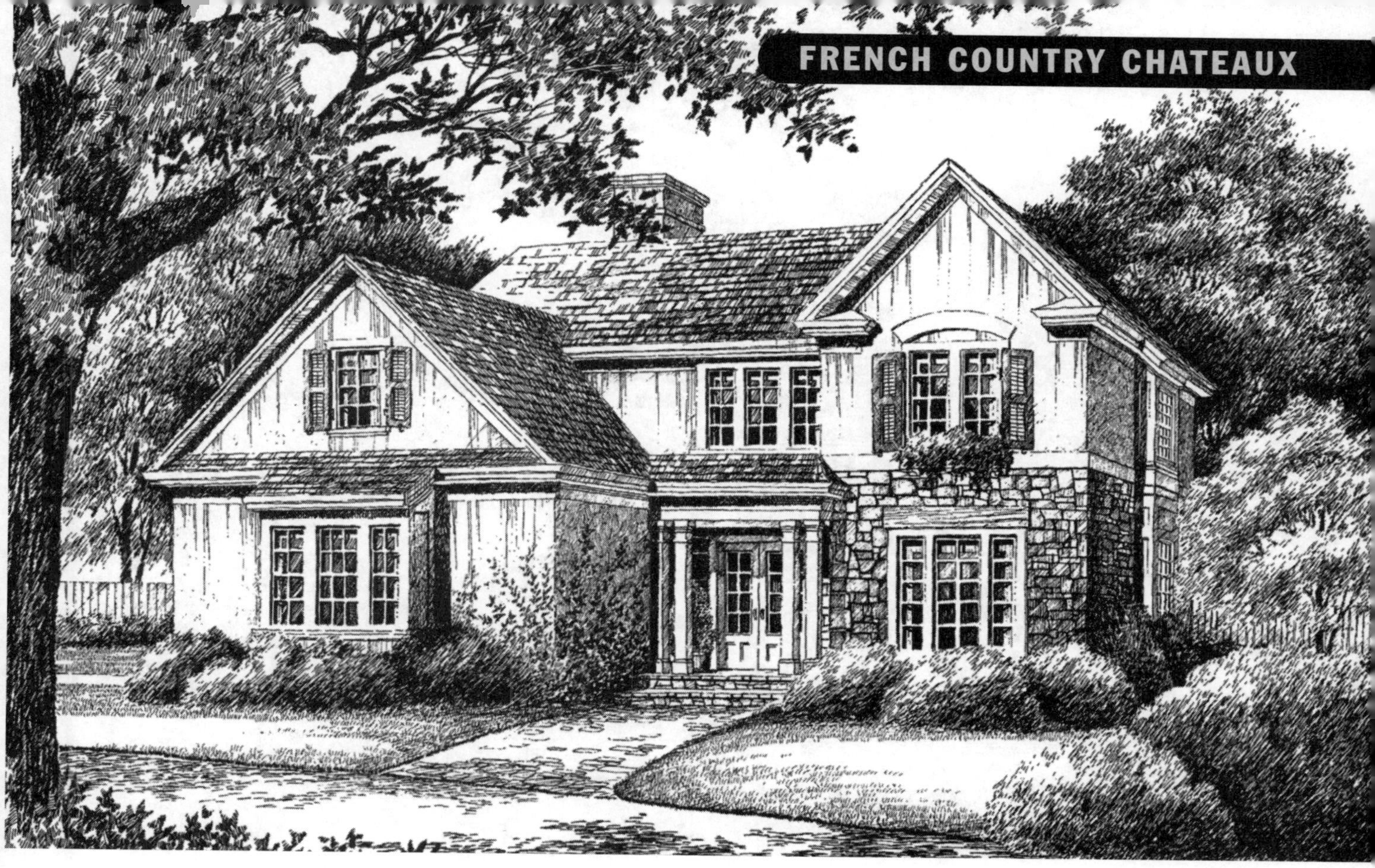

plan# HPT930339

- Style: European Cottage
- First Floor: 1,395 sq. ft.
- Second Floor: 1,210 sq. ft.
- Total: 2,605 sq. ft.
- Bonus Space: 225 sq. ft.
- Bedrooms: 3
- Bathrooms: 2½
- Width: 47'-0"
- Depth: 49'-6"
- Foundation: Basement

SEARCH ONLINE @ EPLANS.COM

The well-balanced use of stucco and stone combined with box-bay window treatments and a covered entry make this English country home especially inviting. The two-story foyer opens on the right to formal living and dining rooms, bright with natural light. A spacious U-shaped kitchen adjoins a breakfast nook with views of the outdoors. This area flows nicely into the two-story great room, which offers a through-fireplace to the media room. A plush retreat awaits the homeowner upstairs with a master suite that offers a quiet, windowed sitting area with views to the rear grounds. Two family bedrooms share a full bath and a balcony hall that has a dramatic view of the great room below.

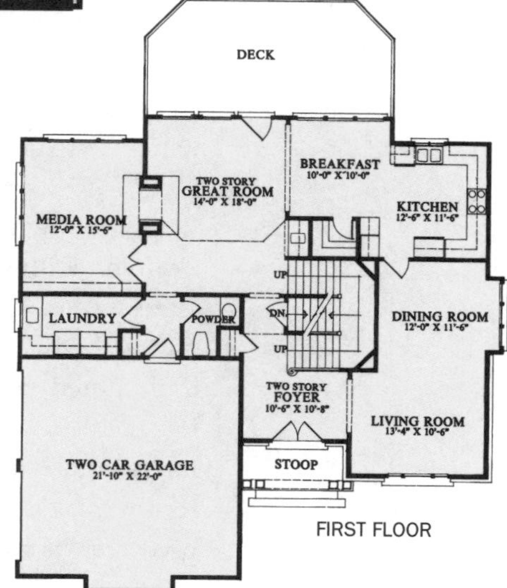

QUOTE ONE®

Cost to build? See page 436 to order complete cost estimate to build this house in your area!

SECOND FLOOR

FIRST FLOOR

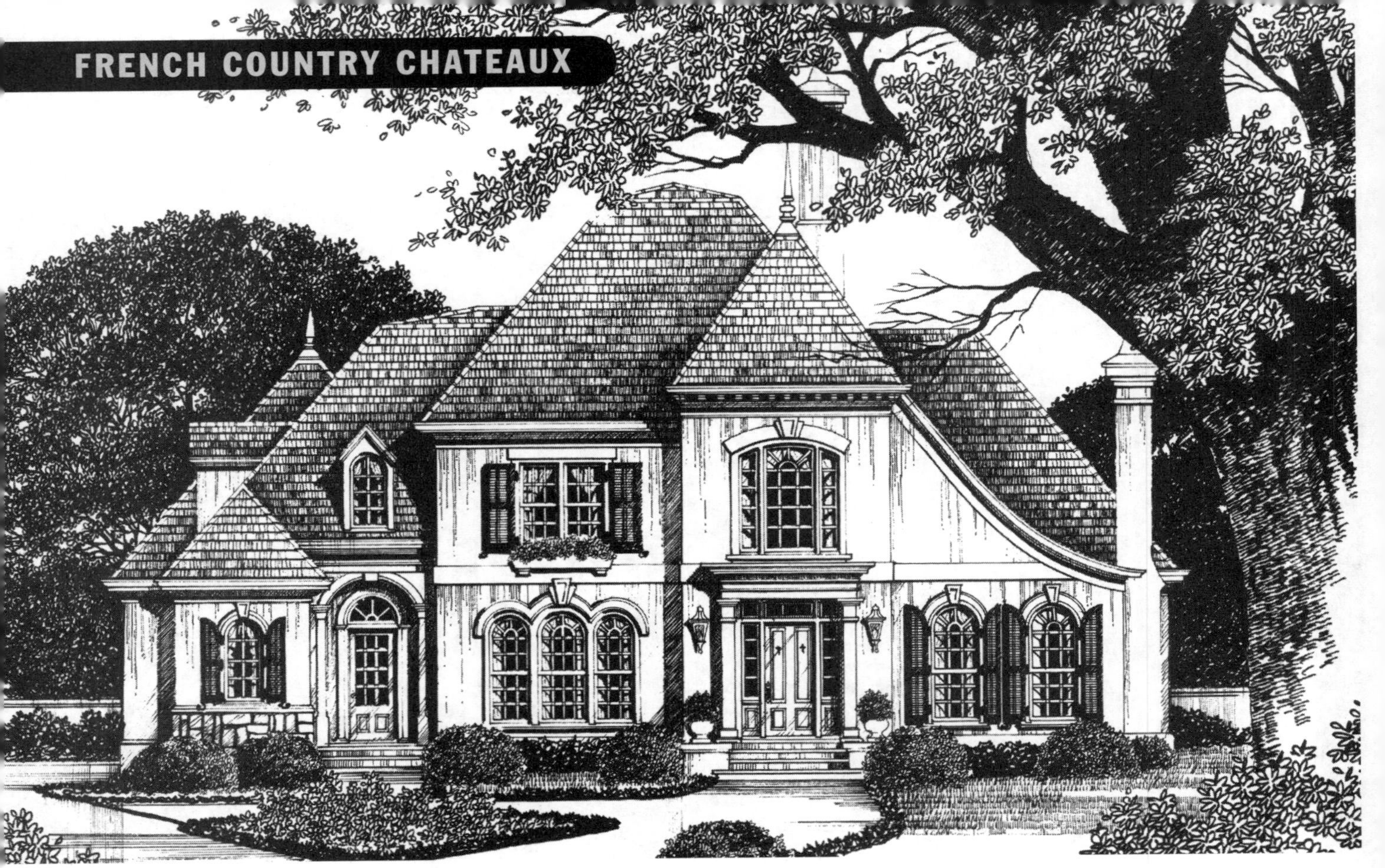

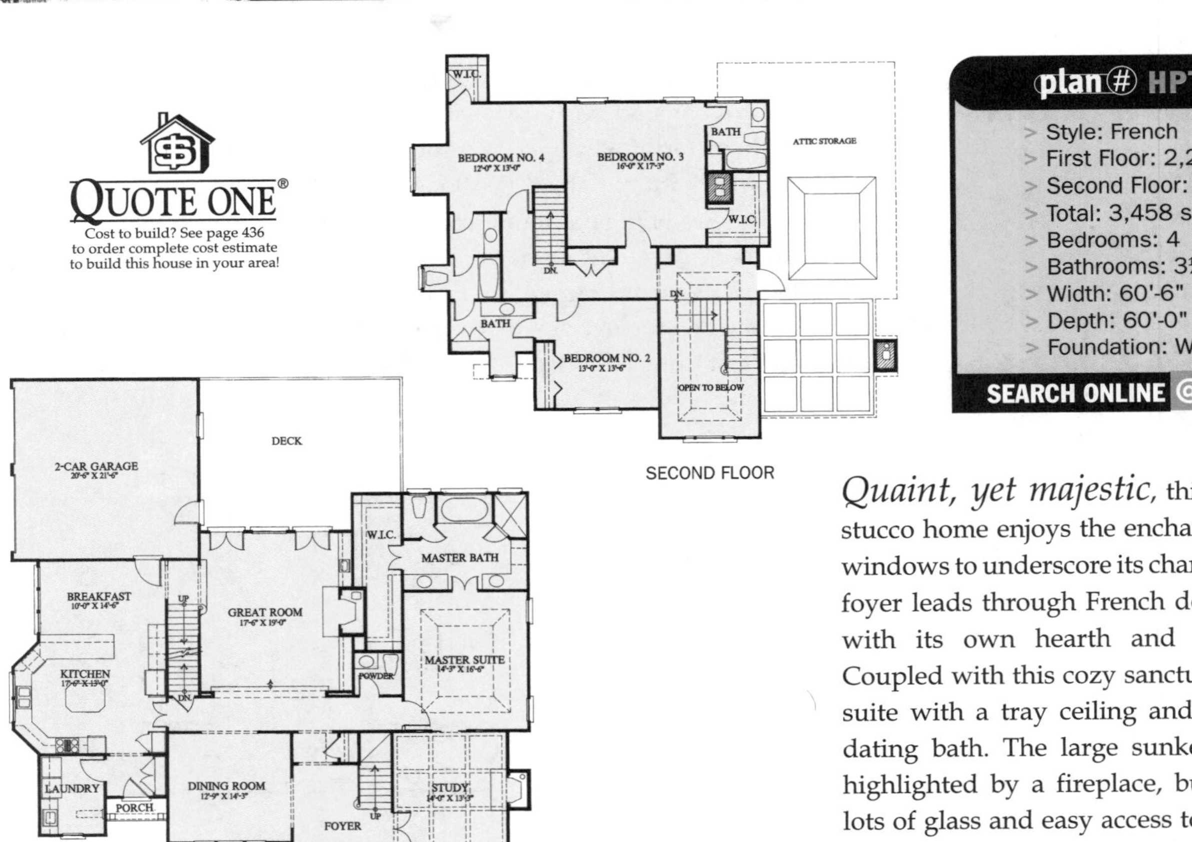

plan# HPT930340

- Style: French
- First Floor: 2,208 sq. ft.
- Second Floor: 1,250 sq. ft.
- Total: 3,458 sq. ft.
- Bedrooms: 4
- Bathrooms: 3½
- Width: 60'-6"
- Depth: 60'-0"
- Foundation: Walkout Basement

SEARCH ONLINE @ EPLANS.COM

Quaint, yet majestic, this European-style stucco home enjoys the enchantment of arched windows to underscore its charm. The two-story foyer leads through French doors to the study with its own hearth and coffered ceiling. Coupled with this cozy sanctuary is the master suite with a tray ceiling and large accommodating bath. The large sunken great room is highlighted by a fireplace, built-in bookcases, lots of glass and easy access to a back stair and large gourmet kitchen. Three secondary bedrooms reside upstairs. One upstairs bedroom gives guests a private bath and walk-in closet.

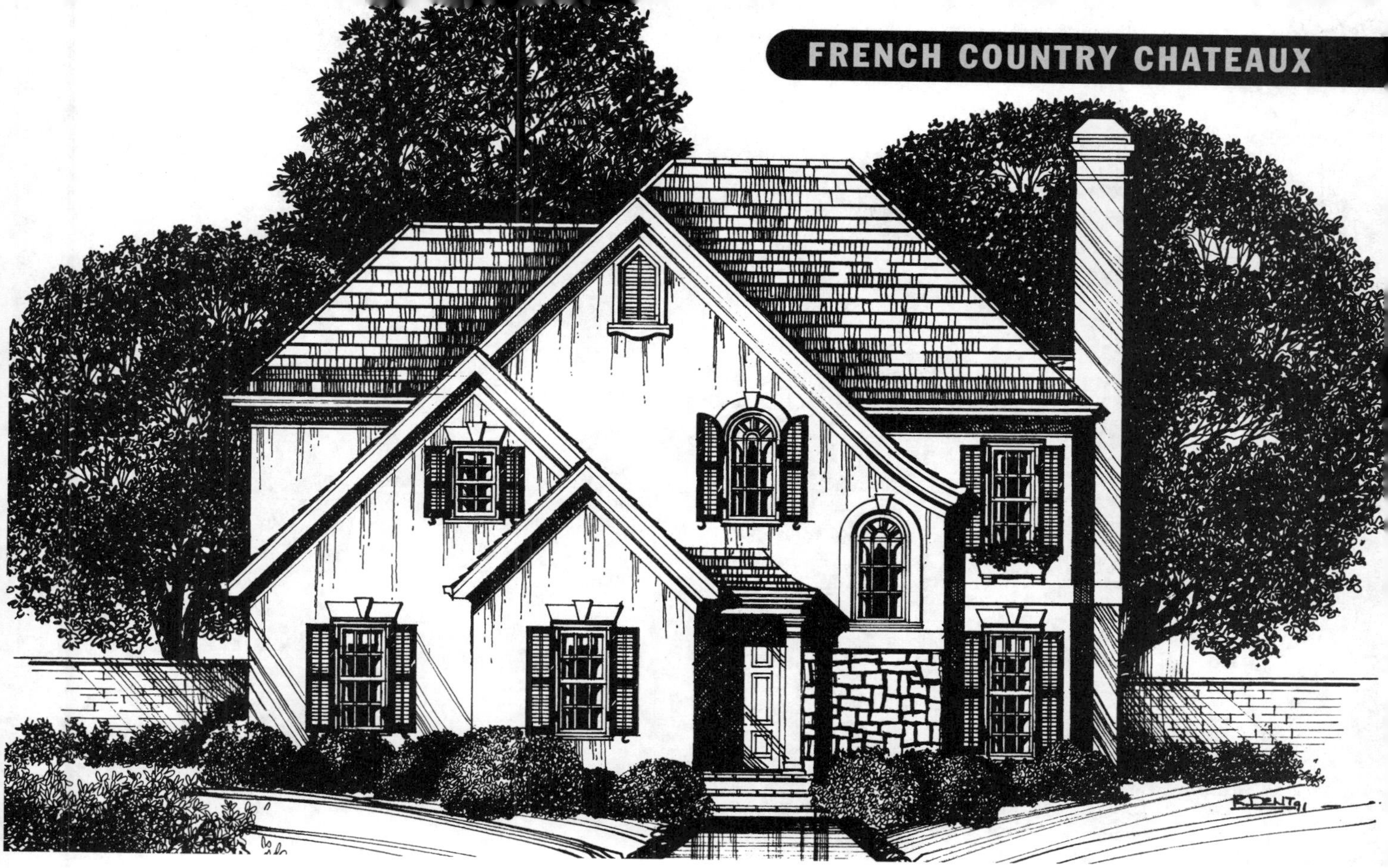

plan# HPT930341

- Style: French
- First Floor: 915 sq. ft.
- Second Floor: 935 sq. ft.
- Total: 1,850 sq. ft.
- Bonus Space: 80 sq. ft.
- Bedrooms: 3
- Bathrooms: 2½
- Width: 40'-6"
- Depth: 45'-0"
- Foundation: Walkout Basement

SEARCH ONLINE @ EPLANS.COM

SECOND FLOOR

Upon entry to this charming cottage, the foyer opens to a hallway leading to the kitchen and the generous great room with a fireplace. The great room acesses a large deck. Columns frame the dining room adjacent to the great room. The staircase off the foyer leads to the second floor where the master suite and two family bedrooms are found. A bonus room completes the second floor.

FIRST FLOOR

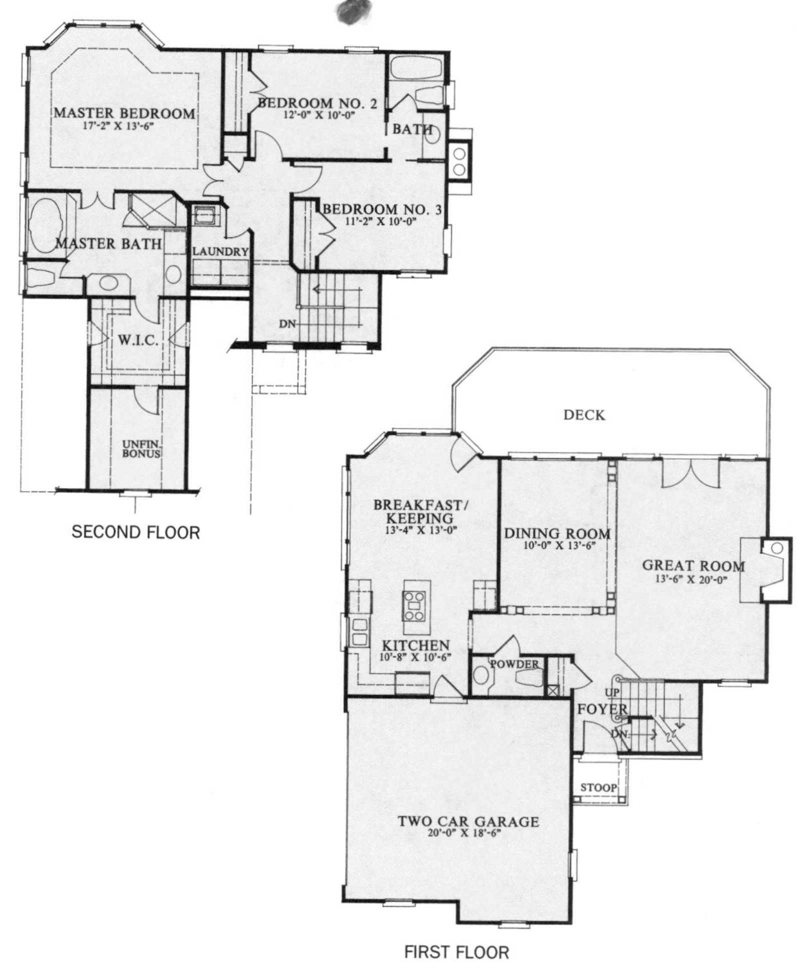

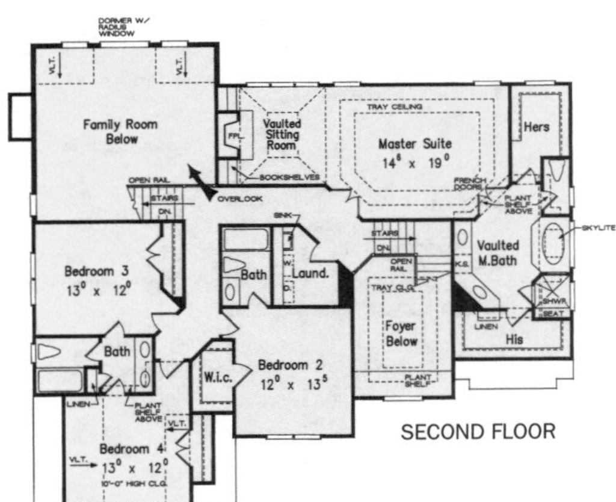

SECOND FLOOR

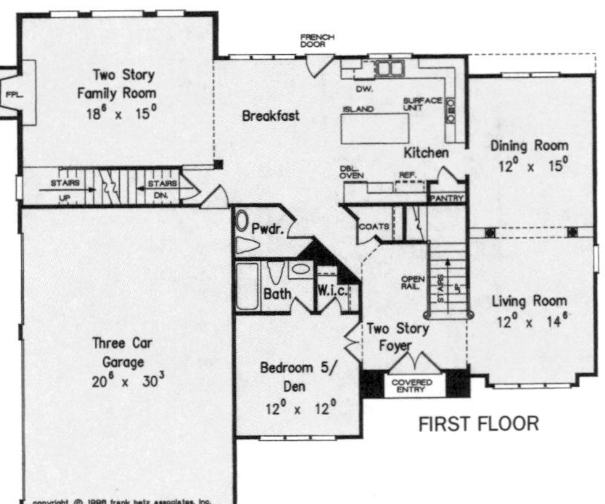

FIRST FLOOR

plan# HPT930342

- Style: French Country
- First Floor: 1,583 sq. ft.
- Second Floor: 1,632 sq. ft.
- Total: 3,215 sq. ft.
- Bedrooms: 5
- Bathrooms: 4½
- Width: 58'-4"
- Depth: 50'-0"
- Foundation: Crawlspace, Basement

SEARCH ONLINE @ EPLANS.COM

From outside to inside, the decorative details on this stucco two-story make it very special. Ceiling adornments are particularly interesting: the two-story foyer and the master bedroom have tray ceilings. The dining room and living room are separated by columns; another column graces the two-story family room. A den is reached through double doors just to the left of the foyer. Use it for an additional bedroom if needed—it has a private bath. There are four upstairs bedrooms in this plan. The master suite includes a fireplace in the vaulted sitting room.

plan# HPT930343

- Style: European Cottage
- First Floor: 1,862 sq. ft.
- Second Floor: 1,044 sq. ft.
- Total: 2,906 sq. ft.
- Bonus Space: 259 sq. ft.
- Bedrooms: 3
- Bathrooms: 3½
- Width: 60'-0"
- Depth: 60'-0"
- Foundation: Crawlspace

SEARCH ONLINE @ EPLANS.COM

SECOND FLOOR

A gently sloping, high-pitched roof complements keystones, arch-top windows and a delicate balcony balustrade and calls up a sense of cozy elegance. The foyer opens to a grand room with a focal-point fireplace and access to a screened room that leads to the veranda. The gourmet kitchen offers a walk-in pantry, acres of counter space and a morning room with outdoor flow. An island wardrobe highlights the master suite, which boasts a secluded lounge with a door to a private area of the veranda. Upstairs, two secondary bedrooms enjoy a balcony overlook to the foyer, and each room has its own access to an outdoor deck.

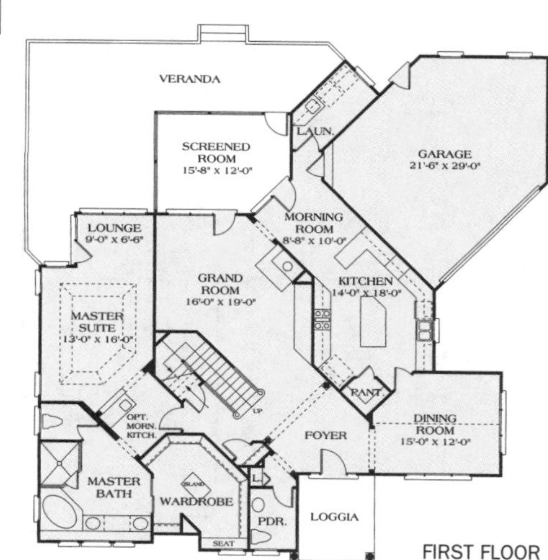

FIRST FLOOR

SECOND FLOOR

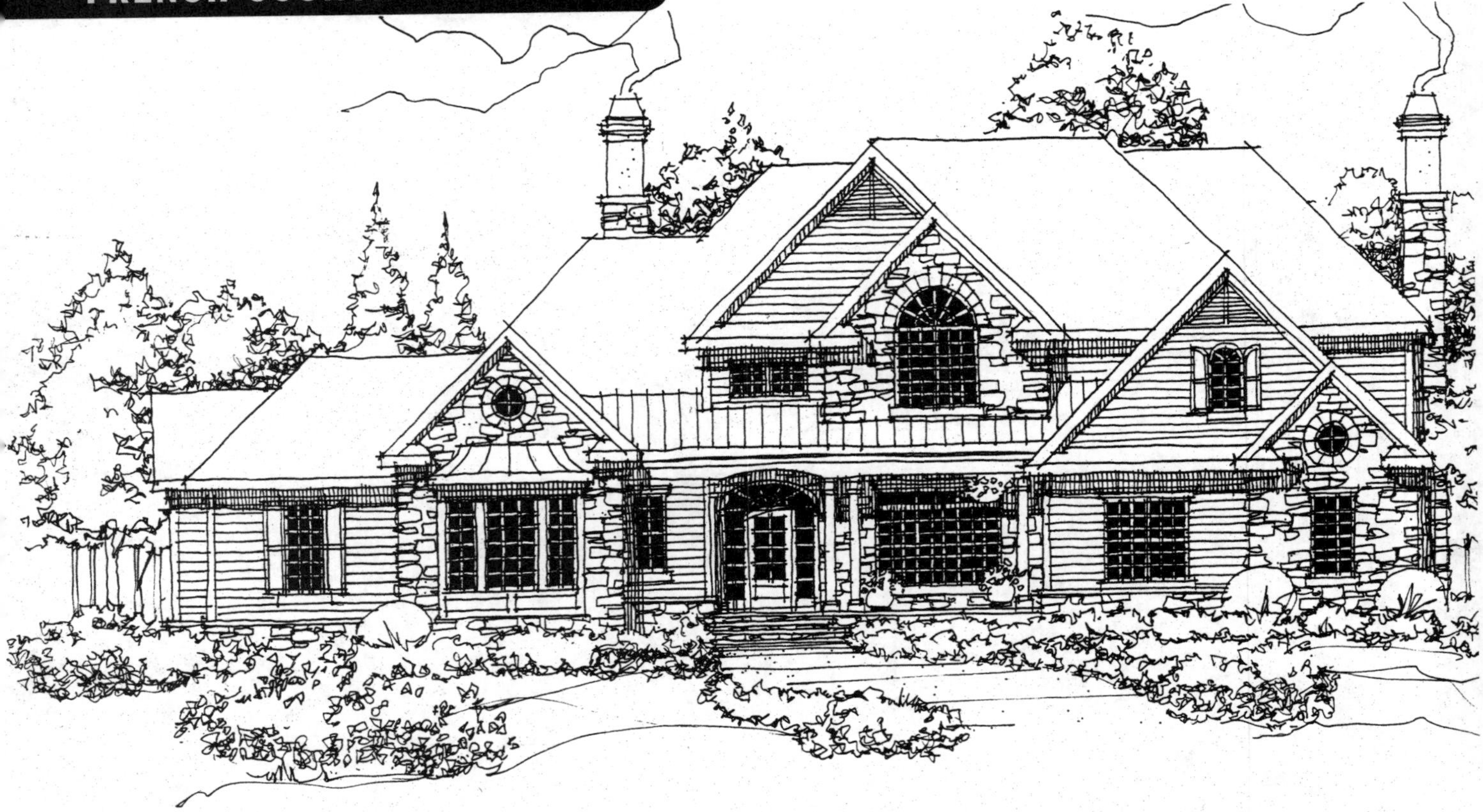

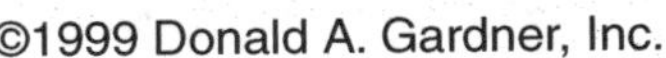

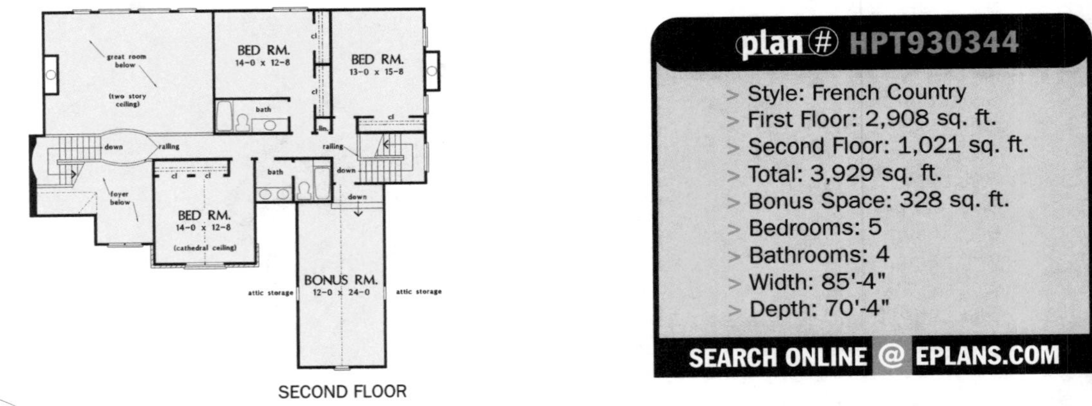

plan# HPT930344

- Style: French Country
- First Floor: 2,908 sq. ft.
- Second Floor: 1,021 sq. ft.
- Total: 3,929 sq. ft.
- Bonus Space: 328 sq. ft.
- Bedrooms: 5
- Bathrooms: 4
- Width: 85'-4"
- Depth: 70'-4"

SEARCH ONLINE @ EPLANS.COM

FIRST FLOOR

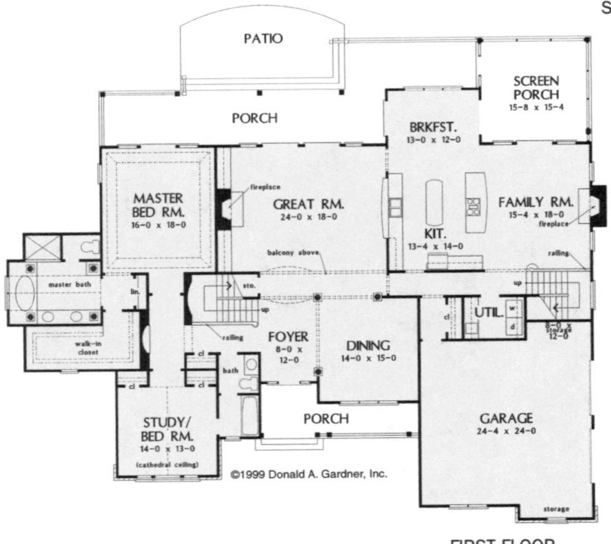

Siding and stone embellish the exterior of this five-bedroom traditional estate for an exciting, yet stately appearance. A two-story foyer creates an impressive entry. An equally impressive two-story great room features a fireplace, built-ins and back-porch access. The first-floor master suite enjoys an elegant tray ceiling, back-porch access and a lavish bath with all the amenities, including an enormous walk-in closet. Down the hall, a second first-floor bedroom easily converts to a study. The island kitchen easily serves the dining and breakfast rooms. A fireplace warms the casual family room. The breakfast room accesses the screened porch. Three additional bedrooms are on the second floor. The bonus room above the garage is great for attic storage, a home office or a guest suite.

plan# HPT930345

- Style: French Country
- First Floor: 3,520 sq. ft.
- Second Floor: 1,638 sq. ft.
- Total: 5,158 sq. ft.
- Bonus Space: 411 sq. ft.
- Bedrooms: 5
- Bathrooms: 4½
- Width: 96'-6"
- Depth: 58'-8"

SEARCH ONLINE @ EPLANS.COM

SECOND FLOOR

This custom-designed estate home elegantly combines stone and stucco, arched windows and stunning exterior details under its distinctive hipped roof. The two-story foyer is impressive with its grand staircase, tray ceiling and overlooking balcony. Equally remarkable is the generous living room with a fireplace and a coffered two-story ceiling. The kitchen, breakfast bay and family room with a fireplace are all open to one another for a comfortable, casual atmosphere. The first-floor master suite indulges with numerous closets, a dressing room and a fabulous bath. Upstairs, four more bedrooms are topped by tray ceilings—three have walk-in closets and two have private baths. The three-car garage boasts additional storage and a bonus room above.

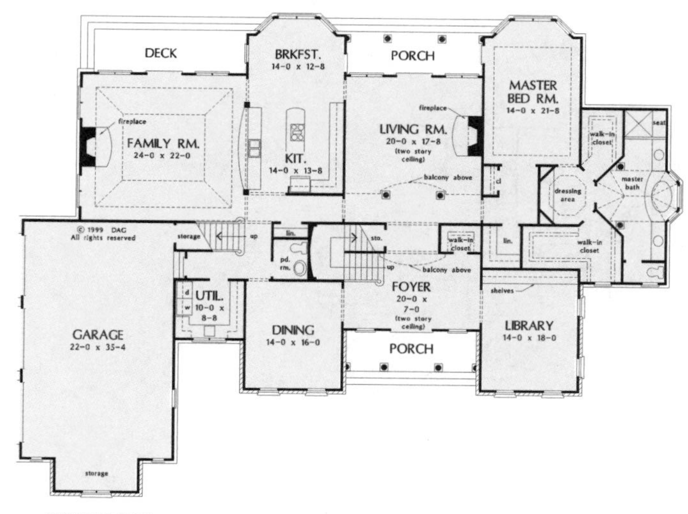

FIRST FLOOR

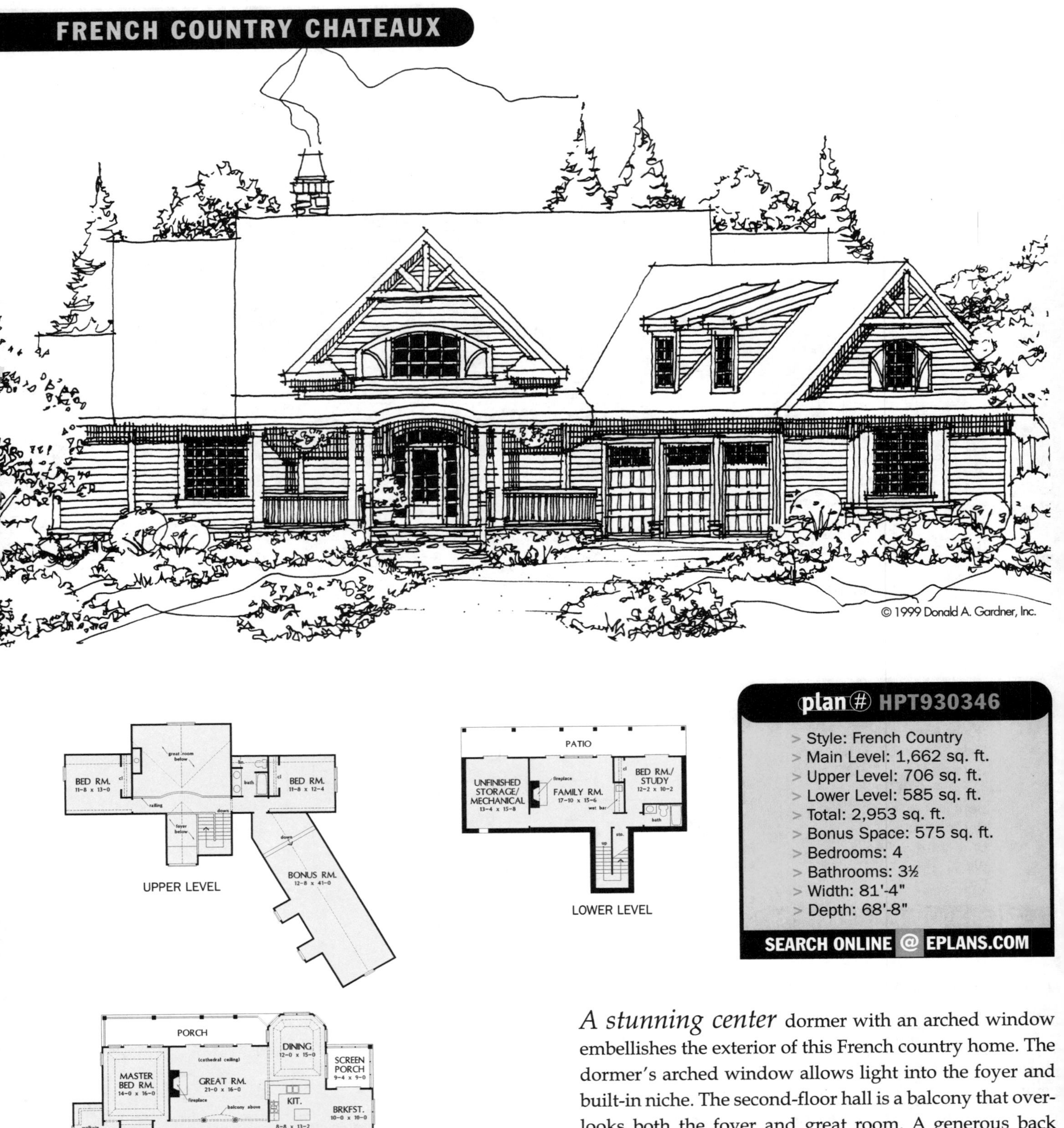

plan# HPT930346

- Style: French Country
- Main Level: 1,662 sq. ft.
- Upper Level: 706 sq. ft.
- Lower Level: 585 sq. ft.
- Total: 2,953 sq. ft.
- Bonus Space: 575 sq. ft.
- Bedrooms: 4
- Bathrooms: 3½
- Width: 81'-4"
- Depth: 68'-8"

SEARCH ONLINE @ EPLANS.COM

A stunning center dormer with an arched window embellishes the exterior of this French country home. The dormer's arched window allows light into the foyer and built-in niche. The second-floor hall is a balcony that overlooks both the foyer and great room. A generous back porch extends the great room, which features an impressive vaulted ceiling and fireplace, while a tray ceiling adorns the formal dining room. The master suite, which includes a tray ceiling as well, enjoys back-porch access, a built-in cabinet, generous walk-in closet and private bath. Two more bedrooms are located upstairs, while a fourth can be found in the lower level along with a family room.

plan# HPT930347

- Style: French Country
- First Floor: 2,477 sq. ft.
- Second Floor: 742 sq. ft.
- Total: 3,219 sq. ft.
- Bonus Space: 419 sq. ft.
- Bedrooms: 4
- Bathrooms: 4
- Width: 100'-0"
- Depth: 66'-2"

SEARCH ONLINE @ EPLANS.COM

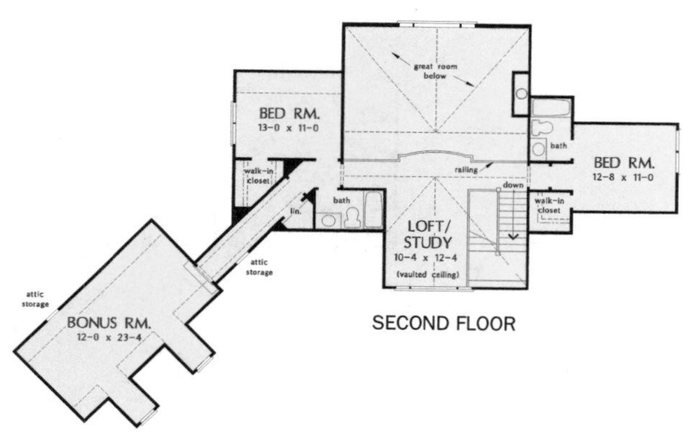

A prominent center gable with an arched window accents the facade of this custom French country home, which features an exterior of cedar shakes, siding and stone. An open floor plan with generously proportioned rooms contributes to the home's spacious and relaxed atmosphere. The vaulted great room boasts a rear wall of windows, a fireplace bordered by built-in cabinets, and convenient access to the kitchen. A second-floor loft overlooks the great room for added drama. The master suite is completely secluded and enjoys a cathedral ceiling, back-porch access, a large walk-in closet and a luxurious bath. The home includes three additional bedrooms and baths as well as a vaulted loft/study and a bonus room.

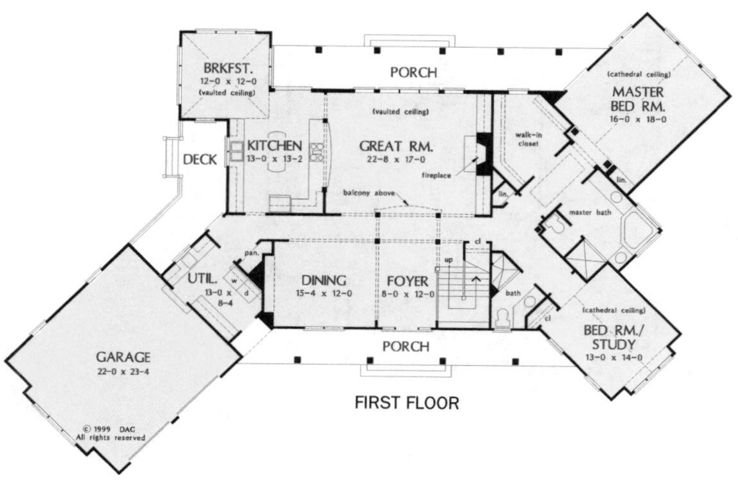

ALLEN

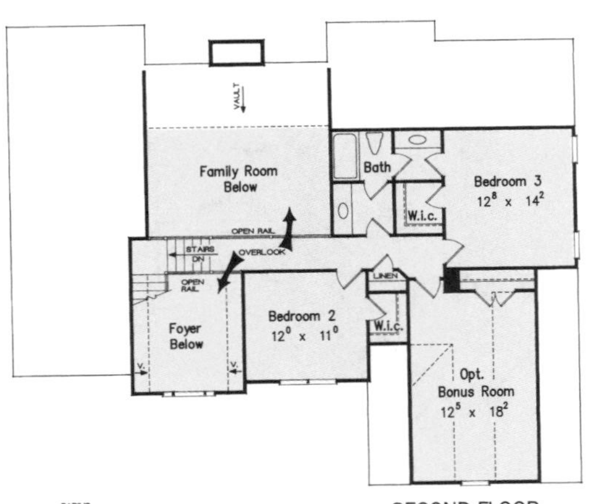

SECOND FLOOR

plan# HPT930348

- Style: French Country
- First Floor: 1,761 sq. ft.
- Second Floor: 580 sq. ft.
- Total: 2,341 sq. ft.
- Bonus Space: 276 sq. ft.
- Bedrooms: 4
- Bathrooms: 3
- Width: 56'-0"
- Depth: 47'-6"
- Foundation: Crawlspace, Slab, Basement

SEARCH ONLINE @ EPLANS.COM

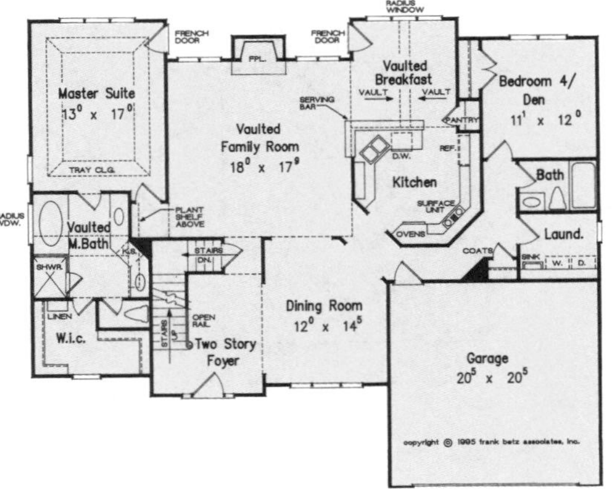

FIRST FLOOR

Decorative arches and quoins give this home a wonderful curb appeal that matches its comfortable interior. The two-story foyer is bathed in natural light as it leads to the formal dining room and beyond to the counter-filled kitchen and the vaulted breakfast nook. A den, or possible fourth bedroom, is tucked away at the rear for privacy and includes a full bath. Located on the first floor, also for privacy, is a spacious master suite with a luxurious private bath. Two family bedrooms and a full bath reside on the second floor, as well as a balcony that looks down to the family room and the foyer. An optional bonus room is available for expanding at a later date.

plan# HPT930349

- Style: French Country
- First Floor: 2,146 sq. ft.
- Second Floor: 878 sq. ft.
- Total: 3,024 sq. ft.
- Bonus Space: 341 sq. ft.
- Bedrooms: 4
- Bathrooms: 3½
- Width: 61'-0"
- Depth: 60'-4"
- Foundation: Crawlspace, Basement

SEARCH ONLINE @ EPLANS.COM

The wood and brick siding, muntin windows with shutters and keystones, and a covered front porch with columns on this traditional home will catch anyone's attention. The two-story foyer leads to a formal dining room with decorative columns and a vaulted living room to the opposite side. The grand room also enjoys a vaulted ceiling, a fireplace and radius windows. The gourmet kitchen features a serving bar and a large pantry. The master bedroom takes over the right wing of the home with its tray ceiling, a sitting room with a bay window, built-in art niche, and French doors leading to the private bath. This private bath includes a vaulted ceiling, an oversized garden tub, and a huge His and Hers walk-in closet. The second floor holds three additional family bedrooms along with an optional bonus room—note all bedrooms include a walk-in closet.

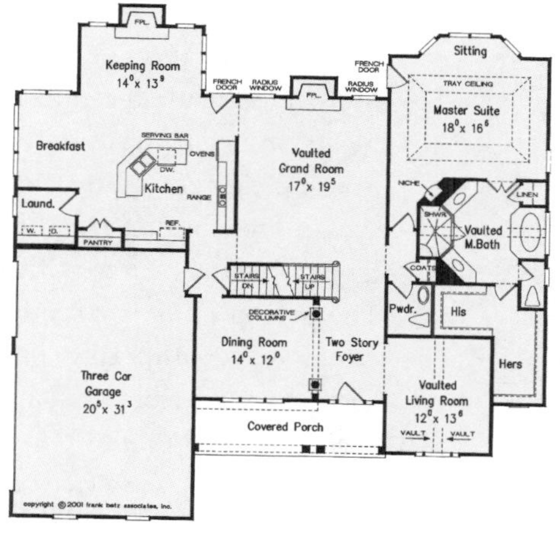

FIRST FLOOR

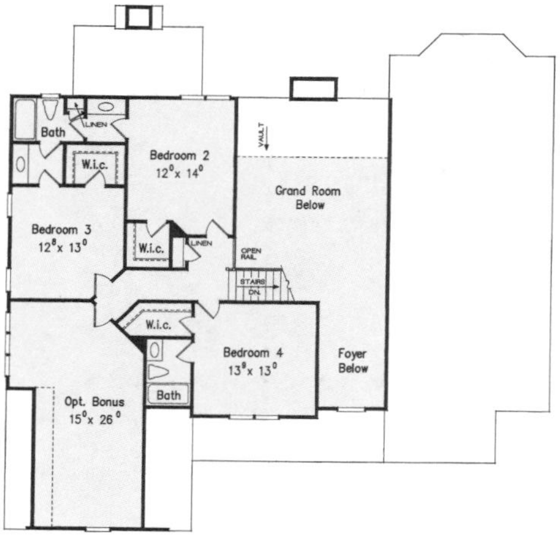

SECOND FLOOR

SECOND FLOOR

FIRST FLOOR

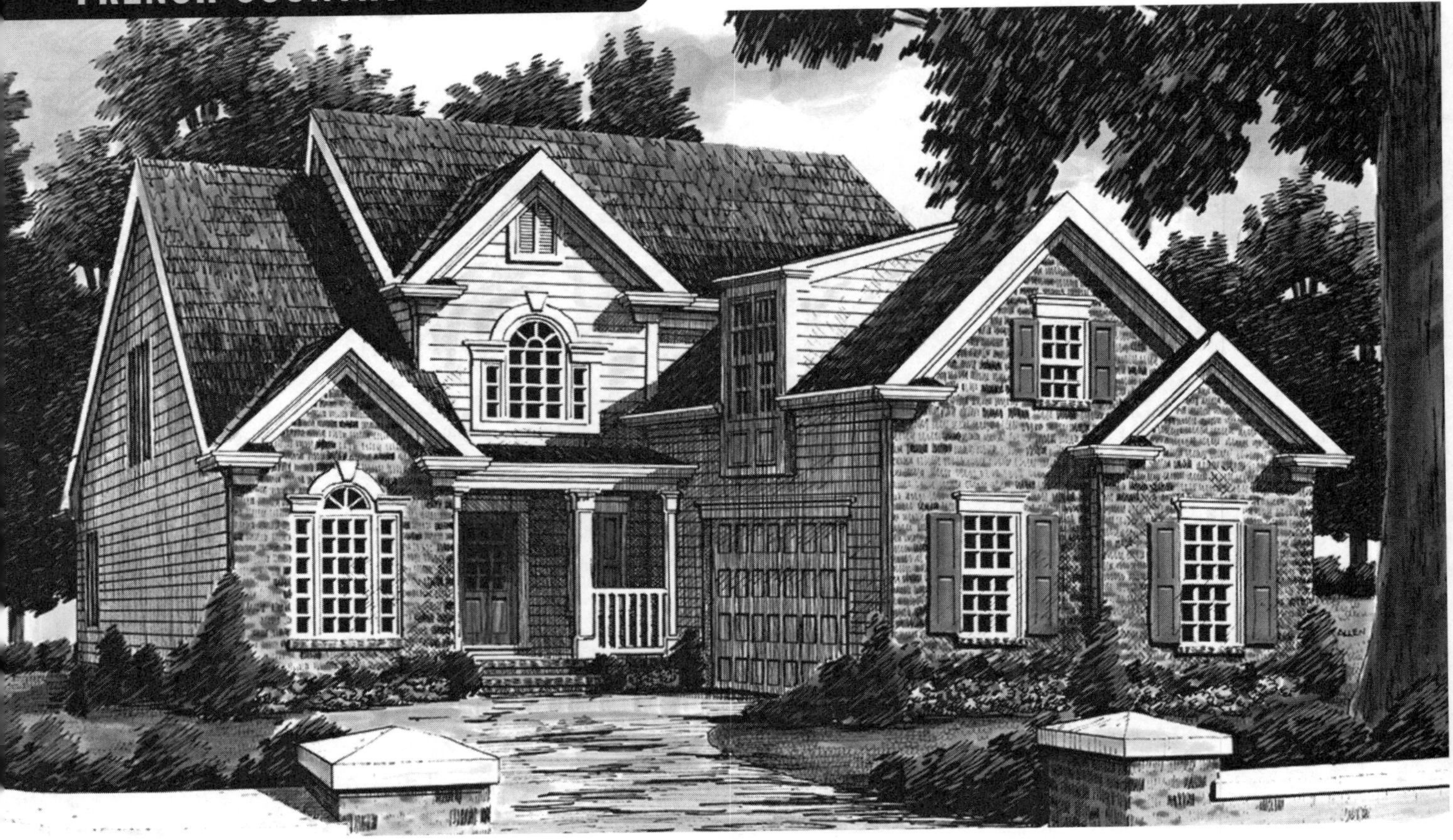

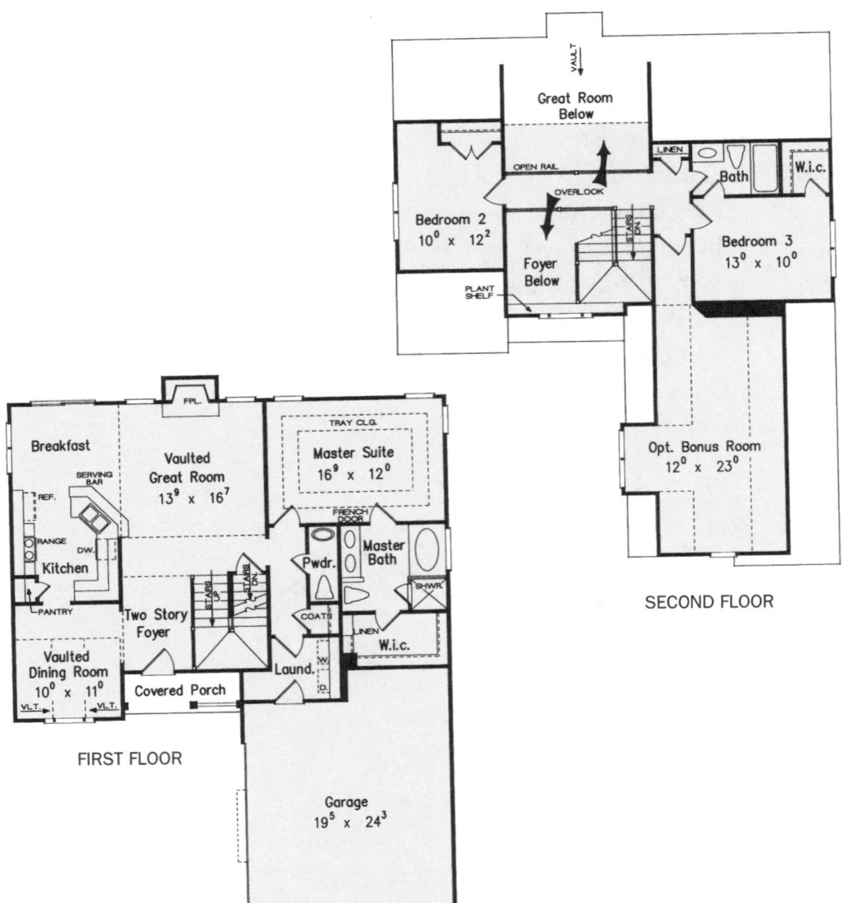

plan# HPT930350

- Style: French Country
- First Floor: 1,179 sq. ft.
- Second Floor: 479 sq. ft.
- Total: 1,658 sq. ft.
- Bonus Space: 338 sq. ft.
- Bedrooms: 3
- Bathrooms: 2½
- Width: 41'-6"
- Depth: 54'-4"
- Foundation: Crawlspace, Slab, Basement

SEARCH ONLINE @ EPLANS.COM

With vaulted ceilings in the dining room and the great room, a tray ceiling in the master suite and a sunlit two-story foyer, this inviting design offers a wealth of light and space. The counter-filled kitchen opens to a large breakfast area with backyard access. The master suite is complete with a walk-in closet and pampering bath. Upstairs, two secondary bedrooms share a hall bath and access to an optional bonus room. Note the storage space in the two-car garage.

plan# HPT930351

- Style: French Country
- First Floor: 1,205 sq. ft.
- Second Floor: 1,277 sq. ft.
- Total: 2,482 sq. ft.
- Bedrooms: 4
- Bathrooms: 2½
- Width: 53'-6"
- Depth: 39'-4"
- Foundation: Crawlspace, Slab, Basement

SEARCH ONLINE @ EPLANS.COM

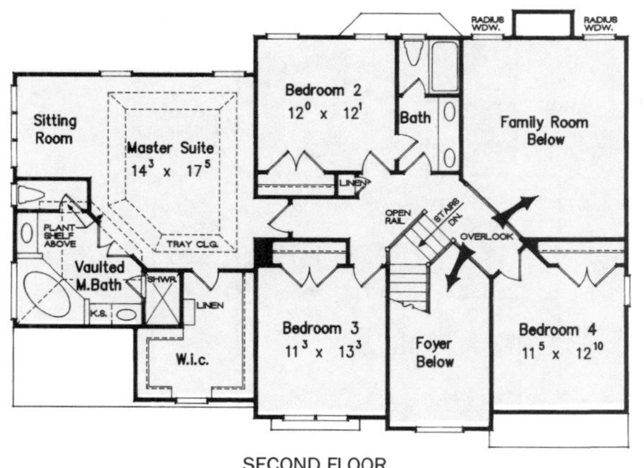

SECOND FLOOR

A taste of Europe is reflected in arched windows topped off by keystones in this traditional design. Formal rooms flank the foyer, which leads to a two-story family room with a focal-point fireplace. The sunny breakfast nook opens to a private covered porch through a French door. A spacious, well-organized kitchen features angled, wrapping counters, double ovens and a walk-in pantry. The garage offers a service entrance to the utility area and pantry. An angled staircase leads from the two-story foyer to the sleeping quarters upstairs. Here, a gallery hall with a balcony overlooks the foyer and family room and connects the family bedrooms. A private hall leads to the master suite. It boasts a well-lit sitting area, a walk-in closet with linen storage, and a lavish bath with a vaulted ceiling and plant shelves.

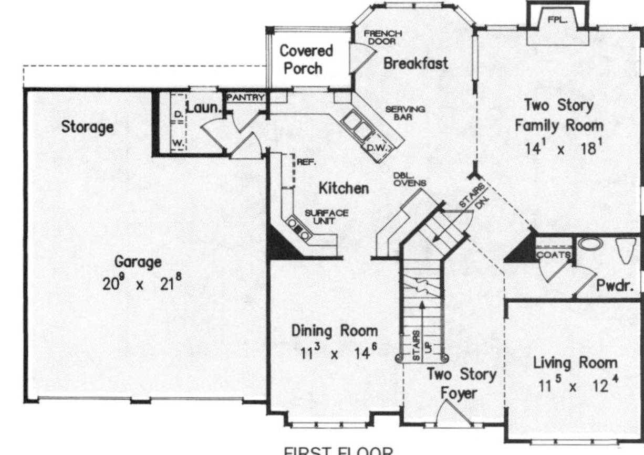

FIRST FLOOR

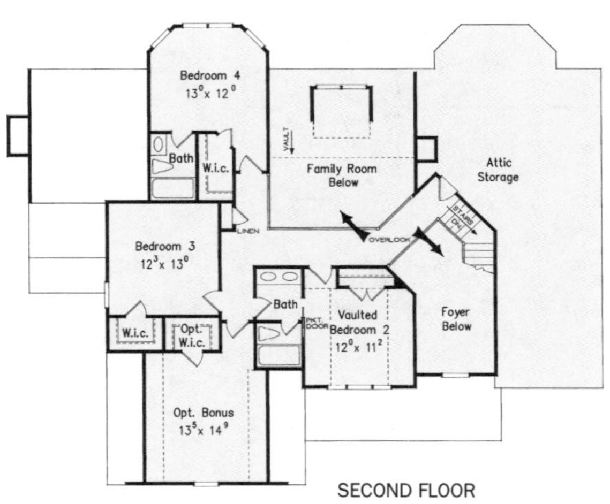

SECOND FLOOR

plan# HPT930352

- Style: Chateau
- First Floor: 2,104 sq. ft.
- Second Floor: 866 sq. ft.
- Total: 2,970 sq. ft.
- Bonus Space: 245 sq. ft.
- Bedrooms: 4
- Bathrooms: 3½
- Width: 65'-10"
- Depth: 53'-0"
- Foundation: Crawlspace, Basement

SEARCH ONLINE @ EPLANS.COM

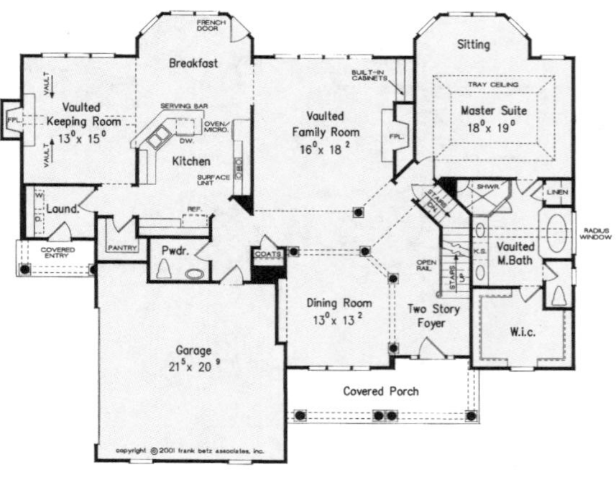

FIRST FLOOR

This quaint, country chateau provides traditional elegance complete with two full levels of luxurious family living. Stone trim, siding, country shutters and a farmhouse-style front porch add rustic accents to the exterior. Inside, a two-story foyer introduces the formal dining room and vaulted family room warmed by a fireplace. Casual areas of the home include the gourmet kitchen, breakfast bay and vaulted keeping room. Amenities are plentiful in the master suite, located to the right of the plan—the suite enjoys a sleeping area brightened by a sitting bay and topped by a tray ceiling. The vaulted master bath boasts a roomy walk-in closet. Three additional bedrooms, two baths and a bonus room reside upstairs—Bedroom 2 is vaulted.

plan# HPT930353

- Style: French Country
- First Floor: 1,448 sq. ft.
- Second Floor: 1,714 sq. ft.
- Total: 3,162 sq. ft.
- Bedrooms: 5
- Bathrooms: 4
- Width: 60'-0"
- Depth: 43'-10"
- Foundation: Crawlspace, Basement

SEARCH ONLINE @ EPLANS.COM

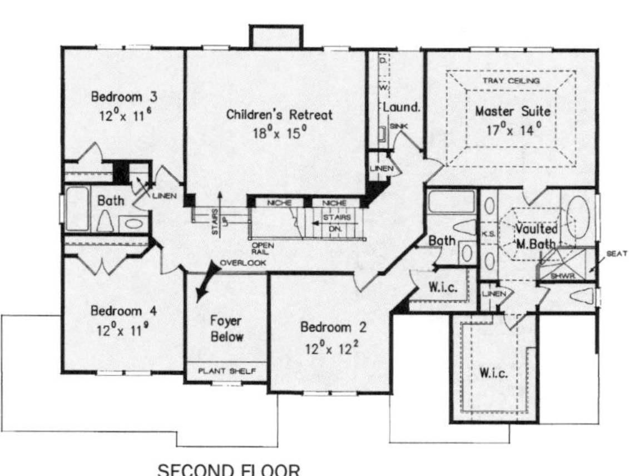

SECOND FLOOR

Stones and clapboard siding adorn this roomy home. Inside, the two-story foyer introduces a private study with double-door entry and a large formal dining room. Straight ahead, decorative columns welcome visitors to the family room, which features a coffered ceiling, fireplace and open planning. The breakfast room and kitchen work well together. A first-floor bedroom is perfect as a guest suite. Upstairs, three family bedrooms—one with a private bath—enjoy a children's retreat that functions as a bonus space. The master suite is the picture of luxury with a sumptuous bath and oversized walk-in closet.

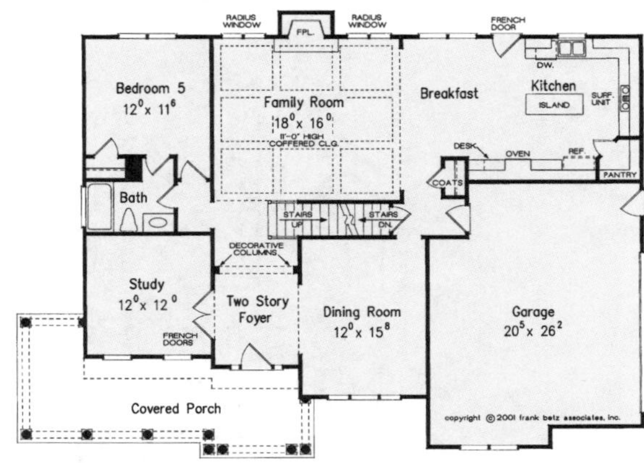

FIRST FLOOR

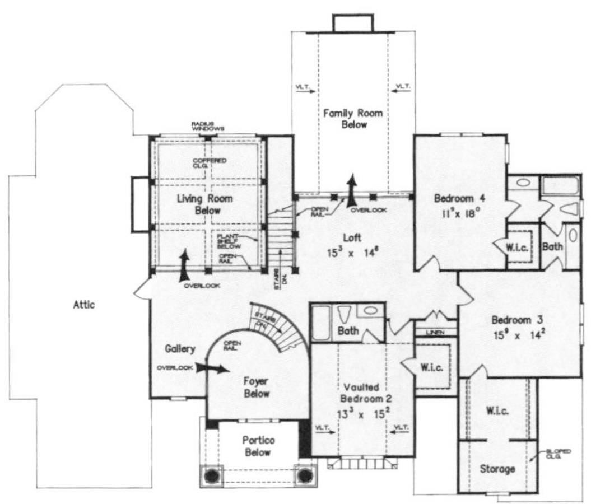

SECOND FLOOR

plan# HPT930354

- Style: French
- First Floor: 2,764 sq. ft.
- Second Floor: 1,598 sq. ft.
- Total: 4,362 sq. ft.
- Bedrooms: 4
- Bathrooms: 3½
- Width: 74'-6"
- Depth: 65'-10"
- Foundation: Crawlspace, Basement

SEARCH ONLINE @ EPLANS.COM

FIRST FLOOR

Decorative detailing adds prestigious beauty to this facade. The portico enters into the foyer where a spiral staircase adds elegance. The heart of this magnificent design is the two-story grand room with its fireplace and built-in bookshelves. Decorative columns and dual French doors demand notice in the two-story living room. The private master wing features a secluded study, bayed sitting area and vaulted bath. Upstairs, Bedrooms 3 and 4 each include a built-in desk.

plan# HPT930355

- Style: French Country
- First Floor: 1,786 sq. ft.
- Second Floor: 1,739 sq. ft.
- Total: 3,525 sq. ft.
- Bedrooms: 5
- Bathrooms: 4½
- Width: 59'-0"
- Depth: 53'-0"
- Foundation: Crawlspace, Slab, Basement

SEARCH ONLINE @ EPLANS.COM

European details bring charm and a touch of joie de vivre to this traditional home. Casual living space includes a two-story family room with a centered fireplace. A sizable kitchen, with an island serving bar and a French door to the rear property, leads to the formal dining room through a convenient butler's pantry. The second floor includes a generous master suite with a sitting room defined by decorative columns and five lovely windows. Bedroom 2 has a private bath, while two additional bedrooms share a hall bath with compartmented lavatories.

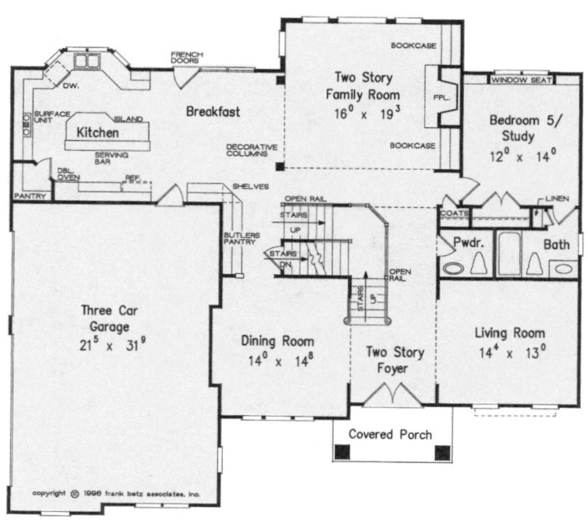

FIRST FLOOR

SECOND FLOOR

SECOND FLOOR

FIRST FLOOR

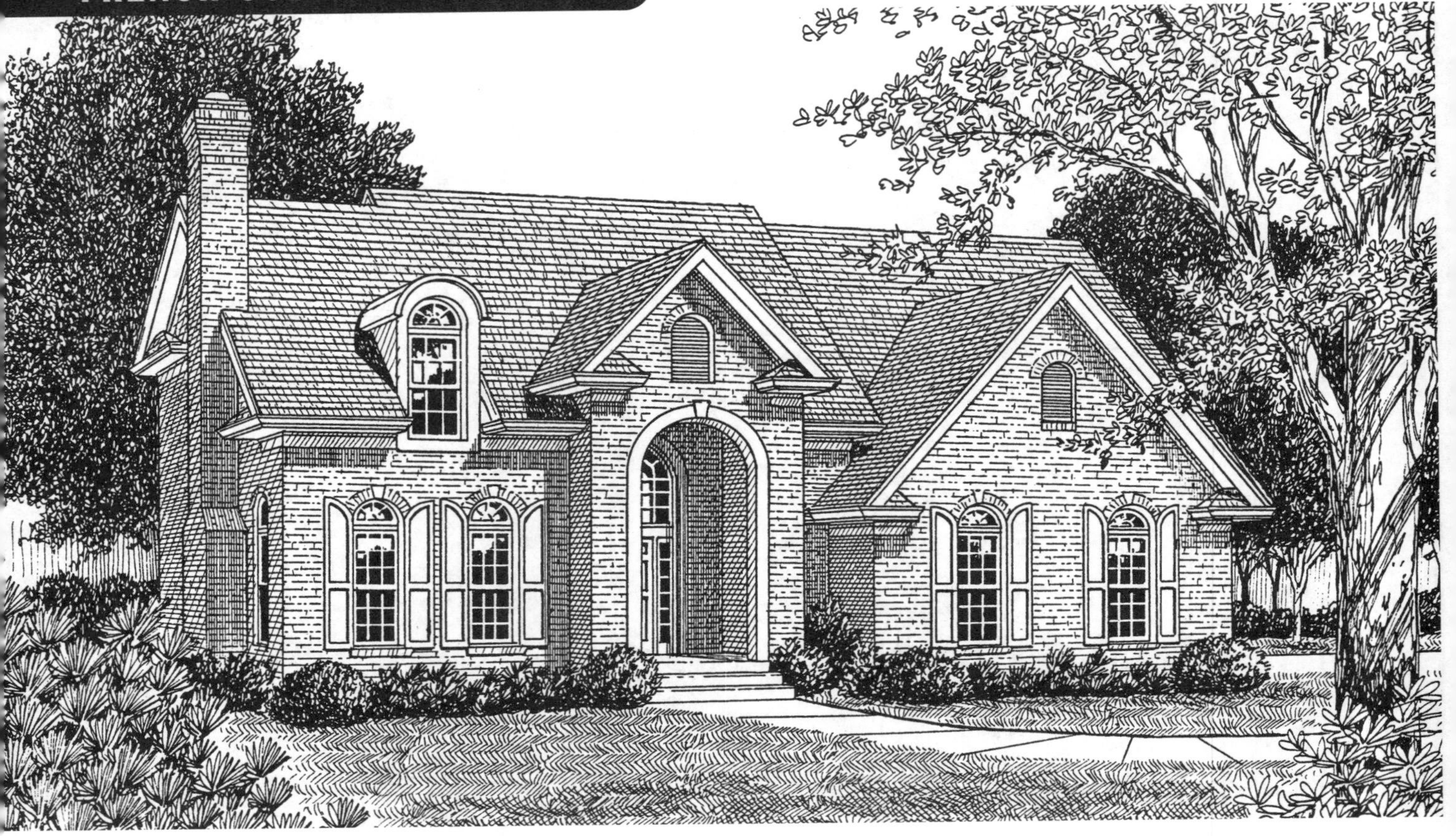

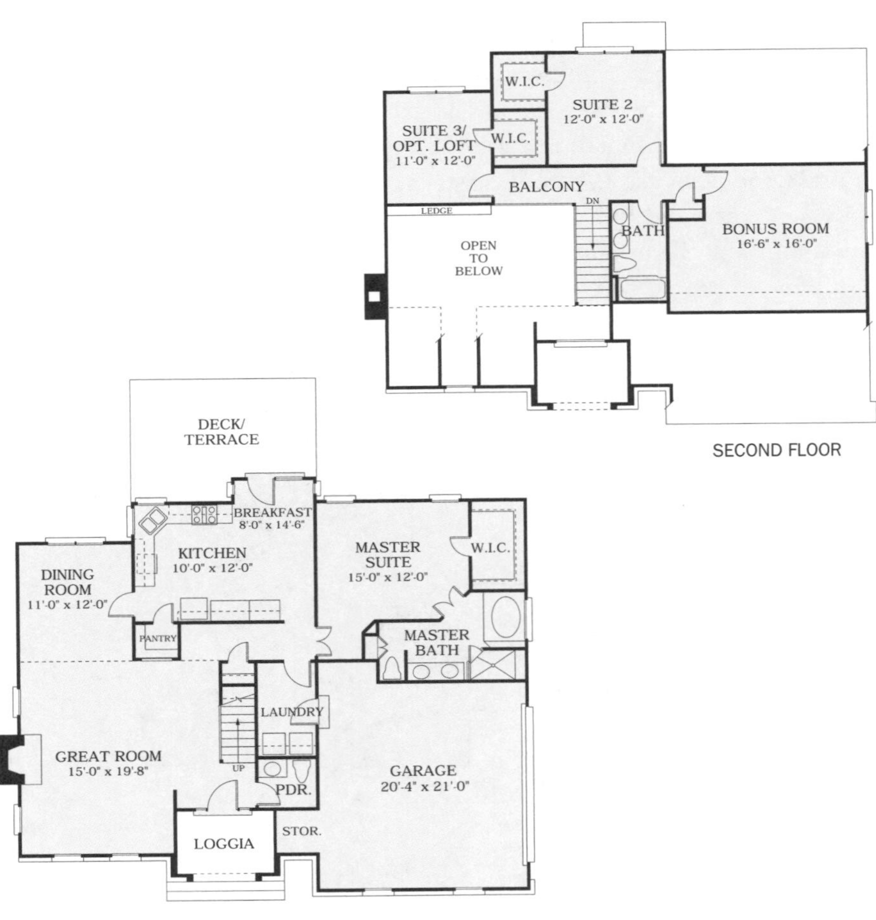

plan# HPT930356

- Style: French Country
- First Floor: 1,383 sq. ft.
- Second Floor: 546 sq. ft.
- Total: 1,929 sq. ft.
- Bonus Space: 320 sq. ft.
- Bedrooms: 3
- Bathrooms: 2½
- Width: 50'-6"
- Depth: 42'-10"
- Foundation: Crawlspace, Slab

SEARCH ONLINE @ EPLANS.COM

This open, airy design is one that seems much larger than it actually is. A large two-story great room opens into the dining room. The roomy master suite boasts a terrific walk-in closet and a bath with dual lavatories. A breakfast area that opens to a deck, and corner windows at the kitchen sink, help bring the outdoors in. There's plenty of storage, including an ample pantry, a two-car garage and a bonus room that can double as a fourth suite.

plan# HPT930357

- Style: French Country
- First Floor: 1,320 sq. ft.
- Second Floor: 554 sq. ft.
- Total: 1,874 sq. ft.
- Bonus Space: 155 sq. ft.
- Bedrooms: 4
- Bathrooms: 2½
- Width: 54'-6"
- Depth: 42'-4"
- Foundation: Crawlspace, Basement

SEARCH ONLINE @ EPLANS.COM

This plan combines a traditional, stately exterior with an updated floor plan to create a house that will please the entire family. The heart of the plan is surely the wide-open living space consisting of the vaulted family room, breakfast area and gourmet kitchen. Highlights here are a full-length fireplace, a French door to the rear yard and an island cooktop. The master suite has a tray ceiling and a vaulted master bath with a garden tub and walk-in closet. The family sleeping area on the upper level gives the option of two bedrooms and a loft overlooking the family room or three bedrooms.

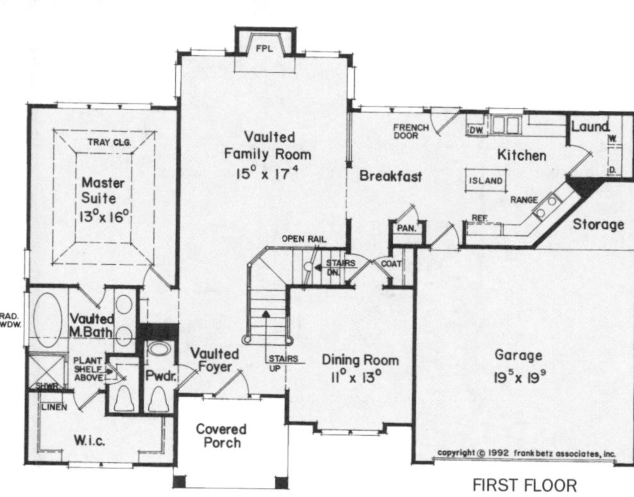

FIRST FLOOR

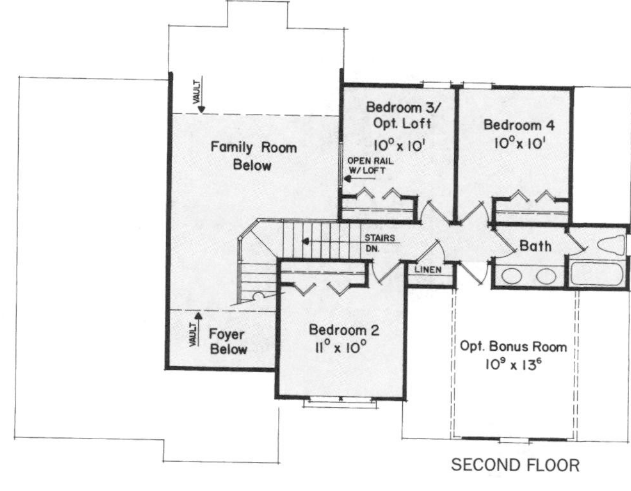

SECOND FLOOR

FRENCH COUNTRY CHATEAUX

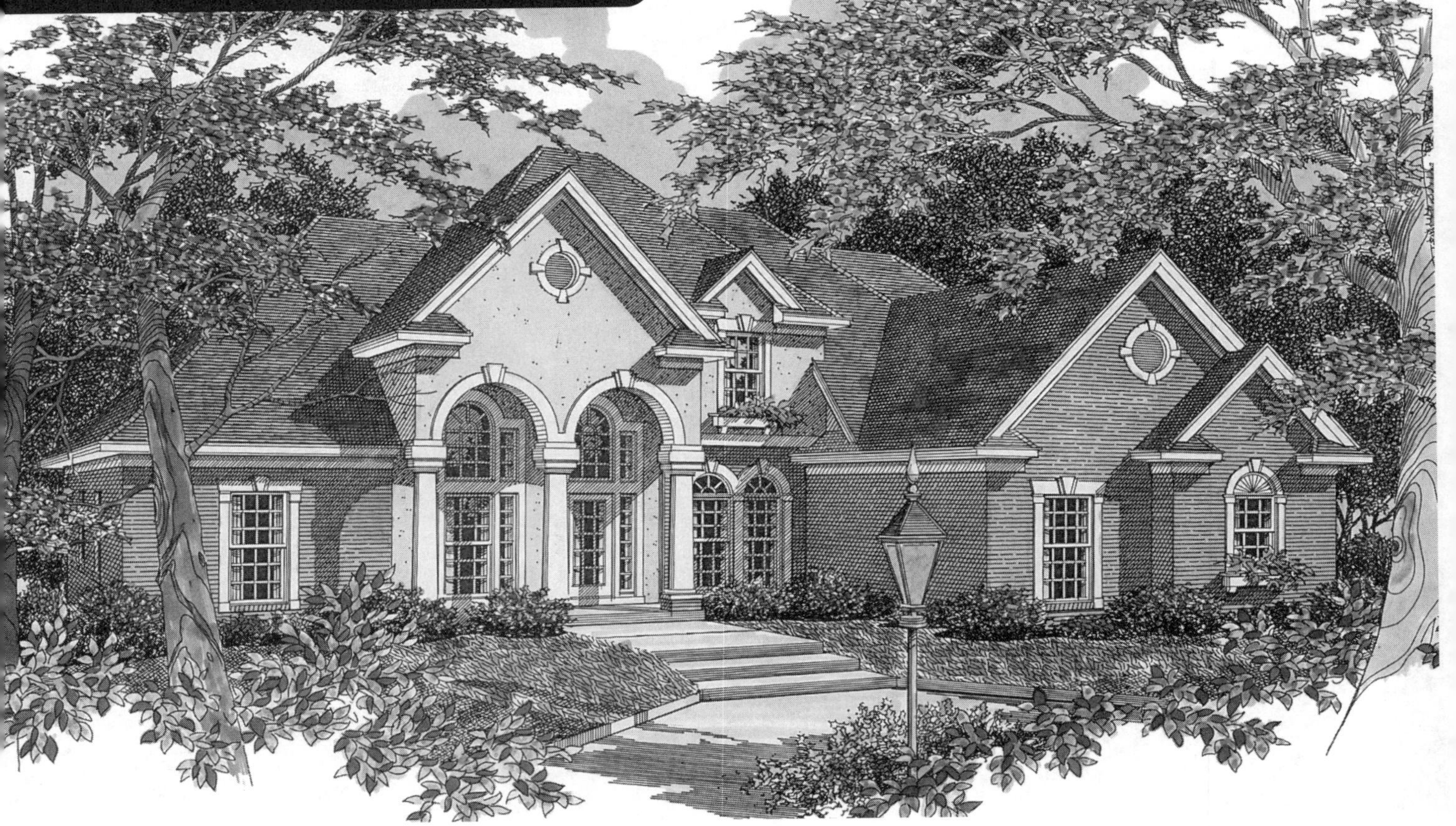

A lovely double arch gives this European-style home a commanding presence. Once inside, a two-story foyer provides an open view directly through the formal living room to the rear grounds beyond. The spacious kitchen with a work island and the bayed breakfast area share space with the family room. The private master suite features dual sinks, twin walk-in closets, a corner garden tub and a separate shower. A large game room completes this wonderful family home.

plan# HPT930358

L

- Style: Norman
- First Floor: 2,469 sq. ft.
- Second Floor: 1,025 sq. ft.
- Total: 3,494 sq. ft.
- Bonus Space: 320 sq. ft.
- Bedrooms: 4
- Bathrooms: 3½
- Width: 67'-8"
- Depth: 74'-2"
- Foundation: Basement, Crawlspace, Slab

SEARCH ONLINE @ EPLANS.COM

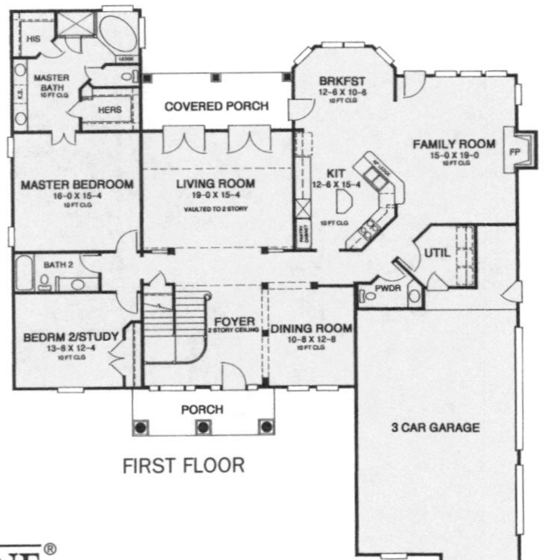

FIRST FLOOR

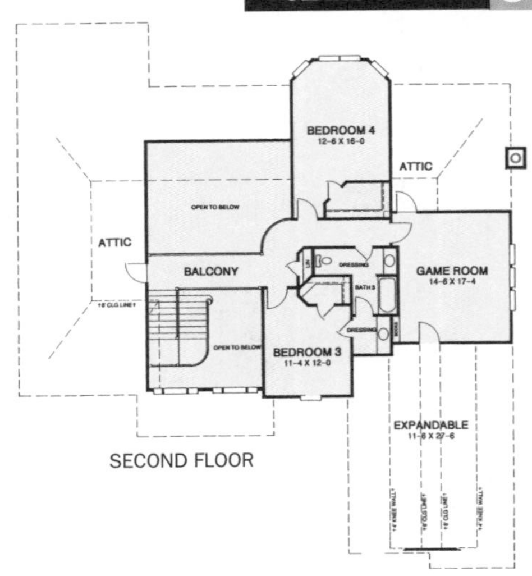

SECOND FLOOR

QUOTE ONE®

Cost to build? See page 436 to order complete cost estimate to build this house in your area!

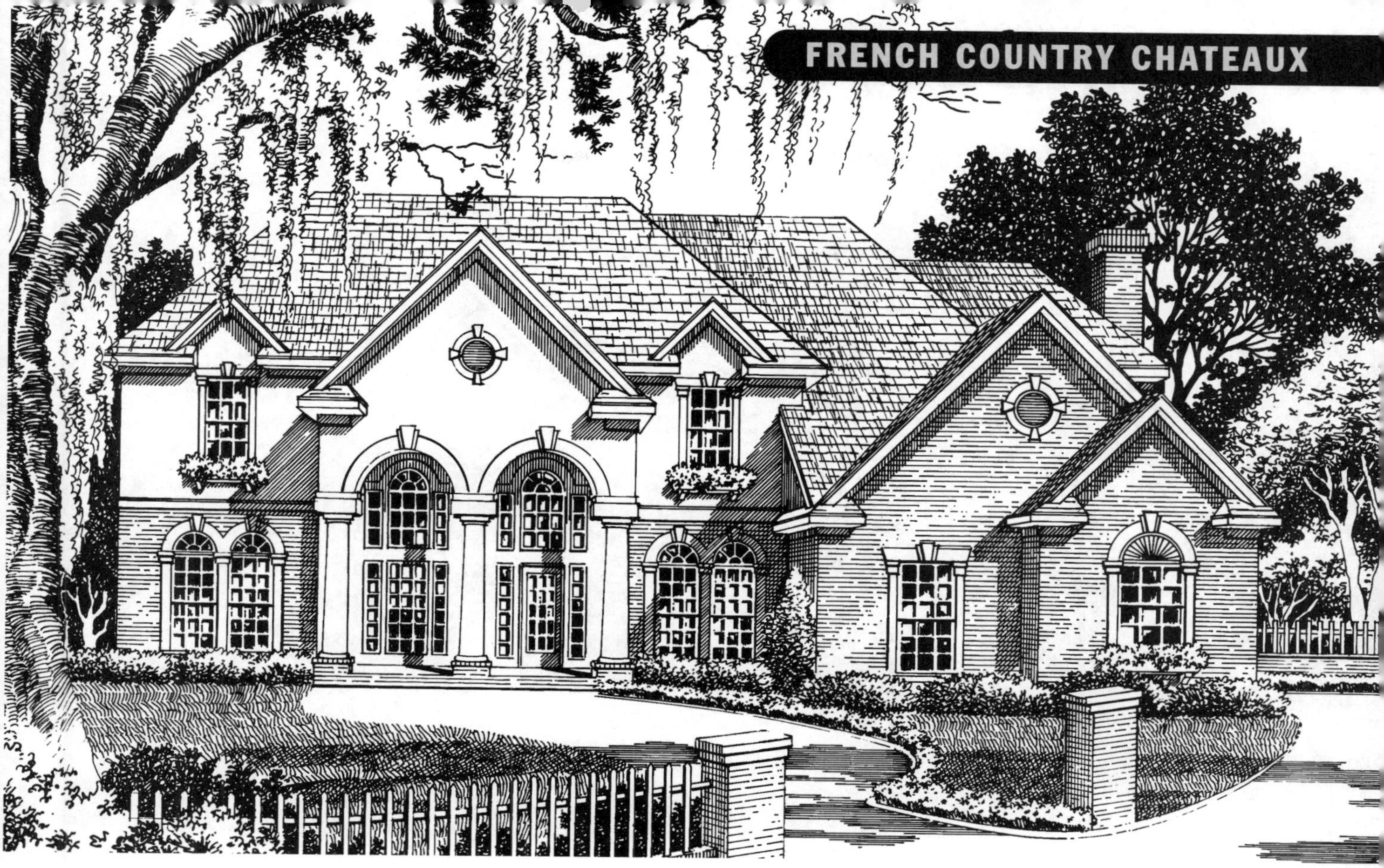

plan# HPT930359

- Style: French Country
- First Floor: 1,919 sq. ft.
- Second Floor: 1,190 sq. ft.
- Total: 3,109 sq. ft.
- Bonus Space: 286 sq. ft.
- Bedrooms: 4
- Bathrooms: 3½
- Width: 64'-6"
- Depth: 55'-10"
- Foundation: Crawlspace, Slab, Basement

SEARCH ONLINE @ EPLANS.COM

Flower boxes, arches and multi-pane windows all combine to create the elegant facade of this four-bedroom home. Inside, the two-story foyer introduces a formal dining room to its right and leads to a two-story living room that is filled with light. An efficient kitchen has a bayed breakfast room and shares a snack bar with a cozy family room. Located on the first floor for privacy, the master suite is graced with a luxurious bath. Upstairs, three secondary bedrooms share two full baths and access a large game room. For future growth there is an expandable area accessed through the game room.

SECOND FLOOR

FIRST FLOOR

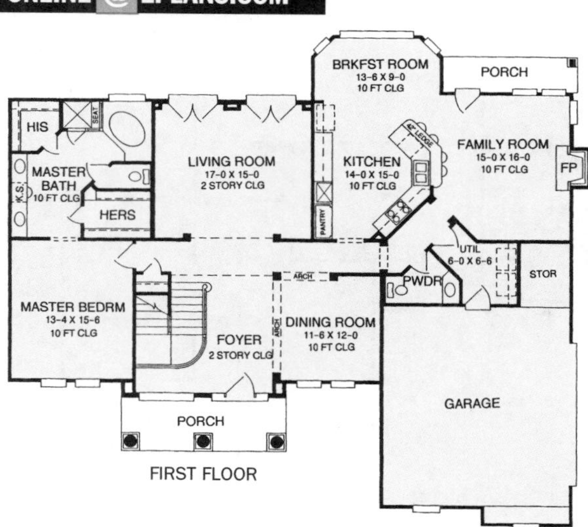

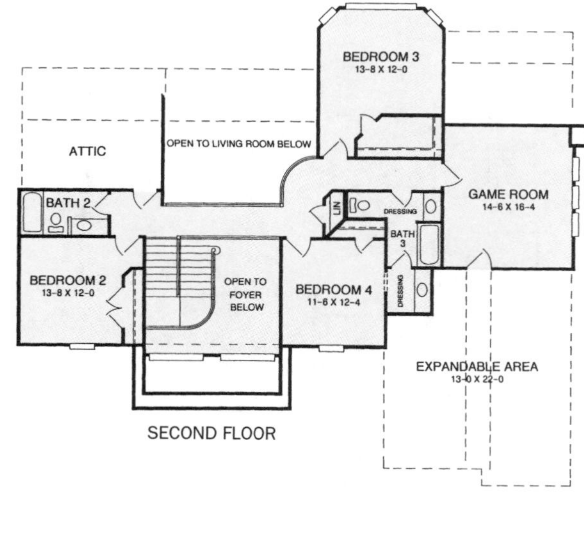

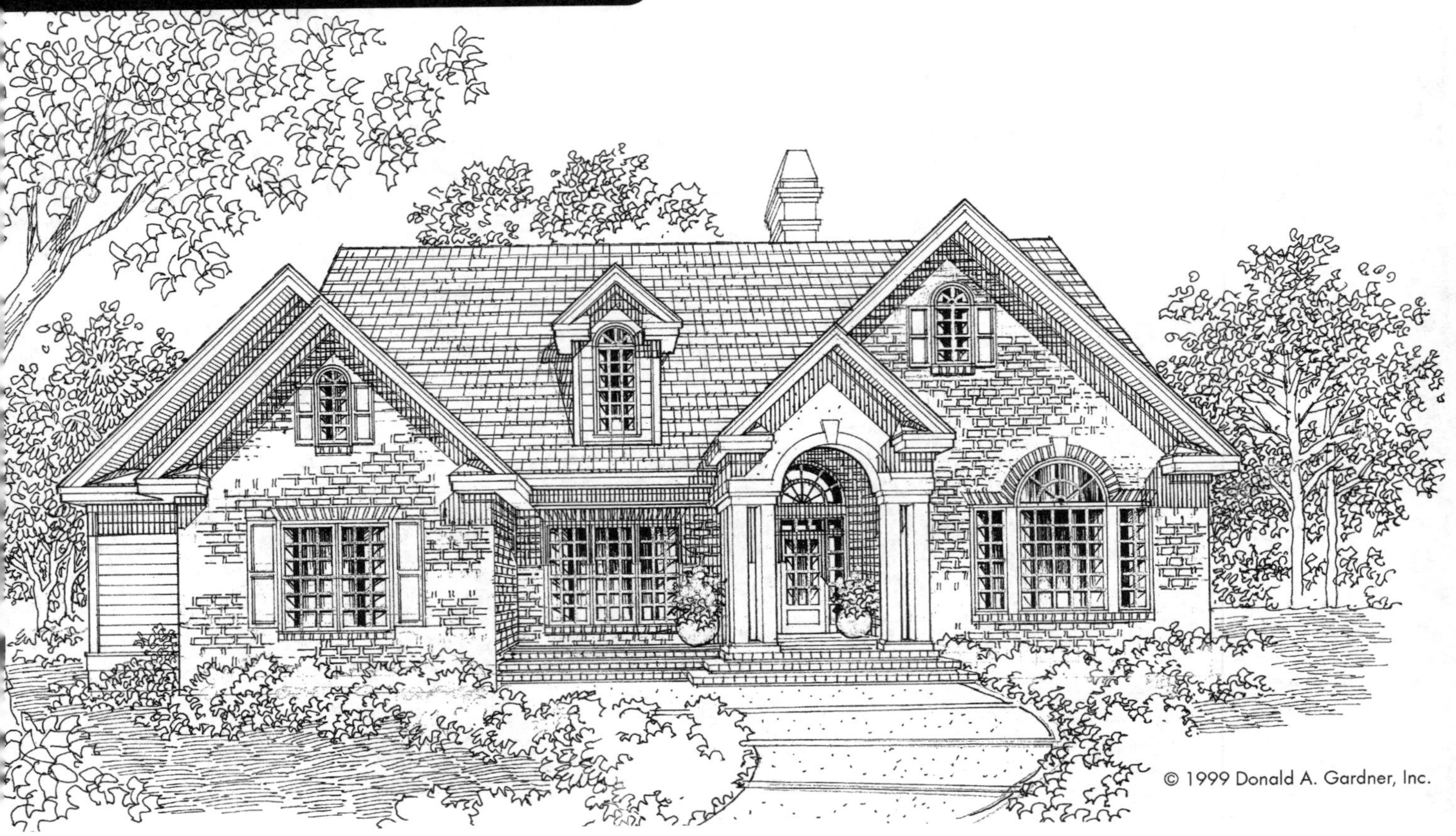

With its dramatic columned entry, arched windows and brick facade with stucco and siding accents, this home offers a dazzling blend of styles. The vaulted great room is open and spacious, illuminated by a rear clerestory dormer and French doors that lead to a back deck. The kitchen is open with easy access to the dining room, great room, breakfast bay and screened porch. The master suite and another bedroom are located on the first floor, while two more family bedrooms, each with a walk-in closet, can be found upstairs. The master suite features a tray ceiling, a linen closet, a walk-in closet and a well-appointed private bath.

plan# HPT930360

- Style: French Country
- First Floor: 1,869 sq. ft.
- Second Floor: 491 sq. ft.
- Total: 2,360 sq. ft.
- Bonus Space: 297 sq. ft.
- Bedrooms: 4
- Bathrooms: 3
- Width: 65'-0"
- Depth: 48'-8"

SEARCH ONLINE @ EPLANS.COM

FIRST FLOOR

SECOND FLOOR

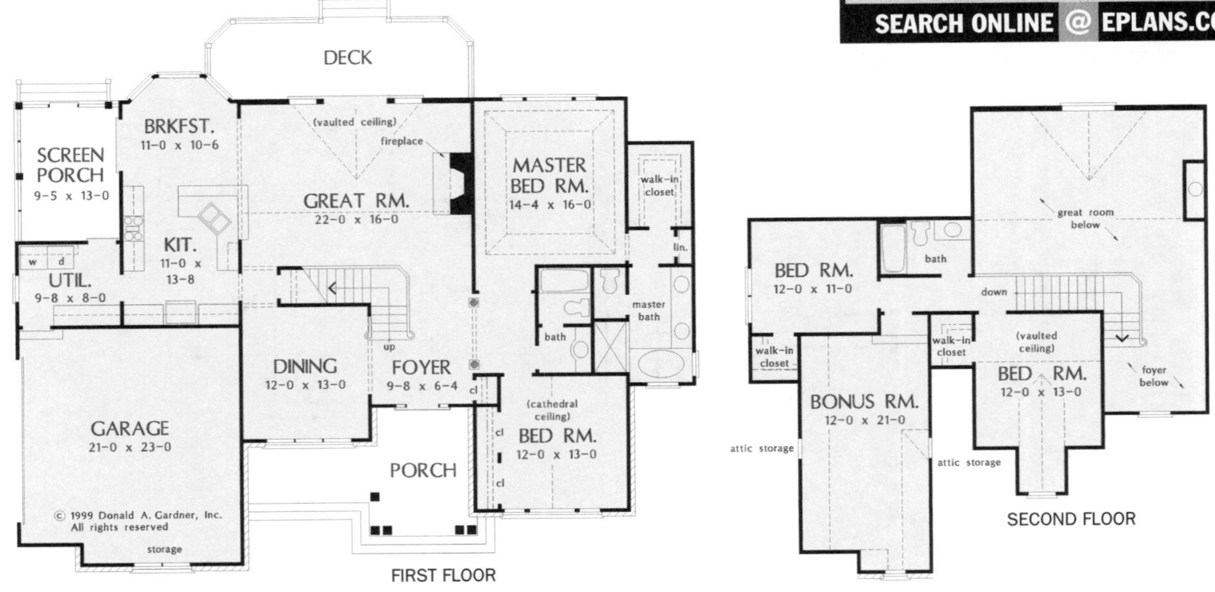

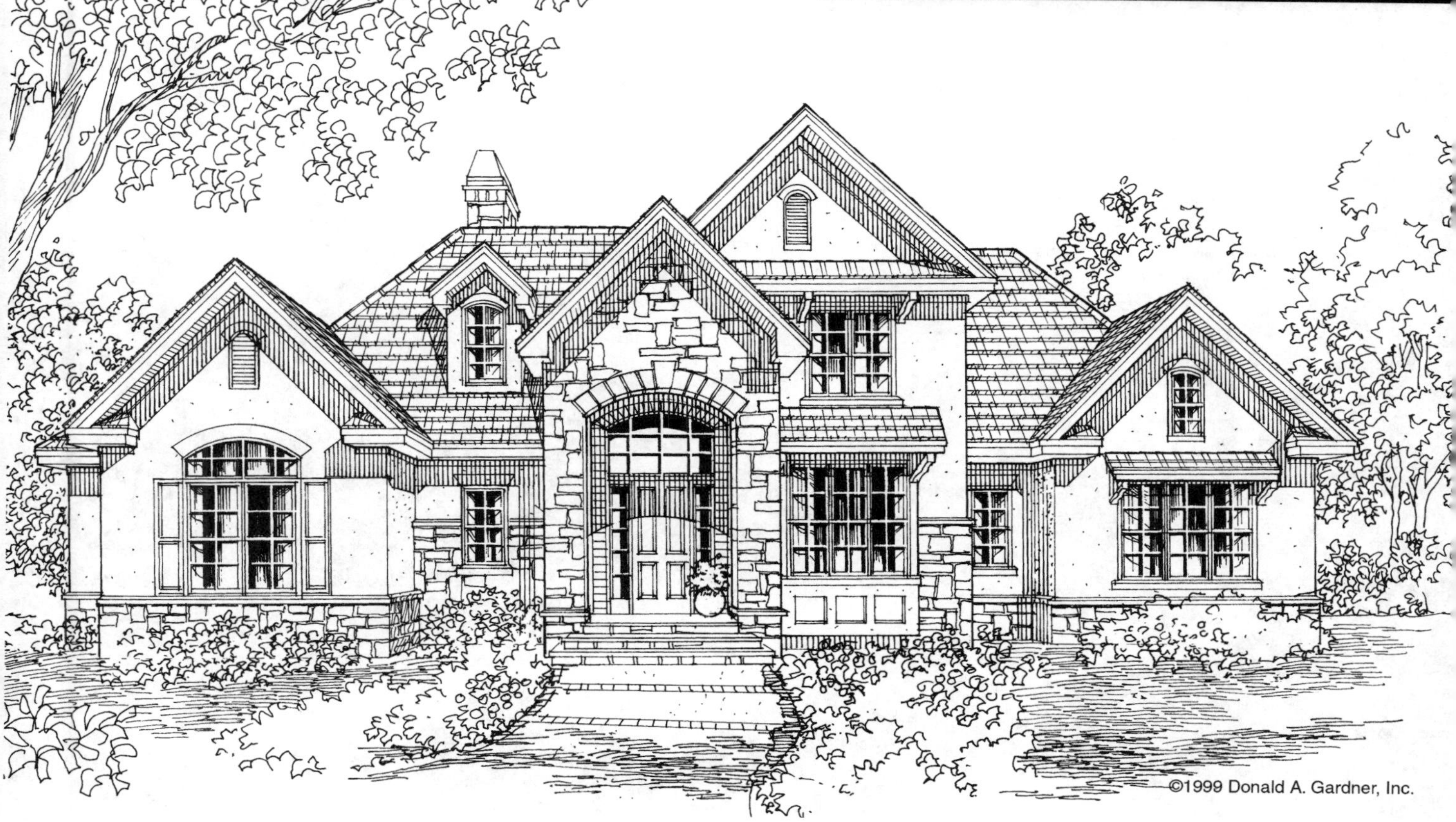

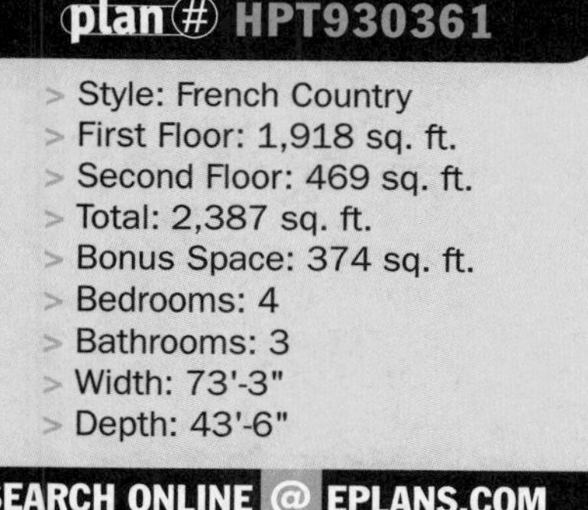

plan# HPT930361

- Style: French Country
- First Floor: 1,918 sq. ft.
- Second Floor: 469 sq. ft.
- Total: 2,387 sq. ft.
- Bonus Space: 374 sq. ft.
- Bedrooms: 4
- Bathrooms: 3
- Width: 73'-3"
- Depth: 43'-6"

SEARCH ONLINE @ EPLANS.COM

Enjoy the elegance of the stone-and-stucco exterior on this amenity-filled, four-bedroom home. An impressive fireplace features built-ins to each side within the great room. The secondary bedroom on the first floor—or make it a study—provides access to a full bath, while the trayed-ceiling master suite includes a sumptuous bath, two walk-in closets and a bay window. Two secondary bedrooms, a bonus room and a full bath reside on the second floor.

SECOND FLOOR

FIRST FLOOR

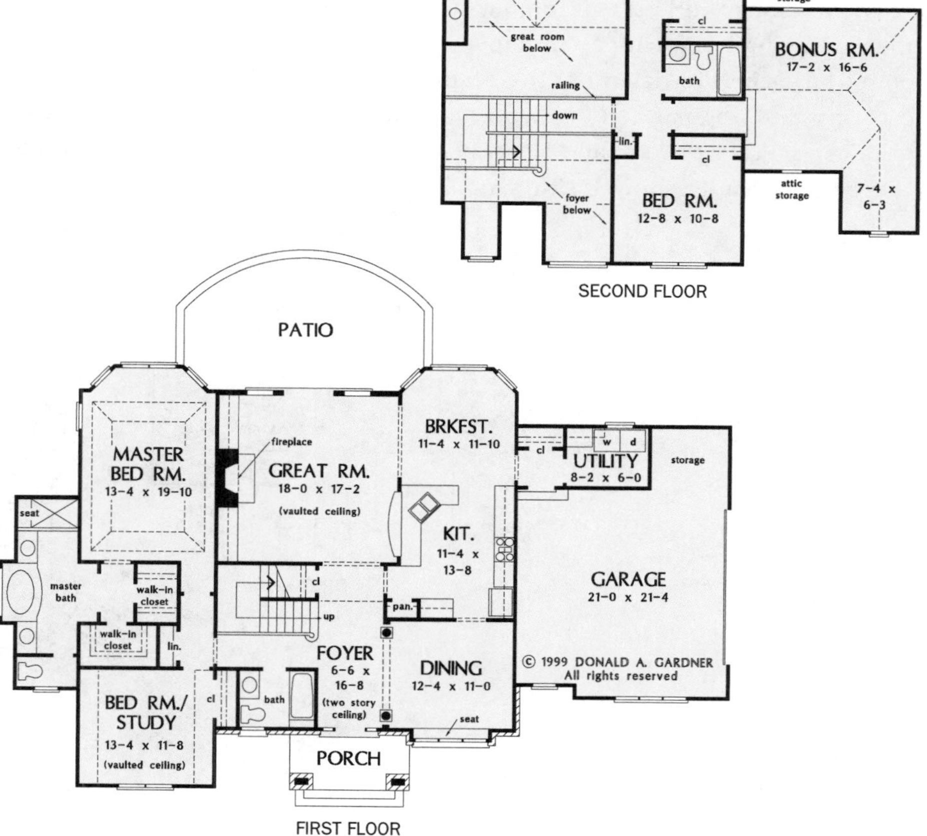

FRENCH COUNTRY CHATEAUX

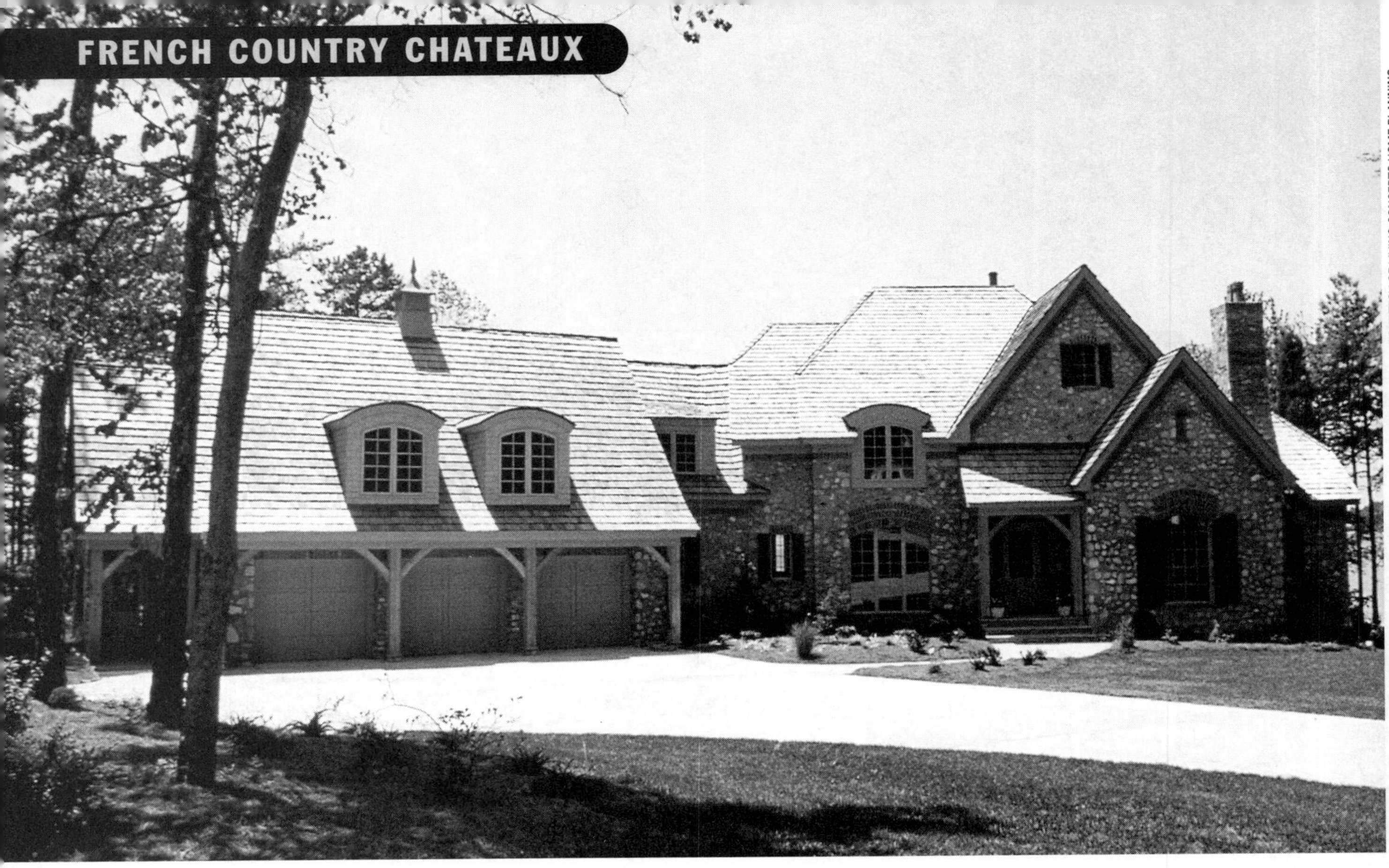

COURTESY OF LIVING CONCEPTS HOME PLANNING

Gently curved arches and dormers contrast with the straight lines of gables and wooden columns on this French-style stone exterior. Small-paned windows are enhanced by shutters; tall chimneys and a cupola add height. Inside, a spacious gathering room with an impressive fireplace opens to a cheery morning room. The kitchen is a delight, with a beam ceiling, triangular work island, walk-in pantry and angular counter with a snack bar. The nearby laundry room includes a sink, a work area and plenty of room for storage. The first-floor master suite boasts a bay-windowed sitting nook, a deluxe bath and a handy study.

plan# HPT930362

- Style: French
- First Floor: 2,660 sq. ft.
- Second Floor: 914 sq. ft.
- Total: 3,574 sq. ft.
- Bonus Space: 733 sq. ft.
- Bedrooms: 3
- Bathrooms: 4½
- Width: 114'-8"
- Depth: 75'-10"
- Foundation: Crawlspace

SEARCH ONLINE @ EPLANS.COM

FIRST FLOOR

SECOND FLOOR

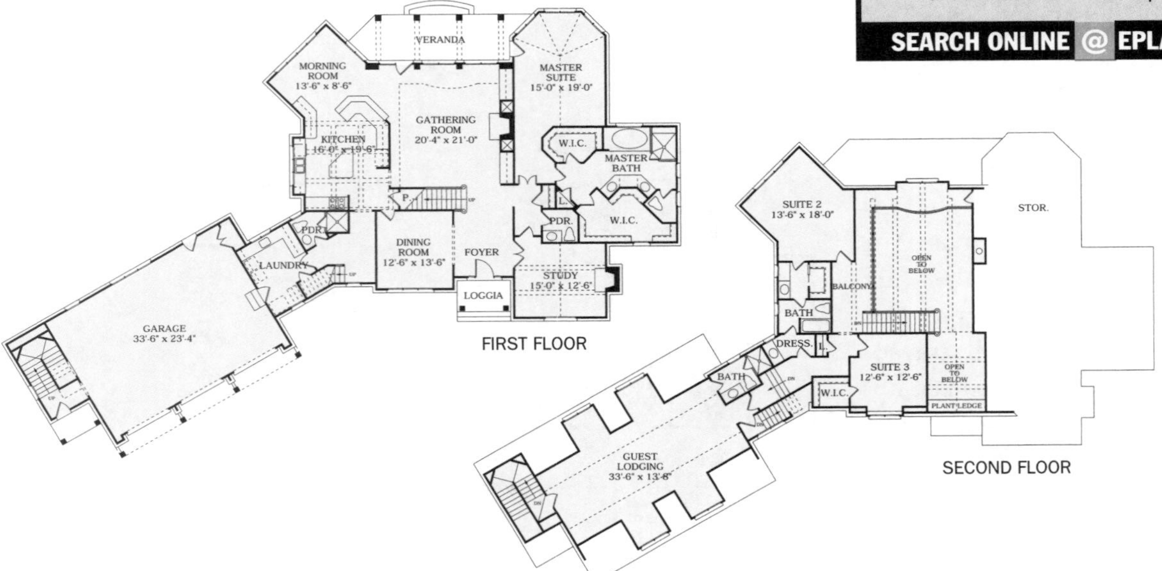

plan# HPT930363

- Style: French Country
- First Floor: 1,746 sq. ft.
- Second Floor: 651 sq. ft.
- Total: 2,397 sq. ft.
- Bonus Space: 283 sq. ft.
- Bedrooms: 3
- Bathrooms: 2½
- Width: 50'-0"
- Depth: 75'-4"
- Foundation: Walkout Basement

SEARCH ONLINE @ EPLANS.COM

At the heart of this home, a gourmet kitchen provides beautiful hardwood floors, a snack counter and a walk-in pantry. Double doors open to a gallery hall that leads to the formal dining room—an enchanting retreat for chandelier-lit evenings. A classic great room—perfect for both formal and casual family gatherings—is warmed by a cozy fireplace and brightened by a wall of windows. The outdoor living area is spacious enough for grand events. The master suite is brightened by sweeping views of the backyard and a romantic fireplace just for two. Upstairs, the third bedroom is easily converted to a home office for the busy entrepreneur.

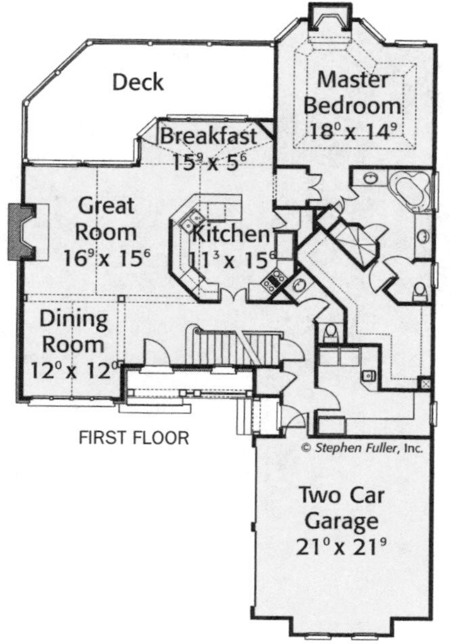

FIRST FLOOR

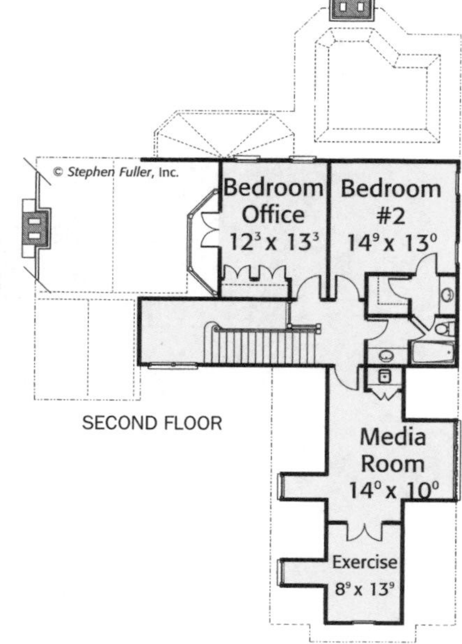

SECOND FLOOR

Multi-pane windows and a natural stone facade complement this French country estate. A two-story foyer leads to a central grand room. A formal dining room to the front offers a fireplace. To the left, a cozy study with a second fireplace features built-in cabinetry. The sleeping quarters offer luxurious amenities. The master bath includes a whirlpool tub in a bumped-out bay, twin lavatories and two walk-in closets. Upstairs, three suites, each with a walk-in closet and one with its own bath, share a balcony hall that leads to a home theater. An apartment over the garage will house visiting or live-in relatives, or may be used as a maid's quarters.

plan# HPT930364

- Style: French Country
- First Floor: 3,560 sq. ft.
- Second Floor: 1,783 sq. ft.
- Total: 5,343 sq. ft.
- Bonus Space: 641 sq. ft.
- Bedrooms: 4
- Bathrooms: 3½
- Width: 121'-2"
- Depth: 104'-4"
- Foundation: Crawlspace

SEARCH ONLINE @ EPLANS.COM

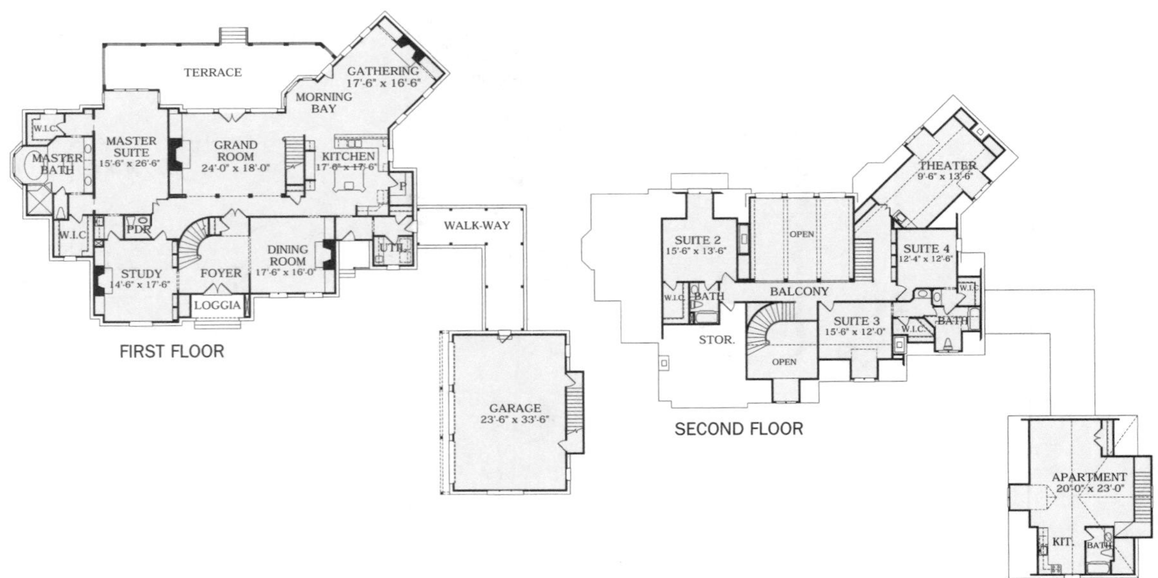

plan# HPT930365

- Style: Mediterranean
- First Floor: 3,307 sq. ft.
- Second Floor: 1,642 sq. ft.
- Total: 4,949 sq. ft.
- Bonus Space: 1,134 sq. ft.
- Bedrooms: 5
- Bathrooms: 4½ + ½
- Width: 115'-4"
- Depth: 68'-10"
- Foundation: Crawlspace

SEARCH ONLINE @ EPLANS.COM

You'll be amazed at what this French country estate has to offer. A study/parlor and a formal dining room announce a grand foyer. Ahead, the living room offers a wet bar and French doors to the rear property. The kitchen is dazzling, with an enormous pantry, oversized cooktop island... even a pizza oven! The gathering room has a corner fireplace and accesses the covered veranda. To the far right, the master suite is a delicious retreat from the world. A bowed window lets in light and a romantic fireplace makes chilly nights cozy. The luxurious bath is awe inspiring, with a roman tub and separate compartmented toilet areas—one with a bidet. Upstairs, three family bedrooms share a generous bonus room. A separate pool house is available, which includes a fireplace, full bath, and dressing area.

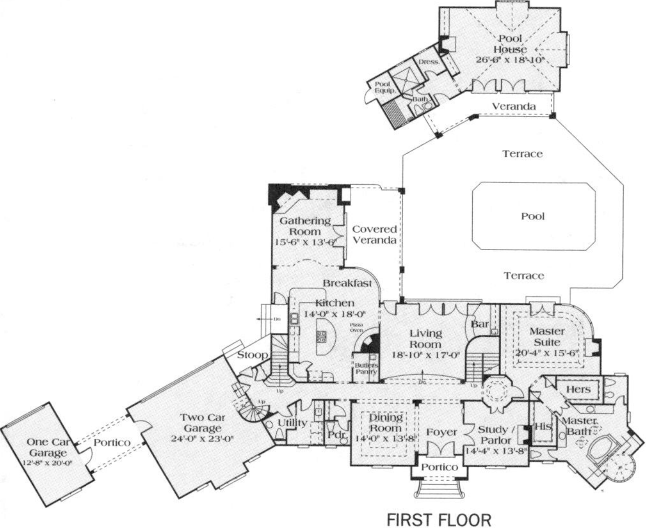

FIRST FLOOR

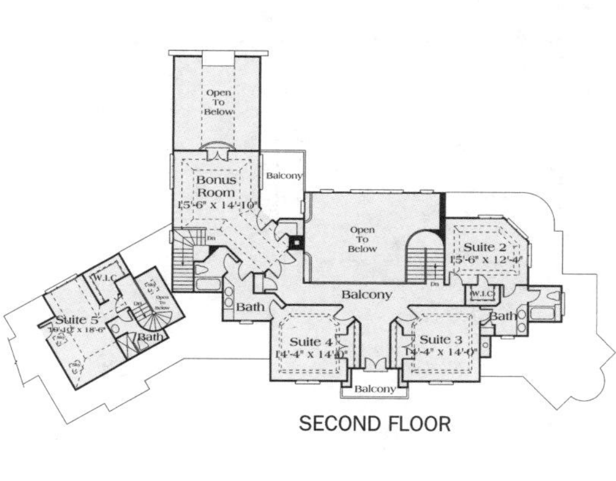

SECOND FLOOR

Sweeping heights lend a grand stroke to this estate in the study, the grand foyer, the dining room and the living room. The living and dining room ceilings are coffered. Upstairs, the master suite enjoys a full list of appointments, including an exercise (or bonus) room, a tub tower with a vaulted cove-lit ceiling, and a private deck. Also on this floor is a guest bedroom with an observation deck (or make this a spectacular study to complement the master suite). Other special details include: a pass-through outdoor bar, an outdoor kitchen, a workshop area, two verandas and a glass elevator.

plan# HPT930366

- Style: Mediterranean
- First Floor: 3,667 sq. ft.
- Second Floor: 1,867 sq. ft.
- Total: 5,534 sq. ft.
- Bonus Space: 140 sq. ft.
- Bedrooms: 4
- Bathrooms: 5½
- Width: 102'-0"
- Depth: 87'-0"
- Foundation: Slab

SEARCH ONLINE @ EPLANS.COM

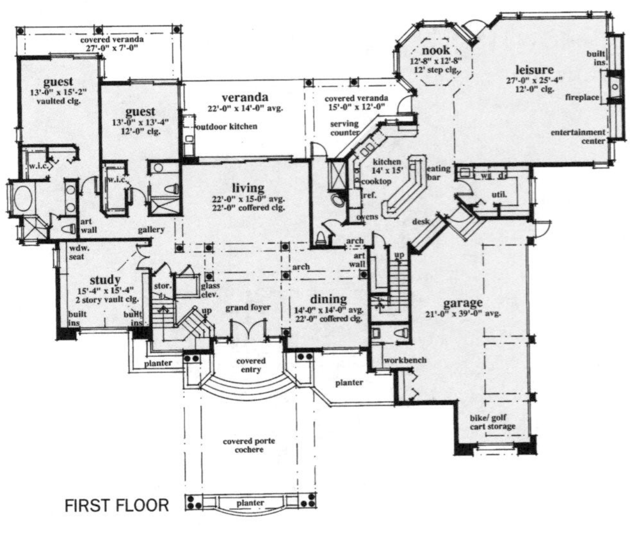

FIRST FLOOR

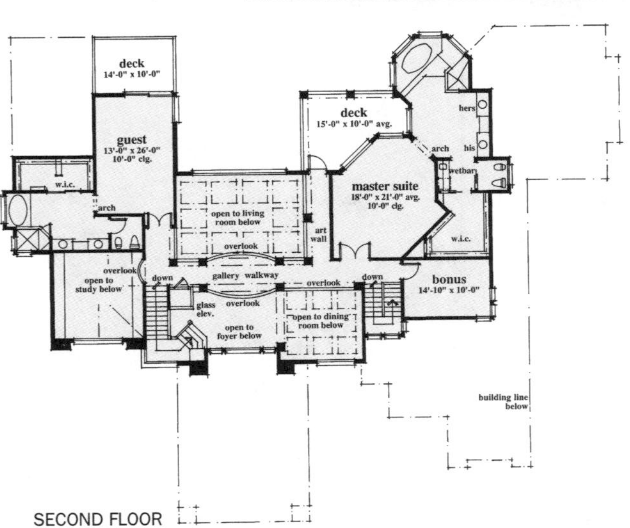

SECOND FLOOR

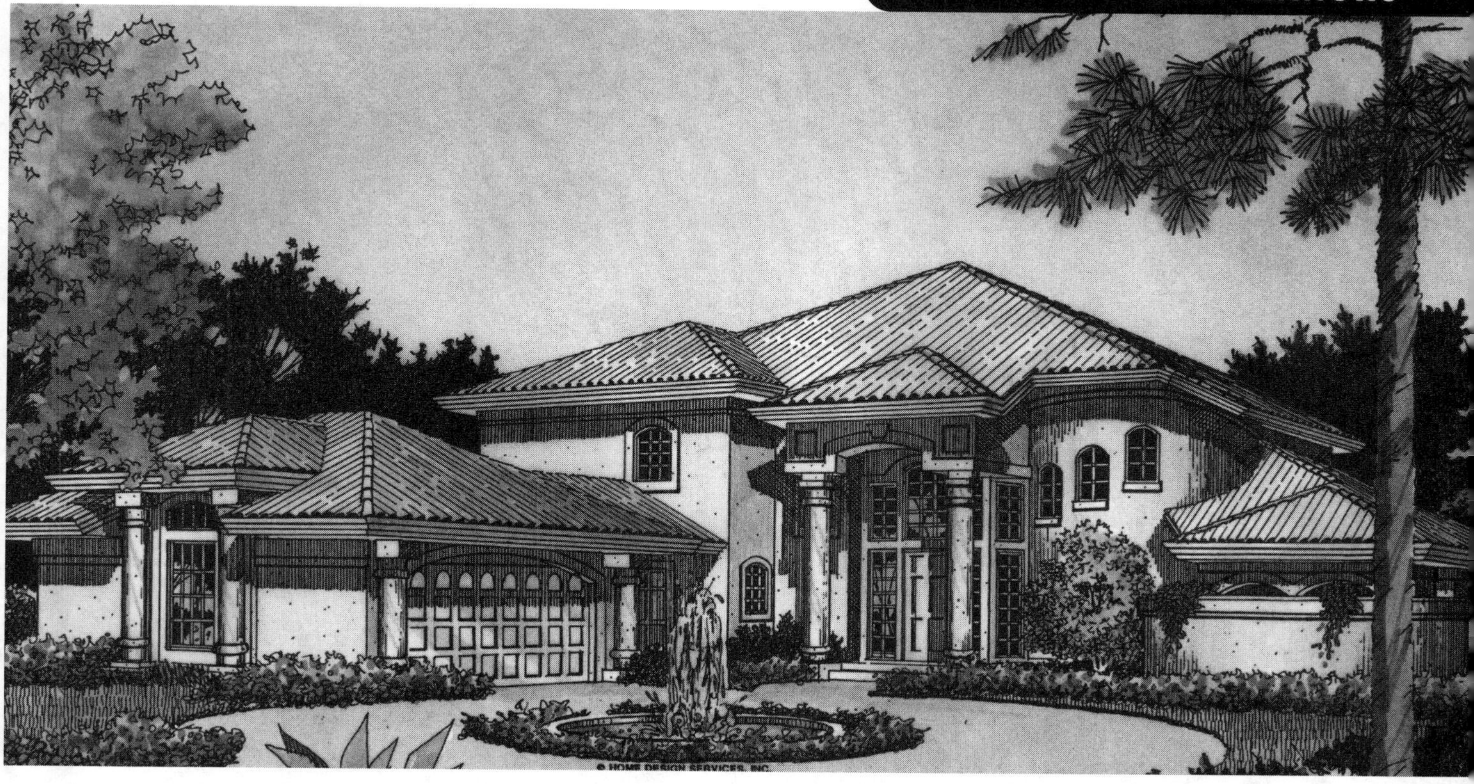

plan# HPT930367

- Style: Mediterranean
- First Floor: 3,236 sq. ft.
- Second Floor: 494 sq. ft.
- Total: 3,730 sq. ft.
- Bedrooms: 4
- Bathrooms: 3½
- Width: 80'-0"
- Depth: 89'-10"
- Foundation: Slab

SEARCH ONLINE @ EPLANS.COM

If you want to build a home light years ahead of most other designs, non-traditional, yet addresses every need for your family, this showcase home is for you. From the moment you walk into this home, you are confronted with wonderful interior architecture that reflects modern, yet refined taste. The exterior says contemporary; the interior creates special excitement. Note the special rounded corners found throughout the home and the many amenities. The master suite is especially appealing with a fireplace and grand bath. Upstairs are a library/sitting room and a very private den or guest bedroom.

FIRST FLOOR

SECOND FLOOR

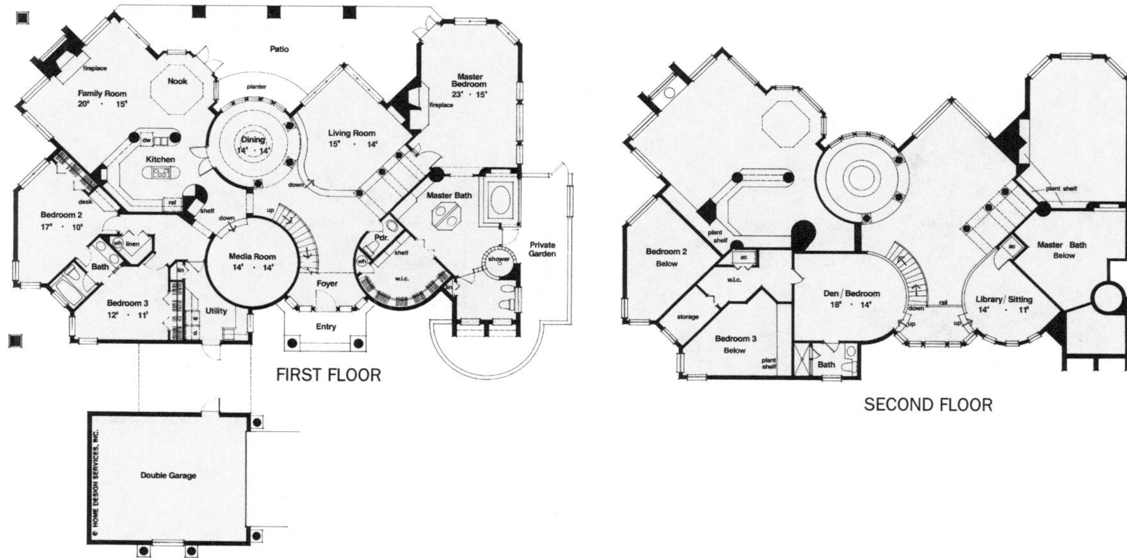

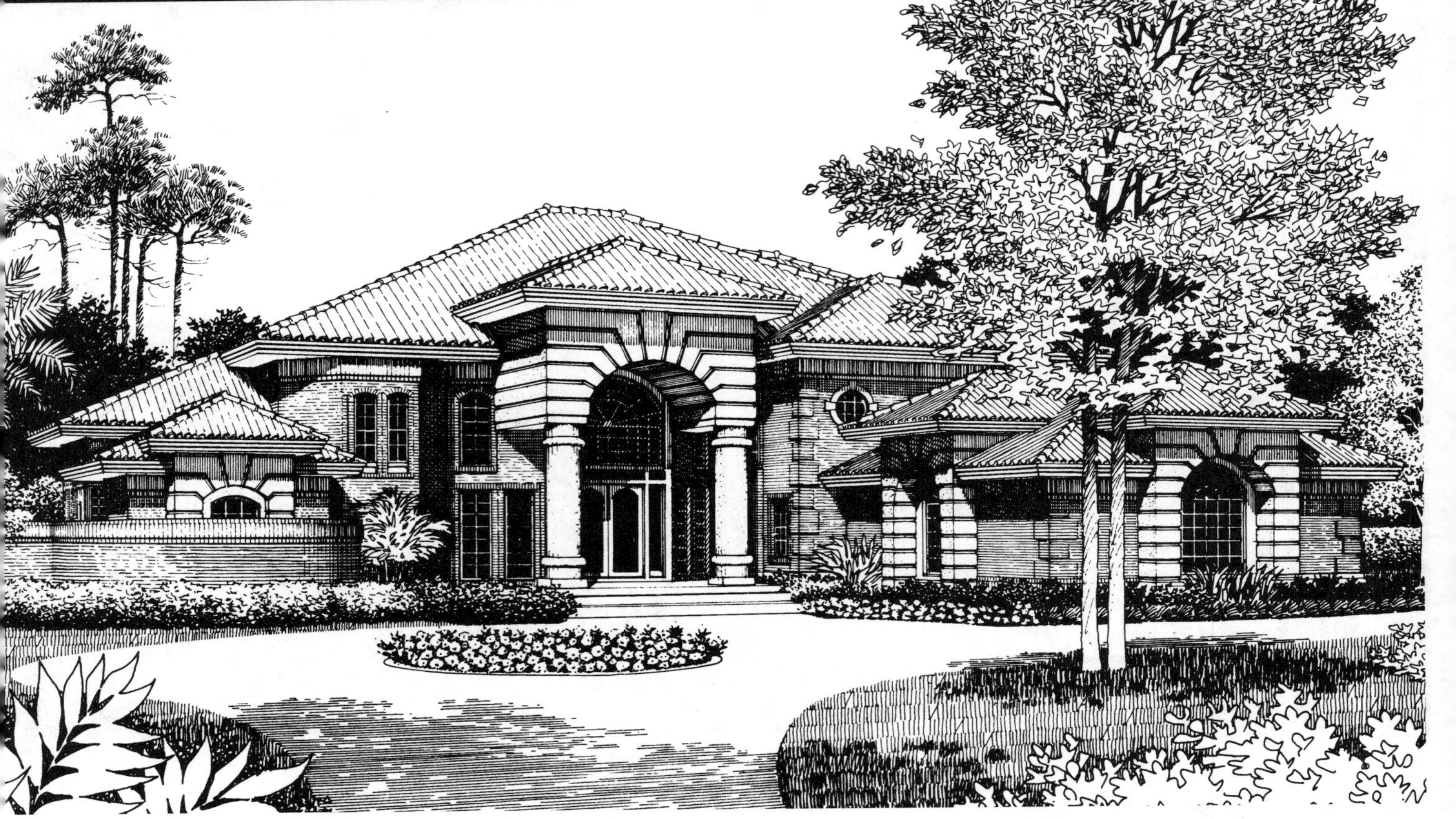

This fresh and innovative design creates unbeatable ambiance. The breakfast nook and family room both open to a patio—a perfect arrangement for informal entertaining. The dining room is sure to please with elegant pillars separating it from the sunken living room. A media room delights both with its shape and convenience to the nearby kitchen—great for snack runs. A private garden surrounds the master bath and its spa tub and enormous walk-in closet. The master bedroom is enchanting with a fireplace and access to the outdoors. Additional family bedrooms come in a variety of different shapes and sizes; Bedroom 4 reigns over the second floor and features its own full bath.

plan# HPT930368

- Style: Mediterranean
- First Floor: 3,770 sq. ft.
- Second Floor: 634 sq. ft.
- Total: 4,404 sq. ft.
- Bedrooms: 4
- Bathrooms: 3½
- Width: 87'-0"
- Depth: 97'-6"
- Foundation: Slab

SEARCH ONLINE @ EPLANS.COM

FIRST FLOOR

SECOND FLOOR

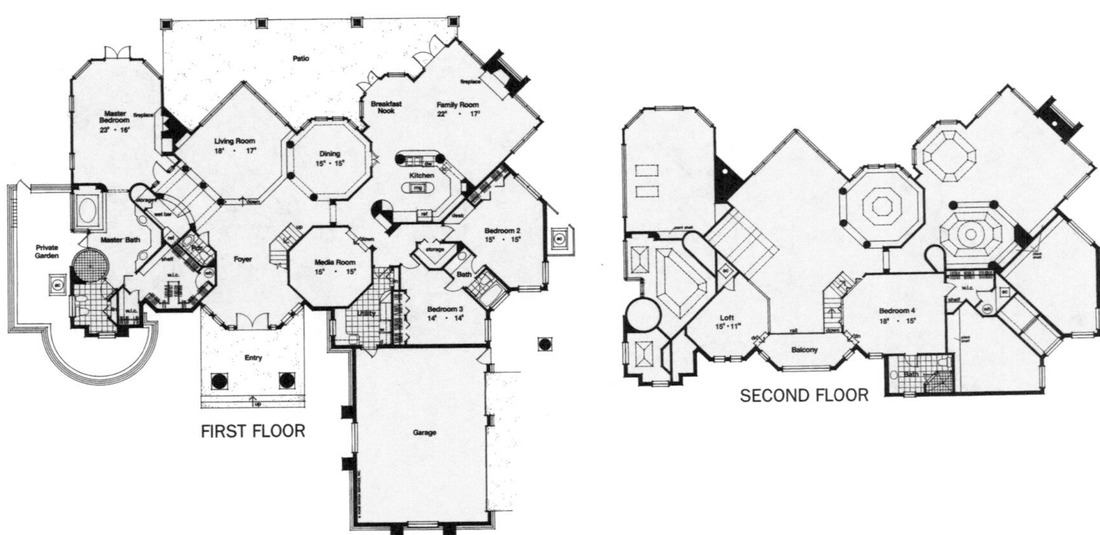

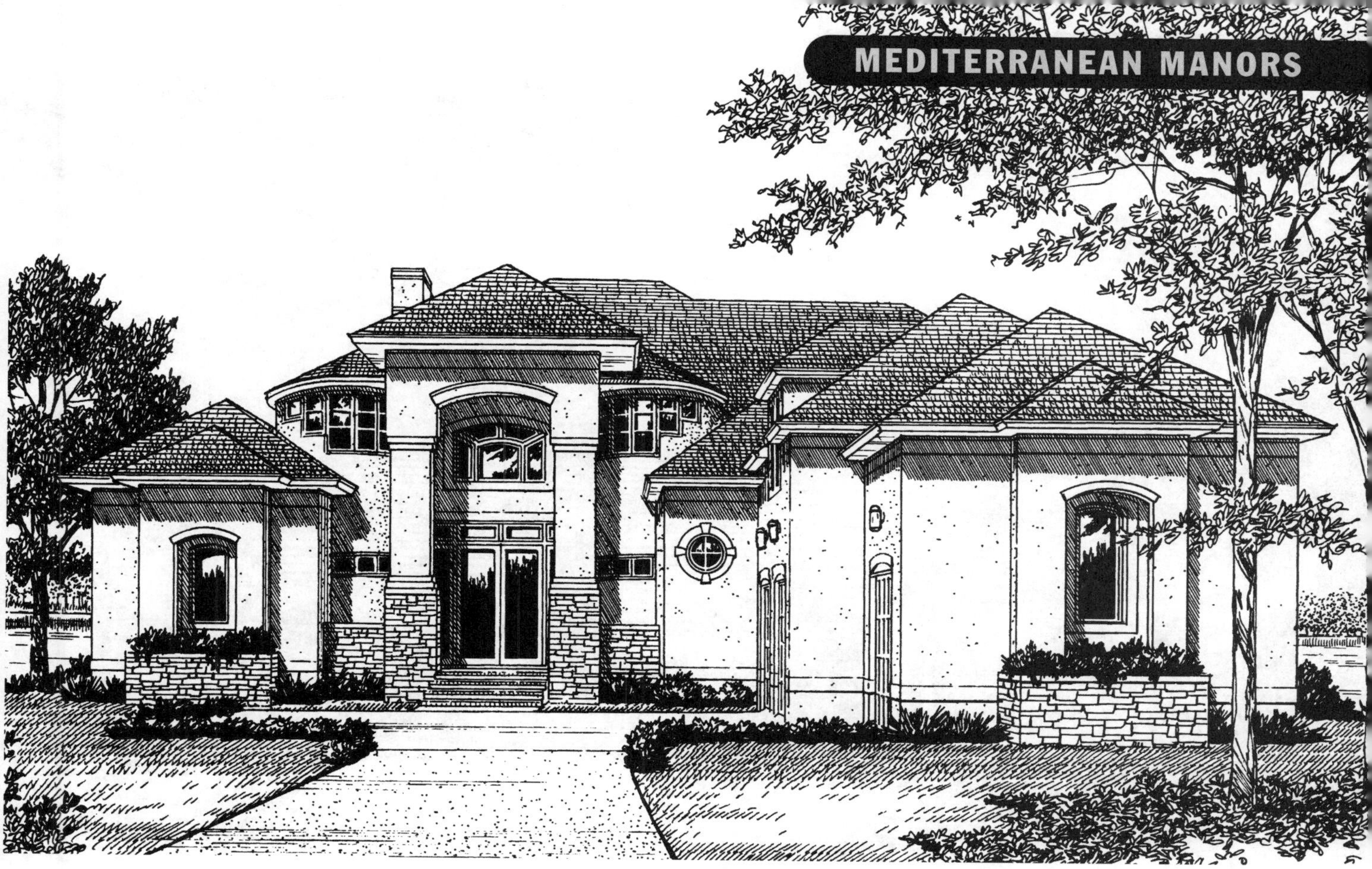

plan# HPT930369

- Style: Mediterranean
- First Floor: 2,391 sq. ft.
- Second Floor: 922 sq. ft.
- Total: 3313 sq. ft.
- Bonus Space: 400 sq. ft.
- Bedrooms: 3
- Bathrooms: 3½
- Width: 63'-10"
- Depth: 85'-6"
- Foundation: Walkout Basement

SEARCH ONLINE @ EPLANS.COM

Here's an upscale multi-level plan with expansive rear views. The first floor provides an open living and dining area, defined by decorative columns and enhanced by natural light from tall windows. A breakfast area with a lovely triple window opens to a sun room, which allows light to pour into the gourmet kitchen. The master wing features a tray ceiling in the bedroom, two walk-in closets and an elegant private vestibule leading to a lavish bath. Upstairs, a reading loft overlooks the great room and leads to a sleeping area with two suites. A recreation room, exercise room, office, guest suite and additional storage are available in the finished basement.

FIRST FLOOR

SECOND FLOOR

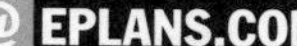

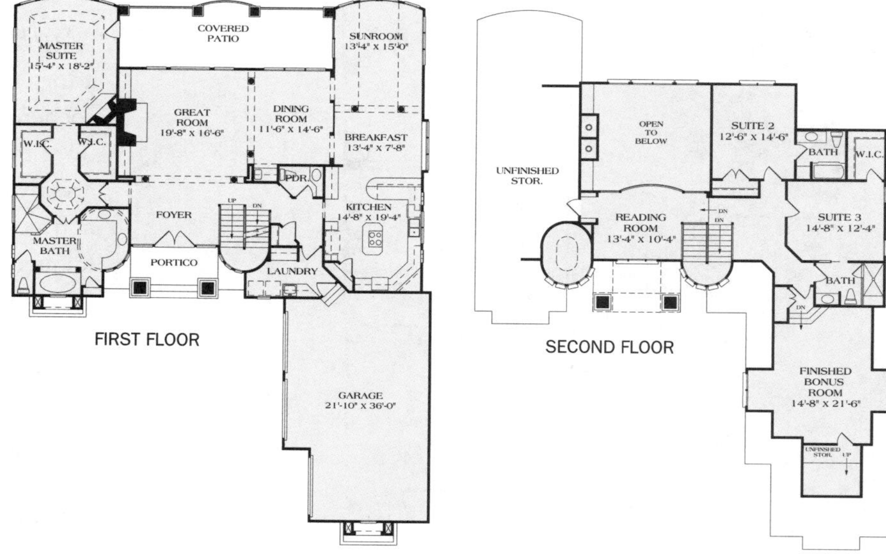

© HOME DESIGN SERVICES, INC.

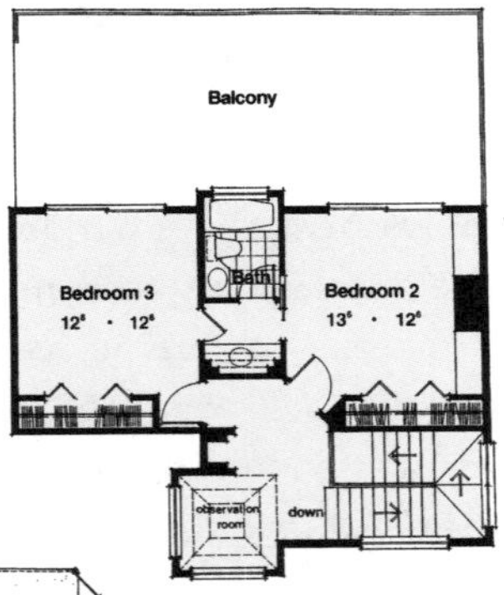

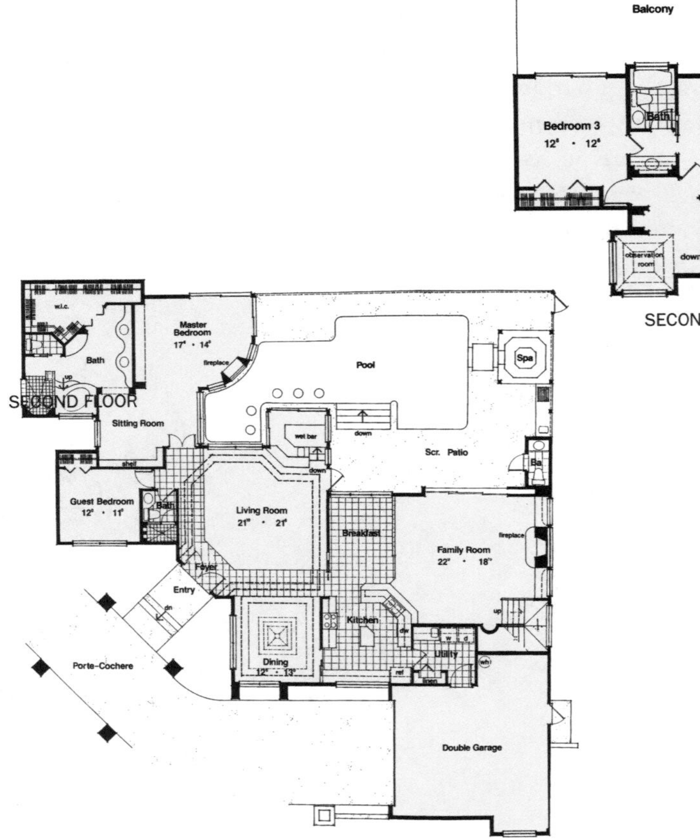

SECOND FLOOR

FIRST FLOOR

plan# HPT930370

- Style: Mediterranean
- First Floor: 2,669 sq. ft.
- Second Floor: 621 sq. ft.
- Total: 3,290 sq. ft.
- Bedrooms: 4
- Bathrooms: 3½
- Width: 78'-0"
- Depth: 84'-6"
- Foundation: Slab

SEARCH ONLINE @ EPLANS.COM

Multiple rooflines, arches and corner quoins adorn the facade of this magnificent home. A porte cochere creates a stunning prelude to the double-door entry. A wet bar serves the sunken living room and overlooks the pool area. The dining room has a tray ceiling and is located near the gourmet kitchen with a food-preparation island and angled counter. A guest room opens off the living room. The generous family room, warmed by a fireplace, opens to the screened patio. The master suite provides a sitting room and a fireplace that's set into an angled wall. Its luxurious bath includes a step-up tub. Upstairs, two bedrooms share the oversized balcony and nearby observation room.

plan# HPT930371

- Style: Mediterranean
- First Floor: 2,051 sq. ft.
- Second Floor: 749 sq. ft.
- Total: 2,800 sq. ft.
- Bedrooms: 3
- Bathrooms: 2½
- Width: 50'-0"
- Depth: 74'-0"
- Foundation: Slab

SEARCH ONLINE @ EPLANS.COM

Only fifty feet in width, this fabulous design will fit anywhere! From the moment you enter the home from the foyer, this floor plan explodes in every direction with huge living spaces. Flanking the foyer are the living and dining rooms, and the visual impact of the staircase is breathtaking. Two-story ceilings adorn the huge family room with double-stacked glass walls. Sunlight floods the breakfast nook, and the kitchen is a gourmet's dream, complete with a cooking island and loads of overhead cabinets. Tray ceilings grace the master suite, which also offers a well-designed private bath. Here, a large soaking tub, doorless shower, private toilet chamber and huge walk-in closet are sure to please. Upstairs, two oversized bedrooms and a loft space—perfect for the home computer—share a full bath.

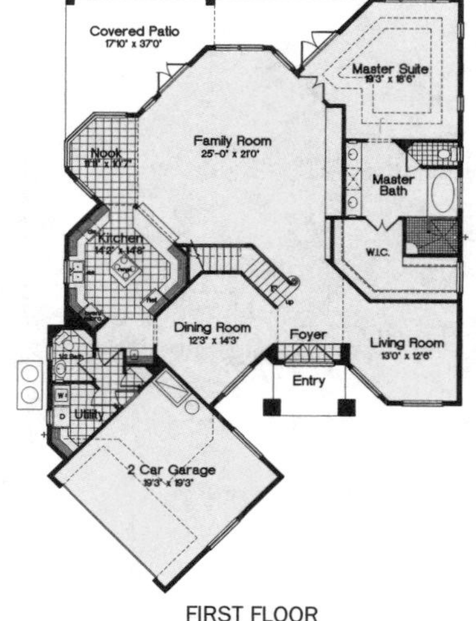

FIRST FLOOR

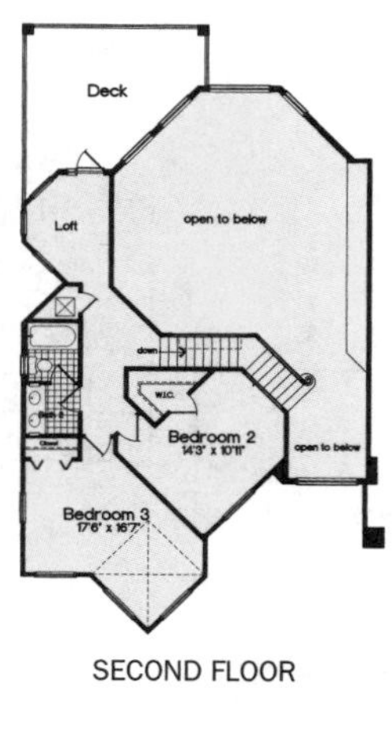

SECOND FLOOR

This Mediterranean estate features palatial elegance with all the comfortable amenities of the modern world. Double doors welcome you inside to a sunlit gallery that introduces a beautiful double staircase. The island kitchen easily serves the formal dining room. A bayed den accesses a rear deck. The gathering room is served by a bar area and is warmed by a fireplace. The study is a quiet retreat accessing a covered porch that extends to an outdoor deck. The second floor offers a plush master suite that includes a sitting area, two walk-in closets and a private bath. Two additional suites and a playroom also reside here. The basement level is an impressive entertainment center that provides a recreation room served by a wet bar, a billiard room, home theater, gym, in-door spa, sauna, guest suite, second kitchen and a mechanical/storage room. An elevator provides easy access to all levels.

plan# HPT930372

- Style: Mediterranean
- Main Level: 2,710 sq. ft.
- Upper Level: 2,784 sq. ft.
- Lower Level: 2,574 sq. ft.
- Total: 8,068 sq. ft.
- Bedrooms: 4
- Bathrooms: 5
- Width: 79'-4"
- Depth: 76'-8"
- Foundation: Walkout Basement

SEARCH ONLINE @ EPLANS.COM

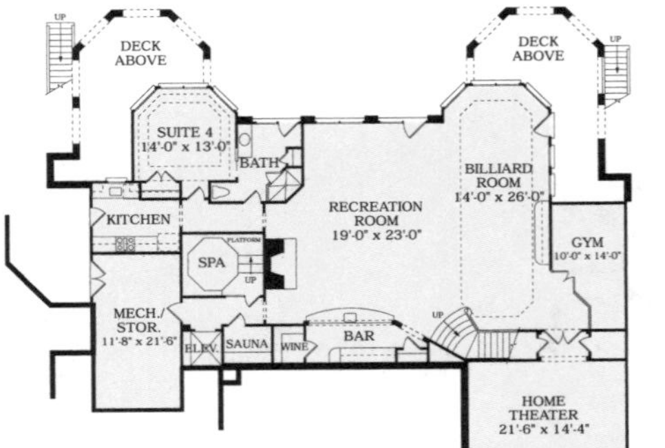

DECK ABOVE
DECK ABOVE
SUITE 4 14'-0" x 13'-0"
BATH
KITCHEN
RECREATION ROOM 19'-0" x 23'-0"
BILLIARD ROOM 14'-0" x 26'-0"
GYM 10'-0" x 14'-0"
SPA
MECH./ STOR. 11'-8" x 21'-6"
ELEV.
SAUNA
WINE
BAR
HOME THEATER 21'-6" x 14'-4"

LOWER LEVEL

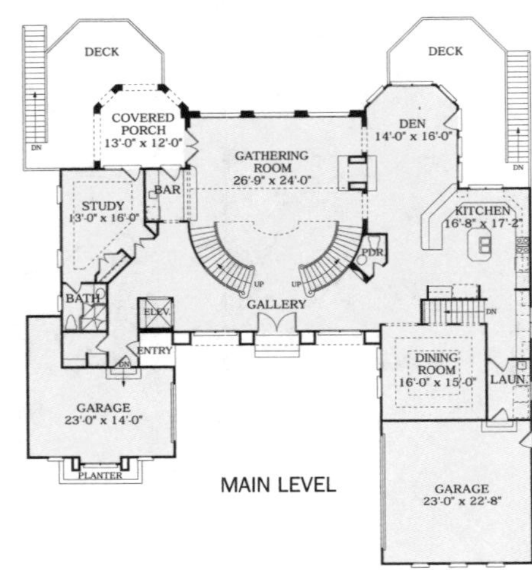

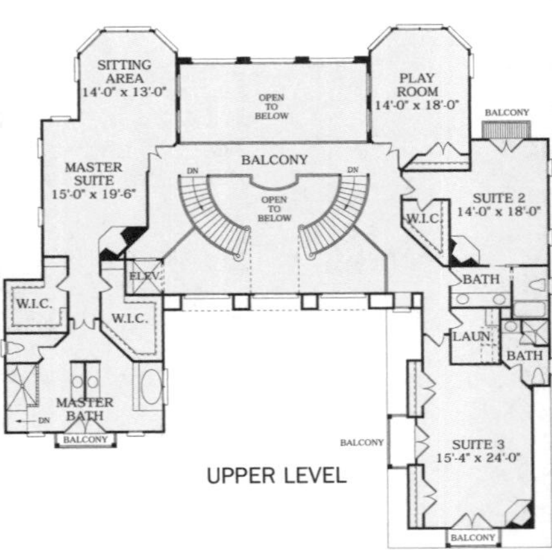

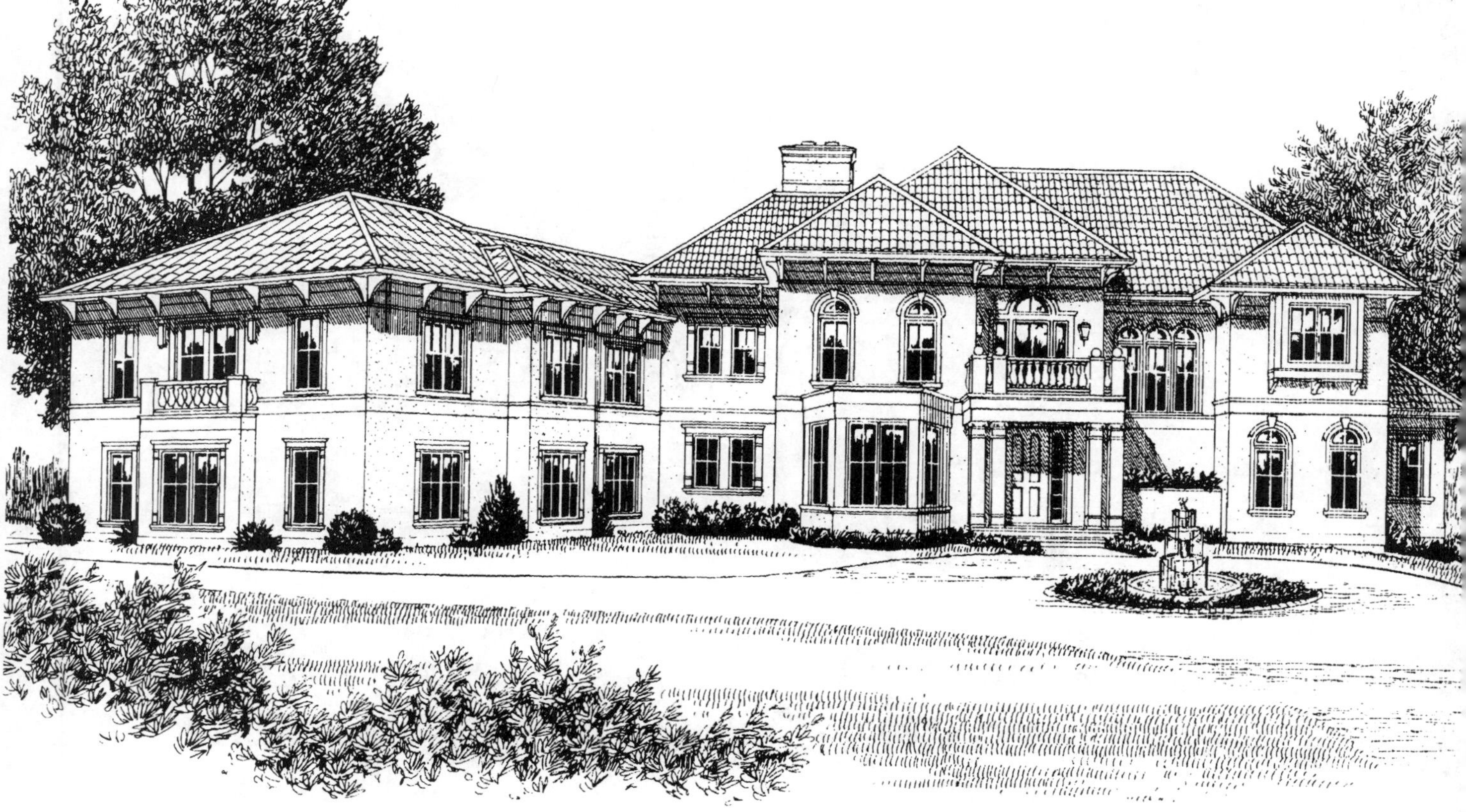

plan# HPT930373

- Style: Mediterranean
- First Floor: 3,300 sq. ft.
- Second Floor: 1,973 sq. ft.
- Total: 5,273 sq. ft.
- Basement: 2,870 sq. ft.
- Bonus Space: 960 sq. ft.
- Bedrooms: 4
- Bathrooms: 5½
- Width: 107'-10"
- Depth: 75'-7"
- Foundation: Walkout Basement

SEARCH ONLINE @ EPLANS.COM

This exciting Mediterranean villa is a lavish design filled with a modern array of amenities. A portico welcomes you inside, where formal rooms offer breathtaking interior vistas. The casual areas of the home include a gourmet island kitchen, breakfast room and family room warmed by a fireplace. The first-floor master suite provides a sitting bay, private bath and two walk-in closets. Three additional family suites reside upstairs, along with an office/suite and spacious recreation room. The basement level is reserved for entertainment, starting with a pool room served by a bar, a sitting room with a fireplace, a media room, an exercise room with a sauna, a guest suite and mechanical/storage room. The elevator is a convenient touch.

FIRST FLOOR

BASEMENT

SECOND FLOOR

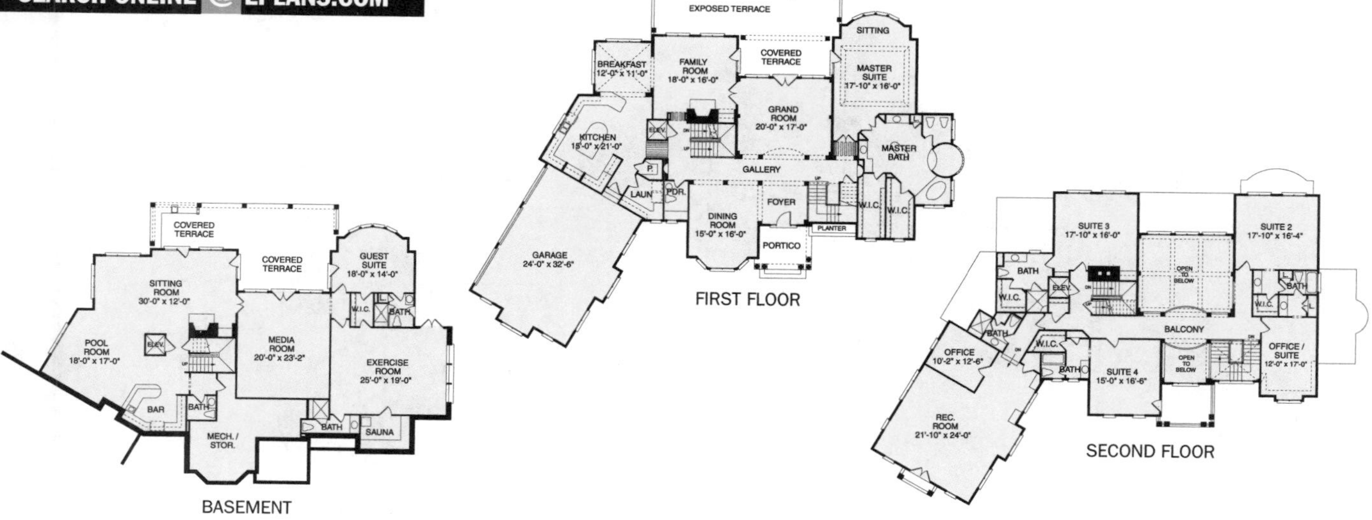

The ornamental stucco detailing on this home creates an Old World charm. The two-story foyer with a sweeping curved stair opens to the large formal dining room and study. The two-story great room overlooks the rear patio. A large kitchen with an island workstation opens to an octagonal-shaped breakfast room and the family room. The master suite, offering convenient access to the study, is complete with a fireplace, two walk-in closets and a bath with twin vanities and a separate shower and tub. A staircase located off the family room provides additional access to the three second-floor bedrooms that each offer walk-in closets and plenty of storage.

plan# HPT930374

- Style: Mediterranean
- First Floor: 3,568 sq. ft.
- Second Floor: 1,667 sq. ft.
- Total: 5,235 sq. ft.
- Bedrooms: 4
- Bathrooms: 3½
- Width: 86'-8"
- Depth: 79'-0"
- Foundation: Walkout Basement

SEARCH ONLINE @ EPLANS.COM

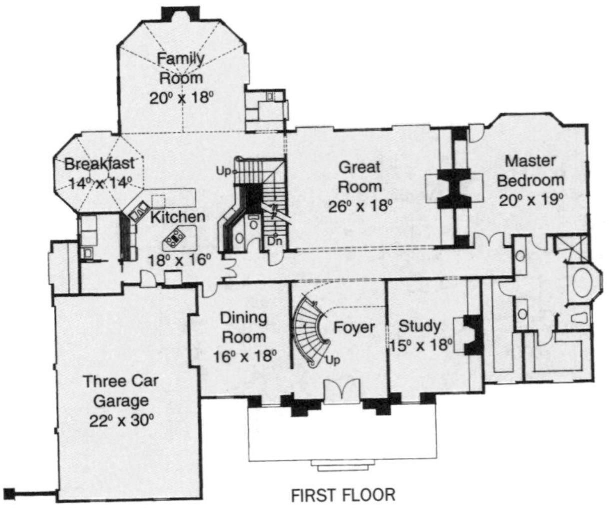

FIRST FLOOR

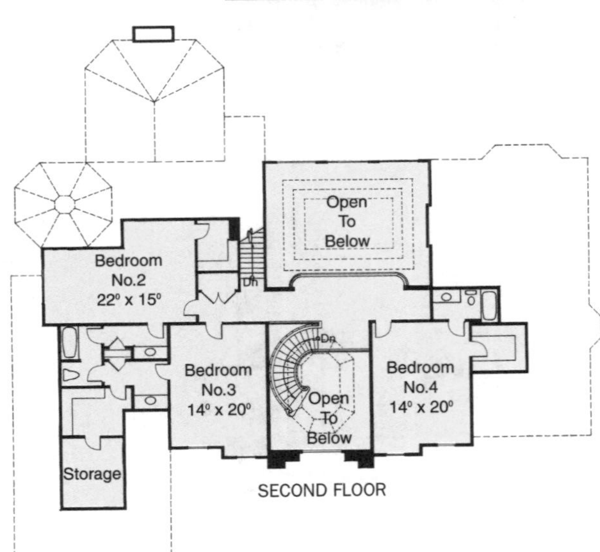

SECOND FLOOR

plan# HPT930375

- Style: Mediterranean
- First Floor: 3,592 sq. ft.
- Second Floor: 2,861 sq. ft.
- Total: 6,453 sq. ft.
- Bedrooms: 5
- Bathrooms: 5½
- Width: 96'-5"
- Depth: 91'-6"
- Foundation: Crawlspace

SEARCH ONLINE @ EPLANS.COM

Stunning Mediterranean style gives this home a sense of palatial elegance. Arches frame the portico, which leads inside to an impressive two-story foyer—a study warmed by a fireplace is to the left, while a formal dining room is introduced to the right. The first-floor master suite enjoys a deluxe whirlpool bath and two walk-in closets. The island kitchen opens to the casual family room, warmed by a second fireplace. Four additional suites reside upstairs for other family members. A romantic overlook views the great room and foyer. A sitting room is placed just outside of the second-floor recreation room.

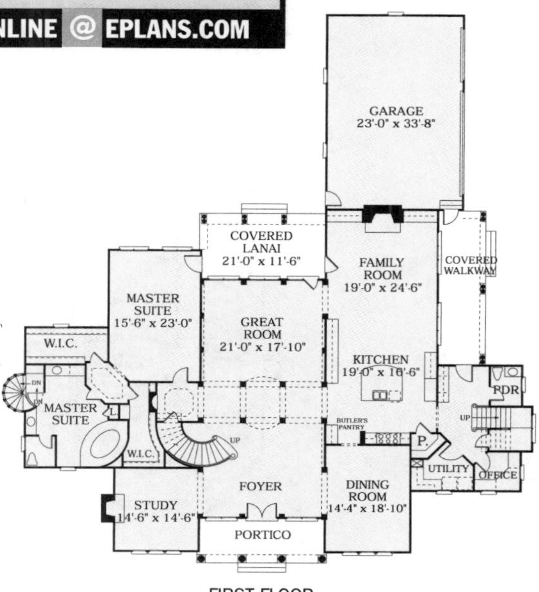

FIRST FLOOR

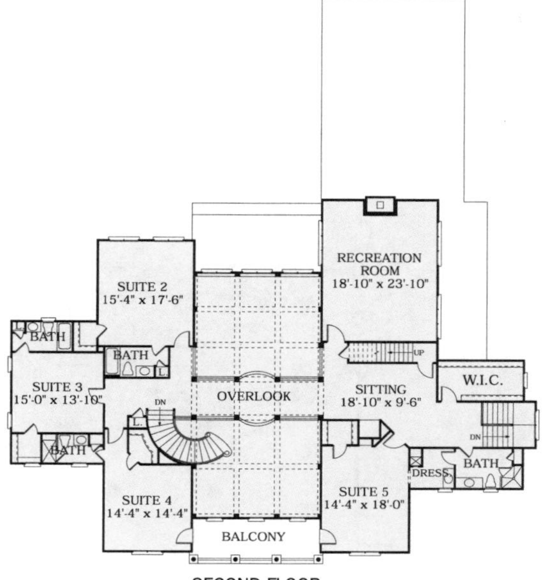

SECOND FLOOR

Ensure an elegant lifestyle with this luxurious plan. A turret, two-story bay windows and plenty of arched glass impart a graceful style to the exterior, while rich amenities inside furnish contentment. A grand foyer decked with columns introduces the living room with curved-glass windows viewing the rear gardens. The study and living room share a through-fireplace. The master suite enjoys a tray ceiling, two walk-in closets, a separate shower and a garden tub set in a bay window. Informal entertainment will be a breeze with a rich leisure room adjoining the kitchen and breakfast nook and opening to a rear veranda. Upstairs, two family bedrooms and a guest suite with a private deck complete the plan.

plan# HPT930376

- Style: Italianate
- First Floor: 2,841 sq. ft.
- Second Floor: 1,052 sq. ft.
- Total: 3,893 sq. ft.
- Bedrooms: 4
- Bathrooms: 3½
- Width: 85'-0"
- Depth: 76'-8"
- Foundation: Crawlspace

SEARCH ONLINE  EPLANS.COM

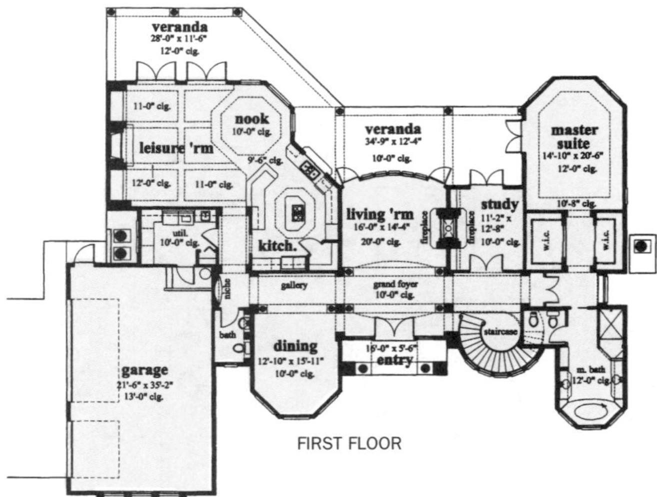

FIRST FLOOR

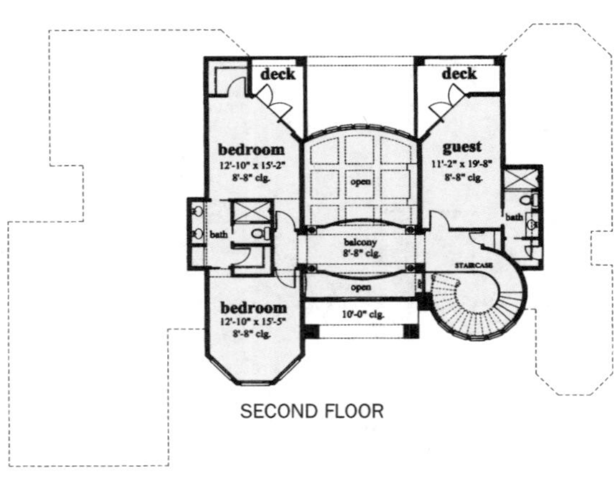

SECOND FLOOR

plan# HPT930377

- Style: French
- First Floor: 2,899 sq. ft.
- Second Floor: 1,472 sq. ft.
- Total: 4,371 sq. ft.
- Bedrooms: 4
- Bathrooms: 3½
- Width: 69'-4"
- Depth: 76'-8"
- Foundation: Slab

SEARCH ONLINE @ EPLANS.COM

Finished with French country adornments, this estate home is comfortable in just about any setting. Main living areas are sunken down just a bit from the entry foyer, providing them with soaring ceilings and sweeping views. The family room features a focal fireplace. A columned entry gains access to the master suite where separate sitting and sleeping areas are defined by a three-sided fireplace. There are three bedrooms upstairs; one has a private bath. The sunken media room on this level includes storage space. Look for the decks on the second level.

FIRST FLOOR

OPTIONAL LAYOUT

SECOND FLOOR

The stone facade and woodwork detail give this home a Craftsman appeal. The foyer opens to a staircase up to the vaulted great room, which features a fireplace flanked by built-ins and French-door access to the rear covered porch. The open dining room with a tray ceiling offers convenience to the spacious kitchen. Two family bedrooms share a bath and enjoy private porches. An overlook to the great room below is a perfect introduction to the master suite. The second level spreads out the luxury of the master suite with a spacious walk-in closet, a private porch and a glorious master bath with a garden tub, dual vanities and a compartmented toilet.

plan# HPT930378

- Style: Mediterranean
- First Floor: 1,383 sq. ft.
- Second Floor: 595 sq. ft.
- Total: 1,978 sq. ft.
- Bonus Space: 617 sq. ft.
- Bedrooms: 3
- Bathrooms: 2
- Width: 48'-0"
- Depth: 48'-8"
- Foundation: Walkout Basement

SEARCH ONLINE @ EPLANS.COM

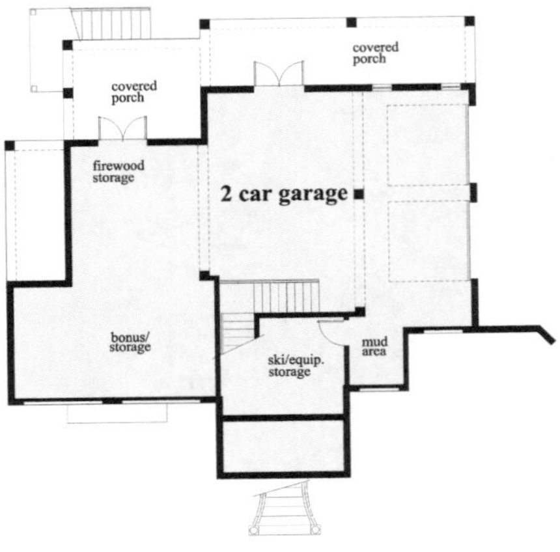

BASEMENT

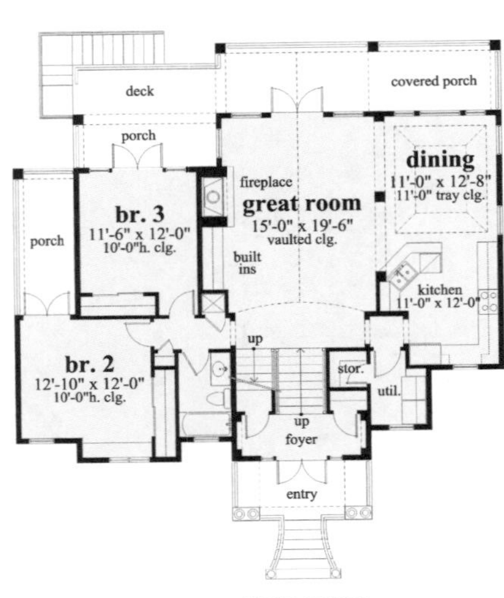

FIRST FLOOR

SECOND FLOOR

plan# HPT930379

- Style: Mediterranean
- First Floor: 1,305 sq. ft.
- Second Floor: 1,215 sq. ft.
- Total: 2,520 sq. ft.
- Bonus Space: 935 sq. ft.
- Bedrooms: 3
- Bathrooms: 3
- Width: 30'-6"
- Depth: 72'-2"
- Foundation: Slab

SEARCH ONLINE @ EPLANS.COM

Louvered shutters, balustered railings and a slate-style roof complement a stucco-and-siding blend on this narrow design. Entry stairs lead up to the living areas, defined by arches and columns. A wall of built-ins and a fireplace highlight the contemporary great room, while four sets of French doors expand the living area to the wraparound porch. Second-floor sleeping quarters include a guest suite with a bayed sitting area, an additional bedroom and a full bath. The master suite features two walk-in closets, separate vanities and French doors to a private observation deck. The lower level offers bonus space for future use and another porch.

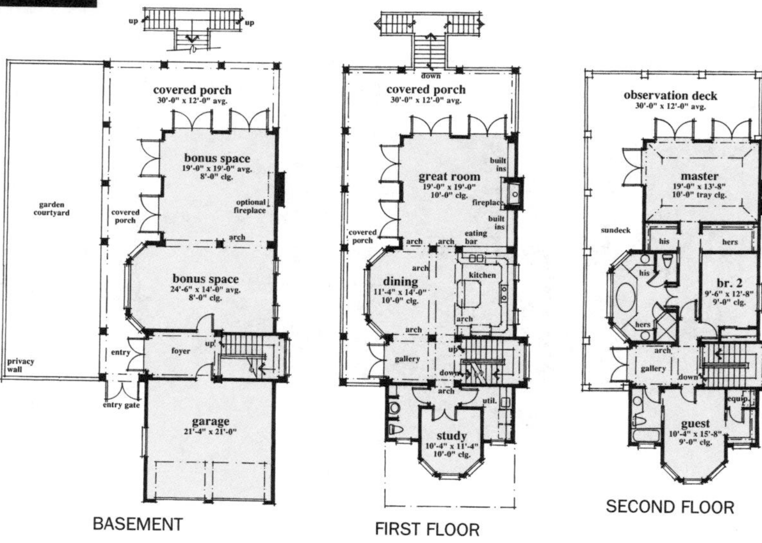

The mixture of grand details with a comfortable layout makes this home a perfect combination of elegance and easy living. Those who prefer a spacious master suite set apart from the rest of the home will love this arrangement. The top story is devoted to a master suite with double doors leading to a private porch and a loft that overlooks the vaulted great room below. On the first floor, each of the two family bedrooms has an adjoining porch. The built-ins and fireplace in the great room give a feeling of casual sophistication.

plan# HPT930380

- Style: Mediterranean
- First Floor: 1,383 sq. ft.
- Second Floor: 595 sq. ft.
- Total: 1,978 sq. ft.
- Bonus Space: 617 sq. ft.
- Bedrooms: 3
- Bathrooms: 2
- Width: 48'-0"
- Depth: 42'-0"
- Foundation: Island Basement

SEARCH ONLINE @ EPLANS.COM

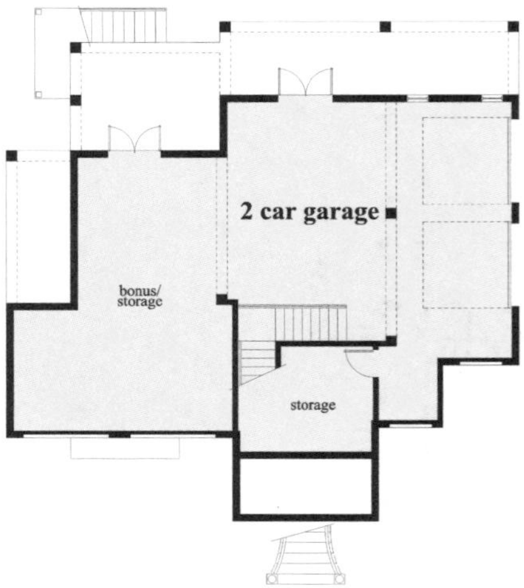

2 car garage
bonus/storage
storage

BASEMENT

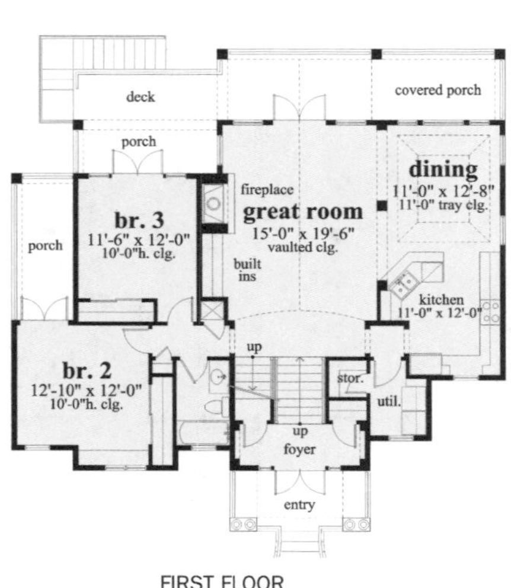

FIRST FLOOR

SECOND FLOOR

plan# HPT930381

- Style: Italianate
- First Floor: 1,266 sq. ft.
- Second Floor: 1,324 sq. ft.
- Total: 2,590 sq. ft.
- Bedrooms: 3
- Bathrooms: 2½
- Width: 34'-0"
- Depth: 63'-2"
- Foundation: Crawlspace

SEARCH ONLINE @ EPLANS.COM

This lovely contemporary home boasts plenty of indoor/outdoor flow. Four sets of double doors wrap around the great room and dining area and open to the stunning veranda. The great room is enhanced by a coffered ceiling and built-in cabinetry, while the entire first floor is bathed in sunlight from a wall of glass doors overlooking the veranda. The dining room connects to a gourmet island kitchen. Upstairs, a beautiful deck wraps gracefully around the family bedrooms. The master suite is a skylit haven enhanced by a sitting bay, which features a vaulted octagonal ceiling and a cozy two-sided fireplace. Private double doors access the sun deck from the master suite, the secondary bedrooms and the study.

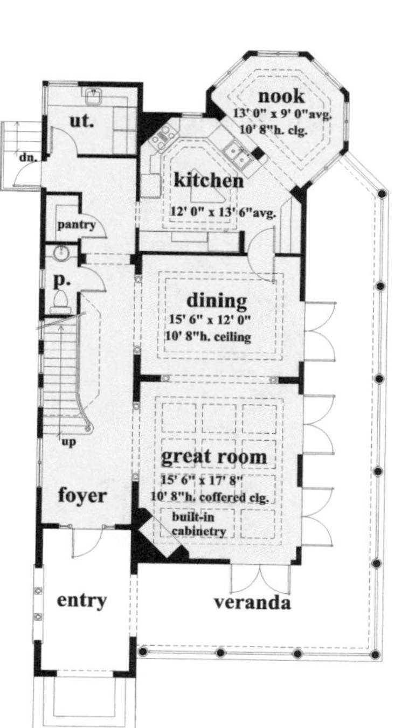

FIRST FLOOR

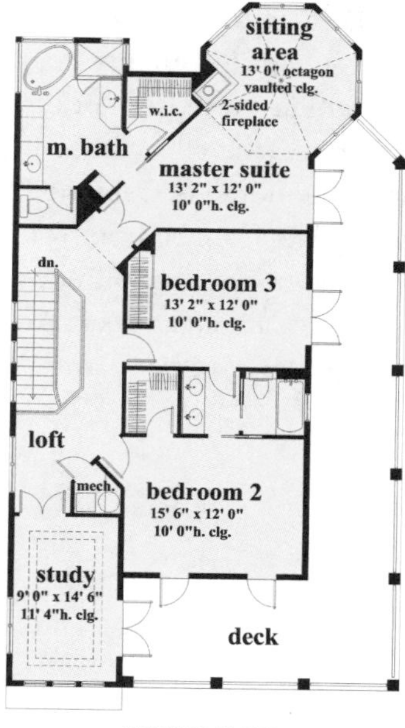

SECOND FLOOR

Clean, contemporary lines, a unique floor plan and a metal roof with a cupola set this farmhouse apart. Remote-control transoms in the cupola open to create an airy and decidedly unique foyer. The great room, sun room, dining room and kitchen flow from one to another for casual entertaining with flair. The rear of the home is fashioned with plenty of windows overlooking the multi-level deck. A front bedroom and bath would make a comfortable guest suite. The master bedroom and bath upstairs are bridged by a pipe-rail balcony that also gives access to a rear deck. An additional bedroom, home office and bath complete this very special plan.

plan# HPT930382

L

- Style: Contemporary
- First Floor: 1,309 sq. ft.
- Second Floor: 1,343 sq. ft.
- Total: 2,652 sq. ft.
- Bedrooms: 3
- Bathrooms: 3
- Width: 44'-4"
- Depth: 58'-2"
- Foundation: Crawlspace

SEARCH ONLINE @ EPLANS.COM

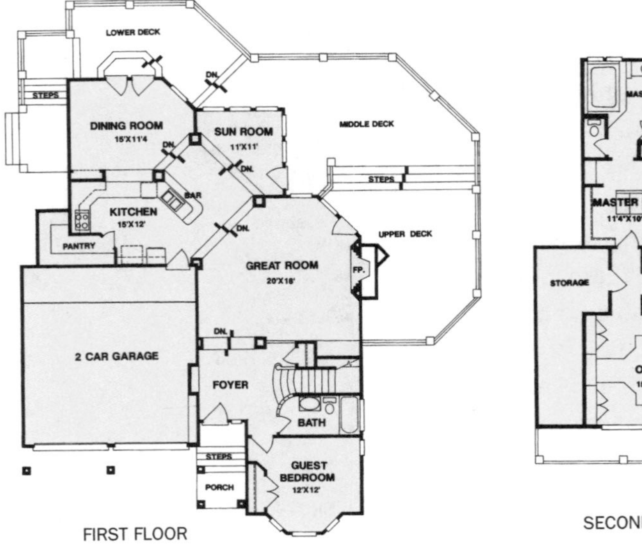

FIRST FLOOR

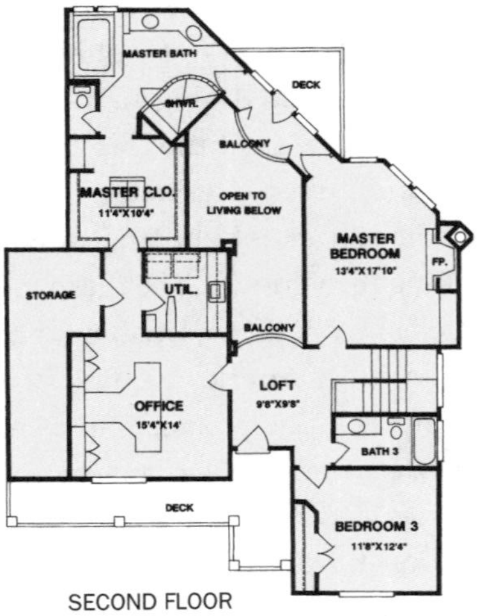

SECOND FLOOR

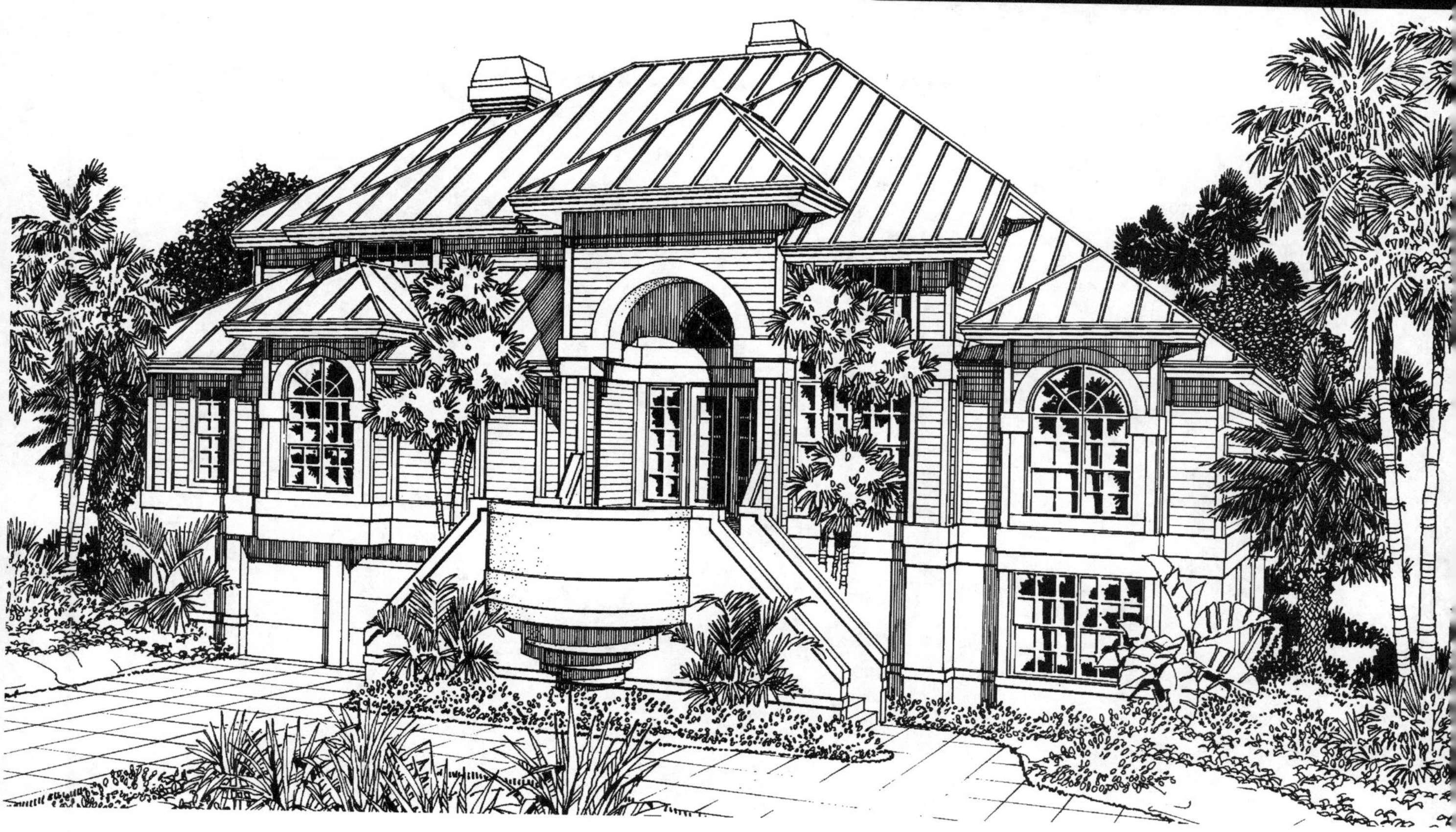

plan# HPT930383

L

- Style: Mediterranean
- First Floor: 2,066 sq. ft.
- Second Floor: 810 sq. ft.
- Total: 2,876 sq. ft.
- Bonus Space: 1,260 sq. ft.
- Bedrooms: 3
- Bathrooms: 3½
- Width: 64'-0"
- Depth: 45'-0"
- Foundation: Slab

SEARCH ONLINE @ EPLANS.COM

If entertaining is your passion, then this is the design for you. With a large, open floor plan and an array of amenities, every gathering will be a success. The foyer embraces living areas accented by a glass fireplace and a wet bar. The grand room and dining room each access a screened veranda for outside enjoyments. The gourmet kitchen delights with its openness to the rest of the house. A morning nook here also adds a nice touch. Two bedrooms and a study radiate from the first-floor living areas. Upstairs—or use the elevator—is a beautiful master suite. It contains a huge walk-in closet, a whirlpool tub and a private sun deck with a spa.

SECOND FLOOR

FIRST FLOOR

BASEMENT

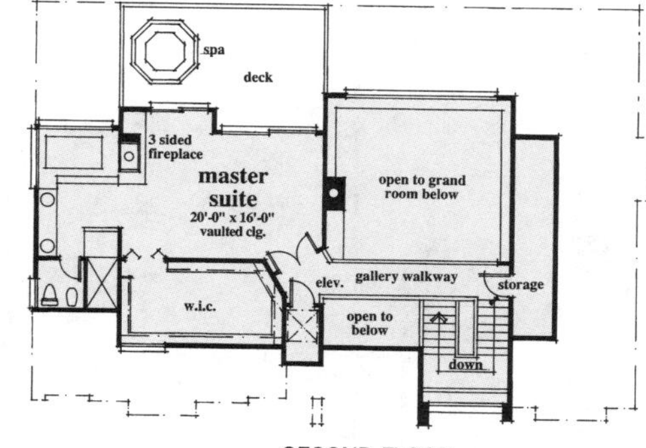

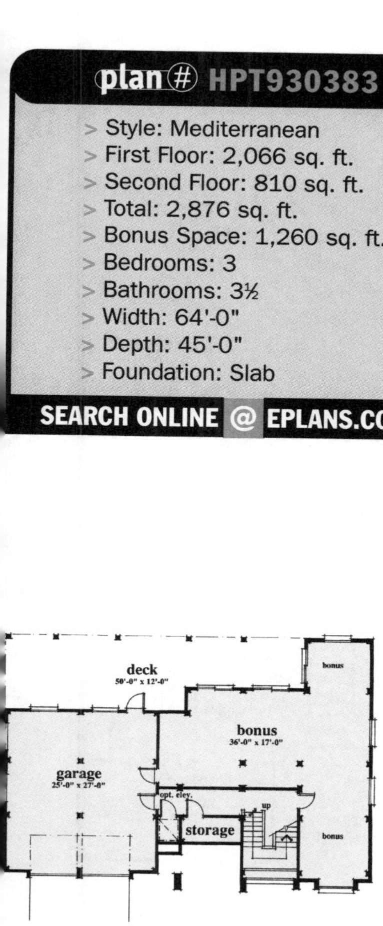

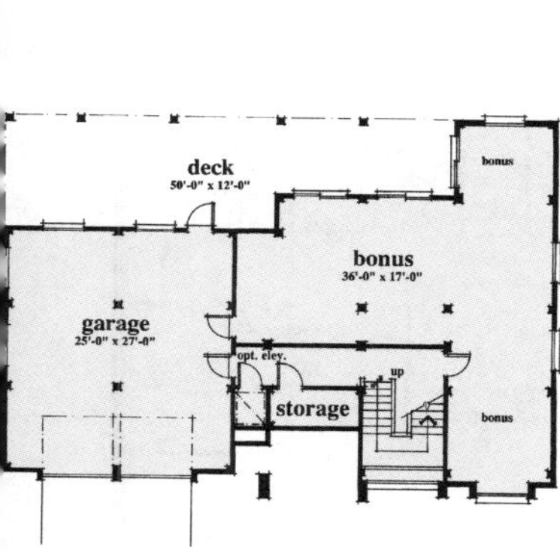

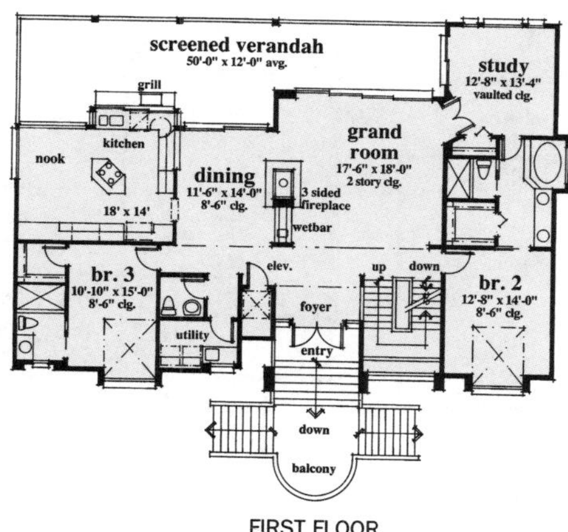

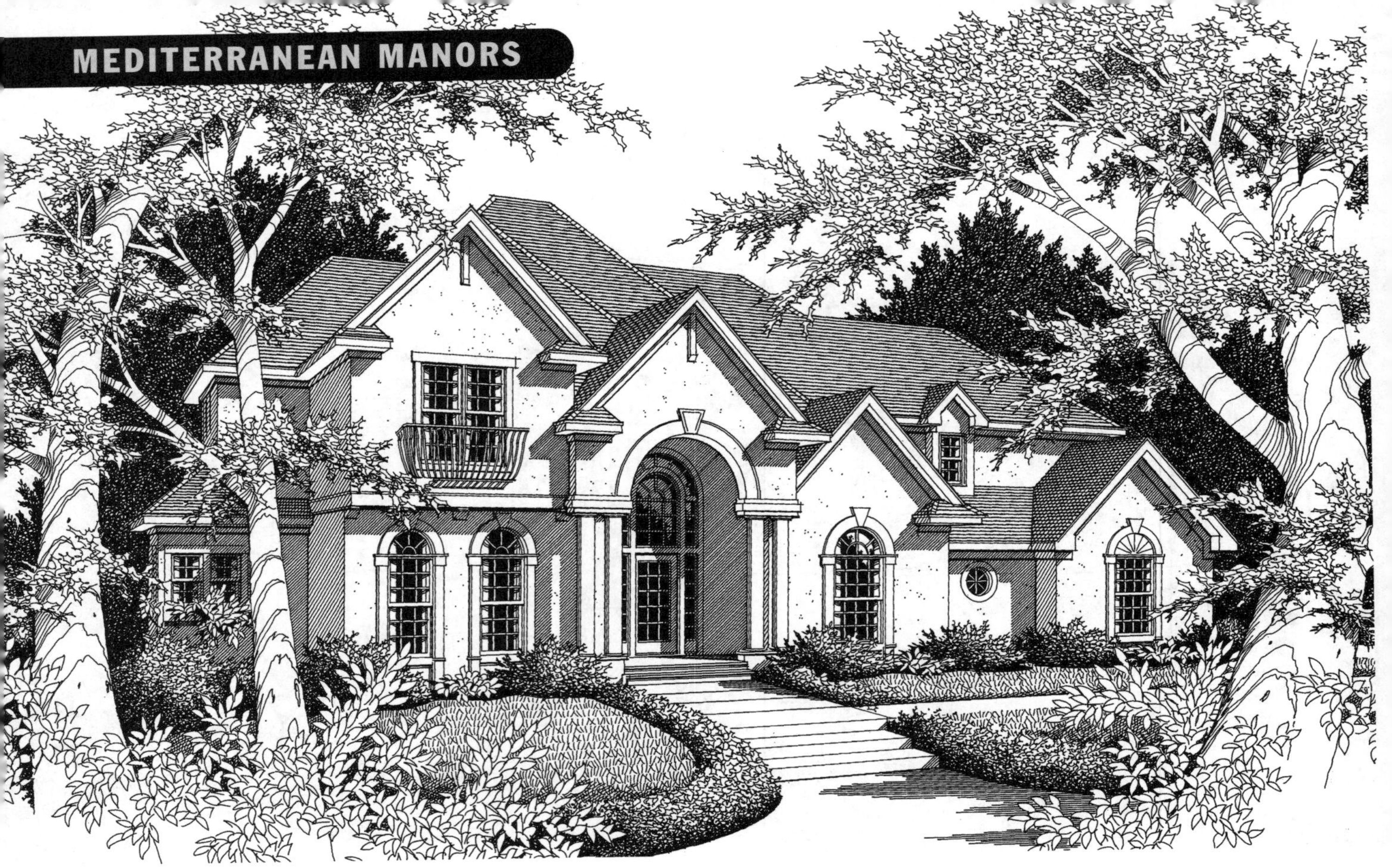

This home speaks of luxury and practicality and is abundant in attractive qualities. A study and dining room flank the foyer, while the great room offers a warming fireplace and double French-door access to the rear yard. A butler's pantry acts as a helpful buffer between the kitchen and the columned dining room. Double bays at the rear of the home form the keeping room and the breakfast room on one side and the master bedroom on the other. Three family bedrooms and two baths grace the second floor. A game room is perfect for casual family time.

plan# HPT930384 L

- Style: Norman
- First Floor: 2,639 sq. ft.
- Second Floor: 1,625 sq. ft.
- Total: 4,264 sq. ft.
- Bedrooms: 4
- Bathrooms: 3½
- Width: 73'-8"
- Depth: 58'-6"
- Foundation: Crawlspace, Slab, Basement

SEARCH ONLINE @ EPLANS.COM

SITTING AREA
11-4 X 5-6
10 FT CLG
MASTER BEDROOM
19-4 X 16-6
10 FT CLG
KEEPING ROOM
11-4 X 16-0
10 FT CLG
BRKFST RM
8-0 X 10-0
10 FT CLG
GREAT ROOM
17-8 X 19-6
2 STORY CLG
KITCHEN
14-0 X 17-0
10 FT CLG
FP
UTIL
8-0 X 8-0
MASTER BATH
10 FT CLG
PWDR
ARCH
PAN
BUTLER'S PANTRY
STORAGE
13-4 X 2-6
GARAGE
22-0 X 21-4
FOYER
2 STORY CLG
STUDY
13-4 X 11-8
10 FT CLG
DINING ROOM
14-0 X 14-4
10 FT CLG
PORCH
FLOWER BOX
FIRST FLOOR

BEDROOM 3
13-4 X 16-6
OPEN TO GREAT ROOM BELOW
BEDROOM 4
13-4 X 17-0
DRESSING
BATH 2
BATH 3
BALCONY
LIN
GAME ROOM
18-6 X 17-0
ATTIC/MECH RM
EXPANDABLE AREA
BEDROOM 2
13-4 X 16-0
OPEN TO FOYER BELOW
SECOND FLOOR

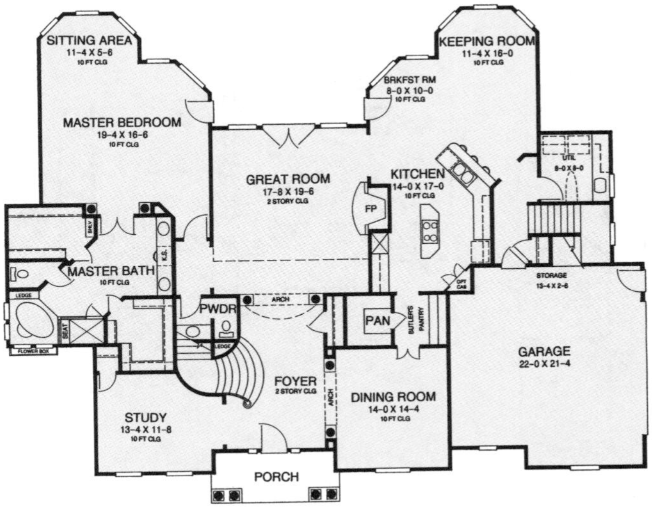

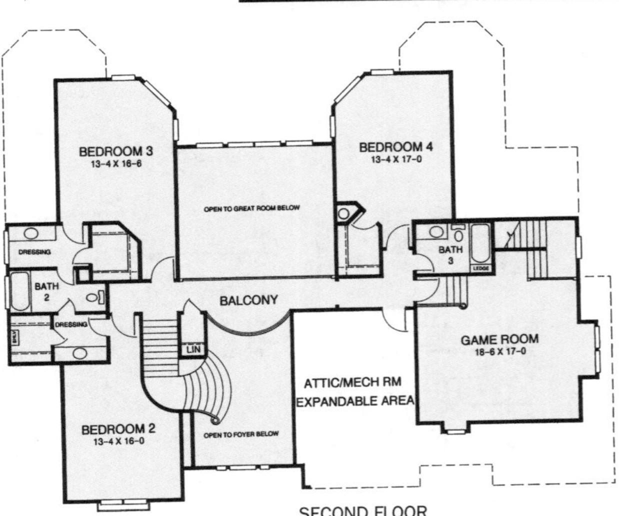

plan# HPT930385

- Style: French Country
- First Floor: 2,384 sq. ft.
- Second Floor: 1,023 sq. ft.
- Total: 3,407 sq. ft.
- Bonus Space: 228 sq. ft.
- Bedrooms: 4
- Bathrooms: 3½
- Width: 63'-4"
- Depth: 57'-0"
- Foundation: Crawlspace, Basement

SEARCH ONLINE @ EPLANS.COM

The covered front porch of this stucco home opens to a two-story foyer and one of two staircases. Arched openings lead into both the formal dining room and the vaulted living room. The efficient kitchen features a walk-in pantry, built-in desk, work island and separate snack bar. Nearby, the large breakfast area opens to the family room. Lavish in its amenities, the master suite offers a separate, vaulted sitting room with a fireplace, among other luxuries. Three bedrooms, along with optional bonus space and attic storage, are found on the second floor.

FIRST FLOOR

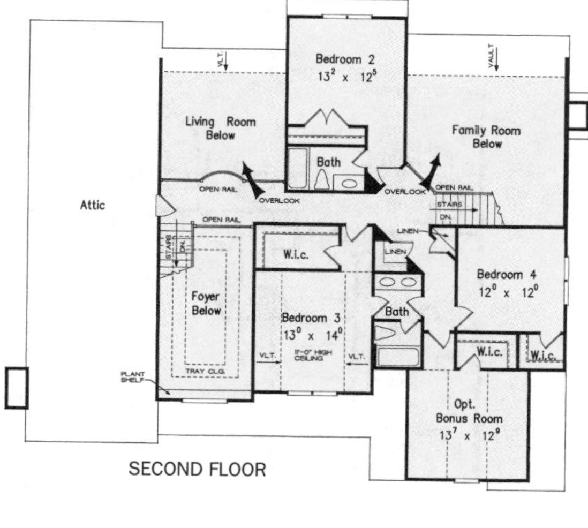

SECOND FLOOR

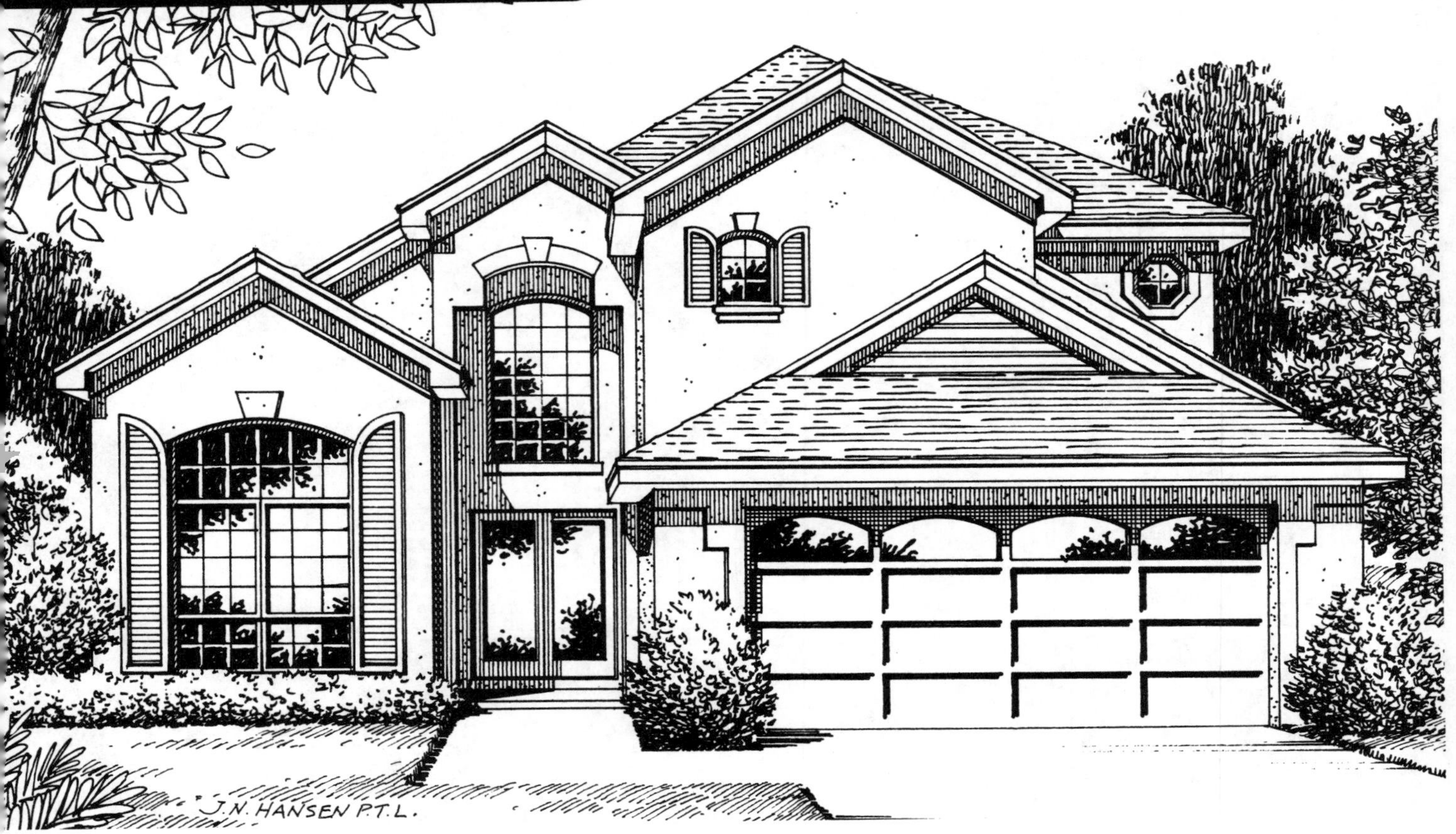

The tiled foyer of this two-story home opens to a living/dining space with a soaring ceiling, a fireplace in the living room and access to a covered patio that invites outdoor livability. The kitchen has an oversized, sunny breakfast area with a volume ceiling. The master bedroom offers privacy with its sumptuous bath; a corner soaking tub, dual lavatories and a compartmented toilet lend character to the room. Upstairs, a loft overlooking the living spaces could become a third bedroom. One of the family bedrooms features a walk-in closet. Both bedrooms share a generous hall bath.

plan# HPT930386

- Style: Contemporary
- First Floor: 1,230 sq. ft.
- Second Floor: 649 sq. ft.
- Total: 1,879 sq. ft.
- Bedrooms: 3
- Bathrooms: 2½
- Width: 38'-0"
- Depth: 53'-6"
- Foundation: Slab

SEARCH ONLINE @ EPLANS.COM

FIRST FLOOR

SECOND FLOOR

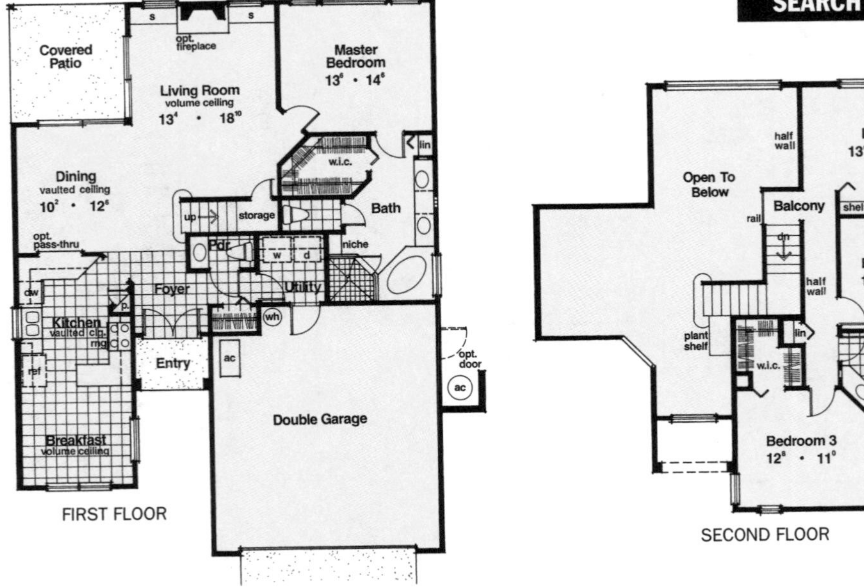

plan# HPT930387

- Style: Mediterranean
- First Floor: 2,190 sq. ft.
- Second Floor: 1,865 sq. ft.
- Total: 4,055 sq. ft.
- Bedrooms: 5
- Bathrooms: 4½ + ½
- Width: 79'-0"
- Depth: 60'-4"
- Foundation: Slab, Basement

SEARCH ONLINE @ EPLANS.COM

This European-style home offers an array of stunning windows that serve both aesthetic and practical purposes. Inside, the foyer leads to the grand staircase and balcony overlook above. A food-preparation island defines the space between the breakfast area and the kitchen. The kitchen also contains dual ovens, extra counter space and a sizable pantry. The rambling master suite features a sitting room, fireplace, full bath and two walk-in closets.

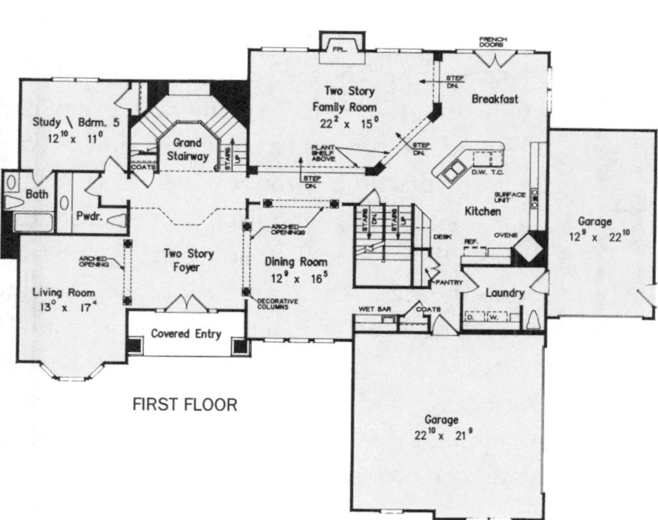

FIRST FLOOR

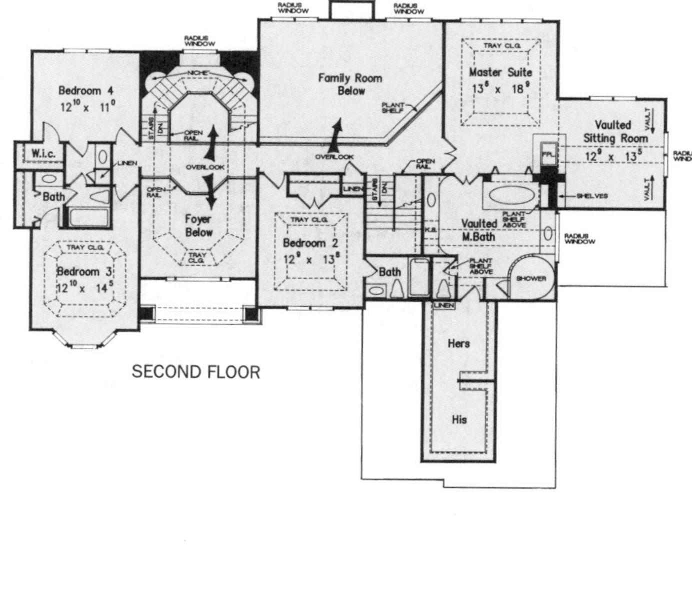

SECOND FLOOR

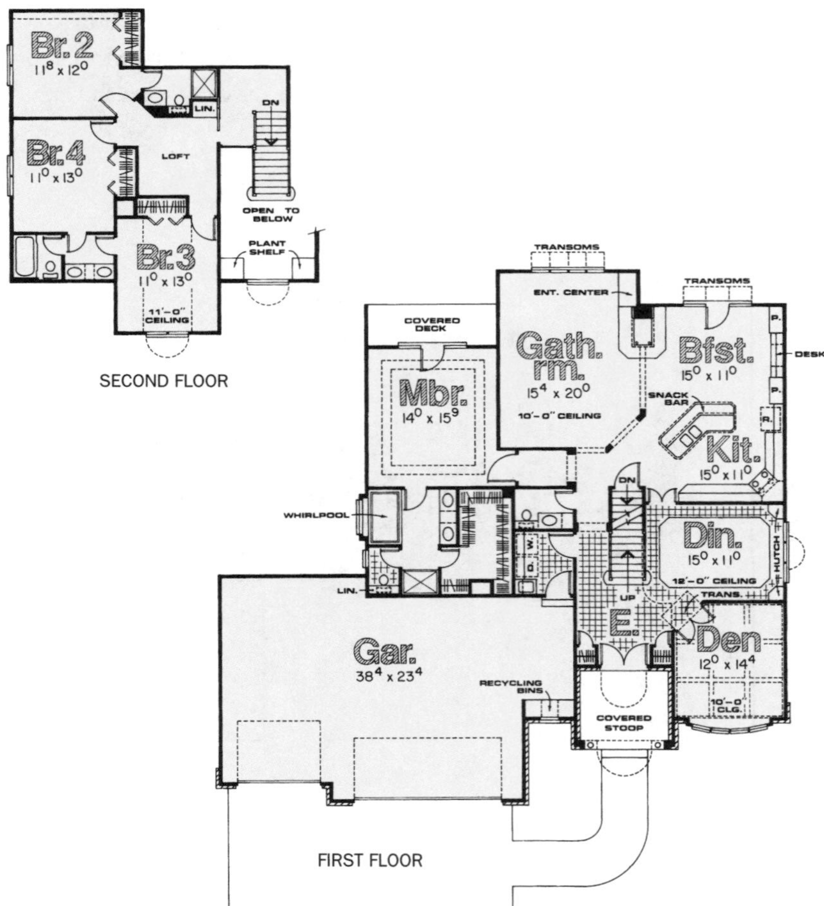

plan# HPT930388

- Style: Mediterranean
- First Floor: 1,800 sq. ft.
- Second Floor: 803 sq. ft.
- Total: 2,603 sq. ft.
- Bedrooms: 4
- Bathrooms: 3½
- Width: 62'-0"
- Depth: 60'-8"

SEARCH ONLINE @ EPLANS.COM

Columns and double doors at the entry create a dash of European flavor for this fine 1½-story home. The tiled entry opens to a dining area with a twelve-foot ceiling and a cozy den with spider-beams and a bowed window. French doors in the dining room allow entry to the island kitchen. The adjacent breakfast area shares a three-sided fireplace with the gathering room. The secluded master suite boasts a private covered deck, whirlpool bath and large walk-in closet. Bedroom 2 has a private bath, while Bedrooms 3 and 4 share a compartmented bath. A popular three-car garage includes a recycling center and convenient laundry room access.

plan# HPT930389

- Style: Mediterranean
- First Floor: 5,120 sq. ft.
- Second Floor: 880 sq. ft.
- Total: 6,000 sq. ft.
- Bedrooms: 5
- Bathrooms: 6½
- Width: 91'-0"
- Depth: 132'-0"
- Foundation: Crawlspace

SEARCH ONLINE @ EPLANS.COM

This sprawling Mediterranean estate is rich with the amenities and extra touches that make a luxurious house a home. Three entrances allow guests to come through the formal entry, and family to use the courtyard or rear porch. Ceilings throughout are ten foot or higher, for grandeur at every turn. The dining room leads to the gourmet kitchen, complete with an island cooktop and plenty of workspace. An adjacent two-story eating area is perfect for casual meals. The sewing room and gym announce three vaulted bedroom suites in an intriguing layout. The master suite is secluded for privacy in the opposite wing. Here, His and Hers closets and a sumptuous bath with an angled tub and a bidet are sure to please. Upstairs, the piano gallery and guest room access the two-story rear porch.

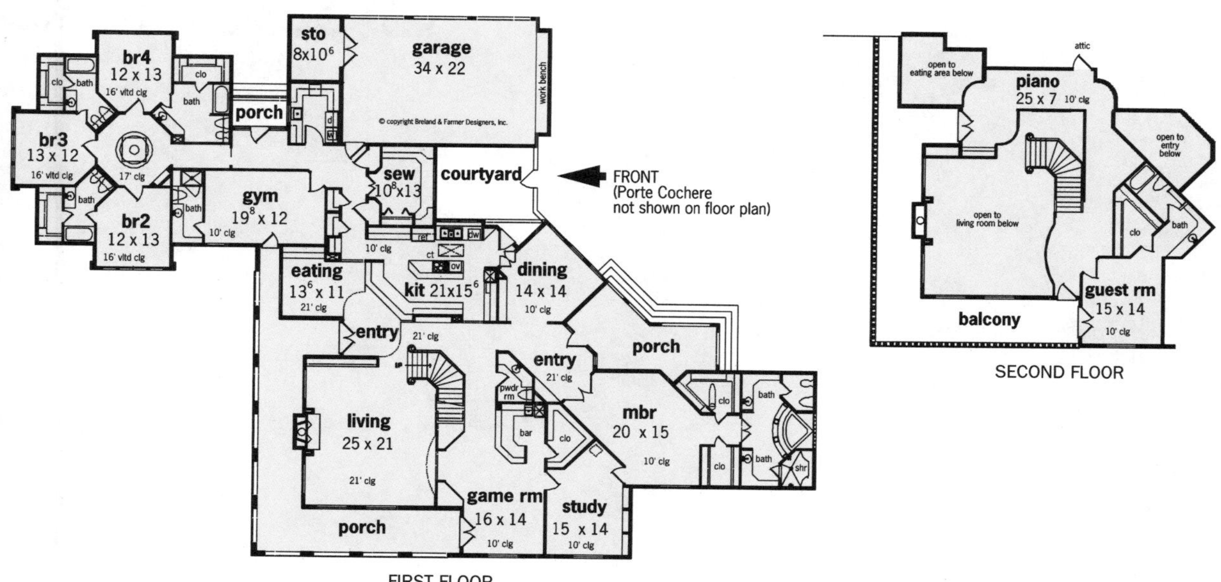

FIRST FLOOR

SECOND FLOOR

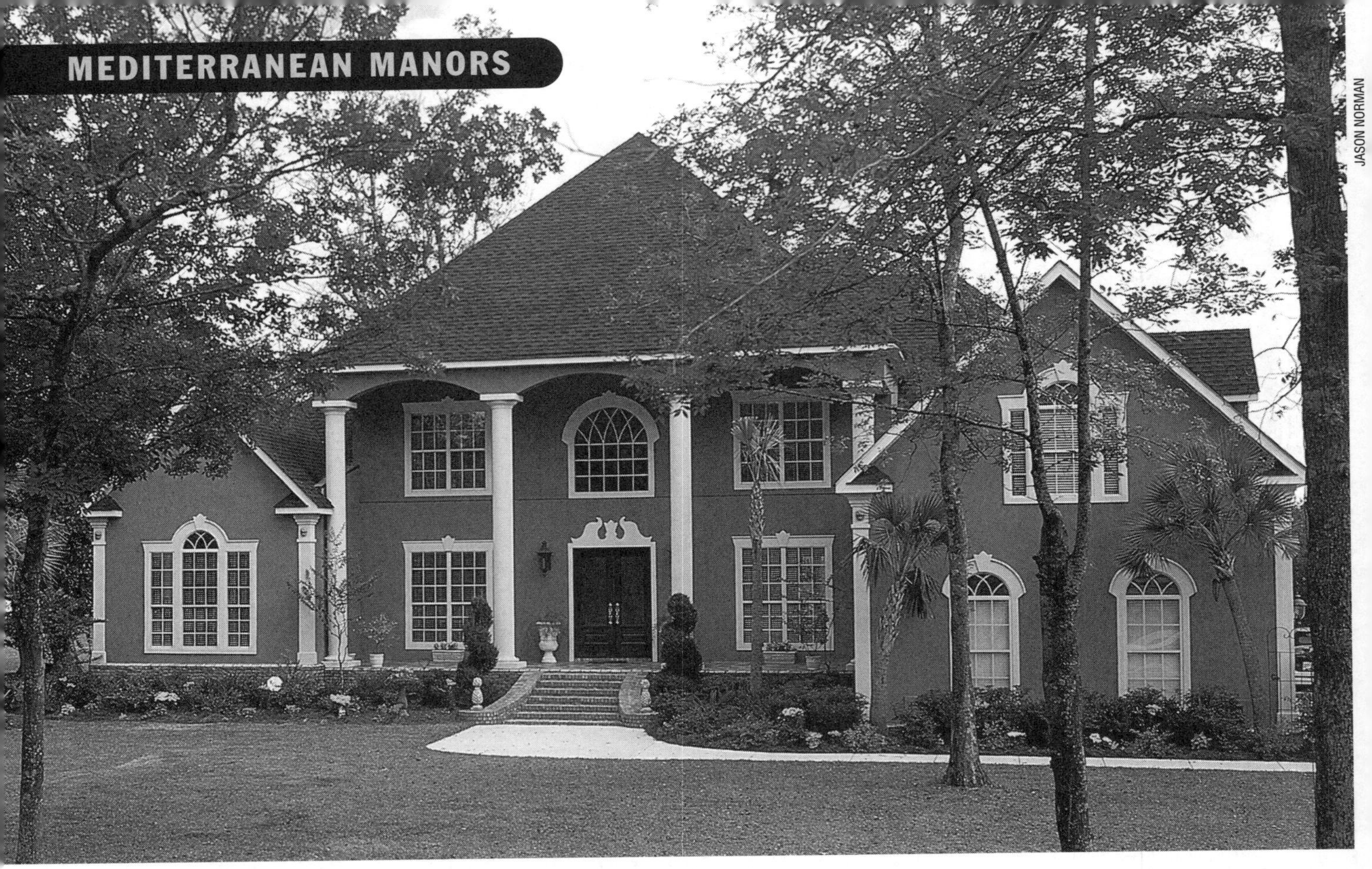

JASON NORMAN

This modern Colonial home exhibits bold style and striking good looks. Historic details inside and out set the tone for a carefully designed plan with today's family in mind. Formal rooms at the front of the home welcome guests; to the rear, the family room basks in the sunlight of wide, tall windows. The well-planned kitchen is equipped with an island and walk-in pantry, and extends into a breakfast bay that is surrounded with natural light. The master wing includes a bayed sun room and lavish bath with a corner whirlpool tub. Three generous bedrooms, a craft room and a future game room inhabit the second floor.

plan# HPT930390

- Style: European Cottage
- First Floor: 3,170 sq. ft.
- Second Floor: 1,515 sq. ft.
- Total: 4,685 sq. ft.
- Bedrooms: 4
- Bathrooms: 3½
- Width: 76'-0"
- Depth: 75'-8"
- Foundation: Slab

SEARCH ONLINE @ EPLANS.COM

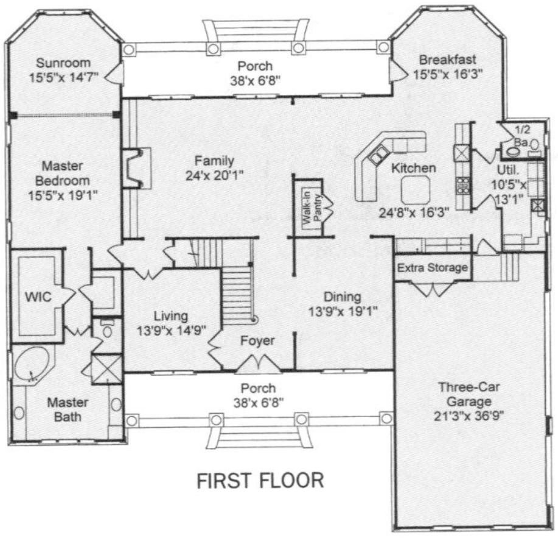

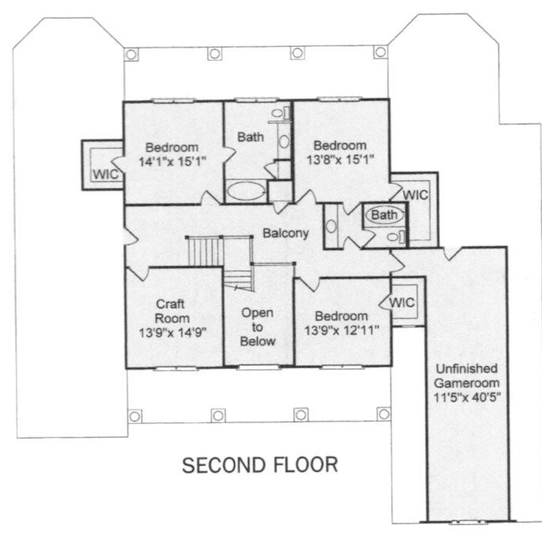

Sunroom
15'5"x 14'7"
Porch
38'x 6'8"
Breakfast
15'5"x 16'3"
Master Bedroom
15'5"x 19'1"
Family
24'x 20'1"
Kitchen
24'8"x 16'3"
Walk-in Pantry
1/2 Ba.
Util.
10'5"x 13'1"
Extra Storage
WIC
Living
13'9"x 14'9"
Foyer
Dining
13'9"x 19'1"
Master Bath
Porch
38'x 6'8"
Three-Car Garage
21'3"x 36'9"

FIRST FLOOR

WIC
Bedroom
14'1"x 15'1"
Bath
Bedroom
13'8"x 15'1"
WIC
Bath
Balcony
Craft Room
13'9"x 14'9"
Open to Below
Bedroom
13'9"x 12'11"
WIC
Unfinished Gameroom
11'5"x 40'5"

SECOND FLOOR

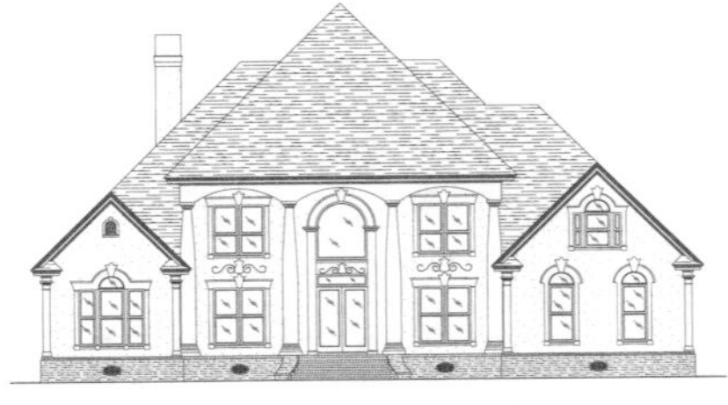

ALTERNATE EXTERIOR

plan# HPT930391

- Style: Mediterranean
- First Floor: 3,010 sq. ft.
- Second Floor: 1,574 sq. ft.
- Total: 4,584 sq. ft.
- Bedrooms: 4
- Bathrooms: 3½
- Width: 74'-0"
- Depth: 96'-0"
- Foundation: Slab

SEARCH ONLINE @ EPLANS.COM

Grecian style and a dramatic presence make this home a neighborhood showpiece. Inside, the foyer gives way to the living room and dining room to the sides; a welcoming family room with a fireplace framed by windows lies just ahead. To the right, a country kitchen with a cooktop island serves the bayed breakfast nook and formal dining room for effortless entertaining. The master wing enjoys privacy and serenity, with no rooms directly above. Here, an exquisite bath includes dual vanities and a corner whirlpool tub. Three bedrooms and a home office share the second floor, easily accessed by front or rear stairs.

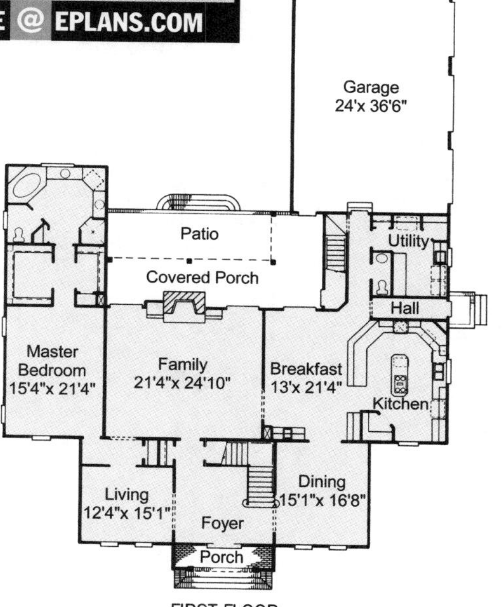

FIRST FLOOR

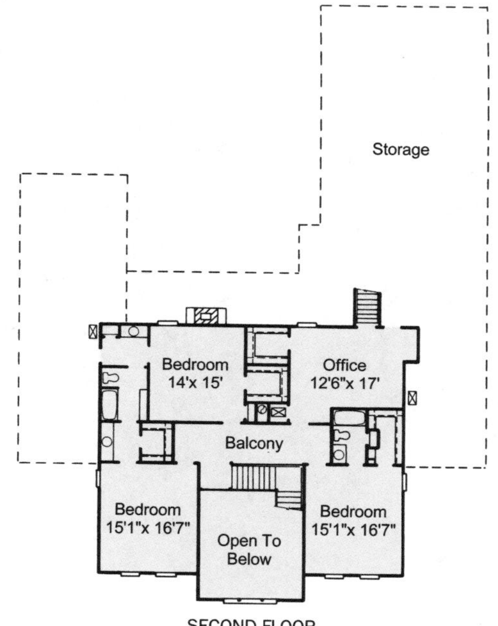

SECOND FLOOR

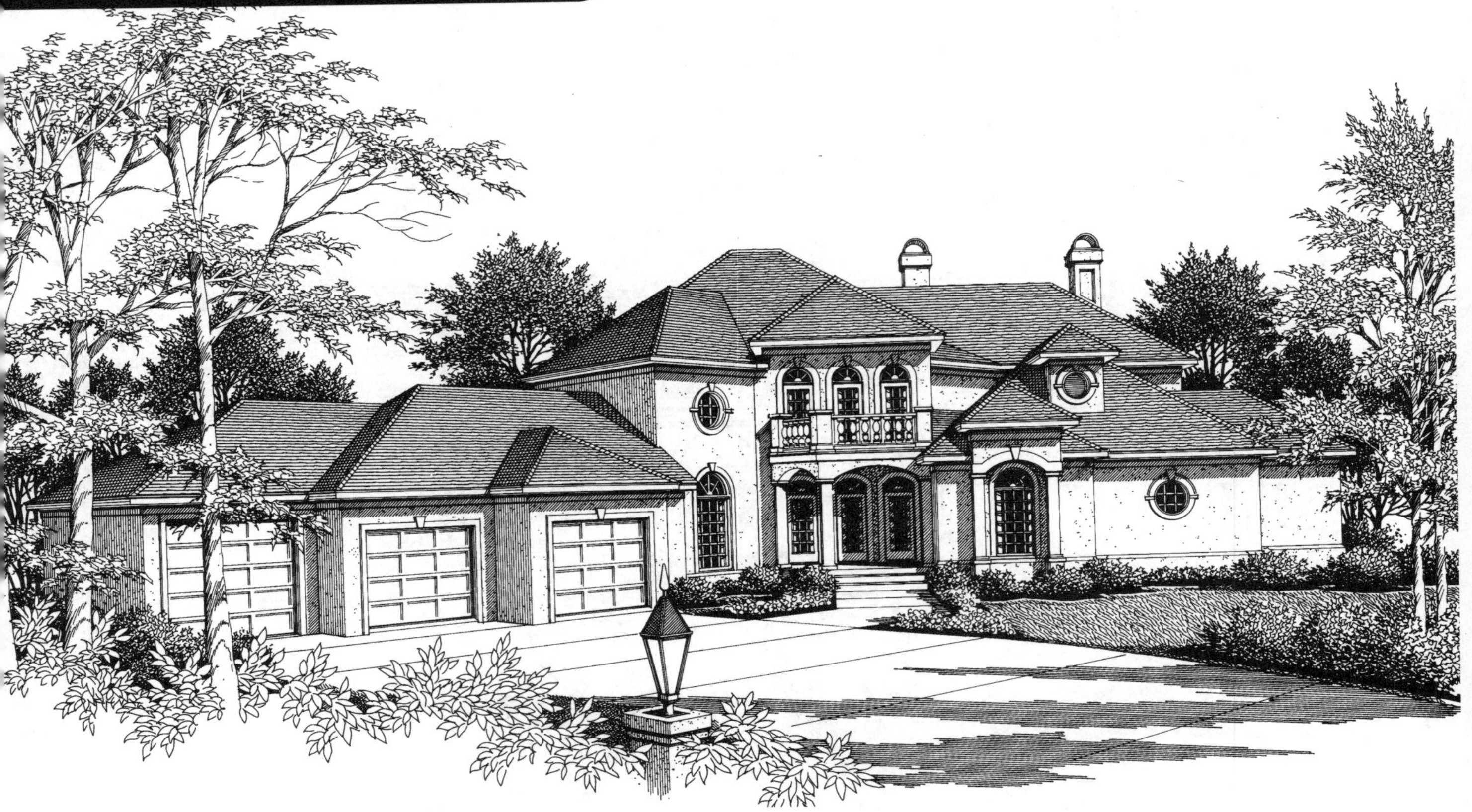

Designed for a sloping lot, this fantastic Mediterranean home features all the views to the rear, making it the perfect home for an ocean, lake or golf-course view. Inside, the great room features a rear wall of windows. The breakfast room, kitchen, dining room and master suite also feature rear views. A three-level series of porches is located on the back for outdoor relaxing. Two bedroom suites are found upstairs, each with a private bath and a porch. The basement of this home features another bedroom suite and a large game room. An expandable area can be used as an office or Bedroom 5.

plan# HPT930392

- Style: Mediterranean
- First Floor: 2,959 sq. ft.
- Second Floor: 1,055 sq. ft.
- Total: 4,014 sq. ft.
- Bedrooms: 3
- Bathrooms: 3½
- Width: 110'-4"
- Depth: 72'-5"
- Foundation: Slab, Basement

SEARCH ONLINE @ EPLANS.COM

FIRST FLOOR

SECOND FLOOR

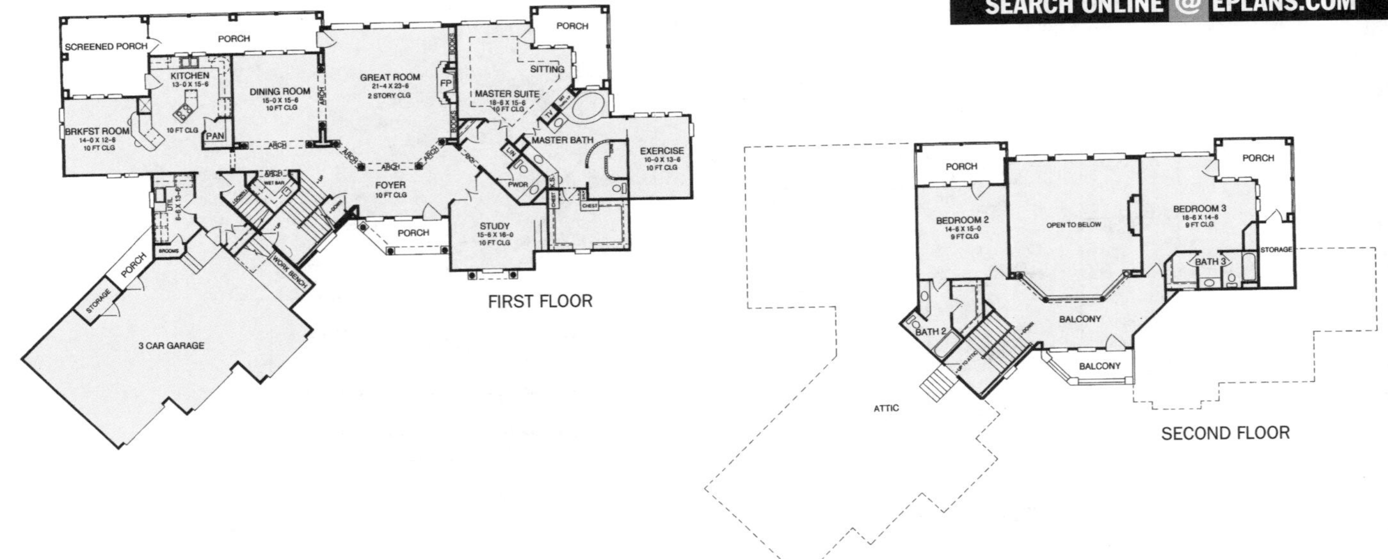

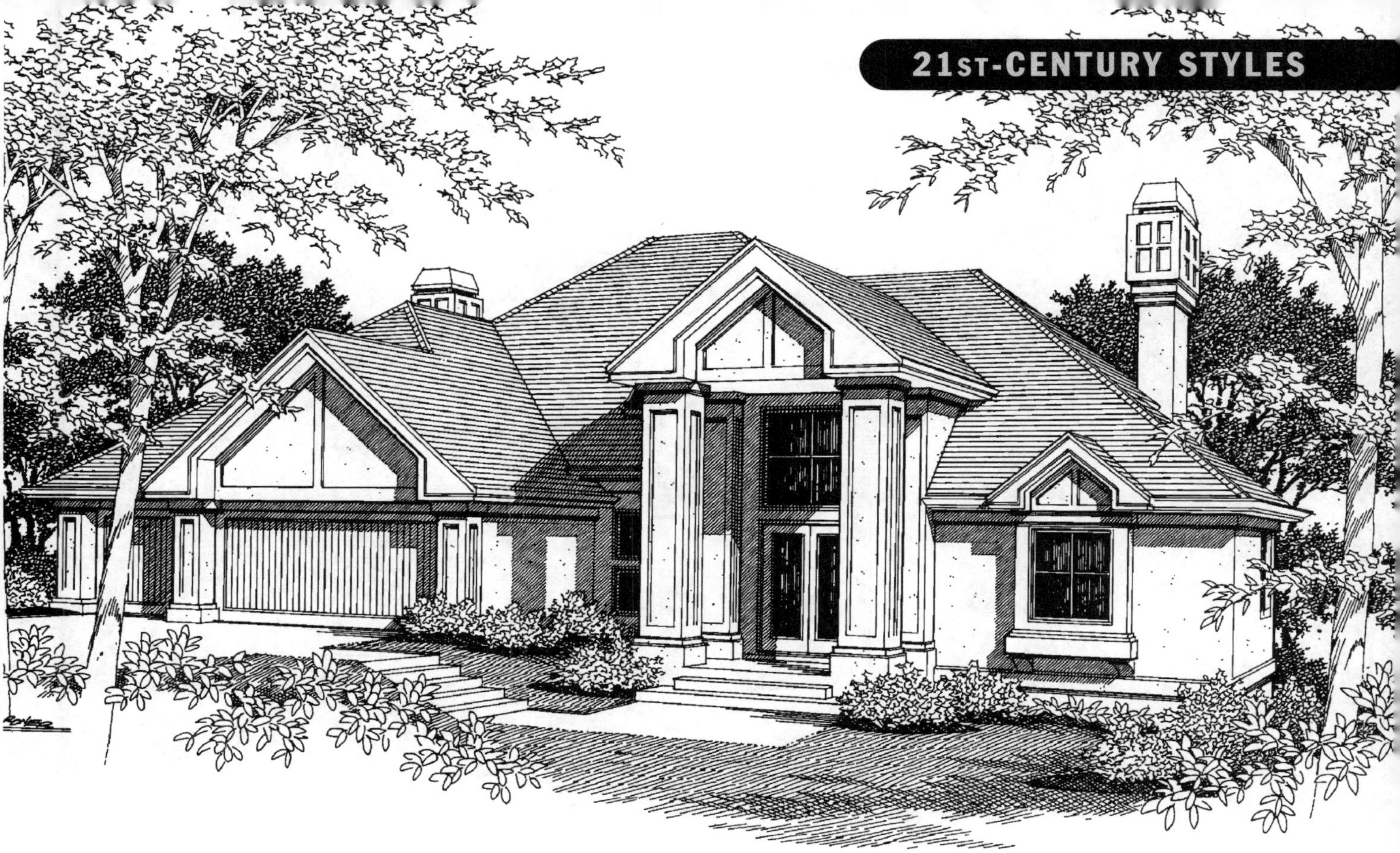

plan# HPT930393

- Style: Contemporary
- First Floor: 1,954 sq. ft.
- Second Floor: 1,308 sq. ft.
- Total: 3,262 sq. ft.
- Bedrooms: 3
- Bathrooms: 2½
- Width: 69'-0"
- Depth: 60'-6"
- Foundation: Crawlspace

L

SEARCH ONLINE @ EPLANS.COM

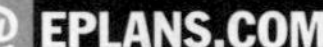

This plan reaps plenty of compliments for the sensational entry. Inside, the floor plan enjoys a large, two-story entry, which leads on to the right to the den with built-ins and a private deck. Straight ahead and down a few steps are the main living areas: the two-story formal living room with a fireplace, the dining room, kitchen and nook, all with tray vaulted ceilings, and the family room with another fireplace and more built-ins. Among three bedrooms on the second floor, the master suite offers a wealth of amenities.

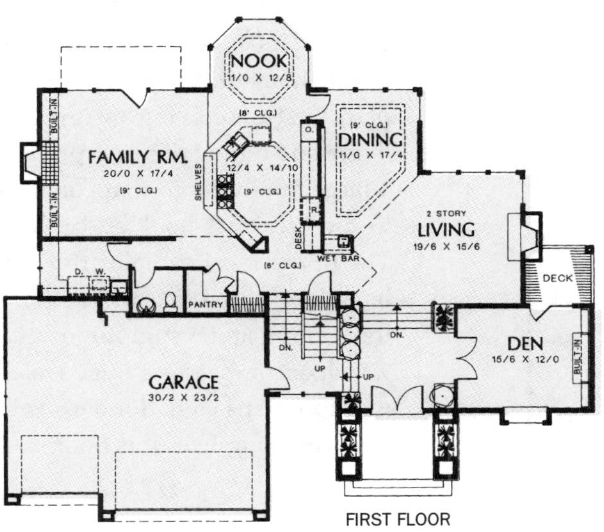

FIRST FLOOR

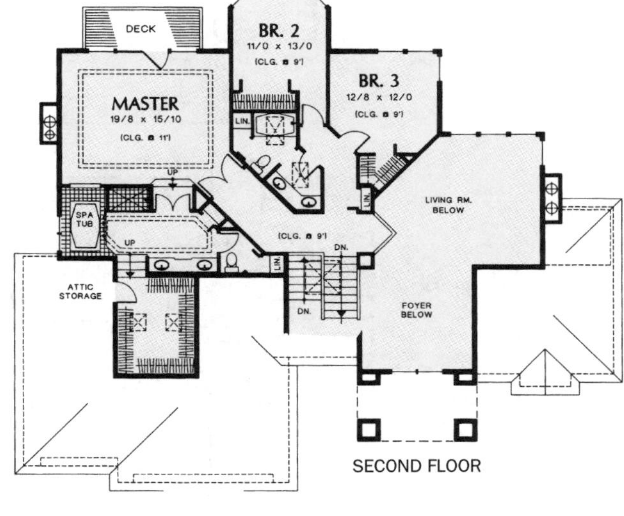

SECOND FLOOR

SECOND FLOOR

FIRST FLOOR

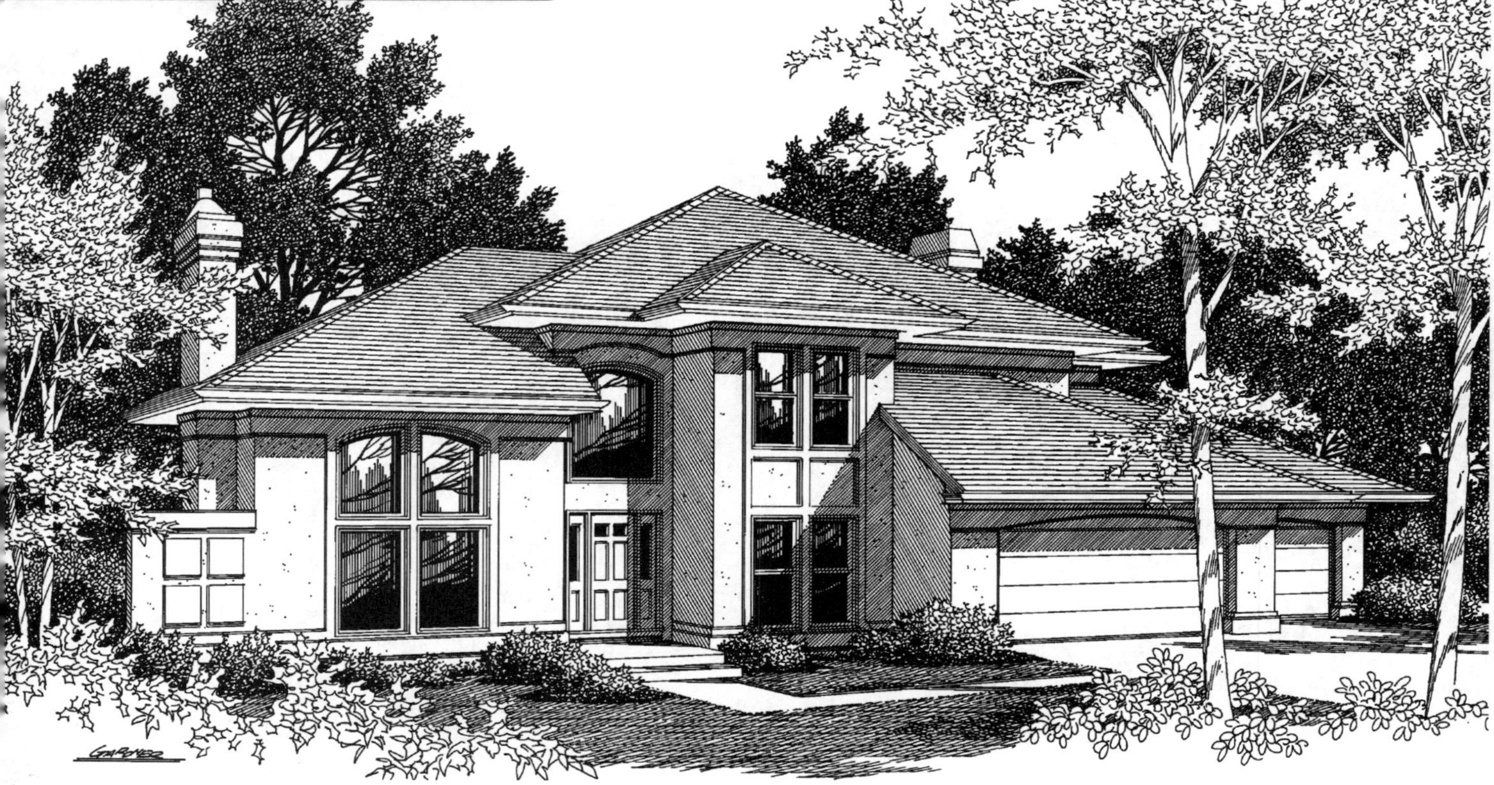

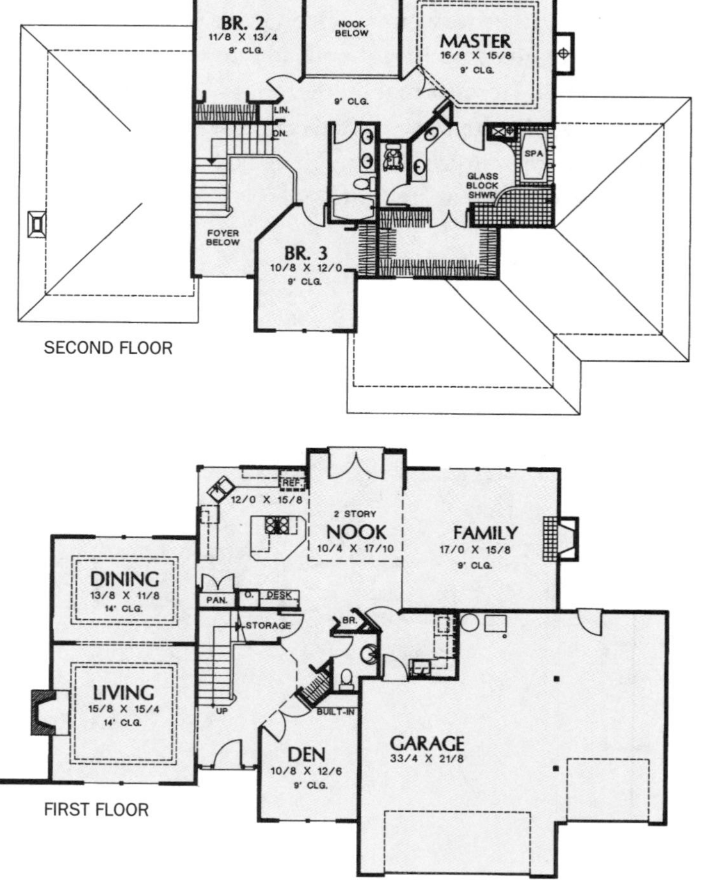

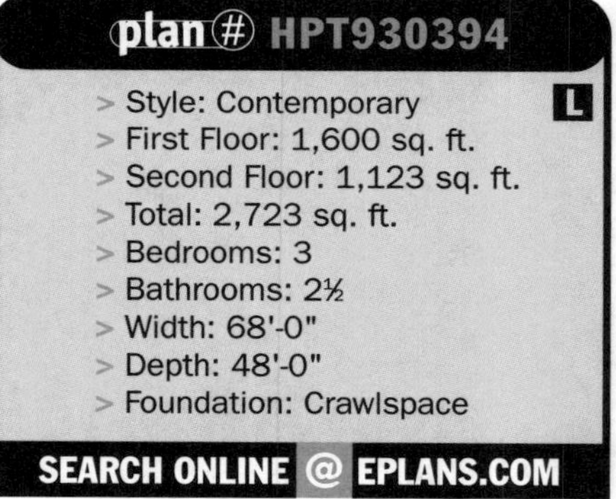

plan# HPT930394

> Style: Contemporary **L**
> First Floor: 1,600 sq. ft.
> Second Floor: 1,123 sq. ft.
> Total: 2,723 sq. ft.
> Bedrooms: 3
> Bathrooms: 2½
> Width: 68'-0"
> Depth: 48'-0"
> Foundation: Crawlspace

SEARCH ONLINE @ EPLANS.COM

Beyond the contemporary facade of this home lies a highly functional floor plan. First-floor living areas include formal living and dining rooms, a private den, and a large family room that connects directly to the breakfast nook and island kitchen. The upper level contains three bedrooms, including a master suite with a nine-foot tray ceiling and a sumptuous master bath, which encompasses a huge walk-in closet, whirlpool spa and double vanity. A fine hall bath completes this floor.

plan# HPT930395

- Style: Contemporary
- First Floor: 1,592 sq. ft.
- Second Floor: 1,178 sq. ft.
- Total: 2,770 sq. ft.
- Bedrooms: 4
- Bathrooms: 2½
- Width: 77'-5"
- Depth: 64'-7"
- Foundation: Crawlspace

SEARCH ONLINE @ EPLANS.COM

The angular placement of this home's three-car garage creates an expansive and very stylish facade. The foyer is punctuated with a dramatic staircase and opens on the right to formal living areas before continuing back into the inviting family room. A fireplace and plenty of windows in the family room are a nice balance to the country kitchen. Amenities here include a breakfast nook, cooktop island and rear access to the formal dining room. Three family bedrooms and a full hall bath join the luxurious master suite on the second floor.

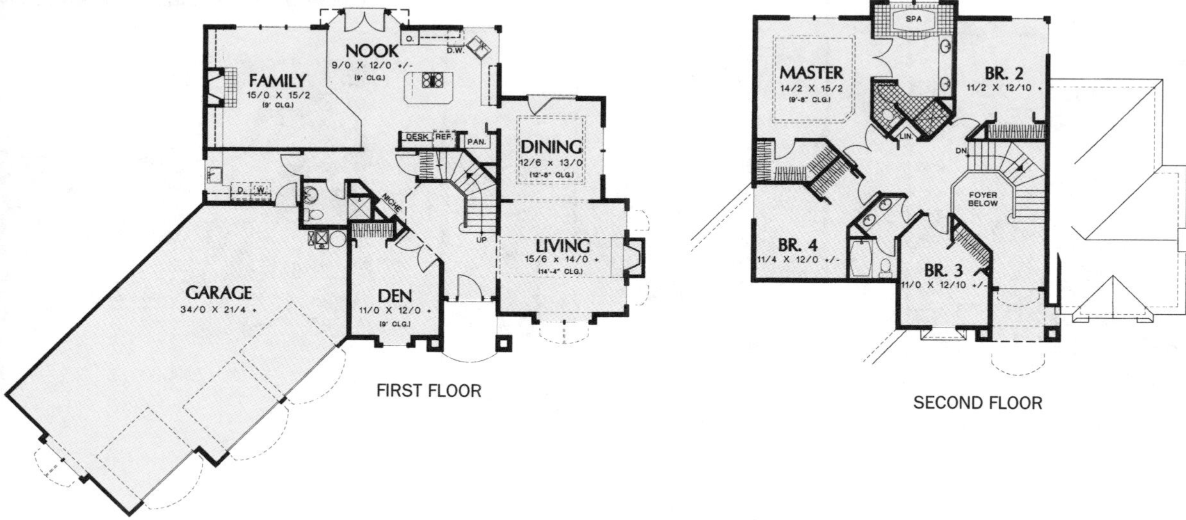

FIRST FLOOR

SECOND FLOOR

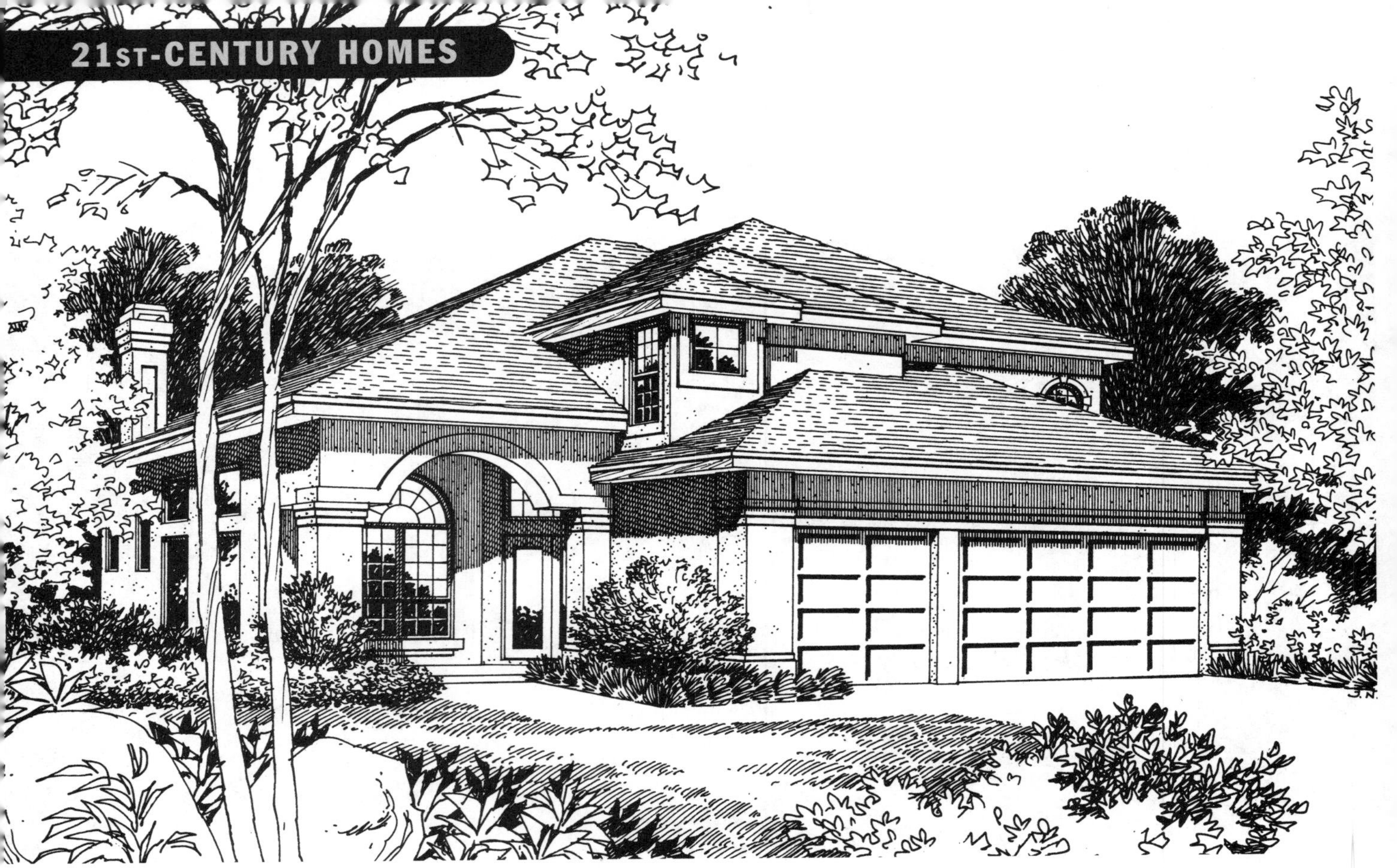

No matter where you're building, this design offers two exteriors to heighten the possibilities. The double-door entry opens to the combined formal living and dining areas. Nearby, the kitchen enjoys ample space for gourmet-meal preparations, as well as an attached breakfast nook. In the family room, a volume ceiling and a fireplace are sure to please. The master bedroom, located at the rear of the first floor, accesses the covered patio. It also sports a bath with a double-bowl lavatory, garden tub and large walk-in closet. On the second floor, three bedrooms enjoy peace and quiet and share a hall bath. An optional loft is included in the blueprints.

plan# HPT930396

- Style: Contemporary
- First Floor: 1,816 sq. ft.
- Second Floor: 703 sq. ft.
- Total: 2,519 sq. ft.
- Bonus Space: 156 sq. ft.
- Bedrooms: 4
- Bathrooms: 2½
- Width: 45'-0"
- Depth: 67'-6"
- Foundation: Slab

SEARCH ONLINE @ EPLANS.COM

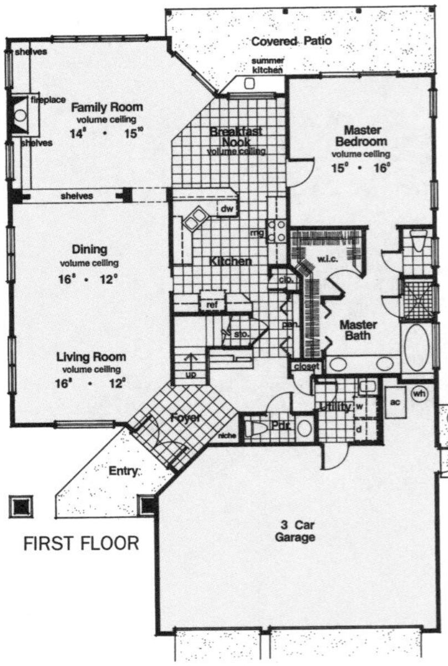

FIRST FLOOR

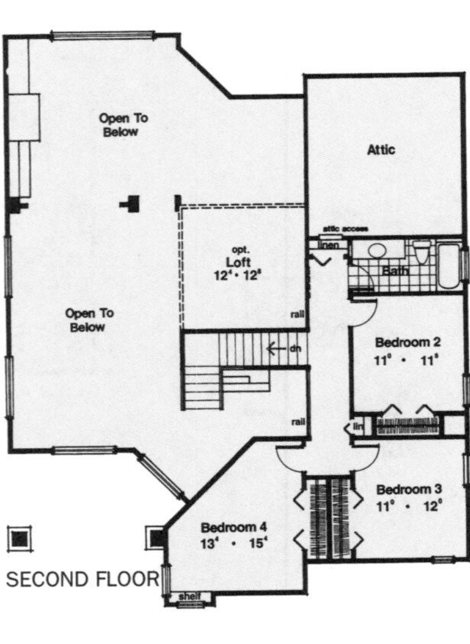

SECOND FLOOR

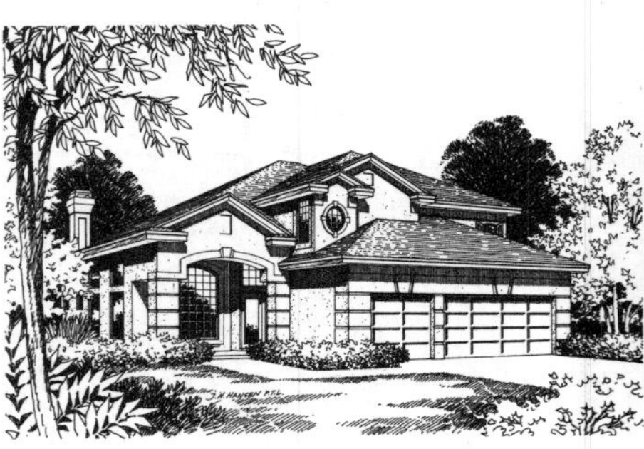

ALTERNATE EXTERIOR

plan# HPT930397

- Style: Contemporary
- First Floor: 1,896 sq. ft.
- Second Floor: 568 sq. ft.
- Total: 2,464 sq. ft.
- Bedrooms: 3
- Bathrooms: 2½
- Width: 45'-0"
- Depth: 64'-0"
- Foundation: Crawlspace

SEARCH ONLINE @ EPLANS.COM

Inside the grand entrance of this contemporary home, a large foyer offers a gracious introduction to the formal living and dining rooms. Nearby, the L-shaped island kitchen serves formal and informal areas with equal ease. A two-story family room with a built-in media center and a corner fireplace shares space with a sunny nook. The private master suite features a walk-in closet and a luxurious bath. The second floor contains two bedrooms and a full bath.

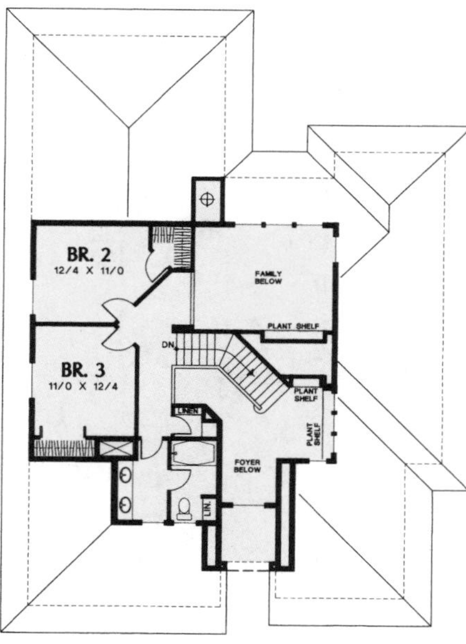

SECOND FLOOR

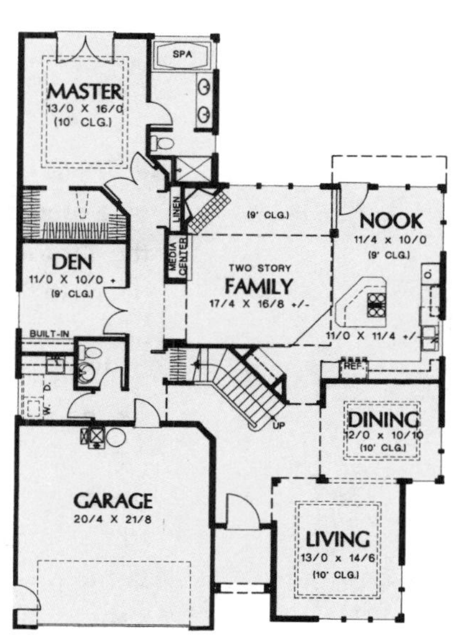

FIRST FLOOR

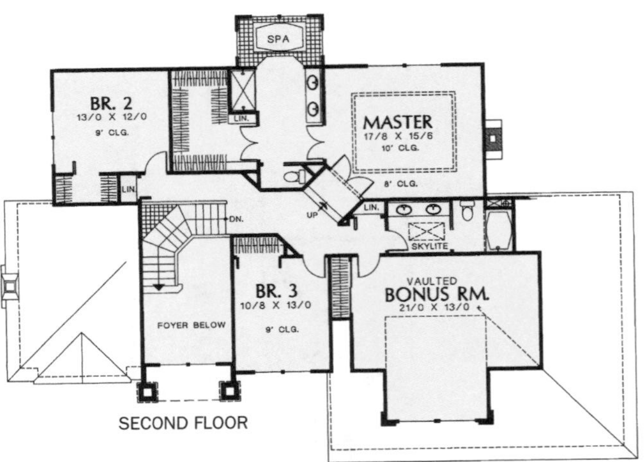

SECOND FLOOR

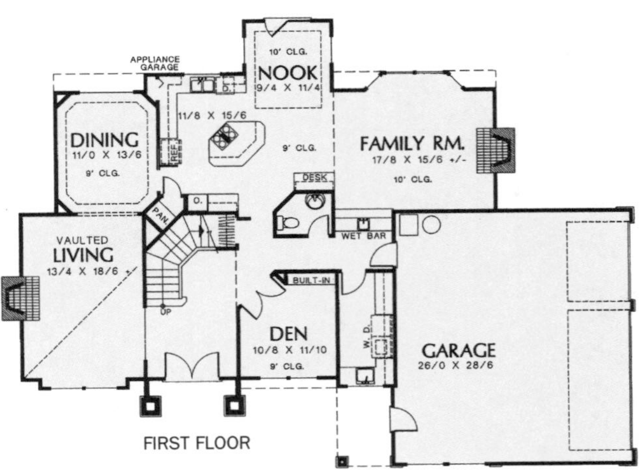

FIRST FLOOR

plan# HPT930398

L

- Style: Contemporary
- First Floor: 1,618 sq. ft.
- Second Floor: 1,212 sq. ft.
- Total: 2,830 sq. ft.
- Bonus Space: 376 sq. ft.
- Bedrooms: 3
- Bathrooms: 2½
- Width: 68'-0"
- Depth: 51'-0"
- Foundation: Crawlspace

SEARCH ONLINE @ EPLANS.COM

This attractive European-styled plan is enhanced by a stucco finish and arched windows complementing the facade. The two-story foyer, with its angled stair, opens to the dramatically vaulted living room on one side and the den with French doors on the other. An efficient L-shaped island kitchen works well with the formal dining room to its left and a sunny nook to the right. A bayed family room with a warming hearth completes this floor. Upstairs, a sumptuous master suite includes a spa tub, shower, twin vanities and a large walk-in closet. Two family bedrooms share a full skylit bath that includes twin vanities. Over the garage is a vaulted bonus room, perfect as a game or hobby room.

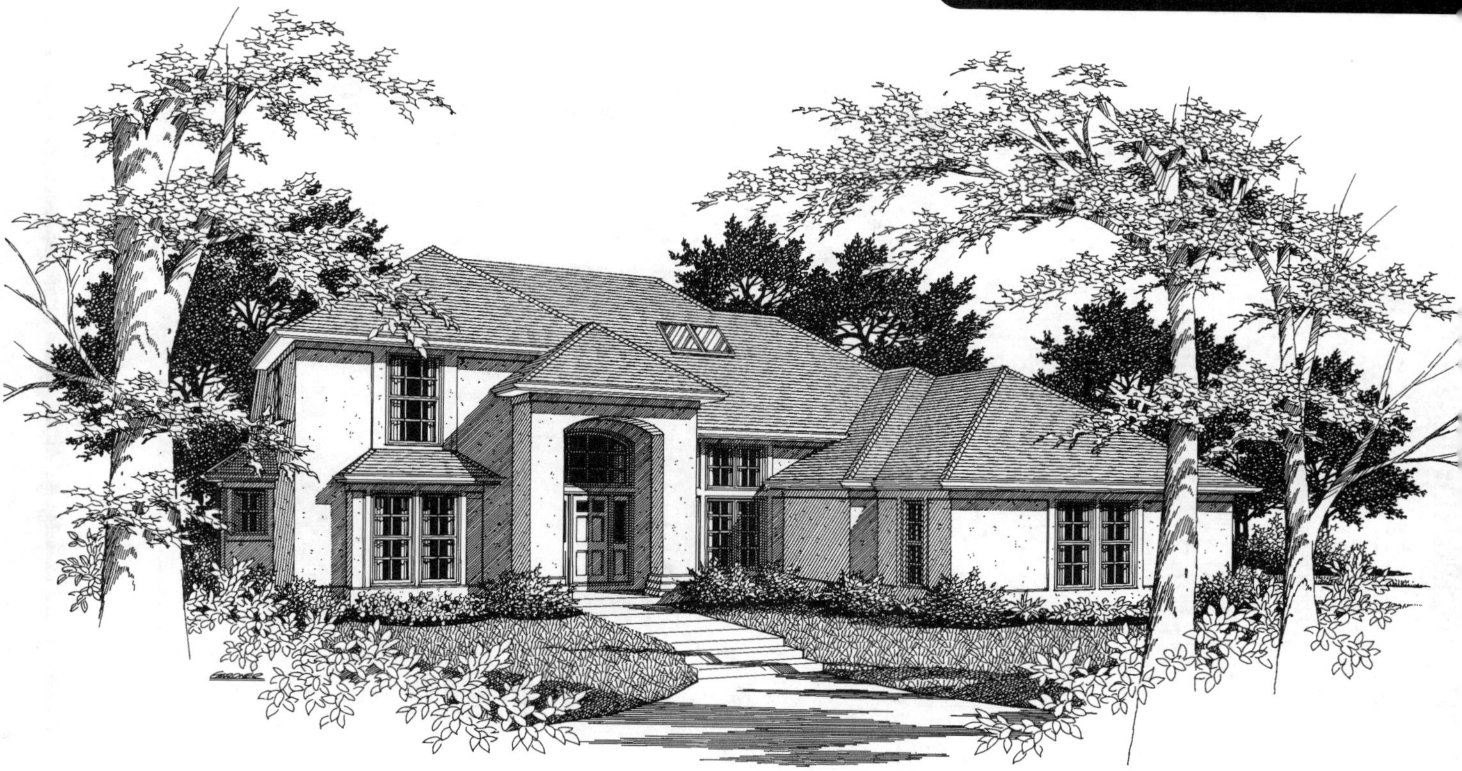

plan# HPT930399

- Style: Contemporary
- First Floor: 1,784 sq. ft.
- Second Floor: 742 sq. ft.
- Total: 2,526 sq. ft.
- Bedrooms: 4
- Bathrooms: 2½
- Width: 64'-0"
- Depth: 60'-0"
- Foundation: Crawlspace

SEARCH ONLINE @ EPLANS.COM

SECOND FLOOR

FIRST FLOOR

This stately contemporary home makes a grand statement inside and out. A volume entry leads to the two-story dining room with a plant shelf and skylights above. The great room with a fireplace flanked by windows is also vaulted. The kitchen provides a desk, a large pantry, an island cooktop and an adjacent breakfast nook with access to a covered porch. Double doors open from the foyer to a den with a built-in cabinet. The master bedroom with a cove ceiling, walk-in closet and amenity-filled bath is conveniently located on the first floor. A two-way staircase leads to the second floor, which includes three family bedrooms and a full bath.

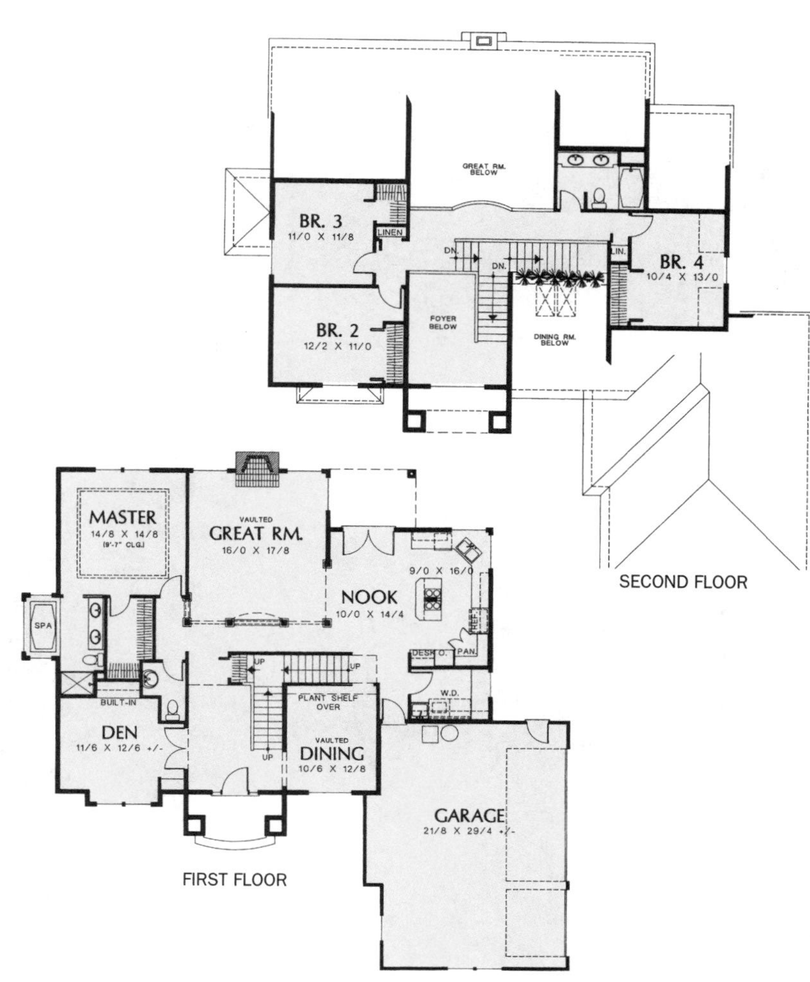

ALTERNATE EXTERIOR

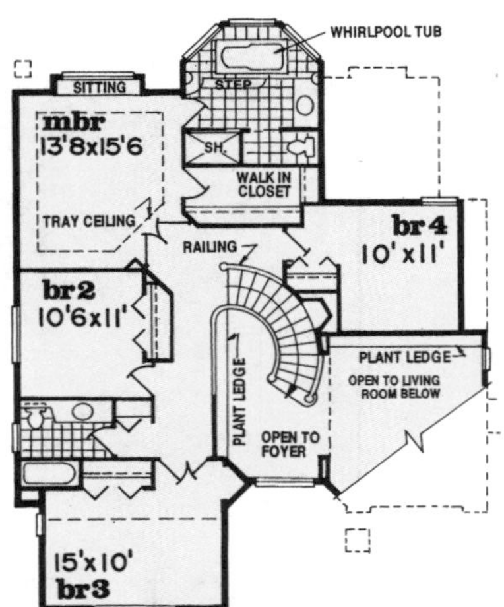

SECOND FLOOR

plan# HPT930400

- Style: Contemporary
- First Floor: 1,383 sq. ft.
- Second Floor: 1,156 sq. ft.
- Total: 2,539 sq. ft.
- Bedrooms: 4
- Bathrooms: 2½
- Width: 40'-0"
- Depth: 59'-0"
- Foundation: Basement, Crawlspace

SEARCH ONLINE @ EPLANS.COM

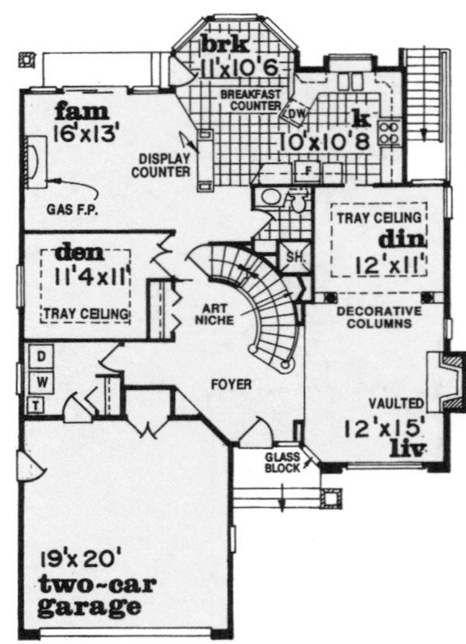

FIRST FLOOR

This well-planned stucco home is suited for a narrow lot. Its interior begins with a two-story foyer that displays a sweeping, curved staircase, an art niche and a plant ledge. The vaulted ceiling in the living room is enhanced by a full-height window and a fireplace. Columns separate the living and dining rooms; the dining room has a tray ceiling. The step-saving kitchen is adjacent to a carousel breakfast room with a French door to the rear yard. A gas fireplace warms the family room, which features a room-divider display counter and sliding glass doors. A den with a tray ceiling rounds out the first floor. The master suite boasts a tray ceiling, window seat, raised whirlpool tub and separate shower. Three family bedrooms share a full bath.

plan# HPT930401

- Style: Contemporary
- First Floor: 1,023 sq. ft.
- Second Floor: 837 sq. ft.
- Total: 1,860 sq. ft.
- Bedrooms: 3
- Bathrooms: 2½
- Width: 47'-0"
- Depth: 47'-0"
- Foundation: Basement, Crawlspace

SEARCH ONLINE @ EPLANS.COM

Plans for this design include both a contemporary stucco exterior and a traditional brick and siding version. The peninsula kitchen blends into a bayed breakfast room and the open family room, which features a fireplace and sliding glass doors to the patio. The second floor includes three bedrooms. The master suite features a bath with arched access, whirlpool tub, separate shower and double vanity. Family bedrooms share a full bath that includes a linen closet.

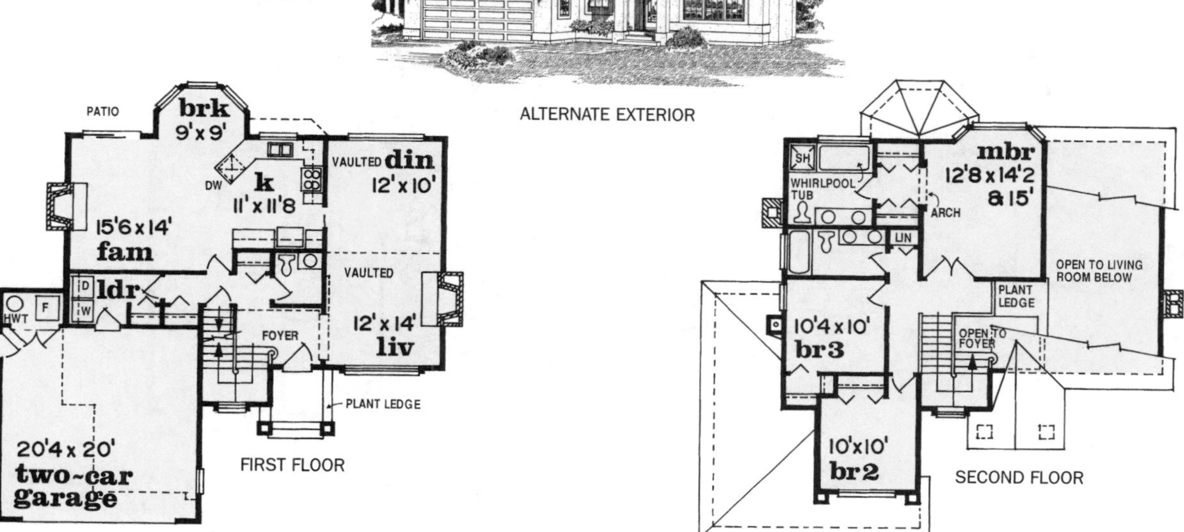

ALTERNATE EXTERIOR

FIRST FLOOR

SECOND FLOOR

This design with lovely contemporary accents features a European silhouette with modern interior spaces. Inside, the combined living and dining area is warmed by a fireplace. Radiant two-story windows illuminate this area. The sharp-angled kitchen features a handy snack bar. A casual family room is located at the rear behind the two-car garage. A convenient laundry room completes the first floor. Four family bedrooms and two full baths are located on the second floor.

plan# HPT930402

- Style: Contemporary
- First Floor: 926 sq. ft.
- Second Floor: 988 sq. ft.
- Total: 1,914 sq. ft.
- Bedrooms: 4
- Bathrooms: 2½
- Width: 42'-0"
- Depth: 34'-0"
- Foundation: Basement

SEARCH ONLINE @ EPLANS.COM

FIRST FLOOR

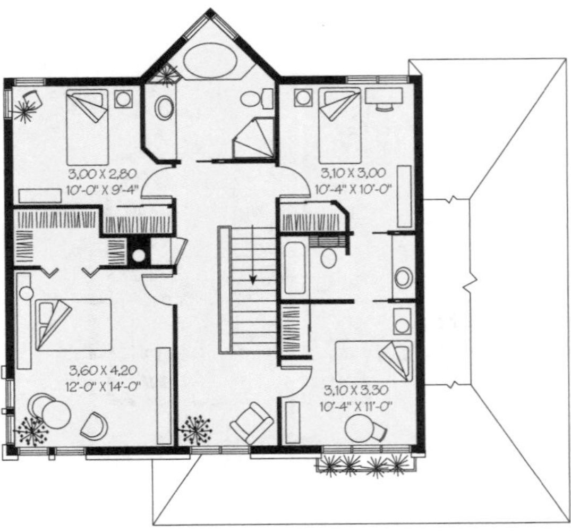

SECOND FLOOR

plan# HPT930403

- Style: Contemporary
- First Floor: 1,290 sq. ft.
- Second Floor: 1,165 sq. ft.
- Total: 2,455 sq. ft.
- Bedrooms: 4
- Bathrooms: 2½
- Width: 42'-0"
- Depth: 41'-0"
- Foundation: Walkout Basement

SEARCH ONLINE @ EPLANS.COM

A distinctive turret-style bay and a floor plan designed for today's family set this contemporary home apart from the crowd. Tile flooring extends from the foyer to utility rooms and a U-shaped kitchen and breakfast nook for low maintenance and beautiful style. The living room is warmed by a fireplace and brightened by a bay window. The dining room is open to the living room for easy entertaining. To the rear, the family room is sure to be a favorite with a gas fireplace, built-in media center and deck access. Upstairs, three bedrooms share a full bath: the master suite enjoys a private bath with dual vanities.

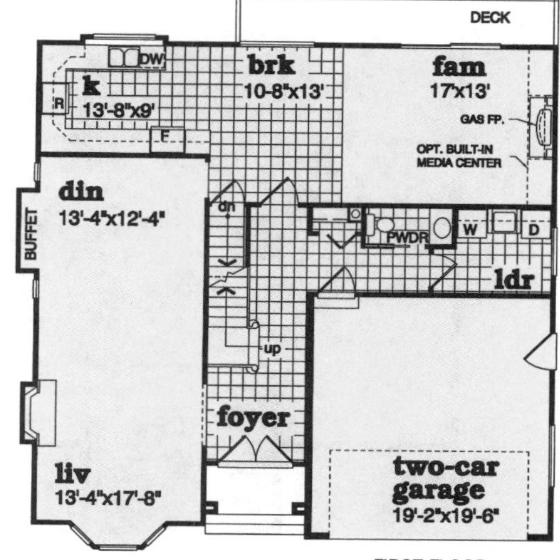

FIRST FLOOR

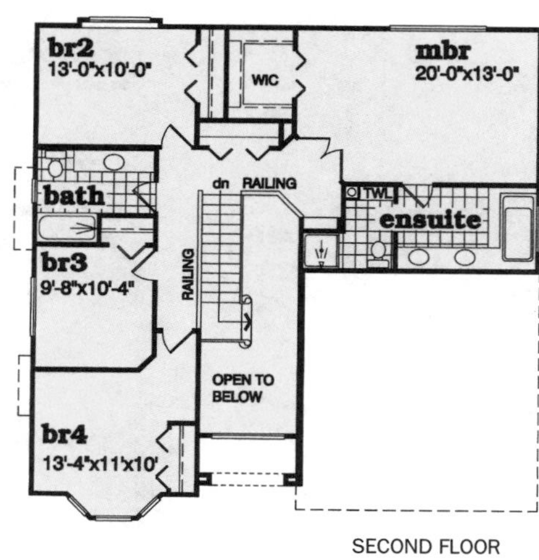

SECOND FLOOR

This Mediterranean home offers a dreamy living-by-the-water lifestyle, but it's ready to build in any region. A lovely arch-top entry announces an exquisite foyer with a curved staircase. The family room provides a fireplace and opens to the outdoors on both sides of the plan. An L-shaped kitchen serves a cozy morning area as well as a stunning formal dining room, which offers a bay window. Second-floor sleeping quarters include four bedrooms and two bathrooms. The master suite opens to a balcony and offers a bath with a double-bowl vanity.

plan# HPT930404

- Style: Mediterranean
- First Floor: 1,065 sq. ft.
- Second Floor: 1,032 sq. ft.
- Total: 2,097 sq. ft.
- Bedrooms: 4
- Bathrooms: 2½
- Width: 38'-0"
- Depth: 38'-0"
- Foundation: Basement

SEARCH ONLINE @ EPLANS.COM

FIRST FLOOR

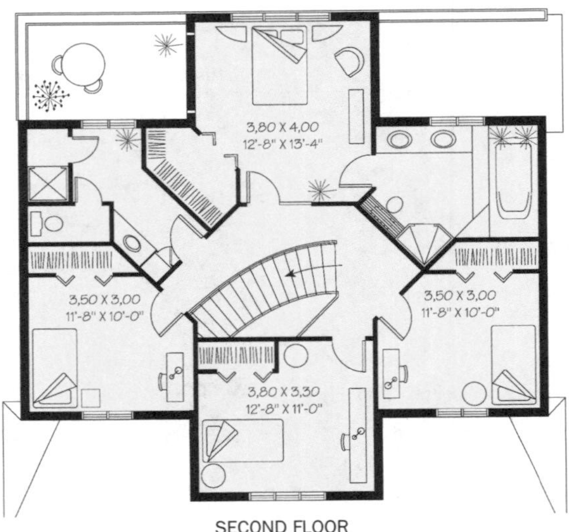

SECOND FLOOR

FOR MORE DETAILED INFORMATION, PLEASE CHECK THE FLOOR PLANS CAREFULLY.

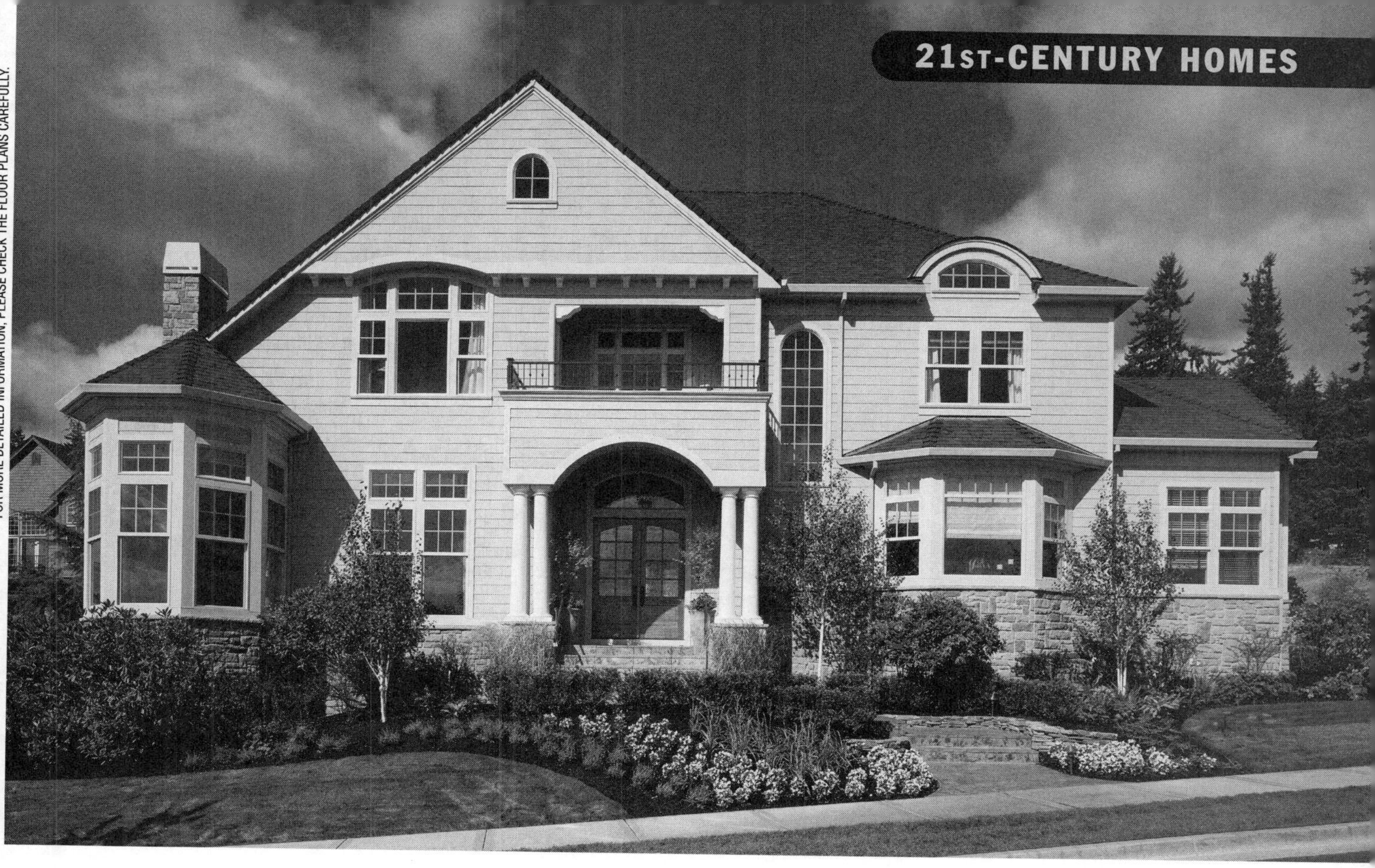

plan# HPT930405

- Style: Contemporary
- First Floor: 2,572 sq. ft.
- Second Floor: 1,578 sq. ft.
- Total: 4,150 sq. ft.
- Bonus Space: 315 sq. ft.
- Bedrooms: 4
- Bathrooms: 4½
- Width: 78'-2"
- Depth: 68'-0"
- Foundation: Crawlspace

SEARCH ONLINE @ EPLANS.COM

SECOND FLOOR

FIRST FLOOR

Craftsman detailing and a hint of French flair make this home a standout in any neighborhood. An impressive foyer opens to the left to the great room, with a coffered ceiling, warming fireplace and a charming alcove, set in a turret. The kitchen is designed for entertaining, with an island that doubles as a snack bar and plenty of room to move. An adjacent porch invites dining alfresco. The bayed study is peaceful and quiet. A nearby guest room enjoys a private bath. Upstairs, the master suite is awe inspiring. A romantic fireplace sets the mood and natural light pours in. A sumptuous spa bath leaves homeowners pampered and relaxed. Two bedroom suites share a vaulted bonus room, perfect as a home gym.

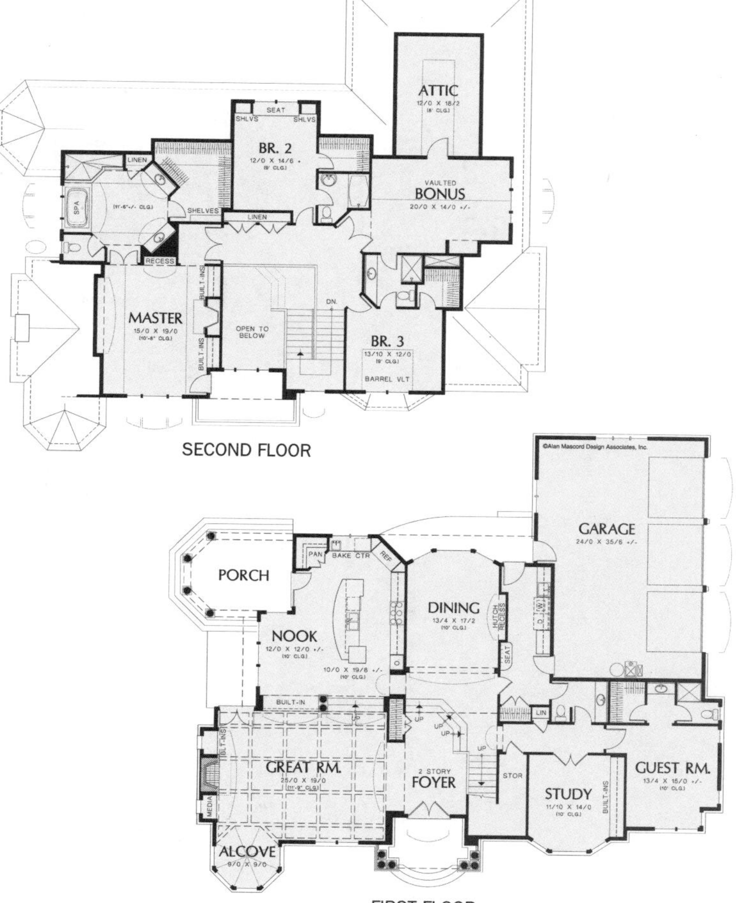

SECOND FLOOR

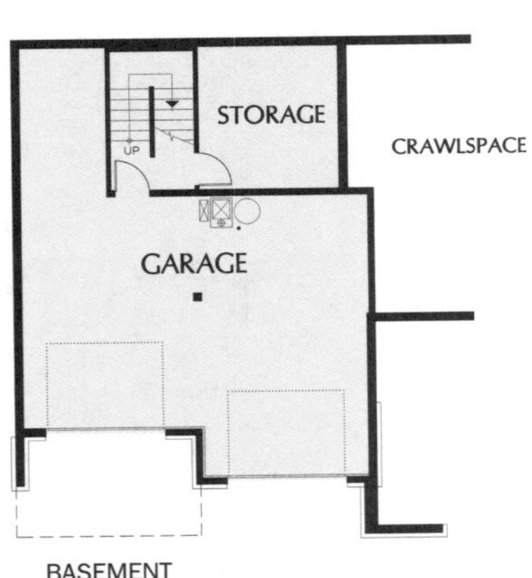

BASEMENT

plan# HPT930406

- Style: Contemporary
- First Floor: 1,501 sq. ft.
- Second Floor: 921 sq. ft.
- Total: 2,509 sq. ft.
- Bedrooms: 3
- Bathrooms: 2½
- Width: 52'-0"
- Depth: 36'-0"
- Foundation: Crawlspace, Basement

SEARCH ONLINE @ EPLANS.COM

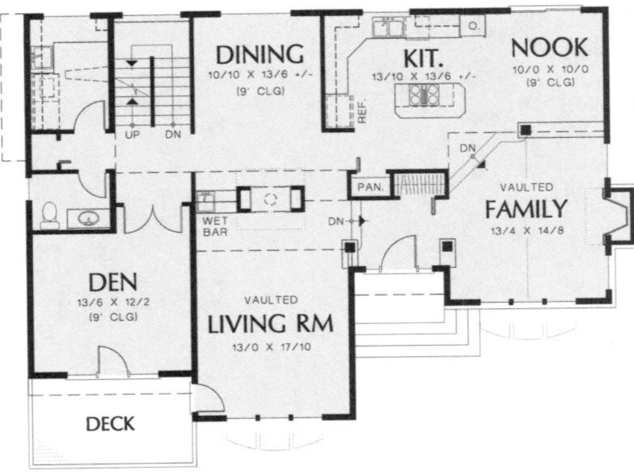

FIRST FLOOR

The contemporary look of this modern country design is both impressive and unique. Enormous windows brighten and enliven every interior space. The vaulted family room features a fireplace, and a two-sided fireplace warms the formal living and dining rooms. The gourmet island kitchen is open to a nook. Double doors open to a den that accesses a front deck. Upstairs, the master bedroom features a private bath with linen storage and a walk-in closet. Two family bedrooms share a Jack-and-Jill bath. The two-car garage features a storage area on the lower level.

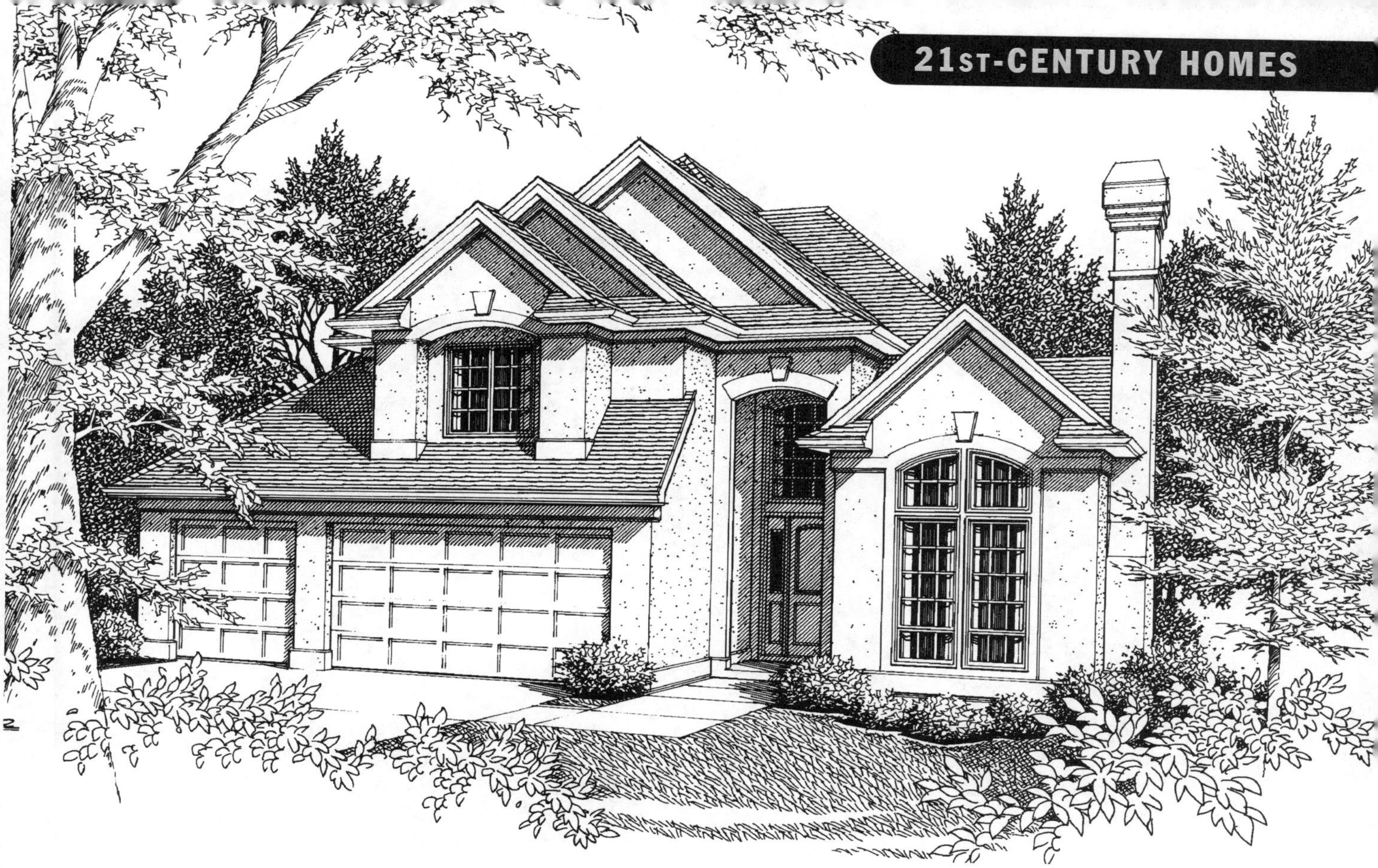

plan# HPT930407

- Style: Contemporary
- First Floor: 1,317 sq. ft.
- Second Floor: 1,146 sq. ft.
- Total: 2,463 sq. ft.
- Bedrooms: 4
- Bathrooms: 2½
- Width: 50'-0"
- Depth: 54'-0"
- Foundation: Crawlspace

SEARCH ONLINE @ EPLANS.COM

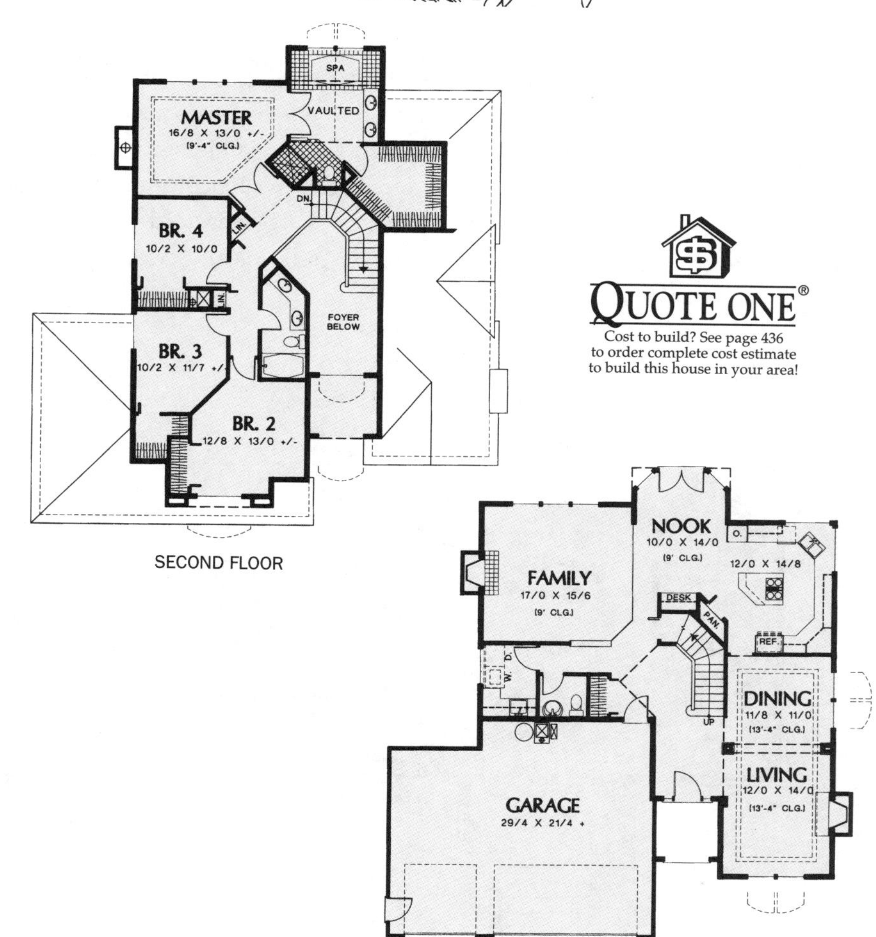

SECOND FLOOR

QUOTE ONE®
Cost to build? See page 436 to order complete cost estimate to build this house in your area!

This striking stucco home incorporates fine design elements throughout the plan, including a columned formal living and dining area with a boxed ceiling and a fireplace. A gourmet kitchen accommodates the most elaborate—as well as the simplest—meals. The large family room is just off the kitchen for easy casual living. A lovely curved staircase leads to a balcony overlooking the foyer. The master bedroom contains many fine design features, including a luxury bath with a vaulted ceiling and a spa-style tub. Three comfortable family bedrooms share a full hall bath.

FIRST FLOOR

This rustic contemporary cottage design is a cozy getaway—perfect for the lake. A petite covered front porch welcomes you inside to the living and dining rooms warmed by a two-sided fireplace. The U-shaped kitchen features a laundry closet. The first-floor bedroom provides ample closet space and is placed near the hall bath. A rear porch completes the first floor. The master bedroom is located upstairs for privacy and offers a private bath, built-ins and closet space.

plan # HPT930408

- Style: Contemporary
- First Floor: 852 sq. ft.
- Second Floor: 374 sq. ft.
- Total: 1,226 sq. ft.
- Bedrooms: 2
- Bathrooms: 2
- Width: 37'-10"
- Depth: 33'-4"
- Foundation: Crawlspace

SEARCH ONLINE @ EPLANS.COM

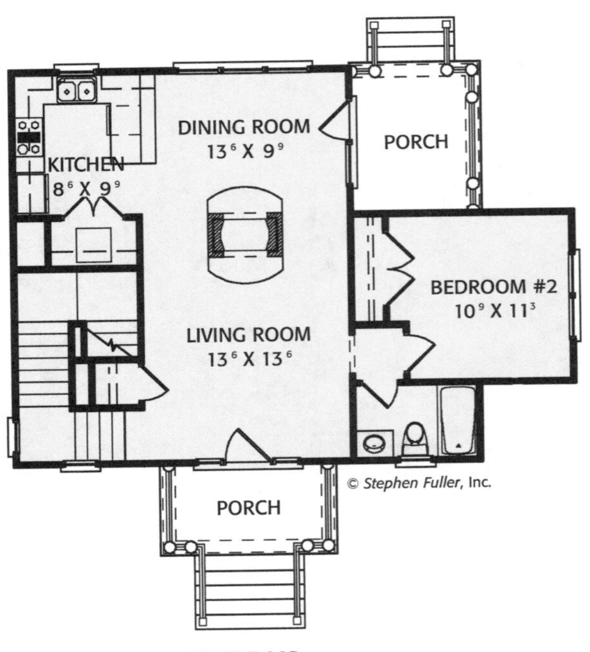

FIRST FLOOR

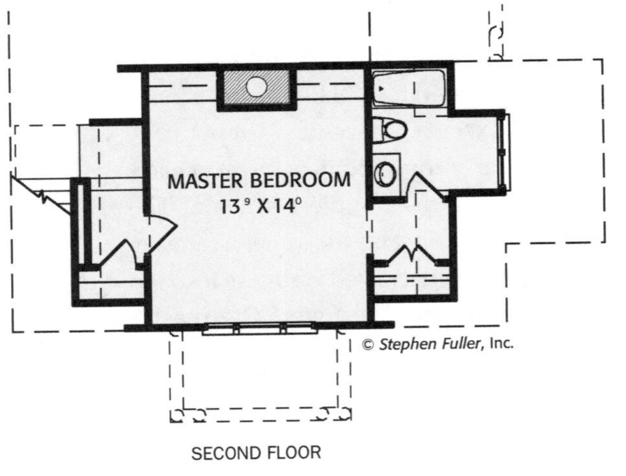

SECOND FLOOR

plan# HPT930409

- Style: Contemporary
- First Floor: 1,170 sq. ft.
- Second Floor: 1,058 sq. ft.
- Total: 2,228 sq. ft.
- Bedrooms: 4
- Bathrooms: 2½
- Width: 30'-0"
- Depth: 51'-0"

SEARCH ONLINE @ EPLANS.COM

A narrow width and front and rear porches make this home perfect for waterfront lots, while its squared-off design makes it easy to afford. The great room, kitchen and breakfast area are all open for a casual and spacious feeling. Numerous windows enhance the area's volume. Flexible rooms located at the front of the home include a formal living or dining room and a study or bedroom with optional entry to the powder room. Upstairs, every bedroom (plus the master bath) enjoys porch access. The master suite features a tray ceiling, dual closets and a sizable bath with linen cabinets.

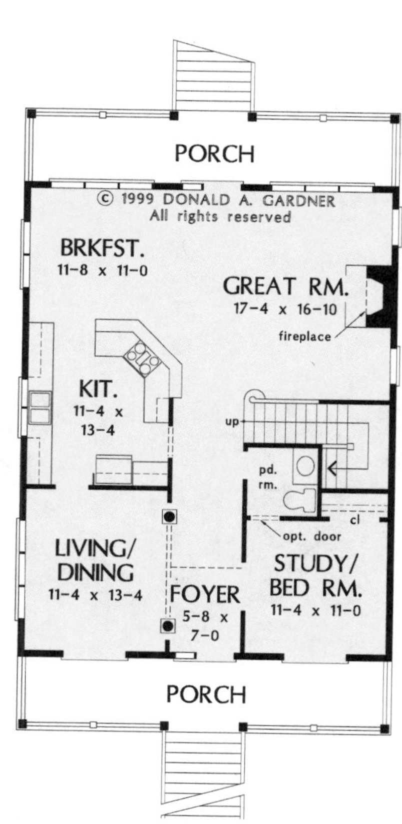

FIRST FLOOR

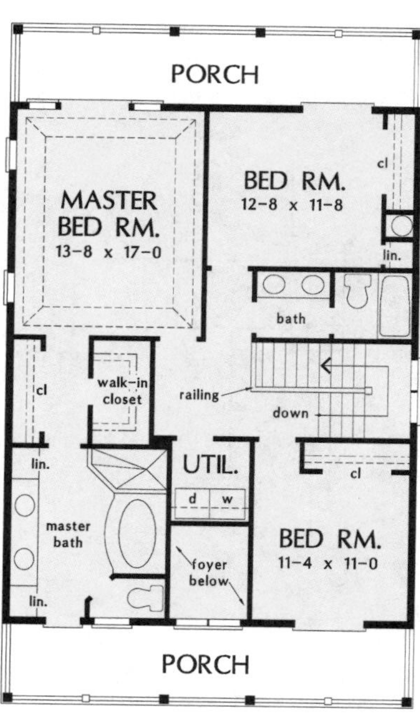

SECOND FLOOR

PHOTO COURTESY OF LIVING CONCEPTS

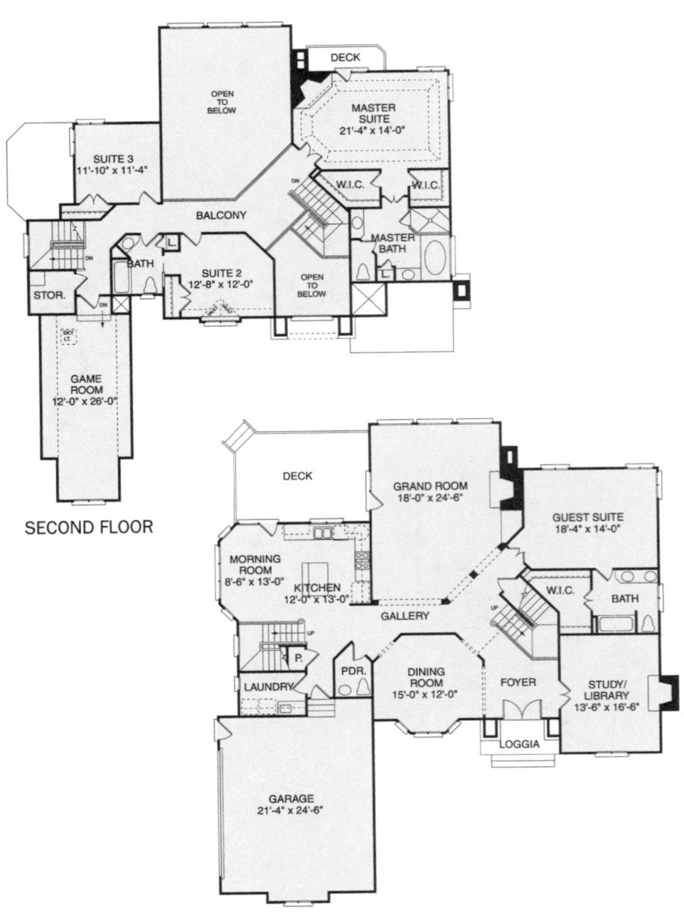

plan# HPT930410

- Style: Contemporary
- First Floor: 2,174 sq. ft.
- Second Floor: 1,241 sq. ft.
- Total: 3,415 sq. ft.
- Bonus Space: 347 sq. ft.
- Bedrooms: 4
- Bathrooms: 3½
- Width: 61'-4"
- Depth: 68'-8"
- Foundation: Crawlspace

SEARCH ONLINE @ EPLANS.COM

An impressive facade of stucco and stone and gabled peaks highlights the exterior of this plan. A loggia welcomes you inside to the foyer flanked by a study/library with a fireplace, and the formal dining room brightened by a bay window. A gallery hall leads to other areas of the home, including a guest suite with a private bath, the grand room warmed by an impressive hearth, and the island kitchen overlooking the morning room. Upstairs, the master suite features a private fireplace, His and Hers walk-in closets and a lavish bath. The second-floor game room is a spacious addition.

© 1998 Donald A Gardner, Inc. B.NATHAN

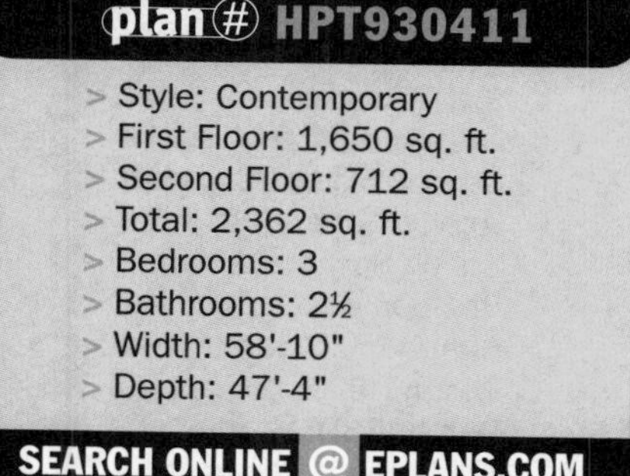

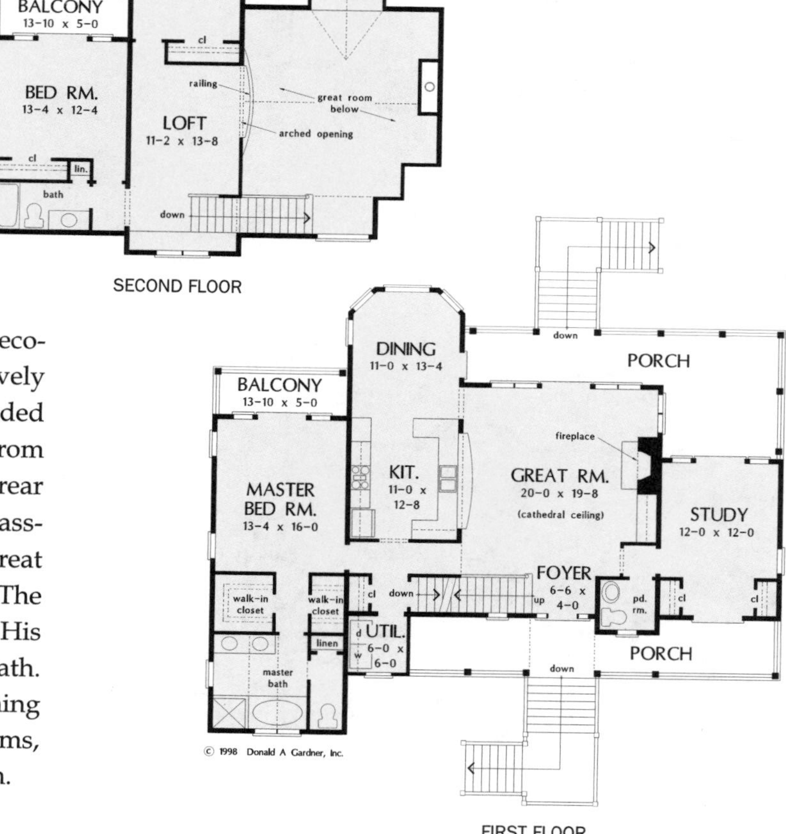

Cedar shakes and striking gables with decorative scalloped insets adorn the exterior of this lovely coastal home. The generous great room is expanded by a rear wall of windows, with additional light from transom windows above the front door and a rear clerestory dormer. The kitchen features a pass-through to the great room. The dining room, great room and study all access an inviting back porch. The master bedroom is a treat with a private balcony, His and Hers walk-in closets and an impeccable bath. Upstairs, a room-sized loft with an arched opening overlooks the great room below. Two more bedrooms, one with its own private balcony, share a hall bath.

SECOND FLOOR

FIRST FLOOR

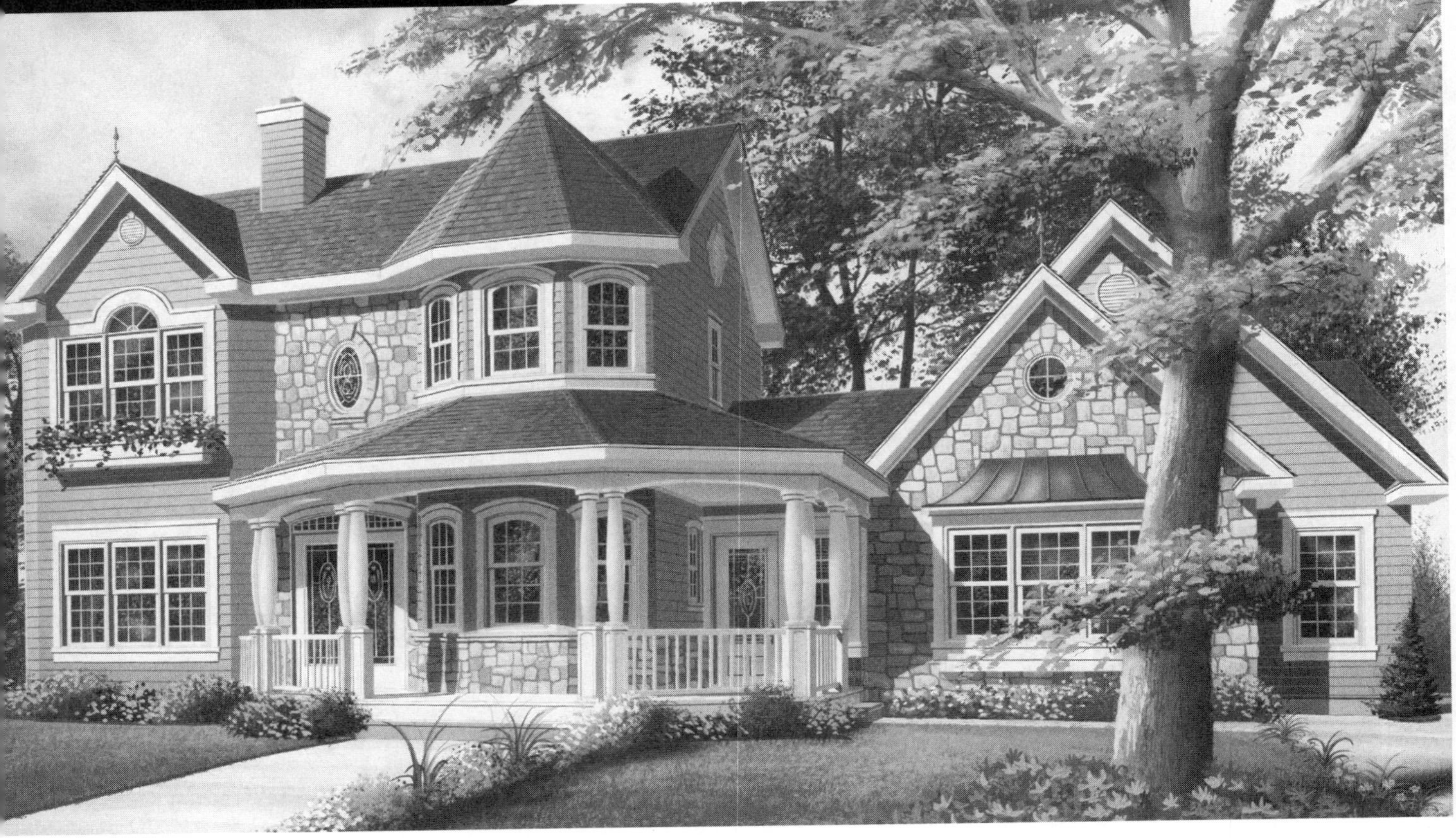

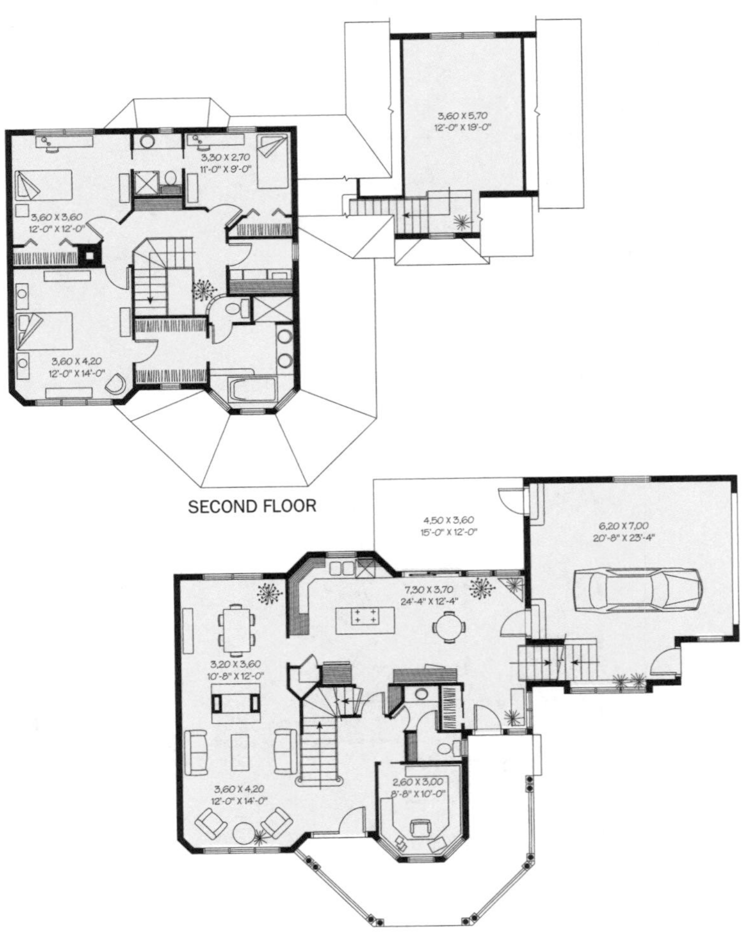

plan# HPT930412

- Style: Contemporary
- First Floor: 1,044 sq. ft.
- Second Floor: 894 sq. ft.
- Total: 1,938 sq. ft.
- Bonus Space: 228 sq. ft.
- Bedrooms: 3
- Bathrooms: 2½
- Width: 58'-0"
- Depth: 43'-6"
- Foundation: Basement

SEARCH ONLINE @ EPLANS.COM

This charming contemporary home provides a well-lit home office, harbored in a beautiful bay with three windows. The second-floor bay brightens the master bath, which has a double-bowl vanity, a step-up tub and a dressing area. The living and dining rooms share a two-sided fireplace. The gourmet kitchen has a cooktop island counter and enjoys outdoor views through sliding glass doors in the breakfast area. A sizable bonus room above the two-car garage can be developed into hobby space or a recreation room.

plan# HPT930413

- Style: Contemporary
- First Floor: 1,186 sq. ft.
- Second Floor: 988 sq. ft.
- Total: 2,174 sq. ft.
- Bedrooms: 4
- Bathrooms: 2½
- Width: 72'-0"
- Depth: 50'-10"
- Foundation: Basement

SEARCH ONLINE @ EPLANS.COM

A Palladian window, fish-scale shingles and turret-style bays set off this country-style Victorian exterior. Muntin windows and a quintessential wraparound porch dress up an understated theme and introduce an unrestrained floor plan with plenty of bays and niches. An impressive tile entry opens to the formal rooms, which nestle to the left side of the plan and enjoy natural light from an abundance of windows. The turret houses a secluded study on the first floor and provides a sunny bay window for a family bedroom upstairs. The second-floor master suite boasts its own fireplace, a dressing area with a walk-in closet, and a lavish bath with a garden tub and twin vanities. The two-car garage offers space for a workshop or extra storage, and leads to a service entrance to the walk-through utility room.

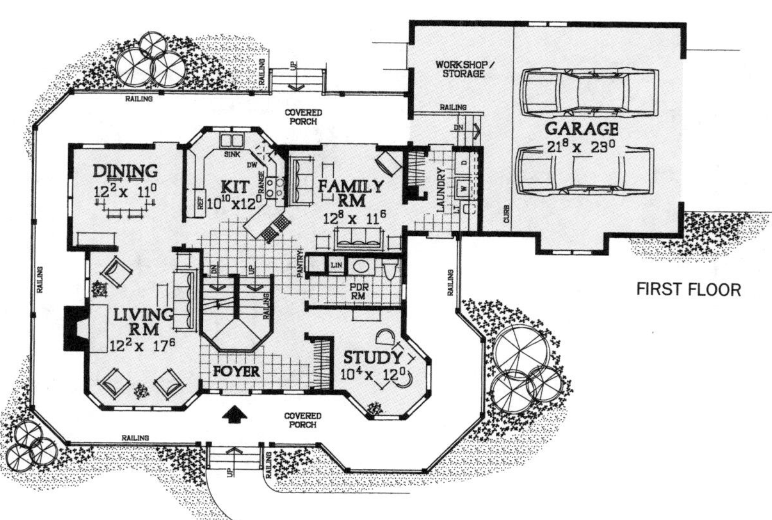

FIRST FLOOR

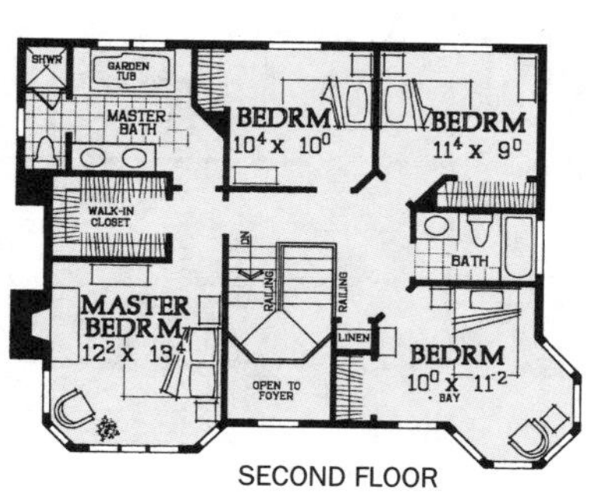

SECOND FLOOR

Traditional charm complements a contemporary interior. A central foyer allows direct access to formal living in the front and casual living in the rear, where the family room, breakfast room and kitchen form a continuous open area. A sun room offers a new dimension to this four-bedroom plan. The master bedroom is located on the first floor for convenience and privacy—and easy access to the covered back porch. A spacious master bath provides a double-bowl vanity, shower and whirlpool tub. Two generously proportioned bedrooms on the second floor share a hall bath; the third has its own bath and a study nook.

plan# HPT930414

- Style: Contemporary
- First Floor: 1,750 sq. ft.
- Second Floor: 977 sq. ft.
- Total: 2,727 sq. ft.
- Bedrooms: 4
- Bathrooms: 3½
- Width: 85'-10"
- Depth: 37'-8"

SEARCH ONLINE @ EPLANS.COM

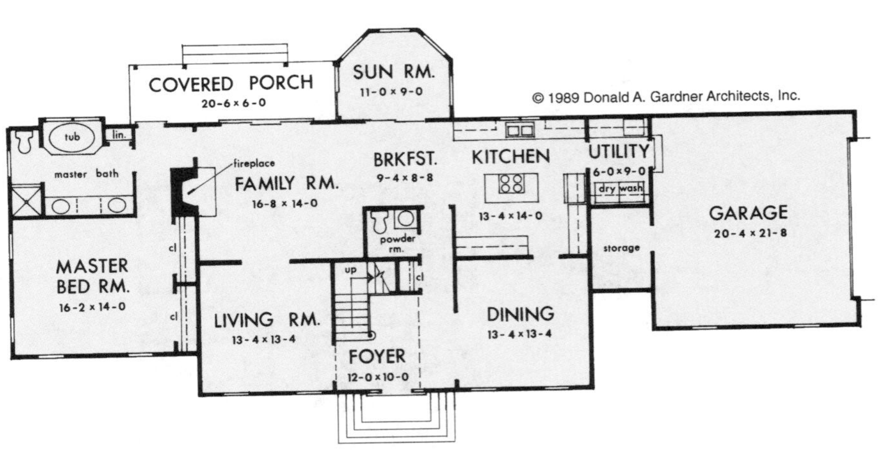

FIRST FLOOR

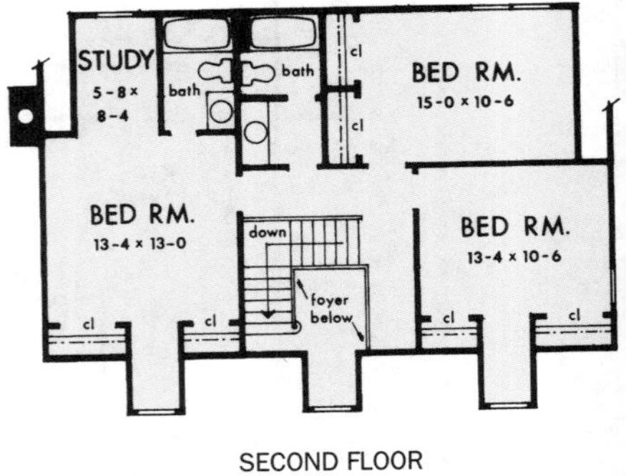

SECOND FLOOR

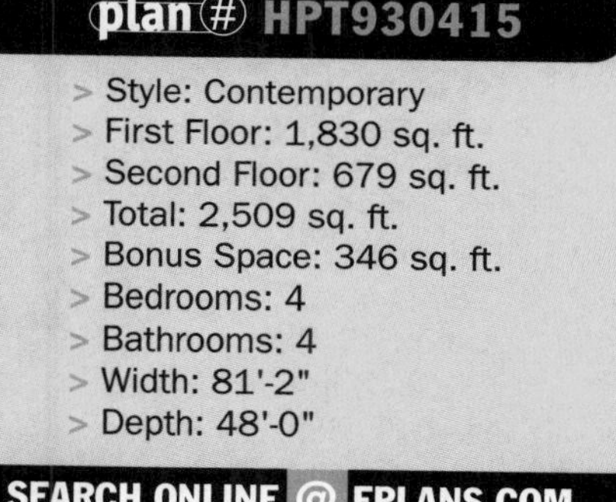

plan# HPT930415

- Style: Contemporary
- First Floor: 1,830 sq. ft.
- Second Floor: 679 sq. ft.
- Total: 2,509 sq. ft.
- Bonus Space: 346 sq. ft.
- Bedrooms: 4
- Bathrooms: 4
- Width: 81'-2"
- Depth: 48'-0"

SEARCH ONLINE @ EPLANS.COM

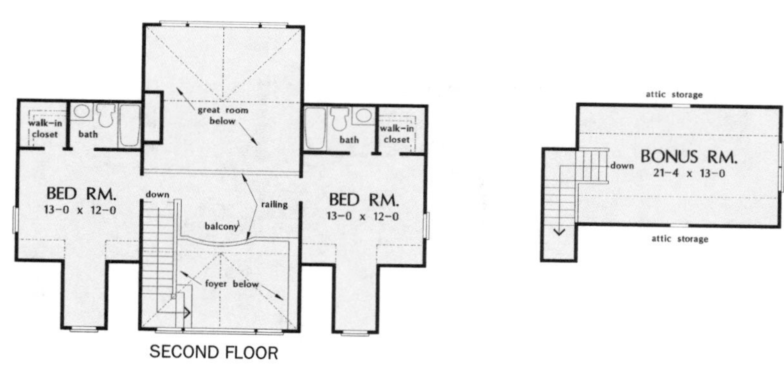

SECOND FLOOR

An expansive, wrapping front porch creates a charming facade for this gracious home. The vaulted foyer receives light from the center clerestory dormer, while an overlooking balcony adds height and drama to the breath-taking entry. A vaulted ceiling heightens the great room. The master bedroom features a tray ceiling for added elegance and a private bath. Both upstairs bedrooms enjoy dormer windows, walk-in closets and private baths. A bonus room above the garage easily converts to a home office or guest suite.

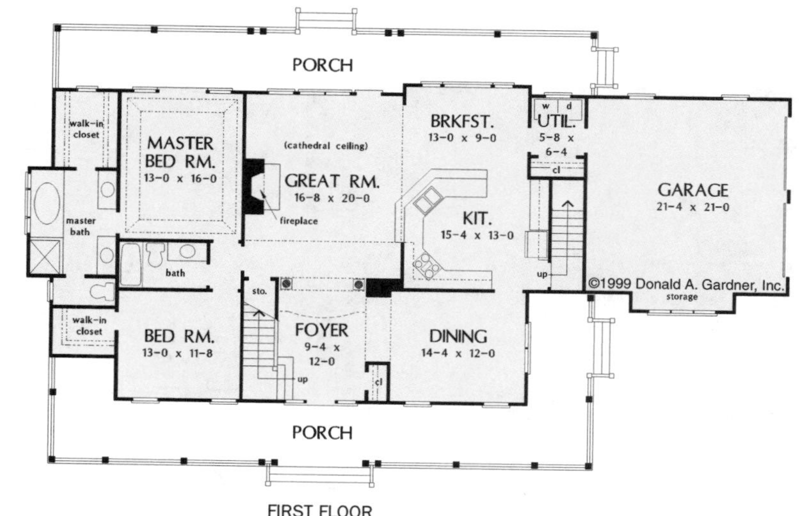

FIRST FLOOR

4,200 x 5,200
14'-0" x 17'-4"
OPEN TO
BELOW

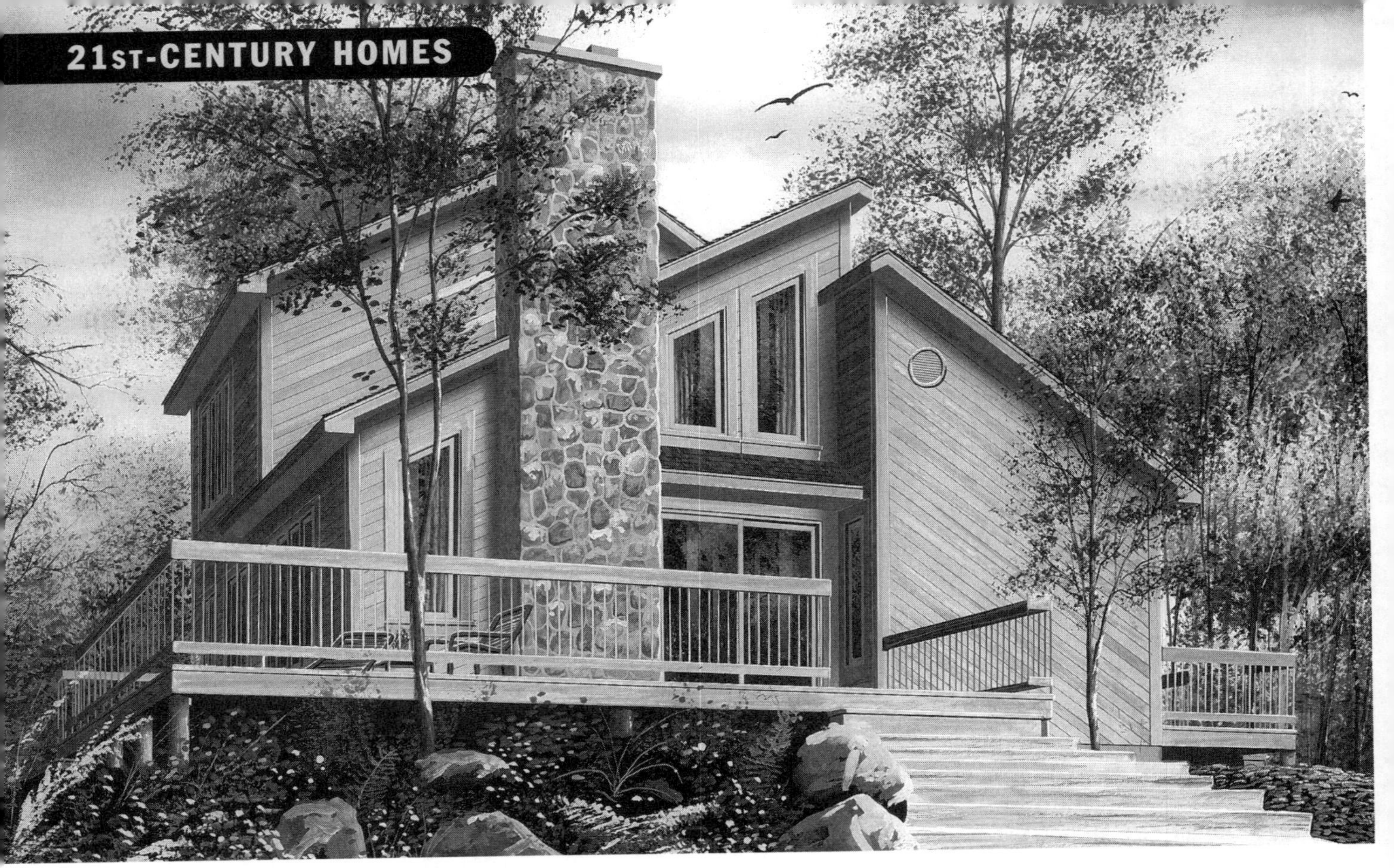

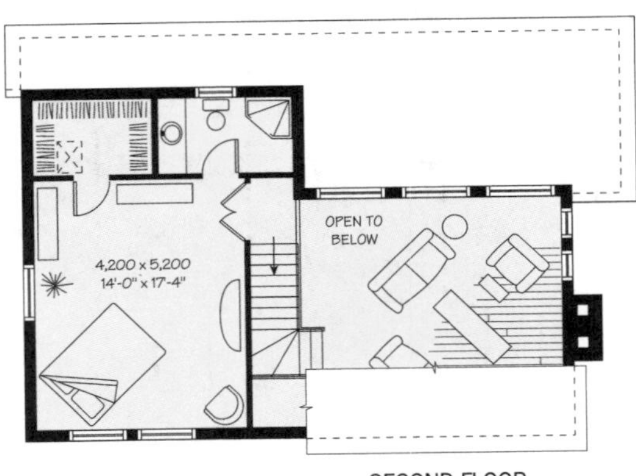

SECOND FLOOR

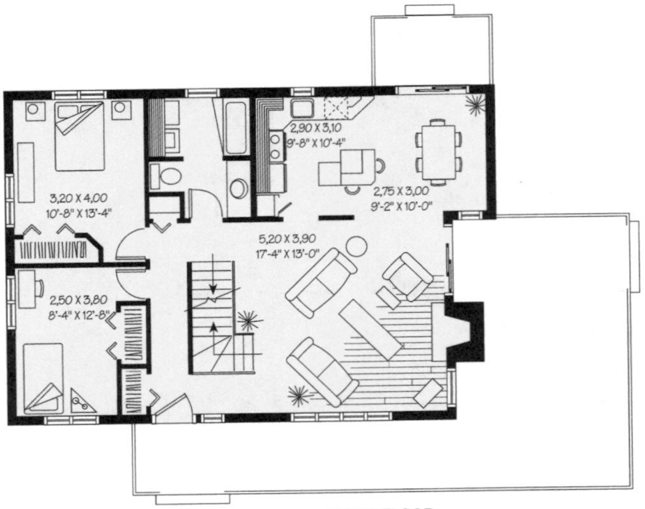

3,20 X 4,00
10'-8" X 13'-4"
2,50 X 3,80
8'-4" X 12'-8"
2,90 X 3,10
9'-8" X 10'-4"
2,75 X 3,00
9'-2" X 10'-0"
5,20 X 3,90
17'-4" X 13'-0"

FIRST FLOOR

plan# HPT930416

- Style: Contemporary
- First Floor: 1,062 sq. ft.
- Second Floor: 454 sq. ft.
- Total: 1,516 sq. ft.
- Bedrooms: 3
- Bathrooms: 2
- Width: 40'-0"
- Depth: 28'-0"
- Foundation: Basement

SEARCH ONLINE @ EPLANS.COM

Contemporary style and modern interior spaces lend this great design dramatic character. The open two-story living room is warmed by a country fireplace. The warmth extends to the island snack-bar kitchen, which is open to the eating area. The large wrap-around deck will provide plenty of outdoor entertainment possibilities. Two first-floor family bedrooms share a hall bath that offers laundry facilities. Upstairs, French doors open to the master bedroom loft, featuring a large walk-in closet and a private shower bath.

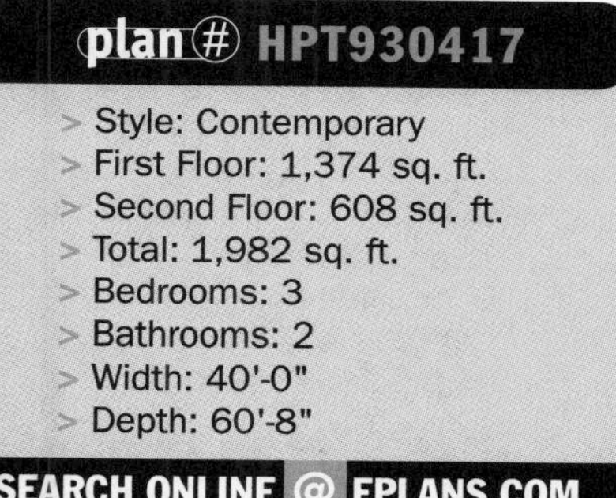
plan# HPT930417

- Style: Contemporary
- First Floor: 1,374 sq. ft.
- Second Floor: 608 sq. ft.
- Total: 1,982 sq. ft.
- Bedrooms: 3
- Bathrooms: 2
- Width: 40'-0"
- Depth: 60'-8"

SEARCH ONLINE @ EPLANS.COM

This rustic three-bedroom vacation home allows for casual living both inside and out. The two-story great room offers dramatic space for entertaining with windows stretching clear to the roof, maximizing the outdoor view. A stone fireplace is the focal point of this room. Two family bedrooms on the first floor share a full hall bath. The second floor holds the master bedroom with a spacious master bath and a walk-in closet. A large loft area overlooks the great room and entrance foyer.

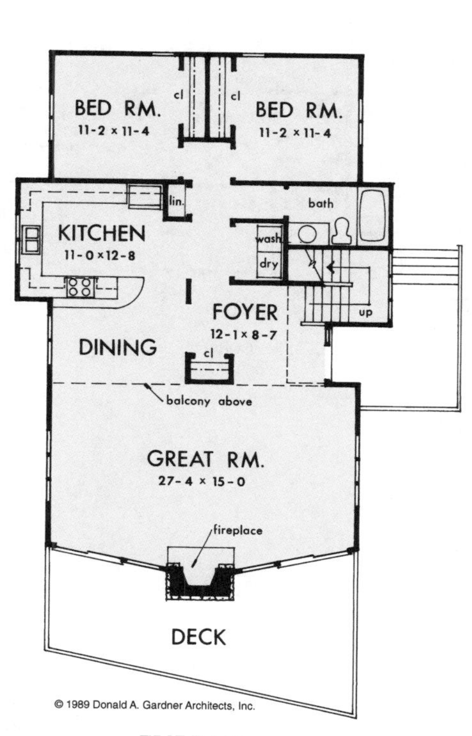

FIRST FLOOR

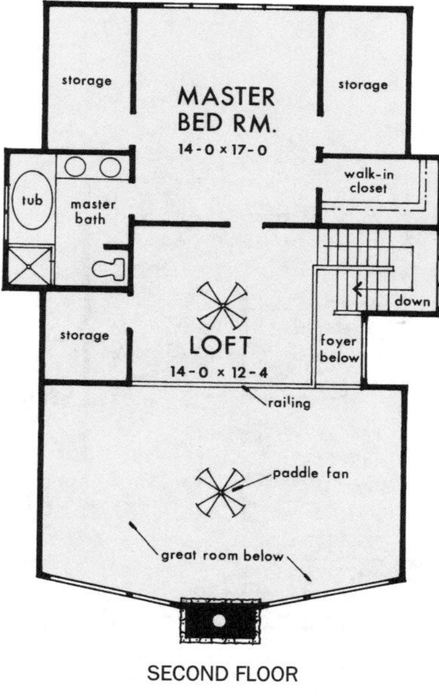

SECOND FLOOR

plan# HPT930418

- Style: Contemporary
- First Floor: 1,340 sq. ft.
- Second Floor: 547 sq. ft.
- Total: 1,887 sq. ft.
- Bedrooms: 3
- Bathrooms: 2
- Width: 45'-4"
- Depth: 60'-0"

SEARCH ONLINE @ EPLANS.COM

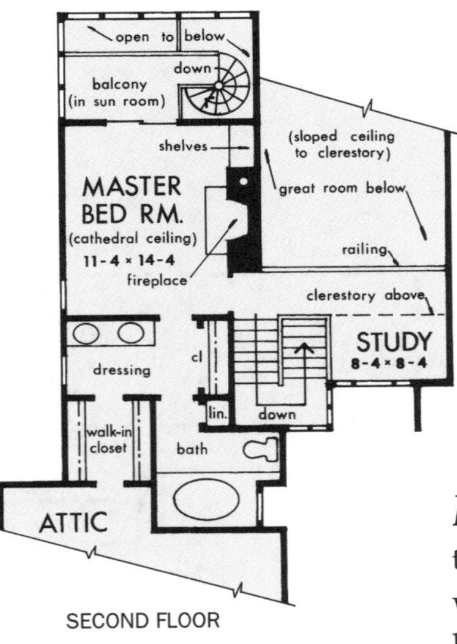

SECOND FLOOR

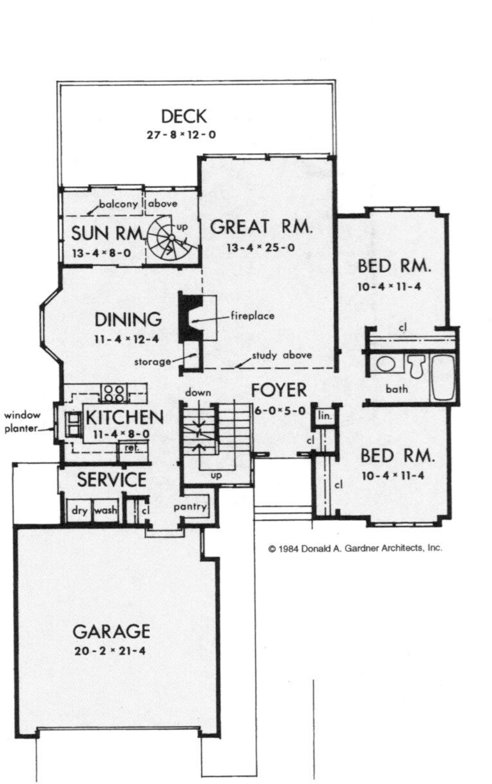

FIRST FLOOR

Because this home's sun room is a full two stories high, it acts as a solar collector when oriented to the south. Enjoying the benefits of this warmth are the dining and great rooms on the first floor and the master suite on the second floor. A spacious deck further extends the outdoor living potential. Special features include: a sloping ceiling with exposed wood beams and a fireplace in the great room; a cathedral ceiling, fireplace, built-in shelves and ample closet space in the master bedroom; a balcony overlook in the upstairs study; and convenient storage space in the attic over the garage.

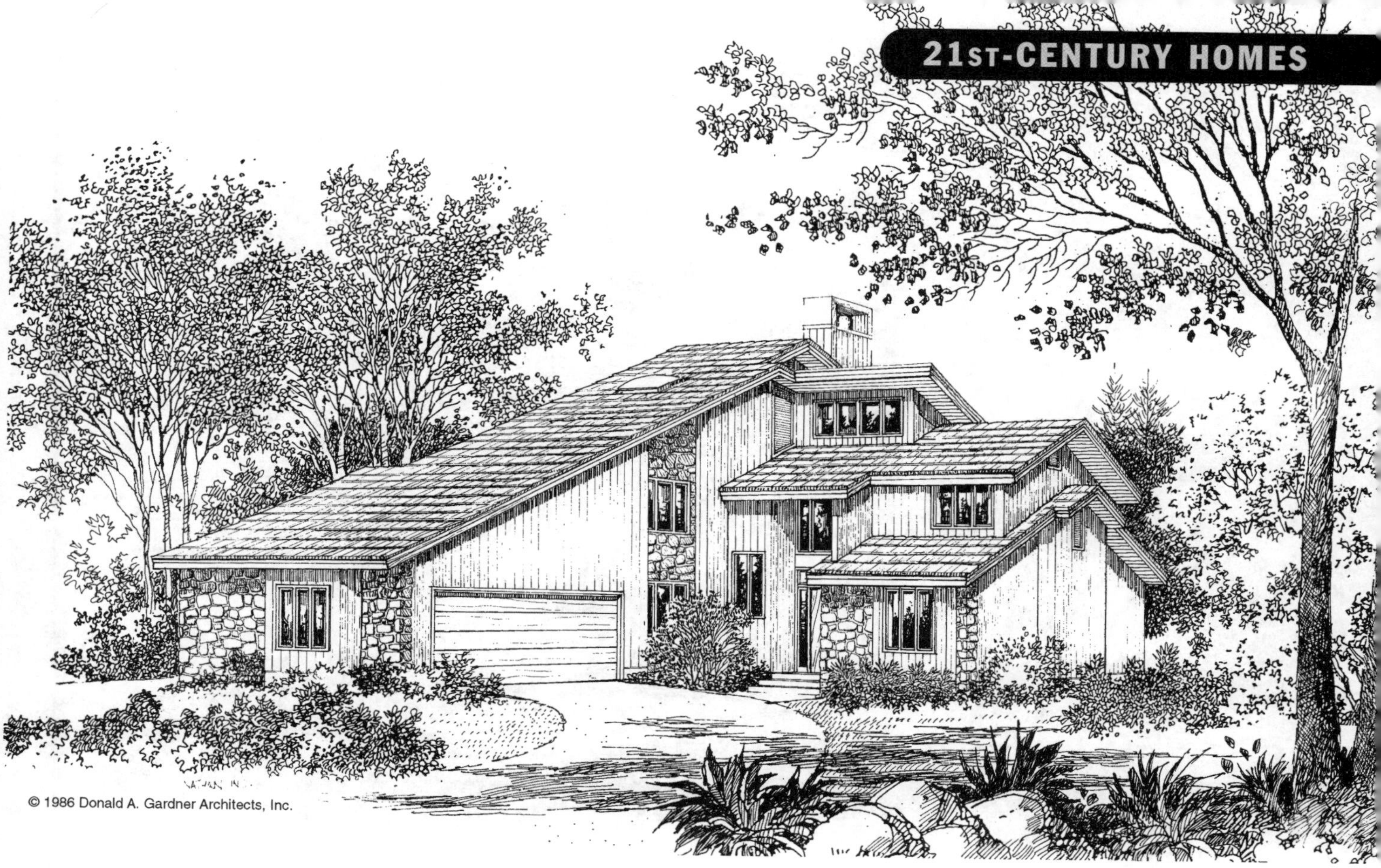

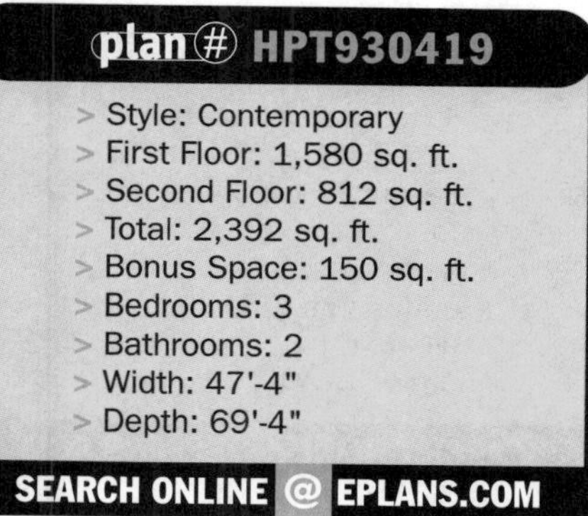

plan# HPT930419

- Style: Contemporary
- First Floor: 1,580 sq. ft.
- Second Floor: 812 sq. ft.
- Total: 2,392 sq. ft.
- Bonus Space: 150 sq. ft.
- Bedrooms: 3
- Bathrooms: 2
- Width: 47'-4"
- Depth: 69'-4"

SEARCH ONLINE @ EPLANS.COM

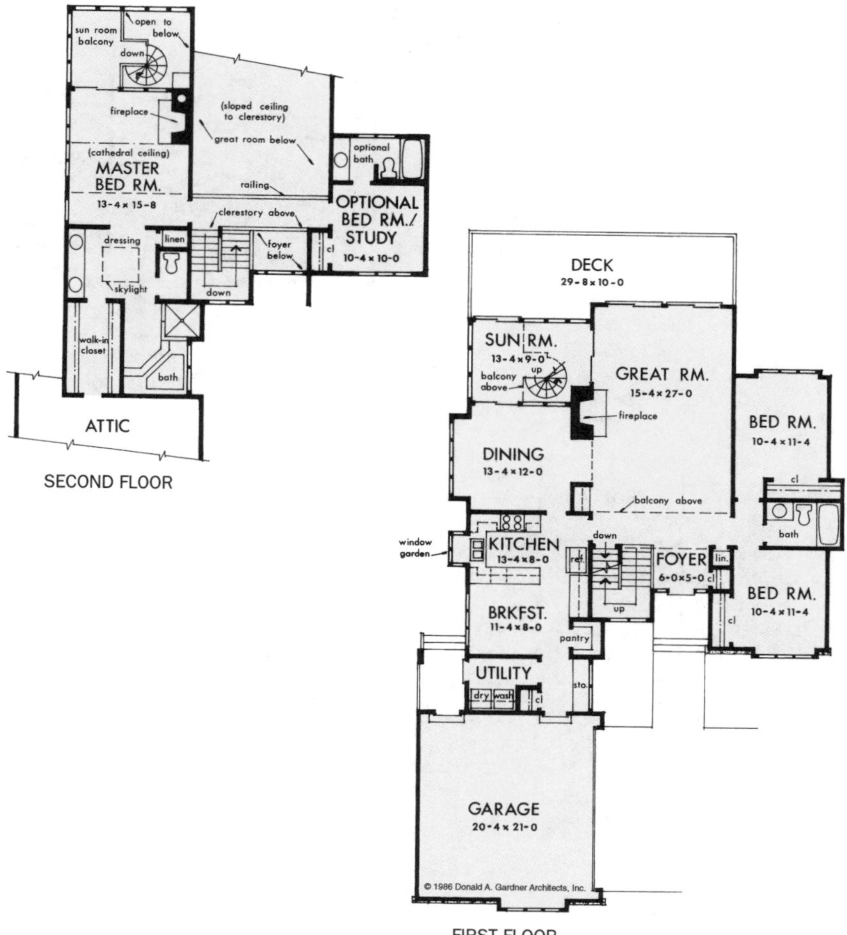

Bold contemporary lines strike an elegant chord in this two-story plan. The foyer leads to a multi-purpose great room with a fireplace and sliding glass doors to a rear deck. The nearby formal dining room connects to the sun room. A U-shaped kitchen features an attached breakfast room and large walk-in pantry. Two bedrooms on this floor share a full bath. The master suite dominates the second floor and features a large walk-in closet, double lavatories, a corner tub and spiral stairs from its private balcony to the sun room below. The upstairs balcony connects it to a study or optional bedroom.

SECOND FLOOR

FIRST FLOOR

SECOND FLOOR

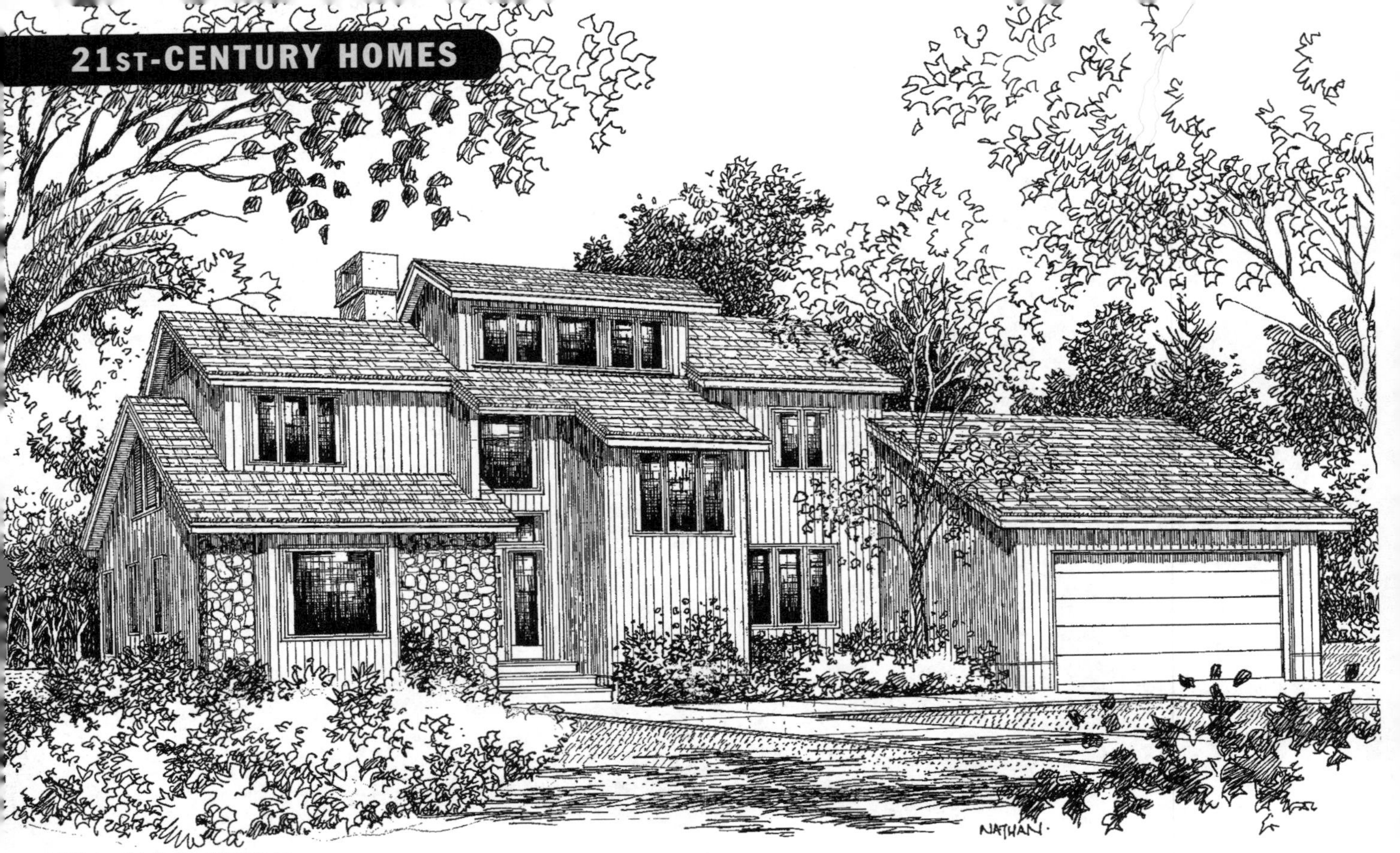

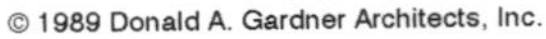

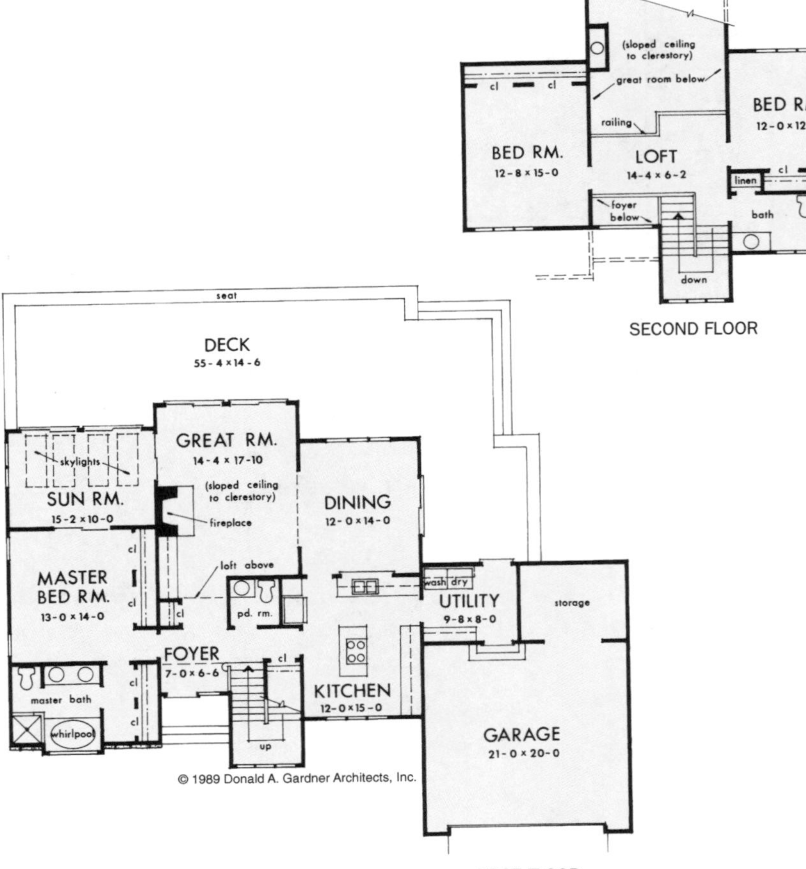

plan# HPT930420

- Style: Contemporary
- First Floor: 1,514 sq. ft.
- Second Floor: 642 sq. ft.
- Total: 2,156 sq. ft.
- Bedrooms: 3
- Bathrooms: 2½
- Width: 64'-4"
- Depth: 46'-4

SEARCH ONLINE @ EPLANS.COM

FIRST FLOOR

Sleek contemporary lines, plenty of windows and a combination of textures give this home a lot of curb appeal. Great for entertaining, the formal dining room has a pass-through to the kitchen for ease in serving. The adjacent great room offers a fireplace, built-ins and access to both the rear deck and the sun room. Located on the first floor for privacy, the master suite features many luscious amenities. Two bedrooms, a full bath and a loft complete the second floor.

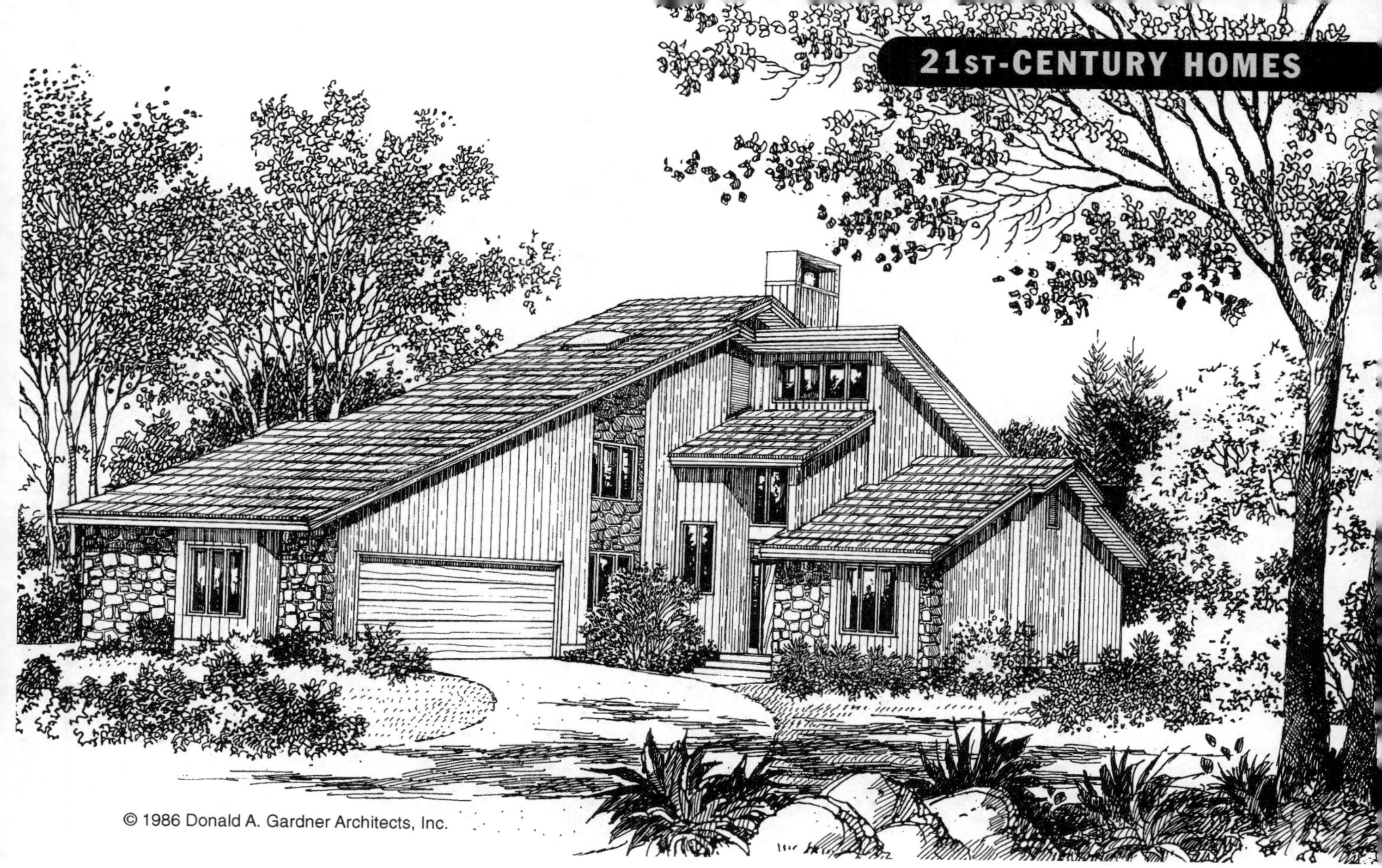

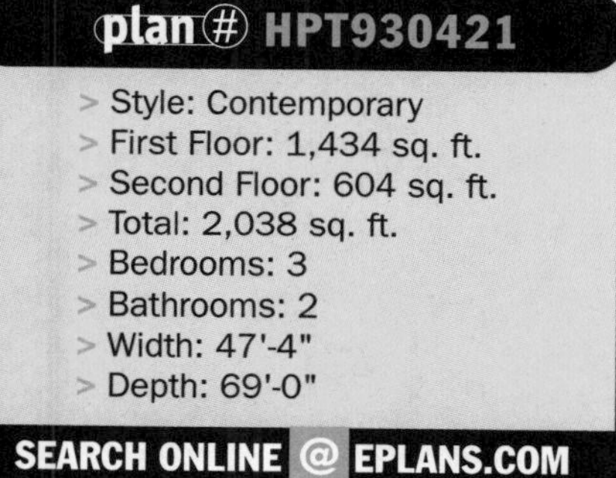

plan# HPT930421

- Style: Contemporary
- First Floor: 1,434 sq. ft.
- Second Floor: 604 sq. ft.
- Total: 2,038 sq. ft.
- Bedrooms: 3
- Bathrooms: 2
- Width: 47'-4"
- Depth: 69'-0"

SEARCH ONLINE @ EPLANS.COM

This home's sun room will delight all with its spiral staircase leading to a balcony and the master suite. The great room enjoys a fireplace and two sets of sliding glass doors leading to the deck. In the kitchen, a U shape lends itself to outstanding convenience. Three bedrooms include two secondary bedrooms and a glorious master suite. Located on the second floor, the private bedroom has a fireplace, a generous dressing area with a skylight, and a lavish bath.

FIRST FLOOR

SECOND FLOOR

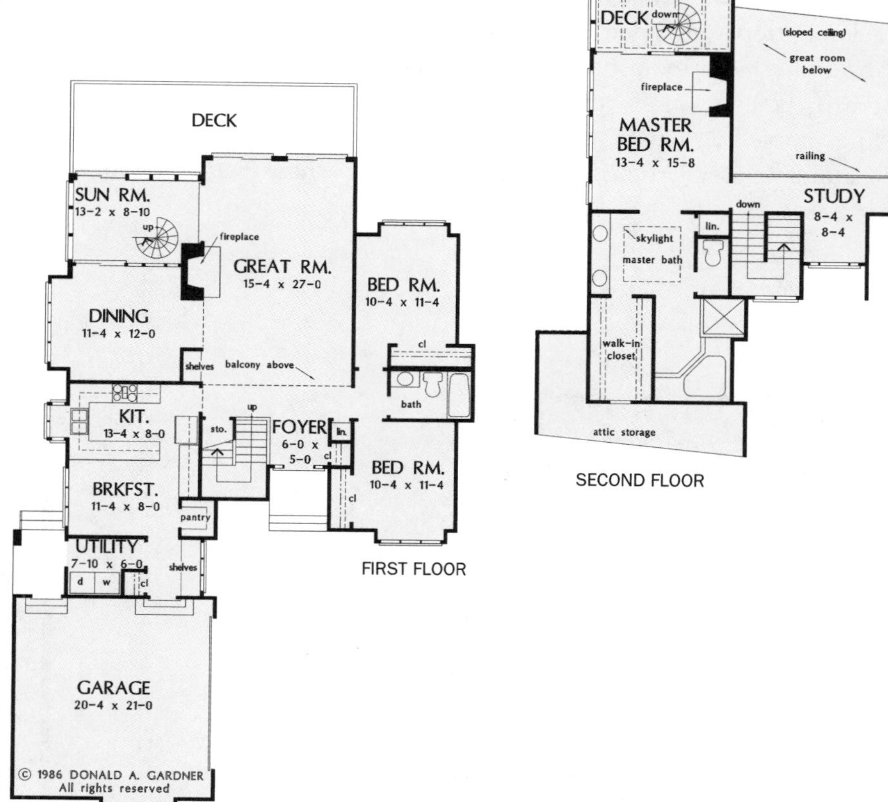

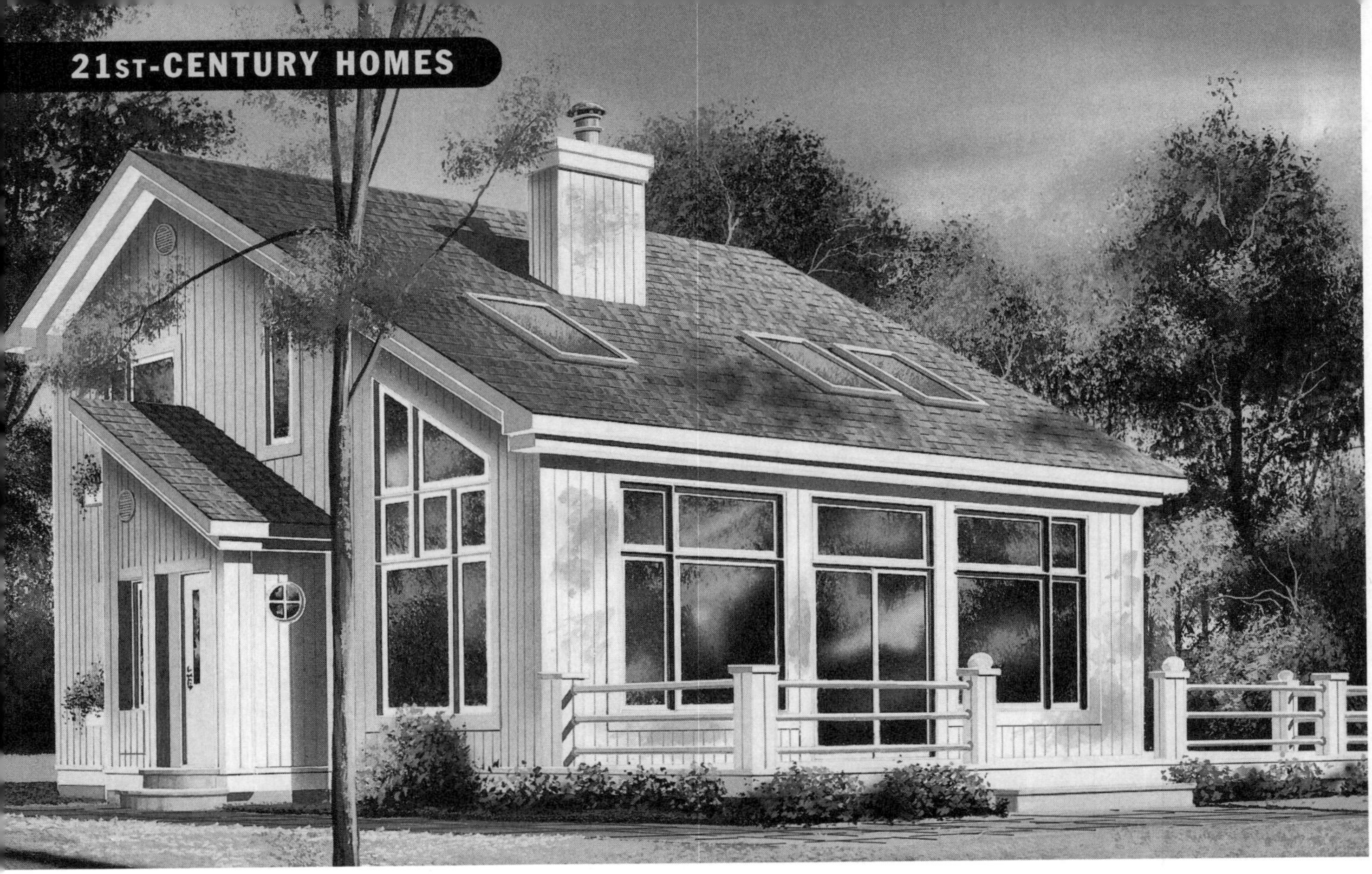

Skylights illuminate the interior of this attractive contemporary design. A large wraparound porch welcomes outdoor activities for warm seasonal events. Inside, the living room, dining room and island snack-bar kitchen are open to each other. The living room is warmed by a fireplace. The first-floor master suite features ample closet space and is placed just across the hall from a spacious bath with a laundry closet. Upstairs, two family bedrooms share a full hall bath.

plan# HPT930422

- Style: Contemporary
- First Floor: 984 sq. ft.
- Second Floor: 560 sq. ft.
- Total: 1,544 sq. ft.
- Bedrooms: 3
- Bathrooms: 2
- Width: 34'-0"
- Depth: 28'-0"
- Foundation: Basement

SEARCH ONLINE @ EPLANS.COM

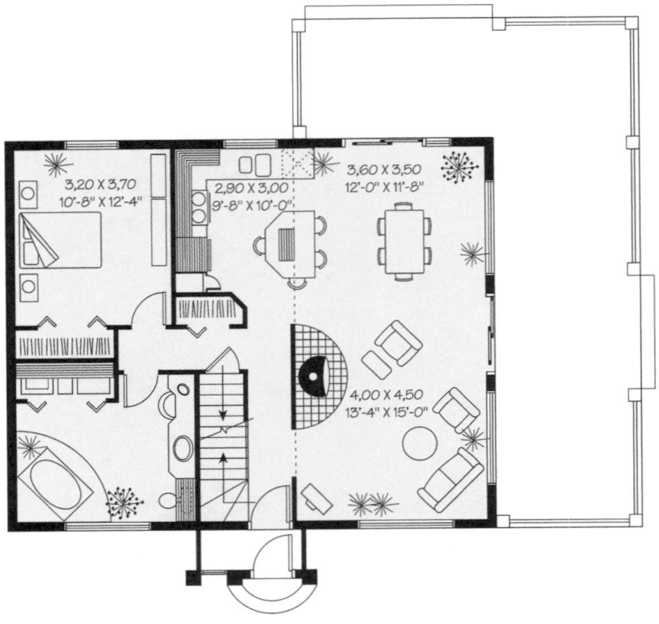

3,20 X 3,70
10'-8" X 12'-4"
2,90 X 3,00
9'-8" X 10'-0"
3,60 X 3,50
12'-0" X 11'-8"
4,00 X 4,50
13'-4" X 15'-0"

FIRST FLOOR

3,60 X 3,00
12'-0" X 10'-0"
3,60 X 2,70
12'-0" X 9'-0"

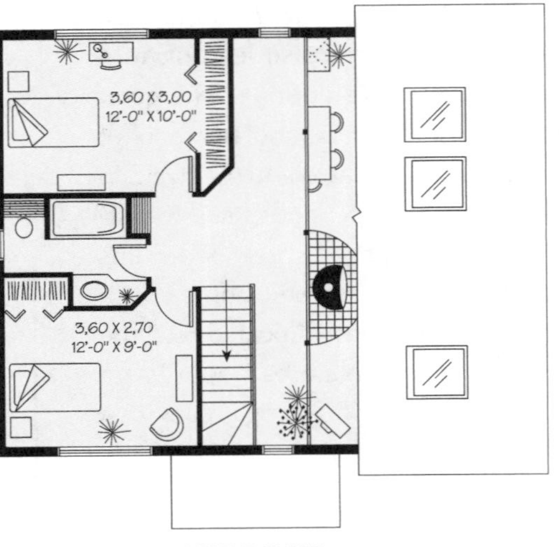

SECOND FLOOR

plan# HPT930423

- Style: Contemporary
- First Floor: 1,165 sq. ft.
- Second Floor: 1,025 sq. ft.
- Total: 2,190 sq. ft.
- Bedrooms: 3
- Bathrooms: 2½
- Width: 40'-0"
- Depth: 44'-0"
- Foundation: Basement

SEARCH ONLINE @ EPLANS.COM

This dramatic contemporary plan features a comfortable family layout, enhanced by modern interior accents. Just inside, a spacious family room is ideal for casual or formal events. The island snack-bar kitchen is open to the dining area, brightened by a box-bay window. Up a few steps to the right, a den quietly resides behind the garage and laundry room. Upstairs, the master suite features a private bath, while two additional family bedrooms share a full hall bath.

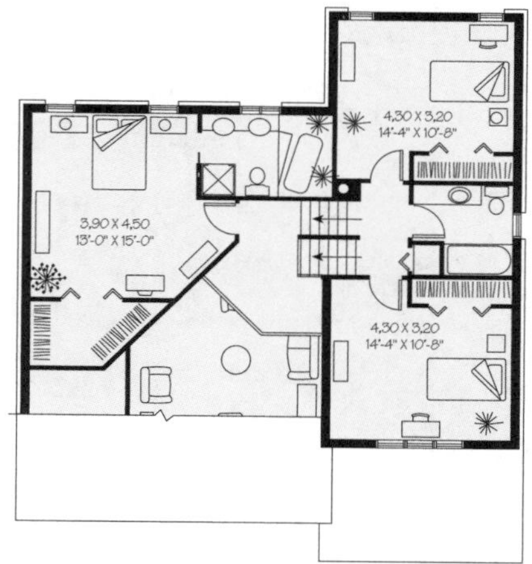

SECOND FLOOR

FIRST FLOOR

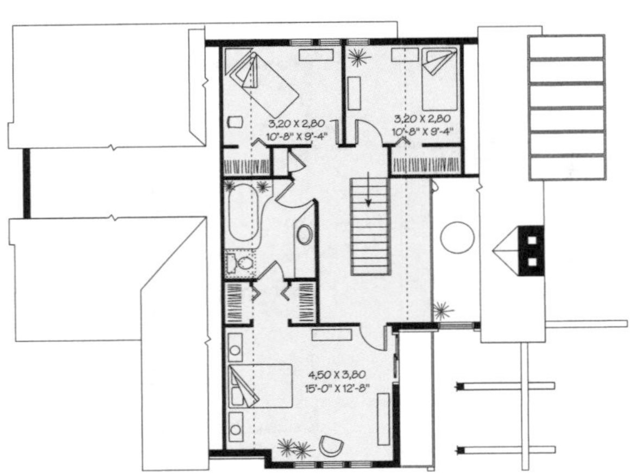

SECOND FLOOR

plan# HPT930424

- Style: Contemporary
- First Floor: 1,062 sq. ft.
- Second Floor: 814 sq. ft.
- Total: 1,876 sq. ft.
- Bedrooms: 3
- Bathrooms: 2
- Width: 46'-0"
- Depth: 40'-0"
- Foundation: Basement

SEARCH ONLINE @ EPLANS.COM

This contemporary home offers all the conveniences of modern luxuries. Just inside, a study sits to the immediate left. The living area opens to the formal dining room for easy entertaining and features a warming fireplace. A sun room is located just off the dining room for quiet escapes. The kitchen opens to a breakfast nook. A laundry room, full bath and garage complete the first floor. The master bedroom, two family bedrooms and a full bath are located upstairs.

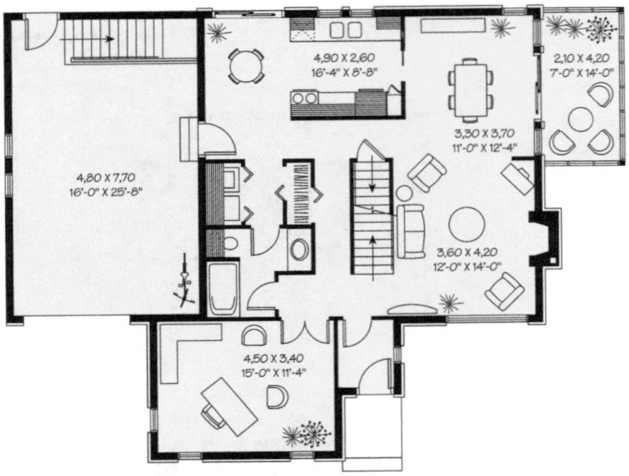

FIRST FLOOR

plan# HPT930425

- Style: Contemporary
- First Floor: 711 sq. ft.
- Second Floor: 539 sq. ft.
- Total: 1,250 sq. ft.
- Bedrooms: 2
- Bathrooms: 1½
- Width: 26'-4"
- Depth: 26'-4"
- Foundation: Basement

SEARCH ONLINE @ EPLANS.COM

This contemporary mountain-cottage design is just right as a vacation home or for a retired couple. A side entry welcomes you inside to the foyer. A two-story bay window brightens the interior. The living room is warmed by a country fireplace and connects through double doors to the dining room. The compact kitchen features an abundance of counter and cabinet space. The second-floor landing overlooks the living room. Two family bedrooms are located upstairs and share a full hall bath.

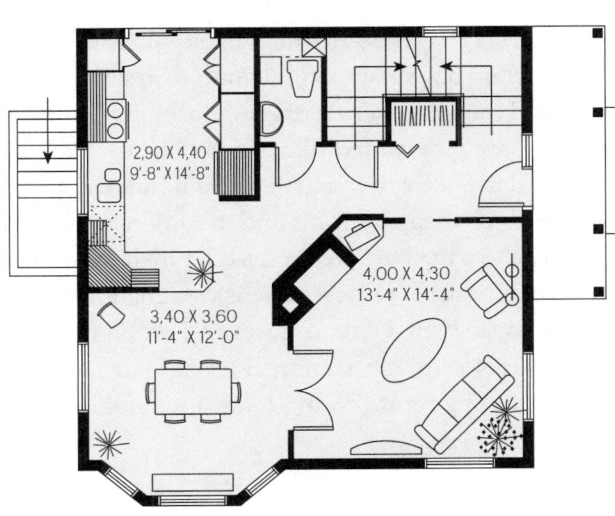

FIRST FLOOR

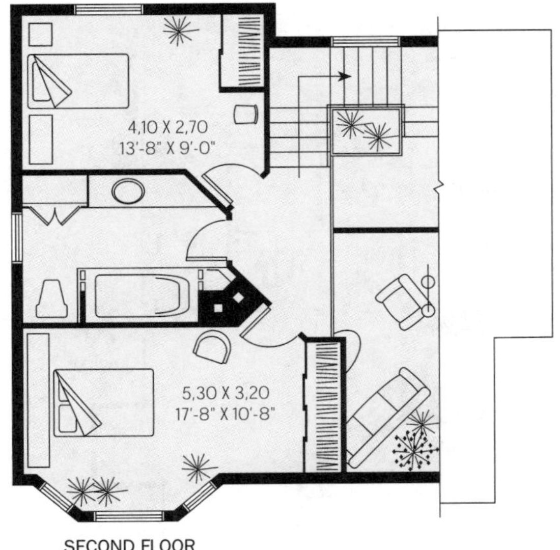

SECOND FLOOR

SECOND FLOOR

plan# HPT930426

- Style: 1,590 sq. ft.
- Second Floor: 756 sq. ft.
- Total: 2,346 sq. ft.
- Bedrooms: 3
- Bathrooms: 3½
- Width: 66'-8"
- Depth: 62'-4"
- Foundation: Basement

SEARCH ONLINE  EPLANS.COM

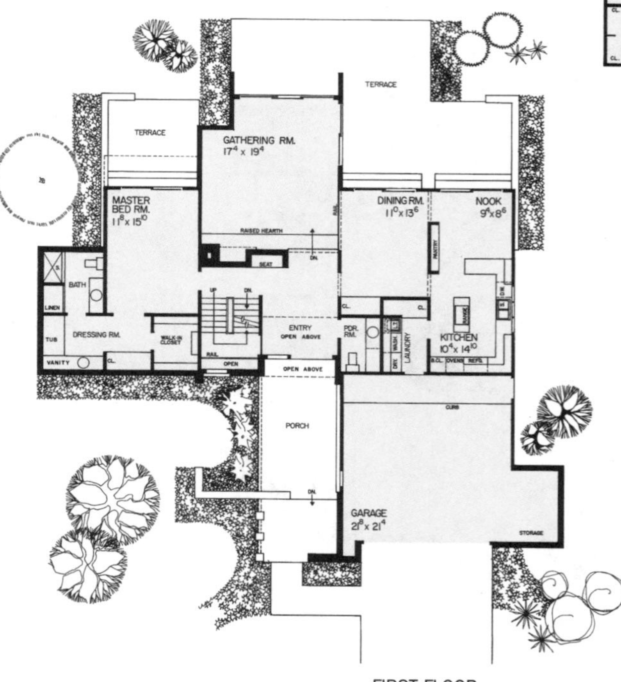

FIRST FLOOR

Entering this home will be a pleasure through the sheltered walkway to the double front doors. The entry hall and sunken gathering room are open to the upstairs for added dimension. There's even a built-in seat in the entry area. The kitchen/nook is very efficient with its many built-ins and the adjacent laundry room. The two upstairs bedrooms offer their own baths, while the first-floor master suite is designed to pamper with a lavish bath, walk-in closet and access to a private terrace. Note the spacious rear terrace with access from the gathering room, dining room and nook.

This exquisite brick-and-stucco contemporary home takes its cue from the tradition of Frank Lloyd Wright. The formal living and dining areas combine to provide a spectacular view of the rear grounds. "Unique" best describes the private master suite, highlighted by a multitude of amenities. The family living area encompasses the left portion of the plan, featuring a spacious family room with a corner fireplace, access to the covered patio from the breakfast area and a step-saving kitchen. Bedroom 2 connects to a private bath. Upstairs, two bedrooms share a balcony, a sitting room and a full bath.

plan# HPT930427

- Style: Contemporary
- First Floor: 2,531 sq. ft.
- Second Floor: 669 sq. ft.
- Total: 3,200 sq. ft.
- Bedrooms: 4
- Bathrooms: 3½ + ½
- Width: 82'-4"
- Depth: 72'-0"
- Foundation: Slab

SEARCH ONLINE @ EPLANS.COM

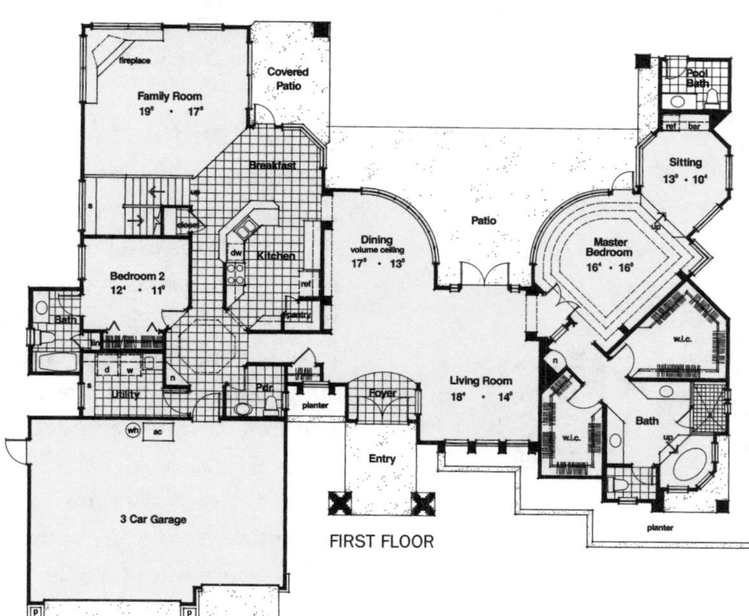

FIRST FLOOR

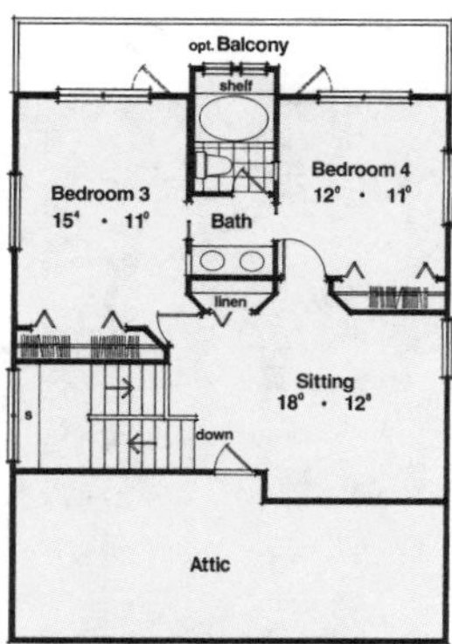

SECOND FLOOR

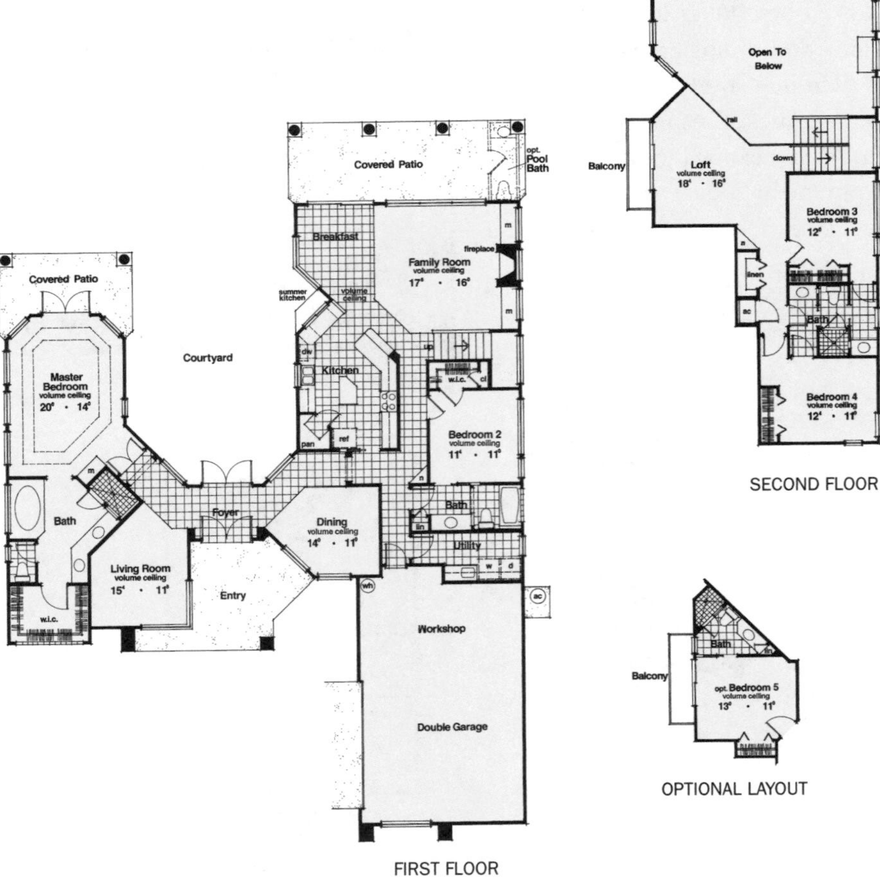

FIRST FLOOR

SECOND FLOOR

OPTIONAL LAYOUT

plan# HPT930428

- Style: Contemporary
- First Floor: 2,254 sq. ft.
- Second Floor: 608 sq. ft.
- Total: 2,862 sq. ft.
- Bedrooms: 4
- Bathrooms: 3
- Width: 66'-0"
- Depth: 78'-10"
- Foundation: Slab

SEARCH ONLINE @ EPLANS.COM

Indoor and outdoor living are enhanced by the beautiful courtyard that decorates the center of this home. A gallery leads to a kitchen featuring a center work island and adjacent breakfast room. To the left, the gallery leads to the formal living room and master suite. The secluded master bedroom features a tray ceiling and double doors that lead to a covered patio. The second floor contains a full bath shared by two family bedrooms and a loft that provides flexible space.

THE GATEWAY TO YOUR NEW HOME

Looking for more plans? Got questions? Try our one-stop home plans resource—eplans.com.

We'll help you streamline the plan selection process, so your dreams can become reality faster than you ever imagined. From choosing your home plan and ideal location to finding an experienced contractor, eplans.com will guide you every step of the way.

Mix and match! Explore! At eplans.com you can combine all your top criteria to find your perfect match. Search for your ideal home plan by any or all of the following:

> Number of bedrooms or baths
> Total square feet
> House style
> Designer
> Cost

With over 10,000 plans, the options are endless. Colonial, ranch, country, and Victorian are just a few of the house styles offered. Keep in mind your essential lifestyle features—whether to include a porch, fireplace, bonus room, or main floor laundry room. And the garage—how many cars must it accommodate, if any? By filling out the preference page on eplans.com, we'll help you narrow your search. And, don't forget to enjoy a virtual home tour before any decisions are set in stone.

At eplans.com we'll make the building process a snap to understand. At the click of a button you'll find a complete building guide. And our eplans task planner will create a construction calendar just for you. Here you'll find links to tips and other valuable information to help you every step of the way—from choosing a site to moving day.

For your added convenience, our home plans experts are available for live, one-on-one chats at eplans.com. Building a home may seem like a complicated project, but it doesn't have to be—particularly if you'll let us help you from start to finish.

COPYRIGHT DOS & DON'TS

Blueprints for residential construction (or working drawings, as they are often called in the industry) are copyrighted intellectual property, protected under the terms of United States Copyright Law and, therefore, cannot be copied legally for use in building. However, we've made it easy for you to get what you need to build your home, without violating copyright law. Following are some guidelines to help you obtain the right number of copies for your chosen blueprint design.

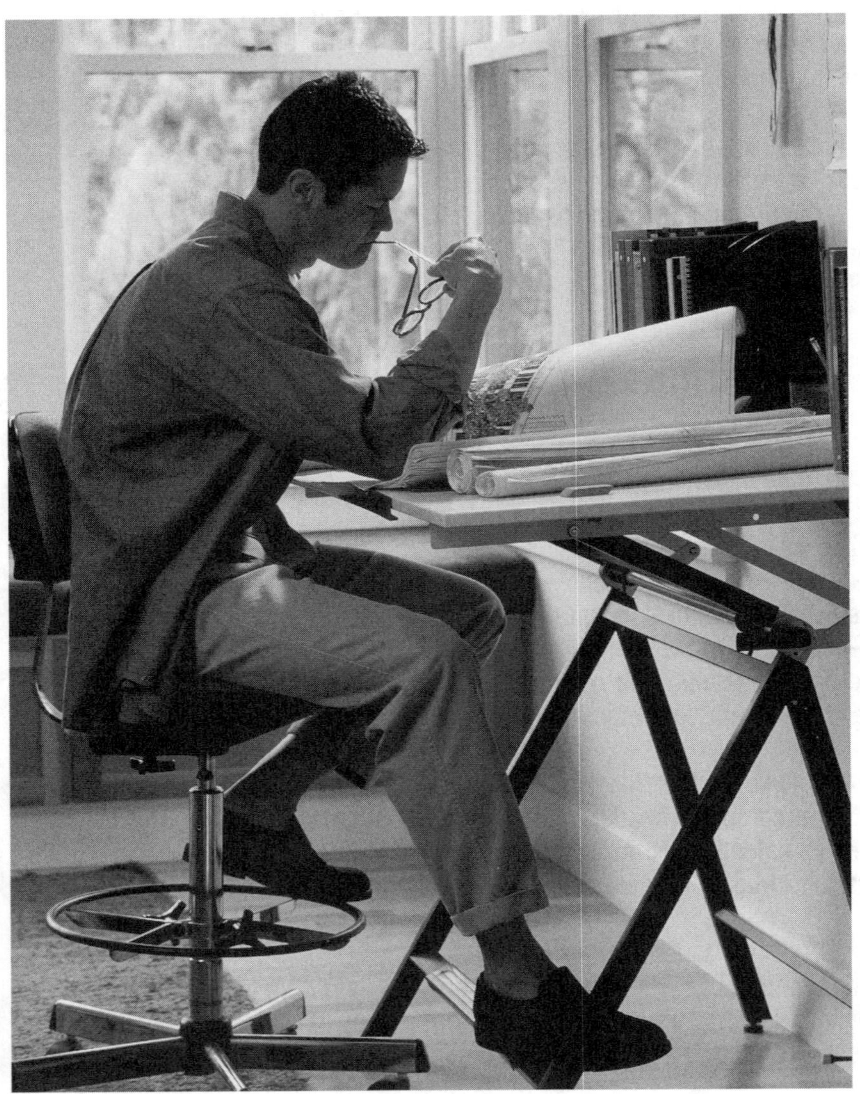

COPYRIGHT DO

- Do purchase enough copies of the blueprints to satisfy building requirements. As a rule for a home or project plan, you will need a set for yourself, two or three for your builder and subcontractors, two for the local building department, and one to three for your mortgage lender. You may want to check with your local building department or your builder to see how many they need before you purchase. You may need to buy eight to 10 sets; note that some areas of the country require purchase of vellums (also called reproducibles) instead of blueprints. Vellums can be written on and changed more easily than blueprints. Also, remember, plans are only good for one-time construction.
- Do consider reverse blueprints if you want to flop the plan. Lettering and numbering will appear backward, but the reversed sets will help you and your builder better visualize the design.
- Do take advantage of multiple-set discounts at the time you place your order. Usually, purchasing additional sets after you receive your initial order is not as cost-effective.
- Do take advantage of vellums. Though they are a little more expensive, they can be changed, copied, and used for one-time construction of a home. You will receive a copyright release letter with your vellums that will allow you to have them copied.
- Do talk with one of our professional service representatives before placing your order. They can give you great advice about what packages are available for your chosen design and what will work best for your particular situation.

COPYRIGHT DON'T

- Don't think you should purchase only one set of blueprints for a building project. One is fine if you want to study the plan closely, but will not be enough for actual building.
- Don't expect your builder or a copy center to make copies of standard blueprints. They cannot legally—most copy centers are aware of this.
- Don't purchase standard blueprints if you know you'll want to make changes to the plans; vellums are a better value.
- Don't use blueprints or vellums more than one time. Additional fees apply if you want to build more than one time from a set of drawings. ■

LET US SHOW YOU OUR HOME BLUEPRINT PACKAGE.

BUILDING A HOME? PLANNING A HOME?

OUR BLUEPRINT PACKAGE HAS NEARLY EVERYTHING YOU NEED TO GET THE JOB DONE RIGHT,

whether you're working on your own or with help from an architect, designer, builder or subcontractors. Each Blueprint Package is the result of many hours of work by licensed architects or professional designers.

QUALITY

Hundreds of hours of painstaking effort have gone into the development of your blueprint plan. Each home has been quality-checked by professionals to insure accuracy and buildability.

VALUE

Because we sell in volume, you can buy professional quality blueprints at a fraction of their development cost. With our plans, your dream home design costs substantially less than the fees charged by architects.

SERVICE

Once you've chosen your favorite home plan, you'll receive fast, efficient service whether you choose to mail or fax your order to us or call us toll free at 1-800-521-6797. After you have received your order, call for customer service toll free 1-888-690-1116.

SATISFACTION

Over 50 years of service to satisfied home plan buyers provide us unparalleled experience and knowledge in producing quality blueprints.

ORDER TOLL FREE 1-800-521-6797

After you've looked over our Blueprint Package and Important Extras, call toll free on our Blueprint Hotline: 1-800-521-6797, for current pricing and availability prior to mailing the order form on page 445. We're ready and eager to serve you. After you have received your order, call for customer service toll free 1-888-690-1116.

Each set of blueprints is an interrelated collection of detail sheets which includes components such as floor plans, interior and exterior elevations, dimensions, cross-sections, diagrams and notations. These sheets show exactly how your house is to be built.

SETS MAY INCLUDE:

FRONTAL SHEET
This artist's sketch of the exterior of the house gives you an idea of how the house will look when built and landscaped. Large floor plans show all levels of the house and provide an overview of your new home's livability, as well as a handy reference for deciding on furniture placement.

FOUNDATION PLANS
This sheet shows the foundation layout including support walls, excavated and unexcavated areas, if any, and foundation notes. If slab construction rather than basement, the plan shows footings and details for a monolithic slab. This page, or another in the set, may include a sample plot plan for locating your house on a building site.

DETAILED FLOOR PLANS
These plans show the layout of each floor of the house. Rooms and interior spaces are carefully dimensioned and keys are given for cross-section details provided later in the plans. The positions of electrical outlets and switches are shown.

HOUSE CROSS-SECTIONS
Large-scale views show sections or cut-aways of the foundation, interior walls, exterior walls, floors, stairways and roof details. Additional cross-sections may show important changes in floor, ceiling or roof heights or the relationship of one level to another. Extremely valuable for construction, these sections show exactly how the various parts of the house fit together.

INTERIOR ELEVATIONS
Many of our drawings show the design and placement of kitchen and bathroom cabinets, laundry areas, fireplaces, bookcases and other built-ins. Little "extras," such as mantelpiece and wainscoting drawings, plus molding sections, provide details that give your home that custom touch.

EXTERIOR ELEVATIONS
These drawings show the front, rear and sides of your house and give necessary notes on exterior materials and finishes. Particular attention is given to cornice detail, brick and stone accents or other finish items that make your home unique.

Important Extras To Do The Job Right!

INTRODUCING IMPORTANT PLANNING AND CONSTRUCTION AIDS DEVELOPED BY OUR PROFESSIONALS TO HELP YOU SUCCEED IN YOUR HOME-BUILDING PROJECT

MATERIALS LIST

(Note: Because of the diversity of local building codes, our Materials List does not include mechanical materials.)

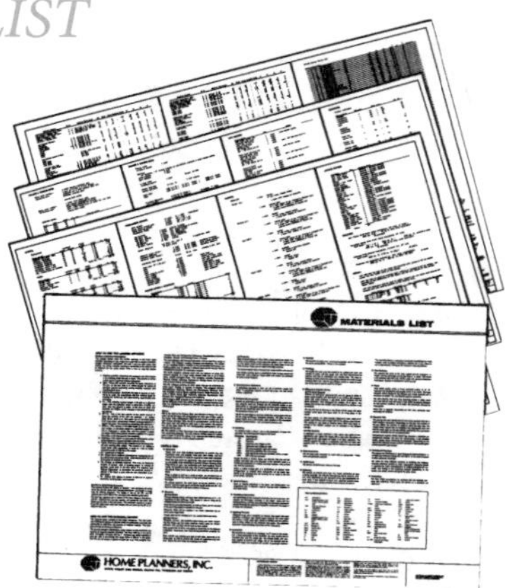

For many of the designs in our portfolio, we offer a customized materials take-off that is invaluable in planning and estimating the cost of your new home. This Materials List outlines the quantity, type and size of materials needed to build your house (with the exception of mechanical system items). Included are framing lumber, windows and doors, kitchen and bath cabinetry, rough and finish hardware, and much more. This handy list helps you or your builder cost out materials and serves as a reference sheet when you're compiling bids. Some Materials Lists may be ordered before blueprints are ordered, call for information.

SPECIFICATION OUTLINE

This valuable 16-page document is critical to building your house correctly. Designed to be filled in by you or your builder, this book lists 166 stages or items crucial to the building process. It provides a comprehensive review of the construction process and helps in choosing materials. When combined with the blueprints, a signed contract, and a schedule, it becomes a legal document and record for the building of your home.

QUOTE ONE®

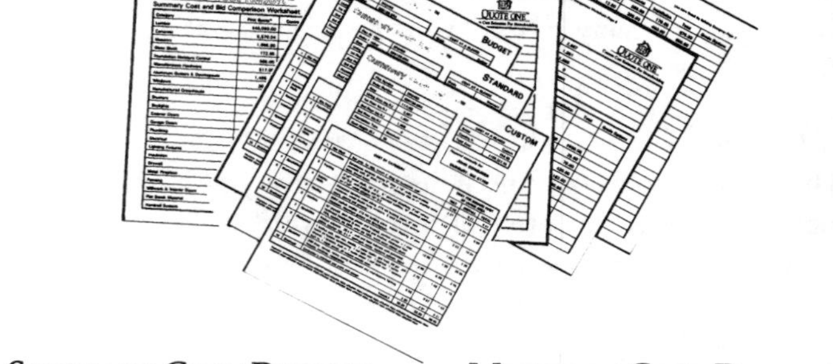

SUMMARY COST REPORT **MATERIAL COST REPORT**

A product for estimating the cost of building select designs, the Quote One® system is available in two separate stages: The Summary Cost Report and the Material Cost Report.

The **Summary Cost Report** is the first stage in the package and shows the total cost per square foot for your chosen home in your zip-code area and then breaks that cost down into various categories showing the costs for building materials, labor and installation. The report includes three grades: Budget, Standard and Custom. These reports allow you to evaluate your building budget and compare the costs of building a variety of homes in your area.

Make even more informed decisions about your home-building project with the second phase of our package, our **Material Cost Report.** This tool is invaluable in planning and estimating the cost of your new home. The material and installation (labor and equipment) cost is shown for each of over 1,000 line items provided in the Materials List (Standard grade), which is included when you purchase this estimating tool. It allows you to determine building costs for your specific zip-code area and for your chosen home design. Space is allowed for additional estimates from contractors and subcontractors, such as for mechanical materials, which are not included in our packages. This invaluable tool includes a Materials List. A Material Cost Report cannot be ordered before blueprints are ordered. Call for details. In addition, ask about our Home Planners Estimating Package.

If you are interested in a plan that is not indicated as Quote One®, please call and ask our sales reps. They will be happy to verify the status for you. To order these invaluable reports, use the order form.

CONSTRUCTION INFORMATION

If you want to know more about techniques— and deal more confidently with subcontractors — we offer these useful sheets. Each set is an excellent tool that will add to your understanding of these technical subjects. These helpful details provide general construction information and are not specific to any single plan.

PLUMBING

The Blueprint Package includes locations for all the plumbing fixtures, including sinks, lavatories, tubs, showers, toilets, laundry trays and water heaters. However, if you want to know more about the complete plumbing system, these Plumbing Details will prove very useful. Prepared to meet requirements of the National Plumbing Code, these fact-filled sheets give general information on pipe schedules, fittings, sump-pump details, water-softener hookups, septic system details and much more. Sheets also include a glossary of terms.

ELECTRICAL

The locations for every electrical switch, plug and outlet are shown in your Blueprint Package. However, these Electrical Details go further to take the mystery out of household electrical systems. Prepared to meet requirements of the National Electrical Code, these comprehensive drawings come packed with helpful information, including wire sizing, switch-installation schematics, cable-routing details, appliance wattage, doorbell hook-ups, typical service panel circuitry and much more. A glossary of terms is also included.

CONSTRUCTION

The Blueprint Package contains information an experienced builder needs to construct a particular house. However, it doesn't show all the ways that houses can be built, nor does it explain alternate construction methods. To help you understand how your house will be built—and offer additional techniques—this set of Construction Details depicts the materials and methods used to build foundations, fireplaces, walls, floors and roofs. Where appropriate, the drawings show acceptable alternatives.

MECHANICAL

These Mechanical Details contain fundamental principles and useful data that will help you make informed decisions and communicate with subcontractors about heating and cooling systems. Drawings contain instructions and samples that allow you to make simple load calculations, and preliminary sizing and costing analysis. Covered are the most commonly used systems from heat pumps to solar fuel systems. The package is filled with illustrations and diagrams to help you visualize components and how they relate to one another.

THE HANDS-ON HOME FURNITURE PLANNER

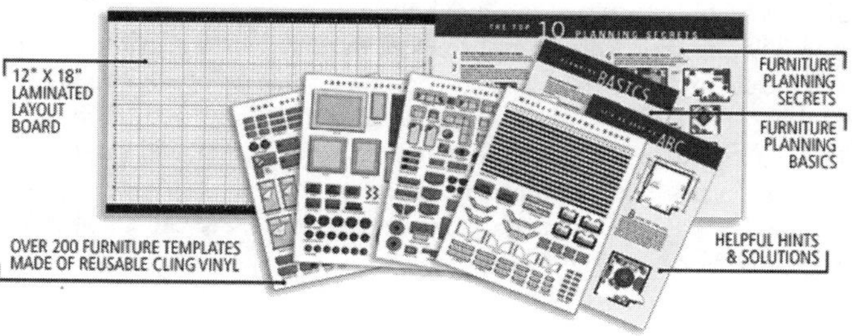

Effectively plan the space in your home using The **Hands-On Home Furniture Planner**. It's fun and easy—no more moving heavy pieces of furniture to see how the room will go together. And you can try different layouts, moving furniture at a whim.

The kit includes reusable peel and stick furniture templates that fit onto a 12" x 18" laminated layout board—space enough to layout every room in your home.

Also included in the package are a number of helpful planning tools. You'll receive:

- ✓ Helpful hints and solutions for difficult situations.
- ✓ Furniture planning basics to get you started.
- ✓ Furniture planning secrets that let you in on some of the tricks of professional designers.

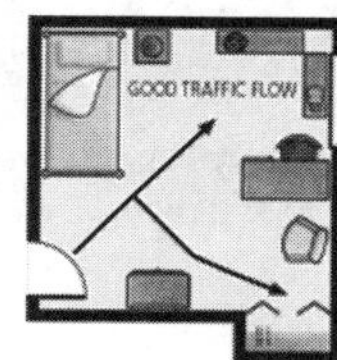

The **Hands-On Home Furniture Planner** is the one tool that no new homeowner or home remodeler should be without. It's also a perfect housewarming gift!

To Order, Call Toll Free 1-800-521-6797

After you've looked over our Blueprint Package and Important Extras on these pages, call for current pricing and availability prior to mailing the order form. We're ready and eager to serve you. After you have received your order, call for customer service toll free 1-888-690-1116.

THE DECK BLUEPRINT PACKAGE

Many of the homes in this book can be enhanced with a professionally designed Home Planners Deck Plan. Those homes marked with a **D** have a complementary Deck Plan, sold separately, which includes a Deck Plan Frontal Sheet, Deck Framing and Floor Plans, Deck Elevations and a Deck Materials List. A Standard Deck Details Package, also available, provides all the how-to information necessary for building *any* deck. Our Complete Deck Building Package contains one set of Custom Deck Plans of your choice, plus one set of Standard Deck Building Details, all for one low price. Our plans and details are carefully prepared in an easy-to-understand format that will guide you through every stage of your deck-building project. This page shows a sample Deck layout to match your favorite house. See Blueprint Price Schedule for ordering information.

THE LANDSCAPE BLUEPRINT PACKAGE

For the homes marked with an **L** in this book, Home Planners has created a front-yard Landscape Plan that is complementary in design to the house plan. These comprehensive blueprint packages include a Frontal Sheet, Plan View, Regionalized Plant & Materials List, a sheet on Planting and Maintaining Your Landscape, Zone Maps and Plant Size and Description Guide. These plans will help you achieve professional results, adding value and enjoyment to your property for years to come. Each set of blueprints is a full 18" x 24" in size with clear, complete instructions and easy-to-read type. A sample Landscape Plan is shown below. See Blueprint Price Schedule for ordering information.

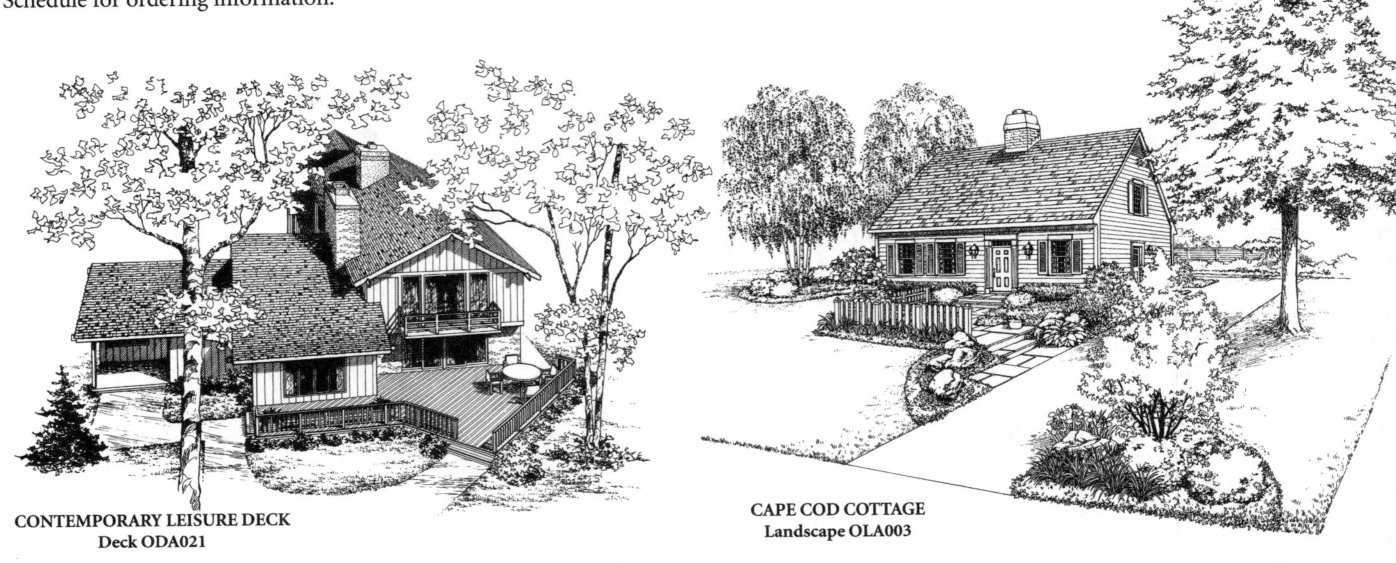

CONTEMPORARY LEISURE DECK
Deck ODA021

CAPE COD COTTAGE
Landscape OLA003

REGIONAL ORDER MAP

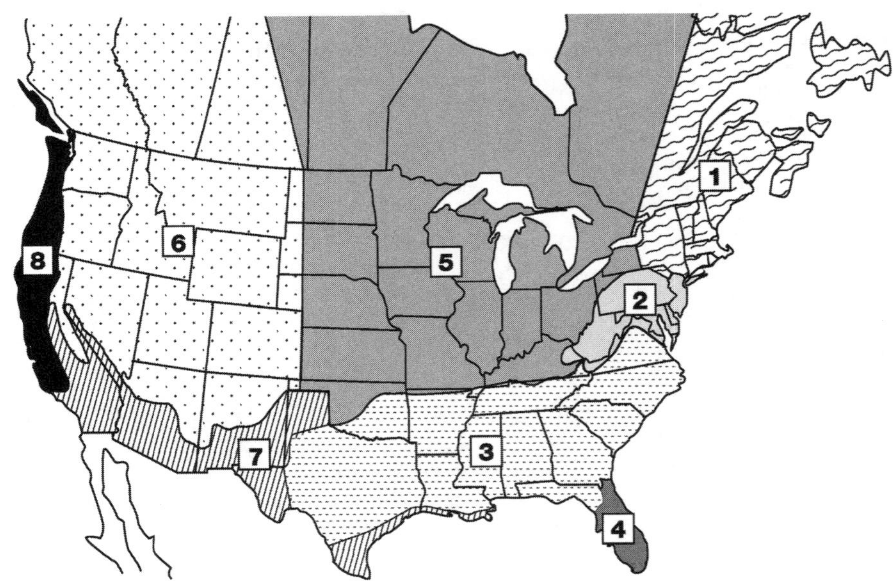

Most Landscape Plans are available with a Plant & Materials List adapted by horticultural experts to 8 different regions of the country. Please specify the Geographic Region when ordering your plan. See Blueprint Price Schedule for ordering information and regional availability.

Region	1	Northeast
Region	2	Mid-Atlantic
Region	3	Deep South
Region	4	Florida & Gulf Coast
Region	5	Midwest
Region	6	Rocky Mountains
Region	7	Southern California & Desert Southwest
Region	8	Northern California & Pacific Northwest

BLUEPRINT PRICE SCHEDULE

Prices guaranteed through December 31, 2003

ERS	1-SET STUDY PACKAGE	4-SET BUILDING PACKAGE	8-SET BUILDING PACKAGE	1-SET REPRODUCIBLE*
P1	$20	$50	$90	$140
P2	$40	$70	$110	$160
P3	$70	$100	$140	$190
P4	$100	$130	$170	$220
P5	$140	$170	$210	$270
P6	$180	$210	$250	$310
A1	$440	$480	$520	$660
A2	$480	$520	$560	$720
A3	$530	$575	$615	$800
A4	$575	$620	$660	$870
C1	$620	$665	$710	$935
C2	$670	$715	$760	$1000
C3	$715	$760	$805	$1075
C4	$765	$810	$855	$1150
L1	$870	$925	$975	$1300
L2	$945	$1000	$1050	$1420
L3	$1050	$1105	$1155	$1575
L4	$1155	$1210	$1260	$1735
Q1				.35/sq. ft.

* Requires a fax number

TIONS FOR PLANS IN TIERS A1–L4

litional Identical Blueprints

ame order for "A1–L4" price plans .... **$50 per set**

erse Blueprints (mirror image)

1 4- or 8-set order for "A1–L4" plans .... **$50 fee per order**

cification Outlines .... **$10 each**

terials Lists for "A1–C3" plans .... **$60 each**

terials Lists for "C4–L4" plans .... **$70 each**

TIONS FOR PLANS IN TIERS P1–P6

litional Identical Blueprints

ame order for "P1–P6" price plans .... **$10 per set**

erse Blueprints (mirror image) for "P1–P6" price plans ....**$10 fee per order**

et of Deck Construction Details .... **$14.95 each**

k Construction Package .... **add $10 to Building Package price**

ludes 1 set of "P1–P6" plans, plus 1 set Standard Deck Construction Details)

PORTANT NOTES

Q one-set building package includes one set of reproducible vellum
nstruction drawings plus one set of study blueprints.

e 1-set study package is marked "not for construction."

ices for 4- or 8-set Building Packages honored only at time of original order.

me foundations carry a $225 surcharge.

ght-reading reverse blueprints, if available, will incur a $165 surcharge.

dditional identical blueprints may be purchased within 60 days of original order.

O USE THE INDEX, refer to the design number listed in numerical order (a elpful page reference is also given). Note the price tier and refer to the Blueprint rice Schedule above for the cost of one, four or eight sets of blueprints or the cost f a reproducible drawing. Additional prices are shown for identical and reverse lueprint sets, as well as a very useful Materials List for some of the plans. Also note the Plan Index those plans that have Deck Plans or Landscape Plans. Refer to e schedules above for prices of these plans. The letter "Y" identifies plans that are art of our Quote One® estimating service and those that offer Materials Lists.

O ORDER, Call toll free 1-800-521-6797 for current pricing and availability rior to mailing the order form. FAX: 1-800-224-6699 or 520-544-3086.

PLAN INDEX

DESIGN	PRICE	PAGE	MATERIALS LIST	QUOTE ONE®	DECK	DECK PRICE	LANDSCAPE	LANDSCAPE PRICE	REGIONS
HPT930001	C1	4	Y						
HPT930002	SQ1	6	Y						
HPT930003	C3	7	Y	Y					
HPT930004	C3	8	Y						
HPT930005	A4	9	Y	Y					
HPT930006	L3	10							
HPT930007	SQ1	11							
HPT930008	C2	12	Y	Y					
HPT930009	C3	13							
HPT930010	C2	14	Y						
HPT930011	C2	15							
HPT930012	SQ1	16	Y				OLA008	P4	1234568
HPT930013	SQ3	17							
HPT930014	C1	18	Y	Y					
HPT930015	A3	19	Y						
HPT930016	C3	20	Y						
HPT930017	A4	21	Y	Y					
HPT930018	C2	22	Y						
HPT930019	C1	23	Y						
HPT930020	C2	24							
HPT930021	C3	25							
HPT930022	C3	26							
HPT930023	L1	27							
HPT930024	L2	28							
HPT930025	C4	29							
HPT930026	L2	30	Y						
HPT930027	L1	31	Y						
HPT930028	C1	32	Y	Y					
HPT930029	C2	33	Y	Y	ODA012	P3	OLA024	P4	123568
HPT930030	A4	34	Y		ODA011	P2	OLA083	P3	12345678
HPT930031	C2	35							
HPT930032	C2	36	Y						
HPT930033	C1	37	Y						
HPT930034	C3	38							
HPT930035	L1	39							
HPT930036	A4	40							
HPT930037	C2	41	Y						
HPT930038	C1	42	Y						
HPT930039	C1	43	Y						
HPT930040	A4	44	Y						
HPT930041	C3	45	Y	Y			OLA014	P4	12345678
HPT930042	A3	46							
HPT930043	C2	47	Y						
HPT930044	C3	48							
HPT930045	SQ1	49	Y	Y					
HPT930046	C2	50							
HPT930047	C2	51							
HPT930048	C2	52							

PLAN INDEX

DESIGN	PRICE	PAGE	MATERIALS LIST	QUOTE ONE®	DECK	DECK PRICE	LANDSCAPE	LANDSCAPE PRICE	REGIONS
HPT930049	A4	53	Y						
HPT930050	SQ1	54							
HPT930051	A3	55							
HPT930052	A4	56	Y						
HPT930053	A4	57							
HPT930054	C1	58	Y						
HPT930055	A4	59							
HPT930056	C2	60	Y						
HPT930057	C2	61	Y						
HPT930058	A3	62	Y						
HPT930059	C2	63	Y						
HPT930060	C1	64	Y						
HPT930061	C3	65	Y						
HPT930062	C2	66	Y	Y					
HPT930063	C3	67	Y	Y			OLA024	P4	123568
HPT930064	C2	68	Y						
HPT930065	C1	69	Y						
HPT930066	C1	70	Y						
HPT930067	C1	71	Y						
HPT930068	C1	72	Y						
HPT930069	A4	73	Y	Y					
HPT930070	A4	74	Y						
HPT930071	C2	75							
HPT930072	A3	76	Y						
HPT930073	A3	77	Y						
HPT930074	A3	78	Y						
HPT930075	A3	79	Y						
HPT930076	SQ1	80	Y						
HPT930077	C3	81	Y						
HPT930078	A4	82	Y	Y	ODA012	P3	OLA083	P3	12345678
HPT930079	A4	83	Y						
HPT930080	C1	84	Y						
HPT930081	A4	85	Y						
HPT930082	A4	86	Y	Y	ODA012	P3	OLA083	P3	12345678
HPT930083	A4	87	Y	Y	ODA011	P2	OLA024	P4	123568
HPT930084	A4	88	Y						
HPT930085	C1	89							
HPT930086	C1	90							
HPT930087	A4	91	Y						
HPT930088	A4	92	Y						
HPT930089	A4	93	Y						
HPT930090	C1	94	Y						
HPT930091	C2	95	Y						
HPT930092	C2	96	Y						
HPT930093	SQ1	97	Y						
HPT930094	C1	98	Y						
HPT930095	C1	99	Y						
HPT930096	C1	100	Y						
HPT930097	C2	101	Y						
HPT930098	A4	102	Y	Y	ODA012	P3	OLA093	P3	1234567
HPT930099	C1	103	Y	Y					
HPT930100	C1	104	Y						
HPT930101	C1	105							
HPT930102	A4	106	Y						
HPT930103	C2	107	Y	Y					
HPT930104	A4	108	Y						
HPT930105	C2	109	Y						
HPT930106	C1	110	Y	Y					
HPT930107	C1	111	Y						
HPT930108	A4	112	Y						
HPT930109	C1	113	Y						
HPT930110	A4	114	Y	Y					
HPT930111	C2	115	Y						
HPT930112	C1	116	Y	Y					
HPT930113	A4	117	Y	Y					
HPT930114	SQ1	118	Y						
HPT930115	C1	119	Y	Y					
HPT930116	A4	120	Y	Y	ODA012	P3	OLA083	P3	1234567
HPT930117	C1	121	Y						
HPT930118	SQ1	122	Y						
HPT930119	C3	123	Y						
HPT930120	A4	124	Y	Y					
HPT930121	C1	125	Y	Y					
HPT930122	C2	126	Y	Y					
HPT930123	C1	127	Y						
HPT930124	C2	128							
HPT930125	A4	129	Y	Y					
HPT930126	SQ1	130	Y						
HPT930127	A4	131	Y						
HPT930128	SQ1	132	Y						
HPT930129	C2	133							
HPT930130	C2	134							
HPT930131	C2	135							
HPT930132	A4	136	Y						
HPT930133	A4	137	Y						
HPT930134	C3	138	Y						
HPT930135	A4	139	Y						
HPT930136	A3	140	Y						
HPT930137	C2	141							
HPT930138	C1	142	Y						
HPT930139	A3	143							
HPT930140	C1	144	Y						
HPT930141	A4	145							
HPT930142	A4	146	Y						
HPT930143	C4	147	Y	Y			OLA024	P4	123568
HPT930144	A3	148							

PLAN INDEX

DESIGN	PRICE	PAGE	MATERIALS LIST	QUOTE ONE®	DECK	DECK PRICE	LANDSCAPE	LANDSCAPE PRICE	REGIONS
930145	A4	149	Y						
930146	C1	150							
930147	A2	151							
930148	A2	152							
930149	A2	153							
930150	C1	154	Y						
930151	A2	155	Y						
930152	A3	156							
930153	C1	157							
930154	A3	158	Y						
930155	A4	159	Y						
930156	C3	160	Y	Y					
930157	C1	161	Y	Y					
930158	A4	162	Y	Y					
930159	A3	163	Y	Y					
930160	A3	164	Y						
930161	A4	165	Y						
930162	A3	166							
930163	C3	167							
930164	A4	168							
930165	C1	169							
930166	A4	170							
930167	A3	171							
930168	C2	172							
930169	A3	173	Y						
930170	A4	174							
930171	A3	175							
930172	A1	176	Y						
930173	A4	177	Y						
930174	C1	178							
930175	C3	179							
930176	C1	180							
930177	SQ1	181							
930178	C2	182					OLA004	P3	123568
930179	SQ1	183					OLA010	P3	1234568
930180	C2	184							
930181	C1	185							
930182	SQ1	186	Y				OLA024	P4	123568
930183	SQ1	187							
930184	C2	188	Y						
930185	C2	189	Y	Y			OLA024	P4	123568
930186	C1	190	Y						
930187	C3	191	Y						
930188	C3	192	Y						
930189	C2	193	Y						
930190	C2	194							
930191	SQ1	195							
930192	SQ1	196							

PLAN INDEX

DESIGN	PRICE	PAGE	MATERIALS LIST	QUOTE ONE®	DECK	DECK PRICE	LANDSCAPE	LANDSCAPE PRICE	REGIONS
HPT930193	C1	197							
HPT930194	C3	198							
HPT930195	SQ1	199							
HPT930196	SQ1	200							
HPT930197	A4	201	Y						
HPT930198	C1	202	Y	Y					
HPT930199	A3	203	Y						
HPT930200	SQ1	204	Y						
HPT930201	A4	205	Y						
HPT930202	C1	206	Y						
HPT930203	C2	207	Y						
HPT930204	C1	208	Y	Y					
HPT930205	C1	209	Y	Y					
HPT930206	C1	210							
HPT930207	SQ3	211	Y						
HPT930208	SQ1	212					OLA017	P3	123568
HPT930209	C3	213							
HPT930210	L1	214	Y	Y					
HPT930211	C3	215							
HPT930212	A4	216							
HPT930213	A4	217	Y						
HPT930214	C3	218							
HPT930215	C2	219							
HPT930216	L3	220							
HPT930217	C3	221							
HPT930218	SQ1	222	Y						
HPT930219	L1	223	Y						
HPT930220	C2	224	Y						
HPT930221	C4	225							
HPT930222	A4	226	Y						
HPT930223	C4	227							
HPT930224	L1	228							
HPT930225	SQ1	229	Y						
HPT930226	C1	230							
HPT930227	C3	231	Y						
HPT930228	SQ1	232	Y	Y					
HPT930229	C2	233	Y						
HPT930230	C2	234							
HPT930231	C2	235							
HPT930232	L1	236							
HPT930233	C3	237	Y	Y					
HPT930234	A4	238	Y	Y					
HPT930235	SQ1	239	Y						
HPT930236	C1	240	Y						
HPT930237	SQ1	241	Y	Y					
HPT930238	A3	242	Y						
HPT930239	C1	243	Y						
HPT930240	L1	244							

PLAN INDEX

DESIGN	PRICE	PAGE	MATERIALS LIST	QUOTE ONE®	DECK	DECK PRICE	LANDSCAPE	LANDSCAPE PRICE	REGIONS
HPT930241	C2	245							
HPT930242	C2	246							
HPT930243	C2	247							
HPT930244	A4	248							
HPT930245	L2	249							
HPT930246	C1	250							
HPT930247	C2	251							
HPT930248	C4	252							
HPT930249	C3	253							
HPT930250	C2	254							
HPT930251	C1	255							
HPT930252	C2	256							
HPT930253	C4	257							
HPT930254	C1	258							
HPT930255	C4	259							
HPT930256	C3	260							
HPT930257	C4	261							
HPT930258	C3	262							
HPT930259	SQ1	263							
HPT930260	SQ1	264							
HPT930261	C3	265							
HPT930262	C2	266							
HPT930263	C3	267							
HPT930264	C1	268							
HPT930265	C3	269							
HPT930266	C3	270							
HPT930267	C3	271							
HPT930268	C3	272							
HPT930269	C3	273							
HPT930270	C3	274							
HPT930271	C3	275							
HPT930272	C3	276							
HPT930273	SQ1	277							
HPT930274	SQ1	278	Y	Y					
HPT930275	L1	279							
HPT930276	C2	280							
HPT930277	C4	281							
HPT930278	C4	282	Y	Y					
HPT930279	A4	283							
HPT930280	C3	284	Y	Y					
HPT930281	C2	285	Y	Y	ODA011	P2	OLA025	P3	123568
HPT930282	C2	286							
HPT930283	C3	287							
HPT930284	A3	288							
HPT930285	C1	289							
HPT930286	C1	290							
HPT930287	C1	291							
HPT930288	C3	292							

PLAN INDEX

DESIGN	PRICE	PAGE	MATERIALS LIST	QUOTE ONE®	DECK	DECK PRICE	LANDSCAPE	LANDSCAPE PRICE	REGIONS
HPT930289	C2	293							
HPT930290	C2	294							
HPT930291	C4	295							
HPT930292	C4	296							
HPT930293	L2	297							
HPT930294	L1	298							
HPT930295	L2	299							
HPT930296	C1	300	Y						
HPT930297	C1	301	Y						
HPT930298	SQ1	302							
HPT930299	C1	303							
HPT930300	C2	304							
HPT930301	C1	305							
HPT930302	C2	306	Y	Y					
HPT930303	C3	307							
HPT930304	C2	308	Y						
HPT930305	C2	309	Y	Y					
HPT930306	C3	310							
HPT930307	L1	311							
HPT930308	SQ1	312							
HPT930309	L1	313							
HPT930310	C4	314							
HPT930311	L1	315							
HPT930312	C1	316	Y	Y			OLA025	P3	12356
HPT930313	L3	317							
HPT930314	C1	318							
HPT930315	C1	319							
HPT930316	A4	320	Y						
HPT930317	C3	321							
HPT930318	C1	322							
HPT930319	C2	323							
HPT930320	C2	324							
HPT930321	C3	325							
HPT930322	C2	326							
HPT930323	C3	327							
HPT930324	C4	328							
HPT930325	L1	329							
HPT930326	C2	330							
HPT930327	C4	331	Y						
HPT930328	C2	332	Y						
HPT930329	C1	333							
HPT930330	C4	334							
HPT930331	C4	335							
HPT930332	C2	336							
HPT930333	C2	337							
HPT930334	C1	338							
HPT930335	C4	339							
HPT930336	C1	340	Y						

PLAN INDEX

DESIGN	PRICE	PAGE	MATERIALS LIST	QUOTE ONE®	DECK	DECK PRICE	LANDSCAPE	LANDSCAPE PRICE	REGIONS
HPT930337	C3	341							
HPT930338	C2	342	Y	Y					
HPT930339	C3	343	Y	Y					
HPT930340	SQ1	344	Y	Y					
IPT930341	C1	345							
IPT930342	C4	346							
IPT930343	C1	347							
IPT930344	C4	348	Y						
IPT930345	L2	349	Y						
IPT930346	C2	350	Y						
IPT930347	SQ1	351	Y						
IPT930348	SQ1	352		Y					
IPT930349	C4	353							
IPT930350	C1	354							
PT930351	C2	355							
PT930352	C3	356							
PT930353	C4	357							
PT930354	SQ1	358							
PT930355	L1	359							
PT930356	A3	360							
PT930357	C1	361							
PT930358	C3	362	Y	Y			OLA008	P4	1234568
PT930359	SQ1	363							
PT930360	C1	364	Y						
PT930361	C1	365	Y						
PT930362	C3	366							
T930363	C2	367							
T930364	L1	368							
T930365	SQ1	369							
T930366	L3	370							
T930367	SQ1	371							
T930368	SQ1	372							
T930369	SQ1	373							
T930370	SQ1	374							
T930371	C1	375							
T930372	L3	376							
T930373	L3	377							
T930374	L3	378							
T930375	SQ1	379							
930376	L1	380							
930377	L1	381	Y						
930378	C1	382							
930379	C1	383	Y						
930380	C1	384							
930381	C3	385							
930382	C1	386					OLA001	P3	123568
930383	C4	387					OLA004	P3	123568
930384	L1	388					OLA008	P4	1234568
HPT930385	C4	389							
HPT930386	A4	390							
HPT930387	L2	391							
HPT930388	C1	392	Y						
HPT930389	L2	393	Y						
HPT930390	SQ1	394							
HPT930391	C4	395							
HPT930392	L1	396							
HPT930393	SQ1	397					OLA001	P3	123568
HPT930394	C1	398	Y				OLA005	P3	123568
HPT930395	C1	399	Y						
HPT930396	A4	400							
HPT930397	A4	401	Y						
HPT930398	C1	402	Y				OLA005	P3	123568
HPT930399	C1	403					OLA008	P4	1234568
HPT930400	C1	404	Y						
HPT930401	A3	405	Y						
HPT930402	A3	406	Y						
HPT930403	A4	407	Y						
HPT930404	C2	408	Y						
HPT930405	SQ1	409							
HPT930406	C1	410							
HPT930407	A4	411	Y	Y					
HPT930408	A2	412							
HPT930409	C1	413							
HPT930410	C2	414							
HPT930411	C1	415	Y						
HPT930412	C1	416	Y						
HPT930413	SQ1	417	Y		ODA011	P2	OLA088	P4	12345678
HPT930414	C2	418	Y						
HPT930415	C2	419	Y						
HPT930416	A3	420	Y						
HPT930417	A4	421	Y						
HPT930418	A4	422	Y						
HPT930419	C1	423	Y						
HPT930420	C1	424							
HPT930421	C1	425	Y						
HPT930422	A3	426	Y						
HPT930423	A4	427	Y						
HPT930424	A3	428	Y						
HPT930425	A2	429	Y						
HPT930426	C1	430	Y				OLA035	P3	12345678
HPT930427	C3	431							
HPT930428	C2	432							

BEFORE FILLING OUT THE ORDER FORM, PLEASE CALL US ON OUR TOLL-FREE BLUEPRINT HOTLINE 1-800-521-6797. YOU MAY WANT TO LEARN MORE ABOUT OUR SERVICES AND PRODUCTS. HERE'S SOME INFORMATION YOU WILL FIND HELPFUL.

OUR EXCHANGE POLICY

With the exception of reproducible plan orders, we will exchange your entire first order for an equal or greater number of blueprints within our plan collection within 90 days of the original order. The entire content of your original order must be returned before an exchange will be processed. Please call our customer service department for your return authorization number and shipping instructions. If the returned blueprints look used, redlined or copied, we will not honor your exchange. Fees for exchanging your blueprints are as follows: 20% of the amount of the original order...plus the difference in cost if exchanging for a design in a higher price bracket or less the difference in cost if exchanging for a design in a lower price bracket. (**Reproducible blueprints are not exchangeable or refundable.**) Please call for current postage and handling prices. Shipping and handling charges are not refundable.

ABOUT REPRODUCIBLES

When purchasing a reproducible you may be required to furnish a fax number. The designer will fax documents that you must sign and return to them before shipping will take place.

ABOUT REVERSE BLUEPRINTS

Although lettering and dimensions will appear backward, reverses will be a useful aid if you decide to flop the plan. See Price Schedule and Plans Index for pricing.

REVISING, MODIFYING AND CUSTOMIZING PLANS

Like many homeowners who buy these plans, you and your builder, architect or engineer may want to make changes to them. We recommend purchase of a reproducible plan for any changes made by your builder, licensed architect or engineer. As set forth below, we cannot assume any responsibility for blueprints which have been changed, whether by you, your builder or by professionals selected by you or referred to you by us, because such individuals are outside our supervision and control.

ARCHITECTURAL AND ENGINEERING SEALS

Some cities and states are now requiring that a licensed architect or engineer review and "seal" a blueprint, or officially approve it, prior to construction due to concerns over energy costs, safety and other factors. Prior to application for a building permit or the start of actual construction, we strongly advise that you consult your local building official who can tell you if such a review is required.

ABOUT THE DESIGNS

The architects and designers whose work appears in this publication are among America's leading residential designers. Each plan was designed to meet the requirements of a nationally recognized model building code in effect at the time and place the plan was drawn. Because national building codes change from time to time, plans may not comply with any such code at the time they are sold to a customer. In addition, building officials may not accept these plans as final construction documents of record as the plans may need to be modified and additional drawings and details added to suit local conditions and requirements. We strongly advise that purchasers consult a licensed architect or engineer, and their local building official, before starting any construction related to these plans.

LOCAL BUILDING CODES AND ZONING REQUIREMENTS

At the time of creation, our plans are drawn to specifications published by the Building Officials and Code Administrators (BOCA) International, Inc.; the Southern Building Code Congress (SBCCI) International, Inc.; the International Conference of Building Officials (ICBO); or the Council of American Building Officials (CABO). Our plans are designed to meet or exceed national building standards. Because of the great differences in geography and climate throughout the United States and Canada, each state, county and municipality has its own building codes, zone requirements, ordinances and building regulations. Your plan may need to be modified to comply with local requirements regarding snow loads, energy codes, soil and seismic conditions and a wide range of other matters. In addition, you may need to obtain permits or inspections from local governments before and in the course of construction. Prior to using blueprints ordered from us, we strongly advise that you consult a licensed architect or engineer—and speak with your local building official—before applying for any permit or beginning construction. We authorize the use of our blueprints on the express condition that you strictly comply with all local building codes, zoning requirements and other applicable laws, regulations, ordinances and requirements. Notice: Plans for homes to be built in Nevada must be re-drawn by a Nevada-registered professional. Consult your building official for more information on this subject.

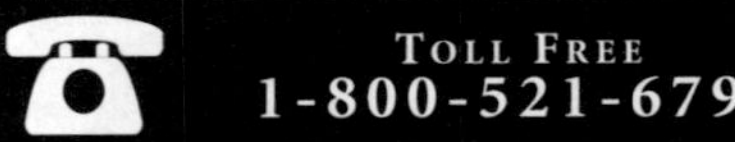

REGULAR OFFICE HOURS:

8:00 a.m.-9:00 p.m. EST, Monday-Friday

If we receive your order by 3:00 p.m. EST, Monday-Friday, we'll process it and ship within **two business days**. When ordering by phone, please have your credit card or check information ready. We'll also ask you for the Order Form Key Number at the bottom of the order form.

By FAX: Copy the Order Form on the next page and send it on our FAX line: 1-800-224-6699 or 520-544-3086.

Canadian Customers
Order Toll Free 1-877-223-6389

DISCLAIMER

The designers we work with have put substantial care and effort into the creation of their blueprints. However, because they cannot provide on-site consultation, supervision and control over actual construction, and because of the great variance in local building requirements, building practices and soil, seismic, weather and other conditions, WE CANNOT MAKE ANY WARRANTY, EXPRESS OR IMPLIED, WITH RESPECT TO THE CONTENT OR USE OF THE BLUEPRINTS, INCLUDING BUT NOT LIMITED TO ANY WARRANTY OF MERCHANTABILITY OR OF FITNESS FOR A PARTICULAR PURPOSE. **ITEMS, PRICES, TERMS AND CONDITIONS ARE SUBJECT TO CHANGE WITHOUT NOTICE. REPRODUCIBLE PLAN ORDERS MAY REQUIRE A CUSTOMER'S SIGNED RELEASE BEFORE SHIPPING.**

TERMS AND CONDITIONS

These designs are protected under the terms of United States Copyright Law and may not be copied or reproduced in any way, by any means, unless you have purchased Reproducibles which clearly indicate your right to copy or reproduce. We authorize the use of your chosen design as an aid in the construction of one single family home only. You may not use this design to build a second or multiple dwellings without purchasing another blueprint or blueprints or paying additional design fees.

HOW MANY BLUEPRINTS DO YOU NEED?

Although a standard building package may satisfy many states, cities and counties, some plans may require certain changes. For your convenience, we have developed a Reproducible plan which allows a local professional to modify and make up to 10 copies of your revised plan. As our plans are all copyright protected, with your purchase of the Reproducible, we will supply you with a Copyright release letter. The number of copies you may need: 1 for owner; 3 for builder; 2 for local building department and 1-3 sets for your mortgage lender.

ORDER TOLL FREE!

For information about any of our services or to order call 1-800-521-6797

Browse our website: www.eplans.com

BLUEPRINTS ARE NOT REFUNDABLE EXCHANGES ONLY

For Customer Service, call toll free 1-888-690-1116.

ORDER FORM

CALL FOR CURRENT PRICING & AVAILABILITY PRIOR TO MAILING THIS ORDER FORM.

HOME PLANNERS, LLC wholly owned by Hanley-Wood, LLC
3275 WEST INA ROAD, SUITE 220 • TUCSON, ARIZONA • 85741

THE BASIC BLUEPRINT PACKAGE

Rush me the following (please refer to the Plans Index and Price Schedule in this section):

___Set(s) of reproducibles*, plan number(s) ________ $________
indicate foundation type ________ surcharge (if applicable): $________
___Set(s) of blueprints, plan number(s) ________ $________
indicate foundation type ________ surcharge (if applicable): $________
___Additional identical blueprints (standard or reverse) in same order @ $50 per set $________
___Reverse blueprints @ $50 fee per order. Right-reading reverse @ $165 surcharge $________

IMPORTANT EXTRAS

Rush me the following:

___Materials List: $60 (Must be purchased with Blueprint set.) Add $10 for Schedule C4–SQ1 plans $________
___**Quote One**® Summary Cost Report @ $29.95 for one, $14.95 for each additional, for plans ________ $________
Building location: City ________ Zip Code ________
___**Quote One**® Material Cost Report @ $120 Schedules P1–C3; $130 Schedules C4–SQ1, for plan ________(Must be purchased with Blueprints set.) $________
Building location: City ________ Zip Code ________
___Specification Outlines @ $10 each $________
___Detail Sets @ $14.95 each; any two $22.95; any three $29.95; all four for $39.95 (save $19.85) $________
___❑ Plumbing ❑ Electrical ❑ Construction ❑ Mechanical
___Home Furniture Planner @ $15.95 each $________

DECK BLUEPRINTS

(Please refer to the Plans Index and Price Schedule in this section)

___Set(s) of Deck Plan ________. $________
___Additional identical blueprints in same order @ $10 per set. $________
___Reverse blueprints @ $10 fee per order. $________
___Set of Standard Deck Details @ $14.95 per set. $________
___Set of Complete Deck Construction Package (Best Buy!) Add $10 to Building Package.
Includes Custom Deck Plan ________ Plus Standard Deck Details

LANDSCAPE BLUEPRINTS

(Please refer to the Plans Index and Price Schedule in this section.)

___Set(s) of Landscape Plan ________ $________
___Additional identical blueprints in same order @ $10 per set $________
___Reverse blueprints @ $10 fee per order $________

Please indicate appropriate region of the country for Plant & Material List. Region ________

POSTAGE AND HANDLING *SIGNATURE IS REQUIRED FOR ALL DELIVERIES.*	**1–3 sets**	**4+ sets**
DELIVERY		
No CODs (Requires street address—No P.O. Boxes)		
•Regular Service (Allow 7–10 business days delivery)	❑ $20.00	❑ $25.00
•Priority (Allow 4–5 business days delivery)	❑ $25.00	❑ $35.00
•Express (Allow 3 business days delivery)	❑ $35.00	❑ $45.00
OVERSEAS DELIVERY	fax, phone or mail for quote	

Note: All delivery times are from date Blueprint Package is shipped.

POSTAGE (From box above) $________
SUBTOTAL $________
SALES TAX (AZ & MI residents, please add appropriate state and local sales tax.) $________
TOTAL (Subtotal and tax) $________

YOUR ADDRESS (please print legibly)

Name ________
Street ________
City ________ State ________ Zip ________
Daytime telephone number (required) (____) ________
* Fax number (required for reproducible orders) ________
TeleCheck® Checks By Phone℠ available

FOR CREDIT CARD ORDERS ONLY

Credit card number ________ Exp. Date: (M/Y) ________
Check one ❑ Visa ❑ MasterCard ❑ American Express

Order Form Key
HPT93

Signature (required)________
Please check appropriate box: ❑ Licensed Builder-Contractor ❑ Homeowner

ORDER TOLL FREE!
1-800-521-6797

BY FAX: Copy the order form above and send it on our FAXLINE: 1-800-224-6699 OR 520-544-3086

HELPFUL BOOKS FROM HOME PLANNERS

1 BIGGEST & BEST

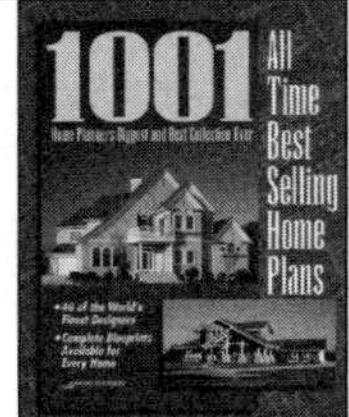

1001 of our best-selling plans in one volume. 1,074 to 7,275 square feet. 704 pgs $12.95 1K1

2 ONE-STORY

450 designs for all lifestyles. 800 to 4,900 square feet. 384 pgs $9.95 OS

3 MORE ONE-STORY

475 superb one-level plans from 800 to 5,000 square feet. 448 pgs $9.95 MO2

4 TWO-STORY

443 designs for one-and-a-half and two stories. 1,500 to 6,000 square feet. 448 pgs $9.95 TS

5 VACATION

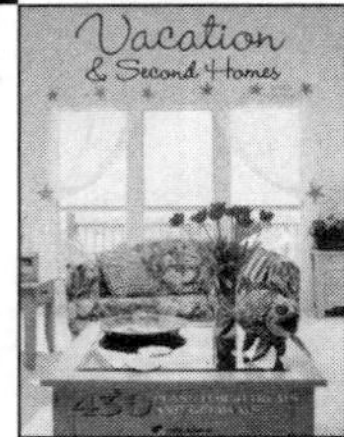

430 designs for recreation, retirement and leisure. 448 pgs $9.95 VS3

6 HILLSIDE

208 designs for split-levels, bi-levels, multi-levels and walk-outs. 224 pgs $9.95 HH

7 FARMHOUSE

300 Fresh Designs from Classic to Modern. 320 pgs. $10.95 FCP

8 COUNTRY HOUSES

208 unique home plans that combine traditional style and modern livability. 224 pgs $9.95 CN

9 BUDGET-SMART

200 efficient plans from 7 top designers, that you can really afford to build! 224 pgs $8.95 BS

10 BARRIER-FREE

Over 1,700 products and 51 plans for accessible living. 128 pgs $15.95 UH

11 ENCYCLOPEDIA

500 exceptional plans for all styles and budgets—the best book of its kind! 528 pgs $9.95 ENC

12 ENCYCLOPEDIA II

500 completely new plans. Spacious and stylish designs for every budget and taste. 352 pgs $9.95 E2

13 AFFORDABLE

300 Modest plans for savvy homebuyers.256 pgs. $9.95 AH2

14 VICTORIAN

210 striking Victorian and Farmhouse designs from today's top designers. 224 pgs $15.95 VDH2

15 ESTATE

Dream big! Eighteen designers showcase their biggest and best plans. 224 pgs $16.95 EDH3

16 LUXURY

170 lavish designs, over 50% brand-new plans added to a most elegant collection. 192 pgs $12.95 LD3

17 EUROPEAN STYLES

200 homes with a unique flair of the Old World. 224 pgs $15.95 EURO

18 COUNTRY CLASSICS

Donald Gardner's 101 best Country and Traditional home plans. 192 pgs $17.95 DAG

19 COUNTRY

85 Charming Designs from American Home Gallery. 160 pgs. $17.95 CTY

20 TRADITIONAL

85 timeless designs from the Design Traditions Library. 160 pgs $17.95 TRA

21 COTTAGES

245 Delightful retreats from 825 to 3,500 square feet. 256 pgs. $10.95 COOL

22 CABINS TO VILLAS

Enchanting Homes for Mountain Sea or Sun, from the Sater collection. 144 pgs $19.95 CCV

23 CONTEMPORARY

The most complete and imaginative collection of contemporary designs available anywhere. 256 pgs. $10.95 CM2

24 FRENCH COUNTRY

Live every day in the French countryside using these plans, landscapes and interiors. 192 pgs. $14.95 PN

25 SOUTHERN

207 homes rich in Southern styling and comfort. 240 pgs $8.95 SH

26 SOUTHWESTERN

138 designs that capture the spirit of the Southwest. 144 pgs $10.95 SW

27 SHINGLE-STYLE

155 Home plans from Classic Colonials to Breezy Bungalows. 192 pgs. $12.95 SNG

28 NEIGHBORHOOD

170 designs with the feel of main street America. 192 pgs $12.95 TND

29 CRAFTSMAN

170 Home plans in the Craftsman and Bungalow style. 192 pgs $12.95 CC

30 GRAND VISTAS

200 Homes with a View. 224 pgs. $10.95 GV

Home Planners wants your building experience to be as pleasant and trouble-free as possible. That's why we've expanded our library of do-it-yourself titles to help you along.

31 DUPLEX & TOWNHOMES

115 Duplex, Multiplex & Townhome Designs. 128 pgs. $17.95 MFH

32 WATERFRONT

200 designs perfect for your waterside wonderland. 208 pgs $10.95 WF

33 NATURAL LIGHT

223 Sunny home plans for all regions. 240 pgs. $8.95 NA

34 NOSTALGIA

100 Time-Honored designs updated with today's features. 224 pgs. $14.95 NOS

35 STREET OF DREAMS

Over 300 photos showcase 54 prestigious homes. 256 pgs $19.95 SOD

36 NARROW-LOT

250 Designs for houses 17' to 50' wide. 256 pgs. $9.95 NL2

37 SMALL HOUSES

Innovative plans for sensible lifestyles. 224 pgs. $8.95 SM2

LANDSCAPE DESIGNS

38 GARDENS & MORE

225 gardens, landscapes, decks and more to enhance every home. 320 pgs. $19.95 GLP

39 EASY-CARE

41 special landscapes designed for beauty and low maintenance. 160 pgs $14.95 ECL

40 BACKYARDS

40 designs focused solely on creating your own specially themed backyard oasis. 160 pgs $14.95 BYL

41 BEDS & BORDERS

40 Professional designs for do-it-yourselfers 160 pgs. $14.95 BB

42 BUYER'S GUIDE

A comprehensive look at 2700 products for all aspects of landscaping & gardening. 128 pgs $19.95 LPBG

PROJECT GUIDES

43 OUTDOOR

74 easy-to-build designs, lets you create and build your own backyard oasis. 128 pgs $9.95 YG2

44 GARAGES

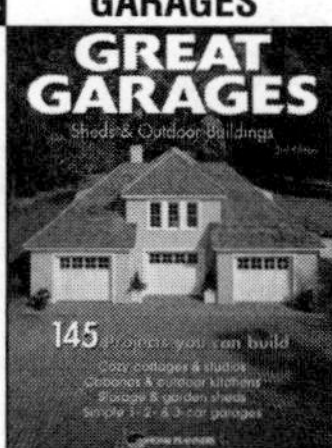

145 exciting projects from 64 to 1,900 square feet. 160 pgs. $9.95 GG2

45 DECKS

A brand new collection of 120 beautiful and practical decks. 144 pgs. $9.95 DP2

46 HOME BUILDING

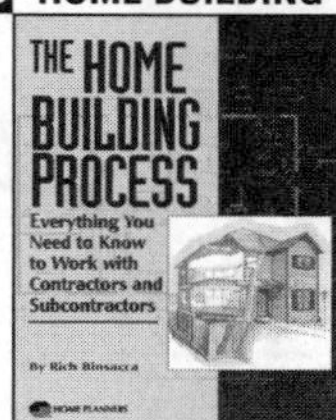

Everything you need to know to work with contractors and subcontractors. 212 pgs $14.95 HBP

47 RURAL BUILDING

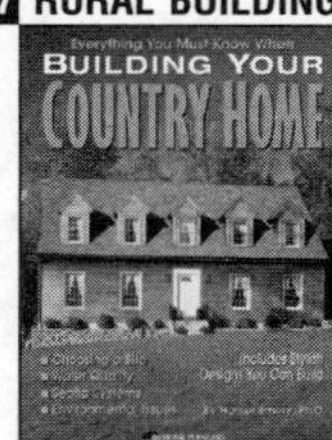

Everything you need to know to build your home in the country. 232 pgs. $14.95 BYC

48 VACATION HOMES

Your complete guide to building your vacation home. 224 pgs. $14.95 BYV

Book Order Form

To order your books, just check the box of the book numbered below and complete the coupon. We will process your order and ship it from our office within two business days. Send coupon and check (in U.S. funds).

YES! Please send me the books I've indicated:

❑ 1:1K1 ....$12.95	❑ 17:EURO ...$15.95	❑ 33:NA $8.95
❑ 2:OS $9.95	❑ 18:DAG......$17.95	❑ 34:NOS......$14.95
❑ 3:MO2 ....$9.95	❑ 19:CTY $17.95	❑ 35:SOD......$19.95
❑ 4:TS $9.95	❑ 20:TRA $17.95	❑ 36:NL2 ....$9.95
❑ 5:VS3...........$9.95	❑ 21:COOL....$10.95	❑ 37:SM2 ....$8.95
❑ 6:HH $9.95	❑ 22:CCV $19.95	❑ 38:GLP $19.95
❑ 7:FCP $10.95	❑ 23:CM2 .....$10.95	❑ 39:ECL.......$14.95
❑ 8:CN $9.95	❑ 24:PN $14.95	❑ 40:BYL $14.95
❑ 9:BS.............$8.95	❑ 25:SH $8.95	❑ 41:BB $14.95
❑ 10:UH........$15.95	❑ 26:SW $10.95	❑ 42:LPBG....$19.95
❑ 11:ENC $9.95	❑ 27:SNG......$12.95	❑ 43:YG2 ....$9.95
❑ 12:E2 ....$9.95	❑ 28:TND $12.95	❑ 44:GG2 ....$9.95
❑ 13:AH2 ....$9.95	❑ 29:CC $12.95	❑ 45:DP2 ....$9.95
❑ 14:VDH2....$15.95	❑ 30:GV $10.95	❑ 46:HBP......$14.95
❑ 15:EDH3....$16.95	❑ 31:MFH $17.95	❑ 47:BYC $14.95
❑ 16:LD3 ......$12.95	❑ 32:WF $10.95	❑ 48:BYV $14.95

Books Subtotal $______

ADD Postage and Handling (allow 4–6 weeks for delivery) $ 4.00

Sales Tax: (AZ & MI residents, add state and local sales tax.) $______

YOUR TOTAL (Subtotal, Postage/Handling, Tax) $______

YOUR ADDRESS (PLEASE PRINT)

Name____________________

Street ____________________

City __________ State______ Zip ______

Phone (______) ______—______

YOUR PAYMENT

TeleCheck® Checks By Phone℠ available

Check one: ❑ Check ❑ Visa ❑ MasterCard ❑ American Express

Required credit card information:

Credit Card Number____________________

Expiration Date (Month/Year) ______/______

Signature Required ____________________

Home Planners, LLC
3275 W. Ina Road, Suite 220, Dept. BK, Tucson, AZ 85741

HPT93

Canadian Customers Order Toll Free 1-877-223-6389

Home Planning Resources

For faster service order online at
www.hwspecials.com

Heat-N-Glo
1-888-427-3973
www.heatnglo.com

Heat-N-Glo offers quality gas, woodburning and electric fireplaces, including gas log sets, stoves, and inserts for pre-existing fireplaces. Now available gas grills and outdoor fireplaces. Send for a free brochure.

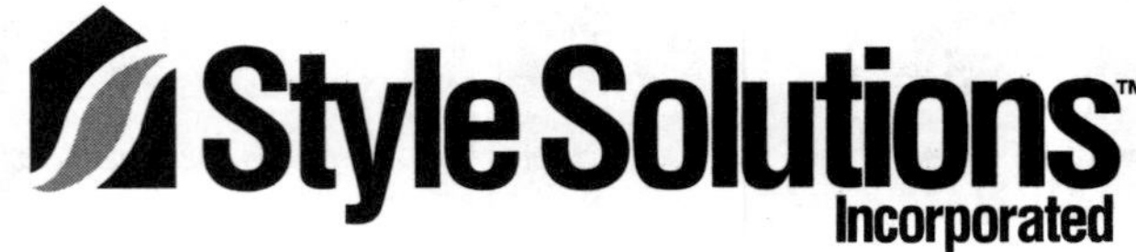

Ideas for your next project. Beautiful, durable, elegant low-maintenance millwork, mouldings, balustrade systems and much more. For your free catalog please call us at 1-800-446-3040 or visit www.stylesolutionsinc.com.

Aristokraft
One MasterBrand Cabinets Drive
Jasper, IN 47546
(812) 482-2527
www.aristokraft.com

Aristokraft offers you superb value, outstanding quality and great style that fit your budget. Transform your great ideas into reality with popular styles and features that reflect your taste and lifestyle. $5.00

Therma-Tru Doors
1687 Woodlands Drive
Maumee, OH 43537
1-800-THERMA-TRU
www.thermatru.com

THERMA TRU® DOORS
THE DOOR SYSTEM YOU CAN BELIEVE IN

The undisputed brand leader, Therma-Tru specializes in fiberglass and steel entry doors for every budget. Excellent craftsmanship, energy efficiency and variety make Therma-Tru the perfect choice for all your entry door needs.

225 Garden, Landscape
and Project Plans
To order, call
1-800-322-6797

225 Do-It-Yourself designs that help transform boring yards into exciting outdoor entertainment spaces. Gorgeous gardens, luxurious landscapes, dazzling decks and other outdoor amenities. Complete construction blueprints available for every project. Only $19.95 (plus $4 shipping/handling).

Have we got plans for you!

eplans.com
Stop dreaming. Start building.

Your online source for home designs and ideas. Find thousands of plans from the nation's top designers...all in one place. Plus, links to the best known names in building supplies and services.